MTV
France

1st Edition

by Anna Brooke, Nathalie Jordi,
Lauren Sommer & Anna Sussman

1807
WILEY
2007

Wiley Publishing, Inc.

Anna Brooke

British-born **Anna Brooke** began her love affair with France on a camping trip in Brittany at age 13. After gaining an honors degree in French and European studies, she moved to Paris in 2000 and has spent the last 7 years becoming a full-fledged bohemian, juggling life between freelance travel writing (*Time Out Paris,* Frommer's, Alastair Sawdays, and Dorling & Kindersley), TV presenting and voiceovers (Discovery Channel and Trivop TV), and acting (3 years singing in a cabaret, short movies, and ads). She is currently writing a one-woman show and dreaming of hosting her own travel program. Any offers are kindly welcome; contact her at annaebrooke@yahoo.fr.

Nathalie Jordi

Nathalie Jordi's appetites keep her bouncing around among County Cork, New York, London, and the French Alps. When not slinging curd as a cheesemaker, she writes for *Travel + Leisure, Condé Nast Traveler, Gastronomica,* and her blog at www.autobiogeography. com. Her dream of a life spent baking, getting baked, and sitting in the sun are gathering steam during her current stint as a waitress in New York City.

Lauren Sommer

Native Californian **Lauren Sommer** is a travel and environmental writer whose work has appeared in *Sierra* magazine, *National Geographic Adventure,* and various online publications. When not living as a downhill ski instructor or pursuing a croissant quest in France, she works in public broadcasting in San Francisco.

Anna Sussman

Anna Sussman studied French and Italian literature at Brown University in adherence to her belief that it is critical to engage with the literature of countries in which one plans to eat and shop. Currently based in Cairo, she keeps her mom, friends, and clothes in New York City while she hops around the Middle East reporting on human rights and women's issues. She has written for the *New York Times, The New York Observer, The Nation,* and *WomensEnews;* and has lived in Brazil, Egypt, France, Italy, Morocco, Tunisia, Turkey, and the United States. (Photo by Christophe Katrib.)

Published by:
Wiley Publishing, Inc.
111 River St.
Hoboken, NJ 07030-5774

ISBN: 978-0-7645-8770-2

Editor: Maureen Clarke

Production Editor: Suzanna R. Thompson

Cartographer: Tim Lohnes

Cover & Interior Design: Eric Frommelt

Anniversary Logo Design: Richard Pacifico

Production by Wiley Indianapolis Composition Services

For information on our other products and services or to obtain technical support, please contact our Customer Care Department within the U.S. at 800/762-2974, outside the U.S. at 317/572-3993 or fax 317/572-4002.

Wiley also publishes its books in a variety of electronic formats. Some content that appears in print may not be available in electronic formats.

Manufactured in the United States of America

5 4 3 2 1

Table of Contents

List of Maps

Acknowledgments

Thanks to everybody—friends, family, and passersby—for your tips and constant stream of support, particularly Kate Antcliff, Anne Bracconi, the Corbel family, Christelle Cotin, Alison Culliford, Sandrine Hamon, Rosa Jackson, Sebastien Joly, Elizabeth Kapour, Nicola Platts, Renaud Serniclay, Andrea Stemler, Emily Vitaud, Juliette Vergez-Honta, Dora Whitaker, Agence Media Presse, and everybody at Woods TV. Thanks also to those who looked after my goldfish while I was away and did my washing up while I finished the final chapters. Thanks to my fellow authors—Anna, Lauren, and Nathalie—and a special thanks to Maureen Clarke, my morale-boosting editor who has the patience of an angel. Last, but not least, thank you to Dawn Postans; to the Middleton family; to the Horrobin family; and to Gail, Bill, and Robin Brooke, for their unconditional love and support.
—Anna Brooke

I would like to thank my family for their hospitality; my coauthors for their patience and good work; and the French for making their cheese, charcuterie, and bread so damn appetizing.
—Nathalie Jordi

Thanks to my fellow authors and to my editor for their unwavering insight; to my family back home for their support; to the wonderful people on the road who opened their doors and shared their lives; and to Toby, who was there to remind me that, in life, a better *patisserie* is always around the corner.
—Lauren Sommer

I would like to thank my mom for pretty much everything. And thanks also to my friends; to the coauthors of this book; to my editor, Maureen Clarke; and to Leif Pettersen, for their encouragement along the way.
—Anna Sussman

An Invitation to the Reader

In researching this book, we discovered many wonderful places—hotels, restaurants, shops, and more. We're sure you'll find others. Please tell us about them, so we can share the information with your fellow travelers in upcoming editions. If you were disappointed with a recommendation, we'd love to know that, too. Please write to:

MTV France, 1st Edition
Wiley Publishing, Inc.
111 River St.
Hoboken, NJ 07030-5774

An Additional Note

Please be advised that travel information is subject to change at any time—and this is especially true of prices. We therefore suggest that you write or call ahead for confirmation when making your travel plans. The authors, editors, and publisher cannot be held responsible for the experiences of readers while traveling. Your safety is important to us, however, so we encourage you to stay alert and be aware of your surroundings. Keep a close eye on cameras, purses, and wallets, all favorite targets of thieves and pickpockets.

A Note on Prices

The MTV Guides provide exact prices in each destination's local currency. The rates of this exchange as this book went to press are listed in the table below. Exchange rates are constantly in flux; for up-to-the-minute information, consult a currency-conversion website such as www.oanda.com/convert/classic.

Euro €	US $	UK £	Canadian $	Australian $	New Zealand $
1€ **equals**	$1.20	£0.68	C$1.35	A$1.60	NZ$1.75

Star Ratings, Icons & Abbreviations

Every hotel, restaurant, and attraction listed in this guide has been ranked for quality, value, service, amenities, and special features using a star-rating system. Hotels and restaurants are rated on a scale of zero (recommended) to three stars (exceptional). Attractions, shopping, and nightlife are rated according to the following scale: zero stars (recommended), one star (highly recommended), two stars (very highly recommended), and three stars (must-see). In addition to the star-rating system, we also use three feature icons that point you to great deals, in-the-know advice, and unique experiences. Throughout the book, look for:

 The most-happening restaurants, hotels, and things to do—don't leave town without checking these places out.

 When cash flow is at a trickle, head for these spots: no-cost museums, free concerts, bars with complimentary food, and more.

 Savvy advice and practical recommendations for students who are studying abroad.

The Best of France

The Best Student Towns

- **Paris:** Gay Paree, the City of Light, City of Romance, is also a city of students—thousands of them, all of whom call the French capital their (often second) home. Several universities and colleges draw in a mix of kids for the arts and the sciences, which explains the eclectic array of student-oriented venues and happy hours. Hang out anywhere near the Sorbonne, in the 5th *arrondissement,* and you'll see hundreds of scarf-clad school kids, cigarettes in hand, debating in cafes. Living in such a big city, students here tend to be very switched-on *(branché),* which can make them somewhat snooty toward visitors or newcomers. Still, hang out in a student bar here, and you'll soon see that a Parisian student drinks, chats, and demonstrates in the street as though the year were still 1968. See p. 66.

- **Bordeaux:** What a looker! Bordeaux is a well-dressed, well-off town that looks a little like a movie set, but students give this chic setting a bit more character and variety. Without them, it would probably feel like a big monument, albeit a pretty one. Anywhere the collegiate crowd hangs (around place de la Victoire, with its myriad cheap watering holes, for example), the youthful energy is palpable. Bordeaux's three universities, with some 60,000 thirsty college kids enrolled, are no exception. They're what make a visit to Bordeaux a fun time—from its cool bar and club scene to its shopping, with everything from cowboy boots to retro threads for sale. See p. 272.

- **Toulouse:** After Paris, the University of Toulouse has France's second-highest student population —count them, more than 100,000 knowledge-thirsty, or just plain thirsty, youths. And that number is constantly growing. But if the college vibe makes you jittery and only reminds you of last semester's freak-out cram sessions, relax: Students don't flood every corner and cafe in Toulouse. The city also attracts lots of travelers (like you) and people from the sprawling suburbs and industrial regions just outside its historical center. See p. 382.

- **Montpellier:** Most of the people out and about in Montpellier aren't locals, nor are they necessarily French—they're students at the University of Montpellier, making the average age here about 25. More than 65,000 students arrive yearly to be enlightened, not only in the world of sciences, but also in literature, flirting, and liberation from *les pères*. College here is a time of expression and lazy days spent wondering how to improve the world, how to live, love, laugh, and be happy. See p. 371.

❍ **Marseille:** This Mediterranean port might not spring to mind as a student town, but between Aix-en-Provence and Marseille, plenty of students (particularly medical students) take advantage of the port city's unrivalled nightlife and cheap prices. Thanks to the sea, beaches, laid-back atmosphere,

relatively exotic populace, and high-strung parties, you'd be hard pushed to find a groovier town. See p. 424.

❍ **Lyon:** Pretty Lyon gives you the big-city feel without the overwhelmingness of Paris, which makes it a great place to get acquainted with French cosmopolitan culture. Its stature as a large city and its two major universities—the imaginatively named Lyon I and Lyon II, whose buildings are scattered along regular city blocks—keep Lyon hip and with-it. When school is in session, the youth scene here is pretty big, and bars, live music, and clubs abound. See p. 561.

The Best Scenes for Hip Youngsters

❍ **Rue Oberkampf (Paris, 11th arr.):** You want to party like a local, but you don't have time to keep crossing the whole of Paris to get from one bar to the next? Fear not—rue Oberkampf, 11th arr. (Métro: Parmentier or Ménilmontant), is Paris's ultimate nighttime venue. The whole strip looks (and is) artfully decayed. There is nothing chic about any of the bars, restaurants, or clubs, but for dusk-till-dawn festivities, you can't do better than here. See p. 104.

❍ **New Morning (Paris, 10th arr.):** Dress down and look cool if you want to fit in with the jazz fans who populate this funky joint, where you'll be able to observe French concert etiquette in action. When do you dance? When is it suitable to tap your toes to the rhythm of the music? How do you stop that Prince look-alike from eyeing you up and down? Wait a minute—that *is* Prince! See p. 107.

❍ **Le Café Chaud (Angoulême):** Angoulême is MTV's big surprise: A small, relatively unknown town with a hot 'n' toasty nightlife scene. To soak up some of the action, a beer in this gay bar is *de rigueur*, whether you're straight or

bent. It is the only place in town with a live DJ, and after a few drinks, you'll be planning your next stint with the friendly locals. See p. 304.

❍ **Place de la Victoire (Bordeaux):** You wanna meet students? Then you wanna come here. The dozens of student bars that surround the square are hot spots of alcohol-fueled hysteria. It'll be tough to find another place in France where you can get chatting to the locals so easily—and maybe latch onto one for an all-night party. See p. 287.

❍ **La Caravelle (Marseille):** It's first-come, first-served on the panoramic balcony of this funky tapas bar—which explains why the place fills up earlier than most. Or is it because the drinks are cheap, the tapas free, and the location to die for (the best spot for views of Notre-Dame de la Garde Church)? If you're cool, you'll come. See p. 436.

❍ **L'Atmosphere Internationale (Dijon):** This is the best bar in which to hook up with a foreign student: There's dancing, billiards, and plenty of international types just waiting to befriend a lonely traveler. See p. 641.

The Best Festivals

○ **Rock en Seine (Paris):** Paris, cultural center of the Hexagon, is never short on festivals. This one, however (in late Aug, in the suburb of St-Cloud), is one of the best—a rock fest on the Seine with wicked big-name acts and thousands of enthusiastic music-lovers who make Glastonbury look uncouth. See p. 106.

○ **Rayon Frais (Tours):** For the last 3 years, Tours has conjured an artistic oasis amid what is otherwise a creative desert—its 3-day festival of theater, contemporary and urban art, and music. Don't miss it if you want to understand what makes youngsters in the sleepy provinces tick. See p. 155.

○ **Film International du Festival (La Rochelle):** So what if it isn't Cannes? Other towns have red carpets, you know, and every year in early July, La Rochelle rolls out theirs for some of the biggest French and international names in showbiz. See p. 327.

○ **Les Francofolies (La Rochelle):** Just when you thought the film festival would steal all the limelight, this week-long music fest takes over, at the end of July, providing everyone with happening concerts by artists of varying degrees of fame and fortune. See p. 327.

○ **Festival d'Avignon (Avignon):** This is the best town in which to say "To be or not to be," before dropping off a bridge: The former cultural, religious, and political center of Christendom (famous for its ruined bridge, pont d'Avignon) is one of the prettiest and most interesting of Provence's cities, with an annual kick-ass theater festival that is the envy of cities the world over. See p. 455.

○ **Jasminade Festival (Grasse):** This is the coolest Grassois tradition around: an August celebration in honor of jasmine, one of the flowers that made the French perfume capital what it is today. Highlight: the town firefighters spraying residents with vast quantities of eau de cologne. For information, call ☎ **04-97-05-57-90** or go to www.ville-grasse.com/jasminade.

○ **Les Eurockéennes (Belfort/Franche Comté):** Join the crowds for the funkiest, loudest, and most famous concerts in France. It's a kind of Woodstock-meets-Glastonbury, with a cool dose of musical *je ne sais quoi,* performed by both international and home-grown artists. See p. 660.

The Best Funky Arts Venues

○ **Point Ephémère (Paris, 10th arr.):** Once your eyes adjust to the cigarette smoke (or perhaps no-smoking laws will have been enforced by then?), you'll see that art galleries don't get much cooler than this one. On the canal St-Martin, it houses a concert space, bar, restaurant, art gallery, and music studio—a veritable magnet for hipsters struggling to survive in Paris's cut-throat creative world. See p. 106.

○ **Centre Pompidou (Paris, 4th arr.):** The blue, red, white, and yellow Centre Pompidou—with its exposed pipes and external escalators—is a controversial piece of art in itself. It houses works by legendary artists such as Picasso, Dalí, Kandinsky, Matisse, Magritte, and Warhol on permanent display. If the Pompidou is too time-honored for you, seek out the new **La Maison Rouge** (10 bd.de la Bastille, 12th arr.), which has exciting contemporary programs. See p. 113.

○ **LU Lieu Unique (Nantes):** Say "LU" to the French, and they'll say "biscuits." Say "LU" to Nantais folk, and they'll say "the old LU biscuit factory–turned–contemporary art platform, for anyone with something to say." See p. 185.

○ **capc Musée Contemporary Art Museum (Bordeaux):** Surrounded by majestic 18th-century houses, this "culcha" temple stands out like a chicken in a steak house. After falling into disrepair in the 1960s, the former 19th-century warehouse narrowly avoided demolition in 1973, and now puts its great expanses to good use as one of the most avant-garde contemporary art museums in France. It also has one of Bordeaux's hottest eateries, the Café du Musée, on its roof. See p. 293

○ **La Friche (Marseille):** This is the best place to get in with the alternatively trendy art crowd. DJ l'Amateur is one of Marseille's funkiest sound maestros, and La Friche is his territory. If boogying is not your forte, come grab a play, test their brand-new restaurant, or join the underground "it" crowd for some cross-media entertainment. See p. 436.

○ **Musée d'Art Moderne (Troyes):** For art lovers and admirers of Fauvist paintings, this museum is a reason in itself to visit Troyes: an Episcopal palace with hundreds of paintings by big names such as Matisse, Roussel, and Modigliani. See p. 688.

The Best Tipple-Tasting

○ **Baud & Millet (Bordeaux):** Pass through what looks like an ordinary wine shop, and you'll find a cheerful little bistro where you can combine your love of the vine with another of France's greatest culinary achievements: cheese—more than 50 varieties, to be exact. It's open from 9am to midnight, so you can satisfy your cravings at almost any time of the day. See p. 285.

○ **St-Emilion:** This is France's best Bacchanalian UNESCO World Heritage site. Its UN-protected medieval core includes a stupendous monolithic church (see below). Every other building is devoted to the world-famous St-Emilion red wine appellation. When tasting, just remember to slurp, swill, and pour the rest into the spittoon. The wine here is so good, and so much of it will pass your lips, that you'll be legless before lunchtime if you swallow. See p. 308.

○ **Otard (Cognac):** You get two for one in this brandy palace: an informative historical visit of François I's **Château de Cognac** plus a fascinating tour around the Otard cognac distillery, finished off by a tasting. It's lipsmackingly good! See p. 307.

○ **Moët & Chandon (Epernay):** It's cold, it's damp, you know the mildew loves it, but so does the champagne, which ferments patiently in vast underground cellars, until the day it can burst into action. The underground tour is one of the best in Epernay and will allow you to sample a glass of bubbly. See p. 678.

The Best Venues for Tracking the Rich & Famous

○ **Kong (Paris, 1st arr.):** If you were a *Sex and the City* fan, no trip to Paris would be complete without visiting this wacky Manga-themed restaurant, where the one and only Carrie Bradshaw (don't faint now) ate a meal. What's more,

Paris's beautiful tribes still eat here today, making it a hot spot for hooking up with someone moneyed. See p. 97.

- **Deauville (Normandy):** Its film festival rivals Cannes, with its promenade of famous names (the beachside catwalk called Les Planches). When you're not star-spotting, you can be busy losing vast quantities of money at the race course or casino. See p. 208.

- **Le Baoli (Cannes):** This painfully hip lounge is packed all the time with the likes of Leonardo (DiCaprio), his posse, and the hot girls who want to meet him. See p. 492.

- **Fairmont Monte Carlo (Monte Carlo):** If you can get there, the best rooftop pool for you to sneak your way into lies on the seventh floor of this tycoon hangout. So you're not on one of the private yachts parked outside. That's okay. At least from here you can see them all, plus the rest of the Mediterranean—making it very obvious why they call this part of the world the Côte d'Azur. Dress nice and act the part. See p. 521.

- **Casino de Monte Carlo (Monte Carlo):** Don't even step inside if you're not ready to play with the big boys and girls; you'll have to pay before you even see a slot machine. That said, if you've come to Monaco to gawk, this is the place to do it. Bigwigs, both literal and figurative, litter the joint. Wear sunglasses to shield yourself from the bling reflecting off the chandeliers reflecting off the bling, and prepare yourself to lose a million dollars. For more info, go to www.casinomontecarlo.com.

- **Cannes Film Festival (Cannes):** We could hardly get away with a "best of" list that excluded the most sophisticated film festival on the planet. Anybody who's anybody in the world of showbiz will tread Cannes's famous red carpet. If you're a star junkie, this is your seventh heaven—the ultimate destination for having your body parts signed in person by your favorite celebrities. See p. 485.

The Best Spots Beside the Sea

- **Fort National (Brittany):** It may look like it's built on an island off the coast, but once the sea rolls back during low tide, a land bridge emerges. Walking out to the fort reveals some stunning views of St-Malo, but keep your eye on your watch. Once the tide comes back in, there's no way back to your hotel bed. See p. 232.

- **Dune de Pilat (Arcachon):** The Bassin d'Arcachon brought mister Sandman his dream, in Europe's largest dune, measuring 3km (2 miles) long, 105m (344 ft.) high, and 500m (1,640 ft.) wide. Mounting the Dune de Pilat's steep slopes is an anti-flab solution that would make Pamela Anderson's personal trainer scream for oxygen.

Besides the free workout and panoramic views, migratory birds flock here in autumn on their way to the nearby ornithological sanctuary. See p. 314.

- **La Rochelle:** If you "like to seafood and eat it," this is the town for you. Bucket loads of fish, shellfish, and other briny delights are cooked to perfection in this historical port. If you'd rather see sea creatures alive and well, don't miss La Rochelle's Aquarium—with a vast collection, plus a brand-new cafe with a great view over the medieval towers and the sea. See p. 316.

- **Ile de Ré (La Rochelle):** Get your bicycle out, as you'll need it to get around this magnificent island, famous for its stunning chalky cliffs, dunes, rich birdlife, and salt pans. Everything about this place, peppered with fishermen's cabins and sleepy villages, is conducive to relaxation. See p. 325.

○ **Plage de Pampelonne (St-Tropez):** Admit it: You've come to the Côte d'Azur to go boob-spotting, and there's nothing shameful about it. Well, knocker yourself out at this beach where Brigitte Bardot's legacy stays aflame. See p. 484.

○ **Cala Francese (Corsica):** Deserted and sandy, with warm, tempting water, this beach also has the exceptional advantage of being backed by a ruined Genovese tower and Roman vestiges. So why don't many people go there? Who cares?! See p. 543.

The Best Moments

○ **Strolling along the Seine (Paris):** Just because thousands have done it before you doesn't mean you shouldn't experience the magic of the River Seine. Painters such as Sisley, Turner, and Monet have all fallen under its spell, and so will you, as you watch lovers walking hand in hand, anglers casting their lines, *bouquinistes* (secondhand-book dealers) peddling their postcards and 100-year-old pornography, and in-line skaters dodging passersby, as the quaysides are closed to cars during the summer months on Sundays. See p. 108.

○ **Mont St-Michel (Normandy):** Can a place get more magical than this? Crowned by a fortified abbey, encircled by the sea, and veiled by mist, the pyramidal silhouette of this medieval island is one's of France's most iconic and handsome sites. The moment you first set eyes on it will prove unforgettable. See p. 216.

○ **Môle des Noires (St-Malo):** Walking around St-Malo's high city walls is breathtaking, but for one of the best views of the city, head to this long stone walkway that extends far onto the water. On your way to the lighthouse at the end, you'll pass fishermen (looking for a bite in the last light of the day) and witness a gorgeous sunset over the ocean (now sigh!). See p. 233.

○ **Le Plan Lumière (Toulouse):** A city-wide initiative to illuminate Toulouse's best-looking buildings by night. Check out the place Saint-Georges, the place du Capitole, the Halle aux Grains, the basilique Saint-Sernin, the Mediatheque Jose Cabanis, the Abattoirs, and the banks of the Garonne, especially the quai Saint-Pierre, the usine du Bazacle, and the bridges: the pont des Catalans, the pont Neuf, and the pont Saint-Pierre. See p. 384.

○ **Hôtel Sube (St-Tropez):** Given its location on the bay, St-Tropez is known for great sunsets. But the balcony seating at Sube, which faces west and overlooks the statue of Suffren and the private yachts in the bay, gives you a special vantage. It's quite possibly the best place from which to watch the sun set on the entire Côte d'Azur. For more info, call ☎ **04-94-97-30-04.**

○ **The N81 Road out of Ajaccio (Corsica):** Follow this route until you get to the Calanches de Piana, an extraordinary micro-environment that looks like Moab, Utah. It's all jutting red rock and green nubbly brush, and the roads are perilous, but it's a thrilling, gorgeous ride. Go hiking or take a picnic into the Foret Communale de Piana. See p. 530.

The Best Regional Produce

○ **Jean-Yves Bordier (St-Malo):** Sure, everyone has been telling you how wonderful French butter is. But until you taste the creamy, light gold miracle sold here, you have no idea what you're missing. Jean-Yves Bordier serves artisan butter that will make you bow down and worship French dairy. In addition to the plain salted kind, he also makes butter with a Breton twist: *beurre aux algues* (seaweed butter). It sounds weird, but the salty, brine-y flavor will rock your world. See p. 235.

○ **Baillardran (Bordeaux):** Bordeaux is famous for scrumptious rum and vanilla cork-shaped cakes called *canelé.* It would be a sin not to try one, so avoid having to repent, and try one. Or two or three. Or four or five (once you start you can't stop). See p. 282.

○ **Ajaccio Market (Corsica):** Ajaccio's market is packed with all manner of fresh produce, delectable charcuterie, hoary cheeses, and, best of all, Ajaccians haggling over their purchases. Try the tarts, *brocciu beigets,* or just munch on a super-fresh fig. It's on **Square Campinchi,** across from the tourist office. See p. 535.

○ **La Petite Friande (Reims):** At the risk of suffering death by chocolate, hurry here and *RIP* open some wrappers. You'll guarantee your place in chocolate heaven. See p. 676.

○ **La Boutique Maille (Dijon):** Buying Dijon mustard in the supermarket just isn't the same as acquiring some from this original boutique, which dates from 1777. See p. 646.

The Best of Freaky France

○ **Catacombs (Paris, 14th arr.):** A little-known fact is that Paris lies over 300km of tunnels (created as Paris's bedrock was mined to build much of the town we see today). The tunnels beneath place Denfert Rochereau can be visited during a tour of the Catacombes—mile upon mile of tunnels lined with human bones, dating from when the city's communal graves burst open. See p. 119.

○ **Les Egouts (Paris, 7th arr.):** A few additional kilometers of Paris's tunnel system contains the smelliest museum in the world—Paris's sewers—an ode to the engineers who turned the insalubrious capital into a hygienic place. Look out for the tunnels marked with a replica of the street name overhead. This is a fascinating Paris experience. See p. 119.

○ **Château de Brézé (Loire):** Even if you think you've seen them all, this château

will wow you with its ancient troglodyte village. Its medieval bakery was last used by the Germans in World War II. See p. 174.

○ **Carnac Megaliths (Brittany):** If aliens inhabited Carnac thousands of years ago, they've certainly high-tailed it by now. But for centuries, theories have abounded as to just how these Neolithic stone arrangements got here. Much like Stonehenge, these megaliths were placed in patterns by ancient people. With more than 4,000 stones, it's a baffling sight. See p. 255.

○ **Toulouse Graffiti:** You can't miss it—graffiti is all over Toulouse. See especially Miss Van, one of Toulouse's most famous graffo progeny, and her followers, such as Kat and Lus. See p. 392.

○ **Village des Bories (Gordes/ Provence):** The main attractions in

Gordes are the panoramic view over the Imergue Valley and the château. The weirdest attraction however, is the Village des Bories—an odd assembly of dry-stone huts with corbel vaults, which were used up until the 19th century, although nobody really knows who put them there. See p. 444.

○ **Palais Idéal du Facteur Cheval (Hauterives/Drôme):** In the 19th century, a French postman named Ferdinand Cheval developed a strange hobby—building the palace of his dreams with his own bare hands from any material he could get his hands on. The Gaudí-esque result is one of France's most obscure and beautiful curiosities. For more info, call ☎ **04-75-68-81-19** or go to www.facteurcheval. com.

The Best Places to Eat Your Heart Out

○ **Angl'Opéra (Paris, 2nd arr.):** Chef Gilles Choukroun is part of France's new cooking movement (Generation.C, set to rival Michelin and Nouvelle Cuisine. His cooking is all the talk of the town, with deliciously deconstructed dishes such as foie gras crème brûlée (a starter), and St-Jacques Scallops with coffee, cacao, and black pudding. You'll have to taste it to believe it, but it works. See p. 99.

○ **Le Petit Prince (Paris, 5th arr.):** Sauce, sauce, and more sauce is what you'll get in this fab gay restaurant, where straights go in droves to sample some of the richest (and most filling) cuisine in Paris. Expect fun bantering from the waiters, decent portions, and refined flavors. See p. 98.

○ **Le Bilboq (Ajaccio):** Langoustine spaghetti is the only thing you can order at this authentic Corsican eatery. But you won't find a meal like it anywhere but here. See p. 533.

○ **Les Crayères (Reims):** We all know the French love revolutions, and they're having a culinary one as we speak. While most French chefs stick steadfastly to tradition, this Reims restaurant is radically reinventing its dishes in line with a new French cooking movement. See p. 99. See p. 671.

○ **Le Germinal (Dijon):** Real frogs' legs: Once they were hopping—now they're sautéed in a wide range of deliciously creamy and oh-so-garlicky sauces. For the ultimate Bourguinon experience, don't miss it. See p. 640.

○ **Au Crocodile (Strasbourg):** Rollin' rollin' rollin', keep that cashflow rollin', and you can sample the fine cuisine of a two-star Michelin restaurant. Alchemy probably best explains what goes on in the kitchen, and pure happiness on a plate is what Chef Emilie Jung presents. Opt for the lunch menu if you want to sample for less—around 57€. See p. 701.

The Best Places for a Good Night's Sleep

○ **Hôtel Amour (Paris, 9th arr.):** Not another dead-trendy hotel in Paris? I'm afraid so, but this isn't like the rest. It's the only trendy "vintage" hotel in Paris, with rooms in *very* cool retro styles designed by artists such as Marc Newson, M/M, or Sophie Calle. If you're lucky, you might spot Britpop star Jarvis Cocker hanging out there, too. See p. 90.

○ **Edouard VII Hotel (Paris, 2nd arr.):** King Edward VII used to stay in this bed of luxury when he was the Prince of Wales in the 19th century. Nowadays, it belongs to the glamorous Corbel sisters (in their family since 1951), whose impeccable taste has rendered it one of the chicest addresses in Paris. Come for cool browns, creams, and oranges; come for the swank but unpretentious service; come for the delicious cocktails in the bar; come for the dining room (**Angl'Opéra,** run by chef Gilles Choukroun; see p. 99); and come for an unforgettable night with a view over the Opéra Garnier. See p. 91.

○ **Petit Hôtel Labottière (Bordeaux):** If the fantasy of leading an aristocratic life has haunted you since high school, you'd better book a night here. The elderly owner is a fervent historian and has reconstituted his house to an exact replica of how it was in the 18th century. You can't pass through Bordeaux without admiring the antiques, several of which are so rare that the only other models are in world-famous museums such as the Louvre. In fact, it's almost like sleeping in a museum. See p. 280.

○ **Auberge de Jeunesse Biarritz (Biarritz):** It's not often that youth hostels offer more comfort than hotels, but this gem of a hostel does. Sea, sex, and sun is the house motto. Hoards of international travelers descend in the summer for fun on the beach, sports activities, and some "fraternizing" with the local talent. See p. 333.

○ **Château de Puymartin (Dordogne):** This is your ultimate chance to kip in a haunted medieval castle. The rooms are rather grand but unpretentious, and don't worry about the ghost; Therese de St-Clar doesn't roam year-round. You, on the other hand, will be roaming around at length in this awe-inspiring Dordogne château, in all its turreted finery. See p. 408.

○ **La Maison du Petit Canard (Marseille):** In the heart of the old Panier district, this Chambre d'Hôte (B&B with evening meals if requested, plus one apartment for rent) is in a prime spot for visiting Marseille on foot. The busy, eclectic decor will give you something different to look at every day of your stay. See p. 430.

The Best Places to Get Down with History

○ **Château du Clos-Lucé (Amboise):** The Renaissance man who made Dan Brown a millionaire **(Leonardo da Vinci)** lived in this manor house. Its cellars display models of Leonardo's inventions, affording a glimpse into the mind of one of the world's greatest geniuses. See p. 163.

○ **D-Day Beaches (Normandy):** June 6, 1944, is now known as "the longest day"—a pivotal moment in World War II, when allied forces landed on the beaches of Normandy to combat Hitler's Nazi army. Some of the bloodiest battles of the war were fought here, on what have come to be called the D-Day beaches—a must-see for anyone interested in modern history. See p. 215

○ **Lascaux (Dordogne):** They've had us all duped, but it turns out that these caves, with their famous painted walls, were never inhabited. Nevertheless, they shelter some of the world's best examples of prehistoric art (dating back as far as 18,000 B.C.). It's worth the trip, even though a fake cave (Lascaux II) has opened to save the originals from the elements and visitors. See p. 413.

○ **The Roman Arena (Nîmes):** The most extreme antiquity in southern France, built in the first century, somehow still stands tall for you to admire and delight in. For another town with Roman ruins, visit Arles (p. 457). See p. 365.

○ **Abbaye de Fontenay (Burgundy):** Eight hundred years ago, St-Bernard (a man, not a dog) decided to found an Abbey for his monks in a lonely valley. Today, the monks are gone, but you can still marvel at how the Cistercians lived back then. See p. 651.

○ **Salle de Reddition (Reims):** Who'd have thought that an old schoolhouse near a railroad track would witness such immortalizing events? It was here, in 1945, that World War II came to an end, terminating Hitler's reign of terror. See p. 674.

The Best Châteaux

○ **Château de Versailles (Ile-de-France):** Boy, did that Sun King, Louis XIV, understand opulence. So did those who designed his château (Louis le Vau, Jules Hardouin Mansart, Jacques Ange Gabriel) and gardens (Charles Le Brun, André Le Nôtre). Versailles was the bijou in the royal crown, and nowadays it is the jewel of anybody's visit to the Ile-de-France. Nothing can beat a warm summer's day spent ambling through the terraced gardens, admiring the fountains, Marie Antoinette's hamlet, and the classical music extravaganzas that take place during les Fêtes de Nuit. See p. 132.

○ **Château d'Ussé (Loire Valley):** It was the romantic white turrets of this castle, coupled with the bucolic views over harmonious meadows, that inspired Charles Perrault's *Belle au Bois Dormant* (Sleeping Beauty). Climb the tower and see *the* spinning wheel that pricked Aurora's finger. See p. 171.

○ **Chambord & Chenonceau (Loire):** These are easily the two best Renaissance châteaux in the Loire—and, thereby, the best ones to pretend you own. Both are so stunning you'll never decide which one you like best, so you'll just have to settle for two. Ah, ain't life tough! See p. 157 and p. 165.

○ **Château de Villandry (Loire):** Yes, it's another Loire castle, any one of which could be deemed a "best of" in its own right. Even so, Villandry stands out from the crowd, thanks to its world-famous 16th-century sculpted gardens. Believe it or not, one of the best bits is the ornamental vegetable plot. Who'd have thought cabbages could look this good? See p. 166.

○ **Château de Foix (Foix):** True, it's the only castle in town, but it's in excellent condition, surviving from when it was first built in the 11th century. It went from castle, to barracks, to prison, leaving layers of history strewn all over the grounds. Keep an eye out for the 18th-century graffiti by prisoners with a lot of time on their hands. See p. 353.

○ **Château de Milandes (Dordogne):** It's not every day you get to visit a castle that was owned by a fascinating 20th-century star. Banana belt–wearing Josephine Baker fell in love with this bite-size, fairy-tale castle and lived there from 1947 until her death in 1975. Today, you can visit restored period rooms, plus a few of Josephine's apartments. See p. 419.

The Best Outlandish Architecture

○ **La Maison Radieuse (Nantes, Loire):** Budding architects must not miss this modern architectural wonder—Le Corbusier's *other* multicolored block of flats (its companion is in Marseille; see p. 438). See p. 185.

○ **Eglise Monolith (St-Emilion):** Nobody said things have to be modern to be outlandish. And you won't find a building more eccentric than this massive medieval underground church. Carved by Benedictine monks from the 9th to 12th century, it's one of the world's best examples of monolithic architecture. See p. 309.

○ **Carcassonne (Languedoc-Roussillon):** Medieval madness (in large portions) is what you get here, in France's best-preserved walled medieval city. Everything is authentic, from the ramparts (home to plenty of bats), to the quaint cobbled streets and houses, to the atmospheric château.

They associate Carcassonne with the Dark Ages, but frankly, the architecture is enlightening. See p. 395.

○ **Pont du Gard (near Nîmes):** There's no doubt about it, those Romans knew their engineering. And none knew it better than Marcus Vipsanius Agrippa, the whiz kid behind this ingenious aqueduct. It's one of the best-preserved Roman monuments in the world. If it weren't for the inevitable weathering, you'd be forgiven for thinking it was a wonder of modern architecture. See p. 369.

○ **Notre-Dame du Haut (Ronchamp, Burgundy):** That dastardly Swiss Corbusier did it again! With daring and flair, he designed one of the most important contemporary religious buildings in modern history, proving that untreated concrete can look downright dazzling. See p. 661.

The Best Religious Buildings

○ **La Grande Mosquée de Paris (Paris, 5th arr.):** Whether you are of Islamic faith or not, a trip to this working mosque should be high on your list. Come here for a sauna (men's and women's days are separate), a mint tea and Arab pastry, or an evening couscous in the pretty tiled courtyard where hungry sparrows swoop down looking for crumbs. See p. 112.

○ **Sacré-Coeur (Paris, 18th arr.) & Notre-Dame de Paris (Paris, 4th arr.):** How does one choose between two such stirring edifices? One doesn't. You should look around both before climbing to the top and comparing the

breathtaking views they provide over the City of Light. See p. 111 and p. 112.

○ **Cathédrale Notre-Dame (Rouen):** Claude Monet and Rouen's cathedral have been through a lot together. The painter used its intricate facade to explore the changing patterns of light. Thirty paintings and more than 100 years later, the world can enjoy emblematic treasures such as *Harmony in Blue and Gold* (on display in the Musée d'Orsay in Paris; see p. 115). This is an architectural gem not to be missed. See p. 203.

○ **Cathédrale Orthodoxe Russe St-Nicholas (Nice):** Is it strange to you that that there's an onion-domed, fili-greed Russian church smack in the middle of Nice? This religious edifice is the most charmingly unusual place in town for you to repent of your sins. See p. 505.

○ **Cathédrale Notre-Dame-de-l'Assomption (Clermand Ferrand):** This is the church most likely to terrorize you into converting: The imposing, black stone strikes the fear of God into visitors. See p. 615.

○ **Cathédrale St-Pierre-et-St-Paul (Troyes):** Want a wow-factor from stained glass? Then you must come here to admire the 16th-century windows. Bold and colorful, they look brand new, even abstract, and way ahead of their time. Look out for the "Mystical Wine Press," which gruesomely depicts Jesus's blood being squeezed out by a press and turned into wine. See p. 688.

The Basics

Barely the size of Texas, France is old Europe at its finest and modern Europe at its most explosive—a place where the past and present coexist amid stinky cheeses, medieval châteaux, sun-drenched cities, and Alpine chalets; where eating is an art form; and where thrill-seekers can cop an adrenaline rush somewhere different every day. Forget the horror stories of Aunt Virginia's lost luggage, rude Parisian waiters, and how the term "freedom fries" came to be; France will enchant your senses, enthrall your mind, and leave you with a photo album so impressive you'll be the envy of all who know you.

But where to start? You've probably been dreaming of coming here for years, so beware: With its snow-topped mountains, rolling hills, sandy beaches, fairy-tale castles, gastronomical delights, and gobsmackingly good wine, this land could creep under your skin and stay there, luring back visitors again and again. It would take a lifetime to get around all of France's regions, though, so unless you plan to get a job, buy a house, and raise your family here, this book will suffice to guide you through the *best* of France.

The aim of this chapter is to provide you with the information you need to get it right, both before your travel and during your trip: When should you go? How will you get there? Should you book a tour or travel independently? What should you pack? How much will it cost? You'll find all the necessary resources, along with addresses, phone numbers, and websites, here.

The Lay of the Land

The French fondly call mainland France the "Hexagon," due to its six-sided shape (sans the island of Corsica, off the Mediterranean coast). It is one of Europe's largest countries, although, at 547,030 sq. km (211,209 sq. miles), it is nary the size of Texas. Nevertheless, mainland France packs more stupefying sights and sounds into one space than any other European country, and it's bordered by six: The United Kingdom lies just across the English Channel to the north; Spain is over the Pyrenees in the southwest; Italy and Switzerland lie on the other side of the Alps in the east; Belgium and Luxembourg are on the northeast border; and Germany is to the east.

Navigating France can seem complicated, but it is simple once you've grasped that the mainland is split into 95 areas called *départements* (four other *départements*—Guadeloupe, Martinique, Guyane, Réunion—are overseas). Each *département* has a corresponding number (from 01 to 95), which makes up its postal code. Paris, for instance, lies in *département* 75, and all Paris postal codes start with that number.

In addition to this, France is also split into 22 regions, all of which straddle several *départements*. For example, the Ile-de-France region covers eight *départements:* Paris (75), Essonne (91), Hauts-de-Seine (92), Seine-Saint-Denis (93), Seine-et-Marne (77), Val-de-Marne (94), Val-d'Oise (95), and Yvelines (78). To help you get the most out of France, we've covered 16 of the 22 regions.

The Regions in Brief

Go ahead—I challenge you to travel the length and breadth of Europe and find another country so utterly rich and diverse in sites and scenery. Where else can you go in just one visit from seemingly endless, flat fertile lands in the north, to the rolling green, château-studded hills of the Loire Valley; the voluptuous vineyards of Burgundy; the east's spectacular snow-spotted Alpine ranges; the rocky outcrops and verdant pastures of the Pyrenees; the Massif Central's wild plateaus; the southeast's arid Mediterranean coast; the never-ending fields of lavender and sunflowers in Provence; and the wild maritime sea-scenes of Brittany. As if that weren't enough, you'll also be wowed by the spectacular cultural and historic differences that define each region. As you travel around, let your imagination run wild, let your senses soar, and let your brain try to find a superlative to describe every wonderful thing you see. I guarantee you'll run out of words.

ALSACE-LORRAINE Between Germany and the forests of the Vosges is the most Teutonic of France's provinces: Alsace, with cosmopolitan **Strasbourg** as its capital. Celebrated for its cuisine, particularly its foie gras and *choucroute,* this area is home to villages with half-timbered designs that make you think of the Black Forest. If you travel the Route de Vin (Wine Road), you'll come across gorgeous **Colmar,** a romantic medieval-cum-Renaissance town with quaint streets and canals. In contrast, **Verdun** is a poignant must-see, where 800,000 soldiers tragically lost their lives in World War I and World War II. The capital of Lorraine, **Nancy,** is the guardian of a grand 18th-century plaza, place Stanislas, and its student population is substantial enough to ensure a hip bar life. See chapter 18.

THE BASQUE COUNTRY & THE PYRENEES Since prehistoric times, the rugged Pyrenees have formed a natural boundary between France and Spain. The Basques, one of Europe's most unusual (and patriotic) cultures, flourished in the valleys here. In the 19th century, resorts such as **Biarritz** and nearby **Bayonne** attracted the French aristocracy (the Empress Eugénie's palace at Biarritz is now a hotel). In villages and towns of the Pyrenees, such as **Foix** and **Jean-Pied-de-Port,** old folkloric traditions, permeated with Spanish influences, continue to thrive. See chapter 8.

BORDEAUX & CHARENTE-MARITIME Flat, fertile, and frequently ignored by North Americans, this region includes towns pivotal in French history (**Angoulême** and **La Rochelle**) as well as wine- and liquor-producing villages (**Cognac** and **St-Emilion**) with names that are celebrated around the world. **Bordeaux,** the district's largest city, has an economy based on wine merchandising, boasts grand 18th-century architecture, and offers a top nightlife alongside both students and glamorous locals. It also makes an excellent base for visiting coastal attractions such as **Arcachon** and its gargantuan sand dune, the **Dune de Pilat.** See chapter 7.

BRITTANY Jutting into the Atlantic, the westernmost region of France is known for its rocky coastlines, Celtic roots, frequent rain, and ancient dialect, akin to the Gaelic tongues of Wales and Ireland. Many French vacationers love the seacoast (rivaled only by the Côte d'Azur) for its sandy beaches, cliffs, and natural beauty. **Carnac** is home to ancient Celtic dolmens and burial mounds, and the walled city of **St-Malo** is one of the most picturesque in the region. **Rennes,** the regional capital and university town, is a fine spot for a party with local students, and **Quimper** is

a quintessential Breton town high on culture and quiet charm. See chapter 6.

BURGUNDY & THE FRANCHE COMTE Few trips will prove as rewarding as several leisurely days spent exploring Burgundy, with its splendid old cities such as **Dijon,** famous for its mustard and fine cuisine (*boeuf* and *escargots à la bourguignonne*). This is also vine country, known for its colored roof tiles and meandering wine trails in and out of hamlets and towns whose names (**Beaune** and Nuits-St-Georges) are synonymous with Bacchus's favorite alcoholic drink. In the Franche Comté, beautiful **Besançon** sits anchored in the ox-box meander of the Rivers Doubs and harbors the region's most vibrant student population; and nearby **Belfort** hosts France's hippest rock festival, Les Eurockéennes, set in the middle of a lake. See chapter 16.

THE CHAMPAGNE REGION Every French monarch since A.D. 496 was crowned at **Reims,** and much of French history is linked with this holy site. In the path of any invader wishing to occupy Paris, Reims and the Champagne district have seen much bloodshed, including the World War I battles of the Somme and the Marne. The mecca of Champagne is the town of **Epernay,** where most of the great champagne houses offer atmospheric cellar tours coupled with *dégustations* (wine-tasting). For fun in the outdoors, the **Forêt de l'Orient** has enough trees and lakes to keep you busy; and if you wish to let rip on sausage, don't miss **Troyes**—home of the smelliest *saucisse* on earth, the *andouillette*. See chapter 17.

CORSICA For many foreign visitors, the island of Corsica (just off the southeast coast) is a forgotten land. Come here for hidden beauty, alternately green and rocky landscapes, azure seas, and a warm welcome that is wholly Mediterranean.

France: Regions at a Glance

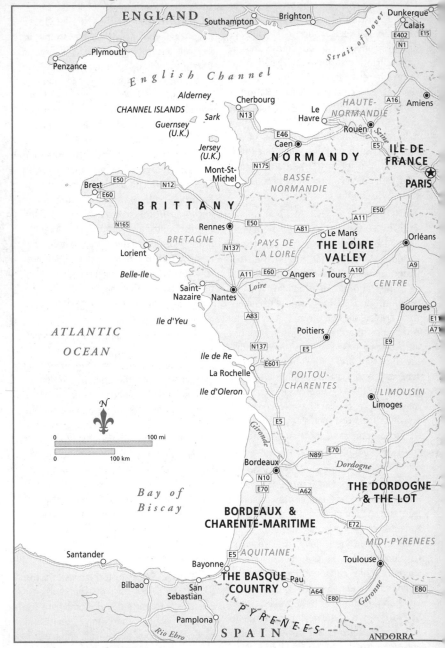

Exquisite settlements such as **Bonifacio, Corte,** and **Bastia** lead you on a journey of historical, cultural, and gastronomical discovery, and make great bases for hiking and cycling around the island. The capital **Ajaccio** is *the* place for hip nighthawks. See chapter 13.

LA COTE D'AZUR (FRENCH RIVIERA)

For some, the fabled Côte d'Azur (Blue Coast) has become quite overbuilt and spoiled by tourism. For others, it still evokes images of the diamond-encrusted jet set. The principality of **Monaco** has only about 2 sq. km (³/₄ sq. mile), of land but more millionaires per capita than anyplace else on earth. The rich, famous, and glamorous descend on **Cannes** each spring for the world's most prestigious international film festival. **Nice** is the biggest city, and most convenient for exploring the area, while **Grasse** is the center of France's renowned fragrance industry. The coast has some sandy beaches. Many are rocky or pebbly, but that doesn't stop sunbathers from whipping out their nipples on the *plage* (beach), which is second nature to most sunbathers in this region, especially in St-Tropez, where bronzing bodies fry in olive oil. And some of the restaurants are citadels of conspicuous consumption. Dozens of artists and their patrons have littered the landscape with world-class galleries and art museums. See chapter 12.

THE DORDOGNE & THE LOT

Also known as Perigord-Quercy, the land of foie gras and truffles is the site of some of Europe's oldest settlements. For biking or indulging in gourmet meals, the region is among the top vacation spots in France, often overlooked by North Americans. In the Périgord, the cave paintings at **Les Eyzies** reveal traces of Cro-Magnon settlements. The Dordogne is the second-largest *département,* with highlights such as the market town **Sarlat-le-Canéda,** and the perched settlements of **Rocamadour** and **Domme. Cahors** is the region's main wine attraction. See chapter 10.

ILE-DE-FRANCE

See "Paris & the Ile-de-France," below.

LANGUEDOC-ROUSSILLON

Languedoc may not be as chic as nearby Provence, but it's less frenetic and more affordable. **Roussillon** is the rock-strewn French answer to Catalonia, just across the Spanish border. While you're here, you can't miss **Toulouse,** the bustling pink capital of Languedoc. **Carcassonne,** a marvelous walled city with fortifications begun around A.D. 500, is also a highlight. With its Roman ruins and bullfights, **Nîmes** exudes an unexpected Spanish air. **Montpellier** is a bumpin' college town with cool nightlife, and there are plenty or smaller wonders for you to get your teeth into, such as the 17m-high (56-ft.) Roman aqueduct **Pont du Gard.** See chapter 9.

LOIRE VALLEY

This area includes two ancient provinces, Touraine (centered on **Tours**) and Anjou (centered on **Angers**). It was beloved by royalty and nobility until Henry IV moved his court to Paris. Head here to see the most magnificent castles in France, many of which look like they've come straight out of a fairy tale. Irrigated by the Loire River and its many tributaries, the valley also produces superb wines for you to taste. The capital of the Loire, **Nantes** is a forward-thinking town with some of the hippest nightlife and art in the region. See chapter 4.

MASSIF CENTRAL & AUVERGNE

The rugged heartland of south-central France, this underpopulated district contains ancient cities, unspoiled scenery, and a cool abundance of black lava, from which many buildings were created. For a real "wow" factor, head to the **Parc Naturel Regional des Volcans d'Auvergne,** where you can walk among more than 200 volcanoes. The largest cities are **Clermont-Ferrand** and **Limoges**—the medieval capitals of the provinces of the Auvergne and the Limousin, respectively. **Bourges,** a gateway to the region and the former capital of Aquitaine, has a beautiful Gothic cathedral and a cool annual music festival. See chapter 15.

NORMANDY This region will forever be linked to the 1944 D-Day invasion. If you're intrigued by World War II, you could find a visit to the D-Day beaches the most emotionally worthwhile part of your trip. Normandy boasts a whopping 599km (372 miles) of coastline and a cool maritime tradition. It's a popular weekend getaway for seaside-craved Parisians, and many hotels and restaurants thrive here, especially around the casino town of **Deauville** and its quaint neighbor **Trouville.** Normandy's great attractions include the **Rouen** cathedral, medieval **Bayeux,** the breathtaking medieval island of **Mont-St-Michel,** and the **Alabaster** and **Flower** coasts. See chapter 5.

PARIS & THE ILE-DE-FRANCE The Ile-de-France is an island only in the sense that a handful of canals and rivers—with weird-sounding names such as Essonne, Epte, Aisne, Eure, and Ourcq—delineate its boundaries (about an 81km/50-mile radius from the center of Paris). France was born in this temperate basin, where the attractions include the **City of Light** (Paris's nickname), **Versailles, Fontainebleau, Chartres, Giverny,** and Mickey's magical kingdom **Disneyland.** See chapter 3.

PROVENCE One of France's most fabled regions flanks the Alps and the Italian border along its eastern end, and incorporates a host of sites long frequented by the rich, famous, and creatively talented. Premier destinations are **Aix-en-Provence,** associated with Paul Cézanne; **Arles,** "the soul of Provence," captured by Vincent van Gogh; **Avignon,** the 14th-century capital of Christendom during the papal schism, now known for its kick-ass theater festival; and **Marseille,** a port city established by the Phoenicians (in some ways more North African than French), now hip as hell for party-goers. Provence's gems are its small villages, such **Les Baux.** And the **Camargue**—the marshy delta formed by two arms of the Rhône River—is rich in bird life, and famous for its white horses and cowboys. See chapter 11.

THE RHONE VALLEY & FRENCH ALPS A fertile area of Alpine foothills and sloping valleys in eastern and southeastern France, the upper Rhône Valley ranges from the French suburbs of Geneva, in Switzerland, to the northern borders of Provence. The district is thoroughly French, unflinchingly bourgeois, and dedicated to preserving the gastronomic and cultural traditions that have produced some of the most celebrated chefs in French history. Only 2 hours by train from Paris, the region's cultural centerpiece, **Lyon,** is France's "second city." In the French Alps, the ski resorts rival those of neighboring Switzerland and boast incredible scenery: snowcapped peaks, glaciers, and Alpine lakes. **Chamonix** is a famous ski resort facing **Mont Blanc,** western Europe's highest mountain. **Chambéry** is a sleepy but stunning base for exploring the area. And during the summer, the restful **Evian** is a peaceful spa resort. See chapter 14.

Smoke Out!

Take away one of the following iconic images of France, and a pillar of Frenchness would topple: a sexy brunette with a breast exposed; lovers kissing on the steps of the Paris Métro; and a moody dude with a cigarette hanging out of his mouth. Breasts and kissing look like they're here to stay (they don't cause cancer), but a new European law to abolish smoking in public places will hit the French especially hard. As of February 2007, smoking will be illegal in offices, universities, and railway stations. Cafes, bars, restaurants, and nightclubs will have until January 2008 to fully comply. Only time will tell how the French react: A frog without a fag is like a snail without the garlic butter; and for the nation that invented the *tabac* (a cafe-cum-bar that specifically sells tobacco), taking away the beloved right to smoke a cigarette wherever, whenever, is practically an infringement of the *Droits de l'Homme (Rights of Man)*. In the meantime, you globetrotting smokers will have plenty to talk about as you strike up a match and a conversation with a stranger—in the street.

Visitor Information

Tourist Offices

Before you go, your best source of information is the **French Government Tourist Office** (www.franceguide.com), which can be reached at the following addresses:

○ **United States:** 444 Madison Ave., 16th Floor, New York, NY 10022 (☎ **212/838-7800;** fax 212/838-7855); 205 N. Michigan Ave., Chicago, IL 60601 (☎ **514/288-1904**); or 9454 Wilshire Blvd., Suite 715, Beverly Hills, CA 90212 (☎ **310/271-6665**).

○ **Canada:** 1981 av. McGill College, Suite 490, Montréal, QC H3A 2W9 (☎ **514/288-2026;** fax 514/845-4868).

○ **United Kingdom:** 178 Piccadilly, London W1J 9AL (☎ **09068/244-123** [60p per min.]; fax 020/7493-6594).

○ **Australia & New Zealand:** 25 Blight St., Sydney, NSW 2000 (☎ **02/9231-5244;** fax 02/9221-8682).

Getting In & Out

Passports, Visas & Customs

All foreign (non-French) nationals need a valid passport to enter France. For an up-to-date country-by-country listing of passport requirements around the world, go to the "Foreign Entry Requirements" page of the U.S. State Department website at **http://travel.state.gov/foreignentryreqs.html**.

The French government no longer requires visas for **U.S. citizens** staying in France for less than 90 days. For longer stays, U.S. visitors must apply for a long-term visa, residence card, or temporary-stay visa. Applications are available from the **Consulate** section of the **French Embassy,** 4101 Reservoir Rd. NW, Washington, DC 20007 (☎ **202/944-6195;** www.consulfrance-washington.org), or from the visa section of the French Consulate at 934 Fifth Ave., New York, NY 10021 (☎ **212/606-3600;** www.consulfrance-newyork.org). Visas are required for students planning to study in France. (Also see "Study Abroad" and "Work Abroad" on p. 49.)

Citizens of **Australia, Britain, Canada, New Zealand, Switzerland, Japan,** and **European Union** countries do not need visas. **South Africans** do need visas. Contact the French Consulate, k78 Queen Victoria St. Gardens, Capetown (☎ **021-423-1575**). Residents of all other countries can check with the nearest French government tourist office.

BORDER CROSSINGS TO MONACO

Stay cool, kids. Tiny Monaco (2 sq. km/ $^3/_4$ sq. mile) is an independent nation, but document requirements for travel to Monaco are the same as those for France, and there are no border patrols or passport formalities. For information, contact the **Monaco Government Tourist and Convention Bureau,** 565 Fifth Ave., 23rd Floor, New York, NY 10017 (☎ **800/ 753-9696** or 212/286-3330; fax 212/286-9890; www.visitmonaco.com); or at The Chambers, Chelsea Harbour, London SW10 OXF (☎ **020/7352-9962;** fax 020/7352-2103).

Frommers.com

The Frommer's website (**www. frommers.com**) offers travel tips, reviews, monthly vacation give-aways, a bookstore, and online booking. The Frommers.com Newsletter posts the latest deals, travel trends, and money-saving secrets; our Community area has message boards, where Frommer's readers post queries and share advice. The Online Reservations System (www.frommers.com/book_a_trip) takes you to Frommer's pre-ferred online partners for booking.

What You Can Bring to France

Customs restrictions for visitors entering France differ for citizens of European Union (E.U.) and non-E.U. countries. Non-E.U. nationals can bring in duty-free 200 cigarettes, or 100 cigarillos, or 50 cigars, or 250 grams of smoking tobacco. This amount is doubled if you live outside Europe. You can also bring in 2 liters of wine and 1 liter of alcohol over 22 proof, and 2 liters of wine 22 proof or under. In addition, you can bring in 60cc of perfume, a quarter liter of eau de toilette, 250cc of coffee, and 200 grams of tea. Visitors age 15 and over can bring in other goods totaling 175€ ($228); for those under 15, the limit is 90€ ($117). Customs officials tend to be lenient about general merchandise, as the limits are very low.

Citizens of E.U. countries can bring in any amount of goods as long as the goods are intended for their personal use and not for resale.

What You Can Bring Home

U.S. CITIZENS

Returning U.S. citizens who have been away for 48 hours or more are allowed to bring back, once every 30 days, $800 worth of merchandise duty-free. You're charged a flat rate of duty on the next $1,000 worth of purchases, and any dollar amount beyond that is subject to duty at whatever rates apply. On mailed gifts, the duty-free limit is $200. Have your receipts or purchases handy to expedite the declaration process.

Note: If you owe duty, you are required to pay on your arrival in the United States, using cash, personal check, government or traveler's check, or money order; some locations also accept Visa or MasterCard.

To avoid having to pay duty on foreign-made personal items you owned before your trip, bring along a bill of sale, insurance policy, jeweler's appraisal, or receipt of purchase. Or you can register items that can be readily identified by a permanently affixed serial number or marking—think laptop computers, cameras, and CD players—with Customs before you leave. Take the items to the nearest Customs office, or register them with Customs at the airport from which you're departing. You'll receive, at no cost, a Certificate of Registration, which allows duty-free entry for the life of the item.

You cannot bring fresh foodstuffs into the U.S—so no fresh foie gras, cheese, or truffles, I'm afraid, but canned foods are allowed.

For specifics on what you can bring back and the corresponding fees, download the invaluable free pamphlet *Know Before You Go,* online at **www.cbp.gov.** (Click on "Travel," and then click on "Know Before You Go.") Or contact the **U.S. Customs & Border Protection (CBP),** 1300 Pennsylvania Ave. NW, Washington, DC 20229 (☎ **877/287-8667**) and request the pamphlet.

CANADIAN CITIZENS

Canada allows its citizens a C$750 exemption, and you're allowed to bring back duty-free 1 carton of cigarettes, 1 can of tobacco, 40 imperial ounces of liquor, and

In-Flight Security Measures

In the light of new terrorism controls, also check with your airline to see exactly what you can take on board the airplane. There is nothing worse than arriving at the airport and having to part with your beloved lipstick or fresh water just because you forgot to check.

50 cigars. In addition, you're allowed to mail gifts to Canada from abroad valued at less than C$60 a day, provided they're unsolicited and don't contain alcohol or tobacco (write on the package UNSOLICITED GIFT, UNDER C$60 VALUE). All valuables, including serial numbers of valuables you already own, such as expensive foreign cameras, should be declared on the Y-38 form before departure from Canada. *Note:* The C$750 exemption can only be used once a year after an absence of 7 days.

For a clear summary of Canadian rules, write for the booklet *I Declare,* issued by the **Canada Border Services Agency** (☎ **800/461-9999** in Canada, or 204/983-3500; www.cbsa-asfc.gc.ca).

U.K. CITIZENS

Citizens of the U.K. returning from an E.U. country such as France go through a Customs exit (called the "Blue Exit") especially for E.U. travelers. In essence, there is no limit on what you can bring back from an E.U. country, as long as the items are for personal use (this includes gifts) and you have already paid the duty and tax. However, Customs law sets out guidance levels. If you bring in more than these levels, you may be asked to prove that the goods are for your own use. Guidance levels on goods bought in the E.U. for your own use are 3,200 cigarettes, 200 cigars, 400 cigarillos, 3 kilograms of smoking tobacco, 10 liters of spirits, 90 liters of wine, 20 liters of fortified wine (such as port or sherry), and 110 liters of beer.

For information, contact **HM Customs & Excise** at ☎ **0845/010-9000** (from outside the U.K., 020/8929-0152), or consult their website at www.hmce.gov.uk.

AUSTRALIAN CITIZENS

The duty-free allowance in **Australia** is A$900 or, for those under 18, A$450.

Citizens can bring in 250 cigarettes or 250 grams of loose tobacco, and 2.25 liters of alcohol. If you're returning with valuables you already own, such as foreign-made cameras, you should file form B263.

A helpful brochure available from Australian consulates or Customs offices is *Know Before You Go*. For more information, call the **Australian Customs Service** at ☎ **1300/363-263,** or log on to www.customs.gov.au.

NEW ZEALAND CITIZENS

The duty-free allowance for **New Zealand** is $700. Citizens over 17 can bring in 200 cigarettes, 50 cigars, or 250 grams of tobacco (or a mixture of all three if their combined weight doesn't exceed 250 grams); plus 4.5 liters of wine and beer, or 1.125 liters of liquor. New Zealand currency does not carry import or export restrictions. Fill out a certificate of export, listing the valuables you are taking out of the country; that way, you can bring them back without paying duty.

Most questions are answered in a free pamphlet available at New Zealand consulates and Customs offices: *New Zealand Customs Guide for Travellers, Notice no. 4.* For more information, contact **New Zealand Customs,** The Customhouse, 17–21 Whitmore St., Box 2218, Wellington (☎ **04/473-6099** or 0800/428-786; www.customs.govt.nz).

Passport Savvy

Allow plenty of time before your trip to apply for a passport; processing can take up to 4 weeks, and even longer during busy periods (especially spring). When traveling around, guard your passport at all times. They're worth a hell of a lot of money on an international black market, and plenty of people out there would love to get their sticky mitts on yours. Keep it tucked away somewhere safe, and keep a separate photocopy of the pages with your photo and passport number. If you lose your passport, contact the nearest embassy as soon as possible.

Money, Money, Money, Money! (Money!)

While you don't need to be rolling in cash to enjoy France, it helps. France is a damned expensive destination, especially where food and drink are concerned. Part of the cost is the value-added tax (VAT in English, TVA in French), which adds between 6% and 33% to everything.

Rental cars (and fuel) are expensive, and flying within France costs more than within the U.S. Train travel is relatively inexpensive, especially with a rail pass. Prices in Paris and on the Riviera are higher than in the provinces, but things are catching up fast. Three of the most visited areas—**Brittany, Normandy,** and the **Loire Valley**—still have bargain hotels and restaurants offering superb food at moderate prices.

Currency

It's a good idea to exchange at least some money before you leave home—at least enough to cover airport incidentals and transportation to your hotel so you can avoid lines at airport ATMs. You can exchange money at your local American Express or Thomas Cook office or at your bank. If you're far away from a bank with currency-exchange services, try **American Express** (☎ **800/637-3782;** www.americanexpress.com) or **Thomas Cook** (☎ **800/223-7373;** www.thomas cook.com), which offer traveler's checks and foreign currency for a $15 order fee and additional shipping costs.

France's old currency, the franc, disappeared on March 1, 2002, and was replaced by the **euro,** whose official abbreviation is "EUR." Euro notes come in denominations of €5, €10, €20, €50, €100, €200, and €500. The euro is divided into 100 centimes; coins come in denominations of €2, €1, 50¢, 20¢, 10¢, 5¢, 2¢, and 1¢. Exchange rates of participating countries are locked into a common currency fluctuating against the dollar. Following are conversion rates that were accurate at the time of writing:

- ○ **U.S. dollar:** US$1 was worth approximately .76€.
- ○ **Canadian dollar:** C$1 equaled approximately .72€.
- ○ **British pound:** £1 equaled approximately 1.46€.

For up-to-the-minute conversion rates, visit **www.xe.com/ucc**. And for more about the euro, check out **www.europa. eu.int**.

ATMs & Credit Cards

The easiest and best way to get cash in France is from a *guiche automatique* (ATM or cashpoint), found in just about any French city or town. The **Cirrus** (☎ **800/424-7787;** www.mastercard.com) and **PLUS** (☎ **800/843-7587;** www.visa. com) networks span the globe; look at the back of your bank card to see which network you're on, then call or check online for ATM locations at your destination. *Note:* If your current PIN is more than four digits, change it to a four-digit (ideally numeric) code. Many European machines do not accept codes that are longer than four digits, and some may not have alphabetic equivalents noted on the keypad. *Also:* Remember that many banks impose a fee every time you use a card at another bank's ATM, and that fee can be higher for international transactions (up to $5 or more) than for domestic ones (where they're rarely more than $2). In addition, the bank from which you withdraw cash may charge its own fee. For international withdrawal fees, ask your bank.

Many places accept credit cards, although not all do. A stash of cash is always a good thing to keep on you, just in case.

When to Go

When it comes to visiting France, timing is everything. A visit to Louis XIV's château in July is about as pleasant as riding the subway during rush hour; go in October or May, on the other hand, and you'll at least have a little more elbowroom while you're checking yourself out in the trippy Galerie des Glaces (Hall of Mirrors). Either do as the locals do and avoid Paris in July and August, when many sites close for two weeks, or come during the summer months to avoid the Parisians; if you time your visit for the spring (Apr–June) or the fall (Sept–Nov), you'll avoid the crunch of the tourist season. Most people avoid the country between November and February, but if dreary, drizzly skies don't dampen your spirits, this time of year has its advantages, in that you'll probably be able to score cheaper airfare and lodgings.

France Calendar of Events

See individual chapters for additional events in each region.

January

Monte Carlo Motor Rally (Le Rallye de Monte Carlo). The world's most venerable car race. For information, call the

Monaco Tourist Office (☎ **377-92-16-61-66**) or the Rally Director (☎ **377-93-15-26-00**; www.acm.mc). See chapter 12. Usually mid-January.

February

Carnival of Nice. Parades, boat races, music, balls, and fireworks are all part of this celebration. The climax is the 114-year tradition of burning King Carnival in effigy, after Les Batailles des Fleurs (Battles of the Flowers), when teams pelt each other with blooms. For details, contact the Nice Convention and Visitors Bureau (☎ **08-92-70-74-07**; fax 04-92-16-85-16; www.nicecarnaval.com). See chapter 12. Late February to early March.

March

Foire du Trône. On the Reuilly Lawn of the Bois de Vincennes (12th arr., Paris), this mammoth amusement park operates daily from 2pm to midnight. Call ☎ **01-46-27-52-29** (www.foiredutrone.com). See chapter 3. End of March to end of May.

April

International Marathon of Paris. Runners from around the world compete. Call ☎ **01-41-33-15-68** or visit www.parismarathon.com. See chapter 3. Early April.

May

Antiques Show. The annual *Cinq Jours de l'Objet Extraordinaire* show features more than 100 galleries and antiques stores displaying their collections in seven streets on the Left Bank, Carré Rive Gauche, Paris. For information, call ☎ **01-42-60-70-10** (www.carrerivegauche.com). See chapter 3. Mid-May to early June.

Cannes Film Festival (Festival International du Film). Movie madness transforms this city into a media circus. Admission to the films in competition is by invitation only. Other films play 24 hours a day. Contact the Festival International du Film, 3 rue Amélie, 75007

Paris (☎ **01-53-59-61-00**; www.festival-cannes.org). Two weeks before the festival, its administration moves to the Palais des Festivals, esplanade Georges-Pompidou, 06400 Cannes. See chapter 12. Mid-May.

Monaco Grand Prix de Formule. Hundreds of cars race through the narrow streets and winding roads in a blend of high-tech machinery and medieval architecture. Call ☎ **377-93-15-26-00** or 377-92-16-61-66, or visit www.acm.mc. See chapter 12. Mid-May.

French Open Tennis Championship (Stade Roland-Garros, 16th arr., Paris; Métro: Porte d'Auteuil). The Open features 10 days of men's, women's, and doubles tennis on the hot, red, slow, dusty courts. For information, call ☎ **01-47-43-48-00** or visit www.fft.fr. See chapter 3. Late May to early June.

Roland Garros French Tennis Open. Come here to spot celebrities and watch the world's top seeds compete for glory at Stade Roland Garros (2 av. Gordon-Bennett, 16th arr.; ☎ **01-47-43-48-00**). Two weeks beginning last Sunday in May.

June

Prix du Jockey Club and **Prix Diane-Hermès,** Hippodrome de Chantilly. Thoroughbreds from as far away as Kentucky and Brunei compete in a race that's talked about in horsy circles around the world. On race days, dozens of trains depart from Paris's Gare du Nord for Chantilly, where racegoers take free shuttle buses to the track. Call ☎ **03-44-62-41-00** for information on these and other Chantilly events. See chapter 3. Early June.

Cinéscénie de Puy du Fou, *son-et-lumière,* Château du Puy du Fou, Les Epesses (La Vendée), Brittany. A cast of 2,500 actors, dozens of horses, and laser shows celebrate the achievements of the

Middle Ages. Call ☎ **02-51-64-11-11** or visit www.puydufou.com. See chapter 6. Early June to early September.

Festival de St-Denis. A surge of music in the burial place of the French kings, a grim early Gothic monument in Paris's northern suburb of St-Denis. Call ☎ **01-48-13-12-10** (www.festival-saint-denis.fr). See chapter 3. Early June to July.

Paris Air Show. France's military-industrial complex shows off its high-tech hardware. Fans, competitors, and industrial spies mob Le Bourget Airport. Call ☎ **01-53-23-33-34** or visit www.paris-air-show.com. See chapter 3. Mid-June in alternate years; next is mid-June 2007.

Fête de la Musique. This celebration of the summer solstice is the only day on which noise laws don't apply in Paris. Musicians and wannabes pour into the streets, where you can make music with anything, even if it means banging two garbage cans together. Musical parties pop up in virtually all open spaces. For details, call ☎ **01-40-03-94-70** or visit www.fetedelamusique.culture.fr. June 21.

Gay Pride Parade, place de la République to place de la Bastille, Paris. A week of expositions and parties climaxes in a parade patterned after those in New York and San Francisco, followed by a dance at the Palais de Bercy. For more information about gay pride and any other aspect of gay, lesbian, and transgendered life in and around Paris, contact Lesbian and Gay Pride Ile-de-France, 3 rue Keller, B.P. 255, 75524 Paris Cedex 11 (☎/fax **01-72-70-39-22;** www.inter-lgbt. org). See chapter 3. Late June.

July & August

Tour de France. Europe's most hotly contested bicycle race sends crews of wind-tunnel-tested athletes along an itinerary that detours deep into the Massif Central and ranges across the Alps. The finish line is on the Champs-Elysées. See chapter 15. Call ☎ **01-41-33-15-00** (www. letour.fr). First 3 weeks of July.

Colmar International Music Festival, Colmar. Classical concerts take place in public buildings in one of the most folkloric towns in Alsace. Call ☎ **03-89-20-68-97** (www.festival-colmar.com). First 2 weeks of July. See chapter 18.

Les Chorégies d'Orange, Orange. One of southern France's most important lyric festivals presents oratorios, operas, and choral works in France's best-preserved Roman amphitheater. Call ☎ **04-90-34-24-24** (www.choregies.asso.fr). See chapter 11. Early July to early August.

Fête Chopin, Paris. Everything you've ever wanted to hear by the Polish exile, who lived most of his life in Paris. Piano recitals take place in the Orangerie du Parc de Bagatelle, 16th arr. Call ☎ **01-45-00-22-19** (www.frederic-chopin.com). See chapter 3. Early July.

Les Nocturnes du Mont-St-Michel. This is a sound-and-light tour through the stairways and corridors of one of Europe's most impressive medieval monuments. Call ☎ **02-33-89-80-00** or check out www.monum.fr for more information. See chapter 5. Performances are Monday through Saturday evenings from early July to late August.

Festival d'Avignon. This world-class festival has a reputation for exposing new talent to critical scrutiny and acclaim. The focus is usually on avant-garde works in theater, dance, and music. Many of the dance and theater performances take place in either the 14th-century courtyard of the Palais des Pâpes or the medieval Cloître (Cloister) des Carmes. For information, call ☎ **04-90-27-66-50** (www.festival-avignon.com). See chapter 11. Last 3 weeks of July.

Bastille Day. Celebrating the birth of modern-day France, the nation's festivities reach their peak in Paris with street fairs, pageants, fireworks, and feasts. In Paris, the day begins with a parade down the Champs-Elysées and ends with fireworks at Montmartre. See chapter 3. July 14.

Paris Quartier d'Eté. For 4 weeks, music rules the Arènes de Lutèce and the Cour d'Honneur at the Sorbonne, both in the Quartier Latin. The dozen or so concerts are grander than the outdoorsy setting; they include performances by the Orchestre de Paris, the Orchestre National de France, and the Baroque Orchestra of the European Union. Call ☎ 01-44-94-98-00 (www.quartierdete.com). See chapter 3. Mid-July to mid-August.

Nice Jazz Festival. The most prestigious jazz festival in Europe. Concerts begin in the afternoon and go on until late at night (sometimes all night) on the Arènes de Cimiez, a hill above the city. Contact the Grand Parade du Jazz, Cultural Affairs Department of the city of Nice (☎ 04-92-14-46-46; www.nicejazzfest.com). See chapter 12. Mid-July.

Cinéma en Plein Air, Paris. Classic movies are projected onto Europe's biggest inflatable screen every day (except Mon) from mid-July to the end of August at Parc de la Villette, 19th arr. (☎ 01-40-02-75-75; www.villette.com; Métro: Porte de Pantin). Pack a picnic, rent a deck chair and blankets, and watch the stars appear in the sky over the screen. How romantic! Mid-July to late August.

Festival d'Aix-en-Provence. A musical event par excellence, with everything from Gregorian chant to melodies composed on synthesizers. Recitals are in the medieval cloister of the Cathédrale St-Sauveur. Expect heat, crowds, and traffic. Contact the Festival International d'Art

cheap Tickets

Global Tickets secures passes to many of the musical and theatrical events at the Avignon festival as well as other cultural happenings throughout France. You'll pay a hefty fee (as much as 20%) for the convenience. Contact Global at 234 W. 44th St., Suite 1000, New York, NY 10036 (☎ **800/669-8687;** www. keithprowse.com).

Lyrique et Académie Européenne de Musique (☎ **04-42-17-34-34;** www. festival-aix.com). See chapter 11. Month of July.

St-Guilhem Music Season, St-Guilhem le Désert, near Montpellier, Languedoc. A monastery hosts this festival of baroque organ and choral music. Call ☎ **04-67-57-44-33** (www.saint-guilhem-le-desert.com). See chapter 9. Month of July.

Festival Interceltique de Lorient, Brittany. Celtic verse and lore are celebrated in the Celtic heart of France. The 150 concerts include classical and folkloric musicians, dancers, singers, and painters. Traditional Breton *pardons* (religious processions) take place in the once-independent maritime duchy. Call ☎ **02-97-21-24-29** or check www.festival-interceltique. com. See chapter 6. Early August.

Festival International de Folklore et Fête de la Vigne (Les Folkloriades), Dijon, Beaune, and about 20 villages of the Côte d'Or. At the International Festival of Folklore and Wine in Dijon, dance troupes from around the world perform and participate in folkloric events in celebration of the wines of Burgundy. Contact the Festival de Musique et Danse Populares (☎ **03-80-30-37-95**). See chapter 16. Late August to early September.

THE BASICS

Rock en Seine, Paris. This annual rock fest in the riverside parkland of the Domaine National de St-Cloud attracts over 50,000 fans with cool lineups such as the White Stripes and the Chemical Brothers. Tickets cost around 40€ for a day, 65€ a weekend. Visit www.rocken seine.com for info. Late August.

September

La Villette Jazz Festival. Some 50 concerts are held in churches, auditoriums, and concert halls in the Paris suburb of La Villette. Past festivals have included Herbie Hancock, Shirley Horn, and other international artists. Call ☎ 01-40-03-75-75 (www.villette.com). See chapter 3. Early to mid-September.

Rendez-Vous Electroniques Festival. A highlight of this 10-day electronic festival featuring techno concerts and art expositions is the **Paris Techno Parade.** Visit www.techopol.net for details. Early September.

Festival d'Automne, Paris. One of France's most famous festivals is one of its most eclectic, focusing mainly on modern music, ballet, theater, and art. Contact the Festival d'Automne (☎ 01-53-45-17-00; www.festival-automne.com). See chapter 3. Mid-September to late December.

Paris Auto Show, Parc des Expositions, Porte de Versailles, 15th arr., Paris. This is the showcase for European car design, complete with glistening metal, glitzy attendees, lots of hype, and the latest models. Check *Pariscope* for details; contact the French Government Tourist Office (see "Visitor Information," earlier in this chapter); call ☎ 01-56-88-22-40; or visit www.mondial-automobile.com. See chapter 3. Late September to mid-October.

October

Perpignan Jazz Festival. Musicians from everywhere jam in what many consider Languedoc's most appealing season. Call ☎ 04-68-35-37-46 (www.jazzebre.com). See chapter 9. Month of October.

Prix de l'Arc de Triomphe, Hippodrome de Longchamp, 16th arr., Paris (☎ 01-49-20-30; www.france-galop.com). France's answer to England's Ascot is the country's most prestigious horse race, culminating the equine season in Europe. See chapter 3. Early October.

November

Armistice Day, nationwide. In Paris, the signing of the document that ended World War I is celebrated with a military parade from the Arc de Triomphe to the Hôtel des Invalides. See chapter 3. November 11.

Les Trois Glorieuses, Clos-de-Vougeot, Beaune, and Meursault. Three Burgundian towns stage the country's most important wine festival. You may not gain access to many of the gatherings, but tastings and other amusements will keep you occupied. Reserve early, or visit as day trips from nearby villages. Contact the Office de Tourisme de Beaune (☎ 02-23-35-58-57; www.beaune.tctourisme.com). See chapter 16. Third week in November.

Beaujoulais Nouveau. November is a traditionally calm month for France—except for the release day of this special type of wine that is best sipped when it is young. Every year, various specials and festivities in bars and restaurants revolve around this festive wine. Connoisseurs compare it with previous years' harvests, and the non-connoisseurs just sip it down and refill all night long. Third Thursday in November.

December

Christmas Fairs, Alsace (especially Strasbourg). More than 60 villages celebrate a traditional Christmas. The events in Strasbourg have continued for some 430 years. Other towns with celebrations are Munster, Sélestat, Riquewihr, Kaysersberg, Wissembourg, and Thann. Call ☏ **03-89-24-73-50** (www.tourism-alsace.com). See chapter 18. Late November to December 24.

The Boat Fair (Le Salon Nautique de Paris). Europe's major exposition of what's afloat, at Parc des Expositions, Porte de Versailles, 15th arr., Paris (☏ **01-41-90-47-22;** www.salonnautiqueparis.com; Métro: Porte de Versailles). See chapter 3. Ten days in early December.

Fête des Lumières, Lyon. In honor of the Virgin Mary, lights are placed in windows through the city. Call ☏ **04-72-07-97-18** (www.lyon.fr). See chapter 14. Early December through early January.

Marché de Noël, Mougins. About 40 merchants, selling all kinds of Christmas ornaments and gifts, descend on this small village in Provence. Call ☏ **04-93-75-87-67** (www.mougins-coteazur.org). See chapter 11. Early December.

Fête de St-Sylvestre (New Year's Eve), nationwide. In Paris, it's most boisterously celebrated in the Quartier Latin. At midnight, the city explodes. Strangers kiss and boulevard St-Michel and the Champs-Elysées become virtual pedestrian malls. See chapter 3. December 31.

Weather

France's weather varies from region to region and even from town to town. Despite its latitude, Paris never gets very cold—snow is rare. The hands-down winner for wetness is Brittany. Brest (known for the mold—probably caused by the constant damp—that adds flavor to its bleu cheeses) receives a staggering amount of rain between October and December. Rain usually falls in a steady, foggy drizzle and rarely lasts more than a day. May is the driest month.

The Mediterranean coast in the south has the driest climate. When it does rain, it's heaviest in spring and autumn. (Cannes sometimes receives more rainfall than Paris.) Summers are comfortably dry—beneficial to humans but deadly to vegetation, which (unless it's irrigated) often dries and burns up in the parched months.

Provence dreads *le mistral* (an unrelenting, hot wind), which most often blows in the winter for a few days but can last for up to 2 weeks.

THE BASICS

Paris's Average Daytime Temperature & Rainfall

	Jan	Feb	Mar	Apr	May	June	July	Aug	Sept	Oct	Nov	Dec
Temp. °F	38	39	46	51	58	64	66	66	61	53	45	40
Temp. °C	3	4	8	11	14	18	19	19	16	12	7	4
Rainfall (in.)	3.2	2.9	2.4	2.7	3.2	3.5	3.3	3.7	3.3	3.0	3.5	3.1

Holidays

In France, holidays are called *jours fériés.* Shops and many businesses (banks, some museums, some restaurants) close on holidays, but hotels and emergency services remain open.

The main holidays include New Year's Day (Jan 1), Easter Sunday and Monday, Labor Day (May 1), V-E Day (May 8), Whitmonday (May 19), Ascension Thursday (40 days after Easter), Bastille Day (July 14), Assumption of the Blessed Virgin (Aug 15), All Saints' Day (Nov 1), Armistice Day (Nov 11), and Christmas (Dec 25).

Health & Insurance

Travel Insurance

France is far from home for most of us. Given the number of things that can go wrong while you're on the road—think lost luggage, stolen passports, medical emergencies, you know—you might want to consider insurance. It's especially useful if you're prone to losing your wallet, missing flights or trains, or forgetting things. Prices vary widely, but expect to pay between 5% and 8% of the trip itself. You can get estimates from various providers through **InsureMyTrip.com.** Enter your trip cost and dates, your age, and other information for prices from more than a dozen companies.

You can also directly contact one of the following recommended insurers:

- **Access America** (☎ 866/807-3982; www.accessamerica.com)
- **Travel Guard International** (☎ 800/826-4919; www.travelguard.com)
- **Travel Insured International** (☎ 800/243-3174; www.travelinsured.com)
- **Travelex Insurance Services** (☎ 888/457-4602; www.travelex-insurance.com)

Medical Insurance

Most U.S. health plans cover you if you get sick away from home, but check—especially if you're insured by an HMO. Most out-of-country hospitals make you pay your bills up front and reimburse you only after you return home and file the paperwork. If you don't have insurance at home, you might want to try one of the following companies for your trip:

- **MEDEX Assistance** (☎ 410/453-6300; www.medexassist.com)
- **Travel Assistance International** (☎ 800/821-2828; www.travel assistance.com; for general information on services, call the company's Worldwide Assistance Services, Inc., at ☎ 800/777-8710)

Health

France is generally a low-risk country to visit: You don't need shots, food is safe, and you can drink the water. It's easy to get a prescription filled, and most destinations have English-speaking doctors at hospitals with well-trained staffs. If you're still concerned, check with one of the following government websites before you go.

- **Australia:** www.dfat.gov.au/travel
- **Canada:** www.hc-sc.gc.ca/index_e.html

Paris or Bust

Airlines go bankrupt, so protect yourself by **buying your tickets with a credit card.** The Fair Credit Billing Act guarantees that you can get your money back from the credit card company if a travel supplier goes under (and if you request the refund within 60 days of the bankruptcy). **Travel insurance** can also help, but make sure it covers against "carrier default" for your specific travel provider. Know that if a U.S. airline goes bust mid-trip, a 2001 federal law requires other carriers to take you to your destination (on a space-available basis) for a fee of no more than $25, provided you rebook within 60 days of the cancellation.

○ **U.K.:** www.dh.gov.uk/PolicyAnd Guidance/HealthAdviceForTravellers/ fs/en

○ **U.S.:** www.cdc.gov/travel

SICK AWAY FROM HOME?

Don't sweat . . . unless you have a fever. Any foreign consulate can provide a list of doctors in the area who speak English. If you get sick, consider asking your hotel concierge to recommend a local doctor—even his or her own. You can also try the emergency room at a local hospital. Many hospitals also have walk-in clinics for emergency cases that are not life-threatening; you may not get immediate attention, but you won't pay the high price of an emergency room visit.

If you have a chronic disease, consult your doctor before your leave. Pack **prescription medications** in your carry-on luggage, and carry them in their original containers, with pharmacy labels—otherwise they won't make it through airport security. Carry the generic name of prescription medicines, in case a local pharmacist is unfamiliar with the brand name.

Safety & Scams

France is a pretty safe country, but use common sense. If you're traveling by car, never leave valuables inside, and never travel with your car unlocked. Don't leave valuables in your room or carry big wads of cash. Keep your money on you in a safe place that's tough for anyone else to access. The most common problem, especially in big cities, is pickpockets and/or gangs of Gypsy kids who surround you, distract you, and steal your purse or wallet. If someone steals your credit cards, call your credit card company right away to report the loss. Here is a list of numbers to call from within France:

○ **American Express (U.S.):** ☎ 08-00-90-08-98
○ **American Express (other countries):** ☎ 01-47-77-72-00
○ **American Express traveler's checks:** ☎ 08-00-90-86-00
○ **Checkbooks:** ☎ 08-92-68-32-08
○ **Diner's Club:** ☎ 08-00-22-20-73
○ **Eurocard/MasterCard:** ☎ 08-00-90-23-90
○ **MasterCard:** ☎ 08-00-90-23-90
○ **JCB:** ☎ 08-00-05-81-11
○ **Visa:** ☎ 08-00-90-20-33

Getting Wired

Nowadays it's hard to find a city of any size that *doesn't* have a cybercafe, and there are plenty all over the Hexagon. Even in very isolated villages, the occasional entrepreneur has added a few computer terminals to a cafe or bar. Most youth hostels and hotels have at least one computer with Internet access, although you might have to pay to use it.

If you've got your laptop with you, you'll soon find that Wi-Fi (wireless fidelity) is not nearly as widespread in France as it is in the U.S. In fact, it's still relatively rare to come across hotels that offer it, and virtually no coffee shops outside of inner-city Starbucks do at this time. Most business-class hotels do have dataports for laptop modems, and quite a few offer high-speed Internet access if you have an Ethernet cable.

Wherever you go, bring a connection kit of the right power, and phone adapters, a spare phone cord, and a spare Ethernet network cable—or find out whether your

Cellphones Abroad

The three letters you want to hear your cellphone company say to you are GSM (Global System for Mobiles). That is the big, seamless network that makes for easy cross-border cellphone use throughout Europe and dozens of other countries worldwide. If your cellphone is on a GSM system, and you have a world-capable multiband phone, you can make and receive calls across the globe. Just call your wireless operator and ask for "international roaming" to be activated on your account, and you're underway. Unfortunately, international roaming charges can be astronomical—usually $1 to $1.50 per minute.

If you're going to be in France for a long time, consider buying an "unlocked" world phone, or just have your own phone unlocked ("locked" phones restrict you from using any other SIM cards than the one your phone company supplies). If your phone is unlocked, you can buy and use a cheap, prepaid SIM card from local cellphone shops in France. You'll get a local phone number—and much lower calling rates.

hotel supplies them to guests. You might want to purchase a phone cord converter at the airport, so you can plug your phone cable into the wall using the two-pronged French plug, which differs from the U.S., U.K., and Canadian phone plugs.

Getting There

By Air

The two Paris airports—**Orly** (airport code: ORY) and **Charles de Gaulle** (airport code: CDG)—are about even in terms of convenience to the city's center, though taxi rides from Orly may take less time than those from de Gaulle. Orly, the older of the two, is 13km (8 miles) south of the center; Charles de Gaulle is 22km (14 miles) northeast. Air France serves Charles de Gaulle (Terminal 2C) from North America. U.S. carriers land at both airports.

Most airlines charge their lowest fares between November 1 and March 13. Shoulder season (Oct and mid-Mar to mid-June) is a bit more expensive, though we think it's the ideal time to visit France.

AIRLINES INTO FRANCE

American Airlines (☎ 800/433-7300; www.aa.com) has daily flights to Paris from Dallas/Fort Worth, Chicago, Miami, Boston, and New York.

British Airways (☎ 800/AIRWAYS; www.britishairways.com) runs flights from 18 U.S. cities to Heathrow and Gatwick airports in England. From there, you can book a British Airways flight to Paris.

Continental Airlines (☎ 800/525-0280; www.continental.com) flies non-stop to Paris from Newark and Houston. Flights from Newark depart daily; flights from Houston depart four to seven times a week, depending on the season.

Delta Air Lines (☎ 800/241-4141; www.delta.com) flies nonstop from Atlanta to Paris every evening and runs daily nonstop flights from Cincinnati and New York. Delta is the only airline offering nonstop service from New York to Nice.

US Airways (☎ 800/428-4322; www. usairways.com) offers daily nonstop service from Philadelphia to Paris.

Air France (☎ 800/237-2747; www.airfrance.com) offers flights daily or several times a week between Paris and Atlanta, Boston, Chicago, Cincinnati, Houston, Los Angeles, Mexico City, Miami, Montréal, New York, Newark, San Francisco, Toronto, and Washington, D.C.

In 2004, Air France bought KLM Royal Dutch Airlines, which led to the creation of **Air France-KLM,** the world's biggest airline in terms of revenue. KLM and Air France have coordinated their schedules and fares to act as a unit. The merger has led to better connections between flights.

FLIGHTS FROM AUSTRALIA & NEW ZEALAND Getting to Paris from Australia is tough, because **Air France** (☎ 02-92-44-21-00; www.airfrance.fr) has discontinued direct flights. Qantas flies from Sydney to Singapore and other locations with service to Paris. Consequently, on virtually any route, you have to change planes at least once and sometimes twice. **British Airways** (☎ 1300-767-177; www.britishairways.com) flies daily from Sydney and Melbourne to London in time for several connecting flights to Paris. **Qantas** (☎ 612/13-13-13; www.qantas.com.au) can route passengers from Australia into London, where you make connections for the hop across the Channel. Qantas also flies from Auckland to Sydney and on to London.

FOR STUDENTS

STA Travel is now the world's leader in student travel. **ELTExpress** (☎ 800/TRAV-800; www.eltexpress.com) has excellent fares to Europe.

Getting There from Europe

BY AIR

From London, **Air France** (☎ 0870/142-4343; www.airfrance.com) and **British Airways** (☎ 0870/850-9850 in the U.K.;

Online Travel Tools

Surfing for Airfare

The most popular online travel agencies are **Travelocity** (**www.travelocity.com**, or www.travelocity.co.uk); **Expedia** (**www.expedia.com**, www.expedia.co.uk, or www.expedia.ca); and **Orbitz** (**www.orbitz.com**). Other helpful websites for booking cheap airline tickets online include:

- → www.biddingfortravel.com
- → www.cheapflights.com
- → www.hotwire.com
- → www.kayak.com
- → www.lastminutetravel.com
- → www.opodo.co.uk
- → www.priceline.com
- → www.sidestep.com
- → www.site59.com
- → www.smartertravel.com

Blogs & Travelogues

To search for blogs about France, check out these sites:

- → www.gridskipper.com
- → www.salon.com/wanderlust
- → www.travelblog.com
- → www.travelblog.org
- → www.worldhum.com
- → www.writtenroad.com

THE BASICS

www.ba.com) fly frequently to Paris; the trip takes 1 hour. These airlines operate up to 17 flights daily from Heathrow. Many travelers also fly out of the London City Airport in the Docklands.

Direct flights to Paris operate from other U.K. cities such as Manchester and Edinburgh. Contact Air France, British Airways, or **British Midland** (☎ 0870/607-0555; www.flybmi.com). Daily papers often carry ads for cheap flights. Highly recommended **Trailfinders** (☎ **0845/058-5858;** www.trailfinders.com) sells discount fares.

You can reach Paris from any major European capital. Your best bet is to fly on the national carrier, Air France, which has more connections into Paris from European capitals than any other airline. From Dublin, try **Aer Lingus** (☎ **800-IRISH-AIR;** www.aerlingus.com), which schedules the most flights to Paris from Ireland. From Amsterdam, try **NWA/KLM** (☎ **800/447-4747;** www.nwa.com).

BY TRAIN

Paris is one of Europe's busiest rail junctions, with trains arriving at and departing from its many stations every few minutes. If you're in Europe, you may want to go to Paris by train. The cost is relatively low—especially compared to renting a car.

Rail passes as well as individual rail tickets are available at most travel agencies or at any office of **Rail Europe** (☎ **877/272-RAIL** in the U.S.; www.raileurope.com) or **Eurostar** (☎ **800/EUROSTAR** in the U.S.; www.eurostar.com) see below.

BY BUS

Bus travel to Paris is available from London as well as many cities on the Continent. In the early 1990s, the French government established incentives for long-haul buses not to drive into the center of Paris. The arrival and departure point for Europe's largest operator, **Eurolines France,** 28 av. du Général-de-Gaulle, 93541 Bagnolet (☎ **01-49-72-51-52;** www.eurolines.fr), is a 25-minute Métro ride from central Paris, at the terminus of line no. 3 (Métro: Gallieni), in the eastern suburb of Bagnolet. Despite this minor inconvenience, many people prefer bus travel.

Long-haul buses are equipped with toilets, and they stop at mealtimes for rest and refreshment.

Because Eurolines does not have a U.S. sales agent, most people buy their ticket in Europe. Any European travel agent can arrange the sale. If you're traveling to Paris from London, contact **Eurolines (U.K.) Ltd.,** 52 Grosvenor Gardens, Victoria, London SW1 0AU (☎ **0870/514-3219;** www.nationalexpress.com for information or credit card sales).

BY CAR

The major highways into Paris are A1 from the north (Great Britain and Benelux); A13 from Rouen, Normandy, and northwest France; A10 from Bordeaux, the Pyrenees, the southwest, and Spain; A6 from Lyon, the French Alps, the Riviera, and Italy; and A4 from Metz, Nancy, and Strasbourg in the east.

BY FERRY FROM ENGLAND

Ferries and hydrofoils operate day and night, with the exception of last-minute cancellations during storms. Many crossings are timed to coincide with the arrival and departure of trains (especially those between London and Paris). Trains let you off a short walk from the piers. Most ferries carry cars, trucks, and freight, but some hydrofoils take passengers only. The major routes include at least 12 trips a day between Dover or Folkestone and Calais or Boulogne.

Hovercraft and hydrofoils make the trip from Dover to Calais, the shortest distance across the Channel, in just 40 minutes during good weather. The ferries may take several hours, depending on the weather and tides. If you're bringing a car, it's important to make reservations—space below decks is usually crowded. Timetables can vary depending on weather conditions and many other factors.

The leading operator of ferries across the channel is **P&O Ferries** (☎ **0870/598-0333** in the U.K.; www.poferries.com). It operates car and passenger ferries between Portsmouth, England, and Cherbourg, France (three departures a day; 4¼ hr. each way during daylight hours, 7 hr. each way at night); and between Portsmouth and Le Havre, France (three a day; 5½ hr. each way). Most popular is the route between Dover, England, and Calais, France (25 sailings a day; 1¼ hr. each way), with a one-way fare of about £18 ($32), free for children under 4.

THE CHUNNEL

Queen Elizabeth II and the late French president François Mitterrand opened the Channel Tunnel (Chunnel) in 1994, and the **Eurostar** has daily passenger service from London to Paris and Brussels. The $15-billion tunnel, one of the great engineering feats of our time, is the first link between Britain and the Continent since the Ice Age. The 50km (31-mile) journey takes 35 minutes, including 19 minutes in the Chunnel.

Eurostar tickets are available through **Rail Europe** (☎ **877/272-RAIL;** www.raileurope.com). In London, make reservations for Eurostar (or any other train in Europe) at ☎ **0870/518-6186.** In Paris, call ☎ **01-70-70-60-88,** and in the United States, call ☎ **800/EUROSTAR;** www.eurostar.com. Chunnel train traffic is competitive with air travel, if you calculate door-to-door travel time. Trains leave from London's Waterloo Station and arrive in Paris at Gare du Nord. The one-way passenger fare between London and Paris averages $150 second class, $375 first class.

Fares are complicated and depend on a number of factors. The cheapest one-way fare is Leisure RT, requiring a purchase at least 14 business days before the date of travel and a minimum 2-night stay. A return ticket must be booked to receive this discounted fare.

The Chunnel accommodates not only trains but also cars, buses, taxis, and motorcycles. Prices start at 80€ ($104) each way for a small car. **Eurotunnel,** a train carrying vehicles under the Channel (☎ **0870/535-3535** in the U.K.; www.eurotunnel.com), connects Calais, France, with Folkestone, England. It operates 24 hours a day, 365 days a year, running every 15 minutes during peak travel times and at least once an hour at night.

Before boarding Eurotunnel, you stop at a booth to show your ticket, and then pass through Immigration for both countries at one time. During the ride, you travel in air-conditioned carriages, remaining in your car or stepping outside to stretch your legs. Less than an hour later, you simply drive off.

THE BASICS

Staying in France: Tips on Lodgings

France is very accustomed to tourists, so you shouldn't have problems finding accommodations to suit your budget, even in some of the remotest areas. The cheapest and most obvious choice is youth hostels. They tend to be clean, well-maintained, and set in very pretty spots. The French government rates hotels on a one-to four-star system. One-star hotels are definitely budget, but not always as horrible as you'd imagine; two-star lodgings are quality tourist hotels; three stars go to first-class hotels; and four stars are reserved for deluxe accommodations. In some of the lower categories, the rooms may not have private bathrooms; instead, many have what the French call a *cabinet de toilette* (hot and cold running water and maybe a bidet, see below). In such hotels, bathrooms are down the hall. Nearly all hotels in France have central heating, but not all have air-conditioning. Our selections generally do, but if you can't possibly survive without it, always check upon reservation. Most rooms are priced per room and not per person, which can make bunking up with a few mates as cheap as a youth hostel. If you're traveling with friends, you could also consider saving money by renting a *gîte* (cottage) an apartment, or by camping.

Youth Hostels

A youth hostel in French is an *auberge de jeunesse*, run by an organization called **FUAJ** (Fédération Unie des Auberges de Jeunesse, 27 rue Pajol, Paris 75018; ☎ 01-44-89-87-27; www.fuaj.org), affiliated with **Hostelling International** (www.hihostels.com). FUAJ ensures that standards are kept up to snuff, so staying in one of their establishments is usually a guarantee of quality. You'll need to buy a membership card from the hostel, however, or from Hostelling International. Hostels in France often have links with local activity centers and can offer cycling, walking, canoeing, horseback riding, skiing, or snow-boarding activities. Most tourist offices can give you the FUAJ guidebook that lists all affiliated hostels around France. If you're already a surfing dude, or you fancy hanging out with a few, try **Ze-Bus** (www.ze-bus.com), a hop-on hop-off bus service designed for independent travelers and backpackers in FUAJ youth hostels, covering surf spots and some of the best historical sites. Check their site for more details.

Self-Catering D.I.Y.

If you can stay for at least a week and don't mind doing your own cooking and cleaning, you may want to rent long-term accommodations. The local French Tourist

Back on the Chain Gang

Okay, so they take the charm and the fun out of sleeping in a foreign country, but a last resort is a last resort, and chain hotels do have a habit of being there when you need them most. If you must resort to a franchise, consider the **Mercure** chain, an organization of moderately priced, modern hotels throughout France. Even at the peak of the tourist season, a room at a Mercure in Paris rents for as little as 80€ ($104) per night. For more information on Mercure hotels and its 100-page directory, call **Accor** (☎ 800/221-4542 in the U.S.; www.mercure.com). **Formule 1** hotels, which tend to group around highways, offer basic but safe rooms for up to three people from around 29€ ($38) per night. Built from prefabricated units, these air-conditioned, soundproof hotels are shipped to a site and assembled, often on the outskirts of cities such as Paris (27 in the suburbs). There are 150 of these throughout the rest of France. Formule 1's low cost makes it unprofitable for the chain to allow customers to reserve rooms from the United States, so you'll have to reserve upon arrival. For a directory, call ☎ 01-69-36-75-00 (www.hotelformule1.com). Other worthwhile economy bets, sometimes with a bit more charm, are the hotels and restaurants of the **Fédération Nationale des Logis de France,** 83 av. d'Italie, 75013 Paris (☎ 01-45-84-83-84; www.logis-de-france.fr). This is an association of 3,000 hotels, usually country inns convenient for motorists, most rated one or two stars. The association publishes an annual directory.

Board might help you obtain a list of agencies that offer this type of rental (which is popular at ski resorts).

For apartment, farmhouse, or cottage stays of 2 weeks or more, **Idyll Untours** (☎ **888-868-6871**; www.untours.com) provides exceptional vacation rentals for a reasonable price—which includes air/ground transportation, cooking facilities, and on-call support from a local resident. Best of all: Untours—named the "Most Generous Company in America" by Newman's Own—donates most profits toward low-interest loans for underprivileged entrepreneurs around the world.

NYHabitat (☎ **212-255-8018**; www.ny habitat.com) brokers sublets in Paris and the south of France (mostly Provence). Properties range from Left Bank studio efficiencies to villas on the Côte d'Azur, with a broad range of prices and rental periods to match (most places rent by the week, but daily and monthly sublets are also available for certain sites). The website includes photographs of all the properties, many of which have cooking facilities and washing machines. They can make for extremely affordable lodgings—especially when you factor in the money you'll save by preparing your own meals. Most of the agents are French, but they're based in New York, which makes transactions particularly easy for North American travelers.

Gîtes de France (59 rue St-Lazare, Paris 75009; ☎ **01-49-70-75-75**; info@gites-de-france.fr; www.gites-de-france.fr) is also one of the best, offering charming villas, cottages, and B&Bs (some with cooking facilities) at a wide range of prices. Dreaming of a quaint cottage or château with a garden, pool, and views to die for? British-based **Alastair Sawdays** (www.sawdays.co.uk) lists some of the most rewarding and beautiful places to rent and B&Bs in France for all budgets. Also, for B&B, apartment, and hotel bookings,

surfing for Hotels

In addition to **Travelocity, Expedia, Orbitz, Priceline,** and **Hotwire,** the following websites will help you with booking hotel rooms online. Just be sure to **get a confirmation number** and **make a printout** of any online booking transaction.

→ www.hotels.com
→ www.quickbook.com;
→ www.travelaxe.net
→ www.travelweb.com
→ www.tripadvisor.com

particularly in Paris, check out **www.venere.com**.

CyberRentals is a worldwide vacation rental website (☎ **512/684-1098**; www.cyberrentals.com) that lists vacation homes, condos, luxury villas, cabins, chalets, and other real estate available for rent by owner.

If you want to rent an apartment in Paris, the **Barclay International Group,** 6800 Jericho Turnpike, Syosset, NY 11791 (☎ **800/845-6636** or 516/364-0064; fax 516/364-4468; www.barclayweb.com), will give you access to about 3,000 apartments and villas throughout Paris (and 39 other cities in France), ranging from modest modern units to the most stylish lodgings. Units rent for 1 night to 6 months; all have TVs and kitchenettes; and many have concierge staffs and lobby-level security. The least expensive cost around $89 per night, double occupancy. Discounts are given for a stay of 1 week or longer. Rentals must be prepaid in U.S. dollars or with a U.S. credit or charge card.

If you can't afford to rent, but you've got a great place back home, you could opt for a **flat exchange.** One good site is http://intervac-online.com. For the occasional

THE BASICS

Baffling Bidets

You've just entered your hotel room, and you're desperate for a wee, but there are *two* toilet-like contraptions in the bathroom. Which one do you baptize? What if you make the wrong choice? And how are you supposed to hover over the wider one with a strange tap in the middle? Well, go relieve yourself in the normal toilet, and then I have three words for you: *"Bidet, bidet, bidet!"* Historically, the French word *bidet* means "pony," and probably derives from the fact that you sit astride a bidet as you would a pony (minus the whip and spurs, we hope, but to each his own). Invented in the late 17th century by an unknown furniture maker, for cleaning your genitalia and anus after toileting, they became a favorite addition to Royal bathrooms; then the aristocratic habit caught on, and fanny flushing has remained a permanent fixture in French toilet etiquette ever since. Some people boast that it is cleaner than using toilet paper (yikes). Others use toilet paper and then pamper their privates over the *bidet.* But it's also a great way to wash feet, bathe babies, and rinse underwear. Strangely enough, even though they're a French invention, *bidets* are not that common in French homes; you'll probably come across them only in hotel rooms.

swap check out www.parisnet.net, and www.switchome.org.

Hotels & B&Bs

Here as everywhere, hotels and B&Bs vary wildly. The spectacularly expensive ones will answer your every desire. They have slamming nightclubs, luscious spas, and amazing restaurants. If money is an object, however, you could land in some grim, run-down, chintzy, cheap place, where particle board seems to be the only kind of wood. You could equally land on a gem, but it is so hard to tell. We're brutally honest in this guide and try to steer you away from the money pits. As a general rule, though, if you're on a budget, B&Bs, campsites, and youth hostels are better options than very cheap hotels.

Getting Around France

By Air

Rail travel is so good here that you probably won't be taking off between cities, and France has few domestic competitors. **Air France** (☎ **800/237-2747**; www.airfrance.com) is the 800-pound gorilla, serving about eight French cities. Air travel time from Paris to almost anywhere in France is about an hour.

By Train

The world's fastest trains (TGVs, Trains de Grands Vitesse) link some 50 French cities, allowing you to get from Paris to just about anywhere else in the country in hours. With 39,000km (24,200 miles) of track and about 3,000 stations, **SNCF** (French National Railroads) is fabled for its on-time performance. You can travel in first or second class by day and in couchette by night. Most trains have dining facilities, but it's cheaper to take food with you.

In the United States: For more information and to purchase rail passes before you leave, contact **Rail Europe** (☎ **877/272-RAIL;** www.raileurope.com).

In Canada: Call Rail Europe at ☎ **800/361-RAIL.**

In London: SNCF has offices at Rail Europe, 179 Piccadilly, London W1V 0BA (☎ **0870/584-8848**).

In France: Tickets can be bought online from www.sncf.com; for information, call ☎ 36-35. If you know exactly where you want to go and read French, a simpler way to buy tickets is to use the *Billetterie Automatique* (ticket machine) in every train station. If you know your PIN, you can use a credit card to buy your ticket.

FRANCE RAIL PASSES

Working cooperatively with SNCF, Air Inter Europe, and Avis, **Rail Europe** offers three flexible rail passes that can reduce travel costs considerably.

The **France Railpass** provides unlimited rail transport in France for any 4 days within 1 month, at $269 in first class and $229 in second. You can purchase up to 6 more days for an extra $35 per person per day.

The **France Rail 'n' Drive Pass,** available only in North America, combines good value on both rail travel and Avis car rentals. It is best used by arriving at a major rail depot, then striking out to explore the countryside by car. It includes the France Railpass (see above) and use of a rental car. A 4-day rail pass (first class) and 2 days' use of the cheapest rental car (with unlimited mileage) is $265 per person (for two people traveling together).

The best deal if you're traveling in France with a friend—or even three or four friends—is the **France Saverpass,** granting 4 days of unlimited travel in a 1-month period. The cost is $230 per person first class or $195 second class. There's also a **France Youthpass** for travelers 25 or under, granting 4 days of unlimited train travel within a month. The cost is $199 in first class or $169 in second class.

By Bus

France's rail system is so efficient and high quality that bus travel is practically non-existent. Our advice is stick to rail or car.

By Car

The most charming châteaux and cool country hotels often seem to lie away from the main cities and train stations. Thus, renting a car is often the best way to travel around France, especially if you plan to explore it in depth.

THE BASICS

Avoiding a Night on the Park Bench

If you are traveling from abroad, you should always have at least your first night's room booked—not just because sleeping on the sidewalk sucks, but also because you will be required to give Immigration an address for where you're staying (if you're not a European passport holder) when you arrive at the airport. Call ahead and reserve a room or book via the Internet (you should look at a property's website anyway, as that's often where the best prices and last-minute deals are posted). If you do arrive in France without a room reservation, first call the hostels listed in this book. If they're booked head to the local tourist office, which can help with their computerized reservation service. Note that in France, room sizes (particularly in Paris where a broom-cupboard would not be an exaggerated description for some accommodations) are often very small. It is not because size doesn't matter in France, more because buildings tend to be very old, and date from an era when people were a lot smaller and needed less space.

Eurail Passes

The **Eurailpass** permits unlimited first-class rail travel in any country in western Europe except the British Isles. Passes are available for purchase online (www.eurail.com) and at various offices/agents around the world. Travel agents and railway agents in such cities as New York, Montréal, and Los Angeles sell Eurail passes. You can purchase them at the North American offices of CIT Travel Service, the SNCF in France, and in other European countries' railroads associations. It is strongly recommended that you purchase passes before you leave home, as not all passes are available in Europe; also, passes purchased in Europe will cost about 20% more. Numerous options are available for travel in France. The pass must be purchased 21 days before departure for Europe by a non–European Union resident. For further details or for purchase, call **Rail Pass Express** (☎ 800/722-7151; www. eurail.com). It's also available from **STA Travel** (☎ 800/781-4040; www. sta.com) and other travel agents. You can also find more information online at www.eurail.com.

But Europe's rail networks are so well developed and inexpensive that we recommend you rent a car only for exploring areas little serviced by rail, such as Brittany, rural Burgundy, and the Dordogne. Or take trains between cities and rent a car on the days when you want to explore independently.

DRIVING TIMES

Driving time in Europe is largely hit or miss (for want of a better expression) and will depend on how much sightseeing you do along the way. Driving time from Paris to Bordeaux is 7 to 8 hours minimum. It's 2½ hours from Paris to Rouen, 3½ hours to Nantes, and 4 hours to Lyon. The driving time from Marseille to Paris (771km/479 miles) is (by some) considered a matter of national pride, and tall tales abound about how rapidly the French can do it. Flooring it, you may conceivably get there in 7 hours, but by TGV you'll make it in just 3.

CAR RENTALS

To rent a car, you'll need to present a passport, a driver's license, and a credit card. You also have to meet the company's minimum-age requirement. (For the least expensive cars, this is 21 at Hertz, 23 at Avis, and 25 at Budget. More expensive cars may require that you be at least 25.) It usually isn't obligatory within France, but certain companies have asked for the presentation of an International Driver's License, even though this is becoming increasingly superfluous in western Europe.

Note: The best deal is usually a weekly rental with unlimited mileage. All car-rental bills in France are subject to a 19.6% government tax. Though the rental company won't usually mind if you drive your car into, say, Germany, Switzerland, Italy, or Spain, it's often forbidden to transport your car by ferry, including across the Channel to England.

In France, **collision damage waiver (CDW)** is usually factored into the overall rate quoted, but you should always verify this before taking a car on the road. At most companies, the CDW provision won't protect you against theft; if this is the case, ask about purchasing extra theft protection. Also automatic transmission is a luxury in Europe, so if you want it, you'll pay dearly. *Note:* France affords so many opportunities to go wine-tasting that the temptation to drink and drive is a constant. This is dangerous and considered a crime in France (subject to 2-year imprisonment), so always ask the local tourist office about organized wine-tasting tours if you desperately want to sample the stuff.

GASOLINE

Known in France as *essence,* gas is expensive for those accustomed to North American prices. At press time, it was about $5.50 a gallon, according to CNN. All but the least expensive cars usually require an octane rating, which the French classify as *essence super,* the most expensive variety. Depending on your car, you'll need either leaded *(avec plomb)* or unleaded *(sans plomb).*

Beware the mixture of gasoline and oil, called *mélange* or *gasoil,* sold in some rural communities; this mixture is for very old two-cycle engines.

Note: Sometimes you can drive for miles in rural France without encountering a gas station; don't let your tank get dangerously low.

DRIVING RULES

Everyone in the car, in both the front and back seats, must wear seat belts. Children under 12 must ride in the back seat. Drivers are supposed to yield to the car on their right, except where signs indicate otherwise, as at traffic circles.

If you violate the speed limit, expect a big fine. Limits are about 130kmph (81 mph) on expressways, about 100kmph (62 mph) on major national highways, and 90kmph (56 mph) on country roads. In towns, don't exceed 60kmph (37 mph).

Note: It's illegal to use a cellphone while you're driving in France; you will be ticketed if you're stopped.

DRIVING MAPS

For France as a whole, most motorists opt for **Michelin map 989.** For regions, Michelin publishes a series of **yellow maps** that are quite good. Big travel-book stores in North America carry these maps, and they're commonly available in France (at lower prices). In this age of congested

Rental Cars

The following car-rental agencies are proven reliable in France:

→ **Avis** (☎ **800/331-1212** in the U.S. and Canada; www.avis. com) has offices at both Paris airports and an inner-city headquarters at 5 rue Bixio, 7th arr. (☎ **01-44-18-10-50**; Métro: Ecole Militaire), near the Eiffel Tower.

→ **National** (☎ **800/CAR-RENT** in the U.S. and Canada; www. nationalcar.com) is represented in Paris by **Europcar,** one office is at 48 rue de Berri, 8th arr. (☎ **01-53-93-73-40**; Métro: St. Philippe du Roule). It has offices at both Paris airports and at a dozen other locations. For the lowest rates, reserve in advance from North America.

→ **Budget** (☎ **800/472-3325** in the U.S., 800/268-8900 in Canada; www.budget.com) has about 30 locations in Paris and at Orly (☎ **01-49-75-56-05**) and Charles de Gaulle (☎ **01-48-62-70-22**).

→ **Hertz** (☎ **800/654-3131** in the U.S. and Canada; www.hertz. com) maintains about 15 locations in Paris, including offices at the city's airports. The main office is at 27 place St-Ferdinand, 17th arr. (☎ **01-45-74-97-39**; Métro: Argentine). Be sure to ask about promotional discounts.

traffic, one useful feature of the Michelin map is its designations of alternative *routes de dégagement,* which let you skirt big cities and avoid traffic-clogged highways. To plot out your route, you could also try www.mappy.fr.

ROADSIDE ASSISTANCE

A breakdown is called *une panne* in France. Call the police at ☎ **17** anywhere in

France to be put in touch with the nearest garage. Most local garages offer towing. If the breakdown occurs on an expressway, find the nearest roadside emergency phone box, pick up the phone, and put a call through. You'll be connected to the nearest breakdown service facility.

Tips for Travel on the Cheap

Student Discounts

Lots of travel discounts are available to students, teachers (at any grade level, kindergarten through university), and youths (ages 12–25). Most attractions have a reduced student-rate admission charge, with the presentation of a valid student ID card.

Two popular student ID cards are the ISE Card (International Student Exchange Card) and the ISIC (International Student Identity Card). For a look at the various travel benefits that come with membership, go to www.isecard.com and www.isiccard.com.

The International Student Identity Card (ISIC) offers a range of benefits for students aged 12 and up, including store discounts and a 24-hour emergency helpline, as well as international recognition of your student status. They cost just $22 and are available through student travel offices, universities, and so forth. Check out the ISIC homepage (www.isic.com); you can also buy them from STA Travel (☎ **800/781-4040** in North America; www.sta.com or www.statravel.com), the biggest student travel agency in the world.

If you're no longer a student but are still under 26, you can get an International Youth Travel Card (IYTC) for the same price from the same group. It entitles you to some discounts (but not on museum admissions). Travel CUTS (☎ **800/592-CUTS;** www.travelcuts.com) offers similar services for both Canadians and U.S. residents.

Tips for Backpackers/Creative Packing

What to Carry

"Backpacker" is a figurative term. You can be a young, carefree, budget-oriented traveler even if you carry a rolling suitcase. In most cases, a rolling bag is just as convenient to carry around as a backpack, if not more so, and it can be easier to organize. However, when it comes to climbing stairs and covering longer distances on foot, the classic backpack can't be beat.

To maximize the space in any bag, the key words are **rolling** and **compartmentalizing.** Rolling your clothes will help you fit more. As for compartmentalizing, you want to be able to access those things that you need most. Put toiletries near the top or in their compartment. Keep film, camera, and so on in a separate compartment that is easily accessible, and make sure you have a separate compartment for dirty clothes.

Another thing to keep in mind is that **you don't have to look like a schlep to be a backpacker.** Nice(r) clothes don't necessarily take up more room in your bag, so ditch the hiking boots and pack some wrinkle-free clothes so that you can look presentable when you hit the town. The reality is, unless you're taking an extreme adventure/ecotourism tour, you won't *really* be hiking too much. Mostly, you'll be traipsing around cities where the locals look effortlessly chic year-round. Lastly, we all know that shoes can take up the most room in bags. Keep this in mind. And when choosing a backpack, make sure there are straps on the outside for larger items such as shoes, sweatshirts, coats, and blankets. Regardless of whatever else you pack, you'll want that favorite, flattering pair of jeans; sneakers (comfortable but cool); comfy, non-skimpy sleepwear (for those shared hostel rooms); and a pair of rubber flip-flops for the shared bathrooms and showers you'll encounter at hostels and other budget hotels. Keep the inside of your bag free for anything fragile that you might need to protect. And remember: Since you may want to bring a few things home, it doesn't hurt to leave a few compartments empty or pack an extra, empty bag for the goodies.

What to Bring

○ **Clothes.** Check the weather, but the key here is a mix of comfortable city clothes and casual country gear; always be prepared for rain, with a rain jacket or windbreaker.

○ **Comfortable shoes and sandals.** You'll be doing endless amounts of walking.

○ **Posh shoes.** If you can squeeze them in, bring them; some French nightclubs can be choosy.

○ **Camera and memory card.** Film and batteries are easy to purchase in France.

○ **Extra bag.** To bring stuff home in.

○ **Electrical plug adapter.** For computers and iPod and cellphone chargers.

○ **Basic medicine kit.** Pack prescriptions, stomach medicine, pain relievers, and diarrhea medicine.

○ **Sun protection.** Don't forget sunblock, sunglasses, and a brimmed hat.

○ **A change of clothes in your carry-on bag.** In case luggage misses its flight, it's better to be safe than sorry.

○ **Passport.** And visa, if necessary.

○ **ATM and/or credit cards.** Also pack some cash to get you going upon arrival.

THE BASICS

Tips for Gay Travelers

France is one of the world's most tolerant countries toward gays and lesbians, and no special laws discriminate against them. "Gay Paree" boasts a large gay population, with many clubs, restaurants, organizations, and services.

A helpful source is **La Maison des Femmes,** 163 rue de Charenton, 12th arr., Paris (☎ **01-43-43-41-13;** http://maisondesfemmes.free.fr; Métro: Charonne). It offers information about Paris for lesbians and bisexual women, and sometimes sponsors informal get-togethers. Call for a recorded announcement that gives the hours when someone will be available that particular week.

Lesbian or bisexual women can also pick up a copy of *Lesbia,* if only to check out the ads. These publications and others are available at Paris's largest, best-stocked gay bookstore, **Les Mots à la Bouche,** 6

rue Ste-Croix-de-la-Bretonnerie, 4th arr. (☎ **01-42-78-88-30;** www.motsbouche. com; Métro: Hôtel-de-Ville; Mon–Sat 11am–11pm, Sun 2–8pm), which carries publications in both French and English.

The **International Gay and Lesbian Travel Association (IGLTA;** ☎ **800/ 448-8550** or 954/776-2626; www.iglta.org) is the trade association for the gay and lesbian travel industry, and offers an online directory of gay- and lesbian-friendly travel businesses; go to their website and click on "Members."

Many agencies offer tours and travel itineraries specifically for gay and lesbian travelers. Among them are **Above and Beyond Tours** (☎ 800/397-2681; www.abovebeyondtours.com); **Now, Voyager** (☎ 800/255-6951; www.nowvoyager. com); and **Olivia Cruises & Resorts** (☎ 800/631-6277; www.olivia.com).

Gay.com Travel (☎ **800/929-2268** or 415/644-8044; www.gay.com/travel or www. outandabout.com) is an excellent online successor to the popular *Out & About* print magazine. It provides regularly updated information about gay-owned, gay-oriented, and gay-friendly lodging, dining, sightseeing, nightlife, and shopping establishments in every important destination worldwide.

The following travel guides are available at many bookstores, or you can order them from any online bookseller: *Spartacus International Gay Guide* (Bruno Gmünder Verlag; www.spartacus world.com/gayguide), *Odysseus: The International Gay Travel Planner* (Odysseus Enterprises Ltd.), and the *Damron* guides (www.damron.com), with separate, annual books for gay men and lesbians.

Tips for Travelers with Disabilities

Most disabilities shouldn't stop anyone from traveling. There are more options and resources out there than ever before.

Facilities for travelers in France, and nearly all modern hotels, provide accessible rooms. Older hotels (unless they've been renovated) may not provide elevators, special toilet facilities, or wheelchair ramps.

The new TGVs (high-speed trains) are wheelchair accessible; older trains have compartments for wheelchair boarding. On the Paris Métro, passengers with disabilities are able to sit in wider seats provided for their comfort. Guide dogs ride free. However, some stations don't have escalators or elevators.

Knowing which hotels, restaurants, and attractions are accessible can save you a lot of frustration. **Association des Paralysés de France,** 17 bd. Auguste-Blanqui, 75013 Paris (☎ **01-40-78-69-66;** www.apf.asso.fr), provides documentation, moral support, and travel ideas for individuals who use wheelchairs. In addition to the Paris office, it maintains an office in each of the 90 *départements* ("mini-states" into which France is divided) and can help find hotels, transportation, sightseeing, house rentals, and (in some cases) companionship for

special needs travelers. It's not, however, a travel agency.

Many travel agencies offer customized tours and itineraries for travelers with disabilities. Among them are **Flying Wheels Travel** (☎ **507/451-5005;** www.flying wheelstravel.com); **Access-Able Travel Source** (☎ **303/232-2979;** www.access-able.com); and **Accessible Journeys** (☎ **800/846-4537** or 610/521-0339; www. disabilitytravel.com). **Avis Rent a Car** has an "Avis Access" program that offers such services as a dedicated 24-hour toll-free number (☎ **888/879-4273**) for customers with special travel needs; special car features such as swivel seats, spinner knobs, and hand controls; and accessible bus service.

Organizations that offer assistance to disabled travelers include **MossRehab** (www.mossresourcenet.org); the **American Foundation for the Blind** (AFB; ☎ **800/232-5463;** www.afb.org); and **SATH** (**Society for Accessible Travel & Hospitality;** ☎ **212/447-7284;** www.sath. org). **AirAmbulanceCard.com** is now partnered with SATH and allows you to preselect top-notch hospitals in case of an emergency.

The community website **iCan** (www. icanonline.net/channels/travel)   has destination guides and several regular columns on accessible travel. Also check out the quarterly magazine *Emerging Horizons* (www.emerginghorizons.com), and *Open World* magazine, published by SATH.

FOR BRITISH TRAVELERS WITH DISABILITIES The **Royal Association for Disability and Rehabilitation** **(RADAR),** Unit 12, City Forum, 250 City Rd., London EC1V 8AF (☎ **020/7250-3222;** www.radar.org.uk). Another resource is **Holiday Care Service,** Sunley House, 7th Floor, 4 Bedford Park, Croydon, Surrey CR0 2AP (☎ **0845/124-9971;** www.holiday care.org), a charity advising on accommodations for seniors and persons with disabilities. Annual membership is £37.50.

Tips for Solo Travelers

In cities, take a cab home at night, and follow all the usual advice of caution you get when you travel anywhere. Don't do anything in France you would not do at home.

Men

Foreign men should encounter few problems traveling in France. The French are very familiar with international travelers, and are generally savvy about tourists and tourism. There is a bit of a macho culture in certain parts—particularly in the South in the Basque regions—and men should avoid getting involved in any local tensions. Otherwise, though, you're likely to find that interactions with local residents are friendly and relaxed. In the end, the simple fact is that being male and foreign will neither hurt you nor help you as you travel around France. While France is a conservative country, it is not backward, and you should feel comfortable striking up conversations with men and women precisely as you would at home. Women may give you funny looks at first, but as soon as they see you're not trying to get into their pants, they'll relax.

Women

Women should expect few if any problems traveling in France. The country's view on women is slightly lagging behind some other countries, but things are much more advanced now than they were even a couple of decades ago. Women traveling alone or in groups are accepted in every environment, although, women drinking lots of alcohol (that is, getting totally rat-arsed) is not looked upon favorably. French men, while not aggressive, do stare at women a lot. If you don't want to engage in a conversation, don't hold their gaze, and don't answer when they talk to you. They'll soon get the message. Pay particular attention to this in Paris and Marseille. If you drink in a bar at night, though, you may well get attention—even if you're reading a book, talking on the phone to your fiancé, and doing su doku at 100 miles per hour. So be prepared to fend them off. French men almost always respond well to polite rejection, though.

Check out the award-winning website **Journeywoman** (www.journeywoman. com), a "real life" women's travel-information network where you can sign up for a free e-mail newsletter and get advice on everything from etiquette and dress to safety; or the travel guide *Safety and Security for Women Who Travel* by Sheila Swan and Peter Laufer (Travelers' Tales, Inc.), offering common-sense tips on safe travel.

THE BASICS

Tips for Minority Travelers

Since the days of the celebrated chanteuse Josephine Baker and, later, the author James Baldwin, France has welcomed African-American travelers. That welcome continues today. A good book on the subject is Tyler Stovall's *Paris Noir*. Another worthwhile resource is the website www.cafedelasoul.com.

Regrettably, anti-Semitism has been on the rise in Europe, especially in France, which has registered a significant increase in incidents against Jews. French Jews (not visitors from abroad) have suffered assaults and attacks against synagogues, cemeteries, schools, and other Jewish property. Officials say they believe that attacks in France are linked to the worsening of the Israeli-Palestinian conflict. Some sources—none official—recommend that travelers conceal Star of David jewelry and other such items to ensure personal safety while traveling in France.

Officially, the government of France welcomes Jewish visitors and promises a vigorous defense of their safety and concerns. The French Government Tourist Office website (www.franceguide.com) has a "Jewish Traveler Guide" section with more information.

Specialized Tours & Resources

Ecotourism

You can find eco-friendly travel tips, statistics, and touring companies and associations—listed by destination under "Travel Choice"—at the TIES website, www.ecotourism.org. **Ecotravel.com** is part online magazine and part ecodirectory that lets you search for touring companies in several categories (water-based, land-based, spiritually oriented, and so on). Also check out **Conservation International** (www.conservation.org)—which, with *National Geographic Traveler*, annually presents **World Legacy Awards** (www.wlaward.org) to those travel tour operators, businesses, organizations, and places that have made a significant contribution to sustainable tourism.

In a country as diverse and popular as France, there are numerous options.

Ballooning

It's a little on the steep side, but if you're looking for something really special, the world's largest hot-air-balloon operator is **Buddy Bombard's Private Europe,** 333 Pershing Way, West Palm Beach, FL 33401 (☎ **800/862-8537** or 561/837-6610; fax 561/837-6623; www.bombardsociety.com). It maintains about three dozen hot-air balloons, some in the Loire Valley and Burgundy. The 5-day tours, costing $7,471 per person (double occupancy), incorporate food and wine-tasting and all meals, lodging in chic-as-hell hotels, sightseeing, rail transfers to and from Paris, and a daily balloon ride over vineyards and fields.

Slightly cheaper, but still expensive is **Bonaventura Balloon Co.,** 133 Wall Rd., Napa Valley, CA 94573 (☎ **800/FLY-NAPA** or 707/944-2822; fax 707/944-2220; www.bonaventuraballoons.com), which meets you in Paris and takes you on the high-speed train to Burgundy, where your balloon tour begins. It carries you over the scenic parts of the region, before dropping you off for the night in a 14th-century mill, now an inn owned by a three-star chef. A 9-day trip is $2,695 per person, including sightseeing in Paris, two balloon trips, lodging, cooking classes, wine-tasting, and at least one meal per day.

Pedal Pushing

....

For an all-inclusive biking tour, try **VBT (Deluxe Bicycle Vacations),** 614 Monkton Rd., Bristol, VT 05443 (☎ **800/245-3868;** www.vbt.com), which offers trips in five of the most scenic parts of France. These range from Burgundy (which combines a barge tour) to the Loire Valley—even Provence and the Normandy Coast. Packages are priced from $2,495 to $3,445 per person, which is pricey but covers everything, including airfare.

→ **Euro-Bike & Walking Tours,** P.O. Box 990, DeKalb, IL 60115 (☎ **800/ 321-6060** or 815/758-8851; www.eurobike.com), offers 10-day tours in the Dordogne ($2,450–$3,575 per person), 11-day tours in Provence ($2,850–$4,050 per person), 6-day tours of Burgundy ($1,795–$2,450 per person), and 8-day tours of the Loire ($2,250–$3,195 per person). All are escorted and include room, breakfast, and dinner.

→ **Go-today.com** (a division of Europe Express), 19021 120th Ave. NE, Suite 102, Bothell, WA 98011 (☎ **800/227-3235** or 425/487-6711; www.go-today.com), has biking and walking tours of Bordeaux, Burgundy, the Dordogne, the Loire Valley, and Provence. An 8-day guided bike tour is $1,289 per person, double occupancy. All tours include overnight accommodations and most meals. Guided tours include van support and a guide; on nonguided tours, you'll always have the name of an English-speaking local contact.

Adventure Tours

If you fancy testing your thigh muscles and cycling around France, contact the **Fédération Française de Cyclotourisme** (12 rue Louis-Bertrand, 94200 Ivry-sur-Seine; ☎ **01-56-20-88-87;** www.ffct.org), which supplies detailed biking itineraries for the whole of France.

If you've always fancied yourself a John Whitaker or a Princess Anne, you might fancy discovering France astride a mighty fine stallion or mare. The **Comité National de Tourisme Equestre** (9 bd. Macdonald, 19th arr., Paris; ☎ **01-53-26-15-50;** www.ffe.com or www.tourisme-equestre.fr) has plenty of information on where to find horseback riding tours and clubs.

France is littered with scenic gorges and rivers for you to canoe or kayak down. For information on clubs and associations contact the **Fédération Française de Canoë-kayak** (87 quai de la Marne, 94340 Joinville-le-Pont; ☎ **01-45-11-08-50;** www.ffcanoe.asso.fr).

Hiking is an excellent way to discover the countryside. Only on foot can you get to the hard-to-reach sites that guarantee some of Frances' most breathtaking views. The national parks are ideal walking ground, but the whole country is littered with indicated "GR" paths (*grande randonnée,* or walking routes). The federation **Française de la Randonnée Pédestre** can provide official maps and information on hiking in France. If you stop by Paris, buy maps from their boutique at 14 rue Riquet, 19th arr. (☎ **01-44-89-93-90**), or if you read French, check out www.ffrp.asso.fr.

If you're the sort who gets a thrill when hanging upside down off a rock face, the chances are you're a climber. France should feel like second heaven to you then, as there are plenty of places for you to scale. Local tourist offices will be able to

THE BASICS

offer you information on where to go (particularly in the Alps, Pyrenees, Massif Central, and Auvergne), but for a list of all the associations across the country, contact the **Club Alpin Français (FFCAM;** 24 av. Laumière, 19th arr., Paris; ☎ **01-53-72-87-00;** www.ffcam.fr).

If you were a fish in a previous life and you feel most at home when surfing the crest of a wave, you should contact the **Fédération Française de Surf** (Plage Nord, BP 28, 40 150 Hossegor; ☎ **05-58-43-55-88;** www.surfingfrance.com) for info on surfing, bodyboarding, longboarding, skimboarding, and Surf Tandem in the Hexagon.

If you think you are a fish now, you might like to dive off France's shores. That means you should contact the French diving association, **Fédération Française d'Etude et de Sports Sous-Marins** (24 quai de Rive-Neuve, 13284, Marseille cedex 7; ☎ **04-91-33-99-31** or 08-20-00-457; www.ffessm.fr).

Cooking Schools

Dig deep into your pockets if you want to learn to cook with the upper-crusts at a **French cooking school.** The famous/infamous Georges-Auguste Escoffier (1846–1935) taught the Edwardians how to eat. Today the Hôtel Ritz maintains the **Ritz-Escoffier Ecole de Gastronomie Française,** 38 rue Cambon, 75001 Paris (☎ **01-43-16-30-50;** www.ritzparis.com), which offers demonstration classes of the master's techniques on Saturdays. These cost 125€ ($163) each. Courses, taught in French and English, start at 980€ ($1,274) for 1 week, up to 5,550€ ($7,150) for 6 weeks.

Le Cordon Bleu, 8 rue Léon-Delhomme, 75015 Paris (☎ **800/457-2433** in the U.S., or 01-53-68-22-50; www.cordonbleu.edu), was established in 1895, and is the most famous French cooking school—

where Julia Child learned to perfect her *pâté brisée* and *mousse au chocolat.* Its best-known courses last 10 weeks, at the end of which the school issues certificates. Many enthusiasts prefer a less intense immersion and opt for a 4-day workshop or a 3-hour demonstration class. Enrollment in either is first-come, first-served; costs are 30€ to 142€ ($39–$185) for a demonstration and 859€ to 889€ ($1,117–$1,156) for the 4-day workshop. Classes are in English.

If you fancy a stint in Nice, you may want to learn real Niçoise cooking in a laid-back environment, with one of the friendliest English/Canadian/almost French people in the country. Contact **Rosa Jackson** (p. 502), the drive behind **Les Petits Farcis** cooking school (7 rue du Jesus, 06300 Nice; ☎ **06-81-67-41-22**). She's a food groupie, author of several cookbooks and guidebooks on the subject. A whiz in the kitchen, she can teach you how to create perfect regional Mediterranean cuisine, before (or after) taking you on a tour of Nice's wonderful markets. Prices range from 100€ to 290€ ($130–$377) per person.

Learning the Lingo

The **Alliance Française,** 101 bd. Raspail, 75270 Paris (☎ **01-42-84-90-00;** fax 01-42-84-91-01; www.alliancefr.org), a nonprofit organization with a network of 1,100 establishments in 138 countries, offers French-language courses to some 350,000 students. The school in Paris is open all year; monthlong courses range from 320€ to 640€ ($416–$832), depending on the number of hours per day. Request information and an application at least 1 month before your departure. In North America, the largest branch is the **Alliance Française,** 1900 L St. NW, Washington, DC 20036 (☎ **800/6-FRANCE;** fax 800/491-6980; www.afusa.org).

A clearinghouse for information on French-language schools is **Lingua Service Worldwide,** 75 Prospect St., Suite 4, Huntington, NY 11743 (☎ **800/394-LEARN** or 631/424-0777; www.linguaservice worldwide.com). Its programs are available in many cities throughout France. They cost $844 to $2,185 for 2 weeks, depending on the city, the school, and the accommodations.

Highbrow Music Tour

One outfit that coordinates hotel stays in Paris with major musical events, usually in at least one (and often both) of the city's opera houses, is **Dailey-Thorp Travel,** P.O. Box 670, Big Horn, Wyoming 82833 (☎ **800/998-4677** or 307/673-1555; fax 307/674-7474; www.daileythorp.com). Sojourns tend to last 3 to 7 days and, in many cases, tie in with performances in other cities (usually London, Berlin, or Milan). Expect accommodations in deluxe hotels such as the Hôtel du Louvre or the Hôtel Scribe, and a staff that has made arrangements for all the nuts and bolts of your arrival in, and artistic exposure to, Paris.

Tennis Tours

Die-hard fans around the world set their calendars by the French Open, at Paris's Roland-Garros stadium. You can book your hotel and tickets to the event on your own, but if you're unsure about scheduling, consider a California-based company, **Advantage Tennis Tours,** 33 White Sail Dr., Suite 100, Laguna Niguel, CA 92677 (☎ **800/341-8687** or 949/661-7331; fax 949/489-2837; www.advantagetennistours. com). They typically book packages including 5 or 6 nights of hotel accommodations in Paris, 2 or 3 days on Center Court, and the skills of a bilingual hostess; rates per person, without airfare, begin at $2,875, double occupancy, depending on your choice of hotel and the duration of your visit.

THE BASICS

I Don't Want to Leave! Staying Beyond Vacation

Study Abroad

Considering the sheer number of language schools, business colleges, and universities in Paris alone, it's not surprising that the country's student population is considerable. If you're interested in **studying abroad in France,** contact your university to find out if they have a partnership program in France. To get basic info on legal and administrative requirements, consult the French government website **www.diplomatie.gouv.fr**. For language and cooking classes, see "Specialized Tours & Resources," above.

The government relies on three associations to recruit foreign students. You could contact these organizations directly:

○ **Agence EduFrance:** 79 ave Denfert-Rochereau, 75014, Paris; www.edu

france.fr. Their website lists other offices in North America, Asia, and Canada.

○ **The CNOUS** (Centre National de Oeuvres Universitaires et Scholaires): Sous-Direction des Affaires Internationales, 6 rue Jean Calvin 75005 Paris; ☎ **01-44-18-53-00;** www.cnous.fr. CNOUS can help find student accommodations and study placements.

○ **EGIDE** (Centre Français pour l'Accueil et les Echanges Internationaux): 28 rue de la Grange aux Belles, 75010, Paris; ☎ **01-40-40-58-58;** www.egide.asso.fr.s.

Work Abroad

As a whole, the job market in France is not as healthy as it is in other western European countries such as Britain and

Guarantee of Quality: The AOC

(Appellation d'Origine Contrôlée)

We bet you've been wondering what all the AOC labels on French foods mean; you've probably spotted them on wines, cheeses, and other edible French products. They signify that the foodstuffs (usually milk products such as cheese) or wine come from a certain region (any region), and have been made using methods that are specific to that region. The National Institute of AOC control ensures that only products that comply with these "regional" production methods get an AOC label. It is therefore a kind of guarantee of quality and tradition. In some ways, the label can be misleading; it doesn't necessarily mean one product is "better" than another. A fine artisanal cheese made on a small farm, for instance, may prove to be some of the best you've ever eaten, even though it hasn't flown under the government radar to win the stamp of approval. If you are a sucker for stickers, however, look out for the AOC sign on over 467 alcoholic drinks, 47 cheeses and milk products, and 25 other foodstuffs. The value of all of these AOC products equates to 17 billion euros.

THE BASICS

Ireland. However, finding work, especially if you speak some French, is not impossible, as long as you don't mind what you do. If you look for work in Paris, grab the English *FUSAC* magazine (free in English bookstores and in some shops and bars), which lists jobs available for English speakers. As a non-citizen student in France (from outside the E.U.), you can legally work 20 hours a week. Non E.U. members will require an *authorisation provisoire de travail* (provisional working permit) from the **DDTEFT** (Direction Départementale du Travail, d'Emploi et de la Formation Professionelle; 109 rue Montmartre, 2nd arr., Paris; ☎ **01-44-84-41-00;** www.travail-gouv.fr; Métro: Bourse), and for that you'll need a **Carte de Séjour** (visitor's permit); see below. The **CROUS** will also find part-time jobs for students (☎ **01-40-51-37-52** to -57; www.crous-paris.fr/emploi).

PERMITS

All non-E.U. citizens staying in France for more than 3 months are supposed to apply for the bane of every foreigner's life in France—the infamous **Carte de Séjour**

(visitor's temporary residence permit), valid for 1 year. The exact documents required to obtain one vary depending upon where you are from, but as a rule be expected to provide proof of a French bank account (a difficult thing to obtain, as many banks require you to have a *carte de séjour* before they'll open an account for you), a certified translation of your birth certificate, a work contract (again, difficult, as you may need a *carte de séjour* in order to get a work permit), or a proof of study in France. The **CIRA** (Centre Interministerial de Renseignements Administratifs; ☎ **08-21-08-09-10**) offers advice on French administrative procedures. To apply for your *carte de séjour,* check procedures with your local *mairie* (town hall) or in Paris. Expect to queue for hours outside the **Préfecture de Police de Paris,** Services Etrangers (7–9 bd du Palais, 4th arr., Paris; ☎ **01-53-71-51-68;** Métro: Cité), to pick up paperwork or hand in your completed dossier for approval. It may seem like a Catch-22 situation, but if you follow the procedures, stay cool, and act patient, you'll get there in the end.

Eating Your Way through France

France is practically synonymous with good food. It has an admirable range of restaurants in all price categories, a gastronomic delight for each region (nay . . . town), and an admirable array of settings that range from old-world hotel dining rooms, country mansions, and castles, to skylit terraces, shop-front bistros, riverside cottages, and converted houses.

Before you book a table, here are a few things you should know:

Upscale Lunch

Restaurant prices in France have gone up dramatically—in many cases by 20% to 25%—in recent years. Nobody is more aware of this than the French themselves, who blame the price hikes on the changeover from the franc to the euro, and general inflation. But if you're hankering after a gourmet meal, and only the best will do, you don't have to splurge your entire week's budget on one evening meal. Instead, opt for your main meal there in the middle of the day by trying the set-lunch menu. You'll experience the same great cuisine at half the price of a nighttime meal.

RESERVATIONS Except for self-service eateries, informal cafes, and some popular seafood spots, most restaurants encourage reservations, and most expensive restaurants require them. In the most popular eateries, Friday and Saturday nights are often booked up a week or more in advance, so have a few options in mind if you're booking at the last minute and want to try out the hot spots in town.

Tip: If a restaurant is booked from 8 or 8:30pm onward, ask if you can dine late, at 10:30pm. Some popular restaurants run two sittings.

PRICES Meal prices at restaurants include whopping taxes (19.60% VAT, TVA in French). Many restaurants include the tip as a service charge added automatically to the bill (marked *service compris* on the bill). When no service charge is added, tip up to 15% depending on the quality of the service. But don't feel that you have to tip if you've had mediocre service (the worst they'll do is think you're a stingy foreign tourist). Do check your bill, as some unscrupulous restaurants do not make it clear that you actually have already tipped, thus encouraging you to accidentally do so twice.

THE BASICS

France Nuts & Bolts

American Express The Paris office is at 11 rue Scribe (☎ **01-47-77-79-28**). It operates as a travel agency, a tour operator, and a mail pickup service every Monday to Friday from 9:30am to 6:30pm, Saturday 9am to 5:30pm. Its banking section, for issues involving American Express credit cards, transfers of funds, and credit-related issues, is open Monday to Saturday from 9am to 6:30pm. In Marseille, there's an office at 39 bd. de la Canebiére (☎ **04-91-13-71-26**); it's open Monday to Friday 9am to 6pm and Saturday 9am to noon and 2 to 5:30pm.

ATM Networks See "Money" on p. 23.

Business Hours Business hours are erratic, as befits a nation of individualists. Most banks are open Monday through Friday from 9:30am to 4:30pm. Many, particularly in small towns, take a lunch break. Hours are usually posted on the door. Most museums close 1 day a week (often Tues), and they're generally closed on national holidays. Usual hours are from 9:30am to 5pm. In Paris or other big French cities, stores are generally open from 9, 9:30, or (often) 10am to 6 or 7pm without a break for lunch. Some shops, delis, cafes, and newsstands open at 8am and close at 8 or 9pm. In some small stores, the lunch break can last 3 hours, beginning at 1pm. This is more common in the south than in the north.

Car Rentals See "Getting Around France" on p. 38.

Cashpoints See "ATM Networks," above.

Currency See "Money" on p. 23.

Driving Rules See "Getting Around France" on p. 38.

Drugstores If you need a *pharmacie* during off-hours, have the front-desk staff at your hotel get in touch with the nearest Commissariat de Police. An agent there will have the address of a nearby pharmacy open 24 hours a day. French law requires that the pharmacies in any given neighborhood display the name and location of the one that remains open all night. In Paris, one of the most central all-nighters is **Pharmacy Les Champs "Derhy,"** 84 av. des Champs-Elysées, 8th arr. (☎ 01-45-62-02-41; Métro: George V).

Electricity Electricity in France runs on 220-volt, 50-cycle AC current. U.S. electricity is 110-volt, 60-cycle current. If you are bringing anything electric, you will need a voltage transformer and a plug adapter. Some appliances have dual voltage, which means that you will only need a plug adapter to run your hair dryer or razor, for example. A switch on the appliance will allow you to change voltages. Adapters and converters are for sale at Radio Shack and luggage and travel stores.

Embassies & Consulates See "Paris Nuts & Bolts" on p. 81.

Emergencies You can get help anywhere by calling ☎ **17** for the police; ☎ **18** for the fire department *(pompiers)* who also run as paramedics; or ☎ **15** for medical emergencies.

Hospitals Dial ☎ **15** for medical emergencies. In Paris, the **American Hospital,** 63 bd. Victor-Hugo, in the suburb of Neuilly-sur-Seine (☎ 01-46-41-25-25; Métro: Pont-de-Levallois or Pont-de-Neuilly; bus: 82), operates a 24-hour emergency service. The bilingual staff accepts Blue Cross and other American insurance plans. Hospitals in other major cities include **Hôpital Rouen,** 1 rue de Germont (☎ 02-32-88-89-90), in Rouen; **Hôpital Bretonneau,** 2 bd. Tonnellé (☎ 02-47-47-47), in Tours; **Hôpital Civil de Strasbourg,** 1 place de l'Hôpital (☎ 03-88-11-67-68) in Strasbourg; **Hôpital Edouard Herriot,** 5 place Arsonval (☎ 08-20-08-20-69), in Lyon; **Hôpital de Avignon,** 305 rue Raoul Follereau (☎ 04-32-75-33-33) in Avignon; **Hôpital St- Roch,** 5 rue Pierre Dévoluy (☎ 04-92-03-33-75), in Nice; **CHU de Rangueil,** av. du Prof. Jean-Poulhes (☎ 05-61-32-25-33) in Toulouse.

Language   English is increasingly understood in France, especially among young people who have studied it in school. People are more likely to understand English in such centers as Paris and the Riviera than in the more remote provinces. Service personnel in hotels tend to speak English, at least at the front desk. A staff member at most restaurants will speak a bit of English. But many people you encounter in France do not speak English, and you may want to carry a Berlitz handbook. For some basic vocabulary, refer to the Survival French chapter.

Liquor Laws   Supermarkets, grocery stores, and cafes all sell alcoholic beverages. The legal drinking age is 16. Persons under 16 can be served an alcoholic drink if accompanied by a parent or legal guardian. Wine and liquor are sold every day of the year. *Be warned:* France is very strict about drunk-driving laws. If convicted, you face a stiff fine and a possible prison term of up to 2 years.

Lost & Found   To speed the process of replacing your personal documents if they're lost or stolen, make a photocopy of the first few pages of your passport and write down your credit card numbers (and the serial numbers of your traveler's checks, if you're using them). Leave this information with someone at home—to be faxed to you in an emergency—and swap it with your traveling companion. Be sure to tell all of your credit card companies the minute you discover your wallet has been lost or stolen, and file a report at the nearest police precinct. Your credit card company or insurer may require a police report number or record of the loss.

If you need emergency cash over the weekend when all banks and American Express offices are closed, you can have money wired to you via **Western Union** (☎ **800/325-6000;** www.westernunion.com). **Travelers Express/MoneyGram** is the largest company in the U.S. for money orders. You can transfer funds either online or by phone in about 10 minutes (☎ **800/MONEY-GRAM;** www.moneygram.com).

If you've lost all forms of photo ID, call your airline and explain the situation; your carrier may let you board the plane if you have a copy of your passport or birth certificate and a copy of the police report you've filed.

Mail   Allow 5 to 8 days to send or receive mail from your home. Airmail letters within Europe cost .50€ (65¢); to the United States and Canada, .90€ ($1.15). Airmail letters to Australia and New Zealand cost .90€ ($1.15).

You can exchange money at post offices. Many hotels sell stamps, as do local post offices and cafes displaying a red TABAC sign outside. The French post is not the most reliable of entities, so if you do need to send anything of value, it could be worth paying for recorded delivery (recommandé, Chronopost, or FedEx).

Measurements   The metric system is used in France. Hand gestures are often more useful for indicating what you want in a shop, but for basic conversions, see below.

For clothing, taille unique means one-size only. T-shirts and knitwear are often sized 1, 2, or 3 (small, medium, or large). Children's clothes are sized by age. Otherwise, follow these conversions:

Size Conversion Chart

Women's Clothing

French	36	38	40	42	44	46
American	6	8	10	12	14	16

Women's Shoes

French	36	37	38	39	40	41
American	5	6	7	8	9	10

Men's Suits

French	44	46	48	50–52	54	56
American	34	36	38	40	42	44

Men's Shirts

French	35	36–37	38	39–40	41	42–43
American	14	14$\frac{1}{2}$	15	15$\frac{1}{2}$	16	16$\frac{1}{2}$

Men's Shoes

French	42	43	44	45	46
American	9	10	11	12	13

Newspapers & Magazines   Copies of the international edition of *The Herald Tribune* are distributed all over France, and are sold at newspaper kiosks and at newsstands in the lobbies of first-class or deluxe hotels. Copies of *Time* and *Newsweek* are also widely sold. A far larger selection of U.K. magazines and newspapers is available. London newspapers arrive in Paris an hour or so after publication.

Police   Call ☎ **17** anywhere in France.

Restrooms   If you're in dire need, duck into a cafe or brasserie to use the lavatory. It's customary to make a small purchase if you do so. Some Paris Métro stations and underground garages usually contain public restrooms, but the degree of cleanliness varies. France still has some "hole-in-the-ground" toilets, so be warned (see "The Turkish Loo" on p. 108). For reviews and recommendations of the tidiest toilets in France and other places, visit **www.thebathroomdiaries.com**.

Taxes   As a member of the European Union, France routinely imposes a value-added tax (VAT in English, TVA in French) on many goods and services. The standard VAT is 19.6% on merchandise, including clothing, appliances, liquor, leather goods, shoes, furs, jewelry, perfumes, cameras, and even caviar. Refunds are made for the tax on certain goods and merchandise, but not on services. The minimum purchase is 184€ ($239) at one time for nationals or residents of countries outside the E.U.

Telephones   The French use a **télécarte,** or phone debit card, which you can purchase at rail stations, post offices, and other places. Sold in two versions, it allows you to use either 50 or 120 charge units (depending on the card) by inserting the card into the slot of most public phones. Depending on the type of card you buy, the cost starts at 10€ ($13) and goes up from there. You must use this card when making calls within France; coins are no longer accepted. You can use a major credit card in much the same way as a télécarte, but there's a catch: To do so involves a minimum charge of 20€ ($26). The phone system gives you 30 days to use up this 20€ credit. If possible, avoid making calls from your hotel; some establishments will double or triple the charges.

To call France:

1. Dial the international access code: 011 from the U.S.; 00 from the U.K., Ireland, or New Zealand; or 0011 from Australia.
2. Dial the country code: 33.
3. Dial the city code, which is always two digits, beginning with a zero, but drop that first zero.
4. Dial the eight-digit number.

For calls within France: You must dial the full 10-digit number, including the area code. For example, even if you're calling next door in Paris, you still must dial 01.

To make international calls: To make international calls from France, first dial 00 and then the country code (U.S. or Canada 1; U.K. 44; Ireland 353; Australia 61; New Zealand 64). Next you dial the area code and number. For example, if you wanted to call the British Embassy in Washington, D.C., you would dial ☏ **00-1-202-588-7800.**

For directory and operator assistance: Dial ☏ **118-000** for assistance in French; in English, dial 0-800/364-775. If you wish to use an operator to call your home country, you dial the toll-free number of ☏ **08-00-99-00** plus the following 10 digits of your country code: Include 08-00-99-00-11 for the U.S. and Canada, and 08-00-99-00-44 for the U.K., or 08-00-99-00-61 for Australia. Other access numbers for long-distance operators include AT&T Direct (☏ **08-00-99-00-11** or 800/222-0300 for information) and MCI WorldPhone (☏ **08-00-99-0019** or 800/444-4444 for information).

Toll-free numbers: For France, numbers beginning with 08 and followed by 00 are toll free. But be careful. Numbers that begin with 08 followed by 36 carry a .35€ (50¢) surcharge per minute.

Time   The French equivalent of daylight saving time lasts from April to September, which puts it 1 hour ahead of French winter time. France is usually 6 hours ahead of U.S. Eastern Time, except in October, when U.S. clocks are still on daylight time; then France is only 5 hours ahead. The rest of the year, when it's 9am in New York, it's 3pm in France.

Tipping   Most bills say *service compris,* which means the total includes the tip. But French diners often leave some small change as an additional tip, especially if service has been exceptional. Some general guidelines: For hotel staff, tip 1€ to 1.50€ ($1.30–$1.95) for every item of baggage the porter carries on arrival and departure, and 1.50€ ($1.95) per day for the maid. In cafes, service is usually included. Tip taxi drivers 10% to 15% of the amount on the meter (but this is not obligatory). In theaters and restaurants, give cloakroom attendants at least .75€ to 1.20€ ($1–$2) per item.

Give cinema and theater ushers about .50€ (65¢). For guides for group visits to museums and monuments, 1.50€ ($1.95) is a reasonable tip.

Useful Phone Numbers   U.S. Department of State Travel Advisory: ☎ **202/647-5225** (staffed 24 hr.); U.S. Passport Agency: ☎ **202/647-0518;** U.S. Centers for Disease Control International Traveler's Hot Line: ☎ **404/332-4559.**

Water   Drinking water is safe. If you ask for water in a restaurant, it'll be served bottled (for which you'll pay) unless you specifically request *l'eau du robinet* (tap water). Your waiter may ask if you'd like your water *avec gas* (carbonated) or *sans gas* (without bubbles).

Paris & Ile-de-France

by Anna Brooke

Few cities evoke so much promise and emotion as the French capital. Myths of romance hang over the city like mist over the Seine, in some ways obscuring the dynamic reality of modern Parisian life and in other ways creating it: The couples lip-locked on park benches; the cult of femininity that Parisian women obsessively cultivate; even the pigeons, exceptionally well fed and plumed, enliven this lore as they give substance to it. Paris cannot shake off the ghosts of its literary and artistic past, either, from the romantic visions of Victor Hugo and the darkness of Emile Zola, to the crazed ravings of Louis Aragon, the depressive ponderings of Sartre, and the intensely intelligent observations of Simone de Beauvoir. In modern times, the cinematic has replaced the literary, and the great Jean-Pierre Melville, Jean-Luc Godard, François Truffaut, and even foreigners such as Woody Allen have used the city as the backdrop for their kaleidoscopic hallucinations.

Once you get over just how damn beautiful it is, however, you start noticing its little "quirks": The romance dims the moment you step in a steaming pile of dog poop (this proper populace spends much time elegantly dodging the ubiquitous *merde*), or kiss death while trying to cross a street besieged by maniacal drivers (always look left and right twice), or catch sight of the many tents distributed by the Red Cross to the city's ever-growing homeless population. A tumultuous contradiction of pleasures and annoyances coexists here: Heavy traffic, pollution, quick tempers, bitchiness, arrogance, an innate unwillingness to comply, and lofty prices lock horns day and night with the unfaltering beauty of the Seine, the attractiveness of Parisian women and men, the attention they devote to their flowers, their hair, their window displays, their shoes (although not always their sidewalks), and their gastronomy. Paris has more history, exquisite food, breathtaking museums, chi-chi boutiques, idyllic cafes, expansive avenues, and beautiful people in one little *rue* than most cities have in their entire square mileage. You could fill a couple of weeks of your time here, easy. Hell, you could spend 2 weeks in the Louvre alone.

Even so, don't confine yourself to the city for the whole of your trip. The **Ile-de-France** (the region in which Paris lies) isn't just about the capital. Enclosed in the circle of four great rivers—the Aube, the Oise, the Marne, and the Seine—the Ile-de-France consists of many small towns and lush landscapes. Since the end of the 18th century, the beauty of the surrounding countryside has attracted legendary artists such as

Claude Monet, who made his home in **Giverny.** And now it soaks up the runoff of millions of travelers who visit Paris each year. It is rife with forests and châteaux (**Fontainebleau, Chantilly, Rambouillet,** and **Vaux-le-Viconte**), medieval towns **(Provins),** and cathedrals **(Chârtres).** All of them are an easy day trip from the capital, and a great way to shed your club gear, *branché*-conscious mindset, and cares for a while.

So go ahead, join the hordes of tourists marching on Louis XIV's fabulous château in **Versailles,** get religious with the pilgrims at the Cathédrale Nôtre-Dame in **Chartres,** or pack some bread crumbs and hike to one of the Hansel-and-Gretel forests outside of town. Just don't expect to find star-studded nightlife on your excursions: The region's towns act as the dark cosmos over which the City of Light's heavenly bodies shine.

The Best of Paris & Ile-de-France

For more of the best of Paris and Ile-de-France, see the "Best of France" chapter.

The Best Nightlife

○ **The Best Lounge Bar: China Club** is a converted mansion done up like a 1930s Hong Kong gentleman's club. Swishly presented with red walls, a black-and-white floor, and a long zinc bar, it's the perfect escape for a cocktail among friends, a romantic dinner with a new beau or belle, a toe-tapping session in the downstairs concert room, or a puff on a cigar in the upstairs *fumoir.* See p. 97.

○ **The Best Place to See and Be Seen:** Looking good is prerequisite to sharing space with the French reality-TV stars, models, platinum-blond heiresses, and

moneyed wannabes who swank around **La Suite.** To ensure entry into this very pink and very selective resto-club, book a table at the penthouse restaurant before slinking down to the bar later on. See p. 105.

○ **The Best Live Music Venue: La Flèche d'Or** has seriously cleaned up its acts and its reputation over the last few years. Today it is one of Paris's most happening live-music venues for rock and electro sounds. There's even a cool brasserie in the annex for those hungry moments between tunes. See p. 105.

○ **The Best Gay Scene:** With an openly gay mayor, you'd expect the capital to have a thriving gay and lesbian scene, and guess what—it does. Most of the action happens in and around the

Marais district, where the rainbow flag flies high and proud. This area is home to myriad gay venues, from quiet bars and trendy restaurants to swinging nightclubs with back rooms. See p. 73.

The Best Sightseeing

○ **The Best Two Museums for Cultural Initiation:** If you've never visited the **Louvre** (p. 116) or the **Musée d'Orsay** (p. 115), get yourself round to either of these iconic museums sharpish. The Louvre is a veritable palace of antiquity that could take weeks to explore. This is where you'll find the pieces that everybody must see at least once in their lifetime: da Vinci's *Mona Lisa*, Milo's *Venus*, the Hellenistic *Winged Victory of Samothrace*, and Michelangelo's *Slaves*. The Musée d'Orsay is the perfect complement to the Louvre. Set in a former railway station, its structure is as impressive as its collections. A whole floor is devoted to Impressionist paintings. Pure eye candy.

○ **The Best Unusual Place to Catch a Film:** Seeing a 19th-century Japanese pagoda in the middle of Paris is interesting enough. But when you learn that it's an arthouse cinema (some films play in English), you've really got to see it with your own eyes. **La Pagode**'s main screen is set in the former ballroom whose walls are decorated with silk tapestries. See p. 120.

○ **The Best Place to Call on the Dead:** You don't have to be a ghoul to be thrilled by a visit to Europe's most famous cemetery, **Père-Lachaise.** You can pay your respects to the earthly remains of Gertrude Stein and her longtime companion, Alice B. Toklas; Oscar Wilde; Yves Montand and Simone Signoret; Edith Piaf; Isadora Duncan; Abélard and Héloïse; Frédéric Chopin;

Marcel Proust; Eugène Delacroix; Jim Morrison; and others. The tomb designs are intriguing and often eerie. Laid out in 1803 on a hill in Ménilmontant, the cemetery offers surprises with its bizarre monuments, unexpected views, and ornate sculpture. See p. 111.

○ **The Best Place to Track Bohemia:** The old **Canal St-Martin,** through central Paris, has plenty of empty warehouses, run-down cafes, and real-estate potential—too much for any self-respecting bohemian to refuse. Once a working class neighborhood, it's now a stretch of shabby-chic bars, restaurants, bistros, and boutiques—the ultimate haunt for anyone looking to study the Parisian breed of Bobos (Bourgeois-Bohemians) and perhaps become one for the evening. See p. 77.

○ **The Best Place to Explore by Candlelight:** Louis XIV's finance minister built **Vaux-le-Vicomte,** a wondrous and most decadent palace. Then the king got jealous and imprisoned him for life—but not before stealing his architect, painter, and gardener for Versailles. For a few months every year, the castle staff switches off the electricity and guides you through the gardens and stately rooms, lit entirely by candlelight. See p. 136.

The Best Dining

○ **The Best Cheap Meal in a Local Haunt:** It's worth the 10-minute uphill walk to sit within the warm, yellow glow of **Ma Pomme**'s four walls (covered in temporary art exhibitions), and to taste their excellent-value 21€ menu. It's one of the best yet cheapest places on the block. See p. 96.

○ **The Best Quick Lunch or Dinner on the Go:** You've got 10€ in your pocket and you're starving. Come to **Chez**

Chartier, a 19th-century former workers' canteen, and soak up the atmosphere. Time here has indeed stood still: Waiters look like they've stepped out of a Renoir painting, the food hasn't changed much since Renoir's era, and the prices have withstood almost 2 centuries of inflation. See p. 95.

○ **The Best Place to Come to Grips with France's New Generation of Young Chefs:** We're all familiar with Nouvelle Cuisine and Michelin stars, but times have changed, and a new generation of young chefs is slogging away to renew France's culinary reputation. Generation.C (the name of the association) is a cultural movement that considers cooking an art form. To sample this New Wave cuisine, try restaurants such as **Angl'Opéra** (39 av. de l'Opéra, 2nd arr.; ☎ 01-42-61-86-25; www. anglopera.com; Métro/RER: Opéra and **La Famille** (41 rue des Trois Frères, 18th arr.; ☎ 01-42-52-11-12; Métro: Anvers or Abbesses). See p. 99.

The Best Hotels

○ **The Best Doable Hotel for a Spot of Romance:** What makes the **Aviatic** so charming? Could it be the bistro-style breakfast room, covered in old Parisian posters? Or is it the location, snuck down an unlikely street between Montparnasse and St-Germain des Près? Nah, it must be the devastatingly sweet empire lounge near the front door; or the cozy rooms, each individually decorated in plush fabrics. Oh, I don't know—it's just entirely romantic. See p. 87.

The Best Shopping

○ **The Best One-Stop Shopping: Colette** was the first to kick off the trend of concept stores. With their fusion of art, fashion, music, and other

creative-designer pursuits, concept stores look set to stick around—at least until the next concept crops up. See p. 128 for a full list.

○ **The Best Places to Shop Like a Local:** If you want to feel Parisian, you must amble through one of the open-air or covered *marchés* to buy fresh food—perhaps a ripe 'n' creamy Camembert or a pumpkin-gold cantaloupe—to be eaten before sundown. For iconic French food–shopping, head to **Saxe-Breteuil Market** (place de Breteuil to av. de Seguri; Thurs–Sat 7am–2:30pm), the only food market with a view of the Tour Eiffel. **Marché des Enfants Rouge** (39 rue de Bretagne; Tues–Sat 8:30am–1pm and 4–7:30pm, Sun 8:30am–2pm) is Paris's oldest market, dating from 1615. And **Marché Moufftard** (rue Moufftard) is a wonderfully typical Parisian street market where you may well spot a few chefs stocking up for the day.

The Best Outdoor Activities

○ **The Best Place to Watch a Movie in Summer:** Every July and August at **Parc de la Villette** (☎ 01-40-03-75-75; www.villette.com), locals turn up by the thousands, with picnic baskets and blankets in tow, to watch outdoor films, projected onto Europe's largest inflatable TV screen. It's the ultimate way to soak up the laid-back atmosphere of summer in Paris.

○ **The Best Place to Picnic:** Park-life in Paris doesn't begin and end in the Luxembourg and Tuileries gardens, beautiful as they are. Plenty of other wide-open spaces are lending a new edge to the city's green-scene. **Les Buttes-Chaumont** (p. 124), high on a hillside in the northeast, is a glorious array of meandering paths and vertical cliffs. **Parc André Citroën** (p. 123) is a modern-day take on formal gardens, with angular paths, glass greenhouses, computerized fountains, and a tapered hot-air balloon that rises up over the city.

○ **The Best Place to Gamble Away a Sunny Afternoon:** Paris boasts eight tracks for horse racing. The most famous and the classiest is **Hippodrome de Longchamp,** in the Bois de Boulogne, the site of the Prix de l'Arc de Triomphe and Grand Prix (p. 124). These and other top races are major social events, so you'll have to dress up (hats recommended, ladies). Take the Métro to Porte d'Auteuil and then a bus from there to the track. The racing newspaper *Paris Turf* and weekly entertainment magazines detail race times.

The Best Experiences

○ **People-Watching in Cafes:** The cafe is where passionate meetings of writers, artists, philosophers, thinkers, and revolutionaries have taken place in Paris for centuries. Parisians still stop by their favorite haunts to meet lovers and friends, to make new ones, or to sit in solitude with a newspaper, book, or laptop computer. For the coolest cafes, see p. 92.

○ **Taking High Tea in Highbrow Haunts:** The English have tea drinking down to a "T," so to speak, but the old school Parisian *salon de thé* is unique: Skip the cucumber sandwiches and delve into luscious desserts such as macaroons from **La Durée** (16 rue Royale, 8th arr.; ☎ 01-42-60-21-79; Métro: Concorde or Madeleine; 75 av. des Champs Elysées, 8th arr.; ☎ 01-40-75-08-75; www.laduree.fr), the best vanilla-cream *millefeuille* in Paris, from **Café de la Paix** (place de l'Opéra, 9th

arr.; ☎ 01-40-07-36-36; Métro: Opéra; RER: Auber), or a rich hot chocolate from the grandest Parisian tea salon, **Angélina** (226 rue de Rivoli, 1st arr.; ☎ 01-42-60-82-00; Métro: Tuileries or Concorde).

○ **Attending a Ballet or an Opera:** When in Paris, one must embrace the literati, and nowhere can you more enjoyably rub shoulders with them (nay, fight for elbowroom) than in Paris's two opera and ballet venues. The **Opéra Bastille** (p. 120) was inaugurated in 1989 to compete with the *grande dame* of the music scene, the 19th-century, rococo **Opéra Garnier** (p. 120), created by Charles Garnier, beneath a controversial ceiling by Marc Chagall. The modern Bastille, France's largest opera house, with curtains by designer Issey Miyake, features opera and symphony performances in four concert halls (its main hall seats 2,700); and Garnier's palace deals mostly with ballet and modern dance. Whether you're attending a performance of Bizet or a male-only *Swan Lake,* dress for the pomp and circumstance.

○ **Climbing to the Top of the Eiffel Tower:** Gustave Eiffel built Paris's ultimate phallic edifice in 1889 for the World Exhibition. Climbing it (1,665 steps or the elevator—hard choice!) never fails to impress. At night, watch it sparkle under 42km (26 miles) of electric bulbs switched on for 10 minutes on the hour; by day, watch the steely blue and cream hues of Paris roll out before your eyes. See p. 110.

○ **Pose for Your Portrait at Place du Tertre:** It's touristy, it's always jam-packed, but it's so damn cute: Place du Tertre is Montmartre's busiest square, filled with houses, cafes, piano bars, and creperies. Painters such as Toulouse

Lautrec once hung out here, but nowadays the artists crowding the streets are there for one thing only—to paint your portrait. And why not create some personalized Parisian memorabilia? See p. 78.

○ **Boating along the Seine:** The Seine is not only the life-force of Paris, it is also a source of beauty. No visit to the French capital would be complete without a boat trip along the river's panoramic stretches. The bridges, beautiful from up above, are stunning from down below, where you can study the statues up close and personal, and see the smaller details visible only from water level. **Bateaux Parisiens** (www.bateauxparisiens.com), **Bateaux-Mouches** (www.bateaux-mouches.fr), and **Batobus** (www.batobus.com) are the three main companies that rule the waves. See p. 80.

○ **Getting Lost in the Château de Versailles and Its Wondrous Gardens:** Boy, did that Sun King, Louis XIV, understand opulence. The bijou in the royal crown, Versailles is still the best way to spend a warm summer day in the Ile-de-France. Amble through the terraced gardens and admire the fountains, Marie Antoinette's hamlet, and the classical music extravaganzas that take place during les Fêtes de Nuit music festival. See p. 132.

○ **Shopping Till You Drop:** You can't visit the world's fashion capital without whipping out a few notes from your wallet at least once. Whether you are a designer junky, love department stores, or are on a mission to find the world's most unique boutique, Paris will satisfy. And it's not just about fashion: Family-run food shops, artisan outlets, and flea markets round out the shopping spectrum. See p. 124.

○ **Sitting in the Audience of a French TV Show:** The insulated world of French television is one of the hardest to penetrate in western Europe. But every studio-based TV program needs a lively audience to create a bit of atmosphere, and that's where you can step in. If you can understand and talk a bit of French, try www.claponline.com or call ☎ **08-25-16-97-97** to register for **France 2** (www.france2.fr) and **France 3** (www.France3.fr) TV channels. For **TF1** (www.tf1.fr), call ☎ **08-25-80-98-10** for a full list of audience-based programs.

○ **Going to the Circus:** Think entertainment in Paris, and nine times out of ten, you'll think glitzy cabaret. But the circus is also very popular and very Parisian. And you can see it all—from lions and tigers and bears (oh, my!) under a traditional Big-Top (Cirque Pinder; www.cirquepinder.com), to avant-garde acrobatics at places such as Parc de la Villette (www.villette.com). See p. 123.

Getting Around the Region

Served by both the **RER** and **SNCF rail lines,** the Ile-de-France is tourist-friendly (perhaps too friendly). The region's sites are best seen on day trips or overnights from Paris. For train departure times and real-time traffic reports around Paris and the Ile-de-France, check the sites **www.ratp.fr**, **www.sncf.com**, and **www.bison-fute.equipement.gouv.fr**, where you can plot routes by road.

When you're in Paris, you have several choices: The **Métro** (subway), which covers the town center; the **RER** (part-subway, part—outside train line), which covers the center and some of Ile-de-France; **buses,** which cover the center and suburbs; **boats,** which run along the Seine; and **taxis.**

The easiest, fastest, and most efficient way to get around is by **Métro** and **RER.** Métro lines are numbered from 1 to 14, RER lines from A to E. The final destination of each line is clearly marked on subway maps, in the underground passageways, and on the train cars. Both run daily from around 5:30am to 1:15am (depending upon the line). It's reasonably safe at any hour, but beware of pickpockets and pay special attention at cross-over stations such as Châtelet, Gare du Nord, and Montparnasse (especially at night), where several TGV, Métro, and RER lines run out to the suburbs, attracting the odd unsavory group of youths. You can buy tickets from a machine in the subway station or from a ticket window. Individual (purple) tickets cost 1.40€, and a package of 10 *(un carnet)* is 11€ (see "Cheap Tickets to Ride" on p. 65). These are valid on the Métro, RER, and buses in the town center. Don't worry that Paris is divided into transport zones; you don't need to understand the zones unless you are planning to travel outside Paris to places such as Versailles or the airport. Central Paris is classed as zones 1 and 2, and a standard ticket is valid in these two zones. For destinations farther afield on the RER, buy a separate ticket. To get through the turnstiles to the Métro and RER, put your ticket in the slot and then take the ticket with you on the train. Don't lose it whatever you do; you may need it to get out, and mean-spirited *controleurs* dressed in uniform can stop you at any time on the trains or in the station and ask to see your ticket; if it's not bona fide, they'll fine you.

To familiarize yourself with the subway system, check out the color map on the inside back cover of this book. Most stations display a map of the Métro at the entrance. To locate the line you should take, find where you are on the map, find your destination (or station change), follow the line to the end of its route, and note the name of the final stop, which is that line's direction. In the station, follow the signs for your direction in the passageways until you reach the platform. Just before you get to the platform, a panel will list the stops served by the train, so you can double-check that you're in the right place. Many larger stations have maps with push-button indicators that light up your route when you press the button for your destination, and others have help points where you can ask directions.

Buses are much slower than the Métro, but they afford views of the city while you're on the move. The majority run from 7am to 8:30pm, a few operate until 12:30am, and several nighttime buses **(Noctilien)** operate from 12:30 to 5:30am (most Noctilien lines start at train stations Châtelet, Gare de Lyon, Gare du Nord, Montparnasse, and Gare St-Lazare). Service is limited on Sundays and holidays for all buses. Bus and Métro fares are the same; you can use the same tickets on both. Most bus rides require one ticket, but some destinations require two (never more than two within the city limits).

At certain stops, signs list destinations and bus numbers serving that point. Destinations are usually listed north to south and east to west. Most stops are also posted on the sides of the buses. If you intend to use the buses a lot, pick up an RATP bus map at any Métro or print one off from **www.ratp.fr.** For detailed recorded information (in English) on bus and Métro routes, call ☎ **01-58-76-16-16.**

PARIS & ILE-DE-FRANCE

The RATP also operates the **Balabus**—big-windowed, orange-and-white motor coaches that run only during limited hours (Mon–Fri 8:30am–5:30pm). Itineraries run in both directions between Gare de Lyon and the Grande Arche de La Défense, encompassing some of the city's most beautiful vistas. It's a great deal—two Métro tickets, for 1.40€ each, will carry you the entire route. You'll recognize the bus and the route it follows by the Bb symbol emblazoned on each bus's side and on bus stops. For more information on all of the above, call ☎ **08-92-68-77-14** (www.ratp.fr).

It's virtually impossible to get a **taxi** at rush hour, so don't even try. (Taxi drivers are organized into a lobby that limits their number to 15,000.) Watch out for common rip-offs: Always check the meter to make sure you're not paying the previous passenger's fare. Beware of cabs without meters, which often wait at airports and outside nightclubs for tipsy patrons. As a rule, only get into cabs labeled TAXI PARISIEN. You can hail them on the street when they have their light on (marked LIBRE), or from ranks found near many Métro stations. From one side of town to another (and we're talking right across town), you can expect to pay around 25€. On airport trips, you're not required to pay for the driver's empty return ride; to or from the center, you should expect to pay around 50€ to 60€. Small luggage is free if it's transported alongside you, but heavier suitcases will need to go in the trunk and cost up to 3€ extra. Tipping is not obligatory, but 10% to 15% will usually elicit a genuine *merci*. For radio cabs, call **Les Taxis Bleus** (☎ **08-25-16-10-10**) or **Taxi G7** (☎ **01-47-39-47-39**)—but note that you'll be charged from the point where the taxi begins the drive to pick you up.

If the idea of crossing Paris by **boat** is too cool for you to refuse, try the **Batobus** (☎ **08-25-05-01-01;** www.batobus.com). The 150-passenger ferry runs along the Seine every day between April and December. It stops at all the main points of interest: **Eiffel Tower, Musée d'Orsay,** the **Louvre, Notre-Dame,** and the **Hôtel de Ville.** Unlike the Bateaux-Mouches (p. 81), the Batobus does not provide recorded commentary, and the only fare option is a pass valid for either 1, 2, or 5 days, each allowing as many entrances and exits as you want. A 1-day pass costs 11€ for adults, 5€ for students; a 2-day pass costs 13€ for adults, 6€ for students; a 5-day pass costs 16€ for adults, 7€ for students. Boats operate daily (closed most of Jan) every 15 to 30 minutes, starting between 10 and 10:30am and ending between 4:30 and 10:30pm, depending on the season.

For many sites in Ile-de-France, you will need to take standard trains run by France's national service the **SNCF** (☎ **08-36-67-68-69** or 08-36-35-35-35 from the U.S., ☎ 36-35 from France; www.sncf.com). **SNCF Transilien** is an Ile-de-France-specific line that covers (among others) Versailles and Fontainebleau, selling combined return tickets and entry to the attractions. Inquire at the ticket desk when you purchase your train tickets and check out **www.transilien.com**.

RENTAL VEHICLES

Once you've seen how Parisians drive, you will not be looking for your own set of wheels in town. Cars are useful, however, for getting out and about in the **Ile-de-France.** Here are a few reliable rental agencies. For road maps and itinerary instructions, check out **www.mappy.fr**.

◌ **Ada:** There are several addresses, but the most useful are 80 av. de Saint-Ouen, 18th arr. (☎ **01-46-27-36-87;** Métro: Guy Moquet); 47 cours de Vincennes, 20th arr. (☎ **08-25-16-96-00;** Métro: Nation); Gare de Lyon, 12th arr. (☎ **08-25-16-96-00;** RER/Métro: Gare de Lyon); and 34 av.

Cheap Tickets to Ride

If you plan to ride the Métro a lot, the **Paris Visite** pass (☎ 08-92-68-77-14; www.parisvisite.com) may be worthwhile. You get unlimited rides for 1 to 5 days depending on the price (8.50€ for 1 day, 14€ for 2 days, 19€ for 3 days, and 27€ for 5 days), all for access to zones 1 to 3, which includes central Paris and its nearby suburbs, but not Disneyland, the airport, or Versailles (available from all RATP desks in the Métro and from tourist offices).

Carte Orange is the most economical option for anyone who arrives in Paris early in the week. Sold at large Métro stations, it allows 1 week of unlimited Métro or bus transit within central Paris and its immediate outskirts for 16€. The pass is valid from any Monday to the following Sunday. It's sold only on Monday, Tuesday, and Wednesday, and you'll have to submit a passport-size photo upon purchase.

Another discount pass is **Carte Mobilis,** which allows unlimited travel on bus, subway, and RER lines during a 1-day period for 5.50€ to 19€, depending on the zone. Ask for it at any Métro station.

If a rendezvous with the world's favorite mouse is in the cards, you can save queuing at **Disneyland Paris** by buying a 1-day passport (44€ adults, 36€ children) at the same time as your RER ticket.

de la République, 11th arr. (☎ 01-48-06-58-13; www.ada.fr; Métro: République).

○ **Europcar:** The most handy addresses are Gare SNCF d'Austerlitz, bd. de l'Hôpital, 13th arr. (☎ 01-44-06-08-96; Métro: Gare d'Austerlitz); 88 rue de la Roquette, 11th arr. (☎ 01-43-57-20-62; Métro: Bastille); Charles de Gaulle Airport terminals 1, 2, and 3 (☎ 08-25-82-54-90); and Gare du Nord, 10th arr. (☎ 08-25-82-54-38; www.europcar.fr; Métro/RER: Gare du Nord).

○ **Avis:** Contact the Paris headquarters at ☎ 01-53-93-73-40 (www.avis.fr). Locations are at Gare Montparnasse, 15th arr. (Métro: Montparnasse); place de la Madeleine (in the underground parking lot), 8th arr. (Métro: Madeleine); 105 rue de Lourmel, 15th arr. (Métro: Lourmel or Boucicaut).

Freescoot (www.freescoot.com) rents bicycles, motorcycles, and scooters. They have two locations: one at 114 bd. Voltaire, 75011 Paris (☎ 01-44-93-04-03; Métro: Voltaire) and the other at 63 quai de la Tournelle, 75005 Paris (☎ 01-44-07-06-72; Métro: Jussieu). **Motorail** (190 rue de Bercy Gare de Lyon, 75012 Paris; ☎ 08-92-35-00-25; www.motorail.fr; Métro: Gare de Lyon) also rents scooters, motorcycles, and bicycles with all the necessary equipment (helmets, gloves, jackets).

Lack of space makes **parking** in Paris a challenge. Just look at the cars strewn across pedestrian crossings and street corners and you'll understand the "anything goes" parking policy upheld by most Parisians. The silly thing is that a parking fine often costs less than the actual cost of parking, so it is not surprising that many Parisians don't worry about tickets. But if you'd rather avoid a fine, seek out one of the city's many underground parking lots (look out for a blue panel with a large white P on it). Several hotels have private parking or deals with nearby parking lots, so don't forget to ask when you book your room. As a last resort, you could look into pre-booking a parking space on www.parkingsdeparis.com.

Paris

The reasons why people come to Paris far outstrip the truth of the French capital, where the clichés are so potent they ultimately become the real thing. Paris has never lost its place in the world as the capital of class, intrigue, and desire. It is here that you can best contemplate what you want from life, and it is here that many people do that very thing.

Some come to chase away the banality of daily life, to repair love that is ailing, or to find love that is missing. Others come to treat themselves to the guilt of calories they deny themselves at home; to re-ingest the buzz of recognizing the details they appreciated, the tastes they recall, or the waiter who charmed them last summer; or to tap into an alternative vibe—one that is different, but no less powerful and creative than the artistic energy thrumming through London, New York, and Tokyo.

The way Paris creeps under your skin and stays there is a phenomenon all of its own. There is the "you" before Paris, and the "you" after Paris. Then there is the return: The tiny thrill and apprehension of re-connecting with the person you were when you were here—the person in you that you'd forgotten existed and can't be anywhere else.

Paris is not surreal, weird, or hedonistic. It is simply inexhaustible in its ability to charm, to seduce, to please, and to invite you to search deeper and with more intensity into everything. The *café noisette* or the flute of kir with a *soupçon* of cassis that you sip on any great boulevard terrace is less about what you're drinking than the time you take to do nothing, the plans you make for the afternoon and the next 30 years. For the visitor in you, Paris is about love, about memory, about the broader history you and the city are both part of, and, of course, the flush of delight that lives in the realization of this.

Paris History 101

You'd need an entire book just to cover the main events of the dense and complex history of Paris, but this timeline highlights the most important moments since the region was first inhabited by humans, in 2000 B.C. (I haven't included my own arrival date, but FYI it was Dec 28, 2000.)

2000 B.C. Lutétia thrives along a strategic crossing of the Seine, the headquarters of the Parisii tribe.

52 B.C. Julius Caesar conquers Lutétia during the Gallic Wars.

A.D. 150 Lutétia flourishes as a Roman colony, expanding to the Left Bank.

200 Barbarian Gauls force the Romans to retreat to Ile de la Cité.

300 Lutétia is renamed Paris; Roman power weakens in northern France.

350 Christianization of Paris begins.

400s The Franks invade Paris, with social transformation from the Roman to the Gallo-Roman culture.

466 Clovis—founder of the Merovingian dynasty and first non-Roman ruler of Paris since the Parisii—is born.

800 Charlemagne, founder of the Carolingian dynasty, is crowned Holy Roman Emperor and rules from Aachen in modern Germany.

987 Hugh Capet, founder of France's foremost early medieval dynasty, rises to power; his family rules from Paris.

1100 The Université de Paris attracts scholars from throughout Europe.

1200s Paris's population and power grow, though it is often unsettled by plagues and feudal battles.

1422 England invades Paris during the Hundred Years' War.

1429 Joan of Arc tries to regain Paris for the French; the Burgundians later capture and sell her to the English, who burn her at the stake in Rouen.

1500s François I, first of the French Renaissance kings, embellishes Paris but chooses to maintain his court in the Loire Valley.

1549 Henri II rules from Paris; construction of public and private residences begins, many in the Marais.

1564 Construction begins on Catherine de Médicis's Palais des Tuileries; building facades in Paris move from half-timbered to more durable chiseled stonework.

1572 The Wars of Religion reach their climax with the St. Bartholomew's Day massacre of Protestants.

1598 Henri IV, the most eccentric and enlightened monarch of his era, endorses the Edict of Nantes, granting tolerance to Protestants; a crazed monk fatally stabs him 12 years later.

1615 Construction begins on the Palais du Luxembourg for Henri IV's widow, Marie de Médicis.

1636 The Palais Royal is launched by Cardinal Richelieu; soon, two marshy islands in the Seine are interconnected and filled in to create Ile St-Louis.

1643 Louis XIV, the "Sun King" and the most powerful ruler since the Caesars, rises to power; he moves his court to the newly built Versailles.

1776 The American Declaration of Independence strikes a revolutionary chord in France.

1789 The French Revolution begins.

1793 Louis XVI and his queen, Marie Antoinette, are publicly guillotined.

1799 Napoleon Bonaparte crowns himself Master of France and embellishes Paris further with neoclassical splendor.

1803 Napoleon abandons French overseas expansion and sells Louisiana to the United States.

PARIS & ILE-DE-FRANCE

1812 Napoleon is defeated in the Russian winter campaign.

1814 Aided by a coalition of France's enemies, especially England, the Bourbon monarchy under Louis XVIII is restored.

1821 Napoleon Bonaparte dies.

1824 Louis XVIII dies, and Charles X succeeds him.

1830 Charles X is deposed, and the more liberal Louis-Philippe is elected king; Paris prospers as it industrializes.

1848 A violent working-class revolution deposes Louis-Philippe, who's replaced by autocratic Napoleon III.

1853 On Napoleon III's orders, Baron Haussmann redesigns Paris's landscapes and creates the Grands Boulevards, completed in 1870.

1860s Impressionist painting emerges.

1870 The Franco-Prussian War ends in the defeat of France; Paris is threatened by Prussian cannons placed on the outskirts of the city; a revolution in the aftermath of this defeat destroys the Palais des Tuileries and overthrows the government; the Third Republic rises with its elected president, Marshal MacMahon.

1878 Several international expositions add monuments to the Paris skyline, including the Tour Eiffel and Sacré-Coeur (through 1937).

1895 Capt. Alfred Dreyfus, a Jew, is wrongfully charged with treason and sentenced to life on Devil's Island. The incident will lead to one of the major French political scandals of the 19th century.

1898 Emile Zola publishes *J'Accuse* in defense of Dreyfus and flees into exile in England.

1906 Dreyfus is finally exonerated, and his rank is restored.

1914 World War I rips apart Europe. The Germans are defeated (through 1918).

1940 German troops invade Paris; the French government, under Marshal Pétain, evacuates to Vichy, while the French Resistance under Gen. Charles de Gaulle maintains symbolic headquarters in London.

1944 U.S. troops liberate Paris; de Gaulle returns in triumph.

1948 The revolt in the French colony of Madagascar costs 80,000 French lives; France's empire continues to collapse in Southeast Asia and equatorial Africa.

1952 The creation, with Germany, of the ECSC (European Coal and Steel Community), the precursor of the modern European Union.

1954 War begins in Algeria and is eventually lost; refugees flood Paris, and the nation becomes divided over its North African policies (through 1962).

1958 France's Fourth Republic collapses; General de Gaulle is called out of retirement to head the Fifth Republic.

1968 Paris's students and factory workers engage in a general revolt; the French government is overhauled in the aftermath.

1981 François Mitterrand is elected France's first Socialist president since the 1940s; he's reelected in 1988.

1989 Paris celebrates the bicentennial of the French Revolution.

1992 Euro Disney opens on the outskirts of Paris.

1994 François Mitterrand and Queen Elizabeth II ride under the English Channel in the new Chunnel.

1995 Jacques Chirac is elected over Mitterrand, who dies the following year; Paris is crippled by a general strike; terrorists bomb the subway.

1997 Authorities enforce strict immigration laws, causing strife for African and Arab immigrants and dividing the country; French voters elect Socialist Lionel Jospin as Chirac's new prime minister.

1998 Socialists triumph in local elections across France.

1999 The euro is introduced; on Christmas Day a violent storm assaults Paris and the Ile-de-France, damaging buildings and toppling thousands of trees.

2001 Bertrand Delanoë becomes Paris's first openly gay mayor, a member of the left-wing PS (Parti Socialiste), and instigator of several annual cultural events (Nuit Blanche, Paris-Plage, Paris's swimming pool on the Seine). He renders access to all state museums in Paris free of charge, campaigns avidly against the spread of HIV and AIDs in the capital, and plans to create 400 Wi-Fi connections around the city's public gardens, streets, and monuments.

2002 France replaces its national currency, the franc, and switches to the euro, the new European currency.

2003 Attacks on French Jews mark the worst anti-Semitism since World War II.

2005 George W. Bush and Chirac meet for dinner (including french fries) to mend relations. Riots explode in the suburbs and students go on strike about an unsatisfactory first-employment bill. France shocks Europe by voting against a European Constitution.

2006 The nation prepares itself for the 2007 general elections.

Getting There

BY AIR

High season on most airlines' routes to Paris is usually June to the beginning of September. This is the most expensive and most crowded time to travel. **Shoulder season** is April to May, early September to October, and December 15 to December 24. **Low season** is November 1 to December 14 and December 25 to March 31. Paris has two main airports: Roissy Charles de Gaulle (north) and Orly (south). It is also served by a small, third airport, Beauvais, a good distance away in Picardie.

Roissy Charles de Gaulle

If you are flying into Paris, you'll most likely arrive at **Roissy Charles de Gaulle** (airport code: CDG; ☎ **01-48-62-12-12,** or 39-50 in France) in the north of the city. The best way to get into the center is to take the **RER B** from the RER station (T1 or T2) at the airport, which travels directly into downtown Paris, stopping at key stations such as Gare du Nord, Châtelet, Notre-Dame/St-Michel, and Luxembourg, from where you can change lines to your final destination. Free shuttle buses *(navettes)* run from each terminal to the nearest RER station, where you can buy a ticket to the center of town (8.10€; Paris Visite and Carte Orange cards are accepted for zones 1–5). The train takes 30 to 45 minutes. If you're traveling from Paris to the airport on the RER, you will need to take a shuttle bus for all terminals except T3 (to which you can walk). Build in extra time for this as the roads around the airport can be congested.

Another option to and from the airport is the **Roissybus** (www.ratp.fr), which departs from a point near the corner of the rue Scribe and place de l'Opéra every 15 minutes from 5:45am to 11pm. The cost for the 50-minute ride is 8.50€.

Taxis from Roissy into the city run about 50€ on the meter. At night (8pm–7am) fares are about 40% higher. Long queues of both taxis and passengers form outside each of the airport's terminals in a surprisingly orderly fashion.

You can also take either of two **Air France** shuttle buses, both of which depart from Roissy for points within central Paris. Line 2 departs at 15-minute intervals every day between 6am and 11pm, charging 10€ each way for the 40-minute transit to the place de l'Etoile (Métro/RER: Charles de Gaulle Etoile), with a stop en route at Porte Maillot (Métro: Porte Maillot). Line 4 departs at 30-minute intervals every day between 7am and 9:30pm, charging 12€ for the 50-minute trip to the Gare Montparnasse (Métro: Montparnasse), making an intermediate stop at the Gare de Lyon (Métro/RER) en route. From any of those points within central Paris, Métro lines can carry you on to virtually any other point within the city.

Orly Airport

Orly (☎ 01-49-75-52-52) has two terminals: Orly Sud (south) for international flights and Orly Ouest (west) for domestic flights. A free shuttle bus links them.

Air France buses leave from Exit E of Orly Ouest and from Exit K, Platform 5, of Orly Sud every 12 minutes from 5:45am to 11pm for Gare des Invalides in central Paris at a cost of 11€ one-way. Other buses depart for place Denfert-Rochereau in the south of Paris at a cost of 12€.

An alternative method for reaching central Paris involves taking a **monorail** (OrlyVal) to the RER station of Anthony and then the RER train into downtown Paris. The OrlyVal makes stops at the north and south terminals, and continues at 8-minute intervals for the 10-minute ride to the Anthony RER station. At Anthony, you'll board an RER train (Line B) for the 30-minute ride into the city. The cost of the OrlyVal monorail plus the RER (Line B) transit into Paris is 9.10€, a fare that might seem a bit high but that offsets the horrendous construction costs of a monorail that sails above the congested roadways encircling the airport.

A **taxi** from Orly to the center of Paris costs about 35€ more at night and on weekends. Returning to the airport, **buses** to Orly leave from the Invalides terminal to either Orly Sud or Orly Ouest every 15 minutes, taking about 30 minutes.

Caution: Don't take a meterless taxi from CDG, Orly Sud, or Orly Ouest. It's much safer (and usually cheaper) to hire a metered cab from the taxi queues, which are under the scrutiny of a police officer.

Beauvais

Paris's third airport is **Beauvais** (www. aeroportbeauvais.com), outside the city in Picardie. It is the base for a bunch of budget airlines that offer cheap flights to cities in France, Europe, and Britain. A shuttle will cost 13€ one-way from Porte

Maillot (tickets are sold onboard; call ☎ 08-92-68-20-64).

BY TRAIN

If you're already in Europe, you might decide to travel to Paris by train, especially if you have a **Eurailpass.** Rail passes or individual rail tickets within Europe are available at most travel agencies, at any office of **Rail Europe** (☎ 877/272-RAIL; www.raileurope.com), or at **Eurostar** (☎ 800/EUROSTAR in the U.S., 0870/584-8848 in London, 08-92-35-35-39 in Paris; www.eurostar.com).

There are six major train stations in Paris: **Gare d'Austerlitz,** 55 quai d'Austerlitz, 13th arr. (serving the southwest, with trains from the Loire Valley, the Bordeaux country, and the Pyrenees); **Gare de l'Est,** place du 11 Novembre 1918, 10th arr. (serving the east, with trains from Strasbourg, Nancy, Reims, and beyond to Zurich, Basel, Luxembourg, and Austria); **Gare de Lyon,** 20 bd. Diderot, 12th arr. (serving the southeast with trains from the Côte d'Azur and Provence to Geneva, Lausanne, and Italy); **Gare Montparnasse,** 17 bd. Vaugirard, 15th arr. (serving the west, with trains from Brittany); **Gare du Nord,** 18 rue de Dunkerque, 15th arr. (serving the north, with trains from Holland, Denmark, Belgium, and Germany); and **Gare St-Lazare,** 13 rue d'Amsterdam, 8th arr. (serving the northwest, with trains from Normandy).

For general train information and to make reservations, call the **SNCF** at ☎ 36-35. Each of these stations has a Métro, RER, or bus service that makes the whole city easily accessible. Taxis are also available at designated stands at every station. Be alert in train stations, especially at night.

BY CAR

Driving in Paris? Are you mad? It is definitely not an easy task. Parking is difficult; traffic is dense; and networks of one-way streets make navigation, even with the best of maps, a problem. If you do drive, however, note that Paris is encircled by a ring road called the **_périphérique_** and that entry into the center is via points called _Portes._ Always obtain detailed directions to your destination, including the name of the exit (Porte) you need on the _périphérique._ Remember that the Portes aren't numbered (they are named; for example, Porte de Vincennes), and the name of your Porte will crop up one exit before you need to leave the périphérique, so that you can get in the right lane. Avoid rush hours if you can (8–9:30am and 5:30–7pm). Few hotels, except the luxury ones, have garages, but the staff will usually be able to direct you to one nearby.

The **major highways** into Paris are the A1 from the north (Great Britain and Benelux); A13 from Rouen, Normandy, and northwest France; A10 from Bordeaux, the Pyrenees, France's southwest, and Spain; A6 from Lyon, the French Alps, the Riviera, and Italy; and A4 from Metz, Nancy, and Strasbourg in eastern France.

BY BUS

Bus travel to Paris is available from London and many other cities on the continent. In the early 1990s, the French government established strong incentives for long-haul buses not to drive into the center of Paris, so the arrival/departure point for Europe's largest bus operator, **Eurolines France,** is a 20-minute Métro ride from central Paris, at the terminus of Métro Line 3 (Gallieni), in the eastern suburb of Bagnolet. Despite this inconvenience, many people prefer bus travel. **Eurolines France** is at 28 av. du Général-de-Gaulle, 93541 Bagnolet (☎ 08-92-89-90-91; www.nationalexpress.com; www.eurolines.fr).

Long-haul buses are equipped with toilets, and they stop at mealtimes for rest and refreshment. The price of a round-trip ticket between Paris and London (a 10-hr. trip) is 36€ to 45€ for passengers 13 or over. Eurolines doesn't have a U.S.-based sales agent, but any European travel agent can arrange these purchases or you can book online. If you're traveling to Paris from London, contact **Eurolines (U.K.) Ltd.,** 52 Grosvenor Gardens, Victoria, London SW1 (☎ 020/7730-8235; www. eurolines.co.uk).

UNDER THE CHANNEL

One of the great engineering feats of our time, the $15-billion Channel Tunnel (Chunnel) opened in 1994. The **Eurostar** now has daily service from London to both Paris and Brussels. The journey from London to Paris takes just under 3 hours (of which just 20 min. is spent in the Chunnel). Stores selling duty-free goods, restaurants, service stations, and bilingual staffs are available to travelers on both sides of the Channel.

Eurostar tickets are available through **Rail Europe** (☎ 877-257-2887 in the U.S.; www.raileurope.com). In Great Britain, make reservations for Eurostar at ☎ 08705-18-61-86 or 0870-530-0003; and from France call ☎ 08-92-35-35-39 (www.eurostar.com). Chunnel train travel is competitive with flying, if you calculate door-to-door travel time. Trains leave from London's Waterloo Station and arrive in Paris at the Gare du Nord.

The tunnel also accommodates passenger cars, charter buses, taxis, and motorcycles, transporting them under the Channel from Folkestone, England, to Calais, France. It operates 24 hours a day, running every 15 minutes during peak travel times and at least once an hour at night. You can buy tickets at the tollbooth

at the tunnel's entrance. With **Le Shuttle** (☎ 08-10-63-03-04 from France; ☎ 08-705-35-35-35 from U.K.; www.eurotunnel. com), gone are the days of weather-related delays, seasickness, and advance reservations.

Before they board Le Shuttle, motorists stop at a tollbooth and pass through British and French immigration at the same time. Then they drive onto a 1km-long (¹/₂ mile) train and travel through the tunnel. During the ride, motorists stay in air-conditioned carriages, remaining inside their cars or stepping outside to stretch their legs. When the trip is completed, they simply drive off. Total travel time is about an hour. Once on French soil, British drivers must remember to drive on the right-hand side of the road.

Orientation

The Seine River runs east-west through the middle of Paris. Beyond that, the city is split into 20 sectors called *arrondissements.* They spiral out like the shell of a snail (fitting for the escargot-loving French), clockwise from the central islands (Ile-St-Louis and Ile de la Cité), finishing in the northeast. The system can appear at first to make as much sense as the scoring system on a dartboard (the 17th is next to the 8th is next to the 1st), but you'll get used to it. We've indicated the *arrondissement* for each venue listed after the addresses throughout this chapter.

Arrondissements

In listings, the Paris *arrondissements* in this book are labeled as follows: The first *arrondissement* (*1er* in French) will be labeled 1st after the street name and number; the second *arrondissement* (*2e* in French) is labeled 2nd; and so forth, up to *arrondissement 20e,* labeled 20th.

Arago Medallion Trail

In homage to François Arago (1786–1804), astronomer and head of Paris's Observatory (1843), the Dutch artist Jan Dibbets laid bronze medallions, 12cm (4¾ in.) in diameter, along the meridian line that Argo traced across Paris. They follow Arago's trail from the Cité Universitaire in the south, to Porte de Montmartre in the north. To see these curiosities, keep your eyes fixed to the floor at 79 rue Lepic (18th arr.), outside 9–11 bd. Haussman (9th arr.), 16 rue du 4 Septembre (2nd arr.), 15 rue Saint Augustin (2nd arr.), 9 rue de Montpensier (1st arr.), place du Palais Royal (rue de Rivoli side, 1st arr.), Jardin Marco Polo near a Ping-Pong table (6th arr.), 2 rue de l'Observatoire (6th arr.), Cité Universitaire in between the Canadian pavilion and the Cambodian pavilion (14th arr.).

The *arrondissements* begin with the 1st on the Right Bank (north) of the Seine, smack-dab in the center of town, and then swing up and out, uncoiling clockwise. The city is bounded by the *périphérique*, a belt-way that runs up against the far ends of the double-digit *arrondissements*. In general, it's best to disregard the linear order of the *arrondissements* and to think, instead, in terms of the neighborhoods associated with the number: The 1st is the Louvre and Les Halles; the 3rd and 4th is the Marais, Beaubourg, and the islands; the 5th is the Latin Quarter; the 6th is St-Germain; and so on.

1ST (1ER) ARRONDISSEMENT (MUSEE DU LOUVRE/LES HALLES)

The **Louvre** lures hordes to the 1st *arrondissement,* on the Right Bank. This area is also home to rue de Rivoli and the **Jeu de Paume** and **Orangerie** museums. Walk through the **Jardin des Tuileries,** laid out by Louis XIV's gardener. Pause to take in the beauty of **place Vendôme.** Zola's "belly of Paris" (Les Halles) is no longer the food-and-meat market; it's now the **Forum des Halles,** an underground (frequently dodgy) shopping center. Cool bars and restaurants line the streets surrounding Le Forum des Halles.

2ND (2E) ARRONDISSEMENT (LA BOURSE)

Home to the **Bourse (stock exchange),** this Right Bank district lies between the *grands boulevards* and rue Etienne-Marcel. On weekdays, the shouts of brokers echo across place de la Bourse. Much of the east end of the 2nd is devoted to the **garment district (Le Sentier).** You'll find gems amid the commercialism, and none finer than the **Musée Cognacq-Jay** (25 bd. des Capucines; ☎ 01-40-27-07-21; www.paris.fr), featuring work by every artist from Watteau to Fragonard.

3RD (3E) ARRONDISSEMENT (LE MARAIS, WHICH STRADDLES THE 4TH)

This district embraces much of **Le Marais (the Swamp),** one of the best loved of the old Right Bank neighborhoods. Kings have called Le Marais home, and its salons have echoed with the remarks of Racine, Voltaire, Molière, and Mme de Sévigné. It enjoyed a renewal in the 1990s, with galleries and boutiques. One of its chief draws is **Musée Picasso,** a cool repository of 20th-century art. Le Marais is also the center of Paris's gay and lesbian scene. Rue des Rosiers, with its Jewish restaurants, preserves the memory of the hundreds of Jewish residents who used to reside in Le Marais. Many still do, of course.

PARIS & ÎLE-DE-FRANCE

Paris Arrondissements

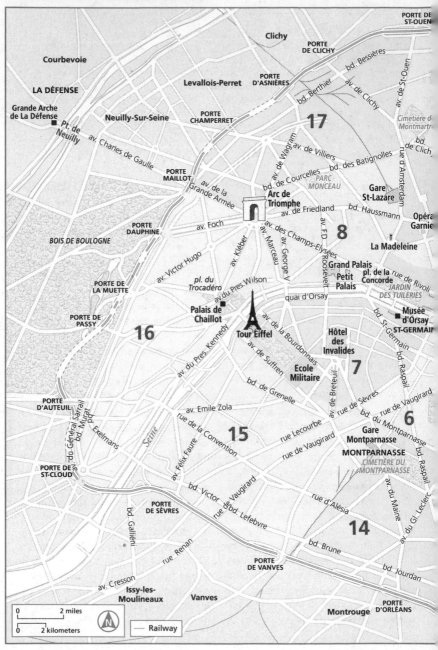

PORTE DE ST-OUEN

Clichy

PORTE DE CLICHY

bd. Bessières

Courbevoie

Levallois-Perret

PORTE D'ASNIÈRES

bd. Berthier

av. de Clichy

av. de St-Ouen

Cimetière de Montmartr

LA DÉFENSE

Grande Arche de La Défense

PORTE CHAMPERRET

Neuilly-Sur-Seine

17

bd. de Clich

rue d'Amsterdam

Pt. de Neuilly

av. Charles de Gaulle

av. de Wagram

av. de Villiers

bd. des Batignolles

PORTE MAILLOT

av. de la Grande Armée

av. de Courcelles

PARC MONCEAU

Gare St-Lazáre

Opéra Garnie

Arc de Triomphe

av. de Friedland

bd. Haussmann

PORTE DAUPHINE

av. Foch

av. des Champs-Elysées

8

La Madeleine

BOIS DE BOULOGNE

av. Victor Hugo

av. Kléber

av. Marceau

av. George V

av. F.D. Roosevelt

Grand Palais

Petit Palais

pl. de la Concorde

rue de Rivoli

PORTE DE LA MUETTE

pl. du Trocadéro

quai d'Orsay

JARDIN DES TUILERIES

PORTE DE PASSY

av. du Pres. Wilson

Palais de Chaillot

Musée d'Orsay

ST-GERMAIN

bd. St-Germain

16

Tour Eiffel

av. de la Bourdonnais

Hôtel des Invalides

av. du Pres. Kennedy

av. de Suffren

Ecole Militaire

av. de Breteuil

7

bd. Raspail

PORTE D'AUTEUIL

bd. Général Sarrail

bd. Murat

Exelmans

av. Emile Zola

bd. de Grenelle

av. de Sèvres

rue de Sèvres

rue de Vaugirard

6

Seine

rue de la Convention

15

rue Lecourbe

bd. du Montparnasse

Gare Montparnasse

bd. Raspail

PORTE DE ST-CLOUD

av. Félix Faure

rue de Vaugirard

MONTPARNASSE

CIMETIÈRE DU MONTPARNASSE

bd. Victor

rue de Vaugirard

bd. Lefebvre

rue d'Alésia

av. du Maine

av. du Gl. Leclerc

PORTE DE SÈVRES

bd. Galliéni

14

bd. Brune

bd. Jourdan

rue Renan

PORTE DE VANVES

av. Cresson

Issy-les-Moulineaux

Vanves

PORTE D'ORLÉANS

Montrouge

0   2 miles
0   2 kilometers

N

— Railway

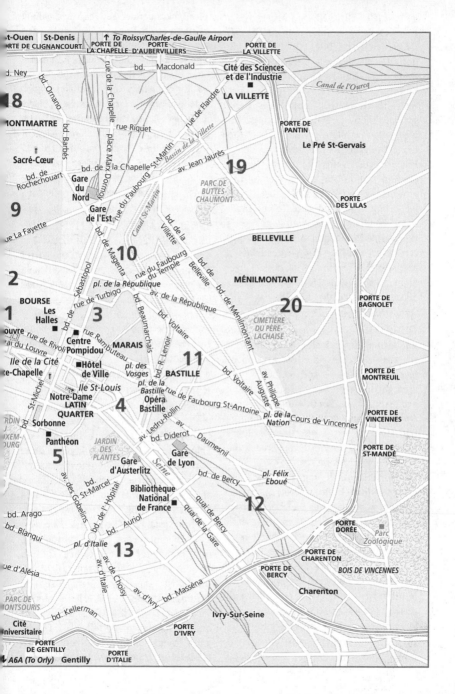

4TH (4E) ARRONDISSEMENT (ILE DE LA CITE/ILE ST-LOUIS & BEAUBOURG) The 4th has it all: not only the Ile de la Cité, with **Notre-Dame,** the **Sainte-Chapelle,** and the **Conciergerie,** but also the Ile St-Louis, with town houses, courtyards, and antiques shops. Ile St-Louis, a former cow pasture and dueling ground, is home to 6,000 Louisiens, its permanent residents. Prepare your arms for some serious elbowing action. The area is touristy and crowded—very crowded. On the islands you'll find some **bird and flower markets,** then back on the Right Bank there's the **Centre Pompidou.** After all this, you can retreat to **place des Vosges** (classed as the Marais), a square of perfect harmony where Victor Hugo penned many masterpieces from 1832 to 1848.

5TH (5E) ARRONDISSEMENT (LATIN QUARTER) The Quartier Latin is Paris's intellectual soul, featuring bookstores, schools, churches, jazz clubs, student dives, Roman ruins, and boutiques. The area got its name because students and professors at the **Sorbonne** (founded in 1253) spoke Latin. As the center of "intellectual Paris," it was the setting for Henry Murger's novel *La Vie Bohème* (later the Puccini opera *La Bohème*). The 5th borders the Seine, so you'll want to stroll along **quai de Montebello,** where vendors sell everything from antique Daumier prints to copies of Balzac's *Père Goriot.* The area also stretches to the **Panthéon,** the resting place of Rousseau, Zola, Hugo, Voltaire, and Jean Moulin, the Resistance leader tortured to death by the Gestapo; and **rue Moufftard**—a wonderful street filled with restaurants and a street market.

6TH (6E) ARRONDISSEMENT (ST-GERMAIN/LUXEMBOURG) This is, for wealthy arty types, the most colorful Left Bank quarter. You can see young artists emerging from the **Ecole des Beaux-Arts.** Strolling the boulevards of the 6th, including **St-Germain,** is interesting enough, but the secret of the district lies in its narrow streets, hidden squares, and the **Jardin du Luxembourg,** by Marie de Médici's **Palais du Luxembourg.** To be authentic, stroll these streets with a loaf of bread from the ovens of **Poilâne,** 8 rue du Cherche-Midi (☎ 01-45-48-42-59). You'll encounter historic and literary associations, as on **rue Jacob,** where Racine, Ingres, and Hemingway lived.

7TH (7E) ARRONDISSEMENT (EIFFEL TOWER/MUSEE D'ORSAY) The capital's most phallic edifice, the **Eiffel Tower** dominates the 7th on the Left Bank. The 7th is also home to the **Hôtel des Invalides,** which contains Napoleon's Tomb and the Musée de l'Armée. Even if you've little time to explore, you should visit the **Musée d'Orsay,** for its sublime 19th-century art.

8TH (8E) ARRONDISSEMENT (CHAMPS-ELYSEES/MADELEINE) Everybody who visits Paris passes through the 8th—home of the **avenue des Champs-Elysées,** linking the **Arc de Triomphe** with the obelisk on **place de la Concorde.** This is fashion-house country, expensive hotel land, rip-off restaurants, and shoppers' corner. But it is also the area known for having France's superlatives: the best restaurant **(Taillevent),** the sexiest strip joint **(Crazy Horse Saloon),** the most splendid square **(place de la Concorde),** the grandest hotel **(Crillon),** the most impressive arch **(Arc de Triomphe),** the oldest Métro station **(Franklin-D-Roosevelt),** and the most ancient monument **(Obelisk of Luxor;** 3,300 years old). Also here is **La Madeleine** church, which looks like a

Greek temple and holds frequent classical music concerts.

9TH (9E) ARRONDISSEMENT (OPERA GARNIER/PIGALLE)

Everything from the Quartier de l'Opéra to the strip joints of Pigalle (the infamous "Pig Alley" for World War II GIs) is in the 9th, on the Right Bank. Baron Haussmann's 19th-century redevelopment radically altered it, and the *grands boulevards* are among the most obvious of his works. The **Opéra,** the final hurrah of Second Empire opulence (now the Opéra Garnier or Palais Garnier), was genuinely built over an underground lake and inspired Gaston Leroux's *Phantom of the Opera.*

10TH (10E) ARRONDISSEMENT (GARE DU NORD/GARE DE L'EST/CANAL ST-MARTIN)

The two stations—along with cinemas, porno houses, and commercial zones—don't make for desirable sightseeing, but the 10th has gradually been infiltrated by Paris's Bobo population, turning certain areas into veritable dens of cool funkiness. The Canal St-Martin falls into this category, with plenty of bohemian bars, restaurants, and shops. Along the north African-influenced rue du Faubourg St-Denis are a couple of the city's best Belle Epoque brasseries: **Brasserie Flo** (7 cour Petites Ecuries; ☎ 01-47-70-13-59) and **Brasserie Julien** (10 rue du Faubourg St-Denis; ☎ **01-47-70-12-06**).

11TH (11E) ARRONDISSEMENT (BASTILLE/OBERKAMPF)

The **Opéra Bastille,** opened in 1989, is the center of this district. The "people's opera house" stands on the **place de la Bastille,** where on July 14, 1789, Parisians stormed the fortress and released the prisoners. This area between the Marais, Ménilmontant, and République is "scruffy-collar chic," and *artistes* walk the sidewalks of rue Oberkampf (one of the hottest nightspots).

Hip Parisians live and work among decaying 19th-century apartments and 1960s public housing with graffiti-spattered walls.

12TH (12E) ARRONDISSEMENT (BOIS DE VINCENNES/GARE DE LYON/BERCY)

The 12th has undergone a renaissance, with new housing, shops, and restaurants. The major attraction is the **Bois de Vincennes,** a sprawling park on the eastern periphery of Paris, with its nearby Château de Vincennes and Parc Floral de Paris, covered in springtime rhododendrons and autumn dahlias. The **Gare de Lyon,** aside from being a mainline station, has an unexpected Art Nouveau restaurant, **Le Train Bleu**—a national treasure. **Bercy,** with its modern park (including vines) and **Cour St-Emillion** (an outdoor mall built in old wine stores with a multiscreen cinema complex) is also worth visiting—especially on Sunday, when the shops open.

13TH (13E) ARRONDISSEMENT (BIBLIOTHEQUE FRANÇOIS MITTERAND/BUTTE AUX CAILLES)

The 13th is not the easiest *arrondissement* to like at first glance, but a load of money was pumped into it over the last few years, and it's beginning to bear the fruits of this investment. In front of the polemical high-rise **Bibliothèque François Mitterrand** (library), the **Batofar** (opposite 11 quai François Mauriac; ☎ **01-53-60-17-30**) is a hip live-music venue and nightclub on an old boat; and the **Butte aux Cailles** is a sweet village-like quarter that teems with student bars and cool restaurants. The 13th also hold Paris's **Chinese quarter**—a must-see during Chinese New Year—and an area where you can eat well on the cheap day or night.

14TH (14E) ARRONDISSEMENT (MONTPARNASSE)

The northern end of this district on the Left Bank is **Montparnasse,** home of the Lost

Generation, and the site of Paris's only downtown skyscraper (go to the top for the great views). Come here to experience **literary cafes** such as La Rotonde, Le Sélect, La Dôme, and La Coupole. Perhaps Gertrude Stein didn't come here (she loathed cafes), but other American expats such as Hemingway and Fitzgerald arrived for a drink or four. Along rue de la Gaîté you'll find the Left Bank hub of Paris's theater scene, and farther south at Denfert Rochereau lies Paris's most morbid attraction, the bone-lined **Catacombes.**

15TH (15E) ARRONDISSEMENT (LA MOTTE PICQUET GRENELLE/PARC ANDRE CITROËN)

The 15th is a vast, mostly residential district that begins near the Eiffel Tower (Ecole Militaire) and stretches southwest to the wonderfully swish Parc André Citroën. You probably won't be exploring this area unless your hotel is here (or you're heading for the park), but should you hang around, check out **rue de Commerce** (near Métro: La Motte Picquet Grenelle) with lots of boutiques and high-street stores.

16TH (16E) ARRONDISSEMENT (TROCADERO/BOIS DE BOULOGNE)

Highlights of the 16th, on the Right Bank, are the **Bois de Boulogne, Jardins du Trocadéro, Musée de Balzac, Musée Guimet** (famous for its Asian collections), and **Cimetière de Passy,** resting place of Manet, Giraudoux, and Debussy. This large *arrondissement* is posh as hell, and loves being so. It's known for its well-heeled bourgeoisie; high rents; expensive boulevards; beautiful people; and prosperous, conservative addresses such as **avenue d'Iéna** and **avenue Victor-Hugo.** The 16th also includes the best place to view the Eiffel Tower: **place du Trocadéro.**

17TH (17E) ARRONDISSEMENT (PARC MONCEAU/PLACE CLICHY)

One of the most spread-out *arrondissements,* the 17th, on the Right Bank, flanks the northern periphery of Paris. It incorporates the northern edge of place Charles-de-Gaulle–Etoile in the west, the place Wagram at its center, and the tawdry place Clichy in the east. Highlights are **Parc Monceau,** the **Palais des Congrès** (of interest only if you're attending a show), and the **Porte Maillot Air Terminal.**

18TH (18E) ARRONDISSEMENT (MONTMARTRE)

The 18th, at the far end of the Right Bank, is associated with such names as the **Marché aux Puces de Clignancourt** flea market, **Moulin Rouge, Sacré-Coeur,** and **place du Tertre** (a tourist trap if ever there was one). Utrillo was its native son, Renoir lived here, and Toulouse-Lautrec adopted the area as his own. Today, place Blanche is a seedy site, full of prostitutes and sex-shops. But head up **rue Lepic** and you'll be surrounded by pure "Montmartrian" bohemia, with cool bars, funky clothes shops, restaurants in windmills (well, one, actually: **Moulin de la Galette** at 83 rue Lepic; ☎ 01-46-06-84-77), arthouse cinemas, and hidden passages that lead to vineyards.

19TH (19E) ARRONDISSEMENT (LA VILLETTE)

Visitors come to what was once the village of La Villette to see the **Cité des Sciences et de l'Industrie,** a science museum and park that is fast turning into a hotbed of creation. There are two avant-garde circus venues here, the **Cité de la Musique** serves as a launch-pad for all sorts of musical genres, and the **Zenith** concert hall is played by most big French and international names. Mostly residential, this district is one of the most ethnic in Paris, home to workers from all parts of the former French Empire. A highlight is **Les Buttes Chaumont** park, where you wander under man-made cliffs and waterfalls, have a picnic, and take in the panorama over Paris.

20TH (20E) ARRONDISSEMENT (PERE-LACHAISE CEMETERY) This district's greatest landmark is the **Père-Lachaise Cemetery,** resting place of Piaf, Proust, Wilde, Duncan, Stein and Toklas, Bernhardt, Colette, Jim Morrison, and many others. The district is home to many ethnic minorities, many of whom fled Algeria or Tunisia in the 1950s; and in true Bobo style, it is also a magnet for trendy bohemians looking to go out on the cheap.

Getting Around

BY PUBLIC TRANSPORTATION

For public transport, see "Getting Around the Region," above. If you're looking for something more organized, why not hop on one of Paris's tour buses? **Cityrama** (149 rue St-Honoré, 1st arr.; ☎ **01-44-55-61-00;** Métro: Palais Royal or Musée du Louvre), operates double-decker red-and-yellow buses with oversize windows and multilingual recorded commentaries giving an overview of Paris's history and monuments. To hop on and hop off an open-top bus, opt for **l'Open Tour** (run in

Right on Time

Lost your watch? Doesn't mean you have to miss your train. The capital has more than 109 sundials, interspersed throughout town. Look out for some at the Hôtel de Ville, in the Jardins des Tuileries, at the bottom of the main courtyard of the Sorbonne, and at the St-Gervais church.

conjunction with Cityrama and the RATP, 13 rue Auber, 9th arr.; ☎ **01-42-66-56-56;** www.paris-opentour.com; Métro: Opéra or Havre-Caumartin; RER: Auber).

BY BICYCLE

You can rent bikes from a number of places in town. **Maison Roue Libre** rents bicycles for about 10€ to 15€ for 1 day in several locations in Paris: near Hôtel de Ville (av. Victoria), in the park (bois de Vincennes), in front of the château (esplanade du Château), and at porte d'Auteuil/Gare Routière RATP. They also have two central offices at **Les Halles:** 1 passage Mondétour, 1st arr. (☎ **08-10-44-15-34;** Montétour is at the intersection of rue Rambuteau and rue Mondétour; Métro: Châtelet Les Halles) and 37 bd. Bourdon, 4th arr. (☎ **01-44-54-19-29;**

Friday Night "Rando" Fever

The Paris Roller Rando takes over the city on Friday nights, "rando" being short for *randonnée,* meaning tour or excursion. The starting time is around 10pm at the foot of the Montparnasse Tower, 14th arr. (also the name of the Métro stop). Roller folk from Paris and throughout Ile-de-France amass here to begin their 3-hour weekly journey through the city on in-line skates. Every Friday three motorcycle policemen lead the way with dome lights flashing, to signal moving cars to get out of the way. First-aid wagons follow the "rollers." On an average night in Paris, some 20,000 rollers show up. Many visitors like to stay up late that night to watch these "mad, mad Parisians" in all their crazed "rollermania." Check out **www.pari-roller.com.**

www.ratp.fr or www.rouelibre.fr; Métro: Bastille).

For an excellent orchestrated bike tour, call **Fat Tire Bike Tours** (☎ 01-56-58-10-54; www.fattirebiketoursparis.com), which offers a variety of visits conducted almost entirely on the pavements, parks, and riverfront quays of Paris, taking in views of the city's most famous landmarks. The cost is 24€ per person (22€ students) for the day tour and 28€ (26€ students) for the night tour. The night tour is more festive than the day tour and includes a complimentary ride aboard the Bateaux-Mouches (see below). Meet at the south leg (*pilier sud*) of the Eiffel Tower (look for their yellow sign at the meeting point).

ON FOOT

The best way to see Paris is to hoof it around town. Walking will let you absorb the city slowly, as it's meant to be discovered.

BY BOAT

Take to the waves (or at least the ripples) for sweeping vistas of the riverbanks and some of the best views of Notre-Dame. Many of the boats have open sun decks, bars, and restaurants. **Bateaux Parisiens** have concocted an excellent commentated 1-hour cruise up and down the Seine (☎ 01-46-99-43-13; www.bateaux parisiens.com). Tickets cost 10€ and boats leave from the quay by the Eiffel Tower (Port de la Bordonnais, Pier 3) year-round, and also from below Notre-Dame Cathedral (Mar 24–Nov 5). April to September tours leave every 30 minutes from 10am to 11pm; October to March, boats go at least once an hour from 10am to 10pm.

Police Stations by Arrondissement

1st	45 place du Marché St-Honoré (☎ 01-47-03-60-00; Métro: Tuileries).
2nd	18 rue Croissant (☎ 01-44-88-18-00; Métro: Sentier).
3rd	4-bis-6 rue Ours (☎ 01-42-76-13-00; Métro: Etienne Marcel).
4th	2 place Baudoyer (☎ 01-44-78-61-00; Métro: Hôtel de Ville).
5th	4 rue de la Montagne Geneviève (☎ 01-44-41-51-00; Métro: Maubert Mutualité).
6th	78 rue Bonaparte (☎ 01-40-46-38-30; Métro: St-Sulpice).
7th	7–9 rue Fabert (☎ 01-44-18-69-07; Métro: Invalides).
8th	1 av. du Général Eisenhower (☎ 01-44-18-69-07; Métro: Champs Elysées Clémenceau).
9th	14 bis rue Chauchat (☎ 01-44-83-80-80; Métro: Richelieu Drouot).
10th	26 rue Lousi Blanc (☎ 01-53-19-43-10; Métro: Louis Blanc).
11th	107 bd. Volatire (☎ 01-44-93-27-30; Métro: Voltaire).
12th	80 av. Daumesnil (☎ 01-44-87-50-12; Métro: Gare de Lyon).
13th	144 bd. de l'Hôpital (☎ 01-40-79-05-05; Métro: Place de l'Italie).
14th	114–116 av. du Maine (☎ 01-53-68-81-00; Métro: Gaîté).
15th	250 rue de Vaugirard (☎ 01-53-68-50-00; Métro: Vaugirard).
16th	62 av. Mozart (☎ 01-55-74-50-00; Métro: Ranelagh).
17th	19–21 rue Truffaut (☎ 01-44-90-37-17; Métro: Place de Clichy).
18th	79–81 rue de Clignancourt (☎ 01-53-41-50-00; Métro: Marcadet Poissonniers).
19th	3–5 rue Erik Satie (☎ 01-55-56-58-00; Métro: Ourcq).
20th	48 av. Gambette (☎ 01-40-33-34-00; Métro: Gambetta).

The second company, **Bateaux-Mouches** (☎ 01-40-76-99-99; www.bateaux-mouches.fr; Métro: Alma-Marceau), has boats that depart from the Right Bank, next to pont de l'Alma. Tours last about 75 minutes, costing around 8€. May to October, tours leave daily at 20- to 30-minute intervals, beginning at 10am and ending at 11:30pm; November to April, there are at least nine departures daily from 11am to 9pm, with a schedule that changes according to demand and the weather.

For a trip into Bohemia and a Paris that still reminisces about the days of Piaf and Mistanguette, jump on one of **Canauxrama**'s (☎ 01-42-39-15-00; www.canauxrama.com) canal boats, which navigate the city's lesser-known waterway—the Canal St-Martin and its underground tunnel—between Port de l'Arsenal at Bastille (12th), where the canal joins the Seine, and the Parc de la Villette (19th). Expect to fork out 14€ adult, 11€ students. Departures leave year-round at 9:45am from both Port de l'Arsenel (Métro: Bastille) and Bassin de la Villette, 13 Quai de Loire, 19th arr. (Métro: Jaurès), and at 2:45pm.

Tourist Offices

Wherever you are, you won't be far from **Paris Convention and Visitors Bureau** (☎ 08-92-68-30-00; www.paris-info.com), which has offices throughout the city. The main one is at 25–27 rue des Pyramides, 1st arr. (Métro: Pyramides; Mon–Sat 10am–7pm, Sun and holidays 11am–7pm). The others are **Gare de Lyon** (20 bd. Diderot, 12th arr.; Mon–Sat 8am–6pm; Métro/RER: Gare de Lyon); **Gare du Nord,** 18 rue de Dunkerque, 10th arr. (daily 8am–6pm; Métro/RER: Gare du Nord); **Anvers Information Point,** opposite 72 bd. Rochechouart, 18th arr. (daily 10am–6pm; Métro: Anvers); **Clémenceau,** corner of Champs Elysées and avenue Marigny, 8th arr. (Apr 3–Sept 15 daily 9am–7pm; Métro: Champs Elysées Clémenceau); **Espace Tourisme Ile-de-France,** in the Carrousel du Louvre, 99 rue de Rivoli, 1st arr. (daily 9am–7pm; Métro: Palais–Royal Musée du Louvre); **Montmartre,** 21 place du Tertre, 18th arr. (daily 10am–7pm; Métro: Abbesses or Lamarck–Caulaincourt). Any of these branches will make hotel reservations for walk-in clients: The service charge is free for hostels and between 2€ and 6€ for hotels, depending on their category and price range. Be warned that these offices are extremely busy year-round, and especially in midsummer, so be prepared to test your queuing etiquette.

PARIS & ILE-DE-FRANCE

Paris Nuts & Bolts

Cellphone Providers & Service Centers The main cellphone providers in France are **France Telecom** (www.francetelecom.com), **SFR** (www.sfr.fr), and **Orange** (www.orange.com). Orange has a pay-as-you-go plan called Idée Nomade, which may be your best bet if you are traveling in France for a while. With this plan, you can buy time in most cellphone shops and tobacco stores (called *un tabac*, pronounced "tah-bah"). Paris has about a million cellphone stores, so you shouldn't have any trouble finding one—check the websites mentioned here for details.

Currency For the best exchange rates, cash traveler's checks at foreign-exchange offices or banks, rather than at your hotel or in a shop. Still, your best bet is to use your ATM to directly withdraw euros. Banks in Paris are generally open Monday to Friday from 9am to 4:30pm. There's a **Citibank** at 125 av. des Champs Elysées (☎ 01-49-05-49-05; www.citibank.fr).

Embassies   The **Embassy of the United Kingdom** is at 35 rue Faubourg St-Honoré, 8th arr. (☎ 01-44-51-31-00; Métro: Concorde or Madeleine), open Monday through Friday from 9:30am to 1pm and 2:30 to 5pm. The consulate is at 18 bis rue d'Anjou, 8th arr. (☎ 01-44-51-31-02; Métro: Concorde or Madeleine), open Monday through Friday from 9am to noon and 2 to 5pm. For the **Embassy of the United States,** head for the heavily guarded 2 av. Gabriel, 8th arr. (☎ 01-43-12-47-08; Métro: Concorde). It is open Monday through Friday from 9am to 6pm. Passports are issued at its consulate at 2 rue St-Florentin (☎ 01-43-12-22-22; Métro: Concorde). The **Embassy of Canada** is found at 35 av. Montaigne, 8th arr. (☎ 01-44-43-29-00; Métro: Franklin-D-Roosevelt or Alma-Marceau), open Monday through Friday from 9am to noon and 2 to 5pm. For the **Embassy of Australia** go to 4 rue Jean-Rey, 15th arr. (☎ 01-40-59-33-00; Métro: Bir-Hakeim), open Monday through Friday from 9:15am to noon and 2:30 to 4:30pm. The **Embassy of New Zealand** is at 7 ter rue Léonard-de-Vinci, 16th arr. (☎ 01-45-00-24-11; Métro: Victor Hugo), open Monday through Friday from 9am to 1pm and 2:30 to 6pm.

Emergencies   The usuals—☎ **15** for an ambulance, ☎ **17** for the cops, ☎ **18** for fire department and paramedics. You can also call **SOS Médecins** (emergency doctors) at ☎ 01-47-07-77-77 or **SOS Dentaire** (emergency dentists) at ☎ 01-43-37-51-00.

Laundromats   Throughout Paris, you'll find *laveries automatiques,* or self-service laundries, dotting the streets. These cost about 3.50€ per load, and about 0.50€ to 0.80€ for 5 to 10 minutes of drying time. If you're near the Louvre, check out **Laverie Libre Service** (7 rue Jean Jacques Rousseau, 1st arr.; daily 7:30am–10pm; Métro: Louvre-Rivoli). In the Latin Quarter, try **Laverie Libre Service** (215 rue St-Jacques, 5th arr.; daily 7am–10pm; Métro: Luxembourg). Also ask at your hotel for the nearest addresses. Some hostels are equipped with clothes washing facilities.

Pharmacies   The city is littered with green neon crosses indicating pharmacies, but if you need drugs out of hours try **Dérhy/Pharmacie des Champs Elysées** (8th arr.; ☎ 01-45-62-02-41) and **Pharmacie Européenne de la place de Clichy** (6 place de Clichy, 9th arr.; ☎ 01-48-74-65-18), which are open 24/7.

Post Office   When you're ready to mail those postcards, head to the main **Bureau de Poste,** 52 rue du Louvre, 75001 Paris (☎ 01-40-28-76-00; Métro: Louvre-Rivoli), which is open 24 hours a day. For a small fee, you can receive mail at this post as well; just bring your passport to do so.

Safety   Paris is a fairly safe city, but beware of pickpockets at all times, especially child thieves. Pickpockets are particularly prevalent around major tourist hubs such as the Louvre, Eiffel Tower, Montmartre, Notre-Dame, and on the Métro. If someone comes up to you and asks if you speak English, always say no. If you say yes, Gypsy women or children will often put some piece of paper or book in front of you with words written in English. While you are reading about how this poor person has no job and needs money, they cut your purse strap or pick your pockets. Should you fall victim, head to the nearest police station (*Commissariat de police;* see box, below). Also see the Basics chapter for numbers to call for stolen credit cards and checkbooks (p. 31). If you are victim of a mugging, and you wish your injuries to be medically certified, you can register a formal complaint, every day, 24 hours a day, at the Hôtel-Dieu hospital, place du Parvis de Notre-Dame (in front of Notre-Dame, also called place Jean-Paul II, 4th arr.; Métro: Cité).

Store Hours   Mostly 9:30pm to 7pm Monday to Saturday. Some shops still close at lunchtime, but this is rare in the capital nowadays (unlike in the provinces). Sunday shopping in Paris is mainly in the Marais (4th arr.), underneath the Louvre (Carousel du Louvre, 1st arr.), Bercy Village (12th arr.), and on the Champs Elysées (8th arr.). Shops usually open late morning or early afternoon

Taxis   If you can't flag one down in the street, try **Les Taxis Bleus** (☎ **08-25-16-10-10**) or **Taxi G7** (☎ **01-47-39-47-39**).

Useful Websites   Check out these babies for the latest lowdown on the capital: **www.culture.fr** (forthcoming cultural events); **www.fnac.com** (online tickets for concerts and museums); **lemonsound.com** (clubbing agenda); **expatica.com** (listings on art, music, and theater events); **www.bparis.com** (a fun, chatty perspective on the great city from an expat's point of view); **www.parisdigest.com** (helpful visitor information); and **www.parisfranceguide.com** (yet more nightlife listings for theater and live music).

Weather   This isn't the French Riviera, but the capital can get mighty hot in summer, especially in recent years, when temperatures have crept up to 40°C (104°F) in August. Winter (Nov–Mar) tends to be cold, around 0°C (32°F), and temperatures can drop to as low as −10°C (14°F). Spring and autumn remain mild (about 18–20°C or 64–68°F), but as global warming worsens, weather is becoming less and less predictable. Rain is frequent in spring and autumn, but nothing can beat the summer thunderstorms, when thunder claps and bangs so loudly that the 19th-century buildings shudder.

PARIS & ILE-DE-FRANCE

Sleeping

Picture this: You wake up to the light poking through the curtains of your cozy hotel room, your nose detects a whiff of freshly baked croissants and freshly ground coffee, and you suddenly remember where you are—that you've made it to one of the most beautiful destinations in the world. Paris—"ahh!"

Well, before you get to that happy stage, you have to choose where it is you'd like to wake up. Do you want a room with a view? Is

central location important? Do you want charm or cutting-edge design? Is price an issue? Do you mind sharing a toilet? Paris is so awash with places to stay (from dives to palaces) that these are genuine questions you should ask yourself, so the wrong choice doesn't put a downer on your whole stay.

Try the places on this list, however, and you shouldn't be disappointed. We've chosen them not for their number of stars—hotels in Paris are government-rated with zero to four stars, which is often based on arbitrary criteria and can be misleading—but for their location, price-quality ratio, and overall appeal. All accept credit cards unless otherwise stated (see websites or call for details).

Note: Air-conditioning in the capital can be rare, so if you're temperature-sensitive, always ask about A/C before you reserve.

Note also: Paris is more expensive than the rest of France, and so the price categories in this chapter differ from elsewhere in this book.

HOSTELS

→**Center International BVJ Paris-Louvre** This 207-bed hostel with modern amenities is run by the Bureau des Voyages de la Jeunesse. Rooms are far and away cleaner than in the average hostel, and you can't beat the location close to the Louvre. On the Left Bank, there's a sister hostel on 44 rue des Bernardins, 5th arr. *20 rue Jean-Jacques Rousseau, 1st arr. ☎ 01-53-00-90-90. bvj@wanadoo.fr. 25€ per person. Rates include breakfast. Métro: Louvre-Rivoli. Amenities: Breakfast room; shared bathrooms.*

→**Le Village Hostel** The best things about Le Village are its common spaces, such as the fully equipped kitchen and bar/lounge, where you'll be sure to meet fellow English-speaking travelers. They also have a good location and everything is fairly clean. The downside? Management kicks you out during the day for cleaning (but, hey, at least there's no curfew). The dorm rooms contain bunk beds with thin sheetless mattresses; be prepared to rent or bring your own. Some rooms have amazing views over the Sacré-Coeur. The maximum stay is 1 week. Look out for the colorful fresco in the lobby by artist Mary Blaque. *20 rue d'Orsel, 18th arr. ☎ 01-42-64-22-02. www.villagehostel.fr. 20€–25€ dorm bed (room for 3–8 people), 25€–27€ double. Métro: Anvers. Amenities: Bar; lounge; Internet; kitchen; lockout (11am–4pm); shared bathrooms; sheets (2.50€); telephone (in common room); towel (1€).*

→**Woodstock Hostel** ★ You'll party like a rock star until bedtime (bar closes at 2am) in this cool hostel (who the hell stuck that car on the wall in the lobby?), which teems with foreigners. It's a clean venue with a kitchen, common spaces for meeting people, and bunk beds with thick mattresses, but the benefits end there. The 2am curfew can be a pain if you're into partying outside of the hostel, and they kick you out between 11am and 3pm for cleaning. Alcohol from the outside isn't allowed either, so if you do party in the hostel bar, be prepared to buy semi-pricey booze. That said, you'll be in a prime spot for visiting Paris's Right Bank, just below Montmartre. *48 rue Rodier, 9th arr. ☎ 01-48-78-87-76. www.woodstock.fr. 21€ dorm bed, 24€ per person for bunk-bed room. Prices decrease 3€ Oct–Mar. Rates include breakfast. Métro: Anvers. Amenities: Breakfast room; curfew (2am); Internet; kitchen; lockout (11am–3pm); luggage storage; shared bathrooms; sheets; telephone (in common room); towels.*

→**Young and Happy Hostel** This hostel has a friendly vibe and a great location in the Latin Quarter, which makes up for a slightly downtrodden decor. The rooms contain four beds maximum. The common area has a bar with cheap beer (reason alone to come, right?), where you can chat up other backpackers. *80 rue*

Paris Sleeping Prices

Cheap	Under 90€
Doable	90€–170€
Splurge	170€

Pick Your Paris

Boho, Romantic, Time-Honored, or Chic?

The French capital means so many things to so many people. To help you find the Paris of your dreams, we've categorized most of the "Sleeping," "Eating," and "Partying" listings in the Paris section as Bohemian, Romantic, Time-Honored, or Chic. Listings are still divided by standard price categories (Cheap, Doable, and Splurge), with the style (where relevant) noted beside each entry.

➜ **Bohemian:** Paris has long been a refuge for avant-garde artists with more style and taste than money. Our boho listings are for those who want to rub shoulders with the city's latest fleet of shabby chic artists, intellectuals, writers, poets, photographers, and filmmakers.

➜ **Romantic:** Paris has a way of warming hearts and filling minds with soppy thoughts. If you're open to its charms, you too can see the most romantic city in the world through rose-tinted glasses. All you need is love—and this guidebook, of course.

➜ **Time-Honored:** You're looking for classic Paris—the Paris that makes you feel like you're in a movie. Don't be ashamed: You want that Belle Epoque brasserie. You want that view of the Eiffel Tower from your window.

➜ **Chic:** Admit it—you're a fashionista. You love nothing more than seeing and being seen. Glamour is the name of your game, you eat the glitterati for breakfast, and you want Paris to show you its swankest addresses.

Mouffetard, 5th arr. ☎ *01-47-07-47-07. www. youngandhappy.fr.* *21€–26€ dorm bed. Rates include breakfast. Métro: Place Monge. Amenities: Breakfast room; bar; curfew (2am); Internet; kitchen; luggage storage; shared bathrooms.*

CHEAP

➜ **Hôtel Beauséjour** ★★ *ROMANTIC* For the price you pay, you can't expect luxury, but this cute hotel is an oasis of calm, with its whitewashed walls (artfully covered in black-and-white photos by local artists), verdant courtyard (a fine spot for breakfast in the shade), and cozy bedrooms. If you want to impress your loved one on a budget, you could do a lot worse than here. *6 rue Lécluse, 17th arr.* ☎ *01-42-93-35-77. www.hbeausejour.com.* *70€–90€ double; 110€ triple. Métro: Place de Clichy. Amenities: Breakfast room, Wi-Fi. In room: TV.*

➜ **Hôtel Bonséjour** *BOHEMIAN* The best deal in Montmartre, this hotel is near

the Sacré-Coeur and many restaurants and bars. You won't find any frills (check out the hideous carpet), but if you're looking for a cheap, clean room with a bed, this place is for you. Rooms have no toilets (one toilet per floor, and there are about five rooms per floor), and almost all have a shower. Shower-less rooms have a sink and access to a shower for 2€. If you want a room with a balcony over the quiet but oh-so-cool rue Burq, request nos. 23, 33, 43, or 53. *11 rue Burq, 18th arr.* ☎ *01-42-54-22-53. www.hotel-bonsejour-montmartre.fr.* *36€ double, 42€–46€ with shower; 49€ triple, 57€ with shower. Métro: Abbesses or Blanche. Amenities: Shared bathrooms (in some).*

➜ **Hôtel Chopin** *BOHEMIAN/ROMANTIC* In the 19th century, when Haussman constructed his *grands boulevards,* he also built lots of covered passages. The upper crust of Paris gathered here to drink tea, visit curiosity shops, and generally look

Internet Cafes & Free Wi-Fi

Wanna get connected? *Pas de problème!* Paris has scores of Internet cafes, and free Wi-Fi points. Here are some of the top hot spots.

Internet Cafes

→ **@Z Net:** Located at 14 rue Descartes; 5th arr. (☎ **01-43-25-32-18;** 3€ per hour; Mon–Thurs 11am–midnight, Fri 11am–7pm. Sun and holidays 1pm–midnight; Métro: Cardinal Lemoine or Maubert-Mutualité).

→ **Cyber world C@fé:** There's a discount (5.50€ an hour) for students and unemployed people (how very socialist). 20 rue de l'Exposition, 7th arr. (☎ **01-53-59-96-54;** www.cyberworld-cafe.com; Mon–Sat noon–10pm, Sun and holidays noon–8pm; Métro: Ecole Militaire).

→ **@bbessesxv3.com:** Grab 1 hour here for 3€. Located at 22 rue Houdon; 18th arr. (☎ **01-42-23-07-05;** www.tatoolagoon.com/sites/abbessesxv3; daily 7am–7pm; Métro: Abbesses or Pigalle).

Cafes & Pubs with Free Wi-Fi

→ **Café du Pont Neuf:** 14 quai du Louvre, 1st arr. (☎ **01-42-33-32-37;** Métro: Pont Neuf).

→ **Le Fumoir:** 6 rue du Amiral Coligny, 1st arr. (☎ **01-42-60-97-54;** Métro: Louvre Rivoli).

→ **Frog and Rosbif:** 116 rue Saint-Denis, 2nd arr. (☎ **01-42-36-34-73;** Métro: Etienne Marcel).

→ **Le Bistrot Marguerite:** 2 quai de Gesvres, 4th arr. (☎ **01-42-72-00-04;** Métro: Hôtel-de-Ville).

→ **Le Café du Métro:** 13 rue du Vieux Colombier, 6th arr. (☎ **01-45-48-58-56;** Métro: St-Sulpice).

→ **Poona Lounge:** 25 rue Marbeuf, 8th arr. (☎ **01-40-70-09-99;** Métro: Franklin-D-Roosevelt).

→ **Café Français:** 3 place de la Bastille, 11th arr. (☎ **01-40-29-04-02;** Métro: Bastille).

→ **Le Sancerre:** 35 rue des Abbesses, 18th arr. (☎ **01-42-58-08-20;** Métro: Abbesses).

fashionable, until World War I and World War II, when they fell into disrepair. Set at the bottom of one of these passageways, the Hôtel Chopin still has simple but terribly atmospheric rooms. You can imagine you're Sherlock Holmes as you fall asleep praying that you won't be woken up by a ghost of Hôtel Chopin's past. They don't believe in them around here, but the heavy ambience in the reception and breakfast room is enough to get me wondering. *46 passage Jouffroy or 10 bd. de Montmartre, 9th arr.* ☎ *01-47-70-58-10. www. hotel-chopin.com. 80€–90€ double; 105€ triple. Métro: Grands Boulevards or Richelieu Drouot. Amenities: TV.*

→**Hôtel du Champs de Mars** ★ This adorable hotel is family-run, and the owners Françoise and Stéphane Gourdal will treat you like honored guests at their impeccably decorated home. Every room is decorated differently (usually featuring bright pastels with rich fabric and tasteful paintings), but they are all clean, cozy, and colorful. Most of the bathrooms have bathtub/shower combinations. *7 rue du Champs de Mars, 7th arr.* ☎ *01-45-51-52-30. www. hotel-du-champ-de-mars.com. 79€ single or double; 84€ 2 twin beds; 100€ triple. Breakfast available for 6.50€. Métro: Ecole Militaire. Amenities: Wheelchair-friendly. In room: TV (satellite), safe.*

➔**Hôtel du Commerce** This budget hotel (in a very central location) boasts the sort of small frills that make the difference to a weary backpacker. The decor is pretty jarring (think bright yellow, mauve, and orange), and the walls are thin. But the free Internet access and printer in the lobby, microwave, fridge, plates, cutlery, and TV in the lounge can cause a tired traveler to weep tears of joy. Some rooms have a private shower and toilet for 20€ extra. *14 rue de la Montagne Ste-Geneviève, 5th arr.* ☎ *01-43-54-89-69. www.commerce-paris-hotel.com. 39€ double with shared bathroom; 49€ with private shower; 59€ triple with private bathroom; 89€ quad with private shower. All prices increase 10€ Mar–June and Sept–Dec. Métro: Maubert-Mutualité. Amenities: Fridge (in common room); Internet; microwave (in common room); shared bathrooms (in some); TV (in common room).*

➔**Hôtel La Tour Eiffel** *TIME-HONORED* If being near the biggest hunk of magnificently engineered iron in Paris is your dream, and you've not got money to burn, shack up in this small hotel with rooms overlooking a quiet street, the Eiffel Tower, or the garden of the Romanian Embassy. It is one of the cheapest options in this expensive neighborhood. The rooms are basic with sparse furniture and minimalist, yet tasteful, decoration. *17 rue de l'Exposition, 7th arr.* ☎ *01-47-05-14-75. www.hotel-tour eiffel.com. 65€–85€ double; 75€–95€ double with twin beds. Breakfast available for 6€.*

Métro: Ecole Militaire. Amenities: Breakfast room; wheelchair friendly; Wi-Fi. In room: TV.

➔**Hôtel Paris France** ★ The name sounds like something you'd tap into an Internet search engine. But read between the lines and this is what you get. Hotel: Yes sir, with no-frills, larger than average rooms (the attic bedroom has views of Montmartre), and typical rococo decor with gold and reds. Paris: In the dead center by the Marais and République, an otherwise expensive spot to kip in. France: Well Paris is in France, the staff members are French, and depending upon what you get up to in the bedroom, you could put this down as being an unforgettable French experience. *72 rue de Turbigo, 3rd arr.* ☎ *01-42-78-00-04. www.paris-france-hotel.com. From 76€ double. Métro: Temple. Amenities: Bar; Internet; free Wi-Fi. In room: TV.*

DOABLE

MTV **Best** ➔**Aviatic** *ROMANTIC* This gem of a hotel is family-run, which is why so much attention goes into every element of your stay here. It's definitely one for historians—the building lies on the site of the former house where Louis XIV's illegitimate children were brought up away from the prying eyes of the court, and it was frequented by pilots during both world wars (hence the name Aviatic). From the moment you step in, you feel like you're in somebody's home rather than a hotel. Rooms are plushly decorated in thick patterned fabrics, and some have parquet floors installed specially for guests with allergies. The breakfast salon feels like a Left Bank institution, covered in old bistro posters. If you fancy a stroll around the romantic Jardin de Luxembourg nearby, ask them to pack you a picnic. *105 rue de Vaugirard, 6th arr. Métro: Montparnasse or St-Placide.* ☎ *01-53-63-25-50. www.aviatic.fr. From 115€ double. Amenities: A/C; bar; elevators; Internet. In room: TV, free water.*

PARIS & ILE-DE-FRANCE

Sleeping & Eating in Paris

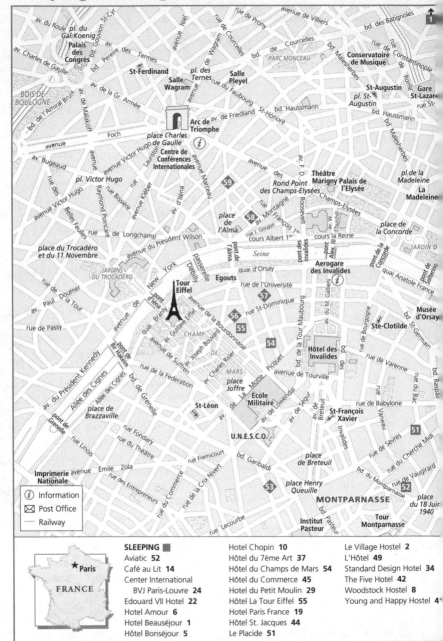

SLEEPING ■

Aviatic **52**
Café au Lit **14**
Center International
   BVJ Paris-Louvre **24**
Edouard VII Hotel **22**
Hotel Amour **6**
Hotel Beauséjour **1**
Hôtel Bonséjour **5**

Hotel Chopin **10**
Hôtel du 7ème Art **37**
Hôtel du Champs de Mars **54**
Hôtel du Commerce **45**
Hotel du Petit Moulin **29**
Hôtel La Tour Eiffel **55**
Hotel Paris France **19**
Hôtel St. Jacques **44**
Le Placide **51**

Le Village Hostel **2**
L'Hôtel **49**
Standard Design Hotel **34**
The Five Hotel **42**
Woodstock Hostel **8**
Young and Happy Hostel **4**

EATING ◆

Alain Ducasse au Plaza Athénée **58**	Chez Chartier **11**	La Boulangerie **17**
Angl'Opera **23**	Chez l'Ami Jean **57**	La Dôme du Marais **28**
Berthillon **39**	Chez Omar **30**	La Famille **4**
Breakfast in America **40**	Chez Prune **13**	La Fourmi **7**
Café Beaubourg **27**	China Club **35**	La Gazetta **36**
Café Constant **56**	De La Ville Café **12**	Le Café Arosé **3**
Café de la Musique **15**	Jean **9**	Le Chateaubriand **18**
	Kong **26**	Le Comptoir du Relais **48**
	La Bonne Franquette **31**	Le Fumoir **25**

Le Petit Pont **47**
Le Petit Marché **32**
Le Petit Prince **43**
Le Pré Verre **46**
Le Tambour **21**
Le Troquet **53**
Les Deux Magots **50**
Les Saveurs de Flora **59**
Ma Pomme **16**
Mon Vieil Ami **38**
Pause Café **33**
Stohrer **20**

MTV Best ● → **Hôtel Amour** ★★

BOHEMIAN/ROMANTIC Ever-present André (cool hotel and bar tycoon) has struck again—this time in partnership with one of the Costes clan (other cool hotel and bar tycoons). Don't expect to extract much info from the website: When places are this hip, they don't need introducing; and how annoying that they're right. All 20 rooms have been designed in a retro style by artists such as Marc Newson, M/M, or Sophie Calle. Most bathrooms are not separate from the sleeping area, which is fine if you're a couple, but if you're sharing with friends you might like more intimacy. Vintage reigns on every floor, a style (or non-style, depending on how you look at it) that carries on through to the sweet, 1950s courtyard where you can have a natter, eat, drink with mates, and watch the goldfish. *8 rue Navarin, 9th arr. Métro: Anvers, Pigalle, or St-Georges. ☎ 01-48-78-31-80. www.hotelamour.com. From 90€ double. Amenities: Restaurant; bar; Wi-Fi.*

→ **Hôtel du 7ème Art** ★ *BOHEMIAN* Film buffs unite: This is the only hotel in Paris to devote its premises to the "seventh art"—cinema. Staying here is almost like being in a movie, surrounded by kitsch memorabilia from flicks and days gone by. Rooms are looking a little tattered, but they're clean and big enough for you to spread out in. The downstairs serves as a themed tearoom by day—a great place for meeting fellow travelers and curious Parisians who pop by to see the decor. It's a great value in the heart of the Marais. *20 rue St-Paul. ☎ 01-44-54-85-00. www.paris-hotel-7art.com. 80€–135€ double. Métro: Bastille or St-Paul. Amenities: Tearoom; A/C; exercise room in basement; Internet. In room: TV, safe.*

→ **Hôtel St. Jacques** *TIME-HONORED* The best value in the Latin Quarter, the Hôtel St. Jacques is perfect for small budgets. Despite the affordable price, it maintains the standards of classic French comfort—check out the marble lobby and Impressionist art that hangs in the rooms and hallways. Murals decorate the room walls, and room no. 30 has a view of Sacré-Coeur. *35 rue des Écoles, 5th arr. ☎ 01-44-07-45-45. www.paris-hotel-stjacques.com. 95€–124€ double. Breakfast 8.50€. Métro: Bastille or Maubert-Mutualité. Amenities: Internet; luggage storage; safe; tourist desk. In room: TV (satellite), hair dryer, Internet, safe, scale.*

→ **Standard Design Hotel** ★ *CHIC* A partygoers paradise, this hotel offers a sleek, cool design that would be at home in any modern city anywhere in the world. As it is, you'll be hitting the pillow near Bastille—a cool but crusty part of town that contrasts refreshingly with the crisp interiors. Some rooms look out over the lively and incredibly Bobo (Bourgeois-Bohemian) streets of rue de la Roquette and rue des Taillandiers. The bold stripes in the breakfast room will challenge your ability to focus, but then you can give your whole body a rest over a massage or a manicure. *29 rue Taillandiers, 11th arr. ☎ 01-48-05-30-97. www.standard-hotel.com. 150€–165€ double. Métro: Bastille. Amenities: A/C; facials; Internet; manicure; massage; Wi-Fi. In room: Satellite TV.*

SPLURGE

→ **Café au Lit** *BOHEMIAN* Fed up with hotels? How about lodging in an art gallery? Café au Lit is a wonderful new concept: an apartment that you can rent with ever-changing art on its walls, open to the public when you're not staying there. This minimalist hybrid guesthouse really feels more New York than "19th *arrondissement*" in Paris. Expect affordable prices (from

250€ for a 3-day weekend). *16 rue de la Liberté, 19th arr.* ☎ *01-46-36-18-85. http:// cafeaulit.com. 250€ for 3 nights (minimum stay), 500€ for 1 week. Métro: Jourdain. Amenities: Fully furnished apartment w/kitchen.*

→ **Edouard VII Hotel** TIME-HONORED/ CHIC I have three words for you: Location, location, location (right in between the Louvre and the Opéra Garnier). And here are some more: wonderful design (cool reds, creams, and browns by F. Foucaut); funky English-style bar (with great cocktails); approachable, smiley staff; views to die for (over the opera house); large, swish bedrooms; luxurious bathrooms; a gym; and one of Paris's hottest restaurants, Angl'Opéra (see "Eating," below). If that isn't enough to make you want to splurge here, you really are too difficult to please. *39 av. de l'Opéra, 2nd arr.* ☎ *01-42-61-56-90. www.edouard7hotel.com. 405€–595€ double. Credit cards accepted. Métro: Bastille or Opéra/Pyramides. Amenities: Restaurant; bar; gym; Internet. In room: A/C, TV (satellite), bathrobes, CD players in some rooms, Internet, minibar, safety box, slippers, sound-proofing.*

→ **The Five Hotel** ★ CHIC This is the newest place in Chic camp—a bijou hotel on the edge of the Latin Quarter with cutting-edge design by Vincent Bastie. Artist Isabelle Emmerique also decorated every room with Chinese lacquer wall sculptures. Rooms are named after the color they're painted (black, orange, green, beige, plum, blue). Lighting is moody, even in the bathrooms, and there is something distinctly Stanley Kubrick about the whole affair— something mysterious yet almost too contemporary. *3 rue Flatters, 5th arr.* ☎ *01-43-31-74-21. www.thefivehotel.com. 150€–270€ double. During special promotions for 3-night and weekly stays, prices drop to 140€ per night. Métro: Bastille or Gobelins. Amenities: Free Wi-Fi; Internet; laundry service. In room: A/C, TV, safety box.*

→ **Hôtel du Petit Moulin** ★★ BOHEMIAN/CHIC This is Lacroix territory, baby—and don't you know it. The world-renowned fashion designer decorated this luxurious, bold, and boutiquelike place with all the extravagance he could muster. No, you haven't got spots in your eyes—it's just the black-and-white dotty carpet, darling. In this former *boulangerie* (the bakery where Victor Hugo apparently bought his baguettes), some period features remain, such as the stairwells, period tapestries, and Flemish frescoes. Lacroix's imaginative touches have transformed them into what can only be described as design-fusion-extraordinaire. *29–31 rue du Poitou, 3rd arr.* ☎ *01-42-74-10-10. www.hoteldupetitmoulin.com. From 180€ double. Métro: Bastille or Filles du Calvaire. Amenities: Bar. In room: A/C, TV, Internet, minibar, Wi-Fi.*

→ **Le Placide** CHIC Another new arrival, this chic-as-hell hotel gives everyone a lesson in how to be cool. Philippe Stark is behind much of the decor, which means you can expect a retro look revisited with 21st-century spunk. The talk of the town is their duplex room, fully equipped for reduced mobility guests, with an upstairs bed for caregivers. Set on the Left Bank near Le Bon Marché department store, it's within easy walking distance of all the sights. There are only 11 rooms—and, trust me, they're going to fill up quickly as word gets out, so book 'em quick. *6 rue St-Placide, 6th arr. www.leplacidehotel.com. 350€–375€ double. Métro: St-Placide. Amenities: Tearoom; A/C; full access for guests w/disabilities; Internet; 24-hr. room service; Wi-Fi. In room: TV, DVD, Wi-Fi.*

→ **L'Hôtel** ★★ ROMANTIC For love-making in St-Germain, you can't get better than this place—one of the most luxurious and quixotic hotels on the Left Bank. Its claim to fame is that Oscar Wilde died here (in room 16), but L'Hôtel has more to brag about than that: a gorgeous domed entrance, 20 exquisite rooms sumptuously decorated according to themes (Napoleon III, Mistinguett, Venice, leopard print), a celebrity A-list (stars such as Johnny Depp appreciate the elegant yet discreet charm and the homey feel), and luxurious fabric wall-coverings and beds that are inviting enough to dive into. The bathrooms are small but stocked with Hermès toiletries. One of the highlights of the hotel is their private spa in the basement, which you can reserve for 1-hour intervals. You have exclusive access to a steam room and a salt-water pool, free of charge. *13 rue des Beaux-Arts, 6th arr.* ☎ *01-44-41-99-00. www.l-hotel. com. 240€–370€ double (depending on view); 640€ deluxe room and suite; 740€ apt. Métro: St-Germain-des-Prés. Amenities: Restaurant; bar; laundry service; room service; spa; steam room; swimming pool; Wi-Fi. In room: TV, data-port, minibar, robe, safe, slippers.*

Eating

Welcome to the city that prides itself on being the world's culinary capital. Only in Paris can you turn onto the nearest little crooked side street; enter the first nonde-script bistro you see; sit down at a bare, wobbly table; order from an illegibly hand-scrawled menu; and get a memorable meal. This is also an exciting time for gourmands, as France undergoes some-what of a gastronomic revolution. As a nation proud of its culinary prowess, France has finally woken up to the fact that Grand-mère's boeuf bourgignon and onion soup (while utterly delicious) are no longer making the headlines on the world food circuit. A new cooking movement, Generation.C (C for cuisine or creation), has united the country's most innovative chefs in an attempt to redefine French cooking and put it back on the map. Paris is a magnet for these new-wave *cusiniers,*

Paris Eating Prices

Cheap   Under 25€
Doable 25€–50€
Splurge 50€

which is great news for your taste buds and your wallet: All are highly "doable," costwise (p. 99).

As in the "Sleeping" section, above, the price classifications for restaurants have been altered to take into account Paris's high prices. Each entry is also classified by style (Chic, Time-Honored, Romantic, Bohemian). All venues accept credit cards unless otherwise stated (see websites or call for details).

CAFES & LIGHT FARE

In autumn and winter, Paris gets gray, dreary, and a little on edge, and people busily withdraw into their newspapers, cafes, and hot chocolates. In summer, however, you should have no trouble find-ing spots in which to do nothing amid the company of locals. Nearly every cafe puts out tables, and most every plaza or park is full of the most jaw-dropping slackers you've seen. With so much of the popula-tion here in cafes so much of the time, the question arises: Don't these people work? The answer to which is: sort of. With three-course lunches, 12% unemployment, and a freshly minted law enforcing a 35-hour-maximum work week, Parisians have a lot of time to dawdle. Join them, day or night, in some of these places.

→ **Berthillon** *TIME-HONORED* One of the world's most famous ice-cream shops since it opened in 1954, Berthillon dishes out decadently good ice-cream cones, filled with flavors made from real fruit, to a mix of tourists and locals. Stop at the ter-race if you want to spy on the boats float-ing down the Ile St-Louis; and if you want to be truly Parisian, head for the nearest quayside and sit on the wall overlooking the Seine. *31 rue St-Louis-en-l'Ile, 4th arr. ☎ 01-43-54-31-61. www.berthillon-glacier.fr. Wed–Sun 10am–8pm. Métro: Pont Marie.*

→ **Café Beaubourg** *CHIC* Next to the all-pedestrian plaza of the Centre Pompidou, this is a trendy cafe with soaring concrete columns and a minimalist decor. Many of the regulars work in the neighborhood's eclectic shops and galleries. You can order salads, omelets, grilled steak, chicken *cordon bleu*, pastries, and daily platters (7€–20€). In warm weather, tables are set up on the sprawling outdoor terrace, providing an appropriate niche for watching the young and the restless go by. *100 rue St-Martin, 4th arr. ☎ 01-48-87-63-96. Sun–Thurs 8am–1am; Fri-Sat 8am–2am. Métro: Rambuteau or Hôtel-de-Ville.*

→ **Café de la Musique** ★★ *CHIC* This cafe's location in one of the grandest of Mitterrand's *grands travaux* guarantees a crowd passionately devoted to music; the recorded sounds that play in the background are refreshingly eclectic. The red-and-green velour setting might remind you of a modern opera house, and you can sample inspired food like lobster-studded risotto, roasted rack of lamb with thyme, very fresh salads of the type you'd find in Italy (food from 15€), and excellent coffee. As the sun sets, listen to the DJs spinning some tunes and watch the urbanized young hipsters emerging from the Métro. *In the Cité de la Musique, place Fontaine Aux Lions, 213 av. Jean-Jaurès, 19th arr. ☎ 01-48-03-15-91. Daily 8am–2am. Métro: Porte de Pantin.*

→ **Chez Prune** *BOHEMIAN* Girls, get out your knee-length boots, floaty dresses, thick-knitted cardigans, and layers of beads. Boys, ruffle your hair, untuck your shirt, buy a woolen scarf. And everybody wear thick-rimmed glasses or shades. You need to look right to fit in at this Canal St-Martin Bobo magnet. Once you make the grade, you'll find yourself alongside artsy types pitching scripts and cool do-littlers supping mojitos or chomping on cold-meat and cheese platters. (12€). *71 quai de Valmy, 10th arr. ☎ 01-42-41-30-47. Mon–Sat 8am–2pm; Sun 10am–2am. Métro: République.*

→ **De La Ville Café** *BOHEMIAN* Paris has a wonderful habit of finding use for its old buildings. This place, once one of Paris's most notorious brothels, is now a cafe-cum-restaurant so cool that it has attracted the (usually unmovable) hip crowd from the nearby Marais to this lesser explored part of town. Decor is distinctly hippie, with distressed walls, funky lighting, and a grandiose staircase that leads to the eating/art expo space near the back. Look out for the pretty painted ceilings and the waiters' aprons, designed by Agnès B. *34 bd. Bonne Nouvelle, 10th arr. ☎ 01-48-24-48-09. Daily 11am–2pm. Métro: Bonne Nouvelle.*

→ **La Fourmi** ★ *BOHEMIAN* This place, on the cusp of the 9th and 18th, caters to laid-back Montmartre folk on their way up and down the steep slopes of the "Butte" (a veritable migration for many people who prefer to stick within the limits of their hill-top village). Within a stone's throw from concert halls Elysée Montmartre and

---

SRO Savings

You'll pay substantially less in a cafe if you stand at the counter rather than sit at a table, partly because there's no service charge and partly because clients tend to linger at tables.

the funky Divan du Monde, it's in a prime spot for a pre-show pick-me-up or a flick through the infinite piles of entertainment flyers. Industrial chic best sums up the decor, with its huge wine-bottle chandelier and an enormous zinc bar. Also come for the lunchtime food, reasonably priced at around 15€ for salads and *plats du jour*. *74 rue des Martyrs, 18th arr.* ☎ *01.42.64.70.35. Mon–Thurs 8am–2am; Fri–Sat 8am–4am; Sun 10am–2am. Food served noon–3pm and 7–11pm. Métro: Pigalle.*

→ **Le Fumoir** *CHIC* An intriguing mix of hip Parisians and Euro-lounger types comes to linger over coffee or eat good (but overpriced) food in a book-lined setting that recalls the great cafes of Mitteleuropa, French colonial Indochina, and the American '30s. If you come, also feel free to join the throngs of new-generation cafe-workers—freelancers who have conned themselves into thinking they'll get more work done by sitting in a cafe, with a laptop, pumping the free Wi-Fi. *Place du Louvre, 6 rue de l'Amiral-Coligny, 1st arr.* ☎ *01-42-92-00-24. Daily noon–2am. Métro: Louvre Rivoli.*

→ **Le Petit Pont** *CHIC/ROMANTIC* This place was a wooden fortress in the 9th century, before Charles VI turned it into a prison. Nowadays, things are less bleak, and Le Petit Pont (Little Bridge) is a great venue for a quick coffee, a lengthy coffee, a brunch, or a snack while you're looking at Notre-Dame Cathedral. For the amorously inclined, the highlight of the drinks list is the lovers' cocktail: One glass with two straws so that you can lock lips while slurping a margarita. *1 rue du Petit Pont, 5th arr.* ☎ *01-43-54-23-81. Daily 6am–4am. Métro: St-Michel.*

→ **Les Deux Magots** *TIME-HONORED/ BOHEMIAN* Don't let the thought of fly larvae buzz in your mind at the Magots; it's Confucian wise men (*magots,* pronounced "mah-go") that give this cafe its name. Sartre and de Beauvoir once sipped coffee here, making it a legendary hangout for the sophisticated residents of St-Germain-des-Prés and flocks of summer tourists. Visitors monopolize the few sidewalk tables as the waiters rush about, seemingly oblivious to anyone's needs. The crystal chandeliers are brightly lit, but the regulars are used to the glare. After all, some read their papers here while drinking coffee (4.50€), eating salads, pastries, ice cream, or one of the (expensive) daily specials. *6 place St-Germain-des-Prés, 6th arr.* ☎ *01-45-48-55-25. 19–29€. Daily 7:30am–1:30am. Métro: St-Germain-des-Prés.*

→ **Stohrer** ★ *TIME-HONORED* Opened in 1730 by Louis XV's personal chef, Stohrer survives as one of Paris's oldest pastry shops for good reason. The wares here are sweet, sophisticated, and almost make you believe that they don't contain any calories (dream on!). Come for some of the city's best croissants and tortes; to admire the pretty murals by Paul Baudry, who designed the foyer at the Palais Garnier; and, of course, to say that you've eaten a cake from the same shop as Queen Elizabeth II, who stopped by in 2004. *51 rue Montorgueil, 2nd arr.* ☎ *01-42-33-38-20. Daily 7:30am–8pm. Métro: Sentier.*

CHEAP

It's very fashionable nowadays to be a member of the F.C.G. (Financially Challenged Gang), and when you're traveling (in homage to writer George Orwell), there is nowhere better to be down and out than in Paris. For a wide choice of cheap French, Italian, and Greek restaurants, head to **rue Moufftard** (5th arr.; Métro: Place Monge). **Passage Brady** (10th arr.; Métro: Strasbourg St-Denis or Château d'Eau) is in a rather unsavory quarter (but quite safe), south of the Gare de l'Est, with a whole strip of flavorsome and low-cost Indian

Pat a Cake, Pat a Cake, Baker Woman

Let's face it, the Fifth Republic may be allegorically represented as a woman, but feminine *je ne sais quoi* has had little effect on the male-dominated world of bread-making—unless your name is **Apollonia Poîlane.** When her parents died in 2002 (in a tragic helicopter crash), Apollonia found herself the 18-year-old CEO of Poîlane, one of the most successful family-run bakeries in the world and favorite among Hollywood movie stars (Bob De Niro has his buns sent direct from Paris via FedEx). The secret is in the *panis perpetuus,* or "heredi-tary" element, of the bread: Upon Grandpa's orders, a small quantity of dough is salvaged from each batch and added to the next, thus linking every Poîlane loaf across the globe to the first ever *miche* (leavened bread, scored with the famous P for Poîlane) to have been lifted out of the oven in 1932! If you too would like to buy your own loaf of *panis perpetuus* or Grandma's shortbread biscuits, *punitions* (punishments), whip your fanny round to the flagship bou-tique at 8 rue du Cherche-Midi, 6th arr. (☎ **01-45-48-42-59;** www.poilane.com; Métro: Sèvres Babylone or St-Sulpice; Mon–Sat 7:15am–8:15pm; no credit cards; bread costs around 3.35€/kilo). Their second branch is at 49 bd. de Grenelle, 15th arr. (☎ **01-45-79-11-49**).

restaurants. On the Left bank, **rue St-André des Arts** and **rue de la Harpe** (5th arr.; Métro: St-Michel) are home to dozens of teeming creperies, Greek, and French restaurants with menus for around 15€.

→**Breakfast in America** AMERICAN DINER Connecticut-born Hollywood screenwriter Craig Carlson opened this replica of a down-home U.S.-based diner in 2003, building it with funds from members of the California film community who donated memorabilia from some of their recent films. Its self-proclaimed mission involves dispensing proper, rib-sticking American breakfasts and diner food to a generation of Parisians who assume, prior to their visits here, that coffee comes only as espresso and that quantities, per meal, are rigidly limited. *17 rue des Ecoles, 5th arr. ☎ 01-43-54-50-28. www.breakfast-in-america. com. Breakfast platters 5.95€–7.50€; fixed-price Sun brunch 15€. Daily 8:30am–10:30pm. Métro: Cardinal Lemoine or Jussieu. There is also a sister restaurant at 4 rue Malher, 4th arr. (☎ 01-42-72-40-21; Métro: St-Paul).*

MTV Best ◯ →**Chez Chartier** FRENCH *TIME-HONORED* This is one of the oldest and cheapest worker canteens in the whole city—a veritable institution and an absolute must. Don't expect elaborate food, but do expect French staples such as Steak-frites, eggs with mayonnaise (oeuf mayonnaise), pâté, onion soup (soupe à l'onion), and beetroot salad, all served in an impressive 19th-century dining room. When the black-and-white clad waiter runs up to your table, order straight away. Who knows when he'll be back again—there is so much hustle and bustle he could get lost in the din. *7 rue du Faubourg Montmartre, 9th arr. ☎ 01-47-70-86-29 (no reservations). Fixed-price 18€. Daily 11:30am–3pm and 6–10pm. Métro: Grands Boulevards.*

→ **La Bonne Franquette** MOROCCAN *BOHEMIAN* Once you've worked up an appetite wandering around Père-Lachaise cemetery, one of the best places for a hearty couscous is this place, run by three handsome, friendly brothers who take pride in their cooking and choice of decor.

You're in Paris, so shabby-chic is par for the course, but the ever-changing art on the terra-cotta walls adds to the general allure of the funky light fittings and objects all around. The couscous is one of the city's best, with lashings of sauce and spicy sausage and chicken (vegetarian options available). If you don't fancy Moroccan food, opt for a French salad or snack; and if you crave a mint tea with Arab pastries, go look at the sweet table and choose your poison! *151 rue de la Roquette, 11th arr.* ☎ *01-43-48-85-88. Prices start at 10€. Mon–Sat 10am–1am. Métro: Voltaire or Père-Lachaise.*

➜ **La Boulangerie** ★ FRENCH *ROMANTIC* In a converted bakery right in the heart of the artist-cum-immigrant quarters around Ménilmontant, this is a real neighborhood bistro. Waiters dash around the period room energetically, cheery-faced regulars absorb more Chinon wine than seems humanly possibly, and dishes arrive piping hot and well presented. If they're on the menu, go for the crab ravioli in lobster sauce, any of the succulent steaks, and almond-apricot tart—pure heaven on a plate. *15 rue Panoyaux, 20th arr.* ☎ *01-43-58-45-45. Mon–Fri noon–2pm and 7:30–11pm; Sat 7:30pm–midnight. Métro: Ménilmontant.*

➜ **Le Café Arosé** ★ BRASSERIE *BOHEMIAN* At first glance there is nothing that makes this brand-new resto-cafe stand out from the crowds. It has red banquettes (like every other bistro in Paris), the menus are written on blackboards (like every other bistro in Paris), and there's a traditional wooden bar (you got it . . . like every other bistro in Paris); yet there is something inexplicably intoxicating about the atmosphere. Yes, the staff members are smiley; yes, the wine list is decent; and yes, the mouth-watering magret of duck and the strawberry cappuccino tiramisu

go down without touching the sides. Yes, that must be it! *123 rue Caulincourt, 18th arr.* ☎ *01-42-57-14-30. Mon–Sat 8am–2am; Sun 8am–7pm. Fixed-price 25€. Food served noon–midnight. Métro: Lamark Caulincourt.*

➜ **Le Pré Verre** FUSION *CHIC* Sleek and contemporary, the walls of this Left Bank restaurant are decorated in CD jackets. It makes for an interesting statement—one that is continued through to the food, with unusual contemporary dishes such as beef cheeks with ginger mash and swordfish with lemongrass. The chefs here don't hesitate to spice up all of their food. If you're strapped for cash but desperately want to come, opt for the cheaper lunch menu—a steal at 13€. *19 rue de Sommerard, 5th arr.* ☎ *01-43-54-59-47. Fixed-price 25€. Tues–Sat noon–2pm and 7–10:30pm. Closed 2 weeks in Aug. Métro: Cluny-La Sorbonne.*

➜ **Le Tambour** ALL-NIGHT/FRENCH BOHEMIAN You've just left a nightclub and you're starving? You've been strolling around Paris all night with your loved one and all that kissing's made you hungry? This is the place for you. Le Tambour is a veritable ode to Paname, with Parisian memorabilia across every inch of wall and in every nook and cranny (look out for the illuminated Métro map). It is open all day and every night until 6am, which makes it popular with an eclectic group of punters, from journalists who have worked late in nearby offices to nightclubbers and general insomniacs with a yen for hearty French food. *41 rue de Montmartre, 2nd arr.* ☎ *01-42-33-06-90. Average 25€. Daily 10am–6am. Métro: Etienne Marcel or Sentier.*

📺 Best ✪ ➜ **Ma Pomme** FUSION FRENCH *BOHEMIAN* The only feasible reason for this restaurant to hide behind half-open shutters is that it wants to keep its excellent-value cooking a secret from all but the locals, who pile in droves into

Picnic á la Parisienne

Whether you're poor and hungry, or just fancy soaking up outdoors Paris *à la parisienne*, you can't beat picnicking. The **Pont des Arts** (1st arr.) is a wicked spot in the summer. This pedestrian bridge has unforgettable views of Ile de la Cité and the top of the Eiffel tower, and fills up with couples and groups of friends sharing elaborate homemade wares, the baker's best baguettes and pastries, and copious amounts of wine. The **Square du Vert Gallant** (1st arr.) opposite Pont des Arts, at the tip of the Ile de la Cité, also echos to the sound of clinking bottles and baguette crunching. At sunset, the slopes of the **Sacré-Coeur** (18th arr.) make an unbeatably romantic location as you watch the day disappear in veils of red, gold, yellow, and mauve over the whole of Paris. For a distinctly Bobo picnic, grab a spot on one of the wrought-iron bridges over the **Canal St-Martin** (10th arr.). This stretch is also lined with bars, so if your wine runs out you can run for a refill. Of course, the most timeless spot has to be on the **Champ de Mars** (7th arr.) overlooking the Eiffel tower.

its yellow dining room, decorated with art that changes regularly. This is possibly the restaurant with the best price-quality ratio, thanks to a 22€ prix-fixe (fixed-price) menu that incorporates delicious dishes such as lamb roasted in comté cheese, curried kangaroo steak, and the best chocolate cake on the Ménilmontant drag. *107 rue de Ménilmontant, 20th arr.* ☎ *01-40-33-10-40. Menu 22€. Mon–Fri 11am–2am; Sat 7:30pm–2am. Métro: Ménilmontant (then a 10-min. walk up a steep hill).*

DOABLE

→ **Café Constant** TRADITIONAL FRENCH *TIME-HONORED* Christian Constant used to be chef at the Crillon (the Palace hotel on place de la Concorde). Then he spread his wings and opened his Michelin-starred restaurant Violon d'Ingres on rue St-Dominique (7th arr.). Feeling a desire to go back to basics, he bought the *tabac* next-door to the Violon, and turned it into this— an excellent local bistro specializing in traditional French grub just like granny used to make. Start with the homemade pâté, and then opt for the just-pink calves' liver and potato purée, and finish it all off with gooey chocolate tarte. Purrrr! *139 rue*

St-Dominique, 7th arr. ☎ *01-47-53-73-34. Average 26€. Tues–Sat noon–2:30pm and 7:30–10:30pm. Métro: Ecole Militaire. RER: Pont d'Alma.*

MTV **Best ●** → **China Club** ★★ ASIAN *CHIC/ROMANTIC* What class, what chic, what a pleasant surprise it's not a private club! From the moment you step in, you feel like you've been transported back into a swish Jackie Chan film set in the 1930s: deep-red walls, black-and-white tile floors, squishy leather chesterfields you can sink into while sipping your Singapore Sling. The food (all Asian) is delicious. If you don't want a sit-down meal, order dim sum with your cocktails. Then there's the dark upstairs *fumoir*, a hideaway for young trendies with romance on their minds. If you're into jazz, you can also slink downstairs for a live set. *50 rue de Charenton, 12th arr.* ☎ *01-43-43-82-02. www.chinaclub.cc. Fixed-price 28€. Daily 7pm–2am (closed Aug). Métro: Bastille or Ledru Rollin.*

MTV **Best ●** → **Kong** FUSION *CHIC* Made famous throughout the world by Carrie in *Sex and the City*, Kong is still one of the hottest restaurants on the Paris drag, set at the top of the Kenzo building at

PARIS & ILE-DE-FRANCE

Pont Neuf. You'll dig the wicked views over the river and wacky Manga-themed details by top-dog Philippe Starck, including Perspex chairs, Pokémon memorabilia, giant Geisha panels, and a pebble-stone carpet. Food is fashionably fusion (think lobster spring rolls and foie gras cooked in miso). There's not a lot of it (bad for the figure, darling), but it's worth the payout for the extravagant, playful surroundings. On Fridays and Saturdays, join the beautiful people as they flock to listen to live DJs. *1 rue du Pont Neuf, 1st arr.* ☎ *01-40-39-09-99. www.kong.fr. Average 40€. Daily 10:30am–2am. Métro: Pont Neuf or Châtelet.*

Ⓜ **Best ⦿** ➜ **Le Petit Prince** ★ CONTEMPORARY FRENCH *BOHEMIAN* On a little side street near the Pantheon, this gay-identified restaurant is a must for even the straightest epicurean. Cozy decor, smiley staff, and delicious food (all covered in wondrously rich sauces) are what make this restaurant stand out. Butter, cream, alcohol—everything sinful has gone into making some heavenly flavors. And then there's the long and eclectic wine list. So what's the downfall? Well, with grub so great it is damned popular with the locals, forcing the owners to enforce two-sittings per night. If you get there for the earlier one (8pm), you'll be hurried away by 10:30pm at the latest. Unless you have some bars to get around, aim instead for the second sitting, when you can stay until closing. *12 rue Lanneau, 5th arr.* ☎ *01-43-54-77-26. Fixed-price menu 25€–55€. Daily 7:30pm–close. Métro: Maubert Mutualité.*

➜ **Le Troquet** ★★ BASQUE *BOHEMIAN* Chef Christian Etchebest learned his tricks from Christian Constant (see Café Constant, above), and boy did he learn 'em well. Food is *tout simplement* wonderful. Try the cheese puff pastry tart covered in avocado purée, smoked eel, and apple—an unusual combination, but one that works perfectly.

Other dishes include delights such as olive-stuffed chicken breast served with cabbage flavored with juniper, pork, and olive oil; and roasted fig meringue turnover (an upside-down gâteau with custard cream). You have no reason to wander down this purely residential street in the 15th other than to come here—so come here. *21 rue François-Bonvin, 15th arr.* ☎ *01-45-66-89-00. Fixed-price menu 30€. Tues–Sat noon–2:30pm and 7:30–11pm. Métro: Sèvres-Lecourbe.*

➜ **Pause Café** ★ BOHEMIAN Need lessons in posing? Come to this place, so renowned for its "look at me—are you looking at me?" clientele that it has earned the nickname "Pose Café." Pop on your dark sunglasses (vintage of course); sidle up to the regular film, music, and journalist crowds; and sup in style (or try one of their hearty lunchtime dishes) on their busy terrace or inside on the scruffy, but oh-so-cool banquettes and wooden tables. *41 rue de Charonne, 11th arr.* ☎ *01-48-06-08-33. Lunch 12€–14€; 3-course dinner menu 28€. Mon–Sat 7am–2am; Sun 9am–10pm. Métro: Bastille or Ledru Rollin.*

SPLURGE

➜ **Alain Ducasse au Plaza Athénée** ★★ CONTEMPORARY *CHIC* If you've a quick 600€ to blow on a meal for two, you too can sup in Paris's most coveted dining room alongside millionaires, royalty, and the world's most famous faces. Even the waiters look like they were born in a diamond-encrusted palace. Remember which knife and fork to use as you tuck delicately into Christophe Moret's finely prepared dishes and feast your eyes on the 10,000 loose crystal drops that dangle from the ceiling—well, this is Paris's fashion avenue. *Hôtel Plaza Athénée, 35 av. Montaigne, 8th arr.* ☎ *01-53-67-65-00. Fixed-price menus 220€–320€. Thurs–Fri noon–2pm and 7pm–close; Mon–Wed 7pm–close.*

Generation.C: changing French Gastronomy

Roll up, roll up—this is the hottest stuff to come out of Paris's oven for almost 3 decades. **Generation.C** (C meaning Cooking or Creation) is an association of young chefs, under 40 years of age, set to redefine French cuisine for generations to come. In the 1970s, Nouvelle Cuisine was a flagstone in France's culinary history, fixing the way in which cooking was perceived and practiced around the world. Today, Generation.C plays as an important role in modern France as Nouvelle Cuisine did 30 years ago.

You could almost think of it as a cultural movement—one that considers cooking an art form, a promoter of experimentation, a means of expression, and guardian of France's reputation on the world food circuit. It also promotes the democratization of fine cuisine by keeping prices comparatively low, and breathing fresh air into the training of young chefs, who are encouraged to invent rather than conform (the antithesis of Old-School Michelin).

Chef Gilles Choukroun is at the cool restaurant 📺 Best● **Angl'Opéra** (39 av. de l'Opéra, 2nd arr.; ☎ **01-42-61-86-25;** www.anglopera.com; Mon–Fri 11:30am–11pm; Métro: Opéra) in the Edouard VII Hotel (p. 91). He's at the forefront of this movement with his fun, contemporary food that embraces influences from world cuisine, giving it fresh flair and flavor. On the menu are astounding inventions such as foie gras crème-brûlée, raw tuna with grapefruit and liquorice, pan-fried pork with oysters and coconut milk, and poached pear with pistachios, almonds, and wasabi—all as surprising as they are delicious.

For other Generation.C restaurants, re-educate your palate at:

➜ **Chez l'Ami Jean:** 27 rue Malar, 7th arr. (☎ **01-47-05-86-89;** count on spending 30€ a head)

➜ **Jean:** 8 rue St-Lazare, 9th arr. (☎ **01-48-78-62-73;** count on spending 35€–70€ a head)

➜ **La Famille:** 41 rue des Trois Frères, 18th arr. (☎ **01-42-52-11-12;** count on spending 35€ a head)

➜ **La Gazetta:** 29 rue de Cotte, 12th arr. (☎ **01-43-47-47-05;** www.lagazzetta.fr; count on spending 30€ a head)

➜ **Le Châteaubriand:** 129 av. Parmentier, 11th arr. (☎ **01-43-57-45-95;** count on spending 13€–36€ a head)

➜ **Le Comptoir du Relais:** 7–9 Carrefour de l'Odéon, 6th arr. (☎ **01-44-27-07-97;** count on spending 50€ a head)

➜ **Les Saveurs de Flora:** 38 av. Georges V, 8th arr. (☎ **01-40-70-10-49;** count on spending 30€–50€ a head)

➜ **Mon Vieil Ami:** 69 rue St-Louis en L'Ile, 4th arr. (☎ **01-40-46-01-35;** main courses 50€)

PARIS & ILE-DE-FRANCE

➜ **La Dôme du Marais** ★ FRENCH *ROMANTIC* Eat here and you'll dine in one of the best examples of 18th-century neoclassical circular architecture in France—the Credit Municipal's pawnbrokers building. The room (lit by natural light) makes you feels as though you're sitting in a medieval corn exchange or eating on the stage of Sheakespeare's Globe Theater. As for the food (all from the local market), try the St-Jacques scallops on a bed of lentils, or the hare stuffed with liver in a red wine sauce served with mushroom ravioli and pumpkin mash. Desserts, like plum and hazelnut crumble, are to die for, but if you don't have room, don't worry—you get little cakes and chocolate with your coffee. If you want to impress your partner, or just splurge somewhere less decadent than *chez* Ducasse (see above), book a table here. *53 rue des Francs-Bourgeois, 4th arr.* ☎ *01-42-74-54-17. Fixed-price 35€–65€, a la carte 70€. Mon–Sat noon–2:30pm and 7:30–11pm. Métro: St-Paul.*

VEGETARIAN

If you don't eat meat, you might just make it through in Paris, where at least a few places will cater to your needs. Try **Le Petit Marché** (9 rue de Béarn, 3rd arr.; ☎ **01-42-72-06-67;** daily noon–3pm and 8pm–midnight; Métro: Chemin Vert), a hip Marais bistro that attracts both the fashion and health conscious. Food is not exclusively vegetarian, but they do have a selection of all veggie goodies. **Chez Omar** (47 rue de Bretagne, 3rd arr.; ☎ **01-42-72-36-26;** Mon–Sat noon–2:30pm and 7–11:30pm, Sun 7–11pm; Métro: Temple or Arts et Métiers) is one of Paris's best Moroccan restaurants (and the only North African one that people queue up for—even in the rain). Here you can chomp on excellent all-vegetable couscous dishes and sticky Algerian pastries.

Partying

The bar scene is the site of Paris nightlife; it is here that Parisians feel most at home, mugging under the dim lights, dangling Gauloises and Marlboros from their puckered lips, and frightening their little dogs. Though Paris has plenty of clubbers and music lovers, it is the "bar" that allows Parisians to show off what they've got going on, and hide away what they don't. Dress codes vary depending on where you're going. Dress up for Chic venues, but

dress down with style for Bohemian places. Jeans are acceptable almost everywhere except in the posh venues. If you're going clubbing, sneakers could cost you entry to some hot spots.

BARS

➜**Andy Wahloo** ★ *BOHEMIAN* What this tiny bar loses in space it makes up for in style. Created by the folks behind Momo and Sketch in London, it is a wonderfully bombastic take on a Moroccan-hippy parlor, with patterned rugs thrown over the banquettes, retro North African food packaging stocked in the bookcase (just for show, man), and stools made from overturned paint barrels. Get there early if you want a seat—the place fills up with a trendy crowd after 9pm. *69 rue des Gravilliers, 3rd arr.* ☎ *01-42-71-20-38. Métro: Arts et Métiers.*

➜**Chez Richard** *BOHEMIAN* This is a fine Marais venue for people-watching, inside a courtyard off rue Vieille-du-Temple. The interior is lined with stone, and the ceiling fans and palm leaves evoke

The Drinking Game

There is no enforced drinking age in France, but neither are there great drunks; people consume moderately and get drunk with great composure. It's only tourists you'll hear shouting, "Yahoooo!" while under the influence. As for narcotics, I would definitely not recommend you head out to the rough streets of the *banlieue,* the dangerous outskirts, the only areas in Paris where drugs are hawked in the street. In most public parks, such as the Champ de Mars, you'll find kids sneaking a toke, though busts are extremely rare.

Garçon Meets Fille

Are the French the seducers and seductresses they're fabled to be? They've got something; there's no denying it. Maybe it's that Paris is in some haunting way a lonelier place than you might have imagined, or maybe it's that political correctness has never crossed the sea, but arts long-lost in the Anglophone countries—such as innuendo, drawn-out flirtation, shameless meaningful looks between strangers, sexy PDA, and the asking-for and giving-out of phone numbers without a lot of to-do—are still alive here, charging almost every exchange with a little *frisson*. The two little kisses upon greeting and parting are not always totally innocent; nor are those lingering looks on the Métro: I heard tell of a friend of a friend, not bad-looking, who sat beside a not bad-looking total stranger, and after a 15-minute wordless ride, the two rose in unison and walked silently back to her place. Or maybe people just tell these stories to make everyone else miserable.

Note: A *préservatif* is a condom, not a food additive. And be careful, because there *are* some weirdoes out there.

old Algiers (once a French colony). The action is on two levels, and hip music is played in the background. Happy hour daily from 6 to 8pm is a reason alone to visit when the tables fill up with after-work loungers. This is a great spot for striking a conversation. *37 rue Vieille-du-Temple, 4th arr.* ☎ *01-42-74-31-65. Métro: Hôtel-de-Ville.*

→ **Harry's New York Bar** *TIME-HON-ORED* At *sank roo doe noo,* as the ads tell you to instruct your cabdriver, is the most famous bar in Europe—possibly in the world. Opened on Thanksgiving Day 1911 by an expatriate named MacElhone, it's where members of the World War I ambulance corps drank themselves silly. In addition to being Hemingway's favorite, Harry's is where the White Lady and Sidecar cocktails were invented; it's also the reputed birthplace of the Bloody Mary and the headquarters of a loosely organized fraternity of drinkers known as the International Bar Flies. Evening crowds include pre- and post-theater groupies and night owls who aren't bothered by the gritty setting and unflattering lighting. A softer, somewhat less macho ambience

reigns in the cellar, where a pianist provides music Tuesday to Saturday from 10pm to 3am. *5 rue Daunou, 2nd arr.* ☎ *01-42-61-71-14. www.harrys-bar.fr. Métro: Opéra.*

→ **La Belle Hortense** *ROMANTIC* There are dozens of other bars and cafes near this one, but none maintains a bookstore in back, and few seem so self-consciously aware of their roles as ersatz literary salons. Come for a glass of wine, a kiss in the corner, and participation in a discussion within what's defined as "a literary bar." It's named after a pulpy 19th-century romance *(La Belle Hortense)* set within the neighborhood. Wine is 3€ to 7€ per glass. *31 rue Vieille-du-Temple, 4th arr.* ☎ *01-48-04-71-60. Métro: Hôtel-de-Ville.*

→ **Le Progrès** *BOHEMIAN* This is a chill neighborhood bar with a friendly staff serving traditional French cuisine daily for lunch. After lunchtime, it morphs into a cool bar that attracts everyone from foreign tourists to neighborhood regulars, poets, would-be artists, and actors. Chessboards are available for people who want to relax with a drink and a game. Drinks are priced fairly; cocktails start at

PARIS & ILE-DE-FRANCE

Partying & Sightseeing in Paris

MONTMARTRE

place Pigalle

Moulin Rouge

bd. de Clichy

Casino de Paris

Ste-Trinité

Notre-Dame de Lorette

bd. Haussmann

Opéra Garnier

place de l'Opéra

place Italiens

bd. des Capucines

place Vendôme

St-Roch

bd. de la Chapelle

Gare du Nord

St-Vincent de Paul

Gare de l'Est

St-Laurent

St-Joseph

place du Colonel Fabien

PARC DES BUTTES-CHAUMONT

Folies Bergère

bd. Montmartre

Bourse des Valeurs

rue du Mail

rue de Cléry

rue d'Aboukir

rue Réaumur

Conservatoire des Arts et Métiers

place de la République

St-Joseph

Palais Royal

place A. Malraux

TUILERIES

place du Carrousel

Musée du Louvre

Bourse du Commerce

Forum des Halles

Théâtre du Châtelet

St-Merri

Ecole Nationale des Beaux-Arts

ST-GERMAIN-DES-PRÉS

ILE DE LA CITÉ

St-Germain

St-Sulpice

Sorbonne

Palais du Luxembourg

JARDIN DU LUXEMBOURG

Université Paris V

Notre-Dame

QUARTIER LATIN

Université Paris VII

JARDIN DES PLANTES

Archives Nationales

LE MARAIS

St-Denis

St-Ambroise

Archives Nationales

St-Gervais

St-Paul

place des Vosges

place de la Bastille

Opéra Bastille

Théâtre de la Bastille

ILE ST-LOUIS

St-Louis

Gare de Lyon

	Hôtel des Invalides/Napoleon's Tomb **42**
	La Grande Arche de La Défense **47**
	La Grande Mosquée de Paris **16**
Bibliothèque Nationale de France, Site Tolbiac/François Mitterrand **15**	La Madeleine **52**
Cathédrale de Notre-Dame **19**	Musée Carnavalet **25**
Center Pompidou **26**	Musée de l'Institut du Monde Arabe **18**
Cimetière du Père-Lachaise **11**	Musée d'Orsay **41**
Cimetière de Montmartre **1**	Musée du Louvre **40**
Cimetière du Montparnasse **36**	Musée National des Arts Asiatiques Guimet **46**
Conciergerie **32**	Musée National du Moyen Age (Musée de Cluny) **34**
Hôtel de Ville **20**	

Musée Picasso **24**
Panthéon **35**
St-Eustache **29**
St-Germain-des-Prés **38**
St-Sulpice **37**
Ste-Chapelle **33**
Tour Eiffel **44**
Musée du Quai Branly **43**
Cité de l'Architecture et du Patrimoine **45**
Cité Nationale de l'Histoire de l'Immigration **12**
Château de Vincennes **13**

The Oberkampf Bar-Crawl

Still hip after all these years, **M** Best❂ **rue Oberkampf** and its neighboring **rue St-Maur** and **rue Jean-Pierre Timbaud** are the main drags of the 11th *arrondissement*. They are home to the cheapest happy hours in Paris and the ultimate destination for a flirt with the debaucheries of French nightlife (aka a bar-crawl). Follow this guide and you should collapse in a happy heap at around 6:30am. *Note:* Most happy hours run 6 to 9pm, and the nearest Métros are Parmentier, Ménilmontant, and Couronnes. Now off you fly.

Rue Jean Pierre Timbaud

1. **Café Cannibale** (no. 93; ☎ **01-49-29-95-59;** beer 2.50€). An intellectual atmosphere lingers around its zinc bar and red-topped tables. A fine spot, therefore, for drink number 1, before you turn into a blabbering wreck.

2. **Le Chat Noir** (no. 76; ☎ **01-48-06-98-22;** house cocktail 6.50€). A favorite for its weekend jazz and Monday night chess tournaments.

3. **La Marquise** (no. 74; no phone; beer 2.50€), over the road, doubles up as a restaurant with regular live music that attracts a mixed crowd of trendies.

Rue St-Maur

4. The **Newport** (no. 114; no phone) is a cool but scruffy pub (step over the cigarette butts on the floor) that pumps out reggae into the wee hours and practically gives beer away (just 1.50€ 6–10pm).

5. Next door, in the **Nun's Café** (no. 112 bis; ☎ **01-58-30-65-48**), a young crowd of students downs alcoholic drinks like there's no tomorrow.

6. For something a little calmer, head to **Les Couleurs** (no. 117; ☎ **01-43-57-95-61**), where locals chill in comfy chairs and pontificate about why beer (2.50€) here costs less than water!

Rue Oberkampf

7. **Café Charbon** (no. 109; ☎ **01-43-57-55-13**) has been hailed as the hippest hangout in Oberkampf for over 10 years. Squeeze through the Bobo crowds to admire the former Belle Epoque dancehall decor and slurp on some of their lush margaritas.

8. **La Mercerie,** over the road (no. 98; ☎ **01-43-38-81-30**), is a grungy-chic haunt that serves Paris's best mojitos to loud groups of friends.

9. The **Quartier Général** (no. 103; ☎ **01-43-14-65-78**), with its industrial chic decor and aluminium pipe lighting, stays open until dawn on Friday and Saturday nights.

10. Newest kid on the block is the fantastic **Oxyd'Bar** (corner of rue Oberkampf at 26 av. Jean Aicard; ☎ **01-48-06-21-81**), which feels more like a sitting room than a bar. Music dudes hang here for the chilled flow of live Jazz and cheap martinis (3€).

11. End the night at Nouveau Casino (see below) or at **Cithéa** (no. 114; ☎ **01-40-21-70-95;** www.cithea.com), a funky club-cum-boudoir that invites streams of trendy DJs.

about 7€, and a pitcher of wine goes for 10€. *7 rue des 3 Frères, 18th arr.* ☎ *01-42-64-07-37. Métro: Abbesses.*

➜**Man Ray** *CHIC* This chic rendezvous off the Champs-Elysées is dedicated to Man Ray, the famous photographer and American Dadaist, who usually felt more comfortable roaming Montparnasse than the 8th. The club is a media favorite, mainly because some of its owners are Johnny Depp, Sean Penn, and John Malkovich. Don't count on seeing them, though—they're hardly ever there. What you will see, however, is a bustling basement restaurant presided over by two winged Indonesian goddesses, and a giant upstairs bar that overlooks the action. Jazz and the occasional classical music concert play Monday to Thursday from 7 to 9pm in the bar, and every night after 11pm a DJ spins (Fri after 11pm, that space becomes a disco that costs 15€–20€, including the first drink). *34 rue Marbeuf, 8th arr.* ☎ *01-56-88-36-36. Métro: Franklin-D-Roosevelt.*

CLUBS & LIVE MUSIC VENUES

➜**Batofar** ★ *BOHEMIAN* Self-consciously proud of its status as a club that virtually everybody views as hip, Batofar sits on a converted barge that floats on the Seine, sometimes attracting hundreds of gyrating dancers, most of whom are in their 20s and 30s. House, garage, techno, and live jazz by groups that hail from (among other places) Morocco, Senegal, and Germany sometimes add to the mix. Come here for an insight into late-night Paris at its most raffish and countercultural, and don't even try to categorize the patrons. Beer is expensive at 9€ a bottle; cover is 12€ to 16€. *Facing 11 quai François Mauriac, 13th arr.* ☎ *01-53-60-17-30. Closed Nov–Mar. Métro: Quai de la Gare.*

📺 Best ♥ FREE ➜**La Flêche d'Or** *BOHEMIAN* New management, new style.

This hotbed of musical creation is Paris's ultimate indie-rock and electro club. Set in a former train station, nightly concerts (from 9pm) shake the walls with sounds from Paris's hottest talent (both up-and-coming and well-established). Two huge bars keep patrons well serviced. A cool brasserie serves standard grub such as salads and pasta (8€–15€). And check out the view over the railway lines. If you want to understand what makes young Parisians trip, a visit to this fun, happening venue is obligatory. *102 bis rue de Bagnolet, 20th arr.* ☎ *01-44-64-01-02. www.flechedor.fr. Métro: Alexandre Dumas or Porte de Bagnolet.*

📺 Best ♥ ➜**La Suite** *CHIC* It's kitsch to the max (everywhere is pink), but it's also cool to the max—and *the* place to be seen if you want to get in with Paris's "it" crowd. If you really want to fit in, dine here beforehand or order a heinously expensive bottle of champagne, then sit back and watch the bold and the beautiful roll in before your eyes. If you can get in that is. This little slice of party heaven is very selective. Madame l'Hôtesse or Monsieur le Bouncer may turn you away if they don't like your face, earrings, or shoes (damn it, you knew you should have worn the pink stilettos). But if you make the grade, you'll be bopping next to TV stars, models, and the capital's most superficial (but oh-so-gorgeous) trendies. It's like totally so worth it, man! *40 av. George V, 8th arr.* ☎ *01-53-57-49-49. Métro: George V.*

➜**Les Bains Douches** *CHIC* The name "The Baths" comes from this hot spot's former function as a Turkish bath that attracted gay clients, none more notable than Marcel Proust. It may be hard to get in if the doorman doesn't think you're trendy and *très chic*. Yes, that was Jennifer Lopez you saw whirling around the floor. Dancing begins at midnight, and a supper-club-like restaurant is upstairs. Meals cost 40€ to 50€. On certain nights this is the hottest party atmosphere in Paris, and Mondays are increasingly gay, although sexual preference is hardly an issue here: "We all walk the waterfront," one DJ enigmatically told me. Cover is 20€. *7 rue du Bourg-l'Abbé, 3rd arr.* ☎ *01-48-87-01-80. Métro: Étienne Marcel.*

➜**Nouveau Casino** *CHIC/BOHEMIAN* Some Paris-watchers consider this the epitome of the hyperhip countercultural scene that blossoms along the rue Oberkampf every night. In a former movie theater adjacent to the Café Charbon, it's a large, drafty space centered on a dance floor and an enormous bar crafted to resemble an iceberg. Live concerts take place nightly between 8pm and 1am; on Friday and Saturday, the party continues from 1am until dawn with a DJ who spins some of the most avant-garde dance music in Paris. Celebrity-spotters have picked out Prince Albert of Monaco and such French-language film stars as Vincent Cassel and Mathieu Kassovitz. For a schedule of bands and singers, visit the (French-language) website. Admission to concerts ranges 12€ to 15€; to get into the disco, you'll pay 5€ to 10€. *109 rue Oberkampf, 11th arr.* ☎ *01-43-57-57-40. www.nouveaucasino.net. Métro: St-Maur, Parmentier, or Ménilmontant.*

MTV (Best ✪) ➜**Point Ephémère** *CHIC/ BOHEMIAN* Canal St-Martin gets hotter by the year, but no place burns brighter than this melting pot—with an arts gallery, concert hall, music studios, bar, and restaurant all under the same roof. From the moment you spy the graffiti-clad exterior from the bridge over the canal, you know you're heading somewhere hip. In fact, despite its "art for all" policy, the people who hang here are almost too hip to handle. Nevertheless it's one of the most exciting venues in the capital, with plenty of progressive and experimental audiovisual and performing arts shows, wild electronic music nights, regular appearances from bands of the underground hip-hop and rock scene, and energetic DJs. What's more, its waterside location and bustling terrace ensure that its vast expanses are always thronging with funky young things from far and wide. Come join them for that ultimate, cool Parisian experience. *200 quai de Valmy, 10th arr.* ☎ *01-40-34-02-48. www.pointephemere.org. Métro: Jaurès.*

➜**Triptyque** ★ *BOHEMIAN* If you like to be the person who says, "I saw him/her before he/she was really famous" take a trip to the oh-so-alternative Triptyque, where many trendsetting DJs are tried and tested by their record labels. The crowd here is switched on *(branché)*, and arrive in (well) dressed-down gaggles to dig the live hip-hop, jazz, funk, drum and bass, and all-night electro parties. There's a chill area, a bar, and a steamy dance floor for you to slink between as you concentrate on looking as cool as everyone

Rock en Seine

For 2 days in August, the Paris suburb of Saint-Cloud swaps its slick, bourgeois attitude for something entirely more funky—a rock festival with a devout following of international cool kids. Bring a blanket and wads of cash (food and drinks—mainly beer—are expensive), and listen to the sounds of bands like Radiohead, Beck, Franz Ferdinand, Massive Attack, Babyshambels, and Morrisey (acts change each year). Tickets are for sale online and in branches of the **FNAC** store (www.fnac.com).

around you. *142 rue de Montmartre, 2nd arr.*
☎ *01-40-28-05-55.* *www.letriptyque.com.*
Métro: Bourse or Grands Boulevards.

JAZZ CLUBS

➜ **Le Bilboquet** *TIME-HONORED/
ROMANTIC* Come here and follow in the
footsteps of David Bowie and ZZ Top. This
restaurant/jazz club/piano bar, where the
film *Paris Blues* was shot, offers some of
the best music in the city. Jazz is featured
on the upper level in the restaurant, a
wood-paneled room with a copper ceiling,
brass-trimmed bar, and Victorian cande-
labra. The menu (a bit of a splurge at 55€)
is limited but classic French. *13 rue
St-Benoît, 6th arr.* ☎ *01-45-48-81-84. Métro:
St-Germain-des-Prés.*

📺 Best ♦ ➜ **New Morning** *BOHEMIAN*
Jazz maniacs come to drink, talk, and
dance at this long-enduring club. It
remains on the see-and-be-seen circuit, so
you might spy Spike Lee or Prince. The
high-ceilinged loft was turned into a nightclub in 1981. Many styles of music are performed, and the club is popular with jazz
groups from Central and South Africa. Call
to find out what's going on the night you
plan to visit. Admission is 16€ to 25€. *7–9
rue des Petites-Écuries, 10th arr.* ☎ *01-45-23-
51-41. www.newmorning.com. Métro: Château-
d'Eau.*

FABULOUS GAY BARS

In a nutshell, gay life is centered around
Les Halles and **Le Marais,** with the great-
est concentration of gay and lesbian clubs,
restaurants, bars, and shops between the
Hôtel de Ville and Rambuteau Métro stops.
Gay dance clubs come and go so fast that
even the magazines devoted to them, like
Illico—distributed free in the gay bars and
bookstores—have a hard time keeping up.
For lesbians, there is ***Lesbian Magazine.***
Also look for Gai Pied's ***Guide Gai*** and
Têtu Magazine, sold at most newsstands.

Café Cox (15 rue des Archives, 4th arr.;
☎ **01-42-72-08-00**) gets so busy in the
early evening that the crowd stands on the
sidewalk. This is where you'll find the most
mixed gay crowd in Paris—from hunky
American tourists to sexy Parisian men.
A hot, fun place in Les Halles is **Le Tropic
Café** (66 rue des Lombards, 1st arr.; ☎ **01-
40-13-92-62**; Métro/RER: Châtelet—Les
Halles), where the trendy, good-looking
crowd parties until dawn. A restaurant
with a bar popular with women is **Okawa**
(40 rue Vieille-du-Temple, 4th arr.; ☎ **01-
48-04-30-69**; Métro: Hôtel-de-Ville),
where trendy lesbians (and some gay men)
enjoy happy hour. The **Banana Café** (13
rue de la Ferronnerie, 1st arr.; ☎ **01-42-
33-35-31**; Métro: Châtelet—Les Halles) is a
popular all-night bar for gays visiting or
doing business in Paris. Occupying two
floors of a 19th-century building, it has
walls the color of an overripe banana, dim
lighting, and a policy of raising the drink
prices after 10pm, when things become
really interesting. On many nights, go-go
dancers perform from spotlit platforms in
the cellar.

Le Pulp (25 bd. Poissonière, 2nd arr.;
☎ **01-40-26-01-93**; Métro: Grands
Boulevards) is one of the most popular lesbian dance clubs, looking like a burgundy-
colored 19th-century French music hall.
The venue, as the French like to say, is *très
cool,* with cutting-edge music played in a
setting that just happens to discourage the
presence of men. And finally there's the
legendary **Le Queen** (102 av. des Champs-
Elysées, 8th arr.; ☎ **01-53-89-08-90**;
Métro: Franklin-D-Roosevelt or George V).
Should you miss gay life *à la* New York,
seek out the flashing purple sign on the
Champs Elysées. This place is mobbed, primarily by gay men and, to a lesser degree,
chic women who work in fashion and
film. Look for drag shows, muscle shows,

PARIS & ÎLE-DE-FRANCE

The Turkish Loo

If I may, I would like to lead you into the strange realms of French paradox.

Paris is a city that prides itself on its gastronomy, fashionable addresses, chic-as-hell hotels, and all that sparkles. Yet somewhere swimming in that sea of sophistication is the oil slick, the stain, the blemish, the killer. It's the most unhygienic toilet known to man, and Paris's ultimate downfall: the Turkish loo.

"The Turkish loo?! What the hell is that?!" you cry. That, my dear friends, is the hole in the ground that Parisian bars and cafes sometimes try to pass off as a suitable toilet for customers. A porcelain contraption, sunk into the floor, with two little footholds on either side of a hole. Ready, aim, fire is the M.O. Good thigh muscles are a necessity. And whatever you do, don't take a dump, and don't flush the thing until your feet are well clear. Sprinkling while you're tinkling (especially if you're a girl) is an unavoidable hazard.

The unpleasantness of the Turkish loo also spreads to other toilet habits. Many bars, for instance, make a huge effort to make their interiors attractive and keep the money rolling in, yet forget to upkeep their water closets. Fanny wiping evidently isn't as important as Visa swiping, and Parisian frogs are at the bottom of the bog on this count.

striptease by *danseurs* atop the bars, and everything from '70s-style disco nights to foam parties.

Sightseeing

Paris is a city where taking in the street life—shopping, strolling, and hanging out—should claim as much of your time as sightseeing in churches or museums. Having a picnic in a park, taking a sunrise amble along the Seine, spending an afternoon at a flea market—Paris bewitches you with these kinds of experiences. For all the Louvre's beauty, you'll probably remember Montmartre's hilly cobbles better than the 372nd oil painting of your visit.

There is so much to get around that it would be impossible to visit everything. The following items therefore cover the main sights, or the coolest sights, accompanied by a short list of other venues you could visit should you wish to overdose on culture.

PUBLIC MONUMENTS

➔**Arc de Triomphe** ★ The largest triumphal arch in the world, the Arc de Triomphe is 49m (161 ft.) high and 44m (144 ft.) wide. Commissioned by Napoleon in 1806 to commemorate the victories of the Grand Armée, it was finally finished in 1836, just 4 years before his coffin passed beneath it on its way to Les Invalides. Since then, it has become the site of many state funerals and it is also where you will find the tomb and eternal flame of the Unknown Soldier. To reach it, *don't try to cross the square*, Paris's busiest traffic hub. With a dozen streets radiating from the "Star," the roundabout has been called by one writer "vehicular roulette with more balls than numbers." Death is certain! Take the underground passage, and live a little longer. If you make it there alive, climb the stairs to the top and admire the linear beauty of Paris's town planning. *Place Charles de Gaulle-Étoile, 8th arr.* ☎ *01-55-37-73-77. www. monum.fr. Admission 4.50€–7€. Daily Apr–Sept 10am–11pm; Oct–Mar 10am–10:30pm. Métro/RER: Charles-de-Gaulle–Étoile.*

➔**Conciergerie** ★★ London has its Bloody Tower, and Paris has its Conciergerie. Even though it had a long regal history before the

Revolution (it looks like a fairy-tale castle), it was forever stained by the Reign of Terror and lives as an infamous symbol of Dr. Guillotin's wonderful little invention. You approach through its landmark twin towers, the **Tour d'Argent** (where the crown jewels were stored at one time) and **Tour de César,** but the **Salle des Gardes (Guard Room)** is the actual entrance. However, architecture plays a secondary role to the list of prisoners who spent their last days here. Louis XVI, Marie Antoinette, Robspierre, and thousands of others were brought here to be tortured or await their trials during the Revolution. *1 quai de l'Horloge, 4th arr. ☎ 01-53-40-60-93. www. monum.fr. Admission 6.10€ adults, 4.10€ ages 18–25. Daily 9:30am–6pm. Métro: Cité, Châtelet, or St-Michel. RER: St-Michel.*

→**Hôtel des Invalides/Napoleon's Tomb** ★ In 1670, the Sun King decided to build this "hotel" to house disabled soldiers, but by the time it was complete Louis XIV was long gone. The best way to approach the Invalides (recognizable for its gilded dome by Jules Hardouin-Mansart) is by crossing over the Right Bank via the pont Alexander-III and entering the cobblestone forecourt, where a display of massive cannons makes a formidable welcome. Napoleon is buried here, but before rushing to his tomb, you could see the military museum, the **Musée de l'Armée,** containing one of the world's greatest collections of weapons, uniforms, and equipment. The collection at **Musée des Plans-Reliefs** shows French towns and monuments done in scale models (the model of Strasbourg fills an entire room), as well as models of military fortifications since the days of the great Vauban. A walk across the Cour d'Honneur (Court of Honor) delivers you to the **Eglise du Dôme,** whose dome is the second-tallest monument in Paris (the Tour Eiffel is the tallest, of course). Napoleon is buried here. Surrounding his tomb are a dozen Amazon-like figures representing his victories. *Place des Invalides, 7th arr. ☎ 01-44-42-37-72. www.invalides.org. Admission to*

cheap Thrills

On the first Sunday of each month, **museums** are generally free. See listings below for specifics. Many museums also offer free admission for people under 18 and discounts for people 18 to 25, with valid student ID. If you plan to hit dozens of sites, you should invest in the **Paris Museum Pass,** which allows you to enter over 60 museums and monuments throughout the region for free, without queuing, and as many times as you like (a godsend, considering you could easily spend 6 days in the Louvre). They are sold at participating museums and monuments, and at the tourist offices. Choose between a 2-day (30€), 4-day (45€), or 6-day (60€) pass; don't forget to write your name and the date of your first visit on the back to validate it. For more information, check out **www.paris museumpass.fr.**

For a panoramic trip around Paris on the cheap (the price of a bus ticket), take the line **no. 95 bus,** which goes from place de Clichy via the Opéra, Louvre, Palais Royal, St-Germain-de-Prés, and Montparnasse. The **no. 69 bus** starts at the Eiffel Tower and ends at Père-Lachaise cemetery. See **www.ratp.fr** for bus information.

Musée de l'Armée, Napoleon's Tomb, and Musée des Plans-Reliefs 7€ adults, 5€ students. Oct–Mar daily 10am–5pm; Apr–May and Sept daily 10am–6pm; June–Aug daily 10am–7pm. Closed Jan 1, May 1, Nov 1, and Dec 25. Métro: La tour-Maubourg, Varenne, Invalides, or St-François-Xavier.

FREE ➜ **Hôtel de Ville** ★ On a large square with fountains and early-1900s lampposts, the 19th-century Hôtel de Ville isn't a hotel, but Paris's grandiose City Hall. The medieval structure it replaced had witnessed countless municipally ordered executions. Henry IV's assassin, Ravaillac, was quartered alive on the square in 1610, his body tied to four horses that bolted in opposite directions. On May 24, 1871, the Communards doused the City Hall with petrol, creating a blaze that lasted for 8 days. The Third Republic ordered the structure rebuilt, with many changes, even creating a Hall of Mirrors evocative of the one at Versailles. For security reasons, the major splendor of this building is closed to the public. However, the information center sponsors exhibits on Paris in the main lobby. *29 rue de Rivoli, 4th arr. ☎ 01-42-76-43-43. Free admission. Information center Mon–Sat 9:30am–6pm. Métro: Hôtel-de-Ville.*

➜ **Panthéon** ★ Some of the most famous men in French history (Victor Hugo, for one) are buried here on the crest of the mount of St. Geneviève. In 1744, Louis XV vowed that if he recovered from a mysterious illness, he'd build a church to replace the Abbaye de St. Geneviève. He recovered but took his time fulfilling his promise. It wasn't until 1764 that Mme de Pompadour's brother hired Soufflot to design a church in the form of a Greek cross with a dome reminiscent of St. Paul's in London. After the Revolution, the church was converted to a "Temple of Fame" and became a pantheon for the great men of France, namely Voltaire,

Rousseau, Soufflot, Zola, and Braille. Only one woman has a place here: Marie Curie, who joined her husband, Pierre. Told you the French were sexist! *Place du Panthéon, 5th arr. ☎ 01-44-32-18-00. www.monum.fr. Admission 7€ adults, 4.50€ students. Apr 1–Sept 30 daily 10am–6:30pm; Oct 1–Mar 31 daily 10am–6pm (last entrance 45 min. before closing). Métro: Cardinal Lemoine, Maubert-Mutualité, or RER: Luxembourg.*

➜ **Public Monument Extras** The **Arènes de Lutèce** (access at rues Monge and Navarre, 5th arr.; no phone; free admission; May–Sept daily 8am–10pm, Oct–Apr daily 8am–5:30pm; Métro: Jussieu) amphitheater is Paris's most important Roman ruin after the baths in the Musée de Cluny (p. 117). The **Palais Royal** ★ (rue St-Honoré, 1st arr.; no phone; free admission; Métro: Palais Royal–Musée du Louvre) was originally the residence of Cardinal Richelieu, but today houses government buildings and the sublime **Jardin du Palais Royal,** surrounded by shop-filled arcades (many designer vintage clothes boutiques and restaurants). To take in some more modern architecture, try **Bibliothèque Nationale de France, Site Tolbiac/François Mitterrand** (quai François-Mauriac, 13th arr.; ☎ 01-53-79-59-59; www.bnf.fr; admission 3€; Mon 2–10pm, Tues–Sat 9am–10pm, Sun noon–7pm; closed Sept 6–19; Métro: Bibliothèque François-Mitterrand), the French National Library with a futuristic design by Dominique Perrault. Built in 1996, it is a quartet of 24-story towers evoking the look of open books.

➜ **Tour Eiffel** ★★ This is without doubt one of the most recognizable structures in the world. Weighing 7,000 tons but exerting about the same pressure on the ground as an average-size person sitting in a chair, the wrought-iron tower wasn't meant to be permanent. The French engineer

Gustave-Alexandre Eiffel built it for the 1889 Universal Exhibition. (He also designed the framework for the Statue of Liberty.) Praised by some and denounced by others (some called it a "giraffe," the "world's greatest lamppost," or the "iron monster"), the tower created as much controversy in the 1880s as I. M. Pei's glass pyramid at the Louvre did in the 1980s. What saved it from demolition was the advent of radio—as the tallest structure in Europe, it made the perfect perch for a radio antenna (now a TV antenna). The tower, including its TV antenna, is 317m high and on a clear day you can see it from 65km (40 miles) away. One of the best spots from which to admire the Eiffel tower is from Trocadéro. Come here at night and watch the tower sparkle for 10 minutes every hour. *Champ de Mars, 7th arr.* ☎ *01-44-11-23-23. www.tour-eiffel.fr. Admission to 1st landing 4.10€, 2nd landing 7.50€, 3rd landing 11€. Stairs to 2nd floor 3.80€. Sept–May daily 9:30am–11:45pm; June–Aug daily 9am–12:45pm. Fall and winter, stairs open only to 6pm. Métro: Trocadéro, Ecole Militaire, or Bir Hakeim. RER: Champ de Mars–Tour Eiffel.*

CEMETERIES

→**Cimetière du Père-Lachaise** ★★ This cemetery has been called the "grandest address in Paris." A free map is available at the newsstand across from the main entrance. Everybody from **Sarah Bernhardt** to **Oscar Wilde** to **Richard Wright** is here, along with **Honoré de Balzac, Jacques-Louis David, Eugène Delacroix, Maria Callas, Max Ernst,** and **Georges Bizet. Colette** was taken here in 1954; her black granite slab always sports flowers, and legend has it that cats replenish the roses (which drugs do they use?). In time, the "little sparrow," **Edith Piaf,** followed. Napoleon's marshals, **Ney** and **Masséna,** lie here, as do **Frédéric**

Chopin and **Molière. Marcel Proust's** black tombstone rarely lacks a tiny bunch of violets (he wanted to be buried beside his friend/lover, composer **Maurice Ravel,** but their families wouldn't allow it). Some tombs are sentimental favorites: Love-torn graffiti radiates 1km (½ mile) from the grave of Doors singer **Jim Morrison.** Eerie monuments also honor Frenchmen who died in the Resistance or in Nazi concentration camps. *16 rue de Repos; 20th arr.* ☎ *01-55-25-82-10. www.pere-lachaise.com. Mon–Fri 8am–6pm; Sat 8:30am–6pm; Sun 9am–6pm (closes at 5:30pm Nov to early Mar). Métro: Père-Lachaise or Phillipe Auguste.*

FREE →**Cemetery Extras** The **Cimetière de Montmartre** ★ (20 av. Rachel, 18th arr.; ☎ **01-53-42-36-30;** Sun–Fri 8am–6pm, Sat 8:30am–6pm; closes at 5:30pm in winter; Métro: La Fourche) is an afterlife hall of fame for novelist **Alexandre Dumas,** Impressionist **Edgar Degas,** composers **Hector Berlioz** and **Jacques Offenbach,** and **François Truffaut,** film director of the *nouvelle vague* (new wave). Another must-see is the debris-littered **Cimetière du Montparnasse** ★ (3 bd. Edgar-Quinet, 14th arr.; ☎ **01-44-10-86-50;** Mon–Fri 8am–6pm, Sat 8:30am–6pm, Sun 9am–6pm, to 5:30pm Nov–Mar; Métro: Edgar Quinet or Raspail), where you'll see the gravesites of **Simone de Beauvoir** and **Jean-Paul Sartre, Samuel Beckett, Pierre Larousse** (famous for his dictionary), **Capt. Alfred Dreyfus,** auto tycoon **André Citroën,** sculptor **Ossip Zadkine,** and photographer **Man Ray.**

RELIGIOUS BUILDINGS

MTV Best◉ →**Basilique du Sacré-Coeur** ★ Sacré-Coeur is one of Paris's most characteristic landmarks and has been the subject of much controversy. One Parisian called it "a lunatic's confectionery dream." An offended Zola declared it "the basilica of the ridiculous." The artist Utrillo, however, never tired of drawing and painting it. Atop the *butte* (hill) in Montmartre, its multiple gleaming white domes and *campanile* (bell tower) loom over Paris like a 12th-century Byzantine church. But it in fact dates from the 1870s, following France's defeat by the Prussians. The interior is brilliantly decorated with mosaics: Look for the striking Christ on the ceiling—visible from practically everywhere. For the best view over Paris, climb the stone steps up to the gallery around the inner dome from where your eyes take in a sweep of Paris extending for 48km (30 miles). *Place St-Pierre, 18th arr. ☎ 01-53-41-89-09. www.sacre-coeur-montmartre.com. Free admission to basilica; joint ticket to dome and crypt 5€ adults. Basilica daily 6:45am–11pm; dome and crypt daily 9am–6pm. Métro: Abbesses or Anvers, and then follow signs to the funicular (funiculaire).*

MTV Best ◉ → **Cathédrale de Notre-Dame** ★★ Notre-Dame is the heart of Paris and even of the country itself: Distances from the city to all parts of France are calculated from a spot at the far end of place du Parvis, in front of the cathedral, where a circular bronze plaque marks **Kilomètre Zéro.** Founded in the 12th century by Maurice de Sully, bishop of Paris, Notre-Dame has grown over the years, changing as Paris has changed, often falling victim to whims of taste. Although beautiful inside, it is arguably more impressive from the outside, so you should walk all around it to fully appreciate its vast proportions. Believe it or not, the cathedral was once scheduled for demolition, but thanks to the popularity of Victor Hugo's *Hunchback of Notre-Dame* and the revival of interest in the Gothic period, a movement mushroomed to restore the cathedral to its original glory—a task completed under Viollet-le-Duc.

One of the most iconic elements of the cathedral are the gargoyles. To visit them, you have to scale steps leading to the twin **towers,** rising to a height of 68m (223 ft.). Once there, you can inspect devils (some giving you the raspberry), hobgoblins, and birds of prey. Look carefully, and you may see hunchback Quasimodo with Esmerelda. This vantage point offers some of the best views over Paris, especially when the skies are moody. *6 place du Parvis Notre-Dame, 4th arr. ☎ 01-42-34-56-10. Free admission to cathedral. Towers 6.10€ adults, 4.10€ students. Cathedral year-round daily 8am–6:45pm. Towers and crypt Apr–Sept daily 9:30am–6pm; Oct–Mar daily 10am–5:15pm. Museum Sat–Sun 2–5pm. Treasury Mon–Sat 9:30–6pm; Sun 2–6pm. Métro: Cité or St-Michel. RER: St-Michel.*

MTV Best ◉ → **La Grande Mosquée de Paris** ★★ This beautiful pink-marble mosque was built in 1922 to honor the North African countries that had given aid to France during World War I. Today, North Africans living in Paris gather on Friday, the Muslim holy day, and during Ramadan to pray. Short tours are given of the building, its central courtyard, and its Moorish garden; guides present a brief history of the Islamic faith. However, you may want just to wander around on your own and then join the students from nearby universities for couscous and sweet mint tea at the Muslim **Restaurant de la Mosquée de Paris** (☎ 01-43-31-18-14; daily noon–3pm and 7–10:30pm), adjoining the grounds, or have a sweat and a massage in the Hamman. Call for details. *2 place du Puits-de-l'Ermite, 5th arr. ☎ 01-45-35-97-33. www.mosquee-de-paris.net. Admission 3€ adults, 2€ students. Sat–Thurs 9am–noon and 2–6pm. Métro: Place Monge.*

→ **Sainte-Chapelle** ★ Countless writers have called this tiny chapel a jewel box. Yet that hardly suffices. Nor will it do to call it "a light show." Go when the sun is shining, and you'll need no one else's words to describe the remarkable effects of natural light on Sainte-Chapelle. You approach the church through the Cour de la Sainte-Chapelle of the Palais de Justice, which, if it weren't for the chapel's 74m (243-ft.) spire, would swallow it up. Begun in 1246, the bi-level chapel was built to house relics of the True Cross, including the Crown of Thorns acquired by St. Louis (the Crusader king, Louis IX) from the emperor of Constantinople. The *chapelle basse* **(lower chapel)** is supported by flying buttresses and exquisite fleur-de-lis designs. The *chapelle haute* **(upper chapel),** one of the greatest achievements of Gothic art (just check out the stained-glass windows), is reached via a narrow spiral staircase. Ste-Chapelle stages **concerts** in summer; tickets cost 19€ to 25€. Call ☎ **01-42-77-65-65** from 11am to 6pm daily for details. *Palais de Justice, 4 bd. du Palais, 4th arr. ☎ 01-53-40-60-80. www. monum.fr. 5.50€ adults, 4.50€ students. Apr–Sept daily 9:30am–6:30pm; Oct–Mar daily 10am–5pm. Métro: Cité, St-Michel, or Châtelet–Les Halles. RER: St-Michel.*

Other Religious Buildings

La Madeleine ★★ (place de la Madeleine, 8th arr.; ☎ **01-44-51-63-00**; free admission; Mon–Sat 8am–7pm, Sun 8am–1:30pm and 3:30–7pm; Métro: Madeleine) is one of Paris's minor landmarks, dominating rue Royale, and resembling a Roman temple. **St-Eustache** ★★ (2 rue du Jour, 1st arr.; ☎ **01-42-36-31-05**; www.st-eustache.org; free admission; daily 9am–7:30pm; Métro: Les Halles) is a Gothic and Renaissance beauty completed in 1637. It was the site of Madame de Pompadour and Richelieu's baptisms, and Molière's funeral. One of Paris's oldest churches, from the 6th century, is **St-Germain-des-Prés** ★★ (3 place St-Germain-des-Prés, 6th arr.; ☎ **01-43-25-41-71**; free admission; Mon–Sat

8am–7:45pm; Sun 9am–8pm; Métro: St-Germain-des-Prés). It was founded as part of a Benedictine abbey by Childebert, son of Clovis, but alas the marble columns in the triforium are all that remain from then. The Romanesque tower, topped by a 19th-century spire, is the most enduring landmark in St-Germain-des-Prés. Recently made famous by Dan Brown in *The Da Vinci Code,* **St-Sulpice** ★★ (rue St-Sulpice, 6th arr.; ☎ **01-46-33-21-78**; free admission; daily 7:30am–7:30pm; Métro: St-Sulpice) is an architectural gem filled with Delacroix frescoes in the **Chapelle des Anges (Chapel of the Angels),** the first on your right as you enter. Painted in his final years, they were a high point in his baffling career.

MUSEUMS

📺 Best → **Centre Pompidou** ★★ The dream of former president Georges Pompidou, this center for 20th- and 21st-century art, designed by Richard Rogers and Renzo Piano, opened in 1977 and quickly became the focus of controversy. Some nicknamed it "the most avant-garde building in the world;" others called the Centre Pompidou an architectural disgrace. Even today, the museum splits Parisians into two groups: those who love it and those who hate it. You'll be hard-pressed to find someone indifferent to its bold exoskeletal architecture and the brightly painted pipes and ducts crisscrossing its transparent facade (green for water, red for heat, blue for air, yellow for electricity).

The Centre Pompidou encompasses five attractions: The **Musée National d'Art Moderne (National Museum of Modern Art),** with its vast collection of 20th- and 21st-century art (Dalí's *Hallucination partielle: Six images de Lénine sur un piano* [1931], with Lenin dancing on a piano, is usually on show). The **Bibliothèque Information Publique** is a public information library that gives free access to a million French and foreign books, periodicals, films, records, slides, and microfilms in nearly every area of knowledge. The **Center de Création Industriel (Center for Industrial Design)** emphasizes the contributions made in the fields of architecture, visual communications, publishing, and community planning; and the **Institut de Recherche et de Coordination Acoustique-Musique (Institute for Research and Coordination of Acoustics/Music)** brings together musicians and composers interested in furthering the cause of contemporary and traditional music. Finally, you can visit a re-creation of the Jazz Age studio of Romanian sculptor Brancusi, the **Atelier Brancusi** ★, a mini-museum slightly separated from the rest of the action. Don't miss the museum's **forecourt** (a free entertainment center featuring mimes, fire-eaters, circus performers, and sometimes musicians) and the nearby **Stravinsky fountain,** containing mobile sculptures by Tinguely and Saint Phalle. *Place Georges-Pompidou, 4th arr.* ☎ *01-44-78-12-33. www.centerpompidou.fr. Admission 10€ adults, 8€ students, free for children under 18. Wed–Mon 11am–10pm. Métro: Rambuteau, Hôtel-de-Ville, or Châtelet–Les Halles.*

➔ **Château de Vincennes** Few people know it, but at the end of Métro line 1 lies a stunning medieval château that has played a central role in the history of France right up to World War I and World War II. The Vincennes château (in Vincennes) has always had the highest medieval *donjon* in France, but today it is also the most beautiful, after 10 years of painstaking restoration work. Visit this national treasure if you fancy seeing Charles V's royal collections and learning about famous prisoners such as Fouquet (see "Vaux-le-Vicomte: Never One-Up the King" on p. 136), the sexually explicit Marquis de Sade, and Mirabeau, who contributed to writing the *Rights of Man (Les Droits de l'Homme). Av. de Paris, Vincennes 94300. RER A Vincennes.* ☎ *01-44-54-19-30. www.monum.fr. Guided tours daily: 45-min. tour 5€ adults, 3.50€ students; 75-min. tour daily 6.50€ adults, 4.50€ students; free for those under 18. Métro: Château de Vincennes.*

➔ **Cité de l'Architecture et du Patrimonie** Set in one wing of the Palais Chaillot at Trocadéro, this is set to be one of the largest architectural centers in the world, showcasing French architecture from the 12th century onward, with a heavy emphasis on contemporary design and regular temporary exhibitions. Besides the permanent collection, which promises to display massive portions of churches, come here to see the fascinating exhibition on Vauban (Louis XIV's builder; see "Besançon History 101" on p. 653) in celebration of his tercentenary. Don't miss the views of the Eiffel tower from the roof tops. *Palais de Chaillot, 1 place du Trocadéro 16th arr.* ☎ *01-58-51-52-00. www.citechaillot. fr. Admission 10€ adults, 6€ students. Métro: Trocadéro.*

➔ **Cité Nationale de l'Histoire de l'Immigration** Since the Musée du Quai Branly stole the Palais de la Porte Dorée's collections, there has been great debate as to what this stunning 1930s colonial palace should become. Well, wonder no more: From April 2007, it will open as Paris's immigration museum, with collections on immigration through the ages. For years crocodiles have lived in the basement aquarium of the building, and they are here to stay, so you can still admire them after your visit. *293 av. Daumesnil, 12th arr.* ☎ *01-53-59-58-60. www.histoire-immigration. fr. Call for admission. Métro: Porte Dorée.*

→ **Les Arts Décoratifs** You get three for the price of one here. Les Arts Décoratifs groups these hip, newly renovated museums: the **Musée des Arts Décoratifs** (decorative arts museum), **Musée de la Mode et du Textile** (fashion and textile museum), and **Musée de la Publicité** (advertising museum). After 10 years of renovations, the Musée des Arts Décoratifs now displays a rich and fascinating collection on French *art de vivre* from medieval times to the present via a series of excellent "period rooms" that show you literally how times have changed. From March 29 to August 12 you will also get a kick out of the futuristic yet highly 1960s creations by Italian designer Joe Colombo (think TV screens on the ceilings, moving walls with minibars). In the Musée de la Mode et du Textile, there is also a trippin' collection of ballet costumes designed by Jean-Paul Gaultier. *107 rue de Rivoli, 1st arr.* ☎ *01-44-55-57-50. www.lesartsdecoratifs.fr. Admission 6€–17€, for a variety of single and joint-museum tickets; see website for details. Métro: Palais Royal Musée du Louvre.*

FREE → **Musée Carnavalet-Histoire de Paris** ★ If you're a secret history geek but history tomes bore you, spend some time here for insight into Paris's past, which comes alive in details such as the chessmen Louis XVI used to distract himself while waiting to go to the guillotine. The building is a Renaissance palace built in 1544 by Pierre Lescot and Jean Goujon, and later acquired by Mme de Carnavalet. Several salons cover the Revolution, with a bust of Marat, a portrait of Danton, and a model of the Bastille (one painting shows its demolition). Another salon tells the story of the captivity of the royal family at the Conciergerie, including the bed in which Mme Elisabeth (the sister of Louis XVI) slept, and the dauphin's exercise book. Don't forget to continue on to the **Hôtel le Pelletier de St-Fargeau,** across the courtyard, where you'll find furniture from the Louis XIV period to the early 20th century, including a replica of Marcel Proust's cork-lined bedroom with his actual furniture, including his brass bed. *23 rue de Sévigné, 3rd arr.* ☎ *01-44-59-58-58. Free admission. Tues–Sun 10am–6pm. Métro: St-Paul or Chemin-Vert.*

→ **Musée de l'Institut du Monde Arabe** ★★ Many factors have contributed to France's preoccupation with the Arab world, but three of the most important include trade links that developed during the Crusades, a large Arab population living today in France, and the memories of France's lost colonies in North Africa. For insights into the way France has handled its relations with the Arab world, consider making a trek to this bastion of Arab intellect and aesthetics. Designed in 1987 by architect Jean Nouvel and funded by 22 different, mostly Arab countries, it includes expositions on calligraphy, decorative arts, architecture, and photography produced by the Arab/Islamic world, and insights into its religion, philosophy, and politics. There's a bookshop on-site, a replica of a Medina selling high-quality gift and art objects, and archival resources that are usually open only to bona-fide scholars. Views from the windows of the on-site Moroccan restaurant encompass Notre-Dame, l'Ile de la Cité, and Sacré-Coeur. *1 rue des Fossés St-Bernard, 5th arr.* ☎ *01-40-51-38-38. www.imarabe.org. Entrance to permanent exhibitions 5€ adults, 4€ students. Tues–Sun 10am–6pm. Métro: Jussieu, Cardinal Lemoine, or Sully-Morland.*

MTV **Best** ⬇ → **Musée d'Orsay** ★★ Architects created one of the world's great museums from an old rail station, the neo-classical Gare d'Orsay, across the Seine from the Louvre and the Tuileries. Don't skip the Louvre, of course, but come here even if you have to miss all the other art museums in town. The Orsay boasts an astounding collection devoted to the watershed years, 1848 to 1914, with a treasure trove by the big names plus all the lesser-known groups (the Symbolists, Pointillists, Nabis, Realists, and late Romantics). The 80 galleries also include funky Belle Epoque furniture, photographs, objets d'art, and architectural models. A monument to the Industrial Revolution, the Orsay is covered by an arching glass roof allowing in floods of light. It displays works ranging from the creations of academic and historic painters such as Ingres to romanticists such as Delacroix, to neorealists such as Courbet and Daumier. The Impressionists and post-Impressionists (including Manet, Monet, Cézanne, van Gogh, and Renoir) share space with the fauves, Matisse, the Cubists, and the expressionists in a setting once used by Orson Welles to film a nightmarish scene in *The Trial,* based on Kafka's unfinished novel. *1 rue de Bellechasse or 62 rue de Lille, 7th arr. ☎ 01-40-49-48-14. www.musee-orsay.fr. Admission 7.50€ adults, 5.50€ students. Tues–Wed and Fri–Sat 10am– 6pm; Thurs 10am–9:45pm (June 23–Sept 28 9am–6pm); Sun 9am–6pm. Métro: Solférino. RER: Musée d'Orsay.*

MTV **Best ❤** → **Musée du Louvre** ★★
The most famous museum in France and possibly in the world, the Louvre was originally built in the 12th century as a royal fortress and palace for Philip II. The grand building contains paintings, sculptures, and graphic art from the Middle Ages as well as Greek, Etruscan, Roman, Oriental, and Egyptian antiquities. People on one of those "Paris-in-a-day" tours try to break track records to glimpse the Louvre's two most famous ladies: the beguiling *Mona Lisa* (called *La Joconde* in French) and the armless *Venus de Milo.* The herd then dashes on a 5-minute stampede in pursuit of *Winged Victory,* the headless statue

discovered at Samothrace and dating from about 200 B.C. But these are three of the roughly 30,000 works on display. So where would you like to start? The collections are divided into seven departments: Egyptian Antiquities; Oriental Antiquities; Greek, Etruscan, and Roman Antiquities; Sculpture; Painting; Decorative Arts; and Graphic Arts. A number of galleries, devoted to Italian paintings, Roman glass and bronzes, Oriental antiquities, and Egyptian antiquities, were opened in 1997 and 1998. If you don't have to do Paris in a day, you might want to visit several times, concentrating on different collections or schools of painting. Those with little time should take a guided tour. When you get tired, consider a pick-me-up at the chic **Café Marly** in the Cour Napoléon. This cafe overlooks the glass pyramid and offers coffees, pastries (by Paris's legendary pastry-maker, Lenôtre), salads, sandwiches, and delicious platters from 15€. One way to avoid the line is to buy from the automatic ticket machine situated just inside the Carousel du Louvre shopping center beneath the museum. From here you can enter directly from underneath the Pyramid, as opposed to the main entrance in the glass pyramid in the Cour Napoléon. *99 rue de Rivoli, 1st arr. ☎ 01-40-20-53-70. www.louvre.fr. Admission 8.50€ (6€ for late-night visits). Free admission 1st Sun of the month. Wed–Mon 9am–6pm (until 9:45pm Wed and Fri). Parts of the museum close at 5:30pm. Métro: Palais-Royal or Louvre-Rivoli.*

→ **Musée du Quai Branly** Opened in 2006, Paris's newest museum was built by architect Jean Nouvel, the brainchild of Paris's Arab Insitute (Institut du Monde Arabe). It's entirely dedicated to the arts and civilizations of Africa, Asia, Oceania, and the Americas. It holds a vast and fascinating collection of over 3,500 objects. The building, a work of art in itself, is worth a gander just for its slick design and unusual mix of materials. Between April and July 8, however, don't miss the Jardin d'Amour (Love Garden) by Nigerian/British artist Yinka Shonibare, which mixes the traditional elements of 18th-century French gardens and African objects and fabrics. *27–37 quai Branly; 206–218, rue de l'Université, 7th arr.* ☎ *01-56-61-70-00. www. quaibranly.fr. Admission 10€. Métro: Alma Marceau, Iéna, or Bir Hakeim. RER: Pont del'Alma.*

→ **Musée National des Arts Asiatiques Guimet** ★★ This is one of the most beautiful Asian museums in the world, and it houses one of the world's finest collections of Asian art. Some 3,000 pieces of the museum's 45,000 works are on display. The Guimet, opened in Lyon but transferred to Paris in 1889, received the Musée Indochinois du Trocadéro's collections in 1931 and the Louvre's Asian collections after World War II. The most interesting exhibits are Buddhas, serpentine monster heads, funereal figurines, and antiquities from the temple of Angkor Wat. Some galleries are devoted to Tibetan art, including fascinating scenes of the Grand Lamas entwined with serpents and demons. *6 place d'Iéna, 16th arr.* ☎ *01-56-52-53-00. www.museeguimet.fr. Admission 6€ adults, 4€ ages 18–25. Wed–Mon 10am–6pm. Métro: Iéna.*

→ **Musée National du Moyen Age (Musée de Cluny)** ★★ Along with the Hôtel de Sens in the Marais, the Hôtel de Cluny is all that remains of domestic medieval architecture in Paris. Enter through the cobblestoned **Cour d'Honneur (Court of Honor),** where you can admire the flamboyant Gothic building with its vines, turreted walls, gargoyles, and dormers with seashell motifs. This collection of medieval arts and crafts is superb. Most people come to see **the Lady and the Unicorn Tapestries,** the

most acclaimed tapestries of their kind. All the romance of the age of chivalry—a beautiful princess and her handmaiden, beasts of prey, and house pets—lives on in them. Downstairs are the ruins of the **Roman baths,** from around A.D. 200. The best-preserved section is seen in Room X, the frigidarium (where one bathed in cold water). The ribbed vaulting here rests on consoles evoking ships' prows. Credit for this unusual motif goes to the builders of the baths, Paris's boatmen. During Tiberius's reign, a column to Jupiter was found beneath Notre-Dame's chancel and is now on view in the court; called the "Column of the Boatmen," it's believed to be the oldest sculpture created in Paris. *In the Hôtel de Cluny, 6 place Paul-Painlevé, 5th arr.* ☎ *01-53-73-78-00. www.musee-moyenage. fr. Admission 5.50€ adults, 4€ ages 18–25. Wed–Mon 9:15am–5:45pm. Métro: Cluny–La Sorbonne, Saint-Michel, or Odéon.*

→ **Musée Picasso** ★★ When it opened at the beautifully restored Hôtel Salé (Salt Mansion, built by a man who made his fortune by controlling the salt distribution in 17th-c. France) in the Marais, the press hailed it as a "museum for Picasso's Picassos." And that's what it is. The state acquired the world's greatest Picasso collection in lieu of $50 million in inheritance taxes: 203 paintings, 158 sculptures, 16 collages, 19 bas-reliefs, 88 ceramics, and more than 1,500 sketches and 1,600 engravings, along with 30 notebooks. These works span some 75 years of the artist's life and ever-changing style. Because the collection is so vast, temporary exhibits featuring items such as his **studies of the Minotaur** are held twice per year. Also here is Picasso's own treasure trove of art, with works by Cézanne, Rousseau, Braque, Derain, and Miró. *In the Hôtel Salé, 5 rue de Thorigny, 3rd arr.* ☎ *01-42-71-25-21. www.paris.org/Musees/Picasso.*

PARIS & ILE-DE-FRANCE

The Heart of the Boy Who Would Be King

In a bizarre twist, following a mass in 2004, the heart of the 10-year-old heir to the French throne, Louis XVII, was laid to rest at **Saint-Denis Basilica** (2 rue de Strasbourg, St-Denis; ☎ 01-48-09-83-54), near the graves of his parents, Marie Antoinette and Louis XVI. The heart was pickled, stolen, returned, and—2 centuries later—DNA tested. Ceremonies recognizing the royal heart put to rest more than 2 centuries of rumor and legend surrounding the child's death. Genetic testing has persuaded even the most cynical historians that the person who might have been the future Louis XVII never escaped prison. The boy died of tuberculosis in 1795, his body ravaged by tumors. The child's corpse was dumped into a common grave, but not before a doctor secretly carved out his heart and smuggled it out of prison in a handkerchief. The heart of the dead boy was compared with DNA from hair trimmed from Marie Antoinette during her childhood in Austria. It was a perfect match. Well, knock me down with a feather!

Admission 5.50€ adults, 4€ ages 18–25. Apr–Sept Wed–Mon 9:30am–6pm; Oct–Mar Wed–Mon 9:30am–5:30pm. Métro: St-Paul, Filles du Calvaire, or Chemin Vert.

Other Museums

Musée Jacquemart-André (158 bd. Haussmann, 8th arr.; ☎ 01-45-62-11-59; www.musee-jacquemart-andre.com; admission 8.50€ adults, 6.50€ students; daily 10am–6pm; Métro: Miromesnil or St-Philippe-du-Roule) is the finest museum of its type in Paris, the treasure trove of a couple devoted to 18th-century French paintings and furnishings, 17th-century Dutch and Flemish paintings, and Italian Renaissance works. Don't miss the tea-room. For a serious dose of Monet head to **Musée Marmottan–Claude Monet** ★ (2 rue Louis-Boilly, 16th arr.; ☎ 01-44-96-50-33; www.marmottan.com; admission 7€ adults, 4.50€ ages 8–24; Tues–Sun 10am–6pm; Métro: La Muette; RER: Bouilainvilliers) where paintings, watercolors, pastels, and drawings allow Monet lovers to trace the evolution of the Impressionist master's work in a single museum. **Musée National Eugène Delacroix** (place de Furstenberg, 6th arr.; ☎ 01-44-41-86-50; www.musee-delacroix.

fr; admission 5€; Wed–Mon 9:30am–5pm; Métro: St-Germain-des-Prés and Mabillon) is for Delacroix groupies, who want to see where he lived, worked, and died. The museum is on one of the Left Bank's most charming squares, with a romantic garden. For a summer stroll or an insight into the "father of modern sculpture," visit the **Musée Rodin and gardens** ★★ (Hôtel Biron, 77 rue de Varenne, 7th arr.; ☎ 01-44-18-61-10; www.musee-rodin.fr; admission 5€ adults, 3€ adults 18–25; Apr–Sept Tues–Sun 9:30am–5:45pm, Oct–Mar Tues–Sun 9:30am–4:45pm; Métro: Varenne, Invalides, or St-François-Xavier), where you'll see famed works such as *The Thinker,* and *Le Baiser (The Kiss).* Music fans will dig the **Musée de la Musique** ★ (Cité de la Musique, 221 av. Jean-Jaurès, 19th arr.; ☎ 01-44-84-45-00; www.cite-musique.fr; admission 6.50€ adults, 5.20€ students; Tues–Sat noon–6pm, Sun 10am–6pm; Métro: Porte de Pantin) in the $120-million stone-and-glass Cité de la Musique, where you can view 4,500 instruments from the 16th century to the present as well as paintings, engravings, and sculptures that relate to musical history. Opposite, the **Cité des Sciences**

(Parc de la Villette, 30 av. Corentin-Cariou, 19th arr.; ☎ 01-40-05-70-00; www.cite-sciences.fr; admission 7.50€ adults, 5.50€ students; Tues–Sat 10am–6pm, Sun 10am–7pm; Metro: Porte de La Villette) is Paris's flagship science museum with everything from a planetarium and giant cinema screen to unusual temporary exhibitions. If you're into sculpture, visit the **Musée Zadkine** ★ (100 bis rue d'Assas, 6th arr.; ☎ 01-55-42-77-20; www.paris.fr/musees/zadkine; free admission to permanent collections; Tues–Sun 10am–6pm; Métro: Notre-Dame des Champs or Vavin), near the Jardin du Luxembourg. Once the home of sculptor Ossip Zadkine (1890–1967), it contains some 300 pieces of his works. The **Musée de l'Erotisme** ★ (72 bd. de Clichy, 18th arr.; ☎ 01-42-58-28-73; admission 7€ adults, under 17 not permitted; daily 10am–2am; Métro: Blanche) is smack-bang in the red-light district but presents a tasteful but risqué collection of erotic art and artifacts. Finally for some funky modern art, don't miss the **Palais de Tokyo** (13 av. du Président Wilson, 16th arr.; ☎ 01-47-23-38-86; www.palaisdetokyo.com; admission 6€ adults, 4.50€ students; Tues–Sun noon–midnight; Métro: Iéna; RER: Pont d'Alma)—easily the most exciting thing to happen to Paris since the Pompidou Center; and the **Jeu de Paume** (1 place de la Concorde, 8th arr.; ☎ 01-47-03-12-50; www.jeudepaume.org; admission 6€ adults, 3€ students; Tues noon–9pm, Wed–Fri noon–7pm, Sat–Sun 10am–7pm; Métro: Concorde), Paris's newest photography and visual arts museum.

UNDERGROUND PARIS

In the 18th century, like an Oklahoma musical, Paris's communal graves started "bustin' out all over," and the government realized that something had to be done to prevent the spread of disease. So, in 1785 over 6 million graves were moved to a series of former limestone quarries underneath Paris, creating the 📺 **Best!** **Catacombes de Paris** (1 av. du colonel Roi-Tanguy, 14th arr.; ☎ 01-43-22-47-63; admission 2.60€–5€; Tues–Sun 10am–5pm; Métro: Denfert-Rochereau). Today you can visit 1.7km (1 mile) of the total 300km (186 miles) of tunnels that lie beneath the city (not all are catacombs). The grossest part (if not the object of your visit) is that the bones are on display, and some are even artistically arranged in patterns or shapes. For a somewhat smellier underground experience, head to 📺 **Best!** **Les Egouts** ★ (pont de l'Alma, 7th arr.; ☎ 01-53-68-27-82; admission 3.80€ adults, 3.05€ students; May–Oct Sat–Wed 11am–5pm; closed Nov–Apr; Métro: Alma-Marceau; RER: Pont d'Alma), or sewers, where you can see how Paris remarkably does away with its waste. *Warning:* This tour is fascinating, but it can get a bit spongy, especially in summer.

GALLERIES

Art galleries abound in Paris. If you're lucky, you'll happen upon an exhibition opening where you can mingle with the Parisian artsy crowd while munching on free snacks and beverages. The 3rd *arrondissement* is the base for many of the city's galleries, but this is no time for old masters—the city's up and coming artists are making waves. **Galerie Emmanuel Perrotin** (76 rue de Turenne, 3rd arr.; ☎ 01-42-16-79-79; www.galerieperrotin.com; Tues–Sat 11am–7pm; Métro: St-Sébastien Froissart) is a well-known, edgy gallery that features big names such as Sophie Calle plus lesser-known creative types in need of display space. The **Galerie Cent 8** (108 rue Vieille-du-Temple, 3rd arr.; ☎ 01-42-74-53-57; www.cent8.com; Tues–Fri 10am–1pm and 2:30–7pm, Sat 10:30am–7pm; Métro: Filles du Calvaire) provides stimulating shows from all the medias including paintings and photography. **Galerie Michel Rein** (42 rue de Turenne, 3rd arr.; ☎ 01-42-72-68-13; www.michelrein.com; Tues–Sat 11am–7pm; Métro: Chemin Vert) showcases weird and wacky pieces by French artists such as Didier Marcel and Delphine Coindet.

The 13th *arrondissement* is also home to many contemporary art galleries, including the very experimental, neo-conceptual **Air de Paris** (32 rue Louise Weiss, 13th arr.; ☎ 01-44-23-02-77; www.airdeparis.com; Tues–Sat 11am–7pm; Métro: Chevaleret), and the classy, but equally avant-garde **Galerie Almine Rech** (127 rue du Chevaleret, 13th arr.; ☎ 01-45-83-71-90; www.galeriealminerech.com; Tues–Sat 11am–7pm; Métro: Bibliothèque François Mitterand or Chevaleret), which exhibits light installations by James Turrell, film, and photos.

CINEMA

If you're desperate to see something in English, want to test your *français*, or just fancy doing something a little different, you're in luck; Paris has plenty of cinemas for you to choose from. The most unusual and beautiful setting has to be 📺 Best ● **La Pagode** (57 bis rue de Babylone, 7th arr.; ☎ 01-45-55-48-48-48; 8€ adults, 6.50€ students and on Mon and Wed; no credit cards; Métro: St-François Xavier), a 19th-century replica of a Japanese pagoda, with a little Asian garden, silk walls, and carved beams. Another great arthouse cinema is **Studio 28** (10 rue Tholozé, 18th arr.; ☎ 01-46-06-36-07; www.cinemastudio28.com; 7.50€ adults, 6:30€ students; no credit cards; Métro: Abbesses or Blanche), known for its eclectic programming, civilized bar that serves snacks, and historic films such as the controversial 1920s *Age d'Or* and more recent *Amélie Poulain*. The quirkiest cinemas in town have to be the **MK2s** on either side of the Canal St-Martin on **Quai de Seine** and **Quai de Loire** (7 Quai de Seine/14 Quai de Loire, 19th arr.; ☎ 08-92-69-84-84; www.mk2.com; 9:30€ adults, 6.70€ students; Métro: Stalingrad or Jaures) linked together by a little boat called *Zéro de Conduite*. For a multiscreen complex surrounded by shops and restaurants, head for the **UGC Ciné Cité** at Bercy Village (2 cour St-Emilion, 12th arr.; ☎ 08-36-68-68-58; www.ugc.fr; 9.20€ adults, 6.50€ students; Métro: Cour St-Emilion). And when all else fails, there are several cinemas up both sides of the Champs Elysées.

HIGHBROW HAUNTS

When in Paris, you need at least one classy night out rubbing shoulders with the literati and impeccably mannered. The opera is an obvious draw, and Paris has got two of them. The original opera, the **Opéra Garnier** (place de l'Opéra, 9th arr.; ☎ 08-92-89-90-90 or 01-40-01-17-89; www.operadeparis.fr; tickets 5€–130€; Métro: Opéra), was designed by Charles Garnier in 1875. The inspiration for Leroux's great *Phantom of the Opera,* it is a rococo marvel adorned with marble and sculpture, including *The Dance* by Carpeaux, a ceiling by Chagall, and even beehives on the roof (buy the Opéra's honey in the gift shop and from Fauchon, see below). It's known for its excellent ballet (leaving most of the opera to Bastille) and makes for one of the most elegant evenings you can spend in the City of Light.

The **Opéra Bastille,** at place de la Bastille (120 rue Lyon, 12th arr.; ☎ 01-40-01-17-89; www.operadeparis.fr; tickets range 8€–130€, depending on what you are seeing and where you want to sit; Métro: Bastille), is set in another of Paris's controversial modern buildings. The "beached whale" (as some call it) was designed by Canadian architect Carlos Ott, with curtains by Japanese designer Issey

Mythbusting

Littered with trite images of Parisians, tourists are often forced to seek out the cliché before the reality. Well I say "no more!" Here are four of the most steadfast clichés on the block plus an analysis of the truth behind them:

1. **All Parisians are rude: True 5/10** The obnoxious, patronizing Paris-dweller is a genuine blot on Paris's landscape, but nice Parisians do exist. They hold the door open for you in the Métro, they apologize for knocking into you as they gracefully sidestep the dog poop, and if they really like you they invite you back to their flat for some rough and tumble.

2. **Parisians are bad drivers: True 10/10** Oh, yes. This is fact. The French hold the title of Europe's most accident-prone nation, statistically having more car accidents per head than any other European country. The busy place de l'Etoile around the Arc de Triomphe is the only place in Europe where 50% responsibility goes to both drivers (whoever's fault it is) when an accident occurs. Many French still drink and drive.

3. **French cinema always shows naked women: True 10/10** *Oui, oui, oui!* The French are obsessed with gratuitous naked breasts. In the French film-maker's guidebook, *How to Be a Successful French Director,* the rules are written out clearly: 1) How to create suspense—show a naked breast. 2) How to liven up any scene—show a naked breast. 3) How to add intrigue to a difficult storyline—show a naked breast. It is the squishy cinematic answer to every French film director's question.

4. **The French are the best lovers in the world: True 5/10** They may speak the language of lurve, but the French are no more love specialists than Chirac was an honest president. They spend far more time intellectualizing love than actually making it. And let's face it, rumpy-pumpy doesn't have anything to do with nationality. Love handles are love handles, and it's the chemistry that counts.

Miyake. This is where all the biggies play: Mozart's *Marriage of Figaro* and Tchaikovsky's *Queen of Spades,* for example. The main hall is the largest of any French opera house, with 2,700 seats.

If you can't get a seat in Garnier or Bastille, try the **Opéra Comique** (5 rue Favart, 2nd arr.; ☎ **08-25-00-00-58;** www.opera-comique.com; tickets 7€–60€; Métro: Richelieu-Drouot), a charming venue for light opera, built in the late 1890s.

If you're a French-speaker, visiting Paris without seeing a Molière at the **Comédie-Française** ★★ would be like going to London without seeing a Shakespeare. Established to keep the classics alive and promote important contemporary authors, it's where you will see the works of Molière and Racine staged most beautifully (2 rue de Richelieu, 1st arr.; ☎ **01-44-58-14-13;** tickets 13€–27€; Métro: Palais-Royal-Musée du Louvre).

Theater

You'll be hard-pressed to find a play in English in Paris. If that doesn't deter you, check out some of these theaters for upcoming plays and dance performances: **Théâtre de la Ville** has two show houses (tickets 12€–23€). The first location is at Théâtre de la Ville (2 place du Châtelet, 4th arr.; Métro: Châtelet) and the second location is in Montmartre (31 rue des Abbesses,

Getting Your Mitts on Cheap Tickets

Book directly at the theaters or, if you don't care what you see, get up to 50% off at the **Kiosque Théâtre** (15 place de la Madeleine, 8th arr.; no phone; www.kiosquetheatre.com; Métro: Madeleine), which offers leftover tickets on the day of performance. Tickets for evening performances are sold Tuesday through Friday from 12:30 to 8pm and Saturday from 2 to 8pm.

18th arr.; Métro: Abbesses). Call ahead or check their website for more information (☎ 01-42-74-22-77; www.theatredelaville-paris.com). The **Théâtre des Champs-Elysées** is a spectacular theater where you can see operas, ballets, orchestras, and plays. From its beautiful exterior to its lavish interior—you sit in red velvet armchairs with gold fringe—this place screams class (15 av. Montaigne, 8th arr.; ☎ 01-49-52-50-50; www.theatrechampselysees.fr; tickets 7€–130€; Métro: Alma-Marceau or Franklin-D-Roosevelt). **Théâtre National de Chaillot** (1 place du Trocadéro, 16th arr.; ☎ 01-53-65-30-00; www.theatre-chaillot.fr; tickets 12€–36€; Métro: Trocadéro) is part of the architectural complex facing the Eiffel Tower and one of the city's largest concert halls. It hosts cultural events and many contemporary dance spectacles that are announced on billboards in front of the theater.

Cabaret & Comedy

All blue **Chez Michou** (80 rue des Martyrs, 18th arr.; ☎ 01-46-06-16-04; cover 95€; reservations required, shows nightly 10:30pm; Métro: Pigalle) is a legend in the cabaret world, known for its veteran impresario Michou (who only wears blue) and his cross-dressing belles who pay tribute to Americans such as Whitney Houston and Tina Turner, or French stars such as Mireille Mathieu and Brigitte Bardot. For something wholly more sophisticated, even beautiful, head for the **Crazy Horse Saloon** ★★ (12 av. George V, 8th arr.; ☎ 01-47-23-32-32; www.lecrazyhorse-paris.com; shows Sun–Fri 8:30pm and 11pm; Sat 7:30pm, 9:45pm, and 11:50pm; reservations recommended; cover 50€, including two drinks at the bar, or 95€, including two drinks at a table; Métro: George-V or Alma-Marceau). Impeccable choreography and a sly, coquettish celebration of the female form (not a pole-dancer in sight—just stunners bathed in light) draw in both men and women. Whatever your sexual preference, I challenge you not to find the show strangely hypnotic. The time-honored must-see is the **Moulin Rouge** ★ (82 bd. de Clichy, 18th arr.; ☎ 01-53-09-82-82; www.moulinrouge.fr; Métro: Blanche). Yes, it's a bit touristy and expensive, but the boobies bounce and the sequins sparkle with so much pizazz that you'll forget the high prices. Choose between three fixed menus with three courses for 140€ to 170€. Dinner starts at 7pm, followed by the show at 9pm. The show only costs 97€ at 9pm and 87€ at 11pm.

With over 1,000 seats, the **Lido de Paris** ★★ (116 bis av. des Champs-Elysées, 8th arr.; ☎ 01-40-76-56-10; www.lido.fr; dinner 7:30pm; shows Sun–Thurs 9:30pm, Sat 9:30pm and midnight; tickets 100€–140€; Métro: George V) is the largest cabaret of the lot. More avant-garde than the Moulin Rouge, the 60 Bluebell Girls slink across stage with explosive panache and wacky costumes.

To have some belly laughs in English, visit **Laughing Matters**—Karl Beer's fantastic comedy club, which brings Britain's and America's funniest comics across the water to play on the stage of the **Java Theatre** (105 rue du Faubourg du Temple, 10th arr.; ☎ 01-53-19-98-88; www.anythingmatters.com; Métro: République). This is the only English language comedy venue in the whole of Paris.

Circus

Admit it. You thought that life in Paris was a cabaret, old chum. Well it is, but sometimes, just sometimes, it plays second fiddle to the city's circuses. The oldest venue in Paris is the **Cirque d'Hiver Bouglione** (110 rue Amélot, 11th arr.; ☎ 01-47-00-28-81; www.cirquehiver.com; Métro: Filles du Calvaire), run by the same family for 70 years, and housed in the wonderful winter circus. For horses, lions, elephants, and monkeys, try the **Cirque Pinder** (Pelouse de Reilly, 12th arr.; ☎ 01-45-90-21-25; www.cirquepinder.com; Métro: Porte Dorée), which finishes its yearly tour in Paris around Christmas. Finally, some of Paris's most avant-garde circus acts (including acrobatic artists Les Arts Saut and surrealist group la Cirque Plume) come out of **Espace Chapiteaux** (at Parc de la Villette, 19th arr.; ☎ 01-42-09-01-09; www.villette.com; Métro: Porte de Pantin).

Playing Outside
PARKS & GARDENS

The French have a rather conservative approach to their parks. When we think "park" we say, "Great, let's go for a quick game of Frisbee." When they think *"parc,"* they say, "Aren't the sycamores and flower beds lovely?" It is not unusual for wardens (lobotomized in the sense of humor department) to blow whistles to tell you to keep off the grass. For some relaxed parklife—somewhere to roll around on the grass and have a picnic—two of the best spots lie just on the outskirts of town. **The Bois de Vincennes** (12th arr.; Métro: Porte Dorée) in the east is a wonderful setting where you can hire boats on the lake and amble around tree-shaded paths that lead to hidden treasures such as a Buddhist temple and an island cafe. The **Bois de Boulogne** (Métro: Les-Sablons in Neuilly; Porte-Maillot, 17th arr.; or Porte-Dauphine; 16th arr.) is often called the "main lung" of Paris. You can traverse it by horse-drawn carriage or car, though you'll see a whole lot more on foot. It contains several lakes, the **Jardin d'Acclimatation** (with a zoo, an amusement park, and a narrow-gauge railway for kids), two **racetracks** (see below), and the **Parc de Bagatelle,** famous for its amazing tulips (Apr) and roses (late May). Some parts of the park require you to pay an entrance fee. Don't come to either "Bois" at night when they turn into hunting grounds for prostitutes.

Two modern additions are **Parc André Citroën** (Métro: Balard or Javel, 15th arr.) and **Parc de Bercy** (Métro: Bercy or Cour St-Emilion, 12th arr.). Different beasts entirely from the well-manicured parks mentioned below, they are newly green spaces created from old industrial ground. Parc André Citroën on the Left Bank is an inventive, decidedly modern park—complete with computerized fountains, waterfalls, and sensory gardens dotted with black tulips. DJs play here in the summer but if the music fails to move you, you can also take a ride on the world's largest tethered balloon. Parc de Bercy transformed a former docking sight off the Seine, famous for its wine warehouses, into a 13 hectare public park, adjoined by Bercy Village—a complex of shops, restaurants, and a cinema.

The spectacular statue-studded **Jardin des Tuileries** ★★, bordering place de la Concorde (Métro: Tuileries or Concorde) and the Louvre, is as much a part of Paris as the Seine. Le Nôtre, Louis XIV's gardener and planner of the Versailles grounds, designed the gardens whose most distinctive statues are the 18 enormous bronzes by Maillol.

Hemingway once told a friend that the **Jardin du Luxembourg** ★★, in the 6th *arrondissement* (Métro: Odéon; RER: Luxembourg), "kept us from starvation." Apparently, in his poverty-stricken days in Paris, he wheeled a baby carriage through the garden because it was known "for the classiness of its pigeons." When the gendarme went across the street for a glass of wine, the writer would eye his victim, preferably a plump one; lure him with corn; "snatch him, wring his neck"; and hide him under the blanket. "We got a little tired of pigeon that year," he confessed, "but they filled many a void."

The Luxembourg has always been associated with artists, though children, students, and tourists predominate nowadays. Come here to see kids sailing toy boats in the fountains, attend an occasional Grand Guignol puppet show, and play *boules* (lawn bowling) with a group of elderly men who wear black berets and have Gauloises dangling from their mouths.

Parc Monceau ★ (Métro: Monceau or Villiers, 8th arr.) is ringed with stunning 18th- and 19th-century mansions. Carmontelle designed it in 1778 as a private hideaway for the duc d'Orléans. Today admire the Roman columns and statues while dodging the American expats pushing their babies round in prams.

Arguably the most striking, manmade park in Paris, 📺 Best 🌢 **Les Buttes-Chaumont** ★★ (Métro: Buttes Chaumont, 19th arr.) is a must for anyone looking for sweeping vistas over the city, hidden lawns for picnics, cliffs, and bridges. Built in 1860 upon a former Gypsum quarry, it adds a welcome stretch of green for residents in the 19th *arrondissement,* who go jogging or partake in a number of free Chinese martial arts classes.

Shopping

You don't have to buy anything to appreciate shopping in Paris—just soak up the art form the French have made of rampant consumerism. Peer in the *vitrines* (display windows), lick them (yes, the French call window-shopping *lêche-vitrine,* which is translated as "licking windows"), absorb cutting-edge ideas, witness new trends, and take home with you a whole new education in style. Some of the best shopping districts are in the 8th around the **Champs Elysées,** in the **Marais** (4th arr.), in the 6th along **rue de Rennes** and near **Métro**

A Day at the Races

The epicenter of Paris horse racing is the **Hippodrome de Longchamp** in the Bois de Boulogne, 16th arr. (☎ 01-44-30-75-00; RER/Métro: Porte Maillot, and then a free shuttle bus on race days only). Established in 1855, during the autocratic but pleasure-loving reign of Napoleon III, it's the most prestigious, boasts the greatest number of promising thoroughbreds, and awards the largest purse in France. The most important events at Longchamp are the **Grand Prix de Paris** in late June and the **Prix de l'Arc de Triomphe** in early October. Another racing venue is the **Hippodrome d'Auteuil,** also in the Bois de Boulogne (☎ 01-40-71-47-47; Métro: Porte Auteuil, and then walk). Known for its steeplechases and obstacle courses, it sometimes attracts more than 50,000 Parisians at a time. Spectators appreciate the park's promenades as much as they do the equestrian events. Races are conducted early March to late November.

Sevres Babylone, in the 1st around and below **Châtelet-les-Halles** (underground shopping mall), behind the Opéra Garnier in the **9th,** in the 18th along **rue des Abbesses,** and in the 2nd around **Métro Etienne Marcel.** For some Sunday shopping, head to the Marais, **Bercy Village** (Métro: Cour St-Emilion, 12th arr.), or the shopping mall beneath the Louvre museum, the **Carousel du Louvre** (99 rue de Rivoli; Métro: Palais-Royal-Musée du Louvre). Elsewhere will be closed.

DEPARTMENT STORES

When La Samaritaine closed its doors, Paris was left with just four department stores. Two of them—Au Printemps and Galeries Lafayette—lie behind the Opéra Garnier. Printemps' customer service is better, but they otherwise differ little.

➔ **Au Bon Marché** Don't be fooled by the name of this department store (meaning "low-budget" or "cheap"). This two-part Left Bank department store is overtly luxurious, selling fashion for men, women, and children; furniture; upscale gifts; and housewares. Also check out the wicked food court. *22–24 rue de Sèvres, 7th arr.* ☎ *01-44-39-80-00. Mon–Wed and Fri 9:30am–7pm; Thurs 10am–9pm; Sat 9:30am–8pm. Métro: Sèvres-Babylone.*

➔ **Au Printemps** ★★ This store is divided into sections: Housewares **(Printemps Maison),** women's fashion **(Printemps de la Mode),** and men's clothes **(Le Printemps de l'Homme).** Check out the magnificent stained-glass dome, through which turquoise light cascades into the sixth-floor **Café Flo,** where you can have a coffee or a full meal. Or for something funkier, head to the Paul Smith–designed **World Bar** at the top of Printemps de l'Homme. Its walls, covered in yellowing newspapers, provide a hip backdrop for great fusion food. *64 bd. Haussmann, 9th arr.* ☎ *01-42-82-50-00. Mon–Wed and Fri–Sat*

9:35am–7pm; Thurs 9:35am–9pm. Métro: Havre-Caumartin or St-Lazare. RER: Auber.

➔ **BHV** ★★ This is the capital's best and most chic all-rounder, selling everything from DIY products and household appliances to men's and women's clothes and books. *52–64 rue de Rivoli, 4th arr.* ☎ *01-42-74-90-00. www.bhv.fr. Mon–Tues and Thurs–Sat 9:30am–7:30am; Wed 9:30am–9pm. Métro: Hôtel-de-Ville.*

➔ **Galeries Lafayette** ★★ With its early-1900s stained-glass cupola, Galeries Lafayette is classified as a historic monument. This store could provision a small city with everything from perfume to fashion. It is even more user-friendly than Au Printemps, with more emphasis on up-and-coming designers. Also in the complex is **Lafayette Gourmet,** one of the fanciest grocery stores in Paris; and if you feel like splurging, hire a stylist for the day, to help you spend your money on clothes (call for details). *40 bd. Haussmann, 9th arr.* ☎ *01-42-82-34-56. Mon–Wed and Fri–Sat 9:30am–6:45pm; Thurs 9:30am–9pm. Métro: Chaussée d'Antin. RER: Auber.*

CLOTHING & ACCESSORIES

➔ **Antoine et Lili** ★ For the bohemian in you girls, this is a mecca of vibrant, neo-hippy skirts, dresses, coats, and accessories. If you really like the designs, you could also pop next door and see if the patterns have been continued on their equally colorful ranges of kitchenware. *95 quai de Valmy, 10th arr.* ☎ *01-40-37-45-55. www.antoineetlili.com. Sun–Mon 11am–7pm; Tues–Fri 11am–8pm; Sat 10am–8pm. Métro: Jacques Bonsergent.*

➔ **BCBG Max Azria** You'll quickly get the sense that someone spent hours meticulously selecting the women's clothing and accessories featured on three floors of this stylish boutique. *BCBG* means *bon chic, bon genre*—a designation for things stylish, restrained, and tasteful. Things here are, indeed, "BCBG" but in brighter colors than you might have expected. They are also expensive, so be prepared to put it all on plastic. *14 bd. de la Madeleine, 9th arr.* ☎ *01-43-12-55-20. Mon–Sat 10am–7pm. Métro: Madeleine.*

➔ **Boutique M Dia** ★ A real rags-to-riches story lies behind this urban sports clothes shop. Mohammed Dia left his under-privileged suburban ghetto of Sarcelles for the U.S., and came back with the idea of the decade: to launch his own clothes label. After a bit of clever marketing, he managed to get NBA Dallas Mavericks to wear his shoe line Tariq, and the rest is history. Today you too can dress like a cool rapper by splurging at this flagship boutique. *5–7 rue des Innocents, 1st arr.* ☎ *01-40-26-03-31. www.mdiawear.com. Mon 1–8pm; Tues–Sat 11am–8pm. Métro: Châtelet. RER: Châtelet-les-Halles.*

➔ **Kiliwatch** ★★ If you're cool and you know it, you shop here, where you can mix 'n' match real vintage clothes with the best of urban street wear to get that true retro-hip look you've been hankering after. G-Star, Diesel, and Kulte are just some of the featured brands for men and women, and if you wondered where your mom's 1970s sequin top or your pop's bell-bottom pants disappeared to, you might just find them at the back of the shop. *64 rue Tiquetonne, 2nd arr.* ☎ *01-42-21-17-37. www. kiliwatch.com. Mon 2–7pm; Tues–Sat 11am–7pm. Métro: Étienne Marcel.*

➔ **Ladies and Gentlemen** This wacky den of cool design is an "experience." First the red dummies catch your eye; then the techno music enters your ears, compelling you to check out the hidden alcoves, in search of the slightly surreal men's and women's creations designed by Isabelle Ballu and Moritz Rogorsky. *4 passage Charles Dallery, 11th arr.* ☎ *01-47-00-86-12.*

Tues–Sat noon–7pm; Sun 2–7pm. Métro: Ledru Rollin.

➔ **Madelios** One for the boys, Madelios is a two-floor mega-store with over 100 different labels. Its decor leaves a lot to be desired. In fact, the shop itself doesn't make you want to enter. But enter it you should if you're looking for well-cut suits (both designer and high-street), shoes, and men's accessories. *23 bd. de la Madeleine, 1st arr.* ☎ *01-53-45-00-00. www.madelios.com. Mon–Sat 10am–7pm. Métro: Madeleine.*

➔ **Zadig & Voltaire** ★★ Wonder how the *parisiennes* get that cool, urban but chic look with faded jeans and cotton tops? Now you know. They shop here. Texture rules, with plenty of simple but wonderfully crafted tops, skirts, and bottoms. Put them together (copy the mannequins), and you can look as Bobo as can be. *42 rue des Francs-Bourgeois, 3rd arr.* ☎ *01-44-54-00-60. www.zadig-et-voltaire.com. Sun–Mon 1:30–7:30pm; Tues–Sat 10:30am–7:30pm. Métro: St-Paul or Hôtel-de-Ville.*

ANTIQUES & CURIOSITIES

➔ **Marché aux Puces de la Porte de Vanves** ★★ The best flea market in Paris, this weekend event sprawls along two streets. There's little in terms of formal antiques and furniture, but it's a winner for used Hermès scarves, toys, ephemera, costume jewelry, perfume bottles, and bad art. On Sunday there's a food market one street over. *Av. Georges-Lafenestre, 14th arr. Sat–Mon 6:30am–4:30pm. Métro: Porte de Vanves.*

➔ **Marché aux Puces St-Ouen de Clignancourt** ★ Paris's most famous flea market is actually a grouping of more than a dozen flea markets—a complex of 2,500 to 3,000 open stalls and shops on the northern fringe of the city, selling everything from antiques to junk, from new to vintage clothing. Vendors start bringing

Going Retro

To find that extra-distressed leather jacket with a cigarette burn made by Mick Jaggar on the first Rolling Stone's tour, dream on. But have a hoot rooting through all the other old wearable stuff at these vintage shops.

→ **Come On Eileen** (16–18 rue des Taillandiers, 11th arr.; ☎ 01-43-38-12-11; Mon–Thurs 11:30am–8:30pm, Fri 11:30am–7:30pm, Sun 4–8pm; Métro: Ledru Rollin) is a three-level fantasia of vintage treasures where you'll find everything from old gala dresses to cowboy boots.

→ **Free 'P' Star** (8 rue ste-Croix de la Bretonnerie, 4th arr.; ☎ 01-42-76-03-72; Mon–Sat noon–11pm, Sun 2–10pm; Métro: St-Paul) is ideal for a fancy-dress party or if you decide your wardrobe needs some retro-glitz with old army jackets, 1950s summer dresses, or any of the other frocks that caught the owner's eye.

→ **Le Mouton à Cinq Pattes** (138 bd. St-Germain, 6th arr.; ☎ 01-43-26-49-26; Mon–Fri 10:30am–7:30pm, Sat 10:30am–8pm; Métro: Odéon). With a chic St-Germain location, you'd expect this place to be posh. Come here for last season's catwalk cast-offs and designer vintage.

→ **A l'Elégance d'Autre Fois** (5 rue du Pas-de-la-Mule, 4th arr.; ☎ 01-48-87-78-84; take your chances or call for exact opening times; Métro: Chemin Vert) is for those with a foot fetish, or at least those who don't mind wearing designer shoes and boots that have already had somebody else's foot in them. If you can't afford to buy a pair (60€–400€), you can rent them for a special occasion.

out their offerings around 9am and start taking them in around 6pm. Monday is traditionally the best day for bargain seekers. Flea-market virgins always want to know two things: "Will I get any real bargains?" and "Will I get fleeced?" It's all relative. Just don't forget to barter. To get to the Marché aux Puces, you have to cross a dodgy street market, so beware of pickpockets and teenage troublemakers. *Av. de la Porte de Clignancourt, 18th arr. Sat–Mon 9am–7pm. Métro: Porte de Clignancourt (turn left and cross bd. Ney, and then walk north on av. de la Porte Montmartre).*

BOOKS

If you like rare and unusual books, patronize one of the *bouquinistes,* the owners of those army-green stalls that line the Seine. This is where tourists in the 1920s and 1930s went to buy "dirty" French postcards. You might get lucky and come across some treasured book, like an original edition of Henry Miller's *Tropic of Cancer,* which sells banned for decades in the United States. For the best English-language bookstores, try **Brentano's** (37 av. de l'Opéra, 2nd arr.; ☎ 01-42-61-52-50; Mon–Sat 10am–7pm; Métro: Opéra or Pyramides), which sells guides, maps, novels, and nonfiction as well as greeting cards, postcards, holiday items, and gifts. **Galignani** (224 rue de Rivoli, 1st arr.; ☎ 01-42-60-76-07; Mon–Sat 10am–7pm; Métro: Tuileries) was Paris's first English bookstore—a venerable wood-paneled venue that has thrived since 1810. Emphasis is on French classics, modern fiction, sociology, and fine arts.

The most famous bookstore on the Left Bank is **Shakespeare and Company** ★ (37 rue de la Bûcherie, 5th arr.; no phone; daily 11am–midnight; Métro: St-Michel), once frequented by Hemingway, Fitzgerald, and Stein. It is a musty old place where expats still swap books and literary gossip. If you fancy a cup of tea while you read, try **Tea and Tattered Pages** (24 rue Mayet, 6th arr.; ☎ **01-40-65-94-35;** Mon–Sat 11am–7pm, Sun noon–6pm; Métro: Duroc). It's out of the way, but worth the trip. For the Brits in Paris, nothing can replace their beloved **W. H. Smith** (248 rue de Rivoli, 1st arr.; ☎ **01-44-77-88-99;** Mon–Sat 9am–7:30pm, Sun 1–7:30pm; Métro: Concorde), which sells books, magazines, newspapers published in English (most titles are from Britain), and BBC DVDs that you can't find anywhere else.

MUSIC & MEDIA

➔ **Blue Moon Music** ★ If you love reggae and raga, you'll love Blue Moon Music for its funky Jamaican sounds and weekly imports. *84 rue Quincampoix, 3rd arr. ☎ 01-40-29-45-60. Mon–Sat 11am–7pm. Métro: Rambuteau.*

➔ **Crocodisc** This shop has a vast range of rock, funk, country, and classical disks. *40–42 rue des Écoles, 5th arr. ☎ 01-43-54-47-95. Tues–Sat 11am–7pm. Métro: Maubert Mutualité.*

➔ **FNAC** FNAC is a large chain of music and bookstores known for its wide selection and good prices. You can also buy tickets to concerts and theater productions here. Eight branches are in Paris, with the largest being at 136 rue de Rennes, and others on rue St-Lazare, av. des Champs-Elysées, Forum des Halles, av. des Ternes, and av. d'Italie. *136 rue de Rennes, 6th arr. ☎ 01-49-54-30-00. Mon–Sat 10am–7:30pm (Champs-Elysées location daily noon–midnight). Métro: St-Placide.*

➔ **Monster Melodies** This shop has more than 10,000 secondhand CDs for you to rifle through. *9 rue des Déchargeurs, 1st arr. ☎ 01-40-28-09-39. Mon–Sat noon–7pm. Métro: Les Halles.*

➔ **Virgin Megastore** ★★ Europe's biggest and most widely publicized CD and record store. The Champs-Elysées branch is the city's largest music store; others can be found at the Carrousel du Louvre and Gare Montparnasse. *52–60 av. des Champs-Elysées, 8th arr. ☎ 01-49-53-50-00. Mon–Sat 10am–midnight; Sun noon–midnight. Métro: Franklin-D-Roosevelt.*

CONCEPT STORES

Why do your shopping in several shops, when you can come to one and get it all? *Voilà,* the "concept" behind Paris's concept stores—although, let's face it, we're talking designer not supermarket. **Colette** (213 rue St-Honoré, 1st arr.; ☎ **01-55-35-33-90;** Mon–Sat 11am–7:30pm; Métro: Tuileries or Pyramides) was first to open and it's still a swank citadel for *à la mode* fashion. Even if you don't buy the zany accessories, designer clothes, makeup, or underground music, patronize the water bar with its three dozen brands of bottled water. For other spin-offs, check out all-white **Castelbajac** (10 rue Vauvilliers, 1st arr.; ☎ **01-55-34-10-10;** www.jc-de-castelbajac. com; Métro: Les Halles); the ever-changing collections at **EspaceLab 101** (44 rue de la Rochefoucauld, 9th arr.; ☎ **01-49-95-95-85;** Métro: Pigalle or St-Georges); the mix of fashion and contemporary art at **Spree** (16 rue de la Vieuville, 18th arr.; ☎ **01-42-23-41-40;** Métro: Abbesses); and finally **Surface to Air** (46 rue de l'Arbre-Sec, 1st arr.; ☎ **01-49-27-04-54;** www.surface2air. com; Métro: Pont Neuf), which offers cult clothing, runs bi-annual fashion salons, and has launched its own menswear label.

Market Madness

Outdoor markets are plentiful in Paris. Some of the better known are the **Marché Buci;** the **rue Mouffetard market,** open Tuesday to Sunday from 9:30am to 1pm and Tuesday to Saturday from 4 to 7pm (6th arr.; Métro: Monge or Censier-Daubenton); and the **rue Montorgueil market,** behind the St-Eustache church, open Monday to Saturday from 9am to 7pm (1st arr.; Métro: Les Halles or Sentier). The trendiest market is **Marché Biologique,** along boulevard Raspail, a tree-lined stretch lying between rue de Rennes and rue du Cherche-Midi, 6th arr. It's open Sunday 8:30am to 6:30pm (Métro: Montparnasse).

FOOD, WINE & LOCAL CRAFTS

➜ **Debauve & Gallais** ★ Once a pharmacy that sold chocolate for medicinal reasons (created in 1800), it is now quite simply one of the best *chocolatiers* in the city. Some of the varieties are most unusual, including tea and honey flavors; the truffles are to die for; and if you want to treat yourself or a loved one, you can't beat the chocolate boxes that look like a book. *30 rue des Sts-Pères, 7th arr. ☎ 01-45-48-54-67. www.debauve-et-gallais.com. Mon–Sat 9am–7pm. Métro: St-Germain-des-Près or rue de Bac.*

➜ **Fauchon** ★★ This is one hyper-upscale mega-delicatessen that plies the wealthy and the greedy with top-notch products from its three divisions: the *épicerie* (for jams, crackers, pastas, and exotic canned goods); the *pâtissier* (for breads, pastries, and chocolates); and the *traiteur* (for cheeses, terrines, pâtés, caviar, and fruits). Prices are steep, but the inventories—at least to serious foodies—are fascinating. *26 place de la Madeleine, 8th arr. ☎ 01-47-42-91-10. Mon–Sat 9:30am–7pm. Métro: Madeleine.*

➜ **Fromagerie Dubois et Fils** Where would we be without cheese? At the Fromagerie Dubois, nowhere, because cheese is more to them than just a food product; it is a way of life and an artform. They stock over 80 types of goat's cheese plus prize-winning others, including a devastating St-Félicien. *80 rue de Tocqueville, 17th arr. ☎ 01-42-27-11-38. Tues–Fri 9am–1pm and 4–8pm; Sat 8:30am–7:30pm; Sun 9am–1pm. Métro: Malesherbes or Villiers.*

➜ **Hédiard** ★ This 1850 temple of *haute gastronomie* has been renovated, perhaps to woo visitors away from Fauchon. The decor is a series of salons filled with almost Disneyesque displays meant to give the store the look of an early-1900s spice emporium. Hédiard is rich in coffees, teas, jams, and spices. The decor changes with whatever holiday (Halloween, Easter, Bastille Day) or special promotion (the coffees of Brazil, the teas of Ceylon) is in effect at the time. *21 place de la Madeleine, 8th arr. ☎ 01-43-12-88-77. Mon–Sat 9am–11pm. Métro: Madeleine.*

➜ **Nicholas** You'll find smaller branches all over the capital, but this is the flagship store, and don't you know it. Scattered over three floors are fairly priced bottles of mainstream wines such as Alsatian Gewürztztraminers and Collioures from Languedoc-Roussillon. Down in the basement you'll find some exceptionally rare vintages, such as a Romanée-Conti from Burgundy, whose 1961 vintage sells for around 7,900€ per bottle. *31 place de la Madeleine, 8th arr. ☎ 01-42-68-00-16. Mon–Sat 9:30am–8pm. Métro: Madeleine.*

Paris for Zip

The chips are down, your credit card has been blocked, and it'll be 2 days before your money gets wired over—what do you do? You go to these places. Paris is a pricey city, but when you know where to look, you can get stuff for practically free.

→ **Free food and drink:** On Fridays and Saturdays, when you buy a drink (5€), you can wolf down delicious free couscous, alongside students, in-the-know tourists, and hungry locals at **Les Fontaines** (153 rue St-Maur, 11th arr.; ☎ **01-43-57-53-14;** Métro: Belleville).

→ **Free music concerts:** Come listen to classical, jazz, or electro concerts one or two Tuesdays a month at the Cité Internationale des Arts. Check their site, **www.citedesartsparis.net**, for more details (18 rue de l'Hôtel de Ville, 4th arr.; ☎ **01-42-78-71-72;** Métro: Pont Marie). Also try the free Sunday-night jamming sessions at **Les 7 Lezards** (10 rue des Rosiers, 4th arr.; ☎ **01-48-87-08-97;** www.7lezards.com; Métro: St-Paul).

→ **Free theater:** On the first Sunday of the month at 6:30pm, don't miss the improvisation matches that go on at **L'Entrepôt** cultural center (7 rue Francis de Pressensé, 14th arr.; ☎ **01-45-40-07-50;** www.lentrepot.fr; Métro: Pernety).

→ **Free sport:** Fancy pretending you're in New York City's Central Park? Then head for les **Buttes Chaumont** park, where Master Thoï gives Qi Gong lessons (exercising one's internal organs) every day at 9am (near the Weber Café below the rue Botzaris). If that's a little too New Age (or early), head for the **bassin de la Villette** (opposite 51 quai de Seine, 20th arr.), where you'll find four table-tennis tables for some Ping-Pong action with the locals.

→ **Free museums:** On the first Sunday of every month, entry to most of Paris's museums is free of charge. Museums that are free year-round include **Musée Carnavalet** (23 rue de Sévigné, 3rd arr.; ☎ **01-44-59-58-58;** Métro: St-Paul), **Maison de Victor Hugo** (Victor Hugo's house; 6 place des Voges, 4th arr.; ☎ **01-42-72-10-16;** Métro: Bastille, St-Paul, or Chemin Vert), and the recently re-opened **Petit Palais** (av. Winston Churchill, 8th arr.; ☎ **01-53-43-40-00;** Métro: Champs-Elysées Clemenceau), housing art from the 16th to 20th century. Check **www.paris.fr** for more details.

→ **Free books: www.bookcrossing.com** is a funky site that lists places in cities all over the world where someone has left a book for someone else to appropriate. Hundreds of books are currently loose in the streets of Paris; just log on to see where to find one.

Festivals

See the France Calendar of Events on p. 24. For more details and exact dates for festivals and events in Paris, go to **www.parisinfo.com**.

Ile-de-France

Paris lies inland, right? So why are its satellite regions called the Island of France (Ile-de-France)? The answer is simple: Paris is the center of a curious

Paris & the Ile-de-France

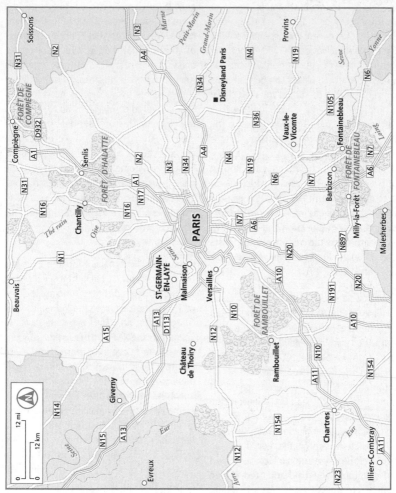

landlocked island, shaped roughly like a saucer, encircled by a thin ribbon of rivers: the **Epte, Aisne, Marne,** and **Yonne.** Fringing these rivers are forests with famous names such as **Fontainebleau,** said to be responsible for Paris's clear, gentle air and the unusual length of its spring and fall. Well, that must have been before global warming, but there's no argument that they still provide the capital with a fine series of day trips, all within easy reach. The **Château de Versailles,** the Sun King's Palace, is obviously the first destination—and, dare I say, "the Ile-de-France must-see." **Chârtres,** gateway to the Loire Valley, with its glorious Cathédrale Notre-Dame de Chârtres, is a draw for Gothic art lovers. The châteaux at **Fontainebleau** and **Vaux-le-Vicomte** are mind-blowing structures that ooze history, charm, and finesse. For kids of all ages, there's **Disneyland Paris,** home of French Mickey and Minnie. Finally, this region is a haven for artists, and you can visit the painted worlds of Claud Monet, one of the masters of Impressionism, at **Giverny.** All these places can be visited as day trips from the capital, so you won't have to pack your bags and go hotel hunting.

If you wish to spend more time in the region, consider visiting **Chantilly,** famous for its exquisite château and stables; **Provins** (gateway to Champagne), known for it's chocolate-box allure, which never quite made it out of the Middle Ages; the seemingly never-ending **Rambouillet** forest; and **Auvers-sur-Oise** and **Barbizon,** which attracted the keen eyes of artists such as Corot, Renoir, Degas, Monet, van Gogh, and Cézanne.

Versailles

Certainly no first-time visit to Paris would be complete without visiting Sun King Louis XIV's posh château at Versailles. The seat of power between 1682 and 1789, it was later the digs of Louis XVI and Marie Antoinette, before they were dragged off to meet the guillotine in Paris. Back in the *grand siècle* (a golden era before the Revolution), all you needed was a sword, a hat, and a bribe for the guard at the gate. Provided you didn't look as if you had smallpox, you'd be admitted to the Château de Versailles, where you could stroll through salon after glittering salon and watch the Sun King, gossiping, dancing, plotting, and flirting. Louis XIV was accorded about as much privacy as an institution. In fact, his legacy still draws in tourists by the millions. During the high tourist season in summer, the halls of the château are like the sidewalks in midtown Manhattan at rush hour. Expect to find yourself standing in lines and wading your way through crowds just to get to the Grands Appartements. Despite the signs reminding tourists that "only the bearers of the official badge are allowed to make commentary," you'll hear many an American Ivy League prepster enjoying the sound of his own voice as he brings his sandal-footed companions up to speed on the château's history. Besides rich kids on their postgrad junket to Europe, there are also herds of obnoxious, squabbling French kids being chaperoned through the halls by their overwhelmed instructors. Your best bet for a successful visit is to come very, very early in the morning or late in the afternoon.

GETTING THERE

From Paris, catch the **RER** line C at the Gare d'Austerlitz, St-Michel, Musée d'Orsay, Invalides, Ponte de l'Alma, Champ de Mars, or Javel, and take it to the Versailles Rive Gauche station. The trip takes 35 to 40 minutes. **SNCF trains** make frequent runs from Gare St-Lazare and Gare Montparnasse in Paris to Versailles: Trains departing from Gare St-Lazare arrive at the Versailles Rive Droite railway station; trains departing from Gare Montparnasse arrive at Versailles Chantiers station. Both Versailles stations are within a 10-minute walk of the château, and directions to the château are clearly signposted from each railway station.

If you're **driving,** exit the *périphérique* (the ringed road around Paris) on N10 (av. du Général-Leclerc), which will take you to Versailles; park on place d'Armes in front of the château.

TOURIST OFFICE

The **Office de Tourisme** is at 2 bis av. de Paris (☎ **01-39-24-88-88;** www.versailles-tourisme.com).

Versailles

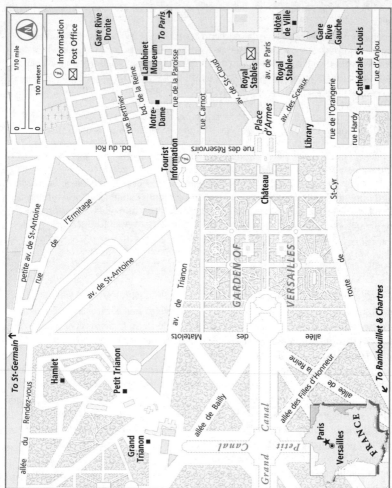

SIGHTSEEING

→ **Château de Versailles** ★★ It took 50 years (from 1661) and some 45,000 workers to transform the Château de Versailles from Louis XIII's hunting lodge into the envy of Europe and a symbol of opulence copied the world over yet never duplicated. (Louis le Vau, Jules Hardouin Mansart, and Jacques Ange Gabriel designed the house; Charles Le Brun and André Le Nôtre landscaped the garden.) Wishing (with good reason) to keep an eye on the nobles of France, Louis XIV summoned them to live at his court. Here he amused them with constant entertainment and lavish banquets. To some he awarded such tasks as holding the hem of his robe. When Louis XIV died in 1715, his great-grandson Louis

Les Fêtes de Nuit de Versailles ★★

Every year between late August and early September, the gardens of Versailles burst into action for the **Les Fêtes de Nuit de Versailles** festival, where onlookers are wooed with an extravaganza of fireworks, prerecorded classical music, and up to 200 players in period costume, portraying the glories of France as symbolized by Louis XIV and the courtiers of the *ancien régime*. If you can't stay for the nighttime performances, try **Les Grands Eaux Musicals de Versailles** on Saturdays and Sundays from late March to early October (usually 11:30am–noon and 3:30–5:30pm), when the warden turns on the fountains and powerful classical music is sounded throughout the park. Inquire at the Château de Versailles (☎ **01-30-83-78-00;** www.chateauversailles.fr) or consult the website for more details and prices.

Passport for all attractions costs 20€ Monday to Friday, and 25€ Saturday and Sunday. Admission to the palace is 14€; to both Trianons 9€. Everything is free for children under 18, and some reductions are made after 3pm. Admission to the gardens is free for everyone. The palace is open April to October, Tuesday to Sunday, 9am to 6:30pm; November to March, Tuesday to Sunday, 9am to 5:30pm. The Trianons are open daily noon to 6pm; the grounds are open daily from dawn to dusk.

XV succeeded him and continued the outrageous pomp, though he is said to have predicted the outcome: "*Après moi le déluge*" (After me, the deluge). His wife, Marie Leszczynska, was shocked by the blatant decadence at Versailles.

The next monarch, Louis XVI, found his grandfather's behavior scandalous—in fact, on gaining the throne he ordered that the "stairway of indiscretion" (secret stairs leading to the king's bedchamber) be removed. The well-intentioned but weak king and his queen, Marie Antoinette, were well liked at first, but the queen's frivolity and spending led to her downfall. Louis and Marie Antoinette were at Versailles on October 6, 1789, when they were notified that mobs were marching on the palace. As predicted, *le déluge* had arrived.

The highlights of Versailles are the magnificent **Grands Appartements** in the Louis XIV style, each bearing the name of the allegorical painting on the ceiling and the 71m-long (233-ft.) **Hall of Mirrors** ★★, begun by Mansart in 1678 and decorated by Le Brun with 17 arched windows faced by beveled mirrors in simulated arcades. On June 28, 1919, the treaty ending World War I was signed in this corridor. The German Empire was proclaimed here in 1871. These wonderful royal apartments were, however, for show. To escape the demands of court etiquette, Louis XV and Louis XVI retired to the lovely and more manageable **Petits Appartements.**

➔ **Jardins de Versailles** ★★ Spread across 100 hectares, these spectacular gardens were laid out by landscape artist André Le Nôtre. At the peak of their glory, 1,400 fountains spewed forth. One fountain depicts Apollo in his chariot pulled by four horses, surrounded by Tritons rising from the water. Le Nôtre created a Garden of Eden using ornamental lakes and canals, geometrically designed flower beds, and avenues bordered with statuary. On the mile-long **Grand Canal**, Louis XV used to take gondola rides with his favorite of the moment. While you're there, don't miss the pink-and-white-marble **Grand Trianon,** designed by Hardouin-Mansart for Louis XIV in 1687. Nixon slept here in the room where Mme de Pompadour died. The original furnishings are gone, replaced today by mostly Empire pieces. Gabriel, the designer of place de la Concorde in Paris, built the **Petit Trianon** in 1768 for Louis XV. In time, Marie Antoinette adopted it as her favorite residence, a place to escape the rigid life at the main palace. Many of the current furnishings, including a few in her rather modest bedchamber, belonged to the ill-fated queen.

Fontainbleau: A Hunter's Paradise

Set within the vestiges of a forest that bears its name (Forêt de Fontainebleau), this suburb of Paris has offered refuge to French monarchs throughout the country's history. Kings from the Renaissance valued it because of its nearness to rich hunting grounds and its distance from the slums and smells of the city. Napoleon loved the place, embellishing it with his distinctive monogram and decorative style. After the glories of Versailles (dripping in gold), a visit to Fontainebleau can be refreshing. It actually looks like a place a king (or maybe even you or I) could live, whereas Versailles is more of a production—a mighty fine production—but a production nonetheless.

GETTING THERE

Trains to Fontainebleau depart from the Gare de Lyon in Paris. The trip takes 45 minutes each way. Fontainebleau's railway station lies 3km (2 miles) north of the château, in the suburb of Avon. A local bus (marked simply CHATEAU and part of line A) makes the trip to the château at 15-minute intervals Monday through Saturday, and at 30-minute intervals on Sunday; the fare is 1.70€ each way. If you're **driving,** take A6 south from Paris, exit onto N191, and follow signs.

TOURIST OFFICE

The **Office de Tourisme** is at 4 rue Royale, Fontainebleau (☎ 01-60-74-99-99; www.fontainebleau-tourisme.com), immediately opposite the main entrance to the château.

SIGHTSEEING

➜**Palais de Fontainebleau** ★★ Looking at this sumptuous, yet somehow understated, hunting lodge, it is not hard to understand why little old Napoleon loved it so much. He followed the pattern of a succession of French kings in the pre-Versailles days who used Fontainebleau as a resort and hunted in its forests. François I tried to turn the hunting lodge into a royal palace in the Italian Renaissance style, bringing artists, including Benvenuto Cellini, there to work for him. Under this patronage, the School of Fontainebleau gained prestige, led by painters Rosso Fiorentino and Primaticcio. The artists adorned the 63m-long (207-ft.) stucco-framed panels of the **Gallery of François I.** You'll also notice that the salamander, the symbol of the Chevalier king, is everywhere. One of the prettiest rooms is the **Ballroom** (or Gallery of Henri II), which displays the interlaced initials H&D, referring to Henri and his beautiful mistress, Diane de Poitiers. Competing with this illicit tandem are the initials H&C, symbolizing Henri and his ho-hum wife, Catherine de Médicis. Look out for the monumental fireplace supported by two bronze satyrs, made in 1966 (the originals were melted down during the Revolution). And don't forget to look up at the ceiling, which displays lovely octagonal coffering adorned with rosettes.

You can wander around much of the palace on your own, visiting sites evoking the Corsican's 19th-century imperial heyday. They include the **throne room** where Napoleon abdicated his rulership of France, his **offices,** his monumental **bedroom,** and his **bathroom.** Some of the smaller Napoleonic Rooms contain his personal mementos and artifacts.

After the palace, visit the **gardens** and especially the **carp pond** (there's always something fishy going on round there), although they are mere preludes to the forest of Fontainebleau and not nearly as spectacular as those surrounding Versailles. *Place du Général-de-Gaulle.* ☎ *01-60-71-50-70. www.musee-chateau-fontainebleau.fr. Combination ticket including private apartments and Napoleonic rooms 11€ adults, 9.50€ students. Main château 6.50€ adults, 4.50€ students. June–Sept Wed–Mon 9:30am–6pm; Oct–May Wed–Mon 9:30am–5pm.*

Vaux-le-Vicomte: Never One-Up the King

Never ever try to outdo your king. That is the lesson to be learned from Vaux-le-Vicomte. Built by Louis XIV's financial minister Nicolas Fouquet, its completion was celebrated in 1661 by means of an extravagant party. Molière wrote a play, Lully composed the music, jewel-encrusted elephants paraded around as Chinese fireworks lit up the skies. All would have been fine except for one key detail: Fouquet invited the king, and the king was disgusted (nay, jealous) of his finance minister's display of grandeur. Louis asked architect Le Vau, painter Lebrun, and gardener Le Nôtre to work their magic on Versailles, and had Fouquet kept in solitary confinement. In fact some conspiracy theorists think Fouquet was the Man in the Iron Mask. Today Vaux-le-Vicomte is one of the most charming châteaux in the Ile-de-France. What a pity it's so damned difficult to get to.

GETTING THERE

By **car,** take N6 southeast from Paris to Melun, which is 6km (3³/₄ miles) west of the château. By **train,** take the 45-minute ride from Gare de Lyon to Melun, then a taxi (call ☎ 01-64-52-51-50) from the station 6.5km (4 miles) to Vaux-le-Vicomte (count 22€ each way). If you time it right on **weekends,** you could arrive at the station in time to take the shuttle (Châteaubus) to the castle. The Châteaubus runs from March 25 to November 12 from the station (av. Gallieni in front of the Café de la Gare). March 25 to May 1 and October 7 to November 12, buses leave at 12:10 and 2:20pm and return from the château at 5:30 and 6:25pm. May 6 to October 1, buses leave the station at 10:10am, 12:10, 2:20, 3:25, and 6:50pm (for the candlelight visits); return from the château at 2:50, 5:30, 6:25, 7:25, and 10:15pm. Tickets cost between 3€ and 4€.

TOURIST OFFICE

The nearest **tourist office** is in the Hôtel de Ville, 18 rue Paul Doumer, Melun (☎ 01-64-52-64-52; www.melun-tourisme.com). It is open Tuesday through Saturday 9am to 12:15pm and 2 to 6pm.

SIGHTSEEING

➜ **Château de Vaux-le-Vicomte** ★★ One of the stateliest French châteaux that's still privately owned, Vaux-le-Vicomte belongs to Patrice, *comte* de Vogüe, whose ownership dates back many generations. He lives in one of the outbuildings, not in the main building, which is open for tours. And before you ask— *non,* he doesn't have any eligible offspring. The view of the château from the main gate reveals the splendor of 17th-century

France. On the south side, a majestic staircase sweeps toward the gardens, designed by Le Nôtre. The Grand Canal, flanked by waterfalls, divides the greenery. The château is furnished with 17th-century pieces. A self-guided tour of the interior includes Fouquet's personal suite, the huge basement and wine cellar, the servants' dining room, and the copper-filled kitchen. Included in the admission fee is entrance to the château's carriage museum **(Musée des Equipages)** in the stables. Some 25 restored 18th- and 19th-century carriages are on display, each accessorized with mannequin horses and people.

If you're looking for romance, don't miss the candlelight evenings **(Des Soirées à Chandelles;** May to mid-Oct Sat 8pm–midnight, July–Aug Fri 8pm–midnight), when thousands of candles illuminate both the château and its gardens. Admission during candlelight evenings is 16€ for adults, 13€ for students. *77950 Maincy.* ☎ *01-64-14-41-90. www.vaux-le-vicomte.com. Admission 13€ adults, 9.90€ students. Mid-Mar to mid-Nov daily 10am–6pm. Closed mid-Nov to mid-Mar.*

Giverny: Impressive Impressionism

Fancy seeing those waterlilies for real? On the border between Normandy and the Ile-de-France, the Claude Monet Foundation preserves the estate where the great painter lived for 43 years. The restored house and its gardens are open to the public, and boy are they beautiful—once you get past the queues of tourists that is. Indeed, learn to ignore the hoards and you'll see where Monet lived, with his mistress and eight kids in 1883, in all its authentic finery. In fact, the pink cottage and flower beds are so enchanting they look like they've been frozen in time in one of his paintings.

While you're here, you should also check out the American art museum. Over 100 American artists sojourned in and painted Giverny, and much of their work is on display here.

GETTING THERE

It takes a morning to get to Giverny and to see its sights. Take the Paris-Rouen **train** from Paris's Gare St-Lazare to the Vernon station, where a taxi can take you the 5km (3 miles) to Giverny. Perhaps the easiest way to get there is on a full-day **bus tour,** for 65€ per person, that focuses on Monet's house and garden. Check with **Cityrama,** 149 rue St-Honoré, 1st arr. (☎ **01-44-55-61-00;** Métro: Palais-Royal– Musée du Louvre.)

If you're **driving,** take the Autoroute de l'Ouest (Port de St-Cloud) toward Rouen. Leave it at Bonnières, then cross the Seine on the Bonnières Bridge. From here, a direct road leads to Giverny. Expect it to take about an hour; try to avoid weekends. Another approach is to leave the highway at the Bonnières exit and go toward Vernon. Once there, cross the bridge over the Seine and follow signs to Giverny or Gasny (Giverny is before Gasny). This is easier than going through Bonnières, where there aren't many signs.

SIGHTSEEING

➜ **Claude Monet Foundation** ★★ Born in 1840, Impressionist Claude Monet was a brilliant innovator, excelling in presenting the effects of light at different times of day. Some have gone so far as to say he "invented light." His paintings of the Rouen cathedral and of waterlilies, which one critic called "vertical interpretations of horizontal lines," are just a few of his masterpieces. When Monet died in 1926, his son, Michel, inherited the house but left it abandoned. The gardens almost became a jungle, inhabited by river rats. In 1966, Michel died and left the house and gardens to the Académie des Beaux-Arts. It wasn't until 1977 that Gerald van der Kemp, who restored Versailles, decided to work on Giverny. A large part of it was restored with gifts from U.S. benefactors, notably the late Lila Acheson Wallace, former head of *Reader's Digest*.

If you visit you'll see Monet's collection of 18th- and 19th-century Japanese prints as well as antique (though not original) furnishings. You can stroll the garden and view all the iconic sights: the thousands of flowers, including the *nymphéas* (waterlilies); the Japanese bridge, hung with wisteria; and a setting of weeping willows and rhododendrons. *84 rue Claude-Monet Parc Gasny.* ☎ *02-32-51-28-21. www. fondation-monet.com. Admission 6€ adults, 4.70€ students. Apr–Oct Tues–Sun 9:30am–6pm. Closed Nov–Mar.*

➔ **Musée d'Art Americain Giverny** ★ About 100 yards from Monet's former house and gardens, this museum showcases the U.S.-born artists, mainly Impressionists, who were influenced by Monet and lived at Giverny. Among the more famous painters were John Singer Sargent and William Metcalf, who often summered at Giverny, writing about "its glories" to other artists. The American painters came from 1887 onward, drawn more by the charm of the village than by the presence of Monet. An estimated 100 artists came to live in Giverny, although they did not have much contact, if any, with Monet, who considered these American painters "a nuisance." He'd turn in his grave if he could see his house nowadays, no doubt. *99 rue Claude-Monet.* ☎ *02-32-51-94-65. www.maag.org. Admission 5.50€ adults, 4€ students. Free admission 1st Sun of the month. Apr–Oct daily 10am–6pm. Closed Nov–Mar.*

Disneyland Paris: Oh, Mickey, You're So Fine!

Hey Mickey! After provoking some of the most enthusiastic and controversial reactions in recent French history, the multi-million-dollar Disneyland Paris opened in 1992. It's one of the world's most lavish theme parks, conceived on a scale rivaling that of Versailles. European journalists initially accused it of everything from cultural imperialism to the death knell of French culture. But the proof is in the pudding, and "Disneyland Paris" has become France's number-one tourist attraction, with 50 million visitors annually. Disneyland Paris looks, tastes, and feels like the ones in California and Florida—except for the cheeseburgers served *avec pommes frites.* In 2002, the Paris park added **Walt Disney Studios,** focusing on the role of movies in popular culture. Take 1 day for the highlights, 2 days for more depth.

GETTING THERE

The **RER** (Line A) has a stop within walking distance of the park. Board the RER in Paris at Charles-de-Gaulle—Etoile, Châtelet—Les Halles, or Nation. Get off at Line A's last stop, Marne-la-Vallée/Chessy, 45 minutes from central Paris. Trains run daily, every 10 to 20 minutes from 5:30am to around 12:30am.

Shuttle buses connect Orly and Charles de Gaulle airports with each hotel in the resort. Buses depart the airports every 30 to 45 minutes. If you're **driving,** take A4 east from Paris, and get off at Exit 14, DIS-NEYLAND PARIS. Parking begins at 8€ per day, but it's free if you are staying at one of the park hotels. A series of moving sidewalks speeds pedestrian transit from parking areas to the park entrance.

SIGHTSEEING

➔ **Disneyland Paris** ★★ Mickey and friends welcome you to five "lands" of entertainment, a dozen hotels, a campground, an entertainment center (**Disney Village,** with six restaurants of its own), a 27-hole golf course, and dozens of restaurants, shows, and shops (gee, thanks, Mickey!). The Disney Village entertainment center is illuminated inside by a spectacular gridwork of lights suspended 18m (59 ft.) above the ground. The complex contains dance clubs, shops, restaurants (one of which offers a dinner spectacle based on the original *Buffalo Bill's Wild West Show*), bars for adults trying to escape their children, a French Government Tourist Office, a post office, and a marina.

Main Street, U.S.A., abounds with horse-drawn carriages and barbershop quartets. Steam-powered railway cars embark from the Main Street Station for a trip through a Grand Canyon diorama to **Frontierland,** with its paddlewheel steamers reminiscent of Mark Twain's Mississippi River. The park's steam trains chug past **Adventureland**—with its swashbuckling pirates, Swiss Family Robinson treehouse, and reenacted Arabian Nights legends—to **Fantasyland.** Here you'll find the **Sleeping Beauty Castle** *(Le Château de la Belle au Bois Dormant)*, whose pinnacles and turrets are an idealized (and spectacular) interpretation of French châteaux. In its shadow are Europeanized versions of *Blanche Neige et les Sept Nains* (Snow White and the Seven Dwarfs), Peter Pan, Dumbo, Alice (from Wonderland), the Mad Hatter's Teacups, and Sir Lancelot's Magic Carousel. Visions of the future are in **Discoveryland,** where tributes to invention and imagination draw from the works of Leonardo da Vinci, Jules Verne, H. G. Wells, the modern masters of science fiction, and the *Star Wars* series.

Next to Disneyland Paris, **Walt Disney Studios** takes guests on a behind-the-scenes interactive discovery of film, animation, and television. The main entrance

Fast Pass Long Lines

Disneyland Paris has instituted a program that's done well at the other parks. With the **Fast Pass** system, visitors to the various rides reserve a 1-hour time block. Within that block, the waiting is usually no more than 8 minutes.

to the studios, called the **Front Lot,** consists of "Sunset Boulevard," an elaborate sound stage complete with hundreds of film props. The **Animation Courtyard** allows visitors to learn the trade secrets of Disney animators, and the **Production Courtyard** lets guests take a look behind the scenes of film and TV production. At **Catastrophe Canyon,** guests are plunged into the heart of a film shoot. Finally, the **Back Lot** is home to special effects and stunt workshops. A live stunt show features cars, motorbikes, and jet skis. If you think you're tough, the Rock 'n' Roller Coaster featuring the music of Aerosmith will prove you ain't. It combines rock memorabilia with high-speed scary twists and turns (completely in the dark); and a reconstruction of one of the explosion scenes in the Hollywood action film *Armaggeddon. Marne-la-Vallée.* ☎ *08-25-30-53-00 (Disneyland Paris Guest Relations office, in City Hall on Main Street, U.S.A.). www.disneylandparis.com. Admission to main park for 1 day, depending on season, 44€ adults; a 1-day ticket to the main park and Disney Studios 54€, a 2-day ticket to the main park and Disney Studios 95€ adults; and a 3-day ticket to the main park and Disney Studios 119€ adults. July–Aug daily 9am–8pm; Sept–June daily 9am–6pm, depending on school and public holidays. Daily 9am–6pm (opens at 10am during certain seasons of the year). Disney Studios tends to close at*

PARIS & ILE-DE-FRANCE

least 1 hr. before the main park. Consult web-
site for up-to-the-minute details.

Chartres: Gateway to the Loire

While Versailles and Fontainebleau attract tourists for their flamboyance, Chartres is a sleepy small town of 42,000 inhabitants, 60 miles southwest of Paris. The main draw here is the Gothic Cathédrale Nôtre Dame, dating back to 1260, which has drawn religious pilgrims from far and wide since the Middle Ages. Today visitors come to gape at its stained glass, which creates a calm, unearthly glow over the stark spires and the various religious relics inside. One especially important one is the famous Voile de la Vierge, or sacred tunic of the Virgin Mary. The robe's history is even longer than the church's: Constantine Porphyrogenitus and Irene presented it to Charlemagne in the fourth century, and Charles the Bald delivered it to Chartres around 876. If time remains after viewing the cathedral, you may want to explore the medieval cobblestone streets of the **Vieux Quartier (Old Town),** with its gabled houses and humped bridges spanning the Eure River. From the pont de Bouju, you can see the lofty spires in the background. Try to find **rue Chantault,** which boasts houses with colorful facades; one is 8 centuries old.

If you're planning a trip to the Loire Valley, Chartres is otherwise known as the "Gateway to the Loire" and makes an ideal stopping-off point.

GETTING THERE

From Paris's Gare Montparnasse, **trains** run directly to Chartres, taking less than an hour. If you're **driving,** take A10/A11 southwest from the périphérique, and follow signs to Le Mans and Chartres. (The Chartres exit is clearly marked.) The

Office de Tourisme is on place de la Cathédrale (☎ 02-37-18-26-26; www.chartres-tourisme.com).

SIGHTSEEING

FREE → **Cathédrale Notre-Dame de Chartres** ★★ Many observers feel the architectural aspirations of the Middle Ages reached their highest expression in the glorious Cathédrale de Chartres. Come to see its soaring architecture; highly wrought sculpture; and above all, its stained glass, which gave the world a new color: Chartres blue. Reportedly, Rodin once sat for hours on the sidewalk, admiring this cathedral's Romanesque sculpture. His opinion: Chartres is the French Acropolis. When it began to rain, a kind soul offered him an umbrella, which he declined, so transfixed was he by this place. The cathedral's origins are uncertain; some have suggested it grew up over an ancient Druid site that later became a Roman temple. As early as the 4th century, there was a Christian basilica here. An 1194 fire destroyed most of what had by then become a Romanesque cathedral but spared the western facade and crypt. The cathedral you see today dates principally from the 13th century, when it was rebuilt with the efforts and contributions of kings, princes, churchmen, and pilgrims from all over Europe. One of the world's greatest high Gothic cathedrals, it was the first to use flying buttresses to support the soaring dimensions within.

Whether you admit to geeky tendencies or not, the glass here is unlike anything else in the world. Most dates from the 12th and 13th centuries and was spared in both world wars by painstakingly removing it piece by piece. See the windows in the morning, at noon, in the afternoon, at sunset—as often as you can. Like the petals of a kaleidoscope, they constantly change. It's difficult to single out one panel or window above the others, but an exceptional one is the 12th-century *Vierge de la Belle Verrière (Our Lady of the Beautiful Window)* on the south side.

After your visit, stroll through the **Episcopal Gardens** and enjoy yet another view of this remarkable cathedral. *16 Cloître Notre-Dame.* ☎ *02-37-21-59-08. www.diocese chartres.com/cathedrale. Free admission to cathedral. Daily 8:30am–7:30pm.*

PARIS & ILE-DE-FRANCE

The Loire Valley

by *Anna Brooke*

Ever wondered where all the Prince and Princess Charmings have gone? It's easy to believe they're here, lost, deep in the heart of the Loire Valley. They've not been flung into dungeons, nor cast under magic spells, *non, non, non*. It's just that there are just so many châteaux to visit it will take them hundreds of years to get out. And when they do, they will probably be full-fledged members of Alcoholics Anonymous, trying to kick the inevitable wine-drinking habit everybody picks up around here (see the Nerd's Guide to French Wine & Culture on p. 731).

The moral of this story: Pass on Monsieur or Mademoiselle Charming, and charm yourself. It won't be hard amid the Loire's many elegant vineyards, winding rivers, and Renaissance glory. Leave the fairy tales to Disney & Co.—even if these parts make you feel like you're starring in one of their movies.

The Loire is the longest waterway in France, at 1,020km (632 miles). Its regal valley is at the heart of French life—a vast, UNESCO-protected region that stretches from the outskirts of Greater Paris through luscious, green countryside, known as the "Garden of France," to the Atlantic coast, between La Rochelle and Brittany. Thanks to its central location, **Tours** is a handy base from which to quench your castle fever. But so too are the château-towns of **Angers, Saumur, Amboise,** and **Blois,** resplendent amid vineyards, hunting forests, and watercourses.

The sheer quantity and beauty of the Loire châteaux make them the region's obvious draw, but there are other attractions to explore. Head west and you'll hit **Nantes,** an arty, forward-thinking river port that opens the region to the Atlantic coast. Not only does it bridge the gap between Brittany and the Loire, it also harbors a cool alternative party scene. Troglodyte dwellings around **Saumur**—including the astounding **Château de Brézé** with an entire subterranean village hidden in its moat—provide some wacky sightseeing. And then there's the wine: Old Bacchus has his grips on yet another part of France, producing some of the country's crispest whites, reds, and rosés.

The problem with the Loire lies not in deciding what to visit, but what to visit first. It all deserves your attention. To ease the difficulty, this chapter covers two cool cities, Tours and Nantes, and the region's top 20 castles, from east to west. Industrial **Orléans** is the Loire region's capital, with an attractive historic core. But unless you have a blazing interest in Joan of Arc, who spent much of her short life there before burning at the stake at age 19, you won't find it as compelling as other places in this chapter. (For more information on Orléans, contact the **Office de Tourisme:** ☎ **02-38-24-05-05;** www.tourisme-orleans.com).

If you want to run free outdoors before you leave, check out "Playing Outside in the Loire" (p. 190), which details the best places to canoe, golf, horseback ride, and hike.

The Best of the Loire Valley

⊙ **The Best Place to Get High on Bubbles: Saumur** has got it all: a fairy-tale château, a cavalry school, mushrooms, and some of the best sparkling wine outside Champagne. See p. 172.

⊙ **The Best Place to Get Creative in an Old Biscuit Factory:** Say "LU" to the French, and they'll say "biscuits." Say "LU" to folk from Nantes, and they'll say **"Lieu Unique"**—the old LU biscuit factory turned contemporary art platform, for anyone with something to say. See p. 185.

⊙ **The Best Festival for Fresh Artistic Talent (Tours):** For the last 3 years, Tours has conjured an artistic oasis amid what is otherwise a creative desert in **Rayon Frais**—its 3-day festival of

theater, contemporary and urban art, and music. See p. 155.

⊙ **The Best Retreat on a Rainy Day (Tours):** The **Musée des Beaux-Arts** houses one of the finest art collections outside Paris. See p. 154.

⊙ **The Best Place to Get Liver Failure (Tours):** Eeny, meeny, miny, mo: Whatever you do, don't drink a pint of every beer at **Le Palais de la Bière,** with more than 260 to choose from. See p. 151.

⊙ **The Best Way to Soak Up City Life (Tours):** Think "France," and you think about abundant **markets.** In Tours, which abounds with 30 of them, you can't forget which country you are visiting. See p. 154.

THE LOIRE VALLEY

Ze Bumpin' Surfer Bus Tour

Ze-bus (44 rue Henri Germain; **www.ze-bus.com**) is a coach transport company that targets surfers on a budget looking for some culture with their sea and sand. For the Loire Valley trip, you start at Angoulême, visit Poitiers, Tours, Blois, Chambord, and then end up in Paris. The coaches pick you up outside your designated FUAJ youth hostel (www.fuaj.org) and provide plenty of occasions for you to hook up with fellow international travelers. Prices run from 99€ for 2 days to 300€ for a week's travel. You also have the option of starting or ending your journeys in the U.K. Check out the website for all destinations.

- **The Best Château to Sleep in (Tours):** It's torture to visit so many castles without sleeping in one—which is why you should stay at the **Château Beaulieu.** See p. 150.
- **The Best Place to Feel Small (Nantes):** Climb a gargantuan model elephant in the old boat hangars at **Les Nefs.** See p. 188.
- **The Best Place to Dine Like You're a 19th-Century Lord (Nantes): La Cigale** is Belle Epoque, it's beautiful, and the grub is damned delicious. See p. 182.

- **The Best Place in Which to Pretend You're in a Quaint Fishing Village (Nantes): Trentemoult** is solid evidence of the fact that Nantais folk wish they were really from Brittany. This former fishing village oozes Breton quaintness. See p. 189.
- **The Best 19th-Century Passageway Filled with Shops (Nantes):** The **Passage Pommeraye** is beautiful and teeming with sightseers and shoppers. See p. 189.

Getting Around the Region

First off, you'll need a set of wheels. Trains from Paris run to Tours (1 hr.), Angers (1½ hr.), and Nantes (2 hr.). There's even TGV access from Lille. But many of the smaller châteaux are accessible only by road. Buses sometimes run from towns such as Chartres and Tours, but otherwise you'll have to take the A11 from Paris for Angers and Nantes, and then the A10 for Blois and Tours. Nantes has a small airport that deals with internal flights around France, plus some European destinations (including Britain), North Africa, and the West Indies.

Tours: The Ultimate Base for Château-Hopping

232km (144 miles) SW of Paris, 113km (70 miles) SW of Orléans; pop. 138,000

Tours is without châteaux but its location, at the junction of the Loire and Cher rivers, makes it the traditional center for exploring the valley. So before you overdose on castles, boost your system with busy streets, cafes, bars, and a thronging nightlife led by a bunch of bubbly students.

There's a strong rivalry here with neighboring Angers. Both are relatively small riverside cities; both rely heavily on their quaint old quarters for tourism; and both offer their share of stained glass and ancient stone. But it's Tours that snatches

THE LOIRE VALLEY

The Loire Valley's Top 20 Châteaux

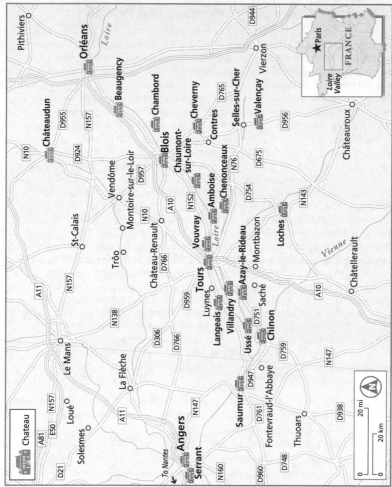

up the bulk of the region's tourists. You've been warned.

The locals can fancy themselves Parisians if the mood strikes. From their wooing tactics to their bar etiquette, members of Tours's younger generation have traditionally behaved like punky kids with chips on their shoulders about being from a picturesque small city on the Loire. Now,

with the increasing number of tourists and ensuing possibilities for diversion, they can have an attitude as well. If you win the trust of a young Tours resident, you can pat yourself on the back, but the initial ice-breaking can daunt the less determined.

Don't give up too soon, though. Obviously not everyone has this aura of "excellence," and there are certainly

A Feudal Exercise: Châteaux Architecture

No, you're not seeing double, triple, or quadruple—there really are that many castles. Exploring the Loire Valley is like working your way through a textbook on Medieval to Renaissance architecture, though it's much more interesting in three dimensions, *bien sûr.*

First up was the Merovingian period, when the first Loire castles appeared in the form of fortified former Gallo-Roman villas (5th–10th c.). Constant unrest led to the design of the Motte castle in the 1100s—a mound of earth, surrounded by a ditch, upon which a square tower (the keep) was built to keep out the enemy (Langeais and Blois châteaux started life this way). By the 12th and 13th centuries, stone had replaced wood, and defensive walls with spherical towers cropped up around the now circular keep. Builders began widening moats, to improve defenses, and adding stone machicolations, new loopholes for archers, and missile-launching platforms, to allow castles to lash back more effectively at attacking enemies. In the 14th and 15th centuries, their function shifted from defense to comfort, with larger living quarters and the first lavatories; but by the Renaissance (16th c.), warfare was so very passé that royal one-upmanship became a serious preoccupation: Keeps, turrets, and moats became decorative additions, windows got bigger, staircases became ornate, and gardens were sculpted. The court of the Valois kings wanted two things and two things only—comfort and aestheticism. But they couldn't decide where to settle. Charles VII liked Chinon and Loches, Charles XIII preferred Amboise, Louis VII liked Blois, and François I (1515–47) spent time in both. The result: châteaux, châteaux, and more châteaux, adorned with breathtaking finery. And wherever the king went, his nobles followed with their own gorgeous structures—some, I daresay, more beautiful than the king's.

plenty of people—both kids and adults—who are more than willing to help out a polite and curious traveler. A good place to start is the tourist office, which employs an overwhelming number of these friendly youth. A good basic guide is available (in French and English), which outlines everything from museums to restaurants to bars.

Another reason to visit is for the food and wine. The Touraine table is one of the best in France, serving specialties from all over the country plus a few delights of its own. Expect to stuff your face with *rillettes* (goose or pork pâté), *andouillette* (tripe sausage; see the Champagne chapter), *coq-au-vin* made with Chinon wine, delicious Ste-Maure goat's cheese, and macaroons made by the monks of Cormery.

Getting There

BY AIR

Nah, not here mate.

BY TRAIN

Most of the trains bound for Tours, including all TGVs (as many as 10 per day), depart from Paris's Gare Montparnasse. A very limited number, including some of the slow and conventional commuter trains, depart from Gare d'Austerlitz. Many, but not all, of the conventional (non-TGV) trains pull into the center of Tours, at the **Gare Tours Centre Ville,** place du

Tours

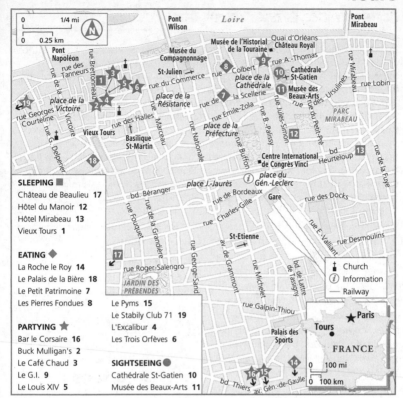

SLEEPING ■
Château de Beaulieu **17**
Hôtel du Manoir **12**
Hôtel Mirabeau **13**
Vieux Tours **1**

EATING ◆
La Roche le Roy **14**
Le Palais de la Bière **18**
Le Petit Patrimoine **7**
Les Pierres Fondues **8**

PARTYING ★
Bar le Corsaire **16**
Buck Mulligan's **2**
Le Café Chaud **3**
Le G.I. **9**
Le Louis XIV **5**

Le Pyms **15**
Le Stabily Club 71 **19**
L'Excalibur **4**
Les Trois Orfèves **6**

SIGHTSEEING ●
Cathédrale St-Gatien **10**
Musée des Beaux-Arts **11**

Maréchal-Leclerc, 3 rue Edouard-Vaillant. Some conventional trains and virtually all the TGV trains, however, arrive at the isolated railway station of **Tours/St-Pierre-des-Corps,** about 6km (4 miles) east of the center of Tours. If you end up here, wait for the next one into Tours Centre, grab a taxi, or await a free *navette* (bus) for ongoing transport to the center of Tours. For information, call ☎ **36-35.**

BY CAR

If you're **driving,** take highway A10 to Tours. As I mentioned, it makes a great base for visiting châteaux, so you could think of renting a car from here (see below).

BY BUS

See "Ze Bumpin' Surfer Bus Tour" on p. 144 and visit www.ze-bus.com.

Orientation

Tours proper is a sprawling maze of residential streets between the two rivers. The heart of town cozies up against the Loire and extends south to boulevard Thiers. In this section, you'll find Vieux Tours—a mismatched assortment of cobblestone streets and amazingly beautiful old buildings (especially around the **place Plumereau,** the main student hangout). The town center is divided on a larger scale into roughly four

Carefree Car-Free Travel

So you're without wheels? Keep cool, man. Car-deprived travelers who want to visit the châteaux of the Loire Valley no longer need to take local buses. The **tourist office** (78 rue Bernard-Palissy; ☎ 02-47-70-37-37) sponsors an armada of eight-passenger minibuses that depart from the office between 9 and 9:30am and between 1 and 1:30pm daily, year-round. Tours visit two to four châteaux, depending on the schedule; destinations change frequently. Morning sessions cost 21€ to 27€; afternoon excursions are 27€ to 33€, depending on the stops and their distance from Tours. The price does not include admission to the châteaux (see individual château listings, below), but participation in the tour qualifies you for reduced group rates. Some visitors combine two half-day tours into a full day of château-hopping. Because trains from Paris take only 55 minutes each way, this makes a worthwhile side trip.

quadrants, split by avenue de Grammont/rue Nationale running north/south and boulevard Béranger/Heurteloup running east/west. The old town is in the northwest quadrant, in the Hôtel de Ville (town hall). Several museums are in the northeast quadrant, the train station is in the southeast, and a largely uneventful residential area is in the southwest. The best neighborhoods for visitors lie between boulevard Béranger/Heurteloup and the river at the place Anatole France and the place Plumereau, as well as the place Jean-Jaures, just south of boulevard Béranger. Shops, cinemas, and restaurants line the congested rue Nationale, which can be a good starting point for exploring Tours since it cuts through the heart of the city.

Getting Around

BY BUS

Public transport is usually unnecessary in the northern quadrants, but to reach other parts of Tours, the bus is your best choice. You can pick up most bus lines near the train station and at place Jean Jaures. They run regularly throughout the day until around 11pm. Tickets are 1.20€, available

for purchase onboard and valid for an hour (**www.filbleu.fr**).

BY BICYCLE

You can rent a bike at **Vélomania,** 109 rue Colbert (☎ 02-47-05-10-11; http://pierre.dumaz.free.fr) for just under 15€ per day. The shop is open Monday 3:30 to 7:30pm, Tuesday to Friday 10:30am to 1:30pm and

Rental Vehicles

Car-rental offices in or near the train station include:

➙ **Avis** in the Tours Centre station (☎ 02-47-44-61-61; daily 8am–noon and 1:15–7pm)

➙ **Hertz,** at 57 rue Marcel-Tribut (☎ 02-47-75-50-00; daily 8am–noon and 2–7pm)

➙ **Ada,** at 136 av. André Maginot (☎ 02-47-42-90-92; Mon–Fri 8am–noon and 2–7pm, Sat 9am–noon and 3–6pm)

If you want to rent a car from St-Pierre des Corps try **Europcar,** on place de la Gare, St-Pierre-des-Corps (☎ 02-47-64-47-76; daily 6am–11pm).

Tours History 101

Those feisty Romans were everywhere, including here—though back then they called the region *Caesarodonum* (Caesar's Hill). From the 1st century A.D. onward, it became the chief town of the Romanized Gauls who called themselves *Turones* (hence the name Tours). A few remnants from this era are near the cathedral.

When the city was Christianized, Tours's bishop, St-Martin, became a veritable star. After his death in A.D. 397, his relics attracted such a crowd that religious pilgrims en route to Santiago de Compostela in northwest Spain stopped here to pay homage.

In the 14th century, the city underwent major expansion, so that by the mid–15th to 16th centuries, it had become a favorite place of refuge for endangered monarchs and, from time to time, the seat of power. Charles VII, Louis XI, Charles VIII, and François I all loved Tours, where their main ministers and advisors chose to live, and where (thanks to Louis XI) the silk industry flourished.

The Renaissance era produced some decadently flamboyant architecture (see the top sections of the cathedral towers). And then the 18th century set in, with new roads and bridges, including the fabulous Pont Wilson.

2:30 to 7:30pm, and Saturday 10:30am to 7:30pm. It is open Sunday at 6pm only for returns.

Tourist Offices

The **Office de Tourisme** is at 78 rue Bernard-Palissy (☎ **02-47-70-37-37**; www.ligeris.com). Daily in July and August, they offer guided old-town walking tours, in a mixture of French and English. The 2-hour excursions depart from the tourist office, usually at 10am or 2:30pm. April to June and September and October tours run only on Saturday, Sunday, and holidays. Reservations are required. Cost is 5.50€.

Tours Nuts & Bolts

Emergencies Ambulance ☎ **15**; police ☎ **17**; fire/paramedic service ☎ **18**.

Internet/Wireless Hot Spots **Le Paradis Vert** (9 rue Michelet; ☎ **02-47-64-78-50**; www.leparadisvert.com; daily 10am–2am; 4€ per hour, ask about student reductions) is a wicked joint with 36 billiard tables, 250 cocktails, 100 beers, ice creams, and a cybercafe (if you can still see the screens by the time you sit down). It's the biggest games bar in France.

Laundromats If you *must* wash your garments in Tours, head to the cheesy-sounding **Lavo-2000** (20 rue Bretonneau; ☎ **02-47-73-14-69**; http://lavo-2000.com) in the Old Quarter, where you can do a load from 3.60€ and sightsee while you wait.

Pharmacies **Pharmacie de l'Avenue** (28 av. de Grammont; ☎ 02-47-05-49-32) is in a handy spot near place J-Jaures for a quick medicine fix.

Post Office Post 'em at La Poste (75 bis rue Marceau; ☎ 02-47-31-11-41).

Taxis **Taxi Radio** is reliable (☎ 02-47-20-30-40).

Websites See **www.tours.onboujoo.com** for bar reviews and soirée ideas.

Sleeping

HOSTELS

➔ **Vieux Tours** ★★ This place gets two stars because it's hard to find youth hostels so close to the city center. It's also just 300m (984 ft.) from place Plumereau, the main student haunt, which makes it the ultimate choice for budget bunking. Rooms are clean, you get free sheets, and if you can't face cooking for yourself, you can eat in the on-site cafeteria or one of the myriad restaurants at your doorstep. *5 rue Bretonneau.* ☎ *02-47-37-81-58. www.fuaj.org. 17€ bed. Rate includes breakfast. Reception daily 8am–noon and 6–10pm. From the station, take bus no. 4 to Vieux Tours stop.*

CHEAP

➔ **Hôtel du Manoir** This 19th-century residence is on a quiet street near the train station, but it's dead comfy and an excellent value for the money. Rooms would not win prizes for their size, but they all have windows that let in lots of light. As you'd expect from budget lodgings in the Loire, furnishings are simple, and bathrooms have typical tub/shower combos or showers only. *2 rue Traversière.* ☎ *02-47-05-37-37. 46€–56€ double. Credit cards accepted. Parking 3€. In room: A/C, TV.*

➔ **Hôtel Mirabeau** ★ Built into a quiet, downtown mansion, this hotel's brochure caters to business travelers, but it's a cozy getaway for anyone. You feel as though you're staying in someone's house: Rooms are individually decorated, beds are made with blankets (most French establishments haven't discovered duvets), and each room has an original marble fireplace and cool period touches such as 1930s mirrors and cute bedside tables. On a sunny day, you can have breakfast on the patio, and guests have Internet access. *89 bis bd. Heurteloup.* ☎ *02-47-05-24-60. www. hotel-mirabeau.fr. 40€–52€ double. Breakfast 6.50€ (7€ in room). Parking 10€. In room: TV.*

SPLURGE

We'll skip the doables here (the cheap options are more than adequate) and jump head-first into a splurge.

➔ **Château de Beaulieu** ★★ You are just about to embark on a journey around some of the world's most mind-blowing châteaux. To fathom what it felt like to live there, you need to stay in one. Plus you might meet a prince or princess from the Charming family, after which money will be no object. There, has that justified this splurge for you? At this 17th-century estate, you can experience what life was like in another era. Beyond the entrance, a double curving stairway leads to the reception hall. Guest rooms have mahogany and chestnut furniture, decorative fireplaces, and limitless hot water. The château proper has only nine rooms, so make sure you reserve one of them; the others are a bit more sterile, in a turn-of-the-20th-century pavilion nearby. Of course, a castle of this caliber has to have a flaw. In this case, it's the fact that you'll need a car to get there from the center of Tours. Take D86 from Tours, then D207 toward Beaulieu, 7km (45 miles); it's southwest of Tours. *67 rue de Beaulieu.* ☎ *02-47-53-20-26.* *www.chateaudebeaulieu37.com.* *85€–132€ double. Half-board 170€–210€ for 2. Credit cards accepted. Amenities: Restaurant; bar; dry cleaning; laundry service; 3 tennis courts (across road). In room: A/C, TV, hair dryer, minibar.*

Eating

CAFES & LIGHT FARE

→**Les Pierres Fondues** CHEESE FONDUES If you're after a quick meal with a difference, you can't beat this place. It's small, but that just adds to the charm as you plunge your skewer of meat or bread into the delicious, spongy, melted-cheese fondues. You can also cook your meat yourself and choose from an array of sauces. For something lighter, opt for a salad or a *tartine* (toasted sandwich). *122 rue Colbert.* ☎ *02-47-05-14-54.* *www.pierres fondues.com. Fondue 16€ per person. Credit cards accepted. Mon–Tues and Thurs–Fri 7–11pm; Sat noon–2pm and 7–11pm.*

CHEAP

→**Le Petit Patrimoine** TRADITIONAL FRENCH This pocket-size, long-established restaurant has a powerful yet quirky appeal. Outfitted in a rustic old-fashioned style that might have been inspired by someone's early-20th-century grandmother's house, it has ceiling beams, old masonry walls, and a sense of respect for diehard French aesthetics and values (retro is back). Depending on the chef's mood, you could end up with dishes that include a savory *matelote* of veal with baby vegetables, a salad of *rillons* (a meat byproduct made from bacon), grilled beefsteaks with goat cheese, and a *tourte*

Tourangelle composed of pastry casing filled with goat cheese and the above-mentioned *rillons.* *58 rue Colbert.* ☎ *02-47-66-05-81.* *Reservations recommended. Fixed-price menu 14€–28€. Credit cards accepted. Mon–Sat noon–2pm; daily 7–10pm.*

DOABLE

📺 Best ● →**Le Palais de la Bière** ★ ALSATIAN BRASSERIE If you ain't got the cash to make it from the Loire to Alsace, come here. Decorated like a Germanic tavern with beams, this place will convince you that you've made it to the German border—before everything goes foggy, that is. The waiters have a sneaky habit of plying you with their 260 beer and 60 whiskey varieties. If you're adventurous and like beer, try flavors such as melon and banana. Whatever you do, line your stomach first with eastern French delights such as mussels, sauerkraut, and grilled meat. And savor them—they might be the last thing you remember about the evening. *29 place Gaston-Pailou.* ☎ *02-47-61-50-48.* *Entrees 9€–13€. Credit cards accepted. Mon–Sat 10am–2am; Sun 10am–3pm.*

SPLURGE

→**La Roche le Roy** ★★ MODERN FRENCH Why is it that the most expensive joints flee the town center? Ask top chef Alain Couturier when you get here. Whatever his response, you'll forgive him once you've tasted treats such as scalloped foie gras with lentils, cod with saffron cream sauce, pan-fried scallops with truffle vinaigrette, and *matelote* (stew) of eel with Chinon or Bourgeuil wine. For dessert, try a slice of warm orange-flavored chocolate served with coffee-flavored sherbet, and then say your prayers, for you will be in dessert heaven. From the center of town, take av. Grammont south (follow signs to

M T V 🛡 Tours de Force

Long a student town, Tours has a lively young population. Even during summer months, when most students have left, a youthful crowd rules the hot spots. Place Plumereau (often shortened to "place Plume"), a square of medieval buildings, houses a riot of restaurants and bars. In the warmer months, the square explodes with tables, which fill with people who like to see and be seen. In addition to the bars and clubs around the place Plumereau, an even trendier street, rue Colbert, has recently emerged as a hip and fashionable strip. Rue Colbert lies in the heart of Tours, midway between the place Plumereau and the cathedral.

A popular site is **Le Louis XIV** (37 rue Briçonnet; ☎ **02-47-05-77-17**), a stylish bar where it's possible for outsiders to meet new friends and companions. The hottest place in town is **L'Excalibur** (35 rue Briçonnet; ☎ **02-47-64-76-78**), with a disco beat and video system. A clientele of all ages, many from the surrounding countryside, heads to **Le Pyms** (170 av. de Grammont; ☎ **02-47-66-22-22**), an alternative disco open Tuesday through Sunday from 10:30pm to at least 4am. A relatively new bar that tends to be loaded with a selection of local students is **Le Stabily Club 71** (71 rue Georges-Courteline; ☎ **02-47-37-01-54**). If you just can't stay away from the overwhelming supply of Irish bars cluttering the streets of France, why not pick a good one? **Buck Mulligan's** (37–39 rue du Grand Marché; ☎ **02/47-39-61-69;** daily 5pm–2am) has the name and the face to go with it. Expect giddy Irish tunes, ample Irish brew, and a slew of Brits and Americans at the bar.

If you're gay, relatively energetic, and like to dance, check out the town's most popular gay bar and disco, **Le G.I.** (13 rue Lavoisier; ☎ **02-47-66-29-96**). Positioned on a dark street in a safe but somewhat run-down neighborhood, it attracts a local, mostly male crowd that packs the place on weekends.

St-Avertin–Vierzon). The road crosses a bridge but doesn't change names. The restaurant is beside that road, on the southern periphery of Tours. *55 rte. St-Avertin.* ☎ *02-47-27-22-00. Reservations recommended. Fixed-price lunch 30€, fixed-price dinner 46€–65€. Credit cards accepted. Tues–Sat noon–1:45pm and 7:30–9:30pm. Closed 1 week in Feb and 3 weeks in Aug.*

Partying

In most quarters of town, best behavior is expected at all times. Any shenanigans—from public drunkenness to simple public loudness—warrant severe looks and mumbles of disapproval. In and around the nighttime place Plumereau, however,

manners are lost and social mores forgotten as everyone slams back the booze and stumbles over the cobblestones. The mood is basically that of a large outdoor party, though the same boisterous behavior during the day is probably not the best idea.

BARS

➜ **Bar le Corsaire** The pirate theme is pushed to the max here: aquariums down below, boat cabin decor when you walk in, barmen with scurvy (only joking, but they *are* dressed as sailors and look like something out of a Village People video), and copious amounts of alcohol! In fact, 500 cocktail varieties make the drinks list look more like a telephone directory. Each cocktail has its own glass. They also do fantastic ice creams. Drinks and cocktails, at 10€, don't break the bank either. *187 av. Grammont.* ☎ *02-47-05-20-00.*

CLUBS & LIVE MUSIC VENUES

📺 (Best ◉) → **Le Café Chaud** What to do when your heart is in Paris but your soul is in Tours? Open a Paris-themed discothèque, of course. Patrons are early 20-somethings who let rip to salsa and jazz before heading downstairs for a mélange of sound in well-reconstituted Paris Métro decor. The cocktails (9€) also have a Paris theme, with names such as Rive Gauche or Rive Droite. Everyone should try the house special—Le Café Chaud—a take on Irish coffee with whiskey, coffee liqueur, and fresh cream. Beers are 3€. At around 11pm, music from downstairs makes its way upstairs, and everyone boogies to electro-funk. *33 rue Briçonnet.* ☎ *02-47-05-64-45.*

→ **Les Trois Orfèves** This place, once steeped in history (it's in a vaulted 15th- to 16th-c. basement that was used by the kings for illicit rendezvous), is now clad, head to toe, in black-and-white photos and throngs to the beat of music-mad party-seekers who come by twice a week to listen to blues, ska, reggae, and rock concerts. Other evenings are more disco-orientated, with lashings of '70s and '80s music. From time to time, they team up with other venues for Les Tremplins Musicaux de Tours—a festival aimed at discovering new young musical talent. This is the cheapest nightclub in Tours at 2€, but you'll have to have a drink, which bumps up the price. Beers are 4€; cocktails run 8€. *6 rue des Orfèvres.* ☎ *02-47-64-02-73.*

Sightseeing

The capital of the Touraine is used more as a center for excursions to the châteaux than as a sightseeing attraction of its own. But there are some nuggets here for those willing to hang around long enough to discover them.

PUBLIC MONUMENTS

(FREE) → **Cathédrale St-Gatien** This cathedral honors the 3rd-century evangelist. Its flamboyant Gothic facade is flanked by towers with bases from the 12th century and tops from the Renaissance. The lanterns also date to the Renaissance. The choir is from the 13th century, with new additions built in each century through the 16th. Sheltered inside is the handsome 16th-century tomb of Charles VIII and Anne de Bretagne's two children. Some of the glorious stained-glass windows are from the 13th century. *5 place de la Cathédrale.* ☎ *02-47-70-21-00. Free admission. Daily 9am–7pm.*

Boy Meets Girl in Tours

Here, 20-something and teen males seem to have forgotten about the dating game, leaving the graceful act of seduction up to older, more socially mature men. (Perhaps that's why you see so many attractive young women on the arms of men who could be their dads at the brasseries and out on the streets.) Tours males will hit on chicks regardless of their age. No one is overly intense in his pursuit, however. If you're not interested, simply ignore it or look bored. Boys, on the other hand, probably won't encounter any overzealous Mrs. Robinsons on a night out, and can instead concentrate on wooing amours from their own generation.

THE LOIRE VALLEY

Arts Scene

Like most of its Loire Valley siblings, Tours's art scene leans heavily on the past for support. Ideas look to the future, however, at the **Centre de Création Contemporaine** (53–55 rue Marcel Tribut; ☎ 02-47-66-50-00; www.ccc-art. com; free admission; Wed–Sun 2–6pm; closed Dec 25–Jan 1; bus: 6 to Champ-Girault). The center, which is near the railway station (a 10-min. walk southeast of the town center), opened in 1985 with the dual mission of bringing new art into the public eye through exhibits and making that art accessible and understandable. Three to five exhibitions take place every year.

MUSEUMS

📺 Best● → **Musée des Beaux-Arts** This fine provincial museum, set in the Palais des Archevêques, is worth a visit just to see its lovely rooms and gardens. It's not all that common to see such treasures outside of Paris, but here you'll find Old Masters such as Degas, Delacroix, Rembrandt, and Boucher. The sculpture collection includes works by Rodin, Houdon, and Bourdelle. And you can tour the gardens for free. *18 place François-Sicard. ☎ 02-47-05-68-73. Admission 4.50€ adults, 2.50€ students. Wed–Mon 9am–12:45pm and 2–6pm. Free admission to gardens daily 7am–8:30pm.*

Playing Outside

With so many châteaux to visit, parks might not be at the top of the list of things to do here, but should you decide to take some time out from city life, you'll find parks aplenty. **Le Jardin Botanique** (on bd. Tonnellé, in front of the Bretonneau hospital) is Tours's oldest public garden. Created in 1843 by the chemist Jean-Anthyme Margueron (1771–1848), it grows many medicinal plants (more than 2,000 species cared for by the chemist faculty). There's also a small animal area, a mini farmyard, pink flamingos, and aviaries. If you want a quick rest before you catch the train, try the **Jardin de la Préfecture,** opposite the station, with a few shaded benches and pristine lawns. The **Parc Mirabeau** near boulevard Heurteloup is an old cemetery with pretty chestnut trees

To Market You Go!

Tours has 📺 Best● **more than 30 markets,** but the following are the most animated. The **Marché Gourmand,** or gourmet market, takes place on the first and third Friday of each month, from 4 to 10pm, on the place de la Résistance. The **antiques market,** on the first and third Friday of the month, is in the pedestrian zone on rue de Bordeaux; on the fourth Sunday of the month, a larger version of the event takes place, with more *brocante* than genuine antiques. The **flower market,** Wednesday and Saturday 8am to 6pm, is on boulevard Béranger. And the **crafts market (Marché Artisanal),** is held on Saturday from 9am to 6pm, on the place des Halles. The covered market, **Les Halles et Grand Marché,** with a huge selection of fresh, local meat, cheese, and produce, is at place Gaston-Pailhou, Monday to Saturday 6am to 7pm and Sunday 6am to 1pm. **Traditional food markets** take place Tuesday to Sunday mornings at various locations; ask at the tourist office.

and a few statues. If you want to combine culture with gardens, head to the **Musée des Beaux-Arts** (see above); its intricate flower beds and topiary demonstrate that the French know a thing or two about gardens.

Shopping

In the pedestrian area of **rue de Bordeaux,** from the magnificent train station to rue Nationale, you'll find dozens of mall-type shops and department stores selling clothes, shoes, jewelry, leather goods, and the like. Up **rue Nationale** toward the river are more stores, more upscale boutiques, and a small mall with chain boutiques. Rue Nationale continues across the river, but turn left on **rue du Commerce** toward the old town center. You'll want to explore the streets and courtyards for regional specialties, books, toys, and crafts. A hotbed for antiques is east of rue Nationale (toward the cathedral), along **rue de la Scellerie.**

Festivals & Events

There comes a time when pent-up artistic talent has to find a way out. With the Loire Valley being a conservative region with a proclivity for the old rather than the new, somebody had to do something fast. The answer came in 2003 with 📺 ❨Best❩ **Rayon Frais**—a young and lively arts festival that covers everything from urban and contemporary art to dance, music, and theater. Over 3 days in early summer (usually July), various venues turn themselves into platforms for bright artists with a voice to be voiced and a sound to be sounded. If you're interested in seeing what the struggling local hipsters get up to, this is a cool time to visit Tours. Check out **www. tours.fr/rayonsfrais** or call ☎ 02-47-21-62-62 for more information.

Top 20 Châteaux of the Loire

Embarking on a journey across the Loire Valley is like crossing the Valley of the Kings who once favored it. It's also a great way to soak up the local culture, fill your belly with delicious local cuisine, and feast your peepholes on wondrous sites that have withstood the hardships of time. Châteaux tend to be well signposted, so grab a worthy steed (see "Rental Vehicles" in "Tours," above), a decent map, and away you fly! Don't forget to build in extra time for wine-tasting.

1. Châteaudun ★★: It's Spooky!

103km (64 miles) SW of Paris, 43km (27 miles) SW of Chartres. Visiting time: 1½ hr.

Any skeletons in your closets? Bring them along to the austere and foreboding Château de Châteaudun, which looks menacing enough to have a few hidden bones of its own. The castle stands on a bluff over a tributary of the Loire, and it's the first one you'll spot coming from Paris. Begun in the Middle Ages, it is a mix of medieval, Gothic, and Renaissance architecture, with towering chimneys and dormers. From the 12th century, the keep is one of the earliest circular keeps in the region. After a fire in the 18th century, Hardouin, Louis XV's architect, directed the town's reconstruction and turned over the castle to the homeless, who stripped it of its finery. In 1935, the government acquired the fortress and launched a restoration. Even today, it's not richly furnished, but you'll dig the fine tapestries, depicting scenes such as the worship of the golden calf, and the two stunning carved staircases. Inside the Ste-Chapelle, dating from the Middle Ages, are more than a dozen 15th-century robed statues (look out for St. Mary the Egyptian, clothed only in her own hair). In 2002, the curators added a permanent exhibit honoring Jean Dunois, the bastard son of Louis I of Orléans and comrade-in-arms to the English-hating Joan of Arc. *Place Jean-de-Dunois.* ☎ *02-37-94-02-90. Admission 6.10€, 4.10€ for ages 18–25, free for kids under 18. Daily Apr–Sept 9:30am–6:15pm (until 7pm July–Aug), Oct–Mar 10am–12:30pm and 2–5pm.*

Getting There

Buses arrive daily from Chartres (trip time: 45 min.), depending on the season. One-way fare is around 12€. For schedules, call the station, Gare Routière, Chartres ☎ **02-37-18-59-00.** Trains from Paris's Gare d'Austerlitz take 90 minutes to Châteaudun. Check with the **SNCF** (☎ **36-35**) or the **Office de Tourisme** (1 rue de Luynes; ☎ **02-37-45-22-46;** www.ville-chateaudun.com) for schedules. If you're **driving** from Paris, head southwest along A10 and exit at Phivars. Then take N10, following signs for Châteaudun.

2. Beaugency: The Seat of Anglo-French Rivalry

150km (93 miles) SW of Paris, 85km (53 miles) NE of Tours. Visiting time: 2 hr.

One of the most important events in medieval history took place here: the 1152 annulment of the marriage of Eleanor of Aquitaine and her cousin, Louis VII. After 10 years of marriage, Eleanor and Louis found themselves in Palestine on the Second Crusade, where Louis grew jealous of Eleanor's flirtations with Raymond de Poitiers. The couple returned to France separately, divorce pending, and once the wedding was annulled for "prohibited kinship," Eleanor ran off with Henry II of England, bringing southwestern France as her dowry. This single union would lead to centuries of Anglo-French tensions, but it also gave the world Richard the Lion-Hearted, their son. (The film *The Lion in Winter* dramatizes these events.)

The best way to enter Beaugency is from the south, over a 14th-century bridge that's unusual for its 26 arches, each in a different style. Cute and cobbled, the town is an archaeological garden called the City of the Lords, named after the counts who enjoyed great power here in the Middle Ages.

On your quest for châteaux, you should visit the 15th-century **Château Dunois,** a brooding, foreboding, and impressive building with historical links that stretch back to almost-mystical medieval antecedents. It was built on the foundations of an earlier château from about A.D. 1000, known as the *Château des Sires de Beaugency* (château of the lords of Beaugency), whose feudal power extended

throughout the region. Astride the street (la rue du Pont) that leads to one of the château's secondary entrances, the Voûte St-Georges (St. George's Vault) is an arched gateway from the earlier château.

Inside is **Le Musée des Arts et Traditions Populaires de l'Orléanais** (Musée Daniel Vannier), which contains a folklore museum of the Orléans district. The collection includes antique toys, hairpieces, furniture, costumes, paintings, and sculpture. *2 place Dunois.* ☎ *02-38-44-55-23. Admission 5.50€ adults. Apr–Sept, admission includes a mostly French-language guided tour that runs 6 times daily during open hours. Wed–Sun 10am–noon and 2–5pm (to 6:30pm in summer).*

Getting There

If you're **driving** from Blois to Beaugency, take D951 northeast. About 20 **trains** (☎ **36-35**) per day run between Beaugency and either Blois or Orléans; each trip takes 20 minutes. From Orléans, about eight **buses** a day make the trip to Beaugency. For bus schedules and information, call the station in Orléans (☎ **02-38-53-94-75**). The **Office de Tourisme** is at 3 place du Dr.-Hyvernaud (☎ **02-38-44-54-42**).

Sleeping & Eating

➜**Abbaye de Beaugency** ★ Go on—treat yourself to this very "doable" hotel and restaurant. It's the oldest hotel in Beaugency, built in 1640 as a monastery. It has an elegant brick facade that makes you think you're actually staying in a château, and it sits beside the Loire with a view of the old bridge. What else can one ask for? The rooms, in the old monks' cells, are poshed up in creams and dark wooden flooring. The restaurant, with its 26€ to 36€ menus, has a cheese board so delicious you'll wish you'd been born a mouse. *2 quai de l'Abbaye.* ☎ *02-38-44-67-35. www.hotel-abbaye-beaugency. com. 92€–108€ double; 98€–128€ suite. Credit cards accepted. Amenities: Restaurant; bar; 24-hr. drinks-only room service; nonsmoking rooms. In room: TV.*

📺 (Best 👍) 3. Chambord ★★: The Renaissance Rocks

191km (118 miles) SW of Paris, 18km (11 miles) E of Blois. Visiting time: 2 hr.

When François I said, "Come on over to my place," he meant the Château de Chambord. And *oh là là*, what a place! Some 2,000 workers began "the pile" in 1519. What emerged 20 years later was the pinnacle of the French Renaissance, the largest château in the Loire Valley. When Charles V of Germany visited, nymphets in transparent veils tossed wildflowers in his path as a welcome. Monarchs such as Henri II and Catherine de Médicis, Louis XIII, and Henri III came and went from Chambord. But none loved it like François I—and it's not hard to see why. Set in more than 5,260 hectares (13,000 acres) of parkland, enclosed by a wall stretching some 32km (20 miles), Chambord is stunning, with its facade dominated by four monumental towers. The three-story keep has a spectacular terrace from which the ladies of the court used to watch their men return from hunting. The keep also encloses a corkscrew staircase, superimposed upon itself so that one person may descend and a second ascend without ever meeting (handy for illicit rendezvous). *41250 Bracieux ☎ 08-25-82-60-88. www.chambord.org. Admission 8.50€ adults, 6€ 18–25. In the summer, the castle comes to life in a musical and lighting extravaganza called Son-et-Lumière. Call for more information. Daily Apr–Sept 9am–6:15pm, Oct–Mar 9am–5:15pm.*

Getting There

Once again, it's best to **drive** to Chambord. Take D951 northeast from Blois to Ménars, turning onto the rural road to Chambord. You can also rent a **bicycle** in Blois and ride the 18km (11 miles) to Chambord, or take a **tour** to Chambord from Blois in summer. From June 15 to September 15, **Transports du Loir et Cher** (☎ 02-54-58-55-61) runs bus service to Chambord, leaving Blois at 9am and 1:30pm with return trips at 1 and 6pm.

The **Office de Tourisme** on place St-Michel, near Bracieux (☎ 02-54-33-39-16), is open mid-June to October. Call them for information on special tours.

Sleeping & Eating

➔ **Hôtel du Grand-St-Michel** If you spend the night here, dine in the on-site restaurant in a fine spot overlooking the château, which is dramatically floodlit at night. Ask for a front room if you want a view over the château, but don't expect anything fashionable. Trends get bypassed in these parts, and accommodations are comfortable but provincial in terms of decor. (Remember this joint was built as a kennel for the royal hounds.) The wicked little restaurant has a huge summer terrace, great grub, and an even greater wine list. *103 place St-Michel, 41250 Chambord, near Bracieux. ☎ 02-54-20-31-31. 49€–79€ double. Credit cards accepted. Closed mid-Nov to mid-Dec. Amenities: Restaurant; tennis court. In room: TV.*

4. Blois: Fit for a King

180km (112 miles) SW of Paris, 60km (37 miles) NE of Tours. Visiting time: 1½ hr. château, 2 hr. town.

For a wee town of 55,000, Blois (pronounced "Blwah") gets a hell of a lot of visitors (more than half a million a year), who flock primarily to the château and then discover a living museum of cobblestone streets, medieval alleyways, and restored white houses with slate roofs and red-brick chimneys.

Getting There

The Paris-Austerlitz line via Orléans runs to Blois in 2 hours, and there are also regular trains from Tours (40 min.). Call ☎ 35-36. The train station is at place de la Gare. From June to September, you can take a **bus** (☎ 02-54-90-41-41) from the Blois train station to tour châteaux in the area, including Chambord, Chaumont, Chenonceau, and Amboise. If you're **driving** from Tours, take RN152 east to Blois. If you'd like to explore the area by

bike, go to **Le Blond Claude,** 44 levée des Tuileries (☎ 02-54-74-30-13), where rentals cost 6€ to 12€ per day. You must leave your passport, a credit card, a driver's license, or a deposit of 250€. The **Office de Tourisme** is at 23 place du Château (☎ 02-54-90-41-41; www.loire deschateaux.com). It provides much info on all the Loire châteaux and organizes tours.

Orientation & Sightseeing

If you have money to spare, invest in a hat or visit the high-end clothes, perfume, shoe, and jewelry shops around **rue St-Martin** and **rue du Commerce.** For the kids back home (or the big kid that is yourself), stop at **Au Paradis des Enfants,** in a 15th-century house at 2 rue des Trois-Clefs (☎ 02-54-78-09-68). You'll find yourself in the middle of an ongoing toy story. To decorate your new château (honestly, you'll feel inclined to call the builders after a day in the Loire), you'll find tapestries at **Tapisserie Langlois,** Voûte du Château (☎ 02-54-78-04-43; www.langlois-blois.com). Biscuit lovers should flock to **La Biscuiterie des Châteaux** (17 place du Château; ☎ 02-54-58-80-97); chocoholics will find their poison at **Max Vauché** (50 rue du Commerce; ☎ 02-54-78-23-55); and on Saturday mornings, a **food market** on rue St-Lubin and place Louis XII lines several blocks in the center of town at the foot of the château. It's ideal for picnic fixings.

→ **Château de Blois** ★ ★ Dig this gruesome story: A wound in battle earned the Duc de Guise the name Balafré (Scarface), but he was nevertheless a ladies' man. Indeed, on the misty morning of December 23, 1588, the Duc de Guise had just left the arms of one of Catherine de Médicis's ladies-in-waiting when his archrival, King Henri III, summoned him. When the duke arrived, however, only the king's minions

were about, and they attacked the duke with daggers. Wounded, he made for the door, where more guards awaited him. Staggering, the duke fell to the floor in a pool of his own blood. Only then did Henri emerge from behind the curtains. "Mon Dieu," he reputedly exclaimed, "He's taller dead than alive!" The body couldn't be shown; the duke was too popular. So he was quartered and burned in a fireplace.

The Duc de Guise's murder is only one of the grisly events associated with the Château de Blois. Blois soon became a palace of exile, when Louis XIII banished his poor mother, Marie de Médicis, to the château. But she escaped by sliding into the moat down a mound of dirt left by the builders.

Standing in the courtyard is like being in that architectural textbook I mentioned in the intro. The Hall of the Estates-General is a beautiful 13th-century work; Louis XII built the Charles d'Orléans gallery and the Louis XII wing from 1498 to 1501. Mansart constructed the Gaston d'Orléans wing between 1635 and 1637. Most remarkable is the François I wing, a French Renaissance masterpiece, containing a spiral staircase with ornamented balustrades and the king's symbol, the salamander.

Like Chambord, the château presents a *son-et-lumière* show in French, from May to September (in English on Wed). ☎ 02-54-90-33-33. www.ville-blois.fr. Admission 6.50€ adults, 5€ students. Oct–Mar daily 9am–12:30pm and 2–5.30pm; Apr–Sept daily 9am–6.30pm.

→ **Maison de la Magie** This is one of the kitschiest magic shows on earth, opposite the château. Unmissable from the outside, thanks to six golden dragonheads sticking out of the windows, it will teach you all about magic through the ages. You can also see a show and pick up a few tricks yourself. *1 place du Château.* ☎ *02-54-55-26-26. www.maisondelamagie.fr. Admission 7.50€ adults, 6.50€ students. Mar 25–Sept 24 and school holidays daily 10am–12:30pm and 2–6pm.*

Sleeping

Some of the best rooms in town are at **Le Médicis** (see "Eating," below).

Two hostels on the outskirts of Blois, **Montlivault** (Levée de la Loire, Vineuil; ☎ 02-54-78-27-21) and **Les Grouëts** (18 rue de l'Hôtel Pasquier, Les Grouëts; ☎ 02-54-78-27-21), provide good, cheap accommodations in the countryside. Beds in both cost 10€. And both are accessible by bus from Blois on Line 1 **(Montlivault)** and Line 4 **(Les Grouëts).** For further details, see **www.fuaj.org**.

→ **Hôtel le Savoie** Okay, it's not like staying in a castle, but this modern 1930s-era hotel is both inviting and livable—from its courteous staff to its guest rooms, which are quiet, cozy, and oh-so vintage. Bathrooms, each with a shower, are tiny but have sufficient shelf space. The breakfast buffet will set you up for the day ahead, with pastries and plenty of toast. *6–8 rue du Docteur-Ducoux.* ☎ *02-54-74-32-21. www.hotel-blois.com. Doubles 45€–57€. Amenities: Bar; nonsmoking rooms. In room: TV.*

Eating

→ **Le Médicis** ★ TRADITIONAL FRENCH Christian and Annick Garanger run a super inn 15 minutes away from the château. The grub is mainly seafood, with gourmet goodies such as asparagus in mousseline sauce, scampi ravioli with saffron sauce, and suprême of perch with morels. Coco addicts will love the chocolate Valrhona mousse dessert. And when your gut's busted, you can sleep it off in one of their air-conditioned rooms upstairs—a steal at 87€ to 92€ a night. *2 allée François Ier.* ☎ *02-54-43-94-04. www.le-medicis.com.*

Reservations required. Fixed-price menu 22€–68€. Credit cards accepted. Daily noon–2pm and 7–9pm. Closed Jan and Sun nights Nov–Mar.

→ **L'Orangerie du Château** ★★★ TOURAINE Next door to the château, one of the castle's former outbuildings holds the swankest and most scrumptious restaurant in the area. This is a hangout for local big-wig foodies. When you take your seat, look debonair, look confident, and look like you know what Sauvignon de Touraine is (one of the best local wines on the menu). You'll delight in chef Jean-Marc Molveaux's filet mignon with truffles, medley of shellfish and nuts in cream sauce, and melted chocolate and pistachio with crème fraîche dessert. *1 av. Jean-Laigret.* ☎ *02-54-78-05-36. Reservations required. Fixed-price menu 31€–65€. Credit cards accepted. Thurs–Tues noon–1:45pm; Thurs–Sat and Mon–Tues 7:15–9:15pm. Closed mid-Feb to mid-Mar.*

Partying

Nightlife isn't booming here, but there's a healthy selection of venues. Mosey on down to the fun and friendly **L'Hendrix Café** (1 rue du Puits-Châtel; ☎ **02-54-78-04-36**), or **The Riverside** (3 rue Henri-Drussy; ☎ **02-54-78-33-79**). If you're a jazz freak but can't stand smoke, try the **Velvet Jazz Lounge** (15 bis rue Haute; ☎ **02-54-78-36-32**)—a hip music den decorated with a deep-orange vaulted ceiling, and Blois's first entirely nonsmoking venue.

5. Cheverny ★★: So Posh!

192km (119 miles) SW of Paris, 19km (12 miles) SE of Blois. Visiting time: 2 hr.

Indulging in aristocratic activities is just so difficult these days. The upper crust heads to the Sologne area for the hunt as if the 17th century had never ended. But 21st-century realities—say, formidable taxes—mean that

THE LOIRE VALLEY

the Château de Cheverny must open some of its rooms to visitors. *Quelle horreur!*

Unlike most of the Loire châteaux, Cheverny is the residence of the original owner's descendants. The family of the *vicomte* de Sigalas can trace its lineage to Henri Hurault, the son of the chancellor of Henri III and Henri IV, who built the first château in 1634. Its history reads like something out of a historical B movie. Upon finding his wife shagging a page, Hurault killed the page and offered his spouse a choice: She could swallow poison or have his sword plunged into her heart. She elected the less bloody method, and he tore down the castle and rebuilt it for his second wife. Designed in classic Louis XIII style, it boasts square pavilions flanking the central pile. If you're an antiques fan, you'll love the furnishings, tapestries, and *objets d'art*. A 17th-century French artist, Jean Mosnier, decorated the fireplace with motifs from the legend of Adonis, the Guards' Room contains a collection of medieval armor, and an ace Gobelin tapestry depicts the abduction of Helen of Troy.

If you've ever read *Tin Tin*, you might have noticed a resemblance between Cheverny and Captain Haddock's Moulinsart château. That is because the Belgium comic strip artist Hergé based Moulinsart on Cheverny, hence the Tin Tin museum, which you should visit in the castle's old *Salle des Trophées*. *Cheverny.* ☎ *02-54-79-96-29. www.chateau-cheverny. fr. Admission is 6.30€ adults, 4.20€ students. Daily Oct–Mar 9:45am–5pm; Apr–June and Sept 9:15am–6:15pm; July–Aug 9:15am–6:45pm.*

Getting There

Cheverny is 19km (12 miles) south of Blois, along D765. It's best reached by **car** or **bus tour** from Blois with **Transports du Loir et Cher** (☎ 02-54-58-55-61). From the railway station at Blois, a bus departs for Cheverny once a day at noon, returning to Blois 4 hours later, according to an oft-changing schedule. If you prefer making your own timetables, hire a car or jump in a **taxi** from the railway station at Blois.

Sleeping & Eating

→ **St-Hubert** TRADITIONAL FRENCH Get your taste buds ready: Here you can munch on the cheap on quail, thigh of roebuck in pepper sauce, cheeses, and a fruit tart. For a splurge, try the lobster, an *aiguillette* of duckling prepared with grapes, or a casserole of seafood with shellfish sauce. It's just about 500m (1,640 ft.) from the château. If you make Cheverny your night-time pit stop, you can stay in one of 20 no-frills rooms with TVs for 50€ to 58€ for a double. *122 rte. Nationale, 41700 Cour-Cheverny.* ☎ *02-54-79-96-60. www. hotel-sthubert.com. Fixed-price menu 15€–38€. Credit cards accepted. Daily 12:15–2pm and 7:30–9pm. Closed Jan, Sun night off season.*

6. Valençay ★★: It's a Looker!

233km (145 miles) SW of Paris, 56km (35 miles) S of Blois. Visiting time: 1½ hr.

If châteaux were supermodels, the Château de Valençay would be splattered over every glossy on earth. It's one of the Loire's most handsome Renaissance châteaux, and boy does it ooze chic. Talleyrand acquired it in 1803 on the orders of Napoleon, who wanted his minister of foreign affairs to receive dignitaries in style. The d'Estampes family built Valençay in 1540, after tearing down a 12th-century château. The dungeon and west tower date to this period, as does the main body of the building. Other wings were added in the 17th and 18th centuries. The effect is seriously grandiose, with domes and turrets.

As was his wont, Napoleon stamped his Empire decor ideas on the château, but in the private apartments you can still admire a few Louis XV and Louis XVI trappings, before ambling around the perfectly pruned French gardens and deer park, which actually contains llamas, peacocks, and kangaroos. ☎ *02-54-00-15-69. www.musee-jacquemart-andre. com/valencay. Admission to the castle, car museum (see below), and park 8.50€ adults, 6.50€ students. Apr–June daily 9:30am–6pm; July–Aug daily 9:30am–7:30pm; Sept–Mar by reservation only.*

Sightseeing

→ **Musée de l'Automobile** If you're motor-mad and love old stuff, don't miss this little gem opposite the castle. It features a collection of more than 60 antique automobiles (mostly French), including a nifty Bédélia (ca. 1914)—a sort of tandem-style vehicle (the driver rode behind the passenger) with a pulley-operated two-speed gearshift. It's the rarest item in the collection. *Rte. du Blois, 12 av. de la Résistance.* ☎ *02-54-00-07-74. Admission 5€ ($6.50) for adults, 2.50€ ($3.25) for children 7–17, free for children under 7. Daily July–Aug 10:30am–12:30pm and 1:30–7:30pm; daily mid-Mar to June and Sept–Oct 10am–12:30pm and 2–6pm. Closed Nov to mid-Mar.*

Getting There

If you're **driving** from Tours, take N76 east, turning south on D956 to Valençay. From Blois, follow D956 south. SNCF operates **rail** service from Blois. Call ☎ **36-35.**

The **Office de Tourisme** is at 2 av. de Résistance (☎ **02-54-00-04-42**).

Eating & Sleeping

→ **Hôtel Le Relais du Moulin** For your money, you can't do better than this cute hotel with a swimming pool. Five minutes from the entrance to the château, it sits adjacent to a stream and the now-disabled water wheel of an 18th-century textile mill, which produced fabrics for curtains, clothing, and upholsteries during the age of Talleyrand and Napoleon. The bedrooms are outfitted with contemporary-looking furniture, tones of pale yellow and soft red, and views that overlook the château, the river, vineyards, and the park surrounding the hotel and the château. As if that weren't enough, you can pork out on decent traditional food for 17€ to 38€. *95 rte. Nationale, 36600 Valençay.* ☎ *02-54-00-38-00. www.hotel-lerelaisdumoulin.com. 60€ double. Credit cards accepted. Closed Nov–Mar. Amenities: Restaurant; bar; exercise room; indoor pool; limited-mobility rooms; sauna. In room: TV, minibar.*

7. Chaumont-sur-Loire ★★: A Sad Old Affair

200km (124 miles) SW of Paris, 40km (25 miles) E of Tours. Visiting time: 2 hr.

Poor Diane de Poitiers! When she first crossed the drawbridge, the Château de Chaumont must have looked grim as hell. Her lover, Henri II, had recently died, and although he had given her Chenonceau, his angry widow, Catherine de Médicis, forced Diane to trade it in for the less ornate Chaumont. By today's standards, you'll see it wasn't that bad a deal. Battlements and pepper-pot turrets are straight out of a Shrek movie, and the interior is full of portraits demonstrating that Diane deserved her reputation as forever beautiful.

The noble Charles d'Amboise built Chaumont ("burning mount") during the reign of Louis XII. Overlooking the Loire, it's approached by a pretty (and very long) walk up from the village through a tree-studded park. The castle spans the period between the Middle Ages and the Renaissance, and its prize exhibit is a collection of medallions by the Italian artist Nini. A guest of the château, he made medallion portraits of kings, queens, nobles, and dignitaries—including Benjamin Franklin, who once visited. In Catherine de Médicis's bedroom, you can see a portrait of the Italian-born queen. The superstitious Catherine housed her astrologer, Cosimo Ruggieri, in one of the tower rooms (you can see his portrait), where he reportedly foretold the disasters awaiting her sons (what a healthy person to have around). In Ruggieri's room, a tapestry depicts Medusa with a flying horse escaping from her head. ☎ *02-54-51-26-26. Admission 6.10€ adults, 4.10€ students. Daily year-round (except Jan 1, May 1, Nov 1, Nov 11, and Dec 25). Mar 15–Oct 18 9:30am–6:30pm and Oct 19–Mar 14 10am–4pm.*

Getting There

Plenty of **trains** run each day between Chaumont and Blois (trip time: 15 min.) and Tours (about 45 min.). The railway station serving Chaumont is in Onzain, 2.5km (2 miles) north of the château, and makes for a nice walk. By **car** from Blois, take the N152 then the D1 left into Chaumont-sur-Loire.

The **Office de Tourisme** is on rue du Maréchal-Leclerc (☎ **02-54-20-91-73;** www.chaumontsurloire.info).

Sleeping & Eating

➜ **Hostellerie du Château** You should-n't need to sleep in town, but if you do, you can't get closer to the château than this renovated, half-timbered inn with a terrace-flanked pool. You'll heave a con-tented sigh when you see that your accommodations open onto the riverbank of the Loire. The on-site restaurant serves replenishing regional specialties. *2 rue Maréchal de-Lattre-de-Tassigny, 41150 Chaumont-sur-Loire.* ☎ *02-54-20-98-04. 58€–141€ double. Credit cards accepted. Amenities: Restaurant; bar; laundry serv-ice; outdoor pool. In room: TV, hair dryer.*

MTV Best❶ 8. Amboise: Good Enough for da Vinci, Good Enough for Jagger

219km (136 miles) SW of Paris, 35km (22 miles) E of Tours. Visiting time: 4 hr.

The good news: This is a real Renaissance town. The bad news: Because it is so beautiful, tour buses overrun it, especially in summer. And many townspeople are still bitter about Mick Jagger's purchase of a nearby château. In any case, long before the time of pop stars, geniuses such as Leonardo da Vinci inhabited this land. Da Vinci spent his last few years here, and you may well make a pact to come back before the Grim Reaper gets you—the mystique of medieval France remains strangely hypnotic. The château visit takes about 1½ hours, but you should allow extra time for ambling around the town and visiting the out-of-town attractions listed below.

Getting There

Amboise is on the Paris-Blois-Tours **train** line. The trip from both Tours and Blois takes around 20 minutes. About five con-ventional trains a day leave from Paris's Gare d'Austerlitz (trip time: 2¹/₂ hr.), and several high-speed TGV trains (trip time: 1¹/₂ hr.) depart from the Gare Montparnasse for St-Pierre-des-Corps, less than a kilometer from Tours. From St-Pierre-des-Corps, you

can transfer to a conventional train to Amboise. For information, call ☎ **36-35.** By **bus,** try **Autocars de Touraine** (☎ 02-47-57-00-44), which operates out of the Gare Routière in Tours just across from the railway station, and runs about six trips a day between Tours and Amboise. The one-way trip takes about 40 minutes and costs less than 4€. By **car** from Tours, take N152 east to D32, then turn south and following the signs.

The **Office de Tourisme** is on quai du Général-de-Gaulle (☎ 02-47-57-01-37). Make it your first port of call. They have piles of leaflets on all sorts of activities in and around Amboise.

Orientation & Sightseeing

➜ **Château d'Amboise** ★★ Old Charlie VIII sure knew how to pick his spot: a rocky spur separating the valleys of the Loire and the Amasse, in the center of vineyards known as Touraine-Amboise. This 15th-century château, which domi-nates the town, was the first in France to reflect the Italian Renaissance, combining both Gothic and Renaissance styles. You enter on a ramp that opens onto a panoramic terrace with amazing river views. At one time, buildings surrounded this terrace, and fêtes took place in the enclosed courtyard. But, alas, it all fell into decline during the Revolution, and today only about a quarter of the once-sprawling edifice remains. You come first to the flamboyant Gothic **Chapelle de St-Hubert,** distinguished by its lacelike trac-ery and rumored to contain the tomb of great Leonardo da Vinci himself. In the rest of the château, mainly the royal chambers, grand tapestries cover the walls. The **Logis du Roi** (king's apart-ment) was built against the **Tour des Minimes** (also known as the Tour des Cavaliers), which once had a ramp for horsemen. The other notable tower is the

Heurtault, which is broader than the Minimes and leads to the town. ☎ 02-47-57-00-98. *www.chateau-amboise.com. Admission 7.70€ adults, 6.50€ students. July–Aug daily 9am–7pm; Apr–Jun daily 9am–6:30pm; Sept–Oct daily 9am–6pm; Nov 1–15 daily 9am–5:30pm; Nov 16–Jan daily 9am–noon and 2–4:45pm; Feb–Mar 15 daily 9am–noon and 1:30–5:30pm; Mar 16–31 daily 9am–6pm.*

→ **Château du Clos-Lucé** ★ You can't come to Amboise and ignore the fact that Leonardo da Vinci lived here. His quaint brick-and-stone building, constructed in the 1400s, served as a retreat for Anne de Bretagne. According to legend, she spent a lot of time there praying and meditating. Later, François I installed "the great master in all forms of art and science," in the house. Da Vinci lived there for 3 years, until his death in 1519. (The paintings of Leonardo dying in François's arms are probably symbolic; the king was supposedly out of town at the time.) Today, the site is a tiny museum, offering insights into Leonardo's life and a sense of the decorative arts of the era. The manor contains furniture from his era; examples of his sketches; models for his flying machines, bridges, and cannons; and even a primitive example of a machine gun.

2 rue de Clos-Lucé. ☎ *02-47-57-00-73. www.vinci-closluce.com. May–Nov admission 12€ adults, 9€ students. Nov–Apr admission 8.50€ adults, 6.50€ students. Jan daily 10am–5pm; Feb–Mar and Nov–Dec daily 9am–6pm; Apr–June and Sept–Oct daily 9am–7pm; July–Aug daily 9am–8pm. Closed Jan 1 and Dec 25.*

Out of Town

The geeky **Parc des Mini-Châteaux,** on the outskirts of Amboise, is like Disneyland revisited for Lilliputians in the Loire—with pint-size replicas of the Loire's most famous castles (built at $^{1}/_{25}$ the size of the originals). Chambord, for example, is less than 3.5m (12 ft.) tall. Admission is 12€ for adults, 8€ for students. Open April to mid-November, with occasional closures based on the school calendar. Hours vary according to the season; call ahead for information. To drive here from Amboise, follow signs to Tours and take RD751 along the Loire's southern bank.

Nearby, the **Pagode de Chanteloup** ★★ is a perfect picnic stop. On the edge of Amboise Forest is a 44m-high (144-ft.) Chinese pagoda commissioned by the Duke of Choiseul (Louis XV's minister) in the 18th century. It is the only remaining part of his château, built as a replica to

Bill Gates's Da Vinci Codex

What is the link between a medieval genius and the 21st century's most prominent tech tycoon? A CD-ROM, of course. When Leonardo da Vinci died in le Clos-Lucé in 1519, he left behind thousands of manuscript pages on engineering, music, sculpture, painting, and the sciences. These all went to his faithful student Francesco Melzi, who, upon his own death in 1570, divided the documents among his heirs into codex. The largest chunk, the *Codex Atlanticus,* is in the Biblioteca Ambrosiana in Milan. Bill Gates managed to get his mitts on the smallest volume, the *Codex Leicester.* It's the only section that's privately owned, and it cost the multibillionaire $30 million. The original pages occasionally work their way around world exhibitions, but their fragility has led Gates to do what he does best—put them on a CD-ROM so that everyone can see them for generations to come.

THE LOIRE VALLEY

Versailles (sinfully demolished in 1823 by estate agents), and a must-see if you get off on architectural eccentricities. *3km (2 miles) south of Amboise via the D31. Chanteloup nr. Amboise.* ☎ *02-47-57-20-97. Admission 6.30€. July–Aug daily 9:30am–7:30pm; June daily 10am–7pm; May and Sept daily 10am–6:30pm, Mar–Apr Mon–Fri 10am–noon and 2–6pm and Sat–Sun 10am–6pm; Oct–Nov weekends and public holidays 10am–5pm.*

Sleeping

→ **Belle-Vue** Okay, so it's not plush. In fact, it's shabby around the edges and exudes the conservatism of the Loire Valley of 25 years ago. But, built of stone in the mid–18th century, in the shadow of the château, it's a great base for touring the castle and befriending others doing the same. The rooms are small and nostalgically furnished. All have en-suite bathrooms. Breakfast is the only meal served. *12 quai Charles-Guinot, 37400 Amboise.* ☎ *02-47-57-02-26. 55€–69€ double. Credit cards accepted. Closed Nov 15–Mar 15. Amenities: Bar; limited-mobility rooms. In room: TV.*

→ **Café des Arts** This little joint is dead central and dirt cheap. You might feel like Ma and Pa built you the bunk beds here (no midnight cuddles for you couples out there), but the rooms are clean and comfortable with a sink and a bidet. WC and bathroom are shared. And did I mention that it's cheap? Very cheap. *32 rue Victor Hugo.* ☎ *02-47-57-25-04. 20€ single; 33€ double; 47€ triple. Credit cards accepted. Closed in Nov. Breakfast 6€. Food and snacks available.*

→ **Le Fleuray** ★ It's out of the center, but if you're lucky, Mick Jagger will be in residence. This well-maintained pink stucco manor house is his retreat when the going gets tough. It will charm you with masses of geraniums, marigolds, and flowering vines that adorn the masonry in warm weather, homelike rooms dotted with antique accessories, and a handy swimming pool. The food's top-notch, too. Locals flock here for delights such as dates stuffed with warm Roquefort cheese, pork pâté with onions and chutney, and Creole-style chicken in curry-flavored cream sauce garnished with pineapples (fixed-price menus 28€–38€). *Rte. Dame Marie, 37530 Cangey, near Amboise.* ☎ *02-47-56-09-25. www.lefleurayhotel.com. 78€–115€ double. Credit cards accepted. Free parking. From Amboise, take N152 northeast of town, following signs to Blois; 12km (7 miles) from Amboise, turn onto D74 toward Cangey. Amenities: Restaurant; bar; limited-mobility rooms; nonsmoking rooms; outdoor pool. In room: TV, hair dryer.*

Eating

The restaurant at **Le Fleuray** is fantastic (see "Sleeping," above).

→ **Brasserie de l'Hôtel de Ville** FRENCH Smack-bang in the middle of the historic core, this is a bustling brasserie that would be more at home in Paris than Amboise. You'll rub shoulders with local office workers, art lovers, and boisterous groups of friends at night. Expect noise, noise, and more noise, all focused on rows of banquettes, hassled waiters, and steaming platters that emerge speedily from the overworked kitchen. Cuisine is deliciously old-fashioned with grandma's favorites such as *sole meunière*, grilled beefsteak with french fries, *pot-au-feu*, calves' liver, and dishes from France's Southwest, including a very savory cassoulet. *3 rue François Ier.* ☎ *02-47-57-26-30. Reservations recommended. Fixed-price menu 11€; a la carte 25€–30€. Credit cards accepted. Daily 10am–3pm and 7–9:30pm.*

🅼🆅 Best⦿ 9. Chenonceau ★★: Renaissance Masterpiece

224km (139 miles) SW of Paris, 26km (16 miles) E of Tours. Visiting time: 2 hr.

Love triangles never work out, and the Château de Chenonceau is proof. In 1547, Henri II gave the château to his beautiful mistress, Diane de Poitiers—who for a time was virtually queen of France, infuriating Henri's dour wife, Catherine de Médicis. When Henri died, Catherine became regent (her eldest son was still a child) and took revenge by forcing Diane to return the jewelry Henri had given her and abandon her beloved home.

Chenonceau is one of the most remarkable castles in France. It spans an entire river, and the way the waters of the Cher surge and foam beneath its vaulted medieval foundations really does look mystical. Inside, you can marvel at yet more Gobelin tapestries (p. 439), including one of a woman pouring water over the back of an angry dragon. The chapel contains a marble *Virgin and Child* by Murillo as well as portraits of Catherine de Médicis in black and white. Catherine added her own touches, building a two-story gallery inspired by her native Florence across the bridge.

The history of Chenonceau is related in 15 tableaux in the **Musée de Cire (wax museum),** in a Renaissance-era annex a few steps from the château. Open the same hours as the château, it charges admission of 3.50€. Diane de Poitiers, who introduced France to the artichoke, among other things, is depicted in three tableaux. One portrays Catherine de Médicis tossing out her cuckold husband's mistress.

Chenonceaux (the village is spelled with a final "x," but the château isn't). ☎ *02-47-23-90-07. www.chenonceau.com. Admission 8€ adults, 6.50€ students. A son-et-lumière show starts at 10:15pm daily July–Aug; admission is 5€. Mid-Mar to mid-Sept daily 9am–7pm; Sept 16–Sept 30 daily 9am–6.30pm; Oct–Feb 9am–5 or 6pm.*

Getting There

Several daily **trains** run from Tours to Chenonceaux (trip time: 30 min.), depositing you at the base of the château from where you can walk or take a taxi. If you're **driving,** take the D31 S from Amboise, then the D40 E.

The **Syndicat d'Initiative** (1 rue du Dr. Bretonneau; ☎ **02-47-23-94-45**) dispenses tourist information year-round.

Sleeping & Eating

➜ **La Roseraie** ★ You can't find a better pit stop in Chenonceaux than La Roseraie. Sleep here and you'll be following in the footsteps of Winston Churchill, Eleanor Roosevelt, and Harry Truman. During World War II, the innkeeper gained fame with the Allies because of his role in smuggling Churchill's nephew out of Vichy-occupied France. The rooms are chintzy and cute (think bold-patterned wallpaper and matching bedspreads), the terraced garden inspires an evening drink, and there's a pool. The excellent dining room serves house-style foie gras, magret of duckling with pears and cherries, and an unusual and delicious invention—*emincée* (a dish made with braised meat) of rump steak with wine-marinated pears. *7 rue du Dr. Bretonneau, Chenonceaux, 37150 Bléré.* ☎ *02-47-23-90-09. www.charmingroseraie.com. 49€–95€ double; 180€ apartment. Credit cards accepted. Closed mid-Nov to mid-Feb. Amenities: Restaurant; bar; dry cleaning; laundry service; outdoor pool. In room: TV.*

Shopping

➜ **Cave des Dômes** Chenonceau also makes some great wines, bottled at the château. Pop along to this place and fill up on some. ☎ *02-47-23-90-07.*

10. Loches ★★: The Most Beautiful Dentures in History

258km (160 miles) SW of Paris, 40km (25 miles) SE of Tours. Visiting time: 3 hr.

Agnès Sorel (Charles VII's mistress) was a stunner, and her legendary beauty is forever linked to Loches—the valley's *cité médiévale,* in the hills on the banks of the Indre. A real "acropolis of the Loire," the château and its satellite buildings form a complex called the **Cité Royale** ★. If you like the early medieval period and dank dungeons, this place is for you. The House of Anjou, from which the Plantagenets descended, owned the castle from 886 to 1205, and then the kings of France occupied it from the mid-13th century until Charles IX became king in 1560.

The Château de Loches is remembered for the *belle des belles* (beauty of beauties), Agnès Sorel, whose tomb is guarded by two sculpted angels. In 1777, the tomb was opened, but all that remained of the 15th-century looker was a set of dentures and some locks of hair. Sorel was maid of honor to Isabelle de Lorraine, before Charles VII singled her out as his mistress, and she had great influence on the monarch until her mysterious death. Afterward, Fouquet painted her as a practically topless Virgin Mary, with a disgruntled Charles VII looking on. (The original is in Antwerp; the château has a copy.) If you're interested in art, you should definitely search out the triptych of *The Passion* (1485) from the Fouquet school, and horror-story fans should check out the *donjon* (see below). *5 place Charles-VII. ☎ 02-47-59-01-32. Admission to château or dungeon 3.80€ adults, 2.70€ students. Combination ticket 5.10€ adults, 3.50€ students. Apr–Sept daily 9am–7pm; Oct–Mar daily 9:30am–5pm.*

Getting There

Buses run daily from Tours; the 45-minute trip costs around 7.50€ one-way. For bus information, call ☎ 02-47-05-30-49. Trains also run from Tours and take 50 minutes. Call ☎ 36-35. If you're **driving** from Tours, take N143 southeast to Loches.

The **Office de Tourisme** is near the bus station on place de la Marne (☎ 02-47-91-82-82; www.lochestourainecotesud.com).

Sleeping & Eating

Loches is short on inns and good restaurants. If you're here for lunch, you could try the 18th-century **Hôtel George-Sand** (39 rue Quintefol; ☎ 02-47-59-39-74; www.hotelrestaurant-georgesand.com). It may look like the sort of place your grandparents would choose, but it's known for its Touraine cuisine. The rooms are equally old-fashioned, but they're cheap and, well, beggars can't be choosers. Menu-fixe starts at 20€. Doubles are 61€ to 67€.

📺 Best ⊙ 11. Villandry ★★: It's Got Green Fingers

253km (157 miles) SW of Paris, 32km (20 miles) NE of Chinon, 18km (11 miles) W of Tours. Visiting time: 2 hr.

The rustle of the trees and twittering of the birds overhead are like music to your ears in this magnificent 16th-century-style garden—one of the rare Loire parks that's more famous than its château.

The grounds contain 17km (11 miles) of boxwood sculpture, which the gardeners cut to style in only 2 weeks each September. Every square of the gardens is like a geometric mosaic. The borders symbolize the faces of love: tender, tragic (represented by daggers), and crazy (with a labyrinth that doesn't get you anywhere). Pink tulips and dahlias suggest sweet love; red, tragic; and yellow, unfaithful. All colors signify passionate love. The vine arbors, citrus hedges, and walks keep six

Feeling Cagey in Loches?

There's nothing like medieval torture to get your blood curdling. Loches' *donjon* (dungeon) was the site of many an unpleasant moment when Louis XI was in town. Cardinal Jean Balue, the king's favorite advisor, invented *le Cage*—a 2 by 2m (7 by 7 ft.) suspended prison that was occasionally modified to prevent prisoners from standing up. You entered *le Cage* and you died in *le Cage*, as Balue knew too well. After the king discovered Balue had been plotting against him with the Duke of Burgundy, he imprisoned him in 1469. He reportedly "hung around" for 11 years before he swung his last in 1480. Another noteworthy prisoner was the duke of Milan, Ludovico Sforza, who was imprisoned in the Martelet and painted frescoes on the walls to pass the time; he died here in 1508 (☎ 02-47-59-07-86).

muscled men busy full-time (calm down ladies). One garden contains all the French vegetables *except* the potato, which wasn't known in France in the 16th century.

A feudal castle once stood at Villandry. In 1536, Jean Lebreton, François I's chancellor, built the present Renaissance Château de Villandry, the buildings of which form a U, surrounded by a lovely moat. Near the gardens is a terrace from which you can see the small village and its 12th-century church. To calm hunger pangs, a handy tearoom on-site, **La Dulce Terrasse** (☎ **02-47-50-02-10**), serves up traditional Loire cooking, freshly baked bread, homemade ice cream, and cocktails made from fresh fruit. *3 rue Principale, 37510 Villandry.* ☎ *02-47-50-02-09. Admission to gardens, including a guided tour of the château, 8€ adults. Admission to gardens only, without a guide, 5.50€ adults. Gardens daily 9am–sunset (5–7:30pm). Château daily 9am–4:30 or 6:30pm, depending on a complicated seasonal schedule; call for details. Tours are conducted in French with leaflets in English.*

Getting There

Villandry has no train service. The nearest connection from Tours is at the town of Savonnières. If you're young legs are bursting with energy, you can walk along the Loire for 4km (2¹/₂ miles) from Savonnières to reach Villandry, rent a **bike** at the station, or splurge on a **taxi.** You can also **drive,** following the D7 from Tours.

Sleeping & Eating

Don't bother staying here. Villandry is best-visited as a day trip from Tours or Chinon.

12. Langeais: *The* Royal "I Do"

259km (161 miles) SW of Paris, 26km (16 miles) W of Tours. Visiting time: 1¹/₂ hr.

Had newspapers been invented, the history of Langeais would have read like this: On December 6, 1491, Anne de Bretagne arrived at Langeais. Carried in a litter decked with gold cloth, she wore a gown of gold cloth ornamented with 160 sables. Her marriage to Charles VIII was Langeais' golden hour.

➜ **Château de Langeais** ★★ The designers of Langeais evidently hadn't heard of the word *jovial* when they built this formidable gray pile that dominates the town. But it was the Middle Ages, and Langeais was originally built as a fortress. Once you get inside, however, all is forgiven. The foreboding facade and drawbridge give way to richly decorated apartments. The castle dates from the 9th century, but the present structure was built in 1465. The interior is well preserved and furnished thanks to Jacques Siegfried, who not only restored it over 20 years but bequeathed it to the Institut de France in 1904. But enough about the decor; let's get to the nitty gritty—the wedding. Anne de Bretagne and Charles VIII tied the knot here (there's a cheesy wax reenactment in one of the chambers), and their symbols—scallops, fleurs-de-lis, and ermine—still set the motif for the Guard Room. Seven tapestries known as the Valiant Knights also cover the walls of the wedding chamber, where the newlyweds would have had sex for the first time, under the eyes of the servants in waiting. No wonder the word *voyeur* comes from France! *37130 Langeais.* ☎ *02-47-96-72-60. Admission 6.50€ adults, 4€ students and under 25. July 14–Aug 20 daily 9:30am–8pm; Apr–July 14 and Aug 21–Oct 15 daily 9:30am–6:30pm; Oct 16–Mar daily 10am–5:30pm.*

Getting There

Several **trains** per day stop here en route from Tours or Saumur. Transit time from Tours is 20 minutes. For schedules and information, call ☎ **36-35.** If you're **driving** from Tours, take N152 southwest to Langeais.

The **Office de Tourisme** is at place du 14-Juillet (☎ **02-47-96-58-22**).

Sleeping & Eating

As with Villandry, you shouldn't bother eating or sleeping here.

13. Azay-le-Rideau: Don't Outdo the King, Please

261km (162 miles) SW of Paris, 21km (13 miles) SW of Tours. Visiting time: 2 hr.

What a whopper! What a beauty! Its machicolated towers and blue-slate roof pierced with dormers shimmer in the moat, creating a reflection like a Monet painting. But don't be fooled—the defensive medieval look is all for show. The Château d'Azay-le-Rideau is actually another idyllic Renaissance structure commissioned by a minister to the king who had the balls to try to outshine His Majesty (p. 136)—and then paid the price. The man in question was Gilles Berthelot, François I's finance minister, and the castle was so elegant that the Chevalier King grew jealous and accused Berthelot of misappropriating funds. Berthelot was forced to flee, and the château reverted to the king, although he didn't live here—he just granted it to "friends of the Crown."

If you're feeling intellectual, here's a tip: Before you enter, circle the château and note the château's perfect proportions—it being Touraine's crowning achievement of the Renaissance. Check out its most fancifully ornate feature—the bay enclosing a grand stairway with a straight flight of steps. The Renaissance interior is a virtual museum.

The best view in the Castle has to be from the second-floor Royal Chamber (believed to have housed Louis XIII), which looks out at the beautiful gardens. You'll also love the adjoining red chamber with a portrait gallery that includes Diane de Poitiers (Henri II's favorite) in her bath. *Admission 9€ adults, 5€ guests under 25. In warm weather, son-et-lumière performances feature recorded music and lights beaming on the exterior of the château. Daily July–Aug, 9:30am–7pm; Apr–June and Sept–Oct 9:30am–6pm; Nov–Mar 10am–12:30pm and 2–5:30pm. The shows last about 1 hr. and begin at 10:30pm May–July, 10pm Aug, and 9:30pm Sept.*

Getting There

To reach Azay-le-Rideau, take the **train** from Tours or Chinon. Trip time is about 30 minutes. Both Tours and Chinon have express service to Paris, call ☎ **36-35.** If you're **driving** from Tours, take D759 southwest to Azay-le-Rideau.

Because trains arrive at Azay-le-Rideau's railway station in relatively small numbers, some visitors prefer to travel to the railway station in nearby Tours and switch to any of the frequent buses between Tours's railway station and Azay, operated by Ste. TER, a subsidiary of the SNCF.

The **Office de Tourisme** is on 4 rue du Château (☎ **02-47-45-44-40;** www.ot-paysazaylerideau.com).

Sleeping & Eating

➜ **Le Grand Monarque** As you've probably noticed by now, most sleeping places in the Loire Valley have decent restaurants. This place is no different. And while there's nothing hip about the decor (the ivy that covers the exterior of this hotel must have magical powers to protect it from the modern world), there is plenty of pizzazz on the plates. Get a load of this: brochette of crayfish with sesame sauce, suprême of *sandre* (a freshwater fish) in shallot-flavored broth, and galette of pig's foot *en confit.* If that doesn't tempt you, this may: terrine of stingray with celery, steak of mullet prepared with the local wine of Azay, and a kettle of crayfish with a bouillon of mushrooms. Considering what you get, the prices aren't so bad: Fixed-price menus range from 28€ to 55€. During warmer months, you can dine out on the courtyard, which looks like something out of a 19th-century romance novel. In February, March, October, and November, the restaurant closes on Sunday night, on Monday, and for Tuesday and Friday lunch. *3 place de la République, 37190 Azay-le-Rideau.* ☎ *02-47-45-40-08. www.legrandmonarque.com. 52€–125€ double. Credit cards accepted. Closed Dec–Jan. Amenities: Parking 6€, Restaurant; bar; laundry service. In room: TV.*

Funky Literary Venue: Buzzin' Balzac

Four kilometers (2½ miles) east of Azay-le-Rideau (take D17), you can visit **Saché,** the hometown of Honoré de Balzac. It was here that he wrote *The Lily of the Valley* and declared that his affection for the Touraine was like "the love of the artist for his art." It's a bit la-dee-dah, but worth a stop if you're into high-brow haunts. The **Musée Balzac** (37190 Saché; ☎ **02-47-26-86-50;** admission 3.80€ adults, 2.70€ students, 2.50€ kids 7–18, free for kids under 7), in the 19th-century Château de Saché, contains the writer's bedrooms, preserved as they were when he lived here. A collection of Balzac's notes, first editions, etchings, letters, and cartoons are also on display, as is a copy of Rodin's sculpture of the writer. Open daily April to September 9am to 7pm, October to March 9:30am to 12:30pm and 2 to 5:30pm.

14. Chinon: Joan of Arc & the Booze

283km (175 miles) SW of Paris, 48km (30 miles) SW of Tours, 31km (19 miles) SW of Langeais. Visiting time: 3 hr.

One of the oldest fortress-châteaux in France, Chinon is where Joan of Arc pleaded with Charles the Dauphin—the future French king Charles VII—to take action against the English in 1429, during the Hundred Years' War. Disinherited by his sister Catherine's marriage to British king Henry V, Charles granted Joan an army during the Siege of Orléans. The decisive victory she won there for the French ultimately led to Charles's coronation as king of France later that year. The seat of French power stayed at Chinon until the end of the Hundred Years' War.

Aujourd'hui, Chinon is a sleepy village known mainly for its scrumptious red wines, which means two things: You can pretend to be French by soaking up the slow pace of life in one of Chinon's terraced cafes; and you can try a spot of wine-tasting in one of the wine capitals of France.

Getting There

The SNCF runs both **trains** and **buses** every day to Chinon from Tours (trip time: about 1 hr.). Call ☎ **36-35** for information and schedules. Both buses and trains arrive at the train station, which lies at the edge of the very small town. If you're **driving** from Tours, take D759 southwest through Azay-le-Rideau to Chinon.

The **Office de Tourisme** is at place Hofheim (☎ **02-47-93-17-85;** www.chinon.com).

Orientation & Sightseeing

No, you haven't been transported into a period movie. People really live in Chinon's winding streets and half-timbered houses, many built in the 15th and 16th centuries during the court's heyday. There is a wicked view of the castle, over the river Vienne, on quai Danton. From this vantage point, you'll be able to see the castle in relation to the village and the river. To see one of the most typical streets in Chinon, head to rue Voltaire, lined with 15th- and 16th-century town houses. Check out no. 44, where Richard the Lionhearted died on April 6, 1199, from a wound suffered during the siege of Chalus in Limousin.

→ **Château de Chinon** ★★ From across the Vienne, the imposing Château de Chinon looks like it fell into ruin long ago. Today it consists of three buildings, two of which have been partially restored (they're still missing roofs). One of the restored buildings, Château du Milieu, dates from the 11th to the 15th centuries and contains the keep and clock tower, which houses a fading museum of Joan of Arc. A cool moat separates Château du

THE LOIRE VALLEY

Getting Your Paws on Chinon Wine

Chinon's famous wines crop up on lists all around the world, and supermarkets sell both lower-grade and top-quality versions, but if you want to buy some from a family that has been in the business longer than anyone can remember, head to **Caves Plouzeau** (94 rue Haute-St-Maurice; ☎ **02-47-93-32-11;** closed Oct–Mar and Mon). Its 12th-century cellars were dug to provide building blocks for the foundations of the château. The present management dates from 1929, and bottles of red or white wine cost around 7€ to 15€.

Milieu from the Château du Coudray, which contains the Tour du Coudray, where Joan of Arc once stayed. If you think that graffiti is a modern phenomenon, think again: In the 14th century, the Knights Templar were imprisoned here and scrawled all over the walls before meeting violent deaths. Some of the grim walls from other dilapidated edifices remain, although many buildings—including the Great Hall where Joan of Arc sought out the dauphin—have been torn down. In light of the pristine, almost flawless appearances of the other châteaux, Chinon offers a refreshingly crude alternative. ☎ *02-47-93-13-45. Admission 6€ adults, 4.50€ students. Apr–Sept daily 9am–7pm; Oct–Mar daily 9:30am–5pm. Closed Jan 1 and Dec 25.*

Sleeping

→ **Hôtel Le Plantagenet** Right in the town center, this great little 19th-century mansion opens onto views of the river Vienne and has dead-easy access to the medieval heart of Chinon. You'll be used to the Loire's untrendy—er, I mean, character-filled—rooms by now. These are a decent size but otherwise no different. The grace note here is the private garden and terrace where you can enjoy a drink. You can also make arrangements with local bike companies should you wish to châteaux-hop by bicycle. Some rooms, just as good as those in the main building,

are in an annex manor house, the Maison Bourgeoise. *12 place Jeanne d'Arc, 37500 Chinon.* ☎ *02-47-93-36-92. www.hotelplantagenet.com. 48€–65€ double. Credit cards accepted. Amenities: Bar. In room: A/C, TV, hair dryer.*

Eating

→ **L'Oceanic** SEAFOOD/FRENCH Let's face it, you've been inland for a while now, so why not indulge in some excellent seafood? Marie-Paule and Patrick Descoubes change the specialties daily, based on what's best at the marketplace (even though it's miles from the nearest beach, the fish is impeccably fresh). A particularly delicious meal may include cassoulet of lobster and scallops with vanilla-flavored butter, carpaccio of sea scallops with fried leeks and herb-flavored vinaigrette, stingray with Camembert sauce, and roasted filets of codfish with Muenster cheese cream sauce. If you're not in a fishy mood, ask the owners to prepare a delicious steak. *13 rue Rabelais.* ☎ *02-47-93-44-55. Fixed-price menu 21€–28€. Credit cards accepted. Tues–Sun noon–2pm; Tues–Sat 7:30–9:30pm.*

Partying

Le Café Français (37 place du Général-de-Gaulle; ☎ **02-47-93-32-78**), behind the Hôtel de Ville (town hall), attracts many good-looking singles. *Pourquoi?* Who knows. Who cares. All I can say is that if you're looking to couple, head on down and check out the lineup over a glass of Chinon or one of the occasional concerts held here.

Shopping

If you love magic mushrooms—sorry, not the hallucinogenic variety—and fancy a shopping trip with a difference, head out of Chinon to the **Champignonnière du Saut au Loup** (rte. de Chinon, Montsoreau 49730; ☎ **02-41-51-70-30;** mid-Mar to Nov daily 10am–6pm) with cave-like galleries overhanging the Loire river. The boutique sells many varieties of mushrooms, and at the end of your visit, you can sample a *galipette*—a regional stuffed mushroom, served in the grotto-like restaurant. Far out, man.

📺 Best● 15. Ussé ★★: Sleeping Beauty's Pad

295km (183 miles) SW of Paris, 14km (9 miles) NE of Chinon. Visiting time: 1½ hr.

Lance? Check. Sword? Check. Fire-breathing-dragon-resistant shield? Check. Thimble against pricks on spinning wheels? Check. Okay, now you're ready to visit Ussé. At the edge of the deep, dark forest of Chinon in Rigny-Ussé, **Château d'Ussé** was *the* inspiration for Perrault's legend of Sleeping Beauty *(La Belle au bois dormant).* Whether or not you're into fairy tales, there's no denying that this château—conceived as a fortress with a complex of steeples, turrets, towers, and dormers overlooking the Indre River—is as beautiful as the girl who fell asleep in it.

The present owner, the marquis de Blacas, has opened many rooms to the public. The guided tour begins in the Renaissance chapel, with its sculptured portal and handsome stalls. Next up are the royal apartments, furnished with tapestries and antiques. Then, for those diehard princes out there, there's a cheese-tastic spiral stairway leading to a tower with Sleeping Beauty waiting for her prince to come. Don't pucker up too soon, though, unless you like to kiss candles. She's as waxwork as the day she popped out of the mould. ☎ *02-47-95-54-05. Admission 10€ adults, 3.50€ students. Feb 14–Nov 11 daily 9:30am–6:30pm.*

Getting There

The château is best visited by car or on an organized bus tour from Tours. By car from Tours or Villandry, follow D7 to Ussé.

Sleeping

Take heed! Nod off here and you might not wake up. Opt for somewhere less enchanted—like Tours.

16. Fontevraud-l'Abbaye: Not Quite a Castle, but Who Cares?

304km (189 miles) SW of Paris, 16km (10 miles) SE of Saumur. Visiting time: 2 hr.

The Abbaye Royale de Fontevraud isn't a castle, but it is linked to the Plantagenet dynasty, buried here. The kings, whose male line ended in 1485, were also the *comtes* d'Anjou, but they wanted eternal rest in their native soil, bless them. Walking around here is like visiting the Hall of Fame for dead French royals. In the 12th-century Romanesque church lie Henry II of England, the first Plantagenet king; Eleanor of Aquitaine, the most famous woman of the Middle Ages; and her crusading son, Richard the Lion-Hearted. The tombs fared badly during the Revolution, when mobs desecrated the sarcophagi and scattered their contents on the floor. But damage aside, they're still pretty impressive.

One other fascinating place is the octagonal **Tour d'Evraud,** the last remaining Romanesque kitchen in France. If you fancy yourself a singer, warble to your heart's content. The acoustics are so amazing, you might attract a crowd as the sound spills out around the gardens. Dating from the 12th century, it contains five of its original eight *apsides* (half-rounded indentations originally conceived as chapels), each crowned with a conically roofed turret. A pyramid tops the conglomeration, capped by an open-air lantern tower pierced with lancets. ☎ *02-41-51-71-41. www.abbaye-fontevraud.com. Admission 6.10€ adults, 4.10€ under 25. Daily June–Sept 9am–6pm; Apr–May and Oct 10am–5:30pm; Nov–Mar 10am–5pm.*

Getting There

If you're **driving,** take N147 about 4km (2½ miles) from the village of Montsoreau. About five **buses** run daily from Saumur;

the one-way fare for the 30-minute trip is 3.50€.

The **Office de Tourisme,** allée Ste-Catherine (☎ **02-41-51-79-45**), within the compound of the medieval abbey, is open only from May 15 to September 30.

Sleeping

Don't sleep here. But if you're feeling rich, you could opt for lunch.

Eating

➡**La Licorne** ★ MODERN FRENCH You've seen enough kings and queens in the Abbey to eat like one here, for this, my *chers amis,* is a worthy splurge: a place that combines medieval history, 18th-century opulence, and culinary sensuality. In summer, grab a table in the refined garden or the elegantly rustic dining room. Chef Jean-Michel Bézille's menu (produced with the help of Fabrice Bretel) almost always includes filet of beef flavored with smoked pork and shallots, roasted *sandre* with Szechuan peppers, crayfish-stuffed ravioli with basil-flavored morel sauce, plus variations on many of the freshwater fish of the Loire Valley. Luscious desserts include warm chocolate tart with pears and lemon-butter sauce. What are you waiting for? *Allée Ste-Catherine.* ☎ *02-41-51-72-49. Reservations required. Fixed-price menu 27€–72€. Credit cards accepted. Tues–Sun noon–1:30pm; Tues–Sat 7–9pm.*

ᴹᵀⱽ Best ♥ 17. Saumur

299km (185 miles) SW of Paris. 53km (33 miles) SE of Angers. Visiting time: 4 hr.

Saumur is a snobby town, but it's another great base for exploring the western Loire Valley—especially if you have a taste for the high life and an undying love of fungi. Not only is it a major wine capital with its own sparkling variety, it also grows 100,000 tons of the mushrooms that make the French go goggle-eyed. To boot, the funky little Château de Saumur watches over the town like a jewel in the crown.

Getting There

Trains run frequently between Tours and Nantes, stopping at Saumur. Some 20 trains per day arrive from Tours (trip time: 45 min.); 11 trains per day pull in from Angers (trip time: 30 min.). The train station is on the north side of town. Most major points of interest, including the château, are on the south bank. From the station, take bus A into town. If you're **driving** from Tours, follow N152 southwest to Saumur.

The **Office de Tourisme** is on place de la Bilange (☎ **02-41-40-20-60**). Its hours vary greatly throughout the year, so call first.

Orientation & Sightseeing

You can thank Saumur for three things apart from wine and mushrooms: One, its bourgeois atmosphere, which inspired Balzac to write *Eugénie Grandet;* two, little black dresses, which started life as a twinkle in the eye of couturière Coco Chanel, who was born here; and three (for you men-lovers out there), the men of Saumur, some of the most testosterone-charged, skilled equestrians in the world. Founded in 1768, the city's riding school, **Cadre Noir de Saumur** ★ (rue de l'Abbaye; ☎ **02-41-53-50-50**), is one of the grandest in Europe, rivaling Vienna's. (Apr–Sept Tues–Sun; 7€ tours begin at 9:30am–11am and 2–4pm).

As you're wandering the streets, don't miss **La Maison du Vin** (quai Lucien Gauthier; ☎ **02-41-38-45-83**), with its vast stock direct from the many surrounding vineyards. Slightly farther afield, deep in the Loire bedrock, **Bouvet-Ladubay** (Saint Hilaire Saint Florent, 49400 Saumur; ☎ **02-41-83-83-83;** www.bouvet-ladubay.fr; call for hours) offers trips through their 8km-long (5-mile) wine cellars. Tickets are an almost symbolic 1€. The winery runs tasting courses and houses a massive permanent contemporary art exhibition. If you still have room for bottles in your suitcase, visit **Veuve Amiot** (21 rue Jean-Ackerman; ☎ 02-41-83-14-14), in Saumur's center. They also run tours and tastings.

➜ **Château de Saumur** ★★ You mustn't let the wine distract you from your castle-hopping: A visit to this castle is mandatory. It exudes both romance (you can tell it was once a fairy-tale castle of bell turrets and gilded weathercocks) and austerity (it's now a stark and foreboding fortress that became a prison under Napoleon, and then eventually a barracks and munitions depot). Inside, you can visit the **Musée des Arts Décoratifs,** which is known for its 16th- to 18th-century ceramics collection. The **Musée du Cheval** ★ is devoted to the history of the horse through the ages, complete with stirrups, antique saddles, and spurs. ☎ 02-41-40-24-40. www.saumur-tourisme. net/chateausaumur_uk.html. Admission 2€. Oct–Mar daily 10am–1pm and 2–5pm; Apr–Sept daily 10am–1pm and 2–6pm; rest of the year Wed–Mon 10am–1pm and 2–5:30pm.

➜ **Musée du Champignon** This museum in Saint-Hilaire takes you deep into dark, dank caverns where colonies of mushrooms sprout, mature, and cry out to be picked. Only accessible by car. Rte. Gennes, 49400. ☎ 02-41-50-31-55. www. musee-du-champignon.com. Call for hours.

Sleeping

➜ **Hôtel Le Canter** ★ Giddy up to the Canter, next to the riding center. It's in a prime spot for sleeping centrally on the cheap. What's more, you get snazzy decor for your money. It looks like it's straight out of an IKEA catalogue, but when every other place in the Loire looks like it hasn't been touched since the 1970s, that's a refreshing change. The bar-cum-breakfast room looks cool in its retro green and wood, and the staff is smiley. An excellent value. ☎ 02-41-50-37-88. www.lecanter.fr. 31€–37€ double; 37€–42€ triple. Credit cards accepted. Amenities: Bar; free Internet access. In room: TV, iron.

Eating

➜ **Le Tire Bouchon** BRASSERIE The name "corkscrew" (tire-bouchon) makes you think of good food and tasty wine, so it's no surprise that's what you get here. Start your meal with a sparkling pink rosé cave de Grenelle (which can't be called champagne because it's from the Loire Valley). Then try the snails cooked in Pastis. The red mullet in orange butter will make you question why French people are thin, as will the chocolate mousse—one of the best in town. 10 place de la République. ☎ 02-41-67-35-05. Fixed-price menus 9.50€, 17€, and 28€. Credit cards accepted. Wed–Mon lunch and dinner (closed Sun evening Jan–Feb).

Partying

Now don't faint, but believe it or not, snobby Saumur has a few worthy nightspots. If you want to shake it with the kool kids, head to **L'Absynthe** (27 rue Molière; ☎ 02-41-51-23-37), which is possibly the most teeming bar in Saumur. They stage regular concerts, have open-mic nights, and diminish everyone's senses with 30 kinds of beer and 40-plus whiskies. **Blues Rock** (7 rue de la Petite Bilange; ☎ 02-41-51-23-37) attracts a chic crowd of all ages and styles, with its rock lineup. To while away the evening outside, trail your tush to the half-timbered **place St-Pierre,** which has four venues (Le Café du Parvis, Le Richelieu, Le Café de la Place, and le Swing) that all seduce passersby with their shady terraces.

THE LOIRE VALLEY

18. ⓂⓉⓋ (Best❶) Brézé ★★: Troglodyte Heaven

304km (188 miles) SW of Paris, 74km (46 miles) W of Tours, 10km (6 miles) S of Saumur, 60km (37 miles) SE of Angers. Visiting time: 3 hr.

Upon approaching the Château de Brézé, you first see an elegant, Renaissance structure surrounded by the oldest vineyards in the Loire. Then you notice that Brézé underwent some fine-tuning in the early 19th century, and that surrounding the courtyard are the main building (where you can visit some apartments), the gallery, and the gatehouse, plus two large round towers. Just off the courtyard, however, a discreet wooden door takes you deep down into the belly of the earth to the **Roche de Brézé,** the château's underground troglodyte village—a vast complex of tunnels, steeped in mystery. When the Grand Condé, Gilles Maillé-Brézé, built the castle fortress in 1448, he dug out more than 1,000m (3,280 ft.) of passageways. Five huge chambers were inhabited by soldiers then later used as wine cellars and a press room. Europe's deepest, the dry moat is 18m (59 ft.) deep and 13m (43 ft.) wide and contains living quarters, a silkworm farm, and a bakery that was last used by the invading German soldiers during World War II. It's mind-blowing. Your visit will conclude with a trip to the **Cathédrale d'images**—a spooky audio-visual experience in three gigantic cellars.

The present owners are descendants of the Brézé nobles. Like their ancestors, they're enthusiastic winegrowers, winning prizes for their fantastic Saumur wines. If you fancy buying a bottle or two from such a cool "domaine," check www.vinsdesaumur.com or ask for a *degustation* during your visit. *Brézé.* ☎ *02-41-51-60-15. www.chateaudebreze. com. Admission 8€–12€ adults and 5.50€–8.70€ students, depending upon the length of the visit. Daily Apr–Sept 10am–6:30pm; Oct–Dec and Feb–Mar Tues–Fri 2–4:45pm, Sat–Sun 10am–6pm.*

Getting There

The château can only be visited by car, but it's only 10km (6 miles) from Saumur, which means that taxi fare isn't too elevated. Take the D93 from Saumur (dir Varrains/Chace).

Sleeping & Eating

Don't bother. Head for Saumur or Angers.

19. Angers ★★★

288km (179 miles) SW of Paris, 89km (55 miles) E of Nantes Visiting time: 4 hr.

Straddling the Maine River at the western end of the Loire Valley, Angers, once the capital of Anjou, is best described like its famous Anjou wines: a blend of provincial charm with a suggestion of sophistication. But that, guys, is by day. By night, some 30,000 college students keep this vital city of 260,000 jumping way into the wee hours with a hip bar scene and a handful of nightclubs. Angers is also a prime base for exploring the château district to the east. And it's a great stop-off point on your way to Nantes. There are plenty of parks and gardens to hang out in, and in July the **Festival d'Anjou** turns the city into a hotpot of drama, music, dancing, poetry, and art (see www. festivaldanjou.com).

Getting There

Trains take 1½ hours from Paris's Gare de Montparnasse to Angers. From Tours, seven trains per day make the 1-hour trip. The Angers train station, at place de la Gare, is a handy walking distance from the château (call ☎ 36-35). From Saumur, there are three **bus** connections a day from Monday to Saturday (1½ hr.). Buses arrive at place de la République. Call ☎ 02-41-33-64-64 for schedules. If you're **driving** from Tours, take N152 southwest to Saumur, turning west on D952.

The **Office de Tourisme,** 7 place du Président-Kennedy (☎ 02-41-23-50-00; www.angers-tourisme.com), is opposite the entrance to the château. It runs excellent discovery tours around Angers.

Orientation & Sightseeing

If you're a shopaholic suffering from the lack of shopping options in the Loire, put aside some time for wandering the pedestrian zone in the center of town. Plenty of nifty boutiques will keep you going, selling all sorts of clothes, shoes, jewelry, and books. For regional specialties (yes, that means wine), head to **La Maison du Vin** (5 place du Président-Kennedy; ☎ 02-41-81-13-00), where you can learn about the area's vineyards and buy a bottle or two for gifts or a picnic.

➜ **Château d'Angers** ★★ This moated château has been there, done that, and bought the T-shirt. Dating from the 9th century, it was originally the home of the *comtes* d'Anjou. In time, the Plantagenet dynasty took up residence. From 1230 to 1238, the outer walls and 17 towers were built, creating a hardy fortress. Good King René (one of the last feudal rulers) favored the château, and a brilliant court life flourished during his reign, in the 15th century, until he was forced to surrender to Louis XI. The Sun-King, Louis XIV, turned the château into a jail (I guess when you've got Versailles, everywhere else looks like prison); and in World War II, the Nazis used it as a munitions depot before the Allies bombed it in 1944.

Today it is an absolute must-see. The **Apocalypse Tapestries** miraculously survived years of use as a canopy to protect orange trees and as a wall-hang to cover the damaged interior of a church. Woven in Paris by Nicolas Bataille from cartoons by Jean de Bruges around 1375 for Louis I of Anjou, the series of 77 pieces illustrates the Book of St. John in 100m (328 ft.) of tasteful scenes such as *La Grande prostituée* (the prostitute) and images of Babylon under invasion by demons. After an eyeful of tapestries, you can tour the fortress, including the courtyard, prison, ramparts, windmill tower, 15th-century chapel, and royal apartments. The guided tour focuses on the architecture and history of the château. Most of the year, guided tours depart daily at 10, 11:30am, 1:15, 2:30, and 3:30pm, but between September and April, departures are usually at 10:15am and 2:15pm. Each tour lasts 90 minutes; docents speak French, English, German, or Italian. *2 promenade du Bout-du-Monde.* ☎ *02-41-86-81-94. www.monum.fr. Admission 7€*

adults, *5€ seniors and guests under 25. Sept–Apr daily 10am–5:30pm; May–Aug daily 9:30am–6:30pm.*

FREE ➜ **Cathédrale St-Maurice** ★ The cathedral dates mostly from the 12th and 13th centuries. Its incredibly ornate portal is covered in statues representing everyone from the Queen of Sheba to David at the harp. Stained-glass junkies will love the windows, which have made the cathedral famous—look out for the unusual one depicting St. Christopher with the head of a dog. For a guided tour in English (usually conducted with much charm and humor in July–Aug: "zis is a bite of stannid-glass zat cums from ze sextinth centeuri"), call the church's presbytery at the number above. *Place Freppel.* ☎ *02-41-87-58-45. Free admission. Daily Nov–Mar 8:30am–5:30pm, Apr–Oct 8:30am–7pm.*

➜ **Musée Jean Lurçat** ★★ The Musée Jean Lurcat is easily the town's most intriguing museum, set in the old St-Jean hospital, founded in 1174 to care for the sick. Yet another tapestry is worth your attention here, *Le Chant du Monde (The Song of the World)*, designed by Jean Lurçat and executed in 10 panels between 1957 and 1966. It depicts an abstract conglomeration of beneficent suns, popping champagne bottles, and life cycles of birth and death. You can also visit a 17th-century dispensary, and see everything from a Romanesque cloister–cum–secret garden to a pewter vessel from 1720 that once contained an antidote for snakebites. *4 bd. Arago.* ☎ *02-41-24-18-45. Admission 3.50€ adults, 1.75€ students. Daily June–Sept 10am–7pm, Oct–May 10am–noon and 2–6pm.*

Sleeping

➜ **Hôtel de Lices** Don't be put off by the name. The hotel rooms aren't anything to shout about, but they are *lice free* and clean. This place is all about low cost and location. Within easy walking distance of the historic center, château, and train station, it's an ideal yet cheap Angers stopover. The hotel is also known for its great brasserie, which serves up low-priced but excellent traditional food. *25 rue des Lices.* ☎ *02-41-87-44-10. 36€— 49€ double. Credit cards accepted. In room: TV.*

Eating

Hôtel de Lices has a great restaurant, the **Brasserie des Lices,** with fixed-menus from 15€ to 20€ (see Hôtel de Lices, above).

➜ **La Boucherie** If you're carnivorous and like noisy restaurants, this place is for you. They cook meat, meat, and more meat, served until late at night amid a cacophony of clanking glasses, plates, animated conversation, and loud-mouthed waiters who only communicate with their colleagues in voices over 400 decibels. Try any steak on the menu—they are prepared to perfection and melt on the tongue. *27 bd. du Maréchal Foch.* ☎ *02-41-25-39-25. Fixed-price menus 24€; a la carte 16€. Credit cards accepted. Daily 10am–11pm (until 11:30pm Fri–Sat).*

Partying

To stalk the best bars, head to **place du Ralliement** or **rue St-Laud,** with their many bars and cafes—the center-point of Angers's nightlife. If you're in Homer-mode

and desperately need "BEER Doh," rush to **Le Kent** (7 place Ste-Croix; ☎ **02-41-87-88-55**), an Irish pub that serves a mind-boggling 50 beers and 70 brands of whiskey.

The ultimate antidote to a day of château gazing is an evening on the dance floor at the **Disco Le Boléro.** It's not quite a meat market, but most of the crowds are groups of friends looking for that Prince or Princess charming gone astray in Angers (38 rue St-Laud, adjacent to the place de Ralliement; ☎ **02-41-88-61-19; beer 8€**).

Playing Outside

Pretty Angers offers four flower-clad gardens to choose from: **Jardin des Plantes, Jardin du Mail,** the **Jardin Médieval** (at the foot of the château in the moat), and the **Parcs de l'Etang St-Nicolas** on the outskirts of town. They are open from 8am to 8pm in summer and close at 5.30pm (or at nightfall) in winter.

20. Serrant ★★: It Took 300 Years to Look this Good!

288km (179 miles) SW of Paris, 82km (51 miles) E of Nantes, 10km (6 miles) W of Angers. Visiting time 1½ hr.

This is one of the lesser-known Loire châteaux. Its beauty doesn't hit you in the face the moment you see it, but take time to explore the Château de Serrant and you'll come away starry-eyed, jealous, wishing it was yours.

A Homerun for the Home Brew: Cointreau

Put your hands up if you've ever ordered a Cosmopolitan, Kamikaze, White Lady, or Sidecar. Well, the often imitated, never duplicated main ingredient of these sinfully delectable cocktails is Cointreau—another libation unique to Angers. Two brothers here were confectioners who set out to create a drink of "crystal-clear purity." They ended up with twice-distilled alcohol from the peels of two types of oranges, bitter and sweet, and a factory that has turned out the drink since 1849. Today, some 13 million bottles of Cointreau are consumed annually, and you too can join the band wagon at **La Distillerie Cointreau** (rue Croix Blanche, bd. des Bretonnières; ☎ **02-41-30-50-50**) in the suburb of St-Barthèlemy, a 10-minute drive east of the town center. You can slurp away and stock up on the fruity liqueur in the showroom (closed in Jan).

Charles de Brie began construction in 1546. According to popular rumor, Philibert Delorme—the same guy behind the château de Fontainbleau near Paris—drew up the plans. But it took more than 300 years to finish. From Charles de Brie, it passed to a succession of others with wacky sounding names: Hercule de Rohan (Duke of Montbazon); Guillaume Bautru, whose granddaughter married the Marquis of Vaubrun (Lieutenants-General of the King's army) and erected the chapel in his memory. Then the place was bought by a noble Irishman, Antoine Walsh, who followed James II into exile and became a ship-owner in Nantes; and then in 1830, one of his descendants married the Duc de la Trémoille, whose family has proudly owned the place ever since—besides during World War II, when the Nazis got hold of it. The Germans painted on the basement walls, which still convey a sense of their daily life.

A tour of Serrant takes you around some sumptuous yet highly livable apartments decked with rare furniture, wooden paneling, and opulent Flemish and Brussels tapestries.

If you love old books, you may want to take up residence in the library, with some 12,000 volumes, including first editions of La Fontaine's *Fables.*

Tourists tend to think of the Loire as a summer destination, but if serendipity sends you to Serrant in winter, try an atmospheric tour of the castle by torchlight. Tours (10€ adults, 6€ students) start at 10pm. *Château de Serrant, St-Georges sur Loire.* ☎ *02-41-39-13-01. www.chateau-serrant.net. Admission 9.50€ adults, 6€ students. Guided tours at 10, 11am, noon, 2:15, 3:15, 4:15, and 5:15pm.*

Getting There

Trains run from Angers to Saint Georges sur Loire, but you'll have to jump in a taxi from the station or walk 2km (1¼ miles) up the road. Serrant is best reached by car. From Angers take the N23 west.

Sleeping & Eating

Not here. Head to Angers or Nantes.

Nantes: A Bridge to Brittany

370km (229 miles) SW of Paris, 91km (56 miles) N of La Rochelle, 160km (99 miles) W of Tours; pop. 280,000

Nantes fought for centuries with Rennes to be capital of Brittany—only to lose and settle for status as capital of the Loire in the 1790s. Many foreigners still consider Nantes to be in Brittany—an image encouraged by the Nantais folk, who never quite came to terms with the fact that Nantes is a river port and not a seaport. But despite its deep Breton roots (or at least their seafaring activities: Nantes was an important shipbuilding city until the yards closed in 1987), it feels very much part of the Loire Valley.

Unlike most other places around here, Nantes has modern buildings, a hip art scene, and a rocking student community of 30,000. It might not look as pretty as other cities (heavy bombing in World War II and heavy industry left scars), but this is one seriously forward-thinking metropolis that hasn't ever stopped reinventing itself. The opening of environmentally friendly

bus lines and a failsafe, ultramodern tramway are just the external signs of an undercurrent of new development. Culturally speaking, this is an exciting time to visit, with a host of creative exhibitions in the works for 2007 (see "Sightseeing" on p. 185).

Desperate to spend your money? You'll find hundreds of places in which to empty your pockets here. Nantes is littered with designer and high-street shops, plus a truckload of independent boutiques; and then there's the great food and nightlife. Honestly, you might wonder why you bothered going anywhere else.

Getting There

BY AIR
Aéroport Nantes-Atlantique (☎ **02-40-84-80-00**) is 12km (7½ miles) southeast of town. **Air France** (☎ **02-51-25-02-78**) offers daily flights from Paris. A shuttle bus

THE LOIRE VALLEY

Nantes History 101

Where there's a gateway to the sea, there's power. The primitive city of Nantes (Namnètes) came to prominence thanks to its location just 48km (30 miles) from the coast. Built on the largest of three islands in the Loire, it became part of the Duchy of Bretagne (Brittany), when the young Breton chef, Alain Barbe Torte (first Duke of Bretagne), chased the Normans away in 937. From then on, the fight to be Brittany's capital ensued, until parliament moved to Rennes in 1561, giving Nantes a kick in the teeth it would remember until it became capital of the Loire just after the Revolution.

You can't mention Nantes and not mention the maritime. From the 13th century on, it used its pole-position, at the mouth of the Loire, as a means of trading with England and the Caribbean. By the 18th century, it had become the biggest slavetrading port in Europe.

The most prominent building from the "Bretagne" dynasty is the **Château des Ducs de Bretagne,** built in 1466 (due to re-open after renovation early 2007). The next big round of urban planning then took place in the 18th century, when much of the medieval city was replaced with stately apartments decorated with wrought-iron balconies (check out the Ile Feydeau). The Belle Epoque also left its mark, with dramatic covered passages, such as le Passage Pommeraye (p. 189). Much of Nantes bit the dust during World War I and World War II, but with true Nantais style and flair, the town is gradually rebuilding itself as one of the most happening spots outside Paris.

between the airport and the Nantes train station takes 25 minutes and costs 6€. A taxi from the airport costs 25€ and takes about 15 minutes.

BY TRAIN

The **TGV** from Paris's Gare Montparnasse takes about 2 hours to get to Nantes. Beware of slower trains, which can take up to 5¹/₂ hours. For information, call ☎ 36-35. Nantes's **Gare SNCF** (train station) is at 27 bd. de Stalingrad, a 5-minute walk from the town center.

BY CAR

If you're **driving,** take A11 for 385km (239 miles) west of Paris. The trip takes 3 hours.

BY BUS

Don't do it. The train's too good.

Orientation

Nantes is dead-simple to get around. From the station, if you crane your head and look left, you can make out the château, which is the gateway to the city center. This is a bite-size city, with a foreigner-friendly transport system and sites close enough for you to walk between them painlessly. If you're in need of a large dose of retail therapy, head along **rue de Verdun** (in front of the cathedral) and keep going in a straight line across **cours des 50 otages,** down rue **d'Orléans** into **rue Crébillon.** Every inch of space has enough shops to keep you salivating until tea time. Crébillon, with its lean towards designer wear, is so famous among locals that the verb to shop (*faire du shopping*) has been replaced with *crébilloner.* Several museums are situated along **rue Voltaire.** Most bars, cafes, and restaurants are in the **Bouffay quarter.** The main park, **Jardin des Plantes,** is opposite the Gare SNCF in the east of town. If you want to meet up with your mates like a local, rendezvous at **place de Commerce.**

Nantes Sleeping, Eating & Partying

SLEEPING ■

Camping du Petit Port	**1**
Hôtel Graslin	**22**
La Manu	**6**
L'Hôtel	**5**
Port Beaulieu	**18**
Porte Neuve	**28**

EATING ◆

Boulangerie Simon	**12**
La Cigale	**23**
L'Atlantide	**26**
la Tritaine	**3**
Le Petit Bacchus	**16**
Le Tashi Delek	**13**
Les Rigolettes Nantaise	**14**
Resto-Revue	**2**

PARTYING ★

La Maison Café	**4**
Le Café Cult	**15**
Le Duplex	**27**
Le Floride	**24**
Le Gout et les Couleurs	**17**
Le Live Bar	**11**
Le Royal Club Privé	**25**
Le Temps d'Aimer	**19**
Le Tie Break	**9**
L'Evasion	**10**
LU Lieu Unique	**7**
L'Universe Café	**21**
Quai West	**20**
Wilton's Club	**8**

Getting Around

BY PUBLIC TRANSPORTATION

Take a deep breath. Nantes's public transport won't pollute your lungs. The tramway system has three main lines. Line 1 is the most handy, running from in front of the train station into the town center along the river. Lines 2 and 3 slice through Nantes from N to S. Tickets cost 1.30€ and last a whole hour (duo ticket: 2.20€; pack of 10: 10€; 7-day ticket: 12€), during which you can hop on and off as many times as you fancy (just remember to validate it in a machine onboard). The buses are also reliable, but you probably won't need to use them. For a hip ride with a difference, try the Navibus boats that take you across the river Erdre or up the Loire (normal tickets valid). The Luciole bus will transport nighthawks around the main nighttime hot spots from 2.30am to 7am. Check out www.tan.fr for more information and see "Tourist Offices," below.

BY BICYCLE

Although the city openly promotes cycling, the busy tramlines and roads don't make for ideal biking conditions. If you head north of the city to the river l'Erdre (just behind the Préfecture on place du Port Morand), you'll find some picturesque cycle tracks. The Canal St-Félix in the east also makes for a cool ride. For bike rental,

Phat Phone Tourism

If you're too cool for the **Petit Train de Nantes** (a mini tourist train that leaves in front of the cathedral every hour from 10am–5pm Apr–Sept; ☎ 02-40-62-06-22) and you're feeling flush or lazy, you could do a guided walk with **Allovist** via your mobile phone. Call ☎ **01-39-04-60-60** (or ☎ 33-139-046-060 for a foreign mobile), follow the map, and you'll find out about the main seven points of interest: Cathédrale St-Pierre, Château des Ducs de Bretagne, place du Bouffay, rue Kervégan, Passage Pommeraye, place Royale, and Cours des 50 Otages. Calls cost 0.34€ a minute, but if you're short on time, you can't do better. I told you Nantes was ahead of its time!

you can get one free for 2 hours from the city's parking lots: **Graslin, Commerce, Bretagne,** the **Gare** (Nord section), the **Cité Internationale des Congrès,** the **Camping du Petit Port de l'Erdre** (Ile de Versailles, summer only), and **NGE** (rue Scribe; ☎ 02-51-84-94-51). All are open daily from 9am to 7pm.

ON FOOT

Feel free to attack Nantes on your own two feet—it's the best way to do it.

Tourist Offices

The **Office de Tourisme** is at 3 cours Olivier de Clisson Commerce (☎ **02-40-20-60-00;** www.nantes-tourisme.com; Mon–Sat 10am–6pm, from 10:30am on Thurs). Here you can buy a **Carte Nantes Découvertes,** which allows you to enter museums and ride any of the city's public conveyances, including buses, trains, and the Navibus boats (some seasonal restrictions). Depending on the season, the pass costs 14€ for 1 day, 24€ for 2 days, and 30€ for 3 days.

Nantes Nuts & Bolts

Emergencies   Call ☎ 17 for the police, ☎ 18 for the fire department, and ☎ 15 for an ambulance.

Internet/Wireless Hot Spots   For a quick e-mail checkup, head to **Cyber Planet** (18 rue de l'Arche Seche; ☎ 02-51-82-47-97; http://cyberplanet.fr; Mon–Sat 10am–2am; 3€ per hour or 1€ per 20 min.).

Laundromats   For that fresh feeling, head to **Laverie Aquamatic** (allée Duguay Trouin; ☎ 06-09-63-59-96; daily 7:30am–10pm).

Parking   Look out for signs marked NGE at the station (Gare SNCF Nord), place Bretagne, place du Commerce, and Graslin among others. The Pass Nantes can also be bought from these parking lots.

Pharmacy   **Pharmacie du Change** (6 place du Change; ☎ 02-40-47-43-22; Mon–Fri 9:30am–7:30pm) is in a practical spot.

Post Office   For some stamp lickin', go to **la Poste** at place Bretagne (☎ 02-51-82-57-04).

Safety Nantes is not particularly dangerous, but there are a few beggars around. Just keep your bags close and don't look anyone in the eye.

Taxis For a reliable service, call ☎ **02-40-69-22-22.**

Sleeping

Nantes offers a mountain of choices for a multitude of budgets.

HOSTELS

This town has not one, not two, but three hostels for you to choose from. All are simple, clean accommodations with cooking facilities. The following are the most central.

➜ **La Manu** Set in a converted tobacco factory, rooms are inaccessible from 6am to 8am and from noon to 5pm. *2 place Manu.* ☎ *02-40-29-29-20. www.fuaj.org. 16€. Tramline 1 Manufacture.*

➜ **Port Beaulieu** Also part of the same association, it's set on the industrial but up-and-coming Ile de Nantes. *9 bd. Vincent Gâche.* ☎ *02-40-12-24-00. www.anfjt.asso.fr. Tramline 2 Vincent Gâche.*

➜ **Porte Neuve** An association for young workers, with a few rooms and studio apartments let out to travelers. *1 place Ste-Elisabeth.* ☎ *02-40-20-63-63. www.anfjt. asso.fr. Tramline 3 Jean-Jaures.*

CAMPING

➜ **Camping du Petit Port** When the great outdoors are calling, but an urban location is all you can hope for, compromise at this place just north of the town center. It's on a tributary of the river Erdre, surrounded by trees, and it's on the tramline, for day and nighttime escapades (Tramline 2 Morrhonnière). Besides campsites under the stars, it has mobile homes to rent, bikes to hire, billiard tables galore, and a swimming pool. *21 bd. du Petit Port.* ☎ *02-40-74-47-94. www.nge-nantes.fr. 2.50€–6.20€*

tent per night (depending upon season and vehicles); 55€–91€ mobile home per night.

CHEAP

➜ **Hôtel Graslin** Get your hill shoes ready—the Graslin is on a steep old street near the harbor, in the center of town. There's a definite lassitude to the place, but the owners and managers, M. and Mme Roche, have given it many homelike touches. You do get more for your money than in most other hotels in this price category. The rooms are comfy, though a tad bland, with small, shower-only bathrooms. *1 rue Piron.* ☎ *02-40-69-72-91. www.ifrance. com/graslin. 55€–65€ double. Credit cards accepted. Amenities: Dry cleaning; laundry service; nonsmoking rooms. In room: TV, dataport, hair dryer, safe.*

DOABLE

➜ **L'Hôtel** Any place that calls itself *The* Hôtel either has delusions of grandeur or a genuinely fantastic location. In this case, I'm pleased to say it's the latter. Within sight of the château and the cathedral, this hotel is, for the price, a perfect base in Nantes. Built in the 1980s, it's retro-cool (if you're into the '80s), and neat and modern (if you're not). Rooms are in rich colors with contemporary furnishings. Ask for one with a private balcony overlooking the château. Breakfast is simple but copious enough to fill you up for a day in the city. *6 rue Henri-IV.* ☎ *02-40-29-30-31. www.nantes hotel.com. 79€–90€ double. Credit cards accepted. Parking 8€. Amenities: Dry cleaning; laundry service; limited-mobility rooms; nonsmoking rooms. In room: TV, dataport, hair dryer, minibar.*

THE LOIRE VALLEY

Eating

Nantes has some pretty hot restaurants and a shedload of regional sweets and biscuits.

CAFES & LIGHT FARE

➔**Boulangerie Simon** PATISSERIE First the window display filled with golden, buttery pastries and glorious sandwiches will catch your attention. Then the intoxicating odor of home-baked bread and cakes will convince you to enter and buy one of the tastiest snacks in town. *19 rue de Verdun.* ☎ *02-40-47-18-38. Snacks and pastries from 2€. Thurs–Tues 7am–8pm.*

➔**Le Tashi Delek** ASIAN Fill your mind with stories of Tibetan nights (and days) as you lie back, mint tea in hand (3€), sticky oriental pastry in mouth, and a *narghilé* (giant tobacco pipe) at your feet. This is where the hip youngsters come for a bout of exotic relaxation (the decor feels like an Eastern boudoir), a flit through the papers, and a chat with bosom buddies. *10 rue Briord. No phone. Tea from 3€. Mon–Wed 3:30pm–midnight; Thurs–Sat 3:30pm–1am.*

CHEAP

➔**Le Petit Bacchus** ★★ TRADITIONAL FRENCH This is the place for gourmet food on a pauper's budget. On a miniscule backstreet in the medieval Bouffay quarter, it is a little-known restaurant with an excellent kitchen that churns out dishes such as duck cooked in red wine with foie gras, seafood sauerkraut, apple crumble, and strawberry soup with mint. As you'd expect from a place named Bacchus, there's a fantastic wine list, with many great regional bottles starting at 10€. *5 rue Beauregard.* ☎ *02-40-35-31-17. Fixed-price menu 8.50€, 11€, 14€, and 24€. Credit cards accepted. Mon–Fri noon–2pm and 7–11pm; Sat 7:30–11:30pm.*

DOABLE

MTV Best❂ ➔**La Cigale** FRENCH/ SEAFOOD You can't get more historic or indeed more Belle Epoque than this breathtaking brasserie, which has hardly changed since it opened in 1895, across from the landmark Théâtre Graslin. Treat yourself to French classics such as platters of fresh shellfish, *confit des cuisses de canard* (duckling), and fresh scallops with green peppers and emulsified butter. The sprawling restaurant is always loud, staff are always overworked, and patrons always walk away happy and full. *4 place Graslin.* ☎ *02-51-84-94-94. www.lacigale. com. Reservations recommended. Fixed-price menu 16€–25€. Credit cards accepted. Daily 7:30am–12:30am.*

It's a Piece of Gâteau!

Of course you need sugar! Everybody needs sugar—and when you're in Nantes, there is nowhere better for a sweet-fix than **Les Rigolettes Nantaise** (18 rue de Verdun; ☎ **02-40-48-00-39;** Mon 2–7pm, Tues–Sat 9:30am–7pm). Named after the deliciously fruity bonbons they produce (*rigolettes* look like miniature multi-colored pillows), they are the ultimate reference in regional candy. If you're not a sucker for hard sweets, try a Monarque, a gorgeous almond cake covered in frosting; a Nez Grille (a grilled nose), a rounded butter-caramel that looks like the dog's nose it's named after; or a few chocolates. The links with Brittany have left a mouthwatering legacy, too—buttery Breton biscuits are perfect dunked in tea, coffee, or hot chocolate, so you should grab a tin or two at **la Tritaine,** in front of the cathedral (4 place St-Pierre; ☎ **02-40-20-33-26;** Mon 2–7pm, Tues–Sat 10am–7pm, Sun 3–7:30pm, closed Wed and Sat 1–2pm.

Veggie Might

It's hard to be a vegetarian in France. Ask for no meat, and they'll offer you chicken or fish. Maybe French chickens and fish grow on trees? Or maybe it's just that meat-eating is such a deep tradition here that even today certain people haven't understood that you can survive on vegetables. Being an open-minded sort of city, however, Nantes has one vegetarian restaurant for you to check out. **Resto-Revue** (2 rue du Refuge; ☎ **02-40-47-42-91**; fixed-price menu 13€; Tues–Sat 7:30–11pm), with its giant fork and knife mural on the facade, serves up excellent helpings of vegetable dishes, and pulses with an exotic twist. The rice pudding with hibiscus and coconut is to die for.

SPLURGE

→ **L'Atlantide** ★ MODERN FRENCH Panorama and great grub are on the menu here, on the fourth floor of the complex that houses the city's chamber of commerce. If you're a decor buff, you may have heard of the world-renowned designer Jean-Pierre Wilmotte. Well, he did the nautical-looking enclave with lots of mirrors, but Jean-Yves Gueho's innovative cooking is what draws patrons. Menu items, steeped in the traditions of both the Loire Valley and the Breton coast, may include lobster salad with yellow-wine sauce, potato and herb tart capped with foie gras, Breton turbot with Cantonese spices, and braised sweetbreads with Anjou wine. An excellent dessert is bananas braised in local beer. The cellar is known for some of the finest vintages of Loire Valley wine anywhere, with an emphasis on Anjous and muscadets. *Centre des Salorges, 16 quai Ernest-Renaud.* ☎ *02-40-73-23-23. Reservations required. Fixed-price dinner 35€–65€. Credit cards accepted. Mon–Fri noon–2:30pm; Mon–Sat 7:30–10pm. Closed first 3 weeks of Aug and Dec 23–27.*

Partying

When the sun goes down, the town turns into one big party led by a seriously switched-on student population. If you want a lowdown of the latest hot spots, a great website is www.leboost.com—a sort of forum-cum-blog, with insiders' advice on what's going down. For a list of all musical events in the region, visit www.44musique.com. If your French ain't up to it, here's an overview.

On **place du Bouffay, place du Pilori,** and **rue Kervagen,** you'll find lots of cafes and pubs, many with live music and fun people. A younger crowd rules **rue Scribe.** Catch some live blues, jazz, or rock at **L'Universe Café** (16 rue Jean-Jacques-Rousseau; ☎ 02-40-73-49-55), or techno and disco at **Quai West** (3 quai François-Mitterrand; ☎ 02-40-47-68-45), open all night. A great piano bar with a dance floor and occasional jazz concerts is **Le Tie Break** (1 rue des Petites-Ecuries; ☎ 02-40-47-77-00). The pump-it-up dance scene has a huge following of everyone from students to seniors. The over-30 crowd heads to the vintage '70s disco **L'Evasion** (3 rue de l'Emery; ☎ 02-40-47-99-84). Other popular dance floors are **Le Duplex** (place Emile-Zola; ☎ 02-40-58-01-04); **Le Royal Club Privé** (7 rue des Salorges; ☎ 02-40-69-11-10); and **Wilton's Club** (23 rue Rieux; ☎ 02-40-12-01-13). Take heed: Jeans are not welcome in any of these places, and be prepared to pay 9€ to 12€ to get in. The

THE LOIRE VALLEY

Five Quirky Facts about Nantes

1. It's one of the first French cities to have its own TV station on the Internet (www.mavilletv.com). Check it out for the latest goings-on if your French is good.
2. One in every two inhabitants is under 40.
3. Nantes is 48km (30 miles) from the coast, making it an important river port.
4. It is one of France's most environmentally friendly towns, with clean air 90% of the year.
5. Nantes receives half a million visitors a year.

favorite with gays and lesbians is **Le Petit Marais** (15 rue Kervégan; ☎ 02-40-20-15-25), where people meet and talk in a friendly atmosphere that welcomes everything from leather to lace. **Le Temps d'Aimer** (14 rue Alexandre-Fourny; ☎ 02-40-89-48-60), is mixed and gay-friendly. This disco with its small dance floor attracts a sophisticated crowd. The most you'll pay to get in is 10€. Newer than either of the above-mentioned bars is a mostly gay pub, **Le Gout et les Couleurs** (2 rue Kervégan; ☎ 02-40-20-58-58).

BARS

➜ **La Maison Café** ★★ La Maison, as its name suggests, looks like a house that was decorated by a psychedelic lord sometime in the 1970s. You can choose to drink in the bathroom, the kitchen, the lounge, the bar, the bathtub (fully clothed, of course), or if you've just met someone from the Charming family, the bedroom. DJs spin into the night from 8pm onward. *4 rue Lebrun.* ☎ *02-40-37-04-12. www.lamaisonet.com.*

➜ **Le Café Cult** This joint could be called Anachronisms R Us: A former medieval pharmacy in a building from the 14th century, with original beamed ceilings and walls covered in the most contemporary art the owners could get their hands on. Curtains are heavy; banquettes are red velvet; old chandeliers, including one

made from bottles, light the bar perfectly; and the mojitos are definitely some of the best in Nantes. *2 place du Change.* ☎ *02-40-47-18-49.*

CLUBS & LIVE MUSIC VENUES

Nantes is happening at night if you know where to go. The live music scene is also kicking, with everything from electro-funk to folk-rock.

➜ **Le Floride** There's nothing vaguely like Florida about the Floride—no sun, sea, or fake boobs, just lashings and thrashings of Rock. In fact this is Nantes's only rock-exclusive nightclub that doubles up as a platform for up-and-coming rock stars. There is an occasional flirtation with electro beats, groove, and soul, but otherwise expect stuff like Metallica, Counting Crows, and French groups like Noir Desir (whose lead singer, Bertrand Cantat, is serving 8 years for killing his girlfriend, the late actress Marie Trintignant). *4 rue St-Domingue.* ☎ *02-40-47-66-80.*

➜ **Le Live Bar** No, the main draw of the Live Bar is neither the cow suspended in the window, nor the handwritten messages on the walls (get your pen out and leave some for your mates), nor the cheap beer (2.50€). The real attractions here are the alternative media nights with projections of short films, and the frequent electro, rock, and jazz performances. *6 rue de Strasbourg.* ☎ *02-40-35-54-01.*

📺 **Best ⚑** →**LU Lieu Unique** ★★ This is one unique venue. When the old LU biscuit factory closed down, the local council fortunately realized that it would be a crime against humanity to destroy such a beautiful 19th-century factory building. The solution? A center for the arts with a national theater, a hip bar (with resident DJ), restaurant, live radio broadcasts and concerts, a sauna, library, art exhibition center, a foldable shop (it rolls out from the wall to reveal its wares), and a time capsule (a whole wing, filled with thousands of personal objects due to be reopened in 2100). If you're into music that's out of the ordinary, contemporary art, and late nights, rush round to LU. *Quai Ferdinand-Favre (canal St-Félix).* ☎ *02-40-12-14-34 (concert reservations). www.lelieu unique.com. (Also see "Sightseeing," below.)*

Sightseeing

After the pristine beauty of the Loire châteaux, the eclectic architecture of Nantes (neo-industrial versus traditional 18th and 19th c.) is a welcome change. Its charms won't be as obvious, but seek and ye shall find. And then you can go off and relax in one of six parks.

PUBLIC MONUMENTS

→**Château des Ducs de Bretagne** ★★ You can't visit the top Loire châteaux and then miss this little beauty, sandwiched between the cathedral and the Loire. The castle was constructed in the 9th or 10th century, enlarged in the 13th century, destroyed, and rebuilt into its present shape by François II in 1466. His daughter, Anne de Bretagne, continued the work. Large towers and a bastion flank the castle, which contains a symmetrical section (the Grand Gouvernement) built during the 17th

and 18th centuries. After 3 years of revamping, the castle will reopen in February 2007 with a brand new museum containing more than 800 exhibits, 32 rooms, and temporary exhibitions covering the history of Nantes from medieval times to the present. Call the tourist office for more information. *4 place Marc-Elder.* ☎ *02-51-17-49-00. Tickets 5€ adults over 26; 3€ adults 18–26. Joint tickets for museum and temporary exhibition 8€ adults over 26, 4.80€ adults 18–26. May 15–Sept 15 daily 9am–8pm; Sept 16–May 14 Wed–Mon 10am–7pm.*

📺 **Best ⚑** →**La Maison Radieuse de Le Corbusier** Here's another one for you architect buffs out there. As you may well know, the architect Le Corbusier (see "Le Corbusier's Cité Radieuse" on p. 438, and "Ronchamp: Le Corbusier's Masterpiece" on p. 661) had his heyday in the 1950s with his idealistic view of living space. He wanted to create a vertical village with room for 2,000 families, and everything they could possibly need on-site. The result? A multicolored block of flats with a school, shops, entertainment facilities, and plenty of gardens. He must have done something right, because people still fight for an apartment here. Call the Rezé Town Hall (near Nantes), which organizes visits. ☎ *02-40-84-43-84. www.maisonradieuse.org. Admission 3.25€.*

→**La Tour LU** ★ You've visited it at night for its bar, restaurants, and concerts; now come for the panorama. From the top of Nantes's iconic **Lieu Unique** tower (see above), you can see the whole of the city. And as if that weren't enough, the only way to the top is in the "Gyroama," a strange contraption that looks like something straight out of a Jules Verne novel. *Entrance quai Ferdinand Favre.* ☎ *02-40-12-14-34. Wed–Sat 1–7pm; Sun 3–7pm.*

→**Le Palais de Justice** ★ If there's one architect making his mark on the world, it's the very bald, very French Jean Nouvel. (Visit www.jeannouvel.com and click on the world map to see just how many structures he has built: The Guthrie theater in Minneapolis is one of his latest, along with Paris's Quai Branly museum; see p. 116.) He is the brainchild behind Nantes's law courts (built in 1993), which were conceived as a vast, black rectangular box with transparent walls and giant windows to represent the transparency of justice. *To visit, call the tourist office at* ☎ *08-92-46-40-44.*

HIGHBROW HAUNTS

→ **Le Théâtre Graslin** When you happen upon a neoclassical building with eight Corinthian columns that would look more at home in Rome than in Nantes, you know you're at the city's hangout for classical music-loving illuminati. This national theater is home to the **Angers Nantes Opéra,** which performs excellent contemporary takes on classics by authorities such as Mozart and Verdi. Check out the program at www.angers-nantes-opera. com or call ☎ **02-40-69-77-18.** If the building interests you more than what's on, consider one of the tourist office's guided tours. *26 av. Montaigne.* ☎ *08-92-46-40-44. www.angers-nantes-opera.com.*

CHURCHES

FREE → **Cathédrale St-Pierre** ★★ If Nantes is at the end of a string of French cities, the last thing you'll want to see is *another* cathedral; but trust me, this one really is worth rushing round. Begun in 1434, it wasn't finished until the end of the 19th century, but you'd never know from the outside or the inside (a rare feat). There are two reasons to venture inside: Michel Colomb's Renaissance tomb of

Arts Scene

PERFORMING ARTS As great as it may be, the Lieu Unique is not the only place that churns out great performances. For some café-théâtre, concerts, and short films, head to **La Terrain Neutre Théâtre (TNT;** 12 allée de la Maison Rouge; ☎ 02-40-12-12-28; Sept–June). **Espace 44** (Maison de la Culture de Loire-Atlantique) is a magnet for live, contemporary stage creations (rue du Général Buat; ☎ 02-51-88-25-25; Oct to mid-June); ONPL (Orchestre National des Pays de la Loire) churns out jam-packed classical and contemporary music at the **Cité Internationale des Congrès** (rue de Valmy; ☎ 02-51-25-29-29); and **La Maison de la Marionnette** (1 rue Dugommier; ☎ 02-40-48-70-19; Sept–June) holds regular puppet shows and workshops explaining how to make and manipulate your home-grown Pinocchio.

FILM If you desperately want to see a film in English, look out for "VO" next to the title and check out the multiscreen **Le Gaumont** (place du Commerce; ☎ 08-92-69-66-96). If you get a *Pass* (Carte Nantes Découverte) from the tourist office, you can get money off your ticket. Otherwise, expect to pay around 8€.

ART Contemporary art fans should check out the **FRAC (Fonds regional d'Art contemporain;** in La Fleuriaye-Carquefou; ☎ 02-28-01-50-00; Wed–Fri 1–6pm, Sat–Sun 3–7pm). More than 700 weird and wacky exhibits cover everything from photography, video, sculpture, and painting. It is out of the center of Nantes, so take tramline 1 (toward Beaujoire) and get off at Haluchère, and then take bus no. 95 toward Souchais and stop at Fleuriaye (on Sun take bus no. 85 toward Bois St-Lys, and stop at Carquefou center; www.tan.fr).

Nantes Sightseeing

François II, duc de Bretagne, and his second wife, Marguerite de Foix, which is hauntingly beautiful; and the rich, leaf-like patterns of the stained-glass windows. There, you can leave now. *Place St-Pierre.* ☎ *02-40-47-84-64. Free admission. Summer daily 8:30am–7pm; off season daily 8:30am–6pm.*

MUSEUMS

➔ **Musée des Beaux-Arts de Nantes ★** This is one of western France's most interesting provincial galleries. You'll find an unusually fine collection of sculptures and paintings from the 12th to the late 19th centuries; and the street level is devoted to mostly French modern or contemporary art created since 1900, with special emphasis on painters from the 1950s and 1960s. *10 rue Georges-Clemenceau.* ☎ *02-51-17-45-00. Admission 3.50€ adults, 1.75€ students and under 26; free admission 1st Sun of the month. Wed–Mon 10am–6pm.*

➔ **Musée Jules Verne de Nantes** Did you know that the novelist Jules Verne (*Journey to the Center of the Earth, Around the World in Eighty Days*) was born in Nantes in 1828? This museum is filled with memorabilia and objects inspired by his writings, from ink spots to a magic lantern with glass slides.

Fans also seek out Verne's house at 4 rue de Clisson in the Ile-Feydeau, which is

Colossal Art

Traditionally, Nantes has had a penchant for puppets. Not your average Punch and Judy revivals—we're talking huge puppets, over 10m (33 ft.) tall, parading through the streets once a year during a festival led by the expert showstoppers **Royal de Luxe.** The success of such events, and the need to regenerate the former industrial Ile de Nantes, has given rise to several equally big ideas—namely, giant objects that visitors can explore. The year 2007 sees the arrival of the first one—a 12m-high (39-ft.) wooden elephant that moves, weighs 40 tons, and can hold 70 people on its back at once. Other upcoming inventions include a giant carousel containing sea creatures (for 2009) and a 22m-wide (72-ft.) city, set in a metallic tree (for 2011). All three creations will be built in 📺 Best❖ **Les Nefs** ★★, the city's old shipbuilding hangars (open July 2007).

Other artworks designed to rescue decaying industrial sites will dot the River Loire between Nantes and the Saint Nazaire estuary. In 2007, 2009, and 2011, 30 artists will be turning specific spots (mostly old factories and shipyards) into pieces of contemporary art you can discover during a relaxing cruise. You'll need to see everything to believe it, so hurry and call the tourist office for more information.

privately owned and not open to the public. That neighborhood is a historic, mostly 18th-century area in the heart of the town. It was named after an island (l'Ile Feydeau) that became part of mainland Nantes after the river was diverted into a series of canals during the 18th century. *3 rue de l'Hermitage.* ☎ *02-40-69-72-52. Admission 1.50€ adults. Wed–Mon 10am–noon and 2–6pm. Closed Sun morning.*

→ **Musée Thomas-Dobrée** Thomas Dobrée, a diehard collector and fervent traveler, built this 19th-century neo-Romanesque mansion in the town center, adjacent to the 15th-century manor of Jean V, where the bishops of Nantes occasionally lived. You'll see Dobrée's eclectic collection, including prehistoric and medieval antiquities, Flemish paintings from the 15th century, ecclesiastical relics, paintings by masters such as Dürer, art objects from India, and the Dobrée family jewels. *18 rue Voltaire.* ☎ *02-40-71-03-50. Admission 3€ adults, 1.50€ students. Tues–Fri 1:30–5:30pm; Sat–Sun 2:30–5:30pm.*

Playing Outside

Nantes has a whopping six parks for you to hang out in with a good book and a picnic. The most well known and beautiful is the **Jardin des Plantes** (☎ 02-40-41-65-09; daily 8am–8pm or sundown), 2 blocks east of the cathedral and opposite the Gare SNCF. The **Parc du Grand-Blottereau** (☎ 02-40-41-65-09; gardens open daily, greenhouses open Wed and Sat–Sun; call for visiting times) with its tropical plants and greenhouses is opposite the château; the **Parc de Procé** in the northeast is famous for its rhododendrons and has a tearoom (entrance rue des Dervallières, bd. Constant, and bd. des Anglais); the **Parc Floral de la Beaujoire** near the exhibition center on the River Erdre has more than 400 species of magnolias (rte. de St-Joseph de Porterie); **Parc de la Chantrerie** (north of town, tramway stop Beaujoire) is great for a roll in the grass, and you can hire an electric boat on the **Ile de Versaille** (in the middle of the Erdre), or admire the Japanese gardens.

Skater Tip

If you can't go anywhere without your board, head to the island in the middle of the road next to Hôtel Dieu hospital in Nantes. It's not huge, but there are plenty of ramps on which to wow onlookers with your tricks, and you may meet some likeminded locals.

MTV **Best ●** → **The Trentemoult Village**
Damn Rennes! Why did it have to be Capital of Brittany? If Nantes had won the battle, all of it would have looked as cute as this place. Set on the Left Bank of the Loire, it is a deliciously colorful fishing village that reels in local folk who want to get away from it all. Admittedly, once you've had a drink on the waterfront, grabbed a bite to eat, and gotten lost in the meandering streets, there's not all that much to do. But that's what quaint fishing villages are all about. An organic market is held here on Saturday mornings. Take the Gare Maritime tramstop on line 1, then the Navibus to Trentemoult all on the same ticket.

Shopping

Nantes overflows with shops and boutiques. The principal shopping streets are rue du Calvaire, rue Crébillon, rue Boileau, rue d'Orléans, rue de la Marne, rue de Verdun, and passage Pommeraye (see "The Passage Pommeraye," below). Most of these encompass the shopping districts around place Graslin, place Royale, the château, and the cathedral. For unique gifts, check out the stores owned by two master artisans: **Maison Devineau** (2 place Ste-Croix; ☎ 02-40-47-19-59), which brings the art of waxworking to a new level, "growing" bushels of fruits, flowers, and vegetables from liquid wax; and **Georges Gautier** (9 rue de la Fosse; ☎ 02-40-48-23-19), a historic boutique established in 1823 with the town's best chocolates—yummy!

CLOTHING & ACCESSORIES

→ **Ben SUD Express** Look around you and you'll notice that the Nantais folk are snazzy dressers. If you want to fit in, girls, this shop will dress you like a chic bohemian student. Expect feminine numbers with chunky wools, light flowing fabrics, and sober colors. *5 rue d'Orléans.* ☎ *02-51-72-78-14. Thurs–Tues 10am–7pm, Wed 10am–1pm and 2–7pm.*

→ **Pieton** ★★ If you love your feet, this is a shoe mecca you should cross the city for. They have everything a young funkster could possibly desire: Vans, Kickers, Clarks, and Converse, to name but a few

The Passage Pommeraye

Ever fancied shopping on a film set? Well, the stunning **MTV** **Best ●** **Passage Pommeraye** has been used in so many films (like *Lola* by Jacques Demy for you buffs out there) that whether you mean to or not, that's what you'll be doing if you buy in the shops here. Built in 1843, in pure neoclassical splendor, it is a living vestige of Nantes's 19th-century glory, with sumptuous columns, allegorical statues (the arts, agriculture, industry, science, and sea trade are all represented), wrought-iron balconies, and elegant glasswork. Nowadays, shops are fashion- or jewelry-oriented (see Salsa Nova, below), with a few secondhand book shops. La Cigale restaurant (built in 1900; see p. 182) is here, too, which means you could combine shopping and eating in the same place.

THE LOIRE VALLEY

biggies. *5 rue d'Orléans.* ☎ 02-40-58-00-92. *Mon 2—7pm, Tues—Fri 10am—7pm, Sat 10am—7:30pm.*

→ **Salsa Nova** ★ This is one of the hippest, addresses in Nantes, with some great urban chic designs for men and women. Whether you're looking for a "look-at-me" coat, a laid-back T-shirt, fantasy jewelry, or a present for your Mom, you won't go away empty-handed. *Passage Pommeraye.* ☎ 02-40-48-70-07. *www.salsanova.com. Mon—Sat 10am—7pm.*

MUSIC, BOOKS & MEDIA

You'll find a great English, Spanish, Russian, and Italian book collection at **Les Affaires Etrangères** (15 rue de Vieilles Douves; ☎ 02-40-75-57-03; www.affaires-nantes.com), some wonderful ancient tomes at **Coiffard** (since 1919, 7 rue de la Fosse; ☎ 02-40-48-16-19; www.coiffard.lalibrairie.com), but otherwise head to forever faithful **FNAC** in the old stock-exchange, where you'll find CDs, books, tickets for concerts, and anything multimedia and electrical (palais de la Bourse; ☎ 02-51-72-47-24; www.fnac.com).

FOOD, WINE & LOCAL CRAFTS

Fill up on wine at **La Fief de Vigne** (16 rue Marceau; ☎ 02-40-47-8-75), with its cool glass and stone architecture, and 2,000-plus different bottles; **Gautier-Débotté** (9 rue de la Fosse; ☎ 02-40-48-23-19; http://gautier-debotte.com) sells a decadent array of delectable chocolates; and **Planète FCNA** is the official store for Nantes's soccer team (nicknamed the canaries), selling scarves, gadgets, and tickets to matches (7 rue des Halles; ☎ 02-51-88-91-91; www. www.fcna.fr).

Festivals

→ **Jumping International de Nantes** The international show-jumping tournament returns with a jamboree of horsy attractions, in the Parc des Expositions de la Beaujoire. *Late Jan.*

→ **La Folle Journée** A 5-day classical music fest at the Cité Internationale des Congrès. Reservations required. ☎ 02-51-88-20-00. *Late Jan and 1st week in Feb.*

→ **Let's Dance** For the fifth year in a row, Le Lieu Unique is holding a cool and competitive dance event. *3rd week in Mar.*

→ **Utopiales** Nantes's science fiction festival features all sorts of media, from cinema and comic strips to video games and new technologies. *Early Nov.*

Playing Outside in the Loire

The region around Nantes can supply hours of joy both on the water and on land. As you've probably realized, the Loire Valley is huge, so the best way to attack the great outdoors is to work out what you want to visit first, and then call a few of the organizations listed below to find out whether you can work a few sporty moments into your itinerary.

Canoeing & Kayaking

Many waterways run through the region; and the most suitable rivers for canoeing or kayaking are the Cisse, Conie, Cosson, Huisne, Indre, Loir, Vienne, and *bien sûr* the Loire. **The Fédération Française de Canoë-Kayak (FFCK;** 87 quai de la Marne, Joinville le Pont, near Paris; ☎ 01-45-11-08-50; www.ffck.org) lists many, including the **Canoe-Kayak Club d'Angers** (http://ckcac.free.fr) in Angers. The **Comité Régionale de Canoë-Kayak du Centre** has a website in English listing all the affiliated clubs (1240 rue de la Bergeresse, 45160 Olivet; ☎ 02-38-49-88-80; www.canoe-regioncentre.org); and the **Ligue Canoë-Kayak des Pays de Loire** gives info on the regional competitions (route s'Angers, 49080 Bouchemaine; ☎ 02-41-73-86-10; www.crck.org/pays delaloire).

Cycling

Whatever the circumference of your thighs, the Loire is ideal cycling terrain: It's flat, varied, and damned pretty. There are the banks of the Loire, the forests, and of course the châteaux, which could (if your energy knows no limits) be visited by bicycle. For recommended cycling tours of various lengths, call the **Fédération Française de Cyclotourisme** or check out their website (12 rue Louis Bertrand, 94200 Ivry-sur-Seine; ☎ 01-56-20-88-88; www.ffct.org).

Golf

The region has several 18-hole courses to choose from, so contact the **Fédération Française de Golf** (68 rue Anatole France, 92309 Levallois-Perret; ☎ 01-41-49-77-00; www.ffgolf.org), the **Ligue du Centre, Golf de Touraine** (37510 Ballan-Miré; ☎ 02-47-67-42-28), or the **Ligue de Golf des Pays Loire** (9 rue du Couëdic, 44000 Nantes; ☎ 02-40-08-05-06; www.ligue-golf-paysdelaloire.asso.fr).

Hiking

For some sightseeing on your own two feet, the **Fédération Française de la Randonnée Pédestre (FFPR)** publishes detailed maps on all regions of France including the Loire (14 rue Riquet, 75019 Paris; ☎ 01-44-89-93-90; www.ffrandonnee.fr). Then there's the **Comité de Touraine pour la Randonnée Pédstre in Tours** (78 rue Bernard-Palissy; ☎ 02-47-70-37-35) and the **Comité Departementale du Tourisme de l'Anjou,** which has five maps on paths for ramblers (place Kennedy, 49021 Angers; ☎ 02-41-23-51-23; www.anjou-tourisme.com).

Horse & Pony Trekking

Horseback riding in the Loire is a coveted activity. For information on exploring France on horseback, contact the **Association Régionale de Tourisme Equestre,** which publishes an annual brochure (9 bd. MacDonald, 75019 Paris; ☎ 01-53-26-15-50). The best regional associations are the **Association Regionale de Tourisme Equestre des Pays de la Loire** (3 rue Bossuet, 44000 Nantes; ☎ 02-40-48-12-27) and the **Association Regionale de Tourisme Equestre Centre Val de Loire** (Maison des Sports, 32 rue Alain-Gerbault, BP 719, 41700 Blois cedex; ☎ 02-54-42-95-60, ext. 411).

Normandy

by Anna Brooke

Amid the rolling meadows, tranquil orchards, half-timbered houses, and striking cliff tops of Normandy, it's hard to imagine the bloody battles that went down here.

In modern times, Normandy is most famous for its role in ending World War II. The Allied invasion of June 6, 1944, ravaged much of the region when the largest armada ever assembled successfully fought to wrest Europe from Nazi power. Today, many visitors come to Normandy just to see the **D-Day beachheads.**

Long before the Allies did battle on this soil, the Scandinavian Vikings were the first to seize the realm. They came and they conquered, but soon they settled on a more constructive activity known as farming. Then came the Normans—none more fearsome than William the Conqueror, a dastardly man who defeated King Harold at the Battle of Hastings in England (aka the Norman Conquest) in 1066. This chapter of history is immortalized at **Bayeux** in a medieval tapestry of the same name.

Despite all the wars and bloodshed, Normandy is a vast, versatile province. One minute it will conjure images of a Millet landscape (with cattle grazing in fields and thatched cottages); then whisk you off on a seafaring voyage through the rugged chalky cliffs of **Etretat** and the **Côte d'Alabâtre (Alabaster Coast);** and then onto the chic resort towns of **Deauville** and **Trouville** (part of the region known as La Côte Fleurie, or "Flower Coast," so called because of the profusion of summer flowers); before dropping you off, in time for tea, in the atmospheric Gothic capital

Rouen; or at one of France's most breathtaking treasures, the fortified monastery of **Mont St-Michel.**

To make the most of your time here, I suggest splitting your trip into three parts: **Rouen,** the beautiful regional capital; our **Sea-Stint,** which takes you along the Alabaster and Flower Coast through Etretat, **Honfleur,** Deauville, and Trouville; and finally our **Historic Trail,** which, as its name suggests, leads you to sites of historical interest—namely Bayeux, the D-Day Beaches, and Mont St-Michel. Although **Caen** (p. 214) does not receive in-depth coverage in this chapter, it makes a handy base for the history trail. Should you wish to hang around longer, the hectic seaports of Dieppe and Cherbourg will fill your days with boats, beaches, and busy harbors.

The Best of Normandy

◯ **The Best Hollow Cliffs to Hunt Gentleman Thieves In:** Writer Maurice le Blanc's character, Arsène Lupin, is France's most elusive and charming criminal. Visit **Etretat** and you'll plunge head first into le Blanc's stories of intrigue and hidden treasures. See p. 211.

◯ **The Best Tapestry to Describe How the French Whipped the English's Asses:** Twenty-one meters (70 ft.) long, the Romanesque tapestry **Bayeux** tells the tale of that fateful day in 1066 when King Harold of England lost his eye and his life to William the Conqueror's arrow. See p. 213.

◯ **The Best Place to See Where Joan of Arc Breathed Her Last:** Joan of Arc was just 19 when the English burned her at the stake on **Rouen**'s place du Vieux-Marché in 1431. But life goes on, and nowadays you can have a coffee or dinner just opposite that spot. Just don't light up! See p. 195.

◯ **The Best Street on Which to Imagine You're a Medieval Tradesman (Rouen):** Cobbled and evocative, the half-timbered **rue du Gros Horloge** is one of the most authentic in Rouen. See p. 198.

◯ **The Best Champagne Bar with Attitude (Rouen):** The newest joint in Rouen, **Des Bulles Plein Les Oreilles,** will get you high on sound and tipsy on bubbles. But beware: Non-trendies should either abstain, or come undercover to observe the Bobos (Bourgeois-Bohemians) in their natural habitat. See p. 202.

◯ **The Best Place to Eat and Splurge in a Historic (If Not Slightly Morbid) Setting (Rouen):** Right by Joan of Arc's final resting place, local bigwigs and stars eat at **La Couronne,** along with fans who fancy being in a showbiz magazine rather than buying one. Who forgot to call the paparazzi? See p. 200.

◯ **The Best Place to Observe a Dying Trade (Rouen):** Rouen is famous for its *faïence*—a ceramic made from a clay-compound and tin-based enamel. It's hard to get your mitts on the real deal these days, and so making a trip to **Faïencerie Carpentier Augy** (even if you don't buy anything for Grandma) is obligatory. See p. 205.

Normandy

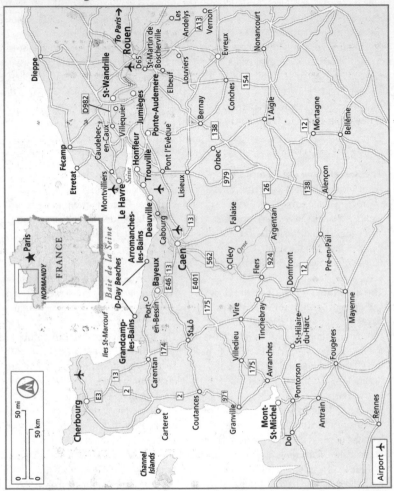

Getting Around the Region

The most painless and efficient way to navigate the region is to combine **rail and car** travel. Taking the train from Paris to any major Normandy hub is easy, but traveling inter-regionally is more difficult, which makes having a set of wheels a priority. For information on **trains,** the old faithful **SNCF** (☎ 36-35; www.sncf.com) provides the best schedule information and lets you book online. For those traveling by **motorcar** or **scooter, www. bison-fute.equipement.gouv.fr** gives up-to-the-minute traffic information; **www.mappy.com** will also help you to map out your road trip. Within the towns of Normandy, **walking** is the fastest way to get around, from the train station to the center of town.

Normandy Nosh & Naughty Tipples

"Normandy" is a synonym for "good cooking." Indeed, Norman folk are renowned for being the country's heartiest eaters—a reputation confirmed by the somewhat rosy-cheeked and rounded local populace. You could be likewise if you'd grown up around apples, pears, seafood, and Jersey cows—the staple requirements for fresh cream, cheese, apple-tarts, butter pastries, veal, seafood platters, cider, calvados (apple liqueur), and a whole host of other delicious dishes that combine the aforementioned ingredients and guarantee a coronary by 30. Here is a list of some of the treats that await you: **Camembert** (the world's most famous cheese, though only the stuff made in Normandy is considered the real deal), **duck** (in Rouen), **shrimp and cockles** from Honfleur, **pork in cider, tripe *à la mode de Caen*** (steamed tripe cooked with vegetables in cider), ***moules marinières*** (mussels in white wine with shallots, parsley, and butter), and the herbal alcoholic pick-me-up **Benedictine** (from Fécamp, see "Etretat: Tracking the Gentleman Thief" on p. 211), first concocted by a Benedictine monk in 1510.

MTV Best❷ Rouen: Joan of Arc's Resting Place

135km (84 miles) NW of Paris, 83km (51 miles) S of Deauville, 235km (146 miles) E of Mont St-Michel; pop. 390,000

The capital of Normandy, Rouen is an important industrial river port (fourth largest in France) that has risen from the ashes on more than one occasion. Victor Hugo may have called it "the city of 100 spires," but "the city of 100 fires" would have been more apt after heavy Allied bombing reduced almost everything to rubble during World War II. Fortunately, the spectacular **Cathédrale de Notre-Dame** and the small but intricately laid out **Vieille Ville (Old Town)** of the beautiful Rive Droite were spared. In true Rouennais spirit, many damaged buildings were also painstakingly rebuilt using revived crafts from the Middle Ages—an admirable feat that makes today's Rouen a pleasure to walk around.

Come here and you'll discover a bustling, vibrant city, bursting with activity generated by the industries connected to the port and the students at nearby universities and art schools. After a few hours in the narrow streets of the Old Town,

you'll wish you had enough money to do more than just window-shop (especially in the expensive antiques quarters around the Cathédrale). But you will undoubtedly take solace, if not in the number of bars, in the beautiful, traditional architecture: old half-timber, white stucco, brown-tile-roofed houses, asymmetrically held together by heavy dark crossbeams.

Walking the streets of Rouen is also like walking through a hall of fame. Former residents include the writers Pierre Corneille and Gustave Flaubert; Claude Monet (who couldn't stop painting the cathedral's fleeting beauty at all hours of the day); Joan of Arc, who was burned at the stake on place du Vieux-Marché in 1431 ("Oh, Rouen, art thou then my final resting place?" *Oui, ma chère Joan, oui*); and William the Conqueror, who died here in 1087.

Today's crowds are extremely varied. You'll see natty white dreads, athletically built sports players, scraggly scrappy-looking intellectuals, and well-to-do

NORMANDY

Rouen History 101

After a day of farming and a hearty meal, those horn-helmeted Viking warriors weren't all that nasty really. Look at King Rollo. He wrangled the title of first Duke of Normandy and a baptism in Rouen, taking on the more French but less tough-sounding name of Robert. He also proved to be a kick-ass town planner by narrowing and deepening the riverbed, building on Rouen's unused marshland, and reinforcing the riverbanks with quays. His works lasted until the 19th century. *Pas mal,* I'm sure you'll agree.

During the Hundred Years' War, Rouen got a serious whipping. In 1418, Henry V of England besieged the town and nearly starved it to death for 6 months. During this reign of terror, the English earned the nickname "the Goddons," derived from their habit of saying "God Damn." The Goddons ruled with an iron fist until 19-year-old Joan of Arc managed to reinstate French Charles VII to the throne in Reims in 1429 (see the Champagne chapter).

For this, however, Joan paid the ultimate price. In May of 1430, the Duke of Burgundy captured her and traded her back to the English for 10,000 gold ducats. The English imprisoned her in Rouen's 13th-century Tower of the Fields, from where she underwent a grueling 3-month trial and torture for heresy. In May of 1431, in the cemetery of the abbey of St-Ouen, they tied her to a scaffold and forced her to recant. She gave in and was condemned to life imprisonment. But that wasn't enough for the infuriated English. In giving up her life as a soldier, Joan had sworn to wear clothes more fitting of a lady. The English took away her women's clothes and forced her to wear men's attire, which subsequently meant that she had broken her pledge. On the 30th of May, she was tied to a pyre and burned alive at place du Vieux-Marché. Her heart, untouched by the fire, was thrown into the Seine for the fish. Her death, however, wasn't in vain. In 1449, Charles VII entered into Rouen victorious as king. Joan was rehabilitated, in 1456, and eventually canonized patron saint of France, in 1920.

professionals all competing for elbow-room in the numerous bars and cafes. And that means one thing—if you can't beat 'em to the table, join 'em!

Getting There

BY TRAIN

From Paris's Gare St-Lazare, **trains** leave for Rouen about once an hour (trip time: 60–70 min.). The station is at place Bernard Tissot, which gives onto rue Jeanne d'Arc. From here, the town center is straight ahead (10 min.). For information, call the **SNCF** (☎ **36-35** within France only) or check **www.sncf.com**.

BY CAR

To **drive** from Paris, take the A13 (the Autoroute de Normandie) northwest to Rouen (trip time: 1¹⁄₂ hr.). The A13 also cuts through most of the rest of the region.

Once you arrive in Rouen, you can park at the following addresses: **Parking Gambetta Maratinville** (43 bd. Gambetta; ☎ **02-32-76-30-08**), **Parking de la Gare** (36–38 rue Verte; ☎ **02-35-98-12-46**), and **Parking de l'Hôtel de Ville** (place du Général de Gaulle; ☎ **02-35-89-92-76**). If you're out at night, don't park on the side of the road. The police are cracking down with heavy fines. Your best bet is one of the underground parking lots on the Right

Rouen

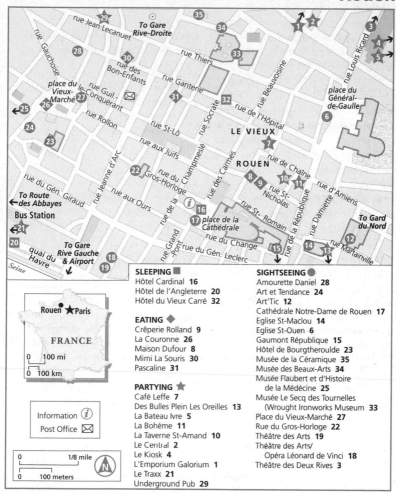

SLEEPING ■
Hôtel Cardinal **16**
Hôtel de l'Angleterre **20**
Hôtel du Vieux Carré **32**

EATING ◆
Crêperie Rolland **9**
La Couronne **26**
Maison Dufour **8**
Mimi La Souris **30**
Pascaline **31**

PARTYING ★
Café Leffe **7**
Des Bulles Plein Les Oreilles **13**
La Bateau Ivre **5**
La Bohème **11**
La Taverne St-Amand **10**
Le Central **2**
Le Kiosk **4**
L'Emporium Galorium **1**
Le Traxx **21**
Underground Pub **29**

SIGHTSEEING ●
Amourette Daniel **28**
Art et Tendance **24**
Art'Tic **12**
Cathédrale Notre-Dame de Rouen **17**
Eglise St-Maclou **14**
Eglise St-Ouen **6**
Gaumont République **15**
Hôtel de Bourgtheroulde **23**
Musée de la Céramique **35**
Musée des Beaux-Arts **34**
Musée Flaubert et d'Histoire
  de la Médécine **25**
Musée Le Secq des Tournelles
  (Wrought Ironworks Museum **33**
Place du Vieux-Marché **27**
Rue du Gros-Horloge **22**
Théâtre des Arts **19**
Théâtre des Arts/
  Opéra Léonard de Vinci **18**
Théâtre des Deux Rives **3**

Information ⓘ
Post Office ✉

Bank, which charge just 1.50€ to park from 7pm to 3am.

BY AIR

Rouen does have an airport (☎ **02-35-79-41-00**), but you're more likely to win the lottery without buying a ticket than find a plane that lands there. The closest alternative airport is Beauvais near Paris (www.aeroportbeauvais.com), which deals with mainly low-cost flights from Ireland

(www.ryanair.com) and eastern Europe (www.wizzair.com).

Orientation

The Seine splits Rouen, like Paris, into a **Rive Gauche (Left Bank)** and **Rive Droite (Right Bank).** The old city is on the right bank, and unless you really dig ugly factory buildings, you'll be spending your time here, far from the cries and smells of the industrial quarters. To reach the old city from the train station, head south along the main north-south route, rue Jeanne d'Arc, which eventually becomes the Pont Jeanne d'Arc and leads into the Rive Gauche. Running through the center of the Vieille Ville, perpendicular to rue Jeanne d'Arc, is the ▣ⓂⓋ ⬭Best❗⬮ **rue du Gros Horloge (Street of the Great Clock),** a wide pedestrian street that connects the **Cathédrale de Notre-Dame,** at its eastern end, to the **place du Vieux Marché.** You should walk down the rue du Gros Horlorge from the Cathédrale de Notre-Dame and check out the ornate gilt medieval timepiece mounted on an archway that bridges the street. Continue another 180m (600 ft.) and you'll see the peculiarly ocean-wave-like **Eglise de Jeanne d'Arc** (think Sydney Opera House meets Le Corbusier during the Middle Ages) on the place du Vieux-Marché. Another main roadway is the east-west rue Jean Lecanuet, with its central **Square Verdel** and the lush **Jardin de l'Hôtel de Ville** at its eastern end.

Getting Around

BY PUBLIC TRANSPORT

To get around the city, you can take your pick from Rouen's underground metro line and extensive bus network. The 5-year-old **Métro** is part of the city's MétroBus system (☎ 02-35-52-52-52). It has one north-to-south line. The most central stations in

Old Rouen are Palais de Justice and Gare (rue Verte). Tickets cost 1.30€ per ride, good for bus transfers within 1 hour of entering the Métro. Buy tickets from kiosks or automated machines.

BY BICYCLE

If, like rock legend Freddy Mercury (R.I.P.), you "want to ride your bicycle," hire one from **Rouen Cycle** (45 rue St-Eloi; ☎ 02-35-71-34-30; Tues–Sat 9am–noon and 2–7pm) for 20€ a day, 30€ a weekend, 50€ a week (deposit required).

ON FOOT

Those feet of yours are a fine form of locomotion, capable of taking you wherever you might want to go in Rouen. Vieille Ville, which is where you'll be spending most of your time, is especially walkable.

Tourist Office

The **Office de Tourisme** is at 25 place de la Cathédrale (☎ 02-32-08-32-40; www.rouentourisme.com; Oct 1–Apr 30 Mon–Sat 9:30am–12:30pm and 1:30–6pm, some Sun 2–6pm; May 1–Sept 30 Mon–Sat 9am–7pm, Sun 9:30am–12:30pm and 2–6pm). Apart from the usual array of tourist brochures, they distribute a neat guide called *Le Viking*. Written in French, it lists all the coolest bars, eateries, and clubs, and details vital information such as emergency numbers. If they've run out, consult Le Viking's website (http://leviking76.free.fr).

Rouen **Nuts & Bolts**

Emergencies The usual emergency numbers are ☎ 15 (ambulance), ☎ 17 (police), and ☎ 18 (fire service plus paramedics). There's a police station, **Poste de Police de l'Hôtel de Ville,** at 19 place du Général de Gaulle (☎ 02-35-07-85-22). You shouldn't have to use it, but it's better to be safe than sorry.

Internet/Wireless Hot Spots To catch up with essentials (friends and family, the state of your bank account, and world politics), **Le coeur.net** will sort you out with

ADSL. They also afford a variety of online games (54 rue Cauchoise; ☎ **02-35-15-45-42;** www.coeur-net.fr.st).

Laundromat **Lavomatic** (56 rue Cauchoise; ☎ **02-35-70-57-58**) is on a central pedestrian-only street. It's open daily 7am to 9pm. If there's no room at the "spin," try the one at 55 rue Amiens (☎ **02-35-88-82-04;** daily 7am–9pm).

Post Office **La Poste,** at 45 rue Jeanne d'Arc (☎ **02-35-15-66-92**), is in a good central location for all your postal needs.

Taxis Who knows, you might meet Vanessa Paradis's favorite "Joe le Taxi" at **Radio Taxis** (☎ **02-35-88-50-50**). If he's not there, try **Taxis Blancs** (☎ **02-35-72-68-99**).

Vehicle Rental No surprise here, the chains have a monopoly, including: **ADA** (34 av. Jean Rondeaux; ☎ 02-35-72-25-88; www.ada.fr); **Avis** (32 av. de Caen; ☎ 02-35-72-64-32; www.avis.fr); **Budget** (14 av. Jean Rondeaux; ☎ 02-32-81-95-00; www.budget.fr); **Europcar** (17 quai Pierre Corneille; ☎ 02-32-08-39-09; www. europcar.com); and **Hertz** (130 rue Jeanne d'Arc; ☎ 02-35-70-70-71; www.hertz.fr).

Sleeping

Being so pretty, Rouen has a disproportionately high number of lackluster hotels. When you know where to look, however, getting some decent shut eye in a central location can be easy as pie.

CHEAP

➔ **Hôtel de l'Angleterre** The traffic noise here can be bad if you leave the window open, but if you sleep like Rip Van Winkle or own a decent pair of earplugs, the front rooms that open onto views of the Seine are reason in itself to stay here. Some have balconies. Rooms are small but comfortable in oranges and reds, there's free Wi-Fi, and bathrooms are clean with a decent shower. Just make sure you reserve well in advance in July and August, when the hotel is packed. *21 quai du Havre.* ☎ *02-35-70-34-95. 55€–60€ double. Credit cards accepted. Parking 9€. Amenities: Bar; dry cleaning; laundry service. In room: TV, Wi-Fi.*

➔ **Hôtel du Vieux Carré** ★★ This restored half-timbered, 18th-century house is easily one of the most charming and tranquil lodgings in Rouen. The enthusiastic and well-traveled owner, Patrick Beaumont,

has tastefully decorated the guest rooms in a cozy, rustic fashion that beckons you to bed down. Unusual for central Rouen, the hotel has a restaurant and tearoom that are as popular with locals as they are with guests. The flower-filled courtyard shelters you from the world outside. *34 rue Ganterie. 76000 Rouen.* ☎ *02-35-71-67-70. 60€ double. Credit cards accepted. Amenities: Restaurant (lunch only); tearoom/cafe; dry cleaning; laundry service; limited-mobility rooms; non-smoking rooms. In room: TV, dataport.*

DOABLE

➔ **Hôtel Cardinal** This hotel is ideally located and affordable. It's across from the cathedral (imagine waking up to a view of the majestic structure and the surrounding half-timbered buildings), in the middle of a neighborhood known for antiques, art galleries, and fine dining. Rooms lack charm (avoid the ones with hideous blue doors and gray walls), but they're clean. There's so much to do in the area, you probably won't be spending much time in them anyway. *1 place de la Cathédrale.* ☎ *02-35-70-24-42. www.cardinal-hotel.com. 58€–76€ double. Credit cards accepted. Parking 5€*

nearby. *Closed mid-Dec to mid-Jan. Amenities: Limited room service; nonsmoking rooms. In room: TV, hair dryer.*

Eating

Rouen offers various dining options, from killer kabobs to innovative cheese and meat combinations, and refined regional cuisine.

CAFES & LIGHT FARE

→ **Crêperie Rolland** FRENCH CREPES When you're hungry but not starving, and you fancy a tasty meal but not a huge one, Rolland's crepes will hit the spot. With everything from the traditional ham, cheese, and egg pancakes to the more innovative varieties (think black pudding and scallops), you're bound to find something to get your stomach juices pumping. You can also stop here for pastry. *22 rue St-Nicolas.* ☎ *02-32-10-19-76. Crepes 5.60€–12€. Lunch Tues–Sat noon–2:30pm; dinner 7.30pm–10.30pm. Mon dinner only 7:30pm–10:30pm.*

CHEAP

→ **Mimi La Souris** CHEESE RESTAURANT You'll be hard-pressed to find something here that doesn't include cheese. You'll also be hard-pressed to spend a lot of money. But don't tell anybody. It's a secret shared only by you, me, and thousands of hungry Rouennais students who pile in for the unbeatable price/quantity ratio. Dishes such as pear with Roquefort and caramelized fruit with Camembert disappear like hot cakes. And Mimi's is the only place in town with a brandy bar, so indulge in a *digestif*. *17 rue des Bons Enfants.* ☎ *02-35-08-45-20. Fixed-price menus 9.80€, 12€, 15€, and 20€. All-you-can-eat lunch buffet 7€. Daily 11:30am–2pm and 6:30–10pm (until 11:30pm Fri–Sat).*

→ **Pascaline** ★ TRADITIONAL FRENCH Hanging here means hanging with the regulars—some of whom look like they've been part of the furniture since the bistro

opened in 1880. The decor hasn't changed much since then either, which is the main attraction—along with some of the cheapest fixed-price menus in town. Menu items include seafood dishes such as *pavé* of monkfish with roughly textured mustard sauce; breast of duck cooked in beer; savory *pot-au-feu maison* (house stew); and, as a *plat du jour,* cassoulet of sausages and lentils. Don't expect graciously presented food; dishes are hearty, time-tested old favorites best enjoyed in generous dollops. *5 rue de la Poterne.* ☎ *02-35-89-67-44. Reservations recommended. Credit cards accepted. Fixed-price menus 13€–22€. Daily noon–2pm and 7–11:15pm.*

DOABLE

→ **Maison Dufour** ★ NORMAN One of Normandy's best-preserved, 15th-century inns has flourished under four generations of the Dufour family since 1906. Dining rooms are decorated with cool copper pots, woodcarvings, and engravings. The food, reflecting local culinary traditions, is so outstanding that it's hard to single out specialties. The home-smoked salmon, *canard* (duckling) *rouennais,* chopped lamb, John Dory in cider sauce, and *sole Normande* are all exemplary. The most fitting Normandy dessert is a Calvados-flavored soufflé or a slice of apple tart. *67 bis rue St-Nicolas.* ☎ *02-35-71-90-62. Reservations required. Fixed-price lunch 16€–38€; fixed-price dinner 25€–38€. Credit cards accepted. Tues–Sun noon–2pm; Tues–Sat 7–9:30pm.*

SPLURGE

MTV **Best** ◗ → **La Couronne** TRADITIONAL NORMAN/FRENCH This institution has seen many stars walk through its doors, including John Wayne, Salvador Dalí, Sophia Loren, Jean-Paul Sartre, and Serge Gainsbourg. But the glamour and sparkle of stardom are not the only attraction. This is the oldest *auberge* in France (open since 1345), which means that it was probably serving food to the bloodthirsty crowd watching Jeanne d'Arc go up in smoke in front of its doors in 1431. Nowadays the only thing smokin' comes from the kitchen—luscious dishes such as salmon stuffed with scallops and cider, foie gras, and their famous Rouennais duck (Dalí's favorite). *31 place du Vieux-Marché.* ☎ *02-35-71-40-90. www.lacouronne. com.fr. Fixed-price menus 23€–45€. Daily noon–2pm and 7–10pm.*

Partying

Rouen has a pretty vibrant bar scene. There's something here for just about everyone—from those who like quiet as they consume their beverages, to sports fans cursing out the TV, to those who can't stop their legs from shaking to the booming beat of house or the staccato of drum 'n' bass. For up-to-date listings, grab *Cette Semaine à Rouen,* a pamphlet that details the week's entertainment offerings and events, available free at the tourist office and most hotels.

BARS

In a nutshell, you'll find much of the nightlife, especially pubs, on place du Vieux-Marché. For a relaxed pint, go to **Café Leffe** (36 place des Carmes; ☎ 02-35-71-93-30), and **La Taverne St-Amand** (11 rue St-Amand; ☎ 02-35-88-51-34), which has a friendly atmosphere, perfect for enjoying a mug of the best Irish, Belgian, or German beer. Across the street, **La Bohème** (18 rue St-Amand; ☎ 02-35-71-53-99), is a hip but tiny discothèque with a cozy, publike ambience. Many students meet at the **Underground Pub** (26 rue des Champs-Maillets; ☎ 02-35-98-44-84), which has a street-level bar and an underground bar fitted with wood and British bric-a-brac.

→ **L'Emporium Galorium** ★ If you believe what you read, this Rouennais hot house has been "helping ugly people have sex since 1987." At least that's the ditty they've adopted to attract crowds of wild party-fiends into their hip and shabby basement bar. Shake your booty two floors underground in medieval cellars (regular concerts and DJ nights are organized each week); and if you see someone you fancy (ugly or otherwise), why not buy him/her a drink? They're criminally cheap (1€ a shooter of flavored vodka, 4€ a glass). Who knows? The ditty just might get you down to some nitty-gritty. *151 rue Beauvoisine.* ☎ *02-35-71-76-95. www. emporium-galorium.com.*

Kabobs: The Ultimate Hangover Prevention

What's so attractive about dubious, oily meat on a stick, roasted on a vertical spit for hours, days, even weeks? It prevents hangovers, of course. Or so you can tell yourself, until you wake up in the morning with onion-breath and a throbbing head. Still, when it comes to eating kabobs, the selectivity of human memory comes into play, and when you've supped a glass too many in Rouen, you'll crave a meatsicle like you've never craved one before. When that happens, head to one of the city's main kabob houses (all open daily until 2am; all for under 5€): **Avenida** (4 place Cauchoise; ☎ 02-35-15-32-54); **Bilel** (61 bd. des Belges); **Aux Bons Enfants** (rue des bons Enfants); **Le Byzance** (32 place des Carmes); **Cappadoce** (85 rue Cauchoise; ☎ 02-35-14-07-83); **Djurdjura** (52 rue de la République; ☎ 02-35-07-34-53); **L'Escale** (80 rue de la République); **Euro Kebab** (12 rue Racine; ☎ 02-35-98-09-82); and **Kantin Izmir** (8 rue Percière; ☎ 02-35-36-15-79), which doubles as a sit-down restaurant with Turkish specialties.

Two Fabulous Gay Bars

Two places should be on your list: **Le Central,** which attracts a *très cool* crowd of mostly gay males in their 20s and 30s who blatantly model themselves on James Dean. They strut their funky stuff to house and techno in the busy bar or grab a game of pinball, billiards, and darts (138 rue Beauvoisine; ☎ **02-35-07-71-97**). The modern **Le Traxx** (4 bis bd. Ferdinand-de-Lesseps; ☎ **02-32-10-12-02**) attracts its share of young, well-connected gays and lesbians. It's known for light shows and techno music. A wild crowd parties here until the wee hours, especially on weekends. You'll pay a 9€ cover, which includes one drink.

MTV **Best ✪** ➜ **Des Bulles Plein Les Oreilles** What a breath of fresh air! An ultramodern bar that radiates trendiness, promotes creativity (regular art exhibitions, stand-up comedy, improvisation nights), and pumps out sleek mixes of electro, house, drum 'n' bass (there's even a VJ who combines film projections with sound). Bartenders serve copious *coupes* of champagne (bottles cost from 35€) to a crowd that would look more at home in the 11th *arrondissement* of Paris than in cutesy old Rouen. If old timber-clad venues are getting a bit too old hat, drop in here for a generous helping of modernity. *24 rue Armand Carrel.* ☎ *02-35-98-49-96.*

CLUBS & LIVE MUSIC VENUES

➜ **La Bateau Ivre** ★★ Don't be fooled by the nondescript decor. This is one of Rouen's most mythical concert-bars with a constant stream of local talent. Although there is an accent on music (rock, hard rock, reggae, and folk get steady lip-service in these parts), all sorts (poets, writers, in fact anybody with something to put on) are given a chance to wow the crowds. Open-mic night on Thursdays can be particularly fun. *17 rue des Sapins.* ☎ *02-35-70-09-05. http://bateauivre.rouen.free.fr.*

➜ **Le Kiosk** With a name like "the kiosk," you might expect something to be for sale here. Love maybe? Not that sort of "love for sale." No, this is more a discothèque—cum—boogie bar, where young singletons congregate on the dance floor and vie for attention, true love, a tongue down their throat—or all of the above. The hard-edged techno music and psychedelic light give everyone a good time—even those who are already loved up, or friends just out for a laugh. Admission is 8€ to 15€. *43 bd. de Verdun.* ☎ *02-35-88-54-50.*

Sightseeing

Ask the tourist office about their audio-guided tours. You can download a map free of charge at **www.rouentourisme.com**. If not, go it alone with our list of main attractions. And don't forget the informative little tourist train (CNA; ☎ **02-32-18-40-23**; tickets 6€; leaves daily Apr–Oct every hour from 10am–noon and 2–5pm from place de la Cathédrale). Go on, you know you want to!

PUBLIC MONUMENTS

FREE ➜ **Hôtel de Bourgtheroulde** Who said banks had to be boring? This one certainly isn't. In fact it's one of Rouen's showcase Gothic buildings. Built in the 15th century by William the Red and enlarged in the Renaissance, it is particularly noteworthy for its interior courtyard (the only part of the building you can visit regularly) with its octagonal stair tower.

The left gallery is entirely Renaissance. The building sometimes opens on weekends for special exhibitions. *15 place de la Pucelle.* ☎ *02-35-08-64-00. Free admission. Courtyard Mon–Fri 8:30am–6:30pm.*

MTV Best ● → **Place du Vieux-Marché** ★ Don't cry now, it was many years ago (1431) that Joan of Arc was executed for heresy here at the Old Marketplace. You wouldn't be able to forget it even if you wanted to. The whole town pays homage to her short, action-packed life; but nowhere is that truer than here, where a bronze cross marks the position of her stake. Nowadays the only stakes around are "steaks" on the plates in the surrounding restaurants, but as thoroughfares go, this pretty square with its modern church has enough activity to spark up everybody's day or night.

MTV Best ● → **Rue du Gros-Horloge** ★ Now a pedestrian street, full of old-world, half-timbered houses, the "Street of the Great Clock" runs between the cathedral and place du Vieux-Marché. It's named after a great, ornate, gilt Renaissance clock mounted on an arch, Rouen's most popular monument. The arch bridges the street and connects to a lovely Louis XV fountain with a bevy of cherubs and a bell tower. Listen for the bells at night that still toll a curfew.

CHURCHES

MTV Best ● FREE → **Cathédrale Notre-Dame de Rouen** You know that when Claude Monet immortalizes something several times over, it has to be worth looking at. Rouen's cathedral (particularly the facade, with its galaxy of statues) will not disappoint. The main door, **Porte Central,** is embellished with sculptures (some destroyed by the Huguenots) depicting the Tree of Jesse. Consecrated in 1063, it is a symphony of lacy stonework

(reconstructed after damage in World War II) with two distinguished towers. The strangely named **Tour de Beurre (Butter Tower)** was financed by the faithful who were willing to pay for the privilege of eating butter during Lent (I told you the Normans liked their butter). Containing a carillon of 56 bells, the **Tour Lanterne (Lantern Tower)**—built in 1877 and utilizing 740 tons of iron and bronze—rises to almost 150m (492 ft.). The cathedral's interior is fairly uniform, but the choir is a masterpiece, with 14 soaring pillars. The Booksellers' Stairway, in the north wing of the transept, is adorned with a stained-glass rose window that dates, in part, from the 1500s. The 13th-century chancel is beautiful, with simple lines. Especially interesting is the **Chapelle de la Vierge,** adorned with Renaissance tombs of the cardinals d'Amboise. And dig this: Richard the Lion-Hearted literally gave his heart to Rouen (it's entombed here) as a token of his affection for the residents. *Place de la Cathédrale.* ☎ *02-35-71-85-65. www.monum. fr. Free admission. Mon–Sat 8am–7pm; Sun 8am–6pm. Closed during Mass and on bank holidays.*

FREE → **Eglise St-Maclou** ★ Another church worth visiting is this one, built in the Flamboyant Gothic style, with a step-gabled porch and cloisters. It is known for the 16th-century panels on its doors (check out the Portail des Fontaines on the left). It was built in 1200, rebuilt in 1432, and consecrated in 1521, and it had a lantern tower added in the 19th century. It sits on a square full of old Norman crooked-timbered buildings. If the cathedral doesn't wear your eyes out, this should be next on your list. *3 place Barthelemy, behind the cathedral.* ☎ *02-35-71-71-72. Free admission. Mon–Sat 10am–noon and 2–5pm; Sun 3–5pm. Closed Jan 1, May 1, July 14, and Nov 11.*

FREE →Eglise St-Ouen ★★ If you're on the trail of Jeanne d'Arc, you have come to the right place. In May of 1431, Joan was taken from here to the cemetery to be burned at the stake unless she recanted. She signed an abjuration, condemning herself to life imprisonment, but that sentence was later revoked (see "Rouen History 101" on p. 196). The church itself is the outgrowth of a 7th-century Benedictine abbey and represents the work of 5 centuries. Flanked by four turrets, its 115m (377-ft.) octagonal lantern tower is called "the ducal crown of Normandy." Its nave is from the 15th century, its choir from the 14th (with 18th-c. railings), and its stained glass from the 14th to the 16th century. *Place du Général-de-Gaulle.* ☎ 02-32-08-31-01. *Free admission. Mar–Oct Tues–Sat 10am–noon and 2–6pm, Sun 10am–noon and 2–5pm (Nov–Feb closed Thurs–Fri).*

HIGHBROW HAUNTS

To gawk at the elegant and muscled bodies of ballet dancers, tap your toes to Tchaikovsky, or serenade your ears with Tosca, attend the **Théâtre des Arts** (7 rue du Dr.-Rambert; ☎ **02-35-71-41-36**), which presents regular ballet, opera, and classical music spectacles. **Théâtre des Deux Rives** (48 rue Louis-Ricard; ☎ **02-35-89-63-41**), presents a wide range of plays in French. **Théâtre des Arts/Opéra Léonard de Vinci** (7 rue du Dr.-Rambert; (☎ **02-35-71-41-36**) has a busy schedule of classical and contemporary opera. If you fancy the way Gothic churches amplify sound, you may want to check out the variety of concerts at **Eglise St-Maclou** and **Eglise St-Ouen** (see above). For information about who's playing, contact the tourist office.

MUSEUMS

The website for the three following museums is **www.rouen-musees.com**.

→**Musée de la Céramique** You can't come to Rouen and not look at what it's famous for—*faïence* (opaquely glazed earthenware). One of the great treasures here is the collection of 17th- and 18th-century Rouen *faïence*, which has a distinctive red hue because of the color of the local clay. The exhibits provide a showcase for Masseot Abaquesne, the premier French artist in faïence, and there's an interesting section devoted to *chinoiserie* from 1699 to 1745. Careful, after an hour here you just might go potty! *1 rue Faucon.* ☎ 02-35-07-31-74. *Admission 2.30€ adults, 1.55€ students. Wed–Mon 10am–1pm and 2–6pm.*

→**Musée des Beaux-Arts** ★★ Get your feet ready. This is one of France's most important provincial museums, with more than 65 rooms of art, ranging from medieval primitives to contemporary paintings. You'll find portraits by David and works by Delacroix and Ingres (seek out his *La Belle Zélie*). A Gérard David retable (altarpiece), *La Vierge et les saints (The Virgin and the Saints)* is a masterpiece. One salon is devoted to Géricault, including his portrait of Delacroix. Other works here are by Veronese, Velásquez, Caravaggio, Rubens, Poussin, Fragonard, and Corot, and by Impressionists such as Monet, including several paintings of the Rouen cathedral. *Esplanade de Marcel Duchamp.* ☎ 02-35-71-28-40. *Admission 3€ adults, 2€ students. Wed–Mon 10am–6pm.*

→**Musée Flaubert et d'Histoire de la Médécine** Gustave Flaubert, author of *Madame Bovary,* was born in the director's quarters of Rouen's public hospital in 1821 (his pop was the director). The room in which he was born is intact, and you can see the glass door that separated the Flauberts from the ward and its patients. Family furniture and medical paraphernalia are also on display. It won't blow your mind, but if you've read *Madame Bovary,* get kicks from 19th-century history, or just want to get out of the rain, you'll spend a happy half-hour here. *51 rue de Lecat.* ☎ *02-35-15-59-95. Admission 2.20€ adults, 1.50€ students. Tues 10am–6pm; Wed–Sat 10am–noon and 2–6pm. Closed holidays.*

→ **Musée Le Secq des Tournelles (Wrought Ironworks Museum)** I bet you never thought you'd be contemplating wrought iron, but here in Rouen things are a little different from everywhere in the world; old Norman crafts are particularly cherished. Housed in the 15th-century Eglise St-Laurent, this museum shows off an eclectic collection (some 14,000 pieces) of what a critic once called "forthright masculine forging to lacy feminine filigree"—including Roman keys and a needlepoint balustrade that graced Mme de Pompadour's country mansion. *2 rue Jacques-Villon.* ☎ *02-35-88-42-92. Admission 2.30€ adults, 1.55€ students. Wed–Mon 10am–1pm and 2–6pm.*

ART SCENE

Just because Rouen is an old-world kind of town doesn't mean that its modern art can't make the grade.

Unexpected Galleries

The Rouennais folk have a special relationship between their town's rich history, and the way they see their future, which is reflected in their art. To see for yourself what that relationship is, rinse your eyes with the stuff on show at **Amourette Daniel** (45 rue des Bons Enfants; ☎ **02-35-70-20-51**); **Art et Tendance** (34 rue du Vieux Palais; ☎ **02-35-15-47-56**; www.art-tendances.com), which sells knick-knacks, originals, and famous copies; and **Art'Tic** (178 rue Martainville; ☎ **06-20-75-22-39**; http://association-art-tic.spaces.live.com), a kind of showroom for on-the-up local artists. Also check out **www.forumdesarts.net**.

Performing Arts

What's good enough for Paris is good enough for Rouen. Paris has a Zenith concert hall, and so it's only fitting that Rouen should have one, too. What's more, the **Zenith** in Rouen (44 av. des Canadeins, 76120 Grand Quevilly; ☎ **02-32-91-92-92**; www.zenith-de-rouen.com) is in one seriously funky building, built in 2001 to look like a giant, silver spaceship. Join the throngs of people (up to 8,000) for big international and French acts.

Film

Whether you're craving something in English, or fancy testing your French without subtitles, grab a flick at **Gaumont République** (28 rue de la République; ☎ **08-92-69-66-96**; 8.50€).

Playing Outside

Had enough of cobblestones, narrow streets, and half-timbered houses? You want wide open spaces, greenery, and panorama? *Pas de problème!* The **Côte St-Cathérine** is a grassy knoll overlooking Rouen that offers pretty vistas of the whole city. You'll have to climb 525 steps to get up there, mind you, but once you do, you'll find yourself in another world—a protected realm of rare urban flora, which you can visit alone, or learn more about on a guided tour (☎ **02-32-08-01-42**; www.cote-sainte-catherine.com; Apr–Sept, one Sun each month). Access the steep path from the Cimetière du Mont Gargan (catch bus no. 20, toward Saint Léger du Bourg Denis, from the *centre ville,* and get off at Cimetière du Mont Gargan, at rue du Mont Gargan).

Shopping

MTV Best ● → **Faïencerie Carpentier Augy** Rouen was once one of France's major producers of the fine decorative

old Stuff

You'd have to be blind not to notice that Rouen is also an antiques capital. The old town has more than 80 vendors, but the best hunting ground is along **rue Eau-de-Robec, place Barthélémy, rue Damiette,** and **rue St-Romain.** The city also has two cool **flea markets,** on Saturday and Sunday at place St-Mare, and on Thursday at place des Emmurés. Medium- and large-scale auctions take place year-round at **Les Salles des Ventes,** 25 rue du Général-Giraud (☎ **02-35-71-13-50**) and 20 rue de la Croix-de-Fer (☎ **02-35-98-73-49**).

ceramic ware known as *faïence de Rouen.* Examples of both antique and contemporary *faïence* abound in town, but the best place to pick up a piece or two is here. It is the last remaining producer and sells both contemporary *faïence* and reproductions of historic styles in an array of colors. *26 rue St-Romain.* ☎ *02-35-88-77-47. www.fayencerie-augy.com.*

→ **La Chocolatière** Lovers of chocolate will discover a veritable paradise here, where the local specialty—a praline-layered *paillardises* rich in velvety chocolate—has attracted local gourmets for as long as anyone can remember. *18 rue Guillaume-le-Conquérant.* ☎ *02-35-71-00-79. http://rouen-chocolat.com. Daily 8am–7:45pm.*

→ **Monique** Where did you get that hat? From Monique, if you please. For millinery, head here, where all the hats are original, running the gamut from funky to refined and elegant. Best of all, you won't pay Paris prices. *58 rue St-Romain.* ☎ *02-35-98-07-03.*

Festivals & Events

In the spring and summer, Rouen bursts into life with some groovy annual events. There's the **International Festival of Nordic Film** (first 2 weeks in Mar; ☎ **02-32-08-32-40**), a **24-hour boat race** (Apr 30—May 1 around Ile Lacroix; ☎ **02-32-08-32-40**), the **Joan of Arc festival** and medieval market (end of May), and **Les Jeudis de Juillet** with live music concerts around the city (July).

The Sea Stint: The Alabaster & Flower Coast

201km (125 miles) NW of Paris, 90km (56 miles) NW of Rouen

There is no better way to see Normandy than by securing yourself a set of wheels and heading cross-country to the pretty seaside destinations along the Alabaster and Flower coastline. Honfleur, probably your first port of call, is the joker of the pack, set at the mouth of the River Seine; but Etretat (with nearby Fécamp) and the chic resorts of Deauville and Trouville all afford cool sea views.

Honfleur: A Painter's Paradise

Budding Picassos, behold Honfleur: one of Normandy's most charming fishing ports, set at the mouth of the Seine opposite Le Havre. There is something about the way the light settles here (especially in the marina where the medieval houses shimmer in the water's reflection) that makes you want to haul out your easel and start experimenting with color. You wouldn't be the first. Artists such as Daubigny, Corot, and Monet have all favored this township, and today, almost every street (some dating back to the 11th c.) is jam-packed with art galleries displaying work by artists who have done just that. Having escaped major damage in World War II, and thanks to the Pont de Normandie, the bridge that links Honfleur to Le Havre (until 2004 the longest in France, measuring 2,143m/7,029 ft.), visitors flock here by the thousands. Come join them, and you won't be disappointed.

GETTING THERE

If you're **driving** from the south (including Paris), D579 leads to the major boulevard, rue de la République. Follow it to the town center. Driving time from Paris is 2¹/₂ hours. If you're relying on public transport, note that there are no direct **trains** to Honfleur. From Paris, you'll have to take one of the dozen or so daily trains from Gare St-Lazare to Deauville. From there, bus no. 20 makes the 25-minute ride to Honfleur. From Rouen, take the train to Le Havre and transfer to bus no. 50 for the 30-minute ride to Honfleur. Several **buses** run daily between Caen and Honfleur (trip time: 2 hr.); the one-way fare is 20€. For information, call **Bus Verts** (☎ 08-10-21-42-14).

TOURIST OFFICE

The **Office de Tourisme** is on quai le Paulmier (☎ 02-31-89-23-30; www.ot-honfleur.fr).

ORIENTATION & SIGHTSEEING

Honfleur is small and can be visited in an hour (unless you opt for a museum). It also has a good supply of eateries, which makes it a hot spot for lunch or dinner. Begin your tour at place de la Porte-de-Rouen and stroll along the **Vieux Bassin,** the old harbor, taking in the fishing boats and narrow, slate-roofed houses. On the north side of the basin, the former governor's house,

Lieutenance, dates from the 16th century. Don't miss the gorgeous **Eglise Ste-Catherine** (place Ste-Catherine; ☎ 02-31-89-11-93; daily 9am–noon and 2–6pm), constructed of timber by 15th-century shipbuilders. Its wooden belfry on the other side of the street is also stunning.

Should you lengthen your visit to more than a stroll and a coffee on the harbor, it's worth stopping at the **Maisons Satie,** the 1866 birthplace of Honfleur's native son, composer Erik Satie (67 bd. Charles V; ☎ 02-31-89-11-11; admission 5.10€ adults; Apr–Sept Wed–Mon 10am–7pm, Oct–Dec and Feb 16–Mar Wed–Mon 11am–6pm, closed Jan–Feb 15). This high-tech museum pays homage to Satie, not just as a composer but as a painter and an inspiration to Picasso, Braque, Cocteau, Débussy, Ravel, and Stravinsky.

If you're interested in Impressionism, drop by the **Musée Eugène-Boudin** (place Erik-Satie; ☎ 02-31-89-54-00; July–Sept admission 5€ adults, 4.30€ students; Oct–June admission 4.40€ adults, 2.70€ students; Mar 15–Sept Wed–Mon 10am–noon and 2–6pm; Oct–Mar 14 Wed–Mon 8:30am–5pm, Sat–Sun 10am–noon and 2:30–5pm). It has a good collection of works by the painters who flocked to this port when Impressionism was new.

SLEEPING

There's no getting away from it; Honfleur is bloody expensive. Finding a bed for less than 100€ is tougher than getting a Frenchman to remain faithful to his wife (just joking). If you are determined to sleep here, try **Les Cascades,** a decent address with a regional restaurant (menus 13€–29€) and 17 simple but excellent-value rooms from 32€ to 56€ a double (17 place Tiers; ☎ 02-31-89-05-83; www.lescascades.com). If you've got a bigger budget, consider **Castel Albertine,** a handsome, redbrick hotel that used to belong to Albert Sorel (a 19th-c. historian and scholar). Its rococo rooms overlook gardens and trees, for 80€ to 145€ a double. (19 cours Albert-Manuel; ☎ 02-31-98-85-56; www.honfleurhotels.com).

EATING

Try any of the restaurants around the old port. **Les Cascades** hotel (see above) also serves plenty of locally caught fish, including excellent *moules marinières*. If you're up for a splurge, try **La Terrasse et l'Assiette.** Outfitted "in the Norman style," with heavy beams and lots of exposed brick, the gourmet citadel of Honfleur attracts an upscale international clientele with dishes that include crayfish with sautéed vermicelli and truffles (8 place Ste-Catherine; ☎ 02-31-89-31-33; reservations recommended; main courses 28€–35€; fixed-price menu 31€–51€; credit cards accepted; Wed–Sun noon–2pm and 7:30–9pm).

📺 Best ◉ Deauville & Trouville: Côte d'Azur of the North

Although they're two different towns, it's hard not to put Deauville and Trouville in the same basket. Both sit on the Flower Coast (separated only by the River Touques), both attract the region's jet-setters (and Parisians looking for escapism), both have a decent nightlife, and both like to think of themselves as being the French Riviera of the north. Well, if Deauville is Cannes (yes, it too has a film festival), Trouville is Nice (slightly quainter and less showy). Are you catching my drift?

DEAUVILLE

206km (128 miles) NW of Paris, 93km (58 miles) NW of Rouen

Deauville has been associated with the rich and famous ever since the duc de Morny, Napoleon III's half-brother, founded it as an upscale resort in 1859. In 1913, it entered sartorial history when Coco Chanel launched her career here, opening a boutique selling tiny hats that challenged the fashion of huge-brimmed hats loaded with flowers and fruit. (Coco's point of view: "How can the mind breathe under those things?"). Since then, it has never looked back, and even today it attracts high-flyers with its sandy beach, casino, and horse races.

Getting There

To **drive** from Paris (trip time: 2¹⁄₂ hr.), take the A13 west to Pont L'Evêque, then follow N177 east to Deauville. There are 6 to 10 daily **rail** connections from Paris's Gare St-Lazare (trip time: 2¹⁄₄ hr.). The rail depot lies between Trouville and Deauville, south of town. Take a taxi from the station. **Bus Verts du Calvados** (☎ 08-10-21-42-14) serves the Normandy coast from Caen to Le Havre.

Tourist Office

The **Office de Tourisme** is on place de la Mairie (☎ 02-31-14-40-00; www.deauville.org).

Orientation & Sightseeing

Coco Chanel cultivated a tradition of elegance that survives in Deauville and in its smaller neighbor Trouville, on the opposite bank of the Toques (see "Trouville," below). As stylish and (by everyone's definition) as *expensive* as it is, you won't see the sort of flashy behavior cultivated on the real French Riviera. Remember that Deauville is just opposite Britain. Somehow, the restrained and ever-so-polite way of its cross-Channel neighbors has rubbed off on the locals, moneyed beings that they are. They also get an annual invasion from Parisians—so much so that Deauville has been dubbed Paris's 21st *arrondissement.* The crowds that come tend to be urban and hip, which means that businesses and entertainment venues have to keep up with the trends if they want to stay afloat. With its golf courses, casinos, deluxe hotels, La

Touques and Clairefontaine racetracks, regattas, a yachting harbor, polo grounds, and tennis courts, Deauville is a formidable playground for the upper classes and those wishing to meet them. Looking for a charming place to stroll? Head for boutique-lined **rue Eugène-Colas, place Morny** (named for the resort's founder), and **place du Casino.** You might not be able to afford anything, but just being there makes you feel you've gone up in the world.

Playing Outdoors & with Money

Whether you're straight, gay, bi, or a hermaphrodite, life's a beach in Deauville. One of the best spots is the town's boardwalk, **Les Planches,** a promenade running parallel to the beach covered with the names of all the film stars who have bathed here. Beaux Arts and half-timbered, Norman-inspired buildings line its edges. In summer, especially August, parasols dot the beach, and oiled bodies cover every inch of sand. (And on windy days, sand covers every inch of oiled bodies, too.) The resort's only other sandy stretch is **Plage de Deauville,** a strip that's part of La Côte Fleurie.

One of the best ways to rub shoulders with the wealthy is to join them in their favorite activity—putting balls in holes. On Mont Canisy, **Golf Barrière de Deauville** (☎ 02-31-14-24-24) offers a tranquil country setting of rapid greens and difficult roughs, with sweeping views of the Auge valley and air tinged by the sea's salty tang. You've got energy? Try the 18-hole course. You've got less energy? Try the 9-hole course (greens fees are half the rates noted below). You just want to practice and see who else is hanging? Opt for the indoor driving range and putting green. Greens fees are 40€ to 80€ Saturday and Sunday, and 30€ to 48€ Monday through Friday.

To get rich quick, buy a wide hat (not one of Coco's numbers), dress smart, and place a bet at one of these horse-racing venues, where you can watch horses every day from late June to early October (races at 2pm or a polo match at 3pm). **Hippodrome de Deauville La Touques** (bd. Mauger; ☎ 02-31-14-20-00), in the heart of town near the Mairie de Deauville (town hall); and the **Hippodrome de Deauville Clairefontaine** (rte. de Clairefontaine; ☎ 02-31-14-69-00), 2km (1¼ mile) west of the center.

Sleeping

Goodness me, it's hard to find a bargain in diamond-clad Deauville, and I'm sorry to say that means you might have to head away from the center. Chain hotel **Ibis** (9–10 quai de la Marine; ☎ 02-31-14-50-00; www.hotelibis.com; 59€–90€ double, 110€–150€ duplex suite for 2–6) is dull and standardized, on the periphery of Deauville about a half-mile from the casino, but it's one of the best bargains in town. If you move like lightening, you might be fast enough for a room at **Hôtel Le Trophée** ★ (81 rue du Général-Leclerc; ☎ 02-31-88-45-86; www.letrophee.com; 69€–114€ double) in the middle of Deauville, 150m (492 ft.) from the beach. Rooms are small but have private balconies overlooking the shopping streets, and there's a sun terrace on the roof.

➜ **Royal-Barrière** ★★ During the Deauville Festival of American Film, the U.S. stars stay here, which means that if you're lucky, you could be sleeping in the same bed as once did Mr. Pitt and Ms. Jolie. This opulent structure with columns and exposed timbers adjoins the casino and fronts a park near the Channel, evoking an Edwardian-era grand palace hotel. The decor of the guest rooms, conceived by mega-designer Jacques Garcia, is a reinterpretation of Directoire and Napoleon III styles. *Bd. Eugène-Cornuché.* ☎ *02-31-98-66-33.* *www.lucienbarriere.com.* *280€–624€ double; 900€–1,475€ suite. Credit cards accepted. Closed Nov to mid-Mar. Amenities: 2 restaurants; bar; dry cleaning; health club; heated outdoor pool; laundry service; 24-hr. room service; sauna. In room: TV, dataport, hair dryer, minibar, safe.*

Eating

→ **Chez Miocque** TRADITIONAL FRENCH It's a bit of a splurge, but this hip cafe will fill you up on hearty brasserie-style food, including succulent lamb stew with spring vegetables, filet of skate with cream-based caper sauce, mussels in white-wine sauce, and steaks. It does a bustling business at its sidewalk tables for lunch, dinner, or just drinks. *81 rue Eugène-Colas.* ☎ *02-31-88-09-52. Reservations recommended. Main courses 20€–40€. Credit cards accepted. July–Sept daily 9am–midnight; mid-Feb to June and Oct–Dec Fri–Mon noon–4pm and 7pm–midnight. Closed Jan to mid-Feb.*

Partying

The **Casino de Deauville** (rue Edmond-Blanc; ☎ **02-31-14-31-14**; www.lucien barriere.com) is one of France's premier casinos (games include roulette, baccarat, blackjack, and poker). Its original Belle Epoque core has been expanded with a theater, a nightclub, three restaurants, and an extensive collection of slot machines (*machines à sous;* daily 11am–2am, until 3am Fri and 4am Sat; no dress code; free admission). The areas containing *les jeux traditionnels* (traditional games) are open daily at 4pm and close between 3am and 4am, depending on business and the day of the week. Entrance is 12€ and you must present a passport or identity card to gain admission. Jackets (but not ties) are requested for men.

If it's a boogie you're looking for, head to the high-energy **Y Club** (14 bis rue Désiré-le-Hoc; ☎ **02-31-88-30-91**). For salsa, merengue, and reggae, visit **Brok Café**

(14 av. du Général-de-Gaulle; ☎ **02-31-81-30-81**). And for cool hits and an indoor swimming pool near the bar, **Dancing Les Planches** (Le Bois Lauret, Blonville; ☎ **02-31-87-58-09**), 4km (2½ miles) is a sleek joint.

Festival

For a week in September, the **Deauville Festival of American Film** (☎ **02-31-14-40-00**; www.festival-deauville.com) gives Cannes's a run for its money. Actors, producers, directors, and writers flock here and briefly eclipse the high rollers at the casinos and the horse-racing and polo crowd. Don't forget your notebook for those autographs!

TROUVILLE

206km (128 miles) NW of Paris, 90km (56 miles) NW of Rouen

Compared to its flamboyant neighbor (Deauville) across the Touques River, Trouville feels more like the fishing port Honfleur (see above). In fact, they're quite similar, really—except Trouville has fewer boutiques and art galleries. Don't expect the grand atmosphere of Deauville; Trouville is wealthy, but it's also low-key and less reliant on resort euros. When the bathers leave its splendid sands, Trouville continues to thrive—its resident population of fishermen sees to that.

Getting There

There are **rail** connections from Gare St-Lazare in Paris to Trouville (see "Deauville," earlier in this chapter). **Bus Verts du Calvados** links Trouville, Deauville, and the surrounding region with the rest of Normandy. For bus information, call the **Gare Routière** (☎ **08-10-21-42-14**). If you're traveling by **car** from Deauville, drive west along the D180.

Tourist Office

The **Office de Tourisme** is at 32 quai Fernand-Moureaux (☎ **02-31-14-60-70**; www.trouvillesurmer.org).

Orientation & Sightseeing

In the heyday of Napoleon III, during the 1860s, *boulevardiers* used to bring their wives and families to Trouville and stash their mistresses in Deauville. A complicated activity, no doubt, but one facilitated by the proximity of the two towns. Well, I reckon that for once the wives got the better deal. In contrast to Deauville's almost clinical town planning, Trouville is a mass of labyrinthine alleyways that hint at its origins as a medieval fishing port. They're far more interesting to look around, but once you've had your fill of cutesy old stuff, you can hop across the water for some glamour in Deauville. Should you happen upon Trouville in the summer, expect lots of flesh sprawled on the sands in various states of undress. There's only one beach, **Plage de Trouville** (though when you've tired of it, you only have to cross the river to reach the Plage de Deauville).

Sleeping

➜ **Le Beach Hotel** If you can't afford Deauville, Trouville is slightly cheaper (but only slightly). You might feel a bit like a poor relation sleeping here (seven floors built in the '80s, yuck), but rooms are a good size, have comfy beds, and views of Trouville harbor. *1 quai Albert Ier.* ☎ *02-31-98-12-00. 67€–95€ double. Credit cards accepted. Amenities: Restaurant; bar; limited-mobility rooms; limited room service; outdoor pool. In room: TV, minibar.*

Eating

➜ **La Petite Auberge** NORMAN Okay, it's not that cheap—but nothing is around here. You should flock to this Norman bistro, a block from the casino, for regional wonders such as cream of cauliflower soup with scallops, or a *pot-au-feu Dieppoise* featuring filet of sole, scallops, monkfish, and salmon beautifully simmered together. Because the bistro seats only 30, reservations are vital in summer. *7 rue Carnot.*

☎ *02-31-88-11-07. Reservations required. Fixed-price menus 26€–44€. Credit cards accepted. July Thurs–Tues noon–2:30pm and 7:15–9:30pm; Aug daily noon–2:30pm and 7:15–9:30pm; Sept–June Thurs–Mon noon–2:30pm and 7–10pm.*

Partying

Living in the shadows of a shinier bigger brother (Deauville), this side of the River Touques has fewer parties. Trouville's **Casino Barrière de Trouville** (place du Maréchal-Foch; ☎ **02-31-87-75-00**; www.lucienbarriere.com), however, is less stuffy than its sibling's though less architecturally distinctive. It has more of a New Orleans–style environment, with a blues and jazz bar that schedules live music Friday and Saturday night, and a small-scale replica of Bourbon Street. Entrance to the slot machines is free. Entrance to the more formal area with roulette, blackjack, and craps costs 11€ (you'll need a passport or identity card to get in). The formal area is open Sunday to Thursday 8pm to 2am, Friday 8pm to 3am, and Sat 8pm to 4am. The rest of the casino is open daily from 10am. Men aren't required to wear jackets and ties, but sneakers are a no-no.

MTV Best ✪ Etretat: Tracking the Gentleman Thief

When you were a kid, did you ever dream about bourgeois crooks, hidden treasures, and hollow cliffs? "What's that got to do with Normandy?" you may well ask. Well, everything, if you come to Etretat. This sleepy fishing town on the Alabaster coast (Côte d'Alabâtre) is famous for spectacular white cliffs, giant archways, and a mysterious chalk needle that inspired the mind of one of France's most famous 19th-century writers, Maurice Leblanc. He based an entire crime novel, *L'Aiguille Creuse (The*

Hollow Needle), on the geography of Etretat. He made it the headquarters of an evasive gentleman thief named Arsène Lupin, who hid his stolen booty within the chalky hollows of Etretat's needle. You might have heard of him: French director Jean-Paul Salomé turned the tale into a box office hit *(Arsène Lupin)* featuring Kristin Scott Thomas and French heart-throb Romain Duris.

The Alabaster coast is renowned for its natural beauty, with smooth, green fields, dramatic white cliffs, clustered villages, 19th-century villas, and a host of flora and fauna. There is also a rich birdlife, so if you're lucky and know what you're looking for, you could see peregrine falcons, kittiwakes, fulmars (a cousin of the albatross), and great cormorants (a feat considering their chicks used to be considered a local delicacy).

The town of Etretat has several picturesque streets, but its real charm lies in its shingle beaches (no sand here, I'm afraid), overshadowed by some of the most dramatic cliffs in Normandy. This is where you'll be spending most of your time—on them, underneath them, and even (in the **Trou de l'Homme**) inside them.

GETTING THERE

If you're **driving** from Paris, take the A13 and exit at Fécamp/Etretat (3 hr.). By **train,** TGVs from Paris St-Lazare go via Rouen to Bréauté, from where you can catch a coach service (**Autocar gris;** ☎ 02-35-27-04-25) to Etretat and Fécamp.

TOURIST OFFICE

The **Office de Tourisme** is at place Maurice Guillard (☎ 02-35-27-05-21; www.etretat.net).

ORIENTATION & SIGHTSEEING

Upon arrival in Etretat, you'll notice it isn't quite the quaint, cobbled fishing village you'd expect to find. The town was small and unremarkable until the 19th century, when Etretat's spectacular views were discovered and then devoured by bourgeois families on vacation. Big-wigs such as writer Maupassant and the Queens of Spain—Marie-Christine de Bourbon Sicile and Isabelle II—sojourned in the nearby **Château les Aygues** (rue Offenbach; ☎ 02-35-28-92-77; July–Aug Wed–Mon 2–6pm), now a museum and *chambres d'hôtes*. The Anglo-Norman architecture in town dates mainly from this era (except for the 14th-c. covered market and 16th-c. Manoir de la Salamandre restaurant, imported from the Norman town of Liseux in the early 20th c.).

If you want to fuel your imagination before you get to the cliffs, go to Maurice Leblanc's pretty 19th-century house, **Le Clos Arsène Lupin** (15 rue G. de Maupassant; ☎ 02-35-10-59-53; www.arsene-lupin.com; daily 10am–5pm; closed Nov to early Feb). It's now a museum devoted to the writer, his lovable rogue Arsène Lupin, and the story of the Hollow Needle.

A few kilometers from Etretat is the 📺 Best❸ **Palais de Benedictine** in Fécamp. Built in 1900 with decadent Gothic and Renaissance-inspired architecture, it is a magical place—a working distillery–cum–art museum. An educational tour explains how the delicious, spicy liquor Benedictine is made (invented by medieval Benedictine monks). Another section is entirely given over to 15th- and 16th-century paintings and a contemporary art exhibition room. *110 rue Alexandre le Grand. ☎ 02-35-10-26-10. www.benedictine. fr. Admission 5.80€. Daily 10:30am–6pm (closed Jan and 1–2pm in low season).*

PLAYING OUTDOORS

Who needs the gym when you can climb cliffs? From the stony beach in town, walk up the muddy track that borders Etretat's

18-hole golf course (deemed the finest on mainland France: **Golf—Route du Havre** ☎ **02-35-27-04-89;** www.golfetretat.com) along the cliff edge for an overall view of the needle. Once at the top, you'll notice the remnants of an old fort with grey-stone steps and an accessible lookout point. According to legend, a chamber known as "La Chambre des Demoiselles" lies beneath the fort. Nobles used it to imprison ill-disciplined women—although nobody has ever found it.

Back on beach level, you can only reach the needle at low tide (don't try it if the tide is rising), by climbing through a natural tunnel known as the **Trou à l'Homme** (man hole). Wear good shoes, as access to the hole is via a dicey, iron ladder. Once you get through the obscurity of the cave, a monumental view opens onto the needle and adjacent arches, the "Porte d'Aval" and the "Manneporte." At the foot of the hole, don't forget to marvel at Marie Antoinette's former oyster farms (the trench-like rectangles, sunk deep into the beach), once used by locals to grow the finest oysters in France.

For somewhere more secluded, head out along the D4, between Etretat and Fécamp, to the tiny hamlet of **Vaucottes,** which harbors one of the area's prettiest and most secluded flintstone beaches around.

SLEEPING & EATING

➔ **La Salamandre** ✶ This medieval and Renaissance-style building will feed you then put you to bed. The 16th-century dining room specializes in seafood, homemade foie gras, and organic meats. There are even several vegetarian options—a rarity in France. The upstairs bedrooms are tastefully decorated with simple period touches and contrast refreshingly with the rest of the town. *Bd. René Coty.* ☎ *02-35-27-17-07. 32€–106€ double. Menus 15€–32€.*

The History Trail

In a country as old as France, it is impossible to separate tourism from history. So much has happened here that even the smallest, most miniscule, and seemingly irrelevant hamlet has probably witnessed some of history's most juicy episodes. Normandy definitely complies with this theory, and the following trail will take you to three of the region's most important and breathtaking historical sites.

▥ Best ☻ Bayeux

267km (166 miles) NW of Paris, 25km (16 miles) NW of Caen

It was the early Dukes of Normandy (Viking Rollo's descendants; see "Rouen History 101" on p. 196) who first sent their sons to this settlement to learn the Norse language. Since then, things have changed somewhat. The Vikings gradually turned into homegrown Normans, and Bayeux exploded in typical medieval splendor with timbered houses, stone mansions, cobblestone streets, and picture-perfect waterways (the River Aure and old tanners district). Bayeux was fortunately spared from bombardment in 1944 and was the first French town to be liberated from Nazi control.

Visitors wanting to explore sites associated with "the Longest Day" flood the town, because many memorials (not to mention the beaches; see "D-Day Beaches," below) are only 9.5km (6 miles) to 19km (12 miles) away. Shops line the cozy little lanes, many selling more World War II memorabilia and postcards than you'll ever need.

Bayeux can easily be covered in a day, so if you'd prefer to stay somewhere more upbeat, head for Caen (see below), which has a wider choice of eateries, bars, and hotels.

GETTING THERE

Trains depart daily from Paris's Gare St-Lazare (2¹/₂ hr.), and many stop in Caen. Travel time between Caen and Bayeux is about 20 minutes. To **drive** to Bayeux from Paris (3 hr.), take the A13 to Caen and the E46 west to Bayeux.

TOURIST OFFICE

The **Office de Tourisme** is at pont St-Jean (☎ 02-31-51-28-28; www.bayeux-tourisme.com).

ORIENTATION & SIGHTSEEING

Pretty medieval Bayeux is good for a stroll. There's a lovely Romanesque cathedral, **Notre-Dame de Bayeux** (rue du Bienvenu; ☎ 02-31-92-01-85; free admission; daily 8:30am–6pm, to 7pm July–Aug). The **Musée Memorial de la Bataille de Normandie** (bd. Fabian Ware; ☎ 02-31-51-46-90; admission 5.50€ adults, 2.60€ students; May–Sept 15 daily 9:30am–6:30pm; Sept 16–Apr 10am–12:30pm and 2–6pm), deals with the military and human history of the Battle of Normandy (June 6–Aug 22, 1944). And the hard-hitting **Commonwealth Cemetery** (☎ 03-21-21-77-00) on the northwestern perimeter houses 4,144 graves of soldiers from throughout the British Commonwealth. The real reason to come here, though, is for the **Musée de la Tapisserie de Bayeux** ★★ (Centre Guillaume-le-Conquérant, 13 rue de Nesmond; ☎ 02-31-51-25-50; admission 7.40€ adults, 3€ students; May–Aug daily 9am–7pm; mid-Mar to Apr and Sept–Oct daily 9am–6:30pm; Nov to mid-Mar daily 9:30am–12:30pm and 2–6pm), which contains the most famous tapestry in the world: The Bayeux tapestry. Contrary to legend, it wasn't made by Queen Mathilda, the wife of William the Conqueror. More likely, it was commissioned in Kent and created by unknown embroiderers between 1066 and 1077. It is actually an embroidery on linen, 70m (230 ft.) long and 5m (16 ft.) wide, depicting in 58 scenes the story of William the Conqueror's takeover of England. Scenes include the coronation of Harold as the Saxon king of England, Harold returning from his journey to Normandy, the surrender of Dinan, Harold being told of the apparition of a comet (a portent of misfortune), William dressed for war, and the death of Harold. The decorative borders include scenes from *Aesop's Fables.*

SLEEPING

It's cute and interesting by day, but you'll be bored at night, so head off to nearby **Caen** for some action before bedtime. One of the best-value sleeps is **Hôtel St-Etienne** ★★ (2 rue de l'Academie, Caen 1400; ☎ 02-31-86-35-82; www.hotel-saint-etienne.com). Set in a tranquil quarter close to the Abbaye-aux-Homme, it has rooms for 28€ to 40€.

EATING

➜**Le Pommier** ★ NORMAN For some good, hearty Norman nosh, you can't get more authentic than 18th-century Le Pommier. As its name suggests (*pommier* means apple tree), much of its cooking uses apples or stuffs that derive from apples, such as cider. But dishes aren't drowned in gravies, and they evolve with the seasons. Duckling foie gras is usually on the menu, as is rabbit stew braised in cider. *38 rue des Cuisiniers.* ☎ *02-31-21-52-10. Reservations recommended. Fixed-price menus 11€–26€ lunch, 14€–26€ dinner. Credit cards accepted. Apr–Sept daily noon–2:30pm and 7–9:30pm; Oct–Mar Thurs–Mon noon–2pm and 7–9:30pm.*

FESTIVAL

The town goes wild on the first weekend in July during **Fêtes Médiévales.** The streets fill with wine and song during 2 days of medieval revelry. For information, call ☎ 02-31-92-03-30.

D-Day Beaches

*Arromanches-les-Bains: 272km (169 miles)
NW of Paris, 11km (7 miles) NW of Bayeux;
Grandcamp-Maisy (near Omaha Beach):
299km (185 miles) NW of Paris, 56km (35 miles)
NW of Caen*

During a rainy week in June 1944, the greatest armada ever—soldiers and sailors, warships, landing craft, tugboats, jeeps—assembled along the southern coast of England. At 9:15pm on June 5, the BBC announced to the French Resistance that the invasion was imminent, signaling the underground to start dynamiting the railways. Before midnight, Allied planes began bombing the Norman coast. By 1:30am on June 6 ("the Longest Day"), members of the 101st Airborne were parachuting to the ground on German-occupied French soil. At 6:30am, the Americans began landing on the beaches, codenamed Utah and Omaha. An hour later, British and Canadian forces made beachheads at Juno, Gold, and Sword.

The Nazis had mocked Churchill's promise in 1943 to liberate France "before the fall of the autumn leaves." When the invasion did come, it was swift, sudden, and a surprise to the formidable "Atlantic wall." Today, veterans (fewer and fewer as time goes by) walk with their children and grandchildren across the beaches where "Czech hedgehogs," "Belgian grills," "pillboxes," and "Rommel asparagus" (all military barriers or structures) once stood and where some of the bloodiest battles of the war took place.

GETTING THERE

Public transportation is as unreliable as President Chirac when he says that he never used the state's money to pay for his holidays. Therefore, the best way to get to the D-Day beaches is to **drive.** The trip takes about 3 hours from Paris. Take A13 west to Caen and continue west along A13 to Bayeux. From Bayeux, travel north along D6 until you reach the coast at Port-en-Bessin. From here, D514 runs along the coastline; most D-Day sites are west of Port-en-Bessin. Parking is not a problem, as most of the designated areas along the roadway are free. If you can, try to visit on a weekday, as weekends can get very crowded with summer tourists and sunbathers.

If you don't have a car, the best way to see the D-Day beaches is on a **tour. Normandy Tours,** Hôtel de la Gare, Bayeux (☎ 02-31-92-10-70; www.normandy-tours-hotel.com), runs a 4- to 5-hour tour (in English) to Arromanches, Omaha Beach, the American Military Cemetery, and Pointe du Hoc for 40€ adults, 32€ students. **Normandy Sightseeing Tours** (618 rte. du Lavoir; ☎ 02-31-51-70-52; www.normandyweb guide.com) offers good half-day trips from 40€ to 45€ for adults and 35€ for students; a full-day trip is 75€ for adults and 65€ for students. The company picks you up at your hotel in Bayeux. A final option, **Battlebus** (☎ 02-31-22-28-82; www.battlebus.fr), conducts a simultaneously riveting, exhausting, and stimulating full-day tour, encompassing all sites and beaches that were pivotal during the D-Day landing and Battle of Normandy. Cost is 80€ per person for 1 day and 150€ for the 2-day American experience tour.

TOURIST OFFICE

The **Office de Tourisme** at Arromanches-les-Bains (4 rue du Maréchal-Joffre; ☎ 02-31-21-47-56) is open year-round.

SLEEPING & EATING

If you can't make it back to Caen in time, kill two birds with one stone in Grandcamp-Maisy, where **Hôtel Duguesclin** (4 quai Crampon, 14450 Grandcamp-Maisy; ☎ 02-31-22-64-22) serves tasty hot grub (the fish soup and grilled scallops are scrumptious) for 14€ to 29€ a menu, and provides 29 comfortable rooms from 45€ to 53€.

NORMANDY

Reliving the Longest Day

Fans of *Saving Private Ryan* or *Band of Brothers,* your 📺 Best❢ **"longest day" tour** starts at the seaside resort of **Arromanches-les-Bains.** In June 1944, the 50th British Division took it and turned the former fishing port into a mammoth prefabricated port known as Winston (it was towed across the Channel to supply the Allied forces). The wreckage of that artificial harbor is just off the beach, **Plage du Débarquement.** In Arromanches, the **Musée du Débarquement** (place du 6 Juin; ☎ 02-31-22-34-31; www.normandy1944.com; admission 6€ adults, 4€ students; May–Sept daily 9am–7pm, Oct to mid-Dec, Feb–Apr daily 10am–12:30pm, 1:30–5pm; closed mid-Dec to Jan) features maps, models, a cinema, photographs, and a diorama of the landing, with English commentary.

Moving along the coast, you'll arrive at **Omaha Beach,** where you can still see the war wreckage. "Hanging on by their toenails," the men of the 1st and 29th American Divisions occupied the beach that June day. The code name Omaha became famous; until then, the beaches had been called St-Laurent, Vierville-sur-Mer, and Colleville. A monument commemorates the heroism of the invaders. Covering some 70 hectares (173 acres) at Omaha Beach, the **Normandy American Cemetery** (☎ 02-31-51-62-00) is filled with crosses and Stars of David in Lasa marble. The remains of 9,386 American military dead were buried here on territory now owned by the United States, a gift from the French nation. The cemetery is open from 9am to 5pm daily.

Farther along the coast, you'll see the jagged lime cliffs of the **Pointe du Hoc.** A cross honors a group of American Rangers, led by Lt. Col. James Rudder, who scaled the cliffs using hooks to get at the pillboxes (gun emplacements). The scars of war are more visible here than at any other point along the beach. Farther along the Cotentin Peninsula is **Utah Beach,** where the 4th U.S. Infantry Division landed at 6:30am. The landing force was nearly 3km (2 miles) south of its intended destination, but Nazi defenses were weak. By midday, the infantry had completely cleared the beach. A U.S. monument commemorates their heroism.

Nearby, you can visit the hamlet of **Ste-Mère-Eglise,** which was virtually unknown outside of France before paratroopers dropped from the sky. In Ste-Mère-Eglise is Kilometer "0" on the Liberty Highway, marking the first of the milestones the American armies reached on their way to Metz and Bastogne.

📺 Best❢ Mont St-Michel

Massive walls measuring more than half a mile in circumference surround one of Europe's great attractions, Mont St-Michel. It is a stunning little summit (78m/256 ft. high), crowned by an abbey, connected to the Baie du Mont St-Michel by a causeway that borders Normandy and Brittany. Once the view from the mainland has taken your breath away, prepare to lose it again as you climb the steep Grande Rue (the main street) past hordes of tourists and schlocky souvenir stands to reach the famous abbey. Look past the tack toward the beautiful 15th- and 16th-century houses (still, for the most part, inhabited by wealthy locals). In fact if you can get into the right mindset, it's rather like a melodramatic Hollywood epic—minus shrieking Mel Gibson and war paint, fortunately.

Visitors from the world over make the trek to visit the abbey, some out of religious curiosity, but most simply to view

Mont St-Michel

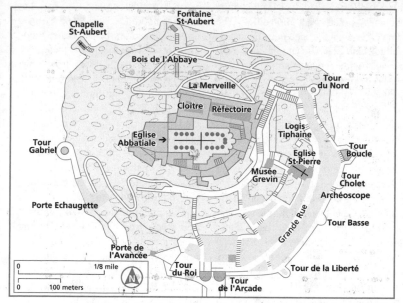

Map labels: Fontaine St-Aubert, Chapelle St-Aubert, Bois de l'Abbaye, Tour du Nord, La Merveille, Cloitre, Réfectoire, Logis Tiphaine, Tour Gabriel, Eglise Abbatiale →, Eglise St-Pierre, Tour Boucle, Musée Grevin, Tour Cholet, Archéoscope, Porte Echaugette, Grande Rue, Tour Basse, Porte de l'Avancée, Tour de la Liberté, Tour du Roi, Tour de l'Arcade

0   1/8 mile
0   100 meters
N

the stunning mix of architectural styles—from the Gothic choir to the pink granite refectory from the early 1200s.

Many think of revolutionary and independent France simply in terms of the 18th-century Revolution. But it was here at Mont St-Michel that the concept of a free-standing France was birthed centuries before that event, during the darkest years of France's occupation by the English.

GETTING THERE

The best way is to **drive.** From Caen, follow A84 southwest to Pontorson, continuing a few more kilometers to Avranches; from there, merge onto D43, following signs to its end at Mont St-Michel. Total driving time from Paris is about 4¹/₂ hours.

There are no direct trains between Paris and Mont St-Michel, but you could catch a high-speed **TGV train** from Paris's Gare Montparnasse to Rennes, from where you can transfer to the **bus** run by the **SNCF** (☎ 36–35) for the 75-minute trip to Mont St-Michel. Another company, Les

Courriers Bretons (☎ 02-99-19-70-70; www.lescourriersbretons.fr), also covers the 75-minute ride to Mont St-Michel from St-Malo two to five times a day for under 10€ per person.

TOURIST OFFICE

The **Office de Tourisme** is in the Corps de Garde des Bourgeois (the Old Guard Room of the Bourgeois), at the left of the town gates (☎ 02-33-60-14-30; www.ot-montsaintmichel.com). The tourist office is open daily year-round except Christmas and New Year's Day.

ORIENTATION & SIGHTSEEING

It may as well be Everest for the huffing and puffing you'll do by the time you get to the **abbey** at the top. In the 8th century, St. Aubert, the bishop of Avranches, founded an oratory on this spot. A Benedictine monastery, founded in 966 by Richard I, replaced it. That burned in 1203 so King Philippe Auguste financed the building of an abbey in the 13th century.

NORMANDY

Ramparts encircle the church and a three-tiered ensemble of 13th-century buildings called **La Merveille (The Marvel)**—one of Europe's most important Gothic complexes, a citadel in which the concept of an independent France was nurtured during the 300 years of English occupation in the Aquitaine.

On the second terrace of La Merveille is one of Mont St-Michel's largest and most beautiful rooms, a 13th-century hall known as the **Salle des Chevaliers.**

Crowning the mountain's summit is the **Eglise Abbatiale** (Abbaye Mont St-Michel; ☎ 02-33-89-80-00; www.monum.fr; 8€ adults, 5€ students and adults 18–25), not to be confused with the parish church, Eglise St-Pierre, which is lower on the mountain. Begun in the 11th century, the abbey church consists of a Romanesque nave and transept, plus a choir in Flamboyant Gothic style. The rectangular refectory dates from 1212, and the cloisters with their columns of pink granite are from 1225. Open daily May to September 9am to 6pm, October to April 9:30am to 5pm. Also open Monday to Saturday in June to September from 9pm to 1am (last entrance at midnight). Mass begins Tuesday to Sunday at 12:15pm.

Archeoscope, at chemin de la Ronde (☎ 02-33-89-01-85), is a small theater that presents *L'Eau et La Lumière (Water and Light)*, celebrating the legend and lore of Mont St-Michel and its role as a preserver of French medieval nationalism (shows begin every 30–60 min. between 9:30am–5:30pm). A cool and unusual diversion is the adjacent **Musée de la Mer** (Grande Rue; ☎ 02-33-89-02-02), which showcases marine crafts throughout history and illustrations of the French government's ongoing project intended to reactivate the tidal cleansing of the nearby marshes. **Musée Grevin (Musée Historique de Mont St-Michel;** chemin de la Ronde; ☎ 02-33-89-02-02), traces

the history of the abbey. Another museum worth dashing around is the **Logis Tiphaine** (Grande Rue; ☎ 02-33-89-02-02), a 15th-century home originally under the control of the Duguesclin family, noted defenders of the fortress from English intrigue. In the building, next to the Eglise St-Pierre, you'll find furniture and accessories from that era, and a sense of pride at the fortress's durability as a bastion of all things French. A combined ticket for all four attractions is 15€ for adults and 12€ for students. Other than the Archeoscope, whose hours are noted above, the museums are open daily from 9am to 5pm.

If you're running short on dough (or even if you're not), you'd do well to simply appreciate the natural beauty of the surrounding area—including the famous and sometimes ferocious tides and quicksand—and the amazing abbey itself, rather than splurging on the museums.

In 2007, some access to the mount may be limited as work begins to reinforce its perimeters. Call the tourist office for more information.

SLEEPING & EATING

➜ **La Mère Poulard** Staying near the Mont is going to cost you—it's best to make this a day trip. But if you miss the last low tide out of town, you could give La Mère Poulard a call. This country inn is a shrine to those who revere the omelet that Annette Poulard created in 1888, when the hotel was founded. Rooms are charming and priced according to the quality of the views. The restaurant (Les Terrasses Poulard) in the adjacent village house serves up regional bests such as *agneau du pré salé* (lamb raised on the saltwater marshes near the foundations of the abbey) and an array of fish, including lobster. It's pricey, but by Jove it's worth the splurge. *Grande Rue, 50116 Mont St-Michel. ☎ 02-33-89-68-68. www. mere-poulard.fr. 60€–280€ double. Credit cards accepted. Restaurant daily noon–10pm.*

Brittany

by Lauren Sommer

Residents of Brittany, in France's northwest corner, like to think of their region as a nation unto itself—with its rugged shores, warm beaches, prehistoric sites, and fiercely independent culture blending Celtic and French traditions. When Brittany finally joined France in 1532, it retained several "privileges" granting them rights to avoid taxes and retain some autonomy, and this spirit of sticking it to authority has endured for centuries. If you're wondering about the second language on the street signs, it's traditional Breton, a language much closer to Welsh than French. Not many people are fluent in it these days; you'll have to work to find the spoken word. But Celtic influence is found elsewhere in Brittany—from its music, food, and traditional dance to its location, snugged under the English Channel on the northwest coast, in direct sight of England.

Brittany is not just famous with English tourists (though their presence guarantees you'll find some English speakers during your travels here). It's also frequented by French vacationers, which means that you won't feel like you're in a French theme park with American tourists, even at the most overrun sights in July and August. With plenty of surf and a bustling beach culture, towns like St-Malo and Carnac heat up during the day and keep going at night with student dive bars and pubs filled with locals. Some seriously old historic sites await visitors, from Stone Age rock formations in Carnac to crooked medieval houses in Rennes and castles in St-Malo. And while Normandy may be the most famous World War II landing zone, Brittany took a brutal battering as well, bearing battle scars all over the region.

Cuisine in Brittany boils down to two categories that you'll get to know well: seafood and crepes.

With so much oceanfront property, Brittany pulls in some of the freshest and tastiest seafood in France. Its cold waters feed world-famous *huitres* (oysters), several of which are local specialties, as well as lobster, fish, and sardines. And you'll find creperies on every corner serving the French version of fast food. Breton crepes are made with traditional black wheat (*blé noir*), much heartier than their fair-colored pancake cousins. While you may expect every French region to specialize in wine, you won't find any grapes in Brittany. Cider is the name of game, and it comes in a vast number of varieties. Finally, no trip would be complete without tasting a *kouign amann*, Brittany's sugary, buttery pastry.

The Best of Brittany

○ **The Best Walk at Sunset (St-Malo):** Walking around St-Malo's high city walls is breathtaking, but for one of the best views of the city, head to **Môle des Noires,** a long stone walkway that extends far onto the water. On your way to the lighthouse at the end, you'll pass fishermen looking for a bite in the last light of the day and witness a gorgeous sunset over the ocean. See p. 233.

○ **The Best Bar Name (St-Malo): Le Café du Coin d'en Bas de la rue du Bout de la Ville d'en Face du Port— La Java,** the corner cafe at the bottom of the road at the end of town across from the port, is *the party*. With a name like that, you know you'll be running into some seriously sarcastic bar staffers inside. And then there's the Moulin-Rouge-gone-mad decor. Even if you don't take a seat on one of the wooden swings by the bar, it's worth peeking in for a jolt of sensory overload. See p. 231.

○ **The Best Place to Feel Patriotic (St-Malo):** You may have seen a lot of World War II movies over the years, but it's nothing compared to walking in someone's footsteps. The **Memorial 39—45** is actually a three-story German bunker built deep into the ground, housing a museum dedicated to St-Malo's liberation. Just seeing the anti-aircraft gun pointing towards the sky gives you one powerful picture of how dire a scene it must have been. See p. 233.

○ **The Best Indulgence (Rennes):** Don't let appearances fool you. The 30 different chocolates in **Chocolaterie Durand** are uniformly shaped squares, labeled only by number in gold lettering on top. But beneath the dark exterior, there's nothing tame about their flavor. This *chocolaterie* uses exotic ingredients such as cardamom, elder blossom, and peppers to make the most outrageous and indulgent flavor combinations imaginable. You won't think of chocolate the same way again. See p. 246.

○ **The Best Medieval Street to Stroll (Rennes):** Right in the heart of Rennes's historic district, the tiny crooked **rue de la Psalette** has some of the best examples of timber-framed houses. Only a few stories tall with colorful beams, the houses are over 500 years old. See p. 246.

○ **The Best 19th-Century Prison to Bust a Move In (Rennes):** Some nightclubs are dark and dank for no reason. But the decor at **Delicatessen** is thanks to centuries of imprisonment. The underground club has modern furniture

Brittany

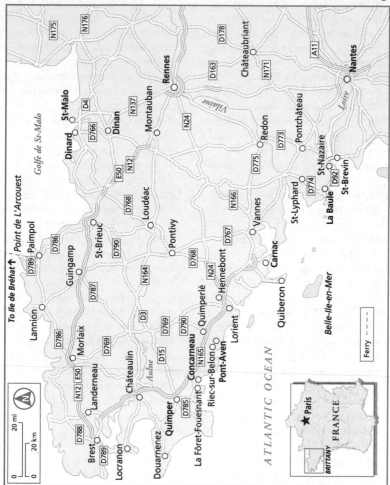

and electronic music whammed into a historic dungeon in the center of Rennes. The location can't be beat. See p. 244.

○ **The Best Gourmet Restaurant that's Downright Cheap (Rennes):** Warm, flavorful, and affordable, **Le Bocal** is everything you want in a neighborhood restaurant. After a meal at this little French place, you'll wish you could transport it home with you. They serve incredibly tasty gourmet dishes, putting a modern spin on traditional French ingredients, at astoundingly reasonable prices. See p. 242.

○ **The Best Culinary Adventure (Rennes):** Known as one of biggest and best farmer's markets in France, the **Rennes Farmer's Market** is an authentic taste of how the French experience food. Locals vehemently discuss and argue about the quality of the vegetables, cheeses, and fruit sold by the vendors. Even if you don't dive in yourself, you'll learn a little something. See p. 247.

○ **The Best Spot to try Mojito, Eucalyptus, or Tomato Ice Cream (Carnac):** As the 2000 Guinness World Record holder for the highest number of flavors, **Igloo** is not a place to visit if you're indecisive. With 170 flavors, it goes way beyond chocolate and strawberry. Adventurous eaters can try violet, potato, cider, or whiskey ice cream, but the trick is actually deciding on one. See p. 252.

○ **The Best Way to Navigate Carnac:** Unless you plan to park on the beach and stay for the duration of your trip, getting around Carnac can be tricky. With Carnac-Ville and Carnac-Plage separated, and kilometers of ancient megaliths to discover, a **bicycle** is the best way to get up close and personal on a schedule. See p. 250.

○ **The Best Kouign Amann (Carnac):** You won't be able to travel far in Brittany without discovering *kouign amann.* It's the buttery, sugary cousin of the croissant—a super decadent pastry rolled like a cinnamon bun. And while some bakeries serve a less than stellar version, **Patisserie Elie** creates a calorically punishing masterpiece. See p. 253.

○ **The Best 17th-Century Manor to Call Home (Quimper):** Most trips to France include a lot of guided tours to 17th-century landmarks. But why only visit

when you can walk the grounds, breakfast in the garden, and tuck yourself in at a 17th-century manor? The stunning **Manoir du Stang,** just outside Quimper, is an unforgettable experience with amazing stone buildings, beautiful grounds, and prices that are about the same as at the average hotel in town. See p. 262.

○ **The Best Creperie (Quimper):** After a few days traveling in Brittany, you may feel like if you've had one crepe, you've had them all. But the authentic black wheat crepes at **La Krampouzerie** are a cut above. Made with organic ingredients, many come in unpredictable and mouthwatering flavor combinations. Crepe with seaweed, anyone? See p. 262.

○ **The Best Museum . . . for Your Grandmother (Quimper):** Be warned: You're entering the realm of the twee. If Quimper is famous for anything, it's handmade painted pottery called *la faïence,* created here for 300 years. The **Musée de la Faïence de Quimper** documents its entire history, from the earliest cups and plates to elaborate hand-painted violins. Be prepared for a lot of cooing collectable-lovers. See p. 265.

○ **The Best Place to Find a Decent Muffin (Quimper):** In the land of croissants and madeleines, it's not often you run across carbo-heavy American-style muffins. But the **C.Com Café** is the best place in town to check your e-mail and indulge in café au lait and piping hot baked goods fresh from the oven. See p. 262.

St-Malo: Surf, Sun & Stone Walls

414km (257 miles) W of Paris, 69km (43 miles) N of Rennes

The walled city of St-Malo presides over Brittany's rugged northern coast, in a spot that looks like a postcard from any angle.

It's at the mouth of the Rance River, with beaches, bays, and port towns surrounding it. Medieval ramparts encircle the

St-Malo

heart of the city and lord it over the crashing waves below. Understandably, St-Malo does not go unnoticed by tourists. Beachgoers lounge on kilometers of open sand with stunning views of the city, nearby islands, and open sea.

The location has been popular for centuries, but not in the same pursuit of bare-skinned sun-worshiping. St-Malo has a rich sea-faring tradition, home to fishermen, military troops, and corsairs—pirates that were given the royal go-ahead to sack and pillage English ships. (These rebels are still a source of pride for the Malouins, so be careful not to call them pirates.) Besides the ramparts, Bretons also built several forts, on small islands connected to the

land only at low tide, to stave off the English navy. St-Malo's military significance continued well into the 20th century.

Most tourists spend their time *"Intra-Muros,"* within St-Malo's walls, where quaint streets hold restaurants, shops, and bars. But not everything you're seeing is as old as you think. By 1945, almost 80% of the city was destroyed in World War II bombing. German troops had taken hold of the city and held it through devastating Allied bombing before finally surrendering. While much of the city was reconstructed, it still has a winning old-fashioned feel.

St-Malo is also home to Brittany's stick-it-to-ya attitude. In 1590, Malouins declared the city its own republic separate from the king, and it stayed that way for a whole 4 years. The town's motto, *ni Français, ni Breton, Malouin suis,* evinces the fierce local pride.

During July and August, the St-Malo crowds can be overwhelming inside the city, and reservations are tight. There are plenty of other options for shacking up along the beach, which extends east from the city walls. The vibe is decidedly calmer, since the walk to St-Malo's nightlife inside the city can be 10 to 15 minutes. But thanks to the beach scene and plenty of Parisian tourists, St, Malo's nightlife is definitely something to write home about. While St-Malo attracts all types, a younger nocturnal set keeps going late into the evening hours. With seashores, sights, and seafood to keep them busy, why stop?

Getting There

BY TRAIN

St-Malo's train station was renovated in 2006, and now serves TGV fast trains from Paris and Rennes. Trains from Paris take around 3 hours (☎ 08-36-35-35-35; www.sncf.com). The station itself is a bit of a leap from the heart of St-Malo, so head directly out the doors to the bus station for transit (see "By Bus," below).

BY CAR

The drive from Rennes is only an hour long. Jump on the N137 heading north towards St-Malo and follow the signs to the city center once you arrive.

BY BUS

St-Malo's local bus service can actually be useful for getting to several sites nearby. **Les Courriers Bretons** (☎ 02-99-19-70-80; www.lescourriersbretons.com) runs buses between St-Malo and Cancale (2€), St-Malo and Mont St-Michel (4.50€), and Rennes and Mont St-Michel (11€). You can buy tickets on the esplanade St-Vincent in St-Malo,

directly next to the tourist office. Prices are 20% cheaper for youth under 26. Depending on the route, there are only a handful of departures each day, so get your hands on tickets ahead of time.

BY FERRY

Hopping a ferry across the English Channel from the U.K. to St-Malo is no trouble. **Condor Ferries** (☎ 08-25-13-51-35; www.condorferries.com) connects two port towns in the U.K., Weymouth and Poole, to St-Malo, with stops on the islands of Jersey and Guernsey along with way. **Brittany Ferries** (☎ 02-99-40-64-41; www.brittanyferries.com) also runs a connection between Portsmouth in the U.K. and St-Malo. For local hops over water, the **Compagnie Corsaire** (☎ 08-25-13-80-35; www.compagniecorsaire.com) runs a short ferry across the bay to Dinard, as well as several other local ports such as Dinan, Iles Chausey, Iles Cezembre, and a scenic tour through the Bay of Cancale. All ferries leave from the port outside the southwest end of the walled city.

Orientation

In St-Malo, you're either in or you're out (of the city walls, that is). Most tourists sleep and hang out *Intra-Muros* (I.M. for short), inside the high stone walls that surround St-Malo's downtown. When it comes to eating, sightseeing, canoodling, and people-watching, *Intra-Muros* is the place to be. But it's not all St-Malo has to offer. Stretching east from the city is a long series of beaches, and with plenty of beachfront space, that means a long line of hotels as far as you can see. The vibe is decidedly calmer, as most hotels are a 10-minute walk or more from the city walls, but the boardwalk fills up with plenty of beachgoers in the summer months.

Getting Around

BY CAR

If you're car-bound *Intra-Muros,* check with your hotel about parking. In July and August, it's almost impossible to drive within the city walls, but if you need to get your car inside, use the Porte St-Louis. During the rest of the year, cars are allowed through the main Porte St-Vincent. Driving is only allowed on one path around the inside perimeter of the walls.

There are several paid parking lots just outside the walls next to the tourist office, but charges can climb quickly. A cheaper option is to use the paid parking lots next to the train station. It's much farther, but during the summer, a free shuttle runs to the walled city from 10am to 10pm for parking patrons only.

For taxi service, call **Allo Taxi Malouins** (☎ **02-99-81-30-30;** www.allo-taxis-malouins.com). In the summer, you'll often find them waiting at a taxi stand outside the Porte Vincent as well.

BY BUS

St-Malo's bus system is efficient and well run. A number of bus lines run between the train station and the walled city, which is the cheapest way to do the 5-minute trip. Look for buses nos. 12, 21, 22, 3, 4, 6, and make sure the driver is heading *Intra-Muros.* Other useful stops take you to many of St-Malo's beaches, the youth hostel, the sights in Cité d'Aleth, and the Aquarium. Tickets are sold onboard for 1.20€ a ride or 3.30€ for a 24-hour pass. During the summer, a limited evening bus schedule runs between 8pm to midnight, but not on all lines. For a detailed schedule, visit the tourist office or check online (http://bus.annuaire-emeraude.com). Die-hard public transportation fans can go by the bus kiosk at the esplanade St-Vincent outside the St-Malo château (☎ **02-99-56-06-06;** Mon–Fri 8:15am–12:15am and 1:45–4:10, Sat 8:15am–noon).

BY BIKE

If you're shacking up down the beach from St-Malo's walled city center, a bike will definitely speed the trip. The closest bike rental shop is not far from the train station. Visit **Les Velos Bleus** (19 rue Alphonse Thébault; ☎ **02-99-40-31-63;** www.velos-bleus.fr; July–Aug Mon–Sun 9am–noon and 2–6pm, Sept–June Mon–Sat) for a variety of bike rentals. The youth hostel (see below) also has bikes available for guests.

Tourist Office

St-Malo's tourist office is hard to miss. Located outside the main entrance to the city walls at Porte Vincent and next to the bus stop, the office gets overrun in the summer. It has all the pamphlets, books, and question-answering staff you might need. There's also a separate counter that handles watersports questions. Office de Tourisme (esplanade St-Vincent; ☎ **08-25-13-52-00;** www.saint-malo-tourisme.com; Oct–Mar Mon–Sat 9am–12:30pm and 1:30–6pm, Apr–June and Sept Mon–Sat 9am–12:30pm and 1:30–6:30pm, Sun 10am–12:30pm and 2:30–6pm, July–Aug Mon–Sat 9am–6:30pm, Sun 10am–6pm).

BRITTANY

St-Malo Nuts & Bolts

Car Rental   To nab some wheels and feel the salt spray in your hair, try **Avis** (located inside the train station; ☎ **02-99-40-18-54;** www.avis.com; Mon–Sat 8am–noon and 1–6:30pm) or a bit farther from the train station, **Europcar** (16 bd. des Talards; ☎ **02-99-56-75-17;** www.europcar.com).

Internet Cafe Internet access is scarce in St-Malo. While many hotels offer wireless or computers in the lobby, the closest Internet cafe is a 15-minute walk down the beach from the tourist office. **Cyberm@lo** (68 chaussée du Sillon; ☎ **02-99-56-07-78; 4€** an hour, 2.50€ for a half-hour) has around a dozen computers and the advantage of beach access. For a quick e-mail check inside the city, try **Le Café Bleu** (see "Eating," below) or **L'Alambic Café** (8 rue du Boyer; Mon–Sun 11am–midnight; 1€ for 10 min.). Both are on the same street and pricey enough to keep your e-mails short and sweet. If you're desperate to get online while hanging out at the train station, try **Cyber'Com** (26 bis bd. des Talards; ☎ **02-99-56-05-83;** www.cybermalo. com; Mon–Tues and Fri 9am–noon and 1:30–6pm, Thurs 10am–noon and 1:30–7pm; 4€ an hour) a 10-minute walk away.

Laundromats You'll find one automatic laundromat inside the city on rue de la Hearse next to the Halle au Blé. You'd have to feel pretty filthy, though, to brave the prices at **Lavomatique** (daily 7am–9pm). With a lock on the suds market, they charge a pretty penny.

Post Office The easiest post office to find is within the city walls at 4 place des Frères Lamennais (Mon–Fri 8:45am–12:15pm and 1:30–5:45pm; Sat 8:45am–noon).

Supermarkets For bottled water and candy bars, **Marché Plus** (9 rue St-Vincent; ☎ **02-99-40-94-14;** Mon–Sat 7am–9pm, Sun 9am–1pm) is the most convenient stop. The underground supermarket is dead center on one of the busiest streets in St-Malo.

Sleeping

Just like the rest of St-Malo, a fine line is drawn between hotels *Intra-Muros* and hotels on the outside. The steepest prices are found within the city walls during high season, but there are still surprisingly good bargains to be found. All other hotels are lined up along the Plage du Sillon, which stretches hundreds of yards. Oceanview rooms can still be steep, but prices are generally lower due to the 10- to 15-minute walk to the heart of St-Malo. If you're traveling with a car, you may consider staying down the beach, for easier parking.

HOSTELS & CAMPING

→ **Camping de la Cité d'Aleth** This small campground is found in St-Servan on a raised hill just near the Memorial 39–45. The location is quiet and not far from some stunning views of St-Malo and the surrounding bay. *Allée Gaston Buy, St-Servan.*

☎ *02-99-81-60-91. 12€ for 1 person with no electricity, 16€ for 1 person with electricity, 5.50€ for each additional person. May–Sept.*

→ **Centre Patrick Varangot** St-Malo's youth hostel does a brisk business in the summer, owing mostly to its location a few blocks from the beach. Rooms come in many different varieties, sleeping two to three with showers or two to five on bunks, with bathrooms down the hall. The atmosphere is relaxed with tennis and volleyball courts outside and a cafeteria that serves small meals. The hostel has no curfew, and if the distance from main St-Malo gets you down, you can rent one of several bikes at 12€ a day. To get there from *Intra-Muros*, take the no. 21 bus to the Châteaubriand stop, or the no. 5 bus to the "Auberge de Jeunesse" stop. *37 av. du R. P. Umbricht.* ☎ *02-99-40-29-80. www.centrevarangot.com. 14€–19€ per person. Amenities: Free Internet; free parking.*

CHEAP

→ **Hôtel Le Nautilus** ★ The nautical theme at this *petit hôtel* is inescapable, but for value, it can't be beat. Both clean and comfortable, Le Nautilus is leagues beyond anything else in St-Malo in this price range. Inside, the rooms can be a bit snug, decorated with bold colors that are intense at times, but they're by far the most modern and up-to-date of any budget hotel in the area. Le Nautilus is also a good choice for single travelers (with single rooms, tucked on the top floor, that are a steal), as well as for groups, who can ask for two adjoining double rooms at a reduced rate. Don't wait to make a reservation, since the 15 rooms fill up fast in the summer. *9 rue de la Corne de Cerf.* ☎ *02-99-40-42-27. www.lenautilus.com. 35€–53€ single; 45€–57€ double; 65€–75€ quad. Credit cards accepted. Amenities: Elevator; free Wi-Fi. In room: Satellite TV w/English channels.*

→ **Hôtel Quic en Groigne** This hotel isn't the newest on the block, but it's extremely well tended. The husband-and-wife team that run it are warmly welcoming with plenty of advice. On a quiet street off the beaten path, the hotel has a homey feel and the rooms are comfortable, if not a little old-fashioned. Breakfast is served in a bright windowed atrium. Overall, it's a solid budget choice. *8 rue d'Estrées.* ☎ *02-99-20-22-20. www.quic-en-groigne.com. 48€–65€ double. Breakfast 7€. Credit cards accepted. Amenities: Parking 8€. In room: TV.*

DOABLE

→ **Hôtel Anne de Bretagne** Another hotel in the heart of St-Malo, Anne de Bretagne is a solid, if not somewhat plain choice. The hotel is split into two buildings across from each other on a small side street, which protects the hotel from noise. Rooms are snug and straightforward in standard hotel style. An added perk is the two computers in the lobby for checking e-mail, as well as Wi-Fi. *10 rue de St-Thomas.* ☎ *02-99-56-18-00. www.hotel-annede bretagne.com. 60€–72€ double. Breakfast 7€. Credit cards accepted. Parking 10€. Amenities: Elevator; paid Wi-Fi. In room: TV.*

→ **Hôtel Bristol Union** ★ Centrally located and renovated in 2005, Hôtel Bristol Union offers some serious value for the money. The hotel is decorated in bold, modern colors with no flowery pastels in sight. The comfortable and clean rooms come in two grades, the slightly larger *Superieur* rooms with a bathtub, and standard Club rooms, which are more than adequate. Even during the summer high season, the hotel offers double rooms for 70€, which is an impressive deal considering how pricey St-Malo hotel rooms can be in July and August. *4 place de la Poissoniere.* ☎ *02-99-40-83-36. www.hotel-bristol-union. com. 49€–80€ single; 59€–96€ double, 120€–150€ family suites. Breakfast 9€. Credit cards accepted. Parking 12€. Closed mid-Nov to mid-Feb. Amenities: Elevator; free Wi-Fi. In room: A/C, TV.*

→ **Hôtel de France et de Châteaubriand** Centrally located on the busiest square in St-Malo, this hotel has an Old Europe feel with "Napoleon III architecture." The main reason to book here is for the eye-catching ocean views from some rooms. Note that it's the only hotel *Intra-Muros* that peeks over the city walls toward the sea. Many rooms offer plenty of elbowroom, but some bathrooms are dated and worn. The restaurant downstairs looks out on a main square and stays busy in the summer with the tourist foot traffic. Unless you're looking to do some seaside gazing in your slippers, it's possible to get a better deal elsewhere. *Place Châteaubriand.* ☎ *02-99-56-66-52. www.hotel-chateaubriand-st-malo.com. 75€–98€ double. Breakfast 10€. Credit cards accepted. Parking 12€. Amenities: Restaurant; elevator; paid Wi-Fi. In room: A/C, TV.*

BRITTANY

BRITTANY

→**Hôtel Les Charmettes** Beach bums, apply here. This hotel, located down the beach from the walled city, has the best deal around for rooms with an ocean view. Cheaper rooms are in the annex behind the main hotel, but the several rooms overlooking the beach are a steal. Either way, you'll have direct beachfront access and a picturesque view for breakfast. Rooms are a bit on the tight side, but simple and comfortable. *64 bd. Hébert-Courtoisville.* ☏ *02-99-56-07-31. www.hotel-les-charmettes.com. 60€–70€ double. Breakfast 7€. Credit cards accepted. Free parking. In room: TV.*

SPLURGE

→**Hôtel Alba** ★ If you're looking for a little luxury outside the city walls, try the Alba, a lavish boutique hotel with an ocean view and only 22 rooms inside. It's worth shelling out the dough for a room with an ocean view or balcony, which more than makes up for the small size of the rooms. Downstairs is an impressive dark-wood bar, and outside the patio leads to direct beach access. As with any hotel outside the ramparts, it's a better choice if you're more of a beach bum than a night owl. *17 rue des Dunes.* ☏ *02-99-40-37-18. www.hotelalba. com. 70€–140€ double. Breakfast 12€. Credit cards accepted. Amenities: Elevator, paid Wi-Fi. In room: A/C, TV.*

→**Hôtel Elizabeth** ★ This cozy hotel has plenty of Breton charm. The main hotel is housed in a 17th-century stone building, whose warm rooms are plush and filled with period furniture. The other set of rooms is in the annex, with more modern decor at less expensive rates. Both options are seriously comfortable but not overpretentious. Another big perk is the breakfast, served in the old stone basement with mega ceiling beams overhead. *2 rue des*

Cordiers. ☏ *02-99-56-24-98. www.st-malo-hotel-elizabeth.com. Main building 120€–165€ double; annex 80€–110€. Rates include breakfast. Credit cards accepted. Parking 10€–15€. In room: A/C, TV.*

Eating

Seaside St-Malo exemplifies Breton cuisine, with superlative crepes and seafood. Most of what you'll find will fall into either of these two categories (sometimes both at the same time). Aside from the wide variety of creperies to choose from, you'll find a lot of mussels and french-fry joints, popular everywhere in France. But St-Malo also offers a bounty of local specialties, including fresh fish, shrimp, and, most famously, oysters. Tourists arrive in droves to gulp trays upon trays of these salty delicacies—but remember, oysters are at their best in the fall.

CAFES & LIGHT FARE

→**Glacier Sanchez** ICE CREAM/CAFE You'll recognize this ice-cream shop by the line of tourists outside at all hours of the day. It's popular not only for its huge selection of flavors but its mega portions, too. The "Super Sanchez" is a stomach-cramping four scoops of chocolate with whipped cream in a giant waffle cone. The "Special Sanchez" is a monstrous 12-scoop sundae with the works (including pyrotechnics). Either way, the trick is to eat fast enough to beat the St-Malo sun, and burn off the calories later by strolling on the city walls. *9 rue de la Vieille Boucherie.* ☏ *02-99-56-67-17. Apr–Nov Mon–Sun 10am–11pm.*

CHEAP

→**La Touline** CREPERIE For variety, this popular creperie is the place to go. In fact, it takes some time to scan the laundry list menu where the ingredients are shuffled around like a game of poker. But it's worth doing due diligence to find the right combination of ingredients to top these light, buttery crepes. Two standouts are the crepes with smoked salmon, cream, and lemon, as well as the goat cheese, salad, walnut, and smoked bacon combination. The outdoor seating is also a choice venue for people-watching in the summer. *6 place de la Poissonerie.* ☎ *02-99-40-10-98. Main courses 2€–8€. Credit cards accepted. Tues–Sun noon–10pm.*

➔ **Le Café Bleu** CREPERIE This small creperie is totally down-to-earth, featuring crepes with organic produce and a warm ambience. As one of the most veggie-friendly joints in town, they serve crepes with spinach, chevre, and tomato and other veggie combos, as well as more traditional, carnivorous fare. Slightly off the beaten trail near the Plage de Bon Secours, it isn't overrun during the height of tourist season. The other big plus is the Internet access, which is a rare find in the city walls. Jump on their computer for 4€ an hour after you finish off that dessert crepe. *12 rue de Boye.* ☎ *02-99-40-98-38. Main courses 6€–8.50€. Credit cards accepted. Thurs–Tues and 10:30am–2:30pm and 6:30–10pm.*

➔ **Ti Nevez** CREPERIE Perhaps the least-flashy address in St-Malo, this creperie has Breton-style down-home goodness. Run by a husband and wife team, the dining room is super cozy with carved wooden chairs and tiny tables. The menu isn't much fancier, with strictly traditional crepe cuisine, but each crepe is high quality and prepared right there in the dining room. Go for a *crêpe flambé* for some sweet dessert-time pyrotechnics, or try their house-made *far breton* pastry. *12 rue Broussais.* ☎ *02-99-40-82-50. Main courses 2€–7€. Credit cards accepted. Mon–Sun noon–10pm.*

DOABLE

➔ **Au Pied du Cheval II** ★ SEAFOOD/ SHELLFISH This is the sister restaurant of the well-liked Au Pied du Cheval nearby in Cancale, and its ties to the port town of Cancale mean one thing—oysters. You'll know this is a real seafood joint by the simple and straightforward shellfish menu. Grab a carafe of Muscadet and chow down on grilled prawns and buckets of shrimp with no fancy preparation—just the good stuff. Of course, oysters come by the platterful, which they crack open nearby with their custom shucking tool. Only the gutsiest diners should try the *bulots* (whelks), salty delicacies that are akin to escargot but from the sea. *6 rue Jacques Cartier.* ☎ *02-99-40-98-18. Main courses 8€–16€. Credit cards accepted. Mon–Sun noon–10:30pm.*

➔ **La Corderie** ★ SEAFOOD If you're in St-Servans to see the sights, be sure not to miss this seafood spot. The restaurant is tucked away on a side street in Cité d'Aleth, which means diners get a full view of the water from both the dining room and the outdoor seating on the terrace. Even better, they specialize in super fresh seafood at slightly lower prices than what's found inside St-Malo's city walls. Their three-course menu changes weekly based on what's fresh and in season, and at 17€ it's a steal. For a lighter meal, they offer a fish of the day at 11€. Without a doubt, it's the best way to satisfy a seafood fix without breaking the bank. *9 chemin de la Corderie, Cité d'Aleth.* ☎ *02-99-81-62-38. www.lacorderie.com. Menu 17€; entrees 11€–22€. Credit cards accepted. Tues–Sun noon–2pm and 7–10pm. Bus: 12 (Alet stop).*

➔ **Le 3 Bis** FRENCH If you've finally had enough mussels and fries, Le 3 Bis is a quieter spot with both surf and turf. With modern decor, it's a much better choice for quiet dinner conversation than the jammed tourist spots down the block. Their menu is short and sweet, based on seasonal ingredients. Many of their dishes are also done *Pierrade*, which means you cook your own meat or veggies on a hot stone (think *shabu shabu*, the French way). *3 rue des Orbettes.* ☎ *02-99-40-82-33. www. le-3-bis.com. Menu 18€, main courses 10€– 15€. Credit cards accepted. Mon–Sun noon– midnight.*

SPLURGE

→ **A l'Abordage** ★ MODERN FRENCH For the sleekest dining address in St-Malo, look no further than A l'Abordage. Decor is modern, in deep purple and cool grays, with nary a single fake fishing net or decorative porthole. More impressively, the cuisine is adventurous and refined with dishes such as pan-fried prawns with cucumber and truffle oil. It incorporates the fresh local bounty of St-Malo's seas, but you'll also find French favorites such as lamb and duck. The restaurant also doubles as a wine bar with an impressive list organized by wine intensity. It's definitely worth trading in your flip-flops to eat here, if you can handle the bill. *5 place de la Poissonnerie.* ☎ *02-99-40-87-53. www. alabordagesaintmalo.com. Menu 50€, main courses 20€–24€. Credit cards accepted. Tues–Fri noon–2pm and 7:15–9:30pm, Sat 7:15–9:30pm.*

→ **Le Chalut** SEAFOOD/FRENCH If you ask around for a good seafood spot *Intra-Muros*, most locals will point you to this restaurant. During the summer, it's hard to get in without a reservation. They specialize in fresh local fish, and put together more refined dishes than the touristy mussels and oyster joints around town. Expect some traditional French preparations with elaborate sauces, but the freshness of the produce, lobster, and fish shines through. The dining room has a traditional feel, but it's one of the only spots inside the city with gourmet cred. *8 rue de la Corne de Cerf.* ☎ *02-99-56-71-58. Main courses 20€–26€, menus 32€–48€. Credit cards accepted. Tues 7–10pm, Wed–Sun noon–2pm and 7–10pm. Reservations recommended.*

Partying

Brittany is a playground of both international and French tourists. And with plenty of Parisians arriving for summer vacation, the demand for nightlife means St-Malo is swinging. With its slew of bars for any taste or preference, it provides plenty of reasons to wash off the salt water and put on something cute after the sun goes down.

How to Order Breton Oysters

Breton oysters are famous throughout France, but St-Malo is next to Cancale, one of the most productive regions. A port town that holds massive beds of oysters year-round, Cancale has the freshest access possible to these brine-y little suckers. The *huitres* come in five sizes, labeled no. 2 through no. 5 on restaurant menus (5s being the smallest and cheapest). Locals slurp 2s or 3s from icy trays by the dozens—except in the summer, when they haven't reached peak flavor yet. Tourists gulp off mountains of them year-round, but Bretons know that oysters are best in fall and winter. (Remember the old rule: Eat oysters only in months that end in "r.") If you're lucky enough to arrive in fall or late summer, keep your eye out for local, flat Belon oysters. You won't see them on the menu in the summer (when oysters make baby oysters), but they're considered the cream of the crop.

FUNKY BARS

→**L'Absinthe Café** ★★ Frequented by young Parisians on vacation, L'Absinthe is a stellar bar with a lounge layout. Its cozy three floors are decorated with red walls and dark wood, and the leather couches and small tables offer plenty of space to chill with a half-pint or cocktail. Expect to hear current indie goodness on the sound system, along with whatever else the bartenders are in the mood for. Overall, it's by far the youngest hangout inside the city walls. *1 rue de L'Orma.* ☎ *02-99-40-85-40.*

→**L'Aviso** ★ Brittany may be cider country, but with 300 beers on the menu, L'Aviso will make you forget all about it. The funky, two-story pub is a laid-back shrine to all things hoppy, and serves everything from the lightest blond beers to the darkest stouts. If reading the whole menu takes too long, ask for a Coreff or Telenn Du, both local Breton brews, or pick from their impressive selection of Belgian ales. Beer adventurers: Be sure to ask if they have Kwak on tap for one impressive beer presentation. *12 rue du Point du Jour.* ☎ *02-99-40-99-08.*

📺 Best ☺ →**Le Café du Coin d'en Bas de la rue du Bout de la Ville d'en Face du Port—La Java** Be prepared before you walk in—this bar is Moulin Rouge on acid. Inside it's overflowing with kitsch, jam-packed with old posters, sultry dark red colors, and a campy antique doll collection scattered all over the walls. The bartender is quick to crack jokes (often at your expense), but it's worth sticking around at this one-of-a-kind joint. (Its name, by the way, means "the corner cafe at the bottom of the road at the end of town across from the port—the party;" *la java* is mid-20th-c. slang for the party.) Plant yourself on one of the wooden swings that serve as bar stools, and sip on a Pelforth strawberry ale or a Le Zizi Coin-Coin cocktail

(Cointreau and lemon on ice). *3 rue Ste-Barbe.* ☎ *02-99-56-41-90. www.lajavacafe.com.*

→**Le Cancalais** This dive bar in St-Servan overlooks a quiet bay. With ample outdoor seating on the deck, it has plenty of space from which to take in the view. Be prepared for a super-casual vibe, since the area isn't pounded by a lot of foot traffic. The bartenders are easygoing, the brews flow freely from beer on tap, and a lonely piano in the back is free for patrons inspired to tickle the ivories. If you're in Cité d'Aleth for the day, grab a pint and while away an hour or two on the deck. *1 quai Solidor, Cité d'Aleth.* ☎ *02-99-81-15-79.*

→**Le Chat'bada** On most nights, this cozy lounge keeps it low-key, but once or twice a week it gets hopping when the club features local live jazz trios and duos. Its location, on a side street off the busiest square in St-Malo, also makes it an easy choice for a quiet cocktail away from the tourist throngs. *3 rue Garangeau.* ☎ *02-99-40-89-32.*

CLUBS & LIVE MUSIC VENUES

→**Le 109** A hybrid club and bar, Le 109 is best described as a lounge with a DJ. In a cavernous underground space inside the city walls, it stays consistently busy during tourist season. Expect to hear house, techno, and other Euro favorites, but the dancing doesn't pick up until late into the night, when the crowd gets a bit looser. Even if you're not in the mood to get down, Le 109 is the best option if you're looking for something more chic and upscale than the funkier bars in town. Cover is 5€. *3 rue des Cordiers.* ☎ *02-99-56-81-09. www.le-109.com.*

Sightseeing

If you can tear yourself away from the sand long enough, you'll find that St-Malo has a fascinating history. From museums to medieval forts to the ramparts, there's enough to keep you away from the surf for days. Here's another tip: If you plan to see

BRITTANY

three of St-Malo's main attractions—the Château de St-Malo, which houses the Musée de l'Histoire de St-Malo, the Memorial 39–45, and the Tour Solidor— you can buy a reduced-price ticket for all three instead of paying for each full price (11€ adults, 5.50€ students). Just ask for the group ticket when you visit the first of any three of them.

MUSEUMS & SIGHTS

➔ **Fort du Petit Bé** Hike down a mussel- and barnacle-encrusted stone path from Ile du Grand Bé, and you'll reach this 17th-century fort. As the farthest point from the mainland, it's the first to be swallowed up by the rising tide, so keep an eye on the sea unless you've trained to swim the English Channel. A guided tour takes you into the fort to see the military quarters and pow-der room. It's a kick to imagine what the English armada must have looked like sailing in to attack. If you've already vis-ited the Fort National, you could skip this one. *Promenade des Bés, facing the Plage de Bon Secours. ☎ 06-08-27-51-20. Tickets 4€. Apr–Nov during low tide only.*

MTV Best ● ➔ **Fort National de St-Malo** If you're looking out to sea from St-Malo, you won't be able to miss this landmark, though you won't be able to get there for a good part of the day. The Fort National was built on an island off the coast, which is linked to St-Malo by a land bridge during low tide only. The location made it a prime defense against English bat-tleships since 1689, and later was used by German troops in World War II to hold French prisoners. The only way to get inside the fort is through the guided tour in French, but they do provide English lan-guage materials to read along with. Several of the guides get to sleep inside the fort dur-ing the summer season, so when all the other tourists scurry back to St-Malo before tide rises, they've got a million-dollar view.

Located off of the Grand Plage. ☎ 02-99-85-34-33 for tour information. www.fort national.com. Admission adults 4€, 2€ under 16. Tours begin on the half-hour. June 1–Sept 30 Mon–Sun 10am–6pm generally; changes daily based on tides.

➔ **Grand Aquarium de St-Malo** The good news is that if you're a die-hard fan of the life aquatic, St-Malo's medium-size Grand Aquarium has hours of fishy fun. The bad news is that it's located way off the beaten path, accessible only by car or bus. As a respite from a beach marathon, the aquarium has a 360-degree-round shark room, ocean creature petting zoo, and a famed 30-year-old lobster (no prom-ises it will still be alive by the time you get here). If you slacked off on making a hotel reservation, you can sleep with the fishes; the aquarium offers a limited number of spots for an overnight stay in the shark room for 110€ per person. *Av. du Général Patton. ☎ 02-99-21-19-00. www.aquarium-st-malo.com. Tickets 14€. Sept–June 10am–6pm, June 1–July 13 9:30am–8pm, July 14–Aug 15 9:30am–10pm, Aug 16–31 9:30am–8pm. Aquarium stop on bus no. 5.*

FREE ➔ **Ile du Grand Bé** This is the closest of the second set of islands off the coast of St-Malo, connected to the main-land during low tide only. The main draw of Ile du Grand-Bé, a rugged windswept hill, is the stunning ocean views it offers. It also is home to the grave of St-Malo's favorite son, François-René de Châteaubriand. A father of the Romanticism movement in French literature, he left St-Malo to seek his fame but upon his death was brought home to score one of the most impressive burial sites ever. The grave is modest, but the blustery romance of it all is right out of *Wuthering Heights. Promenade des Bés, fac-ing the Plage de Bon Secours.*

➔ **Musée d'Histoire, Château de St-Malo** This castle is one of the most central sites in St-Malo. The main spire houses the Musée de l'Histoire, a series of exhibits on the town's illustrious sea history. Sure, it's a lot of old maritime stuff, but it's the best place to get a sense of the area's legacy. You'll come across ship memorabilia, old scrolls, and some pretty gnarly contraptions used by privateers and pirates to board ships. Another perk is emerging outside at the very top of the tower with all of St-Malo and its walls beneath you (after a long winding staircase, of course). The spot was the last stronghold of World War II German troops before they surrendered. *Inside St-Malo's Château, near the Porte Vincent.* ☎ *02-99-40-71-57. Adults 5€, students 2.50€. Apr–Sept Mon–Sun 10am–12:30pm and 2–6pm Oct–Mar Tues–Sun 10am–noon and 2–6pm.*

→ **Musée International de Long-Cours Cap-Hornier-Tour Solidor** The Tour Solidor is a lone 14th-century tower in St-Servan, standing guard over the bay. Like many medieval buildings, it went from military fort to a prison to some kind of museum. Inside is another of St-Malo's maritime museums, which houses old maps, sailing gear, and the odd stuffed albatross. If you're in Cité d'Aleth for the day, you might as well put it on your list, for the views from the top turrets of the fort. Otherwise, rely on the Musée d'Histoire in St-Malo's château for nautical and seafaring satisfaction. *Quai Sébastopol, Cité d'Aleth. 5€ adults, 2.50€ students. Apr–Sept Mon–Sun 10am–12:30pm and 2–6pm Oct–Mar Tues–Sun 10am–noon and 2–6pm. Alet stop on bus no. 12.*

MTV (**Best ●**) → **Musée Memorial 39–45** While the beaches of Normandy command the most World War II recognition, Brittany was also a key front in the war. Just a hop away from the ramparts, this memorial is housed in an old bunker for German troops, built deep into the ground.

While the miles of tunnels they built are now off limits, the bunker tour takes you into three levels of the stronghold, and through the history of the occupation. Even if you don't catch much of the French military vocabulary on the tour, the museum is still worth a visit. You'll see photos, memorabilia, and even the bed-sheet the Germans finally used to surrender to the Allies. You'll walk away with a bit more appreciation for Uncle Sam—seeing just how entrenched German troops were in 1944, and what an incredible feat the U.S. troops accomplished. *End of allée Gaston Buy, Cité d'Aleth.* ☎ *02-99-82-41-74. 5€ adults, 2.50€ students. Visits by guided tours only. Tues–Sun July–Aug tours at 10:15, 11am, 2, 3, 4, and 5pm; Sept–June 2, 3:15, and 4:30pm. Aleth stop on bus no.12.*

MTV (**Best ●**) (**FREE**) → **The Ramparts** Sure, it seems obvious, but walking the perimeter of St-Malo's high stone walls is one of the best experiences the city has to offer. From the Porte St-Thomas you'll have a stunning view of the ocean. You'll eventually arrive at the best picnic spot around, the Bastion de la Hollande, where the wall expands to include grass and benches (climb up near place de Guet for a shortcut). From there you leave the seaside for a view towards the bay. The **MTV** (**Best ●**) **Môle des Noires,** a long stone walkway that leads to a lighthouse, also extends from this corner, and offers a stunning view of the city. You'll need to exit at the Porte de Dinan, underneath the walls, to get out there. If you're determined to walk the whole perimeter, you can continue the rest of the way around, ending near the Porte Vincent. All in all, it's no quick jaunt, but it's well worth it for the photo-snapping opportunities.

MONUMENTS & CHURCHES
(**FREE**) → **Cathédrale St-Vincent of St-Malo** In the center of town, St-Malo's

cathedral is worth a peek. Begun in the 11th century and built up over the centuries, the church went through a final reconstruction after World War II. Inside are many lovely stained-glass windows with very modern patterns, most of which skip the normal storytelling themes about saints and sinners. *Place J. de Chatillion. Mon–Sun 9:45am–6pm.*

Shopping

You can say *merci* again to the influx of Parisian tourists in St-Malo. The demand for designer duds means that the shopping scene is fairly interesting within the city walls, which is surprising for such a small place. From expensive labels to cheap touristy goods, St-Malo has enough browsing options to keep you busy.

CLOTHING & ACCESSORIES

➜ **Jules** With mass-market shirts, jeans, and socks, this chain store is a standard address for essentials for men. For the more fashion adventurous, check out their über-Euro T-shirts, which often have strange English words printed on them for no apparent reason. *12 rue Porcon de la Barbinais.* ☎ 02-99-20-15-20. *Mon–Sun 10am–7pm.*

➜ **Karina** You'll realize that a lot of Parisians vacation in St-Malo from this shop, which houses mega-labels like Sonia Rykiel and Maxmara. This women's boutique deals in the cream of the crop and can outfit you in the most famous French designers around. Expect price tags to match. *5 rue des Merciers.* ☎ 02-99-40-84-43. *Mon–Sun 10am–12:30pm and 2:30–7:30pm. Closed Sun afternoon.*

➜ **LC8 Pret-a-Porter Homme** If you're male with some cash to drop, then LC8 is the right boutique. With labels like Guess? and Calvin Klein, the small shop guarantees that you'll walk out looking sharp, at probably the same price as your hotel room. *8 Grand Rue.* ☎ 02-99-20-23-18. *Tues–Sat 10:15am–12:15pm and 3–7:15pm.*

➜ **Why Not?** For both guys and gals, this shop has a little bit of everything. You'll find a mix of European and international labels such as G-Star and Franklin Marshall, but don't worry about looking too Euro. Plenty of what's on the racks will remind you of home. *5 rue Broussais.* ☎ 02-23-18-69-12. *Mon–Sun 10:30am–12:30pm and 2–7pm.*

FOOD, WINE & LOCAL CRAFTS

➜ **Boulangerie Prime** With few bakeries inside the city walls, this boulangerie doesn't have too much competition, but they turn out tasty baked goods just the same. Aside from baguettes and their brethren, try their raisin, fig, or walnut breads for something less run of the mill. Their homemade *kouign amann* is also good, though it runs the same price as the more touristy kiosks that churn them out by the boatload. *1 Grand Rue.* ☎ 02-99-40-90-79. *Mon–Sat 7:30am–7:30pm.*

➜ **Cave de l'Abbaye St-Jean** No beach picnic would be complete without a bottle of something tucked in your pack, and the friendly, down-to-earth staff at this wine store will help you find one, even if the only word you know is "Bordeaux." Tell them what you like, and they'll find you one just as good for half the price. But the real treat is the many varieties of Breton cider they sell. Just like French wine, French cider tastes differently depending on where it comes from. It goes from super-sweet to downright bitter, so take your pick. You won't even need a bottle opener. *7 rue des Cordiers.* ☎ 02-99-20-17-20. *Mon–Sun 9:30am–8:30pm.*

➜ **Confiserie Guella** This candy shop is front and center on one of the busiest tourist drags in St-Malo, and it's also one of the most well known, founded in 1935. They're most famous for their caramels made with salted Breton butter—*caramels au beurre sale de Bretagne*. Grab a bag for an easy gift to bring home to mom and dad, or for emergency provisions on long train rides. *8 rue Porcon.* ☎ *02-99-40-83-43. Mon–Sun 9am–8pm.*

➔ **Farmer's Market** Found in the indoor Halles au Blé, St-Malo's farmer's market isn't overwhelmingly large. But if you're looking for a light snack and want a bit of local flavor, it's worth taking a quick tour around. *Halle au Blé, rue de la Herse. Tues and Fri 8am–1pm.*

📺 (Best ❂) ➔ **Jean-Yves Bordier** Technically, this is cheese shop, and a darn good one at that, but the real reason to stop by is the butter. Jean-Yves Bordier makes artisan butter the old-fashioned way, with milk from local Breton cows. Ask for a bit of the *demi-sel,* which the staff will carve off in a huge hunk and beat with wooden tools until it reaches the optimal flavor. Their *beurre aux algues* is also incredible—a light, airy, gold butter with tiny flecks of salty seaweed that will blow your mind. Pick up a few local cheeses and add some baguettes, and you've got one unforgettable picnic. Chances are you'll forget you're eating butter and start eating it like cheese. *9 rue de l'Orme.* ☎ *02-99-40-88-79. Sun–Mon 8:30am–1pm, Tues–Sat 8:30am–1pm and 4–7:30pm.*

➔ **Le Roux Charcuterie** For carnivores, this small butcher counter has the essential sandwich fixings, such as dried salami, cured meats, and proscuitto, as well as serious cuts of meat for local patrons. Ask them to slice something up on the spot, nice and thin, and pack it away with the rest of your picnic. *14 rue de l'Orme.* ☎ *02-99-40-84-40.*

➔ **Les 4 Saisons** This address is your produce stop on rue de l'Orme. Their counter is overflowing with fruit and vegetables, and not just apples and oranges. Depending on the season, you can get your hands on gorgeous figs, plums, and *fraises des bois*—real-deal wild strawberries with a decadent fragrance. As in a lot of French produce joints, however, you have to keep your hands to yourself and resist the urge to fondle the peaches. The staff selects your produce for you, once you elbow in between the locals. *10 rue de l'Orme.* ☎ *02-99-40-12-84. Mon 9am–1pm, Tues–Sat 8:30am–1pm and 4–7:30pm, Sun 9am–1pm and 5–7:30pm.*

MUSIC, BOOKS & MEDIA

➔ **Librarie Le Septentrion** Stepping into this small bookstore is a bit of a time warp. Its shelves are stuffed with antique books, posters, and postcards. A quick glance around will reveal scientific manuals from the 1800s, newspapers from the 1940s, and 17th-century letters. You can pick up antique postcards from the 1900s at not much more than the newbies down the street, as well as pricier volumes for serious collectors. Either way, you'll walk away with something out of the ordinary. *2 place Brévet.* ☎ *06-20-10-97-11. Tues–Sat 10:30am–12:15pm and 2:30–7pm, Sun 3–6:30pm.*

FUN BUYS

➔ **Vent de Voyage** ★ This small shop is one of a kind. Everything inside is made from sheer, lightweight racing sails that have already gone around the world. Trash collectors usually charge boaters to get rid of old sails, as they're notoriously hard to destroy. Vent de Voyage salvages them by turning them into unique bags, totes, and sacs. The results are completely unique, in sheer, white, or bright colors. Everything is featherweight but seriously durable and completely modern. *3 rue St-Thomas.* ☎ *02-99-20-17-91. www.ventdevoyage.com. Mon–Sat 10am–12:30pm and 3–7:30pm.*

Playing Outside
BEACHES

With miles of wide beaches, St-Malo has plenty of sand to go around. Most remarkably, St-Malo is known for extreme differences in tidal heights. At low tide, hundreds of yards of beach are exposed, which means instead of walking along the beach, you can simply hike down to the water's edge. The most centrally located beach is the **Plage de Bon Secours,** which lies directly below the ramparts. The small spot gets crowded due to its location, but also due to its semi-natural outdoor swimming pool. It may only be a few stone walls and a diving board, but depending on the tide it can look like a custom built-in pool right on the beach, when it's not submerged by the ocean (which acts a pool cleaning system *au naturelle*).

If you want room to stretch out your beach towel, head east of the walled city. As you walk down Chaussée de Sillon, the large **Plage de Sillon** has plenty of sunbathing surface area and restrooms. The beach is marked by hundreds of tall wooden posts next to the boardwalk wall, which act as breaks against the waves. Much farther down, the beach turns into **Plage de la Hoguette,** and then **Plage de Rochebonne,** both of which stay much less densely populated and are home to some wilder breaking waves.

WATERSPORTS

With so much water around St-Malo and a thriving beach culture, watersports possibilities abound. To get started with some basic windsurfing, contact the **Surf School** (2 av. de la Hoguette; ☎ 02-99-40-07-47; www.surfschool.org). On Plage de la Hoguette, the school leads lessons for kids and adults. If you're looking for a slower pace, go for a kayaking tour around the bay with **Corsaires Malouins** (7 rue de la Clouterie; ☎ 02-99-40-92-04; summer daily 9am–noon and 2–5pm). They offer half-day and full-day kayak trips leaving from the Bon Secours beach. For

more underwater fun, **St-Malo Plongee Emeraude** (☎ 02-99-19-90-36; www.saintmaloplongee.com) leads scuba-diving trips around St-Malo's bay for all skill levels. Trips can also have an archaeological or biological theme. Their diving center is at the Bleu Emeraude, near St-Servan's Plage des Bas Sablons. To really pick up the pace, try kite surfing with **Sensations Kite** (☎ 06-08-94-70-89; www.sensationskite.com). It's a lot like extreme windsurfing, skimming over the waves with a much larger sail that delivers real speed.

Festival

➔**La Route du Rock** ★★ If you're passing through Brittany in early August, you'll kick yourself if you miss this one. La Route du Rock is a three-day music festival featuring some of the best indie bands from home and abroad, making it one of the biggest rock gatherings in France. Past lineups have included Belle & Sebastian, Cat Power, Yo La Tengo, Interpol, Broken Social Scene, and a slew of other bands. The main outdoor venue is held at a killer 18th-century fort, the Fort de St-Père, about 12km (7 miles) from St-Malo. Duck into the tourist office to ask about the transportation options arranged for the event, as well as the very popular campsites near the fort, available only during the festival. The other music venues are beachside, directly outside St-Malo's walls. Tickets are available for one evening or up to 3 days, in case you want to cherry-pick from the lineup. Tickets will also get you a discount on TER trains to St-Malo during the festival. Even if you're skipping it, be aware: The already busy St-Malo hotels get booked solid for the festival, so don't expect to roll into town without a reservation. A smaller 2-day version of the festival is held in February. ☎ 02-99-54-01-11. www.laroutedu rock.com. Tickets 15€–80€.

Rennes: Student Town, Medieval Flair

350km (217 miles) W of Paris, 107km (66 miles) N of Nantes

Young scene, old town—this capital city of Brittany is a bustling university center with a rich history. When school is in session, the wide streets of Rennes look like a college campus, even though the schools are far outside town. With a busy shopping district, scores of restaurants, and riotous nightlife, downtown is a magnet for the younger generation. But Rennes has also got the goods when it comes to sights, with medieval houses, churches, and a few museums. Even so, Rennes is just as much about the city ambience as it is about tourist attractions.

Rennes is a historical hybrid. On one end of the city center, the streets are laid out medieval-style. The tiny, crooked alleys hold traditional timber-framed houses, leaning far over the street and letting in little light and air (couldn't have been too pleasant with horses and no modern plumbing). On the east side of town, it's a different story. After most of the city was destroyed in a massive fire, 18th-century urban planners were brought in with some new ideas. Much like Paris, wide streets were designed for the light-colored stone buildings. Huge public squares were also a fixture for modern living, giving Rennes's shopping district plenty of breathing room.

Keep in mind, Rennes isn't a huge tourist trap, since the city is also an urban center for the region. You'll be rubbing shoulders with locals more often than other tourists. Rennes impresses with its lively cuisine and nightlife. With Rennes's brilliant Saturday farmer's market, local restaurants have a leg up over other cities. And be prepared for the nightlife. Bars are packed wall to wall on the rue St-Michel, which attracts all sorts of characters. The scene is a bit more raucous during the school year, but in summer you'll still find plenty of places to throw back a pint. All told, it's not a bad spot to spend a few nights on your way through the region.

Getting There

BY AIR

Aéroport Rennes-St-Jacques (☎ 02-99-29-60-00; www.rennes.aeroport.fr) is about 20 minutes southwest of town, and serves flights from around France and the United Kingdom. The closest public transportation is through Rennes's local bus network (see "By Bus" under "Getting Around" below), which picks up half a mile away in the hamlet of St-Jacques de la Lande. Head to the Gautrais bus stop for the 57 bus, which drops off in the center of Rennes, at place de la République.

BY TRAIN

Only 2 hours from Paris, Rennes is no trouble to reach on fast **TGV trains** (www.sncf.com). The station also connects with Nantes, which is 1 hour and 20 minutes away, as well as Brest, 2¹/₂ hours away. Rennes is also a hub for getting around the rest of Brittany on local TER trains.

BY CAR

Heading out of Paris, plan on a 3¹/₂-hour trip, and get onto the A11. Continue east and merge onto the A81/E50, and then onto E50/N157 until you reach Rennes.

BY BUS

The **Illenoo** bus network (www.illenoo.fr) serves the Ille-et-Vilaine *département* in Brittany, including cities such as St-Malo, but it's most useful for nearby towns that aren't served by train stations. Buses pick up at the *gare routière* in Rennes

(☎ 02-99-30-87-80; www.gare-routiere-rennes.fr), directly next to the SNCF train station. The *gare routière* website is also helpful in nailing down a trip.

Orientation

Rennes is divided by the Vilaine River, though these days it's more of a tame canal. The train station is on the south side, as are several hotels and restaurants, but the main heart of Rennes is on the north side. Downtown Rennes is divided between two main squares that can serve as your main reference points: place de Sainte Anne on the north end and place de la République on the Vilaine River. In between you'll find the historic medieval neighborhood as well as the main shopping district. At the very center of town are two more public squares, the bustling place de la Marie and the square in front of the *Parlement* building. Nightlife is concentrated in the northeast corner of town between place Sainte-Anne and place des Lices (also where the farmer's market is). While you may see plenty of students, the universities are actually far outside town. All in all, Rennes has a sizable downtown, which can take 15 minutes to cross on foot.

Getting Around

BY BUS

Hoofing it around town by foot is no problem, but for spots on the outskirts, take the Star bus and metro system (☎ 02-99-79-37-37; www.star.fr). The cost is 1.10€ for 1 hour unlimited of bus and metro, or 3.20€ for a day unlimited.

BY METRO

Rennes has a clean and well-run metro system that's heavily trafficked by students. For visitors, though, only one or two stops are useful, since most lines service the suburbs outside town. Look for line A, which connects the *gare SNCF* (Gare station) to the two main squares in town (République and Sainte Anne stations).

BY BIKE

When walking around Rennes, you'll notice random white bikes around town locked in special docking stations. This is part of the city's **Vélo à la Carte** program (☎ 02-99-79-65-88; http://veloalacarte.free.fr), which is sponsored by Clear Channel. Local residents apply for a card that allows them to unlock the bikes and use them for 2 hours at a time. While this doesn't quite work for tourists, there is an alternative. If you stop by the **SABAR** kiosk on place de la République, they'll allow you to rent a bike for 7 hours for a deposit of 76€. If the system sounds too elaborate for you, stop by **Cycles Guedard** (13 bd. Beaumont; ☎ 02-99-30-43-78), just west of the train station.

BY FOOT

Downtown Rennes is expansive, but trekking around to the major sights is no problem. There's plenty to discover on every street, and when your feet fail, you can jump on a metro or bus to speed up the trip.

Tourist Offices

Rennes's **tourist office** (11 rue St-Yves; ☎ 02-99-67-11-11; www.tourisme-rennes.com) is a well-oiled machine. Housed in an old church, it has got all the maps, brochures, and history you can handle. The ticket office inside covers guided tours to the Parliament building, as well as guided tours around town. The city also sells a "Citypass" for 13€, which grants entrance to several museums and a guided tour. Valid for 2 days only, the pass is only a good deal if you plan to visit a lot of places, so do the math before you spring for it. The office is open July to August Monday to Saturday 9am to 7pm, Sunday 11am to 1pm

Rennes

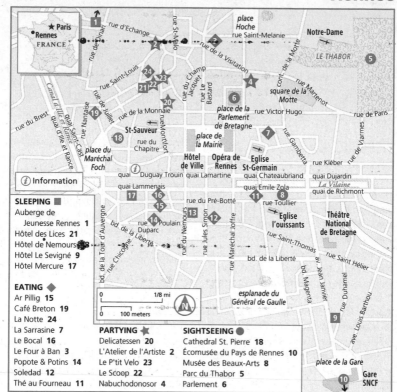

SLEEPING ■
Auberge de
  Jeunesse Rennes **1**
Hôtel des Lices **21**
Hôtel de Nemours **23**
Hôtel Le Sevigné **9**
Hôtel Mercure **17**

EATING ◆
Ar Pillig **15**
Café Breton **19**
La Notte **24**
La Sarrasine **7**
Le Bocal **16**
Le Four à Ban **3**
Popote & Potins **14**
Soledad **12**
Thé au Fourneau **11**

PARTYING 🍸
Delicatessen **20**
L'Atelier de l'Artiste **2**
Le P'tit Velo **23**
Le Scoop **22**
Nabuchodonosor **4**

SIGHTSEEING ●
Cathedral St. Pierre **18**
Écomusée du Pays de Rennes **10**
Musée des Beaux-Arts **8**
Parc du Thabor **5**
Parlement **6**

and 2 to 6pm, September to June 10am to 6pm, Sunday 11am to 1pm and 2 to 6pm.

Recommended Websites

○ **www.tourisme-rennes.com**: The Rennes tourist office website is impressively thorough, and with all the materials published in English as well as

French, it can be a very useful planning tool.

○ **www.bretagne35.com**: This website is a broader travel resource, covering the entire Ile-et-Vilaine *département*. Also translated into English, the site is great for getting a handle on the region, which includes the city of St-Malo.

Rennes Nuts & Bolts

Internet Cafe When looking to do a little Web surfing, Rennes has two very traditional Internet cafes. **Cybernet Online** (22 rue St-Georges; ☎ 02-99-36-37-41; www.cybernetonline.com; Mon–Sat 10:30am–9:30pm) rents computers at 4€ an hour. Slightly farther off the beaten path is **Replay Cybercafe** (22 rue de la Visitation; ☎ 02-23-47-09-67; www.replay-rennes.com; Mon–Sat 11am–10pm, Sun 2–8pm).

Laundromats   If that suitcase is starting to smell less than spring-fresh, visit **Cleanfil** (26 rue Poullain Duparc; ☎ 02-99-78-18-17; Mon–Sun 8am–9pm).

Post Office   You'll find Rennes's main post office in the heart of place de la République (☎ **02-99-78-43-58**; Mon–Fri 8:30am–7pm, Sat 9am–12:30pm). A smaller annex is also found on place Sainte-Anne (Mon 1:45–6:30pm, Tues–Fri 8:45am–12:30pm and 1:45–6:30pm, Sat 8:45am–1pm).

Supermarkets   The best supermarket for a quick bite is the **Galeries Lafayette** (2 rue Rohan; ☎ **02-99-78-49-49**; Mon–Sat 9am–6:30pm), near the heart of town.

Sleeping

Despite being a capital city, Rennes isn't as chock-full of hotels as you might imagine. The center of town is dedicated to shopping, and hotels sit slightly on the outside. If you don't mind walking, you'll find several options clustered around the train station on avenue Jean Janvier, about a 15-minute walk to the town center. Rennes still has some excellent deals, with several hotels that could be charging a whole lot more. In fact, the quality is so high, it levels the playing field completely.

Rennes is one of the French towns that is part of the *Bon Week End en Ville* program, so ask if you can get a two-for-one deal. Many hotels offer 2 nights for the price of one when tourists arrive on a weekend. Most hotels don't give it up during the summer, though, so it's usually only valid from November 1 until March 31. Check the website (www.bon-week-end-en-villes.com) for a list of Rennes hotels that participate, and save some serious dough.

HOSTELS

→ **Auberge de Jeunesse Rennes** In a white building overlooking a canal, Rennes's youth hostel attracts tourists in the summer and students in the fall. Rooms are simple and bare-boned, for between two and four people, and some have a bathroom attached. Downstairs, there's no cafeteria, but breakfast is served and a laundry room is available in case your clothes need a rinse. The atmosphere isn't fancy, but it's comfortable. The hostel is a trek from downtown Rennes. By bus, you can take bus no. 18 from the center of town to the "Auberge de Jeunesse" stop. Then walk to just before the canal and take a right, and you're there. *10–12 Canal St-Martin.* ☎ *02-99-33-22-33. www.hihostels.com. 16€ per person. Rate includes breakfast.*

CHEAP

→ **Hôtel de Nemours** ★★ Just a few years ago, this hotel had a kitschy nautical theme. Since then, it's been completely redone, and now it's one of the best deals in town. With a minimal modern look, in warm grays and white, the decor is simple and hip. Rooms are snug, with clean cutting-edge design, leaving you to wonder why the hotel isn't charging much more. Both young and refined, Hôtel de Nemours is a don't-miss. *5 rue de Nemours.* ☎ *02-99-78-26-26. www.hotelnemours.com. 63€–72€ double. Credit cards accepted. Amenities: Elevator; free Wi-Fi. In room: A/C, TV.*

→ **Hôtel des Lices** ★ Another excellent deal, the comfortable Hôtel des Lices is in the heart of Rennes. Rooms are decorated in bright red, blond wood, and Ikea-esque furniture. Many have small balconies. The hotel is only a hop away from the Saturday farmer's market at place des Lices, and in the heart of the nightlife at place

St-Michel. On the weekend, street noise drifts in, so ask for a quieter room. *7 place des Lices.* ☎ *02-99-79-14-81. www.hotel-des-lices-com. Metro stop: St-Anne station. 59€–64€ double. Breakfast 7.80€. Credit cards accepted. Amenities: Elevator; free Wi-Fi. In room: A/C, TV.*

DOABLE

➜ **Hôtel Le Sevigné** Closer to the train station than the town center, Le Sevigné is a solid choice if you don't mind the distance. Decorated in warm oranges, with a sunny south of France vibe, the rooms are comfortable and clean, but get little sun. Most of Rennes is a 10- to 15-minute walk from the hotel, though plenty of restaurants are on avenue Jean Janvier. *47 bis av. Jean Janvier.* ☎ *02-99-67-27-55. www.hotelle-sevigne.fr. 60€–80€ double. Breakfast 7€. Credit cards accepted. Amenities: Elevator; paid Wi-Fi. In room: A/C, TV.*

SPLURGE

➜ **Hôtel Mercure Place de Bretagne** On the quiet south side of the Vilaine River, this hotel belongs to the larger Mercure chain. Though the rooms have that same hotel chain feel in light yellows and reds, they are comfortable and quiet. Prices depend on room size, so if you're looking for some extra elbowroom, you'll find it. The hotel itself may not provide much charm, but it's a more than pleasant stay. *6 rue Lanjuinais.* ☎ *02-99-79-12-36. www.mercure.com. 108€–132€ double. Breakfast 11€. Credit cards accepted. Parking 10€. Amenities: Elevator; limited mobility access; paid Wi-Fi. In room: A/C, TV.*

Eating

At mealtime in Rennes, plenty of hungry students are on the prowl, which means there are plenty of joints with cheap eats (both good and bad). As with any average Breton town, creperies are a dime a dozen and great for a quick bite. But Rennes also benefits from its super farmer's market, and several restaurants serve up fresh, gourmet cuisine at attainable prices.

CAFES & LIGHT FARE

➜ **Soledad** CAFE/SANDWICHES When you start tiring of the same old *jambon* and *fromage* on a baguette, swing by Soledad for their tasty lunch goods. The small takeout counter uses pesto and tapenades to spruce up their sandwiches, and mixes in other Mediterranean flavors. They also have takeout salads such as mozzarella and tomatoes or tabouleh, making it one of the best places in town for packing a picnic. *1 rue Vasselot.* ☎ *02-99-79-12-73. Dishes 3€–6€. Credit cards accepted. Mon–Sat 9am–7:30pm; Sun 10am–1:30pm.*

➜ **Thé au Fourneau** CAFE/SANDWICHES This tea house is a cozy spot for a lunch or afternoon stop. You'll find locals settling in at homey tables under the low wood ceiling on any given weekday. Thé au Fourneau serves a splendid cup of tea, both regular and iced. With its long list to choose from, it's worth the slightly higher price tag (you need a break from drinking espresso anyway). The lunch menu is simple and satisfying with *tartines*, quiches, and salads. Their desserts and cakes are also a perfect companion to any teatime break. *6 rue du Capitaine Alfred Dreyfus.* ☎ *02-99-78-25-36. Main courses 5.34€–7.62€. Credit cards accepted. Mon–Fri 11am–6:30pm.*

CHEAP

➜ **Ar Pillig** ★ CREPERIE Crepes are the name of the game at this medieval-themed spot (don't worry, no armor or jousting in sight). The cozy restaurant has carved wooden walls and Knights of the Round Table names on the menu, which includes all the basic variations with ham and cheese, and several more adventurous crepes, including ones with goat cheese and apples, or pears and smoked duck breast. It's one of the best creperies in town. *10 rue d'Argentré.* ☎ *02-99-79-53-89. Menus 7.50€. Credit cards accepted. Mon–Sun 11:45am–2pm and 6:45–10:30pm.*

➜ **La Notte** ITALIAN/PIZZERIA Slightly more upscale than your average local pizza joint, La Notte is a favorite among students looking for a meal instead of a slice. The restaurant churns out solid thin crust pizzas with all the trimmings, including veggie-friendly fare. For something out of the ordinary, try the *del pescatore,* with tomatoes, scallops, and prawns cooked in cognac. Other Italian stand-bys are also on the menu, including plentiful salads and pasta dishes. *4 rue des Innocents.* ☎ *02-99-31-79-22. Pizzas and entrees 7.50€–10€. Credit cards accepted. Mon–Fri noon–2pm and 7–11pm; Sat 7pm–midnight.*

➜ **La Sarrasine** CREPERIE Another popular creperie in town, La Sarrasine boasts that they make crepes *à l'ancienne*—the traditional way (though it's not easy to taste the difference). It's comfortably functional on the inside, with outdoor seating in the summer on the quiet rue St-Georges. The street is chock-full of other creperies and restaurants, too, so you can do a little menu comparison before sitting down. *30 rue St-Georges.* ☎ *02-99-38-87-54. Main courses 2€–9€. Credit cards accepted. Tues–Sat 11:30am–2pm and 6:45–11pm.*

DOABLE

➜ **Café Breton** ★ SEAFOOD, FRENCH Fresh market ingredients and affordable entrees keep this joint packed with locals until the late hours. Warm and boisterous inside, Café Breton focuses mainly on seafood, with a menu that changes weekly. At lunchtime you can get hearty salads and lighter dishes. In the evening, look for their fresh fish and market-focused menu. Either way, you'll get a heavy dose of local flavor with a noise level to match. *14 rue*

Nantaise. ☎ *02-99-30-74-95. Entrees 13€–17€. Credit cards accepted. Mon and Sat noon–3pm; Tues–Fri noon–3pm and 7–11pm.*

MTV **Best ◉** ➜ **Le Bocal** ★★ MODERN FRENCH With a simple, down-to-earth vibe, Le Bocal showcases its fresh ingredients. Their straightforward menu, scrawled on a giant blackboard inside, might showcase lamb stew with almonds and figs, cod with chorizo and tomatoes, or filet mignon with pistachios and rosemary. The funky tables and chairs tend to fill up quickly, so don't show up too late. With a reasonably priced carafe of wine, it might just be the best affordable meal you have in Brittany. *6 rue d'Argentré.* ☎ *02-99-78-34-10. Entrees 12€–14€. Credit cards accepted. Tues–Fri noon–3:30pm and 6:15–10:30pm; Sat 6:15–10:30pm.*

➜ **Popote & Potins** MODERN FRENCH "P & P," as this restaurant is known, is a playfully modern take on a classic brasserie. With deep purple walls and a logo in golden Gothic letters, the decor is a funky mishmash of modern and traditional. Unlike the ornamentation, the atmosphere is laid-back, with fresh cuisine. They serve large salads for main courses, with either seafood or foie gras, as well as more traditional dishes like their pork with a lemon and balsamic vinegar reduction. *30 rue Poullain Dupare.* ☎ *02-99-78-22-49. Entrees 12€–16€. Credit cards accepted. Tues–Fri noon–2pm and 7–10:30pm; Sat 7–10:30pm.*

SPLURGE

➜ **Le Four à Ban** ★ MODERN FRENCH For a high quality and upscale experience in Rennes, Le Four à Ban has a serious chef who is serious about food. The cuisine is said to mix his Mediterranean origins with local Breton ingredients. Housed in a former community bakery, the restaurant has a warm stone fireplace and white tablecloths. You're pretty much guaranteed a

Getting a Sugar High in Brittany

Every region in France has its specialty sweet pastry. In Brittany, though, don't expect anything light and flaky. Breton pastries are a serious caloric investment.

→ **Kouign Amann** This classic pastry could also be known as the evil sibling of the croissant. Layers of flaky pastry are rolled into a flat cinnamon bun shape, equally as buttery as a croissant. But a *kouign amann* is denser and sweeter, often with a thick coating of hardened sugar around it. Once you have one, you won't stop until you leave the region.

→ **Le Parlementin** A specialty from Rennes, this cake is perfumed with cider and apples topped with almonds and nougat. They usually come individually sized and wrapped in a special Parlementin label.

→ **Far Breton** These are guaranteed to weigh you down. Far Breton is a dense, custard cake with a consistency much like Spanish *flan*. Inside are brandy-soaked plums or raisins, making it incredibly rich. This is one to share with a friend.

BRITTANY

delectable meal, as long as you finish it off with the famous caramelized apple and salted butter caramel mousse. *4 rue St-Melaine. ☎ 02-99-38-72-85. www.lefouraban. com. Menus 25€–49€, main courses 17€–25€. Credit cards accepted. Mon–Fri noon–2pm and 7–10pm. Closed for Sat lunch and Mon dinner.*

Partying

Thanks to the bustling student population in Rennes, nightlife is quite a scene. From rollicking pubs to outdoor cafes and wine bars, Rennes has a little bit of everything. The main drag for nightlife is on the place St-Michel. In fact, rue St-Michel is nick-named *rue de la soif* (street of thirst) for that very reason. One end is filled with outdoor seating, where a young crowd parks to people-watch. Heading up rue St-Michel, indoor pubs are packed wall-to-wall for pint-drinking, dart-throwing types. Still, there are several other more bohemian spots around town if you're looking for a quieter cocktail or glass of wine. These bars are better suited for the brief philosophical conversation, or any kind of audible exchange, for that matter.

Summer can be a bit quieter than the school year, when the influx of students can turn place St-Michel into a raging party.

FUNKY BARS

→ **L'Atelier de l'Artiste** ★ This popular neighborhood dive has a warmer ambience than its neighbors on rue St-Michel. You'll mostly find students sitting with a pint or glass of wine in the evenings, but it fills up as the night goes on. The bar also acts as an informal exposition space, showing local artists on the walls. On the main square of Sainte-Anne, directly between the nightlife on rue St-Malo and rue St-Michel, it's a good option if you're a pint sipper, instead of a chugger (drinks run 2.50€–5€). *2 rue St-Louis. ☎ 02-99-79-60-98.*

→ **Le P'tit Vélo** This mostly outdoor bar is one of four packed in a row on place St-Michel, with seating pushed together so tightly it's hard to tell where one bar begins and another ends. In warm months, the outdoor spots fill up quickly and the people-watching begins. Afternoons start off low-key, but the scene gets rowdy in the evening as tipsy students fill the square and start bar-hopping. Le P'tit Vélo isn't a remarkable bar, but a spot to visit for the prime real estate. Drinks are 3€ to 7€. *8 place St-Michel.* ☎ *02-99-78-23-98.*

→ **Le Scoop** This is another of the outdoor bars in place St-Michel, the main square to see and be seen in Rennes. Le Scoop pours a standard drink menu—wine, beer, and mixed drinks (3€–7€)—but the real reason to stop by is to park yourself outside for a few hours and raise a glass with the rest of Rennes's student population. *1 place du Haut des Lices.* ☎ *02-99-79-10-39.*

→ **Nabuchodonosor** Everyone in town calls this wine bar "Nabu" for short. It's French for Nebuchadnezzar (think flying ship in *The Matrix*). On any given night you'll find a young, coffeehouse crowd here, seeking refuge from the nighttime zoo at rue St-Michel and perusing the wine list on chalkboards across the walls. Funky wooden chairs and cafe tables also make this a good spot for conversation. During the day, they serve *tartines* and other light food. Glasses and bottles of wine are both easy on the wallet (2€–5€), but they also pour Coreff, a local Breton beer, just in case. *12 rue Hoche.* ☎ *02-99-27-07-58.*

NIGHTCLUBS

MTV Best 🔊 → **Delicatessen** ★ This nightclub is worth seeing for the location alone, and the rest is just icing on the cake— or dungeon, in this case. Delicatessen is underground in the ancient St-Michel prison. The dark archways and stone walls are offset by lounge-y couches and bumping electronic and house music. The spot fills up with students and young Rennais after the bars in town start closing down. Don't get confused and think you're on a guided tour. Delicatessen is for rump-shaking only. Cover is 5€ to 14€ (depending on weekend or weeknight, before 1:30am or

after), and drinks are 5€ to 7€. *7 allée Rallier du Baty.* ☎ *02-99-78-23-41.*

Sightseeing

Rennes won't overwhelm with an astounding number of sights. Part of the city's charm is lurking around street corners in the historic neighborhoods. Even when you have a map, some tiny medieval street always seems to reveal itself. Visiting the museums won't take more than a day if you stick to the main list. If the weather is nice, Parc Thabor's gardens are a beautiful place to relax.

MUSEUMS

→ **Ecomusée du Pays de Rennes** Get a little bit country (Breton-style, that is) at this museum on an old farm just south of town. The old buildings are dedicated to all things rural, with exhibits portraying what life used to be like for Breton farmers. On the surrounding grounds, you'll find a medieval petting zoo where the museum raises ancient breeds of Breton farm animals, including horses, cows, and goats. Don't miss the world's smallest breed of sheep, too—no bigger than a toy poodle. Getting to the Ecomusée is no problem with a car. On public transit, it's more of a commitment, but worthwhile if you have some time on your hands. Take the metro to the "Triangle" stop. Once you're out of the station, hang a left and walk across the bridge over the highway (if it looks like you're in the middle of nowhere, keep going). Once you see the La Bintinais bus stop, hang a right and walk through the private vegetable gardens. During the summer, the buildings are closed from noon to 2pm, but the grounds stay open for picnics. *Ferme de la Bintinais—rte. de Châtillon-sur-Seiche.* ☎ *02-99-51-38-15. Apr–Sept Mon–Fri 9am–6pm, Sat 2–6pm, Sun 2–7pm; Oct–Mar*

Mon–Fri 9am–noon and 2–6pm, Sat 2–6pm, Sun 2–7pm.

→ **Le Parlement** Before you start calling this the Parliament building, be aware that it's actually a superior courthouse. But the Parlement building is nonetheless a serious source of pride and protectiveness for Rennes's residents. After a tragic fire in 1994 (see "Rennes's Fiery Past," below), the city took elaborate care restoring the building and interior to its previous glory. No sconce or pillar was overlooked. Luckily, many of the elaborate ceiling murals were saved during the fire. The only way to get inside is by guided tour through the tourist office, which takes you through the courtrooms and room of the *pas perdus* (lost steps), so named because it was where plaintiffs and attorneys paced while waiting for a verdict. The 1¹/₂-hour tour is available Monday through Friday in French, and once a week in English on Wednesday at 5:30pm. Admission is by guided tour only at the

tourist office (p. 238). *Tickets 6.10€ adults, 3.05€ students.*

→ **Musée des Beaux-Arts** Rennes's Musée des Beaux-Arts is like the movie preview version of the Louvre. Its collection ranges from Greek and Egyptian artifacts to 16th-century art, all the way up to the 20th century. With pieces from Rubens, Picasso, and Brittany's Pont-Aven school, you'll get a taste of the greats without any major burnout. *20 quai Émile Zola.* ☎ *02-99-28-55-85. www.mbar.org. 5.30€–4.20€ (depending on the exhibition), 2.65€–2.15€ students. Tues–Sun 10am–noon and 2–6pm.*

MONUMENTS & CHURCHES

FREE → **Cathédrale St-Pierre** This is Rennes's most elaborate cathedral, with a gilded neoclassical interior and elaborate facade. The one currently standing, however, is the third built on the site. Two before it crumbled under structural problems (one while the chorus was singing

Rennes's Fiery Past

Like most medieval towns, Rennes was built completely out of wood. And like most medieval towns, one little mishap with a candle meant that half the townspeople were left with piles of smoking rubble. In 1720, a fire broke out in Rennes that destroyed 33 streets and 900 timber-framed houses. Most buildings were rebuilt from stone, in large part by the famous Parisian architect Jacques Gabriel, who worked heavily on Versailles. If the public squares and rooftops downtown remind you of Paris, it's not just your imagination.

Rennes's Parlement building escaped the fire, and the residents of Rennes breathed a sigh of relief for the elaborate murals and tapestries inside. Unfortunately, in 1994 a group of Breton fishermen gathered to protest in the square in front of the building. A wayward flare caught the roof of the building, causing another fire. Heroic local firemen worked hard to save the art, and several paintings and tapestries were preserved. Suffering damage from smoke and water, however, they were sent to a Paris workshop for restoration. In the tragic punch line of a comedy of errors (or pure tragedy for the Rennais), the Paris workshop caught fire, destroying the tapestries for good.

If you see a lot of fire extinguishers around Rennes, you'll know why.

inside). This version, completed in the 19th century, is worth stepping into. *Rue de la Monnaie. Mon–Sun 9:30am–noon and 3–6pm.*

Ⓜ Best● HISTORIC NEIGHBORHOODS

While most of Rennes's medieval buildings went up in smoke during the 1720 fire, Rennes's **historic district** is still full of crooked timber houses over 400 years old. The best place to start is near the tourist office on rue St-Yves. Many of the streets nearby, including rue des Dames and rue de Griffon, hold several examples of medieval timber houses, still leaning heavily on each other. On **rue du Chapitre,** look for nos. 3, 5, 20, and 22. Continuing across place Maréchal Foch, you'll reach the **Portes Mordelasies,** the former gated drawbridge that led into the heart of the city. For some of the best examples, visit the tiny street of Ⓜ Best● **rue de la Psalette.** The houses at nos. 8 and 10 were choir schools for altar boys, and the house at no. 12 is one of the oldest examples of a 15th-century building (though it has undergone some upkeep since then).

PARKS & GARDENS

FREE → **Parc du Thabor** ★ Just northeast of the town center is Rennes's massive public garden, designed in the 19th century. Amid its massive walkways, statues, and staircases, you can ramble through the manicured hedges like an aristocrat. The benches and large, grassy fields make excellent picnic areas. In the summer, the city hosts "Les soirées du Thabor" on Wednesday nights, which feature evening performances of Breton dance or music near the rue de la Palestine entrance. When strolling along, keep your eye out for random Ping-Pong tables. *Entrances on place St-Melanie, rue de Paris, rue de la Palestine, and rue de la Duchesse Anne. Mon–Sun 7:15am–9:15pm (summer) and 7:30am–6pm (winter).*

Shopping

Rennes has a vibrant shopping scene, attracting locals from all over. The main district hosts mostly clothing stores, sandwiched between place de la République (where Galeries Lafayette is) and place de la Marie. French chain stores and one-of-a-kind boutiques are condensed in all the streets in between. Rennes has plenty of other places to shop, but they're more spread out. If you're looking to do some international damage to the credit card, come to the center of town.

CLOTHING & ACCESSORIES

→ **Topkapi** This charming women's boutique mixes funk and refinement. All the pieces—including jewelry, clothing, and scarves—are unique with a distinguishing French flair. Prices are a bit steep, but you won't find stuff like this at home. *10 rue de Bertrand. ☎ 02-23-21-13-99. Tues–Sun 11am–2pm and 3–6pm.*

FOOD, WINE & LOCAL CRAFTS

Ⓜ Best● → **Chocolaterie Durand** Despite its tame decor, there's nothing ordinary about this chocolate shop. With 30 different kinds of handmade chocolate truffles to choose from, you'd do well to pick up their buying guide. Each chocolate is decorated in gold numbers on top, since they're all the same shape and size. Inside, however, the differences are mind blowing. The shop owner uses only fresh ingredients in the ganache fillings. You won't find any liquid essences; lemon means real lemon. With so many decadent flavors, it won't be easy to choose. If you're stumped, consider these three standouts: the #28 (made with white chocolate, basil, and lemon zest), the #15 (made with dark chocolate, coffee, and green cardamom from India), and the Absinth, lucky #13 (made with dark chocolate and fresh leaves of wormwood).

As the shop owner says, it's impossible to have a favorite. *5 quai Châteaubriand.* ☎ *02-99-78-10-00. Mon 3–6:30pm, Tues–Sat 10am–7pm.*

→ **Histoires de Vins** When it comes to organic French wines, Histoires de Vins is the spot, with almost a complete stock of "bio wines." Don't think that will break the bank—the shop specializes in affordable bottles. The owner also gives great advice about their well-organized selection. Make sure to grab some authentic Breton cider, too, for a perfect picnic sidekick. *47 rue Vasselot.* ☎ *02-99-79-18-19. Mon–Sat 9:30am–1pm and 2–8pm, Sun 10am–1pm.*

→ **Pâtisserie Bouvier** ★ This sweets shop sells a delicate and colorful collection of *maracons* (a light sandwich cookie). With flavors such as cassis and salted caramel, it's definitely the place to give one a try. They offer plenty of other buttery goodies as well, including the famous Parlementin cake found only in Rennes (see "Getting a Sugar High in Brittany," above). *5 rue la Parcheminerie.* ☎ *02-99-78-14-08. Mon–Fri 9am–noon and 2–7pm; Sat 2–7pm.*

📺 (Best ✪) → **Rennes Farmer's Market** ★ On Saturday mornings, almost everyone in town heads to the market, or so it seems. It's one of the biggest markets in Brittany, and you'll be blown away by the quality and variety of produce and food available. Even more so, it's amazing to watch the care with which locals select and talk about their food. Even if you're simply picking up an apple, don't expect the line to move too quickly. Though the selling pace is frantic, no one will back down from a good discussion. *Place des Lices. Sat 7am–1pm.*

MUSIC, BOOKS & MEDIA

→ **Rockin' Bones** This record shop is difficult to spot on the street, especially because it doesn't quite fit in with the preppy shopping neighborhood around it. Once you duck under an archway, you'll find it at the end of a short driveway. As the name suggests, this shop specializes in rock on vinyl, including current stuff, classic American, and French bands. With new and used records, it offers plenty of bins to flip through. *7 rue de la Motte Fablet.* ☎ *02-99-79-36-49. Mon–Sun 2–7pm.*

FUN BUYS

→ **La Poste du Village** For one-of-a-kind books, postcards, and maps, this small antiques shop has plenty of options. Don't be fazed by the owner's collection of tiny military models. The store holds all kinds of goodies—perfect if you're looking for something unique to take home. Prices can be high, so ask where the affordable sections are. *6 rue Edith Cavell.* ☎ *02-99-79-27-02. Mon–Sat 10am–noon and 2–6pm.*

Festivals

In early July each year, Rennes hosts **Les Tombées de la Nuit** (www.tdn.rennes.fr). The festival is packed with original street performances, musical events, operas, and plays. Shows are both avant-garde and traditional. Street performances are free, and tickets for other events are sold at the tourist office. If you're around for the first weekend in December, head for **Les Transmusicales** (www.lestrans.com). The festival showcases 3 days of music, but only from up-and-coming and breaking artists. You'll hear a lot of rock, but the lineup is decidedly international. You can buy tickets for the full 3 days, or for individual events. Don't forget that the Parc Thabor hosts **Les Soirées du Thabor** on Wednesdays during the summer, featuring traditional Breton dance and music. Visit the tourist office for more information.

King Arthur's Forest

Never in your dorkiest dreams could you imagine a park as brilliantly kitschy as this tribute to all things Arthurian. Legend has it that this was King Arthur's forest, where he hung out with Merlin and his knights and sought the Holy Grail (if you don't remember, brush up on some Monty Python). The good knights and welcoming wenches at the **Centre de L'imaginaire Arthurien (Center for the Arthurian Imagination)** take their swords and shields very seriously, and will welcome you to the Brocéliande forest.

This place is Medieval Times to the 20th degree. So bust out the cape you packed "just in case" and get down to exploring these misty woods. You don't have to be a complete Ren-Fair geek to get a kick out of this campy getaway, though some of the sights, such as Merlin's tomb, take a serious amount of imagination to enjoy (it's a pile of rocks). At 5€ (4€ for students), it's a cheap price for time travel, but special activities such as guided group tours or fairytale sessions will cost you a pretty penny. You can't get here via public transportation, and even getting around the forest requires a car, so it's best to call the Centre to get directions.

The Château de Comper-en-Brocéliande is in Concoret (☎ **02-97-22-79-96**; www.centre-arthurien-broceliande.com).

Carnac: Brittany's Jekyll & Hyde

142km (88 miles) E of Rennes, 492km (305 miles) E of Paris

Carnac is a town with split personality disorder. On one hand, Carnac is a sunny beachside resort populated by sunbathers, body surfers, and ice cream–eaters. On the flip side, Carnac is a quaint French countryside town with a chiming church bell, farmer's market, and historical sights. Luckily, Carnac doesn't attempt to reconcile these two sides in one small space. The town comprises two areas that are 15 minutes apart. Carnac-Plage is the bustling seaside hub with sand, sun, and tourist traps. Carnac-Ville is the small downtown, just inland from the ocean, with shops and local flavor. That makes Carnac a two-for-one experience, with a taste of summer beach fun and local Breton charm.

But Carnac's biggest draw is just north of town: one of the largest Neolithic stone arrangements in western Europe. Much like a bigger and more disorderly Stonehenge, the area holds thousands of megaliths, arranged in long rows and patterns. It covers kilometers of ground, so there's plenty more to discover, by bike or car, than the heavily trafficked spots favored by tourists. In the summer, the main sites are fenced off from the public, thanks to too much tourist traffic. It doesn't stop them from coming, though; in July and August, Carnac is still overrun with foot traffic. The beaches fill up, restaurants get packed, and touristy shops open their doors along the coast. In the winter, of course, Carnac is a ghost town, and most businesses close up shop for the colder months.

Expect to find some painfully high hotel prices during the summer, although crowds tend to be younger than elsewhere in Brittany. Tourists hit the beach by day and the town by night, with its vibrant bar and club scene. If sand and crowds aren't your thing, visit Carnac-Ville, with its small town charm, neighborhood shops, and locals happy to give you directions. Prices are understandably lower in this area, and there are plenty of bargains to be found even during the summer.

The word is definitely out on Carnac, so don't expect to roll into town without reservations. But for sand, Stone Age fun, and local flavor, it's worth the effort.

Getting There

BY TRAIN & BUS

Head's up: There is no train station in Carnac, so don't be surprised when you have to jump the tracks elsewhere. No need to panic, though; getting to town is still easy. The closest train station is in Auray, just north of Carnac. From there, take the **Réseau Tim** (☎ 02-97-21-28-29), a local bus service that drops off at two locations in Carnac. When exiting the train station, take a right turn and head for the buses. Look for line 1, the Auray-Crach-Locmariaquer route. Tickets are sold on board for 4€ a trip; but if you buy a ticket to Carnac at the train station, your bus fare will already be included as well as the scheduling information. During the summer, these buses leave nine times a day, and drop off in front of the tourist office at Carnac-Plage, or in front of the Gendarmerie in Carnac-Ville, west of the main square on rue St-Cornely.

In the summer, a local train called the **Tire-Bouchon** also runs near Carnac, though not exactly to the town itself. Departing from Auray, it drops off at the Plouharnel-Carnac station, which is a 10€ to 15€ taxi ride to Carnac. The Tire-Bouchon continues on to the coastal town of Quiberon from there. Keep in mind, it only runs from June 24 to August 27 at 2.80€ one-way. See the SNCF website (www.sncf.com) for details.

BY CAR

Driving is another convenient way to get to Carnac, if you have the means. From Rennes, take the N24 in the direction of Vannes and Lorient, then join the N166 following the signs to Vannes. Continue east towards Lorient on the N165 until you reach Auray, then turn south on D768 to Carnac.

Orientation

As stated earlier, Carnac is divided into two main regions: Carnac-Plage near the beach and Carnac-Ville in the heart of town. Both areas have hotels, shops, and restaurants, but with completely different vibes and sights. Carnac's beaches extend west of town a bit, and there's a lot more turf to explore if you have the wheels and gumption. Several kilometers north of town are more sights, where fields of Neolithic stone arrangements spread across the countryside. The tourist office hands out several maps of the area, including one that maps several day hikes or afternoon jaunts.

Getting Around

BY PUBLIC TRANSPORTATION

To accommodate the vacation crowds, Carnac runs two different public buses during the summer. From July 10 to August 27, the **Carnavette** follows the straight line between Carnac-Plage and Carnac-Ville. Shuttles pick up beachside at the Grande Plage (near the Base Nautique) and drop off at the main square in Carnac-Ville. The free ride will save you a 20-minute walk, 7 days a week, from 1:30pm to 8:30pm.

For trips farther afield, the **Tatoovu** bus runs in a continuous loop from the beaches to the megaliths. Several stops along the way serve Carnac's many campgrounds, but be aware that the loop runs only in one direction, so you're in for the full ride. Shuttles run only from June 12 to

BRITTANY

September 16, from 9:30am to 1:30pm and 2:30pm to 7:15pm. Tickets are sold onboard for 1.10€.

BY BIKE

Unless you've got a rental car, searching out some of Carnac's best spots can be cumbersome. Stone Age megaliths extend far north of Carnac, and some of the best ones are far off the beaten path. **MTV Best** **Traveling Carnac by bike** is the easiest and most reliable way to get from the beach to lunch, to the sights, and back to your hotel in time for dinner. Plenty of bike rental shops rent everything from mountain bikes (*VTT* in French) to street and road bikes. In Carnac-Plage, visit **Cyclo Tours** (89 av. des Druides; ☎ **02-97-52-06-51;** Apr–Nov Mon–Sun 9am–6:30pm) or **A Bicyclette** (93 bis av. des Druides; ☎ **02-97-52-75-08;** Apr–Oct Mon–Sun 9am–7pm). In Carnac-Ville, visit **Besrest** (2 bis av. des Salines; ☎ **02-97-52-88-92;** Apr–Oct Mon–Sun 9am–6pm). For the most bang for your euro, go for a multiday rental.

BY FOOT

Carnac is only a foot-friendly town for beach bums. If your horizons are broader, consider renting a bike. Getting from Carnac-Plage to Carnac-Ville on foot is no problem, but it is a 20-minute walk each way. Walking from Carnac-Ville to the megaliths north of town is also feasible, but it's another 20-minute walk and it only takes you to one particular area of stone arrangements. If you have no choice, getting around on foot is possible if aided by some public transportation. Just be sure to plan in advance.

Tourist Offices

With two locations to serve your touristic needs, Carnac's tourist offices do a brisk business in the summer. This is the go-to joint for maps, as well as brochures on the surrounding area. If you're traveling the coast, stop by for information and ferry reservations as well. In Carnac-Place, swing by 74 av. des Druides (☎ **02-97-52-13-52;** www.carnac.fr; July–Aug 9am–7pm, Sun 3–7pm, Sept–June Mon–Sat 9am–noon and 2–6pm). In Carnac-Ville, head just across from the cathedral at place de l'Eglise (July–Aug Mon–Sat 9:30am–1pm and 2–7pm, Sun 10am–1pm, low season Mon–Sat 9:30–12:30pm and 2–6pm).

Recommended Websites

- ○ **www.carnac.fr**: The tourist office site is the most thorough English language site on Carnac. The listings aren't exhaustive, but it's a good place to get started.
- ○ **www.carnac.info**: If you have a little French under your belt, this site is a cinch. It lists most of Carnac's bars and restaurants with photos, addresses, and reviews.

Carnac **Nuts & Bolts**

Internet Cafe Since Carnac is a raging summer town that quiets downs to silence in the winter, Internet is hard to come by. The most central place to log on is **Le Baobab** (see "Eating," below). The cafe has free wireless in the mornings only, and two computers inside at 2€ for 30 minutes. Expect to wait inline during busy summer months.

Laundromats   To wash that salt water out of your duds, stop by **La Laverie M.R. Prado,** Carnac-Plage (8 allée des Alignements; ☎ **02-97-52-25-19;** July–Aug Mon–Sat 9am–7pm, Sun 9am–noon, Apr–June and Sept–Oct Mon–Sat 9am–noon and 2–6pm, Sun 9am–noon).

Post Office   The main post office is just outside Carnac-Ville at 18 av. de la Poste (☎ **02-97-52-03-82;** Mon–Fri 9am–noon and 2–6pm, Sat 9am–1pm).

Supermarkets   Tourists know to head to **Marchéu** (68 av. des Druides; Mon–Sat 8:30am–8pm, Sun 8:30am–noon) to stock up on drinks and snacks for beach picnics. This central supermarket, right next to the tourist office, sells food and snacks galore, as well as wine, beer, sunscreen, and beach mats.

Sleeping

If you listen closely during the summertime in Carnac, you'll hear the faint chorus of cash registers chiming. That's because most hotels rake in the cash during high season, charging steep prices the closer you get to the beach. Hotels get so booked that in August it's difficult to find an open bed in town. If you're looking for anything with an ocean view, then hopefully you have some extra euros burning a hole in your pocket. The best deals are found in Carnac-Ville, which, thanks to its tamer location, can still offer value when prices go way up in July and August.

CHEAP

→ **Auberge le Ratelier**   On a quiet side street in Carnac-Ville, Le Ratelier is a picturesque ivy-covered stone house with eight guest rooms. The inn is best known for its popular restaurant, which serves homey, Breton cooking for lunch and dinner. Simple rooms are upstairs from the restaurant and almost make you feel like you're shacking up in a family country home. Some rooms have bathrooms en suite, but they can be very small; it's better to go for the cheaper rooms if you can deal with walking to toilets and showers down the hall. *4 Chemin du Douet, Carnac-Ville.* ☎ *02-97-52-05-04. www.le-ratelier.com. 43€–55€ double.*

→ **Chez Nous** ★   Staying in this cozy bed-and-breakfast is almost like visiting the French aunt you never knew you had. Before you can say "bonjour," the owner will make sure you're checked in and comfortable. Housed in a cozy stone building with ivy covering the front, the rooms are warm, clean, and simple. Stays are informal, and guests receive a key to the front door, which means the most popular rooms fill up quickly in the summer. *5 place de la Chapelle, Carnac-Ville.* ☎ *02-97-52-07-28. chez.nous56@wanadoo.fr. 37€–49€ double. Breakfast 5.50€. No credit cards. Apr–Nov.*

DOABLE

→ **Hôtel Celtique**   If you're looking to stay near the beach but avoid beachfront prices, Hôtel Celtique, part of the Best Western chain, is a good option, just a block from the beach. Management says an extensive renovation should take place in spring 2007, so be sure to ask for a renovated room. Currently, the building has simple, chain hotel-style rooms and a pool. *17 av. de Kermario or 82 av. des Druides (front and back entrances), Carnac-Plage. www.hotel-celtique.com. 75€–152€ double. Breakfast 9€–11€. Credit cards accepted. Amenities: Restaurant; fitness center; Indoor heated pool; sauna; steam room. In room: A/C, TV.*

→**Hôtel La Marine** This cozy hotel's nautical theme isn't something you can ignore. You walk in and immediately see the downstairs bar, which is shaped like a boat. If you don't mind a little kitsch, though, it offers a solid value. The rooms are simple, if slightly worn, and decorated in the blue colors that dominate the hotel. There's also a restaurant downstairs. *4 place de la Chapelle, Carnac-Ville.* ☎ *02-97-52-07-33. www. la-marine-carnac.com. 49€–79€ double. Credit cards accepted. Amenities: Restaurant/ bar. In room: TV, hair dryer.*

→**Plume Au Vent** ★ This *chambres d'hôtes* (bed-and-breakfast) is a pet project of the owner, Elisabeth Rabot, who moved from Paris a few years ago to spend time in Brittany. Staying in one of the two quiet rooms at the Plume Au Vent is like staying with a relative, but one who stays out of your hair. On a quiet side street, the house is recently renovated with modern furnishings, and the rooms are exceptionally large compared to those in other Carnac hotels. Since the rooms share a large bathroom, Elisabeth only rents out both rooms if the parties know each other, so getting a reservation for yourself means you'll have plenty of privacy. *4 Venelle Notre-Dame, Carnac-Ville.* ☎ *06-16-98-34-79. www.fleursdesoleil.fr. 65€ double. Breakfast included. No credit cards.*

SPLURGE

→**Hôtel Le Diana** With a prime location on the most popular beach in town, Le Diana is over-the-top extravagant. The resort hotel has ocean views, poolside bar, and a pricey restaurant. Rooms are eclectic and opulent with crazy prints and designs, but it's definitely one of the most comfortable options in town. Several rooms have balconies that overlook the ocean, but be prepared to shell out the dough for the privilege. *21 bd. de la Plage,*

Carnac-Plage. ☎ *02-97-95-05-38. www.le diana.com. 162€–242€ ocean-view double. 120€–172€ no view. Breakfast 19€. Apr 15– Nov 5. Amenities: Restaurant/bar; exercise room; paid Wi-Fi; pool. In room: A/C, satellite TV, hair dryer, minibar, safe.*

Eating

You won't forget while you're in Carnac that Brittany is crepe country. In addition to a slew of solid creperies, Carnac has a lot of restaurants that cater to tourists with greasy fried things. While there are a few standouts, Carnac falls into the trap that most tourist hot spots do, with cuisine that's more cheesy than authentic.

CAFES & LIGHT FARE

→**Chez Céline** CREPERIE Whether you're biking or walking through miles of megaliths, all that Neolithic fun can certainly work up an appetite. Luckily, Chez Céline is a small snack shack nestled in the rocks themselves, along with a local products store by the same name. They serve Breton fast food (crepes, of course) made with black wheat and all the fixings. Tourists also stop by for a scoop of sorbet and a rest stop at their outdoor picnic tables. Even if you just need a swig of Breizh Cola (the Breton version of Pepsi) to keep you going for the next half-mile of stone arrangements, Chez Céline is your best bet this far from town. *Center of the Kermario Megaliths.* ☎ *02-97-52-17-31. www. chezceline.com. Crepes 2€–5€. Summer only, Mon–Sun noon–9:30pm.*

📺 Best ♦ →**Igloo** ★★ ICE CREAM It's already a challenge to get past the mesmerizing automatic waffle cone machine at Igloo, but the real difficulty lies in choosing from their 170 different flavors of ice cream. With flavors like whiskey, chewing gum, and even Roquefort cheese, Igloo is not the place to order an average cone.

The store makes all their ice cream from local Breton milk and has several other locations around Brittany. Don't worry if your taste runs toward vanilla; there are plenty of staple flavors like chocolate and raspberry. *56 av. des Druides, Carnac-Plage.* ☎ *02-97-52-03-06. 1.50€ for 1 scoop. Credit cards accepted. Apr–Nov Mon–Sun 10am–12:30pm.*

MTV (Best ♥) → **Patisserie Elie** ★ PATIS-SERIE This bread and pastry counter is heavily trafficked by locals picking up their daily baguettes. But just next door is their espresso bar, where you can sit down and have your buttery snack. In addition to their traditional French breakfast, don't miss their *kouign amann,* a dense, flaky sugar-encrusted pastry. Their version puts the others in town to shame. *1 rue St-Cornély, Carnac-Ville.* ☎ *02-97-52-06-10. Main courses 2€–6€. Credit cards accepted. Mon–Sat 7am–8pm; Sun 7am–7pm.*

CHEAP

→ **Crêperie St-Georges** CREPERIE You'll realize how brisk business is for this restaurant when you see the waitstaff taking orders wirelessly on handheld PDAs. With a huge outdoor seating area on one of Carnac's busiest thoroughfares, this creperie fills with crowds during high season. On busy nights, you may feel shuttled to a table like it's a crepe feeding lot. More often, though, it's a good place to put down a few classic crepes and watch the crowds. With a fixed-price menu of a ham crepe, dessert crepe, and glass of cider for *12€,* it won't break the bank. *8 allée du Parc, Carnac-Plage.* ☎ *02-97-52-18-34. Main courses 3€–8€. Mon–Sun noon–10pm.*

→ **La Potion Magique** CREPERIE To find this homey, family-run creperie, look up toward the second floor of a small shopping area. It's slightly out of the way, but during the height of tourist

season, that can also be a very good thing. The menu is simple and straightforward, with many crepes made from the traditional black wheat. With indoor and outdoor seating, it's a good place for a quieter meal. *10 rue St-Cornély, Carnac-Ville.* ☎ *02-97-52-63-46. Main courses 2€–8€. Credit cards accepted. Mon–Sun noon–2pm and 7–9pm.*

DOABLE

→ **La Transat** ★ PIZZERIA This central restaurant is much more up-to-date than your traditional checkered tablecloth pizzeria. It has a hip, modern decor, with sleek tables, a bright white bar, and deep purple walls. They serve up thin crust pizzas with all the traditional toppings, as well as seafood and vegetarian options. Directly across from the bar L'O, the restaurant is on one of Carnac's trendiest blocks. *62 av. des Druides, Carnac-Plage.* ☎ *02-97-52-73-19. Main courses 9€–13€. Credit cards accepted. Mon–Sun noon–3pm and 6pm–midnight.*

→ **Le Baobab** BRASSERIE This restaurant is Carnac's full-service stop. A diner, Internet cafe, bar, and more, Le Baobab is one of the busiest addresses in town. They serve two menus, the first for lunch and dinner with fish, salads, and sandwiches. The second menu is right out of an international diner, with *croque monsieurs* and several types of burgers, served all afternoon. The bar next door is known as Le Modjo, where drinks and appetizers are available. It also houses two very popular computers where access is 2€ for 30 minutes. The cafe has free wireless access, but it's only available in the mornings since the restaurant likes to maintain a high turnover. *3 allée du Parc, Carnac-Plage.* ☎ *02-97-52-29-96. www.baobab-cafe.net. Main courses 5€–15€. Credit cards accepted. Mon–Sun 9am–11pm.*

BRITTANY

SPLURGE

➜**Restaurant La Côte** ★ MODERN FRENCH In the heart of the megaliths and down a small path, this restaurant is tucked far off the beaten trail. But if you're looking for countryside charm and stunning cuisine, La Côte is worth the detour. Housed in a restored farmhouse, the dining room has warm stone walls and an extensive garden and terrace outside. The menus make inventive use of many traditional French ingredients, but also rely heavily on local Breton fish. The special seafood menu, with local lobster, must be ordered 2 days in advance, but it's a deluxe way to sample classic Breton flavors. Finish off the meal with their famous crepes Suzette with crystallized orange. *Center of the Kermario Megaliths.* ☎ *02-97-52-02-80. www. restaurant-la-cote.com. Menus 33€, 43€, and 53€; main courses 20€–25€. Credit cards accepted. July–Aug Tues–Sun 12:15–2:15pm and 6:15–9:15pm, no Tues lunch; Sept–June Tues–Sun 12:15–2:15pm and 6:15–9:15pm, no Sat lunch, no Sun dinner.*

Partying

FUNKY BARS & LOUNGES

➜**La Baignoire de Joséphine** The name of this bar refers to the infamous note Napoleon wrote his wife Josephine while he was traveling abroad: "Coming home soon, don't bathe." But what's in a name? There's nothing so saucy about the location itself. The interior has a beach hut feel with old surfboards and wooden picnic tables, as well as a small terrace out front. Mojitos flow freely all evening, though the crowd can be a bit older than the 20-something bar-hoppers around the rest of town. *16 allée des Alignements, Carnac-Plage.* ☎ *02-97-52-88-95.*

➜**L'Amazone** This is another of Carnac's colorful lounges. On warm summer nights, its spacious terrace fills up with a young crowd sipping cocktails (3€–7.50€). The open interior is decorated with bold colors and curvy velvet couches and chairs. Bartenders keep busy shaking vibrantly colored cocktails and mysterious looking shooters, which young Carnac tourists sip deep into the night. *44 av. de Port en Drô, Carnac-Plage.* ☎ *02-97-52-24-85.*

➜**Le West Pub Company** ★ Half–dive bar, half-lounge, the West Pub is a bit more imaginative than the other nightspots in town. A hybrid of modern and classic, it's a two-story bar with serious character. The funky wooden interior is decorated in old books, wooden doors, carved pillars, and stuff from your grandparents' attic. Mixed in are modern touches such as plush suede couches and hip tables amid the outdoor seating. Stop by for a pint or glass of wine (3€–6€) for a unique experience. *14 allée des Menhirs.* ☎ *02-97-52-90-80.*

➜**L'O** With elaborate drinks piled high with umbrellas and limes, L'O is a lounge with an exotic flair and a place in which to see and be seen. The bar has a decidedly downtown vibe, heavily into electronic music and often hosting DJs on summer nights. While the drinks are tropical, the dark-red interior is Eastern-inspired with Buddhas and Ganeshas freely intermingling. The bar is mostly made up of an outdoor terrace with comfortable tables, where a young crowd kicks back and picks from a long menu of cocktails and shooters (5€–8€), heavy on the rum. You can get the classics such as mojitos and cuba libres for only 5€ during their 5pm to 7pm happy hour. *62 av. des Druides, Carnac-Plage.* ☎ *02-97-52-22-38. www.lo-carnac.com.*

CLUBS

➜**Les Chandelles** ★ Carnac draws a far younger crowd than the rest of Brittany, so you can breathe a sigh of relief and bid adieu to wrinkles on the dance floor. If you've been hankering to blow off some steam and burn off some of that butter, Carnac is one stop where the French kids will not let you down. Les Chandelles is a perennial hot spot packed with generations of spring and summer breakers in its laser-lit interior. A recent face-lift has given this clubbing institution a deliciously ultramodern aesthetic. Now it caters to young fiends of house music, ably spun by DJs flown in from across Europe. Be advised that they can be persnickety about appearance at the door, so don't expect to roll by the rope in the bathing suit and sandals you've been rocking all day. Cover is 10€. *Av. Atlantique.* ☎ *02-97-52-90-98. www. chandelles-carnac.com.*

➔ **Le Whiskey Club** Smoky lighting, old stone walls, and a decadent interior complete with posh leather couches give this clubbing mainstay the feel of a speakeasy. But that's just the first floor—ideal for tipping a pre-game whiskey on the rocks or smoking a cigar. But with the raucous energy of the dance floor upstairs, there's no mistaking this club for an old boy's retreat. The music is as disco-fied as you'd expect, but you'll hardly notice when the place gets jumping. This might be the right time to start getting to know the youth of Carnac. At a club called Le Whiskey, you can pretty much get away with striking up a conversation that goes something like: *"Aimes-tu le whiskey?"* Who said you didn't remember any French? *8 av. des Druides.* ☎ *02-97-52-10-52.*

Sightseeing

MTV **Best ✿** ➔ **The Megaliths** ★
Whether you believe they're filled with an interstellar healing power or that they look like a bunch of random rocks, Carnac's megaliths are one of the most impressive Stone Age sites in western Europe. The site extends for acres north of town, with more than 4,000 stones arranged in patterns and long rows called alignments. Rumors and theories of how they arrived have circulated for centuries. According to Catholic myth, Roman troops pursuing the pope were turned into stone. Other historians thought a glacier deposited them. Today, archaeologists know local Neolithic people arranged them over centuries, from 4,500 B.C. onward.

While the stones are separated into several large groups now, most were thought to have been completely connected. Throughout the millennia, however, they've been moved and borrowed for building materials around town. Even early archaeologists had their way with them (one of whom removed stones and then forgot exactly where they were).

The megalith's popularity could also be their downfall. From April to September each year, the fields are now fenced off from the public. Too much foot traffic for the past several decades has killed the surrounding vegetation, and the ensuing erosion threatened to topple the giants. If you see sheep inside the fences, don't worry. They aren't alien megalith guardians; they're just encouraging the plants to grow again. You may wish you could run through the alignments and invoke extraterrestrials to come visit, but the only way to get inside during the summer is to take a guided tour. From October to March, however, the fences are removed, and tourists can wander at will.

If you're touring the megaliths in the summer and feel discouraged by the fences, visit the many un-fenced stones farther afield. You'll need a bike or car to find them, but pick up a map at the tourist office or visitor center (see Maison des Megaliths, below) and start exploring. Smaller spots aren't as impressive, but they allow for a much closer encounter of the third kind.

BRITTANY

Wanna Rock?

The closest field of megaliths is the **Alignements du Ménec,** which are a short bike ride or longer walk from Carnac-Ville. The visitor center (see Maison des Megaliths, below) is also just across from these alignments. Made up of 1,050 stones in long wavering rows, this group is the farthest west in Carnac. At the far end, a small hamlet was built in an enclosure of 70 stones arranged in an oval shape. Several of the houses have a prehistoric fence of the stones, which blocks off their backyard.

Farther east is the small group of **Toul-Chignan,** with small clustered megaliths. Next comes another large group of megaliths known as the **Kermario Alignements.** This group has some of the largest individual stones, as well as several dolmens, thought to be ancient tombs. With several disjointed groups within the larger group, you can wander around on the marked footpaths, though this group is fenced off.

Continuing east, the next group is known as **Le Manio,** which also holds one giant stone that stands almost 6m (20 ft.). The final large group is called the **Kerlescan Alignments,** a well-preserved group that holds rows of stones and the remnants of a square enclosure, as well as a dolmen.

→**Maison des Megaliths (Visitor Center)** If you're taking a guided tour or need detailed maps, this visitor center is the place to start. They arrange several types of tours, which in the summer are the only way to get near the main megaliths. Guided tours in French are offered April through September, and tours in English are offered sporadically in July and August at 3pm. The center also sells postcards and history books. *On the rue des Alignments, across from the Ménec Alignments.* ☎ *02-97-52-89-99. www.monum.fr. Tours 4€ adults, 3€ 25 and under. May–Aug Mon–Sun 9am–7pm; Sept–Apr Mon–Sun 10am–5:15pm.*

MUSEUMS

→**Musée de Préhistoire** Paleolithic, Mesolithic, Neolithic—the collections here range from 450,000 B.C. to the 8th century, displaying archaeological finds from around the area. The museum holds glass case after glass case of old beads, arrowheads, pottery shards, and carved stones. Eventually you'll start running into hatchets, hoards of Roman coins, and remains of several prehistoric guys and gals. Touring the museum certainly reveals the rich history of France's ancestors (and the ass-kicking power of the Romans), but unless you have a serious hankering for moderately Indiana Jones–style booty, you may be a bit underwhelmed. *10 place de la Chapelle, Carnac-Ville.* ☎ *02-97-52-22-04. www.museedecarnac.com. Admission 5€ adults, students 2.50€. July–Aug Mon–Sun 10am–6pm; May–June and Sept Mon, Wed–Sun 10am–12:30pm and 2–6pm; Oct–Apr Mon, Wed–Sun 10am–12:30pm and 2–5pm.*

CHURCHES

FREE →**Eglise St-Cornély** Built in 1639, this small church in Carnac-Ville is worth a quick peek. It's a bit on the musty side, but holds several stained-glass windows and 18th-century paintings and murals that aren't often seen in churches. It's worth a short detour, but not a long one. *Place St-Cornely, Carnac-Ville. Free admission. Mon–Sun 9am–noon and 2–7pm.*

Schoolhouse Rocks

The stone arrangements in Carnac are among the most extensive in western Europe. They may not be as neatly piled as Stonehenge, but they cover miles of ground, often arranged in long lines that run as far as the naked eye can see. The alignments were erected around 4,500 B.C., though no one quite knows how or why. Here's your archaeological vocabulary guide for visiting *les alignements*.

→ **Menhir** A large stone (megalith), standing vertically in the ground.

→ **Neolithic** The period when the megaliths were placed in Carnac. It's the end of the Stone Age, when farming and polished stone tools first showed up.

→ **Dolmen** Thought to be an ancient tomb, it's a structure with stone walls and a large stone ceiling resting on top.

→ **Cairn** Basically an ancient tombstone, made up of a pile or mound of stones.

Shopping

CLOTHING & ACCESSORIES

→ **Le Minor** You won't be able to travel around Brittany for long without noticing all the blue-and-white striped shirts. A little bit traditional, a little bit high seas, they might be a bit much to throw into your daily wardrobe. Still, if you're looking for authentic Breton goods to bring home, stop at this shop, for all sizes. *22 place de l'Eglise, Carnac-Ville.* ☎ *02-97-52-71-04. Apr–Nov Mon–Sun 10am–1pm and 3–6:30pm.*

FOOD, WINE & LOCAL CRAFTS

→ **Farmer's Market** ★ Just outside the main square in Carnac-Ville, the farmer's market bustles during the summer months. Stalls crowd with tourists seeking a taste of the local flavor, from local wares and gifts to vegetables and specialties. If you're looking for a bit of fruit or some Breton sea salt for mom and dad, this is the place to find it. *On rue du Tumulus, east of place de l'Eglise in Carnac-Ville. Wed and Sun 9am–noon.*

→ **La Belle-Iloise** If you're looking for a way to bring home Brittany's rich sea tradition, look no farther than the tins at this shop. This famous cannery has been packing up sardines and anchovies since 1932. All the tins are decorated with retro advertising and art, and come with a wide variety of flavors, such as sardines with sun-dried tomatoes, or lemon and capers. If little silver fish aren't your thing, try the canned tuna, including sandwich spread and mousses, which make for an excellent picnic lunch. *77 av. des Druides, Carnac-Ville.* ☎ *02-97-50-08-77. Mar–Nov Mon–Sun 9:15am–12:30pm and 2:30–8pm.*

→ **Le Comptoir Florentin** This gourmet grocery sells Brittany's finest, from salt to biscuits to wine. It's much higher quality than some of the cheesy tourist traps around town. They also sell *cidre brut de Carnac,* a local organic cider that isn't super-sweet—a steal at 3.90€ a bottle. *8 rue St-Cornely, Carnac-Ville.* ☎ *02-97-52-29-97. Mon–Sat 10am–7:30pm; Sun 10am–1pm and 5–7:30pm.*

Playing Outside

BEACHES

There's no doubt about it, Carnac is a magnet for sun-worshipers and beach-bathers. The largest and most popular beach is, not surprisingly, found closest to the town center. The **Grand Plage** boasts plenty of

BRITTANY

real estate for spreading out your beach towel, but during the tourist high season, it's busting at the seams. The beach has a very gentle drop-off, so waves stay fairly small. Farther west are two more sheltered beaches, **Plage de Légenèse** and **Plage de Ty Bihan**. They stay much less crowded, and the layout is basically the same. Farthest from town is **Plage de St-Colomban,** which is next to its own limited set of shops and restaurants. For windsurfers, this is the beach to choose.

WATERSPORTS

Thanks to its gently sloping beaches, Carnac is a popular place to learn windsurfing. The water depth doesn't drop off for a hundred yards, so yanking up that sail when you fall off the board is no trouble. For windsurfing lessons and rentals, as well as kayaking, visit **Nautic Sport** (near the Carnac Yacht Club at the Port en Dro;

☎ 02-97-52-88-02; www.nautic-sport. com), which is located on the west end of the Grand Plage.

Road Trip: The Wild Coast

Just south of Carnac lies the port town of **Quiberon** (www.quiberon.com), a picturesque town on an "almost island"—a peninsula connected to the mainland by an isthmus (remember junior high geography?). The coast around this area is known as the Côte Sauvage (Wild Coast), named for the drama of its rocky cliffs, crashing waves, and turbulent seas. From the Port Maria in Quiberon, tourists continue the trip by taking a ferry to **Belle-Ile-en-Mer** (www.belle-ile.com), an island just off the coast. The ferries, run by **SMN** (☎ 08-20-05-60-00; www.smn-navigation.fr), take 45 minutes to reach the rocky island, where tourists hang out to enjoy the rugged beauty and beaches.

Quimper: Quaintness in the Country

560km (347 miles) W of Paris, 233km (144 miles) NW of Nantes, 214km (133 miles) W of Rennes

With its picturesque streets, local charm, and mountains of precious ceramic pottery, Quimper (pronounced "Kem-pair") is a slice of Breton culture, served up supersweetened. If you planned on a whirlwind French vacation with beach bunnies and blinding electronic beats, Quimper is not a city to put on your list. But for authentic Breton charm, Quimper has the local flavor that tends to get drowned out in Brittany's beach towns.

And now for the disclaimer: Quimper's claim to celebrity is a local pottery known as la faïence. Created in town for the past 300 years, the plates, bowls, and mugs are hand-painted with traditional scenes of Breton life and flowery patterns. Many of the high-quality wares are works of art, but the embellishment borders on overkill,

especially given the huge number of shops shelling out the goods to eager tourists. Every collector from France and the U.K. stops by Quimper to fill their bags with the real thing straight from the source. If you're down with country-style ceramics, you'll definitely find something to write home about. If not, consider it part of the overall ambience and try to ignore the glaze-loving zoo.

Since the pottery-collecting crowd tends to represent your grandparents' demographic more than yours, don't be surprised that Quimper doesn't boast a very happening nightlife. While the streets are crowded by day as tourists visit the shops and historical sights, the town empties out after dinner, and you won't find much of a scene even during the busiest summer months. There are a few modern restaurants and a handful of pubs, but after you put down a pint or two, the only things keeping you company during summer nights in Quimper are crickets and ceramics.

Still, Quimper's business is history, culture, and festivals. If you arrive with that in mind, you'll get what you're looking for. The city has shopping, a bustling farmer's market, and picturesque stone streets, a Gothic cathedral, several warm cafes, and authentic Breton restaurants. The coast is nearby, which means you can still beach hop. And even when skies are gray, the museums will keep you busy.

Getting There

BY AIR

The small **Aéroport Quimper-Cornouaille** (☎ 02-98-94-30-30; www.quimper.cci.fr) is 7km (4 miles) from Quimper. Air France runs four shuttle flights to Paris daily, but considering how close Brittany is to Paris, the train is an equally convenient option.

BY TRAIN

Both speedy **TGV** trains and slower **TER** trains serve Quimper, but if your starting destination is Rennes or Paris, it's worth shelling out the extra euros for the fast train. The TGV trip is only 4¹/₂ hours, but the TER trains take 7 hours. On avenue de la Gare, the station is a 10- to 15-minute walk to the center of Quimper along the Odet River. Two bus lines can also shuttle you into town (see "By Bus," below).

BY CAR

From Rennes, take E50/N12 west until you're just outside the town of Montauban. Then continue west on N164 to Chateaulin, and then south following N165 all the way to Quimper.

BY BUS

For regional trips to places that trains don't visit, use **Le Réseau Penn-ar-Bed** (☎ 02-98-90-88-89; http://info transports.cg29.fr; tickets 2€–6€). The network serves cities such as Brest, Quimperlé, and Morlaix. You can pick up buses at the *gare routière*, directly to the right of the train station exit. Tickets are sold onboard.

Orientation

Quimper, like many French towns, is built on the banks of a river. Now more of a tamed canal, the Odet River bisects Quimper with the tourist office and several hotels on the south side and the heart of Quimper on the north. If you need to orient yourself, look for the massive spires of the cathedral above the rooftops, which will lead you to the main square, place St-Corentin. West of the square is Quimper's historic district, also the busiest shopping area in town.

Getting Around

RENTAL CARS/DRIVING TIPS

Parking on the outskirts of Quimper isn't too difficult, and there are several lots available, both free and paid. Head north of the town center, to where rue Fréron and rue des Douves intersect, for several options. Most rental car spots are clustered directly across from the train station. If you need some wheels, try **Hertz** (19 av. de la Gare; ☎ 02-98-53-12-34; www.hertz.com) or **Eurocar** (place de la Gare; ☎ 02-98-90-00-68). For taxis, call **Radio Taxi Quimperois** (☎ 02-98-90-21-21).

BY BUS

Quimper's **QUB** bus network (☎ 02-98-95-26-27; www.qub.fr; tickets 1€) is fairly extensive, but unless you're staying far out of town, none of the lines will be particularly helpful. The most useful are lines 4

BRITTANY

and 6 (line A on Sun), which connect the train station to several stops in the center of town along boulevard Amiral Kerguelen. In summer, special buses shuttle tourists to the beach towns of Bénodet and Fouesnant (see "Watersports" on p. 267).

BY BIKE

Getting around town without wheels is no problem, but if you're looking for more mobility, the closest bike rental shop is north of the town center at **Torch VTT** (58 rue de la Providence; ☎ **02-98-53-84-41;** Tues–Sat 9:30am–12:30pm and 2:30–7pm).

BY FOOT

Scooting around Quimper by foot is easy, as most major sights and restaurants are clustered around the town center. Even sights on the outskirts are a 10-minute walk at most.

Tourist Office

Just across the Max Jacob Bridge on the south side of the River Odet, Quimper's tourist office is stocked with travel brochures and leaflets galore. The staff gives helpful travel information, but lines become long during the summer. This is the address for bus schedules, ferry recommendations, or summer festival information. They also organize several guided tours (5€) of Quimper's old town and cathedral. Lasting 90 minutes, most are conducted in French, but one or two a week are in English. The office gives out small town maps for free. Larger ones are 1€. They also sell the "cultural passport," which gets you into four of Quimper's sights for 12€ (see "Sightseeing" on p. 264). *Place de la Résistance.* ☎ *02-98-53-04-05. www.quimper-tourisme.com. Oct to mid-Mar Mon–Sat 9:30am–12:30pm and 1:30–6pm; mid-Mar to June and Sept Mon–Sat 9:30am–12:30pm and 1:30–6:30pm; July–Aug Mon–Sat 9am–7pm and Sun 10am–1pm and 3–5:45pm. Also Sun in June 10am–12:45pm.*

Quimper **Nuts & Bolts**

Internet Cafe   For a traditional online hookup, the **Eixxos** (10 bd. Dupliex; ☎ **02-98-64-40-56;** Mon–Sat 1–10pm; 4€ an hour) has numerous computers, printers, and other technical gear. On the south side of the Odet, the Internet cafe also has the advantage of staying open late. For lunch and e-mail, visit the centrally located **C.Com Café** (p. 262), about a stone's throw from the farmer's market. With three computers and fresh salads, it's a comfortable place to write home from.

Laundromats   For the closest suds spot, visit the **Laverie de la Gare** (2 bis av. de la Gare; Mon–Sun 8am–9pm), between the train station and the heart of town.

Post Office   For all your air mail and stamp collecting needs, Quimper's post office is halfway between the train station and town center, at 37 bd. Amiral de Kerguelen (Mon–Fri 8am–6:30pm and Sat 8am–noon).

Supermarket/Drugstore   For food, socks, bandages, or envelopes, try **Monoprix** (1 rue René Madec; ☎ **02-98-95-17-37;** Mon–Sat 9am–7pm), France's answer to Target and Kmart. It's the one-stop shop for sunscreen and chocolate emergencies.

Sleeping

For a town that's so heavily trafficked by tourists, Quimper has surprisingly limited hotel options. While most are functional, only a handful stand out. Hotels are clustered together in two areas, neither of which is in the heart of Quimper. Most budget options are lined up directly across from the train station on avenue de la Gare. Though it's a pretty uninspiring area, it's only a 10- to 15-minute walk to the center of town. The second area is found on the quiet side of the Odet River, along boulevard Dupleix.

HOSTELS

➜ **Auberge de Jeunesse Quimper** In a quiet wooded area just outside town, Quimper's youth hostel is in a light, homey building. Though not large or as elaborate as other hostels, it's adequate if you're looking for the basics. Room sizes vary, so be sure to ask for a smaller room if you don't want to bunk with a crowd. The hostel is 3km (2 miles) from the train station, but there's no direct bus line from there. From the center of town, take bus line 1 "Kermoysan" and descend at the Chaptal stop. The trip takes only 5 minutes, but be aware that buses stop running around 8pm. *6 av. des Oiseaux. ☎ 02-98-64-97-97. www.fuaj.org. 40€ per person per night (FUAJ card required). Apr to Oct 14.*

CHEAP

➜ **Hôtel de la Gare** Among the string of budget hotels across from the train station, this is one of the better choices. The rooms are divided between two buildings, one overlooking the street and a quieter one behind it, separated by a courtyard. The rooms are simple and adequate, if not a little run-down, but have all the basics. While it's a very short walk from the train station (big surprise), it's about a 10-minute walk to the center of Quimper.

17 av. de la Gare. ☎ 02-98-90-00-81. www. hoteldelagarequimper.com. 43€–80€ double. Breakfast 6€. Credit cards accepted.

DOABLE

➜ **Hôtel Dupleix** One of a handful of Quimper's mid-range hotels, Hôtel Dupleix is about 5 minutes from the heart of the city. The hotel has a very standard, if not slightly unimaginative feel, with a bold color scheme of reds and blues, but the rooms are clean and comfortable. For a place to catch some Zs, the hotel is more than functional, as long as you're not looking for charm. *34 bd. Dupleix. ☎ 02-98-90-53-35. www.hotel-dupleix.com. 79€–96€ double. Breakfast 9€. Credit cards accepted. Amenities: Restaurant; free Wi-Fi; parking. In room: AC, TV.*

➜ **Hôtel Escale Oceania** This is another hotel along boulevard Dupleix. Formerly known as Hôtel Mascotte, it's part of the Oceania hotels network and offers the comfort and predictability of a chain. Off the main street, the hotel is free of traffic noise, but don't expect stunning city views. Rooms are clean, with bright color schemes. If you're looking for a more parking-friendly and swimming-friendly option, choose the other Oceania hotel on the outskirts of town, recently renovated in 2006 and equipped with a swimming pool. *6 rue Théodore Le Hars. ☎ 02-98-53-37-37. www.oceaniahotels.com. 68€–98€ double. Breakfast 9€. Credit cards accepted. Amenities: Elevator; limited mobility access. In room: A/C, TV.*

➜ **Hôtel Gradlon** Only 5 minutes from Quimper's main square, Hôtel Gradlon is one of the best choices in town. Rooms are simple and stately, and many overlook a small central courtyard. The hotel lobby has an informal bar and sitting area, as well as a cozy breakfast room. Better yet, the staff is extremely helpful in answering any clueless tourist questions you may

BRITTANY

have. *30 rue de Brest.* ☎ *02-98-95-04-39.* *www.hotel-gradlon.com.* *69€–105€ double. Breakfast 11€. Credit cards accepted. Garage 8€. In room: A/C, TV.*

SPLURGE

MTV Best ♥ →**Manoir du Stang** Don't mistake this estate for another tourist attraction when you walk under the stone entryway. Built in 1664, the Manoir du Stang was the heart of the surrounding agricultural estates for several centuries. But don't call it a château (even though it may look like one), as the owner is quick to remind you. Though the manor is a regal size, it has a warm and intimate feeling. The 24 rooms are filled with antiques, but are bright and airy. Outside, you can leisurely walk in the rose garden or around the backyard lakes as if you happen to have castles and titles of your own. And breakfast takes the cake, served either downstairs or outside on a charming terrace overlooking the grounds. The only trick is that with peacefulness this remote, you'll need a rental car unless you're a serious road biker. It might be worth it for a stay this unforgettable. *La Forêt Fouesnant.* ☎ *02-98-56-97-37.* *www. manoirdustang.com.* *75€–140€ double. Breakfast 10€. No credit cards. Apr–Sept. Amenities: Elevator.*

Eating

CAFES & LIGHT FARE

→**Le Bistro à Lire** ★ CAFE This small store hasn't quite decided whether to be a bookstore or a coffee shop, but the combination works out perfectly. The front is stocked with plenty of books, catering mostly to sleuth-y, whodunit-loving readers. Aside from the crime and spy novels, a few English paperbacks are thrown in. The coffee counter in back whips up espresso drinks and serves desserts and sweet things to nibble on. Keep heading back and

you'll find a seat in their outdoor space, a quiet yard that overlooks stone buildings. *18 rue des Boucheries.* ☎ *02-98-95-30-86. Main courses 3€–7€. Credit cards accepted. Tues–Sat 9:30am–6pm.*

→**Les Comptior des Tapas** SPANISH You'll find this informal counter in the heart of Quimper's farmer's market, serving up tapas and other mini dishes. The best time to park yourself on one of their stools is at lunch, when the busy Quimper crowds are checking out the produce and bantering with the stall owners. You can try a little of everything: plates of chorizo, vegetables, and small sandwiches. *Inside the farmer's market, place St-François.* ☎ *02-98-98-00-87. Tapas 2€–6€. No credit cards. Mon–Fri 10am–2:20pm and 5–8pm; Sat 9am–8pm.*

CHEAP

MTV Best ♥ →**C.Com Café** SANDWICHES/SALADS Half lunch cafe, half Internet cafe, the C.Com serves up fresh baked goods, salads, and sandwiches throughout the day. If you get past the line out the door, you can choose between mixed couscous salad, berry crumble, or the mega-size muffins that are cooked fresh in the morning. Lunch salads hit the spot with heaping piles of fresh vegetables and meats. The seating and tables are on the second floor, along with free Wi-Fi and several computers (including an elusive Mac, not commonly found around France). It's the perfect spot to stop in for a quick bite, or camp out for a half-day when necessary. *9 Quai du Port au Vin.* ☎ *02-98-95-81-62. Main courses 6€–10€. Internet access 3€ an hour. Credit cards accepted. Mon 10am–8pm; Tues–Fri 8am–8pm; Sat 8am–7pm.*

MTV Best ♥ →**La Krampouzerie** CREPERIE The interior of this creperie is unassuming at most, but it matches the food completely: warm, comfortable, and satisfying, La Krampouzerie is a local favorite. Their crepes are made from authentic black wheat, which makes for a much heartier and flavorful mouthful, and many of the ingredients are organic. They're also known for several specialties, including a crepe made with *algues d'Ouessant,* a light taste of seaweed, and another made with a Roscoff onion jam. Don't miss a dessert crepe made with black wheat, which you can enjoy outside on the terrace seating. Its location on place au Beurre obviously couldn't be more apt. *9 rue du Sallé.* ☎ *02-98-95-13-08. Main courses 2€–8€. Credit cards accepted. Mon–Sat 11:45am–3:45pm and 5:45–11pm.*

→ **Le Cosy** ★ FRENCH A sign out front of this small restaurant says, "no frites, no crepes." So while you won't find any of the ubiquitous crepes and fries here, you will find seriously satisfying tartines, salads, and other home cooking. The actual restaurant is up a steep staircase from the gourmet shop below, L'Eau à la Bouche, but it's all in the family. It's run by a mother/daughter team; the younger generation runs the kitchen upstairs, and mom is downstairs in the local products store. There's nothing misleading about the name, either—the funky upstairs restaurant is a tight space, but the atmosphere is warm and boisterous. Stop by for a homey meal, and pick up some local Breton goodies downstairs on your way out. *2 rue de Sallé.* ☎ *02-98-95-23-65. Main courses 6€–14€. Credit cards accepted. Mon–Sat noon–2:30pm and 7–9:20pm.*

DOABLE

→ **Erwan** BRETON When you spot a funky purple facade, you'll know you've arrived at Erwan. The restaurant serves satisfying, homey cooking, Breton-style. Along with hearty meat and fish dishes, you can also order the Breton specialty, *kig ha farz.* It's a traditional stew made with vegetables, corned beef, other meats, and a boiled buckwheat dumpling that's crumbled over the top. It's a rib-sticking farmer's supper. If you're game for it, visit the restaurant on Tuesday or call ahead and mention you'd like it, in order to ensure you get a taste. *1–3 rue Aristide Briand.* ☎ *02-98-90-14-14. Main courses 15€–17€. Credit cards accepted. Tues–Fri noon–2pm and 7–10pm; Sat 7–10pm.*

→ **Le Jardin d'Eté** CLASSIC FRENCH This restaurant aims to please a slightly upscale clientele, serving fish and meat in very traditional ways. Portions are small at times, and several of the fish dishes arrive swimming in heavy sauces, but overall the cuisine is satisfying. Better choices include scallops or *entrecôte* (beef). They also offer a moderate-size 19€ menu that combines either an appetizer and main course, or main course and dessert. Still, if you're looking for fine dining, it's worth saving up your espresso money and heading to L'Ambroisie. *12 rue de Sallé.* ☎ *02-98-95-33-00. Main courses 20€–30€. Credit cards accepted. Tues–Sat noon–2pm and 7–10pm.*

SPLURGE

→ **L'Ambroisie** ★ BRETON/FRENCH For a fine dining experience, L'Ambroisie serves up haute cuisine that blends French cooking and Breton ingredients. The menu is short but complex, and dishes are equally as intricate. In addition to French favorites such as lamb and pigeon, seafood also features heavily. Try the pâté of langoustines and asparagus or a killer chocolate tart for dessert. Despite the fancy platings, the dining room isn't intimidating but rather cozy and warm. *49 rue Elie Fréron.* ☎ *02-98-95-00-02. www.ambroisie-quimper.com. Main courses 27€–32€, menus 22€–46€. Credit cards accepted. Tues–Sat noon–2pm and 7–9:30pm; Sun noon–2pm.*

BRITTANY

Partying

During summer months, the daytime streets of Quimper are bustling with tourists. You'll find yourself elbowing past the slow-walking, map-clutching crowds quite often, especially on weekends. However, the nightlife in Quimper is a completely different story. As restaurants start thinning out, the bars presumably would start filling up, but past 10pm the streets of Quimper resemble a ghost town. This is somewhat predictable given the audience Quimper attracts. Between the picturesque streets and famously collectable town pottery, visitors to Quimper consist mostly of families and grandparents. Still, there are a few spots that are good for the nocturnal, if not low-key, going-out crowd.

FUNKY BARS & PUBS

➔ **Café XXI** ★ As one of the most chic establishments in Quimper, Café XXI is a magnet for the young and hip. In addition to the bar, it's also a full restaurant for lunch and dinner. Located on Quimper's main square, it stays consistently busy. The inside is laid out like a lounge, with modern furniture, light wood, and low tables. A daytime crowd parks outside on the terrace seating, munching sandwiches, salads, and pasta dishes. The mood stays low-key as the after-dinner crowd filters in, sipping glasses of wine and cocktails through the evening. *38 place St-Corentin.* ☎ *02-98-95-92-34.*

➔ **Céili** For a taste of local life, Céili is the neighborhood watering hole with Celtic flair. Pronounced "kelli," the pub is home to the local drinking crowd who puts away pints all afternoon and into the night. You won't find any cosmopolitans or mint garnishes here, since the bar specializes in beers, both local from Brittany and from their neighbors up north, across the English Channel. On some weekend evenings, the bar hosts live music, most often of the Celtic variety. In fact, if you plan to swig a pint here, be ready to roll with the strong Celtic pride. *4 rue Aristide Briand.* ☎ *02-98-95-17-61.*

➔ **Klimax Café** On a pleasant side street off Quimper's main square, this small gay bar stays quiet through the afternoon. As the evening wears on, the scene picks up, with house and electronic music. You'll find a diverse crowd, gay and straight, mingling with a cocktail and spilling out into the courtyard. As one of the younger establishments in town, the Klimax Café attracts all types. *26 rue de Front.* ☎ *02-98-95-34-24.*

Sightseeing

Sightseeing in Quimper generally falls into two categories: ceramics and history. On the historical side, Quimper offers several satisfying museums, a grand cathedral, small historic streets, and other spots that offer a taste of Breton history. The list, however, doesn't end up being very long, and you could easily cover the sights in a day. As for the second category, Quimper's historic pottery, it draws an equally heavy amount of foot traffic. Most places for buying, touring, or looking at *la faïence* are in a separate part of town, 10 minutes down Allée de Locmaria from the tourist office. All in all, the pottery-fest could last up to half a day, especially during crowded summer vacation months.

If you plan to visit more than one or two of Quimper's sights, the tourist office offers a "cultural passport." For 12€, the ticket grants you admission to four out of six of Quimper's attractions (the four museums, the H.B. Henriot factory, or a tourist office–hosted guided tour through old town Quimper).

MUSEUMS

➔ **Faïencerie H.B. Henriot** Founded in 1690, H.B. Henriot became the Microsoft of earthenware pottery, acquiring the other *la faïence* factories in town over centuries of competition. Now the factory is known for putting out the finest quality goods. The factory tour covers the techniques of molding and firing the pieces, as well as the *coup de pinceau de Quimper,* the heralded painting brush stroke used by artists for decoration. Keep in mind, a dedicated love for colorful housewares and collectables is a prerequisite for this tour (otherwise, snore). Both this factory and the museum are a 10-minute walk from the tourist office along the Odet River. *2 rue Haute.* ☎ *08-00-62-65-10. www. hb-henriot.com. Admission 3.50€. July–Aug Mon–Sat 9am–11:45am and 1:30–5:15pm; Sept–June Mon–Fri 9am–11:45am and 1:30–5:15pm. Guided tours every 15 min., in English and French.*

➔ **Le Quartier** ★★ In complete contrast to the preciousness of Quimper, this contemporary art space is edgy and modern. It features well-edited exhibitions of paintings, photography, collage, and video by living artists. The museum isn't an overwhelming size and can provide a much-needed break from the Beaux Arts paintings in every French town you visit. While tickets already cost next to nothing, it's also free for students and free for everyone on Sundays. *10 esplanade François Mitterrand.* ☎ *02-98-55-55-77. www. le-quartier.net. Admission 1.50€, free for students, free on Sun. Tues–Sat 10am–12:30pm and 1:30–6pm; Sun 2–5pm.*

MTV Best ◗ ➔ **Musée de la Faïence de Quimper** Located in the *la faïence* neighborhood of Quimper, this museum caters to pottery lovers. Starting with the earliest plates and cups, the collection traces the evolution of the craft through colors, technique, and difficulty. Most pieces depict scenes of traditional Breton life, though some later examples pull in some interesting Art Deco patterns. Still, as you pass the

hand-painted *la faïence* violin, you'll start thinking that maybe this is a tour only a grandmother could love. *14 rue Jean-Baptiste Bousquet.* ☎ *02-98-90-12-72. www. quimper-faiences.com. Admission 4€. Apr–Oct Mon–Sat 10am–6pm.*

➔ **Musée des Beaux-Arts** ★ A lot of French Beaux-Arts museums are chock-full of any random 18th-century art they can get their hands on, but the Beaux Arts Museum in Quimper, thankfully, has shown more restraint. Built in 1995, under the shadow of Quimper's cathedral, the museum is extremely well laid out with rooms that are modern and warm at the same time. They specialize in Breton art, which is a very good thing considering that the Pont-Aven School, known for artists such as Paul Gauguin, is just nearby. There's also a tribute to famous Quimper poet and painter Max Jacob, a buddy of Picasso. With a very well-edited collection, the Musée des Beaux-Arts is definitely worth a look. *40 place St-Corentin.* ☎ *02-98-95-45-20. http://musee-beauxarts. quimper.fr. Admission 4€, 2.50€ under 26 and students. July–Aug Mon–Sun 10am–7pm; Sept–June Wed–Mon 10am–noon and 2–6pm; closed Sun mornings Nov–Apr.*

MONUMENTS & CHURCHES

➔ **Cathédrale St-Corentin** ★ There's no way to ignore this massive church in the heart of Quimper, with its 74m (245-ft.) towers that loom high over the town. Much like Notre-Dame in Paris, the cathedral has buttresses, flying buttresses, gargoyles, and all that Gothic goodness. But the real reason to walk inside is the stunning stained-glass windows. With more than 40 of them created in the 15th century, the windows tell the intricate stories of saints, angels, and sinners. The rest of the interior is downright gloomy compared to the brightness of the frescoes. *Place St-Corentin.* ☎ *02-98-95-06-19.*

BRITTANY

Mon–Sun 8:30am–noon and 1:30–5:30pm;
Sun 8:30am–noon and 2–5:30pm.

HISTORIC NEIGHBORHOODS

To spot the highest concentration of Quimper's historical buildings, mosey down **rue Kéréon,** directly in eyeshot of the cathedral. As the busiest shopping street in Quimper, it's hard to miss, but you'll see plenty of colorful wooden medieval houses. From there, walk up **rue des Boucheries** to continue through the old town, and turn right onto **rue du Sallé.** Once the former home of sausage shops, the street is home to the impressive Mahault de Minuellou family home at number 10. Once back on the main square, you head north up **rue Elie Fréron** for more historic homes, or go south and turn on **rue du Guéodet** for a picturesque view.

Shopping

Though Quimper's shopping district isn't huge, it packs in a little bit of everything. Several major French clothing chain stores are interspersed around the old streets, tempting tourists away from the museums. Wander around the main drag of rue de Kéréon for most of the shopping finds, as well as the several side streets that lead off it.

CLOTHING & ACCESSORIES

→**Princesse Tam-Tam** When it comes to French lingerie, this is the place to pick up a little something special. From classic black lace to magenta and flirty, Princesse Tam-Tam lingerie is a little saucy, but very elegant. Prices can be a bit steep, but the goods are high quality. And if you miss this shop, look for Princesse Tam-Tam boutiques in other French cities. *4 rue Kereon.* ☎ *02-98-95-62-27. www.princessetam-tam. com. Mon–Sat 10am–7pm.*

FOOD, WINE & LOCAL CRAFTS

→**Au Chat Bleu** This chocolate house was founded in 1912 (although it came to Quimper later). Upon stepping inside, it appears that they have a chocolate for every year they've been open. With a huge selection of chocolates and truffles in a small space, it's difficult to find one that doesn't hit your sweet tooth. They also sell more than 40 kinds of jams and jellies from a local artisanal producer, which range from apricot to mint to plum to persimmon. One way or another, you'll get your sugar fix. *5 rue de Gueodet.* ☎ *02-98-64-32-31. Tues–Sun 10am–12:30pm and 2–7pm.*

→**Halles St-François** ★ Quimper's farmers market is a firm fixture in town, in a large indoor space. Inside, local purveyors of fruits, cheese, meat, charcuterie, veggies, and fish show off their freshest goods for locals and tourists alike. Several food counters serve up great snacks: prepared crepes, salads, sandwiches, and even sushi. If you're into doing it your way, you can grab some bread, cheese, and fruit. Even if you're walking in on a full stomach, it's worth a look around to see local ingredients in their natural form and local residents arguing over prices. *Place St-François. No phone. Mon–Sun 8am–1pm and 4–7pm.*

→**Les Saveurs de Bretagne** For local and regional goodies to bring home to mom and dad, this store has the works. They've got boxes upon decorative boxes of cookies, known as *palets au beurre* and *gallettes au beurre,* much like shortbread cookies. Other regional products include caramel made with salted butter, and the famous *fleur de sel,* finely crystallized sea salt from Brittany. If you're looking for a gift just precious enough to prove that you've been on Breton soil, this is the place. *12 rue St-François.* ☎ *02-98-95-68-61. www.saveurs-de-bretagne.com. Mon–Sat 9:30am–1pm and 2–5pm; Sun 2:30–7pm.*

→**Nicolas** This wine store is part of a French chain, founded in 1822. And while you may want to throw your business to the little guy in town instead of this place, Nicolas does have one distinct advantage. Aside from the normal assortment of wines from austere appellations, they also sell "Les Petites Récoltes," a store brand of French wines that are a bargain. At between 2€ to 3€ each, you can't afford not to get them. Look for the bottles with bright colored labels and black cursive writing. Just a stone's throw from the farmer's market, the store is also in optimal territory for a picnic shopping trip. *7 rue de l'Amiral de la Grandière.* ☎ *02-98-95-11-22. www.nicolas. com. Mon–Sat 9am–noon and 1–5pm.*

MUSIC, BOOKS & MEDIA

➜ **Keltia Musique** This music and record label is home to all things Celtic. From classic Celtic ballads to more modern albums, the store features CDs from artists up north, as well as local Breton groups that are keeping traditions alive. Even if you can't understand the words, you'll be surprised at the range you can find. *1 place au Beurre.* ☎ *02-98-95-45-82. www.keltiamusique.com. July–Aug Mon–Sat 10am–7pm; Sept–May Tues–Sat 10:30am–12:30pm and 2–7pm.*

➜ **La Boutique du Dr. Scratch** If you guessed this shop sells records, well, you're right—both used and new vinyl, as well as CDs and comic books. They have a mix of French and American artists singing rock, soul, with some French pop thrown in. Vinyl lovers may find a gem or two, though the selection isn't huge. *3 rue du Front.* ☎ *02-98-95-47-05. Tues–Sun 9:30am–1pm and 3–7:30pm; Mon 3–7:30pm.*

FUN BUYS

➜ **Boutique de H.B. Henriot** This boutique, directly around the corner from the factory tour, sells new and secondhand pottery. In the summer, the store is stuffed to the brim with French and English tourists buying up collectable mugs, plates, and cups by the bagful. Even the secondhand prices are still pretty steep, but if you can elbow past the throngs, there are interesting modern pieces to be found. *Place Bérardier—Locmaria.* ☎ *02-98-52-22-52. www.hb-henriot.com. June–Sept Mon–Sun 9:30am–7pm; Oct–May Mon–Sun 9:30am–6:30pm.*

Playing Outside
PARK ACTIVITIES

Mount Frugy is only 70m (230 ft.) high but reveals some impressive views of Quimper. The trip takes only 30 to 40 minutes, but can be a nice afternoon jaunt. You can pick up the switchbacks directly behind the tourist office and leave the city traffic behind you.

Quimper's small and quiet **Jardin de la Retraite** is another spot good for a picnic or for simply kicking back. On rue Elie Fréron, just north of the cathedral, the garden is open April 15 to October 15 from 9am to 7:15pm.

WATERSPORTS

It may be easy to feel land-locked in Quimper, but the coast isn't far at all. The Odet River connects Quimper to the sea, and several river and boat tours will take you to where the water turns salty. The **Vedettes de l'Odet** (☎ 02-98-57-00-58; www.vedettes-odet.com; tickets 17€ one-way, 23€ round-trip) have several daily departures from Quimper to the port town of Bénodet from June through September. The 1¼-hour trip takes you on a largely untrammeled route through Brittany.

Quimper's bus system also runs to the beach. From July 5 to September 3, the Ligne des Plages picks up at the Résistance stop at the center of Quimper and shuttles tourists to two destinations. One line heads to Bénodet on a 35-minute trip, dropping off in the town center and two

BRITTANY

more beach stops just past it. The second line heads to Fouesnant, driving through the town to four beachfront stops. It's wise to plan out your departure and return, because there are only eight options a day. Check out the **QUB** network for more information (☎ **02-98-95-26-27;** www. qub.fr; tickets 3€ round-trip).

Festival & Events

If you're visiting in July, try to aim for the third week for the **Festival de Cornouaille** (☎ **02-98-55-53-53;** www. festival-cornouaille.com). For 9 days straight, Quimper is home to a mega-celebration of all things Breton. Held to commemorate Brittany's cultural heritage, the festival hosts live music, shows, art, and a huge number of traditional dance events and Breton games. Expect bagpipes, singers, high-stepping dancers, classic Breton duds, and shout-outs to Celtic heritage. Some events are ticketed, while others are free. Of course, the whole thing gets going with a giant parade, a smorgasbord of Breton flair that could win over even the most jaded bystander.

Held for 3 weeks in August, the **Semaines Musicales de Quimper** (☎ **02-98-52-22-52;** www.semaines-musicales-quimper. org) are a series of classical music concerts offered around town. The performances range from large groups to more intimate affairs, spread across Quimper's theaters and churches. Tickets prices depend on the event, and can be bought through the tourist office.

Bordeaux & Charente-Maritime

by *Anna Brooke*

They may not have the Côte d'Azur's glitterati allure, but what the Bordeaux and Charente-Maritime wine regions have is an expanse of long sandy beaches; enough châteaux to start a theme park; a fine seafood tradition that will hook your taste buds, line and sinker, for the rest of your days; and—drumroll, please—some 800 million bottles of wine a year. The wine capital of the world, the Bordeaux region produces 57 distinct appellations, and it's laced with vineyards that run wine-tasting tours (p. 285). The ancient river-town of Cognac—where black lichen stains on the buildings betray the locals' boozy activities (p. 305)—is the very place where, you guessed it, cognac was invented. And brandy is another regional specialty.

Nighthawks will love the laid-back party atmosphere along the Atlantic coastline. In summer, the distant sounds of tam-tam drums and clinking bottles puncture the air from sand bashes in Arcachon and illicit *kumbaya* campfire gatherings near Europe's biggest sand dune (Dune du Pilat). Festivities continue farther inland: By day the Aquitaine capital of Bordeaux and the pretty port of La Rochelle ooze sophistication as university towns; but, come sundown, cafes and brasseries fold away chairs and tables and transform into nighttime hot spots that will keep you going well into the wee hours.

The Aquitaine region (south of Charente-Maritime) has left a dazzling legacy of cultural sites besides the châteaux. Dozens of medieval Romanesque churches line Bordeaux's portion of the Santiago de Compostela pilgrimage route to Spain (p. 293), and Europe's largest monolithic church is in St-Emilion.

Last but not least, there's the great outdoors. Along the mid-Atlantic coast—from La Rochelle down to the Bassin d'Arcachon, passing inland toward Cognac, Angoulême, and Bordeaux—the peaceful, green landscape makes for spectacular sightseeing. Bordeaux claims a long stretch of shoreline (one quarter of France's Atlantic edge); several nearby islands, such as the fun-packed Ile de Ré near La Rochelle; and rich bird life, including several rare species. If you have any energy left after partying, you can burn it off with horseback riding, biking, and watersports in the region.

The Best of Bordeaux & Charente-Maritime

○ **The Best Eccentric Artists' Haunt:** Ever heard of an antiques shop—cum—restaurant where you can buy the decor? At **Café Brocante du Couvent,** in Bordeaux, your cutlery, your plate, and even your chair are for sale. Conceptualist artist Olivier Caban—who has a fetish for Queen Elizabeth II and tractor tires—designed the little garden here. If you like the outlandish, don't miss this haven of nonconformity. See p. 282.

○ **The Best Place to Impress Your Loved One at Night:** Splurge for a night at **La Maison Bord'eaux.** An 18th-century courtyard, a converted stable, cutting-edge interior design, and orgasmic French cuisine make for an unforgettable night. It might cost you *la peau des fesses* (the skin off your ass, as the French say), but after weeks in youth hostels, you couldn't splurge anywhere more worthwhile. See p. 280.

○ **The Best Street for Filling Hungry Bellies:** Just off the stunning place de la Bourse, Bordeaux's **rue St-Rémi** offers myriad eating possibilities. Whether you fancy seafood, French, Indian, Chinese, or pizza, you'll find it at a reasonable price, in a pretty setting. During the summer months, the street teems with tourists, but the large dose of locals and students that hang out there is a sure sign that you get good food for your money. See p. 283.

○ **The Best Places to Observe Bordeaux Beautiful People in their Natural Habitat:** The lounges and bars on the brand new **Bassins à Flot** complex (p. 286) are draws for the trendiest and the wannabes. When all the posing and preening there gets to be a bit much, make a break for the more student-oriented pubs and bars around **place de la Victoire.** See p. 287.

○ **The Best Photo Op in the Region:** Most people overlook the 14th-century **St-Michel Basilica,** but the view from the top is well worth the climb, allowing you to take in the whole of the city in one go. The St-Michel quarter is also known for its bric-a-brac; if you want to write home with a pen used by Napoleon's own hand or buy Marie Antoinette's dinner service, this is the place to hang out. See p. 292.

○ **The Best Place to Whip Out Your Worst Moves: Calle Ocho**'s key ingredient is salsa—plenty of it, pumped into every nook and cranny of all danceable space. After a few cocktails, and some clever lighting, everyone looks good, so don't be surprised if you end up boogying on down with a new Latino lover before the night is through. See p. 278.

○ **The Best Place to Imagine You're a 17th-Century Prisoner: Tour de la Lanterne** is actually a medieval lighthouse from the 15th century, but its thick walls, covered in graffiti by soldiers and political prisoners, betray its

The Bordeaux Region & Atlantic Coast

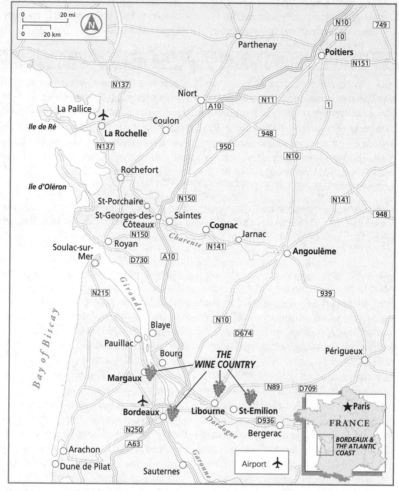

gloomy history (it served as the town's makeshift jail in the 17th–19th c.). See p. 324.

○ **The Best Place to Act Like You're in a TV Game Show:** Okay, so you can't actually visit medieval **Fort Boyard,** but that's because it really is used for a TV game show. Jump on one of the boats touring the offshore attractions and you can imagine what it would be like to be

captured inside what is essentially a 200-year-old Alcatraz. See p. 325.

○ **The Best Place to Bop with Rochelais Students:** You can't get cheesier than **Oxford.** Nor can you pack more people onto one dance floor. Maybe that's why the students flock here—so they can smooch with a stranger, knowing that he or she can't escape without a fight through the crowds. See p. 323.

○ **The Best Place to Be at One with Nature:** Get your bicycle out. You'll need it for getting around **Ile de Ré**, famous for its stunning chalky cliffs, dunes, rich birdlife, and salt pans. Peppered with fisherman's cabins and sleepy villages, everything is conducive to relaxation. See p. 325.

Getting Around the Region

From Montparnasse station in Paris, the high-speed Poitiers–Angoulême–Bordeaux TGV *Atlantique* line will get you there faster than the crow flies (from Paris to Bordeaux, it's 3 hr.). Trains from Montparnasse also run to La Rochelle in 3 hours, and from La Rochelle you can catch a bus to the Ile de Ré. From Bordeaux, trains run to Cognac via Angoulême. Bordeaux has an international airport (Aéroport Bordeaux-Mérignac). If you decide to take the wheel, you'll get there fastest on the main regional highway—the A10 from Paris via Orléans, Tours, and Poitiers (trip time: about 5 hr.). See "Getting There" on p. 273.

Bordeaux: Palatable & Happening

583km (361 miles) SW of Paris, 244km (151 miles) W of Toulouse, 183km (113 miles) S of La Rochelle; pop. 661,000

Capital of the Aquitaine region, Bordeaux sits majestically on the arc of the Garonne River (Bordeaux literally means "on the edge of the water"). If the city itself were bottled, like its famous wine, you would proclaim it a fine vintage—highly palatable, with a strong personality. With its Renaissance charm, spiked with cosmopolitan vitality, Bordeaux has an inexplicable sophistication. After just a few days among its elegant facades, don't be surprised if you ditch your backpack for some Vuitton (darling), struck by a penchant for life's little luxuries—oysters, opera, say, or the elated language of Henry James-in-France.

If posh turns you off, you may want to pick another town, but bear in mind that there's much more to do there than meets the eye. There is no denying it's a wealthy city. Evidence of money is everywhere, from the pristine squares and designer shops to the ornate detail in its perfectly preserved 18th-century facades. You could say money literally grows on trees here.

One in six residents works in the local vine business, which produces some of the world's most expensive *Premier Cru* vintages, including Médoc, Graves, and Pomerol. But if you can see past the stunning architecture, perfect lawns, and litter-free sidewalks, you'll spy hip restaurants, jam-packed bars, and tourist attractions for every age and taste.

Three universities endow Bordeaux with a thriving community of 750,000 students. They're the ones who keep everything well grounded and ensure that a constant flow of cheap booze and loud music remain accessible to anyone looking for a good time. Squeeze past the crowds in any of the student haunts around **place de la Victoire** (p. 287), and you'll find mountains of flyers and independent magazines on Bordeaux's latest hot spots, making it easy for you to dig out the funkiest places or latch onto the more alternative music or party scenes. Just watch where you're going when you're out and about—a brand new state-of-the-art tramway now slinks silently across roads and sidewalks. Looking both ways—twice—is *de rigueur* if you don't want to end up a booze-laced human pancake.

Bordeaux itself could keep you hopping for days, but it is also an ideal base from which to explore other towns in the region. If you've found accommodations at the right price, leave your bags behind and zip around on day trips.

One of my favorite nearby towns is Cognac. Two hours by train from Bordeaux, it is a top spot for brandy amateurs who can visit big-name distilleries such as Hennessy, Otard, and Martell. The small town of Angoulême, an hour away, is a must for anyone who has ever read *Tin Tin*. The only town of its kind in the country, it is entirely devoted to comic strips (*bande désinée* in French) with a whole museum, school, and library given over to them. The nightlife there is also pretty bad-ass and might convince you to stop over. Beach bums will love the sandy delights and watersports opportunities around Arcachon and the Dune de Pilat (45 min. by train), and then there are the great regional wine tours. Bordeaux's tourist office can organize some visits, but if you fancy going it alone, don't miss the stunning, medieval town of St-Emilion; it will get you sizzled ... um, I mean, sophisticate your palate in chocolate-box surroundings.

Getting There

BY AIR

Bordeaux-Mérignac airport (☎ **05-56-34-50-50;** www.bordeaux.aeroport.fr) is

Bordeaux History 101

Poor Bordeaux! Its fertile soils, sunny weather, and excellent maritime position have made it *the* place to invade ever since the Romans first massacred a few Gauls there in 56 B.C. Since very early on, the favorite local pastime (besides killing Christians) was cultivating wine. And it wasn't long before the trading port of *Burdigalato* (as Bordeaux was called then) became one of the most important in Europe.

From the 12th to the 15th century, Bordeaux was part of the English realm, following Eleanor of Aquitaine's marriage in 1154 to the French-speaking Henri Plantagenet, later King Henry II of England. She bore him three daughters and five sons—one of whom became crusading champion, Richard the Lion-Hearted. Three hundred years of English rule came to an abrupt end in 1453, when the English lost the Hundred Years' War (p. 752) and saw Bordeaux fall back to the French.

By the 18th century, the wine trade (encouraged by the English, who couldn't get enough of the stuff back at home or in their colonies) was enjoying a golden era. Today, visitors can still admire 5,000 of the buildings constructed during this period in this city renowned throughout Europe for its beauty.

Baron Haussman, the 19th-century architect responsible for turning medieval Paris into a "modern" city under Napoleon III, used Bordeaux's 18th-century plans as a model for the French capital. And during the Prussian wars of 1870, in World War I and in World War II, the French government withdrew to Bordeaux to govern at a safe distance from the enemy.

Five Quirky Facts about Bordeaux

1. Bordeaux's sister city is Los Angeles.
2. It was the first city in France to have an American consulate.
3. It is aiming to become the world leader in laser and plasma technology. By 2010 it hopes to develop the most powerful laser ever.
4. Place des Quinconces is the largest square in Europe (p. 290).
5. Bordeaux wine country has the oldest and largest number of vineyards in the world.

served by Amsterdam, Barcelona, Brussels, Dublin, Geneva, Lisbon, Madrid, and London. Paris is just 1 hour away by air. **Jet'Bus** (☏ **05-56-34-50-50**) shuttles between the airport and the city center every 45 minutes; the ride takes 40 minutes (Mon–Fri 7:45am–10:45pm; Sat 8:30am–10pm; Sun 8:30am–10:45pm). Tickets cost about 7€ one-way, and stops include place Gambetta, quai Richelieu, and Gare St-Jean. Taxis are also available, parked in front of the airport. The journey takes 30 minutes and costs about 35€. (See "Nuts & Bolts," below, for phone numbers.)

BY TRAIN

Rail is undoubtedly the best way to reach Bordeaux, thanks to France's high-speed TGV train service and reliable regional lines. Because of its southwestern location, near the Spanish border, it's accessible from many points in Europe. Paris and Lille run regular services to Bordeaux, which make it accessible from London via Eurostar, and most trains bound for smaller towns pass through Bordeaux. The railway station, Gare St-Jean, is in the south of town, a 30-minute walk (or 10-min. cab ride) from Vieux Bordeaux (the main center). Ticket prices vary according to your age and when you book them. See "Getting Around France: By Train" in chapter 2, or call ☏ **36-35.**

BY CAR

Driving is a pleasant way to explore the region, and the trip from Paris takes only 5 hours. The A10 highway from the French capital links the city with much of the Charente Maritime region and the rest of Aquitaine. If the purse strings are tight and you don't want to fork over the highway *péage,* you can fall back on the free Routes Nationales or "N" roads (see "Getting There: By Car" and "Getting Around France: By Car" in the Basics chapter). The N10 serves many places along the A10. Driving in the Bordeaux center isn't advisable. The streets are fraught with hazards: narrow 18th-century alleys, massive traffic jams on the quays beside the Garonne, and way too many cars and people. Parking space in the historic core is scarce. If you must drive, look for the blue-and-white P signs that indicate underground public garages. But beware of the fact that the slope down is steep and curved, and any heavy treading could lead to disaster.

BY BUS

Skip the bus. They're uncomfortable and slow, and it's practically impossible to find any that go to Bordeaux. **Citram** (☏ **05-56-43-68-43;** www.citram.com) runs a service around the Gironde region, but it will take you only as far as St-Emilion on our list (302 from Bordeaux to Libourne, and then 318 to St-Emilion; see p. 308).

Orientation

The center of Bordeaux follows the bend of the Garonne River. Like all French cities, it's split into quarters. The **Victoire** quarter in the South is the main student draw, with myriad watering holes distributed conveniently around the place de la Victoire. They stay open all day and serve cheap snacks and beer well past bedtime. In the **Chartrons** district around rue Notre-Dame, many of the 18th-century wine merchants' houses have been renovated, including some sumptuous mansions. There you'll find any antique or old curiosity your heart could desire. The **Quartier des Grands Hommes** is known as the golden triangle due to three expensive streets: Cours Clemenceau, Cours de l'Intendance, and the Allées de Tourny. Dating back to the French Revolution, this area is adorned with typical Bordeaux architecture, within walking distance of the pretty Jardin Public (park) and natural history museum. It is also the city's main highbrow hangout, thanks to the imposing Grand Théâtre and surrounding posh shops and restaurants. The **old town** (Vieux Bordeaux) is the most central part of Bordeaux and, as its name implies, one of the oldest; some buildings date back as far as the 13th century. Its southerly tip, the **St-Michel** district, is dominated by the tapered bell tower of the 📺 Best● **St-Michel Basilica.** It's great for a stroll and a rummage through yet more bric-a-brac. On Sundays, a flea market pulls in the punters, before making way for a bustling food market the rest of the week. Boutiques and stores line the **rue des Trois Conils** and **rue Sainte Catherine.** Farther north, around the lovely place de la Bourse, locals while away the afternoons on 📺 Best● **rue St-Rémi,** with its never-ending rows of restaurants. The same goes for the exquisitely pretty **place du Parlement,** where the cafes afford excellent people-watching and pigeon-feeding opportunities. It may seem unlikely, but the Bordelais (as Bordeaux residents are called) have only just started milking the Garonne's party potential. Downstream, to the north of the city (yep, La Garonne flows south to north), a new complex of restaurants and nightclubs at **Les Bassins à Flot** reel in Bordeaux's most *branché* for

Rental Vehicles

If you're staying in the center, the need for wheels is practically nil; the brand new tram system has made getting around easy and rather enjoyable. Much of the center is one-way and confusing, so navigating the narrow side streets can be very stressful. However, if the idea of road rage *à la française* doesn't scare you off, and you plan to whiz around the surrounding wine country by car or motorbike, try one of these rental agencies. Most have offices in the Gare St-Jean station or at the airport. You should expect to fork out around 50€ per day, although several offer decent weekend promotions: **Holiday Bikes** is your best bet for two-wheelers with 50cc to 100cc scooters at 40€ to 50€ a day. They have an office just 5 minutes from the train station (47–49 rue de Tauzia; ☎ **05-57-59-10-18;** www.holiday-bikes.com) and another at the airport (☎ **05-56-34-67-67**). For cars, **Ada** has good rates (Gare St-Jean arrivals; ☎ **05-56-31-21-11;** www.ada-location.com) as does **Hertz,** also at the station (☎ **08-25-00-24-00;** www.hertz.fr). At the airport, try **Avis** (☎ **08-20-05-05-05;** www.avis.fr) or **National Citer** (☎ **05-56-34-20-68;** www.citer.fr).

nightlong fiestas at the water's edge. Once you've done full circle up there, a few more nightclubs are worth visiting a taxi ride away on the **quai de Paludate** behind the Gare St-Jean.

Getting Around

BY PUBLIC TRANSPORTATION

It's sleek, it's clean, it runs from 5am to 1am, and it's as efficient as it is good-looking. In fact, forget train spotting; tram spotting is now the official Bordelais geek activity, since the spanking new tram system hit the rails in 2006. Against the ornate backdrop of Bordeaux's historical buildings, its space-age appearance looks anachronistic, but its three lines—the A, B, and C—have made getting across the city pain-free and simple (www.infotbc.com). Each tram stop is linked to a bus route or the electric shuttle bus (*navette éléctrique,* which runs between place de la Victoire and place des Quinconces). If you have a transport map and a street plan (the tourist office can supply both), you should be able to navigate your way around with ease. The main tram lines cross at Quinconces (lines B and C), Porte de Bourgogne (lines A and C), and Hôtel de Ville (lines A and B). Tickets *(tickartes)* are valid on all types of transport and cost 1.30€ for 60 minutes of travel, 5€ for 5 journeys, or 10€ for 10 trips. These are sold in *tabacs,* on buses (coins only), or from the gray ticket distributors at most tram stops. Once aboard, don't forget to validate your *tickarte;* if you forget, you could face a hefty fine.

BY BICYCLE

Bordeaux boasts a whopping 1,000km (621 miles) of cycle paths. To discover the city like a true Frenchy, rent a bike. **Holiday Bikes** (47–49 rue de Tauzia; ☎ **05-57-59-10-18;** www.holiday-bikes.com) start their rental prices at 10€ day or 50€ per week; they also rent scooters (see "Rental Vehicles," above). **Le 63** (63 cours d'Alsace et Lorraine; ☎ **05-56-51-39-41**) and **Macadam Sport** (27 quai des Chartrons; ☎ **05-56-51-75-51;** www.macadamsport. com) will rent you wheels for about the same price and help you blend into the throngs of students zipping in and out of the backstreets like Tour de France desperados.

The main **tourist office** (12 cours du XXX juillet; ☎ **05-56-00-66-00;** www. bordeaux-tourisme.fr) offers a 2-hour bike tour around the city for 7€ on the first Sunday of each month at 3pm.

ON FOOT

Bordeaux is one of those awkward-size cities: It's slightly too big for walking everywhere, but too small for using public transport every time you go out. After clever analysis of local habits, you will see that the solution lies in a combination of both: Use the tram to get you to the part you want to explore and then walk as much as your two legs will carry you around each quarter. The map provided by the tourist office is well detailed and lists most street names as well as essential services and cultural sites. On it, you may notice how the city follows the bend of the river, and most attractions fall inside a boomerang-shaped segment of town bordered by five boulevards (cours de la Marne, which links the station to place de la Victoire, cours Aristide Briand, cours d'Albert, cours Georges Clemenceau, and cours de Verdun in the north). Stick to anywhere between these boulevards and the river, and you really can't get lost.

The key to being a perfect pedestrian in Bordeaux is to look where you are going. French drivers aren't always hell-bent on squashing unsuspecting tourists, but Bordeaux features lots of blind corners that motorists, cyclists, tram drivers, and pedestrians negotiate simultaneously.

Unless you're a PlayStation champion with reflexes of steel, watch where you walk.

Finally, keep your eye out for the blue panels on street corners (particularly in the old town). They give a brief explanation of street names and the history behind the area in both French and English.

Bordeaux Nuts & Bolts

Crisis Centers The confidential Women's Rape/Crisis Center number is ☎ **08-00-05-95-95** (www.cfcv.asso.fr; Mon–Fri 10am–7pm). For other crises, call the French Red Cross (Croix Rouge; 74 cours St-Louis; ☎ **08-20-16-17-77**).

Emergencies Call ☎ **17** for the police, ☎ **18** for the fire department, and ☎ **15** for an ambulance.

Internet/Wireless Hot Spots To check your e-mail, update your blog, or check train schedules, stop by **L'Héroïque Sandwich** (17 rue de Candale; ☎ **05-57-59-15-00**; daily 9:30am–2am) near place de la Victoire. There's no squabbling for space here, with its 65 computers. The same goes for its sister cafe **Cyberstation** (23 cours Pasteur; ☎ **05-57-59-15-00**; daily 9:30am–2am).

Laundromats Freshen your threads in **Lavomatique Bordeaux** (203 cours de la Marne; ☎ **06-08-51-20-40**).

Post Office *La Poste* is conveniently located at 58 rue St-Rémi (☎ **05-57-14-32-00**; Mon 2–6pm, Tues–Fri 10am–6pm, Sat 10am–12:30pm) in the old town. While you're there, expect a crash course in French queuing tactics.

Safety Bordeaux is not particularly dangerous, but beware the usual culprits of petty crime (pickpockets and beggars), especially around the train station. Common sense rules here, as in any city: Keep your bags closed, hide your wallet, and don't dilly-dally down dark alleys or talk to men waving pickaxes.

Taxis Taxis are relatively expensive in Bordeaux (they certainly cost more than in Paris), but they're also efficient and generally trustworthy. The main companies are: **Mérignac** (☎ 05-56-97-11-27); **Taxis Girondins** (☎ 05-56-80-70-37); **Taxis Télé** (☎ 05-56-96-00-34); **Allo Bordeaux Taxis** (☎ 05-56-31-61-07); **Aquitaine Taxis Radio** (☎ 05-56-86-80-30); and **Taxis 33** (☎ 05-56-74-95-06; www.taxi33.fr), which runs 24/7. Note that if three or four of you are traveling from the airport into town, it is cheaper to share a taxi than to catch the JetBus.

Tourist Offices General information is available by phone at ☎ **05-56-00-66-00** or online at www.bordeaux-tourisme.com. If you'd prefer to chat with someone three-dimensional or flick through some brochures, head to one of two tourist offices: There's a small one at **Gare St-Jean train station** (☎ **05-56-91-64-70**; Nov–Apr Mon–Fri 9am–noon and 2–6pm; May–Oct Mon–Sat 9am–noon and 1–6pm, Sun 10am–noon and 1–3pm). The **main office** is in Vieux Bordeaux at 12, cours du XXX juillet (☎ **05-56-00-66-00**; Nov–Apr Mon–Sat 9am–6:30pm, Sun 9:45am–6pm; May–Oct: Mon–Sat 9am–7pm [until 7:30pm July–Aug], Sun 9:30am–6:30pm). The Office de Tourisme organizes excellent guided tours around the city and surrounding wine country. They also list accommodations and can help you book them. The **Centre D'information Jeunesse** (5 rue Duffour-Dubergier; ☎ **05-56-56-00-56;** Mon–Thurs 9:30am–6pm, Fri 9:30am–5pm) is also very useful, with information on travel and health, free Internet access, and various travel assistance services.

Sleeping

Whether you're looking for a place to dump your bags or 420-thread-count beauty sleep, Bordeaux has plenty of choices for all budgets. As with many French cities, it was at the back of the queue for air-conditioning, and even though things are catching up (most places listed here have A/C), the summer months can get quite stifling. A great advantage though is that cheap here doesn't necessarily mean "miles out from the center." There are economical options in the heart of the town, although they do tend to get booked quickly. Failing that, the area around the train station is not as grotty as you would expect, and it's just a 10-minute walk from the student-oriented place de la Victoire, or a short tram ride from other sites.

HOSTELS

➔**Auberge de Jeunesse** Bordeaux's only youth hostel is in a handy spot near the Gare St-Jean. There are plenty of reasons to stay here: Staff members wear genuine smiles; breakfast (included in the price) is copious; wannabe chefs can fry up their fantasies in the fully equipped kitchen; and guests (often students looking for more permanent lodgings or European travelers) can relax, chat, or whip out their iPods in the comfy *salle de détente* (lounge). Most importantly, rooms are light, airy, and clean. Just don't stay out past 2am; management locks the front doors from then until 5am. Also: Guests must vacate their rooms between 10am and 4pm, so plan your schedule around this. *22 cours Barbey.* ☎ *05-56-33-00-70.*

www.auberge.jeunesse@centres-animations. asso.fr. 21€ double. Rates include bed linens and breakfast.

CHEAP

➔**Hôtel Acanthe** ★ If your chief priority is being able to stumble to your room after a few bevies and a major pig-out, this is the place for you. Hôtel Acanthe is right by the river, near place de la Bourse on rue St-Rémi (otherwise known as the belly of Bordeaux, after the rows of restaurants and bars that line its sides). But its location is not its only asset. The recently renovated rooms are comfortable, with huge French windows that drench everything with light. And the staff is more than helpful. *12–14 rue St-Rémi.* ☎ *05-56-81-66-58. www.acanthe-hotel-bordeaux.com. 36€–71€ single or double; triple 66€–76€. Breakfast 6.50€. Credit cards accepted. Amenities: Elevator. In room: TV, free Wi-Fi, wake-up call.*

➔**Hôtel Clémenceau** ★ This place has just changed owners, and the new proprietor, who also owns Le Grand Café next door (see "Cafes & Light Fare," below), has given it more than a well-needed lick of paint. Many of the 45 rooms were redecorated in light shades and equipped with—drum roll, please—air-conditioning. The staff is very friendly and the clientele young and adventurous, from all over the globe. *4 cours Clémenceau.* ☎ *05-56-52-98-98. www. hotel-bordeaux.com. 35€–45€ single or double; 59€ triple. Breakfast 6.50€. Credit cards accepted. Parking 7€. Amenities: Bar; elevator. Internet; elevator. In room: A/C, TV, minibar.*

➔**Hôtel Notre-Dame** This place has a bit of a 1980s feel—witness the marble-effect

Bordeaux

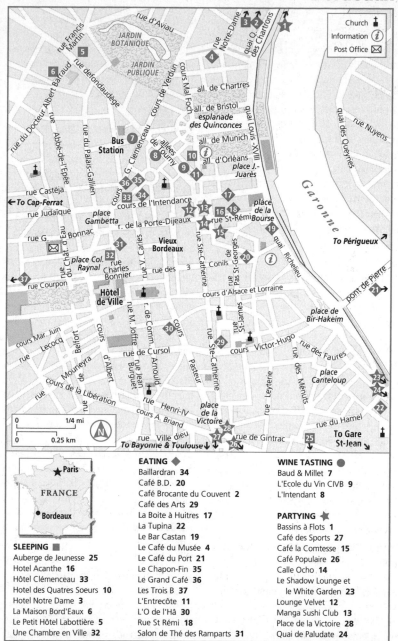

Church ✝
Information ⓘ
Post Office ✉

EATING ◆
Baillardran **34**
Café B.D. **20**
Café Brocante du Couvent **2**
Café des Arts **29**
La Boite à Huitres **17**
La Tupina **22**
Le Bar Castan **19**
Le Café du Musée **4**
Le Café du Port **21**
Le Chapon-Fin **35**
Le Grand Café **36**
Les Trois B **37**
L'Entrecôte **11**
L'O de l'Hâ **30**
Rue St Rémi **18**
Salon de Thé des Ramparts **31**

WINE TASTING ●
Baud & Millet **7**
L'Ecole du Vin CIVB **9**
L'Intendant **8**

PARTYING ✭
Bassins à Flots **1**
Café des Sports **27**
Café la Comtesse **15**
Café Populaire **26**
Calle Ocho **14**
Le Shadow Lounge et
  le White Garden **23**
Lounge Velvet **12**
Manga Sushi Club **13**
Place de la Victoire **28**
Quai de Paludate **24**

SLEEPING ■
Auberge de Jeunesse **25**
Hotel Acanthe **16**
Hôtel Clémenceau **33**
Hotel des Quatres Soeurs **10**
Hotel Notre Dame **3**
La Maison Bord'Eaux **6**
Le Petit Hôtel Labottière **5**
Une Chambre en Ville **32**

★ Paris
FRANCE
● Bordeaux

wallpaper, for starters. But the '80s were cool, right? If you can ignore the grape stencils in the breakfast room (charming though they are), the warm atmosphere of this friendly hotel will win you over. Rooms are individually decorated in bright colors, and staff members will help you carry your bags up the magnificent stone staircase (you've got it: There's no elevator). The Chartrons district is one of the most interesting in Bordeaux, so this makes an ideal base from which to explore the city's more eccentric side, including rows of curiosity shops. *36–38 rue Notre-Dame.* ☎ *05-56-52-88-24. www.hotelnotredame.free.fr. 40€ single; 45€–50€ double. Breakfast 6€. Credit cards accepted. Amenities: Bar; laundry; paid parking. In room: TV, Internet modem point.*

DOABLE

→ **Hôtel des Quatres Soeurs** ★ The ground floor of this long, thin, lovingly decorated hotel is old-school French, with plenty of dark wood, painted panels, and red carpet. The rooms, done in creams and yellows, have a country mansion feel. Wine lovers should flock here. The hotel partners with the nearby **Maison de Millésimes** (37 rue Esprit des Lois; ☎ **05-57-81-19-20;** www.jackswines.com), which runs excellent wine-tasting tours into the Bordeaux region. *6 cours du XXX Juillet.* ☎ *05-56-48-16-00. http://4soeurs.free.fr. 65€ single; 75€–90€ double; 105€–115€ triple (up to 5 people). Breakfast 8€. Credit cards accepted. Amenities: Babysitting; elevator; laundry. In room: A/C, cable TV.*

→ **Une Chambre en Ville** ★★ The attention-grabbing objects and furnishings at this small guesthouse betray its former life as a furniture gallery. The communal areas are particularly swish, with black-and-white walls and funky purple chairs. The five rooms (all air-conditioned) are more traditionally clad in less showy colors. If

you judge a hotel by the cleanliness of its bathrooms, you'll deem this place to be next to godliness. If a balcony is your "thang," request a front room. *35 rue Bouffard.* ☎ *05-56-81-34-53. www.bandbbx. com. 79€–89€ single and double. Breakfast 8€. Credit cards accepted. In room: A/C, TV, Internet access, minibar, safe.*

SPLURGE

MTV Best ● **La Maison Bord'Eaux** ★★ This discreet B&B feels like Bordeaux's best-kept secret. By the looks of the near-invisible entrance (the only indicator from the street is the white, ivy-clad wall and a miniscule plaque), the owners want to keep it that way. Step into the cobbled courtyard, and enter another dimension— a world where cutting-edge contemporary design and traditional 18th-century architecture create a stunning poetic harmony. Especially exquisite are the red and gold wine cabinets in the lounge. The owners are among the region's biggest winegrowers, so you can opt for exclusive wine tours and dinners at some of their châteaux, or delve into a wine-orientated meal *sur place* in the super-sleek dining room (menus 25€ and 45€). Guest rooms are just as swell, decorated in bold, unified colors. Each has a large bed that takes pride of place—*parfait!* *113 rue Dr. Albert Barraud.* ☎ *05-56-44-00-45. www.lamaisonbord-eaux. com. 120€–190€ single or double. Rates include buffet breakfast, which is otherwise 15€. Credit cards accepted. Amenities: Gourmet restaurant; wine bar; parking. In room: Satellite TV, bathrobe, Internet, minibar, safe, slippers.*

MTV Best ● **Le Petit Hôtel Labottière** ★★ If you've had your fill of partying and long to stay somewhere refined, historical, and unique, you can't do better than Le Petit Hôtel Labottière. The place has only two rooms, and both feel like they belong to another era. Owners Liliane and

Michel Korber have spent the last 40 years restoring their city mansion to its former 18th-century glory. Everything, from the floor to the ceiling—including paint color (which was matched perfectly by scraping away 300 years' worth of layers) is textbook authentic. The furniture and knickknacks are of museum quality; many items are so rare the only other known versions live in world-class museums in Paris, London, and Madrid. Breakfast is served in an exquisite walled garden, and guests are encouraged to help themselves to whatever they want from the fridges, free of charge. Don't forget to look at the painting by Pierre Lacour (1774) in the guest entrance—it's the same one as in Bordeaux's Grand Théâtre (p. 290). *14 rue Francis Martin.* ☎ *05-56-48-44-10. www. chateaux-france.com/labottiere. 180€ double. Rates include breakfast. Credit cards accepted. Amenities: Parking. In room: TV. Private tours around the hotel are available for 8€ per person; inquire at Office de Tourisme.*

Eating

So you've found a place to stay, now let's get to the real reason you probably came to France: the food. Eating out in Bordeaux is a great experience. The wine is brilliant, for starters, and thanks to a rich maritime history and links with the nearby Basque country, nosh is well varied and worth getting up in the morning for. France is renowned for being expensive, so don't feel slack if you revert to snacking. It is by no means looked down upon; in fact, it is standard practice in the student quarters. Many bars and restaurants provide quick, cheap options well into the night. Don't forget to try Bordeaux's specialty pastry—a vanilla and rum bread cake called *canelé* (see "Pop a Cork—in Your Mouth!" below).

CAFES & LIGHT FARE

➔**Café B.D.** CAFE   It's hip to be geeky in France, and this concept cafe is proof. Techy-speckies, grunge kids, and families flock here to partake in a now-cool activity that was once practiced in solitary confinement (preferably under the bedclothes with a pocket torch): comic book reading. Café B.D has hundreds of *bande desinées* (comic strips) to choose from. If you're not sure what to pick, the barman (alias: Comic Guru) will recommend something according to your taste. When your eyes are tired and your stomach cries out for more than just a belly laugh, try the sugary muffins, savory tarts, or more substantial fare. *15 rue Maucoudinat.* ☎ *05-56-44-80-23. www. cafebd.com. Main courses 15€–20€. Credit cards accepted. Mon–Tues noon–4pm; Wed noon–7pm; Thurs–Fri noon–4pm and 7:30–10:30pm.*

➔**Le Bar Castan** ★ CAFE   This joint may have been founded in the 19th century, but it's right up-to-date, with an eclectic mix of period and contemporary decor that you could describe as troglodyte-chic. Original Art Deco tiles are set off against giant, fake limestone overhangs that make the place feel like a surreal Belle Epoque grotto. Had Fred Flintstone time-traveled to the 19th-century, he and Barney certainly would have smoked a few cigars here. And why not? The terrace looks out across the river; the *croque monsieurs*, at just 4.50€, are the largest in Bordeaux. The yummy house cocktails (9€) make for the ultimate post- or pre-dinner drink. Yabba dabba do come here! *2 quai de la Douane.* ☎ *05-56-44-51-97. www.grand-bar-castan.com. Croque monsieur (house special) 4.50€. Credit cards accepted. Mon–Sun 8am–2am.*

➔**Les Trois B** ★★ BRASSERIE   This 500-sq.-m (5,382-sq.-ft.) hall of games—with billiards, darts, pool, and snooker, to name a few activities—is away from the main center (about a 10-min. walk from place Gambetta). At first glance, it looks like the community hall that time forgot, somewhere between the 1950s and 1980s; but moving swiftly past the plastic chairs and fake grass carpet, you'll realize that you've turned up somewhere as cultish as it is coveted. When you're tired of play, settle down in the brasserie or on the covered terrace, and tuck into one of their famous *tartines* (a French take on pizza). This is probably one of the best places in Bordeaux for striking up a chat with a local. *175 rue Georges Bonnac. ☎ 05-56-24-06-29. www.lestroisb.com. Main courses 5.50€–7.50€. Credit cards accepted. Mon 6–2pm; Tues–Sun 3pm–2am.*

→ **Salon de Thé des Ramparts** TEA HOUSE There's nothing like a nice cup of tea and a sticky bun to keep you going when you're out and about in a big city. This is certainly the opinion of the hoards of shoppers and students who flock to this cozy corner of exoticism to try one of the 100 teas (all Chinese, Indian, or Ceylon), and masses of homemade cakes, pastries, savory tarts, and scrumptious ice creams (4€–10€). The terrace, which looks out onto a pedestrian street, gets a lot of traffic, particularly on a sunny day, but if you've got time, it's worth waiting for a table. Tea fanatics can also buy their favorite leaves by the kilo. *19 rue Remparts. ☎ 05-56-90-03-03. Pastries 4€–10€. Credit cards accepted. Tues–Sat noon–6:30pm (food); Tues–Sat 11am–7pm (shop).*

CHEAP

MTV Best ◗ Café Brocante du Couvent ★★ FRENCH The Chartrons district is full of antiques shops, but this one stands out from the crowd. Bruno, the owner, is a friendly, eccentric type who gets a kick out of meeting interesting people, serving them food, and then selling then something from his shop. Olivier Caban is a young conceptualist artist who has the habit of attracting interesting people to his exhibits. It works like this: You wander in from the street for lunch (Tues–Sat) or for dinner (Thurs) but don't have anyone to share a meal with. Not to worry—there is a big table for lone travelers. Then as you eat your delicious meal (Bruno invites a chef around to cook), you realize that your plate belongs to a set your Aunt Virginia once had, and you're compelled to buy it. *Pas de problème*—Bruno will make you an offer. Once dinner is over and you've made a few new friends, you can head out to the little garden in the back of the shop and admire Olivier's creations,

Pop a Cork—in Your Mouth!

If you have been blessed with a sweet tooth like mine, your trip to Bordeaux, and quite possibly your life, will never be complete unless you try a *canelé*—little cork-shaped cakes, flavored with rum and vanilla, that crack when you bite into them, before their light, fluffy innards stick to your teeth—beautiful! They first appeared in Bordeaux in the 1600s, and since then they've gone through more names than centuries (*cannelet, canelet, millas-canelet, millason, canaule, canaulé,* and *canaulet*). *Canelé* didn't stick, so to speak, until the 1980s. If you're feeling decadent, try the best ones, made by **Baillardran** (55 cours de l'Intendance; ☎ **05-56-52-92-64;** www.baillardran.com). They also have a stall (for emergency fixes) in the departures area of the Gare St-Jean (ground and lower-ground floors).

Rue St-Rémi ★★

When the chips are down and hunger strikes, who you gonna call? One of the restaurants on [MV][Best] **rue St-Rémi,** probably. Indian, Chinese, Japanese, French, Italian, and Thai cuisines are among the world foods represented. For no-frills French, grab a table at **Les Provinces** (no. 43; ☎ **05-56-81-74-30**), where menus start at 12€ for three courses. **Chez Thibeaud** (no. 53; ☎ **05-56-44-52-43**) — with its exposed stone walls and (oh, so tasteful) nautical-themed wall hangings — is great for some quick seafood on the cheap (three courses start at 12€). If cash is really low (or you've got post alcoholic-binge munchies), let the greasy kabobs and fries at **Cooky's Sandwicherie** (no. 36; ☎ **05-56-44-96-45**) clog your arteries for under 4€. For a slice of Italy, Napoli style, try **Pepperoni** (no. 57; ☎ **05-56-51-78-70**), with its old Italian film memorabilia and excellent, crunchy-crust pizza (8€). In the unlikely event that nothing here tickles your fancy, head to the nearby **place du Parlement** for more choices around a pretty square.

which often feature the Queen of England and tractor tires. Try it; you'll be glad you came to Bordeaux. *23 rue du Couvent.* ☎ *05-56-44-15-20. http://cafe-brocante.info. Menus 20€, including wine. Credit cards accepted. Tues–Fri 12:30–2:30pm and 7–11pm (must reserve in advance).*

→ **Café des Arts** ★ FRENCH/BRASSERIE This Belle Epoque cafe is steeped in history, having survived many of France's most momentous events: World War II (1939–45), the Liberation in 1945, and the student uprising in May 1968, when it functioned as a hospital for wounded activists. The current owners, Jean-Dominique Gracia and Colum Crichton-Stuart, have spent a fortune restoring the cafe to its early-20th-century splendor, and the magnificent marble and huge period mirrors you can see today were all unearthed during the process. Jazz concerts are a permanent fixture, as are delicious dishes such as roasted Camembert cheese, *andouillette* (a smelly tripe sausage), and oysters from nearby Arcachon. *138 cours Victor Hugo/184 rue Ste-Catherine.* ☎ *05-56-91-78-46. www.cafe-des-arts.com. Lunch menu 11€; a la carte*

20€–25€. *Credit cards accepted. Daily noon–12:30am.*

→ **Le Grand Café** FRENCH This is a Bordelais melting pot, where locals, tourists, and students all mingle on the massive terrace, which extends onto the pedestrian-only Cours de l'Intendance. Food tends by be hit-or-miss, but the salads are copious, drenched in vinaigrette and rarely disappointing (11€–15€). On a sunny weekend, the terrace attracts a young crowd, made up of those who didn't get up early enough to go to the beach at Arcachon. Just make sure you have plenty of time to kill. The waiters certainly do, and you should follow their example. *65 cours de l'Intendance.* ☎ *05-56-52-61-10. Lunch menu 11€; a la carte 25€. Credit cards accepted. Daily 8am–2am.*

DOABLE

→ **La Boite à Huitres** ★ SEAFOOD *Mmm!* Oysters — the ultimate aphrodisiac. This chic little fisherman's shack behind the Grand Théâtre serves them up good and fresh year-round, either inside the quaint blue-and-white restaurant or as takeout. The clientele tends to be an assortment of young and old thespian types, united by three common loves: theater, shellfish, and local wine, all consumed in equally large portions. The good news is that a large portion won't break the bank: Prices range from 7.50€ to 19€ for a dozen, depending on size and quality. Expect to pay around 30€ for meals a la carte. *36 cours Chapeau Rouge.* ☎ *05-56-81-64-97. Main courses 7€–16€. Credit cards accepted. Daily noon–2:30pm and 7–11pm (or just after the last performance in the theater).*

📺 Best ● **Le Café du Musée** ★★ FRENCH FUSION Even if you were the spotty kid in school, you can hang out like one of the bold and the beautiful when you visit this trendy new restaurant, nestled in the roof of the city's contemporary art museum. The food is gobsmackingly good (try the pork stuffed with apples or the foie gras terrine with vanilla), and the decor is sleek. Its arched ceilings and low-lighting make you feel like you're in some sort of New York penthouse. On a sunny day, the terrace is *the* place to be, but don't forget to take your shades. It is a major sun trap, and your poor eyes might have difficulty adjusting to the comparable darkness of the dining room on your way to the toilets (I tumbled over a raised floorboard on the way). Sunday brunches (23€ for pastries, cheese, fruit, eggs, smoked salmon, sausage, and bacon) are a popular draw and a prime opportunity for you to study the bourgeois bordelaise family in its natural habitat. *Musée d'Art Contemporain. 7 rue Ferrère.* ☎ *05-56-44-71-61. www.chezgreg.fr. Menu 18€–25€; a la carte 35€. Credit cards accepted. Tues–Sun noon–6pm.*

→ **Le Café du Port** CONTEMPORARY FRENCH Set on the opposite side of the river from the main town, this chic restaurant provides a glimpse of what foreign sailors must have seen when they first cruised up the estuary into Bordeaux in the 18th century. The view hasn't changed much after 300 years, but the food has. Seafood rather predictably takes up a large chunk of the menu, but everything, including some delicious meat dishes, is worth ordering. Try the Mediterranean octopus salad, followed by veal's liver (cooked to Hannibal Lector's standard of pink), and finish everything off with a mouthwatering tiramisu with apricots. *1 quai Deschamps.* ☎ *05-56-77-81-18. www.lecafeduport.com. Lunch menu 16€; a la carte 35€. Credit cards accepted. Tues–Sat noon–2:30pm and 7–10:30pm.*

→ **L'Entrecôte** ★ FRENCH STEAKHOUSE Steak and fries *(steak frites)* are the closest you'll ever get to French fast food, but the concept will seem purely ironic once you've queued up for over an hour at L'Entrecôte. The steak here is so legendary that it is nearly impossible to get a table straight off, particularly as they don't take reservations. But once you've felt these tender morsels melt on your tongue, all will be forgotten. The quality of meat isn't the only thing to write home about: The sauce, a secret recipe that has been handed down from mother to offspring since 1966, is a veritable culinary conundrum, and it's tasty as can be. *4 cours du XXX juillet.* ☎ *05-56-81-76-10. www.entrecote.fr. Steak 16€; a la carte 25€. Credit cards accepted. Daily noon–2pm and 7:15–10:45pm.*

→ **L'O de l'Hâ** ★ FRENCH/INTERNATIONAL The owners got the inspiration for this smart eatery during a visit to New York and the ground-breaking French restaurant Bouley. Miles away from its muse, L'O de l'Hâ provides a backdrop of antique masonry, roughly textured plaster, and polished concrete for intriguing dishes such as crabmeat lasagna with coconut flakes; *brandade* of sweet potatoes with sweet peppers; and a platter that artfully combines raw, sushi-grade fish and pan-fried foie gras with fava beans. Main courses would excite even Anthony Bourdain: roasted sea bream with morel-studded risotto; large Dover sole with spinach, walnuts, and chanterelles; and braised lamb chops with tomato marmalade. From Thursday to Saturday, a DJ spins the evening away from 8 until around 11pm. *5 rue de l'Hâ.* ☎ *05-56-81-42-21. Reservations recommended. Fixed-price lunch 15€; a la carte 30€. Credit cards accepted. Tues–Sat noon–2pm; Tues–Thurs 8–10pm; Fri–Sat 8–11:30pm.*

SPLURGE

→**La Tupina** ★★ BASQUE One of Bordeaux's most talented chefs runs this cozy spot with a desirable summer terrace near quai de la Monnaie. It has been called "a tribute to country kitchens and the grandmothers who cooked in them." I'd call it "a tribute to ducks and the ingredients that go with them." Your meal may typically begin with croutons spread with duck *rillettes,* and the kitchen often uses duck giblets, skin, and livers in salads (*bonjour* the coronary). Other specialties are roasted shoulder of lamb *en confit* with garlic and white beans, lamprey eel *à la Bordelaise,* and steaks grilled and barbecued at the table. Desserts usually include pears marinated in red bordeaux wine. *6 rue de la Porte de la Monnaie.* ☎ *05-56-91-56-37. Reservations recommended. Lunch 32€; dinner 48€. Credit cards accepted. Daily noon–2pm and 7–11pm.*

→**Le Chapon-Fin** ★★ MODERN FRENCH One of the city's most prestigious restaurants occupies an early-20th-century monument that critics have referred to as "organic rococo." Designed by architect Alfred Duprat and crafted from distressed rocks into an Art Nouveau–style grotto, it soars almost 7.5m (25 ft.) to a skylight that floods the interior with light. Owner Nicolas Frion features artful renditions of fresh foie gras of duckling; lobster salad; Pauillac lamb grilled with peppers and mushrooms; sea bass with pecans, celery leaves, and cream; and succulent crayfish and scallops braised in spices and wine. Dress to impress if you decide to splash out here: The restaurant is in one of the city's most upscale neighborhoods, between place Gambetta and the Marché aux Grands Hommes, and you'll be expected to look the part. *5 rue Montesquieu.* ☎ *05-56-79-10-10. Reservations required. Lunch 27€–76€; dinner 48€–76€. Credit cards accepted. Tues–Sat noon–1:30pm and 7:30–9:30pm.*

Wine-Tasting

It would be a waste to leave Bordeaux before tasting its most famous product, and wine shops are the best places to do it. Many restaurants have prodigious *carte de vins,* but hefty commissions make it hard to pop more than one or two corks over dinner. But wine shops abound, and some even offer wine-tasting lessons. The Office de Tourisme can also supply a list of private tours.

MTV Best ❤ **Baud & Millet** Everyone knows that wine goes with cheese, but Baud & Millet have perfected the partnership better than most. Eye up the bottles in the front shop, then follow your nose to your table in the back to marvel at nature's ability to turn something as fundamentally unappetizing as lactose and mold into foodstuff so delicious and varied. Back in the wine shop and downstairs cellar, you can choose from more than 600 bottles, and the seriously knowledgeable staff will happily talk you through what you're tasting. *19 rue Huguerie.* ☎ *05-56-79-05-77. Menus 15€–30€. Credit cards accepted. Mon–Sat 9am–midnight.*

BORDEAUX & CHARENTE-MARITIME

➜ **L'Ecole du Vin CIVB** ★★ This wine school is everyone's cup of *rouge* whether you're an aspiring oenological whiz or just curious to understand what you've been drinking for the past week. There are all sorts of formulas to choose from (in English). The cheapest is a 2-hour lesson (20€) in which you'll receive an overview of winemaking in Bordeaux (soil, grape varieties, language of tasting) before getting your mitts on one dry white, three reds, and a dessert wine. Every Thursday, providing enough people have signed up, you can opt to pay an extra 65€ and have lunch with your teacher in a Bordeaux restaurant before visiting the cellars of two Medoc châteaux (see the Nerd's Guide to French Wine & Culture chapter).

Weekend courses are also popular. They're costly (640€) but include a full-time guide, three lunches, two dinners, and 2 nights in a three-star hotel in the Bordeaux city center. *1 cours du XXX juillet.* ☎ 05-56-00-22-66. *www.ecole.vins-bordeaux.fr. 2-hr. lesson: May 1–Nov 3, Tues–Wed and Fri 10am–noon, Mon, Thurs, and Sat 3–5pm. Weekend option: 3 days in May and Oct (call to check exact dates).*

➜ **L'Intendant** ★ If Bacchus were to build a shrine to wine, he'd do well to model it after the multistory, spiral-shape Intendant, inspired by the Guggenheim museum in New York. No other place in Bordeaux shows off its bottles in such an impressive and original manner. What's more, tasting is free, and prices are very reasonable, with

Rockin' on the Dock of the Bay

Bassins à Flots

Until recently, the 📺 **Best** ❾ **Bassins à Flots** docks were a bleak expanse of industrial wasteland. No one wanted to go there, and no one ever did. Then some bright spark decided it was time for an urban renewal program and managed to entice big-name club owners to move in. Today the Bassin is the ultimate destination for Bordeaux's most *branché.* An ample array of bars, clubs, and restaurants ensure you'll have fun from dusk till dawn. **La Dame de Shanghai** (quai Armand Lalande; ☎ 05-57-10-20-50; www.damedeshanghai. com) is an exclusive, vintage riverboat doubling as a restaurant (menus 25€) and *discothèque.* Decor is a sexy take on a 1930s Shanghai gentleman's club. Chicago-born Paul Johnson is one of many international DJs to have spun some numbers here. When there's not a star behind the wheel, local maestros play excellent house and garage. **Pier 6** (Bassins à Flots; building G2, quai Armand Lalande; ☎ 05-56-50-61-31) is another classy joint whose bouncers will look you up and down twice before letting you in. If you make the grade, you will be rubbing shoulders with designer label junkies amid minimalist decor worthy of a Parisian fashion shoot. Electro pop, house, and dub are particularly coveted here, as are champagne and martini cocktails. Cover is 15€; drinks are around 8€. **Le Poppy's** (Building H34, 1 rue Gironde; ☎ 05-56-69-86-59) is where the Parisian "it" crowd gathers when they leave the capital for some fresh southwesterly air. Music is distinctly electro house with a dash of pop. Cover is 10€; drinks are 7€. The youthful pack that frequents the **Dream Beach Club** (**DBC**; Hangar G2, Bassins à Flots; ☎ 05-56-11-04-46) tends to surf the waves of R&B, hip-hop, and reggae. At the bar, where champagne runs from a tap, you can imagine yourself being filmed in a Beach Boys clip. Cover is 8€; drinks are 7.50€–15€.

ᴍᴛᴠᵁ scholarly slurping

Nowhere is the beer cheaper or the music louder than around **place de la Victoire.** Motley student-oriented crowds flock to every single one of the bars around this square—several times over if they can manage it—to vary their alcohol intake according to what's on offer. The narrow **Bar de la Victoire** (no. 23; ☎ **05-56-91-43-90**) doesn't look like much from outside, but their themed parties (three times a month) are known as the wildest around (beer 3€). The much larger and cheesier **Bodegon** (no. 14; **05-56-94-74-02**) is a must if you love to boogie to kitsch Euro pop. Happy hour is from 6pm to 8pm every evening; a drink and some tapas are as little as 3€. On the opposite side of the square, the **St-Aubin** (no. 6; ☎ **05-56-91-28-15**) dresses all its waiters in sexy black kilts. Nine plasma TV screens broadcast nothing but sports and MTV, and the *International Herald Tribune* is always on hand. **Les Tontons Flinguers** (named after George Lautner's cult 1963 movie) is a small bar that plays reggae and pop into the early hours. Snacks are served morning to night and drinks generally cost less than 4€ (no. 4; place de la Victoire; ☎ **05-56-94-15-61**). For some post-bar clubbing, walk 20 minutes to the **Quai des Paludates** on the other side of the Station (see "Clubs & Live Music Venues," below).

bottles ranging from simple table wine (under 6€), right up to the pricey (we're talking hundreds of euros) but highly toothsome *premier crus* (best vintages). *2 allée de Tourny.* ☎ *05-56-48-01-29. www.chateau primeur.com. Mon 2:30–7:30pm; Tues–Sat 10am–7:30pm.*

Partying

A massive population of 18- to 30-year-olds makes Bordeaux one mean dream of a party scene. Most bars stay open until 2am (3am in spring and summer), then the flow continues to clubs, and if you're lucky, to an after-hours venue. The fashion police don't patrol the town in general (especially around place de la Victoire and in Vieux Bordeaux), but some of the more posh clubs around the Bassin de Flot complex have an unofficial, super-snooty dress code. So dress up or be shot down. Several bars and clubs distribute free magazines on Bordeaux's nightlife. Try *Anatomik* (www.anatomikmag.com) for listings on concerts, clubs, and general goings-on. Another great website for finding out

about the latest nights, DJs, and student soirées is **www.tillate.com**.

BARS

➜**Café des Sports** This is the ultimate sports bar, though in Europe sports means rugby and football—football as in soccer. Jocks and team flags fly everywhere. Run into international football fans, beer in hand, or zone out on one of the 16 plasma screens seen from any table. Polos, dockers, or rugby shirts are not required, but wear one and you'll feel more at home here. Bar snacks such as pizza and burgers (under 15€) will help you soak up the beer. Just don't cheer with your mouth full! *5 cours de l'Argonne.* ☎ *05-56-31-42-24. www. cafedessports-bordeaux.com. Credit cards accepted.*

➜**Café la Comtesse** This arty bar buzzes jazz (acid and non), world music, and funky electronic remixes to help you sink into the red velvet and wooden chairs. It's anything but stuffy, despite the chandelier, fireplace, and paintings on the walls; rather it's a classic bar to chill in and strike

Fun Venues Upstream

Quai de Paludate

Le Comptoir du Jazz ★ If you're into live jazz, you can't leave the city without stopping at this bar adjacent to the restaurant Le Port de la Lune. The artists are excellent (no skiddly bopping wannabes in sight) and more than willing to chat with fans after the show. *59 quai Paludate.* ☎ *05-56-49-15-55.*

Pollux Psychedelic decor, kitschy furniture, and '80s music: What more could you want after the faultlessly chic clubs in the Bassins à Flots. The mixed gay and straight clientele here know this is the maddest club in Bordeaux. It's also one of the friendliest. *48 quai du Paludate.* ☎ *05-56-49-36-93.*

up a chat with funky 20- and 30-somethings. No cocktails are served, just liquor (5€–9€), beers (3€), and hot drinks; after 9pm, prices rise a few centimes, but it's still a great place to wind down in after sightseeing. *25 rue du Parlement.* ☎ *05-56-51-03-07. Credit cards accepted.*

Five Clubbers' Commandments

Before you embark into the mysterious realms of Bordelaise nightlife, follow our Clubbers' Commandments and you should last until morning.

1. **Thou shalt not wear sneakers.** They're often used as a pretext to deny entry.
2. **Thou shalt not arrive in a large group**—unless you are scantily clad girls, in which case you may be admitted for free.
3. **Thou shalt speak English.** The bouncers will think you're easy money.
4. **Thou shalt not look intimidated.** Play it cool and act like you've been there before.
5. **Thou shalt reserve a table in the club restaurant beforehand.** It's the surest path to the dance floor after dinner.

→ **Café Populaire** ★★ Whatever your age, the "Pop," as locals fondly call it, is one of Bordeaux's most popular nightspots. On weekends, anyone lucky enough to find a half meter of space near the oval bar (beer 4€) just might defend it to the death. But as the old proverb says, "The more the merrier." If you smile and shout "pardon" when you step on your neighbor's foot, everything should go swimmingly. The music is 1980s pop and disco. If you get there early enough, you can eat some decent French cuisine for around 25€. *1 rue Kleber.* ☎ *05-56-94-39-06. Credit cards accepted.*

MTV (Best ❂) **Calle Ocho** ★ When the rhythm starts to sway and you're hip to hip with a mysterious Latino (or at least a salsa fan), this vibrant little club, bedecked in yellowing posters and neon lights, will set your pulse racing and your bottom swinging. Crowds of young party animals congregate around all three of the bars to slurp on Bordeaux's finest mojitos (4.50€) and eye up future dance partners. Free salsa classes make sure that everyone looks good on the dance floor (Thurs). You can pocket the rhythm and practice back at home with one of Ocho's two compilation albums, for sale on site. *24 rue Piliers de Tutelle.* ☎ *05-56-48-08-68. www.calleocho.fr.*

→ **Manga Sushi Club** Next door to Calle Ocho, this trendy new bar looks more like something out of a Pokémon comic book than a Bordelaise hot spot. Cute Japanese cartoon folk cover most of the wall space, and you need a degree in looking cool to get served at the bar, but all the preening and hair flicking will be worth it once you've tasted the house cocktail, "Lynchao." Made from Lychees, Soho, tonic, lime, and ice, it is a party pick-me-up to beat all others. Music here is varied with a funky mix of R&B, Japanese hip-house, soul, rap, and the odd big-name DJ. *20 rue Piliers de Tutelle.* ☎ *05-56-90-15-83.*

CLUBS & LIVE MUSIC VENUES

FREE ➔**Le Shadow Lounge et le White Garden** ★ Coming to this select club is a bit like admitting that you're a fashion victim. But dressing up like a mon-eyed youngster from Bordeaux when you're actually a foreign tourist can be great fun. The decor is elegant and refined right down to the marble toilets. Thursday nights are pop-rock; on Fridays a new evening called "Seven Stages" hosts seven DJs and their seven different sounds; and Saturday nights feature live jazz, soul, funk, and house. *5 rue Cabannac.* ☎ *05-56-79-36-93. www.leshadowlounge.com.*

➔**Lounge Velvet** Settle into one of the cocoon-shaped chairs at Lounge Velvet, sip a house cocktail, pontificate over the interesting artwork, and you'll fit right in at this relaxed, trendy gay bar. It's easy to chat with locals here, and the barmen offer you sweets. Happy Hour runs from 7pm to 10pm on Tuesdays. Some nights ring out to the sound of electro house. There's no cover; cocktail are 6.50€; beers are 3.50€. *6 rue Louis Combes.* ☎ *05-56-51-00-79. www.levelvet.net.*

Sightseeing

On your marks, get set, go! There is so much to see that you'll have to plan your days with Olympic precision. Walking around Bordeaux is like traveling through time. You can jump from the 18th to the 19th century, hop back to Roman times, and skip forward to the 21st century just between your hotel and the local cafe. For more targeted sightseeing, try a museum, shop until you drop, or attend the theater or an art gallery. When all that gets to be too much, picturesque public gardens and the Garonne River offer a welcome change of scenery from the urban landscape.

PUBLIC MONUMENTS

➔**Hôtel Frugès** ★ It's not really a tourist "sight," per se, but you can visit it upon special appointment. And if you're into Art Nouveau and the Orient, it's well worth the detour. What is it, you ask? Well, it's one of Bordeaux's few architectural hybrids, built between 1913 and 1927 in an attempt to break with the harmonious (but repetitive) look of the city's buildings. And, by jove, it works. The bold, intricate characteristics of Art Nouveau mix awe-inspiringly well with Oriental details, and nowhere better than in the mosaic bathroom. Designed by the owner, Henry Frugès (a famous indus-trialist), the loo is an ostentatious explo-sion of color and floral design that makes you want to rip all your clothes off and bathe like a king. *63 place des Martyrs.* ☎ *06-07-60-09-55. Small admission fee. May and June by appointment only.*

➔**Palais Gallien** As time goes by only one thing is sure: Gravity is gonna get ya. Nothing can escape its greedy grips—not even a structure as well built as the Palais Gallien Roman amphitheater. Not much of it is left, but the bits that remain are enchanting. Saved in medieval times, thanks to locals who erroneously thought it was a palace that Charlemagne built for his wife Galiene (hence the name), it later became a haunt for 17th-century prostitutes, and then a stone quarry. Today it's the only Roman monument visible in Bordeaux and, for this reason, should be high on your list of stops. *Rue du Dr. Albert Barraud.* ☎ *05-56-00-66-00 for details. Admission 2.50€.*

FREE → **Place des Quinconces** ★★
Architects seemingly wanted to prove that bigger is better when they built this monumental, tree-lined expanse, creating the largest square in Europe. Apart from its size, place des Quinconces is famous for a humungous decorative fountain—a 43m-high (141-ft.) ode to the "genius of liberty" and the best metaphoric summary of French pomp and circumstance I've ever come across. On the river side of the monument, you can make out a proud cockerel (the symbol of France) plus a few representatives of history, justice, and eloquence. On the town side, three voluptuous women allegorize Bordeaux, the Garonne River, and the Dordogne. The fountain portrays the Triumph of the Republic alongside three little children who remind us that education and military service are obligatory. Bless their cotton socks!

FREE → **Pont de Pierre** ★★ Forget Oz! If you want to meet the wizard of wine, follow the redbrick road across the Garonne. The emblematic pont de Pierre is famous for its red brickwork (*pierre* meaning stone). Jutting out over the waters opposite the St-Michel quarter in Vieux Bordeaux, it's easily one of France's prettiest bridges. Commissioned by Napoleon in 1822, so that he could march his army across the river during his invasion of Spain, it is 500m (1,640 ft.) long. For many years, it was a toll bridge. National property since 1861, it's an illustrative part of Bordeaux's river life.

→ **Porte Cailhau** When you've got so much wine to protect, you need a few defensive gates. Built in 1495, the Porte Cailhau keeps ill-wishers out and still looks good enough, 500 years later, to draw well-wishers in by the droves. Like something out of a Hans Christian Andersen story, it offers today's visitors a panoramic view over the river from a height of 23m (75 ft.). *Entrance in place du Palais. No phone. Admission 2.50€. Daily tours 2–7pm.*

HIGHBROW HAUNTS

→ **Le Grand Théâtre** Built next to an old Gallo-Roman forum (now invisible), Bordeaux's theater and opera house is the brainchild of 18th-century architect Victor Louis, who decided to adorn his edifice with phallic Corinthian-style columns. Twelve statues top the facade; nine represent the muses, and three represent the goddesses Juno, Venus, and Minerva. Inside, the main staircase will impress you. It struck 19th-century architect Charles Garnier so deeply he modeled his Paris Opéra after it in 1862. Don't be surprised if visiting it during the day makes you want to come back at night and watch a show. Opera and anything baroque gets a good thrashing here, but contemporary works, classical dance, and hip-hop are also scheduled frequently to ensure that everybody can feel part of Bordeaux's intelligentsia. Tickets can be reserved online; expect to pay at least 35€ a seat, depending upon what's on. *Place de la Comédie.* ☎ *05-56-00-85-20. www.opera-bordeaux.com. For tours, call the tourist office* ☎ *05-56-00-66-00. Admission 5€; 3€ for travelers under 26.*

CHURCHES

Wherever you find authority you'll find religion, and Bordeaux—always a magnet

Bordeaux Sightseeing

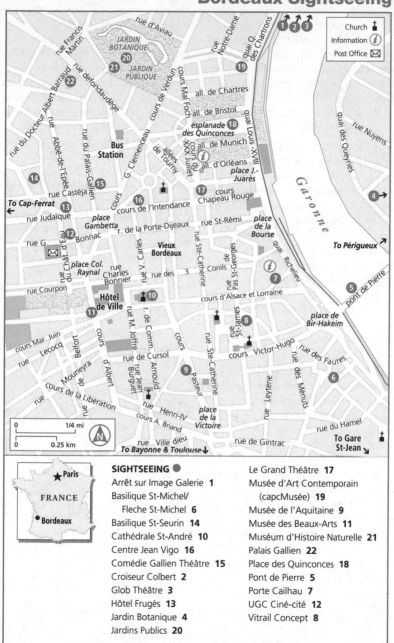

Church	✝
Information	ⓘ
Post Office	✉

SIGHTSEEING ●

Arrêt sur Image Galerie **1**
Basilique St-Michel/
    Fleche St-Michel **6**
Basilique St-Seurin **14**
Cathédrale St-André **10**
Centre Jean Vigo **16**
Comédie Gallien Théâtre **15**
Croiseur Colbert **2**
Glob Théâtre **3**
Hôtel Frugès **13**
Jardin Botanique **4**
Jardins Publics **20**

Le Grand Théâtre **17**
Musée d'Art Contemporain
    (capcMusée) **19**
Musée de l'Aquitaine **9**
Musée des Beaux-Arts **11**
Muséum d'Histoire Naturelle **21**
Palais Gallien **22**
Place des Quinconces **18**
Pont de Pierre **5**
Porte Cailhau **7**
UGC Ciné-cité **12**
Vitrail Concept **8**

for power, money, and ecclesiastical zeal—won't let you down on the church front. Entry is free, but you may have to buy tickets to visit the towers or the crypts. As a sign of respect you are expected to keep your shoulders covered inside. For information about the churches described below (except the St-André Cathedral), call the **Presbytère de l'Eglise St-Michel** (☎ **05-56-94-30-50**); most of the people who answer, however, speak only French.

FREE → **Basilique St-Michel** ★ This church oozes charm. It was constructed in stages from the 14th to the 16th century, and walking around and through it is like reading a history book that spans 200 years' worth of architecture. Its north door is crowned with shells, and the chapel is dedicated to St-James—including a central painting of *The Apotheosis of Saint James* (1631). The whole Basilica is worth seeing, but if your index finger is itching to snap some pictures, don't miss the Fleche St-Michel, across the street. *Place St-Michael. No phone.*

FREE → **Basilique St-Seurin** This is a real oldie. Its most ancient sections, such as its crypt, date from the 5th century. A section of porch displaying some capitals from the Romanesque era is left over from an earlier church. The *Pilgrims' Guide to Santiago de Compostela* (p. 293) advised pilgrims to visit the body of Seurin en route to see St. James in Spain. Look out for the 13th-century statue of St. James, with a staff in his right hand, by the South Door. *Place des Martyrs de la Résistance.* ☎ *05-56-93-89-28. Admission 2.50€. Church: Summer Tues–Sun 8:30am–11:30am, 2–6:30pm; off season Tues–Sun 7:30am–11:30am and 2–5pm. Crypt: June daily 2–7pm.*

FREE → **Cathédrale St-André** ★★ You must visit the largest and most ostentatious church in Bordeaux (124m/406 ft.

long by 18m/59 ft. wide). It is a gorgeous structure on place Pey-Berland, near the southern perimeter of the old town, made of two different sections: an early 14th-century Roman-style nave, and a High Gothic–style chancel, considered to be one of the most beautiful specimens of its kind. Construction began under English rule in 1300, but work was interrupted by a small Franco-British misunderstanding known as the Hundred Years' War. When the French finally chased out the English, building resumed, and the two existing parts of the edifice were linked together. Separate from the rest of the church is the 47m (154-ft.) **Tour Pey-Berland** (☎ **05-56-81-26-25;** www.monum.fr). Built in 1440, the belfry's spire was destroyed by a hurricane in the 18th century and replaced by a gargantuan gilded copper statue of Our Lady of Aquitaine. *Place Pey-Berland.* ☎ *05-56-52-68-10. Admission 5€ adults, 3.50€ guests under 25. Church: Jul–Sept daily 7:30–11:30am, 2–6:30pm; Oct–Jun daily 8:30am–11:30am, 2–5:30pm. Tower: daily 10am–5pm (to 6pm Apr–June and Sept; to 7pm July–Aug). Organ recitals are sometimes held July–Aug Thurs at 5pm.*

[MTV] Best ❂ → **Fleche St-Michel** ★ Built in 1472, it's the second-tallest stone tower in France (after the cathedral at Strasbourg), rising 112m (367 ft.) off the ground. Its 228 steps will give your thighs a workout they're likely to remember for the next few years, and the sweeping views from the top are the ultimate Bordeaux panorama. *Place Canteloup. No phone. Tower: June–Sept daily 2–7pm. Admission 5€. The rest of the year, unless you receive permission from the tourist office, you'll have to appreciate the tower architecture from the ground. July–Aug, every Fri 5–7pm, the bells in the tower are part of a free carillon concert that's audible throughout the neighborhood.*

M T V 🅤 Santiago de Compostela Pilgrimage

Whether you majored in history or skipped school, it is impossible to visit a French city without noticing the huge volume of religious buildings. Bordeaux is no exception, but what makes its churches more interesting than secular buildings is their historical link with a small Spanish university town called Santiago de Compostela. The cathedral there is said to be the final resting place of the Apostle Saint James, martyred by Herod. Throughout the Middle Ages, so many devout Christians trekked across France to pay homage at his shrine that Romanesque ecclesiastical architecture had to evolve (that is, get bigger) in order to accommodate the foot traffic. It's an amazing undertaking, given that enlarging one of these babies would have taken decades. France has around 800 of these medieval structures, and Bordeaux has three (all protected by UNESCO)—the **Saint-André Cathedral,** the **Basilique Saint-Michel,** and the **Basilique Saint-Seurin.** In 1140, a monk called Picaud immortalized the four official pilgrimage routes across France in one of the world's first travel guides, so today you too can follow the road to redemption and admire the ancient villages along the way. (For more information, contact Prieuré de Cayac; 257 A cours du Général de Gaulle, 33170 Gradignan, France; ☎ 05-56-97-22-30.)

MUSEUMS

➔ *Croiseur Colbert* ★★ Hold on to the helm! It's not everyday that you get to climb aboard the seafaring pride of the French nation. Weighing 10,600 tons and measuring 180m (590 ft.) long, the *Colbert* was France's most fearsome battleship; from 1957 to 1991, it was a major war deterrent and missile-launcher. Nowadays you can visit more than 75 rooms of this veritable floating town, including the old hospital, dentist's quarters, the bakery, hairdressers, back engine room, and the admiral's apartments. It's also the ultimate place from which to write home, thanks to the *Colbert* own postal agency—the only one of its kind in the world. The shop sells themed gifts, and the restaurant's regional cooking makes it a revered address for lunch (book ahead; ☎ 05-56-44-96-11). Just hurry here: The government wants to retire the ship for good. *Quai des Chartrons.* ☎ *05-56-44-96-11. http://colbert.croiseur.free. fr. Admission 7€ adults, 6€ students under 25. Oct–Mar Sat–Sun and school holidays*

1–6pm; Apr–May, Sept daily 10am–6pm (until 7pm weekends); June–Aug daily 10am–6pm.

MTV Best ☺ FREE ➔ **Musée d'Art Contemporain (capcMusée)** ★★ Less conformist and somehow snappier than equivalent museums in Paris, Bordeaux's contemporary arts temple is worth a stop whether or not you follow current art. Housed in an old harbor warehouse, its tall walls and lofty vaulted ceilings provide an awesome space for both permanent and temporary collections from the 1960s onward. More than 600 works by 100-plus artists are a permanent fixture, including French painting from the '70s and '80s, and myriad audio-visual exhibitions and eerie projections. On the way in, look out for the rows of leaflets on your left. Here you can pick up a useful brochure called *Dans les Musées de Bordeaux,* which lists the city's major temporary exhibits. You should also stop in the museum's buzzing roof cafe (p. 284), the latest hangout for those wanting to see and be seen. *7 rue*

Speak Softly & Carry a Big Stick?

Ever wondered why French baguettes are long and thin? The answer lies in Napoleon's pants. Well not exactly in *his* pants but in his soldiers'. When he invaded Russia, he knew that the winter would be long and hard, and troops would need extra space in their knapsacks for clothes. The bread they carried was too bulky, so he ordered it made in the shape of a sausage, so soldiers could insert it down their trouser legs and attach it to their socks. The baguette may have been a stroke of genius, but the invasion of Russia definitely was not, and soon the few surviving soldiers were sent home, heads down, their bread between their legs.

Ferrère. ☎ *05-56-00-81-50. www.bordeaux.fr. Free admission to permanent collections; temporary collections 5€ adults, 2.50€ students. Tues–Sun 11am–6pm (until 8pm Wed); closed bank holidays.*

FREE ➜ **Musée de l'Aquitaine** ★
History buffs: Don't miss this jewel in the crown of regional archaeology and ethnology. The Aquitaine museum follows the history of the Bordeaux region from prehistory to the 21st century via eight distinct sections: Prehistoric, Gallo-Roman, Medieval, Renaissance, 19th century, 20th century, ethnology, and iconography. Highlights include a magnificent 14th-century window in the form of a rose and Ossip Zadkine's 20th-century angular statue of Bordeaux-born François Mauriac, one of France's greatest writers of the 19th and 20th centuries. *20 cours Pasteur.* ☎ *05-56-01-51-00. www.bordeaux.fr. Free admission to permanent collections; temporary collections 5€ adults, 2.50€ students. Wed–Mon 11am–6pm.*

➜ **Musée des Beaux-Arts** ★★ France has a lot to thank Napoleon Bonaparte for: state schools, baguettes (see "Speak Softly & Carry a Big Stick?" above), the occasional war against neighboring countries. As if all that wasn't enough, he democratized culture by opening 15 national museums, including this one. It must be said that

Bordeaux's Beaux Arts museum (fine arts museum) is particularly attention-grabbing, thanks to an outstanding collection from the 15th to the 20th centuries, with works by Perugina, Titian, Rubens, Veronese, Delacroix, and Marquet. All are displayed with a great sense of space, allowing you room to discover the paintings up-close and personal. *20 cours d'Albret, Jardin du Palais-Rohan.* ☎ *05-56-10-20-56. www.culture.gouv.fr/culture/bordeaux/index.htm. Admission 4.50€ adults, free for students. Wed–Sun 11am–6pm.*

FREE ➜ **Muséum d'Histoire Naturelle**
You may not have traveled all the way to Bordeaux for a lesson in 200-year-old taxidermy, but this National History museum has charms somewhat more palpitating than stuffed animals—well, almost. Exhibitions trace the history of living things, from the dinosaurs onward; collections feature vertebrates, invertebrates, fossils, mollusks, and a host of other delights that once walked, swam, flew, or slid across Mother Earth. Outside, you can admire the architecture of the building (constructed in 1778 for the parliamentarian Nicolas Lislelerme) from its stately public gardens. In case hunger strikes, the museum has a little snack bar that sells basic refreshments. *Hôtel de Lisleferme.*

Art Happenings

In light of Bordeaux's many fountains, harmonious architecture, and trimmed gardens, you may expect the art scene to be equally pruned. But it's not. Although various galleries show old rugs, china, 16th-century decorative art, and landscape paintings, it's not all still lifes and fogie fodder.

UNEXPECTED GALLERIES   Admit it—you've gazed up at so many stained-glass windows during your whirlwind tour of French churches and cathedrals that they're all looking the same. Well fear not as you can now see how they're made at **Vitrail Concept** (24 rue St-James; ☎ 05-56-51-32-80; free admission; Mon–Fri 9am–noon and 1–6pm). It's a workshop and gallery where artists create new and repair old stained-glass art. Chat with the restorers about the contrasting styles from then and now and how the materials have changed. **Arrêt sur Image Galerie** (Hangar G2, Quai Armand Lalande; ☎ 05-56-39-06-21; www.arretsurimage.com; Mon–Sat 2:30–6:30pm), in the redeveloped Bassin à Flots complex, exhibits all the big and up-and-coming regional names in contemporary art. The emphasis is on collage, photography, sculpture, and engravings.

PERFORMING ARTS   In the Gambetta neighborhood, **Comédie Gallien Théâtre** (20 rue Rolland; ☎ 05-56-44-04-00; www.comediegallien.com; tickets 17€, 15€ reduced, 9€ students, 17€ on Sat) stages creative French comedies and stand-up comedians (a manifestly Anglo-Saxon form of comedy that the French have only just tapped). You'll have to understand French, though, without the help of subtitles. The same goes for Bordeaux's avant-garde performing arts center, the **Glob Théâtre** (69 rue Joséphine; ☎ 05-56-69-06-66; www.glob-theatre.net; tickets 12€, 8€ reduced; shows always start at 9pm), with off-the-wall contemporary performances that often push the boundaries of visual theater. If your French is spotty, opt for a dance or music performance—equally wacky, but comprehensible.

FILM   **Centre Jean Vigo** (6 rue Franklin; ☎ 05-56-44-35-17; www.jeanvigo.com; first session 2:15pm daily; admission 3.80€; Mon and Wed and for students, 4.60€ full-price; no credit cards) shows only original-version films in theme or director-based seasons, including big box-office hits, classics, and international cinema from *Blair Witch* to Hitchcock to Tatsumi Kumashiro. Every so often the cinema hosts lectures before the film, and once a year (usually late May to early June), they turn back the clocks to the era of silent movies with live musicians.

Just want to veg out on a movie that has no cultural significance whatsoever? Go to the 15-screen **UGC Ciné-cité** (13–15 rue Georges Bonnac; ☎ 08-92-70-00-00; first session 11am; 8.50€ adults, 6.50€ students) in the center of the old town. Sometimes they show both French and original versions, but no matter the language you choose, Jim Carrey will always pull the same stupid faces.

Jardins Publics. 5 place Bardineau. ☎ 05-56-48-26-37. www.bordeaux.fr. Free admission to permanent collections; temporary collections 5€ adults, 2.50€ students. Mon and Wed–Fri 11am–6pm; Sat–Sun 2–6pm; closed bank holidays.

Playing Outside

Bordeaux's only playgrounds are the **Jardins Publics (public gardens),** north of the esplanade des Quinconces (access cours de Verdun; daily 8am–8pm; until 6pm winter), and the remarkable **Jardin Botanique (botanical gardens;** access quai des Queyries; ☎ 05-56-52-18-77; daily 8am–8pm; until 6pm in winter), on the opposite side of the river. The public gardens, around since the 18th century, are a draw for families with small kids who come to feed the beautiful swans and dirty their designer clothes on the climbing frames and swings. If such a picture of urban harmony leaves you begging for something less contrived, head over to the Botanical Gardens whose innovative design garnered them a 2005 display at New York's MoMA. Much more interesting in terms of flora, they contain thousands of varieties (including several carnivorous species in the futuristic greenhouses) and have gorgeous views over the quays. On the second Saturday and last Sunday of June, July, and August, sign up for a free guided tour (meeting point: allée Jean Giono quai de Queyries; ☎ 05-56-52-18-77; 10am).

I know, I know; when it comes to wine, I sound like a stuck record, but if the weather is fine, there is no greater way to befriend the great outdoors than walking through the vineyards along the Garonne. The tourist office runs a great rambling tour every Sunday from May to October, which will take you into the **Entre-deux-Mers** region (east of Bordeaux) where you'll visit two properties, go tasting, and picnic on regional produce (reserve via tourist office; ☎ **05-56-00-66-00;** www.entredeuxmers.com; meeting point: Lestiac church; 19€). If you're up for more sporty activities, you should check out **www.entredeuxmers.com** for several cycling tours as well as horseback riding and weekend breaks in the region.

Shopping

If you want old stuff, concentrate your search around **rue Bouffard, rue des Remparts,** and **rue Notre-Dame,** where you'll find a market area known as **Village Notre-Dame** (☎ 05-56-52-66-13 or 05-56-79-01-95), housing all sorts of unusual ye olde shoppes.

For fashion, go to the couture quarter around **place des Grands Hommes** or the **cours Georges-Clemenceau,** with its many upscale, trendy, and classic emporiums. The greatest concentration of shops is on **rue Ste-Catherine,** the longest pedestrian street in France, and **rue des Trois Conils.** Together they have more than 100 boutiques, ranging from the most luxurious to the cheapest, and the **St-Christoly shopping mall,** with plenty of popular French brands.

If your euros are weighing you down, spend them in the **Galerie Condillac** (24 rue Condillac; ☎ 05-56-79-04-31), a classy arthouse that specializes in mostly local artists who paint with strong and vibrant colors. Or for an expensive sugar rush, head to **Cadiot Badie** (26 allées de Tourny; ☎ **05-56-44-24-22**), where the specialty for many decades has been sinfully flavorful chocolates, chocolate truffles, and pralines.

If you want to go home with a bag full of French CDs, you can't do better than at **FNAC** (50 rue Ste-Catherine; ☎ **05-56-00-21-30;** Mon–Sat 10am–7:30pm; credit cards accepted). It might be a chain, but it'll have everything you need to get to grips with the mainstream French music scene.

In the area surrounding rue Ste-Catherine, you'll find pharmacies, small grocers, and other conveniences. For a bigger shop, head to **Auchan** (☎ **05-57-81-74-62**) in the **Centre Commercial Meriadeck** near place Gambetta, which literally sells everything you can think of. Should you wish to tempt the culinary daredevil in you, have lunch at the deli counter and try those snails.

Whether you're a guy or a gal, if you're looking to revive tired tresses, **Toni & Guy** will give you a kick-ass look for around 50€ (114 cours d'Alsace et Lorraine; ☎ **05-56-81-00-50**; www.toniandguy. com). The same goes for **Le Petit Salon** (38 rue du Pas St-Georges; ☎ **05-56-44-54-02**) where stylists snip away to the beat of loud electro-funk. It's the ultimate place for a French haircut.

Store hours are another thing. Bordeaux is in the south, where shops often close for lunch, although there's no hard and fast rule. When the FERME sign is up, slink off to a restaurant for a couple of hours, and then max out your credit card again after 2pm. Just one word of warning: August is quiet here, so some shops may close for a couple of weeks at the start of the month.

CLOTHING & ACCESSORIES

➡**Be You K** ★ Be You K is a subtle play on words to highlight a Franco-British connection that lends a markedly spirited and multicultural flavor to the clothes in this fashionable boutique. Clothes range from denim with unusual cuts and washes, to more feminine, floaty numbers that tastefully clash colors and textures to create a hodgepodge of utterly wearable yet unconventional outfits. *1 rue de la Merci.*

☎ *05-56-52-49-31. Credit cards accepted. Mon–Sat 11am–7:30pm (from 1pm Mon).*

➡**Friperie Docks Caviar** Probably the only place in town to sell T-shirts saying "My girlfriend sucks," this hip outfitter attracts a wild crowd. The concept is simple: You mix 'n' match authentic vintage wear (a real '60s mod jacket, say) with modern retro brands (Pepe Jeans, Doc Martens, and Converse trainers), then throw in the occasional Hello Kitty or Porn Star T-shirt for good measure. *183 rue Ste-Catherine.* ☎ *05-56-91-69-56. Credit cards accepted. Mon–Sat 10:30am–7:30pm.*

➡**IDK Lé** ★ Lets' face it, girls, French women have a reputation for being snazzy dressers. But if you ask me, it's all in the accessories. Give a chick some heels, a matching handbag, and some chunky jewelry, and she'll look sassy whether she's in Chanel or family hand-me-downs. In Bordeaux, IDK Lé is the ultimate accessory purveyor—with every bit of budget bling a young woman could desire. Once you get past the shining trinkets, head for the shoes, and then choose a brightly colored bag to set it all off. Prices range from affordable to splurge-worthy. *19 rue du pas St-Georges.* ☎ *05-56-79-25-18. Credit cards accepted. Tues–Sat 10:30am–7:30pm.*

➡**Sapasousakas** Any self-respecting bloke should have at least one item from this urban-chic label whose clothes, mostly cotton T-shirts and slacks, stand out thanks to quirky details and first-rate cuts. Loud bags, wild sneakers, must-have men's jewelry, and hats top off the look with a zing that has made this young Bordelais brand the talk of many a French town. Buying here won't break the bank either, with plenty of goods from between 30€ and 120€. *11 place du Parlement.* ☎ *05-56-44-77-52. www.sapasousakas.com. Mon 2–7:30pm; Tues–Sat 10am–7:30pm.*

Bordeaux Street Parties

Bordeaux hosts festivals and special events year-round, but these are the principle biggies. For a full list and further details, contact the **tourist office** (☎ **05-56-00-66-00**).

→ The **Carnaval des Deux Rives** is a massive street music festival partly organized by the CAPC art museum with rock, rap, techno, traditional Basque music, and anything else that gets the crowds moving. Late February to early March.

→ **Fête le Vin,** Bordeaux's 4-day wine festival (www.bordeaux-fete-le-vin.com), draws hundreds of producers for wine-tasting and regional food, in the esplanade des Quinconces. Late June to early July.

→ The **Marathon du Médoc** is an addictive way to over-eat, over-drink, and convince yourself you're being healthy by running a 3-day marathon (www.marathondumedoc.com). Early September.

→ Just when you thought you'd tasted everything the region has to offer, they hit you with **Fête du Vin Nouveau.** This one features young wine, to be drunk straight away. Late October.

→ **Wap Doo Wap** If the underground is your playground (or you're in Bordeaux over Halloween), you'll love the alternative clothes in this unconventional little boutique. They cater to the punk, Gothic, cyber, and electro market with an eclectic mix of clothes that combine the occasional bright color with (you've got it) black. There are plenty of kilts, corsets, black boots, and a whole pink and black polka dot range called Crazy Doll. *216 rue Ste-Catherine.* ☎ *05-56-94-67-24. Credit cards accepted. Mon–Sat 10:30am–1pm and 2–7pm (closed Mon morning).*

MUSIC, BOOKS & MEDIA

→ **Mollat** If you fancy French literature or an illustrated coffee-table book to help you recall your trip around France when you get home, you can't do better than at Mollat. A bookstore *par excellence,* it covers an encyclopedic range of subjects, holds regular signing sessions with authors and photography and painting exhibitions, and even distributes its own range of music. *15 rue Vital Carles.* ☎ *05-56-56-40-40. www.mollat.com. Credit cards accepted. Mon–Sat 9:30am–7:30pm.*

FOOD, WINE & LOCAL CRAFTS

→ **La Maison D'Artigua** The last place you may want to be seen is a shop selling tea-towels, aprons, and tablecloths, but when you've got presents to buy, your image has to take second place. Think how happy Aunt Virginia will be when she unwraps some fine Basque linen. Buying something here will undoubtedly win you brownie points with the old folks back home. *73 rue des Trois Conils.* ☎ *05-56-52-02-76. Credit cards accepted. Mon–Sat 10am–7pm.*

Angoulême: Cartoon Central

443km (275 miles) SW of Paris, 116km (72 miles) NE of Bordeaux; pop. 46,000

The old town of Angoulême hugs a hilltop between the Charente and Aguienne rivers. You could visit it on the same day as Cognac, but if you decide to stay somewhere

Angoulême History 101

Angoulême's desirable position—high on a plateau, near a major source of water—has caused more than one squabble over the centuries. Clovis (p. 750) was first to stake his claim on the town, when he robbed it from the Visgoths in the early 6th century, before the Normans got their sticky mitts on it in the 9th. Next in line, in 1200, was dastardly King John, who enlarged the English kingdom with a backhand stroke: He snuck in and married Isabella—heir to the Count of Angoulême and great granddaughter of Louis VI of France—when she was already betrothed to a French count. When King John died, Isabella returned to Angoulême and married Hugh X (part of the noble Lusignan family). When Huge XIII died in 1302 without an heir, Angoulême reverted to the French Crown. King François I raised it to the title of duchy in favor of his Mother Louise of Savoy in the 16th century, and the last duke ever to claim title over Angoulême was Louis-Antoine (Louis XIX), who died in 1844.

overnight, make sure it's here. The town looks deceptively quaint and contained by day, but come sundown, the Diesel jeans sneak out and youngsters prowl the streets like soma-crazed party loons. Being out in the sticks, Angoulême's nightlife has to cater to all ages, but that won't take the edge off your nocturnal escapade. Whatever your birth date, you can get around at least 20 bars without walking more than 200m (656 ft.), and dozens of restaurants are poised to ply you with regional wares.

Another cool reason to visit is for the likes of Tintin, Astérix the Gaul, and Lucky Luke the cowboy, demagogues of French comic strips. Their latest adventures not only sell faster than they roll off the presses, they decorate many buildings in town (ask the tourist office for a list of murals); and for 3 days in January, Angoulême metamorphoses into the site of the **Festival de la Bande Dessinée (International Comic Festival),** the centerpiece of which is the **Centre National de la Bande Dessinée et de l'Image** (**CNBDI;** see p. 301). During its run, cartoon artists from around the world gather to present examples of their work and lecture about their art. For more information, contact the festival (☎ **05-45-97-86-50;** www.bdangouleme.com), **CNBDI** (☎ **05-45-38-65-65;** www.cnbdi.fr), or the tourist office (see below).

If two-dimensional heroes don't get your pulse racing, it's still worth stopping here to see the St-Pierre Cathedral, with its Romanesque-Byzantine facade, and the 19th-century Town Hall, with its 13th- and 15th-century towers. The Rampart walk yields views that stretch over the hills flanking the River Charente almost 75m (246 ft.) down below. For something more hip, check out the program at **La Nef,** Angoulême's hottest concert house.

GETTING THERE

Twelve regular **trains** and 8 to 10 TGV trains (55 min.) run daily from Bordeaux. From Paris's Montparnasse Station, there are seven daily TGV trains (2 hr.). For train information and schedules, call ☎ **36-35. Cartrans,** place du Champ de Mars, Angoulême (☎ 05-45-95-95-99), runs eight **buses** per day between Cognac and Angoulême. The trip takes 1 hour and costs 8.25€ each way. If you're **driving** from Bordeaux, take N10 northeast to Angoulême.

TOURIST OFFICE

The **Office de Tourisme** is at 7 bis rue du Chat (☎ 05-45-95-16-84; www. angouleme.fr). They have the usual information on local events and sites, as well as a map of the cartoon street murals, and they can help find accommodations.

ORIENTATION & SIGHTSEEING

For starters, Angoulême is not huge. You can easily walk across the whole *centre ville* in 15 minutes. The train station is at the bottom of a steep hill, so if you're lazy you can catch the line 2 bus (direction Fléac Sazaris, just out front), which will drop you off near the town hall in less than 5 minutes (get off at Hôtel de Ville). Tickets are sold on board for 1.20€ (buses run Mon–Sat around 7am–8pm every 25 min.). If you brave it on foot, follow avenue Gambetta until the Rampe d'Aguesseau, which leads to place Marengo, rue Hergé, and then to the town hall. Once in town, everything you need to visit (except the **CNBDI** and some street murals) is contained within the old rampart walls, so you really will be able to do it all on foot. **Place Francis Lovel** (in front of the neoclassical **Palais de Justice** law courts; see "Monuments & Churches," below) is a great central point for discovering most daytime and nighttime places of interest. A pretty fountain of sea-serpents gracefully snorts water from their noses, and three cafes provide ample choice for breakfast, lunch, or dinner. **Vieil Angoulême (old town),** spreads out from around **St-Pierre Cathedral.** It's a cute residential area that could be likened to a Disney village, were it not for the blatantly *authentic* medieval buildings. But don't say that to a local if you value your life or your good looks!

Monuments & Churches

➜ **Cathédrale St-Pierre** ★★ One of France's most startling examples of Romanesque-Byzantine style, this stunning structure was begun in 1128 and restored in the 19th century. Flanked by towers, its facade boasts 75 statues, each in a separate niche, representing the Last Judgment. The 19th-century architect Abadie Junior tore down the north tower, and then rebuilt it with the original materials in the same style. (Abadie was also the light behind the Sacré-Coeur in Paris; see p. 111.) Inside, you can wander under a four-domed ceiling and try to stand in the spots of natural light that project through the windows when the sun shines. *4 place St-Pierre.* ☎ *05-45-95-76-02. Mon–Sat 8am–7pm; Sun 9am–6:30pm.*

➜ **Hôtel St-Simon** When you're passing down rue de la Cloche Verte, pop your head around the archway at number 15 and you'll see an awe-inspiring Renaissance facade. The Hôtel St-Simon was built in the first half of the 16th century by the Souchet family, and served for years as the region's contemporary art foundation. The latter has closed down, and there's a lot of hand-wringing over what to do with the building. Let's just hope they don't replace it with iron and glass! *15 rue de la Cloche Verte. No phone.*

➜ **Les Halles Covered Market** Sometimes you have to wonder why people tear down old buildings. I supposed it would have been hard to convert a medieval fortress into a covered market, but imagine if they'd pulled it off. Instead, they built an iron and glass structure in 1886. It's not bad looking really, and the market itself is a sheer delight for the senses, but you can't help but wonder "what if." In any case, you can salivate over all the wonderful fresh produce, including some of the area's most delicious cheeses made by *fromager* extraordinaire, Jean-Louis Bouyer at La Ferme Charentaise (☎ **06-61-41-95-16;** Tues–Sat 7am–1pm, and Mon in July).

➔ **L'Hôtel-de-Ville** ★ Place de l'Hôtel de Ville is the hub of town, easily recognizable thanks to the unexpected appearance of the town hall, which looks more like a castle than an administrative building. It was erected from 1858 to 1866 on the site of the palace of the ducs d'Angoulême, where Marguerite de Navarre, sister of François I, was born. All that remains of the palace are the 15th-century Tour de Valois and 13th-century Tour de Lusignan (*merci,* Hugh X and Hugh XIII), which look attractively incongruous next to the stately Napoleonic architecture elsewhere. *Place de l'Hôtel de Ville.*

➔ **Palais de Justice** The law courts here are out of bounds unless you're a lawyer or a criminal, but don't go stealing baguettes so you can see the inside. A picture of neoclassical tranquillity from the outside (the sun-craving pigeons certainly love it), it was built in 1826 by Mr. Abadie Senior (you guessed it: father of Abadie Junior) and makes a pretty backdrop for slurping espresso in the shade of an elm tree. *Place Francis Louel.*

Museum & Art Scene

➔ **Centre National de la Bande Dessinée et de l'Image (CNBDI)** ★ As the European capital of the cartoon industry, with strong historic and creative links to many of the pop-art and cartoon themes that are part of the French cultural experience, Angoulême needs a focal point. And this is it: a museum devoted to famous cartoons and their creation, cum cafe, library, and unique bookshop. Droves of young creative types flock here for insights into the

entertainment industry, Internet access (free with an admission ticket), and the annual cartoon summer-school organized by the museum for those trying to improve drawing and storyboard skills (see www. cnbdi.fr or contact the tourist office angoulemetourisme@wanadoo.fr for more info; prices start at 300€). The permanent collection is given over to the imaginary worlds of cartoonists. The giant, eerie cardboard decor makes you feel as though you've been sucked into a comic strip. The display of leaflets next to the cash desk at the entrance includes free magazines such as *Sortir,* with listings on concerts and events, and the program for La Nef, Angoulême's major music venue (see below). *121 rue de Bordeaux.* ☎ *05-45-38-65-65. www.cnbdi.fr. Admission 5.50€ adults, 3.50€ students. Jul–Aug daily 10am–7pm; Sept–June Tues–Fri 10am–6pm, Sat–Sun 2–6pm.*

➔ **La Nef** ★ If you crave live music, don't miss this concert venue, which is surprisingly happening for such a small town. Many of the latest regional, national, and sometimes international bands (Placebo staged a show here during their 2006 French tour) take center stage here at least five times a month. La Nef also houses recording studios, and every act supplies an MP3 sample for the website, so you can check them out before you buy a ticket. *Rue Louis Pergaud. Ticket and program info* ☎ *05-45-25-97-00, Tues–Sat 2–7pm;* ☎ *05-45-25-41-11 (info line). www.dingo-lanef.com. Access by car only: Follow signs to Angoulême Sud along the N10 and take the exit Hôpital de Girac/St-Michel. At the Hôpital de Girac roundabout, head for Angoulême Centre Ville, which puts you on the rte. de Bordeaux. At the next roundabout (look out for the Elf petrol station), take the 4th exit, direction Marché de Gros—Centre de Grelet and La Nef.*

Room at the Inn

When all else fails, here are a few fail-safe lodging options: **Hôtel Terminus** (1 place de la Gare; ☎ **05-45-92-39-00**) is a cheap and cheerful place opposite the train station. Rooms run from 39€ a double. Its neighbor **Hôtel d'Orléans** (133 av. Gambetta; ☎ **05-45-92-07-53**) also offers clean and tidy lodgings (many with a balcony) from around 40€ a double. Nearer to the center is the **Hôtel Européen** (1 place Gérard Perot l'Epéron; ☎ **05-45-92-06-42**; www. europeenhotel.com; 59€–66€ double). Rooms have period features and air-conditioning. Near Les Halles, the **Mercure Hôtel de France** (1 place des Halles; ☎ **05-45-95-47-95**; www.mercure.com; 90€–140€ double; credit cards accepted) is a grand hotel on such extensive grounds that you can pretend you're a wealthy 19th-century landowner. This hotel features a restaurant and bar; in-room amenities include air-conditioning, TV, hair dryer, limited mobility rooms, minibar, and some nonsmoking rooms. Parking is available for 6.50€.

PLAYING OUTSIDE

→ **Croisières Angoumois** If you haven't been wine-tasting in Bordeaux—a near-criminal offense if you're in the region—redemption is nigh, thanks to **la Croisière de Bacchus,** a boat trip along the Charente river to some nearby producers of wine, cognac, and *pineau* (a mixture of wine and cognac). For something sweeter, choose the chocolate cruise **(Croisière Gourmande),** which floats you gently into cacao heaven, where you can watch regional masters at work in the **Chocolaterie Letuffe.** *Departure: Port l'Houmeau. For dates, contact the tourist office* (☎ *05-45-95-16-84). Croisière Gourmande 15€ (cruise time: 5 hr.). Croisière de Bacchus 13€ (cruise time: 3 ½ hr.).*

→ **Promenade des Remparts** For a breath of fresh air, walk along the unkempt path that flanks the site of the long-gone fortifications that once surrounded the historic core of Angoulême. The most panoramic section of the 3km (5 miles) walkway is the slice that connects the cathedral with Les Halles covered market. Every third weekend in September, a massive car rally takes place all around the ramparts. If you have any interest in

hotrods or vintage sports cars, it's a scene worth checking out.

SLEEPING

Being a wee place, Angoulême doesn't offer much choice in lodgings, and most hotels lie outside the main center. That said, there is something for everyone's budget. And, let's face it; you've either come for the nightlife, the cartoons, or as a stop en route to Cognac, so you'll hardly need more than a night here anyway. If you do pass by for the cartoon festival in January, make sure you book well in advance if you don't want to bivouac on the wild and freezing ramparts.

Hostels

→ **Auberge de Jeunesse d'Angoulême** ★ Angoulême's youth hostel is the cheapest option and also one of the best. You won't be slap bang in the town center, but you will be just 15 minutes away by foot (10 min. from the station), and you'll get the added excitement of sleeping on an island in the middle of the Charente. The building, an unabashed 1970s throwback, has the occasional groovy charm (white, Corbusier-like chairs in the front lot, for instance), and rooms are bright and clean with single bunk beds. Other facilities include parking, laundromats, kitchen, and cafeteria. The hostel also runs some trips out into the surrounding area. *Ile de Bourgines. ☎ 05-45-92-45-80. www. angouleme@fuaj.org. 12€ per person. Rate includes bed linens and breakfast. Bus: 7 and 9; stop Port de l'Houmeau.*

Cheap

→**Hôtel du Palais** ★★ You can't get more central than the Hôtel du Palais on the pretty place Francis Louvel. It is literally around the corner from most bars and restaurants so you can crawl straight into bed after your 1-night bender. The management is gradually renovating all rooms, but request one of the new ones, with bright walls and attractive curtains. One day they're getting an elevator, but until then you'll have to climb the creaky wooden staircase to slumberland. You can access the Internet (Wi-Fi in late 2007) in the lobby for an extra 12€. *4 place Francis Louvel. ☎ 05-45-92-54-11. www.hoteldupalais. angouleme@wanadoo.fr. 46€–75€ double. Amenities: Parking; Internet. In room: TV.*

EATING

Angoulême sizzles with waves of tempting smells that waft along the narrow backstreets, teasing saliva glands, and activating stomach acids. Don't fight nature—give in to one of these places.

Cheap

→**Angolo d'Italia** ★★ ITALIAN It ain't quite French, but it's a great spot for a change of taste and a step up from the cheap but unreliable pizza places down the surrounding streets. Gabriele the owner is from Rome, and her recipes are either her own inventions or typical Romana. The constant stream of locals is a sure sign that the penne is *molto bene!* A classic bellyfiller (concocted by Gabriele) is pasta served with tomatoes, Parma ham, and

Cognac. *43 rue de Genève. ☎ 05-45-90-51-74. Fixed-price menus 15€, 18€, and 20€–26€. Credit cards accepted. Thurs–Mon noon–2pm and 7:30–10pm.*

→**Balcon Paradis** ★ HEALTHFUL This is a relaxing nonsmoking hangout with an emphasis on healthy food and tea. Sink into a comfy wicker armchair upstairs, tap your index finger to the rhythm of contemporary jazz (Blues Beat Sensation gets regular air time), and admire the photography and paintings over brunch or a giant platter of cheese, meat, or smoked salmon. The terrace is small, but it's a great vantage onto the euphoric crowds that pass by on their way out for the night. Friday nights feature a hilarious quiz. You might not understand a lot of it, but it's a sure way to make friends, test your cartoon skills (there is a drawing competition), and score a free bottle of wine if you win. *14–16 rue Trois-Notre-Dame. ☎ 05-45-39-25-52. Brunch menu 8.40€–19€. Platters 6.50€–8.50€. Credit cards accepted. Tues–Sat 10am–7pm (until 1am Fri).*

Doable

→**Le Lieu-Dit** CONTEMPORARY FRENCH Locals frequent this place, despite its touristy location. Once you get past the aloofness of the efficient waiters, the bustling terrace will relax you with the lulling sound of cheerful banter and clinking crockery. The house specialties are brochettes of beef or chicken (served with masses of fries and salad), hung from a strange table contraption that resembles a medieval torture device. The interior is warm and cozy with dark wood, deep red walls, and zinc tables. Boys, be warned of the Turkish loo (a hole in the ground for you to pee into; see p. 108). Approach it with military precision to avoid the horrors of splash-back. *44 rue Genève/place du Commandant Raynel. ☎ 05-45-95-17-17. About 25€ for 3 courses. Credit cards accepted. Tues–Sat noon–3pm and 7–11pm.*

Splurge

➜ **La Ruelle** ★ ★ FRENCH This first-class restaurant in the oldest part of town is among Angoulême's best. Christophe Combeau and his wife, Virginie, serve brilliant classic French recipes with a modern twist. The best specialties include ravioli stuffed with confit of duckling, served with vegetable bouillon with herbs; oysters in puff pastry in red-wine sauce; filet of fried red snapper with polenta and star-fruit sauce; shoulder of lamb cooked with herbs and baby vegetables; and semi-soft warm chocolate cake served with coffee liqueur and orange essence. If that's not convincing enough, come to see the vestiges of a 17th-century house, still visible in the dining room's stone masonry and painted ceiling beams. *6 rue Trois-Notre-Dame.* ☎ *05-45-95-15-19. Reservations recommended. Fixed-price lunch 22€–50€; fixed-price dinner 28€–50€. Credit cards accepted. Tues–Fri noon–2pm; Mon–Sat 7:30–10pm.*

PARTYING

So you've seen the sights. Now retrace your steps and watch the party unfold. The coolest places are clustered in the narrow streets surrounding Les Halles covered market; these few are especially good.

➜ **Hacienda** Come here to get sizzled with a capital *S*. This hacienda has live bands, thronging crowds of rock types and rapsters, and what's that? An underwear dispensing machine by the bar? Yep that's right—one can never be too prepared! Beer goes for the lowly price of 2.20€, and you can grab a bite to eat if you need to soak up some excess liquid (daily special salads and dishes are around 8€). Festivities happen on two floors: The band plays in the lower part, and the upper mezzanine has a cast iron balcony overlooking the bar. *6 rue de Genève.* ☎ *05-45-39-08-95.*

➜ **La Girafe Café** With its surreal, tribal-themed bar with Dalí-like paintings, sculptures of African Giraffe women, and vividly painted table tops, this cafe is a favorite rendezvous for up-and-coming cartoonists. Mojitos (5.50€) are perfection in a glass, with just the right balance of sugar and mint, beer is cheap at 2.40€ a half, and the music is just rootsy enough that you can sit back in an old movie-theater chair and feel cut off from the rest of the world. *23 rue de la Cloche Verte.* ☎ *05-45-90-91-20.*

➜ **Le Café Chaud** ★ ★ The play on words in the name—*café chaud* means "hot coffee" or "sexy cafe"—befits this small, fantastic gay bar, known as the trendiest locale in Angoulême. It is the only place to hear a DJ on Friday and Saturday nights, and boy does he know how to splice the vinyl. House and house-tek pump into the street as a reminder that this is the place to be. Beer is dirt-cheap at 2:30€ a half. The house punch is even cheaper at 1.50€, and the owner keeps the punters in his bar over dinnertime with free platters of *saucission* (cured, salami-like sausage) and finger food. The nonsmoking section upstairs has an eclectic mix of modern art in a medieval setting and a romantic balcony area with rooftop views over Angoulême. *1 rue Ludovic Trarieux.* ☎ *05-45-38-18-24.*

➜ **Le Kennedy** Irish pubs in France rarely pull it off as well as Le Kennedy has with this bona-fide Irish beer temple. Leprechauns could be lurking in the nooks and crannies, you'll find yourself softening your Ts, and you'll half-think you're pissing in a pot of gold, with the specially imported Irish urinals. Okay, so there's no pulling the wool over your eyes, but believe me, the decor and the homely smell of old Guinness are the most authentic I've ever come across outside the Emerald Isle. A pint of Guinness will set you back 6€, fish and chips for hungry traditionalists are 7€, and when a live band isn't playing, you can

entertain yourself with darts, dominos, billiards, and Internet games (.50€ for the connection, then 2€ for every half-hour). *10 rue Tison d'Argence.* ☎ *05-45-94-12-41.*

Cognac

478km (296 miles) SW of Paris, 37km (23 miles) NW of Angoulême, 113km (70 miles) SE of La Rochelle; pop. 22,000

Ever noticed how the French have a habit of naming culinary specialties after the places where they were invented? Champagne is from Champagne; Brie cheese is from Brie. If Coca Cola had been a French invention the world would be drinking a sugary brown liquid called Atlanta. The reason I say this is that many visitors don't realize that the unassuming town of Cognac is a community and not just a drink. The world enjoys 100 million bottles of the stuff a year, and all of it

comes from here. Cognac from anywhere other than Cognac just ain't cognac. Clever proprietary buggers, the French.

The town itself has its charms: namely two beautiful parks (**Parc François-Ier** and **Parc de l'Hôtel-de-Ville**) and a 12th-century Romanesque-Gothic church, **Eglise St-Léger** (rue de Monseigneur LaCroix; ☎ **05-45-82-05-71;** free admission; daily 8am–6:30pm). But the real reason to visit is for the great Cognac bottlers **Martell, Hennessy,** and **Otard,** who will take you

Cognac History 101

Medieval Cognac was a prosperous, fortified river port for the salt and wine trade. The English and the French loved to fight over its wealth (big surprise) in struggles that were to become emblematic of the Middle Ages in this region. Luckily the feuding simmered down by the Renaissance, and Cognac enjoyed notoriety as a center of art and thought. During this time of political peace, François I—one of France's most important kings—was born, in the château de Cognac (now the **Otard** distillery), on September 12, 1494.

By the 17th and 18th century, many persecuted Huguenots with family ties in England and Holland had fled to the area, keeping the wine trade with northern Europe alive as the salt trade petered out. The only hitch was that wine traveled badly by sea, and so the merchants decided to "burn" the liquor—or, in other words, distil it. And thus was born cognac from Cognac.

But, the "drink of the gods," as Victor Hugo liked to call it, is not the town's only legacy. Three other geezers from Cognac made their mark on world history. First up is **Jean Monnet,** son of a cognac merchant (born 1888), who founded the European Union, along with his German partner Robert Schuman. **Louis Delage** (born 1884) was the motor-mind behind Delage automobiles, which were voted a mark of good (French) taste in the 1937 New York Universal Exhibition. And finally there's **Claude Boucher** (born 1898), who spent 6 years inventing an automatic glassblowing machine that would revolutionize the glass industry forever.

around their distilleries before plying you with liquor at the end of the tour.

While you're out and about, notice the gray film on the buildings around you. Cognac may be beautiful to drink, but it's not beautiful to make, and a black fungus that lives on the vapors released by the cognac factories has spattered many houses and warehouses. While the fumes discolor the brickwork, they also fill the air with sweetness. There's a silver lining to every black cloud of lichen spores.

Getting There

Cognac's rail station is just south of the town center. Seven **trains** per day arrive from Angoulême (trip time: 1 hr). For train information and schedules, call ☎ **36-35.** **Bus** travel is scarce and impractical in this part of France. **Driving** is a better option. The best route is along the A10 highway and the N141 east.

Tourist Information

The **Office de Tourisme,** at 16 rue du 14-Juillet (☎ **05-45-82-10-71;** www.tourism-cognac.com; July–Aug Mon–Sat 9am–7pm, Sun 10am–4pm; Jan–Apr and Oct–Dec Mon–Sat 10am–5pm; May–June and Sept Mon–Sat 9:30am–5:30pm), can advise on all the cognac houses and give information on the **Festival du Film Policier,** a 4-day explosion of crime films held in mid-March and early April (☎ **05-45-35-60-00;** www.festival.cognac.fr).

Orientation & Sightseeing

Whether you're visiting Cognac and Angoulême in 1 day or spending a day in each, head straight to the Cognac distilleries. The rest of the town makes for a picturesque stroll, but it's not a happening place. I'm not saying you'll get bored, but your presence may lower the average age by 20 years.

From the station, take avenue Maréchal Leclerc and turn right down rue Elisée Mousnier to place Martell (Martell Cognac tour is here); then follow rue Aristide Briand and look out for place du Canton on your left. At the place, take the Grande Rue to rue du Château, where you'll find the Château de Cognac and your first tipple at **Otard.** The whole journey should take 20 minutes.

➜ **Hennessy** Hennessy's tour is not as atmospheric as Otard's, but you do get to cross the Charente River by boat. On the Right Bank, the tour begins with an introduction to some of the techniques used in Hennessy's particular cognac-making process: the sophisticated double-distillation, the art of wine-making, and the lost art of barrel-making known as cooperage. The second half of the tour takes place on the Left Bank, in a new, state-of-the-art building where multimedia installations guide you through the company's rich heritage. Once they've whetted your appetite, they whisk you to the boutique for some slurping and purchasing. *1 quai Hennessy.* ☎ *05-45-35-72-68. www.hennessy.com. Tours last just over an hour and cost 6€ for adults over 16; under 16 free. Tours run daily Mar–Dec but frequency varies according to language and demand, so it's best to phone beforehand. June–Sept tours run 10am–6pm; Mar–May and Oct–Dec 10am–5pm.*

➜ **Martell** The oldest of the Cognac houses takes you on a voyage around its beautiful 18th-century mansion—or more precisely deep beneath its mansion, in the musty cellars where the cognac ages patiently for 6 to 8 years in oak demijohns. Oak is used in the aging process, because the tannin in the wood gives the brandy its golden hue. One of the most interesting parts of the tour is the blending room, where brandies from different origins are mixed to perfection. If you're lucky, before you taste Martell's amber elixir, you'll steal a glimpse of so-called "purgatory" and "heaven"—the rooms where for more than a century Martell has been aging its cognac in barrels. *Place Édouard-Martell.* ☎ *05-45-36-33-33. www.martell.com. Tours last an hour and cost 5.50€ adult. June–Sept daily 10am–5pm (from 11am at weekends). Apr–May and Oct, visits are at 10, 11am, 2:30, 3:45, and 5pm Mon–Fri, and noon–5pm weekends. In winter, tours are available by appointment only.*

➔ **Otard** ★★ This tour is tops. Not only is it the most informative and insightful of the brandy visits, it's also in the best building: the late-medieval and oh-so-majestic **Château de Cognac.** Once you've explored the castle and marveled at its different styles (parts of the château are appropriately baronial, and other sections are enormous, holding tens of thousands of bottles of cognac), you'll move on to a technical explanation of cognac production and the tasting—probably the reason you came here in the first place. There are six types to choose from, but one of the best is the **1775 Extra,** crafted from champagne *eaux-de-vie* in a separate cellar

Last Call

Two other châteaux are worth the detour: **Rémy-Martin** (domaine de Merpins, route de Pons; ☎ **05-45-35-76-66;** www.remy.com) and **Camus** (29 rue Marguerite-de-Navarre; ☎ **05-45-32-28-28;** www.camus.fr). If you're short on time and can't do a tour, **La Cognathèque** (8 place Jean-Monnet; ☎ **05-45-82-43-31**) is a good retail outlet that prides itself on having the widest selection from all the distilleries—though you'll pay for the convenience of having all the goods under one roof.

from the rest. It is best enjoyed neat or straight up, heated by the warmth of your hand. With a bit of luck (and imagination), you'll get a lovely lingering taste of dried fruit, honey, and tobacco. *127 bd. Denfert-Rochereau.* ☎ *05-45-36-88-88. www.otard.com. 1-hr. tours cost 5€ for adults, 2.50€ for students 12–18. Apr–June and Sept–Oct tours daily 11am–noon and 2–6pm; July–Aug tours Sun and holidays 11am–noon and 1:30–7pm; Nov–Dec Mon–Thurs 11am–2:30pm and 3:45–5pm, and Fri 11am–4pm; Jan–Mar by appointment only. Call the tourist office or the company several days in advance to check times, which rotate according to the number of visitors and availability of guides.*

Sleeping

➔ **Hôtel Héritage** ★★ You shouldn't need to spend a night in Cognac, but if you have a tipple too many and miss the train, you could do a lot worse than this audacious and surprisingly funky hotel. Was it possibly the cognac fumes that gave the owners their idea for the hallucinogenic color scheme? A lime-green bar, a red-and-purple dining room, and individually decorated bedrooms each more wacky than the next. What's more, it works brilliantly. The restaurant serves excellent French cuisine with a modern twist, and there's an adorable terrace for long summer nights (fixed-price menu 24€). *25 rue d'Angoulême.* ☎ *05-45-82-01-26. www.hheritage.com. 60€ double. Breakfast 6€. Credit cards accepted. Amenities: Restaurant; bar. In room: Wi-Fi.*

Eating

The restaurant at **Hôtel Héritage** (see "Sleeping," above) serves excellent meals.

➔ **Le Coq d'or** BRASSERIE This typical 1920s brasserie is Cognac's most famous restaurant, specializing in tasty regional seafood and sauerkraut 7 days a week from midday to midnight. Pick your dish blindly on the menu—it's all pretty good, whether you're a meat or a fish lover. *Moules frites* (mussels and fries) are a favorite, and locals flock here for the impressive house ice creams that come smothered in deliciously gooey chantilly. *33 place François Ier. ☎ 05-45-82-02-56. About 25€ for 3 courses.*

Ⓜ Best❾ St-Emilion ★★: Thank Bacchus You Made It

35km (22 miles) NE of Bordeaux, 550km (341 miles) SW of Paris, 150km (93 miles) S of La Rochelle; pop. 2,400

If Bordeaux is the city that Bacchus built, St-Emilion has to be his favorite holiday destination. And boy does he know how to choose his vacations. Set on a limestone plateau overlooking the Dordogne valley, it is surrounded by vineyards as far as the eye can see. Inside the town, ancient ramparts, UNESCO-protected monuments, a maze of cobbled streets, and steep stone stairways enchant visitors—and that's even before they've tasted any wine. While we're on the subject, prepare yourself for some *serious* tasting. The wine made in this district has been called "Wine of Honor;" British sovereigns nicknamed it "King of Wines," and with such a noble appellation you will be expected to use enlightened words such as *bouquet, aroma, legs,* and *caudilie* (the number of seconds the flavor of the wine stays in your mouth once swallowed; one *caudilie* is equal to 1 second). St-Emilion also maintains the unusual tradition of La Jurade, a society dedicated to maintaining the highest standard for the local wine and promoting and honoring it around the world. Each spring, the members (who look like Harry Potter extras with silk hats and scarlet robes edged with ermine) parade through town to attend a solemn mass, before pronouncing their judgment on the new wine from the apex of the **Château du Roi (King's Tower;** see below).

Macaroons are another St-Emilion specialty, and you should definitely try one or four. In fact, between you and me, the best way to enjoy them is to dip them in red wine. Yes, okay, it's a recipe I invented by accident when my macaroon slipped into my glass of St-Emilion, but everything happens for a reason, and you shouldn't knock it until you've tried it.

Getting There

Trains from Bordeaux make the 45-minute trip to St-Emilion three times per day (call ☎ **36-65**). **Citram** (www.citram.com) runs a **bus service** from Bordeaux, but its takes well over an hour and you have to change at Libourne (302 from Bordeaux [Quinconces] to Libourne, then 318 to St-Emilion). The only advantage to Citram is that by presenting your ticket at St-Emilion's tourist office you get a reduced rate for their excellent subterranean tour of the hermitage, ossuary, catacombs, and underground church (Eglise Monolithe). By **car,** take the N89/E70 toward Libourne, then the D670. From there the route is signposted.

Tourist Office

The **Office de Tourisme** should be the first place you visit. They organize most of St-Emilion's guided tours, including some excursions into the wine lands from

St-Emilion History 101

Who'd have thought that a Breton baker called Emilion would become a saint and then inadvertently give his name to one of the most famous wine colonies in the world? After leaving his family in search of religious piety, he joined the order of the Saujon monks in nearby Royan, but soon found his clerical social life too demanding. Withdrawing deep into the Combes forest (which formerly covered the area of St-Emilion), he found a cave with a natural spring and lived there alone until his death in A.D. 767. "What's so amazing about that?" you cry. Well, nothing, except that the cave is in the epicenter of St-Emilion (the town). It was here that St-Emilion (the man) is believed to have performed miracles, thus inciting fervent medieval Christians to build the houses and religious buildings you see around his home today. The local wine industry doesn't really have anything to do with the story as such, but it has adopted the appellation *St-Emilion,* and many of the wineries sell their wares exclusively in St-Emilion boutiques.

65€ per person. For outdoor types, there are also biking, horseback riding, and ballooning options (place des Créneaux; ☎ 05-57-55-28-28; www.saint-emilion-tourisme.com; daily 9:30am–12:30pm and 1:45–6pm; until 7pm June–Sept).

Orientation & Sightseeing

St-Emilion is the sort of place that takes your breath away—not just because it's utterly exquisite, but because it is so bloody steep. The medieval streets are so narrow and undulating that walking along them can feel like riding a roller coaster, which means that the best and only way to attack this open-air museum is on foot. St-Emilion is snuggled in a horseshoe shape between two hills, at the junction of which teeters a mammoth belfry looking out earnestly onto the vineyards beyond. From the outside it all looks solid as a rock, but on the inside, the rocks aren't as robust as you might think: The stone ridge is actually honeycombed with caves, St-Emilion's hermitage, catacombs, a chapel, and an underground **Monolithic church** (see "Monuments & Churches," below), placing tremendous strain on the sections

that hold everything up. The heart of the town lies beneath the Belfry in the medieval **place du Marché,** recently renamed **place de l'Eglise Monolithe.** Here you'll find plenty of shops and restaurants, and most other streets wind their way round to the square.

If you'd like a whirlwind tour around the surrounding vineyards and châteaux, you may have to put a paper bag on your head and let the dweeb in you shine through, because the mini–tourist train is *the* best way to take in the sights and learn about the various wines you'll be tasting in town. *Le Train des Grands Vignobles.* ☎ 05-57-51-30-71. *www.visite-saint-emilion.com. Departure is on the north side of the city by the ramparts and dry moat. Summer: 10:30, 11:15am, noon, 2, 2:45, 3:30, 4:15, 5, 5:45, 6:30pm. Call for winter hours. Admission 5€.*

MONUMENTS & CHURCHES

→**Eglise Monolithe** ★ This whopper is the largest underground church in Europe, carved by Benedictine monks during the 9th to 12th century. Three 14th-century bay windows mark its facade, and a 14th-century sculpted portal depicts the Last

Escalettes

You don't have to be a brainiac to see that St-Emilion is so steep in parts it could be used as a training ground for climbing Everest. But it is thanks to this natural gradient that the French have the word *escalier* meaning staircase. *Permettez moi* to explain: The medieval townsfolk created four sloping street sections covered with large, irregular granite stones to facilitate moving around the village. These were called *tertres,* and the stones used to build them were ballasts from the ships that had delivered barrels of St-Emilion wine to the English King via Cornwall in the 12th century. In order to link the *tertres* with the houses (built above one another because of the acute incline), they constructed a series of landings and steps known as *escalettes.* Over time the word changed into *escaliers,* thus giving birth to the modern French word for stairs (copied by the Spanish *escalera;* the Italian *scala;* and the Portuguese *escada*).

Judgment and Resurrection of the Dead. The church is 11m (36 ft.) high, 20m (66 ft.) wide, and 38m (24 ft.) long. It remains standing thanks to massive steel braces that evenly distribute the weight from the belfry up above. Don't worry, it's not about to fall on you; but you can visit it only as part of an organized tour (ring the tourist office for details), which will take you deep into the belly of the Benedictine catacombs, the 13th-century Chapelle de la Trinité, and its underground grotto—a site known as the Hermitage. St-Emilion reportedly sequestered himself there during the latter part of his life. *Place de l'Eglise Monolithe.* ☎ 05-57-55-28-28. *Tickets: 5.50€ adults, 3.60€ students. Tour: 45 min. from tourist office.*

You can visit two additional monuments without an organized tour. The first is the **Belfry** (*clocher*) of the Eglise Monolithe (see above). It rises on place des Créneaux, near place de l'Eglise Monolithe. Built between the 1100s and the 1400s, it's the second-highest tower in the La Gironde region, and for years after its construction was the only aboveground landmark that indicated the position of the underground church. You can climb the bell tower and take in the panoramic view daily between

9am and 6pm for 1€. To do this, go to the tourist office, where someone will entrust you with a key to the tower door in exchange for an ID card. (When you return the key, you'll get your ID back.) The second is the **Château du Roi** (☎ 05-57-24-61-07), founded by Henry III of the Plantagenet line in the 13th century. Don't expect a full-fledged castle. The tower was the first section built, and the construction that followed was either demolished or never completed. Until 1608, this building functioned as the town hall. From its summit, you can see as far away as the Dordogne. You can climb the tower (the procedure is the same as for visiting the Bell Tower) during daylight hours every day except Christmas and New Year's Day (10am–12:30pm and 2–6pm, to 6:30pm Apr–Sept), for 1€.

WINE-TASTING

"Spit, spit I said, don't swallow!" Ah, too late. Let's face it: If you have a craving for the red grape in its alcoholic form, St-Emilion is one liquid ecstasy you won't be able to taste without swallowing. But before you embark on the tasting adventure of your lifetime, here are a few things you should know:

Unlike other French wines, St-Emilion isn't endemic to the town that gave it its name. Nine communes are entitled to call their wine St-Emilion. What this means for you is that there is a wide variety of wines called St-Emilion for you to wash down your gullet. Each has its own special personality, but as a general rule, young wines tend to have aromas of black currant, raspberry, vanilla, and French toast. Older wines tend to smell more powerful, with a bouquet of leather and venison (don't go there!). Since the 1980s, St-Emilion has had eight noteworthy vintages: 1982, 1985, 1988, 1989, 1990, 1994, 1995, and 1998. Now you know, before you taste them in front of the experts.

➜ **La Grande Cave** ★★ From the tourist office, this is the first wine shop you'll come across and possibly the best. The experts here are so knowledgeable and passionate about the wines they sell that you may actually contemplate a career change before you leave the premises. They get all their bottles in directly from the surrounding châteaux and will open whatever you'd like to try—as long as you respect the unwritten tasters' etiquette (see the Nerd's Guide to French Wine & Culture). In short: If you try some things, buy something. *Place du Clocher.* ☎ *05-57-24-14-24. Daily 9am–7pm.*

➜ **L'Essentiel** ★★ Yeah baby, yeah! This swish, funky lounge all glitzed out in pink, lime green, and chrome gives a groovy edge—or should I say curve—to wine-tasting and cheese-eating. You could say that in such a medieval setting, this trendy zone is an *essentiel* breath of fresh air, with its rows of wines, champagnes, and spirits, and delectable cheese platters from 9€. If you're into table art, you'll also appreciate the madcap glassware used to serve the drinks, which incidentally won't break

the bank; wine by the glass starts at a mere 2€. *6 rue Guadet.* ☎ *05-57-24-39-76. www.lessentielvin.com. Daily 10am–10pm (sometimes later).*

Sleeping

It's unnecessary to spend a night here—unless you've had one too many.

CAMPING

➜ **Domaine de la Barbanne** ★ With so many bottles to buy, you might need to cut corners on lodging. Here, cutting corners means that you get to stay in the middle of vineyards, next to a heated pool, near a lake with canoeing and fishing opportunities. You'll need a car to get here (for a taxi call Robert Faustin; ☎ **06-77-75-36-64** or 06-10-34-41-23; www.taxi-st-emilion.com), but once you've pitched your excellent tent, you can take a shuttle bus to and from the village, so you don't need to worry about driving after tasting. Camping lots range from 16€ to 28€ depending on the season and the amenities in your tent, plus there's a launderette, a restaurant, mini-golf, a fitness trail, and bike-renting facilities. *Rte. de Montagne.* ☎ *05-57-24-75-80. www.camping-saint-emilion.com. Access: In Saint-Emilion, in the upper part of the village at the roundabout, take D122 toward Montagne. Le Domaine de la Barbanne is 2.5km (4 miles) on your right.*

HOSTELS

Finding a hotel in the center of St-Emilion—it being a chic kind of place—is nearly impossible on a budget. However, the **Auberge de la Commanderie** (2 rue Porte Brunet; ☎ **05-57-24-70-19;** www.aubergedelacommanderie.com; 65€–95€; closed Dec 20–Feb 24) is in a great spot with some of the cheapest rooms in town. It also has Wi-Fi access and a pretty view over the vineyards.

Eating

Decent grub is always on the menu to accompany the wickedly good wine in St-Emilion. The **Bistrot le Clocher** (3 place du Clocher; ☎ **05-57-74-43-04**; menus from 16€; daily for lunch and dinner) is across the street from the tourist office, in the shade of the monolithic church tower, with views over St-Emilion's red-tiled rooftops. Food is scrum-tiddly-umptious, with excellent confit of duck, lamb roasted in rosemary, and crèmes-brûlées to die for. Down the almost vertical *escalette* behind the place du Clocher sits the **Bar de la Poste**. They do delicious crepes and will make you chuckle with the nation's most badly translated English menu. Fancy some "believed ham," "salad with plugs," or "duck lobe"? How mouthwatering!

For some of those macaroons I mentioned, head to **9 rue Guadet** (☎ **05-57-24-72-33**), where Madame Blanchez has been lovingly baking her prizewinning versions for the last 40 years. Don't forget to dunk them in red wine.

The Bassin d'Arcachon & 📺 Best 🟡 Dune de Pilat

633km (302 miles) SW of Paris, 50km (31 miles) SW of Bordeaux, 230km (143 miles) S of La Rochelle; pop. 11,500

Go on, admit it. You've had your fill of old towns and wine (well, maybe not the wine), and now you're looking for some real action—adrenaline pumping action, heart-wrenching action—the kind that makes your Mom wail and your friends yell "Wow!" You want to see the waves and feel them crash beneath you. You want it? You got it, here on the silvery sands of the Bassin d'Arcachon. And as if that weren't enough, Arcachon is famous for its oysters, and there will be countless opportunities for you to sample morsels so fresh they'll practically be climbing up your esophagus to get out again.

Geographically speaking, the region is very special indeed. For starters, it is the only lagoon on the otherwise straight

Arcachon History 101

It's only 150 years old, which makes Arcachon a young whippersnapper by French standards. Had the nation's rich and powerful of the 19th century not nurtured an obsession for sea air and railways, it may well have remained an anonymous salt marsh. But the saline air here proved too strong a temptation for the Bordelaise wine folk and led to the construction of a new train line between Bordeaux and La Teste on the coast. In turn, a deep-water landing stage was constructed to the north of La Teste, linked by a road along the marshes. Several bricks later, posh villas cropped up along the road, and the town we call Arcachon was born. In the 1860s, it was already a popular summer resort, yet it surprisingly came into its own in the winter, when tuberculosis patients flocked to its shores in hope of respite or a cure (the fragrance of balsam from the surrounding pine trees was considered beneficial). Nowadays, visitors aren't coughing up anything but money, and the old tuberculosis-ridden area—now the disease-free Winter town—displays some of the prettiest and most sumptuous villas in Arcachon.

shoreline; it houses kilometers of salt marshes; it is a natural magnet for endangered birds that astonishingly flock to the **Teich Bird Sanctuary,** as if they know they'll be pampered there (see "Playing Outside," below); and it's home to the **Dune de Pilat,** the mother of all sand dunes and the largest one in Europe (see "La Dune de Pilat," below).

The town of **Arcachon** sprung up as a seaside resort in 1845, and many of its buildings date from this era. The rest, particularly along the Ville d'Eté (Summer town) seafront are classically more modern and ooze the sort of cool glamour you typically find on the French Riviera. What a pity residents here don't have the equivalent bank balances, right? Wrong! Arcachon bubbles with jet-setters, mostly retired but still filthy rich, who hop over to the lagoon's northern headland in Cap Ferret via luxury yacht. Back in the real world, what Arcachon loses in superficial bourgeoisie it gains in beautiful, activity-filled coastline. After playing hard, locals need to party hard, and at night sun-kissed bodies carry on the fun in a variety of nighttime hot spots, namely in the local discothèques or around forbidden campfires on the nearby beaches.

Getting There & Around

Trains running from Paris travel to Arcachon all day (usually via Bordeaux) and take 3 hours direct, and 4¹/₂ hours through Bordeaux. From Bordeaux, the trip takes 45 minutes, and trains leave roughly once an hour from 8am to 9pm (☎ **36-65**). By **car,** make the hour-long journey from Bordeaux via the A63 and then the A660 toward Arcachon (no toll). From Paris take the ever faithful A10 toward Bordeaux.

Once you've arrived, getting around town is quite simple. Just look for a blue line on the ground; where you find blue lines, you can flag down one of the free **Eho** buses (☎ 05-57-52-98-98), which run from the four sectors of town (see "Orientation & Sightseeing," below) to the station. Line A runs along Péreire and Moulleau beaches, Line B serves the Winter town and the Abatilles area behind the Parc Péreire, and Line C covers the Autumn town (Mon–Sat every 20–40 min. from 8:15am–noon and 3–6:55pm).

Tourist Office

The **Office de Tourisme** (esplanade Georges Pompidou; ☎ **05-57-52-97-97**; www.arcachon.com or www.bassin-arcachon.com) has masses of information on everything there is to do around the Bassin d'Arcachon, including some of the smaller towns not in this list. As Arcachon is more a summer destination, they will advise you on what's open should you visit off season, and their street map is detailed enough to keep you from getting lost. It's open October to March Monday to Friday from 9am to 6pm (until 5pm Sat), April to June and September Monday to Saturday from 9am to 6pm (Sun 10am–1pm and 2–5pm), and July to August daily from 9am to 7pm.

Orientation & Sightseeing

Arcachon is famous for its four seasons, but they have nothing to do with weather, Vivaldi, or five-star hotels. Arcachon's four seasons refer to its four districts: Winter, Summer, Spring, and Autumn—named after the seasons during which they historically come into their own.

Fittingly, the 5km-long (3-mile) **Summer town (Ville d'Eté)** is where you'll find the jetties, the beaches, the seafront promenades, and the boat trips out into the Bassin. If your pockets are bogged down with coins, head to the stunning Château

La Dune de Pilat ★★

Europe's Biggest Sand Dune

Somebody, somewhere, is running out of sand, and 📺 **Best** **La Dune de Pilat** just keeps getting bigger. It's already 105m (344 ft.) tall, 500m (1,640 ft.) wide, and 3km (5 miles) long, but dominant westerly winds keep piling on the layers, sculpting the dune with creamy-colored undulations so continuous you'll feel humbled by the experience. Needless to say the vista from the top—across pine forest and over the alternately inky blue and turquoise sea—is awe-inspiring. The climb calls for super human leg muscles, but where else can you get such a workout for zip? And if you're still *au fait* with your inner kid, try rolling back down, provided someone is there to catch you at the bottom. If standing on top of the dune isn't enough for you, release the beast with **Sand Fly** (☎ **06-63-21-27-82;** www.sand-fly.com), which runs parascending lessons from 80€ per person from nearby Camping La Forêt along the Route de Biscarosse. To get to the dune, the **611 Bus du Pyla** runs from June to September. You can catch the bus once an hour between 9am and 7:30pm from the train station. The last bus back from the dune to Arcachon is at 7:55pm. Tickets cost 2.70€. If all else fails try **Arcachon Taxis** (☎ **05-56-83-88-88**), which run 24/7.

Deganne. Now a **Casino,** it's laden with hungry slot machines ready to gobble up your loose change (163 bd. de la Plage; ☎ 05-56-83-41-44; www.partouche.fr; daily 10am–4am, until 3am Sun–Thurs; games tables open from 9:30pm).

Farther inland around the **Parc Mauresque** is the pine-lined **Winter town (Ville d'Hiver),** frequented by grandees from all around the world. Napoleon III, Elisabeth (Sissi) of Austria, and Europe's most highflying literati (and their dogs, obviously) sojourned here with or without TB. The resulting architecture looks miscellaneously grandiose with huge Swiss chalets, English cottages, Moorish villas, and neo-Gothic manors.

If you smell something fishy, you've probably come to the **Autumn town (Ville d'Automne),** which engulfs the port area and St-Elme's college, France's first-ever fisherman's school. The most easterly tip, la Pointe de l'Aiguillon, shows what pre-19th-century Arcachon would

have looked like with its authentic fisherman's houses.

The more temperate **Spring town (Ville de Printemps)** has three beaches (Arbousiers, Moulleau, and Péreire) and the relaxing Péreire park. It's quiet except in June, when the Péreire stretch of sand hosts a wild horse jumping competition, the **Jumping des Sables** (www.etrier-arcachon.com). **Les Tchanquetas**'s 4-day bash is also in June. Food, booze, and jazz are available in gluttonous portions to anyone willing to rumba past sundown (call the tourist office for details on both: ☎ 05-57-52-97-97).

Playing Outside

Cyana Diving School will let you bob along the bottom of the beautiful briny sea whatever your level of experience for around 60€ a day (Port de Plaisance, 74 bd. de la Plage; ☎ 06-09-73-25-22; www.cyana-arcachon.com). Budding parachutists can test their bladder control through **Wafou**. They'll hurtle you out of a moving plane strapped to a strapping instructor for 200€ a jump (12 av. Ste-Marie; ☎ **05-56-83-20-71**, 06-63-16-33-43, and 06-28-04-85-30; www.wafou.com). If you've got a licence, **Espace Gliss** (Arcachon Marine; ☎ **05-57-72-23-23**; www.espacegliss.fr) will hire you a jet ski for the extortionate price of 165€ a half-day (plus 1,000€ deposit!). For some ocean waves at a quarter of the price (albeit without an engine), try **Arcachon Kayak Adventure,** which runs excellent kayak tours around the whole of the Bassin, including one to the Dune de Pilat. Prices start at 25€ for a half-day (24 rue Alfred Dejean; ☎ **06-25-08-44-37**; http://arcakayakaventure.free.fr). Trek along the beaches on horseback at **Etrier Sportif** (25 av. Pierre Frondaie; ☎ **05-56-83-21-79**; www.etrier-arcachon.com). For biking, try **Dingo Vélos** (1 rue Grenier; ☎ **05-56-83-44-09** or 06-87-27-39-86; www.dingo-velo.com). If your **skateboard** is getting rusty, take it for a glide on the designated slopes at **Plage Péreire** (☎ **05-57-52-98-98**).

Finally if you're into chicks, go spot a few at the **Parc Ornithologique du Teich** bird sanctuary and nature reserve. There are several walks to follow, all with concealed observation points from which you and your inner voyeur can watch the rare and beautiful wild fowl without disturbing them (Le Teich; ☎ **05-56-22-80-93**; www.parc-ornithologique-du-teich.com; from Arcachon trains leave roughly once every hour from 8am and take 15 min.; daily 10am–6pm, until 7pm summer; tickets 6.80€).

Sleeping

CAMPING

➜ **Camping Club d'Arcachon** ★ If you're old enough to remember *Dirty*

The Scoop

Here's the scoop: The best ice cream in Arcachon is near the Moulleau beach. Two parlors split the territory: **Le Cornet d'Amour,** with unusual flavors such as tea, yoghurt, and *frommage blanc* (5 av. N-D des Passes, near the Moulleau Jetty); and **Les Délices Glacées** (257 bd. de la Côte d'Argent), renowned for its nougat flavor.

Dancing with Patrick Swayze, you'll love this campsite: the balmy odor of pine trees, log steps, sand that stays in your shoes for weeks, a pool with a rad slide, a restaurant, a bar—in fact forget Arcachon, just stay here. The site is a 20-minute walk from the main center, but they organize tours, and nowhere else—and I mean nowhere else—will rent you a pitch for this price. *5 allée de la Galaxie.* ☎ *05-56-83-24-15. www.camping-arcachon.com. 3€ a night. Closed Nov–Dec.*

DOABLE

➜ **Le Dauphin** You can't come to Arcachon and not stay in a typical villa, which is why you should book this place. Had Hansel and Gretel been French, they would have tried to eat the pretty orange and white gingerbread brickwork. Magnolias surround the building and fill the air with a sweet scent when they're in bloom. Rooms look slightly dated, but as you've probably noticed by now, that's par for the course in France. Proximity to the beach makes up for any other shortcomings. *7 av. Gounod.* ☎ *05-56-83-02-89. www. dauphin-arcachon.com. 52€–87€ double. Credit cards accepted. Amenities: Swimming pool. In room: AC, TV.*

Eating

CHEAP

➔ **Pizzeria Vila Roma** PIZZA There are some moments in life when only pizza will do. Should you get a pepperoni pang in Arcachon, this joint, with its *excellent* 16€ menus, should hit the spot without sinking your finances. The restaurant is smack bang in the Summer town between the casino and Eyrac Jetty. It has A/C but sells takeout for those who prefer the fresh salt air by the beach. *161 bd. de la Plage.* ☎ *05-56-83-54-54. Sept–June Thurs–Sun noon–3pm, 7–10:30pm; July–Aug daily Mon–Thurs 7–11pm, Fri–Sun noon–3pm and 7–11pm.*

DOABLE

➔ **Chez Yvette** ★ SEAFOOD Many of those freshly caught oysters I mentioned end up here. Yvette has been plumping up her regulars with seafood specialties for the last 30 years. In case shellfish don't do it for you, there's plenty more to choose from, including the most deliciously roasted turbot in town. And then there's the wine—some of the best bordeaux blancs in Arcachon. *59 bd. du Général Leclerc.* ☎ *05-56-83-05-11. Fixed-price menu 19€, a la carte 23€–50€. Credit cards accepted. Daily lunch and dinner.*

Partying

The Moulleau quarter (south of the Spring town) is chic and showy with plenty of trendy bars for you to crawl around. Otherwise three clubs share the night zone in the *centre ville:* **Le Scotch** attracts a moneyed and wannabe-moneyed crowd—but then what else do you expect from a casino? **Le Cotton,** near the port in the Autumn town, promotes '80s and house euphoria. **L'Escorida** is an intimate, underground club with cool French pop. Dress up if you want to get in.

If you're looking to boogie, head to the beaches south of the Dune de Pilat, where many youngsters camp out under the stars. Just be prepared to run for it if the cops come. And, whatever you do, *don't* light a flame near any trees.

📺 Best❾ **La Rochelle** ★★**: An Unmissable Port of Call**

467km (290 miles) SW of Paris, 161km (100 miles) N of Bordeaux, 145km S of Nantes; pop. 140,000

If you'd much rather embrace the winds off the sea than spend hours slathered in Banana Boat oil reading a romance novel, consider a trip to the port city of La Rochelle. It offers all the mystique of *la mer* without the trappings of a typical seaside resort. Although some tourist brochures try to hype its location as a beach bum's dream, its true charm lies in rugged fishermen and windy days, rather than sea, sex, sun, and ice cream. Nowhere is that more true than on the 📺 Best❾ **Ile de Ré** (www.iledere.com), the stunning island just off La Rochelle. Even into early summer, the salty winds tunnel through the narrow whitewashed streets, and push residents along on their bicycles, as they rush home with their catch from a local fish market (p. 325).

Back on the mainland, things are no less idyllic. La Rochelle's harbor is the biggest yachting center on the coastline, and the old port, framed by medieval towers, looks so picture perfect that you'll wish you'd paid more attention in art class. You may also notice that your average Rochelais (La Rochelle resident) isn't short of a centime or two. Like most of the Atlantic coast, La Rochelle is as chic as hell, and this is reflected in the types of shops you'll find,

La Rochelle

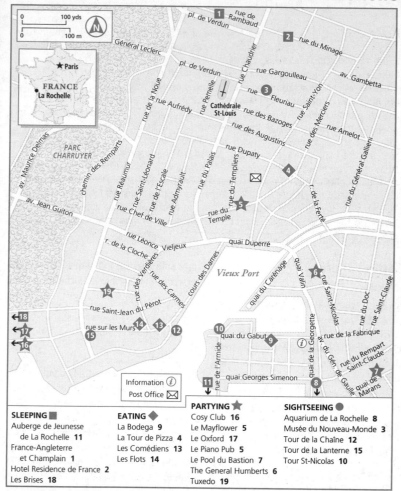

SLEEPING ■
Auberge de Jeunesse
  de La Rochelle **11**
France-Angleterre
  et Champlain **1**
Hotel Residence de France **2**
Les Brises **18**

EATING ◆
La Bodega **9**
La Tour de Pizza **4**
Les Comédiens **13**
Les Flots **14**

PARTYING ★
Cosy Club **16**
Le Mayflower **5**
Le Oxford **17**
Le Piano Pub **5**
Le Pool du Bastion **7**
The General Humberts **6**
Tuxedo **19**

SIGHTSEEING ●
Aquarium de La Rochelle **8**
Musée du Nouveau-Monde **3**
Tour de la Chaîne **12**
Tour de la Lanterne **15**
Tour St-Nicolas **10**

then swiftly avoid. That said you can sense an undercurrent of rebellion among the kids here—not so much in dress or musical tastes, but in their attitude of defiance toward the older locals, with their penchant for cheesy cover bands and brightly colored scooters.

Don't forget that La Rochelle is a university city, so you'll find plenty of young folk to make friends with, especially after twilight in one of the fun bars. There's a flirty pickup scene here too, so with a bit of luck you'll be French kissing before the night is through.

Should you come to town in July, don't miss the yearly music extravaganza **Les Francofolies** (www.francofolies.com; see p. 327). It makes Woodstock look like a boondocks.

La Rochelle History 101

If La Rochelle could talk it would say, "Been there, done that, and bought the T-shirt." Once known as the French Geneva, it was founded as a fishing village in the 10th century on a rocky platform in the center of a marshland. Then our friend Eleanor of Aquitaine gave the town a charter in 1199, freeing it from feudal dues, which allowed the port to capitalize on the wars between France and England. Its profiteering soon paid off and it became the departure point for the founders of Montréal. By the 14th century La Rochelle was one of France's great maritime cities. As a hotbed of Protestant factions, it armed privateers to prey on Catholic vessels but was eventually besieged by Catholic troops. Two men led the fight: Cardinal Richelieu (with his Musketeers) and Jean Guiton, formerly an admiral and then mayor of the city. When Richelieu blockaded the port, La Rochelle bravely resisted, but on October 30, 1628, Richelieu wangled his way in, and out of the 30,000 citizens of the proud city, he found only 5,000 survivors. Today La Rochelle is the cultural and administrative hub of the Charente-Maritime *département*. Fortunately, the only kind of fighting you'll see is for space in the largest pleasure-boat basin in Europe.

Getting There

BY AIR

The La Rochelle–Laleu **airport** (☏ 05-46-42-86-70) is on the coast, 4km (2½ miles) north of the city. Local bus company RTCR runs a shuttle (bus no. 7) to and from place de Verdun in the town center. Buses run from roughly between 7am to 7pm from the airport to place de Verdun, and from 7am to 7:45pm from place de Verdun to Laleu, but call to check or consult their site (**www.rtcr.fr**). You can purchase tickets in most *tabacs* or onboard.

BY TRAIN

Rail connections from Bordeaux and Nantes are frequent. Six to eight trains make the 2-hour journey each day. From Paris five to seven high-speed TGV trains leave from Paris's Gare Montparnasse (trip time: 3 hr.). For information, call ☏ **36-35.**

BY CAR

From Paris, follow the A10 south from Poitiers to exit Niort/St-Maixent, then take N11 west to the coast and La Rochelle. From Bordeaux take the A10 northbound until Saintes, then follow the A837 (which turns into the N137) to La Rochelle.

BY BUS

Trust me and give buses a miss round here. Trains are more reliable and a lot swifter.

Orientation

The layout of La Rochelle is dead simple. The center of town and all its events are concentrated around the Vieux Port (Old Port), and you're never more than a 20-minute walk from the next spot you want to visit. There are two sides to La Rochelle: the old and unspoiled town inside the Vauban defenses, and the tawdry, built-up suburbs, which you won't be seeing unless you're into urban photography and enjoy snapping industrial sites. Being a fortified port, La Rochelle has **fortifications** for you to walk round (or at least trace the outline of), so if you need to burn off excess energy, 5.5km (3 miles) and seven gates later, you'll be satisfactorily pooped. The historic town, with its arch-covered streets, is also great for strolling. The best *rues* with their 17th-century arcades are

Talk of the Town

Five Conversation Starters

1. **Scooters.** They are everywhere—pumped up, brightly colored beasts that tear around the port, occasionally taking out a tourist or two.

2. The gentrification of the bars around the **Vieux Port.** During the day, these outdoor brasseries are crowded with all types of La Rochelle youth and adults, but at night the older folks are sucked into bars with awful cover bands or bad DJs.

3. **The tourists during the film festival.** Sure, every town resents events that draw in millions of pic-snapping outsiders, but when the festival plays second fiddle to the one in a certain other French city on the Riviera, feelings can get pretty nasty.

4. **Film, in general.** At the same time that they rue their silver medal in the French film festival race, these people are French and do love their indie films. Mention Gerard Depardieu for instant laughter and the ensuing lengthy conversation on the merits and demerits of his career, love life, and rapport with his son Guillaume.

5. **The Atlantic.** Especially if you hail from the American East Coast or any place touching a great body of water, this can be an easy conversation starter. People here are proud of their seashore, from the old forts and fishing ports to the beaches and fresh seafood.

rue du Palais, rue du Temple, rue Chaudrier, and **rue des Merciers,** with its ancient wooden houses (the prettiest are at nos. 3, 5, 8, and 17). Four harbors have grown up over the centuries, each rich with local nuance and lore. They are the historic **Vieux port,** the **Port des Minimes** (a modern yacht marina), the **Port de Pêche** (fishing port), and the **Port de Commerce** (used by container ships), so if boats float your . . . um, boat, you can drool over them here (see "Boat Trips" on p. 325). The Vieux Port also makes for some splendid pre- or post-dinner drinking, before you dance the night away in a legendary Rochelais *boîte de nuit.*

Getting Around

BY PUBLIC TRANSPORTATION

RTCR's main bus line 10 passes (☏ 05-46-34-84-58; www.rtcr.fr) from the place de Verdun, a 10-minute walk from the port, to the train station, the Auberge de Jeunesse in Les Minimes, and the Aquarium (via the university). Tickets cost 1.20€. Line 1 runs to the Ile de Ré, also from place de Verdun (tickets cost 1.50€), but for the most part, unless your tootsies are throbbing, it's a better idea simply to have a good pair of walking shoes or a bike.

BY BICYCLE

Bikes are by far the best way to cut across town, and what's more, you can hire one for free at **Vélos Autoplus** ★★ (place de Verdun and quai Valin; ☏ 05-46-34-02-22). Just leave some ID, and the next 2 hours are yours *gratis* (anything over 2 hr. is charged).

BY TAXI

Abeilles Taxis (☏ 05-46-41-22-22 or ☏ 05-46-41-55-55; www.taxi-la-rochelle.com) are reliable and run 24/7 in La Rochelle and its surroundings.

BORDEAUX & CHARENTE-MARITIME

Tourist Offices

The **Office de Tourisme** is on place de la Petite-Sirène, Le Gabut (☎ **05-46-41-14-68**; www.larochelle-tourisme.com; Jul–Aug Mon–Sat 9am–8pm, Sun 10:30am–5:30pm; June and Sept Mon–Sat 9am–7pm, Sun 10:30am–5:30pm; Oct–May Mon–Sat 10am–6pm, Sun 10am–1pm). They organize some great boat trips along the coastline (see "Boat Trips" on p. 325).

La Rochelle Nuts & Bolts

Emergencies　For an ambulance call ☎ **15**, police ☎ **17**, and fire/paramedic service ☎ **18**.

Hospitals　For medical emergencies, call the paramedics on ☎ **18**, or go to the ER at the **Centre Hospitalier de La Rochelle** (bd. Joffre; ☎ **05-46-45-66-26**; www. ch-larochelle.fr; there is also an entry on rue du Docteur Schweitzer; ☎ **05-46-45-50-50**).

Internet/Wireless Hot Spots　On the Bassin des Chalutiers (opposite side from the Aquarium), you can get online for .05€ a minute, or buy a card at 2.50€ for an hour at **Aquacyber** (10 quai Seinac de Meilhan; ☎ **05-46-50-29-21**). They are open daily from 10am to midnight (from 2pm on Sun).

Laundromats　You've probably heard enough jokes about washing your clothes in the sea by now, so I'll cut to the point and say that the **Laverie des Minimes** (Résidence Must, 1 rue Lucile; ☎ **05-46-44-69-20**) isn't too far from the Auberge de Jeunesse or the beach.

Pharmacies　**Pharmacie Asselin** is a short stroll away from the Vieux Port (48 rue des Merciers; ☎ **05-46-41-30-40**).

Post Office　Send your postcards from **La Poste** (6 rue de l'Hôtel de Ville; ☎ **05-46-30-40-00**; Mon–Fri 8am–5pm).

Vehicle Rental　**Europacar** runs some decent deals. Cars can be picked up at La Rochelle's Gare SNCF (158 bis bd. Joffre; ☎ **08-25-35-83-58**).

Websites　**www.ville-larochelle.fr** is an alternative to the tourist office. **www. ulysse-transport.fr** has information for reduced mobility travelers. **www.univ-lr. fr** is the university website. **http://ubacto.com** will keep you abreast of the latest goings on in clubs, restaurants, theaters, cinemas, and bars.

Sleeping

It's difficult to be far from the action when kipping in La Rochelle, which makes generating a few Zs far less of a headache than in larger, more spread-out cities. Try any of the places in this selection and you won't go far wrong.

HOSTELS

→ **Auberge de Jeunesse de La Rochelle** ★ Clearly everyone on a budget wants to be here, south of the old port, on the modern marina, with clean beds and a great atmosphere, for just 14€ a night. At that price, so what if you're not actually on one of the boats parked out front? At least from here you could accidentally bump into an owner, befriend him, and get a tour. Nah, don't listen to me—talking to strangers can be dangerous. If a yacht owner tempts you with sweets or offers to show you his puppies, decline politely and stay land-logged at the Auberge. *Av. des Minimes.* ☎ *05-46-44-43-11. www.fuaj.org. 14€ double. Rates include sheets and breakfast. Amenities: Restaurant (open for breakfast, lunch, and dinner); garden; Internet; laundromat.*

DOABLE

➜**France-Angleterre et Champlain** ★
Close to the major parks, the town hall, and the old port, this establishment is a winner. The most gracious choice in La Rochelle, it was formed by uniting two smaller hotels many years ago, and feels more like the home of a distant, wealthy relative than a hotel. The communal quarters are furnished with an endearing combination of antiques and art objects, and rooms are tasteful and dignified; many with colossal 19th-century armoires, which would certainly have an anecdote or two to share if they could talk. One of the best aspects of the hotel is its romantic garden, brimming with flowers, shrubbery, and trees. *20 rue Rambaud.* ☎ *05-46-41-23-99. www.bw-fa-champlain.com. 56€—100€ double. Parking 8€. Credit cards accepted. Amenities: Nonsmoking rooms. In room: A/C, TV, beverage maker, dataport, hair dryer, iron/ironing board, minibar.*

➜**Les Brises** This hotel boasts that sleeping here is like climbing aboard a cruise ship. Well no one should knock imaginative prose, but the only thing "cruise ship" about the joint is the view right over the sea. From a lounger on the parasol-shaded patio or from your balcony, you can watch the maritime world go by in real time and admire the soaring 19th-century column dedicated to the Virgin. The immaculate

rooms have cherrywood furniture, comfortable beds, and compact, neatly organized bathrooms with shower units. *Chemin de la Digue de Richelieu.* ☎ *05-46-43-89-37. www.hotellesbrises.com. 62€—115€ double. Credit cards accepted. Amenities: Laundry service; limited-mobility rooms. In room: A/C, TV, dataport, hair dryer, minibar, safe.*

SPLURGE

➜**Hôtel Residence de France** ★★
There's something winkingly comforting about staying at this benchmark of quality and impeccable service. It's like slipping on a pair of silk slippers or supping on a smooth, creamy cocktail. Maybe it's the tasteful decor—with its white walls, calico fabrics, and wicker furniture—that subtly reminds you that you're at the seaside. Then there's the art exhibition on the ground floor, displaying work by local artists, and the cute garden equipped with a patio. As if that weren't enough, rooms are spacious with whizzy, free Internet access. *43 rue du Minage.* ☎ *05-46-28-06-00. www.hotel-larochelle.com. Double 105€—155€; suite 135€—220€. Credit cards accepted. Amenities: Laundry; parking. In room: TV, minibar.*

Eating

This stretch of Atlantic churns up some of the country's most delicious and succulent seafood, so you shouldn't dare pass by without trying some (unless you're a vegetarian, of course, in which case you're off the hook!). When you've swallowed one shrimp too many, head away from the port and scout around through the backstreets. With a little diligence, you can easily beat out the mainstays for both quality and value.

COFFEE BARS & LIGHT FARE

➜**La Tour de Pizz** It's 3pm, you're short on money, and you'll keel over if you don't eat something soon. The name La Tour de Pizz (the Tower of Pizz) is admittedly a bad play on words, but any of the 23 pizzas on the menu fortunately aren't a bad play on food. They also do sandwiches, panini, salads, and cakes to take away so you have no excuse for going hungry. *Rue de la Ferté (next to the Hôtel de Ville).* ☎ *05-46-41-06-06. Pizza 6.40€–9.40€, sandwiches from 3.60€ (20% off with a student card). No credit cards. Daily 7am–10pm.*

CHEAP

➔ **La Bodega** Off the beaten tourist track, this is a must for energetic young things looking to eat and drink with like-minded party-people. Bright colors warm the room, while rum cocktails, cool sangria, and Spanish tapas warm the soul. If the tapas don't fill you up, order *una plancha*—an individual BBQ so copious you'll feel like you've eaten a whole cow. This is a fine venue for chatting with locals, and it's the booziest restaurant in town. *21 quai Du Gabut.* ☎ *05-46-30-55-36. Main course 12€; tapas from 2.50€. Credit cards accepted. Daily noon–3pm and 7pm–11pm.*

DOABLE

➔ **Les Comédiens** ★★ You want seafood but your mates want something that comes from dry land—what do you do? Why, go to Les Comédiens, of course. Not only do they serve excellent fish dishes, they provide traditional regional cuisine and seat diners in surroundings that look like they've come straight off stage at *La Comédie Française*. In fact, much of the decor really did start out life in the theater, and the theme is given extra acreage on weekends when live cabaret, magic shows, and hilariously tacky ventriloquists give everyone a Gallic giggle. *15 rue de la Chaîne.* ☎ *05-46-50-51-98. A la carte menu 21€–30€. Credit cards accepted. Daily noon–2pm and 7:30pm–10:30pm.*

Summer Hot Spots

From July to September, head for **quai Duperré, cours des Dames,** and **cours des Templiers.** Come sundown, they mutate into bustling platforms for street performers. The ambience is heartwarming and it's a cool way to set the tone for the rest of the night. Later you may find yourself at **The General Humberts** (14 rue St-Nicolas; ☎ **05-46-37-01-08**), a raucous, Irish pub with a first-rate selection of beer and, of course, Guinness. At cour du Temple, two little hotbeds provide the entertainment. The proudly French-style **Le Piano Pub** (no.12; ☎ **05-46-41-09-52**) books regular rock concerts that keep whipper-snappers like yourselves coming back for more. With its staunchly English decor of wood and leather, **Le Mayflower** (no.14; ☎ **05-46-50-51-39**) is popular with Anglo-mani-acs. Don't be surprised if the bois-terous crowds try to speak English with you. **Tuxedo** (21 place du Maréchal Foch; ☎ **05-46-50-01-22**) is a great gay venue that attracts mixed crowds.

SPLURGE

➔ **Les Flots** ★ Grégory Coutanceau causes quite a stir in his kitchen—not only because he's the son of the famous French chef Richard Coutanceau, but because he's one guy who knows how to have his wicked way with every fish that swims through his door. You need to have a lot of "sole" to do his job, but Grégory knows it's worthwhile when he sees the constant flow of locals ordering his generous and iconoclastic seafood dishes. Set at the foot of the Tour de la Chaîne, the setting is dreamy, and the wine list is fabulous. *1 rue de la Chaîne.* ☎ *05-46-41-32-51. Menus*

30€–100€. *Credit cards accepted. Daily 12:15–2pm and 7:30–10pm.*

Partying

→ **Le Pool du Bastion** Are you listening girls? This is a boy's bar: purple, red, and gray walls; 9 billiard tables (*attention:* French billiards); darts; and baby-foot, the game played by every frustrated French soccer fan under 30. This means that if you come here, your feminine presence (or should I say assets) will not go unnoticed. Boys, I've told the girls to come, so get down here and start strutting. *13 quai de Marans.* ☎ 05-46-41-60-91.

CLUBS & LIVE MUSIC VENUES

→ **Cosy Club** *Mon cher,* "'zis is La Rochelle's flashiest nighttime 'ot spot." Adjoined to the casino, the Cosy Club lives up to its name, wooing punters with leather armchairs, dark woods, and gold—lots of gold. A small stage holds frequent live music concerts, and the dance floor never lies empty once the tunes start a pumpin'. During les Francofolies music festival, the club's bay windows are opened out onto the sea, and some big-name DJs splice away into the night. *Allée du Mail.* ☎ 05-46-34-12-75. *www.lucienbarriere.com.*

MTV **Best** ♥ → **Oxford** ★ You can't get more French than this red hot student draw. For a start, the entry policy is wholly un-PC—with girls getting in for free before midnight (boys, you'll be forking out).

Secondly, the music is seriously retro with a heavy accent on '80s French pop, techno, and reggae. You may well recognize the remix of Vanessa Paradis's (Johnny Depp's wife) *Joe le Taxi,* but when it comes to Etienne Daho or Téléphone, your guess is as good as their dancing. That said, joviality rules, the alcohol flows like a river to the sea, and there's nowhere quite like it for observing Rochelais students on a bender. Women get in free before midnight (except Sat), and everyone catches a break on Mondays and Wednesdays (except bank holidays and July–Aug). Otherwise tickets are 10€, including one drink. Student night is on Thursday. *Plage de la Concurrence.* ☎ 05-46-41-51-81. *www.club-oxford.com.*

Sightseeing

Whether the sun is blazing, or a fine, romantic drizzle has drifted in from the Atlantic Ocean, La Rochelle is a bonbon for the eyes—with its fortified port, arcade-lined streets, ancient wooden homes, and stately mansions.

PUBLIC MONUMENTS

→ **Tour de la Chaîne** During the 1300s, this tower was built as an anchor piece for the large forged-iron chain that stretched across the harbor, closing it against hostile Catholic warships. Most of the exhibits focus on the history of medieval naval warfare. *Quai du Gabut.* ☎ 05-46-34-11-91.

Local Favorites

Old As the Stones, but Boy Do They Rock

If you can't quite grasp what makes the local populous tick, log on to **Les Binuchards**'s website: http://lesbinuchards.free.fr/binuchards.htm. They now have the allure of aging rock stars, but they are the protégés of the Charente-Maritime song world. They're a little bit rock and a little bit folk; a third of their tunes are sung in *patois Charentais,* the local dialect; and even though you won't understand a word, you'll get a kick out of watching the locals get their kicks. If they're playing when you're in town, don't miss them.

Admission 4.60€ adults, 3.10€ students and ages 18–25. July–Aug daily 10am–7pm; May 15–June and Sept 1–15 Tues–Sun 10am–1pm; Sept 16–May 14 Tues–Sun 10am–12:30pm and 2–5:30pm.

📺 Best 🔵 **Tour de la Lanterne** ★ From the glazed turret of this spooky monument, built between 1445 and 1476, a beacon shone every night in order to guide ships. When it wasn't doing duty as a lighthouse, it was used as a jail, well into the 19th century. From the top hold, reached via 162 steps, the panoramic view extends all the way to Ile d'Oléron on a clear day. On the way up, don't forget to think of the 13 poor priests who were tossed from its summit during the Wars of Religion. And remember to study the creepy graffiti scrawled by former prisoners. *Opposite Tour St-Nicolas, quai du Gabut.* ☎ *05-46-34-11-81. Admission 4.60€ adults over 25, 3.10€ students and ages 18–25. July–Aug daily 10am–7pm; Sept 16–May 14 Tues–Sun 10am–12:30pm and 2–5:30pm; May 15–June and Sept 1–15 Tues–Sun 10am–1pm.*

➜ **Tour St-Nicolas** ★ Built between 1371 and 1382, Tour St-Nicolas is the oldest tower in La Rochelle, originally used to guard the town against surprise attacks. From the top, only the old town and the offshore Ile d'Oléron are visible, but from the second floor, you can enjoy a view of the town and harbor. *Quai du Gabut.* ☎ *05-46-34-11-81 or 05-46-41-74-13. Admission 4.60€ adults over 25, 3.10€ students and ages 18–25. July–Aug daily 10am–7pm; Sept 16–May 14 Tues–Sun 10am–12:30pm and 2–5:30pm; May 15–June and Sept 1–15 Tues–Sun 10am–1pm.*

MUSEUMS

➜ **Aquarium de La Rochelle** ★ La Rochelle's blockbuster crowd pleaser rises from a portside position near the Port des Minimes. Inside, guided walkways stretch over two floors of massive and bubbling seawater tanks loaded with approximately 10,000 species of flora and fauna from the oceans of the world. It's hard to miss this place: There are signs for it all over town. If you have any interest in marine zoology, it can be genuinely appealing for a visit of a couple hours, and their cafe affords a fantastic panorama of the old port. *Bassin des Grands Yachts, B.P. 4, Le Vieux Port.* ☎ *05-46-34-00-00. www.aquarium-la rochelle.com. 12€ adults, 9€ students. Use of English-language audioguide 3.50€. July–Aug daily 9am–11pm; Apr–June and Sept daily 9am–8pm; Oct–Mar daily 10am–8pm. Bus: 10.*

➜ **Musée du Nouveau-Monde** ★ If rain has put a dampener on your sightseeing, come and learn about the history of La Rochelle and how this relatively anonymous port played a prominent role in the colonization of Canada. The 18th-century town house is rich with architectural details, and the displays trace the port's 300-year history with the New World. Exhibits start with LaSalle's discovery of the Mississippi Delta in 1682 and end with the settling of the Louisiana territory. *Hôtel Fleuriau, 10 rue Fleuriau.* ☎ *05-46-41-46-50. http://perso.wanadoo.fr/musees-la-rochelle/ n-monde. Admission 4€. Mon and Wed–Sat 10:30am–12:30pm and 1:30–6pm; Sun 3–6pm.*

A SPECIAL TOUR

Treat yourself to an unforgettable 10 minutes in a chopper. It's not that long a trip, but given La Rochelle's magnificent seascape, it'll be a memorable 10 minutes. Call **Heliocean** (La Rochelle Aéroport; ☎ **05-46-43-82-87**; www.jet-systems.fr; prices from 60€ per person).

Playing Outside

La Rochelle practically demands that you fill your lungs with all that fresh sea air. Try a boat trip, cycling, watersports, or horseback riding on the Ile de Ré.

BOAT TRIPS

Grab your sea legs, a lifejacket, and your striped fisherman's pullover: It's all aboard for some nautical sightseeing. La Rochelle has four harbors and masses of coastline for you to investigate. The tourist office (☎ **05-46-41-38-38**) acts as a clearinghouse for the outfitters Croisières Inter-Iles, Navipromer, Cap à l'Ouest, and Ré Croisières, which run a multitude of excursions. The harbor rides combine a look at the modern facilities of one of France's largest ports with a waterside view of the historic ramparts. The other tours run around La Rochelle's neighboring islands, Ile de Ré (see below), Ile d'Oléron (France's second biggest island after Corsica), and the 19th-century offshore prison Fort Boyard (see below).

📺 **Best** ● → **Fort Boyard** From the air, this fort looks like a floating donut; from sea level, it looks like a place where you wouldn't want to be left alone at night. Between the islands of Ré and Oléron, the fort was originally conceived in 1805 as a 74-cannon fortress to protect the two islands and La Rochelle itself. The difficulties of building a military compound on a man-made sandbank, however, continuously delayed construction. Nearly 50 years later, the stunted fort still stood only 2m (7 ft.) above the water. Construction was finally complete in 1857, but by that time, its defensive uses were obsolete, and the fort became a military prison. Now, France 2 TV uses it as the set for a celebrity game show in which teams undergo grueling activities in search of a hidden crystal.

📺 **Best** ● → **Ile de Ré** This luminous, unspoiled island—famous for its salt marshes, wildlife, and fishing shacks—is criminally overlooked by tourists who tend to opt for the bigger Ile d'Oléron. But it's an ideal place in which to relax, play watersports, or ride horses. Sixty-nine

kilometers (43 miles) of white, sandy beaches ring this island a few kilometers off the coast of La Rochelle. Bicycle and hiking paths crisscross its nature preserves. Although a bridge now links it to the mainland, it retains an insular character and feels unscathed by technology. Here, the only kind of net is found on fishing boats, and the only surf is on the crest of a wave.

For a bumping tour, grab a bicycle or a scooter from one of these places: **Cycland** (☎ 05-46-09-97-54; www.cycland.fr); **Cycles & Pêche Neveur** (☎ **05-46-29-20-88**; www.cycles-neveur.com); **Cyclo-surf** (☎ **05-46-30-19-51**; www.cyclo-surf.com); **Locasud** (scooters; ☎ 05-46-29-83-30; www.loscaud.com); then follow this mini-guide for the main sights and sounds:

Whether you arrive by land or sea, you'll hop ashore near **Sablanceaux** (download a map of the island at www.iledere.fr/bonus). From here, navigate counterclockwise toward **La Flotte,** stopping off briefly at **Rivedoux Plage,** for a paddle on the beach, and at the 12th-century **Abbaye de Chateliers,** a mysterious Cistercian abbey ruin, which the Brits desecrated during the wars of religion in 1623. At La Flotte, you'll find a labyrinth of snaking, whitewashed streets, a medieval market, and a cutesy fishing port with a 19th-century jetty.

Next up: **Saint-Martin-de-Ré,** the island's capital. You'll need time here, as it is so damned pretty and interesting. There's the port, marooned on an islet, lined with pleasure boats and buzzing cafe terraces; and then there are the hidden alleys, 17th-century houses, and magnificent fortifications built by Vauban in the 1600s. The monumental clock tower offers the best vistas of the island, especially at night when everything twinkles (visits organized by the tourist office, quai Nicolas Baudin; ☎ **05-46-09-06-18**).

North-facing **Loix** houses the island's last-standing tidal mill and a working salt museum where you can buy some of the most organic "white gold" in France (Ecomusée du marais salant, rte. de la Passe; ☎ **05-46-29-06-77**; www.marais-salant.com). **Ars-en-Ré,** farther south, is another salt-marsh village famous for its black-and-white church tower and delectable oysters (L'Huîtrière de Ré, Le Martray; ☎ **05-46-29-44-24**). While you're there, impress your mates with this little snippet: According to tradition, Ars women should wear a long, narrow headdress called a *Quichenotte.* It is said that the name derives from "Kiss Not," because its shape discouraged the amorous advances of attacking English soldiers.

The last stop in the North, **Les Portes-en-Ré,** is cherished by artists who flock here for contemplative peace and quiet. Then it's on to **St-Clement des Baleines** (Le Phare des Baleines; ☎ **05-46-29-03-11;** closed Nov–Dec), on the farthest tip of the island. Named after the whales that frequently washed up on its shores, it is mostly famous for its lighthouse, which soars 57m (187 ft.) from the ground.

Bordered by dunes and pines, south-central **La Couarde en Mer** is one of Ré's prettiest villages. It boasts 5km (3 miles) of golden sands (open to watersports), a market, and some nifty little lanes.

Given the name **La Bois Plage en Ré,** you'd expect to find a beach and some woods here, and I'm pleased to say you won't be disappointed. What's more, the village is surrounded by vineyards and vegetable gardens, and it harbors Gallo-Roman vestiges.

The last stop, before you collapse from physical and cultural overload, is **Sainte-Marie de Ré** (Bieres de Ré, 11 ZAC des Clémorinants; ☎ **05-46-43-82-63**). It's

famous not only for its Gothic bell tower, but for four unexpectedly palatable beers.

What? You want more? Oh, all right then: For sailing, contact **La Cabane Verte** (☎ **05-46-09-94-73;** www.lacabane verte.com). To ride the waves, call the **Ecole du Surf** (☎ **06-30-08-12-81;** www.re-surf.com). For water-skiing and wakeboarding, check out (☎ **06-79-53-00-26;** www.re-wake.com). And to giddy-up on horses with names like Hollywood and Love Me, the **Ecuries du Moulin** do pony treks (rte. de la Noue, La Flotte-en-Ré; ☎ **05-46-09-32-34;** www.moulin-moreau. com).

Croisières Inter-Iles (see "Tourist Offices," above) serves the island. If you're carless and want to visit during July or August, we recommend the ferry. Round-trip fare is 20€ to 30€, depending on the itinerary and whether the tour involves guided commentary. The bridge that connects the Ile de Ré to the French mainland is accessible from a point 3km (miles) south of La Rochelle. The toll is 11€ in summer, 20€ in winter, and free by bike or on foot.

Shopping

CLOTHING & ACCESSORIES

→ **Matlama** ★★ Before wrapping up your travels, you should always buy one item that makes you the envy of everyone at home. This wild and wacky *lieu de création* has some fun fashion accessories that may foot the bill. How about a hot-water-bottle bag, or "Le Rochelais," a conical pouch you can wear around your waist, on your arm, or over your shoulder? It's La Rochelle's answer to a fanny pack, but it's got 1,000 times more street cred. Prices range from 18€ for a wallet to 169€ for a priceless hand bag. *Case no. 61 quai Louis Prunier.* ☎ *05-46-50-12-84. http://matlama.fr. Tues–Sat 1:30–7pm (morning by appointment only).*

➜ **Sirocco** La Rochelle's purveyor of skateboarding and surfing gear is also great for funky street wear. Bags, T-shirts, shoes, pants—just baggy enough for your Calvins to peek out from underneath, but not so large you can't dish some moves—all are there. Plus they've got brands you can't find elsewhere (Loreak, Volcom, We Closing). Certain models can be bought online. *6 rue Gambetta.* ☎ *05-46-29-27-17. www.siroccosk8.com. Mon 2–7pm, Tues noon–7pm, Wed and Sat 10am–7pm, Thurs–Fri noon–2pm.*

MUSIC, BOOKS & MEDIA

If you need a good read and fancy trying some French, head to **Les Saisons** bookstore, which holds regular lectures by famous authors (*2 rue St-Nicolas;* ☎ **05-46-37-64-18;** http://lessaisons. ubacto.com). Four music shops keep La Rochelle's kids up-to-date. **Fetish Records** is *the* heavy metal institution (*8 rue Bletterie;* ☎ **05-46-50-65-79**). **Harmonia Mundi** is a good source for classical music, jazz, and world sounds (*63 rue des Mercier;* ☎ **05-46-41-17-63**). **Paris Musique** covers all the latest pop hits, new releases, and standards (*22 rue du Palais;* ☎ **05-46-41-66-63**), and **Salam** is a must for anything techno, drum & bass, house, and electronique on CD and on vinyl (*3 rue des Templiers;* ☎ **05-46-41-68-36**).

FOOD, WINE & LOCAL CRAFTS

➜ **Cave Marli** If you've already polished off the bottles you bought in Bordeaux, Marli wine store can replace them all—plus give you a few gift ideas for the folks back home. *22 rue Thiers.* ☎ *05-46-45-38-68. http://ubactu.net/marli. Mon 3:30–8pm, Tues–Sat 9:45am–12:30pm and 3:30–8pm, Sun 9:45am–12:30pm*

Festivals & Events

The busiest month is July. At the start of the month, mix with *la crème de la crème* of French and international actors, directors, and, of course, paparazzi at the [MTV] Best ✪ **Festival International du Film de La Rochelle.** Screenings are held around town; tickets cost 6€ to 15€. For information, contact the festival office in the Maison de la Culture, rue St-Jean de Perot (☎ **05-46-51-54-00;** www.festival-larochelle.org). For a week in mid-July, La Rochelle is rocked by some of the most diverse French and world musical acts around during **Les Francofolies** music festival. It caters to nearly every musical taste with big names and not-so-famous groups, most of them international pop musicians. Groupies and fans overrun the town, and a party atmosphere prevails. Tickets are 20€ to 28€. Call ☎ **05-46-28-28-28** for details (www.francofolies. fr). The Office de Tourisme can also provide details on both festivals.

La Rochelle is also the site of Europe's biggest showcase of boats and yachts: **Le Grand Pavois Salon Nautique.** It's a 5-day extravaganza in late September based around the Port de Plaisance (better known as the Bassin des Yachts, or Yacht Basin). Sellers and buyers of boats and marine hardware, as well as weekend sailors from everywhere, usually attend. If you've ever wanted to reel in a fisherman, there is no better place. For information about dates and venues, call ☎ **05-46-44-46-39** (www.grand-pavois.com).

The Basque Country & the Pyrenees

by Lauren Sommer

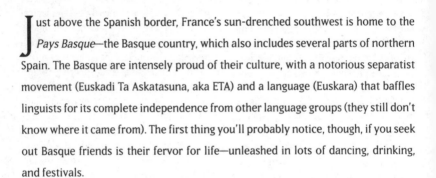

Just above the Spanish border, France's sun-drenched southwest is home to the *Pays Basque*—the Basque country, which also includes several parts of northern Spain. The Basque are intensely proud of their culture, with a notorious separatist movement (Euskadi Ta Askatasuna, aka ETA) and a language (Euskara) that baffles linguists for its complete independence from other language groups (they still don't know where it came from). The first thing you'll probably notice, though, if you seek out Basque friends is their fervor for life—unleashed in lots of dancing, drinking, and festivals.

With Spain so close, Castilian flavors and cuisine have crept across the border, meaning you'll find plenty of tapas bars in these parts. But the Southwest has an incredible menu of its own. The Atlantic Coast is a major fishing port delivering fresh tuna, cod, mussels, and merlu (a type of white fish). The Bearn region is known for its duck and its foie gras. (Goose liver fans are in for a mind-blowing event if they try some of the foie gras sold fresh here.)

Biarritz is the region's most popular stop, not far from San Sebastian in Spain. France's surfing mecca, its coast attracts an international crowd looking for the best breaks. Even if you're not into battling waves, you won't mind the gorgeous miles of shoreline. At higher elevations, the rugged and breathtaking Pyrenees mountains are a playground for hikers and skiers. In summer, the Tour de France races through each year for some of the most grueling climbs of the competition.

If you have a choice, though, head inland for the most authentic taste of life in the Basque countryside—in towns, farms, and markets tucked into the sunny foothills. Sure, there are more famous places to visit in France, but if you're looking to get away from tourist traps and cheap souvenirs, the Basque Country is a rewarding detour.

The Best of the Basque Country

○ **The Best Hotel to Fantasize about Staying In:** It's no understatement to describe the **Hôtel du Palais** as the jewel in Biarritz's crown. The stunning luxury hotel is actually a former palace, built as a royal getaway in 1854 on a bluff overlooking the ocean. Amid the finest quality money can buy, you'll inherit a royal air just walking in the door. You just better hope you're actually an heir, though, with an inheritance that will help pay the mighty bill. See p. 334.

○ **The Best Place for a Post-Beach Drink:** Summer nightlife in Biarritz can be a zoo, but the hippest surfers and beach bunnies head out to **100 Marché.** This laid-back outdoor dive is all about location—high above the Côte des Basques beach. The young clientele sticks around until late into the night, slamming back cocktails and forecasting the surf. See p. 337.

○ **The Best Place to Eat Like a Local (Biarritz):** With local food, free-flowing sangria, and a laid-back vibe, **Bar Jean** packs in a young local crowd for tapas and drinks. Their small plates mix together Basque and Spanish cuisine and can act as a culinary tour of the region, accompanied by boisterous conversation. See p. 336.

○ **The Best Surfing Beach (Biarritz):** Well, "best" could be a bit of an exaggeration; predictably, locals jealously guard the finest spots, so serious surfers will have to win them over with a few free pints. But if you're a beginner or intermediate, **Côte des Basques beach** can be a good place to test your skills while soaking in the scene. See p. 339.

○ **The Best Hot Chocolate Ever (Bayonne):** Forget those powdered packets of Swiss Miss—you've never had hot chocolate like they make it at **Chocolat Cazenave.** So rich it's mind altering, the *chocolat mousseux* is pure and dark, whipped the traditional way into a frothy mousse. You'll realize how serious they are when you see that it's served with a glass of water. See p. 343.

○ **The Best Romantic Dinner that Won't Break the Bank (Bayonne):** Even if you aren't wining and dining your special someone, don't miss **François Miura.** The cuisine is modern, focused on flavor. It's a gourmet experience that won't confuse or shock you with crazy preparations. And at their prices, you'd be crazy to miss it. See p. 344.

○ **The Best Place for Schooling in Basque Culture (Bayonne):** Of course, you won't be able to live it up Basque-style here, but the **Musée Basque** is the primer you'll need to understand how the Basque people tick. From its historic artifacts to its songs and games, it will help you figure out what to talk about when you sit down with your new Basque friends. See p. 345.

○ **The Best Time to Dance in the Streets:** If you're in town at the right time of year, **Les Fêtes de Bayonne** is reason enough to pack differently. When it comes to the multiday party, everyone wears white clothing and red bananas for the dancing, drinking, and bullfighting extravaganza. You'll learn to party the Basque way in no time. See p. 348.

○ **The Best Place to Forget that the French Make Cheese (Foix):** In the land of cheese and duck, the word *vegan* doesn't come up very much. But at **Le Guerrat,** a small bed-and-breakfast outside Foix, they serve up vegan food grown on the grounds that will make you forget that brie even exists. See p. 352.

○ **The Best Spot to Argue over Vegetables:** No fancy tricks here. **Foix's farmer's markets** each week are the local's turf, where they grab vegetables, meat, and cheese in the early morning. Swing by for the local flavor, but get there too late and you'll miss it. See p. 352.

○ **The Best Room with the British Relatives You Always Wanted (Foix): Chapeliers,** in an incredible medieval house beneath Foix's château, run by British owners Kim and Mike, is almost like a home away from home. Just don't get too comfortable or you won't want to leave. See p. 352.

○ **The Best Castle:** True, **Château de Foix** is the only castle in town, but it's in excellent condition, surviving from when it was first built in the 11th century. It went from castle, to barracks, to prison, leaving the layers of history all over the grounds. Keep an eye out for the 18th-century graffiti all over the walls from prisoners with a lot of time on their hands. See p. 353.

Biarritz: Surf's Up on the Atlantic Coast

785km (487 miles) SW of Paris, 193km (120 miles) SW of Bordeaux, 8km (5 miles) W of Bayonne

It may not be as legendary as France's swank Riviera, but Biarritz is the Atlantic version of a stunning beachfront playground, without the pretension. Just above the Spanish border, the city is smack in the middle of Basque country, though you wouldn't know it. Around Biarritz, beach culture trumps all. Sand, surfing, and bronzed bodies are what it's all about, and during the summer it's a full-fledged resort town with all the trimmings.

Biarritz isn't just hot now; it has been an in-crowd hangout for quite some time. Biarritz became established when Empress Eugénie, a longtime fan of the area, convinced her husband, Napoleon III, to build a palace there in 1854. The palace still stands to this day as the Hôtel du Palais, an ultra-luxurious hotel that caters to old money and jet-setters. Since then, other hip crowds have filtered through town. Ernest Hemingway was known to hang out, and later Gary Cooper and Frank Sinatra swung through.

Today, Biarritz's claim to fame is as a surfing mecca. Professional and beginner surfers alike come from around the globe for the waves, and the coast north and south of Biarritz is chock-full of surf spots fiercely protected by locals. The story goes that a Hollywood producer actually imported surfing to Biarritz in the 1960s. Even if you're brand new to the sport, Biarritz is a friendly place to learn (or at least watch other people learn). With all the surf shops and gear shops, it almost feels like being in a surf town in the U.S.

The Basque Country

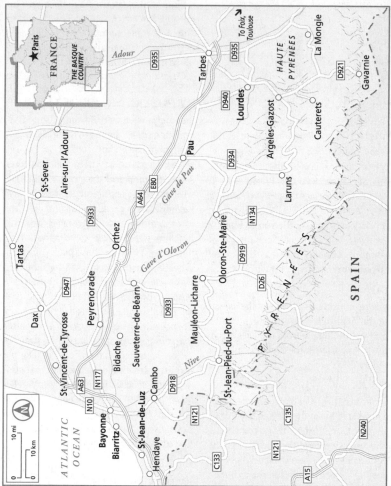

With so many sides, Biarritz is still a mix of old refinement, new attitude, and local flavor. Plenty of cheesy tourist traps are to be found, but when it comes to restaurants and nightlife, Biarritz doesn't fail to please. Local wines and food, especially fresh seafood, are heavily represented. The tricky thing is to get away from the crowds. During the busy summer months, Biarritz's streets are jammed with visitors, and the beaches are packed with frying flesh, packed elbow to elbow. If the scene gets to be too much, cultural Bayonne is a short bus ride away and will remind you that there's plenty more to this region. All too often, though, Biarritz gets left off the list of great beach towns to visit. If you're looking for chill beach fun, this is the spot.

Getting There

BY AIR

Biarritz's small airport is just south of town, connected to town by local bus. The **Aéroport de Biarritz-Anglet-Bayonne** (www.biarritz.aeroport.fr) connects with other cities in France through Air France and cities like London by discount carrier Ryanair.

BY TRAIN

Several trains arrive daily from Bayonne, which is the main link to cities throughout southern France. Head's up: Biarritz's train station isn't in the center of town. In fact, it's not even close to walking distance. Plenty of buses can shuttle you to Biarritz or Anglet, but if you're coming from Bayonne, it makes more sense to take the local bus system instead of the train.

BY CAR

If you're cruising south down the coast, take the A63 from Bordeaux for a 2-hour trip. If you're coming from the east, drive west on N117 from Tarbes, which will take 1¹/₂ hours.

BY BUS

If you're arriving from Bayonne, check out the local Stab bus network (see "By Public Transportation," below). If you're heading to the Spanish side of the border, use the **PESA** bus network (see www.pesa.net for schedules), which can shuttle you to Bilbao or to the nightlife in nearby San Sebastian. Ask about tickets at the Biarrtiz tourist office, since buses leave directly from there.

Orientation

Understandably, most of Biarritz is laid out along the coastline to capitalize on the sea views and beach access. The center of Biarritz spreads out from the coast with streets that slope upward from the beach. Several beaches, including the Côte des

Basques, are far below the city itself and require walking down stairs built into the hillside. The train station, youth hostel, and most campgrounds are actually south of town and inland, just out of walking distance from the heart of town.

Getting Around

BY PUBLIC TRANSPORTATION

Biarritz, Anglet, and Bayonne (the "BAB" region) are all served by the **Stab** bus system (tickets 1.20€, or 4€ for 24 hr.; ☎ **05-59-52-59-52**; www.bus-stab.com). A broad number of lines connect Biarrtiz with the beaches at Anglet and central Bayonne, as well as the airport and the local train stations. From Biarritz to Bayonne is only a 20- to 30-minute ride, depending on the bus line you take. Weekday buses are marked by numbers, while Sunday and holiday buses are marked by letters. Schedules and frequency also fluctuate based on the season. Keep your eye on the clock, since after 9pm only one night bus runs until 5am.

For the beach-combing crowd, take the **Navette des Plages,** a bus line that connects the beaches from Biarritz to Anglet. From early July to early September, the line runs from around 6am to 8pm and can shuttle you from beach to beach until you find a patch of sand that suits you.

BY BIKE

If you plan on systematically visiting every beach in town, a bike would certainly be helpful, but it's by no means necessary. For rentals, visit **Sobilo** (24 rue Peyroloubilh; ☎ **05-59-24-94-47**; www.sobilobiarritz. com; daily 9am–7pm; 12€ a day).

Tourist Office

Biarritz's tourist office functions as a one-stop information kiosk and ticket stand as well. Most people stopping by are looking for tickets to head to Spain, but if you have questions about hotels or other simple travel matters, they can help as well. (1 square d'Ixelles; ☎ **05-59-22-37-10;** July–Aug daily 8am–8pm; Sept–June Mon–Sat 9am–6pm, Sun 10am–5pm).

Recommended Websites

○ **www.ville-biarritz.fr**: This is the town's official site, and it can be useful

for getting all the basics. Check out their surf webcams and live swell maps.

○ **www.surf-report.com**: Yeah, it's pretty self-explanatory. Log on to get the 411 on waves and surf conditions when you're in town.

Biarritz Nuts & Bolts

Internet Cafes   The most complete Internet hot spot is **Form@tic** (15 av. de la Marne; ☎ **05-59-22-12-79;** Mon–Sat 9am–8pm, winter hours 9am–7pm; 1€ for 15 min.). With its 15 computers, including one Mac and wireless, your chances of getting online during busy months are high.

Laundry   For something more heavy-duty than a wash in your hotel room sink, stop by **Compagnie des Lavoirs.** Check out their two locations, 4 rue Jaulerry or avenue de la Marne, both open from 7am to 9pm.

Sleeping

HOSTELS

➜ **Auberge de Jeunesse Biarritz** ★ This is the fully loaded, deluxe youth hostel. Nicer than some hotels in town, Biarritz's hostel is a bustling international clubhouse in summer, with plenty of activities. The spacious and newly constructed building has a cafeteria, laundry, and Internet. The beach is a 15-minute walk, and they team up with a local surf school to provide quality lessons on hanging ten. Rooms come with two, three, or four bunks (along with a sense of camaraderie). The only downside is its distance from the heart of Biarritz. While the hostel is cozied up in a small valley, it's closer to the train station than the center of town, and you'll need to take a car or bus to get there. Take bus nos. 2 or 9 (or on Sun, B) to the "Bois de Boulogne" stop, which drops off on avenue du Président J.F. Kennedy. From there, look for rue Philippe Veyrin and take a right. Walk 5 minutes until you see the hostel on the right. *8 rue Chiquito de Cambo.*

☎ *05-59-41-76-00. www.hihostels.com. 17€ per night. Rates include sheets and breakfast. Hostel card required. Amenities: Bike rental; free parking; Internet access 1€ for 20 min.; laundry.*

CHEAP

➜ **Hôtel Atalaye** As the straightforward owners of this hotel will tell you, it's the cheapest ocean view in town. A handful of the rooms peek over the rooftops at Biarritz's lighthouse and high seas, some of which also have a small balcony. Hôtel Atalaye boasts a central location, yet it's also slightly off the main drag, minimizing noise. Rooms are comfortable and flowery, if not slightly worn down, but overall make for a solid budget option. *6 rue des Goélands.* ☎ *05-59-24-06-76. www.hotel atalaye.com. 42€–70€ double. Breakfast 5.50€. Credit cards accepted. Jan 15–Nov 15. Amenities: Elevator. In room: TV.*

➜ **Hôtel Gardénia** ★ Despite its bright-pink facade, Hôtel Gardénia is actually understated. On a quiet street, the hotel is in better shape than most of Biarritz's heavily trafficked budget hotels. It has a cozy lobby with a computer for checking e-mail (2€) and simple but comfortable rooms, some of which have a shower down the hall. Another perk is the location, equidistant from central Biarrtiz and the Côte des Basques beach, which somehow still keeps the hotel in a quiet area. Excellent budget choice. *19 av. Carnot.* ☎ *05-59-24-10-46. www.hotel-gardenia.com. 35€–59€ double. Breakfast 6€. Credit cards accepted. March–Nov. Amenities: Wireless Internet and computer available.*

→ **Hôtel Palym** For budget digs close to the beach and nightlife, Hôtel Palym is one of the better compromises around. Rooms are small but comfortable, and most have bathrooms en suite. There are a few with facilities in the hall if you're looking to cut your budget. If you're sensitive to ruckus in the streets, ask for a room away from it all, too, since the hotel is on a main drag that sees plenty of summertime foot traffic. If you're nice to the owners, they'll let you check your e-mail on the hotel computer. *6–7 rue du Port-Vieux.* ☎ *05-59-24-16-56. 40€–60€ for 2 people; 70€ for 3. Credit cards accepted. In room: TV.*

DOABLE

→ **Maison Garnier** ★ In a regal house on a quiet corner, Maison Garnier is loaded with charming comfort. The hotel yields a simple and satisfying experience. Large, immaculate rooms have a clean white color scheme. The house is warm and informal. Breakfast is served in a bright dining room, and entrance is granted by a code at the front door. Directly between central Biarritz and the Côte des Basques beach, the hotel is a piece of quiet in the storm. *29 rue Gambetta.* ☎ *05-59-01-60-70. www.hotel-biarritz.com. 90€–115€ double. Breakfast 9€. Credit cards accepted.*

SPLURGE

→ **Carlina Lodge** ★ With surfboard and bike storage right in the lobby, the Carlina is more like a beach dorm than a hotel. But with an unbeatable location touching the Côte des Basques beach, it's a more upscale joint than it appears to be. The vibe mixes minimalism with the '60s California surf scene. Rooms are very simple, with light woods and few embellishments. But each one is suited for beach die-hards, with its own terrace for unadulterated ocean gazing. The hotel also has five apartments with kitchenettes. Tourists check in for weeks at a time, and reservations fill fast. The hotel is on a cove below central Biarritz; nightlife is a 10-minute walk away. *Bd. Prince de Galles.* ☎ *05-59-24-42-14. www.carlina.net. 95€–160€ double; 110€–220€ apt. Breakfast 7€–12€. Credit cards accepted. Amenities: Paid parking (5€).*

→ **Mercure Plaza Biarritz Centre** Of the pricey hotels on avenue Edouard VII, this one is your best bet. The Plaza has been known for decades as Biarritz's Art Deco hotel, but significant renovation in 2004 has seriously updated it. The Deco touches are still there, but they're more understated and mixed in the hotel's bold color scheme. With close access to Biarritz's busiest beach, the location can't be beat. Many rooms have full or partial ocean views, even though they're in the heart of town. Expect to pay for the privilege, though, especially during high season. *10 av. Edouard VII.* ☎ *05-59-24-74-00. www. mercure.com. 125€–260€ double. Breakfast 15€. Parking 12€. Credit cards accepted. Amenities: Bar, parking. In room: A/C, satellite TV, free Wi-Fi, hair dryer, safe.*

SUPER SPLURGE

MTV Best ♥ → **Hôtel du Palais** ★★ There's no ignoring this one. The hotel sits directly next to Biarritz's Grand Plage,

Biarritz

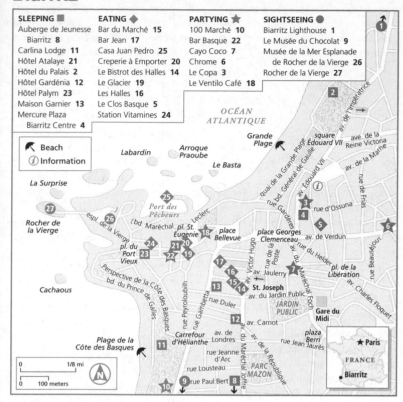

SLEEPING ■	EATING ◆	PARTYING ★	SIGHTSEEING ●
Auberge de Jeunesse Biarritz **8**	Bar du Marché **15**	100 Marché **10**	Biarritz Lighthouse **1**
Carlina Lodge **11**	Bar Jean **17**	Bar Basque **22**	Le Musée du Chocolat **9**
Hôtel Atalaye **21**	Casa Juan Pedro **25**	Cayo Coco **7**	Musée de la Mer Esplanade
Hôtel du Palais **2**	Creperie à Emporter **20**	Chrome **6**	de Rocher de la Vierge **26**
Hôtel Gardénia **12**	Le Bistrot des Halles **14**	Le Copa **3**	Rocher de la Vierge **27**
Hôtel Palym **23**	Le Glacier **19**	Le Ventilo Café **18**	
Maison Garnier **13**	Les Halles **16**		
Mercure Plaza	Le Clos Basque **5**		
Biarritz Centre **4**	Station Vitamines **24**		

★ Beach
ⓘ Information

OCÉAN ATLANTIQUE

★ Paris

FRANCE

● Biarritz

0   1/8 mi
0   100 meters

---

right on the ocean, and while you may not realize it from a distance, it's one of the most luxurious hotels in southern France. The terms "international elite" and "old money" may come to mind. With gorgeous ocean views, a heated saltwater pool, world-class restaurants, and a brand new spa, you'll be living like royalty, which is appropriate given the hotel was a former royal palace. Unless you have "international playboy/playgirl" on your resume, chances are this one is just out of reach. At least you can dream. *1 av. de l'Impératrice.* ☎ *05-59-41-64-00. www.hotel-du-palais.com. 470€–550€ double; 600€–1,500€ suite. Breakfast 30€. Credit cards accepted. Amenities: Bar; elevator; fax; laundry; paid*

Wi-Fi; pool; wheelchair friendly. In-room: A/C, TV, hair dryer, safe.

Eating

CAFES & LIGHT FARE

→**Creperie à Emporter** This small crepe place fits the bill for late-night munchies or pre-dinner snacks. They serve everything from the most basic plain crepes to fancier versions with fixings like eggs or chocolate. Get a taste of the French version of fast food. *22 rue Mazagran.* ☎ *06-62-35-76-19. Crepes 1.50€–5€. Credit cards accepted. Daily noon–1am.*

→**Le Glacier** ★ There's no shortage of ice-cream joints in Biarritz, but the homemade flavors at this one are worth a stop.

With taste combinations like orange and ginger, and *fleur de cactus,* you'll get much more than something sweet on a hot day. *31 rue Mazagran.* ☎ *05-59-22-20-68. Credit cards accepted. Daily 1pm–1am.*

→ **Les Halles** Biarritz's farmer's market isn't overwhelmingly large, but it's stocked full of all the goods for a beach picnic. Pick up sandwiches, bread, fruit, and cheeses in the morning, and stop by the espresso bar on one end to cap off the trip. *Halles centrales, off of rue Gambetta. No phone. No credit cards. Mon–Sat 8am–1pm.*

→ **Station Vitamines** This small grocery store features regional products and more, but the main reason to stop by is their freshly squeezed fruit juices. Made from oranges and other fresh fruit combos, they're the perfect companion for that early morning beach walk. *8 rue de Port-Vieux.* ☎ *06-03-55-80-44. Daily 9am–noon.*

CHEAP

→ **Bar du Marché** ★ FRENCH After too much sun and salt water, sometimes all you want is good food and no attitude. Bar du Marché is a wine bar and dinner joint that is just what the lifeguard ordered. They serve salads and *tartines;* open-face sandwiches with toppings like brie, honey, and walnuts; or chorizo and tomatoes. Even if you aren't looking for dinner, you'll find the wine list is full of regional varieties worth exploring. *8 rue des Halles.* ☎ *05-59-24-16-91. Main courses 4€–10€. Credit cards accepted. Mon–Sat noon–2pm and 7–11pm.*

→ **Casa Juan Pedro** SEAFOOD For grilled seafood right on the water, this informal spot is right on. Found in the tiny cove of Port de Pecheurs (once the real port where fishermen dropped off their catches), Casa Juan Pedro is the least pretentious of the three restaurants here. With only outdoor tables, you'll notice the outdoor grill first. Entrees like prawns,

tuna, mussels, and sardines are served up searing hot with no extra frills. If it weren't for the wine, sangria, and ambience, you'd think you'd stumbled upon a fisherman's lunch spot. *Port de Pecheurs.* ☎ *05-59-24-00-86. Entrees 6€–12€. Credit cards accepted. Daily noon–3pm and 7–11pm.*

DOABLE

📺 Best ♦ → **Bar Jean** ★ TAPAS This tapas bar is packed with locals at all hours, who jam in for conversation and Basque and Spanish flavors. With so many small dishes to order, you can taste a range of Basque favorites such as *piquillos,* roasted red peppers stuffed with cod or other goodies; grilled shrimp; Serrano ham; and *merlu espagnol*—a whole grilled fish made for two. With plenty of sangria to boot, this is one restaurant where you'll want to stick around. *5 rue des Halles.* ☎ *05-59-24-80-38. Entrees 7€–16€. Credit cards accepted. Apr–Sept daily 10am–3pm and 6:30pm–midnight; Oct–Mar Thurs–Mon 10am–3pm and 6:30pm–midnight.*

→ **Le Bistrot des Halles** FRENCH This cozy bistro packs in the locals for hearty regional and Basque fare. Decorated in old bullfighting memorabilia and posters, the restaurant takes advantage of its proximity to les Halles to show off local produce along with serious main courses such as sea bass, rack of lamb, and duck (of course). Finish off your meal with one of three flavors of crème brûlée. *1 rue du Centre.* ☎ *05-59-24-21-22. Entrees 15€–19€. Credit cards accepted. Mon–Sat noon–2pm and 6:30–11pm.*

SPLURGE

→ **Le Clos Basque** ★ BASQUE/FRENCH Locals in the know flock to this spot where rustic local and regional specialties reign supreme, such as cod crusted in chorizo and artichokes. Their three-course 24€ menu is by far the biggest draw, but other prices are reasonable. The place is so popular that during the summers you need to make a reservation 2 to 3 days in advance. Call as soon as you get into town. *12 rue Louis Barthou.* ☎ *05-59-24-24-96. Entrees 12€–16€. Credit cards accepted. Tues–Sun noon–1:30pm and 7:45–9:30pm.*

Partying

FUNKY BARS

➜ **Bar Basque** For a modern take on Basque flavor, this comfortable bar has the goods. Though it sits in the center of Biarritz's nightlife, it maintains an intimate feel with an enclosed outdoor space and warm interior. In the late evening, the crowd chills out with cocktails (4€–7€) and tapas, including cheese plates and small sandwiches. Later on, the pace picks up as the cider- and wine-drinking crowd fills in for some spruced up Basque attitude. *1 Port Vieux.* ☎ *05-59-24-60-92.*

MTV Best ❂ ➜ **100 Marché** ★ This outside bar attracts surfers and beach hounds galore, positioned high on the bluff above the Côte des Basques beach. Unlike the jam-packed joints in town, this place is super laid-back. The bar itself is like a drink shack more than a bar, and the young crowd wanders freely, taking in the stunning views of the water and swapping tips about the conditions and weather. It may be a stroll from the center of town, but it's worth checking out the scene. *Bd. du Prince de Galles. No phone.*

➜ **Le Ventilo Café** This spot is an all-hours magnet for the youngest crowd in Biarritz. During the day, the beach crowd filters in for a salad or sandwich and a break from the Biarritz sun. At night, the space gets packed with the same young sun-worshippers looking to cut loose. With a long menu of cocktails and plenty of house and trip-hop, the scene spills onto the sidewalk during high season. It's definitely a spot to hit if you're looking to see and be seen. Drinks run 6€ to 8€. *30 bis rue Mazagran.* ☎ *05-59-24-31-42.*

NIGHTCLUBS & LIVE MUSIC VENUES

➜ **Cayo Coco** As Biarritz's only salsa bar, the Cayo Coco is home to those who want to dance to a different beat. Dedicated regulars dominate the dance floor with some serious hip shaking, but they're ready to help out any newbies. The rhythm-impaired can also swing by on Thursday nights from 10 to 11pm for a free salsa lesson. The Cuban theme pervades throughout, with rum drinks and mojitos (5€–6€) at the ready. On summer weekends, the bar features a live salsa band that gets the room shaking. *5 rue Jaulerry.* ☎ *05-59-22-53-31.*

➜ **Le Copa** Essentially open 24 hours a day, Le Copa is a restaurant and club that strives to be an all-hours hot spot. The most popular side of it is definitely the club, which opens up at midnight as the bars in town slow down. The underground space is brightly colored, though not too big. Expect a summertime crowd to be getting down to house and techno beats. *24 av. Edouard VII.* ☎ *05-59-24-65-39. www.lecopa.fr.*

GAY BARS

➜ **Chrome** The heart of the gay scene in Biarritz, Chrome is a cozy space with an ultramodern lounge feel. The minimal, urban bar inside is light years ahead in design compared to other spots in town. You'll find a local crowd sharing cocktails (3€–6€), but tourists also pile in on the weekends. Their website also has a helpful guide to gay-friendly spots in town. *49 av. de Verdun.* ☎ *05-59-22-39-94. www.chromelounge.com.*

Sightseeing

MUSEUMS

➜ **Musée de la Mer** Out on a rocky point near Rocher de la Vierge, Biarritz's petit aquarium is home to tanks of local fish, seahorses, sharks, and other life aquatic. On the upper floors, you can get close to their well-fed seal population; when not sleeping, they put on a bit of show for the tourists. They're at their most vivacious at chow time, 10:30am and 5pm each day. The marine museum can be a welcome break on a hot day, but it won't take more than an hour to get through. *Esplanade de Rocher de la Vierge.* ☎ *05-59-22-33-34. www.museedelamer.com. 7.30€, 4.60€ students. Oct–May 9:30am–12:30pm and 2–6pm; June and Sept 9:30am–7pm; July–Aug 9:30am–midnight. Closed Mon Nov–Mar.*

➔ **Le Musée du Chocolat** Put those Hershey's bars away. The motto at this museum is that chocolate should not be tainted by milk or flavorings. It's the pure dark chocolate they're dedicated to here. Like wine, it can have undercurrents of flavor that make each type taste differently. The tour (conducted in French, though they make due for English speakers) takes guests through the different origins of cocoa beans and passes out samples to illuminate the stages of chocolate making. You'll find the museum and its chocolate store by walking past the Côte des Basques beach outside the town center. *14–16 av. Beau Rivage.* ☎ *05-59-41-54-64. www.lemusee duchocolat.com. 5€ for tour and tasting. July–Aug Mon–Sat and Sept–May Tues–Sat 10am–noon and 2–6pm (5pm last entry). Closed Sun.*

MONUMENTS & CHURCHES

➔ **Biarritz Lighthouse** Built in 1834, this lighthouse stands on the north end of town and informally marks the boundary between Anglet and Biarritz. You can climb the 234 steps to the top for a stellar view of the ocean and surrounding town. ☎ *05-59-22-37-10. July 1–Aug 31 daily 10am–12:20pm and 2:30–7pm.*

➔ **Rocher de la Vierge** Head through a stone tunnel at the farthest point off Biarritz and follow a footbridge for one of the best views in town. The "Rock of the Virgin" is named for the statue that was placed there in the 1800s to protect sailors and fishermen. Now you can head out for one sea-blown view of Biarritz and the crashing waves around you. *At the end of esplanade des Anciens Combattants, near the Musée de la Mer.*

Shopping
CLOTHING & ACCESSORIES

➔ **Lily of the Valley** For gals seeking designer duds to hit the town in, the tiny Lily of the Valley boutique can't be beat, with exclusively French designers and hard-to-find originals. If you've got the spare change, you're guaranteed to walk out with more style than you had when you walked in. *2 rue Simon Etcheverry, near place Clemenceau.* ☎ *05-59-22-34-50. Tues–Sun 10am–12:30pm and 3–6:30pm.*

FOOD, WINE & LOCAL CRAFTS

➔ **La Maison Arosteguy** This small grocer is the place to go for gourmet gifts that will travel safely in your suitcase. They've been in operation since 1875 and specialize in all-local products. Pick up Basque specialties, as well as foie gras, wine, and other things that aren't quite recognizable. *5 av. Victor Hugo.* ☎ *05-59-24-00-52. www. arosteguy.com. Mon–Sat 9:30am–1pm and 3–6:30pm, Sun 10am–1pm.*

➔ **Mille et Un Fromages** If the name of this store—meaning "a thousand and one cheeses"—doesn't get you excited, you probably should skip it. But if you want to experience both stinky and creamy varieties from the country that knows cheese best, definitely stop by. They'll set you up with something you've never tried, as well as other goodies to eat it with. *8 av. Victor Hugo.* ☎ *05-59-24-67-88. Mon–Sat 8:30am–1pm and 3:45–8pm.*

FUN BUYS

➔ **Michel Pujol** ★ This small postcard shop has an immense collection of antique posters, documents, and hundreds of postcards from the early 1900s. You can sort through the owner's boxes covering Biarrtiz, Bayonne, and all the coastal attractions, which look a lot like the postcards you can buy at the tourist shops, but a whole lot cooler. Discover you're less original than you thought—people have been writing home about Biarritz for 100 years. *1 rue Champ Lacombe.* ☎ *05-59-24-62-62. Mon–Sat 10am–noon.*

Playing Outside

SURF SCENE & BEACHES

Biarritz is home to six beaches, all of which vary greatly in terms of the scene and the friendliness of the waves. The main hot spot is the **Grande Plage,** found between the Hôtel du Palais and the Casino. As the most accessible beach from the center of town, this is where crowds gather to hang out. Surfing is allowed on one half of the beach, which is marked by flags. Farther south, the tiny **Port Vieux** beach is the most sheltered, meaning that waders and families gather there. Directly south from there is the 🆎 Best● **Côte des Basques** beach, by far the most popular surfing beach. Surfing is best a low tide, since the sand disappears at high tide. Two beaches south of there, **Marbella** and **Milady,** are too far to walk to if you're staying in town, but they're often less crowded in summer. The beach directly north of the Grande Plage, **Miramar,** has very strong currents. Biarritz's beaches are posted with lifeguards from June to September. For a surf report, call ☎ **08-92-68-13-60.** When on the beach, watch for the flags, which mark where swimmers are free to go and where surfing is permitted.

Almost every main beach has a surf school of its own. If you head down to the sand, you'll find them stationed out there. Most teach at the Côte des Basques beach.

The Biarritz youth hostel recommends **Ecole de Surf Hastea** (☎ 05-59-24-23-89; www.hastea.com); basic lessons start at 30€.

For rentals, stop by **Boutique Quiksilver** (☎ **05-59-22-03-12;** www.biarritz-boardriders.com; July–Aug daily 10am–8pm; April–Oct Mon–Sat 10am–7pm, Sun 2:30–6:30pm; Nov–Mar Mon–Sat 10am–12:30pm and 2:30–7pm), directly facing the Grande Plage. They can hook you up with board rentals and gear, and direct you to a surf school and give you advice about conditions. Other surf gear shops include **Rip Curl** (2 av. de la Reine Victoria; ☎ **05-59-24-38-40;** daily 10am–8pm), not far from the Grande Plage.

Anglet

Directly north of Biarritz, Anglet is the sandy home of die-hard surfers and beach-seekers. The glam factor drops several notches here, compared to Biarritz. Anglet is more down-home and rustic, and life here is centered around 5km (3 miles) of shoreline, which is far less developed than the beaches in Biarritz. For beach die-hards, Anglet has plenty of space and far more breaks. Surfers concentrate here for the best surfing. Anglet lacks a large town center on the coastline, and most of the shops and restaurants are clustered around the main Chambre d'Amour beach. It's best to think of Anglet as a long strip of sand with beach outposts dotted along the way.

SLEEPING & EATING

→ **Anglet Youth Hostel** ★ Forget hostel; this place is an international surf camp. With only a 5-minute walk to the waves, surfers and boarders flock here in the summer and camp out for weeks. The hostel offers outdoor camping or four bunk rooms with shared bathrooms. The dining

THE BASQUE COUNTRY & THE PYRENEES

room has long wooden picnic tables, like summer camp, where surfers and travelers dig in after a long day. With surfboard, boogie board, and bike rentals as well, you won't be running around town for your gear. Expect to find an international crowd in the summer, when most folks are in relentless pursuit of the best swells and breaks. Even if you're a novice or if sunbathing is more your speed, you'll find plenty of comrades. *19 rte. des Vignes.* ☎ *05-59-58-70-00. www.hihostels.com. 17€ a night with hostel membership card, breakfast included; 10€ for camping. Dinner 9€; surfboards, boogie boards, and bikes 10€ a day; wet suits 6€ a day. Internet access 5€ an hour. Plages or Marinella bus stops.*

→ **Mojito** You won't find a shortage of greasy spoons around Anglet's central beach, but Mojito is one of the more popular joints that serves up quality seafood. With main dishes like tuna and calamari and other choices like salads, chances are you'll find something to fuel up on after a long day in the water. Mojito is also a good place for a post-beach cocktail. *13–15 av. du Rayon Vert on the Chambre d'Amour.* ☎ *05-59-03-56-31. Entrees 7€–22€. May–Sept daily noon–3pm and 7pm–2am.*

BEACHES & SURFING

Given the major crowds on Biarritz beaches during the high season, Anglet is where you'll find the most serious sunbathers and surfers in the area. If you're thinking of miles of open sand, think again. The word is out on Anglet. But definitely head here if you're looking for a full day of surf, swimming, and relaxing. Don't forget the picnic lunch.

A good place to start is Anglet's tourism website (www.anglet-tourisme.com), which breaks down the turf (in English, too). The main hub is the **Chambre d'Amour** beach, which is the closest to Biarritz. Rumor has it the beach was named for a pair of lovers who escaped here for an interlude only to be swallowed by the rising waves. This is where you'll find several surf schools, as well as bars, restaurants, and surf shops. In summer, it can be quite a scene. North from there, several more beaches can be accessed from the road by bus or car. The northernmost beach is **Plage de la Barre,** which is nestled right near a sailing port and has relatively small waves due to the port's protections.

Bayonne: It's All About Food & Culture

770km (477 miles) SW of Paris, 184km (114 miles) SW of Bordeaux

It may be only a hop, skip, and jump away from the beach crowd in Biarritz, but Bayonne is a city that's remarkably surfer- and bikini-free. Located about 20 minutes east of the Atlantic coast, its star quality is actually found in its culture and food, not in its proximity to the ocean. Bayonne is Basque to the core and is chock-full of the flavors and attitude you might expect.

Get ready—Bayonne locals have two obsessions: chocolate and ham. Bayonne was one of the first chocolate-making cities in France, after Jewish refugees fleeing the Spanish and Portuguese Inquisition in the 15th century brought the trade with them. Dozens of small chocolate houses were born, though only seven main ones exist today. They can teach you everything you didn't know you wanted to know about eating the sweet stuff. As for the *jambon de Bayonne,* as it's known throughout France, it has nothing to do with ham sandwiches from home. The ham is much like prosciutto—salt-cured and always sliced thin. Don't worry about finding lunch in this town.

With Bayonne's historical sights and cultural museums, it's best to think of the town as the perfect counterpart to Biarritz. Many tourists arrive in town expecting to find the ocean on their doorstep, but land-locked Bayonne is no beach town. However, with a local bus system that easily connects Biarritz and Bayonne, there's no excuse not to spend at least a day in Bayonne, tasting the food and getting schooled in some culture.

Getting There

BY AIR

The closest airport option is nearby in Biarritz, accessible via the main local bus system for a cheap fare (p. 332).

BY TRAIN

Bayonne's train station is just across the river from the heart of town in the Saint Esprit district. A number of trains pass through on their way to Irun, the last stop on France's SCNF system before you get to Spain. Walking from the train station to town will cost you 15 minutes, but it's definitely possible. Keep your eye out for the free public transport, though (see "By Public Transportation," below).

BY CAR

If you're traveling west from the south of France, follow the N117 from Toulouse. If you're heading down from Paris, take the A10 south to Vierzon, then N20 south to Limoges. Continue on the N21 until you reach Tarbes, when you'll turn west on the N117.

BY BUS

Forget about the train—if you're traveling to Biarritz or any of the beaches in the region, look no further than the **Stab** bus network (see "By Public Transportation," below).

Orientation

Bayonne is a city carved up by rivers. The large Adour River separates central Bayonne from the Saint Esprit district, where the train station is found. The smaller Nive River is perpendicular to the Adour, and bisects the heart of town into two other districts, Petit Bayonne and Grand Bayonne. On the south end, Petit Bayonne is known for its nightlife. Most shops, restaurants, and other sights are in Grand Bayonne, which has the most hustle and bustle. The Saint-Esprit district is where many locals live, and it was developed much later than the historic center.

Getting Around

BY PUBLIC TRANSPORTATION

Bayonne, Biarritz, and Anglet are all served by the **Stab** bus system (tickets 1.20€ or 4€ for 24 hr.; ☎ 05-59-52-59-52; www.bus-stab.com). A broad number of lines connect Bayonne with the beaches at Anglet and central Bayonne, as well as the airport and the Biarritz train station. From Bayonne to Biarritz, it's only a 20- to 30-minute ride, depending on the bus line you take. Weekday buses are marked by numbers, while Sunday and holiday buses are marked by letters. Schedules and frequency also fluctuate based on the season. Considering how much turf they cover, the buses are extremely helpful. Just keep your eye on the clock, since after 9pm only one night bus runs until 5am.

Bayonne also has **La Navette,** a series of three free shuttle buses that serve the town. The two main ones run from Grand Bayonne to Petit Bayonne and back. They run Monday to Saturday 7:30am to 7:30pm (no Sun, no holidays) at no charge to the public. They are also useful for those parking on the outskirts of town. The third navette, Pass Adour, runs from the train station to two stops in Grand and Petit

Bayonne from 6:30am to 9:30pm Monday to Saturday. This puppy is also free. Navettes run every 15 minutes (give or take), so be aware that it may take you less time just to walk.

For taxi service, call **Taxi Bayonne** (☎ 05-59-59-48-48) or **Taxi Gare** (☎ 05-59-55-13-15), both of which offer 24-hour service.

BY BIKE

Traveling through town on two wheels would be no problem if there were convenient places to rent bikes. The only place close to the center of town is at the **Adour Hotel** (p. 343), which has around half a dozen bikes for rent. Needless to say, they go quickly.

Tourist Offices

Bayonne's tourist office is in the Grand Bayonne district, toward the end of avenue du 11 Novembre (place des Basques; **05-59-46-01-46**; www.bayonne-tourisme. com; Sept–June Mon–Fri 9am–6pm, Sat 10am–8pm; July–Aug Mon–Sat 9am–7pm, Sun 10am–1pm). The main reason to stop by is to pick up the local bus maps and schedules if you're beach bound. The staff can help with questions about the entire region.

Recommended Websites

- **www.ville-bayonne.fr**: This site is the central hub for the town and provides links to plenty of useful information, also in English translation.
- **www.bayonne-tourisme.com**: This is Bayonne's main tourism site and is a good place to start when looking for hotels and restaurants.

Bayonne Nuts & Bolts

Internet Cafes   If you're coming straight from the train station, the closest Internet cafe is in the Saint Esprit district. Stop by **Cyber Net Café** (9 place de la République; ☎ **05-59-50-85-10**; Mon–Sat 7am–8pm and Sun 10am–8pm), which is a bar with a small Internet cafe attached. In the center of town, drop by the **B@b Café** (see "Partying," below) for all e-mail surfing needs.

Laundromats   For a quick suds break, try the **Laverie d'Espagne** (6 rue d'Espagne; ☎ **05-59-59-54-03**; daily 8am–8pm).

Pharmacies & Grocery Stores   For much-needed sunblock, water, snacks, and more, visit **Monoprix** (8 rue Orbe; ☎ **05-59-59-00-33**; Mon–Sat 8:30am–7:30pm), France's own version of Target.

Post Office   To get stamps on all those postcards, try the Post Office near the tourist office (11 rue Jules Labat; Mon–Fri 8am–6pm).

Sleeping

Travelers looking for a bargain often think that Bayonne has cheaper options than Biarritz in the summertime. But with a small number of hotels for the size of the city, Bayonne's prices run about the same. If you're looking for comfortable digs, book early. The good ones go fast.

CHEAP

➜ **Hôtel des Basques** If you're looking for basic digs and need to keep the cost down, this hotel is probably your best bet. The main complaint here is noise given that the hotel is not far from the heart of nightlife in Bayonne. Rooms are also a bit worn down and small, but they get the job done for the price, and the owner is currently in the process of re-doing them. *Place Paul Bert, 4 rue des Lisses.* ☎ *05-59-59-08-02. 32€–38€ double with bathroom, 25€–32€ with shared bathroom. Breakfast 7€. Credit cards accepted.*

➜ **Hôtel Monbar** If you're not into basic amenities (like soap and light bulbs), then this budget joint is for you. Hôtel Monbar features the bare bones—plain rooms with a bed and bathroom and nothing else. Only a few have windows looking outdoors, while most have windows looking inward at the stairwell. Guests check in with the bartender downstairs, so don't expect much service. They do offer a standard French breakfast in the morning. If you're simply looking for four walls, it should fit the bill. *24 rue Pannecau.* ☎ *05-59-59-26-80. 30€ double. Credit cards accepted.*

DOABLE

➜ **Adour Hotel** ★★ Found just across the river from central Bayonne, this hotel is one of the best picks in town. The 12 cozy rooms are clean and bright, each with its own Basque theme. The hotel has a low-key vibe, owing to its small number of rooms and location off Bayonne's main drags. At this price, the hotel is the best value in town. Plan ahead, as rooms book quickly. An added bonus is the bike rentals in town for 13€ at day. It's the only convenient place in town to rent bikes, and those go quickly as well, so make a reservation. *13 place Sainte-Ursule.* ☎ *05-59-55-11-31. www. adourhotel.net. 60€–90€ double. Breakfast 7€. Credit cards accepted. Amenities: Restaurant; bike rental; free Wi-Fi; paid parking. In-room: A/C, TV.*

➜ **Hôtel des Arceaux** ★ Right in the heart of Bayonne, des Arceaux has a prime location. Rooms are quaint and colorful, the best of which have large windows on the upper floors. Each room is decorated in a different color, and some have shared

bathrooms in the hallway. Overall, the hotel is a solid choice, and one of only a limited number in town. *26 rue Port Neuf.* ☎ *05-59-59-15-53. www.hotel-arceaux.com. 30€–74€ double. Breakfast 7€. Credit cards accepted. In room: TV.*

SPLURGE

➜ **Best Western Le Grand Hôtel** There's no doubt that this is the most comfortable lodging in town. Built in 1835 on the site of a medieval convent, the hotel has a long history in Bayonne and brags to have hosted Ernest Hemingway and other personalities. Most rooms are spacious and more than comfortable, and breakfast is served in a bright room downstairs. Summertime price tags are high for what you're getting, so consider looking for fewer stars or simply stay in Biarritz. *21 rue Thiers.* ☎ *05-59-59-62-00. www.bw-legrand hotel.com. 68€–140€ double. Breakfast 12€. Credit cards accepted. Amenities: Restaurant/ bar; bike rental; elevator; golf; paid parking (13€); tennis courts. In room: Satellite TV.*

Eating

In addition to all the samples of chocolate and ham around town, Bayonne offers a slew of gourmet experiences. From tapas to haute cuisine, you'll find some unforgettable experiences. If you'd like to do some picking and choosing, head over to the Quai Amiral Jaureguiberry alongside the Nive River, which has many options. For the more upscale establishments, be sure to make reservations in the summer.

CAFES & LIGHT FARE

➜ **Chocolat Cazenave** ★ CAFE This chocolate *maison* has been in operation since 1854. Aside from offering a catalogue of chocolate bars, they also operate a small tea salon. This is where most people come for the famous 📺 Best● *chocolat mousseux,* a hot chocolate drink so indulgent that it should come with a warning not to operate heavy machinery after drinking it. The price of 5€ may seem a little steep, but it's worth it. The chocolate is foamed with a traditional wooden tool, as it has been for a century. They also serve ice cream and pastries, and a very tasty breakfast that includes the *chocolat mousseux*. It's hard to find a better way to start the day. *19 Arceaux Port Neuf.* ☎ *05-59-59-03-16. Chocolate 5€. Credit cards accepted. Tues–Sat 9am–noon and 2–7pm.*

→ **Les Halles** MARKET Bayonne's farmer's market is full of the region's best fruit, cheeses, seafood, and charcuterie. If you need a baguette or if you are putting lunch together on the fly, stop by here in the morning. Just be careful to make it before 1pm. *Quai Roquebert. No phone. Mon–Thurs 7am–1pm; Fri 7am–1pm and 3–7pm; Sat 6am–2pm.*

CHEAP

→ **Kalaka Café** CAFE With outdoor seating in front of the cathedral, this cafe keeps it simple by serving savory and sweet tartes for lunch only. As the afternoon wears on, it stays open to serve drinks to the tourist crowd and offers a quieter and shadier spot than many of the other cafes around. *7 place Pasteur.* ☎ *06-80-68-94-14. Main courses 4€–7€. Daily 9:15am–7:15pm.*

→ **Le Bistrot de l'Huitre** OYSTER BAR For true seafood lovers, this small oyster bar shucks some of France's best. While most of their oysters come from Brittany, they peddle several other Atlantic Coast varieties, depending on the season. Even if the brine-y creatures aren't your thing, it's still a good place to drop by for a glass of wine. *Halles Centrales, near the pont Pannecau.* ☎ *05-59-46-10-10. http://lebistrot delhuitre.fr. 6 oysters with a glass of white wine 6.90€. Credit cards accepted. Tues–Sun 10am–2pm and 6–9pm. No Sun dinner.*

DOABLE

→ **Ibaia** ★ TAPAS This popular bodega on the banks of the Nive River fills up quickly in the summer. They serve a broad range of Basque and Spanish tapas, from simple cheese and charcuterie plates, to more elaborate dishes such as cod omelets. Since they're all small plates, you can take a chance on many of the traditional dishes. With outdoor tables and a solid wine list, locals stick around for hours. *45 quai Amiral Jaureguiberry.* ☎ *05-59-59-86-66. Entrees 7€–10€. Credit cards accepted. High season daily 12:30–2:30pm and 7:30pm–2am; closed Sun–Mon in low season.*

→ **Itsaski** SEAFOOD Though you can't see the Atlantic, the fact that it's so close-by means there's plenty of fresh seafood for the taking. This restaurant serves up some of the best, from tuna to langoustines. Be sure to stick to what's locally caught. *43 quai Amiral Jaureguiberry.* ☎ *05-59-46-13-96.*

SPLURGE

→ **Au Cheval Blanc** ★★ BASQUE/FRENCH This famed restaurant mixes Basque flavor with haute cuisine. In a historic 1715 house, they focus on regional ingredients and traditional Basque preparations with a gourmet touch. Try their crepinettes if you're feeling adventurous, or stick to the fruits of the sea, like their *merlu* with glazed onions. In any case, it will be a unique experience. *68 rue Bourgneuf.* ☎ *05-59-59-01-33. Reservations recommended. Entrees 24€–36€. Credit cards accepted. Tues–Sun noon–1:30pm; Mon–Sat 8–9:30pm.*

[MTV] (Best) → **François Miura** ★★ MODERN FRENCH You might miss this restaurant in passing. The front is completely inauspicious with clean, frosted glass. Inside, though, the food is far from unremarkable. Served in a warm, modern dining room, the menu at François Miura blends local ingredients with a gourmet touch. With tuna, langoustines (like large prawns), pigeon, and much more, their dishes are refined and full of flavor. Their best deals are by far the several-course menus for 20€ and 31€. Don't miss their rich soufflé with pear liqueur and crème anglaise. *24 rue Marengo.* ☎ *05-59-59-49-89. Entrees 14€–22€. Credit cards accepted. Reservations recommended. Mon–Tues and Thurs–Sun noon–2pm and 8–10pm; no dinner on Sun.*

Partying

The nightlife in Bayonne is found almost exclusively in Petit Bayonne. Visit the streets of rue des Cordeliers and rue Pannecau by day and there's nothing much to see. At night, it's a whole different game, with bars popping up as if from nowhere. The weekends are by far the busiest, when bar crowds spill out into the street.

FUNKY BARS

➜ **Chai Ramina Pub** For decades, Chai Ramina has been the place to go for a dose of Basque attitude and party-hardiness. This funky hole-in-the-wall might be a bit dark for afternoon drinking, but it's worth popping in just to see all the memorabilia hanging from the ceiling. Old junk, copper tins, posters, and photos evince the bar's history. Expect a slow stream of regulars during the day. On Friday and Saturday, they stay open late and get a little rowdy. Drinks are 3€ to 5€. *11 rue Poissonerie.* ☎ *05-59-59-33-07.*

➜ **Katie Daly's Pub** Sure, it's a little strange to see an Irish pub in the south of France. But it's worth seeing beyond the faux–Irish pub decor, because this is actually one of the most popular watering holes in town. The comfortable bar has plenty of tables, and it fills up with locals even though it's a few blocks from the nightlife in Petit Bayonne. On some weekend nights, a live '80s cover band plays all the favorites—and in English, too, so feel free to sing along. Drinks run 4€ to 6€. *3 place de la Liberté.* ☎ *05-59-59-09-14.*

➜ **Le B@b Café** Bayonne's Internet cafe also doubles as a bar, which means you can check your e-mail either with an espresso or beer in hand. The B@b Café stays consistently busy because of this, acting as Bayonne's information hub and meeting place. Even though it's part of Petit Bayonne, the location is still convenient no matter where you are in town. Drinks are 2€ to 4€. *4 rue des Cordeliers.*

➜ **Le Patio** This bar in Petit Bayonne is known for its live music, most often on weekend nights. The room itself is cozy, but draws in a crowd that puts away the pints (2€–4€). When bands are crammed in as well, the place gets jamming. *38 rue Pannecau.* ☎ *05-59-59-36-85.*

➜ **Le Petit Vélo** When Petit Bayonne gets rowdy, you'll find one of the most hardcore bunches here. Le Petit Vélo is home to flaming concoctions with names like Che and Mao. With shooters, shots, and lighters in-hand, the bartenders here aren't pouring any wine, so don't even ask. *45 rue des Cordeliers.*

Sightseeing

MUSEUMS & SIGHTS

MTV Best ➜ **Musée Basque** ★ This recently renovated museum is a library of all things Basque. From art and culture to the objects of everyday life, the exhibition is loaded with artifacts and antiques. It's a good crash course in the history of the area and what Basque culture is built on. One of the coolest aspects is the 1930s documentary *Au Pays des Basques,* which runs continually. It includes footage of tiny Basque villages the way they were in the early 1900s, and gives you a chance to hear the Basque language, which is a whole lot easier than asking someone to speak to you in it. *37 quai des Corsaires.* ☎ *05-59-59-46-61-90. www.musee-basque.com. Admission 5.50€ adults, 3€ students. Free admission 1st Sun of the month. Joint admission including Musée Bonnat 9€ adults, 4.50€ students. May–Oct Tues–Sun 10am–6:30pm; Nov–Apr Tues–Sun 10am–12:30pm and 2–8pm.*

➜ **Musée Bonnat** This art museum is home to all the European heavy-hitters. With works from Rubens, to Ingres, Degas, and Goya, their collection is one of the most complete in France. There are some amazing works to be found here, though few famous ones if you're looking for something you've seen before. Overall, it's a well-edited trove and won't take up too much of an afternoon. *5 rue Jacques-Laffitte.* ☎ *05-59-59-08-52. www.musee-bonnat.com. Admission 5.50€ adults, 3€ students. Free admission July–Aug Wed 5:30–9:30pm and Sept–June on 1st Sun of the month. Nov–Apr Wed–Mon 10am–12:30pm and 2–6pm; May–Oct Wed–Mon 10am–6:30pm.*

FREE ➜ **Cloisters** Directly behind the cathedral, this square was formerly the medieval center of communal and religious life in Bayonne. It's almost a secret garden, hidden from the main streets around it. Begun in the 13th century, the Gothic architecture is worth a look, as are the gravestones that serve as the walkway around the square. *Place Pasteur. Free admission. June–Sept 9am–12:30pm and 2–6pm; Oct–May 9am–12:30pm and 2–5pm.*

FREE ➜ **Le Choco-Musée Puyodebat** For a taste (literally) of the chocolate making tradition in Bayonne, the free guided tours at this factory are the place to start. You'll see antique chocolate equipment and learn more about the origins of cacao. The tour is in French, but you'll still get something out of it even if you miss most of the vocabulary. *9 rue des Gouverneurs.* ☎ *05-59-59-48-42. Free 30-min. tours. Tues–Sat 10am–noon and 3–6pm.*

FREE ➜ **Saloir et Séchoire à Jambon Pierre Ibaialde** Bayonne's pride over their ham is off the charts, and if you've tried the prosciutto-like delicacy, you'll probably understand. The Pierra Ibaialde house sells their own ham, but also offers guided tours for those of you wondering how the heck they make it taste so darn good. Tours are in French, but for pork enthusiasts, it's still interesting to see the drying hams and taste the products, even if you don't understand a word. Food is an international language, after all. *41 rue des Cordeliers.* ☎ *05-59-25-65-30. www.pierre-ibaialde.com. Free 30-min. tours. Daily 9am–12:30pm and 2–6:30pm.*

MONUMENTS & CHURCHES

FREE ➜ **Cathédrale Sainte-Marie** As in most French towns, you can spot the cathedral spires from just about anywhere in town. The large cathedral was built beginning in the 13th century. Much of the original work was destroyed during the French Revolution, but the stained-glass windows still make a spin around the interior worthwhile. *Rue Notre-Dame.* ☎ *05-59-59-17-82. Free admission. Mon–Sat 7:30am–noon and 3–7pm; Sun 3:30–6pm.*

PARKS & GARDENS

FREE ➜ **Jardin Botanique** This botanical garden, housed inside the old city walls, is a throwback to a whole different culture. The structure is laid out like a Japanese garden and features hundreds of different species of plants. Just outside the garden is a large grassy area that offers one of the quietest and most comfy picnic spots in town. *Allée de Tarides (entry near av. de 11 Novembre). Free admission. Apr 15–Oct 15 Tues–Sat 9:30am–noon and 2–6pm.*

Shopping

CLOTHING & ACCESSORIES

➜ **Blue Birds** This women's boutique has modern flair with clean dresses, tops, and

Basque Attitude

Here's a cheat sheet on Basque life:

Euskara This is the Basque language, and if you have the chance to hear it, it's like nothing else you've heard. Scholars believe it's an isolated language, with little relation to other tongues. Heads up, though, since everyone in Basque country says *Adio* (pronounced "a-*dioo*") to say goodbye.

Pelota This traditional Basque game is squash made into an extreme sport. Though there are many varieties, the fastest and most dangerous is *cesta punta.* Players wear a *chistera,* a large curved mitt on their hand, which they use to fling a tiny ball against a faraway wall. With the balls traveling at speeds of over 241kmph (150 mph), there's no time to hit the refreshment stand; it's that fast. Some of the best competitors in the world gather in Biarritz each year for a master tournament (www.cestapunta.com).

Espadrilles You've seen them before—the rope-bottomed, canvas-topped sandals. But espadrilles actually come from the Basque region, and wearing them around here will help you get in with the in-crowd.

ETA This stands for **Euskadi Ta Askatuasuna (Basque Homeland and Liberty),** the main Basque separatist group. They're classified as a terrorist group by the UN, and most of their activity happens in Spain, but even in France, you'll see the acronym graffitied on walls and buildings in deep Basque country.

Fromage de Brebis This local sheep's milk cheese is a traditional favorite, most often served with black cherry jam on the side—*confiture de cerise noire.*

more. The look is more sophisticated than funky. It's on a main shopping drag, with plenty more shops like this one. *12 rue Theirs.* ☎ *05-59-59-15-96. Mon–Sat 9:45am–7pm.*

➔ **Oze Lingerie** With the beaches of Biarritz so close, you might feel unprepared without a super-chic bikini. Oze has the designer labels, with designer prices to match. The other half of the store features French lingerie at its best—lacy bustiers, frilly brassieres, and lots of pink and black. If you wanted to play the part, now's your chance. *2 rue de la Salle.* ☎ *05-59-59-46-60. Daily 10:30am–1pm and 2–7pm.*

FOOD, WINE & LOCAL CRAFTS

➔ **Chocolatier Puyodebat** This store is the retail outpost of the Puyodebat chocolate factory, which conducts free tours (see "Museums & Sights," above). Aside from pounds upon pounds of chocolate in every form (including a bubbling chocolate fountain), the specialty here is *les craquinettes,* hazelnut chocolates with a crunchy outside layer. Be sure to pick up plenty, because it won't last you long. *66 rue d'Espagne.* ☎ *05-59-59-20-86. Mon–Sat 9:30am–12:30pm and 2:30–7pm.*

FUN BUYS

➔ **Philatélie Schneider** ★ This small store is mostly dedicated to stamp collecting, but that's not the reason to visit. It also holds a good collection of used books and records. Roll up your sleeves and check out the old French science fiction and crime novel paperbacks, as well as 45s from French groups of the 1950s and 1960s. Keep an eye out for boxes of old letters and inexpensive stamps, which are also for sale. *3 bis rue Marengo.* ☎ *05-59-59-85-64. Tues–Sat 9:30am–noon and 2:30–6pm.*

Festival

Les Fêtes de Bayonne ★
Beginning the first Wednesday in August, this crazy Basque festival is basically an excuse for a 5-day all-hours party. The only code of conduct is that everyone wears white outfits with red bandanas tied around their necks, which means the center of Bayonne becomes a churning sea of red and white. The festival features a running of the bulls (though less extreme than in Pamplona) and authentic bullfights. If you're looking for pursuits less bovine in nature, there are also plenty of cultural events, including traditional Basque dancing and, of course, drinking. More than any particular happening, this one is worth your time, just to be part of the scene and witness Basque energy at its most unhinged. *Grand Bayonne, the heart of downtown. www.fetes.bayonne.fr. 1st Wed in Aug.*

St-Jean-Pied-de-Port: A Day in the Basque Country

52km (32 miles) SE of Bayonne

In the deep core of Basque country, Saint-Jean-Pied-de-Port is a small mountain town steeped in history. For 1,000 years, the town has been a main stopover on an important Christian trek—the Chemin de Saint-Jacques. Part of the town's name, *Pied-de-Port,* which literally means "foot of the pass," hints at its historical role. Pilgrims making the trek to Santiago de Compostela, in Spain (p. 293), stopped here before heading over the mountains. Today, hikers follow the same trail from France to Spain, but for more recreational reasons.

Saint-Jean-Pied-de-Port is known for its medieval ramparts surrounding a small section of town. It's lorded over by a large citadel that's now a school. The walled city is small but has plenty of character, with charming cobblestone streets and historic houses. The Nive River, trussed with footbridges, divides the whole scene, which affords awesome photo opportunities.

Getting There & Getting Around

By car from Bayonne, hop on the D932, which will get you there in less than an hour. Saint-Jean-Pied-de-Port is the end of the line for trains arriving from Bayonne, and there are only a few trips a day. To get to town from the train station, follow avenue Renaud directly outside. It's only a 10-minute walk to town.

Tourist Offices

For travel information on the region, as well as tips on the town, stop by this small tourist office just outside the city walls (14 place du Général de Gaulle; ☎ **05-59-37-03-57;** www.pyrenees-basques.com; July–Aug Mon–Sat 9am–7pm Sun 9:30am–1pm and 2–5pm; Sept–June Mon–Sat 9am–noon and 2–6pm). Keep in mind, if you want to learn about walking the Chemin de Saint-Jacques, they have a visitor center of their own (p. 350).

Internet Cafe

If you're coming from the train station, stop by the only Internet cafe in town, **Alimentation Paris** (33 av. Renaud; ☎ **05-59-37-01-47;** 7:15am–12:30pm and 3–8:30pm; 2€ for 30 min.). It's not just a cafe; it's also a grocer and the local watering hole for Basque old-timers. By midafternoon, the wine starts flowing for the older gents swapping stories (and wearing authentic Basque berets), while backpackers wander in and wait to get online (there's only one computer in back). You may not understand a word of what's being said, but rest assured; they understand "cheers."

Sleeping

Most of the options for shacking up in Saint-Jean-Pied-de-Port are actually dedicated to the pilgrims who are trekking, so don't be surprised if you're turned away. There are still a few good choices though.

➔ **Maison E. Bernat** ★ This comfortable B&B in the heart of the old town keeps things informal, with only a few rooms available. The atmosphere is warm, and the rooms are large and spacious, though you'll have to share a bathroom. An added plus is the fact that you're staying in a historic house that's part of the town's legacy. *20 rue de la Citadelle.* ☎ *05-59-37-23-10. www.ebernat.com. 57€–68€ double. Breakfast 7€. Credit cards accepted. Mar–Nov.*

DOABLE

➔ **Hôtel Continental** This standard hotel lies just outside the walled city, and offers a good value for the price. Many of the quieter rooms facing away from the street have small terraces and mountain views. The hotel is also connected to Hôtel Central down the street (which is slightly pricier). *3 av. Renaud.* ☎ *05-59-37-00-25. 66€ double. Credit cards accepted. Breakfast 8€. Apr–Nov. Amenities: Elevator. In room: TV.*

Eating

➔ **Cave des Etats de Navarre** WINE BAR For an afternoon snack or light meal, this wine bar has the goods. You can share a cheese or charcuterie plate while getting a walk-through of wines produced locally in the region. Chances are you won't find them often back home. *23 rue d'Espagne.* ☎ *05-59-49-10-48. www.cavedes etatsdenavarre.com. Plates 4€–8€. Credit cards accepted. Daily noon–9:30pm.*

➔ **Hurrup eta Klik Restaurant-Cidrerie** BASQUE Tucked away on the cobbled main drag in the old town, this modern Basque restaurant will ease you into Basque cuisine. They've put a modern spin on old favorites. *3 bis rue de la Citadelle.* ☎ *05-59-37-09-18. Entrees 9€–14€. Menu 25€. Credit cards accepted. Tues–Sun noon–2:15pm and 7–9:15pm. Feb–Nov.*

SPLURGE

➔ **Les Pyrénées** ★★ BASQUE This gourmet restaurant seems slightly out of place in such a small town, but that definitely makes it the star. They specialize in carefully prepared regional foods, and most dishes are small packages with big flavors. For heavyweights, they have a dead serious four-course menu that showcases every facet of the region. For a more reasonable price tag, stop by for a decadent lunch. Their chocolate soufflé is good enough to knock a person out. *19 place du Général de Gaulle.* ☎ *05-59-37-01-01. www.hotel-les-pyrenees.com. Entrees 18€–30€. Credit cards accepted. Mon–Sun noon–2pm and 7–9pm. Closed Mon evening and Tues fall–spring.*

Sightseeing

➔ **Prison des Eveques** The most popular story behind "the Bishop's prison" is that it was used to hold unscrupulous crooks who would dupe willing pilgrims out of their money. It was later used as a prison in World War II. A quick tour reveals the old chambers and the earth-floored dungeon, where you can still see the remnants of a chain and shackle. *41 rue de la Citadelle.* ☎ *05-59-37-03-57. July–Aug daily 10am–6:45pm, mid-Apr to May and Sept to mid-Nov Wed–Mon 11am–12:15pm and 2:30–6:15pm.*

➔ **Porte d'Espagne, Porte St. Jacques & Porte Notre-Dame** It's not too hard to find these doors to the walled city, since you'll have to use them to enter. Remarkably, the large bolts and handles are still in excellent condition. Next to the Porte Notre-Dame you'll find a stone bench built into the city walls where poor pilgrims would wait for medical treatment or a handout from the church.

The Basque Stretch of the Chemin de Saint-Jacques de Compostelle

Nope, you're not the first. The town of Saint-Jean-Pied-de-Port has been trafficked by visitors for almost a millennium. The town was a central stop on "the Way of St. James" to Santiago, Spain, to pay tribute to the apostle's resting place. For more information, see p. 293.

Today the trail is much less religious, but trekkers come internationally to hike it. By day, walkers travel through the Pyrenees and arrive, at sundown, at small towns where bunkhouses take them in, often for free or a token sum. At every joint where pilgrims are welcome, a scallop shell is usually hung over the door, symbolizing the trek.

You'll often see backpackers head straight from the train station in Saint-Jean-Pied-de-Port to the trail headquarters. The **Association des Amis du Chemin de Saint-Jacques** is where they get their pilgrim's passport and a bed assignment for the night (39 rue de la Citadelle; ☎ **05-59-37-05-09;** www. aucoeurduchemin.org; Mar–Oct). There are several starting points for the hike, though it generally takes 30 days to walk the entire way. For the best combination of weather and small crowds, they recommend you hike the trail in May or September, though most walkers hike in the summer months. It's not a bad way to brush up on French and Spanish at the same time.

Foix

86km (53 miles) S of Toulouse

The small town of Foix may look like a tiny dot on the map of the Pyrenees mountains, but with picturesque streets and cozy places to stay, Foix can be a solid home-base for exploring the region. The pace of life in town, which has remained somewhat sheltered over the centuries, is laid-back. Neighbors greet each other as they shop at the farmer's market or hang out at a local cafe. The town center is a mishmash of crooked medieval streets and historic houses.

The one thing you can't miss in Foix (or ignore for that matter) is the massive MTV (Best) **château** built directly above town on a large hill. The castle dominates the view at all times, looking blindingly bright in the morning and mysteriously golden against the night sky. So few people visit the Foix château that, compared to

other ones in France, it's in excellent condition and culturally authentic.

Foix is definitely a little on the sleepy side, so don't expect a raging nightlife. Visiting the town is about taking it in on foot, and slowing down a little. Even if you can cover Foix in only a day or two, the surrounding countryside is a much larger playground. The rolling hills, outdoor sports, and seriously charming towns are there for the taking if you're traveling by bike or car.

Getting There

BY TRAIN

The train line in Foix connects straight to Toulouse, a major hub for elsewhere in France. The station is on **rue Pierre Sémard** (☎ **05-34-09-29-00**), just across the river from town. When you get in, take a right outside the front doors of the station and following a curved road. Once you see the river and Foix's château, you'll take a right across the bridge to the center of town. The walk takes around 10 minutes.

BY BUS

Like most French cities, Foix is more easily reached by train than by bus. However, a local bus service run by **Salt Autocars** runs between Toulouse, Pamiers, Foix, and Ax-les-Thermes, a spa resort town. Swing by the tourist office in Foix to pick up the erratic schedule, or call Salt Autocars's Toulouse office (☎ **05-61-48-61-51**).

Orientation

The most interesting parts of Foix are in the medieval town center, which is a maze of tiny crooked streets with historic houses. The center is bordered by the Ariège River on the north side of town, which you'll cross when you arrive from the train station. Streets in Foix can be a bit tricky, even though they don't take up too much ground. Swing by the tourist office for a map to avoid being stuck in the maze like a mouse.

Getting Around

BY PUBLIC TRANSPORTATION

Aside from taxis (and you don't really need those, anyway), there's no need for public transportation in Foix. You can pick up **taxis** near the Halles aux Grains, on Cours Gabriel Fauré, or by calling ☎ **05-61-65-12-69.**

BY FOOT

The easiest way to get around by far is on foot, as there's not too much terrain to cover.

Tourist Offices

Foix's small tourist office (45 cours Gabriel-Fauré; ☎ **05-61-65-12-12**) can direct you around town, or around the whole region. They're open Monday to Saturday 9am to 7pm, Sunday 10am to noon and 2 to 6pm in July and August, and for the rest of the year Monday to Saturday 9am to noon and 2 to 6pm.

Recommended Website

○ **www.tourism.midi-pyrenees.org**: This site is a great resource if you're exploring the entire region and want to know what to see.

Foix **Nuts & Bolts**

ATMs   Head down the Cours Gabriel Fauré between the Halles aux Grains square and rue St. Jammes, and you'll find several ATMs.

Internet Cafes   To stay connected, visit **Cyberland** in the center of the old town. They've got six computers, a completely informal attitude, and a bit of techno or French hip-hop to keep you company (13 rue Marchand; Mon–Fri 10am–12:30pm and 2–7pm, Sat 11am–12:30pm and 2–7pm; 1€ for 15 min., 3€ for 1 hr.).

Laundromats   **Laverie la Lavandiere** is right in the heart of the old town, affording you the chance to get a snack while your stuff soaks (32 rue de la Faurie; ☎ **05-61-01-72-15;** daily 8am–8:30pm).

Post Office   The main post office is on the Allées de Villotte, just across the Cours Gabriel Faure from the old town. It's also a good place to grab a calling card, with public telephones just outside (4 allées de Villotte; ☎ **61-02-01-23;** Mon–Fri 8am–7pm and Sat 8am–noon).

Sleeping

CHEAP

📺 Best 🔊 → Le Guerrat ★★ This *chambre d'hôte* outside Foix is actually a working organic farm. Sue Morris and Trevor Warman, both English speakers, restored the barn on their property near Rimont to be a warm and cozy guesthouse. Though the inside is thoroughly modern, the old wooden beams and stone walls remind you that you're really in the countryside. They serve a three-course dinner for 18€ that's all vegan (though you wouldn't know it), and breakfast includes their homemade jams. Head here to get a taste of what the French countryside is really like, but it's best if you have some wheels of your own to get around with (it's 30 min. from Foix). For an added fee, Sue and Trevor can pick you up if you can't make the trip on your own. *09420 Esplas de Sèrou.* ☎ *05-61-96-37-03. www.leguerrat.org. 40€ single; 50€ double; 60€ triple. Rates include breakfast. No credit cards.*

DOABLE

📺 Best 🔊 → Chapeliers ★★ If you ever wished you had British relatives who owned a gorgeous house in the south of France, this B&B is probably as close as you're going to get. The location can't be beat, with a view of the château above and the backyard garden. Owners Kim and Mike live upstairs, leaving two downstairs rooms available. Expect a warm welcome from them and a bountiful breakfast. If you like to travel with iPod speakers in your pack, then chances are it's not for you. But for a warm and comfortable stay on the quiet side, this is the spot. *15 rue des Chapeliers.* ☎ *05-34-09-05-48. www. chapeliers.com. 60€ double. Rate includes breakfast. No credit cards.*

→ Hôtel Eychenne Directly in the center of town, this budget hotel is low on frills but high on value. Rooms are small, but well kept and more than adequate for a short-term stay. The hotel has a downstairs bar that sees a fair amount of action from time to time. *11 rue Peyrevidal.* ☎ *05-61-65-00-44. 45€ for 2 people. Breakfast 6€. Credit cards accepted.*

→ Hôtel Lons Well known as Foix's most comfortable hotel, Hôtel Lons overlooks the Ariège River. They have two styles of rooms, some more modern and others very classic, but it's best to request a room with a river view if you're willing to spend the extra money. They also have an annex building, which is a bit colder, but if you ask for a room on the top floor facing the château, you'll have a million-dollar view at bedtime. Their main restaurant also overlooks the river in a sunny atrium. *6 place Georges Dutilh.* ☎ *05-34-09-28-00. www. hotel-lons-foix.com. 50€–57€ double; 66€ for 3–4 people. Breakfast 7.70€. Credit cards accepted.*

Eating

CAFES & LIGHT FARE

→ Boulangerie Hebrard BAKERY This neighborhood spot is where the locals grab their bread in the early hours. Boulangerie Hebrard will tell you that they still do their baking the old-fashioned way—in a wood-burning stone oven. Pick up a baguette or two, or for heartier fare, try their bread with gruyere cheese, ham, and crème fraiche baked right in. *18 rue de la Faurie.* ☎ *05-61-65-10-52. No credit cards. Mon–Sat 7:15am–1pm and 3–8pm.*

📺 Best 🔊 → Farmer's Market ★ MARKET Foix's weekly *marché* actually takes place in two locations. Under the covered Halles au Grain, you'll find mostly meat, cheese, and other goods. Across town (though it's not a big town, remember), it's mostly vegetables and fruits near the Saint-Volusien church. Take a few laps around and see how the pros do it, before you venture forth to get a few samples of local cheese. *Halles au Grain and place St-Volusien. Wed and Fri mornings.*

CHEAP

→**Croustades Martine Crespo** FRENCH SOUTHERN   This English-speaking cafe is a laid-back place to grab a slice of quiche and a salad for lunch, but their real local specialty is *croustade*—a flaky pastry that encloses either savory or sweet goodies. All the ingredients are found locally; for best results, go for a mountain cheese or pear *croustade*. There are plenty of vegetarian options, too. In the summer, their outdoor seating is a good place for some ice cream. *21 rue des Marchands.* ☎ *05-34-09-34-27. www.croustade.com. Menus 10€–12€. Credit cards accepted. Mon–Thurs 10am–7pm Fri–Sat 9am–7pm.*

DOABLE

→**Des 4 Saisons** CREPERIE   This cheery restaurant serves up both crepes and *galettes*—buckwheat crepes with savory fillings. Less predictable are the entrees *à pierrade,* where you're given a hot stone to cook the meat for your dish. Think *shabu shabu,* the French way. *11 rue de la Faurie.* ☎ *05-61-02-71-58. Menus 8€–17€, crepes 3€–7€. Credit cards accepted. Mon–Fri 11:45am–2pm; Fri–Sat 7–10pm.*

→**Restaurant le 19eme** FRENCH SOUTHERN   Don't miss the daily special at this riverside lunch spot. You'll find the *plat du jour* scrawled on a blackboard outside and a list of upcoming specials inside, so you can plan for the week. But arrive right at 12; their savory tarts and *croûte paysanne* tend to go fast. At press time, the balcony overlooking the river was being repaired, but be sure to ask if it's possible yet to have lunch over the Ariège. *2 rue Delcassé.* ☎ *05-61-65-12-10. Menus 10€–16€. Credit cards accepted. Mon–Sat noon–2:30pm.*

Partying

Let's just hope you came to Foix for a break from nightlife. Even during the tourist high season, the most you'll find is a few cafes and restaurants open late, with a few rowdy locals and tourists here and there. But for a laid-back drink after dinner, there is one place that hits the spot.

→ **Halle aux Grains** This covered square next to Cours Gabriel Fauré houses open-air seating for two bar/restaurants nearby. Both offer somewhat forgettable food, but in the warm months, there's no better place to drink your way into the afternoon hours. The bars remain local watering holes into the evening, and the outdoor tables stay open late, offering a quiet place to kill a carafe of wine. Drinks run 2€ to 6€. *Bar le Central: place de la Halle.* ☎ *05-61-65-03-35. No credit cards. Café de la Halle: place de la Halle.* ☎ *05-61-65-01-76.*

Sightseeing

MONUMENTS & CHURCHES

MTV Best ● → **Château de Foix** ★ Built high on a bluff, Foix's château lords over the town below. It's not hard to imagine the Medieval counts peering over at the downtrodden villagers. The earliest mentions of the château came in the 11th century, and the towers were constructed in the 12th and 14th centuries. As happened with many châteaux, the cost of maintenance got to be too much, and it became an army barracks. Later it served as Foix's prison, as the bars on all the windows attest. Many of the walls are covered in prisoners' graffiti, scratched straight into the stone. Even if the history doesn't get you going, the view from the château grounds is worth seeing. ☎ *05-34-09-83-83. www.sesta.fr. Admission 4.20€, students with ID 3.10€. July–Aug daily 9:45am–6:30pm; June and Sept daily 9:45am–noon and 2–6pm; Jan–Apr and Oct–Dec Mon–Fri 10:30am–noon* and 2–5:30pm; May Mon–Fri 10:30am–noon and 2–5:30pm, Sat–Sun 9:45am–noon and 2–6pm.

Shopping
CLOTHING & ACCESSORIES

→ **Cache Cache** For a town as sleepy as Foix, Cache Cache is a surprisingly modern spot for women's fashion. You can pick a summer dress or sandals for the intense southern heat, or a light sweater for when the mountain air cools things down in the evenings. *10 rue des Marchands.* ☎ 05-61-65-45-13. *Daily 9:30am–7pm.*

FOOD, WINE & LOCAL CRAFTS

→ **Aux Saveurs et Délices** There's no way to travel through this region without running into hoards of pâté. And if you're wondering if there's anything that can't be put into pâté form, you'll satisfy your curiosity at Aux Saveurs et Délices. They make their own pâtés, and their *pâté du campagne* (country style) is not for the faint of heart. Vegetarians can opt for the jarred *ratatouille,* but a word of advice: In rural France, it's good to keep asking what's in the "vegetarian" food. *37 rue Labistour.* ☎ 05-61-03-18-28. *www.aux saveursetdelices.com. Daily 9am–8pm.*

→ **Charcuterie Rouch** You know a butcher is serious about meat when he hangs photos of the meat source—by that I mean the cows, pre-slaughter—on a poster outside the shop. If you're not in the market for a whole duck, at least go for their dried salami and sausages for your lunchtime picnic. *Place St. Volusien.* ☎ 05-61-65-04-62. *www.charcuterie-rouch.fr. Mon–Sat 7am–12:30pm and 3–7pm.*

→ **Mazas** Aside from the mouthwatering tarts and cakes displayed at this patisserie, Mazas also makes a traditional local candy—*les flocons de l'Ariège.* It's a hazelnut cream candy, covered by powdered sugar. Ask for a sample from behind the counter—it only takes a few to satisfy your sweet tooth. *29 rue Labistour.* ☎ 05-61-65-01-83. *Daily 8am–7:30pm.*

→ **Mirabelle** Get your picnic goods at Mirabelle—a small organic grocery where you can stock up on fruit, yogurt, cheese, and other staples. Make sure you swing through their local products section, where you can browse local organic jams and jellies as well. *20 rue St. Vincent.* ☎ 05-61-03-66-57. *Tues–Sat 9am–1pm and 2–7pm.*

MUSIC, BOOKS & MEDIA

→ **Majuscule** This two-story bookstore is right across the street from the tourist office, and when it comes to local outdoor guidebooks, it's much more helpful. Head upstairs to pick up books on hiking or climbing in the region, including several books just about Foix. This is also your spot for hoarding Clairefontaine notebooks for your travel journaling. *40 rue Théophile Delcassé.* ☎ 05-61-05-05-80. *Mon–Sat 9:30am–12:30pm and 2–7pm.*

FUN BUYS

→ **M. Slami** ★ There's no sign on this tiny antiques shop, and chances are the proprietor is sitting down the street sharing local gossip. In fact, "antiques shop" is a nice way of saying "a whole lot of old stuff," piled on two tables inside. But if you're willing to start digging, you'll find a treasure trove of old keys, clocks, and boxes of postcards from the early 1900s that begin with *ma chère.* And the price is right. *26 rue de la Faurie. Mon–Sun 8am–noon and 2–6pm*

→ **Sarl des Ets Savignac** Chances are your airline won't be particularly psyched if you take something home from this shop, but if you're looking for a 4-inch knife with an antler handle, or just like the look of cold steel, you've finally found the right place. Foix has an extensive hunting history, and these knives are traditional craft. The store also features a geographical survey of knives from all around France. *15 rue des Marchands.* ☎ *05-61-02-90-70. www. sarl-savignac.fr. Tues–Sat 9:30am–noon and 2:30–7pm.*

Playing Outside

➔ **Grotte de Niaux** These caves hold some of the best prehistoric drawings in the surrounding region, and word has gotten out. They're now so popular you can only visit by guided tour. The 45-minute trek, led by flashlight, reveals paintings of bison and horses created more than 14,000 years ago, as well as other traces from the Cro-Magnon folk who were hanging out then. Be advised: It's almost impossible to get here on public transportation; this is a sight reserved for travelers on wheels. *2km (1¼ miles) southwest of Tarascon.* ☎ *05-61-05-10-10. www.sesta.fr. 3–11 tours offered each day. 9.40€ per person, reservations mandatory.*

Languedoc-Roussillon

by Nathalie Jordi

The Languedoc-Roussillon is dreamer's country. The swelling sand dunes that line the long stretch of coast are dotted, lace-like from above, with marshy lagoons in which meander indolent flamingoes, wild horses, and fierce black bulls. Farther inland, hectares of black grapes (40% of France's total wine production) grow fat on the vines, the sugars inside them boiling sweet under a torrid sun. In more arid regions, such as the Gard, olive trees—in groves originally planted by the Romans, who left other artifacts all over the landscape—spread roots down as they continue their search for the thin waters underground. Whatever terrain is left unplanted reverts to *garrigue,* spread like a rocky blanket between the mountains and the limestone coast. This calcareous network of stony plateaus and half-hearted vegetation represents the last vestiges of the primordial forest that would have covered the land had humans not cleared it to spread their seeds and let loose their animals.

Then there are the region's cities—joyous and bustling (with lots of rugby fans), yet ancient, regal, proud. While unemployment in the Languedoc-Roussillon is 4% higher than elsewhere in France, the aerospace and biotech industries have taken off, and the universities in Montpellier and Toulouse attract young people who often stay.

Some of the earliest Europeans roamed the Languedoc-Roussillon, half a million years ago. Later on, the region saw Greeks, Gauls, a glorious epoch of the Roman Empire, and a benign rule by the Visigoths, who stopped Attila the Hun from getting any farther. Most of all, it saw trade—in the form of Spaniards on their way east, Italians on their way west, and ships from all over the Mediterranean and beyond, coming to trade in fish, wool, pastel, and oil.

The antique language of Oc *(langue d'oc)* still survives in a quaint, reliquary way. Although there are stirrings to bring it back in schools and literature, it is mostly honored on street signs, and pulled from the closet and dusted off for traditional festivals. If you have the chance to attend a local festival, by all means do. Some of the most fun, original, and ancient in all of France happens in this region, such as the boat races in Sete, the Feria in Nîmes, and the Paillasses of Cournonterral, which have been celebrated every Ash Wednesday since 1346.

We've saved the best for last: the food. Hoo, boy. You want seafood or meat? Try the anchovies from Collioure; or the morass of Mediterranean fish fairly leaping from the sea onto your plate; or the gut-busting bean *cassoulet,* best eaten in Toulouse; tender *vivarais* lamb; or garlicky escargots. Or what about Cevennes' selection of charcuterie and cheeses (pelardon, bleu de Causses, fourme d'Aubrac, Roquefort)? And did we already mention that 40% of the wine produced in France comes from the Languedoc-Roussillon?

The Best of Languedoc-Roussillon

◯ **The Best Visual Reminder of History in Progress (Nîmes):** The awesome juxtaposition of the ancient Maison Carrée and the modern Carré d'Art. See p. 365.

◯ **The Best Hostel in the Region (Nîmes):** It's 2km (1¼ miles) from the town center and a decent uphill walk, but the **Nîmes Youth Hostel Chemin de la Cigale** is still one of the best things about Nîmes. Its big, clean, adequately equipped rooms, super-friendly staff, and congenial atmosphere are a welcome relief. See p. 362.

◯ **The Most Extreme Antiquity in Southern France (Nîmes):** The Roman **arena** was built in, oh, the first century, and still somehow stands. See p. 365.

◯ **The Biggest Town Party You Should Do Your Best to Be Around For (Nîmes):** During the **Feria de la Pentecôte,** bulls die and everyone drinks heartily to their very good health. See p. 368.

◯ **The Best Tip with Regard to the Feria (Nîmes): Book ahead.** The Feria sounds fun to a lot of other people, too. See p. 368.

◯ **The Most Likely to Elicit Animated Discussion at the Café (Montpellier):** The neoclassical **Antigone** neighborhood, built in the late 1970s on reclaimed Army land. See p. 376.

◯ **The Street that Sort of Makes Us Wish We Were Still Living in the Middle Ages (Montpellier):** The still-adorable **rue Embouque d'Or.** See p. 378.

◯ **The Monument That Reminds Us That, Actually, We'd Rather Be Living Today (Montpellier):** Sure, we'd like a church like **L'Eglise Saint-Roch** named after us too, but spending a lifetime as a self-denying pilgrim healing others of the plague while simultaneously suffering from it? No thanks. See p. 379.

○ **The Moment You May Give Up Cabernet Forever (Montpellier):** Tasting some divine Languedoc wines with the sweet and good-looking staff at **Le Comptoir.** See p. 376.

○ **The Best Reminder That We're Actually in Southern France (Montpellier):** Watching the old men play *boules* at the Parc Rimbaud. See p. 378.

○ **The Best Solid Sud-Ouest Meal (Toulouse):** Friendly, brash, lively, and best of all, delicious, **Le J'Go**—the local outpost of Paris's equally well-loved southwestern eating house—serves up unabashedly rustic, generous portions of the food that makes this region legendary. See p. 387.

○ **The Best Guardian of the Patrimony (Toulouse): Le Père Louis** does its country proud by having served terrific wine and charcuterie since 1889 around a breathtaking zinc-bar base surrounded by wine barrels. See p. 388.

○ **The Best Surprisingly Excellent Concert to Catch (Toulouse):** The Wednesday-night organ concert at the **Musée des Augustins.** The museum is open until 9pm on Wednesday nights and puts on a half-hour concert at 8pm that's free with proof of a museum ticket. Wandering through the illuminated Gothic cloisters at night, after the sounds of the organ have subsided, is mystical and transformative. See p. 390.

Getting Around the Region

SNCF trains crisscross this area pretty comprehensively, and buses run where the trains don't. The trains can be late, though (what is it about the south, in any country?), so have a backup plan if you have to hold to a tight schedule for some reason.

When the train is obscenely late, the SCNF will refund you up to one-third the price of your reservation. (If you're touring France on a Eurail pass, though, that refund will amount to around 2 bucks.)

Nîmes: French, Roman, or Spanish?

721km (447 miles) directly S of Paris, 43km (27 miles) W of Avignon, 246km (153 miles) S of Lyon

It's warm, even at night, the tapas bars are world-class, and everyone's quaffing sangria and eating dinner at 10pm. Where are we, Barcelona? Madrid? Not quite. But Nîmes, the capital of the Gard, is more than just a lily-livered imitator of fun Catalonian towns.

Every year this town gets better, though it's still a bit quieter than its Langeudocien counterpart, Montpellier. Its Roman ruins get sprinkled with face powder, while its modern art and architecture scene show

off new and daring haircuts. Its classic restaurants keep on pumping out solid Languedocien fare, as new ones experiment with flavor and regionality. All in all, it's an interesting town, well worth a visit.

Getting There

BY AIR

The **Aéroport de Nîmes-Arles-Camargue** is 8km (5 miles) south of Nîmes on the route de Saint-Gilles. Lots of low-cost airlines come here from abroad. Shuttles can take

Languedoc-Roussillon

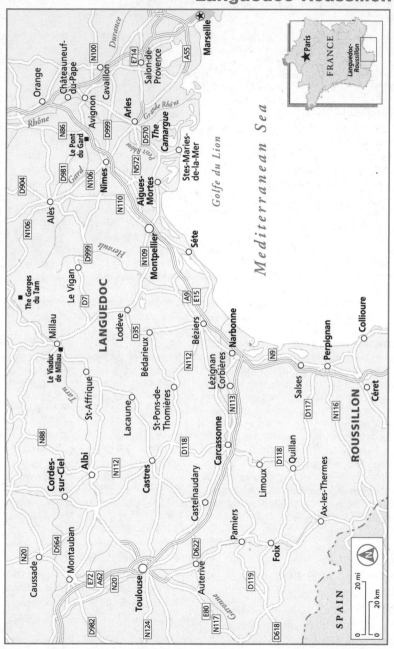

Wines of the Languedoc-Roussillon

Because it produces nearly half the wine in France, the Languedoc is often unfairly maligned as little more than a table or cooking wine region, with the exception of muscats, banyuls, and other liquorous wines. It's true that much mediocre wine has come from L-R soil, but that has been changing over the last 10 to 15 years; the region's potential—with its long summers, good soil, strong sun, and ocean breezes—is enormous, and it's finally being put to good use. Local vinters ripped out many acres of high-volume grapes in favor of "nobler" varieties, such as the traditional picpoul, bourboulenc, grenach, viognier, mourvedre, and muscat, which are either vinified purely or blended to good effect.

Corbieres, for example, the biggest (in terms of volume) AOC in the Languedoc and the fourth-biggest in France, is produced between Carcassonne, Narbonne, and Perpignan, and benefits from both *garrigue* conditions and breezes off both the Mediterranean and the Atlantic. The wines from this small region—where the reds are made principally from Carignan, black Grenache, Syrah, Mourvedre, and Cinsault grapes; and the whites from Grenache, Maccabeu, Bourboulenc, Marsanne, and Roussanne—are spicy and full-bodied. When young, they give off black-fruit flavors and, when more mature, peppery, spicy, anise-like, and herbal flavors. They go well, as you might imagine, with local food: calamari for the rosés, duck *à l'orange* for the reds, and seafood for the whites.

The grapes for **Coteaux du Languedoc,** on the other hand, are grown on some of the oldest soil ever to have bred vines—the Greeks, Romans, and monks who followed them made wine there. The climate here is hot and dry, and the soil pebbly and calcareous, making the wine, when older, redolent of leather, coffee, cocoa, and game.

The **Minervois** region makes what I think are some of the best wines to come out of the L-R, and you can probably find them once you get back home. The terrain here is also pebbly and calcareous, but some of the more elevated vineyards in the Causses give a different flavor to those farther south and closer to the Mediterranean. The younger wines are beautifully structured and elegant, with aromas of black currant, vanilla, violets, and cinnamon. Later, they elicit more stone-fruit tones, with silky tannins and a long finish.

Touring the wineries in the Languedoc-Roussillon is one of the most pleasant ways to spend a couple of days. We could waste a lot more space telling you where to go, but we'll let **Crème-de-Languedoc (www.creme-de-languedoc. com/Languedoc/activities/wine-tasting.php)** do the job for us.

And remember, if you're thinking about drinking and driving: They put people in jail for that here, too.

you to town; they stop at the Palais de Justice. Call ☎ **04-66-70-49-49.**

BY TRAIN

The train station is on the boulevard Sergent-Triaire, 10 minutes from the coliseum. Renovations to prepare it for TGV access (Paris is now only 3 hr. away, and nine trains run daily) has brought the spanking modern inside into the 21st century, while the lovely 19th-century facade hews to the past. Call ☎ **36-35** for details.

BY CAR

Take the A7 south from Lyon to Orange, and then the A9 toward Nimes. There are parking lots at the arena, on the boulevard Gambetta, at les Halles, and at the Maison Carrée, all open 24 hours a day.

BY BUS

The bus station is on the rue Sainte-Felicité (☎ **04-66-29-52-00**), right behind the train station. The whole of the Gard region is really well connected by bus. Obviously they all make it through Nîmes at some point.

Orientation

The partly pedestrianized center of Nîmes is small enough to walk around, with most of the interest located inside a triangle known as "l'Ecusson," or the shield, formed by the boulevard Victor Hugo, the boulevard Gambetta, and the boulevard Amiral Courbet. Via Domitia, one of the original Roman Gates, is between the covered Halles market and the Porte Auguste. At the southern end of l'Ecusson is the preserved Roman amphitheater known as the Arenes. West of l'Ecusson, the quai de la Fontaine will take you toward the Jardin de la Fontaine, a lovely 18th-century garden replete with statues, terraces, and canals. Climb to the top of the Tour Magne for a view of Nîmes, old and new.

Getting Around

BY PUBLIC TRANSPORTATION

The **TCN** network (☎ **04-66-38-15-40**) has 10 lines, which circulate from 6am to 9pm every day of the year besides May 1. You can buy tickets at the Station Esplanade, among other locations.

BY TAXI

Taxi Nîmois (☎ **04-66-29-40-11**) is the agglomeration of all 40 of the small operators in town, and functions 24 hours a day; they have a stand at the train station. Other stations include the Esplanade, Saint Paul, Jean Jaures, Imperator, Ville Active, Caremeau, Coupole, Gambetta, and Le Parnasse. By night (7pm–7am), the prices go up slightly.

Tourist Office

The office (6 rue Auguste; ☎ **04-66-58-38-00**; www.ot-nimes.fr.) is in front of the Musée Carrée, which makes things super simple. If you're there at the right time of year, it may interest you to buy a **Pass Romain,** for which you pay 75€ and receive in return 1 night in a two-star hotel, breakfast, a "Roman dinner," and entry to any of the monuments or museums of Nîmes, including the pont du Gard. You can have a three- or four-star hotel if you pay a supplement. The office is open October to Easter Monday to Friday 8:30am to 7pm, Saturday 9am to 7pm, Sunday and holidays 10am to 5pm; July to August Monday to Friday 8:30am to 8pm, Saturday 9am to 7pm, Sun and holidays 10am to 6pm.

Languedoc-Roussillon Nuts & Bolts

Car Rental   Most of the operators have an office at the train station and one on the avenue du Marechal-Juin: **Avis** at the train station (☎ **04-66-29-66-36**), at 1800 av. du Marechal-Juin (☎ **04-66-29-05-33**). **Budget,** 2000 av. du Marechal-Juin (☎ **04-66-38-01-69**).

Emergencies   For a doctor, call ☎ **04-66-76-11-11**.

Hospitals   **Centre Hospitalier Universitaire de Nîmes** (☎ **04-66-68-68-68**).

Internet/Wireless Hot Spots   There is a Wi-Fi hot spot on the avenue Languedoc at the Exhibition park of Nîmes.

Pharmacies   **Pharmacie de la Croix Bleue** (2 place Salamandre; ☎ 04-66-67-21-51); **Pharmacie Grangette Carles Bernard et Roles** (9 bd. Prague; ☎ 04-66-67-21-51); **Pharmacie Mutualiste** (3 rue Marchands; ☎ 04-66-67-58-62).

Post Office   Post offices are on the boulevard Gambetta (☎ **04-66-36-32-60**) and at 1 bd. de Bruxelles (☎ **04-66-76-69-50**).

Sleeping

If you're coming for the Feria, book a year ahead. Prices below do not reflect Feria inflation.

HOSTELS

MTV Best ◉ → **Nîmes Youth Hostel Chemin de la Cigale** Are you sick of hostels yet? Well, this hostel rocks, so save the splurge for another city. You need to walk a ways uphill to get there, and it's 2km (1¼ mile) from the city center, but there's a bus. Each of the rooms has a bathroom, and many even have a little patio. There's a big garden with tables, and the staff will bend over backward to help you. The social scene is warm, and eggs are served for breakfast, which you'll know is a plus if you've been a stalwart on the hostel circuit. There's Internet access, too. The cost is 10€ for a space in a two-, four-, six-, or eight-bed room. Get there by taking bus 1 (the letter, not the Roman numeral) and ask for the Auberge de Jeuness stop. Once you take the side street in front of the supermarket (on the left), follow the signs. *257 Chemin de l'Auberge de Jeunesse.* ☎ *04-66-68-03-20. www.hinimes.com. 10€ for bed in shared room.*

CHEAP

→ **Cat Hotel** This is probably the cheapest joint in town, but it's clean and cute. And did we mention it's probably the cheapest in town? *22 bd. Amiral Courbet.* ☎ *04-66-67-22-85. 27€–45€ double. Credit cards accepted. In room: Satellite TV.*

→ **Hôtel Amphiteatre** This 15-room hotel used to be a private home in the 18th century, when life was good if you were a successful merchant. The rooms still have an old-school vibe, with antiques (some real, some fake) and funky beds. The whole thing comes off as charming if you squint your eyes a bit. *4 rue des Arenes.* ☎ *04-66-67-28-51. 45€–60€ double. Credit cards accepted. Amenities: Nonsmoking rooms. In room: TV.*

DOABLE

→ **Royal Hotel** Small whitewashed rooms center around an old town house stairwell. The mix of old and new is tasteful, with a gorgeous view and location on the place d'Assas near the quais de la Fontaine. The decorators are all *nîmois,* and you might run into one of them in the Bodeguita (hotel tapas bar) downstairs, which has live tango or flamenco on Thursdays in season and one Thursday a month off season. *3 bd. Alphonse Daudet.* ☎ *04-66-58-28-27. 60€–90€ double. Credit cards accepted. Amenities: Restaurant/bar; fitness center w/sauna; indoor pool. In room: A/C, satellite TV, hair dryer, minibar, safe, Wi-Fi.*

SPLURGE

→ **New Hôtel la Baume** ★★ La Baume, call us. We're ready to move in. Right in the center of town, this beauteous *hôtel particulier* has been gorgeously preserved; were it not for all the modern touches, such as freestanding design sinks, groovy bar stools in the classy vaulted bar, and recessed lighting, we could still imagine ourselves to be in the 17th century. *21 rue Nationale. ☎ 04-66-76-28-41. www.new-hotel. com. 120€–190€ double. Credit cards accepted. Amenities: Restaurant/bar; fitness center w/sauna; game room; parking; pool; tennis. In room: A/C, TV, hair dryer, minibar.*

Eating

People say Nîmes has better tapas bars than its Catalonian neighbor, and it may be true. Drink up the sangria, eat up the paella, and stay out late. Are we really still in France?

CHEAP

Those really low on flow should scoop the sandwich stand *(kiosque)* right by the train station, on the boulevard Feucheres. The sandwiches are good and freaking cheap. Open Sunday to Friday 7:30am to 10:30pm.

Or, as always, just go to the market. Although the building it's in is, to my mind, butt-ass ugly, **Les Halles** ★ is one of the most beautifully presented major markets in southern France, and the products are top-notch. If it isn't a reflex already, make it one: For good, cheap food, head to the market rue Général Perrier, open daily 6:30am to 1pm.

➔ **La Truye qui Filhe** The oldest restaurant in town, open only for lunch, seems to have kept its prices at 19th-century rates. For 8€ for a hot meal and dessert you could feed me anything, so it's all the better to see *rouille* and paella on the menu. ("Menu" is a somewhat inaccurate term, given that this is more of a canteen—although it feels similarly incongruous to be eating off plastic trays under vaulted stone ceilings.) *9 rue Fresque. ☎ 04-66-21-76-33. Menu 8€. Credit cards accepted. Mon–Sat lunch. Closed Aug.*

DOABLE

➔ **Le Jardin d'Hadrien** ★★ FRENCH Enjoy fresh cod or zucchini flowers filled with the famous Nîmes *brandade* in Alain Vinouze's chic, ancient white stone building. If it's summertime, eating in the beautiful hidden garden is a must. But you're

Delicacies Nîmoises

L'agneau de Nîmes Nîmes lamb, always sacrificed at 3 months or less, yielding fine, tender meat.

Le croquant Villaret The mystery recipe hasn't changed since 1775. It's quite possible that the evolution in dental science was spurred on by the legions of people who must have broken teeth on this cracker.

Le petit pate nîmois Just what it sounds like—a little local meat-in-pastry pate.

La fraise de Nîmes The first two varieties of spring strawberries in France, the Gariguette and Ciflorette, only available after the Ides of March (Mar 15).

Les costieres de Nîmes An AOC wine that grows south of town.

Tapenade An olive paste, often blended with anchovies, olive oil, and herbes de Provence.

L'olive de Nîmes Green, firm, fleshy, and fruity—the Picholine variety is picked young (when it's still green; all olives are green before turning black), in December and January. It makes for terrific olive oil, too.

La brandade de Nîmes Salt cod cooked into a puree, with olive oil and a bit of milk. See "Why Is Cod a Local Specialty in Nîmes?" below.

ode to cod

Nîmes and *brandade de morue,* or the salt cod puree that has been made there for 300 years, go hand in hand—to the extent that this apocryphal story about the famous *nîmois* Alphonse Daudet (1840–97) on his deathbed gets recounted often, with an affectionate grin. Apparently the dying novelist had only one thing on his mind: writing an ode to *brandade,* meant to be read aloud at the annual dinners of the literary club he'd founded, also called La Brandade (and so they did until 1960). But cod doesn't swim near Nîmes, so how did this come to be? The salt route is the likely answer: Cod fishermen from Marseilles who came to buy salt from the marshes in Aigues-Mortes probably traded cod for salt. The *nîmois* salted the fish to preserve it. Then 24 hours before they were ready to eat, they soaked it to remove the salt, changed the water a few times, took the bones out, and cooked it with olive oil and milk until it became a smooth paste, which one could eat on toast, with potatoes, by itself, or in any number of other tasty ways.

The *brandadiers* of Nîmes, which once numbered over 20, were so successful at making Nîmes the capital of *brandade* that at one point they fixed the price per kilo of cod to avoid being outbid. Eating *brandade* became a tradition on Fridays and at Easter, not only in Nîmes but all over France. Sadly, after World War II, *brandade* fell out of favor, what with cod being considered poor people's fodder, and cod liver oil—well, no one ever liked cod liver oil.

Today, however, what with the whole "Mediterranean diet" and "French paradox" being on everyone's lips, *brandade,* whose constitutional ingredients are after all fish and olive oil, is back in vogue.

Now, where's that ode to cod?

not the first to hear about it—make a reservation if you want to dine here. *11 rue Enclos Rey. ☎ 04-66-21-86-65. Menus 18€ and 27€. Credit cards accepted. Daily in the morning; Thurs–Mon at night.*

→**Wine Bar Chez Michel** ★ BISTRO Awesome beef and fresh grilled fish in a mahogany-leather setting. Try the wines from the owner's family vineyard, plus any of the 300 others on the list. The lunch menu includes two glasses of wine rather than one, and you're on vacation, so why not? *11 place de la Couronne. ☎ 04-66-76-19-59. Lunch menu 12€–21€; dinner 18€–22€. Credit cards accepted. Tues–Fri noon–2pm; Mon–Sat 7pm–midnight.*

Partying

Nîmes isn't a student town in the same way Montpellier or Toulouse are, but that just means you'll have to share the cafes with people a few years older. Hey, that's okay; there are plenty to go around. Try the boulevard de l'Amiral Courbet, for starters. Or if you want a particularly wild night, head to the coast.

→**La Movida** This usually sedate joint in the gypsies' neighborhood mostly plays flamenco music, but on the weekend everyone comes out, and it gets a little crazier. *2 la Placette. ☎ 04-66-23-33-68.*

→**Le Fresque** Longtime Parisian club owners came down to Nîmes to open up a joint that's relaxed, convivial, and attractive. Listen to live local music, dance, and sip your mojito. This is the kind of place that'll make you go, "Holy shit, I'm on vacation!" *8 rue Fresque. ☎ 04-66-67-83-96.*

✦ **Le Victor Hugo** All of Nîmes's young'uns congregate here, sipping their coffees for hours as they talk Rimbaud and Rambo. At night the music switches on and whoa! it starts bumpin' all of a sudden. *36 bd. Victor Hugo.* ☎ *04-66-21-20-90.*

Sightseeing

Look into buying a *billet global* from any of the museums and monuments. It buys you access to all of them for 3 days. *10€ or 5€ for students.*

PUBLIC MONUMENTS

✦ **Jardins de la Fontaine** At the foot of the Mont Cavalier, these gardens were built around the sacred water source Nîmes, which has hydrated the *nîmois* ever since the early days. Benedictine nuns occupied the temple of Diana during the Middle Ages, but during the 17th century, as the city grew rapidly due to the textile trade, the river was overexploited, so in 1738 officials decided to enlarge the source. That was when the exhumators discovered all the Roman vestiges that had been covered up over time. The classical period was very fashionable then, so it was inconceivable to further bust it open. Louis XV personally assisted in the fantastic discovery, and so his engineer Jacques-Philippe Marechal and a nîmois architect, Gabriel Dardailhon, proposed to turn it into a park—the grandest and most ambitious in France to serve a city rather than a castle. Thank goodness. The results are really lovely. *Daily in summer 9am–7pm, in winter 7:30am–6:30pm.*

📺 (Best ♔) (FREE) ✦ **La Maison Carrée** Inspired by the temple of Apollo in Rome, this "tiny" version is another one of Nîmes's admirably preserved Roman relics. At different points in its history, it has been a court, a consulate, a house, a stable, and a church. *Place de la Maison Carrée. Mid-Mar to mid-Oct daily 9am–7pm; mid-Oct to mid-Mar 10am–5pm.*

📺 (Best ♔) ✦ **Le Carré d'Art** The opinions of the Nîmois are divided on this British-designed mediatheque and contemporary art museum. Some thought it was expensive and pretentious, others that it reflected the Maison Carrée across the square, perfectly. *Place de la Maison Carrée.* ☎ *04-66-76-35-70. Free entry the first Sun of every month. Tues–Sun 10am–6pm.*

📺 (Best ♔) ✦ **Les Arenes** Nîmes's arena, along with Arles's and Rome's, is one of the best-preserved coliseums in the whole world, and it's a mind-blower. Built in the 1st or 2nd century (like the Coliseum in Rome), this arena served as Nîmes's Roman social center and later as a fortress against invaders. Villagers under siege built a veritable village in there, complete with a well, houses, streets, two churches, and even a castle. There were still 230 houses and close to 2,000 inhabitants in the amphitheater in the 18th-century. (Impossibly, out of the 75 amphitheaters still standing in the world, the one in Nîmes is only the 20th biggest, even though it seated 24,000.) Ill-advised restoration efforts in the 19th century pillaged the amphitheater in Arles for missing parts, but thank goodness, that stopped. They started running *courses camarguaises* in there in 1813, and Spanish-style *corridas* in 1863. (They were a huge scandal at the time, but they've happened every year since.) If you can, see a bullfight in there, *do.* Otherwise, Nîmes stages many concerts, circuses, and theater acts there—minor consolation prizes. *Place des Arenes.* ☎ *04-66-76-72-77. 7.70€, but bring your student card. Mid-Mar to mid-Oct daily 9am–7pm, otherwise from 10am–5pm.*

✦ **Tour Magne** This Nîmois "skyscraper" is visible from all the roads that lead into the city, even if it lost its third level some time ago. Once 80 of these surrounded the city; today, the Tour Magne is the only one left. *Mont Cavalier.* ☏ *04-66-67-65-56. Admission 2.40€ adults, 1.90€ students.In summer daily 9am–7pm, in winter Mon–Fri 10am–5pm.*

HISTORIC NEIGHBORHOODS

→ **La Vieille Ville** Today's old town center is originally medieval, but what will be most obvious are the 17th- and 18th-century facades of the old houses.

MUSEUMS

All the museums in Nîmes are open Tuesday to Sunday 9am to 6pm and closed on holidays. When entrance isn't free, it costs 4.65€, or 3.40€ for students.

→ **Musée d'Art Contemporain** Two levels of permanent and temporary collections are housed in the Carré d'Art. *Place de la Maison Carrée.* ☏ *04-66-76-35-70. Admission 4.65€ adults, 3.40€ students. Tues–Sun 10am–6pm.*

→ **Musée du Vieux-Nîmes** ★ Crammed with paintings, engravings, and documents, not to mention ceramics, textiles, furniture, household items, and clothes, this museum tells you everything about the life of the *bourgeoisie nîmoise* of the last few centuries. *Place aux Herbes.* ☏ *04-66-76-73-70. Admission 4.65€ adults, 3.40€ students. Oct–Mar Tues–Sun 11am–6pm; Apr–Sept Tues–Sun 10am–6pm.*

CHURCHES

→ **La Cathédrale Notre-Dame-et-Saint-Castor** The original Romanesque building, consecrated in 1096, mostly disappeared during the violent struggles between Catholics and Protestants in 1567. As soon as it was rebuilt, it was sacked during the Revolution. Note, however, the "new" 19th-century portal that had to be rebuilt after a bishop ordered the old one broken so he could move his new

dais in. Inside, a lovely frieze depicts biblical scenes, and some of the tombs are admirably carved. *Places aux Herbes. No phone. Daily 8:30am–6:30pm (Sat until 8pm).*

TWO SPECIAL TOURS
Maison Carrée

Start at the Maison Carrée, and then walk toward the rue Général Perrier. Two blocks later, pop into Les Halles market and check out the food section. Maybe grab a baguette and some charcuterie while you're at it. Make a left down the rue des Halles, then take your second right, the rue Nationale, to the big boulevard at the end. On your left is Nîmes's original gate, the Porte Auguste. Walking south of this will take you to the Musée Archeologique, where you can scope the Roman artifacts. After that, swing right on the rue des Greffes and peep at the Philippe Starck–designed city arms on the pavement.

Old City

Start at the cathédrale Notre-Dame-et-Saint-Castor and pop in to admire the biblical scenes, then come out to the place aux Herbes. On it is the Musée du Vieux-Nîmes, which I highly recommend if you're interested in how people lived their lives in Nîmes. Once you come out, find the rue de la Madeleine. The streets you'll be walking through are rife with historical and aesthetic details such as gargoyles, balconies, and little courtyards, but you'll have to look up to see them. Pay attention. The first house you'll come across, 1 rue de la Madeleine, has the most elaborate facade in town, with carvings of vines, animals, and people. The *presbytere* on the rue Saint-Castor (no. 9) has a beautiful 17th-century facade, too. Number 14 on the rue de l'Aspic has an amazing staircase, and the Hôtel de Ville on the south side of the street has four stuffed crocodiles in it, plus

P.C. French Bullfighting: The course camarguaise

In case you hadn't noticed, Languedociens take their bull seriously—really seriously. The *culte du taureau*—literally, cult of the bull—has taken root in this region, lending it a richness and flamboyance less observed in cooler northern regions. Each village has its own bullring, and the lads adept at maneuvering their way around the hulking beasts receive the same kind of local adulation that cowboys do in rodeo country.

Camargue bulls are smaller than Spanish bulls, weighing in around 400 kilograms (882 lb.). Apparently, Camargue bulls were useless as work animals, so the *course* evolved with farmhands chasing bulls inside a ring of carts. Unlike the Spanish *corrida,* where the bulls are put to death, no bulls die in the *course camarguaise.* Defenders of the *course* also note the emphasis placed on the bull, which is evident from the publicity posters: The bull's name appears in bigger letters than the *raseteur*'s (unlike the *corrida* posters, which favor *toreadores*). Famous bulls are buried upright in their tombs (as are some famous horses).

The *course camargaise* starts with the *abrivado,* when the bull runs through the streets of town surrounded by *gardiens* riding horses that lead the bull to the ring. The *raseteurs,* or bull-runners, follow them through the streets for an emotional parade known as the *capelado.*

Six bulls go through the ring, each for 15 minutes (there is also a calf for teenagers to chase at the end of events). The bulls are wearing a *cocarde,* or rope, tied between their horns, to which tassels known as *glands* are attached (*ficelles* are also tied around the base of the horns).

First a long-sounding trumpet announces the exit of the bull *(le biou),* and the judge announces its name, the herd it comes from, and the prize at stake. A short trumpet blast indicates the beginning of the 15 minutes, and a *tourneur,* or ex-*raseteur,* taunts the bull in order to make it start running toward the *raseteur.* The bull and the *raseteur,* running at oblique angles toward one another, meet at a figurative point called the *raset,* at which point the *raseteur* uses a hook to remove first the *cocarde,* then *glands,* and finally the *ficelles* from the bull's horns, ideally without maiming anyone. Whether his attempt succeeds or fails, the poor man now has to haul ass to the fence and jump over it before the bull plants its horns into his meaty thigh, fragile ribs, or fleeing back. Cue the theme from *Carmen.* A third trumpet blast announces the end of the 15-minute period.

After the *course* comes the *bandido,* when the bulls are released into the streets. Notice that a lot of these words are in Spanish? Don't be surprised. Remember, at various points in history the whole region belonged to Spanish speakers.

iron-wrought crocodiles in the balcony. North of the Hôtel de Ville is the rue Doree, with imposing *hôtels particuliers* at numbers 3, 4, 5, 7, 9, and then some. Go ahead and poke into the courtyard; it's allowed. When you find the rue des Marchands, look for the passage des Marchands and note the *hôtels particuliers* at nos. 15 and 17, on the way to the eglise Sainte-Eugenie. At the end of the rue des Marchands is the place aux Herbes—and you're back!

ᴍᴛᴠ**U** olé! The French *Feria*

The **Feria** in Nîmes celebrates the fierce spirit of both the bull and the bull-fighter; it's this region's answer to David Beckham. Bulls die, but if that freaks you out, you can always just come to enjoy the atmosphere. The most popular party in Europe after the beer festival in Munich is the ᴍᴠ Best **Feria de la Pentecôte,** in June (there's also the Feria de Primavera in Feb, and the Feria des Vendanges in Sept). For 5 days, the streets resound with the sound of clattering bull hooves, the smell of blood, and nights spent singing, dancing, and boozing it up. The Pegoulade, or carnival procession, departs from the boulevard Jean Jaures and ends at the entrance to the Jardins de la Fontaine; there are fireworks in the lower part of the gardens. The next day is the procession of the bulls down the boulevard Gambetta, and at night music at Jean Jaures. The *novilladas,* or horse *corridas,* happen at around 11am, and the *corrida* itself begins around 6pm. As the week goes on, bullfights alternate with pageants, which alternate with folk music, dancing, and loads of drinking *vino* and sangria. A number of the bars and hotels in town organize private parties that go on until late into the night, providing meals, Spanish dancing, musical shows, and the like. This is known as a *bodega,* and it's a good idea to reserve ahead. Other than the *corridas* (expensive), the *bodegas,* and your hotel room, marked up 5,000%, most events are free. A tip about the *corrida:* You can buy a spot at the very top of the amphitheater at the last minute for 15€. Then, 5 minutes before the matadors enter, you can jump the fences to join the crowds if room remains.

Shopping

MUSIC, BOOKS & MEDIA

→ **Le Carré d'Art** This 13,000-sq.-m (139,931-sq.-ft.) mediatheque and bookstore is Sir Norman Foster's modern counterpart to the 2nd-century Roman Maison Carrée. *Place de la Maison Carrée.* ☎ 04-66-76-35-35.

FOOD, WINE & LOCAL CRAFTS

→ **Maison Raymond-Geoffroy** This adorable boutique opened in 1879, when Jules Raymond first began potting his *brandade* (still a Nîmes specialty today). *34 rue Nationale.* ☎ 04-66-67-20-47.

→ **Patisserie Moyne-Bressand** Fresh products and artisanal methods combine to make superlative candies. Come for the sage-flavored caramels, sweet confited

Nîmes Markets

Check out the following local markets for great prices on everything from fresh produce to vintage records.

→ **Les Halles de Nîmes** (rue Général Perrier; Mon–Sun 6:30am–1pm)

→ **Boulevard Jean Jaures Sud** (Fri 7am–1pm)

→ **Saint Cesaire** (place du Griffe; Sat 8am–1pm)

→ **Esplanade Charles de Gaulle,** for books and records (third Sat of the month 9am–6pm)

→ **Boulevard Gambetta** for art (every other Sun 9am–5pm)

olives wrapped in marzipan, and other *delices. 20 bd. Victor Hugo.* ☎ *04-66-67-35-12.*

Festivals & Events

➔ **Les Jeudis de Nîmes** In July and August, droves of artists and musicians gather on squares to meet, greet, and sell their wares—especially on the place du Marché, place aux Herbes, place de la Maison Carrée, and the place de l'Horloge. *Thurs in July and Aug.*

Farther Afield of Nîmes: Le Pont du Gard

23km (14 miles) NE of Nîmes

Do you ever think about the Romans? I mean, *really* think about them? "Listen here, Marcus Vipsanius Agrippa," Roman emperor Claudius probably said, sometime around the middle of the first century, "Nemauses (the huge Roman city that later became Nîmes) is growing at an astonishing rate, and their springs just aren't cutting the mustard anymore. The city needs more water, and you're in charge. Do something, my good man—fast!"

He probably sounded slightly less like a character from a bad British Bible epic, but regardless, what could Marcus Vipsanius Agrippa do? He racked his brain—disobeying an order like this could mean fresh meat for the man-hungry lions used to feeding on gladiators. And then he came up with the plan for an aqueduct 50km (31 ft.) long that would stretch between the springs at Uzès and Nîmes. An aqueduct that only descended 17 vertical meters over its entire length. An aqueduct that, nonetheless, could deliver 20,000 cubic meters (44 million gal.) of water to Nîmes daily (that's 100 gal. per second). Water that started in Uzès would get to Nîmes 24 hours later.

Well, we're guessing Claudius found someone else to feed his lions, because the evidence that Agrippa (if that's indeed who built it) did a snap-up job still remains today. Over 90% of the aqueduct runs underground, but the bridge that spans the canyon carved out by the river Gard is one of the most remarkable surviving Roman ruins anywhere. It has 6 arches at the bottom, 11 on the second level, and 47 at the top. The main arch is the largest the Romans ever built—80 feet wide. The bridge stretches 24m (160 ft.) in the air, and was originally about 330m (1,100 ft.) long; today, with 12 arches missing, it still spans an impressive 237m (790 ft.). A stone lid hides a 1.2m (4 ft.) wide, 1.8m (6 ft.) tall chamber lined with waterproof mortar for the water to pass through; it carried water through it for more than 400 years.

Over 3 years, 800 to 1,000 workers constructed the aqueduct entirely without mortar—just stones, some of them up to 6 tons heavy, held with iron clamps. The stones were pulled from a quarry half a kilometer away—and thank goodness, because they needed more than 50,000 tons of them. They lifted them into place by block and tackle—a system of two or more pulleys with a rope threaded through them, developed by Arichmedes to lift or pull heavy loads (and still used today; you'll have seen this in shipyards or on sailboats). The mechanical advantage of block and tackle (pronounced take-el) is equal to the number of lines running between the 2 blocks, so that a tackle consisting of three fixed and three moving pulleys has a mechanical advantage of six, enabling the lifting of weights six times heavier. It's useful when you're moving one 6-ton rock.

The remnants of the scaffolding erected to support the aqueduct as it was being built are still in evidence today, in the form of protruding scaffolding supports and ridges from the wooden frames on which the arches were constructed. Some writing is evident—on the places where dressed stones were to be placed, one can vaguely make out *FRSII* (for *frons sinistra II,* or front left 2). Some of the other writing on the stones comes from the *Compagnons du Tour de France,* a medieval association of French journeymen masons who traveled around the country during their apprenticeship—the pont du Gard was seen as an essential stop.

Between the 4th and the 9th centuries, the aqueduct slowly became unusable, as the conduits filled up with sediment. People began using its stones to build their own houses, and between the Middle Ages and the 18th century, the aqueduct was used as a footbridge. Eventually, it was restored and UNESCO named it a World Heritage Site in 1985. Today the French government has spent 32 million euros building a museum, parking lots, and a gift shop nearby. The pont du Gard is now one of France's top five tourist attractions, with over 1.5 million visitors reported per year.

Getting There

It's easy to visit this marvel by **car,** but you can also take a **bus.** By car, drive west of Avignon toward Nîmes, or northwest of Arles via Tarascon, or northwest of Nîmes with the N86, or southeast of Uzès on the D981. In any case, you'll rejoin the D981, which goes from Remoulins to Uzès and takes you to the Rive Gauche parking lot. Otherwise, take a bus from Nîmes, Uzès,

Collias, Alès, or Avignon. From Nîmes, take line 168 toward Collias or 169 toward Avignon to the pont du Gard—it'll cost you about 10€. Buses run daily, though there are fewer on Sundays and during the off season. The ride is 45 minutes long—call ☎ 04-66-29-27-29 or visit www.stdgard.com. Catch the bus back at the traffic circle 250m (820 ft.) from the pont.

Sleeping

It's easy enough to sleep in Avignon or Nîmes, but there's also a campsite in Remoulins: **Camping La Sousta** (av. du pont-du-Gard; ☎ 04-66-37-12-80; www.lasousta.com; Mar–Oct).

Otherwise, try the **Hôtel-restaurant Le Colombier** (rte. du pont-du-Garde, Remoulins; ☎ 04-66-37-05-28; about 50€ double; credit cards accepted) nearby, on the *rive droite.* This is the closest hotel to the bridge, with about 10 comfortable rooms.

Sightseeing

→ **Le Grand Expo du Pont du Garde** This museum on the Rive Gauche (Left Bank) describes how the aqueduct was made, and there is a rad scenic video of a helicopter ride along the whole 30-mile course between Uzès and Nîmes; it's 3€ and totally worth it. If you buy an all-inclusive 10€ ticket, parking is included, so that is probably the best deal. You can walk to the aqueduct using a path that goes from the museum, and pass under the ridge heading for the riverbank for a better view. Incidentally, this is the second-highest standing Roman structure—the Coliseum in Rome is six feet taller. A sound-and-light show plays against the pont du Gard at night in the summertime—perfect if you've managed to pick up a baggie of *beuh* off the streets in Nîmes. You can definitely see the bridge without going to the museum as long as you get there by 10pm when the parking lot closes. The modern-looking complex comprises a cafeteria, ticket booth, toilets, and shops. *B.P. 7, Vers pont du Gard.* ☎ *08-20-90-33-30. Admission 6€; parking 5€. Museum: Apr–Sept Tues–Sun 9:30am–7pm, Mon 1–7pm; Feb–Mar and Oct daily until 6pm; Nov–Jan daily until 5:30; it might be closed in Jan, so call ahead.*

If **canoeing** sounds appealing, call **Collias Canoes** (☎ **04-66-22-85-54**) or **Association Kayak Vert** (☎ **04-66-22-80-76**). You need a reservation.

Montpellier: Bumpin', Gritty College Town

736km (456 miles) directly S of Paris, 371km (230 miles) S of Vichy, 53km (33 miles) W of Nîmes

Compared to ancient, vestigial-Roman neighbors such as Nîmes, **Montpellier** is just a baby, its history stretching back a mere thousand years. In fact, most of the glory-buildings in town date back "only" to the 16th century or afterwards. This makes it one of the only big cities in France without a Gallo-Roman heritage. Nearby Maguelonne, on the coast, was the first settlement, but after pirates attacked it one too many times, villagers settled farther inland in the hills—hence, perhaps, Montpellier's name (*mont pelé* means naked hill). It was nearly guaranteed prosperity due to its protected location between the hills; its proximity to Nîmes, Beziers, and Narbonne; close and easy access to the sea; and its position on both the Camino de Santiago (Way of St. James) pilgrimage route as well as the salt route. A 12th-century Jewish traveler wrote of its streets, crowded with traders from Spain, Gaul, Greece, Egypt, Genoa, and Pisa.

Today's Montpellier no doubt looks different, but along with Toulouse, it is one of the most happening cities in the south. What can we say about a city midway between Paris and Barcelona with two-thirds of its population under the age of 40? We love it. Sure, it's a little ragged, its politics are tense, and what industry it has is much less glamorous than Paris's or Nice's.

But whatever—it's sunny, it's fun, and it's full of festivals and students.

Despite its relative youth, Montpellier has a long tradition as an education center. William VII of Montpellier founded its hallowed medical school way back in 1180. The university, which today boasts more than 60,000 students, was established in 1220. It also has a rich tradition of religious tolerance. While the Jews in Nice were forced to wear a yellow star and were locked in their ghettos at sundown (see Nice), Montpellier supported a rich Jewish cultural life, and tolerated Muslims, Cathars, and later Protestants as well.

It's hard to imagine today's European nations as anything but the distinct cultural and political entities they are, though the seemingly inflexible boundaries we take for granted have been mutable for centuries. Montpellier, for instance, belonged at one time to the kings of Aragon, which is logical considering its proximity to Spain.

Want a lesson in complicated family dynamics? Pay close attention: Marie of Montpellier (1182–1213) was all set to inherit the lordship after the death of her father, William VIII. But the first man she married, Raymond of Marseille, died too quickly. She then married Bernard IV of Comminges, but he had two other living wives, so she annulled that one lickety-split. In the meantime, her half-brother had taken control of Montpellier, but Marie wouldn't have that, so she married Peter II of Aragon, which restored her title of "Lady of Montpellier" by making Montpellier Aragonian. Once married, Peter tried to divorce her (in order to marry the Queen of Jerusalem) but keep Montpellier for himself. It didn't work, and eventually Marie's son by Peter inherited Montpellier—*and* Aragon.

Yeah, and you thought your family fights were hard-scrabble?

Eventually (in 1349), Montpellier was sold to the French. During the 19th century, the city developed its industry, but what really put it on the map was the resettlement of Algerians there in the 1960s, following Algeria's independence from France. In just a few years, it has grown from France's 25th-largest city to its 8th, making it the key player in the south.

P. S. Montpellier is twinned with Louisville, Heidelberg, and Chengdu. (Dang, we love Wikipedia.)

Getting There

BY AIR

Montpellier-Mediterranée Airport (☎ **04-67-20-85-00**) is in Mauguio. The shuttle between the airport and the center of town takes 15 to 20 minutes.

BY TRAIN

Twenty trains come in every day from Avignon, 20 from Perpignan, 8 from Marseille, and 1 every 2 hours from Toulouse. From Paris it's about 8 to 10 hours, and you might have to change in Lyon. The **gare SNCF** (☎ **36-15**) is on the place Auguste-Gilbert.

BY CAR

Montpellier is off the A9.

BY BUS

Two buses run every day from Nîmes. To get around the region, use Herault Transport—they go to more than 70 destinations, including Palavas, Carnon-la-Grande-Motte, Sete, Agde, and Beziers.

Orientation

Montpellier is nestled between hills about 20 miles north of the coast. The center of town is the place de la Comedie, known locally as *l'Oeuf* (the egg). The breezy, pleasant Esplanade abuts just north of it; new mall spaces, Le Polygone and Le Triangle, are to the east. The new neoclassical neighborhood Antigone is laid out east of them, and the north-south Lez River is east of Antigone. The rue de la Loge west of the place de la Comedie leads to the grand Arc de Triomphe and elegant Promenade de Peyrou, where Montpellier residents take walks before *l'heure de l'apéritif,* admiring the views of the Med and Cevennes National Park.

Getting Around

BY PUBLIC TRANSPORTATION

Thirty bus lines run across Montpellier's municipality. They have more non-polluting buses than almost any other city in France, and two lines run at night: the Rabelais, which goes from Mas de Bagneres to Mosson (through the gare Saint Roch) every night from 9pm to 1am; and L'Amigo, the line to take if you're going out clubbing. Every Thursday, Friday, and Saturday from midnight to 5am, L'Amigo goes from the Gare Saint Roch to the Palladium and back. More info is available on **tam-way.com**.

Montpellier also has a 15km (9 miles) tramway with 27 stations between Mosson and Odysseum. It takes 45 minutes to get from one side to the other. By 2007, Tramway Line 2 will be operational; it will have 35 stations between Saint-Jean-de-Vedas and Jacou.

BY BICYCLE

Montpellier has enacted a pilot program to offer its citizens free bicycles in the summer to get to the beach. It got off the ground in 2005, and in 2006, they were offering 100 bikes to anyone who had a TaM ticket and ID card. Find them at the "Pilou" stop at the end of line 32 at Villeneuve les Maguelone. The service is available from June to September from 10am to 8pm, although in June it's only Saturday and Sunday. Call ☎ **04-67-22-87-82.**

You can rent bikes at one of four TaM Vélo locations: 27, rue Maguelonne (Gares tramway stop), at the Euromedecine tramway stop, at Occitanie, and Odysseum. A deposit of 150€ is required.

BY TAXI

Call **Taxi Radio du Midi** (☎ 04-67-10-00-00) or **Taxi Bleu** (☎ 04-67-23-20-00).

ON FOOT

Luckily, Montpellier's center is mostly pedestrian. See the place de la Comedie for an example—it was pedestrianized in 1985, and it looks much better for it.

Tourist Offices

The tourist office is on the **Esplanade Comedie** (☎ **04-67-60-60-60**). It's open Monday to Friday 9am to 6:30pm, Saturday 10am to 6pm, and Sunday and holidays 10am to 1pm and 2 to 5pm. They do guided walks of the city with themes such as famous Montpellierians, the medieval city, or the *hôtels particuliers*, every Wednesday, Saturday, and Sunday.

They run a temporary space at the station in the summer (June–Sept Mon–Fri 10am–1pm and 2–6pm). You can get a City Pass for Montpellier for discounts in a number of tourist sites; it costs 10€ to 20€; ask the tourist bureau about it.

Montpellier **Nuts & Bolts**

Car Rental   Call **Ada** (☎ 04-67-58-34-35); **Budget** (☎ 04-67-92-69-00); or **Hertz** (☎ 04-67-06-87-90).

Emergencies   Call ☎ **15.**

Hospital   **Hôpital Lapeyronie** (191 av. Doyen Gaston Giraud; ☎ **04-67-33-81-67**).

Internet/Wireless Hot Spots   **Station Internet** (6–8 place du Marché aux Fleurs; take the tram to Comedie); **Cyberzine** (4 rue Bonnier d'Alco); **Cyberforum** (24 cours Gambetta); **Aux Mille et une Fleurs d'Or** (20 place du Nombre d'Or Antigone).

Police   ☎The police station is at 206 rue du Comte-de-Melgueil (☎ **04-99-13-50-00**).

Post Office   4 place Rondelet (☎ **04-67-34-50-00**); l'Ecusson in front of the flower market (☎ **04-67-60-03-60**); place de la Comedie (☎ **04-67-60-07-50**); Antigone at 275 rue Leon Blum (☎ **04-67-20-97-00**). Open Monday to Friday 8am to 7pm and Saturday 8am to noon.

Sleeping

Most of the hotels in town are within an easy walk between the train station and the old center. Three roads to check out in particular: boulevard Victor Hugo, rue Magueione, and rue de Verdun. You can also go straight to the tourist office, and they will make a reservation for you. Most of the hotels will charge a nominal tax on top of your room rate, but it's usually less than 1€ per day.

HOSTELS

→ **Auberge de Jeunesse Montpellier** This is the only hostel in Montpellier, and it's dirty and inhospitable. With that said, it's worth noting that lots of young French travelers stay there anyway. It's cheap, so if you don't mind going grotty, give it a try. You'll need a FUAJ card. *Rue des Écoles Laiques Impasse Petite Corraterie.* ☎ *04-67-60-32-22. 15€ bed (with FUAJ card). Amenities: Bar; pool table; TV.*

CHEAP

→ **Abasun Hotel** Clean, simple, and only slightly tacky, this hotel is really close to the train station, the Corum, and the place de la Comedie. Unlike the Hôtel des Etuves, where you'll wake someone up if you're coming in late, this hotel is open all the time. It also has air-conditioning. *13 rue Magueione.* ☎ *04-67-58-36-80. 51€ double. Credit cards accepted. Amenities: Safe. In room: A/C.*

→ **Hôtel des Etuves** Two blocks from the place de la Comedie, on a cute little pedestrian street right between the opera, the Corum, the tramway, and the train station, this hotel has 15 rooms with private bathrooms. And the prices are *right:* 25€ to 45€. The same family has been in charge since 1920, but the building dates back to the beginning of the 19th century. *24 rue des Étuves.* ☎ *04-67-60-78-19. www.hoteldes*

etuves.fr. 23€–36€ single; 37€–42€ double. Credit cards accepted. Amenities: Bar; limited room service; nonsmoking rooms. In room: A/C in some, TV, Internet, minibar.

→ **Hôtel le Strasbourg** This sweet little family establishment is close to the Corum, the train station, and Antigone. The rooms, which all have bathrooms, are air-conditioned, insulated against noise, and warmly decorated in Mediterranean colors or a marine theme. *39 bd. de Strasbourg.* ☎ *04-67-65-19-00. www.le-strasbourg.com. 48€–55€ double. Credit cards accepted.*

DOABLE

MTV **Best** → **Hôtel des Arceaux** Each of the rooms are decorated with impeccable taste—the best in Montpellier. Some have a wrought-iron theme, others are modern and sleek, others have terra-cotta color schemes. You can eat breakfast in your room or in the adorable little garden outside. Ask for a "standing" room; they're slightly pricier but worth it. *35 bd. des Arceaux.* ☎ *04-67-92-03-03. www.hoteldes arceaux.com. 60€–95€ double. Credit cards accepted. Amenities: Parking. In room: A/C, satellite TV, minibar, terrace, Wi-Fi.*

→ **Hôtel Ulysse** In the center of town, rooms here are cute, comfortable, and clean. Each one is decorated differently, with wrought-iron beds, color TV, and minibar. You can also relax in the common room or garden. *338 av. Saint-Maur.* ☎ *04-67-02-02-30. www.hotel-ulysse.com. 24 units. 58€–68€ double. Breakfast 7.20€. Credit cards accepted. Amenities: Paid parking 5€. In room: TV, minibar.*

Eating

The Languedoc has good eating, and Montpellier is at the heart of it. Go wild in the little neighborhood bistros; it's hard to go wrong if you pick places that are packed.

A Pinch of Salt?

Sete, the biggest fishing port in France, is only about 20 miles from Montpellier, so the fish is freaking fresh. It's still expensive, but try *bouillabaisse a la Montpellieraise* anyway. They throw dried ham, pork fat, and leeks into the traditional French recipe, binding the lot with pureed mini-fish (it's better than it sounds, we promise). *Bouillinade* is similar to bouillabaisse but without the puree or aioli, with potatoes on the side. Anchovies are another local delicacy, either grilled or ground into an *anchoiade*—a mix of garlic, onion, basil, and oil.

Adventurous eaters might order *cabassols,* or lamb heads oven-roasted in pork fat. Snails are another local specialty, sometimes popped into the bouillabaisse.

Other Montpellier foodstuffs include *l'amande ferrastar,* a type of almond considered to be among the world's finest; *petit pate de Penezas,* little pork-fat pastries enveloping roasted mutton with brown sugar; *mourtayrol,* a chicken-saffron stew; *olives aux chocolat,* chocolate-dipped almonds that look like olives; or *la grisette de Montpellier,* little gray candies made from honey and licorice, dating back to the Middle Ages.

Local desserts—and there are many—include *le delice des trois graces,* gingerbread-flavored dark chocolate; *l'ecusson,* a chocolate stuffed with Grand Marnier and confited orange; *touron,* a sort of soft nougat made of almonds and pine nuts; and *millas,* cake made from corn flour and pork fat. Yum.

CHEAP

➜**La Creperie des Deux Provinces** CREPERIE This place serves big and good crepes and salad, and you can leave sated for less than 10€. What else can we say? *7 rue Jacques Coeur.* ☎ *04-67-60-68-10. Main courses 13€. Credit cards accepted. Mon–Sat noon–2pm and 7–11:30pm.*

➜**Mac Khalid** NORTH AFRICAN In a city with so many North African immigrants, you can expect to find good kebabs. And here they are, with the crowds to prove it. *10 rue Daru.* ☎ *04-67-92-70-84. Main courses under 10€. Credit cards accepted. Daily 11am–midnight.*

DOABLE

➜**L'Arboisie** SEAFOOD Terrific, sparkling-fresh seafood in a crazy-tacky dining room with a festive and joyous atmosphere. Nice local cheeses, too. *12 bis, rue Jules Ferry.* ☎ *04-67-92-02-55. Menus 28€ and 48€. Credit cards accepted. Mon–Fri noon–2pm; Mon–Sat 7–11pm.*

➜**L'Assiette aux Fromages** FONDUES If you're sick of the beach and want to pretend you're in the Alps for a little while, escape to L'Assiette and regale yourself with fondues and dried hams. They have cheeses from all over France but specialize in Alpine cheeses and dishes. Dinner will cost you about 25€. *17 rue Gustave.* ☎ *04-67-58-94-48. Main courses 9€–14€. Credit cards accepted. Mon–Fri noon–1:30pm; Mon–Sat 7–10:30pm.*

➜**Le Grain de Sel** BISTRO This is the kind of French bistro you'll wish you had in your neighborhood back home. The owners are sweethearts, and the food is terrific—hearty and refined, in generous portions. Make sure you end with the cheese plate. *10 rue du Pyla-Saint-Gely.* ☎ *04-67-60-85-82. Menus around 20€. Credit cards accepted. Mon–Sat noon–2:30pm; Tues–Sat 7–11pm.*

SPLURGE

→ **Le Jardin des Sens** FRENCH Brothers Laurent and Jacques Pourcel have made it their mission to blow all of your preconceptions about food and flavor, from this small hotel-restaurant in the middle of Montpellier. Recently Michelin knocked its three stars down to two, but *Restaurant* magazine still named it one of the 50 best restaurants in the world. Taste the pig's trotters, foie gras ravioli, monkfish mousse, or rabbit filet, and decide for yourself. *11 av. Saint-Lazare.* ☏ *04-99-58-38-38. Main courses 40€–51€; lunch menu Thurs–Fri 50€; dinner menu and Sat lunch menu 125€–190€. Credit cards accepted. Thurs–Sat noon–2pm; Tues–Sat 7:30–10pm. Closed 2 weeks in Jan.*

Partying

Unlike most other French cities, which come to life in the summer, Montpellier quiets down. Such is life in a college town, but you may be psyched to have the place all to yourself. Most bars in Montpellier stop letting people in after 1am, but (lean in close now) that doesn't mean everyone has to leave right away.

CAFES

Montpellier is a cafe city, and you'll see people glued to their seats all day and long into the evening. They start with coffee, they move onto wine, and by the end of the night they're sipping digestifs or espressos. Most of the action happens on the place Jean-Jaures.

→ **Fitzpatrick's** If you're jonesing to speak English, come to this Irish pub, where the Guinness is as syrupy as Dublin's, and you can watch the footy on the telly. *5 place Saint-Come.* ☏ *04-67-60-58-30.*

→ **Le Café Joseph** Classics are always in, and this one's no exception. You'll find lots of Montpellier youth here. *3 place Jean-Jaures.* ☏ *04-67-66-31-95.*

MTV **Best** ● → **Le Comptoir** A tiny Montpellierain wine bar that's hip and sexy without trying too hard. Get your server to recommend some local wine, and order some cheese and charcuterie to go with it. The DJ nights are super popular. *5 rue du Puits du Temple.* ☏ *04-67-60-94-55.*

CLUBS & LIVE MUSIC VENUES

As befits a student town, Montpellier has one of the most amazing nightlife scenes in the south. There is always something on, whether it's a costume party, a seventies party, or an all-night shindig. And it's not nearly so expensive or pretentious as nightlife in the east, on the Riviera. Thank goodness. To find out where the top booty-shakin' joints are, pick up *Out Next* or the *Coca'Zine,* free monthlies distributed all over town.

→ **Antirouille** This hip venue features new talent, reggae, French *chanson,* rap, ska, blues, cabaret, exhibitions, open stage, *table d'hôte,* and rock concerts. Which is to say, you can find anything here. *12 rue Anatole France.* ☏ *04-67-06-51-60. www.anti.rouille.org.*

→ **Le Bec de Jazz** This teensy little bar hosts lots and lots of different music acts. *9 rue des Gagne Petit.* ☏ *04-67-02-18-83.*

→ **Le Sax'Aphone** This concert cafe with a dining area features jazz, blues, rock, salsa, world music, and a gospel brunch on the first Sunday of every month from noon to 3pm. *24 rue Ernest Michel.* ☏ *04-67-58-80-90.*

Sightseeing

PUBLIC MONUMENTS

MTV **Best** ● → **Antigone** Technically, this is a neighborhood, but it looks like a monument, so we're listing it here. The town municipality bought over 90 acres of land from the army, and architect Ricardo Bofill designed a new world there. In theory, it emulates classical architecture—columns and pilasters and the like—but uses prefab concrete to make it happen. Some people hate it, some love it, but everyone should at least go see it. *Place de la Comedie, esplanade de l'Europe.*

➔ **Arc de Triomphe** Built on the city's old ramparts, this arch is a replica of the one in Paris erected in honor of Louis XIV. It's not any better than the one in Paris, but it was just recently restored. If you take the tourist office's guided tour, you can climb the 103 steps to the top for a bird's-eye view of Montpellier and its surroundings. *Promenade du Peyrou and rue Foch.*

➔ **The Faculty of Medicine** In 1180, Lord Guilhem VIII signed an edict decreeing that anyone, regardless of religion or background, could teach medicine in Montpellier. His friends laughed at him, but what he founded became the oldest operating medical school in the Western world, natch. It was also the first university in France permitted (in 1366) to dissect cadavers. Nostradamus attended; so did Rabelais. The medieval monastery and Episcopal palace that houses the Faculty are open to visitors. *2 rue de l'Ecole de Médecine.* ☏ 04-67-66-27-77.

➔ **L'aqueduc Saint-Clement** Fourteen kilometers (9 miles) long, it stretches from Saint-Clement-de-la-Riviere, north of Montpellier, to the promenade du Peyrou in the middle of it. Eight hundred meters of this megastructure cross the Arceaux neighborhood—a graceful nod to the pont du Gard, that granddaddy of bridges not too far from this neck of the woods. This aqueduct nourishes a number of fountains in Montpellier, among them the one in Pyla Saint Gely, in the neighborhood of Lates, and the Putanelle. Other places to spot it: in the Croix-Verte neighborhood,

north of the city, and on the boulevard de la Lironde in Saint-Clement. *Promenade du Peyrou.*

➔ **Le Palais de Justice** This palace replaced the old castle of the Guilhems of Aragon, once the French bought Montpellier back. It looks like every other Palais de la Justice in France, but that means it's pretty impressive. *On the Promenade du Peyrou.*

➔ **The Medieval Mikve** ★★ Historically, Jews in Montpellier were much more influential and enjoyed more freedom than they did in other parts of France. The 13th-century mikve, in the old Jewish quarter, is one of the best-preserved ceremonial Jewish baths in Europe. Don't miss it. *Guided visits of the Montpellier Mikva available Wed and Sat afternoons through the local tourist office.* ☏ 33-467-58-67-58.

HÔTELS PARTICULIERS

They're spread out all over town, but keep an eye out for the *hôtels particuliers* built by Montpellier's rich. They're often closed, which is why the tourist office's guided tours are such a good idea. The following are among the best, listed by street:

La rue Saint-Guilhem: **L'hôtel de Castries,** at no. 31, is the most extravagant, built in 1640 by Simon Levesville. **L'hôtel Ricard,** at no. 35, has a fine 17th-century facade surrounded by molding. **L'hôtel de Campan** (no. 45) was built in the 1660s.

La rue des Tresoriers-de-la-Bourse **L'hôtel de Ginestous** is at no. 15. **L'hôtel des Tresoriers de la bourse** (no. 4) is stunning and the biggest house in the old city. Farther down is the tiny vaulted medieval **rue du Bras-de-fer.**

The **rue de la Loge:** One of Montpellier's major streets in the Middle Ages was called Gold Street for all the jewelers on it. At no. 11b is the **Hôtel Pont-de-Gout,** built in 1667, which is open for visitors. At no. 19b, you can see the house where **Saint Roch** (see "Churches," below) was born. There's a well at the end of the house that is only open on August 16, when pilgrims come to take water from it, which purportedly treats all sorts of ailments, including the plague. They also use the water to make bread, which is distributed in Montpellier's churches later that day.

La rue **Draperie-Rouge** intersects with the rue de la Vieille and the rue Saint-Ravy. Two palais there, the **palais des rois de Majorque** and the **palais des rois d'Aragon,** belonged to Montpellier's rulers in the 13th century, although they never lived there (they lived in the building that used to be on the site of the current *palais de justice*). They dropped in from time to time, however. Legend has it that Jacques d'Aragon killed his page in the *palais des rois d'Aragon,* because the poor sod had stained his vest.

On the **rue Foch, Hôtel Paul,** at no. 6, was built at the end of the 17th century, making it much older than anything else around. The **Palais de Justice** is across the street.

The 🔳 Best❢ **rue Embouque-d'Or** is so very pretty. At no. 1 is the **Hôtel de Baschy-du-Cayla;** note the wonky width of the door, designed to let in the horse carriages. Jacques de Manse lived at no. 4, the **Hôtel de Manse.**

MUSEUMS

FREE → **Carré Saint-Anne** This 19th-century deconsecrated church hosts exhibitions of contemporary plastic arts. *Place du Petit Scel.* ☎ 04-67-60-82-11. *Free admission. Tues–Sun 1–6pm; until 7pm in summer.*

FREE → **FRAC Regional Contemporary Art Foundation** This foundation owns 750 works by 350 French and international artists but exhibits them on a rotating basis in various spaces throughout the Languedoc, so that as many people as possible can get to the art. That said, there's always something interesting going on at their exhibition space in the city. *4 rue Rambaud.* ☎ 04-99-74-20-35. *www.fraclr.org. Free admission. Tues–Sat 2–6pm.*

→ **Montpellier History Museum** We've avoided putting history museums into other chapters, for want of space. This one rates because it's in a crypt. The Romanesque structure, in the crypt of the Notre-Dame des Tables, was built in the 10th century, but the more modern light projections and video and sound commentaries bring Montpellier's past back to the future. *Place Jean Jaures (in the crypt of the Notre-Dame des Tables).*

Green Places to Squat

Crammed in too many museums? Here are a few great spots in Montpellier in which to take a breather; hopefully you won't have to walk too far to find one. The **Peyrou Royal Promenade,** on the outskirts of the Ecusson, is right near the classically beautiful Arc de Triomphe and the aqueduct. **The Potter's Garden** (tram stop: Corum) is a medieval archaeological garden that served as a meeting point for pilgrims in the 13th century. It was discovered during excavation work on the new tram line. In the Antigone neighborhood, check out the fountain on the **place du Nombre d'Or,** which dances and waves as if magically controlled by gnomes underground. The **Esplanade Gardens** stretch between the place de la Comedie to the Corum, with pools, fountains, and benches, all covered by shady plane trees. Watch the Montpellierains cavort by the banks of the **Lez River,** a neighborhood that is slowly filling up with restaurants and bars. Watch the old men play boules in the 🔳 Best❢ **Parc Rimbaud** (rue Saint-Andre de Novigens).

☏ 04-67-54-33-16. Admission 1.50€. Tues–Sat 10:30am–12:30pm and 1:30–6pm.

➜ **Musée Languedocien** Want to see how Languedociens have lived these past 2,000 years? Gallo-Roman art, Greek ceramics, Romanesque sculptures, and the post-Renaissance decorative arts bring the past to life in this historic private mansion (an amazing structure, worth a visit in and of itself). 7 rue Jacques Coeur. ☏ 04-67-52-93-03. 6€ or 3€ for students. Mon–Sat 2:30–5:30pm (3–5pm Jun 15–Sept 15).

FREE ➜ **The Photo Gallery** Montpellier photographer Roland Laboye runs this gallery with lots of classic photography. Salle Dominique Bagouet, esplanade Charles de Gaulle. ☏ 04-67-60-43-11. Tues–Sat 1–7pm.

CHURCHES

➜ **La Cathédrale St-Pierre** Built in 1364 by pope Urban V, this gigantic and impressive structure officially became a cathedral in 1536, when the bishopric of Maguelone transferred to Montpellier. 6 bis, rue Abbe-Marcel-Montels. ☏ 04-67-66-04-12. Daily 9am–noon and 2:30–7pm.

MTV Best ● ➜ **L'Eglise de Saint-Roch** Come see the faithful get their pilgrims' passports stamped, at one of the stops on the holy road to Santiago de Compostela. Only the hard-core or impossibly starry-eyed pass through, because from here they have more than 1,300km (806 miles) to go. Saint-Roch was a Montpellierain born around 1350 to a family of rich merchants. He fled his parents to become a religious pilgrim and settled in the Appenines, where he caught the plague. He was cured, however, and went on to miraculously cure quite a few others in his travels. When he finally returned to Montpellier, in 1373, locals took him for a spy disguised as a pilgrim and jailed him. Ironically, he died in his hometown prison in 1379. His vindication came in the 17th century, however, when he

was canonized. Today, he's the patron saint of epidemics—how's that for a title? 4 rue Vallat. ☏ 04-67-52-74-87. Mass Tues–Fri 8am; Sun 11:30am; Gregorian chants Tues–Fri 10am.

TWO SPECIAL TOURS

Tour of Old Montpellier
The place St. Roch, place Edouard-Adam, and rue de la Mediterannée are in the process of being painted over with optical illusion frescoes.

Start at the place de la Comedie, the heart of both old and new Montpellier. North of this you'll find the **Esplanade,** a popular summer hangout; east of it is the **Polygone complex.** Take the rue de la Loge and make a right onto the rue Jacques-Coeur. No. 7 is the Hôtel des Tresoriers de France, alternately known as the **Hôtel Jacques Coeur,** named for its 15th-century resident. Right of it is the **chappelle des Penitents Blancs,** an old 17th-century church with even older structures underneath. Make a left on the rue Valedeau, and follow it until the rue Embouque d'Or, where you should turn right. You'll see the **Hôtel de la Manse** and the **Hôtel Baschy de Cayla,** with its Louis XV facade. Now make a right onto the rue de l'Aiguillerie, another right on the rue de Girone, and then the rue Fournarie. It you then take the rue de la Vieille Intendance, you'll get to the **place de la Canourge,** the 17th-century center of Montpellier. Lovely hôtels particuliers surround the garden and its fountains. From there, the rue Astruc will get you to cross the rue Foch, which puts you smack in the middle of the **Ancien Courrier** neighborhood, the very oldest part of Montpellier, now inhabited by its poshest boutiques. Take the rue Jacques d'Aragon, where you'll pass the **Hôtel St. Come,** whose tenant left part of his fortune to the surgeons of Montpellier, so they could build an anatomical theater. The grand-rue Jean Moulin will bring you back to the place de la Comedie.

Tour of Antigone: New Montpellier

Take an hour to wander Antigone and decide whether you side with those who love it or those who want it banished. Start on the east side of the place de la Comedie, then walk past Le Polygone into Antigone. You'll first pass the place du Nombre d'Or, which is followed by the place du Millenaire. Next is the place de Thessalie, then the place du Peloponnese. Finally, you'll reach the Esplanade de l'Europe, and finally the *hôtel de région,* near the river and the port Juvenal. While you're there, be sure not to miss the municipal library and the Olympic pool.

Playing Outside

FREE ➔ **The Botanical Garden** Planted in 1593, this garden is one of the oldest in Europe. It became a model for the rest of the botanical gardens in France, including the one built in Paris 40 years later. *Bd. Henri IV.* ☎ *04-67-63-43-22. Free admission. Tues–Sun noon–6pm in winter, noon–8pm in summer.*

➔ **Vegapolis Ice-Skating Rink** Yes, yes, we're dorks; and it doesn't count as outside, but it gets hot here sometimes, all right? This ice rink is huge (3 sq. km/1 sq. mile), with a sports track and game arena, complete with giant screens, music, and light shows. *Odysseum complex.* ☎ *04-99-52-26-00. www.vegapolis.net. 6.90€. Daily 10am–9:30pm.*

Shopping

MUSIC, BOOKS & MEDIA

➔ **Librairie Sauramps** Debates, lectures, protests, book signings—they all happen here. Remember, student town? *Place de la Comedie.* ☎ *04-67-06-78-78. Daily 10am–7pm.*

FOOD, WINE & LOCAL CRAFTS

➔ **Au Croquants de Montpellier** The city's favorite candy shop, where you can find all the weird local specialties. *7 rue du Faubourg-du-Courreau.* ☎ *04-67-58-67-38. Mon–Sat 7am–7pm (closed for lunch on Mon).*

➔ **Fromagerie Puig** Have you been inside a French cheese shop yet? Smelled the smells of real, non-vacuum-packed, living, stinking cheese? Puig is clean without being sterile, and the staff will provide tastes. *23 rue Saint-Guilhem.* ☎ *04-67-66-17-32. Tues–Thurs 7am–1pm and 4:30–7:30pm; Fri–Sat 7am–7pm.*

➔ **Guy Auzier** Montpellier residents love their sweets, and it's to Auzier's that they flock to satiate their habit. Come and taste. *3 rue du Faubourg-du-Courreau.* ☎ *04-67-92-63-35. Tues–Sun 8am–noon and 2–7pm.*

Tambourine Tennis & Other Local Sports

Tambourin This is the underground national Languedocien sport—like tennis except that players hit the ball with a tambourine. It's played in villages around Montpellier by two teams of five players. It's more popular in Italy, where they have a semi-professional league, but it's still ensconced in Languedocien tradition.

La Course aux Taureaux *Raseteurs* (runners) try to remove the *rasets* (pom-poms) from a bull's horns. Only occasionally does someone die.

Les Joutes Languedociennes "Knights of the lance" stand on a platform on a boat as their team rows it past another boat. The knight, protected only by a shield, uses a lance to push the other knight into the water. It's pretty spectacular, as everyone's pimped out in white gondolier-type outfits, and the crowd gets into it.

Les Paillasses de Cournonterral This game has gone on in Cournonterral every Ash Wednesday since 1346, celebrating the eviction of an annoying neighboring community. People dress up as wild men (Paillasses) and beat each other with rags soaked in stale wine and dregs.

→ **Le Marché Aux Puces** The flea market in Montpellier is humongous, crowded, and filled with crap and treasures. It may be less picturesque than some of the other markets in France, but it will remain an indelible experience in your memory. Make the trek. *Station Mosson, at the end of the railway. Sun until 1pm.*

→ **Maison Regionale des Vins et Produits du Terroir** This former *hôtel particulier* stocks more than 1,200 wines, plus cassoulet, honeys, truffles, chocolates, and then some—all from Languedoc-Roussillon. If you come on a Saturday, you can meet some of the producers. *34 rue Saint-Guilhem. ☎ 04-67-60-40-41. Mon–Sat 9:30am–8pm.*

Festivals & Events

→ **Battle of the Year** Europe's main gathering for break-dancing and hip-hop culture, this festival aims "to help people discover the richness and energy of the hip-hop movement." *Zenith Auditorium. www.attitude asso.com. ☎ 04-67-60-43-89. Apr.*

→ **Local Wine-Tastings** Every Friday 6pm to midnight on the Esplanade. *July–Aug.*

→ **Festival de Radio France et de Montpellier** More than 100 jazz, opera, and other live music performances. *☎ 04-67-02-02-01. July.*

→ **The Tour de France** The international bike race comes to Montpellier! *July.*

→ **Wine Festival** More than 40 producers gather in the place de la Comedie to taste a bunch of Montpellier wines. *☎ 04-67-13-60-00. Dec.*

→ **Montpellier Christmas Market** Takes place on the place de la Comedie. *☎ 04-67-60-60-60. Dec.*

Local Markets

→ **Marché aux Fleurs** This flower market takes place every day on the esplanade Charles-de-Gaulle.

→ **Marché des Arceaux** This organic food market takes place on the boulevard des Arceaux from Tuesday to Saturday from 7am to 1pm.

→ **Marché des Bouquinistes** This used-book market runs every fourth Saturday of the month, on the rue des Etuves.

→ **Marché Paillade** This flower market is open on the avenue d'Heidelberg every day from 7am to 1pm.

→ **Marché Paysan** This farmer's market runs every Sunday morning on avenue Saumel-Champlain.

→ **Marché Place Castellane** This market happens Monday to Saturday from 7:30am to 7:30pm; Sundays from 7:30am to 2pm.

→ **Marché Place de la Comedie** This December Christmas market takes place Monday to Thursday from 7am to 1pm, and Friday to Saturday from 7am to 7pm.

→ **Marché Place Jacques Coeur** This market on the boulevard d'Antigone is open Monday to Saturday from 8am to 9pm, Sundays and holidays from 8am to 3:30pm.

→ **Marché Place Laissac** This market runs Sunday to Friday from 7am to 1pm, Saturday from 7am to 3pm.

→ **Marché Quatre Saisons** This flea market is open on the avenue d'Heidelberg daily from 7am to 1pm.

Farther Afield: Montpellier's Follies

With everyone in town building their *hôtels particuliers,* things kinda crowded, so the more lofty-minded rich city-dwellers lifted up their fine Montpellierian noses and moved out of town—just. Inspired by the villas outside Venice, they built pseudo-châteaux as testaments to their wealth. Some still remain, and those that do are worth a gander. Check out:

→ **Château de Flaugergues** (☎ **04-99-52-66-37;** 4.50€ to see the gardens, 7€ to see the castle), one of the first, overlooking a terraced garden bordered by vines. You can go inside. 1744 av. Albert Einstein. Find the allée du Nouveau-Monde (D2), which is an extension of the avenue Jacques Cartier. At the place Christophe-Colomb, take the avenue Albert Einstein toward Mauguio (D24). The bus no. 12 goes there. Open July and August Tuesday to Sunday 2:30 to 6:30pm.

→ **Château de la Mogere,** whose grounds became an English-style garden, with a 55m aqueduct and Italianate *buffet d'eau.* Gardens are open daily; the château is open daily in summer Sunday to Friday 2:30 to 6:30pm; 2€ to 5€.

→ **Château de la Mosson,** the most famous. You'll need a car to reach it, which is too bad because it's the prettiest of all the follies. Begun in 1723 and completed in 1729, it was broken up in 1744 and its wings were removed. Very little remains. If you don't make it out there, check out the colorful polyester-resin Allan McCollum reinterpretations of mutilated statues found at the Château de la Mosson, on display at the Corum in town. Take the N109 to the Impasse du pont-du-Jour, then the chemin Joseph Bonnier de la Mosson (on foot). Park is open daily 8am to 5:45pm.

→ **Château de la Piscine** (☎ **04-67-75-73-56**—and speak your best French), which faces onto a fantabulous French-style garden with vases and statues galore. Built in 1770 for Joseph-Philibert de Belleval, today this building is totally surrounded by other people's mediocre architecture, but the *cour d'honneur* conveys a sense of what it must've looked like in days of yore. Av. de Lodeve. You'll need an appointment to visit the inside.

→ **Château d'O,** with an amazingly landscaped garden, a living museum of 18th-century landscape architecture. You won't be able to visit the inside, but go for the gardens by finding the avenue des Moulins.

Toulouse: Vibrant, Airy, Pink & Pastel

705km (437 miles) SW of Paris, 245km (152 miles) SE of Bordeaux, 97km (60 miles) W of Carcassonne

A major metropolis during the Roman Empire, Toulouse sank into sleepy provinciality during the 18th and 19th centuries, bypassed by the Industrial Revolution before resurfacing in the 1900s as a critical military, biotech, and aerospace center and bustling university town. Today Toulouse is France's fourth-largest metropolitan area, with the **second-biggest student population after Paris.** It's growing at breakneck speed and shows no signs of slowing down.

Toulouse's earliest inhabitants were a small Celtic tribe called the Tectosages, who settled in the Garonne valley in 300

B.C. The Romans made it a colony in the second century, because of its strategic position between the Mediterranean and the Atlantic, and the colony prospered from the wine trade. Saint Saturnin, after whom one of the most beautiful churches in the city is named, brought Christianity to Toulouse before a crazed mob of heathen tied him to the tail of a bull and killed him. The rue du Taur and Matabiau train station, not to mention the basilica, all recall poor Saint Saturnin in their names; *taur* is an old word for bull, and *matar bios* means "to kill the bull." The city changed hands a few times over subsequent centuries, but it wasn't until after a dark period in the 14th century (plague, the Hundred Years' War, famine, fire, floods) that Toulouse began to proper. Pastel merchants (sellers of blue dye that comes from a plant) built glorious town houses, fine arts flourished, and Charles VII instituted a Parliament. In the 16th century, however, when inexpensive indigo arrived from the New World, it nullified the pastel trade. The 17th century also saw plague, famine, a huge fire, and a civil war between Catholics and Calvinists, which peaked with the scandal of Jean Calas, who was burned alive in 1762, accused of murdering his son for wanting to become a Catholic. Eventually, the uproar calmed down and Toulouse plodded along until the 20th century. Then a flood of immigrants fleeing the fascist regimes in Italy and Spain caused a population surge, forcing Toulouse to finally undergo a much-delayed Industrial Revolution.

All French cities must necessarily marry old and new—traditions, architecture, and infrastructure. Toulouse has done this beautifully, with the pink *hôtels particuliers* that earned the town its nickname (Ville Rose), interspersed with some of the most cutting-edge graffiti art in France; and opera vying for seat space in concert halls with hip-hop and French folk music. The ancient Occitan language (or *langue d'Oc*—get it?) is still evident on street signs in Toulouse, but you're just as likely to hear Gnarls Barkley pumping through an open window.

The man held most responsible for rocketing Toulouse from its sluggish past is Dominique Baudis, who served as mayor from 1983 to 2001. Succeeding his father, Pierre, the younger Baudis strengthened Toulouse's industries (Airbus among them—you'll pass the inverted-pyramid factory on your way from the airport). He also buffeted its cultural heritage. Baudis, who wrote historical novels about the ancient counts of Tolouse, restored the Occitan cross (which had served as the flag of Languedoc) as the new flag of the city. He also restored the city's concert hall, founded a Museum of Modern art, built a huge pop venue, a space museum and educational park, and dug a subway underground. Most incredibly, Baudis announced in 1999 that Toulouse had repaid its debt, making it the only large city in France ever to switch its books from red to black. Indeed, the tax burden in Toulouse is one of the lowest in Europe.

Toulouse sits right on the Pyrenean borderlands before France starts turning really Spanish, but Toulouse itself remains assertedly French. Its cuisine is one of the richest and most delectable in an already rich and delectable region, though you'll find plenty of crap if you're not careful. Toulousains are rabid sports fans (especially for rugby—in fact Toulouse will be hosting some of the games at the 2007 Rugby World Cup). And citizens are very proud of Toulouse's most famous native son Antoine de Saint-Exupéry, author of *The Little Prince* (and several other lesser-known but beautiful books about the author's times as a pilot in the war, during which he ultimately perished). His cute

Second City of Light

Le Plan Lumière is Toulouse's citywide initiative to illuminate its best-looking buildings by night. Check out the place Saint-Georges, the place du Capitole, the Halle aux Grains, the basilique Saint-Sernin, the Mediatheque Jose Cabanis, the Abattoirs, and the banks of the Garonne, especially the quai Saint-Pierre, the usine du Bazacle, and the bridges: the pont des Catalans, the pont Neuf, and the pont Saint-Pierre.

little character even graced the 50-franc note, before the advent of the euro. If you look hard enough, you can still spot him on notebooks, pencil cases, and tattooed skin all over town.

Getting There

BY AIR

The **Toulouse-Blagnac International Airport** is in the city's northwestern suburbs 11km (7 miles) from the center (☎ **08-25-38-00-00**). You can take a shuttle into town, which comes every 20 minutes. It takes 20 minutes (3.70€), and stops at the Gare SNCF Matabiau and the bus station.

BY TRAIN

SNCF Matabiau Gare is on the boulevard Pierre Semard (☎ **08-36-35-35-35**). Take bus 14, 19, 21 or the Métro to Marengo SNCF. Toulouse is the big local hub, so you can catch a TGV here from Paris, Bordeaux, and Marseilles. The train station is a 5-minute Métro ride from the proper city center—take the Métro to Capitole. Or just walk; it's 20 minutes.

BY CAR

The city has recently built many underground parking lots, which has the environmentalists huffing and the in-town shop and business owners laughing all the way to the bank. Leave the boulevard péripherique at exit 15 and park in town.

BY BUS

The *gare routière* (bus station) is right next to the Gare Matabiau on the boulevard Pierre Semard. It's open daily 8am to 7pm. The region is fairly well connected by bus, with Toulouse at the center of it all. Both public (TISSEO) and private companies run services within the province.

Orientation

To get into town from the train station, head left, cross the canal, and head straight down Jean-Jaures, through the place Wilson and into the place du Capitole, the main square in town. In front of it are the beautiful shady gardens of the square Charles-de-Gaulle. The part of the city you'll be interested in is approximately hexagon-shaped and wraps itself around the brown River Garonne. The Canal du Midi, which joins the Garonne, creates an outer ring enclosing inner 19th-century boulevards such as the boulevard Strasbourg, Carnot, and Jules-Guesde.

Getting Around

BY PUBLIC TRANSPORTATION

Métro and Semvat **bus tickets** cost 1.25€ and cover you for an hour within the city center. They're mostly useful during the day, though, so call a **taxi** (☎ **05-34-25-02-50**) if you need to circulate past nightfall. The **Métro** goes until midnight, but covers much less ground than the buses.

Your other option is the **free electric shuttle** that tours the center of town. Call ☎ **05-61-41-70-70.**

BY BOAT

Toulouse's most salient feature is the river Garonne. A cruise tour is a pleasant way to while away a few hours. Call **Peniche Baladine** on ☎ **05-61-80-22-26** or **Toulouse Croisieres** at ☎ **05-61-25-72-57.**

BY BIKE

You can rent bikes from the bus station **TISSEO** (☎ **05-61-41-70-70**) or from **Holiday Bikes** (9 bd. des Minimes; ☎ **05-34-25-79-62**).

ON FOOT

Although it's a big city, the parts of Toulouse you'll want to see are easy to explore on foot. You can cross the old town in about half an hour in either direction.

Tourist Offices

Toulouse's **tourist office** (Square Charles de Gaulle; ☎ **05-61-11-02-22**) is in a 16th-century tower redecorated to resemble a castle keep, on the square Charles de Gaulle, right by the Capitole Métro stop in the center of town. Call them and ask about the English-language guided tours of museums, churches, and the city. You can also buy tickets to some city festivals there. The office is open June to September Monday to Saturday 9am to 7pm, Sunday 10am to 1pm and 2 to 6:30pm; October to May Monday to Friday 9am to 6pm, Saturday 9am to 12:30pm and 2 to 6pm, Sunday 10am to 12:30pm and 2 to 5pm.

Additionally, ask about **Arthemis,** the city's best tour guide organization, which employs 15 overqualified, bubbly founts of knowledge to organize personal or group tours of the city's architectural, artistic, and cultural sights.

The best way to figure out what's going on in Toulouse are the weekly listings magazines, *the Flash* and *the Hebdo,* or the free monthly *Toulouse Culture* magazine, available from the tourist office or newsstands.

Toulouse Nuts & Bolts

Emergencies Dial ☎ **15** for an ambulance, ☎ **17** for the cops, or ☎ **05-61-50-10-80** for emergency doctors.

Hospitals The most centrally located hospital is the **Hôpital de la Grave,** on the place Lange. Take bus 1, 3, 14, or 66, or the Métro to St. Cyprien République.

Pharmacies   **Pharmacie de Nuit** (13 rue Senechal; ☎ **05-61-21-81-20;** daily 8am–8pm). Take Métro Capitole, or bus nos. 10, 22, 24, or 38.

Post Office La Poste, the main branch, is in the center of town (Métro: Capitole) on 9 rue Lafayette (☎ **05-62-15-33-51**).

Sleeping

The city center is the best place to stay, with a variety of offerings from budget to cracklingly upper-crust. The triangle between the Capitole, place Victor Hugo, and place Wilson should have everything you need. Otherwise, try the neighborhood around the train station. It's slightly seedier, but you won't be far from the center; it's a 5-minute Métro ride or 20-minute walk. If you haven't reserved ahead of time, ask the tourist office for a catalogue of accommodations, which comes with a map.

CHEAP

➜ **Hôtel Des Ambassadeurs** This classic two-star is set in the dubious neighborhood near the train station, but it's friendly and congenial. Rooms are spare, but given the price, complaining isn't allowed. *68 rue Bayard.* ☎ *05-61-62-65-84. 32€–37€ double. Credit cards accepted. Amenities: Bar. In room: TV.*

➜ **Hôtel d'Orsay** This tiny little gem is right by the train station, with a great garden in the back where you can have breakfast. The rooms won't blow you away, but you can choose Earth, Water, Air, or Fire as your color scheme. They all include bathrooms, televisions, and modem plugs. *8 bd. Bonrepos.* ☎ *05-61-62-71-61. http://hotel dorsay.free.fr. 45€–60€ double. Credit cards accepted. Amenities: Parking. In room: Satellite TV, hair dryer, Internet.*

➜ **Hôtel Saint-Sernin** This is a perfect choice if you're here over a weekend, when a great little market takes place on the square. Some of the rooms have a beautiful view of the exquisite basilica (and the market, obviously), and all are comfortable and cute. *2 rue Saint-Bernard.* ☎ *05-61-21-73-08. 50€–90€ double. Credit cards accepted. Amenities: Elevator; parking. In room: TV, minibar.*

DOABLE

➜ **Grand Hôtel Raymond IV** Between the town center and the train station, this brick building is a quaint example of Toulouse's *ville rose*. The rooms are all decorated differently, the ornamental theme apparently being "of the period" (the period remaining unspecified but vaguely turn-of-the-20th-c.). *16 rue Raymond IV.* ☎ *05-61-62-89-41. www.hotelraymond4-toulouse.com. 90€–145€ double. Credit cards accepted. Amenities: Bar/ restaurant; laundry service; limited-mobility rooms; parking. In room: A/C, satellite TV, hair dryer, Internet, laundry, minibar, room service, safe.*

SPLURGE

➜ **Hôtel des Beaux-Arts** Sedate, stately, and serene, the Beaux-Arts is to Toulouse what foie gras is to the cuisine of the southwest—the glorious epitome of locality, set right on the river. The 19 rooms are fresh and creatively decorated. If you'll be here two consecutive nights including a Sunday, that night is 30% off. *1 place du pont Neuf.* ☎ *05-34-45-42-42. www.hoteldesbeaux arts.com/GB/default.htm. 100€–200€ double. Credit cards accepted. In room: A/C, satellite TV, hair dryer, safe, Wi-Fi.*

Eating

If you're on a diet, don't come to Toulouse. Better yet, come to Toulouse, but forget your diet; there are plenty of carrot sticks back home. Where else, after all, can you find a foie gras market? If you're still not convinced—well, stay home.

The best places to hunt for meals are the **place Arnaud-Bernard** and the tiny place behind it, the **place des Tiercerettes** (north of Saint-Sernin), as well as the fashionable **rue de la Colombette.** Or just follow the students. They know where the good, cheap eats are.

You'll note that many of the places below serve foie gras, cassoulet, or other much-appreciated southwestern dishes. A word of warning: In Toulouse just as elsewhere, there's more ersatz than genuine good stuff. Purists argue that a proper cassoulet takes a few days to prepare, so if you've had a bad one, it's probably because you didn't find the right place. The joints that have made their name on it are a safer bet than some no-name tourist trap. And even if you've had a bad one (I have), it's worth trying until you find a good one.

COFFEE BARS & LIGHT FARE

By all means, run, don't walk, to the **food market in place Victor Hugo** (off the bd. de Strasbourg; lunch menus 12€–16€, including wine; Tues–Sun), for a tasty, cheap breakfast or lunch (*magret de canard* at under 13€ a kilo made tears spring to my eyes). If you want something a bit more serious than fast food from a stall, try the little row of tiny restaurants in the mezzanine above the market (open only for lunch) that will rival the best in Lyon or even Paris. The most famous is called Atila.

CHEAP

➜ **Jean-Louis Cave** DELI   This deli sells classic French preparations such as eggs in aspic, quiches, veal stew, grilled rabbit, and a terrific *gâteau basque*. *81 rue Riquet.* ☎ *05-61-62-87-78. Menu 7€. Credit cards accepted. Mon–Sat 8:30am–1:30pm and 4–8pm. Métro: Jean Jaures.*

➜ **La Faim des Haricots** VEGETARIAN It's pretty incredible that Toulouse of all places—oligarchy of goose fat and duck liver—would have a decent vegetarian restaurant, but here it is. It's cheap, cute, and simple, and almost everything is homemade. *3 rue du Puits-Vert.* ☎ *05-61-22-49-25. Menus 10€–14€. Credit cards accepted. Mon–Sat noon–2:30pm; Thurs–Sat 7:30–10pm.*

➜ **L'Air de Famille** ★★ CUISINE DU MARCHE   Georges Camuzet trained with the best of them, but decided along with his partner to forsake fancy and keep things simple. They cook delicious, fresh, refined *cuisine du marché* that changes daily, in a convivial, artsy setting. Best of all, the terrific local wine list has glasses that start at 3€. We love it. *12 rue Jules Chalande.* ☎ *05-61-29-85-89. Lunch menu 12€–15€; dinner 15€–20€. Credit cards accepted. Mon–Fri noon–2:30pm and 8–10:30pm.*

➜ **Le May** BISTRO   The food changes daily, and it's cheap, convivial, and filled with locals. If you can't get a table today, come back tomorrow. *4 rue du May.* ☎ *05-61-23-98-76. Menus about 8€ lunch,*

15€ dinner. Credit cards accepted. Mon–Sat noon–2pm; Mon–Sun 7–11pm.

DOABLE

📺 Best ♦ ➜ **Le J'Go** SOUTHWESTERN FRENCH   In general, we hate restaurants that pun with their names, but we're making an exception for Le J'Go (*gigot* means leg, as in "of lamb"). They focus on southwestern specialties, paired with southwestern wines—everything from housemade terrines to lamb shoulders for two (delicious). The specials change daily, posted on their very comprehensive website (www.lejgo.com), which features interviews with their producers, lengthy essays local ingredients, and pictures of all their cute waiters. Things to try: *l'agneau fermier Quercy* (farmhouse lamb from Quercy), *porc noir de Bigorre* (rockin' pork), and their pork *rillettes*. (Incidentally, if you check out the one in Paris, you'll think you're back in Toulouse—everyone still has their southern accent.) *16 place Victor Hugo.* ☎ *05-61-23-02-03. www.lejgo.com. Main courses 17€–23€. Credit cards accepted. Daily 11am–12:30am.*

➜ **Restaurant Emile** FRENCH   This is *the* place to go for cassoulet—they bake it for 7 hours. There's more, like Catalonian fish or foie gras, but we recommend the cassoulet. Emile is set in an old house in a beautiful Toulousien square, where you can eat on the flowered terrace in summer or upstairs overlooking the square in winter. *13 place Saint-Georges.* ☎ *05-61-21-05-56. www.restaurant-emile.com. Lunch menus 18€–30€; dinner menus 40€–50€. Credit cards accepted. Daily noon–1:45pm and 7–9:45pm.*

SPLURGE

➜ **Le 19** FRENCH   Nineteen steps down from the street is what many consider to be the best restaurant in town, set in the high-ceilinged cellar of the 16th-century

Hôtel Garonne. Allegedly it was once used to store salt and fish, but today the menu's much more varied—changing with the seasons. It has (of course) foie gras, but also other duck dishes, or *topinambour* soup with roasted scallops, truffled mashed potatoes, and a "rustic" cabbage and bacon tart that has little of the vulgar about it. *19 Descente de la Halle aux Poissons.* ☎ *05-34-31-94-84. www.restaurantle19.com. Fixed-price lunch 19€–23€, fixed-price dinner from 35€. Credit cards accepted. Tues–Fri noon–2pm; Mon–Sat 8–10:30pm.*

Partying

Befitting a student town, Toulouse has a terrific party scene. Between the hectic trendiness of Paris and the late-night *java* in Barcelona, it makes its peace by starting late but staying mellow.

If you like to make an art out of lounging around in cafes, the place Arnaud Bernard is best for daytime, the place du Capitole better at night. Place Wilson and place Saint-Georges are excellent alternatives as well. You'll find droves of the *jeunesse toulousaine* on the place de la Daurade and then a bit later on the place Saint-Pierre, too.

BARS

→ **La Tantina de Burgos** So the tapas ain't too special—this isn't *quite* Spain, after all—but what better way to spend a warm evening than by drinking sangria in a loud but friendly bar? *27 av. de la Garonnette.* ☎ *05-61-55-59-29.*

→ **La Tireuse** Fancy a beer? Look no farther than the Tireuse, quite a hit among English speakers and the French people coming to hit on them ("what eez your name?"). The only thing in here better-looking than the long handsome wooden counter are the 15 beers on tap.

Try something new. *24 rue Pargaminieres.* ☎ *05-61-12-28-29.*

MTV **Best** ● → **Le Père Louis** You gotta love a country that classifies its wine bars as historic monuments. Papa Louis has been historic since 1889, but only recognized as such in 1991. And it's protected, so that no one can touch the zinc bar or oak barrels. Not only is the wine terrific, with more obscure vintages on display, but the charcuterie plate is just the thing to go with it, and the desserts are homemade. *45 rue des Tourneurs.* ☎ *05-61-21-33-45.*

CLUBS & LIVE MUSIC VENUES

Toulouse has a very active cultural scene, one of the best in the southwest, showcasing everything from opera to slam poetry, from ballet to break-dancing. Check one of the numerous event weeklies to see what's going on while you're there.

→ **Le Classico** It's modern and hip—concrete, steel, and figurative art—without devolving into the boring. Good DJs, who spin hip-hop, house, groove, and techno, save the day. They play every night but Sundays and Mondays from 11pm on. *37 rue des Filatiers.* ☎ *05-61-53-53-60.*

→ **Le Mandala** It's best known for jazz but actually good for everything they do. The tiny brick room is intimate, making everybody in it fall in love with the musicians and each other. *23 rue des Ammidonniers.* ☎ *05-61-21-10-05. www.lemandala.com.*

Night Cap

Finish your night at **Le Frigo,** which stays open until dawn (2 rue des Trois-Journées; ☎ **05-61-21-75-25**) or at **L'Ubu** (16 rue St-Rome; ☎ **05-61-23-26-75;** Mon–Sat 11pm–dawn), an equally supportive pillar of Toulouse nightlife.

Langue d'oc

If you look at a language map of France following the end of the Roman empire, you'll notice the country split in half: the south is covered by a wide swath of "Oc" and the north is swaddled in *Oïl*—both Latin-based Romance languages heavily influenced by the languages of the original pre-Roman tribes that evolved independently, entering literature separately by the 10th century. The names of both languages derive from their word for "yes," and if you notice how closely modern French's *oui* resembles *oïl*, it'll be kind of clear which dialect won out.

Provençal, often conflated with Oc itself, is actually just one of its dialects; it was common in courtly literature of the 12th century and spread by the troubadours, who traveled the land with stories set to music and poetry. In fact, Provençal, along with Latin, was the written administrative language of Southern France and the one spoken at the pontifical court at Avignon. Supposedly, Dante almost wrote his *Divine Comedy* in Oc. He wrote the line *nam alii oc, allii si, alii vero dicunt oïl,* which is to say, "some say *oc,* others say *si,* others say *oïl,*" classifying the Romance languages into their constituent regions. (Waverley Root, several hundred years later, would divide France into three again in his excellent 1958 book *The Food of France,* by the fats used in cooking: butter in the north, oil in the south, and animal fats in the southwest. It's funny to see how closely the demarcations in both language and food parallel each other.)

The 1539 Edict of Villers-Cotterets decreed that the Parisian dialect, evolved from the Langue d'Oïl, would be used for all French administration. But literature in the langue d'Oc continued until the French Revolution, when diversity of language was seen as a threat and discouraged, and during the world wars, when Occitan speakers spent time alongside French speakers. Today there still exist supposedly over 600,000 native speakers of Occitan, although we'd bet that most of them are over the age of 85. Revival efforts are visible—such as posting street signs in Occitan and offering it in schools—but you'll be lucky to hear it on the streets.

In case you do, here are a few useful words: key is *clau,* night is *nuech,* cheese is *formatge,* goat is *cabra,* and church is *glèisa.*

Sightseeing

PUBLIC MONUMENTS

➜ **Le Canal du Midi** ★★ The oldest canal in Europe is still in use, running for 240km (149 miles) between Sete and Toulouse before continuing to the Atlantic, 193km (120 miles) away. The point of the project was to connect Atlantic-facing Gascony and Mediterranean-facing Languedoc in order to avoid detouring through Gibraltar. Construction began in 1666 under Louis XIV and utilized the work of 12,000 people before its completion in 1856. It's a beautiful place for a walk, shaded by plane trees and flanked by cyclists and strollers. You can even take a boat ride through it (see "By Boat," above). *Port de l'Embouchure (ponts Jumeaux).*

➜ **Le Capitole** ★★ This is the most imposing building in Toulouse, no doubt. Its eight marble colonnades and pink facade look out onto the enormous place du Capitole, itself probably one of the most imposing plazas in France. The assassination of the duke of Montmorency happened here, but today you're more likely to see folk-dancing in the summer. Don't miss the inside, especially the "Salle des Illustres," with its gold mouldings and painted frescoes. *Place du Capitole.* ☎ 05-61-22-29-22.

→ **Le Donjon du Capitole** This 16th-century tower, which today houses the tourist office, is one of the only relics of the old town that wasn't destroyed by Haussmann in the 19th century. The slate roof and Flemish style are somewhat at odds in this town of brick and sloped tile roofs, but we like it. *Square Charles de Gaulle.* ☎ 05-61-11-02-22.

MUSEUMS

Note that museums are **free the first Sunday of every month**, or **with a student card.** You can also buy a **museum passport** that allows you access to three museums for 5€ or six for 8€.

→ **Les Abbatoirs Espace d'Art Moderne et Contemporain** ★ On the left bank of the Garonne, which is becoming richer and richer in cultural capital, architects Antoine Stinco and Remi Paipillault have designed a huge art space with library, bookstore, and auditorium, from the city's former slaughterhouse. *76 allées Charles de Fitte.* ☎ 05-34-51-10-60. *Admission 6.10€. Tues–Sun 11am–7pm.*

FREE → **Le Centre de l'Affiche, de la Carte Postale et de l'Art Graphique** Each year the theme or artist changes; each year the museum gets better. This is the best place in town to buy lithographs, decorative stamps, or other deco-geek street cred. *58 Allées Charles de Fitte.* ☎ 05-61-59-24-64. *Free admission. Mon–Fri 9am–noon and 2–6pm. Métro: St. Cyrien-République.*

→ **L'Hôtel Pierre d'Assezat** This 16th-century *hôtel particulier* was built by Nicolas Bachelier for Assezat, a pastel merchant. Today, it houses the Bemberg Foundation, which has a collection of bronzes and paintings. *Place d'Assezat.*

MTV Best ● → **Musée des Augustins** This collection includes outstanding Romanesque and Gothic sculpture and religious paintings, along with a medley of newer (but still classical) paintings: Ingres, Delacroix, Monet, Toulouse-Lautrec, and local Toulousains who painted over the centuries. The marble figures—gargoyles, saints, and martyrs—are stunning, cut mainly out of gray marble from the Pyrenees by anonymous religious artists. The interior garden is a great place to recharge before going back into the city. On Wednesday nights, the museum stays open late and puts on a half-hour organ concert starting at 8pm. *21 rue de Metz.* ☎ 05-61-22-21-82. *Admission 3€. Credit cards accepted. Daily 10am–6pm (Wed until 9pm). Métro: Esquirol.*

FREE → **Musée des Instruments de Médecine des Hopitaux de Toulouse** Medical instruments? More like torture instruments. But if you're into this sort of thing, by all means, go. Just don't blame your nightmares on us. *Hôtel-Dieu Saint Jacques. 2 rue de la Vignerie.* ☎ 05-61-77-82-72. *Free admission. Thurs–Fri 1–5pm, 1st Sun of the month 10am–6pm. Métro: St-Cyrien République.*

→ **Musée Saint-Raymond** ★ This museum, which you'll visit from top to bottom, houses the most important collection of Roman busts discovered in France—some are still being excavated. Visits are narrated by art historians in French. *Place Saint-Sernin.* ☎ 05-61-22-31-44. *Admission 3€. Daily 10am–6pm in off season, 10am–7pm in winter.*

CHURCHES

→ **Basilique Notre-Dame La Daurade** This unconventional 18th-century white and terra-cotta church sits on the base of what was once a pagan temple and, later, a Benedictine monastery. The beautiful mosaics on a gold-leaf background reference the church's name (*doré* means gold), but the real reason to come here is to see Toulouse's *Black Madonna*. *1 place de la Daurade. ☎ 05-61-21-38-32. Hours vary; call for details.*

FREE → **Basilique St-Sernin** ★★ The biggest Romanesque church in the west, built in the 16th century, allegedly holds the remains of 128 saints. It's an important stop for the pilgrims on the road to Santiago de Compostela. Located on place Saint-Sernin, open daily, with a terrific (famous) flea market on the square on Sunday mornings. *Place St-Sernin. No phone. Free admission. Crypts 3€, with slightly shorter hours. Basilica Oct–May Mon–Sat 8:30am–11:45am and 2–5:45pm, Sun 8:30am–12:30pm and 2–7pm; slightly later during the week in June; July–Sept daily 8:30am–6:15pm (Sun until 7:30pm).*

→ **Cathédrale St-Etienne** This church took 4 centuries to build, which means it's a jangle of different styles and themes. Hey, when you're incorporating 17 chapels, you've got to be creative. *Place Saint-Etienne. ☎ 05-61-52-03-82. Daily 8am–7pm.*

→ **Convent of the Jacobins** ★ Monastic life starts looking pretty good when you flee the hot hustle-bustle city for this peaceful in-town oasis. Considered a jewel of Gothic Languedocien art and architecture, the 13th-century structure is built entirely out of bricks. *Parvis des Jacobins. ☎ 05-61-22-23-82. Admission 3€; free admission 1st Sun of the month. Daily 10am–7pm.*

TWO SPECIAL TOURS

Old Toulouse

Start at the **place Saint-Sernin,** where you can admire the gorgeous basilique and the archaeological museum of **Saint-Raymond** (if you're around on a Sunday morning, don't miss the flea market). Walk to the **Capitole**—the quintessence of the "pink city"—via the rue du Taur. Walk slightly east on the rue Lafayette until you get to the place Wilson, with its panoply of cafes and brasseries. Then follow the rue Saint-Antoine-du-T to come upon the old **place Saint-Georges,** with its restaurants and large terraces. You'll have been parallel to the long shopping street known as the rue d'Alsace-Lorraine or rue du Languedoc, which crosses about five 19th-century streets until it hits the rue de Metz, which runs east-west onto the pont Neuf and across the Garonne. This intersection is the most clearly delineated of all the ones in town; the others wind around churches and take a pause for small squares. Note the *hôtels particuliers* you'll pass as you stroll around town: the **Hôtel d'Assezat** on the place d'Assezat, the **Hôtel Dieu Saint Jacques** over the pont Neuf bridge, the **Hôtel de Police,** and **the Hôtel Vieux Raisins** on the rue Ozenne off the place de Carmes. Right on this intersection is the place Esquirol, which is a wet dream for food lovers, with the Comtesse du Barry, Pillon, and Domaine de Lastours food shops. You can double back to the place du Capitole by walking north on the rue des Changes (the old medieval Main St.), passing posh shops as well as classical Toulousain architectural masterpieces such as the **Hôtel d'Astorg, Hôtel de Comere,** and the **Hôtel Dumay,** and then rejoining the rue St. Rome.

Nature Walk

If you're looking for green space and a breath of air, direct yourself to the Garonne river or walk the towpath on the Canal du Midi. You can join it southeast of the Jardin des Plantes, the oldest green area of town, near the Moorish-looking pavilion of the Georges Labit Museum, where you can stop in for a look at some Egyptian and Oriental art. Wander through the three gardens (Jardin des Plantes, Jardin Royal, and Grand-Rond), or the gardens of the Grand-Rond and the Jardin des Plantes. Take the foot-bridges over the

Feminist Graffiti

Miss Van was born in 1973 in Toulouse and started scrawling on its walls at the age of 18. Today, her work shows in galleries all over the world, but she lives and works in Toulouse and Barcelona, and the streets here bear her mark. Her frescoes and paintings offer a feminine alternative to the predominantly male realm of street art. Instead of painting her name—"graffiti has a very megalomaniac side," she says—she decided to represent herself through dolls. Miss Van names among her influences Japanese *manga*, 1950s pin-ups, and comic strips, and tends to paint dolls that are innocent but sexy, bursting with colors and voluptuousness. Miss Van (short for Vanessa) was the first female graffist in Toulouse, but her success has spawned dozens of imitators, which you'll see if you wander the streets. Just make sure you look up, as the graffs can be in unexpected places, like barges, trains, roofs, traffic circles. A few highlights of the Toulouse graffito are the urban scenes on rue Saint Panteleon, rue Baour-Lorman, and rue Gramat. These are in constant state of flux, so the best way to spot good ones is to wander around.

road to look at the palais Niel on the corner of the place Montoulieu. Then, walk northeast up the wide avenues of the allées Jules Guesde until the place du Salin and the place du Parlement (public executions used to take place here). Walking even farther north will take you to the pretty, peaceful place de Carmes; from there, you can keep walking north until you've rejoined the rest of the city.

Playing Outside

One lovely green space is the jardins de la Daurade near the river; take the rue Clemence Isaure and look for the basilique de la Daurade, overlooking the water. Have a breather on the banks of the Garonne, and pose for a cheesy shot with the pont Neuf in the background. Follow the quays toward the pont Saint-Pierre, shaded by plane trees. Alternately, check out the Japanese gardens in the jardin Compans-Caffarelli—there's a big lake too.

Shopping

BOOKS & MEDIA

➜ **The Bookshop** When you've run out of Agatha Christies, this is the place to stock

up. They peddle bestsellers, children's books, and reference works in English. *17 rue Lakanal.* ☎ *05-61-22-99-92.*

FOOD, WINE & LOCAL CRAFTS

➜ **Busquets** Probably the most famous fine food shop in Toulouse is lined with traditional foie gras and beans for cassoulet, smoked salmon, and caviar. *10 rue Remusat.* ☎ *05-61-21-22-16. Mon–Sat 9:30am–1pm and 2:30–8pm. Métro: Capitole.*

➜ **Galerie Daudet** This stylish art gallery stocks painting, sculpture, and jewelry, set amid the other excellent shops on the rue de la Trinité that carry lampstands, glasses, porcelain, and so on. *10 rue de la Trinité.* ☎ *05-34-41-74-84.*

➜ **La Pipe** The strangest smokeshop you'll ever see sells pipes and ashtrays, but it also has a good dose of local charm and character and about 10 years' worth of dust. *6 place du pont-Neuf. No phone. Daily 8:30pm–3am. Métro: Esquirol.*

➜ **Saveurs et Harmonies** Did you know that the only thing that can technically be called tea is water steeped with the leaves of the tea plant, which precludes mint, chamomile, and other herbal "teas"? These must be called *tisanes* or something else. This place also sell good coffee and terrific little munchies from specialized producers all over France, such as honey-sweetened jams, Ile de Ré–salted caramels, and old-style cookies. *24 rue de la Colombette.* ☎ *05-61-99-32-98. Métro: Jean Jaures.*

→**Violettes et Pastel** This shop sells everything violet, the emblem of Toulouse: sweets, jams, tea, liquors, perfume, pot-pourri, candles, incense, soap, and per-fume. *10 rue Saint-Panteleon.* ☎ *05-61-22-14-22. Nearest Métro: Capitole.*

MARKETS

→**Halle Victor-Hugo** On the place Victor Hugo from Tuesday to Sunday 6am to 1pm.

→**Marché de la Basilique Saint-Sernin** This very cute market sells herbs and flow-ers alongside the rue des Trois Piliers. It takes place on Saturday and Sunday morn-ings, but come on Sunday mornings to see the Toulousains out in full force.

→**Marché de la Place du Parlement** This foie gras and poultry market runs from October to March on Wednesday and Friday mornings.

→**Marché de Saint-Aubin** This farmer's market takes place on Sunday mornings.

Perpignan: Straddling Catalonia

905km (561 miles) SW of Paris, 369km (229 miles) NW of Marseille, 64km (40 miles) S of Narbonne

What was once Catalonia's second city after Barcelona and the capital of the king-dom of Majorca has been French since 1659. But that's just a matter of semantics. Perpignan's attitude, its weather, food, and architecture all point south. Now that the advent of the European Union has relaxed borders, you could even pop into Spain from here. Between the sea and the moun-tains, Perpignan has it all. Its promenades are shaded by plane trees, its cafes are bursting with sangria and tapas, and its afternoons are siesta-slow.

Getting There

Trains come from Paris, Montpellier, Marseille via Narbonne, and other local stations. The **Perpignan Rivesaltes Airport** is at ☎ **04-68-52-60-70.** The town is crossed by the **A9** bus between Narbonne and Perpignan. Buses arrive at the gare routière in the Espace Mediterrannée (☎ **04-68-35-29-02**).

Tourist Offices

The tourist office (Palais des Congrès, place Armand Lanoux; ☎ **04-68-66-30-30;** mid-June to mid-Sept Mon–Sat 9am–7pm, Sun and holidays 10am–4pm; mid-Sept to mid-June Mon–Sat 9am–6pm, Sun and holidays 10am–1pm) offers 4€ guided tours that run 90 minutes to an hour.

Another tourist office is at the Espace Palmarium, on the place Arago (mid-June to mid-Sept Mon–Sat 10am–7pm, mid-Sept to mid-June Mon–Sat 10am–6pm, and closed Sun).

Sleeping

→**Auberge de Jeunesse** Halfway between the bus and train stations (can you hear them?), this is one of the old-est youth hostels in France. Put some bougainvillea flowers in your hair and go romance that Barcelonan—just remember to speak your Spanish with a lisp (say Barthelona). *Allée Marc-Pierre, parc de la Pepiniere.* ☎ *04-68-34-63-32. 13€ double.*

→ **Hôtel Alexander** This cute three-story hotel has balconies, and it's clean and tidy. Stay for breakfast. *15 bd. Clemenceau.* ☎ *04-68-35-41-41. www.hotel-alexander.fr. 40€–60€ double. Credit cards accepted. Amenities: Restaurant/bar; parking. In room: TV.*

→ **Hôtel Mondial** Each of the rooms is decorated in a different style by the eccentric proprietress. Do you want to sleep in Egypt or China tonight? Come to Perpignan. Kidding aside, we like its artsy feel, from the cute men in berets walking around to the schizophrenic color scheme. F-U-N-K-Y. *40 bd. Clemenceau* ☎ *04-68-34-55-07. www.hotel-mondial-perpignan.com. 45€–60€ double. Credit cards accepted. In room: TV.*

Eating

→ **Au Vrai Chic Parisien** FRENCH   Is the name of this place meant to be ironic? Because as much as we like it, there's nothing chic or Parisian about it—to its great advantage. It's chaotic, congenial; the owners have adopted the Bennigan's school of decor, only they've pulled it off way better. We love the raw vegetables dipped in *anchoiade,* steak tartare, and potatoes cooked in goose fat. *14 rue Grande la Monnaie.* ☎ *04-68-35-19-16. Menus 10€, or a la carte. Credit cards accepted. Mon–Fri noon–2pm; Fri–Sat 8-10:30pm.*

→ **Restaurant Casa Sansa** FRENCH-CATALAN   Any place this busy has got to be good. Fresh, ample French-Catalan cuisine includes more tapas than you can shake a crucifix at. It's right down the street from the Castillet. *2 rue Grande des Fabriques.* ☎ *04-68-34-21-84. Menus 12€–30€. Credit cards accepted. Daily breakfast starts at 9:30am; dinner starts at 6pm.*

Partying

Head for the place Gambetta and the streets around the Castillet.

Sightseeing

FREE → **La Cathédrale Saint-Jean** Built during the 14th and 15th centuries to commemorate Saint Jean, it's considered one of the most spectacular examples of meridional (southern) Gothic architecture. Inside the chapelle du Devot-Christ is a 14th-century crucifix so pained looking it will strike pity into the heart of any Christian. According to local legend, Christ's inclined head gets closer and closer to his chest every year—once they touch, the world will self-destruct! If you're lucky, you'll catch an organ concert (and you'll leave before the world has a chance to self-destruct). *Place Gambetta.* ☎ *04-68-51-33-72. Free admission. Daily 8am–noon and 3–6:30pm.*

→ **La Place de la Loge** The heart of the old town is always busy despite its tiny size. See especially the Hôtel de Ville, a 14th-century building with 15th-century iron-wrought balconies and bronze arms sticking out of the facade. These symbolize the three types of citizens then allowed to vote. Inside is a bronze sculpture by local son Aillol.

→ **Le Castillet & the Casa Pairal** This tall brick building with two distinctive towers is the former gate into Perpignan, and a good place to start your tour. It was built after Pierre IV dismantled the kingdom of Majorca in 1368, and Louis XI added the porte Notre-Dame, also known as the Petit Castillet, a century later. The Casa Pairal houses the Musée d'Arts et de Traditions populaires du Roussillon, full of household items that depict life in the Roussillon. *Place de Verdun.* ☎ *04-68-35-42-05. May–Sept Wed–Mon 10am–7pm; Oct–Apr 11am–5:30pm.*

→ **Le Jardin de la Miranda** Right next to the eglise Saint-Jacques, this garden, which in medieval times had *hortas*, gardens, and orchards, has a beautiful view.

→ **Le Palais des Rois de Majorque** This is the oldest royal palace still in existence in France, built in the 13th century and surrounded by eight imposing towers. It's remarkably well preserved and offers a beautiful view over Perpignan. The tour of the palace is pretty boring, but the gardens are gorgeous. *Rue des Archers.* ☎ *04-68-34-48-29. 4€, but bring your student card. Daily 10am–6pm from June–Sept and from 9am–5pm the rest of the year.*

→ **The Old Streets of Perpignan** Walk down the rue des Fabriques-Nabot and note la maison Julia at no. 2, built in the 15th century. Then find the rue de la Main-de-Fer, specifically no. 8, la maison Xanxo, built by the workmen diverted from their work on the cathedral by one of the site administrators in 1507. The place des Orfevres, on which resides the palais des Corts, or the medieval courts, is also worth a detour.

Festivals & Events

→ **Festival de Musique Sacrée** Holy music in the old church of Dominicans. *Mid-Mar.*

→ **Procession de la Sanch** A parade between Saint-Jacques and the Cathedral, when black-hooded penitents carry icons and sing. If you're here the week before that *(Semaine Sainte),* you'll find religious celebrations then too. It sounds funky but it's actually pretty cool. *Good Friday.*

Carcassonne—Medieval Disneyland

Do you like to fantasize about the days of knights in shining armor, and maidens with long hair cascading down stone turrets, and the days when exhaust smelled like horseshit rather than petrol? Well, there was more to the Middle Ages than that. There was the plague, and barbarian invasions, and chastity belts, and torture chambers, and compulsory religion. If you prefer thinking of history in the first set of terms, however, come to Carcassonne. And do your best to ignore the hordes who've come to do the same.

Carcassonne, don't get us wrong, is stunning—a 13th-century world of turrets and towers and winding cobblestone alleys. It has a great music festival in the summer, the Festival de la Cite (www.carcassonne-festivaldelacite.com), which features everyone from Sting to opera divas. Allegedly, its name comes from the fact that when Charlemagne besieged the town for several years, a Madame Carcas threw the citizens' last fat pig over the wall. The troops, shocked that the villagers still had so much food that they could afford to waste pork, gave up and took off. Carcas *sonne*-d (sounded) the joyful bells, and the town lived happily ever after.

Historians suspect that Carcassonne is just a Frenchification of the town's original name, Carcas, but this is one of the myriad myths for sale in the city. They'll sell you plastic swords that light up and make whooshing sounds, like medieval light sabers, bad cassoulet, medieval helmets, shot glasses, key chains, commemorative spoons, ugly T-shirts.

We love Carcassonne—at night, from far across the other side of the pont Vieux, over the Aude river, when the city's all lit up, and we can keep our fantasies sacrosanct, devoid of tourists and souvenir stalls.

→ **Feux de la Saint Jean and Festa Major de Saint Jean** Concerts, shows, a ceremony that celebrates breaking bread, bonfires—it's a big one. *June.*

→ **Les Estivales** Big party celebrating all the artists of the South and the Mediterranean—with music, dancing, the works. *July.*

→ **Les Jeudis de Perpignan** Thursday concerts, mimes, and street theater. *Mid-July to mid-Aug.*

→ **Les Sardanes** Traditional Catalonian dance concerts. *July–Aug.*

→ **Visa Pour L'image** Gigantic photojournalism festival, with big names and big pictures. *First 2 weeks of Sept.*

→ **Fête du Vin Primeur** It's kind of like when the Beaujolais Nouveau comes out, but with local wine. ☎ *04-68-66-30-30. Mid-Oct.*

→ **Jazzebre** A jazz festival of increasing significance. *Oct.*

→ **Noël a Perpignan** Catalan singing and *pessebres,* or nativity scenes, are set up around town. *Dec 25.*

Le Viaduc de Millau

On the A75, 641km (397 miles) S of Paris; 86km (115 miles) N of Toulouse

Two thousand years post–pont du Gard (p. 369), what do we have to show for ourselves? In some areas, not much. In others, quite a bit, such as the Viaduc de Millau (www.viaducdemillau.com), opened in 2004. (To get there, take the A75 north or south and get off at exit 45; the bridge is 70 miles northeast of Albi. It's open 24 hr. a day.)

Although we no longer struggle to move water along in modern times, we now have trouble moving people. The Viaduc de Millau was built to assuage the traffic that coagulated around the town of Millau in the summer as people drove south on the A75 toward their vacation, or north to go home; the jams were becoming intolerable. So in 1989, the government built a bridge that traversed the whole valley, high above it.

Millau's advantageous position on the RN9 also brought the town money, as travelers stopped for gas, food, and sleep. The construction of the viaduc, then, is a double-edged sword for Millau—it has removed the more organic traffic the town naturally received before its construction while drawing people to the area to see the bridge.

The bridge's architects included Lord Norman Foster, who designed the big gherkin in London and the Reichstag in Berlin; its engineer was Frenchman Michel Virlogeux; the builders were the Eiffage group, the third largest French group in public works and the sixth largest in Europe, who also built the Tour Eiffel in 1889. Construction costs came to nearly 400 million euros—Eiffage has the rights to collect the approximately 5€ tolls until 2080. The project necessitated 127,000 cubic meters of concrete, 19,000 metric tons of steel, and 5,000 metric tons of pre-stressed concrete for the cables. As a result, the bridge is nearly 2.5km (2 miles) long, the shortest of its piers is 77m (253 ft.) high, and the tallest is 343m (1,125 ft.)—higher than the Eiffel Tower and only slightly shorter than the Empire State building. This, incidentally, makes it the tallest vehicular bridge in the world, nearly twice as tall as the second, Austria's Europabrücke. An estimated 10,000 to 25,000 cars cross the bridge daily.

McDonald's Versus Roquefort

Before the Viaduc de Millau, the most famous thing to come out of Millau had been **José Bové,** the farmer who set the McDonald's there aflame in 1999 as a protest against their use of hormone-treated beef. Europe's response, once alerted to the controversy: restrict hormone-treated beef. The U.S.'s response? Place tariffs on the importation of Roquefort, which Bové used to make for a living. Bové's response, once he served his 44 days in jail? Travel to the U.S. with 30kg of Roquefort in his luggage. Millau was also a famous center of leather refining—first boots, horse harnesses, and leather armor for the army, then products for the Church, aristocrats, and the bourgeoisie, especially gloves. Local sheep farmers gave up their lambs for skin, and in the 1960s, Millau was still producing nearly five million pair annually.

The Gorges du Tarn

615km (381 miles) S of Paris; 232km (144 miles) N of Toulouse

For millions of years, the river Tarn has eroded the calcium deposits through which it runs, sometimes digging canyons up to half a kilometer deep. At times serene, at times violent, the water whorls its way around reddish and orange caves, crevasses, and rock formations for 83km (51 miles) between Florac and Millau. Kayak down it, or hike around, admiring the resilience of the villages clinging impossibly to cliffs.

Or drive. Start at **Ispagnac,** 10km northwest of Florac, driving on the D907. (On Tues and Sat mornings, check out the fruit and vegetable market in town.) This Gallo-Roman village has an elegant 12th-century church, dedicated to St. Pierre, which serves as a lovely example of the meridional, or southern, style of French architecture. One wonders how people even made it here, much less built churches like this or bridges like the Gothic one in **Quezac,** a village 2km (1¼ mile) east. Next, you'll pass the imperious 16th-century château de **Rocheblave,** which you'll have to admire from the outside. Next is **Montbrun,** the château de Charbonnieres, nestled in a

curve of the river. Eighteen kilometers (11 miles) west of Quezac, you'll hit the village of **Sainte-Enimie.** Enimie was a beautiful princess, sister of Merovingian king Dagobert (about whom a rude French rhyme was written during the French Revolution that is still taught to children today), who had been promised to a man she didn't want to marry. She made a vow of chastity, and then asked God to make her unattractive. She got leprosy. After months of suffering, the poor girl bathed in a fountain near Tarn and recovered. She suffered a relapse once back home, and recovered again after another bath. Today we might conclude that she just needed a lesson or two in personal hygiene, but Enimie took this to mean that she was meant to stay and found a convent—which she did.

Here's a pretty detour: nearly 6km (4 miles) west of Saint-Enimie, now on the D986, is **Saint-Chely-du-Tarn**, which you'll reach by crossing an old stone bridge. It is absolutely beautiful.

If you follow the normal road, it will take you to the **château de La Caze,** 8km

(5 miles) southwest of Saint-Enimie, and then to **La Malene,** another 6km (4 miles) away. It's from here that you can catch a ride with **the bateliers de la Malene,** who use traditional boats and techniques to shuttle you down the 8 narrowest and most spectacular kilometers (5 miles) of the Gorges du Tarn. Rides cost 19€, last about an hour, and run from April to October; a shuttle brings you back to the starting point. Unforgettable (Bateliers de la Malene; ☎ **04-66-48-51-10**).

Once you're back in La Malene, stay on the D907 through the windy road of the cirque des Baumes until the **Pas de Soucy,** where the Tarn disappears. Allegedly, the earthquake of 580 caused the river to disappear in the rubble. Continue until **Vignes,** and then take a right onto the D995 for 5km (3 miles) until joining the D46. Making a right at **Saint-Georges-de-Levejac,** which will take you to the so-called "Point Sublime," which affords a spectacular view of the canyon. Returning to Vignes, 12km (7 miles) south, will get you back on track to continue your journey.

The **tourist office** is in Sainte-Enimie (☎ **04-66-48-53-44;** Apr Mon–Sat 9:30am–noon and 2–5:30pm; May to mid-Sept daily 9:30am–12:30pm and 2–6pm; mid-Sept to Mar Mon–Fri 10am–noon and 2–5pm).

Walking

The GR6a, a hiking path that splits off from the GR6 path through the *causses,* climbs out of Le Rozier onto the Causse Mejean between the crossing of the Tarn with the gorges of the river Jonte. Then it follows the rim of the Tarn gorges before rejoining the GR6 at Les Vignes. It will take you 4 to 5 hours.

Sleeping

The Gorges tend to get crowded in the summer, but you'll find additional options for accommodations up the Causse Mejean, including *chambres d'hôtes.*

➜ **Hôtel Voyageurs** All 21 rooms here have bathrooms; some even have televisions. ☎ *05-65-62-60-69. 30€–40€ double. Credit cards accepted. In room: TV (in some).*

CAMPING

For campsites, try the **Municipal Campsite in La Malene** (☎ **04-66-48-58-55;** closed mid-Oct to Mar) or **La Blanquiere** in Vignes (☎ **04-66-48-54-93;** closed mid-Sept to May).

The Dordogne & the Lot

by Anna Brooke

The Dordogne and the Lot are France's best-kept secret for travelers. But don't come here seeking nightlife, social opportunities, or sunny weather (it rains here even in summer). Come instead for authentic village markets, dramatic countryside, châteaux (the Dordogne is also known as "the country of 1,001 castles"), and local delicacies—including truffles, foie gras, succulent meats, and fine wines.

The region is a motherlode for budding archaeologists and geologists, with some of Europe's most impressive cave systems, inhabited by humans tens of thousands of years ago **(Lascaux),** and vast caverns displaying cathedral-like rock formations **(Gouffre de Padirac).** The stunningly verdant and voluptuous countryside, dotted with châteaux, ruined keeps, ramparts, hamlets, and medieval bastides, affords limitless opportunities for sightseeing and outdoor sports.

In fact, this region has so much to offer, it is hard to understand why so relatively few people come here. Tourists as well as the 20th century seem to have bypassed many areas of the Dordogne, which lacks even an efficient transport system. Indeed life goes on here much as it has for the last few hundred years. Local farmers seem happy with their subsistence living, far from the cries of ultramodern technology; the closest they come to pod-casting is shelling peas. Modernity is not inexistent: Internet, TV, and hot running water are part of daily life, but a distinct old-world charm prevails.

Medieval **Sarlat-la-Canéda** (known simply as Sarlat) is one of the prettiest towns around. It's a great base for exploring the region (including the prehistoric caves around **Les Eyzies** and Lascaux). Two other must-see towns are **Rocamadour** (a historic, chocolate-box village, mounted precariously over a precipice) and **Cahors** (world-famous for its wine and medieval bridge). A drive along the Valley of the Dordogne River is also de rigeur, with its postcard-perfect villages (**Domme** is a heart-stopper) and châteaux (including Josephine Baker's **Château de Milandes**).

Périgueux, capital of the Dordogne, also has a pleasant medieval core. The modern town is relatively unattractive, but it makes a great base for outdoor activities such as biking and canoeing. You can bike, hike, or canoe along the Garonne, Dronne, and Vezère rivers, where campsites are plentiful, and B&Bs and inns are rustic. Spring and autumn are the best times for cycling, canoeing, and avoiding inclement weather or the traveling hordes of August.

The Best of the Dordogne & the Lot

○ **The Best Village in Which to Pretend You're an Imprisoned Templar Knight:** The poor Templar Knights were everybody's scapegoats—even in a small place such as **Domme,** where they were banged up for 11 years, deprived of the village's breathtaking panorama over the valley. See p. 418.

○ **The Best Town to Bust Your Gut In:** The motto in **Sarlat** is "food, glorious food"—from what's in the bustling markets to what's on the tables in gastronomic restaurants. See p. 402.

○ **The Best Place to Drink Wine and Then Cross a Freaky Bridge:** In the Lot *département* and region of Quercy, **Cahors** makes kick-ass red wine and woos its visitors with one of the best-preserved fortified Gothic bridges in Europe. See p. 417.

○ **The Best Place to See a Whole Town Erupting from a Rock Face:** All right—it's not quite erupting, but some of the buildings in **Rocamadour** are balanced so precariously on the edge of the rock-face they look like they never could have been built by humans alone. See p. 415.

○ **The Best Place to Guzzle Beer in a Historic Building:** Concerts, billiards, beer, ice cream, salads, and did I mention beer? **Le Pub** (in Sarlat) is one groovy club in an exquisite medieval mansion with a terrace overlooked by a balcony that could have belonged to star-crossed Shakespearean lovers. See p. 409.

○ **The Best Way to See the Countryside without Wheels:** The Dordogne is a bummer to get around if you are "W.W." (Without Wheels), so the SNCF has set up **L'Autorail Espérence**—a low-budget Orient Express–type train that provides food and great views between Bergerac and Sarlat. See p. 411.

○ **The Best Truffle Grub:** If you want to see what pig-hormone emitting fungi tastes like when it's prepared with love and culinary expertise, there is no place better than **Le Présidial** (in Sarlat). Here, according to the season, truffles get more than just lip-service. See p. 409.

○ **The Best and Most Romantic Topiary in the Dordogne:** High on a rocky plateau lies a discreet 18th-century château, in front of which lies **Marqueyssac:** This breathtaking 6km (4 miles) network of fancifully shaped hedges is so pretty that seeing them could make your thumbs turn green with envy. See p. 412.

The Dordogne & the Lot

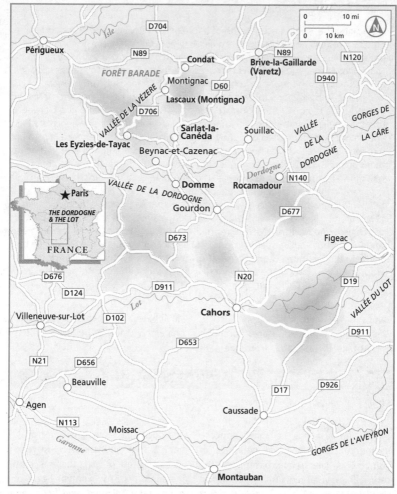

Getting Around the Region

The Dordogne is actually one of the most difficult corners of France to reach and to navigate. It will be nearly impossible for you to see the countryside attractions without a car or motorbike. Although trains travel to the main towns of Sarlat, Périgueux, and Cahors, you should expect long journeys and changes. One of the most direct routes is from Bordeaux. From Paris by TGV, most changes take place at Bordeaux. You can also reach Périgueux directly from Paris or from Bordeaux. You can visit Cahors from Paris, Bordeaux, or Toulouse (change at Montauban). By car, the A89 is a handy highway linking Sarlat to Périgueux and Bordeaux. The A10

Getting a Grip on the Geography

Navigating the length and breadth of a foreign country is never easy; and in France, the task becomes doubly difficult when you're faced with the complicated and nonsensical way they split up their territory. If you've made it down to the Dordogne, you will know by now that France is split into areas called *départements* (see the Basics chapter). All's well so far. But, within each *département* are *régions* that don't stick to the borders of the *départements*. For instance, the *région* of the **Périgord** straddles two *départements* (the Dordogne and the Lot). The same goes for the region of **Quercy.** And just when you think you've got that one sorted out, they go and tell you that the Périgord is also split into four sub-regions that have been color-coded according to the stuff they're famous for! "What?" Well don't get your knickers in a twist—it's quite simple really. The **Périgord Noir (Black)** is so called thanks to the very dark color of its oak trees and the truffles (black diamonds; see "Swine & Black Diamonds," below) that grow here. This is where you'll be spending most of your time, amid pretty stone villages, mind-blowing prehistoric caves, and the town of Sarlat. In the north is the **Périgord Vert (Green),** named after the masses of green forests and Périgod-Limousin national park. The chalky soil around Périgieux gave its name to the **Périgord Blanc (White Périgord)** in the center. The **Périgord Pourpre (Crimson),** in the south, derives its appellation from the red wine grown around Bergerac. Get a grip on that lot and you can join MENSA!

comes down from Paris (6-hr. drive). Bergerac is the nearest airport, although most of its flights come from the U.K. via low-cost companies **Ryanair** (www.ryanair.com) and **Flybe** (www.flybe.com).

📺 Best❶ Sarlat: Art, Foie Gras & Truffles

530km (310 miles) SW of Paris, 180km (117 miles) E of Bordeaux, 60km (37 miles) NW Cahors; pop. 10,000

It's official: Sarlat has the highest concentration of listed medieval buildings in France. This claim to fame has made it the setting for several movies (see "Sarlat on the Silver Screen," below) and given it serious street-credentials in a country where medieval-mania is a huge source of income for the tourist industry.

Almost everything you look at is of some historical importance. But don't think that means you'll be walking around a museum. Sarlat positively bursts, bubbles, and oozes life (a little too much in summer). Between its lively markets (both covered and open-air), teeming cafe terraces, and annual film and theater festivals (see "Festivals" on p. 414), there is hardly a moment's rest. You won't be jiggin' on the dance floor till 6am, and you won't be downing tequila slammers with strangers in cool, shabby-chic bars, but you will be having a damned fine time soaking up the infectious atmosphere, and sampling the first-rate food and wine.

It's not a big town (you can easily walk around it in an hour), but there is something authentically enchanting about

Regional Delicacies

It would be a waste not to taste at least one truffle dish while you're in the Dordogne, but don't neglect the other local specialties. The region is famous for *confit de canard* (duck preserved in fat—calorific but, boy, is it tasty), *cassoulet* (white beans cooked with meat and sausages in a tomato sauce), *foie gras* (the finest of French pâtés), walnuts, capers, strawberries, cheeses (such as Rocamadour Goat's cheese), and wine (Bergerac and Cahors).

meandering in and out of the creamy, narrow streets and cobbled squares. In fact, don't be shocked if, after an hour here, you start calling girls "fair maidens" and boys "sires" (or "ruthless dragon killers," depending on how medieval you're willing to go). The turreted buildings, tiled roofs, and half-timbered houses do make you think you're in days of old. And the crowded markets make you think you want to part with your money.

If you've ever dreamt of being a French chef, now is your chance to buy as much fresh produce as you can fit in your basket.

On Wednesdays and Saturdays, one of the region's most wonderful and varied open-air markets sells everything from organically grown fruits and vegetables (including truffles), to sausages, pâtés, meats and cheeses, jams, honeys, breads, biscuits, walnut cakes, liquors, and a host of other produce you never knew existed. Even if you're bent on partying, I challenge you to come here and experience the paradox of how sleepy French backwaters can provide enough activity to make you want to stay.

Swine & Black Diamonds

What do pigs have in common with bling? Truffles, of course! Known as "black diamonds," this Périgord-grown subterranean fungus (*Tuber Melanosporum* for you biologists out there) is so rare and so delicious that for many gastronomes it is worth its weight in diamonds. Buying even a few will set you back a pretty packet (they can cost more than 386€ a pound). "Okay," you say, "but what about the pig link?" Well, truffles—being dark in color and growing in woods beneath the soil—are nearly impossible to detect with the naked eye. Pigs, however, have sensitive snouts and an insatiable appetite for truffles, which emits a steroid similar to the pheromone of a sexually stimulated boar. This is to say that pigs can sniff them out faster than the hunter can shout "Oy, hog-brain! Don't eat that truffle!" Indeed the problem with pigs is that, as efficient as they are, they are also greedy, forcing many truffle-hunting farmers to replace them with dogs.

Sarlat History 101

Oh, what a surprise: Like most places in France, Sarlat started life as a Gallo-Roman settlement. But it nestled its way into history books in the 8th century, when it became a prosperous town under King Pepin le Bref (whose name literally translates as "Pip the Brief"—no staying power obviously) and the legendary Charlemagne, founder of modern France (see "French History 101" in the Nerd's Guide to French Wine & Culture).

Sarlat's history gets juicy from the 12th century onward. Built up around a well-established Benedictine abbey of Carolingian origin (the only one of its kind spared by the Vikings), it benefited from direct papal security from Rome. A piece of cross from Jesus's crucifixion supposedly made its way here, and during the plague of 1147, St-Bernard reportedly cured the villagers with blessed bread that he administered at the foot of the church. In 1318, the abbey became the seat of a new bishopric created by Pope John XXII, and the church became the Cathédrale Saint-Sacerdos (restored in the 16th–17th c.).

Once that chapter of history was over, in came the spirited old English, fuelled by the desire to conquer and the promise of a Hundred Years' War with their favorite enemy. By this time, Sarlat was a fortified Episcopal city, but that didn't stop the *rosbifs* (as the English were known, pertaining to their national dish of roast beef) from seizing control over much of the area. The French kicked them out once and for all in 1453, and as a reward for Sarlat's efforts against the Brits, Charles VII granted the town enough tax concessions for it to prosper.

Respite was short, however, and Sarlat soon underwent upheaval from the wars of religion, defending Catholicism to the very last. Peace didn't reign again until King Henry IV arrived in the 16th century. From the 16th to the 18th centuries, Sarlat underwent much reconstruction, reflected in many of the mansions you can see today. Geographically too far removed from the main goings-on, it fell asleep for over 150 years, only to re-awaken with the arrival of highways and train lines. Saved from demolition in 1962, thanks to a law passed by politician André Malraux, its handsome architecture has been preserved for the entire world to admire.

Getting There

BY TRAIN

Sarlat is best reached by train from Bordeaux or Toulouse. If you do find yourself traveling there from Paris, you should expect to change in Bordeaux, Soulliac, or Brive. From here you can either take the train to Sarlat or catch a bus (see below). For train information, call ☎ **36-35** or consult **www.sncf.com**. The station lies about 1km (½-mile) south of the old town, which makes for a 15-minute walk or a short taxi ride into the center, depending on how pooped you're feeling from the inevitably long journey.

BY CAR

Many of this region's treasures lie in small, out-of-the way places you can only reach by car or motorbike, so a set of wheels can be vital for getting the most out of your stay. The A10 highway runs from Paris via Poitiers, Angoulême, and Périgueux to Sarlat; the A89 goes from Bordeaux one way and from Lyon the other; and the A20

Sarlat

SLEEPING ■
Camping les Perières **1**
Château de Puymartin **17**
Hotel des Récollets **11**
La Couleuvrine **2**

EATING ◆
La Couleuvrine **2**
Le Présidial **3**
Le Regent **13**
Le Relais de Poste **4**
Roland Mertz **10**

PARTYING ★
Club 24 **16**
Le Pub **14**

SIGHTSEEING ●
Bishop's Palace **8**
Galerie-Atelier Catherine
    de Cressac **15**
Gorodka **7**
Lanterne des Morts **5**
Maison de la Boétie **9**
Musée de la Noix **6**
Place aux Oies **12**

runs from Toulouse via Soulliac. Once you're in Sarlat, the old center is mainly pedestrian only (June–Sept), so visitors are advised to park their vehicles either for free along the ring roads around the old center (except bd. Eugène-Le-Roy in the west) or on avenue Général de Gaulle; or in the pay-parking at the handy place de la Grande Rigaudie, just outside the old town, near rue Tourny.

BY BUS

From Soulliac and Brive, you can get information on bus times and prices at **Voyage Belmons** (☎ 05-65-37-81-15), or **CFTA** (☎ 05-55-17-91-91; www.cftaco.fr).

BY AIR

Unless you're flying in to Bergerac from the U.K. (see "Getting Around the Region," above), you'll be giving the airspace a breather.

Orientation

Sarlat has modern suburbs; but once you're in the cute and bite-size medieval core, you'll forget that anything post-18th century ever existed. Sarlat is a spaghetti-like agglomeration of narrow, labyrinthine streets and hidden squares, dissected by the long, stately **rue de la République** built in the late 18th century. Most sights lie to the east of this street, and almost all

Sarlat on the Silver Screen

Sarladais folk love movies, and the movies love Sarlat. Besides hosting a wonderful annual film festival in November, Sarlat has been the setting for dozens of pictures. Ridley Scott shot his first film, *The Duelists,* here in 1977 (with Harvey Keitel), followed by Robert Hossein's *Les Misérables* in 1982, Danny Huston's *Becoming Colette* in 1991, and Luc Besson's *Joan of Arc* (starring his wife, Milla Jovovich) in 1998. In 2000, Johnny Depp and Juliette Binoche took to Sarlat's streets in Lasse Hallström's *Chocolat,* and in 2001 Peter Hyams's *D'Artagnan* gave the locals more to talk about. Watch them and look out for the film locales when you visit.

roads lead to **place de la Liberté,** where the huge Wednesday and Saturday markets tempt passersby with hundreds of appetizing, multicolored stands. There is also a great covered market on the other side of the *place* in the former church **Eglise Saint-Marie** (adorned in gargoyles). Once you're in the square, don't miss the beautiful **Hôtel de Maleville,** with its combination of French and Italian Renaissance styles, or the focal point of Sarlat's theater festival, the atmospheric **Hôtel de Gisson.** On the outer edge of the center, **rue Landry** and **rue Présidial** mark the seat of the former 17th-century law quarters. Just behind the **Cathédrale St-Sacerdos** lies the spooky 12th-century tower **Lanterne des Morts;** and on the opposite side of town past picturesque **place du Marché aux Oies** (look out for the cute bronze geese statues) lies **rue des Consuls,** lined with dapper town houses.

Getting Around

BY PUBLIC TRANSPORT

Public transportation here is designed to take you to towns near Sarlat, rather than to ferry you from points A to B within town. If you can't walk to your hotel or campsite from the station, you have just one option—Mr Taxi (see "Sarlat Nuts & Bolts," below).

BY BICYCLE

If you're game to whiz around on leg power, bikes are the ideal way to explore sights farther afield. To rent two-wheelers, go to **Cycles Sarladais** (av. Aristide Briand; ☎ 05-53-28-51-87; Tues–Sat 9am–noon, 2–7pm except Aug, when it's open Mon–Sat). They rent bikes from 13€ a day (3 days 35€, 5 days 50€, 7 days 63€). For a motored variety, grab a scooter from **MC Moto** (4 av. de Selves; ☎ 05-53-30-25-44; Mon–Fri 9am–noon and 2–7pm; Sat 9am–6pm). Call for prices.

ON FOOT

Unless it's raining, Sarlat is a joy to walk around. Just put your best foot forward and soak up the sights and the sounds.

Tourist Office

The **Office de Tourisme** is on place Peyrou/rue Tourny (☎ 05-53-31-45-45; www.ot-sarlat-perigord.fr). Here you can grab a free English-language walking guide. From April to September, tag onto one of their guided tours (inquire for costs). They also sell good maps of hiking and biking trails in the Périgord Noir.

Sarlat Nuts & Bolts

Books & Periodicals   If you're desperate to read something in English, **Barrachin—La Maison de la Presse** (no. 34; ☎ 05-53-59-03-28) and **Librairie Majuscule** (no. 43; ☎ 05-53-59-02-54) on avenue de la République, will kit you out with reading fodder.

Emergencies   For police call ☎ 17, fire/paramedics ☎ 18, ambulance ☎ 15. For anything else, call the **Centre Hospitalier,** in the northeast of town (rue Jean Leclaire; ☎ 05-53-31-75-75).

Internet/Wireless Hot Spots   You'd hardly expect an old town like Sarlat to have modern things like cybercafes, but the democratization of technology knows no limits, even in a French backwater. Great news for you, as you can get connected at **Easy Planet,** just north of the old town, at 17 av. Gambetta (☎ 05-53-29-23-48; www.easy-planet.net; Mon–Thurs 10am–7pm, Fri–Sat 10am–midnight, Sun 6pm–midnight). The first 20 minutes are .20€ per minute; then it drops to .05€ per minute.

Laundromat   Freshen your threads at any time of day or night at **Laverie le Lavandou** (10 place de la Bouquerie; ☎ 05-53-59-25-96; open 24/7).

Post Office   Buy your stamps at **La Poste** (place du 14 Juillet; ☎ 05-53-31-73-10).

Taxis   Joe le Taxi left, but his successor, Philippe at **Allo Philipp Taxi,** will run you around (☎ 05-53-59-39-65). If he's not in, give **Brajot** a call (☎ 05-53-59-41-13).

Vehicle Rental   Near the SNCF station, **Europcar** is in a handy spot for picking up a car, on place de Lattre-de-Tassigny (☎ 05-53-30-30-40; www.europcar.fr).

Sleeping

If you're going to be here between June and August, or during one of the annual festivals, book well in advance; rooms go like hotcakes. The Office de Tourisme provides a decent list of accommodations and campsites, so between their listings and ours, you should be catching some Zs without too much hassle. If all else fails, there are always the rampart ruins—just kidding!

CAMPING

→ **Camping les Perières** Not only is this a fine place in which to lay your knapsack down to rest, you can also give your knickers a good rinse; grab a game of tennis, billiards, or volleyball; have a barbecue; go swimming; and even change your currency. And you'll be just 15 minutes away from the old center on foot (it's the nearest campsite to Sarlat). *Rue Jean Gabin, Sarlat.* ☎ *05-53-59-05-84. www.lesperieres.com. 7€– 40€ tent pitches; from 50€ cottage for 1 day, 290€–820€ for 1 week.*

CHEAP

→ **Hôtel des Récollets** ★ Stay in a typical Sarladais building without breaking the bank. This family-run hotel on a quiet street in a former cloister, west of rue de le République, is as charming as it is cheap. The ample breakfast (served, on sunny days, in a quaint and flowery courtyard) somehow eases the pain of getting up in the morning. Rooms are old-fashioned but bright and airy (some with exposed stone walls), and the welcome is easily one of the warmest in town. *4 rue Jean-Jacques-Rousseau.* ☎ *05-53-31-36-00. www.hotel-recollets-sarlat.com. 43€–63€ double; 69€ triple; 79€ 4-person room. Credit cards accepted. Amenities: Free parking. In room: TV, Internet port.*

➜ **La Couleuvrine** ★★ The Couleuvrine (meaning cannon) was Sarlat's last defense tower during the English attacks and the wars of religion. If you get off on history and have a tight budget, you won't find better value elsewhere. This hotel has one of Sarlat's best gastronomic restaurants (see "Eating," below). Bedrooms are cute and character-filled, with textured fabrics, wooden beams, exposed stone walls, and old furniture. The wine and piano bar is very cool, with 100 wines on the list and live music every Wednesday and Saturday. And the history of the place is to die for, so to speak. *1 place de la Bouquerie.* ☎ *05-53-59-27-80. www.la-couleuvrine.com. 45€–60€ double. Credit cards accepted. Amenities: Restaurant, bar. In room: TV.*

DOABLE

MTV **Best** ☻ ➜ **Château de Puymartin** ★★ Okay, it's away from the center (8km/5 miles from Sarlat), but even in the *département* of 1,001 châteaux, it is rare to sleep in a castle at once so imposing, eerie, and beautiful. The Countess de Montbron opens her family's magical fairy-tale home to the public from April to October. Two guest rooms are so princely you'll want to stay within their four walls forever more. Or will you? Back in the 16th century, Therese de St-Clar was in the arms of her lover when her husband walked in. As punishment, he imprisoned her in the same room for 15 years, before sealing her in upon her death. Today, she allegedly

roams the château's covered passageways before entering her old room. Poor Therese—and poor you if she decides to visit you at night! Even if you don't sleep here, you should come to admire the stunning period rooms, all perfectly preserved, and learn about its fascinating history during the Hundred Years' War. *Château de Puymartin.* ☎ *05-53-59-29-97. www.best-of-perigord.tm.fr. 115€ double. Credit cards accepted. Amenities: Museum (6.50€ adults, 4.50€ students). Apr–Nov 10am–noon and 2–6pm (until 6:30pm in Jul–Aug).*

Eating

Sarlat has many great restaurants—and the best news is that they're cheap. There isn't even a single splurge on this list.

CAFES & LIGHT FARE

➜ **Roland Mertz** ★ CAKES First, the mouthwatering window display at this cake shop will catch your eye. Then, as you open the door, wafts of vanilla, caramel, and chocolate will hypnotize you. Next, you'll be mopping up your slobber from the display case. And finally, before you know it, you'll have devoured something sticky, forgotten your name, and wonder how you ended up in a Périgodian tearoom with chocolate down your top. That, my friends, is CCED (compulsive cake-eating disorder)—and you can expect a lot of that around these parts. Don't miss the Lauze—a delicious local chocolate-and-walnut nougat. *33 rue de la République.* ☎ *05-53-59-00-85.*

CHEAP

➜ **Le Regent** FRENCH/SARLADAIS On bustling place de la Liberté, the terrace here is always packed—even in winter, as long as a ray of sunshine peaks out from behind the clouds. But its prime position is not the only draw; the food is top-notch, too. With menus from just 14€, you can sample a host of Sarladais specialties, such as *confit de canard* (duck preserved in fat). If you opt for the slightly more expensive *terroir* menu, you get a free *apéritif* of walnut wine. On market days you might have to wait for a table, but it's worth it. *6 place de la Liberté.* ☎ *05-53-31-06-36. Fixed-price menus 14€–22€. Credit cards accepted. Daily noon–2:30pm and 7–10pm.*

DOABLE

→ **La Couleuvrine** ★ DORDOGNE Along with the Présidial, this wonderful hotel-restaurant (see "Sleeping," above) is one of Sarlat's best eating places. This is where you can pork out on wondrous regional dishes such as *foie gras*, smoked duck, veal, and truffles. If you're feeling adventurous, you could go for the *Flognarde* (snails and pigs' feet served in nettle juice). If budgets are tight, their separate bistro provides scrumptious menus from just 16€. The main dining room looks like something out of a film set, with lots of gold mirrors, velvet seats, beamed ceilings, and a huge stone fireplace. *Coté Bistrot. 1 place de la Bouquerie.* ☎ *05-53-59-27-80. www.la-couleuvrine.com. Fixed-price menus from 19€–45€. Credit cards accepted. Daily noon–1:30pm and 7–10pm.*

📺 Best ♥ → **Le Présidial** FRENCH/DORDOGNE This fantastic restaurant serves lots of truffles and other gourmet grub in a historical setting. The building looks like a mini-château (get a load of the polygonal tower on the roof, supported by wooden stilts), but it was in fact Henri II's royal court of justice, edified in 1553. Eat here in summer, and you'll have to make a hard decision: sit inside in the cool, period dining room or outside in the flowery, walled gardens? Either way, you'll be hard-pressed to find another place that makes kidneys with sweetbreads and fresh pasta taste like such a dream! Also check

out the quality wine list. *6 rue Landry.* ☎ *05-53-28-92-47. Lunch menu 20€; fixed-price from 24€. Credit cards accepted. Tues–Sat noon–2pm and 7–10pm; Sun–Mon evening only (closed mid–Nov to Mar).*

→ **Le Relais de Poste** ★★ CONTEMPORARY FRENCH Husband and wife combo Luc and Catherine Abraham put a contemporary spin on brightly colored, delicious regional dishes with an occasional Mediterranean flourish. Think warm mussels in parsley cream, or medallions of veal in basil cream with potato cakes and sun-dried tomatoes, or triple-chocolate *mille-feuille* with vanilla cream. That's a lot of cream! But once the wine starts a-flowing, and the open fire starts a-cracking, and you're lapping up the rustic charm of the 16th-century dining room, calories will be the last thing on your mind. *Impasse Vieille Poste.* ☎ *05-53-59-63-13. Fixed-price menus 24€–34€. Credit cards accepted. Thurs–Mon noon–2pm and 7–10pm.*

Partying

Put that disco ball away! I've already told you that Sarlat is not a party palace. The best you can expect are a few atmospheric bars with the occasional live band. But if you're dead set on going out anyway, check out the listings on **www.guidedenuit.com**.

BARS

📺 Best ♥ → **Le Pub** "Romeo, Romeo, wherefore art thou, Romeo?" On your way into the bar, look up at the romantic balcony on your left and thank Shakespeare that he didn't write about this place. Romeo would certainly have forgotten to woo Juliette, with cool distractions like live bands, billiards, crackling winter fires, and—last but not least—80 types of beer, 60 cocktails, 10 champagnes, and 30 whiskeys. The setting, an old four-storey mansion (Hôtel Gérard), is to die for, and the promise of late-night entertainment draws in punters of all ages year-round—so come join the throngs. *1 passage Gérard Barry (access vie rue Fénelon).* ☎ 05-53-59-57-98.

CLUBS & LIVE MUSIC VENUES

Despite the limited options, avoid Sarlat's only discothèque, **Le Griot,** at all costs—unless you get off on cheesy, uncouth golden oldies enjoyed by unsavory locals who remember the golden oldies from the first time around, and dance with one eye in the mirror.

→ **Club 24** Skip Le Griot and follow the hip kids out of town to Club 24, in nearby St-Crépin Carlucet (a 10-min. drive from Sarlat). Up to 600 people can bop to house, techno, electro-pop, and electro funk in unison. Because you have to make an effort to get here, clubbing at Club 24 is somewhat of a special occasion for the locals—an event they mark by putting on their glad rags. An on-site tapas restaurant is open from 6pm until 1am (1 meal = free club entry). *La Valade (campsite).* ☎ 05-53-28-92-62. www.leclub24.fr. *Entry 8€ Fri (1 free drink); 10€ Sat (1 free drink). Tapas restaurant Fri–Sun 6pm–1am.*

Sightseeing

This is what Sarlat is really all about—meandering in and out of quaint cobbled backstreets and marveling at the fabulous architecture, before stopping for a coffee or a spot of lunch. Once you've had your fill of the old town, head into the stunning countryside and step back to days gone by, when prehistoric humans lived in Périgordian caves.

PUBLIC MONUMENTS

→ **Bishop's Palace** ★★ The Office de Tourisme (place du Peyrou) has set up shop in this dazzling Gothic and Renaissance building. The upper gallery, which rounds itself off elegantly in a pint-sized turret, is enchanting. In summer, the tourist office holds temporary exhibitions, which give you a chance to explore more than just the main showroom.

→ **Lanterne des Morts** ★★ On the outskirts of the historic quarters just behind the cathedral, this "lantern of the dead" was reputedly erected in the 12th century to commemorate St-Bernard's visit to Sarlat. Nobody knows if this is true, but it does offer some of the prettiest views of Sarlat, and it's an exceptional example of early medieval sepulchral architecture.

→ **Maison de la Boétie** ★ On place du Peyrou, just opposite the cathedral, have a peek at the elegant facade of this Renaissance town house. The upper stories

---

Election Pole

Despite Christianized Charlemagne's efforts to repress all acts of pagan worship in France, one forbidden custom, L'arbre du 1er Mai (The May Day Tree), survives today under the most unlikely of circumstances. Whenever a new member is elected into the local government, a tall tree (usually a pine) is erected in the square, stripped of most of its needles (except at the top), and decorated with ribbons (a sign of purification), crowns (signs of victory), paperchains, flags, and the inscription "In Honor of the elected one." Originally a spring festival organized in honor of Mother Nature (*Maia* to the ancient Greeks and Romans, hence the French name Mai, or May in English), the same ceremony takes place elsewhere in southwest France when new buildings are finished or somebody gets a promotion at work. Any excuse for a pagan party!

Not Your Average Tourist Train

You haven't passed your driving test? You've left your driver's license home? You're scared of mad French drivers who speed like Michael Schumacher on a suicide mission? Whatever the reason you're W.W. (Without Wheels), you too can get out of Sarlat, aboard the 📺 (Best 💡) **Autorail Espérence**—a special tourist train that runs between Sarlat and the pretty town of Bergerac, farther west. Forget the crappy mini choo-choos that drive you around tourist attractions; this is the real deal: a retro wagon where you can dine on local cuisine (think pâtés, foie gras, walnuts, chestnuts, apple juice, prunes, and Bergerac wine) while listening to your tour guide's commentary on the sights outside your window. Tours run in July and August and cost around 15€ all inclusive—a total steal! Reservations are compulsory so call ☎ **05-53-59-55-39** or check with the tourist office.

are decorated with mullioned windows and ornately carved pilasters, which may sound like gobbledygook to you, but it is a typical example of Sarlat's Renaissance architecture. *Place du Peyrou (opposite the cathedral).*

→ **Place aux Oies** ★ Sarlat's most iconic square is recognizable thanks to a bronze statue of three geese (by Lalanne), placed there in memory of the live fowl market that occupied the square for centuries. Have a gander, while you're there, at the **Hôtel de Vassal** and the **Hôtel Chassaing,** two Renaissance beauties.

MUSEUMS

(FREE) → **Musée de la Noix** Unless you were a squirrel in a previous life, a museum dedicated to walnuts may not make your pulse race. This one, however, is free and worth the trip for its boutique, where you can stock up on regional specialties such as chocolate-covered walnuts, walnut oil, cakes, jams, and walnut vinegar. *12 av. Aristide Briand.* ☎ *05-53-29-60-47. Mon–Sat 9am–6pm.*

ART SCENE

→ **Galerie-Atelier Catherine de Cressac** ★ The building itself—the

Renaissance-era Hôtel de Gérard—is a work of art. Then there are Catherine's paintings—wonderful, naively theatrical representations of imaginary worlds and people. Cats and kissing crop up quite a lot, but then who doesn't like animals and a good cuddle? She also runs occasional workshops. *1 passage Gérard de Barry.* ☎ *05-53-59-47-90. http://catherine-decressac. monsite.wanadoo.fr.*

→ **Gorodka** ★★ What are the words one uses to describe a place such as Gorodka? Sensual explosion? Pure eccentricity? A realm where fiction and fantasy meet? Whatever the words you choose, you can't deny that Pierre Shasmoukine had a stroke of genius when he set up this artists' kingdom in a forest, 4km (2½ miles) south of Sarlat, in 1970. The visit includes curiosities such as the Folies Plastiques (plastic madness), a jungle of plastic sculptures in the garden; the Galeries Za, where artists can expose their creations; and Oper-Sexi, a multidisciplinary exhibition on communication between men and women. Visits take place all day, but Pierre strongly advises you to arrive at 5pm, with a picnic, so you can see the lighting installations after nightfall. You can even stay here for

Prehistoric Sites outside Sarlat

Les Eyzies-de-Tayac ★★, an unremarkable market town in the Vézère Valley (known as Les Eyzies), became an archaeologist's dream when prehistoric skeletons were unearthed here in 1868. This area of the Dordogne proved to be one of the world's richest in terms of ancient sites and deposits. Some of the caves contain primitive drawings made 30,000 years ago.

Note: Many of the caves in this area limit the number of daily visitors, but you can call for reservations up to a year in advance. I recommend that you do so, especially if you plan to visit in the summer. Once you've secured your tickets, grab a set of wheels and a map, and journey into this ancient world.

Musée National de la Préhistoire ★★ (1 rue de Musée; ☎ **05-53-06-45-45;** admission 4.50€ adults, 3€ students and ages 18–25; July–Aug daily 9:30am–6:30pm; June and Sept Wed–Mon 9:30am–6pm; Oct–May Wed–Mon 9:30am–12:30pm and 2–5:30pm) is a great starting point for your prehistoric sightseeing. It contains one of the greatest collections in the world, hailed for its treasure trove of Ice Age artifacts. Highlights include a small 15,000-year-old bison carved in bone, 30,000-year-old stone engravings (among the world's most ancient objects of art), the statue of the 3.2-million-year-old "Lucy" (a fake resin composition skeleton of a 3-year-old child from 50,000 years ago), and the first replicas of the first-known human footprints, dating from around 3.6 million years ago.

One of the world's earliest examples of a fish can be seen in the cave of **L'Abri du Poisson** (☎ **05-53-06-86-00;** admission 2.50€; Sun–Fri May to mid-Sept 9:30am–7:30pm, mid-Sept to Dec 9:30am–12:30pm and 2–5:30pm). The monumental frieze of prehistoric sculptures at **Abri du Cap Blanc** (☎ **05-53-59-21-74;** admission 6.40€; daily Apr–Oct 10am–noon, 2–6pm; all day July–Aug) is the only one of its kind open to the public in the world. And **La**

25€ a night. Gorodka is signposted from the center of Sarlat. Take the south exit (Souillac, Gourdon) toward Village La Canéda. ☎ *05-53-31-02-00. www.gorodka. com. Admission 7.50€. Jun 15–Sept 15 daily 10am–midnight; Sept 16–Jun 14 reservation only.*

Playing Outside

→ **Gabares Norbert** It's a sunny day, and you fancy a lazy day on the river, drinking in the dramatic panorama of the Dordogne Valley. Well, you're in luck, because that's just what you can do in the riverside village of La Roque Gageac, 10km (6 miles) south of Sarlat (see "Cool Circuit: Villages & Châteaux" on p. 418). Replicas of 18th- and 19th-century *Gabare* boats (traditional in the area) offer three cruise types along the river, allowing you to recharge your batteries in whatever way you please. *La Roque Gageac.* ☎ *05-53-2940-44. www.gabarres.com. Prices 7.50€ for a 1-hr. trip to 45€ for 6 hr. with lunch included).*

MTV (Best ♪) → **Les Jardins Suspendus de Marqueyssac** ★ If hairdressers Toni & Guy were to chuck in the towel and become gardeners, they would work here, in this vast garden where privet and Mediterranean Cyprus trees are trimmed

Grotte de Font de Gaume (by reservation only; ☎ **05-53-06-86-00;** admission 6.50€) is one of the last remaining painted Paleolithic sanctuaries open to the public. For information on other caves around Les Eyzies, check with the **Office de Tourisme** (19 rue de la Préhistoire, at place de la Mairie; ☎ **05-53-06-97-05;** www.leseyzies.com).

The 📺 (Best♦) **Caves at Lascaux,** 2km (1¼ miles) from the Vézère River town of Montignac, house the most beautiful and famous cave paintings in the world. Unfortunately, you can't view the actual paintings; the caves, discovered by four boys looking for a dog in 1940, closed to the public in 1964 to prevent atmospheric deterioration. But in Lascaux II, a short walk downhill from the real caves, you'll find impressive reproductions, with displays of some 200 paintings so that you'll at least have some idea of what the "Sistine Chapel of Prehistory" (as scientists like to call it) looks like. You can see majestic bulls, wild boars, stags, "Chinese horses," and lifelike deer, the originals of which were painted by Stone Age hunters 15,000 to 20,000 years ago. Try to show up as close to opening time as possible—the number of visitors per day is limited to 2,000, and tickets usually sell out by 2pm. In winter, you can buy tickets directly at Lascaux II, but from April to October you must purchase them from a kiosk adjacent to the Montignac tourist office, place Bertran-de-Born. For information, call ☎ **05-53-51-95-03** (admission 8€ adults, 4.50€ students; July–Aug daily 9am–8pm; mid-Apr to June and Sept–Oct 3 daily 9:30am–6:30pm; Oct 4–Nov 11 daily 10am–12:30pm and 2–6pm; early Feb to mid-Apr and Nov 12–Dec Tues–Sun 10am–12:30pm and 2–5:30pm; closed Jan–early Feb). The **Office de Tourisme** in Montignac can also give you details (place Bertrand-de-Born; ☎ **05-53-51-82-60;** www.bienvenue-montignac.com).

to perfection. You could argue that the hedges here, many shaped like lollipops, are the most beautiful gardens in the Dordogne. Sitting on a 6km-long (2-mile) rocky outcrop near the village of Vézac (along the Dordogne Valley; see "Cool Circuit: Villages & Châteaux" on p. 418), the magical dominion stretches out into the distance via a network of interconnected walkways that look out over the lush, green valley. *Vézac.* ☎ *05-53-31-36-36. www. marqueyssac.com. Daily July–Aug 9am–8pm (by candlelight, until midnight, on Thurs); Apr–May, Jun, and Sept 10am–7pm (until 6pm Feb–Mar, Oct until 11 Nov); Nov 12–Jan 2–5pm.*

Shopping

Many shops close for lunch at noon and reopen around 2:30pm, so plan your day around this.

FOOD, WINE & LOCAL CRAFTS

➔ **Julien de Savignac** Don't let the local truffle mania make you forget the other thing the region's famous for—wine. Indeed, what's a good truffle dish without a glass of fine claret to wash it all down? The enthusiastic and knowledgeable staff in this wine shop would answer "nothing." And how right they are, which is why you should shimmy on down here and buy a

Biking through the Dordogne

The Dordogne's rivers meander through countryside that's among the most verdant and historic in France. Since the 11th century, architects and builders have added greatly to the visual allure of their water sides, and even though this area is underpopulated, it is dotted with more gorgeous monuments, châteaux, 12th-century villages, and adorable churches than you'll have time to visit. As you bike around, the rural character of the area unfolds before you like a vintage picture book. If you're ever in doubt about which way to turn, remember that you'll rarely go wrong if your route parallels the riverbanks of the Lot, the Vézère, the Dordogne, or any of their tributaries.

Local infrastructure supports cycling. Châteaux, hotel, and inn staff treat you respectfully even if you show up on two wheels splattered in mud; they'll even offer advice on suitable bike routes. The SNCF makes it easy to transport a bike on the nation's railways, plus you'll find plenty of rental shops throughout the region. I recommend renting in Sarlat or from the Les Eyzies-de-Tayac tourist office (see "Getting Around: By Bike," above, for details).

Le Comité Départemental du Tourism (25 rue du Président Wilson, 24000 Périgueux; ☎ **05-53-35-50-24;** www.dordogne-perigord-tourisme.fr), provides information about all the towns in the *département* and will help you organize biking, hiking, kayaking, and canoeing trips. Two of the best outdoors outfitters are **Canoé Loisir,** La Riviére, in Vitrac (☎ **05-53-29-05-07;** www.canoes-loisirs.com) and **Explorando,** in Grolejac (☎ **05-53-28-13-84;** www.canoedordogne.com).

bottle or two. *Place Pasteur.* ☎ *05-53-31-29-20. Sept–June Tues–Sat 9:15am–noon and 2.30–6.30pm; July–Aug daily 9:15am–noon and 2.30–6.30pm; closed Jan 15–31.*

Festivals

In July and August, the streets come alive with the region's largest theater festival, le **Féstival des Jeux de théâtre de Sarlat** (☎ **05-53-31-10-83;** www.festival-theatre-sarlat.com). Throughout August until the first week of September, the whole region, including Sarlat, lets its highbrow hair down to the sounds of classical music concerts during the **Féstival de Musique du Périgord Noir** ☎ **05-53-51-61-61.** And finally in cold, wintry November, everybody warms their souls with the country's third most important film festival (after Cannes and Deauville), **Le Féstival de Film de Sarlat** (☎ **05-53-29-18-13;** www.ville-sarlat.fr/festival).

Sarlat's Truffle & Foie-Gras Market

Most people visit Sarlat in summer, but there is a very good reason to come in winter: **Le Marché aux Truffes et au Gras (Truffle and Foie-Gras market)** in place Boissarie. Without the aid of a pig, you can acquire a black diamond straight from its homeland every Saturday between December and February, from 9am until noon.

Rocamadour & Cahors

MTV Best❊ Rocamadour: a Miracle Town

541km (335 miles) SW of Paris, 66km (41 miles) SE of Sarlat

Get you're camera ready, because Rocamadour's setting is one of the most unusual in Europe: Towers, ancient buildings, and oratories cling in stages to the side of a cliff on the slope of the usually dry gorge of Alzou. There must have been Kryptonite in the mortar they used when they built the place, for the whole town is still teetering on the edge, as it has done for over 8 centuries.

Rocamadour reached the zenith of its fame in the 12th century, when an undecayed body, belonging to St-Amadour (a Christian hermit), was found in an ancient grave here. It also became a cult center of the black Madonna, supposedly founded by Zacchaeus, who entertained Christ at Jericho. He reputedly came here with a black wooden statue of the Virgin, although some authorities have suggested that the statue was carved in the 9th century. Either way, the faithful have never stopped visiting, and as a pilgrimage site, Rocamadour (literally means the Rock of St-Amadour) is billed as "the second site of France" (Mont St-Michel ranks first).

Summer visitors descend in droves, and vehicles are prohibited, so you'll have to park in one of the lots and make your way on foot.

The most photogenic entrance to the Basse Ville is the **Porte du Figuier (Fig Tree Gate),** through which many of the most illustrious Europeans of the 13th century passed; and the whole town is best seen when approached from the road coming in from the tiny village of L'Hospitalet.

GETTING THERE

The best way to reach Rocamadour is by **car.** From Bordeaux, travel east along N89 to Brive-la-Gaillarde, connect to N205 east into Cressensac, and continue on N140 south to Rocamadour. From Sarlat, take the D47, then the D12, D141, N20, D673, D36, and D32 into Rocamadour. Rocamadour and neighboring Padirac share a **train station, Gare de Rocamadour-Padirac,** that isn't really convenient for anyone besides taxi drivers—it's 4km (2½ miles) east of Rocamadour on the N140. Trains arrive infrequently from Brive in the north and Capdenac in the south. Call ☎ **36-35** for more information.

TOURIST OFFICE

The town maintains two separate tourist offices in the Hôtel de Ville, rue Roland-le-Preux (☎ **05-65-33-62-59**); and another well-signposted branch office within l'Hospitalet, in the old town (☎ **05-65-33-22-00;** www.rocamadour.com).

ORIENTATION & SIGHTSEEING

The **site** of this gravity-defying village rises abruptly across the landscape. Make sure you wear decent footwear; the only way to reach the town's medieval ramparts or **Cité Réligieuse**—a cluster of chapels and churches halfway up the cliff—is up, along a single, steep street lined with tacky souvenir shops. To help you negotiate the precipitous inclines, the town maintains two elevators. One goes from the Basse Ville (lower town) to the Cité Réligieuse (2€ one-way, 3€ round-trip). The other goes from the Cité Réligieuse to the ramparts *(le château),* near the hill's summit (2.50€ one-way, 4€ round-trip).

You can reach the 14th-century **Château de Rocamadour** *(le château)* by way of the curvy chemin de la Croix. Although it was restored by the local bishops in the 19th century, its interior is off-limits except for guests of the church officials who live and work here. You can, however, walk along its **ramparts** (2.50€), which afford some wicked vistas over the spectacular surroundings (daily 8am–8pm, to 6pm Oct–Apr).

Against the cliff, the **Basilique St-Sauveur** was built in the Romanesque-Gothic style from the 11th to the 13th century. It's decorated with paintings and inscriptions recalling visits of celebrated persons, including Philippe the Handsome. In the **Chapelle Miraculeuse,** the "holy of holies," St. Amadour is said to have carved out an oratory in the rock. Hanging from the roof is one of the oldest known clocks, dating to the 8th century. The Romanesque **Chapelle St-Michel** is sheltered by an overhanging rock and contains two 12th-century frescoes. The venerated **Black Madonna** occupies a chapel—**Chapelle de Notre-Dame**—lying adjacent to the Basilique St-Saveur (☎ **05-65-33-23-23;** free admission; daily 9am–7pm).

FREE ➔ **Cité Religieuse** This cluster of chapels and churches is the town's religious centerpiece, visited by both casual tourists and devoted pilgrims—many of whom make the effort to climb the **Grand Escalier,** a stairway of 216 steps. A recent devotee was the French composer Francis Poulenc, who remained in Rocamadour after a religious conversion he experienced here, and in honor of which he composed his *Litanies à la Vierge Noire.* The weathered steps will lead you to the **parvis des Eglises,** place St-Amadour, with seven chapels. Tour schedules change frequently, based on saints' holidays and local church schedules, but as a rule of thumb, three to five tours take place each day (depending on the season). Times are prominently posted at the entrance. *Place de la Carreta.* ☎ *05-65-33-23-23. Free admission; donations appreciated.*

EATING

The problem with sites such as Rocamadour is that once you're here, you're hostage to the restaurants catering to tourists. For painless, simple grub, try one of these two addresses on rue de la Couronnerie. **Chez Anne-Marie** (☎ **05-65-33-65-81**) serves a cheap mix of omelets, salads, and steaks from 12€. They even have a vegetarian

No Greater Crater: Le Gouffre de Padirac

Did the earth move for you, darling? Well, it did at **Padirac** (☎ **05-65-33-64-56;** www.gouffre-de-padirac.com; admission 8.50€; Apr–Nov daily 9am–6pm, closed noon–2pm Apr–July), when a gigantic cave collapsed 10,000 years ago, exposing a vast crater, incredible rock formations, and a rainwater river. After a 103m (338-ft.) descent, deep into the belly of the earth, you start your expedition with an underground boat trip into the caves, followed by a 500m (1,640-ft.) walk around the rock formations, before emerging underneath the 94m-high (58-ft.) Great Dome, with its awe-inspiring collection of giant stalagmites. Don't drift away from your guide; there are 9km (5½ miles) more of tunnel for you to get lost in. And don't forget your winter woolies; the cave is a constant 55°F (13°C) year-round. If you're in Rocamadour, this natural phenomenon is an absolute must, whether you flunked geology or not.

menu—a rarity in France, especially in the meat-eating Dordogne. Farther along, **La Table des Celtes** (☎ 05-65-33-67-73) serves excellent crepes from 5€, from February to November.

ⅣⅤ Best❂ Cahors in the Lot

541km (335 miles) SW of Paris, 217km (168 miles) SE of Bordeaux, 89km (55 miles) N of Toulouse

The ancient capital of Quercy, Cahors, in the Lot *département,* was a thriving university city in the Middle Ages, and many antiquities from its illustrious past (including the austere Valentré bridge) are still here for you to ogle. Today Cahors is best known for the almost-legendary red wine that's made principally from the Malbec grapes grown in vineyards around this old city. Firm but not harsh, it is one of the most deeply colored fine French wines.

Since the mid-1990s, the city has funded the redesign and replanting of at least 21 municipal gardens. The locals are very proud of them, many of which have been laid out in medieval patterns, using historically appropriate plants. The most spectacular of these gardens lie immediately adjacent to Town Hall, but don't get too excited; overall, they function as a magnet for horticultural societies throughout France. Cahors can be covered in half a day—slightly longer if you go wine-tasting. One of the best times to visit is mid-July, during their annual blues festival, when talented musicians crawl out of the woodwork or fly over the great Atlantic Ocean to perform.

GETTING THERE

To **drive** to Cahors from Toulouse, follow A62 north to the junction with N20 and continue on N20 north into Cahors. From Sarlat, the journey will take just over an hour, and you should take the D46 south, the D6, and then the D911 into Cahors.

Trains serve Cahors from Toulouse, Brive, and Sarlat, although you may have to transfer in neighboring towns. For train information and schedules, call ☎ **36-35.**

TOURIST OFFICE

The **Office de Tourisme** is on place François-Mitterrand (☎ 05-65-53-20-65; fax 05-65-53-20-74; www.mairie-cahors.fr).

ORIENTATION & SIGHTSEEING

Set on a rocky **peninsula,** almost entirely surrounded by a loop of the Lot River, Cahors grew up near a sacred spring that still supplies the city with water today. At the source of the spring, the **Fontaine des Chartreux,** stands the ⅣⅤ Best❂ **pont Valentré** (also called the pont du Diable, or devil bridge), a spooky-looking bridge with a trio of towers. It's a magnificent example of medieval defensive design erected between 1308 and 1380 and restored in the 19th century. The pont was the first medieval fortified bridge in France and remains the most eye-catching site in Cahors, with crenellated parapets, battlements, and seven pointed arches.

Dominating the old town, the **Cathédrale St-Etienne** (30 rue de la Chanterie; ☎ **05-65-35-27-80)** was begun in 1119 and reconstructed between 1285 and 1500. It was the first cathedral in the country to have cupolas, giving it a Romanesque-Byzantine look. It's open daily from 9am (the scheduled hour for daily Mass) to 6 or 7pm, depending on the season. Adjoining the cathedral are the remains of a Gothic cloister from the late 15th century, which are worth seeing if you have nothing better to do. The cloister is open only May to October, Monday to Saturday 10am to 12:30pm. Admission to the cloister is 3€ adults, 2€ students (closed Dec–Apr).

Cahors for Bacchanalians

For wine-tasting in Cahors, put on your best accent and glad rags, and learn to repeat this to your friends: "A robustness that mellows over time characterizes the wines of Cahors." Three wineries of exceptional merit, all within a short drive of Cahors, are **Domaine de Lagrezette,** in Caillac (☎ **05-65-20-07-42**); **Domaine de Haute Serre,** in Cieurac (☎ **05-65-20-80-20**); and **Domaine de St-Didier Parnac,** in Parnac (☎ **05-65-30-78-13**). Their dark wines are of consistently high quality, and they easily hold their own against any of the region's rich, hearty dishes. The Office de Tourisme (see "Tourist Office," above) provides detailed information and maps to these wineries.

EATING

→**Au Fil des Douceurs** FRENCH If Cahors has begun to float your boat, come float in theirs. It's a barge moored on the far side of pont Cabessut, and it's one of the coolest restaurants in the city. Prices are reasonable, and you can expect unusual takes on regional cuisine (foie-gras lasagna, for instance). And you should definitely leave space for dessert; the chef is an ex-*chocolatier* who knows how to make a cacao bean purr. *90 quai de la verrerie.* ☎ *05-65-22-13-04. Tues–Sat noon–2pm and 7–11pm. Fixed-price menus 13€ (lunch), 20€–47€ (dinner).*

FESTIVALS

Blues groups, including some from the United States, turn this town upside down for 3 days in mid-July during the **Festival du Blues.** Most performances are open-air affairs, and many are free, by bands playing at cafes along the boulevard Gambetta. Formal concerts are usually at the **Théâtre des Verdures,** an open-air courtyard in the heart of the medieval city. Tickets are 15€ to 40€. For exact dates and information, contact the Office de Tourisme (see "Tourist Office," above). For tickets, contact **Cahors Blues Festival** (☎ **05-65-35-99-99;** www.cahorsblues festival.com).

Cool Circuit: Villages & Châteaux

Like sheets of molten hematite, the Dordogne River meanders in and out of the Dordogne Valley's hillsides, reflecting the sky and sunlight in its inky depths, like a serpentine mirror. Several of the Dordogne's finest châteaux line this stretch of river, along with villages that hug the cliff tops, and rolling plains and forests that suddenly drop off into precipitous rocky outcrops.

For the best views, grab a bike or a car and follow the D703 westward from Montfort, where from the ox-bow loop of the river, you can admire the pretty Château de Montfort before following the trail to the following sites of intrigue:

MTV Best ◉ →**Domme** ★★ This beautiful 13th-century bastide holds an array of architectural bonbons, including the famous Porte des Tours, covered in graffiti made by Knights Templar prisoners during 11 years of captivity, the Renaissance Governor's house, and a slightly foreboding church with a belfry. Tunnels lead from the church to caves with stalactites and stalagmites. But the real reason to come is for the views—sweeping panoramas, 150m (492 ft.) over the valley, from where you can make out your next stop, La Roque-Gageac, and the Parc de

Marqueyssac (see "Playing Outside," above). *Tourist office, place de la Halle.* ☎ *05-53-31-71-00.*

→ **La Roque-Gageac** ★ From here, you can sail on a traditional boat called a Gabare (see "Playing Outside," above). The village's other attractions include toy-like, ocher-colored houses that line the riverside; the oh-so elegant Manoir de Tarde, with its exotic plant garden; and a troglodyte fort, high on the cliff top, with views to make you forget your legs ache from walking up a nearly sheer 40m (131-ft.) hill.

→ **Château de Castelnaud** ★★ On the opposite side of the river from La Roque-Gageac (off the D57) lies the most visited château in the region. According to history books, Castelnaud, perched high over the valley, belonged to the Cathar nobleman Bernard de Casnac in the 12th century. He was a cruel man, infamous for his hatred of Catholics. In those days, even the smallest suspicion of heresy was enough to kick up a fuss, and soon brave Simon de Montfort led a siege on the castle and restored peace and tranquillity to the valley—until Bernard took it back 1 year later, hanging Montfort's entire garrison. During the Hundred Years' War, Castelnaud sided with the English and then with the Heuguenots during the Wars of Religion. Today, highlights include a 46m-deep (29-ft.) well in the inner courtyard, an austere looking barbican pierced with gun holes, and a cool artillery tower. ☎ *05-53-31-30-00. www.castelnaud.com.*

→ **Château de Beynac** ★ On the opposite side of the river from Castelnaud, just before the village of St-Vincent de Cosse, Beynac is another panoramic paradise with sweeping views over the valley. One enters the castle over a double moat. The way the light falls mysteriously over the hillsides attracted the Impressionist painter Pissarro; and writers such as Henry Miller spent many a contemplative moment amid Beynac's narrow streets. The owners are desperately trying to restore the building to its former medieval glory. No, they don't have any eligible sons or daughters—I already asked. (For detailed schedules, contact the tourist office in La Balme at ☎ **05-53-29-43-08;** www.cc-perigord-noir.fr.)

At the foot of the castle, don't miss the **Parc Archéologique** (☎ **05-53-29-51-28;** July to mid-Sept), which showcases a Bronze-Age settlement. ☎ *05-53-29-50-40. Admission 7€ adults, 3€ kids 5–11. Mar–Sept daily 10am–6:30pm; Oct–Feb daily 11am–sundown.*

→ **Château de Milandes** ★ Everyone remembers Josephine Baker for her risqué dancing and evocative banana belt. But there was another side to the star—a side that believed in fairy tales and the sort of magic that was missing from her own, unhappy childhood. The U.S.-born dancer visited the Château de Milandes in 1937, rented it in 1947, and then acquired the funds necessary to turn it into her very own Sleeping Beauty castle. It was here, in the 1950s, that she adopted and raised 10 different-race children. Her "Rainbow Tribe," as she liked to call them, was a message to the world that we all belong to one race—the human race.

In addition to the castle's restored rooms and collections of Baker's costumes and memorabilia, you can also view some excellent Bird of Prey shows in front of the château. *On the D53 just before Envaux village.* ☎ *05-53-59-31-21. www.milandes.com. 7.80€ adults, 6€ students. April to late Oct.*

Provence

by Anna Brooke

If you could walk through rainbows, I imagine it wouldn't be dissimilar from exploring Provence—with its endless fields of lavender and sunflowers, reflected in the region's traditional bright fabrics, colorful window shutters, and the paintings of Vincent van Gogh and Paul Cézanne, the artists most famously inspired by the landscape.

Provence has its own language and customs within France. While you'd be hard pressed to meet someone who can speak more than just a few words of Provençal, you can't help but notice the locals' cheery, twangy accents, with drawn-out vowels that taper off into nasal sounds. The way of life tends to be drawn out likewise, to match the accent. Locals tend to be friendlier, more relaxed, and generous with their time. The warm summer sun only heightens the vacation atmosphere.

The typical Provençal town is small with a *vieille ville* (old town), often enclosed within walls. Many cities, like Arles, were originally built during the Roman Empire, so you can visit countless Roman amphitheaters, arenas, baths, arches, and aqueducts here. Alongside the inevitable Roman ruins are winding, cobblestone streets and cafes under wide canopies of trees.

Arles has some of the best-preserved Roman ruins around, and it's also famous as the former home of van Gogh. The town is small and quaint, much of it painted a warm yellow color—from the buildings and window shutters to the paintings, umbrellas, and even the napkins in restaurants. **Avignon**'s ramparts enclose one of

France's most culturally impressive towns. Named one of the European Capitals of Culture for the millennium, Avignon's festivals, art museums, and progressive, contemporary attitude toward film and theater are renowned. **Aix-en-Provence,** the birthplace and home of Cézanne, is another artistically significant university town. The bustling port of **Marseille** stands apart from the rest of the region, with its distinct North African influence and fast pace. France's second largest city, it fights constant rumors that it's dark and dangerous, but it's also a happening city, brimming with life, a trippin' music scene, a long list of museums and monuments, cheap shops, and some of the region's best seafood. Beyond the cities, the rocky outcrops in les **Baux de Provence** and the **Camargue,** the marshland near Arles that edges up to the Mediterranean, also lure visitors.

Cuisine in Provence has come a long way over the years. No longer can it be reduced to anything cooked with tomatoes, garlic, and olive oil, although you'll inevitably come across these ingredients. The most famous dishes are *bouillabaisse,* a delectable fish stew that takes hours to prepare when cooked properly, and *ratatouille,* a stew of eggplant, zucchini, tomatoes, and bell peppers. Olives and olive oil are locally grown and pressed, and bread is often served with an olive paste called *tapenade.*

Of course, Provence also has its own wines. The best-known are the Côtes du Rhône and the Côtes du Provence—both light-bodied reds. The most typical Provençal drink, however, is *pastis,* a thick, licorice-flavored liquor that turns white and cloudy when mixed with water.

The Best of Provence

○ **The Best Former Roman Romping Ground:** Nowhere are the relics of a lost empire more visible than in the charming ancient town of **Arles,** complete with a Roman circus and emperor's palace. See p. 456.

○ **The Best Place to Say "To Be or Not to Be" Before Dropping off a Bridge:** The former cultural, religious, and political center of Christendom, **Avignon** is one of the prettiest and most interesting of Provence's cities, with an annual kick-ass theater festival and its famous ruined bridge, the pont d'Avignon. See p. 443.

○ **The Best City in Which to Strut Your Stuff till Sunrise: Marseille,** Provence's busiest working fishing port, is a 24-hour affair, with the stuff for a whole day and a night's entertainment with the friendly locals. See p. 424.

○ **The Best Place to Cry "Yee-Ha!" before Lassoing a Wild Pony: La Camargue** is France's answer to the Wild West, where real cowboys gallop across lagoons, salt-flats, and horse-filled marshes. Look out for the pink flamingoes, too! See p. 463.

○ **The Best Panoramic Provence Village on a Limestone Crag:** Ah, how times change. What was once the finest court in medieval Provence—**Les Baux**—is now the finest regional draw for international tourists, with its ruined castle and dramatic views onto distant mountains. See p. 464.

○ **The Best Spot for Wine & Views of Notre-Dame de la Garde (Marseille):** It's first-come, first-served on the panoramic balcony of **La Caravelle,** a funky tapas bar—which explains why the place fills up earlier

PROVENCE

than most. Or is it because the drinks are cheap, the location to die for, and the tapas free? See p. 436.

○ **The Best Place to Meet Local Creative Types (Marseille):** The climb up the world's smelliest steps (an unofficial urinal for Marseille menfolk) is worth the effort when you catch the funky vibe that radiates from the bars, restaurants, and unusual shops in **Cours Julien.** See p. 441.

○ **The Best Way to Spend Very Little on Food & Watch the Sunset over the Port of Marseille:** A **picnic.** Nicolas wine shop sells cheap bottles, the fast-food cabin on quai de Rive Neuve just opposite sells cones of deep fried seafood and burgers, and the port's quaysides are free to sit on. What more can a poor traveler ask for? See p. 434.

○ **The Best Place to Get in with the Alternatively Trendy Art Crowd:** DJ l'Amateur is one of Marseille's funkiest sound maestros, and **Cabaret Aléatoire de la La Friche** ("La Friche") is his territory. If boogying is not your forte, come grab a play, test their brand-new restaurant, or join the underground "it" crowd for some cross-media entertainment. See p. 436.

○ **The Best & Most Eclectic Museum:** In one of Marseille's prettiest quarters, **Musée de Vieille Charité** showcases a fine Egyptian collection, Cypriot pottery, a morbidly fascinating display of shrunken heads, and other artifacts. See p. 438.

○ **The Best Religious Edifice Visible from Miles Around, from Where You Can See for Miles Around (Marseille):** A church has stood here at **Notre-Dame de la Garde**'s site since the 16th century, although this building dates from the 19th century, in Romano-Byzantine style. Climb to the top for the best views over Marseille and onto its offshore islands. See p. 428.

○ **The Best Reality TV Historical Attraction (Avignon):** You've heard about the **pont St-Bénézet,** and now you can come and dance on it, just like in the song. You can even record your rendition of it on DVD, or watch your mates walk across the bridge (and fall off) live on Earth TV. See p. 451.

○ **The Best and Most Important Religious Site in Provence (Avignon):** First you should sit in a cafe on the opposite side of the square and admire **Palais des Papes** from the outside; then you should spend a few hours looking at the fascinating collections on the inside, before heading back outside to the palace gardens (Rocher des Doms), where you can admire the resident swans. See p. 450.

○ **The Best Splurge on a Bed (Avignon):** You're tired of backpacking? If you see one more tent or communal bathroom you'll explode? Well all that scrimping and saving will be momentarily forgotten when you see the rooms that await you in **La Mirande,** a nest of opulence. See p. 448.

○ **The Best Period to Recite Shakespeare's "All the World's a Stage, and All the Men and Women Merely Players" (Avignon):** During the **Festival d'Avignon,** the whole of Avignon is a stage for 3 weeks. And practically all the men and women you meet there are players, dead set on attracting the attention of the many TV, film, and theater producers that scowl the streets for new talent. See p. 444.

○ **The Best Place to Escape Medieval Mania:** It ain't no Centre Pompidou (see the Paris & Ile-de-France chapter), but art dealer Yvon Lambert certainly gave the **Musée d'Art Contemporain** in Avignon a big present when he lent

Provence

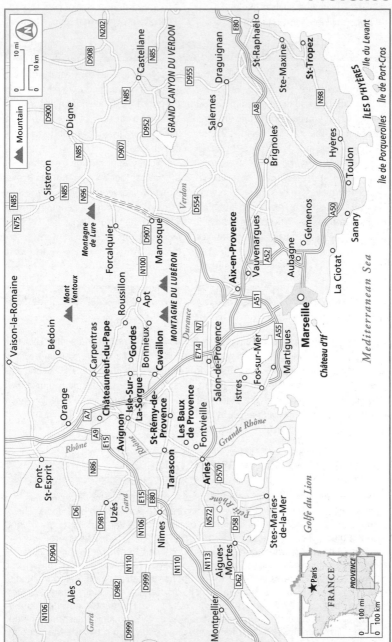

them the Collection Lambert for 20 years. Movements such as Minimal Art, Conceptual Art, Land Art from the '60s and '70s, painting from the '80s, photography and video from the '90s all receive precious wall space. See p. 452.

Getting Around the Region

God bless **TGVs** (and the English for inventing the train), for they make getting to the main cities so damned painless—so much so, that you can practically give the buses a miss. The train station in Marseille is the largest and has connections to everywhere else in France. It's also one of the more notorious train stations in France for thieves, so be sure to keep your eyes and your hands on your valuables. Avignon and Aix-en-Provence also have a TGV connection to Paris, which makes travel in and out of Provence simple. The countryside in Provence is great to explore on a bike—consider renting one in a smaller town, where you'll be closer to the backdrop of lavender fields. You could also hire a car to get to some of the more out-of-the-way villages and stretches of coastline.

If you're approaching from the Riviera, the easiest loop to take through Provence is from Marseille up through Aix-en-Provence and Avignon, ending in Arles. If you're coming from Paris, the TGV stops in Avignon. You then might want to cruise through Arles on your way to Marseille and Aix.

Marseille

771km (479 miles) S of Paris, 187km (116 miles) SW of Nice, 31km (19 miles) S of Aix-en-Provence

Suddenly you're caught in a colorful crowd of people, all speaking animatedly with different accents and drawls. The sun blinds your eyes as it glints off rows of bright, shining fishing boats, and the smells of Bouillabaisse, car fumes, and a nearby fish market fill your nostrils: You can be nowhere else but Marseille. This unique and fast-paced city, with more than a million inhabitants, is the second-largest city in France and distinctly unlike the rest of golden, laid-back Provence—or anywhere else in France for that matter.

Men & Their Balls: Petanques

You just can't get a man to take his hands off his balls in Provence: *Boules,* sometimes known as *petanques,* is an extremely popular regional sport. The principles are simple. Pretend you are over 60, find a flat, sandy stretch of land, grab a glass of Lou Reed's favorite brand of *pastis* (Pernod), split into two teams of three *(triplettes)* or four *(quadrettes),* and throw a small colored ball weighted with iron *(le cochonnet)* as far it will go. The aim now is to throw your heavy balls as close as possible to the *cochonnet,* dislodging the opposition's balls if necessary. It's not as painful as it all sounds—especially after several glasses of *pastis.* And if you really want to fit in, start a heated debate about the state of the world today, shrug your shoulders while making a raspberry noise with your mouth, and chase after your ball, encouraging it to wipe the opposition out of the game.

M T V 🚇 **Marseille**

Number One among the Young & the Restless

To the astonishment of their elders, French people under 25 years voted Marseille the number-one French city in which they'd like to live. Montpellier came second, and Paris tied third with Bordeaux. And when it comes to partying, the funky young things of France certainly know what they're on about; Marseille has a fearsome youth scene with a fantastic focus on music and contemporary art.

It has been called France's New Orleans, and (by Dumas) "the meeting place of the entire world." And it's not hard to see why. It has been a crossroads and a center of immigration since the Phoenicians founded it in 600 B.C.—a gateway to a new world for those who braved the seas from Algeria, Greece, Turkey, Italy, and Spain in hope of a new life or new trading opportunities. This melting pot of cultures and races explains why it has always been a freethinking city—one that dares to deviate from France's accepted status quo, and one that has inevitably been labeled as rebellious.

Perhaps Marseille's most common association is with the national anthem of France, "La Marseillaise." During the Revolution, 500 rebels marched to Paris, singing this rousing song along the way. And the rest, as they say, is history.

Although Marseille is sprawling, dirty (dog-poo hopping is an unofficial sport), and slumlike in many respects, it also exhibits much elegance and charm. The **Vieux-Port,** the lively old harbor, compensates for the dreary industrial dockland nearby. Walking up the main drag from the station down to the port, the

Canebière (known as Can o' Beer to U.S. sailors in World War II), you can still imagine docked Navy ships and immigrant boats in the port.

A lively medley of races and creeds coexist relatively happily here, although in an age of international terrorism and rising racial tensions throughout Europe, the extreme-right has gained popularity. But, before you believe horror stories of drug smuggling, corruption, the Mafia, and racial attacks, come see the city for yourself. Yes you should be careful, and yes, you should use common sense, but it's nonetheless a fascinating place.

The government is investing hefty sums in the city, and by 2007, a brand new tram system should be up and running, relieving some of the traffic from the roads and underground Métro. This is an exciting year to visit, and a great way to get a flavor of things to come.

Getting There

BY AIR

The **airport** (☎ 04-42-14-14-14), 27km (17 miles) northwest of the city center, receives international flights from all over Europe. From the airport, blue-and-white minivans *(navettes)* make the trip to Marseille's St-Charles rail station, a 10-minute walk from the Vieux-Port (or a short Métro ride), for around 9€. The minivans run daily every 20 minutes from 6am (hourly) or to the arrival of the last flight.

BY TRAIN

Marseille has **train** connections from all over Europe, with especially good connections to and from Italy. The city is the terminus for the TGV bullet train, which departs daily from Paris's Gare de Lyon (trip time: 3 hr.). Some Parisians plan a day trip to Marseille, returning to the City of Light for dinner. For information, call ☎ **36-35** or check www.sncf.com.

Marseille History 101

When you're on the coast, chances are your shores will be invaded at some point or another. In Marseille's case, it was more for business than actual blood-spilling when several Phocaean galleys turned up in 600 B.C. in Lacydon Creek, the current Old Port, in search of trading opportunities. They proved a deft hand at business and soon created a prosperous settlement, until the Persians nabbed power in 540 B.C., setting up trading posts in places such as Arles and Avignon, and controlling the seas from Marseille's shores.

Next up came the Romans, who waged a 3-year battle with the locals, won, and went off in togas to create colonies in Aix and Narbonne, turning Marseille into an independent settlement allied to Rome. But status quos are never eternal. Soon, when the rivalry between Caesar and Pompey reached its peak, Marseille had to choose which one to support. Needless to say, it backed the wrong horse (Pompey), and Caesar waged war on the city, stripping it of its fleet and treasures. The silver lining? Marseille kept its independence, its university, and its right to trade with the Far East.

By the 18th century, Marseille was a great port of around 90,000 people that thrived through the importation of textiles, food, drugs, and anything else that 18th-century French folk had a penchant for. It was just about to embark on trading ventures with the West Indies and the rich New World when disaster struck in 1720, in the form of the Great Plague. A ship from Syria brought it ashore despite quarantine measures. The locals were so terrified that the Parliament in Aix outlawed all communication with the city, upon pain of death. They even built a 28km (17 miles) long "Plague Wall," but to no avail. In 2 years, 100,000 people died, 50,000 from Marseille.

But Marseille bounced back with a vengeance, and by 1765, it was back to its old tricks, having established trade with the New World. All this coincided with a decent bout of industrialization, and soon the port began making soap *(savon de Marseille)* and glass. In 1789, the locals fervently backed the Revolution. In fact they were the first town to demand the abolition of the royal family, and volunteers set about going to the capital, singing their "Marseillaise," today France's national anthem.

Under Napoleon, many grand boulevards and theaters were created, but during World War II, Marseilles suffered heavy bombing by German-Italian bombs. Mass reconstruction after the war saw the arrival of many new buildings, including Le Corbusier's famous **Cité Radieuse**—a veritable town in a tower block (p. 438).

BY CAR

If you're **driving** from Paris, follow A6 south to Lyon, then continue south along A7 to Marseille. The drive takes about 7 hours. Once in Provence, take A7 south to Marseille.

BY BUS

Buses serve the **Gare Routière,** place Victor Hugo (☎ **04-91-08-16-40**), adjacent to the St-Charles railway station. Eurolines run coaches from some European countries via Paris to Marseille. Get more info on **www.eurolines.com** or call ☎ 01-49-72-51-51. Be warned that road travel (especially coaches that have to obey strict speed restrictions) is exceedingly slow in comparison to TGVs.

Marseillaise Slang

Fed up of sticking out like a sore thumb? Well get out your note pad. Here are a few words than only the locals knows.

→ **furer** (fu-reh)   To French kiss

→ **méchant** (meh-shan)   Really good (literally, "wicked")

→ **mia** (mee-ah)   A showoff

→ **tè** (tuh)   Who'd have thought that!

→ **vé** (veh)   Look at that!

→ **vier** (vee-eh)   A prick (as in "you prick")—to be used sparingly, unless you like fistfights

BY BOAT

If you're traveling from Corsica, you could take the boat back to France via Marseille. **SNCM Ferryterranée** (61 bd. des Dames, 2nd arr.; ☎ 04-91-56-35-86; www.sncm.fr) run regular crossings. This is one of most fun and exciting ways of traveling to the city.

Orientation

I hope you're reading attentively—there's a lot of info to get through. Marseille is a sprawling mass with an inner city and rapidly growing suburbs. If you don't want to make a mistake and find yourself in these suburban expanses, you need to concentrate on its inner core, for that is where all the fun is to be had; indeed it's the reason you're visiting in the first place.

Split into 16 districts called *arrondissements* (or arr., which, rather like in Paris, are numbered in a spiral beginning in the center from the Vieux Port), the city is quite simple to navigate. Many travelers never visit the museums, preferring to absorb the life of the city on its busy streets and at its cafes, particularly those along the main street, **La Canebière**—the heart and soul of Marseille, and possibly the seediest main street in France. Lined with hotels, shops, and restaurants, it fills with sailors from every nation and people of every nationality. There is a large Algerian populace, and many of the side streets off the Canebière have a distinct North African souk feel to them.

The spectacular **Vieux-Port (1st arr.)**, dominated by the massive neoclassical forts of St-Jean and St-Nicholas, is filled with fishing craft and yachts and ringed with seafood restaurants. For a panoramic view, head to the **Parc du Pharo (7th arr.)**, a promontory facing the entrance to the Vieux-Port. From a terrace overlooking the Château du Pharo, built by Napoleon III for his Eugénie, you can clearly see Fort St-Jean and the old and new cathedrals.

North of Gare Saint-Charles is the **4th arrondissement**, an area known as **Les 5 Avenues**, which is home to wide, tree-lined boulevards and the **Palais Longchamp**, with its **park, Musée des Beaux-Arts,** and **Musée d'Histoire Naturelle.**

The **2nd arrondissement** is the area along the water just north of the Vieux Port, and has good port-side restaurants that are slightly less hectic than those near the Canebière. The hill that rises from behind these attractions should also be explored. It is a cute, medieval district known as **le Panier**—one of the quaintest parts of town, filled with artisan boutiques, several museums, and narrow streets.

Incognito (Again) on the Tourist Train

You got it—another chance to hop on the nerd vehicle extraordinaire. The **Petit Train de la Bonne Mère** (☎ 04-91-40-17-75; Métro: Vieux-Port), makes two circuits around town. Year-round, train no. 1 makes a 50-minute round-trip to **Basilique Notre-Dame-de-la-Garde** (a great way to avoid the huffing and puffing involved if you climb up to the top) and **Basilique St-Victor.** From Easter to October, train no. 2 makes a 40-minute round-trip of old Marseille by way of the cathedral, Vieille Charité, and the Quartier du Panier. The trains depart from quai des Belges at the Vieux-Port. Each trip costs about 5€.

East of the Vieux Port is the **6th** *arrondissement* where the city's coolest bars tend to cluster around the **Cours Julien** and **place Jean Jaurès,** colorfully decorated in wild murals and graffiti. And in between the 6th and 7th *arrondissements* lies the opulent hilltop cathedral of MTV Best❢ **Notre-Dame de la Garde.** On the southwestern edge of town, along the coast, are the best beaches. This area, **the 8th *arrondissement*** makes for a quieter stay than in the center of town, with reasonably priced hotels and mellow sandy beachside bars.

Rental Vehicles

Get some locomotion at the following:

→ **Ada** (Gare St-Charles; ☎ 04-91-64-90-59; www.ada.fr)

→ **Europcar** (121 av. Prado; ☎ 08-25-82-54-21; www.europcar.fr)

→ **Avis** (Gare St-Charles; ☎ 08-20-61-16-36; www.avis.fr)

→ For scooters: **Big Store Moto Centre** (28 cours Lieutaud; ☎ 04-91-55-66-14; www.go2rent.fr)

To park your vehicle, try **Parking du Vieux Port** (cours Etienne d'Orves; ☎ 04-91-54-34-38) or **Parking Julien** (96 cours Julien; ☎ 04-91-47-23-53).

Getting Around

BY PUBLIC TRANSPORTATION

Métro lines 1 and 2 both stop at the main train station, **Gare St-Charles,** place Victor Hugo. Two brand new **tramlines** link the Canabière near the Vieux Port to rue de la République in the 2nd *arrondissement,* boulevard Chave in the 5th *arrondissement,* and boulevard Longchamp in the 1st *arrondissement* near the station. Individual tickets are for sale at Métro, tram, and bus stops for 1.60€ each; they're valid on all transport for up to 60 minutes after purchase. If you plan to take public transport several times during your stay, you get a discount if you buy a **Carte Liberté,** valid for either five rides for 6.50€ or 10 rides for 14€. Information and public-transit maps are available at the main office, **Espace Info,** 6 rue des Fabres (☎ **04-91-91-92-10;** www.metro-tramway-marseille.com). Parking and car safety are so problematic that your best bet is to garage your car and rely on public transportation. Public transport will help you get around the sprawling city without the hassle of traffic.

BY BICYCLE

Are you on a death wish? Why do you want to cycle around such a busy, hilly city? Well if you must risk life and limb, visit **Team Bike** (131 cours Lieutaud; ☎ **04-91-92-76-73;** Tues–Sat 9am–7pm).

ON FOOT

Certain quarters such as **Le Panier, le Vieux Port,** and the shopping areas around **Cannabière** are perfect for walking around. In fact, from the station, you can easily get into the town center in 15 minutes. Walking back is the trouble, which is when public transport comes in handy.

Tourist Offices

The **Office de Tourisme** is at 4 la Canebière (☎ 04-91-13-89-00; www.marseille-tourisme.com; Métro: Vieux-Port). Don't forget to ask about **Le City Pass** that costs 18€ (1 day) or 25€ (2 days) and gives free entry into 14 museums as well as a free boat trip and 10% off at Galeries Lafayette department store.

Marseille **Nuts & Bolts**

Emergencies The usuals—☎ 15 for an ambulance, ☎ 17 for the coppers, ☎ 18 for firemen and paramedics. In case of rape, call **SOS Viols Femmes (Rape crisis;** ☎ 04-91-56-04-10).

Internet/Wireless Hot Spots One of the nicest places to check your e-mail or write your blog is **Info Café,** right on the Vieux Port (1 quai de Rive-Neuve; ☎ 04-91-33-74-98; www.info-cafe.fr). If they're full, grab a cuppa at **Cyber@Thé** (44 rue des Trois-Mages; ☎ 04-91-48-29-72).

Laundromats Take your togs for a whirl at **Lav'éclair** (34 rue Mazagran, 1 arr.; ☎ 04-91-92-69-37).

Post Office **La Poste** at place de l'Hôtel-des-Postes (1st arr.) is in a good central location and stays open Monday to Friday 8am to 7pm.

Safety You shouldn't run into any problems in the city center, but the usual rules apply: Keep your bag well zipped, don't flash money around, look like you know where you're going (if you're lost, stop in cafe or a shop and ask), and don't make unnecessary eye contact with strangers, particularly if you're a girl (as Marseille menfolk can be hot-blooded animals who like chatting up women in the street).

Taxis Call ☎ 04-91-02-20-20 or 04-91-05-80-80.

Sleeping

You'll be needing that rendezvous with Monsieur Sandman after Marseille's vast sightseeing and partying opportunities. Being on the hot and sunny Mediterranean, most hotels have air-conditioning, but always check when you book if you want to avoid sleepless, sweaty nights. Equally, the summer months can get very busy, so booking ahead is vital. If you're caught out, **Allotel** (☎ 08-26-88-68-26; 15¢ per minute) is a great last-minute hotel reservations service. There's no guarantee where you'll end up, but anything's better than sleeping rough, eh?

HOSTELS

Right then, you can either choose a charming building 5km (3 miles) out of the *centre-ville,* or a soulless modern building by the beach. If you opt for architectural style, jump on Métro line 1 (toward La Rose), get off at Les Chartreux, take bus 6 (to Marius-Py) or line 8 (to Bois-Luzy), and head for the **Auberge de Jeunesse de Bois Luzy** (Allée des Primevères, 12th arr.; ☎ 04-91-49-06-18; beds from 12€, sheets included but not breakfast). The building is a pretty 19th-century mansion, set in a park with tennis, volleyball, basketball courts, and an area laid out for the *crème de la crème* of all Provence games—*boules*. Rooms are old but clean. If you're lucky, you'll get one with a sea view.

For the beach option, jump on Bus 44 (get off at Bonnefon) or take Métro line 2 to Rond-point Prado, and go to **Auberge de Jeunesse Bonneveine** (Impasse du Dr Bonfils, av. J. Vidal, 8th arr.; ☎ **04-91-17-63-30;** beds from 15€; sheets and breakfast included). Rooms are simple, there's a communal terrace, Internet access, billiards, and the chance to book sea canoeing or kayaking excursions in the nearby *calanques* (Marseille's pretty coastline coves).

CHEAP

→ **Hôtel Lutetia** At just 200m (656 ft.) from Gare St-Charles, this Empire building is in a great spot for dumping your bags straight off the train, then hitting the *centre-ville*. Rooms aren't huge, but they're dolled up nicely in pretty lavenders and blues. The entrance has a cool mural of a galleon, plus a handy little seating area. Bathrooms are clean, breakfast is copious, and the staff is helpful. Overall, it's great value for the money. *38 Allée Léon Gambetta.* ☎ *04-91-50-81-78. www.hotelmarseille.com. 60€ double. Credit cards accepted. Parking 10€. Amenities: Computer center w/Internet. In room: A/C, TV, nonsmoking rooms available.*

→ **La Maison du Petit Canard** ★★ Smack bang in the old Panier district, near La Vieille Charité museum, the House of the Little Duck is no ugly ducking. It positively bursts with character and charm, with a distinct Oriental-cum-French influence (the embodiment of Marseille, in other words). Some decor looks like it's from a local souk, the rest from Grandma's country cottage. The friendly owners

Stéphanie and Yousef fatten you up with the biggest breakfast on earth, served in their busily decorated dining room. You can rent either a bedroom or an apartment with a kitchen. They serve meals for 14€, in case you can't be bothered to cook or go out for dinner. *2 Impasse Sainte Françoise, 2nd arr.* ☎ *04-91-91-40-31. http://maison. petit.canard.free.fr. 30€–46€ double; from 55€–75€ studio, depending upon the number of people. No credit cards.*

DOABLE

→ **Hôtel Bellevue** ★★ This is the hippest place to stay in Marseille. You get the location (right on the old port), you get the views (looking across the sea to Notre-Dame de la Garde), you get the funky bar (La Caravelle, one of the hottest joints in the city—see "Bars," below), and you get reasonable prices. The rooms are small, but kitted out in block colors (fresh mauves, greens, and blues) with period touches, such as marble fireplaces and fabrics with shell prints. The best bit happens at night, though, when you can rush down the red staircase into the bar and be first onto the balcony for a panoramic slurp with the locals. *34 quai du Port, 2nd arr.* ☎ *04-96-17-05-40. www.hotel-bellevue-marseille.fr. 92€–122€ double. Credit cards accepted. Amenities: Bar. In room: A/C, TV.*

→ **Hôtel Hermès** ★ This wicked joint (same owners as Hôtel Lutetia) has just been renovated, so it has a crisp new feel about it (which can be a godsend in insalubrious Marseille). Many rooms have balconies overlooking the port—perfect for a quick glass of wine (or, to hell with it—champers) before you head out partying or sightseeing. Despite its central location, it is actually quite calm, and there's Wi-Fi. *2 rue Bonneterie.* ☎ *04-96-11-63-63. www.hotel marseille.com. 63€–90€ double. Credit cards accepted. Amenities: Restaurant; Internet (and Wi-Fi); solarium. In room: A/C, TV.*

Marseille

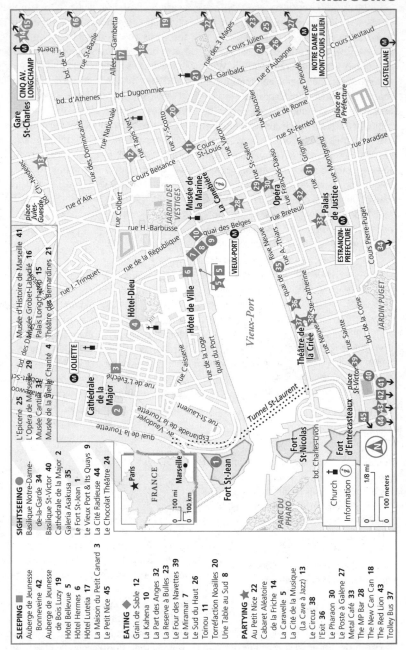

SLEEPING ■
Auberge de Jeunesse Bonneveine **42**
Auberge de Jeunesse de Bois Luzy **19**
Hôtel Bellevue **5**
Hôtel Hermes **6**
Hôtel Lutetia **17**
La Maison du Petit Canard **3**
Le Petit Nice **45**

EATING ◆
Grain de Sable **12**
La Kahena **10**
La Part des Anges **32**
La Reserve à Bulles **23**
Le Four des Navettes **39**
Le Miramar **7**
Le Sud du Haut **26**
Toinou **11**
Torréfaction Noailles **20**
Une Table au Sud **8**

PARTYING ★
Au Petit Nice **22**
Cabaret Aléatoire de la Friche **14**
La Caravelle **5**
La Cité de la Musique (La Cave à Jazz) **13**
Le Circus **38**
l'Exit **36**
Le Pharaon **30**
Le Poste à Galène **27**
Metal Café **33**
The MP Bar **28**
The New Can Can **18**
The Red Lion **43**
Trolley Bus **37**

SIGHTSEEING ●
Basilique Notre-Dame-de-la-Garde **34**
Basilique St-Victor **40**
Cathédrale de la Major **2**
Galeria Asakusa **35**
Le Fort St-Jean **1**
Le Vieux Port & Its Quays **9**
Le Chocolat Théâtre **24**

L'Epicerie **25**
L'Opéra de Marseille **29**
Musée Cantini **31**
Musée de la Vieille Charité **4**
Musée d'Histoire de Marseille **41**
Musée Grobet-Labadié **16**
Palais Longchamp **15**
Théâtre des Bernardines **21**

SPLURGE

➜ **Le Petit Nice** ★ ★ This is *the* posh hotel of Marseille. It opened in 1917, when the Passédat family joined two villas in a secluded area below the street paralleling the beach. The spacious Marina Wing across from the main building offers rooms individually decorated in an antique style, opening onto sea views. The rooms in the main house are more modern and avant-garde. Four rooms were inspired by the Cubist movement, with sleek geometric appointments and bright colors. The apartments are good but get a load of the dining room. The hotel restaurant is beautiful, with a view of the shore and the rocky islands off its coast. In summer, dinner is served in the garden facing the sea. *Corniche Président J. F. Kennedy/Anse-de-Maldormé, 7th arr.* ☎ *04-91-59-25-92. www. petitnice-passedat.com. 210€–490€ double; 400€–850€ suite. Credit cards accepted. Free parking. Métro: Vieux-Port. Amenities: Restaurant; bar; babysitting; free use of bikes; dry cleaning; laundry service; limited-mobility rooms; limited room service; nonsmoking rooms; outdoor pool. In room: A/C, TV, dataport, hair dryer, minibar, safe.*

Eating

It is impossible to go hungry in Marseille, even if you're on a very low budget. Bouillabaisse is Marseille's specialty, but you generally can't go wrong in any seafood restaurant that uses locally caught fish. The ethnic and cultural diversity of its residents also means that it's easy to find great, cheap foreign cuisine—particularly Tunisian and Moroccan. There are dozens of eateries around Cours d'Estienne d'Orves, near the Vieux Port, and Cours Julien just above it. **Here's a tip:** Carry cash; some restaurants don't take credit cards.

CAFES & LIGHT FARE

➜ **Grain de Sable** VEGGIE Pierrick and Nicolas worked in international business before they realized that the cut-throat world of capitalism didn't fit in with their personal convictions. Taking the bull by the horns and putting all their eggs (free-range ones obviously) in one basket, they opened this environmentally friendly snack bar that sells all sorts of delicious organic, vegetarian dishes. There is nothing flower-power about the joint. It is sleek, warm, and modern—the only difference being that the alcohol you order is organic beer or wine. The cakes are to die for (try the carrot and poppy-seed one if it's available), and if you fancy a quick smoothie, they have some of the most original recipes in Marseille. *34 rue Baignoir, 1st arr.* ☎ *04-91-90-39-51. Main courses 7€–12.50€. No credit cards. Mon–Fri 10am–8pm.*

➜ **La Reserve à Bulles** ★ CAFE The French love of cartoon strips (BD, pronounced *Beh-deh* short for *Bande-Dessinée*) is ever present, even in Marseille, where this library-cafe sells hundreds, nay, thousands of BDs. There is a definite male slant to the clientele, so girls, if you're looking for a beau Marseille macho, with geek-like tendencies, who laughs at cartoon people, this could be good flirting ground. Although the accent is on the BDs, there are a few tables where you can sit back and chat around a decent cup of tea or coffee and snacks. *76 rue des Trois Frères Barthélemy.* ☎ *04-91-53-28-91. www.reserveabulles.com. Coffee 1.20€; cartoons 10€–15€. Tues–Sat 10am–8pm.*

➜ **Torréfaction Noailles** TRADITIONAL CAFE You fancy coffee, but your mates want tea and hot chocolate? *Pas de problème.* You want biscuits but your mates want cakes and sweets? *Pas de problème.* Torréfaction Noailles is a Marseille-grown coffee shop–cum–tea shop that sells a wide range of naughties, best enjoyed with a cup of their finest ground coffee (12 varieties) or tea (50 types). Their success has

Say Three Hail Marys & then Stuff Your Face

Since medieval times, Marseille has thrived on the legend of Les Trois Maries—three saints named Mary, including everyone's favorite ex-sinner, Mary Magdalene. Assisted by St. Lazarus, freshly awakened from the dead, they reportedly came ashore near Marseille to Christianize ancient Provence. To commemorate their voyage, small boat-shaped cookies *(les navettes),* flavored with secret ingredients that include tons of orange zest, orange-flower water, and sugar, are forever associated with Marseille. They're sold throughout the city, most notably at **Le Four des Navettes** (136 rue Sainte; ☎ **04-91-33-32-12**). Opened in 1791, it sells the cookies for 7.20€ per dozen and does very little else besides perpetuate the city's most cherished (and dubious) medieval myth.

led them to open several addresses around the city, but this one on La Canebière is the original shop from 1927. *56 La Canebière, 1st arr.* ☎ *04-91-55-60-66. www.noailles.com. Coffee from 6€; biscuits from 4€. Credit cards accepted. Mon–Sat 7am–7pm.*

CHEAP

➔ **La Kahena** ★ TUNISIAN   This is one of the busiest and most-respected Tunisian restaurants in a city that's loaded with worthy competitors. Established in 1976 and set close to the Vieux-Port, it's a two-room enclave of savory North African aromas: minced or grilled lamb, tomatoes, eggplant, herbs, and couscous, so beloved by Tunisian expatriates. The menu lists 10 varieties of couscous, including versions with lamb, chicken, fish, the savory sausages known as *merguez,* and a complete version that includes a little bit of each of those ingredients. Also look for *méchoui,* a succulent version of roasted lamb. The restaurant's name, incidentally, derives from a 6th-century-B.C. Tunisian princess who was legendary for uniting all the Berber tribes of North Africa. The fixed price menu is at 23€, but it's in the "cheap" category because dishes are so bountiful you probably won't need more than a main course. *2 rue de la République.* ☎ *04-91-90-61-93. Reservations recommended. Main*

courses 11€–15€. Daily noon–2:30pm and 7:30–11pm. Métro: Vieux-Port.

DOABLE

➔ **La Part des Anges** ★ FRENCH WINE BAR   This is where the trendy folk come to savor decent wine, and hearty cheese and meat dishes. The decor is not in your face; in fact it is pleasantly understated with the odd baroque touch, interesting painting, or clock on the wall. The wine cellar is the reason most people stop by, with over 250 types, 70 of which can be enjoyed by the glass. Music is chilled lounge, and the regulars are as laid-back as the stuff they listen to. If you've liked what you've tasted, click on the *liens* section of their website to get a listing of their many local wine producers. *33 rue Sainte.* ☎ *04-91-33-48-18. www.lapartdesanges.com. Daily 9am–2am (closed Sun 1–6pm).*

➔ **Le Sud du Haut** PROVENÇAL FUSION   This great restaurant looks more like it sells bric-a-brac than food, but the food is indeed the reason why the locals pile in every night of the week. On sunny days, the semi-shaded terrace is a godsend, and the whole place has a more relaxed feel than many other restaurants on Cours Julien. The mother-daughter duo in the kitchen create wonderful traditional dishes, revisited with contemporary flair. The only downer is the service, which

PROVENCE

Picnic by the Port in Summer

When the chips are down, you can still have a memorable meal 📺 (Best❗) **picnicking by the port.** And even if the chips aren't down, it's a fine way to watch the sun set over the sea, while sipping on a fine wine and chomping on deep-fried seafood.

The key to saving money is all in the planning. You won't look elegant, or indeed couth, but follow this guide and you'll be gut-busted for almost zip.

1. In the morning at breakfast, nab an extra serviette or two for your meal.
2. During the day, save your empty bottles of water.
3. When you're hungry (before 6:30pm), head over to Nicolas wine shop (3 quai de Rive Neuve; ☎ **04-91-55-66-40**) and pick up a bottle of their own label wine. It is the cheapest in the shop (from 3€), noticeable by its brightly colored labels. Ask them to open it for you, replacing the cork in a way so that you can open it again.
4. From here, cross the road to the waterside and look for the white fast-food cabin (on your right). Here you can buy fries, hot dogs, crepes, and the most wonderful deep-fried mussels, cockles, and squid for under 5€.
5. Once you've bought your catch, head away from *centre-ville* along the edge of the port, and sit down on the first available bench, or with feet dangling over the quayside. Pour the wine into your water bottles (who needs glasses), and swig and eat away to your heart's content.

Note: The food shack is only open during the summer, so check that it's serving before you go into Nicolas; otherwise, you'll be drinking on an empty stomach.

makes you feel like you're more in Paris than friendly Marseille. *80 cours Julien, 6th arr.* ☎ *04-91-92-66-64. Reservations recommended. Fixed-price menu 15€ lunch, 30€ evening. Credit cards accepted. Wed–Sat noon–2:30pm and 7:30–11pm. Closed mid-Aug to early Sept.*

➜ **Toinou** SEAFOOD In a massive building that overshadows every other structure nearby, this landmark restaurant serves more shellfish than any other restaurant in Marseille. Inside, a display of more than 40 species of shellfish is laid out for inspection by some of the canniest judges of seafood in France—Toinou's customers. Dining rooms are on three floors, served by a waitstaff who are very entrenched in their *marseillais* accents and demeanors. Don't come here unless

you're really fond of shellfish, any species of which can be served raw or cooked. The wine list is extensive, with attractively priced whites from such regions as the Loire Valley. *3 cours St-Louis, 1st arr.* ☎ *04-91-33-14-94. Reservations recommended. Main courses 12€–42€; fixed-price shellfish platter for 2 42€. Credit cards accepted. Daily 11:30am–2:30pm; Sun–Thurs 6:30–10:30pm; Fri–Sat 6:30–11:30pm.*

SPLURGE

In addition to the listings below, check out the expensive restaurant at **Le Petit Nice** (see "Sleeping," above).

➜ **Le Miramar** ★ SEAFOOD Except for Le Petit Nice, Le Miramar offers the grandest dining in Marseille. Bouillabaisse aficionados flock here to savor a version that

PROVENCE

will surely be a culinary highlight of your trip. It's hard to imagine that this was once a rough-and-tumble recipe favored by local fisherfolk, a way of using the least desirable portion of their catch. *Bouillabaisse* comes from the words *Bouillir* (to boil) and *Baisse* (to turn the heat down); the cooking method. Actually, it's traditionally two dishes, a saffron-tinted soup followed by the fish poached in the soup. It's eaten with *une rouille,* a sauce of red chiles, garlic, olive oil, egg yolk, and cayenne. The version served here involves lots of labor and just as much costly seafood. The setting is a room with frescoes of underwater life and big windows that open onto the Vieux-Port. It's linked to a terrace that overlooks Marseille's most famous church, Notre-Dame-de-la-Garde. *12 quai du Port. 1st arr.* ☎ *04-91-91-10-40. Reservations recommended. Main courses 30€–50€; bouillabaisse from 50€ per person (minimum 2). Credit cards accepted. Tues–Sat noon–2pm and 7:15–10pm.*

➜ **Une Table au Sud** ★★ MODERN PROVENÇAL One floor above street level, in a modern dining room with views of the Vieux-Port, this is the place to be seen in Marseille. Chef de cuisine Lionel Levy (part of Generation.C, France's new culinary movement; see p. 99) and his wife, Florence, the *maître d'hôtel,* serve some of the most creative cuisine in town. Dishes change daily according to the ingredients available at local markets. Menu items include a creamy soup made from chestnuts and sea urchins, and a thick slice of a local saltwater fish known as *denti,* which local gastronomes compare to a *daurade royale* (sea bream) served with flap mushrooms and chicken stock; mullet served with saffron and herb risotto; and roasted squab with Arabica coffee–flavored juices. Depending on the mood of the chef, desserts may include pineapple *dacquoise* (stacked meringue

dessert) served with vanilla-flavored whipped cream. *1 quai du Port. 1st arr.* ☎ *04-91-90-63-53. Reservations recommended. Fixed-price lunch 30€–55€; fixed-price dinner 43€–55€. Credit cards accepted. Tues–Thurs noon–2pm and 7:30–10:30pm; Fri–Sat noon–2pm and 7:30pm–midnight. Closed Aug and Dec 23–27.*

Partying

In a nutshell: A free magazine, **Le Ventilo** (found in Virgin Megastore and some bars) offers a lowdown of nocturnal goings-on; as does **Le Citadingue** (ask at the tourist office or check out www.citadingue.com), and **www.liveinmarseille.com** provides up-to-the-minute concert information. For an amusing and relatively harmless exposure to the town's saltiness, walk around the **Vieux-Port,** where cafes and restaurants angle their sightlines for the best view of the harbor.

Unless the air-conditioning is powerful, Marseille's dance clubs produce a lot of sweat. Pile on the deodorant and try the **Trolley Bus** (24 quai de Rive-Neuve, 7th arr.; ☎ **04-91-54-30-45;** www.letrolley.com)—a fantastic venue, set in four arched cellars that each play different music (techno, house, hip-hop, jazz, rock, and salsa). Close to the Vieux-Port, you can dance and drink at the **Metal Café** (20 rue Fortia; ☎ **04-91-54-03-03**), where a mixed crowd bops to R&B, house, and techno music recently released in London and Los Angeles.

If you miss free-form modern jazz and don't mind taking your chances in the less-than-savory neighborhood adjacent to the city's rail station (**La Gare St-Charles**—take a taxi there and back), consider dropping into **La Cité de la Musique** (also known as **La Cave à Jazz;** 4 rue Bernard-du-Bois; ☎ **04-91-39-28-28**). Other nightlife venues in Marseille evoke Paris, but with

PROVENCE

lots of extra *méridional* (southern) spice thrown in for extra flavor. **Le Pharaon,** for instance, on place de l'Opéra (☎ **04-91-54-09-89**), has a cozy enclave of deep sofas and armchairs, soft lighting, and usually a sense of well-being. **l'Exit** (12 quai de Riveneuve; ☎ **04-91-54-09-89**) is somewhat more bustling and animated, with a terrace that makes the most of Marseille's sultry nights, and two floors of seething nocturnal energy. A place that's loaded with razzmatazz, and appealing for both its dance floor and its cabaret acts, is **Le Circus** (5 rue du Chantier; ☎ **04-91-33-77-22;** admission 15€), with both cabaret acts and a dance floor.

BARS

➔**Au Petit Nice** ★ Not to be confused with the gourmet restaurant *Le* Petit Nice, this Jean-Jaurès institution is one of the most laid-back bars on the strip. Whether you fancy a quick drinkypoo after a stroll around the market, or you want to listen to live jazz on a Saturday night, the owner, an ex-European-boxing champion, knows how to spoil his regulars. Oh, and look out for the strange object sheltering the terrace. The Air Force gave it to the bar—I'll say no more. *28 place Jean-Jaurès 1st arr.* ☎ *04-91-48-43-04.*

MTV Best ● ➔**La Caravelle** ★ You fortunately don't have to be resident in the upstairs hotel Bellevue (see "Sleeping," above) to come to this gem of a watering hole. Decorated in distressed cabaret style, with old boating scenes on the walls (there's even a model galleon on the ceiling—a caravelle), the room hasn't changed since the 1930s. There's a whopping choice of drinks from only 2.40€, and to keep you going before dinner (or even instead of dinner), the waiters bring out dishes of delicious tapas such as potato omelette, Provençal mushrooms, and

chorizo sausage in wine. As if that weren't enough to make you come, their small, wrought-iron balcony is officially the best spot in town, with views over the port onto Notre-Dame de la Garde. If you can't come at night, visit during the day for breakfast or an afternoon coffee. *34 quai du Port, 2nd arr.* ☎ *04-91-90-36-64.*

CLUBS & LIVE MUSIC VENUES

MTV Best ● ➔**Cabaret Aléatoire de la Friche** ★ If you want to be part of the "it" gang, you have to become *Frichiste* (the name given to those who have made this nest of artistic creation their hangout). Anyone can become one; all you have to do is spend a few hours within its neo-industrial walls during the day, looking at their boutique on contemporary art, and eating in their brand new restaurant (Les Grandes Tables de la Friche; **www.restau friche.net**). Then, once digestion is complete, come back at night to boogie to DJ l'Amateur's (aka Olivier) wicked mixes of funk, acidhouse, techno, and pop. There are also regular live concerts, so pick up a program while you're there. *41 rue Jobin, 3rd arr.* ☎ *04-95-04-95-04. www.lafriche.org.*

➔**Le Poste à Galène** ★★ For a decent helping of alternative rock, whip your fanny round to this bed of cool entertainment, where underground bands and on-the-up trendies fight it out for stage supremacy, while you sip on frothy beer. When there aren't live bands, Mr. DJ puts a record on—usually good old '80s pop-rock along the lines of the Cure, Depeche Mode, and Madonna. *103 rue Ferrari, 5th arr.* ☎ *04-91-47-57-99. www.posteagalene.com.*

➔**The Red Lion** ★ This very English pub sticks out like a red balloon at an all pink party. There is something anachronistic about its wooden paneling, fine English beers, and boozy happy hours that would be more at home in the rolling, green countryside of northern England than in the 8th *arrondissement* of Marseille alongside a beach. Still, The Red Lion is happy where it is, and so are the customers who drop by in droves to listen to jam sessions (Tues), blues, rock, and country concerts (Wed and Sun) and live DJ mixes (Thurs–Sat). *Les Plages, 231 av. Mendès-France, 8th arr.* ☎ *04-91-25-17-17.*

FABULOUS GAY BARS

The gay scene in Marseille isn't as crowded or as interesting as the one in Nice, but its premier gay bar, **The MP Bar** (10 rue Beauveau; ☎ **04-91-33-64-79**) benefits from a long history of being the town's gay bar of record. It's open nightly from 6pm to sunrise. An equally cool, and equally gay, option is **The New Can Can** (3–5 rue Sénac; ☎ **04-91-48-59-76**), a broad and sprawling bar-and-disco venue that, at least in Marseille, seems to be everybody's favorite dance-club venue. Officially it's gay, but frankly, it gets so many heterosexuals that the gender-specific definitions that dominate many of the town's other nightclubs are—at least here—practically moot. It closes nightly at around 5am. Cover charge, depending on the night of the week, is between 8€ and 15€.

Sightseeing

Do you have a year to spare? There is so much to explore here it would take that long to see it all. Many people have a great time in Marseille and don't ever step into a church or a museum. Between the bustling streets, shops, bars, cafes, offshore islands, and dramatic *calanque*-filled (cove) coastline, there is something for everybody, so if you're short on time here, you'll be making some harsh decisions.

PUBLIC MONUMENTS

➔ **Le Fort St-Jean** A great spot for a stroll, le Fort St-Jean flanks the Pharo gardens. Its foundations date from the 12th

century, before it was enlarged in the 16th and 17th centuries. Looking out across the sea, it has a 13th-century chapel that is under restoration, and cellars that exhibit objects retrieved from sea wrecks. In 2010 a brand-new, futuristic-looking museum should appear here—the **Musée des Civilisations de l'Europe et de la Méditerranée (MUCEM),** a museum on European civilization.

➔ **Le Vieux Port & Its Quays** ★★ Ask any Marseillais and he'll say that this is the most beautiful port in the world. You can make up your own mind about that—but there's no denying there's something hypnotic about the seemingly eternal rows of fishing boats and yachts. But why are the buildings mostly modern at the foot of the Panier? The answer, my dear friends, is Adolf Hitler, who blew up Louis XIV's buildings to enlarge the port. Over 2,000 homes went up in smoke, and today only a few monuments, such as the 17th-century Hôtel-de-Ville (Town Hall) survive.

HIGHBROW HAUNTS

➔ **L'Opéra de Marseille** This is a superb Art Deco structure with neoclassical columns, and a program to make any literati's brain tick on overtime (check out the culture section of **http://opera. mairie-marseille.fr**). It was initially built in 1787, but it burned down in 1919, only to be rebuilt as you can see it today. The area used to be a red light district—in fact, there are still the odd few seedy joints—but nowadays, the only knicker-pinging you're really likely to see is in Offenbach's operetta of *La Vie Parisiènne. 2 rue Molière.* ☎ *04-91-55-00-70.*

CHURCHES

📺 Best ● FREE ➔ **Basilique Notre-Dame-de-la-Garde** Get your oxygen masks ready—this landmark church crowns a limestone rock overlooking the southern

Le Corbusier's Cité Radieuse

In the 1950s, when Marseille was undergoing serious post-war redevelopment, one man, Le Corbusier, changed the face of modern architecture by building this multicolored tower-block—a veritable all-in-one village, equipped with all things modern that families might require. The first of its kind, it reshaped the way in which housing is conceived all over the world. Everything, from 350 duplex apartments, a school, shops, sports and leisure facilities (including a theater), and even a hotel (☎ **04-91-16-78-28;** www.hotellecorbusier.com; 50€–110€ double) is here. The inside is often dark, with spotlights directed at colored doors, casting an eerie multicolored hue along the corridors. The roof, with its paddling pool and concrete stage, looks like something from Dalí's surrealist paintings, and the views are tremendous. People still live in La Cité Radieuse today. In fact, a cool crowd of young doctors, lawyers, journalists, and anyone with money enough to afford the 300,000€ cost of one of these apartments have places here. If you want to look around an apartment, ask at the hotel (5€ for a half-hour tour). Otherwise, if you're quiet and respectful, you shouldn't have any problems going alone, without a guide. To get there, go to Métro Castellane, then take bus nos. 21 or 22 and get off at Le Corbusier. And take a camera—the sea views are tremendous.

side of the Vieux-Port. If you make it to the top, you'll see that it was built in the Romanesque-Byzantine style popular in the 19th century and topped by a 9m (30-ft.) gilded statue of the Virgin. Visitors come for the view—best at sunset—from its terrace: Spread out before you are the city, the islands, and the sea. *Rue Fort-du-Sanctuaire.* ☎ *04-91-13-40-80. Free admission. Daily 7am–7pm. Métro: Vieux-Port.*

➔**Basilique St-Victor** This semi-fortified basilica was built above a crypt from the 5th century, when St. Cassianus founded the church and abbey. You can visit the crypt, which also reflects work done in the 10th and 11th centuries. *Place St-Victor.* ☎ *04-96-11-22-60. Admission to crypt 2€. Church daily 9am–7pm. Crypt daily 10am–7pm. Head west along quai de Rive-Neuve (near the Gare du Vieux-Port). Métro: Vieux-Port.*

FREE ➔**Cathédrale de la Major** This was one of the largest cathedrals (some 135m/443 ft. long) built in Europe in the 19th century. It has mosaic floors and red-and-white marble banners, and the exterior is

in a bastardized Romanesque-Byzantine style. The domes and cupolas look a lot like Istanbul's famous place of worship. This vast pile has almost swallowed its 12th-century Romanesque predecessor, built on the ruins of a Temple of Diana. *Place de la Major.* ☎ *04-91-90-52-87. Free admission. Hours vary. Métro: Vieux-Port.*

MUSEUMS

➔**Musée Cantini** Don't forget to look at the temporary exhibitions of contemporary art here, as they're often as good as the permanent collections. This museum is devoted to modern art, with masterpieces by Derain, Marquet, Ernst, Masson, Balthus, and others. It also owns a selection of works by important young international artists. *19 rue Grignan.* ☎ *04-91-54-77-75. Admission 3€ adults, 1.50€ students. Oct–May Tues–Sun 10am–5pm; June–Sept Tues–Sun 11am–6pm.*

MTV Best 👍 ➔**Musée de la Vieille Charité** This is a three-in-one center of interest in one of Marseille's most gorgeous settings. Amid Le Panier's medieval backstreets, you can visit either the Mediterranean Archaeological Museum (Musée d'Archéologie Méditerranéenne); the African, Oceanic, and American-Indian Art Museum (Musée d'Arts Africains, Océaniens et Amérindien); or just the baroque chapel—one of the best in France. The archaeological museum contains a fabulous collection of Eyptian art, including mummies and sarcophagi, and the new Mexican section in the Oceanic museum is strangely haunting. In one part there is even a showcase of shrunken heads. The 17th-century **Vieille Charité** is one of the rare buildings of its sort to have survived. It almost disappeared entirely until Le Corbusier attracted attention to it, and had it classed as a historic monument. *2 rue de la Charité, 2nd arr. ☎ 04-91-14-58-80. Admission 3€ adults, 1€ students. June–Sept Tues–Sat 11am–6pm, Oct–May Tues–Sat 10am–5pm.*

➔ **Musée d'Histoire de Marseille** Visitors can sometimes wander through an archaeological garden where excavations are going on (cool, man!), as scholars learn more about the ancient town, founded by Greek sailors. They've discovered a medieval quarter of potters, now open to the public. You can also see what's left of a Roman shipwreck excavated from the site. *Centre Bourse, sq. Belsunce. ☎ 04-91-90-42-22. Admission 2€ adults, 1€ students. Mon–Sat 11am–7pm. Métro: Vieux-Port.*

➔ **Musée Grobet-Labadié** ★ This collection was bequeathed to the city in 1919, and includes Louis XV and Louis XVI furniture, as well as some funky medieval Burgundian and Provençal sculpture. Other exhibits showcase 17th-century Gobelin tapestries; 15th- to 19th-century German, Italian, French, and Flemish paintings; and 16th- and 17th-century Italian and French faïence. *140 bd. Longchamp. ☎ 04-91-62-21-82. Admission 2€ adults, 1€ students. June–Sept Tues–Sun 11am–6pm; Oct–May Tues–Sun 10am–5pm. Closed public holidays. Métro: Cinq av. Longchamp.*

Arts Scene

Marseille is a beehive of creativity. Look out for these addresses.

Unexpected Galleries

Galeria Asakusa (16 place aux Huiles, 1st arr.; ☎ **04-91-33-86-59**; www.galerie-asakusa.net) is a serious, grownup place with fantastic contemporary sculpture and painting creations; and **L'Epicerie** (17 rue Pastoret; ☎ **04-91-41-16-33**; www.epicerie-marseille.org) is a magical *lieu de création* just off the Cours Julien, where art almost comes alive thanks to creative installations. You can also have a coffee here and get chatting with the artists.

Performing Arts

If you're fond of cabaret, and if your French is extremely fluent, consider a few hours within the all-comic ambience of **Le Chocolat Théâtre** (59 cours Julien; ☎ **04-91-42-19-29**; Métro: Cours Julien). Shows begin at 9pm every night, last 1 hour and 45 minutes, and, depending on the night of the week, cost from 14€ to 18€ with one drink included, and from 34€ to 38€ per person if you want dinner as well as the show. If your French isn't up to scratch, you might be lucky enough to catch some contemporay dance or music shows at the **Théâtre des Bernardines** (17 bd. Garibaldi, 1st arr; ☎ **04-91-24-30-40**; Mon–Fri 10am–1pm and 2–6pm for tickets).

Playing Outside

Get your suntan cream out because you're going to be spending lots of time outside. There are plenty of parks and dozens of beaches for you to sprawl out in. Here's a quick list of the best spots. To get to all of the beaches, catch the no. 83 bus from the old port and hop off when their name crops up:

➔ **La Plage des Catelans** This beach is the nearest to the center and therefore the most crowded. If it's open (they have had a few problems recently), you might have to pay an entry fee. For white sand encircled by rocks (if you can make out the sand from underneath the bronzing bodies), head to **La Plage du Prophète** at Endoume Blottie below the Corniche Kennedy. Three beaches make up **Les Plages du Prado:** Plage Gaston-Deffere, which is enjoyed by soccer players and kite flyers; Plage Borély is for sunbathing, with parasols and mattresses for hire (there's also the nearby castle Borély and botanical garden); and la Plage de l'Huveaune, which attracts surfers. The **Jardin du Pharo** makes for a perfect stroll or a sit-down thanks to its great sea views (bd. Charles-Livon, 7th arr.), and finally, you could join the throngs of joggers in le **Jardin Public** behind the

---

Calanques & Island Trips

The coastline between Marseille and Cassis is a wildly beautiful array of hidden coves and sheer cliff-faces called **Les Calanques.** Also off the shores of the city lie several remote islands, **Iles du Frioul** and the foreboding **Château d'If.** All can be visited by boat, and make for an exciting day out.

The **Groupement des Armateurs Côtiers (GACM;** quai des Belges; ☎ **04-91-55-50-09;** Métro: Vieux-Port), runs daily trips (9am–6:30pm) to all three destinations. For the **Château d'If** and the **Frioul islands** (where you can bathe) boats leave every 60 to 90 minutes, depending on the season. You should expect to pay around 10€ round-trip for each place. A 4-hour commentated cruise takes you along the **Calanques,** from 25€, twice-daily from June to September; and at 2pm on Wednesday, Saturday, and Sunday from September to October, according to the weather. On the sparsely vegetated island of **Château d'If** (☎ 04-91-59-02-30 for information), François I built a fortress to defend Marseille. The site later housed a prison, where you can still make out the eerie carvings made by Huguenot prisoners. French writer Alexandre Dumas used the château as a setting for the fictional adventures of *The Count of Monte Cristo.* The château's most famous association—with the legendary Man in the Iron Mask (who was he?)—is also apocryphal. The château is open Tuesday to Sunday 9am to 5:30pm (until 6:30pm Apr–Sept). You'll pay 4€ for entrance onto the island.

Diving

Three certified scuba diving centers rule the waves. All three are very safety conscious and won't take you down below unless you're fit for the ride. Try **Les Plaisirs de la Mer** (1 quai Marcel-Pagnol, 7th arr.; ☎ **04-91-33-03-29;** http://plmclam.free.fr), **Atoll Club** (31 traverse Prat, 8th arr.; ☎ **04-91-72-18-14** or 06-11-54-71-40; www.atollplongee.com), and **No Limit Plongée** (109 av. Madrague-Montredon, 8th arr.; ☎ **04-91-25-32-77;** www.nolimitplongee.com). All cost between 38€ and 45€.

The Locals call it cour Ju

MTV Best⚑ **Cours Julien** lies on a hill (like much of Marseille). If you climb up from the port side, you'll have to ascend a flight of steps that would be pretty were it not for the potent smell of human urine. But alas, until Marseille's men learn bladder control, the steps are a disgusting though necessary obstacle if you are to get to the hippest part of town. Cour Ju unites many elements for sightseers and residents alike. There are dozens of cool bars and restaurants, and a **market** with fruits, vegetables, flowers, and other foods (daily 8am–3pm). At the same location, vendors sell stamps (Sun 8am–1pm) and secondhand goods (every other Sun 8am–7pm). There are also old-book vendors every other Saturday (8am–3pm). But the real reason to come is for the off-the-wall shops. Arty folk have taken over almost every side street with their unique and trendy boutiques. Many people make their own clothes, or design their own objects. One excellent shop is **Ici ou Là** (7 rue pastoret, 6th arr.; ☎ 04-91-47-54-53) for woman's clothes with a difference. You can have some wild and wacky tattoos done at **Maya Tattoo** (18 rue Pastoret; ☎ 04-9-47-98-28). And **Kaabeche** (14 rue Pastoret; ☎ **04-91-42-05-95;** www.kaabeche.net) sells some bizarre and wonderful creations (many made from fake skin) that are often bought by theater productions, or eccentrics looking to stand out from the crowds. **L'Entrepôt** (13 rue Pastoret; ☎ **04-91-92-61-81**) sells hip household items. **L'Araignée à 3 Pattes** (11 rue Michel; ☎ **04-91-47-23-96**) will ensure you look original; **Gsus store-Circoloco** (57 rue de la Palud) will blast your ears with mixes while you kit yourself out in urban wear; and Marseille's first concept store, **Oogie,** like Colette in Paris (see "Music, Books & Media," below), is also here.

magnificent Palais Longchamp (4th arr.), or just sit down on a bench with a picnic.

Shopping

Only Paris and Lyon can compete with Marseille for its breadth and diversity of merchandise. Your best bet is a trip to the **Vieux-Port** and the streets surrounding it, where folkloric objects cram the boutiques. You may not think of Marseille as a place to shop for fashion, but the local industry is booming. Its center is along **cours Julien** and **rue de la Tour,** where you'll find many boutiques and ateliers. Some of the cheapest shops, if you've got a good eye are on **rue d'Aubagne.** Here you'll find all the latest trends at low, low prices.

CLOTHING & ACCESSORIES

Vintage is becoming all the rage in Marseille. At **Felio** (4 place Gabriel-Péri; ☎ 04-91-90-32-67), you'll find large-brimmed hats that would have thrilled ladies of the Belle Epoque, as well as berets and other styles of *chapeaux.* But the most fabulous shop of all is **Space** (2 rue de la Grande Armée, 1st arr.; no phone), run by an ex-Hollywood *costumier* (he did *Titanic*), homesick for his native Marseille. Here you will find classics from every era, including ball dresses, wacky men's ties, old Gucci sunglasses, and anything else that was deemed trendy over 20 years ago.

➜ **Le Marseillais** Dress up yourself or your man as a real Marseillais resident. That means cool long-sleeved T-shirts, funky bob hats and anything blue—yes,

PROVENCE

Birthplace of Soap

Oh, the irony that France's dirtiest town should be the homeland of the world's cleanliest washing product: soap. Soap-making began here in the 17th century, when 15 manufacturers set up shop in Marseille, making it the largest soap production center in the Mediterranean. By 1789, there were 65 soap makers, with 280 soap boilers capable of churning out 22,000 tons a year. In the early 19th century, new oils from the colonies appeared (coconut and palm), which were added to the mixtures, making them whiter, frothier, and sweeter smelling. It was said that only soap from Marseille was good enough to be used by housewives to clean their clothes, houses, and children's faces. The tradition for top-quality soap continues here today. If you fancy grabbing a few blocks to take home, visit **Au Père Blaize** (4–6 rue Méolan; ☎ 04-91-54-04-01), which has been selling the stuff (along with herbs and spices) in the same shop since 1790. For somewhere more hip, try **La Companie de Provence** (1 rue Caisserie, 1st arr.; ☎ 04-91-56-20-40; www.lcdpmarseille.com), which sells nifty liquid soap packs.

lots of blue. You could say this shop caters to a small market. Indeed, how many people do you know who dress like they're from their hometown? But the Lacoste-cum-Diesel mix of this patriotic clothes line may well catch on all over France. Next stop the world! *12 rue Glandèves 1st arr.* ☎ *04-91-33-20-45. Mon–Sat 10am–7pm.*

➔**Plums** ★ Plums offers elegant and original creations. You can buy everything a girl needs to look different: clothes that you can't find anywhere else, unique fantasy jewelry, accessories, bags, and even a few things to spruce up your home. This is a one-stop store for out-of-the-ordinary purchases. *66 rue Breteuil.* ☎ *04-91-37-02-87. Tues–Sat 10am–1pm and 3–7pm.*

MUSIC, BOOKS & MEDIA

➔**Oogie Lifestore** ★★ Drum roll, please. Marseille's first concept store has opened its doors! It's no surpise it has chosen the Cours Julien as its home. It is the trendiest place in town (if not on earth). Still, it is pleasantly surprising to see so much variety under one roof. You can have your hair cut, your makeup done, buy the latest fashions, grab some vintage gear, spin a few vinyls, surf the Internet, watch videos on a giant screen, and have a drink. This is much more friendly than the Parisian equivalents (Colette, for instance; see "Shopping" in the Paris & Ile-de-France chapter), and quite frankly, no funky young thing should be allowed to pass through Marseille without stepping foot inside. *55 cours Julien.* ☎ *04-91-53-10-70. www. myspace.com/oogielifestore.*

FOOD, WINE & LOCAL CRAFTS

Bring a photo to the artists at **Amandine** (69 bd. Eugène-Pierre; ☎ 04-91-47-00-83) and they'll frost a cake with an amazing likeness. If you don't have a snapshot with you, choose from their images, which include scenes of the Vieux-Port. More traditional pastries and chocolates are at **Puyricard** (25 rue Francis-Davso [☎ 04-91-54-26-25] or 155 rue Jean-Mermoz [☎ 04-91-77-94-11]). The treats include chocolates stuffed with *pâté d'amande* (almond paste) and *confits de fruits* (candied fruit). One well-stocked emporium that carries virtually every kind of Provençal foodstuff is **Ducs de Gascogne**

Market Madness

Here's a sampling of the best markets in Marseille:

→ The **Capucins Market** (daily 8am–7pm), place des Capucins, has fruit, herbs, fish, and food products.

→ **Quai des Belges** (daily 8am–1pm) is a fish market on the old port.

→ **Allées de Meilhan,** on La Canebière (Tues and Sat 8am–1pm), sells flowers year-round.

→ **Cours Julien** has a fruit-and-vegetable market plus a few stamp collectors stands and antique book sellers (see "The Locals Call It Cour Ju," above).

(20 cours Estiennes d'Orves; ☎ **04-91-33-87-28;** Métro: Vieux-Port). Everything is beautifully packaged, including *calissons* (sugared almond confections; see Aix-en-Provence), foie gras, jams, honey, olives and olive oil, tapenades, and spices known for centuries throughout the region.

Festivals

Between May and September, Marseille comes alive with music, film, and theatrical creations.

First up in May is the contemporary music festival, **Festival International de musique d'Aujourd'hui.** The **Festival de Marseille** in July showcases an eclectic display of dance, music, and theater productions. Open-air classical music concerts take place during the **Musique à Bagatelle** in June and July. The Longchamp palace gardens *(jardin public)* shake to the rhythm of the **Festival de Jazz des 5 Continents** in July. And between June and August the silver screen sets itself up in open-air cinemas for the **Féstival Ciné Plein Air.**

684km (424 miles) S of Paris, 81km (50 miles) NW of Aix-en-Provence, 106km (66 miles) NW of Marseille; pop. 85,000

Set on the Rhône River, ancient ramparts and turrets enclose the *centre-ville* of Avignon, which was the capital of Christendom in the 14th century. You might recognize the city's name from the children's song *"Sur le pont d'Avignon."* Come here and you'll see that very same bridge—well, half of it. The other half of the 12th century **pont Saint Bénezet** washed away during floods several hundred years ago, and for some strange reason, was never put back. The *pont* is impressive, but it plays second fiddle to the particularly imposing **Palais des Papes.** The pope lived here during what the Romans called the Babylonian Captivity, and the legacy left by that court makes Avignon one of the most beautiful of Europe's medieval cities.

Against this medieval backdrop is a bohemian, artsy culture that attracts travelers old and young, French and international. You'll see tourists cooling off in numerous cafes, you'll see locals chatting on park benches, and you'll find an avant-garde, non-conformist youth culture coexisting happily with the town's more bourgeois and conservative culture-goers. In 2000, Avignon was voted cultural capital of Europe—a title that remains fitting seven years on, thanks to museums such as the **Musée du Petit Palais** and the **Musée Angladon,** which highlight Provence's unforgettable artistic

PROVENCE

achievements. Experimental theaters, galleries, and cinemas have also brought real diversity to the inner city—so much so, that the town plays host to a number of festivals, including France's most famous theater-oriented **Festival d'Avignon** (created by actor Jean Vilar in 1947 and known throughout the land as merely "the festival"). Its alternative fringe festival, the **Festival Off** (held simultaneously) is also a crowd puller, and both make contemporary culture accessible and familiar. This is *the* time to visit (if you can find a hotel room), when for 3 weeks in July, every inch of available show space (including sidewalks and parking lots) is turned into a stage.

The city contains enough attractions to keep you going for days, but it is also a fantastic base for exploring other sites in the area. The nearest attraction, just across the Rhône, is the sleepy village of **Villeneuve-lez-Avignon,** which contains some architectural gems built by the Pope's cardinals (p. 453). The art connoisseur in you may help you recognize **St-Rémy de Provence,** where van Gogh spent much of his tortured life painting olive groves. Antiques lovers will dig **Isle-sur-la-Sorgue,** an entire town given over to *brocantes* (antiques dealers and flea markets). The hilltop village of **Gordes** is a must-see for its panoramic views across the Imergue Valley. And don't miss MTV Best ✿ **Village des Bories**—a strange collection of stone huts that were used up until the 19th century.

Avignon History 101

Like most places in Provence, Avignon (or Avenio as it was called) flourished during the Gallo-Roman period, but sadly fell into obscurity after the barbaric invasions of the 5th century. But, when you're destined to be great, you'll be great—even if you have to wait 600 years. For in the 11th century, the town was able to take advantage of feudal rivalries between the Houses of Toulouse and Barcelona and set itself up as an independent state. It lost its independence to Louis XIII in 1226, but continued to prosper under the Counts of Anjou; and then the popes arrived.

In the 14th century, the popes of Rome just couldn't settle their political differences. When the Frenchman Bertrand de Got was elected Pope, under the name of Clement V in 1305, he decided to set up the court in Avignon. After Clement, seven popes continued the line, of which Benedict XII built the Papal Palace we see today. The arrival of the popes brought tremendous change to the city. Churches, convents, monasteries, and cardinal palaces (especially in Villeneuve-lez-Avignon) popped up like mushrooms, a university was established, and the population doubled, then quadrupled to 40,000. Avignon became a liberal city, attracting many communities marginalized in the rest of France, including Jews. However, it also attracted a range of nasty souls, rogues, and escaped criminals. Soon, the popes tried to move back to Italy, but hostility with Rome created a vast rift in the Christian world as papal courts fought for the church's wealth. The election of Pope Martin V finally ended the crisis, and until the Revolution, Avignon was ruled by a papal legate. Even after the revolution, Avignon wasn't sure where its loyalties lay, but it finally voted to become part of the French Republic in 1791. Phew! The last thing you want to do is change currency on the ramparts!

Getting There

BY AIR

The fastest and easiest way to get here is to **fly** from Paris's Orly Airport to **Aéroport Avignon-Caumont** (☎ 04-90-81-51-51), 8km (5 miles) southeast of Avignon (trip time: 1 hr.). Taxis from the airport to the center cost 20€ to 25€.

BY TRAIN

From Paris, **TGV trains** from Gare de Lyon take 2 hours and 38 minutes. Trains also arrive frequently from Marseille, taking just 70 minutes, and from Arles, taking 30 minutes. For train information, call ☎ 36-35.

BY CAR

If you're **driving** from Paris, take A6 south to Lyon, then A7 south to Avignon.

Orientation

Set on the east side of the Rhône river, the beautiful center of Avignon is walled in and small—great news, as you won't have far to walk between the vast number of attractions. The main **cours Jaurès** runs north from the train station through **Porte de la République** (a door through the ramparts), before turning into rue de la République, which slices through the center of town. This stretch is home to several boutiques, department stores, and the tourist office, and leads to Avignon's centerpiece square **place de l'Horloge.** On a hot day, plane trees provide some welcome shade over the cafe terraces that look onto the **theater** and **Hôtel de Ville (City Hall);** and in the little streets around place de l'Horloge, many windows are painted with images of film stars who have passed through Avignon's walls for its many festivals. Just beyond the square, you get to Avignon's *pièce de résistance*— **le Palais des Papes,** whose little garden **(Rocher des Doms)** just above the steps houses swans and picknickers feeding them leftover baguette. To get to the pont d'Avignon, head toward the river from the Palais de Papes and exit the ramparts via the **Porte du Rocher** gate.

If you've money to burn, you should head southeast to the pedestrian shopping district where you can pick up regional specialties like olive oil, lavender sachets, and *herbes de Provence.* Nearby **place Carnot** and **place Pie** (two other main squares) open out onto the main pedestrian street of **rue Bonneterie** (in fact, all the cutesy pedestrian streets around here are fun to explore), which eventually leads to Avignon's ultimate bohemian street, **rue des Teinturiers,** teeming with artists and students.

Getting Around

BY PUBLIC TRANSPORTATION

Unless you're visiting Villeneuve-lez-Avignon (see "Stepping Back in Time," below), you shouldn't have to hop on anything other than your own two feet (although hopping on those can get pretty tiring—not to mention embarrassing, given the strange looks you'll get from passersby).

BY BICYCLE

If you'd like to explore the area by **bike,** the tourist office recommends two places: **Provence Bike** (52 bd. St-Roch; ☎ 04-90-27-92-61) and **Holiday Bikes** (20 bd. St-Roch; ☎ 04-32-76-23-50), which both rent all sorts of two-wheelers, including scooters and mountain bikes. A deposit of cash or a credit card imprint is required.

BY FOOT

Walking is by far the best (and sometimes only) way to see the old town. Only on foot will you take in the sheer beauty of Avignon's ancient back streets, their labyrinthine layout and hidden churches, Italian-style squares, and regal mansions.

Tourist Offices

The **Office de Tourisme** is at 41 cours Jean-Jaurès (☎ 04-32-74-32-74; fax 04-90-82-95-03; www.ot-avignon.fr). Ask here about **Avignon Passion** Pass—a fantastic way of seeing all the sights (including minibus tours to out-of-town sites) at a reduced rate.

Avignon **Nuts & Bolts**

Emergencies   ☎ **15** SAMU (ambulance), ☎ **17** police, ☎ **18** fire and paramedics.

Internet/Wireless Hot Spots   16 computers are at your disposal at **Webzone** (3 rue St-Jean le Vieux; ☎ **04-32-76-29-47**; www.webzone.fr; Mon–Sat 10am–9pm, Sun noon–8pm; 3.50€ hr. or 2€ 30 min.).

Laundromats   There's no excuse for not smelling sweet in Avignon as there are plenty of washhouses for your clothes. *Intra-muros*, try **Savom** (9 rue du Chapeau-Rouge, place des Corps-Saints, or 27 rue du Portail Magnanen; ☎ **04-90-27-16-85** for all three).

Post Office   Send your snapshots home from **La Poste** at cours Président-Kennedy (Mon–Fri 8am–7pm, Sat from 8am–noon; ☎ **04-90-27-54-10**).

Taxis   Call **Taxi-Radio-Avignonnais** (☎ **04-90-82-20-20**).

Vehicle Rental   For scooters, see "By Bicycle," above. For a car, try **Avis.** They have an office at the SNCF station (Gare SNCF; ☎ **08-20-05-05-05**).

Sleeping

Night night, sleep tight, angels watch you all the night—in Avignon at least, where there are plenty of places for you to K.I.P. (Kip in Peace), except during the Festival d'Avignon, when everywhere is booked, and prices rise. If you own a tent, one of the cheapest accommodations during this period is camping.

CAMPING & HOSTELS

Both of these campsites are also in an ideal location for exploring Villeneuve-les-Avignon.

→**Camping du Pont d'Avignon** As its name suggests, this top campsite looks out over the Rhône from an island, onto the famous bridge. Shaded by trees, and with all sorts of fun activities (swimming, tennis, volleyball, Ping-Pong, bike rental), it is a great option for being close to the center without actually being trampled by the masses during the festival. It's almost a shame the pont d'Avignon only stretches halfway across the river, as it could have been a great shortcut into the campsite from the center. *10 chemin de la Barthelasse.* ☎ *04-90-80-63-50. www.camping-avignon. com. 10€–22€ tent pitch and car space. 320€–440€ per week bungalow tent hire. End of Mar to end of Oct.*

→**Le Bagatelle** This place doubles as a campsite and a youth hostel, so depending on the weather, you can sleep inside or out. The campsite is open year-round and provides wash facilities (it can get busy in the summer), laundromats, and Internet access, as well as bike rental and other sports activities. The youth hostel has 180 beds with rooms for two, four, six, or eight people—a fine way to, er, get to know a new friend. Rooms are plain and simple but livable. *Ie de la Barthelasse.* ☎ *04-90-86-30-39. www.campingbagatelle.com. Hostel*

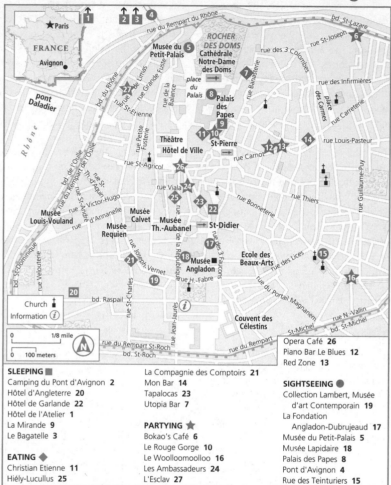

Opera Café **26**
Piano Bar Le Blues **12**
Red Zone **13**

SLEEPING ■
Camping du Pont d'Avignon **2**
Hôtel d'Angleterre **20**
Hôtel de Garlande **22**
Hôtel de l'Atelier **1**
La Mirande **9**
Le Bagatelle **3**

EATING ◆
Christian Etienne **11**
Hiély-Lucullus **25**

La Compagnie des Comptoirs **21**
Mon Bar **14**
Tapalocas **23**
Utopia Bar **7**

PARTYING ★
Bokao's Café **6**
Le Rouge Gorge **10**
Le Woolloomoolloo **16**
Les Ambassadeurs **24**
L'Esclav **27**

SIGHTSEEING ●
Collection Lambert, Musée
   d'art Contemporain **19**
La Fondation
   Angladon-Dubrujeaud **17**
Musée du Petit-Palais **5**
Musée Lapidaire **18**
Palais des Papes **8**
Pont d'Avignon **4**
Rue des Teinturiers **15**

11€–13€ bed; camping prices vary according to the season and number of people, but expect to fork over 5€–20€ a night.

CHEAP

➔ **Hôtel d'Angleterre** This three-story Art Deco structure in the heart of Avignon is the city's best budget hotel, with the advantage of being located inside the city ramparts. It was built in 1929 of gray stone, emulating the style that local builders imagined was characteristic of English houses. The rooms are a tad wee, and really old-fashioned, but comfortable (most with compact shower-only bathrooms). Breakfast is hearty. *29 bd. Raspail, 84000 Avignon.* ☎ *04-90-86-34-31. www.hotel dangleterre.fr. 40€–78€ double. Credit cards accepted. Free parking. Closed Dec 17–Jan 17. Amenities: Dry cleaning; laundry service. In room: TV.*

➜ **Hôtel de l'Atelier** ★★ Now this is more like it. Romantic, nostalgic style in a 16th-century house bursting with charm (the name translates as "the workshop," deriving from the weaving machines that produced fabrics here during the 1950s). Owners Gérard and Annick Burret outfit their rooms in soft, pale colors, high beams, and neatly tiled bathrooms with shower or bathtub. It is nestled in the heart of Villeneuve-lez-Avignon, a 2-minute walk from the Pierre de Luxembourg museum. To add to the experience, a rear garden with potted orange and fig trees provides fruit for breakfast. On cold winter nights, a stone fireplace in the duplex lounge warms your toes and your heart. *5 rue de la Foire, 30400 Villeneuve-lez-Avignon.* ☎ *04-90-25-01-84. www.hoteldelatelier.com. 50€–99€ double. Credit cards accepted. Parking in nearby garage 8€. Amenities: Bar; bike rental; garden; Internet; parking. In room: Satellite TV, hair dryer.*

DOABLE

➜ **Hôtel de Garlande** ★ You can't ask for anything more central, not far from the Palais des Papes and place de l'Horloge. Nor can you ask for anything more charming for your money. This old mansion has just 12 rooms, all dressed in warm and cozy tones. You feel more as though you're staying in someone's house than in a hotel—in fact the friendly staff members do tend to make you feel like you're an old family friend. Breakfast pastries and toasts are delicious, and if you're feeling indulgent, they'll bring them up to your room. *20 rue Galante.* ☎ *04-90-80-08-85. www.hotel degarlande.com. 70€–110€ double. Closed Sat night and Sun in off season.*

SPLURGE

📺 Best ✪ ➜ **La Mirande** ★★ What a splurge. In the heart of Avignon, behind the Palais des Papes, this 700-year-old town house is one of France's grand little

luxuries. In 1987, Achim and Hannelore Stein transformed this place into a citadel of opulence. The hotel displays 2 centuries of decorative art, from the 1700s Salon Chinois to the Salon Rouge, with striped walls in Rothschild red. Room no. 20 is the most sought-after—its lavish premises open onto the garden. All rooms are stunning, with exquisite decor, hand-printed fabrics on the walls, antiques, bedside controls, and huge bathtubs. The restaurant, among the finest in Avignon, deserves its one Michelin star. You can even take cooking lessons (80€–460€). If Avignon is your destination of indulgence, you can't spoil yourself anywhere better. *4 place de la Mirande.* ☎ *04-90-85-93-93. www.la-mirande.fr. 295€–520€ double; 620€–1200€ suite. Credit cards accepted. Parking 25€. Amenities: Restaurant; bar; dry cleaning; laundry service; limited-mobility rooms; nonsmoking rooms. In room: A/C, TV, dataport, hair dryer, minibar, safe.*

Eating

Avignon has plenty of fine eateries, and the good news is they won't leave you penniless.

CAFES & LIGHT FARE

➜ **Mon Bar** "My" bar is indeed that for many Avignonnais who stop by for a quick coffee or a snack on one of their long leather banquettes. Step in from the street and you'll step back to the 1940s and 1950s, the era that most of the decor and indeed the folk propping up the bar have never left. The efficient, smiley staff set the tone for a relaxed moment that is more than conducive to chatting with the people at the next table. *17 rue Portail-Matheron. No phone. Daily 8am–8pm.*

➜ **Utopia Bar** ★ The artsy crowds all come here before or after catching a film (usually of an intellectual nature) in the attached cinema. And you too should pass by when hunger or thirst calls, and try some of their delicious tartines (pizza-like snacks) and quiches. There are always photo or painting exhibitions for you to fix your eyes on while you munch, plus the occasional sax or jazz concert. *4 rue Escaliers St-Anne.* ☎ *04-90-27-04-96. Mon–Sat 11.45am–midnight; Sun 2–11pm.*

CHEAP

➔**Tapalocas** ★ SPANISH Groups of friends looking for fun, loud music, Latino ambience and likeminded partygoers love this place—where the constraints of being an impoverished young person are understood by owners who keep the prices down, way down. Indeed for just 10€ you can eat a decent pile of tapas (over 50 are on the list). They won't win any prizes from Michelin, but after a few glasses of tequila and Spanish wine, everything slides down with astonishing ease. *15 rue Galante.* ☎ *04-90-82-56-84. Daily noon–1am.*

DOABLE

➔**Hiély-Lucullus** ★ FRENCH The Belle Epoque decor of this chic joint enhances grand, innovative cuisine such as crayfish-stuffed ravioli flavored with fresh sage and served with pumpkin sauce, filet of female venison with tangy honey sauce, and escalope of sautéed foie gras on toasted rye bread. Lots of fresh fish is imported daily and cooked to perfection. The *pièce de résistance* is *agneau des Alpilles grillé* (grilled Alpine lamb). If you've a sweet tooth and you're feeling lucky, their vanilla-bourbon cream in puff pastry just might be on the menu. Carafe wines include Tavel Rosé and Châteauneuf-du-Pape. *5 rue de la République.* ☎ *04-90-86-17-07. Reservations required. Fixed-price menu 28€–45€. Credit cards accepted. Daily noon–2pm and 7–10pm.*

➔**La Compagnie des Comptoirs** ★ MEDITERRANEAN Part of the charm of this place derives from the contrast between its contemporary cuisine and the grandeur of its medieval setting, a 10-minute walk from the Palais des Pâpes. The menu is an ode to France's many colonial influences—spices and techniques from North Africa, Egypt, India, Canada, Louisiana, and parts of Africa. Prepare your taste bubs for sensations like tart with confit of onions, thin-sliced smoked swordfish, and orange-flavored vinaigrette; giant prawns slowly cooked with confit of lemons, coriander, cucumbers, and onions; roasted flank of Provençal bull with anchovy sauce, potato purée, and olive oil; and chicken breasts dredged in pulverized hazelnuts, served with prunes and exotic mushrooms. History lovers can get their kicks too: The long, narrow, high-ceilinged dining rooms were originally the hallways and courtyards of a 1363 Benedictine convent that was dissolved during the French Revolution. For those with energy to burn, the restaurant doubles up as a nightclub and bar, and the action spills into the gracefully proportioned interior courtyard, where guest DJs spin tunes every evening in the bar-lounge from 6pm to 1am. *83 rue Joseph-Vernet.* ☎ *04-90-85-99-04. Reservations recommended. Main courses 14€–33€. Credit cards accepted. Tues–Sun noon–2pm; Tues–Sat 7:30–11pm.*

SPLURGE

➔**Christian Etienne** ★★ PROVENÇAL Owner Christian Etienne reaches new culinary heights in his dining room that contains early-16th-century frescoes honoring the marriage of Anne de Bretagne to the French king in 1491. In fact the stone house containing this restaurant was built in 1180, around the same time as the Palais des Papes (next door), so it stands witness to practically all of Avignon's history. Several of the fixed-price menus feature themes along the lines of seasonal tomatoes,

PROVENCE

mushrooms, or other vegetables; one offers preparations of lobster; and the priciest relies on the chef's imagination *(menu confiance)* for unique combinations. In summer, look for the vegetable menu entirely based on ripe tomatoes; the main course is a mousse of lamb, eggplants, tomatoes, and herbs. Be warned—the dishes are vegetarian by name, but not by nature, as they're flavored with fish or meat drippings. A la carte specialties include filet of perch with Châteauneuf-du-Pape, rack of lamb with fresh thyme and garlic essence, and a dessert of fennel sorbet with saffron-flavored creamy vanilla sauce. *10 rue Mons.* ☎ *04-90-86-16-50. Reservations required. Fixed-price lunch 30€–105€; fixed-price dinner 55€–105€. Credit cards accepted. Tues–Sat noon–1:30pm and 8–9:30pm. Closed first 2 weeks in Aug and Dec 20–Jan 6.*

Partying

Avignon is more about culture and history than partying till dawn, but that doesn't mean that you have to live like a puritan. In a nutshell, these are the places you should try:

On place de l'Horloge, brand new trendy **Opéra Café** (☎ **04-90-86-17-43**) is a restaurant-bar-cafe that just may become your favorite watering hole. The danceclub standby is **Les Ambassadeurs,** 27 rue Bancasse (☎ **04-90-86-31-55**), where you'll rub shoulders with lots of posh kids spending Mommy and Daddy's money; it's more animated than its competitor, **Piano Bar Le Blues** (25 rue Carnot; ☎ **04-90-85-79-71**), where you can also test out your capacities as a singing diva on Mondays and Tuesdays. Nearby is a restaurant, **Red Zone** (27 rue Carnot; ☎ **04-90-27-02-44**), that books live performances in the bar area by whatever band happens to be in town. There's also music and dancing at **La Compagnie des Comptoirs.** Winning the award for most unpronounceable name is

Le Woolloomoolloo (16 bis rue des Teinturiers; ☎ **04-90-85-28-44**), which means "black kangaroo" in an Australian Aboriginal dialect. The bar and cafe complement a separate room devoted to the cuisine of France and a changing roster of cuisines from Asia, Africa, and South America. An alternative is **Bokao's Café** (9 quai St-Lazare; ☎ **04-90-82-47-95**), a restaurant and disco. The only cabaret outside of Paris is **Le Rouge Gorge** (10 bis rue de la Peyrolerie; ☎ **04-90-14-02-54**). I can't promise great food or *Quadrille Réaliste* (the French Can Can), but I can promise a laugh and some live blues concerts when the cabaret's not playing. The most viable option for lesbians and gays is **L'Esclav** (12 rue de Limas; ☎ **04-90-85-14-91**), a bar and disco that are the focal point of the city's gay community.

Sightseeing

You can't miss the incredible architecture in Avignon—Le Palais des Papes and the pont d'Avignon are unique sights in France. At the very least, you should plan a stroll past the Palais des Papes at night, when its grand exterior is illuminated. Avignon's art museums keep the town up to par with the rest of Provence and the area's overwhelming emphasis on the visual arts. It is possible to buy a joint ticket for the Palais des Papes and the pont d'Avignon, which will save you a few euros.

PUBLIC MONUMENTS

MTV Best ● → **Palais des Papes** ★★ Dominating Avignon from a hilltop, this is one of the most famous, or notorious, palaces in the Christian world. Headquarters of a schismatic group of cardinals who came close to destroying the authority of the popes in Rome, this fortress-showplace is the monument most frequently associated with Avignon. The guided tour (usually lasting 50 min.) can be monotonous, because most of the rooms have been stripped of their finery. The exceptions are the **Chapelle St-Jean,** known for its frescoes, which are attributed to the school of Matteo Giovanetti and were painted between 1345 and 1348. These frescoes present scenes from the life of John the Baptist and John the Evangelist. More Giovanetti frescoes are in the Chapelle St-Martial. They depict the miracles of St. Martial, the patron saint of Limousin.

The **Grand Tinel (Banquet Hall)** is about 41m (135 ft.) long and 9m (30 ft.) wide; the pope's table stood on the south side. The **Pope's Bedroom** is on the first floor of the Tour des Anges. Its walls are decorated in tempera foliage on which birds and squirrels perch. Birdcages are painted in the recesses of the windows. In a secular vein, the **Studium (Stag Room)**—the study of Clement VI—was frescoed in 1343 with hunting scenes. Added under the same Clement, who had a taste for grandeur, the **Grande Audience (Great Audience Hall)** contains frescoes of the prophets, also attributed to Giovanetti and painted in 1352. Until June 2007, you can visit the Pope's private chambers as part of a special tour that includes brunch for 30€. *Place du Palais des Papes.* ☎ *04-90-27-50-00. www.palais-des-papes.com. Admission (including tour with guide or recording) 9.50€ adults, 7.50€ students, July daily 9am–8pm; Apr–June and Aug–Oct daily 9am–7pm; Nov–Mar daily 9:30am–5:45pm.*

MTV **Best ❂** ➔ **Pont d'Avignon** ★★ Even more famous than the papal residency is the song *"Sur le pont d'Avignon, l'on y danse, l'on y danse"* ("On the bridge of Avignon, we dance, we dance"). **MTV** **Best ❂** **pont St-Bénézet** (☎ **04-90-27-51-16**) was far too narrow for the *danse* of the rhyme, however. Spanning the Rhône and connecting Avignon with Villeneuve-lez-Avignon, the bridge is now a ruin, with only 4 of its original 22 arches. According to legend, it was inspired by a vision that a shepherd named Bénézet had while tending his flock (we'd all like to know what he was smoking, *n'est-ce pas?*). The bridge was built between 1177 and 1185 and suffered various disasters. In 1669, for instance, half of it fell into the river. On one of the piers is the two-story **Chapelle St-Nicolas**—one story in Romanesque style, the other in Gothic. The local council has recently modernized the tour, and today you can record your version of the song *sur le pont d'Avignon* on DVD (5€) and watch the bridge on **www.earthtv.com** 24/7—an activity that brings sense to the phrase "watching paint dry." Once you pay to walk on the bridge, the small chapel on the bridge can be visited as part of the overall admission fee. Here's a tip: Get the audio-guide as it really makes the visit more interesting. *Admission 3.50€ adults, 3€ students. The remains of the bridge open daily Nov to mid-Mar 9:30am–5:45pm; mid-Mar to June and Oct 9:30am–6pm; July 9am to 9pm; and Aug–Sept 9am–8pm.*

➔ **Rue des Teinturiers** ★★ Artists love rue de Teinturiers, and it's not hard to see why: There's a little river with water wheels, bridges that link the street to the houses, and a charm that changes with the seasons. Don't be surprised if you get camera-happy or whip out your paint brushes—you'll want to immortalize this part of town. It was named after the textile-working Indians who lived on the street in the 13th century, and if you're into numinous coincidences, you'll dig this scoop: Seven is a mystical number, and in the middle of the street lies the Chapelle des Pénitents Gris, home to the last of seven Avignonnais brotherhoods. The city is split into seven parishes, seven letters make up the name Avignon, and the city had seven popes—spooky!

MUSEUMS

MTV Best ❢ →**Collection Lambert, Musée d'art Contemporain** ★ Oh, how wonderful it must be to have so much modern art that you can lend pieces out for 20 years and not even notice they're missing. Yvon Lambert created the Collection Lambert in 2000 with more than 350 works from his collection. Yvon's star pieces includes works by Carl Andre, Christian Boltanski, Nan Goldin, Douglas Gordon, Anselm Kiefer, Brice Marden, Gordon Matta-Clark, Robert Ryman, Andres Serrano, and Cy Twombly—a testimony to his passionate engagement in Minimal Art, Conceptual Art, Land Art from the '60s and '70s, painting from the '80s, and photography and video from the '90s. *5 rue Violette.* ☎ *04-90-16-56-20. www.collectionlambert.com. July daily 11am–7pm; Aug daily 11am–6pm; Sept–Jun Tues–Sun 11am–6pm.*

→**La Fondation Angladon-Dubrujeaud** ★ Come here to see the magnificent art collection of Jacques Doucet (1853–1929), the Belle Epoque dandy, dilettante, and designer of Parisian haute couture. When not designing, Doucet collected the early works of a number of artists, among them Picasso, Max Jacob, and van Gogh. You can wander through Doucet's former abode viewing rare antiques; 16th-century Buddhas; Louis XVI chairs designed by Jacob; and canvases by Cézanne, Sisley, Degas, and Modigliani. At Doucet's death, his fortune was so diminished that his nephew paid for his funeral—but his rich legacy lives on here, fortunately for you. *5 rue Laboureur.* ☎ *04-90-82-29-03. Admission 6€ adults, 4€ students Wed–Sun 1–6pm.*

→**Musée du Petit-Palais** Overshadowed by its giant neighbor (Palais des Papes), this museum contains an important collection of paintings from the Italian schools of the 13th to 16th century, with works from Florence, Venice, Siena, and Lombardy. Salons display 15th-century paintings created in Avignon, and several galleries contain Roman and Gothic sculptures. *Place du Palais des Papes.* ☎ *04-90-86-44-58. Admission 6€ adults, 3€ students. June–Sept Wed–Mon 10am–1pm and 2–6pm; Oct–May Wed–Mon 9:30am–1pm and 2–5:30pm.*

→**Musée Lapidaire** A 17th-century Jesuit church houses this collection of Gallo-Roman sculptures, but you would be forgiven for calling the place a junkyard of antiquity: Gargoyles, Gallic and Roman statues, and broken pillars confront you at every turn, and most of the pieces have known greater glory and placement (often in temples); use your imagination to conjure up their lost splendor. *27 rue de la République.* ☎ *04-90-86-33-84. Admission 2€ adults, 1€ students. Wed–Mon 10am–1pm and 2–6pm.*

Three Cool Side Trips

ST-REMY-DE-PROVENCE—A TOWN OF TWO VISIONARIES

Nostradamus, the physician and astrologer, was born here in 1503, but nowadays St-Rémy is more closely associated with the painter **van Gogh.** He committed himself to an asylum here in 1889 after cutting off his left ear (sorry, what did you say?). Between moods of despair, he painted such works as *Olive Trees* and *Cypresses.* You should come to sleepy St-Rémy not only for its memories and sights but also for a glimpse of small-town Provençal life. It is a center for home decorating. Loads of antiques shops and fabric stores line the narrow streets of the old town and the boulevards surrounding it. **Portes Anciennes,** along the route d'Avignon (☎ **04-90-92-13-13**), sells a good selection of antiques and flea-market finds, but St-Rémy's real fame is its great **markets.** On Wednesday morning on the streets of

Stepping Back in Time

Villeneuve-Lez-Avignon ★

The modern world is impinging on Avignon, but across the Rhône, the Middle Ages slumber on. When the popes lived in exile at Avignon, cardinals built palaces *(livrées)* across the river. If you're looking for more calm than the bustling streets of Avignon can offer, this is a good spot to stay or dine. Villenueve-lez-Avignon lies just across the Rhône from Avignon, and it's easiest to reach on bus no. 11, which crosses the larger of the two relatively modern bridges, the **pont Daladier. Office de Tourisme,** 1 place Charles David (☎ **04-90-25-61-33;** www.villeneuvelesavignon.fr/tourisme).

Cardinal Arnaud de Via founded the **Eglise Notre-Dame** (place Meissonier; ☎ **04-90-25-46-24;** free admission; Apr–Sept daily 10am–12:30pm and 2–6:30pm; Oct–Mar daily 10am–noon and 2–5pm) in 1333. Aside from its architecture, you should come to see an antique copy (by an unknown sculptor) of Enguerrand Charonton's *Pietà,* the original of which is in the Louvre.

Inside France's largest Carthusian monastery, the **Chartreuse du Val-de-Bénédiction** (rue de la République; ☎ **04-90-15-24-24;** admission 6.10€ adults, 4.10€ students; Apr–Sept daily 9am–6:30pm; Oct–Mar daily 9:30am–5:30pm), built in 1352, you'll find a church, three cloisters, rows of cells that housed the medieval monks, and rooms depicting aspects of their daily lives. Part of the complex is devoted to a workshop (the Centre National d'Ecritures et du Spectacle) for painters and writers, who live in the cells rent-free for up to a year to pursue their craft. You can see photo and art exhibits throughout the year.

Crowning the town is **Fort St-André** (Mont Andaon; ☎ **04-90-25-45-35;** admission 4.60€ adults, 3.10€ students; Apr–Sept daily 10am–1pm and 2–6pm; Oct–Mar daily 10am–1pm and 2–5pm) founded in 1360 by Jean-le-Bon, to serve as a symbol of might to the pontifical powers across the river.

The **Musée Pierre de Luxembourg (Musée de Villeneuve-lez-Avignon)** is Villeneuve's most important museum (rue de la République; ☎ **04-90-27-49-66;** Admission 3€ adults, 1.80€ students; Apr–Sept Tues–Sun 10am–12:30pm, 2–6:30pm; Mar and Oct–Jan Tues–Sun 10am–noon, 2–5pm; closed Feb). It occupies a 14th-century home constructed for a local cardinal and contains the richest repository of medieval painting and sculpture in the region.

Philippe the Fair constructed the **Tour Philippe le Bel** (rue Montée-de-la-Tour; ☎ **04-32-70-08-57;** admission 1.60€ adults, .90€ students; Apr–Sept daily 10am–12:30pm and 2–7:30pm; Mar and Oct–Nov Tues–Sun 10am–12:30pm and 3–7pm) in the 13th century, when Villeneuve became a French possession. If you have the stamina, you can climb to the top of the tower for a cool view of Avignon and the Rhône Valley.

PROVENCE

the old town, vendors spread out their wares, including spices, olives, fabrics, and crafts. On Saturday morning, a small vegetable market is held near the Eglise St-Martin on boulevard Marceau. It is a wonderfully winning market town that draws the occasional visiting celebrity trying to escape the spotlight.

Getting There

Local **buses** from Avignon (four to nine per day) take 40 minutes and cost around 5.50€ one-way. In St-Rémy, buses pull into the place de la République, in the town center. For bus information, call ☎ **04-90-82-07-35.** If you're **driving,** head south from Avignon along D571.

The **Office de Tourisme** is on place Jean-Jaurès (☎ **04-90-92-05-22;** www.saintremy-de-provence.com).

Sightseeing

Sights in an around St-Rémy include the **Monastère St-Paul-de-Mausolée** (av. Edgar-le-Roy; ☎ **04-90-92-77-00;** admission 3.40€ adults, 2.25€ students; Apr—Oct daily 9:30am—7pm; Nov—Mar daily 10:30am—4:45pm), the 12th-century cloisters of the asylum that van Gogh made famous in his paintings—now a psychiatric hospital for women (a short drive north of Glanum long the D5); and the **Ruines de Glanum** (av. Vincent-van-Gogh). From St-Rémy, take D5 1.5km (1 mile) south, following signs to LES ANTIQUES (☎ **04-90-92-23-79;** admission 6.10€ adults, 4.10€ students; Apr—Sept daily 9:30am—7pm; Oct—Mar Tues—Sun 10am—5pm). These vestiges of a Gallo-Roman settlement include a triumphal arch from the time of Julius Caesar, along with the oldest cenotaph in Provence called the Mausolée des Jules (a mausoleum raised to honor the grandsons of Augustus), and some remains from a Gallo-Greek town of the 2nd century B.C.

ISLE-SUR-LA-SORGUE—FLEA MARKET HEAVEN

In France, there's a big difference between antiques and fun old junk. They even have different names. For serious purchases, you may want to stick to well-established antiques stores, found in great abundance all over France. But if you prefer something more affordable, and your idea of fun is a flea market, then what you really want is a *brocante*—which means that you should visit **Isle-sur-la-Sorgue** (23km/14 miles east of Avignon), The *brocante* market, **Foire à la Brocante,** is on Saturday,

Sunday, and Monday mornings (Sun also holds a food market). In fact get there by 9am as everything is over by 1pm. If you're driving, try for a parking space in the free outdoor lot, Parking Portalet, adjacent to the fairgrounds. The *brocante* is on the near side of the river, a little farther downstream. Every building on the side of the street facing the river is a warehouse filled with dealers and loot.

Isle-sur-la-Sorgue has an **Office de Tourisme** at place de la Liberté (☎ **04-90-38-04-78;** www.ot-islesurlasorgue.fr). Go on, have a good rifle through it all!

GORDES—STRANGE, STRANGE BORRIES

Gordes is another pretty, perched settlement. Its Renaissance castle, narrow cobbled streets, and ochre buildings cling to the steep hillside, creating what is considered to be one of the most enchanting villages in France. But perhaps *enchanted* would be a better adjective: The Gordes you see today has miraculously survived two earthquakes and World War II bombing—no mean feat for such a small village. The magic that has kept the village alive also seems to keep the visitors a-flowing, as tourists arrive in the summer to soak up the authentic atmosphere of its *calades* (paved back streets with vaulted passageways), rampart ruins, craft shops, and lively markets. The Renaissance **Château** (☎ **04-90-72-02-75;** daily 10am—noon and 2—6pm), with its austere machicolated towers, stands on the highest point of the village and should be visited for its collection of paintings by the contemporary Dutch artist Pol Mara. Frequent summer music concerts take place in the castle courtyard (check with the tourist office). One of the most unexpected sights is the **Cave du palais Saint-Firmin** (go to place Genty-Pantaly and head towards rue de l'Eglise and then towards the *point de vue*), the vast, vaulted cellars of a mansion that contain cisterns, stairwells, and the relics of an ancient 15th-century oil mill (apparently most Gordien houses contain similar cellars). However, for historic reasons, the most remarkable aspect of Gordes is the extraordinary **Village des Borries** (stone huts) that lies just out of the town center (leave Gordes on the D15 towards Cavaillon, and just before a fork with the D2, turn right). It is believed that the Borries date back to the Ligurians who lived in the region between 200 and 500 years ago. They built their houses of drystone, without mortar, upon the principle of the Corbel vault, and they were used right up until the 19th century. This is one of the only places in France you'll see such structures, and nobody really understands why they were built here. (☎ **04-90-72-03-48;** daily 9am–dusk).

For more info, contact the **Office de Tourisme de Gordes—La Château** (☎ **04-90-72-02-75;** www.gordes-village. com).

Shopping

CLOTHING & ACCESSORIES

➔ **Elite Boutik** ★ Set on trendy rue des Teinturiers, this is one of Avignon's hippest addresses—a place to live out your girly or manly fantasies of being able to try on all the clothes in the shop and then sit down and have a coffee. Clothes are urban cool with a bohemian twist, and there are plenty of funky accessories to help set your outfits off and ensure that no one back home have the same look. When you're tired, sit back and refuel in the coffee shop before hitting the boutiques elsewhere. *59 rue des Teinturiers.* ☎ *04-90-85-53-78. Mon 2–7pm, Tues–Sat 10am–7pm.*

FOOD, WINE & LOCAL CRAFTS

Budding fashion designers will dig **Les Indiens de Nîmes** (19 rue Joseph-Vernet; ☎ **04-90-86-32-05**), whose aim is to duplicate 18th- and 19th-century Provençal fabric patterns that can be bought by the meter and in the form of clothing for men, women, and children. There are also a few bits and bobs for the house inspired by Provence and the steamy wetlands west of Marseille.

The clothing at **Souleiado** (5 rue Joseph Vernet; ☎ **04-90-86-47-67**) derives from traditional Provençal costumes (mostly for women) and also sells its fabrics by the meter. The name means "first ray of sunshine after a storm."

If you think Granny yearns for a Provençal table set, **Hervé Baume** (19 rue Petite Fusterie; ☎ **04-90-86-37-66**) sells a little bit of everything—from Directoire dinner services to French folk art to hand-blown crystal hurricane lamps. **Jaffier-Parsi** (42 rue des Fourbisseurs; ☎ **04-90-86-08-85**) is known for its copper saucepans from the Norman town of Villedieu-les-Poêles, which has been making them since the Middle Ages. If you're seeking new perspective on Provençal pottery, go to **Terre è Provence** (26 rue de la République; ☎ **04-90-85-56-45**), where you can pick up kitsch-cool terracotta plates decorated with three-dimensional cicadas. Quick—someone call the fashion police!

MARKETS

Most markets in Avignon are open 6am to 1pm. The biggest covered market, with 40 different merchants, is **Les Halles** (place Pie; Tues–Sun). Other smaller **food markets** are on rampart St-Michel on Saturday and Sunday, and on place Crillon on Friday. The **flower market** is on place des Carmes on Saturday, and the **flea market** is in the same place on Sunday.

Festivals

The festival to beat all other festivals is the ▣ **Best**● **Festival d'Avignon.** The event is held during the last 3 weeks in July and the first week in August, and it metamorphoses the city into a seething mass of street performers, arts critics, actors, singers, and thronging crowds of theater lovers. The air is positively electrified by all the creativity that flows and pulsates around the **Old Center.** Place de l'Horloge, and indeed many of the surrounding streets become almost unrecognizable beneath the layers of posters advertising plays, and the sea of passersby. The international festival was set up in 1947 by actor Jean Vilar, so 2007 marks its 60th anniversary. You should expect some powerful avant-garde theater,

dance, comedy, and music. Don't forget to hang around at night. Part of the fun is the bacchanalia nightly in the streets. And if you can't get enough of the stuff, you could also check out the official unofficial festival, **Avignon Public Off,** which programs many theater troops for shows during July (www.avignon-festival-off.com). Prices for rooms and meals skyrocket, so make reservations far in advance (a year if you can).

For information, contact the **Bureaux du Festival,** Espace Saint-Louis (20 rue du Portail Boquier; ☎ **04-90-27-66-50;** www.festival-avignon.com).

📺 Best ☻ Arles

725km (450 miles) S of Paris, 35km (22 miles) SW of Avignon, 89km (55 miles) NW of Marseille; pop. 52,000

This ancient town on the Rhône—with its little alleys, wrought-iron lampposts, yellow buildings with blue shutters, and window boxes filled with pink geraniums—is where you'll find the subjects of van

Gogh's celebrated works the *Café la Nuit* (lit by the pale Provençal light he described as "soft and welcoming"), *Starry Night, The Bridge at Arles, Sunflowers,* and *L'Arlésienne.*

Arles History 101
....

The Greeks are said to have founded Arles in the 6th century B.C., but Julius Caesar made the biggest mark by establishing a prosperous Roman colony here in 49 B.C. when he conquered Marseille. In another 350 years, Constantine the Great named it the second capital of his empire, nicknaming it "the little Rome of the Gauls." It remained a successful industrial center, cashing in on textiles, gold, and silver work for several centuries until the Franks and the Saracens began fighting over the land in the 8th century. By the 9th century, it was a mere shadow of the town it had been; but its position along the Rhône kept some trade alive so that by the 12th century, it had regained its former wealth and was able to pay for the construction of the Romanesque Cathedral of St-Trophine in time for the Germanic emperor Frederick Barbarossa to be crowned there in 1178. But in 1239, Arles became the property of the Counts of Provence, and from then on it gradually lost its status as trade capital to Aix en Provence and Marseille. Arles officially became part of France in 1481, but lack of decent transport lines for many years left it cut off from the rest of the country. It was a godsend for roving historians, because Arles today contains unique sites and has maintained its quirky traditions.

Van Gogh's "Different Light"

Dutch-born Vincent van Gogh (1853–90) moved to Arles in 1888. "What strikes me here," he wrote, "is the transparency of the air." He spent 2 years in the historic towns of Les Baux, St-Rémy, and Stes-Maries, recording, through the filter of his neuroses, dozens of Impressionistic scenes now prized by museums and collectors, though the work was spurned during his lifetime. The artist's search, he said, was for "a different light." When he found it, he went on to create masterpieces such as *Starry Night, Cypresses, Olive Trees,* and *Boats Along the Beach.*

You can take a walking tour of van Gogh's subjects—there are little signs marking each place he once set up his easel—and although none of Arles's museums display van Gogh originals, you can see a great collection of the paintings and drawings Picasso did during his stint here at the **Musée Réattu** (see "Museums," below). Ironically, despite its rich art and history, there isn't much of a contemporary arts scene in Arles. Maybe it's because the summer tourists tend to give in to van Gogh mania and the renowned, well-preserved ruins that date back to the town's beginnings as a Roman port city.

The **Roman Arena** is still used on spring and summer weekends for bullfights. Arles hosts some of the biggest bullfights in France—a brutal activity that often ends in the death of the bull. Nearby is the slightly more deteriorated **Roman amphitheater,** which in the summertime is the setting for plays and concerts. Its impressive marble columns are a good landmark to use as you navigate the town.

Arles, like most of Provence, runs wild with tourists during the summer months. This certainly doesn't mean that you shouldn't come—it is frequently visited for good reason. But it does make it hard to blend in with the local scene and meet young French people. You'll have no trouble meeting other travelers at the Roman ruins and in the Jardin d'Eté, however, and the locals, who are very accustomed to visitors, will treat you royally, with that friendly Provençal smile and striking accent.

Getting There

Trains from Paris's Gare de Lyon arrive at Arles's Gare SNCF, avenue Paulin-Talabot, a short walk from the town center. You may have to change lines in Avignon. There are hourly connections between Arles and Avignon (15 min.), Marseille (1 hr.), and Aix-en-Provence via Marseille (1 hr. 45 min.). For rail schedules and information, call ☎ **36-35.** There are about four **buses** per day from Aix-en-Provence (trip time: 1 hr., 45 min.). For bus information, call **La Boutique des Transports** ☎ **08-10-00-08-16.** If you're **driving,** head south along D570 from Avignon.

Tourist Office

The **Office de Tourisme,** where you can buy a museum pass (see "Sightseeing," below), is at 43 bd. Craponne (☎ **04-90-18-41-20;** www.tourisme.ville-arles.fr).

If you'd like to get around by bicycle, head for **Europbike,** 1 rue Phillipe-le-Bon (☎ **04-90-49-54-69;** www.europbike-provence.com). It rents six-speed road bikes for around 16€ per day, and requires a deposit of 250€.

PROVENCE

Sleeping

HOSTELS

→ **Auberge de Jeunesse d'Arles** When you're down and out in Arles, you can still find somewhere pleasant to rest your weary head, just 10 minutes from the *centre-ville*. Bedrooms take up to eight people. They look a little tired, but the hostel's in a calm neighborhood away from the droves of summer tourists. It offers bike rental and other sports facilities, and has a bar where all the international residents congregate at the end of the day. *20 av. Foch.* ☎ *04-90-96-18-25. www.fuaj.org. 15€ bed. 2.90€ extra if you're not an International Youth Hostel card holder. Rate includes sheets and breakfast.*

CHEAP

→ **Hôtel Le Cloître** ★ This hotel, between the ancient theater and the cloister, is one of those old buildings where you can experience the spirit of the people who lived and worked there, and the events that went down inside. The walls don't need to talk for you to know that some interesting stuff has gone on beneath the 12th-century Romanesque vaultings of this former cloister—every corner and every stone pulsates with history. Throughout, you'll find a rich Provençal atmosphere, pleasant rooms with high ceilings, and subtle references to the building's antique origins. Guest rooms are lean on amenities, except for phones and small, shower-only bathrooms. Still, it's an excellent value for the money. There's also a TV lounge. *16 rue du Cloître. www.hotelcloitre.com.* ☎ *04-90-96-29-50. Fax 04-90-96-02-88. 30 units. 47€–60€ double. Credit cards accepted. Parking 8€. Closed mid-Nov to Mar 15.*

DOABLE

→ **Hôtel Calendal** ★ Because of its reasonable rates, the Calendal is a bargain hunter's paradise: You can't get closer to the arena; it offers high-ceilinged accommodations decorated in bright colors, some with views of the hotel's garden filled with palms and palmettos. Although you'll only get a shower in the bathroom, the price and location make up for any shortcomings. The hotel also doubles as a decent little restaurant that offers buffet lunches and dinner from 15€. *5 rue Porte de Laure.* ☎ *04-90-96-11-89. www.lecalendal. com. 84€–99€ double. Credit cards accepted. Parking 10€. Amenities: Restaurant; bar; laundry service; limited-mobility rooms; limited room service; nonsmoking rooms. In room: A/C, TV, hair dryer, Wi-Fi (ask about prices).*

→ **Hôtel d'Arlatan** ★ Since 1920, the same family has lovingly managed this hotel in the former residence of the *comtes* d'Arlatan de Beaumont, and it shows. Built in the 15th century on ancient Roman foundations, the place bursts with character. Rooms (all gorgeous) are furnished with authentic Provençal antiques with tapestry-covered walls. If you can, wangle a room overlooking the garden. If size is an issue, ask for one on the ground floor. If you have a penchant for life's little luxuries, you'll love the swimming pool, tucked in a pretty corner of a walled courtyard. *26 rue du Sauvage.* ☎ *04-90-93-56-66. www. hotel-arlatan.fr. 85€–153€ double; 173€–243€ suite. Credit cards accepted. Parking 14€. Closed Jan. Amenities: Bar; babysitting; laundry service; limited-mobility rooms; swimming pool. In room: A/C, TV, dataport, minibar.*

SPLURGE

→ **Grand Hôtel Nord-Pinus** ★ Few other hotels in town evoke Provence's charm as well as this one, which originated as a bakery at the turn of the 20th century. Occupying a town house on a tree-lined square in the heart of Arles, it has rooms filled with antiques, an ornate staircase with wrought-iron balustrades, and many

Arles

SLEEPING ■
Auberge de Jeunesse d'Arles 5
Grand Hotel Nord-Pinus 14
Hôtel d'Arlatan 18
Hôtel Calendal 3
Hôtel Le Cloître 10

EATING ◆
Cuisine du Comptoir 16
La Charcuterie 19
La Gueule du Loup 20
Restaurant Lou Marquès 8

PARTYING ★
Le Café van Gogh 15
Le Cargo de Nuit 6

SIGHTSEEING ●
Amphitheater 2
Eglise St-Trophime 11
Les Alyscamps 4
Museon Arlaten 13
Musée de l'Arles et
   de la Provence Antiques 7
Musée Réattu 1
Place de la République 12
Place du Forum 17
Théâtre Antique 9

Information ⓘ

★ Paris

FRANCE

Arles ●

---

of the trappings you'd expect in an upscale private home. Expect glamour in the bedrooms, even theater; they come in a range of shapes, sizes, and decors, and are filled with rich upholsteries and draperies arranged artfully beside massive French doors. Lots of bullfighters and artists have stayed here, and you can contemplate their photographs, as well as a collection of safari photos by Peter Beard that decorate the public areas. *14 place du Forum.* ☎ *04-90-93-44-44. www.nord-pinus. com. 137€–275€ double; 412€ suite. Credit cards accepted. Parking 15€. Amenities: Restaurant; bar; dry cleaning; laundry service; limited room service; nonsmoking rooms. In room: TV, dataport.*

Eating

Restaurants and cafes abound in this tourist haven. The best things on most menus are the big Provençal seafood and vegetable salads—and don't forget to do the local thing and cool off with a *pastis* before you eat. The gardens and ruins are, of course, great places for picnics, especially for budget-watchers.

CAFES & LIGHT FARE

→ **Cuisine du Comptoir** The few cool kids who hang around in Arles come here for the cheap grub and trendy setting. It's tucked beneath the arch of a rampart. Inside, the decor is uncomplicated, with white walls and dark furniture. Food includes excellent toasted sandwiches (all on famous Poîlane bread; see the Paris chapter) and homemade cakes that you can watch being prepared in the kitchen right in the middle of the room. If you're fed up with seeing middle-aged waiters, you may identify better with the young, dynamic crowd at this place. *10 rue de la Liberté.* ☎ *04-90-96-86-28. Menus from 8.50€–10€. Credit cards accepted. Mon 10pm–midnight; Tues–Sat 8:30pm–midnight.*

CHEAP

➜**La Charcuterie** LYONNAIS Pigging out on pig is a venerable pastime in Lyon (where practically every dish includes a sausage), so why not in Arles? The cheery owner is proud of his Lyonnais origins and proud of the top-class, pork-oriented offerings his restaurant cooks so well. Come here for all sorts of sausage, andouillette, saucisson, pigs' trotters, and hams, accompanied by great regional wine. Non–meat lovers (or non–pork eaters) may refrain. *51 rue des Arènes.* ☎ *04-90-96-56-96. www.lacharcuterie.camargue.fr. Tues–Sat for lunch and dinner (plus Sun and Mon in May and July–Aug); closed Aug 1–15 and Dec 23–Jan 6.*

DOABLE

➜**La Gueule du Loup** FRENCH/ PROVENÇAL   Named for its founder, who, according to local legend, grew to resemble a wolf as he aged (don't tell Miss Riding Hood), this cozy, well-managed restaurant occupies a stone-fronted antique house in the historic core of Arles, near the ancient Roman arena. Today it's the Allard family who prepare serious gourmet-style French food that's more elaborate than the cuisine at many competitors. The best examples include hearty filet of bull braised in red wine, monkfish in saffron sauce, roasted cod with green and sweet red peppers in saffron sauce, and superb duckling cooked in duck fat and served with flap

mushrooms. Reservations are important— the cozy room seats only 30. *39 rue des Arènes.* ☎ *04-90-96-96-69. Reservations recommended. Fixed-price menu 25€. Credit cards accepted. Easter–Oct Tues–Sat noon–2:30pm, Mon–Sat 7–9:30pm; Nov–Easter Tues–Sat noon–2:30pm and 7–9:30pm. Closed 1 week in Nov and mid-Jan to mid-Feb.*

SPLURGE

➜**Restaurant Lou Marquès** ★★ PROVENÇAL   Pile on your glad rags, because Lou Marquès, at the Hôtel Jules-César, has the best reputation in town. Cuisine features creative twists on Provençal specialties. A first course could be *queues de langoustine en salade vinaigrette d'agrumes et Basilque* (crustaceans and salad with citrus-and-basil vinaigrette) or *risotto de homard aux truffes* (lobster risotto with truffles). As a main course, try *pavé de loup en barigoule d'artichaut et à la sauge* (a thick slice of wolf fish with sage-stuffed artichokes) or *filet mignon de veau et ragoût fin de cèpes et salsifis* (veal with a stew of mushrooms and *salsify*, a long-forgotten oyster-flavored vegetable). For light dessert, there's *biscuit glacé au miel de lavande* (a small cake glazed with lavender honey). You can sit either in the formal dining room or on the terrace. *Hôtel Jules-César, 9 bd. des Lices.* ☎ *04-90-52-52-52. Reservations recommended. Fixed-price lunch 29€; fixed-price dinner 40€–80€. Credit cards accepted. Daily noon–1:30pm and 7:30–10:30pm. Closed Nov 12–Dec 24.*

Partying

Because of its relatively small population (around 50,000), Arles doesn't offer a particularly mad nightlife, but if you fancy slurping in an immortalized setting, head to **Le Café van Gogh** (11 place du Forum; ☎ **04-90-96-44-56**), which inspired the one-eared artist's *Café la Nuit*. Thanks to this legacy, it's one of the town's most animated cafes and a great haunt for singles (hint, hint).

One of the trendiest choices is the bar-cafe-music hall **Le Cargo de Nuit** (7 av. Sadi-Carnot; ☎ **04-90-49-55-99;** www.cargodenuit.com). Open only on Friday and Saturday night, it's a supper club with cool live music—salsa, jazz, and rock, with a spot of disco or electro, until 3am. Expect to pay between 8€ to 20€. This is the most *super-chouette* (super cool) joint on the block.

Sightseeing

At the tourist office, you can buy two museum passes that allow free entry into Arle's museums and monuments: *The Pass Monuments* costs 14€ for adults, 12€ for students, and gives entry to almost all of the attractions (including the Roman monuments); the Pass Circuit Romain is specifically for the Roman monuments and costs 9€ for adults, and 7€ for students. Both passes are valid for 3 months.

PUBLIC MONUMENTS & CHURCHES

➜ **Eglise St-Trophime** ★ On the east side of place de la République, this church is noted for its 12th-century portal, one of the finest achievements of the southern Romanesque style. Frederick Barbarossa

Raving Romans

Arles is full of Roman monuments. **Place du Forum,** shaded by plane trees, is around the old Roman forum. The Café de Nuit, immortalized by van Gogh, once stood on this square. You can see two Corinthian columns and fragments from a temple at the corner of the Hôtel Nord-Pinus. Three blocks south of here is **place de la République,** dominated by a 15m-tall (49-ft.) blue porphyry obelisk. On the north is the **Hôtel de Ville (town hall)** from 1673, built to Mansart's plans and surmounted by a Renaissance belfry.

One of the city's great classical monuments is the Roman **Théâtre Antique** ★★ (rue du Cloître; ☎ **04-90-49-36-25;** admission 3€ adults, 2.20€ students; May–Sept daily 9am–6pm; Mar–Apr and Oct daily 9am–11:30am and 2–5:30pm; Nov–Feb daily 10am–11:30am and 2–4:30pm). Augustus began the theater in the 1st century, but only two Corinthian columns remain. The *Venus of Arles* was discovered here in 1651. Take rue de la Calade from city hall. Nearby is the **Amphitheater (Les Arènes)** ★★ (rond-point des Arènes; ☎ **04-90-49-36-86;** admission 4€ adults, 3€ students; May–Sept daily 9am–7pm; Mar–Apr, Oct daily 9am–6pm; Nov–Feb daily 10am–4:30pm), also built in the 1st century. Sometimes called Le Cirque Romain, it seats almost 25,000 and still hosts bullfights in summer. Watch your step: The stone steps are uneven, and much of the masonry is worn. For a good view, you can climb the three towers that remain from medieval times, when the amphitheater was turned into a fortress.

Les Alyscamps ★ (rue Pierre-Renaudel; ☎ **04-90-49-36-87;** admission 3.50€ adults, 2.60€ students; Nov–Feb daily 10am–5pm; Mar–Apr and Oct daily 9am–6pm; May–Sept daily 9am–6:30pm; closed Jan 1, May 1, Nov 1, and Dec 25) is possibly the most memorable sight in Arles: a Christian graveyard that was once a Roman necropolis. After being converted into a Christian burial ground in the 4th century, it became a setting for legends and was even mentioned in Dante's *Inferno.* Today, it's lined with poplars and studded with ancient sarcophagi. Arlesiens escape here to enjoy a respite from the heat, and you should follow suit.

Cruelty Rules in *Le olé*

Bullfights, or *corridas,* are held about 5 weekends a year, between Easter and late September. The bull is killed only during the Easter *corridas* (perhaps a reference to the death of Christ?); otherwise, the bull is not killed, making the ritual less bloody than the Spanish version. The Easter event begins at 11am, the others around 5pm. A seat on the stone benches of the Roman amphitheater costs anything from 14€ to 80€. Tickets are usually available at the amphitheater a few hours beforehand. For advance ticket sales, call ☎ **04-90-96-03-70.** *Be warned:* If you are an animal lover you will not enjoy the spectacle. Arles is one of the only cities in France to have its own bullfighting school, and it really is part of the local culture; but when blood is spilled, it is really spilled, and there ain't no crying over spilled bull blood in Arles.

was crowned king of Arles here in 1178; and in the pediment, Christ is surrounded by the symbols of the Evangelists. You should have a gander at the cloister, which is in Gothic and Romanesque styles and noted for its medieval carvings. *Place de la République.* ☎ *04-90-49-33-53. Free admission to church; cloister 3.50€ adults, 2.60€ students. Church daily 8:30am–6:30pm. Cloister Nov–Feb daily 10am–5pm; Mar–Apr, Oct daily 9am–6pm; May–Sept daily 9am–6:30pm. Closed Jan 1, May 1, Nov 1, and Dec 25.*

MUSEUMS

➜**Musée de l'Arles et de la Provence Antiques** ★★ Against Arles's ancient backdrop, this shiny modern building, constructed in 1995, stands out like an Eskimo on a beach or a toga-clad Roman in a shopping mall. Inside, it reverts back in time again, with one of the world's most famous collections of Roman Christian *sarcophagi,* plus a rich ensemble of sculptures,mosaics, and inscriptions from the Augustinian period to the 6th century A.D. Don't miss the 11 detailed models showing ancient monuments of the region as they existed in the past. *Presqu'île du Cirque Romain.* ☎ *04-90-18-88-88. Admission 5.50€ adults, 4€ students. Mar–Oct daily 9am–7pm; Nov–Feb daily 10am–5pm. Closed Jan 1, May 1, Nov 1, and Dec 25.*

➜**Musée Réattu** ★ In a town devoted to van Gogh, this collection, which belonged to the local painter Jacques Réattu, is a breath of fresh air, with several works by Picasso, including etchings and drawings. Other pieces are by Alechinsky, Dufy, and Zadkine; and you should make particular note of the Arras tapestries from the 16th century. *10 rue du Grand-Prieuré.* ☎ *04-90-49-37-58. Admission 4€ adults, 3€ students. May–Sept daily 10am–noon and 2–6:30pm; Mar–Apr and Oct daily 10am–noon and 2–5pm; Nov–Feb daily 1–5:30pm.*

➜**Museon Arlaten** ★ Are you a cunning linguist? Then you'll be lapping this place up like there's no tomorrow. The poet Frédéric Mistral led a movement to establish modern Provençal as a literary language, and the museum's name is rendered in Provençal style. He founded this place using the money from his Nobel Prize for Literature in 1904. It's a folklore museum, with regional costumes, furniture, dolls, a music salon, and a room devoted to mementos of Mistral. *29 rue de la République.* ☎ *04-90-93-58-11. Admission 4€ adults, 3€ students. June–Aug daily 9:30am–noon, 2–6:30pm; Sept daily 9:30am–noon; Apr–May Tues–Sun 9:30am–noon, 2–6pm; Oct–Mar Tues–Sun 9:30am–12:30pm and 2–5pm.*

Two Side Trips

THE CAMARGUE: WHO'S GONNA RIDE YOUR WILD HORSES?

If ever there were a place to fall in love it is here, in this giant botanical and zoological nature reserve—one of France's most wild and romantic areas. You'll have to abandon all preconceptions about French landscapes, for this is France's only "cowboy country"—an alluvial plain inhabited by wild horses (brought here by the Arabs in the Dark Ages), fighting black bulls, salt marshes, lagoons, pink flamingos, wetlands, gluttonous mosquitoes, and roaming gypsies.

The Camargue's fragile ecosystem has been a national park since 1970, and although a whole host of flora and fauna flourish here, the stars of the show are the small horses who roam wild, guarded by the French cowboys known as *gardiens* (guardians), who wear large felt hats to protect themselves from the fierce sun. There is no more evocative a sight on the landscape than watching these beautiful snow-white beasts running through the marshlands, with hoofs so tough they don't need shoes. It is said that they evolved their long manes and long bushy tails over the centuries to slap the mosquitoes who descend on the Carmague in autumn like blood-sucking vampires (forget your insect repellant at your own risk). The *gardiens* do everything from caring for sick horses to selecting black bulls used in *corridas* in Provençal towns such as Arles. To bridge waters, cover marshy ground where black bulls graze, and see wild birds nest from on the back of one of these noble creatures (even if you've never been in the saddle before), call l'**Association de Tourisme Equestre** (☎ 04-90-97-10-40), the **Office de Tourisme** at **Saintes-Maries-de-la-Mer,** the capital of the Camargue (5 av. Vincent-van-Gogh; ☎ 04-90-97-82-55; www.saintesmaries. com) or consult **www.cdte13.com**, which lists all the dependable horseback riding centers in the Camargue, which often provide accommodation.

As you've probably gathered, exotic flora and fauna abound in this region, where the delta of the mighty Rhône River empties into the Mediterranean. Bird life here is the most luxuriant in Europe, known especially for its colonies of elegant pink flamingos, called *flamants roses* in French. Evoking their counterparts in the Florida Everglades, the flamingos share living quarters with some 400 other bird species. An excellent way to see our feathered friends is to check out the bird sanctuary **Parc Ornithologique** (pont du Gau, rte. des Ste-Maries-de-la-Mer; ☎ 04-90-97-82-62; www.parcornithologique.com; admission: 6.50€ adult, 4.50€ student; daily 9am–sunset, 10am–sunset in winter), a 60-hectare microcosm and home to a variety of birds from geese, swans, ducks, kingfishers, ibisis, and the ubiquitous pink flamingo, to more aggressive birds of prey such as hawks, buzzards, and eagles. Off the D570, about 5km (3 miles) north of **Les Sainte-Maries-de-la-Mer,** you can also opt for a pleasant 6km (3.5-mile) walking trail that allows you to experience this ecological wonder firsthand.

Bike touring is another popular means of getting about, but there are problems with difficult, sandy trails. Before setting out on any tour—bike, horse, or otherwise—pick up a series of trail maps from local tourist offices. These maps not only mark the best rides, but indicate length and difficulty, and, most importantly, point out danger spots. In other words, know before you go. For bike rental in Saintes-Maries-de-la-Mer go to: **Le Vélociste** (rte. d'Arles; ☎ 04-90-97-74-56), or **le Vélo Saintois** (19 av.

PROVENCE

de la République; ☎ 04-90 97-74-56). You can expect to pay around 15€ a day.

If you absolutely have to get into the thick of it, you could opt for a boat tour. **Kayak Vert Carmague** offer a variety of tours that let you paddle your own canoe, from their base in Mas de Sylvéréal (30600 Vauvert; ☎ 04-66-73-57-17; www.kayakvert-camargue.fr; 10€–40€). For a boat trip that doesn't require you to do your own paddling, **Les Quatres Maries** (☎ 04-90-97-70-10; bateaux-4maries@camargue.fr) launches boats from Port Gardian at Saintes-Maries that go deep into the Petit Rhône river district. This gives you a close encounter with the wild birds in the area, and you'll also get to watch the black bulls roaming the river's marshy shorelines. The first boat leaves daily at 10:30am (tickets 10€), but we'd hold out for the final departure at 4:15pm (or 6pm July–Aug) so that you can catch the dramatic rose-colored sunset.

Much of the thrill of exploring the Camargue is based on variables that can't be known in advance: Wild creatures have their own priorities and don't wait around for someone to come along and photograph them. So it's a toss-up—you'll either have a lot of fun with Mother Nature or end up wondering "what was that all about?" You won't know before you go, but the best times to visit are spring or early summer. Mosquitoes are a curse in the autumn, and in winter, the Mistral, the constantly blowing ill wind, will make you think the name surely translates as "miserable."

[MTV] Best ● LES BAUX

Cardinal Richelieu called Les Baux "a nesting place for eagles," and boy was he observant. On a wind-swept plateau overlooking the southern Alpilles, 20km (12 miles) from Arles, Les Baux may be a ghost of its former self, but it is still very dramatic and very high. It was once the citadel of seigneurs who ruled with an iron fist and sent their armies as far as Albania. In medieval times, troubadours from all over the continent came to this "court of love," where they recited western Europe's earliest-known vernacular poetry. Eventually, Alix of Baux, the "Scourge of Provence," ruled Les Baux, sending his men throughout the land to kidnap people. If no one was willing to pay ransom for one of his victims, the poor wretch was forced to walk a gangplank over the cliff's edge. Fed up with the rebellions against Louis XIII in 1632, Richelieu commanded his armies to destroy Les Baux. Today, the castle and ramparts are mere shells, though you can see remains of Renaissance mansions. Vertical ravines lie on either side of the town, giving in to dry, foreboding countryside and vineyards—officially classified as Coteaux d'Aix-en-Provence—facing the Alpilles. If you follow the signposted *route des vin,* you can motor through the vineyards in an afternoon, perhaps stopping off for a tipple at growers' estates.

Head to the northern edge of town to see the feudal ruins, called **La Ville Morte (Ghost Village)** ★★—a vast citadel that covers an area at least five times that of Les Baux itself. Rather fittingly, from the ghost village, you can swipe a look over the Val d'Enfer (or Valley of Hell), and even see the Mediterranean in the distance. The castle ruins, **La Citadelle** ★★, sit at the bottom of the town, and can be reached by

The First Cowboys

Ancestors of the Camargue's *gardiens,* who still live in thatched huts called *cabanes,* may have been the first American cowboys. They sailed on French ships to the port of New Orleans and there rode the bayous of Louisiana and East Texas, rounding up cattle (in French, no less).

walking up rue du Château, which leads into the **Château des Baux** (☏ 04-90-54-55-56). You should put aside at least an hour to explore. You enter the citadel by going through the **Hôtel de la Tour du Brau,** which houses the Musée du Château. The building was the residence of the powerful Tour de Brau family and should be visited if you fancy seeing objects related to the history of Les Baux, which will help you understand the ruins in the compound. While you're there, don't miss the former chapel of St-Blaise (now home to a little museum devoted to olives), replicas of medieval siege engines, grottoes used for storage or lodgings in the Middle Ages, the skeleton of a hospital built in the 16th century, and a cemetery. Finally, the **Tour Sarrazin (Saracen Tower)** offers a view of the village and the citadel. Admission to the castle (July–Aug daily 9am–8:30pm; Mar–Jun, Sept–Oct daily 9am–6:30pm; Nov–Feb daily 9:30am–5:30pm), including the museum and the ruins, is 7€ for adults, 5.50€ for students.

The Renaissance-era **Hôtel de Manville,** on rue Frédéric Mistral, was built in the 16th century as a private mansion. Today, it is the **Mairie (town hall)** of Les Baux. You can visit its courtyard. It's open the same hours as Musée des Santons (below). **Fondation Louis Jou** lies in the Renaissance-era **Hôtel Jean-de-Brion,** rue Frédéric Mistral (☏ **04-90-69-88-03** or 04-90-54-34-17). You can visit, but only by appointment; but if you gain admission, you can dig engravings and serigraphs by the Barcelona-born artist Louis Jou (1861–1968), as well as a few small-scale works by Rembrandt, Dürer, and Goya. Jou frequently visited Paris but considered Les Baux his home from 1917 until his death. He is considered the most important contemporary artist to come out of Les Baux.

Back in the village, you can visit the **Yves Brayer Museum** (at the intersection of rue de la Calade and rue de l'Eglise; ☏ 04-90-54-36-99; admission 4€ adults, 2€ students; Apr–Sept daily 10am–12:30pm and 2–6:30pm; off season Wed–Mon 10am–12:30pm and 2–5:30pm, closed Jan to mid-Feb), a 16th-century Hôtel de Porcelet, devoted to the works of figurative painter Yves Brayer (1907–90).

Musée des Santons (free admission; Apr–Oct daily 9am–7pm, Nov–Mar daily 9am–5pm) is in the town's **Ancien Hôtel de Ville,** place Louis Jou (no phone). Built in the 16th century as a chapel, **La Chapelle des Pénitents Blancs**, the museum displays antique and idiosyncratic woodcarvings, each representing a different saint or legend.

For yet more panoramic vistas, climb to the **place St-Vincent** for a sweeping view over the Vallon de la Fontaine. This is also the site of the much-respected **Eglise St-Vincent** whose campanile is spookily called **La Lanterne des Morts (Lantern of the Dead).** The modern windows were a gift from Rainier of Monaco, when he was the Marquis des Baux during the 1980s. Today, Albert of Monaco fulfills the honorary/ceremonial duties associated with the title, but I doubt you'll bump into him now; he has several love children, dotted round the globe, to take care of. Royal seeds are scattered in Monaco like pebbles on a beach, you know.

Baux is best reached by car, but if you can't get one, grab a **taxi** in Arles (☏ **06-80-27-60-92;** see "Getting Around," above), which will take you there for around 35€; be sure to agree upon the fare in advance, and in the summer months brace yourself for the masses of tourists. The **Office de Tourisme** (☏ **04-90-54-34-39;** www.lesbauxdeprovence.com) is on Maison du Roy, near the northern entrance to the old city.

Aix-en-Provence

755km (468 miles) S of Paris, 81km (50 miles) SE of Avignon, 32km (20 miles) N of Marseille; pop. 150,000

This faded **university town** is cracking a bit around the edges, but it remains *the* most charming center in Provence—a difficult title to maintain when you're up against all the beautiful towns in this region. Nevertheless, it warrants the praise, drawing in thousands of visitors every year. Many come to tred in the footsteps of Impressionist painter Paul Cézanne (see "Paul Cézanne in Aix," below), the celebrated son of this old capital of Provence, who immortalized the countryside in his paintings.

Like the rest of Provence, Aix (pronounced "ex") is an inspirational place for artists and writers. Aside from Paul Cézanne, author Emile Zola lived here. The University of Aix-en-Provence has also infused the town with intellectual energy for 600-plus years, and the current student population includes a number of international students, particularly Americans.

No one can ever accuse the citizens of Aix-en-Provence of resembling Parisians. They may be city-dwellers, but they escape into their rugged countryside whenever they can. They are a Mediterranean people who have traditionally made a living from the sea and from their much-painted landscape. It is said that Marseille is the most anti-Parisian city in France; in the same stalwart sprit, Aix-en-Provence is anti-Marseille. In the tradition of a long-standing rivalry between the two cities, the inhabitants of Aix dismiss Marseille today as a virtual colony of North Africa. For the most part, the people of Aix are more homogeneous and Provençal bourgeois than the seaport-dwellers. They are haughtily proud of their culture and taste

Aix-en-Provence History 101

Roman general Caius Sextius Calvinus founded Aix-en-Provence in 122 B.C. as a military outpost. Later it became a civilian colony, the administrative capital of a province of the late Roman Empire, the seat of an archbishop, and official residence of the medieval *comtes* de Provence. Louis II of Anjou founded the University of Aix in 1409. Then Good King René (Louis II's second son) brought real medieval prosperity in the latter part of the 15th century. Réné was an exceptional man, and for any potential queen, the catch of the century. He spoke Latin, Hebrew, Greek, Italian, and Catalan. He wrote poetry, composed music, grasped astronomy, maths, astrology, and geology. He legislated commerce, encouraged agriculture, introduced the Muscadet grape to Provence. He even set up a free health service for his subjects and a sanitary system. In fact, the only thing he could actually be criticized for were the coins he minted from base alloy. After the union of Provence with France, Aix became an important judicial and administrative center. The wealthy men and women of law (that is, the barristers and their wives) built many of the sumptuous 17th- and 18th-century villas you see today. Their influence was maintained until the Revolution, after which Aix fell into decline as Marseille took over as regional capital—undoubtedly the basis of Aix-Marseille rivalry even today.

Paul Cézanne in Aix

Considered the pioneer of the 20th-century school of modern art, Paul Cézanne (1839–1906) is the most celebrated resident of Aix-en-Provence, the city where he was born, lived most of his life, and died. Many of the local museums are dedicated to displaying his paintings, and you can still visit his studio on the northern edge of town.

Cézanne started out studying law at the University of Aix to please his father (don't we all?), but preferred the art classes he took at night. In 1861, he finally convinced his father to let him go to Paris, where he met the Impressionist Camille Pissarro, who in turn introduced Cézanne to Manet and others in the Impressionist circle. Cézanne considered himself part of the Impressionist movement, although his style really began the newer 20th-century trends. From 1864 to 1869, he moved back and forth between Paris and Aix, eventually settling here to paint the landscapes he grew up in.

In 1896, he wrote, "When I was in Aix, I was sure I'd be better off elsewhere. Now that I am here, I regret Aix . . . when one is born there, that's it, nothing else appeals." Indeed, some of his most famous paintings (44 oils and 43 watercolors) are studies of the large mountain visible from town, the Mont Saint-Victoire.

in food and art. Their critics claim they are basking in an "aristocratic grandeur" of yesteryear. The defenders of Aix counter that their university, now six centuries old, instructs foreign students in the fine art of French civilization. I say (lovingly of course): Is there no end to French pride and their ability to debate about it?

The student population and the tourists (particularly in summer) dominate the atmosphere of Aix, and, as you'd expect, there are lots of popular cafes and bars that cater to them. The big ones along the main street, cours Mirabeau, are the most popular with travelers, while the smaller places on the narrow streets of the old town have personalities that have developed more in tune with the students who hang out there. The party scene is largely the purview of the university students, so any bar or club you go to is a good place to meet the French as well as internationals.

Getting There

The city is easily accessible by train from Marseille (35 min.). You can also catch trains from Nice (3–4 hr.) or Cannes (3 ¹/₂ hr.). High-speed TGV trains arrive at **Aix-en-Provence TGV**, 5.5km (3¹/₄ miles) west of Aix, linked to the center by bus (4.10€ one-way). For more information, call ☎ 36-35. If you're **driving** to Aix from Avignon or other points north, take A7 south to RN7 and follow it into town. From Marseille or other points south, take A51 north into town.

To explore the region by bike, head for **Cycles Zammit** (27 rue Mignet; ☎ 04-42-23-19-53), a short walk northeast of the cours Mirabeau. Here you can rent 10-speed racing bikes or more durable mountain bikes for around 14€ a day. You'll have to leave a deposit—your passport or driver's license, or cash or monetary objects worth the value of the bike (usually 350€–400€).

Orientation

Aix's main street, **cours Mirabeau** ★★, has to be one of Europe's most beautiful. Plane trees stretch across the street like umbrellas, shading it from the hot

Provençal sun and filtering the light into shadows that play on the rococo fountains below. Shops and sidewalk cafes line one side of the street; sandstone *hôtels particuliers* (mansions) from the 17th and 18th centuries fill the other. The street begins at the 1860 fountain on place de la Libération, which honors Mirabeau, the revolutionary and statesman. A ring of streets, including **boulevard Carnot** and **cours Sextius,** circles the heart of the old quarter (Vieille Ville, or old town). Inside this périphérique is the pedestrian zone.

Tourist Offices

The **Office de Tourisme** is at 2 place du Général-de-Gaulle (☎ **04-42-16-11-61;** www.aixenprovencetourism.com). They provide two excellent themed street maps for you to follow if you'd like to see the city through the eyes of Cézanne or Zola.

If you've brought your MP3 along, you can also download a walk around town (free of charge) by logging onto the tourist office website.

Sleeping

HOSTELS

→**Auberge de Jeunesse** This big, modern building is practically a city with 140 beds available. That's 140 potential new mates when you stay here. Friend-making activities include volleyball, basketball, baby foot (table soccer), and who knows who you'll meet in the TV lounge, in front of the fireplace in the sitting room, or outside while you're contemplating how the Montagne St-Victoire has changed since Cézanne painted it. Rooms are clean and simple, and the staff friendly and helpful. *Le Jas de Bouffan, 3 av. Marcel Pagnol.* ☎ *04-42-20-15-99. www.fuaj.org. 20€ bed. Rate includes sheets and breakfast. Take bus no. 4 toward Mayanelle and get off at Vasarely-Auberge de Jeunesse.*

CHEAP

→**Hôtel La Caravelle** If you're on a tight budget, you'll have to opt for the non-renovated rooms—the only ones under 60€. If not go for any of the bedrooms in this conservatively furnished hotel, situated just a 3-minute walk away from the center of town. It offers warm hospitality, and one nice touch is the breakfast served in the stone-floored lobby. The rooms have double-glazed windows to help muffle the noise, but most bathrooms contain showers only. *29 bd. du Roi-René (at cours Mirabeau).* ☎ *04-42-21-53-05. www.lacaravelle-hotel.com. 30 units. 46€–70€ double. Credit cards accepted. Amenities: Dry cleaning; laundry service; limited room service; nonsmoking rooms, Wi-Fi. In room: A/C, TV, dataport, minibar.*

DOABLE

→**Grand Hôtel Nègre Coste** This hotel in a 17th-century former town house is so popular with the musicians who flock to Aix for the summer festivals that it's difficult to get a room at any price. Such popularity is understandable. Flowers cascade from *jardinières,* and 18th-century carvings surround the windows. Inside, there's a wide staircase, marble portrait busts,

When the Hôtel Nègre Coste Is Full

Give these two places a call. **Hôtel Cardinal** (24 rue Cardinale; ☎ **04-42-38-32-30;** 70€ double) is set in an 18th-century town house loaded with personalized quirks, and **Hôtel des Quatre Dauphins** (54 rue Roux-Alphéran, ☎ **04-42-38-16-39;** 60€–85€ double) is a short walk from place des Quatre Dauphins and the cours Mirabeau.

Aix-en-Provence

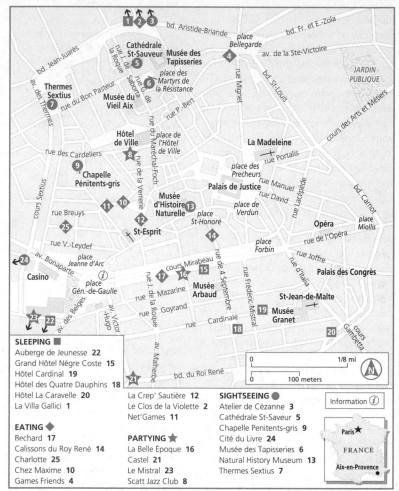

SLEEPING ■
Auberge de Jeunesse **22**
Grand Hôtel Nègre Coste **15**
Hôtel Cardinal **19**
Hôtel des Quatre Dauphins **18**
Hôtel La Caravelle **20**
La Villa Gallici **1**

EATING ◆
Bechard **17**
Calissons du Roy René **14**
Charlotte **25**
Chez Maxime **10**
Games Friends **4**

La Crep' Sautière **12**
Le Clos de la Violette **2**
Net'Games **11**

PARTYING ★
La Belle Epoque **16**
Castel **21**
Le Mistral **23**
Scatt Jazz Club **8**

SIGHTSEEING ●
Atelier de Cézanne **3**
Cathédrale St-Saveur **5**
Chapelle Penitents-gris **9**
Cité du Livre **24**
Musée des Tapisseries **6**
Natural History Museum **13**
Thermes Sextius **7**

Information ⓘ

and a Provençal armoire. The medium-size soundproof rooms contain interesting antiques. The higher floors overlook cours Mirabeau or the old city. Each unit comes with a compact bathroom with shower; some have tubs as well. *33 cours Mirabeau.* ☎ *04-42-27-74-22. 85€–140€ double. Credit card accepted. Parking 10€. Amenities: Laundry service; limited room service; non-smoking rooms. In room: A/C, TV, hair dryer, minibar, safe.*

SPLURGE

➔ **La Villa Gallici** ★★ Pull out your Gucci, Prada, LVMH—whatever bling you can bring—because this is one elegant, relentlessly chic inn. It originated in the 18th century as a private home, and nowadays it's the most stylish hotel in town. The rooms, richly infused with the decorative traditions of Aix, are subtle and charming. Some rooms boast a private terrace or garden, and some even have freestanding baths (go, man!). The villa sits in a large enclosed garden in the heart of Aix, close to one of the best restaurants, Le Clos de la Violette (see "Eating," below). The swimming pool is surrounded by loungers from where you can observe the wealthy tourists from behind your sunglasses. It's a 5-minute walk to the town center. *Av. de la Violette (impasse des Grands Pins). ☎ 04-42-23-29-23. www.villa gallici.com. 220€–740€ double; 420€–900€ suite. Credit cards accepted. Amenities: Restaurant; bar; dry cleaning; laundry service; limited-mobility rooms; outdoor pool; 24-hr. room service. In room: A/C, TV, dataport, hair dryer, minibar, safe.*

Eating

The cuisine of Aix ranges from internationally influenced restaurants, to late-night kebab and pizza stands, to Provençal vegetable salads (artistically arranged platters of raw vegetables such as carrots, cucumbers, tomatoes, and corn, typically with additions such as olives and tuna, topped with a typically Provençal mustard dressing). On the **cours Mirabeau,** you'll find upscale student-filled cafes serving designer pizzas; on the outskirts of town, outside of the ramparts, you'll find a number of plain, white, windowless kidnapper vans cooking pizzas in brick-fire ovens. They're only about a 5- to 10-minute walk out of town, and have surprisingly excellent food. The vans have unpredictable hours and locations, but they're definitely worth the search.

CAFES & LIGHT FARE

Opened more than a century ago, **Bechard** (12 cours Mirabeau; ☎ 04-42-26-06-78), is the most famous bakery in town. It takes its work so seriously that it refers to its underground kitchens as a *laboratoire* (laboratory). Most of the delectable pastries are made fresh every day.

Cybercafes

Aix's two main hotbeds of cyberspace are **Net'Games** (52 rue Aumône Vielle; ☎ **04-42-26-60-42;** www.netgames.fr; daily 10am–midnight; 1€ 15 min., 3€ hour) and **Games Friends** (46 rue du Puits Neuf; ☎ **04-42-63-10-74;** www.games-friends.com; Mon–Sat 10:30am–12:30am, Sun 2pm–12:30am; 3€ hour).

CHEAP

➜**Charlotte** ★ PROVENÇAL   Don't be put off by the nondescript front door: This is an oasis of green in the middle of town. Had your granny been from Aix, she could have done the cooking here, where all the dishes are lovingly prepared with traditional local flavor. The cuisine changes with the seasons, and the jovial boss will undoubtedly sit down beside you to help you choose from the menu. *32 rue des Bernardines. ☎ 04-42-26-77-56. Fixed-price menus from 13€. Credit cards accepted. Tues–Sat 12:30–2:30pm and 8–11pm.*

➜**La Crêp' Sautière** ★ CREPE   The thing about France is that you never quite know when you'll get an urge for a crepe. Brittany and Normandy have so many creperies that you can't pass through the regions without visiting one. But in Aix, the smell of cooking pancake mixture is replaced with fragrant olive oils, peppers, Mediterranean tomatoes, and Provençal herbs—unless you come to this corker of a creperie, that is. Set in an old mill, it offers every sort of crepe your greedy heart could desire—and all in a cozy setting with exposed-stone walls, and atmospheric candlelight at night. *18 rue Bédarrides. ☎ 04-42-27-91-60. Crepes 4€–10€. Tues–Sun noon–2pm and 7–11pm.*

DOABLE

➔**Chez Maxime** PROVENÇAL GRILL Set in the heart of Aix's pedestrian shopping zone, this likeable restaurant offers an all-Provençal ambience of bordeaux-colored banquettes, salmon-colored walls, and tables, shaded by an enormous linden tree, that spill out onto the pavement during clement weather. There's a succulent array of a dozen grills, including roasted shoulder of lamb, beefsteaks, and fresh fish, as well as a main course laced with saffron and the flavors of the sea, a *marmite* (stewpot) *de la mer*. If it's on the menu, you have to try the house-made foie gras of duckling, a kind of pâté made from beef and Provençal herbs known as *caillette de province*, and desserts such as a *fondant au chocolat*. The wine list features dozens of vintages, many of them esoteric bottles from the region. *12 place Ramus.* ☎ *04-42-26-28-51. Reservations recommended. Fixed-price lunch 16€; fixed-price dinner 25€–29€. Credit cards accepted. Tues–Sat noon–2:30pm; Mon–Sat 7:30–10:30pm.*

SPLURGE

➔**Le Clos de la Violette** MODERN FRENCH You must have won the lottery if you're contemplating this innovative restaurant, a few steps from La Villa Gallici (see "Sleeping," above). A stellar example of the innovative cuisine you should expect is the appetizer *mousseline* of potatoes with sea urchins and fish roe. The sea wolf with crisp fried shallots and a "cappuccino" of spicy Spanish sausages is lip-smackingly good, as is the rack of suckling lamb, stuffed with carrots and chickpeas, and served under an herb-flavored pastry crust. For dessert, try multilayered sugar cookies with hazelnut and vanilla-flavored cream sauce and thin slices of white chocolate, or a "celebration" of Provençal figs—an artfully arranged platter containing a galette, tart, parfait, and sorbet. *10 av. de la Violette.* ☎ *04-42-23-30-71. Reservations required. Fixed-price lunch 54€; tasting menu 120€. Credit cards accepted. Tues–Sat noon–1:30pm and 8–9:30pm. Closed 2 weeks in Aug.*

Almonds & Olives

Along with the usual Provençal specialties, Aix is famous for its olives and almonds; in fact, it is called both the olive capital and the almond capital of France. Olive trees are everywhere in the surrounding countryside, and the local markets always have impressive displays of barrels filled to the rim with olives. Aix has an olive festival every June, most of the artisan shops in town sell homemade olive oil, and most Aixois restaurants serve a delicious olive tapenade with your bread.

The famous almonds go into making *Calisson d'Aix,* a favorite gourmet specialty in town. Shaped like a little white flower petal about three times the size of an almond, the *calisson* is a combination of almond paste and candied fruit. According to legend, it was the dessert served at Good King René's wedding in 1473 to Jeanne. To buy the royal snack, try **Calissons du Roy René** (10 rue Clémenceau; ☎ **04-42-26-67-86;** www.calisson.com) or **Maison L Béchard** (12 cours Mirabeau; ☎ **04-42-26-06-78**), which has been making the babies for over a century.

Partying

Aix's ultimate student haunt is **Le Castel** (2 bis bd. Victor Hugo; ☎ **04-42-93-10-18;** Tues–Sat 7pm–4am)—a pub-cum-gallery that mixes culture (monthly art exhibitions) with nighttime debauchery (loud music and decently priced drinks). A bar for trendies in need of a large terrace is **La Belle Epoque** (29 cours Mirabeau; ☎ **04-42-27-65-66;** daily; happy hour 7–8pm except Sat) with a live DJ pumping up the volume with cool lounge and electro-funk.

The "it" crowds lap up the animated bar scene and loud electronic music at **Le Mistral** (3 rue Frédéric-Mistral; ☎ **04-42-38-16-49**). This is the realm of "fashion attitude" (as the French say), where you get in free if you're gorgeous and female (and, depending on the mood of the staff, even receive a free glass or two of champagne), but have to pay a cover charge of around 15€ if you're a bloke. Don't miss the **student night** on Thursdays.

For great jazz that's produced by a changing roster of visiting musicians, head for the **Scatt Jazz Club** (11 rue de la Verrerie; ☎ **04-42-23-00-23;** Tues–Sat from 11pm), a smoky den that maintains notoriously late hours (music often doesn't begin until around midnight) in a wicked setting under medieval vaults. **La Joia Glam Club** (Chemin de l'Enfant, 13290 Les Milles; ☎ **06-80-35-32-94;** www.joia-club.com; Thurs–Sat), is out of town (free shuttle buses run to the nightclub from La Rotonde fountain on place du Général de Gaulle), but that's the price to pay when nightclubs are this cool. Aix's newest body-shop bar is modeled on an oriental villa. It has a restaurant and a patio with an outdoor swimming pool (the kind where you may opt to jump in topless). And it's notorious for its Magic Bubbles evenings, when the terrace is filled with foam. Dress up if you want to get in, and know in advance that long lines await on Fridays and Saturdays. Entrance usually costs 11€ to 20€, unless you're a star or self-enchanted enough to convince the doorman that you are—in which case the velvet ropes may miraculously open, without charge, like the Red Sea before Moses.

Sightseeing

MUSEUMS

➜ **Atelier de Cézanne** ★ Cézanne, the major forerunner of Cubism, lived and worked in this house, surrounded by a wall and restored by American admirers. Repaired in 1970, it remains much as Cézanne left it in 1906, "his coat hanging on the wall, his easel with an unfinished picture waiting for a touch of the master's brush," as Thomas R. Parker wrote. *9 av. Paul-Cézanne (outside town).* ☎ *04-42-21-06-53. www.atelier-cezanne.com. Admission 5.50€ adults, 2€ students. Apr–June and Sept daily 10am–noon and 2:30–6pm; July–Aug daily 10am–6pm; Oct–Mar daily 10am–noon and 2–5pm. Closed Jan 1, May 1, and Dec 25.*

➜ **Musée des Tapisseries** To some, they are just a pile of old drapes, but to others this former archbishop's palace houses three series of important tapestries from the 17th and 18th centuries, including the world's only example of *The History of Don Quixote,* by Natoire (1735). Other attractions that line the gilded walls are *The Russian Games,* by Leprince; and *The Grotesques,* by Monnoyer. The museum also exhibits rare furnishings from the 17th and 18th centuries. *28 place des Martyrs de la Résistance.* ☎ *04-42-23-09-91. Admission 2.50€. Wed–Mon 10am–12:30pm and 1:30–5pm. Closed Jan 1, May 1, and Dec 25.*

➜ **Natural History Museum** Compared to Paris, this is a jot of a natural history museum, yet there is something special you should make the detour for. Way before Roman leader Caius Sextius Calvinus gave his name to the town, Aix-en-Provence was indeed a "Sex-en-Provence"—a veritable **breeding ground for megaloolithid dinosaurs.** In fact you could say that the town was literally sitting on a nest egg—over 1,000 Titanosaurus dinosaur eggs to be exact—the greatest number in the world. Five hundred fifty-three are on show here today. If you loved *Jurassic Park*, you'll love Aix. *6 rue Espariat.* ☎ *04-42-27-91-27. www.museum-aix-en-provence.org. Admission 2.50€; free admission for those under 25. Wed–Mon (daily on school holidays) 10am–noon and 1–5pm.*

HIGHBROW HAUNTS

➜ **Cité du Livre** ★ So it's highbrow—but it's also cool. Set in an old match factory, the City of Books (get a look at the giant book statues out front) is a meeting point for all art forms. It showcases an international video library of Lyric art, holds regular festivals, and is the official headquarters of the Preljocaj Ballet (www.preljocaj.org)—a mind-blowing contemporary ballet troupe that performs all over the world under the direction of Angelin Preljocaj. Check out their website, or rendezvous at the Cité du Live for details of their program and other events. *8–10 rue des Allumettes.* ☎ *04-42-91-98-88. www.citedulivre-aix.com. Opening hours vary.*

RELAXATION

➜ **Thermes Sextius** ★ Montagne St-Victoire isn't just the pretty face of Cézanne's paintings, it is also the site of a 10,000 year-old water source, enriched in calcium and magnesium—that provided baths in 122 B.C. to Caius Sextius. Today, on the site of Mr. Sexy's very spa, you too can rejuvenate your body (or at least make it feel younger) by opting for any of the wonderful massage and beauty treatments on offer in this chic-as-hell setting. Expect to fork out between 82€ and 120€ for the basic treatments (even more for a beauty

treatment), but rest assured that the pampering will fulfill its purpose. *55 av. des Thermes.* ☎ *04-42-23-81-82. www.thermes-sextius.com. Basic treatments 82€–120€. Mon–Fri 8:30am–8:30pm, Sat 9:30am–7:30pm, Sun 9:30am–2:30pm.*

CHURCHES

FREE ➜ **Cathédrale St-Sauveur** ★ The cathedral of Aix is dedicated to Christ under the title St-Sauveur (Holy Savior or Redeemer). Its baptistery dates from the 4th and 5th centuries, and the complex as a whole has seen many additions. It contains a 15th-century Nicolas Froment triptych, *The Burning Bush.* One side depicts the Virgin and Child; the other, Good King René and his second wife, Jeanne de Laval. *Place des Martyrs de la Résistance.* ☎ *04-42-23-45-65. Free admission. Daily 9am–noon and 2–5pm. Mass Sun 10:30am and 7pm.*

FREE ➜ **Chapelle   Penitents-gris (Chapelle des Bourras)** This 16th-century chapel honoring St. Joseph was built on the ancient Roman Aurelian road linking Rome and Spain. Herbert Maza, founder and former president of the Institute for American Universities, restored the chapel. M. Borricand, rector of a group of local ecclesiastics, arranges visits. *15 rue Lieutaud.* ☎ *04-42-26-26-72. Free admission; donations welcome. Visits by reservation only. 17€–19€ bed. Take bus no. 4.*

Playing Outside

ROUTE DE CEZANNE

One of the best experiences in Aix is a walk along the well-marked **route de Cézanne** (D17), which winds eastward through the countryside toward Ste-Victoire. From the east end of cours Mirabeau, take rue du Maréchal-Joffre across boulevard Carnot to boulevard des Poilus, which becomes avenue des Ecoles-Militaires and finally D17. The stretch between Aix and the

PROVENCE

hamlet of Le Tholonet is full of twists and turns, where Cézanne often set up his easel. The entire route makes a lovely 5.5km (3¹/₃-mile) stroll. Le Tholonet has a cafe or two where you can refresh yourself while waiting for one of the frequent buses back to Aix.

Shopping

Santons Fouque (65 cours Gambetta, route de Nice; ☎ 04-42-26-33-38) is for nerds, but it stocks the largest assortment of *santons* (regional wooden figurines of saints) in Aix. More than 1,900 figurines are cast in terra cotta, finished by hand, and painted according to an 18th-century model (medieval shoemakers, barrel makers, coppersmiths, and ironsmiths, poised to welcome the newborn Jesus—ain't that sweet). Figurines range in price from 7€ to 900€. If you don't buy any (let's face it, where are you going to put them?), they are at least worth a photo. **Carré d'Artsistes** (20 rue de la Glacière; ☎ 04-42-27-60-64; Mon 2–7pm, Tues–Sat 10am–1pm and 2–7pm) is an art shop where you can finally afford to buy the paintings. More than 1,000 are for sale, by various artists, from 45€ to 300€.

Whether you're looking for the latest video game for your PS2 or a mega-rare 1980 version of your favorite New York rock band, the guys at **Compact Club** (16 rue Tanneurs; ☎ 04-42-91-30-43) can kit you out. The coolest hairdressers in Aix, at **Pearl** (rue d'Italie; ☎ 04-42-93-20-90; Mon–Sat 9am–6pm), will cut and smooth your locks while you listen to their resident DJ scratch some vinyls at the bottom of the shop. (Cuts start at 33€.) If you're desperate for a new bag, **Un Jour un Sac** (Galerie François Rénier, 30 rue Espariat; ☎ 04-42-91-36-86; Mon–Sat 10am–7pm), has some unusual designs, created by François Rénier, with funky interchangeable handles. **Glamlab** (7 rue Paul Bert; ☎ 04-42-21-96-81; www.glamlab.fr; Tues–Sat 10am–1:30pm

and 2:30-7pm) is a laboratory of glamour for Aix's girls, with unusual cuts and trendy little feminine numbers. And finally for the boys, you should head to the concept store **Plus** (18–20 rue Fauchier; ☎ 04-42-38-55-82; Mon–Sat 10am–1pm and 2–7pm), which sells all sorts of skate-inspired urban wear, sports accessories, and gadgets you can't find elsewhere; there's even a section on graphism in the 1980s.

Festivals

Aix celebrates the performing arts, particularly music, more than any other city in the south of France. It offers at least four summer festivals that showcase music, opera, and dance, including the **Aix en Musique** (☎ 04-82-21-69-69; www.aixenmusique.fr), all summer long, which focuses on symphonic and chamber music; and **Festival International d'Art Lyrique & de Musique** (☎ 04-82-17-34-34; www.festival-aix.com) in late July, which attracts musicians from all over the world. You should also come along for the **Festival International de Danse** (3 weeks in late July and early Aug), which attracts classical and modern dance troupes from throughout Europe and the world. For information, call ☎ 04-42-96-05-01.

To Market We Will Go

Aix has the region's best markets. Place Richelme holds a **fruit and vegetable market** every morning. Come here to buy the exquisite products of Provence, such as olives, lavender, local cheeses, and fresh produce. There's a **flower market** Tuesday, Thursday, and Saturday morning on place de l'Hôtel-de-Ville. The **fish market** is Monday through Saturday morning on place Richelme.

La Côte d'Azur (French Riviera)

by Nathalie Jordi

There's a reason we fantasize about the Côte d'Azur: It's sunny, the water's warm, and a lot of rich, famous, and beautiful people go there—just the sort of place to inspire winter daydreams or exam-time reveries. But you're not the only one who was freezing your ass off in Topeka or procrastinating away as the hours until the Econ test ticked down. Come June, you'll meet everyone else who had the same fantasy, and you'll fight them for space on Nice's plage de la Californie or for passage through the velvet rope at St-Tropez's Le Baoli. Let's face it; if you've bought a guidebook to the French Riviera, you're not likely to run into Brigitte Bardot at a party anytime soon.

You don't have to be a millionaire, though, to enjoy the beach, sip a *pastis,* shop your pants off, or rock the clubs (not that we're saying money doesn't help). The Côte offers some stunning scenery, in both the Mediterranean and the mix of habitués that strut the boardwalk, whether they're obscenely bejeweled old women walking tiny little dogs in Nice or obscenely bejeweled old men walking tiny little women in Monaco. Enough! I'm being harsh. While they often get lumped together, each of the towns on the Côte d'Azur has its own particular character and deserves exploration. I'd suggest sampling them in the off season, unless you like paying through the nose just because it's hot out.

Post-Romans, Visigoths, Franks, and others, the Côte was mostly knit with provincial fishing villages that split their time being "Italian," "Spanish," and "French" (my use of quotes relating to the fact that these nations hadn't yet occurred to anyone as an idea—the people calling the shots weren't presidents or parliaments but rather the counts of Provence, the House of Barcelona, the princes of Anjou). It wasn't until a few British aristocrats, including Queen Victoria, came down to spend the odd winter—this being the preferred season then, as too much sun was considered unhealthy—that the Côte saw the first stirrings of the tourist mecca it was to become.

Things aren't always sunny on the Côte d'Azur, though. While hoteliers and restaurateurs might live a year on the profits they suck out of the unsuspecting during the 3 months of high season, the region still has to look after its elderly and create jobs. If, on average, 10% of French people are unemployed, the figure is as high as 40% among certain sectors on the Côte d'Azur. The only major industry is tourism, and while the Côte certainly makes a fair profit entertaining, the skyrocketing price of local housing, which shows no signs of abatement, means that anyone who actually needs to be there (nurses, teachers, garbage men) can't afford it. Souvenir shops and art galleries that can afford the high rents squeeze out local businesses; young married couples looking to buy their first house face property prices that rival those of tony Parisian neighborhoods. So people take off in search of greener pastures. Who's left? Wealthy foreigners, whose often-empty houses don't do the economy any good, and a disproportionately jobless population living on welfare. Any wonder fascists like Jean-Marie Le Pen are so popular in these parts?

Didn't mean to ruin your buzz. We know it's pretty easy to get blinded by the sun.

The Best of La Côte d'Azur

○ **The Best Place to Stop Thinking You're in L.A. and Come Back to Southern France for a Few Minutes (St-Tropez):** The *boulodrome* on the **place de Lices,** where old men and watercolorists take a break to play a few games of *petanque.* See p. 480.

○ **The Best Venue for Boob-Spotting (St-Tropez):** Admit it already; this is why you came to the Côte d'Azur. Well, knocker yourself out at the **plage de Pampelonne,** where Bardot's legacy stays aflame. See p. 484.

○ **The Best Reason to Skip St-Tropez:** The month of **August.** It's been said before, but it's worth belaboring. See p. 478.

○ **The Best Oysters in Cannes:** Never mind **Astoux et Brun**'s boring decor; what you're after are the *huitres* (oysters), in every guise you can think of. Make sure you gulp down a couple of

fresh ones before you do anything else. See p. 491.

○ **The Most Imposing Facade (Cannes): The InterContinental Carlton,** with its cupolas supposedly modeled after the breasts of a bewitching Gypsy the architect admired. See p. 493.

○ **The Best Place to Repent for Your Sins in Case You Skipped the Cinematheque (Nice):** The **Cathédrale Orthodoxe Russe St-Nicholas,** off the boulevard Tzarewich. Is it strange to you that that there's an onion-domed, filigreed Russian church smack in the middle of Nice? If so, time to brush up on your history. See p. 505.

○ **The Best Place For a Quiet, Trendy Drink (Nice):** The **Bar at the Hi Hotel** is unassuming from outside; nevertheless, walk through the magenta sliding doors of the Hi and *sirote* your cocktail from inside the chill outdoor courtyard

La Côte d'Azur (French Riviera)

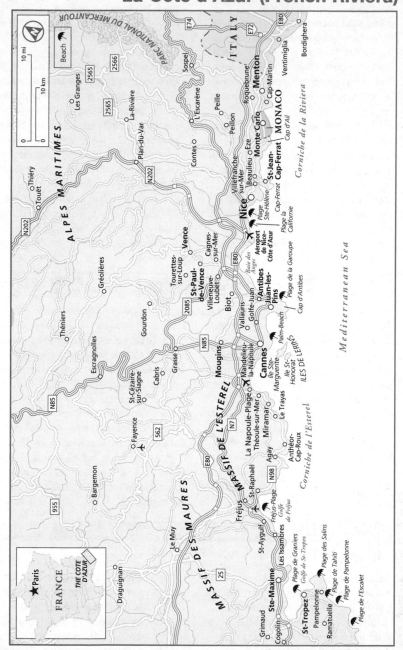

before hitting up the clubs in town. It won't disappoint. See p. 500.

○ **The Best Socca in Nice: Therese,** at the market, is threatening to retire, but if she's still around when you read this, seek her out for the ultimate example of Nice's creamy, nutty chickpea pancake, cooked on an upended oil drum. See p. 507.

○ **The Best Grassois Specialty:** Grasse's *fougassette* is a pillowy, tender take on the *provençal fougasse* bread, but with delicate notes of orange blossom. Is anyone surprised? See p. 478.

○ **The Best Unexpectedly Excellent Museum (Gourdon):** The **Musée des Arts Decoratifs** is a small medieval citadel-village high in the mountains, 14km (9 miles) from Grasse. See p. 517.

○ **The Best Souvenir to Bring Home from Monaco (Monte Carlo):** Stamps, and we're not being lame. This *principalité* is actually a country in and of itself, meaning that it has its own stamps and currency. Stop by the **Comptoir Philatelique de Monaco.** Technically speaking, it's still euros (formerly francs), but they are still Monaco-specific, which is pretty cool. Also check out the coins at the Musée des Timbres et des Monnaies and send postcards home from the Office des Emissions (Timbres-Poste). Both at the Centre Commercial de Fontvieille, 11 Terrasses de Fontvieille (☎ 377-93-15-41-50). Open daily 10am to 5pm (to 6pm in summer). See p. 524.

Getting to the Region

The biggest airport is in Nice, although there are plenty of helipads and smaller runways dotted along the coast. If you'd rather go by rail, the TGV goes from Paris Gare-de-Lyon towards Cannes, Nice, Toulon, and Antibes for about 100€, depending on where and when you're going. It's about 4 hours to Toulon, 5¹/₂ to Cannes, and 6 to Nice. Night trains are also an option; trains go every day and every night. Night trains are also available from Nantes, Strasbourg, Bordeaux, and Metz to Nice. Locally, the SNCF is more developed than nearly anywhere else in France, with stations in every biggish town and an extensive, frequent network of shuttle buses. To get south from Paris in a car, take the A6 Autoroute du Soleil to Lyon and the Rhone Valley, or that A10, A71, and A75 through Bourges and Clermont-Ferrand. From Bordeaux, take the A62 until Toulouse and then head for Narbonne on the A61, Nîmes on the A9, and Salon-de-Provence on the A54. From there you can take *la provençale,* the A8, which spreads west-east and hits Nice. Paris-Toulon is about 850km (527 miles) and costs about 55€ in tolls.

St-Tropez: Clichéd but Still Beautiful

874km (542 miles) S of Paris, 76km (47 miles) SW of Cannes

Old movies of long-limbed brown French women, wearing little besides big sunglasses and floaty headscarves? Think St-Tropez. Painters rhapsodizing about the light and squinting at their canvases as they daub a little more rose—no, cerise—to capture it? Think St-Tropez. Cute little cobblestoned streets with the lovely smells of bouillabaisse bubbling out from the kitchen window? Think St-Tropez. A roiling mass of rude wannabe starlets, fat French citizens, a passel of Teutonic tourists in neon Speedos, and you—all trying to share 10 square feet of beach space? You got it: St-Tropez.

Nevertheless we have to admit this town is still charming and deserves its reputation as one of the most together spots on the French south coast. But like most of the Côte d'Azur, it has fallen victim to its own success, and once the mercury hits 85, it doesn't take long for paradise to turn into a purgatory that smells too much of coconut suntan oil.

Despite the endless floods of visitors who come here, St-Tropez retains its quintessentially French character. If you have the good fortune to come in the off season, you'll find the little fishing village that drew travelers here to begin with, and prices there will fall within reach.

Legend has it that the "little fishing village" started out as a memorial to a Christian martyr named Torpes. He refused to give up the faith in A.D. 68, and was chopped up and thrown onto a dinghy along with a rooster and a dog that were meant to eat the pieces. The dinghy floated to one of the beaches in St-Tropez, and local Christians found it, hid the remains, and built a chapel (today, Pisa, Genoa, and St-Tropez share pieces of the skull). If you check a map, you'll note Cogolin and Grimaud, the nearby villages whose Olde Frenche names recall the cock and the dog that accompanied M. Torpes to Saint Trop'.

Although painters including Matisse, Bonnard, and Signac had discovered the bay by the late 19th century, it wasn't until 1920 that St-Tropez started attracting fashionistas. After a short break for World War II, when it served as the landing platform for the Allied invasion of southern France, it became popular among the French existentialists, movie stars, and everyone else

who decided they wanted a piece of the action. Oh, what? You, too?

Getting There

BY AIR

The closest airport is **Toulon-Hyeres.** You can take buses into town from there.

BY TRAIN

The closest train station is in **St-Raphael.** From the Gare Maritime there (rue Pierre-Auble), you can take a boat for St-Tropez, a highly recommended beautiful 50-minute ride. These leave four or five times a day from April to October and cost 11€.

BY CAR

From Cannes, drive southwest along the RD98 coastal highway, turning east when you see signs for St-Tropez. Be warned: Parking in St-Tropez, especially in high season, is hellish. Some of the better hotels have a parking lot; otherwise, you can park in the **Parking des Lices** beneath the place des Lices if you enter on avenue Paul-Roussel. The lot is free for the first hour, 1€ the second hour, and .50€ for each subsequent hour. If you're going to be there for a whole day, expect to pay a 15€ per day rate in the summer; this drops down to 13€ in the wintertime.

BY BOAT

If your first view of the city came from the water, wouldn't that be pretty sweet? You can make it happen, even if you're not coming in on a private yacht. The **MMG** excursion line takes people on the 20-minute ride from St. Maxime, a town across the cove, between April and November. Boats leave every hour in both directions in midsummer, and about four times a day from April to June and from September to October (no service Nov–Mar). Other boats make the St-Raphael–St-Tropez trip, which takes about 50 minutes (☏ **04-94-82-71-45**).

BY BUS

From St-Tropez, you can take buses to Toulon, Nice, Ramatuelle, Gassin, Grimod, and St. Raphael. Likewise, you can travel from those cities to St-Tropez. The **SODE-TRAV** buses come in and out of the Gare Routière on the avenue du 8 Mai 1945. Call ☎ **04-94-97-88-51;** in the off season, call the office in Hyeres at ☎ 08-25-00-06-50.

Orientation

St-Tropez is small enough to walk around, but you have to tear yourself away from the beaches long enough to do it. The quays of the old port are beautiful, if a little intense, with all the private yachts and Ferraris tooling around. If you walk from there towards the towering Citadelle, you'll pass a bunch of adorable back streets lined with little pastel houses where the fishermen used to live, though they're now crammed with boutiques and watercolor artists. The ▓▓ Best place des Lices, with its restaurants, bars, and *boulodrome,* will tell you you've come to the south end of the neighborhood.

Getting Around

BY PUBLIC TRANSPORTATION

Use the good old **SODETRAV bus** (av. du 8 mai 1945; ☎ **04-94-97-88-51**), which runs buses around the region. For cabs, find the stand on the quai H Bouchard in front of the Musée de l'Annonciade, or call ☎ **04-94-97-05-27.** There are also shuttles that will take you to various beaches; these leave from the places des Lices.

BY BICYCLE

Tool around in style with a bike from **Jean-Louis Mas** (5 rue Josef-Quaranta; ☎ **04-94-97-00-60;** June–Sept Mon–Sat 9am–7pm, Sun 9am–12:30pm; Oct–Apr Mon–Sat 9am–12:30pm and 2–7pm and Sun 9am–12:30pm). Or check out **Holiday Bikes** (14 av. du Général Leclerc; ☎ **04-94-97-09-39;** off season closed Sun–Mon).

ON FOOT

St-Tropez is small enough to get around on foot—unless it's noon and you've finally made your way up the stairs to the top of the Citadelle. Then you'll wish a cab could take you home. No luck, though; you'll have to go all the way down again.

Tourist Offices

The **St-Tropez tourist office** is on quai Jean Jaures (☎ **04-94-97-45-21**). It's open Monday to Saturday 7:30am to 1pm and 2 to 7pm in the summer, and Monday to Saturday 9am to noon and 2 to 6pm during the rest of the year.

St-Tropez **Nuts & Bolts**

Hospitals The local hospital is the **Clinique de l'Oasis** (☎ **04-94-79-07-07**). For emergencies at night, call ☎ **04-94-79-07-20.** For emergencies during the day, call ☎ **04-94-79-47-30.**

Pharmacies Pharmacies will reveal themselves by flashing green neon crosses. If you need one at night *(pharmacie de garde),* call ☎ **04-94-07-08-08.**

Post Office La Poste is on, whaddya know, the rue de la Poste (☎ **04-94-55-96-50**). If you need something mailed to you lickety-split, there's always FedEx. Call them at ☎ **08-00-12-38-00.**

Sleeping

The nearest campground is in Ramatuelle, so if you're looking to sleep on the cheap, St-Tropez ain't the place to do it. Booking in advance is a good idea, given that all the good spots go quickly.

CHEAP

➔**Hôtel Lou Cagnard** What a location, what a price: 5 minutes from the port and just behind the place des Lices, and under 60€ for a basic double room, even in season—although you might have to pay more if you want a toilet that isn't in the hallway. The garden is gorgeous, with a 100-year-old fig tree and lovely smelling lilac and bougainvillea. Garden-facing rooms are probably the best bet, given that the street can be noisy. The rooms are spare but clean and fresh. Best of all: Breakfast is huge. The excellent quality-price ratio of this hotel means that rooms fill up fast, so book quickly. They have parking. *18 av. Paul Roussel. ☎ 04-94-97-04-24. www.hotel-lou-cagnard.com. 48€–78€ double low season, 60€–112€ high season. Credit cards accepted. Closed Nov–Dec. In room: TV.*

DOABLE

➔**B. Lodge Hotel** At the foot of the gardens of the citadel, this hotel can be a bit noisy, but it's still a steal, all things considered. The rooms are simple, chic, and modern, ranging from 70€ to 100€, depending on the room and the season. They have free Wi-Fi and a very cool wooden bar where guests can relax near the end of the day. *Rue de l'Aïoli. ☎ 04-94-97-06-57. www.hotel-b-lodge.com. 80€–110€ double. Credit cards accepted. Amenities: Bar. In room: Safe, Wi-Fi.*

SPLURGE

➔**La Ponche** ★ This tiny little luxury hotel, cobbled together out of old fishermen's cafes in the old alleys near the port, is absolutely the cutest place to stay in St-Tropez, if you want to splash out. Romy Schneider stayed here, as did Boris Vian, Picasso, and even La Bardot, when she was filming *And God Created Woman*. From the balconies, there's a soaring view of the village's pink-tile roofs, the Citadel, and the clock tower. There are only two or three rooms on each floor (18 total), each decorated in the kinds of subtle hues that say, "This color doesn't exist at Target." *Port des Pecheurs, 3 rue des Remparts. ☎ 04-94-97-02-53. www.laponche.com. 145€–350€ rooms overlooking the street or inside patio, 215€–425€ balconied or terraced rooms, 295€–540€ suites with a sea view. Breakfast 19€. Credit cards accepted. Amenities: Restaurant; elevator; paid parking (21€). In room: A/C, satellite TV, minibar, safe.*

Eating

COFFEE BARS & LIGHT FARE

➔**La Tarte Tropezienne** This light brioche-style pastry, scented with orange blossom and stuffed hyper-generously with cream, has been an emblem of St-Tropez since its founding in 1955. *36 rue Georges-Clemenceau. ☎ 04-94-97-71-42. Daily 6:30am–7pm (until 11pm July–Aug). Closed Mon in winter.*

➔**Sorelle** The two sisters who run this joint offer the best coffee in the old port: It's cheap, it's decent, and boy will you enjoy the eye candy (and I'm not talking about the sisters). You won't spend more than 10 or 15 euros on the tasty sandwiches and salads, which you can either eat on-site or take away to nibble on the beaches. *23 quai Suffren. ☎ 04-94-43-87-78. Sandwiches and salads under 10€. No credit cards. Daily 8:30am–noon.*

CHEAP

➔**Le Café** From your post here, smack-dab on the 📺 ⓑⓔⓢⓣ● **place de Lices,** you can watch the old men play *boules* as you savor light meals, salads, or the daily special for as little as 13€ ("cheap" only relative to St-Tropez). A full meal will cost you more like 20€–30€. The old-school bistro tables and zinc bar are evocative of Paris, but if you actually believe this place is for real, get thee to Cannes where you belong. *Place des Lices.* ☎ *04-94-97-44-69. Main courses 15€–25€. Credit cards accepted. Daily 8am–closing (at owner's discretion).*

DOABLE

→ **Auberge des Maures** This place feels like a splurge, but the prices are surprisingly decent, considering it's St-Tropez and you can sit under the stars here in a sculpted garden. Watch the black-clad chefs dance a masterful kitchen ballet that sends waiters out holding aloft smoking platters of lovely smelling grilled fish, deep-fried zucchini blossoms, stuffed vegetables, and other Provençal fare. *4 rue du Docteur Boutin.* ☎ *04-94-97-01-50. Main courses 10€–25€, fixed menu 42€. Credit cards accepted. Daily 7:30pm–1am. Closed Dec–Mar.*

SPLURGE

→ **L'Oasis** Stephane Raimbault, who took over the kitchen from the world-famous, now-retired Louis Outhier, spent 9 years cooking in Japan before coming to this medieval-looking, plane-tree-shaded house and kitchen, making his food très Saint-Trop-meets-Osaka. Try the crayfish "cooked in the fires of hell," accompanied by beautiful baby vegetables, or the traditionally grilled (presumably, not in the fires of hell) Mediterranean fish. The *maison* boasts one of the finest Provençal cellars on the Côte d'Azur. *Rue Honoré-Carle.* ☎ *04-93-49-95-52. Fixed-price lunch 50€, fixed-price dinner 70€–150€. Credit cards accepted. Closed for lunch Apr–Oct, closed Sun dinner and Mon Nov–Mar.*

Partying
BARS & CLUBS

Ho, boy. If this is the section to which you inevitably skip first, you're in luck, because St-Tropez won't disappoint where nightlife is concerned. If you think the crowds, heat, and smell of burning flesh during the day was intense, just wait until nighttime. Why do you think everyone rolls up en masse in the summer? To party, *bien sûr!*

Start the night off with a cheap drink at **La Bodega** (quai de l'Epi; ☎ **04-97-02-25**), then move upstairs to the gay-friendly **Papagayo** (☎ **94-97-07-56**), its three bars and two floors decorated like it's been a St-Tropez classic since the '60s. Although it had a heyday in the '60s too, **Le Bar du Port** (quai Suffren; ☎ **04-94-97-00-54**) has been revamped sleekly to see more glory days. The DJ is always hot in the summer, but during the off season, the weekend is the time to hit this place up.

So you want to hit up a gay club or two? Head straight for rue Sibille, where you'll find **Nano Bar** (2 rue Sibille; ☎ **04-94-97-72-59**) and **Chez Maggy** (5 rue Sibille; ☎ **04-94-97-16-12**). St-Tropez is cool enough that you shouldn't have any problem strutting your stuff in most places, though.

Just try and get into the **VIP Room** (Residences du Nouveau Port; ☎ **04-94-97-14-70**). There's food, but nobody wants it. There's Warhol and Basquiat hanging on the walls, but nobody's looking at it. Bring sunglasses, so as not to get blinded by the neon lights—or recognized.

Sightseeing

If you came here to roast on the beaches and pickle in the nightclubs, you may not have time to explore St-Tropez's more *haute* attractions, but you'd be missing out.

PUBLIC MONUMENTS

➜ **La Citadelle** ★★ Unless you're about to touch down on a helipad, it's from the top of the 16th-century Citadelle that you'll get the absolute best view of St-Tropez. That said, it's quite a way to the top, so we won't blame you for bailing halfway. Then again, there are peacocks up there. Are you convinced yet? ☎ 04-94-97-59-43. *Admission 2.50€–4€. Daily May–Sept 10am–12:30pm and 1:30–6:30pm (summer 10am–10pm). The rest of the year, it closes at 5:30pm.*

MUSEUMS

➜ **La Maison des Papillons** It's a little random to walk into an old typical Tropezian house and be confronted by the sight of 20,000 butterflies pinned to the wall, but the effect is actually pretty cool. Hard-core local explorer Dany Lartigue flitted around the world collecting them, and put them up alongside old family photographs. It's bizarre but cool, especially considering that 15,000 more butterflies are stashed in the closets. *9 rue Etienne Berny.* ☎ 04-94-97-63-45. *3€. Apr 1–Oct 31 Mon–Sat 2:30–6pm. Oct–Mar by appointment only (closed in Nov).*

➜ **Musée de l'Annonciade** An amazing collection of modern art housed inside a 16th-century chapel, this museum is a veritable polyphony of beautiful superpositions. Most of the art is St-Tropez-related (views of the bay both literal and abstract) or just rendered by artists who drew inspiration here. The Matisses and Picabias and Braques used to belong to a rich Tropezian, Georges Grammont, who donated them to the city in 1955. It's well worth a look, on Place Grammont (they did right to name the plaza after him!). *Le Port.* ☎ 04-94-17-84-10. *5.50€ in season, 4.50€ in winter. June 1–Sept 30 Wed–Mon 10am–noon and 3–7pm; Oct 1–May 31 Wed–Mon 10am–noon and 2–6pm.*

TWO SPECIAL TOURS

Old City

Start out in the Old City, on the rue de la Misericorde and wander its ivied medieval arcades. Walk towards the old Ponche neighborhood next, with its little fishing port, crumbling ramparts, and the 15th-century portique du Revelen. Rue Allard has a bunch of cute old whimsically decorated dwellings; check out the maison du Maure, with its turbaned Moor's head looking down on the street. The 17th-century *chapelle* de la Misericorde on the rue Gambetta has a lovely tiled roof that glints gold, green, and blue in the sun. Finish the walk by passing before the place de l'Hôtel-de-Ville with its gorgeous sculpted wooden lintel, and end with a glass of pastis on the place des Lices.

Old Port

Alternately, start at the Château de Suffren, east of the old port. It's the oldest building in town, built in 972. Although it is closed to the public, they sometimes show art there. It's worth asking if anything's going on. Towards the fishing port, a bunch

Something Smells Fishy

Whether you're staying in a ratty hostel or sleeping on 500 thread-count Pakistani cotton sheets, your digs probably don't boast a kitchen. Come check out the 📺 Best ● **fish market on the place aux Herbes** anyway. If you get puckish, you can always sample the fruit and vegetables, and this may be your only chance to see the citizens of St-Tropez wheel and deal what was once its most important asset: fish. Even if you do speak French, just try and decipher the accents you hear.

of cute galleries are clustered near the quai Jean Jaures, and we've already mentioned the place aux Herbes as a great place to see Tropezian life and eat something tasty. You'll have to pass a street of crappy restaurants to get to the citadel, but the view from the top is unparalleled and worth the sweat.

Playing Outside

The closest public beach to the old port, the **plage des Graniers,** takes about 15 minutes to reach, along the Chemin des Graniers, but you might want to walk a little farther to the **baie des Canebiers.** It attracts just as many people, but they're a little more relaxed by the time they get there. Another option is the **plage de la Bouillabaisse,** 15 minutes west from the center of town (you can take a St. Raphael or Toulon bus from the station on avenue Général Leclerc, but get off after just 5 min.).

Otherwise, consider venturing even farther afield. The walk to the next public beach, the **plage des Salins,** is lined with the amazing homes (*grosses baraques*) of the rich and lucky. It's actually pretty empty come wintertime. There is a gay beach called **Coco Beach** in Ramatuelle, about 4 miles from the center of St-Tropez.

You'll need to take the shuttle (which leaves from the place des Lices and takes about 20 min.), the SODETRAV bus (which leaves from the *gare routière*), or rent a bike to get to beaches, such as the enormous 🎔 Best❗ **plage de Pampelonne** and **plage de Tahiti** slightly north.

If you're getting tired of the endless scenery of hundreds of bronzed buttock-hills, board a boat for the afternoon. You can cruise towards Esterel, the islands of Lerins and Hyeres, Cannes, and other points on the French Riviera. Find the **Excursions**

Maritimes Tropeziennes office on the port, or call them at ☎ **04-94-54-53-54.**

Shopping
CLOTHING & ACCESSORIES

Like the high-flying center of luxury that it is, St. Trop has all the requisite trappings: Hermes, Dior, and so on, scattered throughout the city streets, in addition to the shops mentioned here.

➜**Atelier Rondini** Even my grandpa had shoes from here. The famous *tropeziennes* sandals have been made in this very workshop for three generations, and they are probably the most classic emblem of summers in St-Tropez. The *mille-pattes* don't come cheap, but given that grandpa's still wearing his, you know they'll last. They come in standard sizes, but if you're a giant or a dwarf they'll custom-make them for you. *16 rue Georges-Clemenceau.* ☎ *04-94-97-19-55. Apr–Sept Mon–Sat 10am–12:30pm and 3–8pm; July–Aug daily. Seasonal closures.*

➜**Galeries Tropeziennes** For more plebeian fare, visit Galeries Tropeziennes, which carries all things Mediterranean, crowded into showrooms near the place des Lices. It's a good place for gift shopping if you're near the end of your trip. *56 rue Gambetta.* ☎ *04-94-97-02-21.*

➜**Le Dépot** For secondhand glam gear, check out Le Dépot, which sells fabulous secondhand Hermes, Moschino, and Chanel. *Bd. Louis Blanc.* ☎ *04-94-97-80-10.*

FOOD, WINE & LOCAL CRAFTS
➜**Provençal Market** Check out the awesome open-air market on Tuesdays and Saturday mornings on the place des Lices. More than 100 vendors sell everything from clothes to old furnishings to plates to tasty-looking food. Wander, wander. *Place des Lices. Summer daily 8am–noon; winter Tues–Sun 8am–noon.*

Cannes: More than Just a Film Festival

904km (560 miles) directly S of Paris, 445km (276 miles) S of Lyon, 42km (26 miles) W of Nice

What do people say about Cannes? "Sure, they have a sandy beach, but the sand is all trucked in," scoffed one lady. "It's the prettiest town on the Riviera, full of flowers and quaint architecture," said a girl from nearby Cagnes-sur-Mar admiringly. "It's dead boring all year except for during the film festival, and totally overrun in the summer," said yet another. Well, we'll let you make up your own mind. Like other Riviera towns, it *is* overrun in the summer, but that doesn't seem to bother the people that pick that time of year to go. The film festival is one of the most exciting times to find oneself on the French Riviera, along with the Formula One race. But Cannes has charm in spades in any case. You could spend your entire time sunning yourself on the beach at the boulevard du Midi or La Croisette, then throw on a pair of pants and spend the rest of the evening sipping your aperitifs there. But we encourage you to trek a bit farther afield. Discover the pine-lashed avenues de la Californie, the shady piazzas on the Cannet, the îles de Lerins. And try coming in January.

But how did this all come about? How did a village named after the reeds that grew in nearby bogs turn into a town, even today smaller than you'd expect, whose name carries cultural capital the whole world round? Well, like most of the other towns on the Riviera, Cannes started out as a fishing village, albeit one whose fortunate location brought it loads of unwanted attention from invaders until the 18th century. Napoleon spent some time camping in the dunes outside town in 1815, but the man who really changed the fate of Cannes was Lord Chancellor Lord Peter Brougham,

The Cannes Film Festival

One of the most effective vehicles for political propaganda before and during World War II was cinema, as you'll know if you ever took a film class. And so intellectuals at that time dreamed of cinematic freedom, of screening movies that were about something other than subliminal messages turning people into sheep. So they dreamed up the Cannes Film Festival, but they weren't able to put it on until 1946, after the war had ended. The first winners were Rene Clement for *La Bataille du rail* and Roberto Rossellini for *Rome, ville ouverte*. In the following years, Cocteau, Pagnol, Godard, Warhol, Nico, and their glamorous entourages passed through, presiding triumphantly over the town.

If you're here for the festival, better hope you have a press pass or other suitable golden key to get you through the sometimes invisible, often very visible gates. But if you're happy to soak up the scene from the outskirts, you can go to the **Cinéma de la Plage** (Plage de la Croisette; free admission; tickets distributed at the Office du Tourisme), wherein the official movies are shown on the plage de la Croisette. To hunt for autographs, head for the Palais and wait by the red carpet on la Croisette. At around 7pm, the limos pull up to spill out their sequined cargo. Arrive early for a good spot. If you want to sneak up on the stars in their natural habitat, try the Eden Roc, the Martinez, the Carlton, the Noga Hilton, or the Majestic.

Cannes

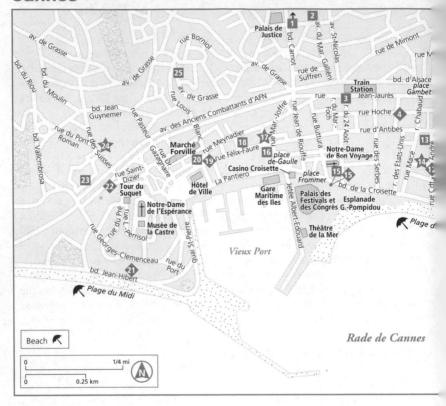

av. de Grasse
bd. du Riou
bd. du Moulin
av. de Grasse
rue Borniol
rue de Suffren
Palais de Justice
bd. Carnot
av. du Mar. Galliéni
av. St-Nicolas
av. du Mar.
rue de Mimont
rue M
av. de Grasse
25
bd. Jean Guynemer
av. de Grasse
rue Louis Blanc
rue Pasteur
av. des Anciens Combattants d'AFN
rue de Grasse
rue du Pont des Suisses
rue des Suisses
rue du Pont Roman
rue Jean de Riouffe
rue Mar.-Joffre
rue Meynadier
rue Jean-Jaurès
rue Hoche
Train Station
bd. d'Alsace
r. du Mar.-Foch
r. du 24 Août
rue Buttura
rue d'Antibes
place Gambet
r. Chabaud
3
4
rue des Serbes
r. des États-Unis
rue Macé
13
André
14
r. Cdt.
24
Marché Forville
20
19
rue Félix-Faure
18
17
16
place de-Gaulle
Notre-Dame de Bon Voyage
23
rue Saint-Dizier
22
Tour du Suquet
Hôtel de Ville
La Pantiero
Casino Croisette
place Frommer
15
15
bd. de la Croisette
rue du Pré
rue L.-Perrisol
Notre-Dame de l'Espérance
Musée de la Castre
rue St-Pierre
rue St-Dié
Gare Maritime des Iles
Palais des Festivals et des Congrès G.-Pompidou
Esplanade
jetée Albert-Édouard
Plage d
rue Georges-Clemenceau
rue du Port
Théâtre de la Mer
21
bd. Jean-Hibert
Vieux Port
Plage du Midi

Beach 🏖

Rade de Cannes

0   1/4 mi
0   0.25 km
N

one of the first among the legions of fortunate Englishmen who summered on the French Riviera. An outbreak of cholera in Nice kept him from getting all the way there, so he settled in Cannes for the night and, seduced, built a palatial residence called the château Eleonore, after his daughter. Brougham spent the next 34 years inviting friends over to enjoy it with him, and more often than not, they had the same reaction. His political chops helped him develop the town, and soon the rest of the British aristocrats transformed a little fishing village into the summer equivalent of Gstaad or St. Moritz. In 1853, once the railroad had arrived, the Croisette was

built, and by 1870, the town already boasted 35 hotels and 200 villas.

Sadly, some ill-advised golden handshakes between hasty developers and palm-rubbing bureaucrats allowed the pouring of far too much cement, and some ugly buildings scar the otherwise beautiful marriage of landscape and architecture.

Remember the Opéra on the waterfront in Nice, which turns its back on the sea to face the Cours Saleya, because no one cared about the ocean or even liked the sun 150 years ago? It was Coco Chanel's vacation to Cannes that changed that—on her bronzed return to Paris, she outshone all the lily-white Parisians. Today, we'd probably agree

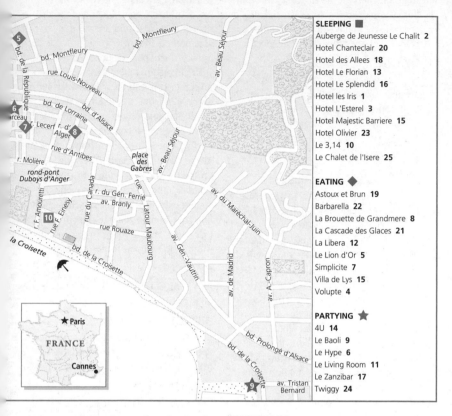

SLEEPING ■
Auberge de Jeunesse Le Chalit **2**
Hotel Chanteclair **20**
Hotel des Allees **18**
Hotel Le Florian **13**
Hotel Le Splendid **16**
Hotel les Iris **1**
Hotel L'Esterel **3**
Hotel Majestic Barriere **15**
Hotel Olivier **23**
Le 3,14 **10**
Le Chalet de l'Isere **25**

EATING ◆
Astoux et Brun **19**
Barbarella **22**
La Brouette de Grandmere **8**
La Cascade des Glaces **21**
La Libera **12**
Le Lion d'Or **5**
Simplicite **7**
Villa de Lys **15**
Volupte **4**

PARTYING ★
4U **14**
Le Baoli **9**
Le Hype **6**
Le Living Room **11**
Le Zanzibar **17**
Twiggy **24**

that some of them have taken the trend a leeetle too far. Remember your suntan lotion, kids. You don't want to end up looking like an Oompa-Loompa.

Getting There

BY AIR

Fly into the **Nice airport** (☎ 08-20-42-33-33), the second largest in France, and take a shuttle; the ride lasts about 30 minutes and they run every half-hour from 8am to 8pm, hourly early in the morning and after 6pm. A taxi will cost you about 60€. There is also the small **Cannes-Mandelieu Airport** (☎ 08-20-42-66-66; cannes-mandelieu.aeroport.fr).

BY TRAIN

The **SNCF** is on place de la Gare, which you can call by dialing ☎ **35-36.** Thankfully, the station is bang in the middle of everything, near the Croisette. After Nice, what a relief! Both the TGV and TER get there.

BY BOAT

You can take a **hydrocruiser** from Nice or St-Tropez; boats leave from Cannes every day at 9:30am and 4:45pm. To St-Tropez one-way: 60€; round-trip 80€.

BY BUS

There are two bus stations: one next to the train station, the other at the Hôtel de Ville. You can travel easily to any other town on the Côte d'Azur or *arriere-pays*, but if you're trying to reach the iles de Lerins, you'll have to go via the quai Laubeuf, on the other side of the port.

BY CAR

You can get there on the A8 or on the N7 around l'Esterel by the north, or on the N98, which has a gorgeous view of Cannes on the way in. If you're coming from Grasse, take the N85, or route Napoléon, to Cannes.

Orientation

Cannes is an easy little city to figure out. At the top is le Suquet, where Cannes began its life. Le Suquet looks down on the port, the rue Meynadier, and the Marché Forville. East of le Suquet, you've got the sexy rue d'Antibes, parallel to La Croisette, where you'll find all the shopping merchandise your heart desires. La Croisette, which stretches from the palais des Festivals to the casino Palm Beach, is 3km (2 miles) long, and it's where all the action happens when The Festival comes to town. The "magic square," or hippest part of town, is right inside, running the length of the rue du Commandant-Andre and spilling over to the streets around it. The neighborhoods of La Croix-des-Gardes and la Californie are where the extraordinary villas built by the English and Russian aristocrats still preen.

Getting Around

BY PUBLIC TRANSPORTATION

There are seventeen **Bus Azur** lines that make the rounds from 7am to 7pm (during The Festival, lines A, B, C, and D keep running after midnight). If you see it (and you can't miss it), grab bus number 8, the one with the open second story. Barring a Lamborghini, it's a great way to see the town with the wind blowing through your hair. Finally, there is the electric shuttle,

which only circulates on the Croisette and rue d'Antibes. You can just hail the driver; tickets cost .50€ and are valid all day. If you parked in town, your ticket is free upon proof of parking ticket.

Or, if you don't mind looking like a dork, take the little tourist train, which leaves every hour from La Croisette in front of the Hôtel Majestic or the colline du Suquet. You can get the commentary in French, English, German, Spanish, Italian, Russian, Arabic, and Japanese. The one for La Croisette goes from 10am to 11pm in the summer, and costs 6€. The one for le Suquet, which covers the beaches and the hill, goes from 10:30am to 11pm in the summer and costs 6€. You get a discount if you want to do both: 9€ for the double run.

BY TAXI

Allo **Taxi Cannes** (☎ 08-90-71-22-27) is open 24 hours a day.

BICYCLE

Rent one at **Alliance Location** (9 rue des Frères-Pradignac; ☎ 04-93-38-62-62); or **Mistral Location** (4 rue Clemenceau; ☎ 04-93-99-25-25).

Tourist Information

○ **Bureau du Palais des Festivals** (esplanade Georges-Pompidou; ☎ 04-92-99-84-22; www.cannes.com; daily July—Aug 9am—8pm; off season 9am—7pm)

○ **Bureau Gare SNCF** (rue Jean-Jaures/place de la Gare; ☎ 04-93-99-19-17; Mon—Sat 9am—7pm)

○ **Cannes La Bocca** (1 rue Pierre-Semard; ☎ 04-93-47-04-12; Tues—Sat 9am—noon and 2:30—6:30pm)

Recommended Website

○ **Cannes-on-line.com:** A great website with lots of city service information.

cannes **Nuts & Bolts**

Car Rental   Try **Avis,** on 69 la Croisette (☎ **04-93-94-15-86**); **Ada,** on 91 bd. Carnot (☎ **04-93-38-38-93**); **Europcar,** on 3 rue Commandant-Vital (☎ **04-93-06-26-30**); or **Hertz** on 147 rue d'Antibes (☎ **04-93-99-04-20**).

Emergencies   Call ☎ **15** or 04-93-69-71-50.

Hospitals   **L'Hôpital des Broussailles** is on 13 av. des Broussailles (☎ **04-93-69-70-00**).

Internet/Wireless Hot Spots   Log on at **Cyber Internet,** which has two locations: one at 32 rue Jean-Jaures; ☎ **04-93-38-49- 97**) and the other at 12 rue du 24 août (☎ **04-93-38-85-63**).

Laundromat   Try the **Laverie Club** (36 rue Georges Clemenceau; ☎ **04-93-38-06-68;** Mon–Fri 8:30am–6:30pm, Sat 8:30am–12:30pm; bus: 8 to Palais des Congrès).

Post Office   Located at 78 av. Francis Tonner in La Bocca (☎ **04-93-48-70-00**).

Sleeping

Other than the week of The Festival, when the inflation is too ridiculous to mention, Cannes is surprisingly affordable. It's a convention city, so crowds ebb and flow. You should make a reservation if you want to guarantee a room. The prices mentioned below do not cover the festival week.

HOSTELS

→**Auberge de Jeunesse Le Chalit** Conveniently located a few minutes away from both the train and beach (although you'll exercise your leg muscles walking there), Le Chalit is unaffiliated with the FUAJ, so you won't need a card. But it looks, smells, and feels like a hostel anyway. There are two four-person rooms and one room with four bunk beds, although they squeeze in 27 people in the summer somehow. You can rent bedding, but they'll lock you out from 11am to 3pm. Rooms vary from 18 to 20€ off season and up to 30€ during the festival. You have to stay for at least 2 nights, and they turn the power off at midnight. Hopefully your coordination is good enough that you won't break anything. *27 av. du Marechal Gallieni.* ☎ *04-93-99-22-11. 18€–30€ bed. Closed Nov and Jan. Amenities: Kitchen, laundry, Wi-Fi.*

→**Iris Hostel** Seven minutes from the train station and beach, this hostel is slightly bigger than the Auberge, and it's open year-round. Sheets are included, and rooms sleep two to six people. The funky Mexican restaurant next door runs salsa lessons and Latino nights with a DJ. *77 bd. Carnot.* ☎ *04-93-68-30-20. www.Iris-solola. com. 20€ per person per night (except during the festival and congrès). Amenities: Internet access; no curfew; no need for a FUAJ card.*

CHEAP

→**Des Allées** The Côte d'Azur's first non-smoking hotel has 10 rooms, all of them renovated, with bathrooms, TV, and Wi-Fi; some even have a balcony with a view of the old port. *6 rue Émile Negrin.* ☎ *04-93-39-53-90. www.hotel-des-allees.com. 60€–90€ Credit cards accepted. In room: A/C, satellite TV, free Wi-Fi, hair dryer, safe.*

→**Hôtel Chanteclair** The rooms are small, the beds even smaller, but the place is clean and has a pretty orange tree-clad

LA CÔTE D'AZUR (FRENCH RIVIERA)

courtyard. You can leave your bags in a locker without a problem if you're leaving later than checkout, and Monsieur Deflene will turn his head if you want to squeeze more people than beds into a room. But beware, during some periods you'll have to reserve for 2 nights. *12 rue Forville.* ☎ *04-09-33-96-88. 40€–50€. No credit cards. Bus: 5 to La Ferrage. In room: Safe.*

→ **Hôtel L'Esterel** Fifty-five modernized rooms at the right price are air-conditioned and noise proof. The top floor has a terrace with a gorgeous view of the bay and the mountains. The location is terrific too, just a few steps away from the Croisette. *15 rue du 24 aout.* ☎ *04-93-38-82-82. www.hotel-esterel-cannes.cote.azur.fr/page_en_1.html. From 50€–80€ double. Credit cards accepted. Amenities: Fax; free parking. In room: A/C, satellite TV, free Wi-Fi, hair dryer, safe.*

DOABLE

→ **Le Chalet de l'Isere** The former home of Guy de Maupassant has turned itself into a cute little hotel, with small rooms and attractive, kind staff members of the sort you want to kiss on the forehead for being so hospitable. Ain't much of the chalet about this place, but the eight rooms are comfortable and pretty. *42 av. de Grasse.* ☎ *04-93-38-50-80. From 60€–80€ double. excellent fixed-price menu 20€–34€. Credit cards accepted. Amenities: Bar/restaurant. In room: TV, Internet.*

SPLURGE

→ **Hôtel Le Florian** Does the decor in this one scream Bates Motel to you, too? Okay, good. Otherwise, no problem: It's clean, modern, comfortable, and really well located, practically astride la Croisette. *8 rue Commandant-André.* ☎ *04-93-39-24-82. www.hotel-leflorian.com. 50€–75€ double. Credit cards accepted. Closed Dec to mid-Jan. In room: A/C, TV, hair dryer.*

→ **Hôtel Majestic Barriere** At the *summum bonum* of hip Cannesian hotelerie, you'll be treated like a VIP as long as you pay up like one. It's got almost 300 classy, sophisticated rooms on top of the Croisette, with its own private beach. It's also got a great brasserie (Fouquet's), a smoking room, and a funky bar. Even the pool is adorned with Murano glass. *10 la Croisette.* ☎ *04-92-98-77-00. 220€–900€ single, 430€–850€ double. Credit cards accepted. Closed mid-Nov to late Dec. Amenities: Bar; 3 restaurants; babysitting; beauty salon; casino; elevator; fitness center; golf; laundry; parking; pool; tennis; watersports. In room: A/C, satellite TV, minibar, safe.*

→ **Hôtel Olivier** All 24 rooms have bathrooms and color TVs, air-conditioning, and sound protection. Built more than a hundred years ago as someone's plush pad, this place takes you away from the roaring crowd without dumping you too far away. More than fifty restaurants lie within stumbling-home distance, and you can read and burnish yourself by the lovely pool. *5 rue des Tambourinaires* ☎ *04-93-39-53-28. www.Hotelolivier.com. 70€–90€ double in off season. Credit cards accepted. Amenities: Bar; dry cleaning; laundry service; limited room service; nonsmoking rooms; outdoor pool. In room: A/C, TV, dataport, hair dryer.*

→ **Hôtel 3,14** Holy moly. What were they smoking when they came up with this place? And can we get some, please? You'll be greeted by a fountain made of Murano glass and a garden dwarf named Shanty. Walk past the water curtain toward reception and put down your bags. Maybe sit down and order a cocktail—you might need one. Every floor is continent-themed, and rooms are decorated to match: pearly curtains and embroidered cushions for the Middle East, Parisian cabarets on the European floor, pop art for America. It's creative, peppy, fun, and we love it—

especially the amazing rooftop pool. *5 rue François-Einesy.* ☎ *04-92-99-72-00. From 170€–300€ double. Credit cards accepted. Amenities: Restaurant; 2 bars; babysitting; fitness center; gift shop; outdoor pool; parking; whirlpool. In room: A/C, TV, hair dryer, minibar, safe.*

➔ **Le Splendid** It looks like a ship, or maybe a wedding cake, but inside, the owner Annick Cagnat will take care of your every last little need. La Splendid has beautiful rooms and majestic balconies (for which you'll pay more), and everything is in place for you to spend the most romantic night of your life. Canoodle with breakfast in bed, take a luxurious bath in the tub, and you'll emerge feeling like one of the movie stars on the Croisette when you come out. *4–5 rue Felix-Faure.* ☎ *04-93-99-55-02 www.splendid-hotel-cannes.fr. 124€–160€ double, depending on the season and the room. Credit cards accepted. Rates include breakfast (a significant perk). Amenities: Babysitting; limited-mobility rooms; limited room service; nonsmoking rooms. In room: A/C, TV/VCR, hair dryer, Internet, safe.*

Eating

The Suquet has lots of places to eat, as does the *carré magique* (magic square), around the rue du Commandant-Andre. The closer you are to the top of the rue d'Antibes towards la Californie, the more expensive the places get; farther west, the prices drop gradually.

COFFEE BARS & LIGHT FARE

➔ **La Cascade des Glaces** Ice cream and cocktails with a sea view—what could be better? This adorable little place sources all its wines from the vineyards without jacking up the prices. Their giant salads are just what salads should be—fresh and made with quality products. They make all their own ice creams and change the menu; check the chalkboard for

it. Expect to pay 20€ for a copious meal. *12 bd. Jean-Hibert, on the plages du Midi.* ☎ *04-93-39-85-18. Main courses 12€–20€. Credit cards accepted. Daily 7am–2:30pm in summer, 8am–7pm in the winter; closed Nov.*

➔ **Volupte** If you're a tea freak, this is your place. Owner Teresa makes a bunch of different teas, and sources the best from all over the world. Everything is homemade, presented beautifully, and served with a smile. It's a great place for breakfast, or come for brunch on Saturday mornings, when the *jeunesse cannoise* flirt and canoodle over the little Italian *patisseries.* *32 rue Hoche.* ☎ *04-93-39-60-32. Main courses 15€–20€. Credit cards accepted. Mon–Sat 8:30am–7:30pm.*

CHEAP

➔ **Le Lion d'Or** In business for 60-plus years, they still make everything themselves, just like mom (not mine, not yours, but maybe theirs) used to. Try the *osso buco de laperau, fenouil, et basilic,* the house specialty. *45 bd. de la République.* ☎ *04-93-38-56-57. Menus 12€–20€. Credit cards accepted. Closed Sun nights and Wed; otherwise open lunch and dinner.*

➔ **Simplicité** Simplicity's the word, from the decor to the food, but they could just as well have called it elegance. The wife of renowned Cannesian restaurateur-slash-institution Noel Mantel has opened a great little joint right behind La Croisette. She serves the best of the regional cuisine: stuffed sardines, aioli, pistou, and the like. Reservations are definitely a good idea. *5 rue Jean-Daumas.* ☎ *04-93-68-27-40. Menus 9€–15€. Credit cards accepted. Mon–Tues and Thurs–Sat noon–2pm and 7–10:30pm.*

DOABLE

MTV Best ➔ **Astoux et Brun** An all-call to seafood lovers everywhere: Astoux et Brun is where you'll find the best *fruits de mer* on the Côte d'Azur, no doubt about it. Splurge on the seafood platter, or just content yourself with oysters. The decor ain't why everyone and their mother flocks here, that's for sure. *27 rue Felix Faure.* ☎ *04-93-39-21-87. Menus 30 €–45€. Credit cards accepted. Daily noon–11pm.*

➜ **La Brouette de Grand-Mère** You may need "grandmother's wheelbarrow" (the translation of this restaurant's name) to cart you out of here, after sampling their gigantic portions of things like *poulette a la bière brune* and *pot-au-feu aux cinq viandes.* And you heard right: no choices. But trust them to do you well. The welcome glass of champagne should put you at ease. *9 bis rue d'Oran.* ☎ *04-93-39-12-10. Menu 35€. Credit cards accepted. Mon–Sat 7–11pm.*

SPLURGE

➜ **Barbarella** Everything here exudes finesse: the Starck furniture, the flowers, the sober-chic lighting, and especially the food. If the confited oranges with the exceptional house-prepared foie gras is on the menu, take it! *16 rue Saint-Dizier.* ☎ *04-92-99-17-33. Menus 30€–40€, excluding wine. Credit cards accepted. Tues–Sun noon–2pm and 7–11pm.*

➜ **Villa de Lys** Have your caviar with green beans on a glamorous terrace alongside La Croisette, surrounded by Jacques Garcia's ostentatious decor. This is one of the most famous and well-respected restaurants on the Côte d'Azur, and rightly so. *Majestic Barriere, 10 La Croisette.* ☎ *04-92-98-77-41. Menus from 65€–125€. Credit cards accepted. Tues–Sat 7:30–10pm.*

Partying

Cannes, especially during The Festival, redefines P-A-R-T-Y-I-N-G. The nightlife here rivals that of any other nightspots in the world. Whether you're into your house, your hip-hop, or your jazz, there's something here for you. But while you

Très Gay!

Cannes has the best gay bars on the Côte d'Azur. For a complete listing of them—and all else queer on the French Riviera—look for the zines in the tourist office.

might get away with looking scruffy in Nice or St-Tropez, it won't be tolerated in Cannes. Don't expect to get in if you don't look the part. Of course, if you're not looking for the hottest clubs, you can wear whatever you want.

Most of the action goes down in the magic square around the rue du Commandant-Andre.

CLUBS & LIVE MUSIC VENUES

➜ **4U** Come for pre-dinner aperitifs at 6pm, when you can much on a little tapa with your first cocktail, but then stay to dance the night away. And it's not just the liquid; the music *is* getting progressively louder as time goes by. Look good, baby. *6 rue des Frères Pradignac.* ☎ *04-93-39-71-21.*

MTV Best ➜ **Le Baoli** You'll have something to tell the grandkids if you get into this club, the hottest in Cannes. Look good, because they'll judge you at the door. And don't take it personally if you don't pass—I didn't get in either. *Bd. de la Croisette Port Canto.* ☎ *04-93-43-03-43.*

➜ **Le Hype** Cannes's friendliest gay club has a different theme every night: Wednesdays are for jazz, or come in bell bottoms for '70s Sundays. Whatever you do, don't wear your vinyl pants, unless they're chaps—you'll stick to the seats. *52 bd. Jean-Jaures.* ☎ *04-93-39-20-50.*

➜ **Le Living Room** Ever had champagne in a Burgundy glass with ice cubes? Robert Parker would pass out, but try it and see how you like it. *13 rue du Docteur Gerard Monod.* ☎ *06-26-17-25-82.*

➔ **Le Zanzibar** This bar has been around forever and become a Cannes classic. It's laid-back, relaxed, and the music won't blow the skin off your face. *85 rue Felix Faure.* ☎ *04-93-39-30-75. No credit cards.*

Sightseeing

HISTORIC NEIGHBORHOODS

➔ **La Californie** This was a Russian colony at the end of the 19th century, and lots of pretty and weird houses still stand there. See the villa Excelsior at no. 9, the palace of la Californie. The château Louis XIII on the avenue de la Tropicale is typical of the *troubadour* style *très en vogue* at the turn of the century. The **Villa des Lotus** (42 av. du Roi Albert Ier) has some ridiculous chimneys and colors. Finally, seek out the medieval-esque château Scoot on 151 av. du Marechal—Juin.

PUBLIC MONUMENTS

➔ **L'allée des Etoiles du Cinéma** This ain't Planet Hollywood, it's the real thing! More than 200 stars have left their hand-prints here. Come and see whose fits yours most comfortably, then write them a creepy letter about it. *Esplanade Georges-Pompidou and around the Palais des Festivals.*

MUSEUMS

➔ **Le Palais des Festivals** We couldn't decide whether Le Palais was a church or a museum, but our moms don't like it when we blaspheme, so here it is—the place where it all goes down, come The Festival. Le Palais looks like a bunker, but inside is a 2,500-person auditorium, a theater that seats 1,000, and a reception room fit for 3,000 people—although most of the people who make it in here are about half an average person's size. The red carpet stays outside all year, so get your new Danish backpacker friends to snap a picture. *Esplanade Georges Pompidou.* ☎ *33-04-93-39-01-01. www.palaisdesfestivals.com. Ticket prices vary; sold daily 10am–7pm (until 8pm in summer).*

TWO SPECIAL TOURS

The Suquet is where most of Old Cannes lies, and it's a good spot to start your exploration of the city. Check out the church of **Notre-Dame d'Esperance,** on the place de la Castre, for an example of Provençal Gothic. The rue St-Antoine has what looks like (but thankfully isn't) every restaurant in Cannes—it has its share of bad, but some of the best in town are here too. Climb up to the place de la Castre, in front of the museum. It's a hike, but what a view when you're up there: the Croisette at your feet; la Californie, with its crazy villas; and in between, the town hall, the old port, and the rue d'Antibes. Farther off is the beautiful iles de Lerins.

➔ **La Croisette** It's hard to believe that what unimaginative villagers once called *le chemin du Bord-de-Mer* has turned into one of the most glamorous streets in the world—and one of the most expensive spots in the universe to buy real estate. Walk by the Art Deco Majestic, the Belle Epoque Malmaison, the 🅜 Best❷ **InterContinental Carlton**'s 150m (492 ft.) elaborate facade—its cupolas inspired, supposedly, by the breasts of a beautiful gypsy by the name of la Belle Otero. The Art Deco Martinez is a worthy distraction from the topless sunbathers, and then near the Port Pierre-Canto, you can stop under the rosebushes for a breather. If you walk all the way to the end of the Croisette, you'll see an amazing view of the *golfe de la Napoule,* the cap d'Antibes and the Prealpes east, and the iles de Lerins. Keep walking until the end of shady, refreshing Palm Beach, and watch the old-schoolers play petanques near the place de l'Etang. Walk back up the way you came, but one street parallel, on the rue d'Antibes—the best place in Cannes to see and be seen.

Playing Outside

→ **Le Cimetière du Grand Jas** Don't think us morbid, but the cemetery is the biggest and best park in Cannes. It's a multilevel expanse of trees, flowers, gorgeous views of the bay, and, yes, graves. *205 av. de Grasse.* ☎ *04-93-99-48-18.*

→ **Les Plages** If the rocky beaches in Nice disappointed you, Cannes's will do you right. The public beaches are along the boulevard du Midi, west of the port, but if you spend a little (20€, say), you can get a beach mattress and plop down on one of the private stretches of sand on la Croisette. We like Ecrin, on the port Canto.

→ **Une Plage Deserte** For the same 20€, you can take a boat to a beach where you'll have the water and sand almost all to yourself. *Bijou Plage, next to the Port Canto.* ☎ *06-14-42-50-42. Mid-June to mid-Sept.*

Shopping

La Croisette and the rue d'Antibes host most of the shopping, and Cannes is a shopper's dream, befitting a celebrity town.

CLOTHING & ACCESSORIES

→ **Mercedeh Shoes** An astonishing Côte d'Azur institution for women who love blisters, credit card bills, and envious looks from other women with the same predilections. *130 rue d'Antibes.* ☎ *04-93-68-21-28.*

MUSIC, BOOKS & MEDIA

If you want to collect movie posters and you're here during the Festival, you'll find merchants selling them near the port, the esplanade Malmaison, or on the rue des Belges.

→ **Cannes English Bookshop** Hey look at that, it ain't just romance novels! Open for more than 20 years, this place sometimes hosts book signings with famous authors. But if no one's there, at least 3,000 books are. *11 rue Bivouac Napoléon.* ☎ *04-93-99-40-08. Mon–Sat 10am–6:45pm.*

→ **Cine Folies** If you came to Cannes because you *luuurve* the stars, this tiny, charming boutique's for you. Crammed full with photos, posters, collectors' celluloid, and dreams. *14 rue des Freres-Pradignac.* ☎ *04-93-39-22-99. Daily 10:30am–12:30pm and 2:30–7:30pm.*

MARKETS

→ **Marché Forville** This stunning covered market sells produce every morning except Monday, when it turns into a *marché de brocantes* (flea market). *Behind the old port on rue de M Forville. Tues–Sun produce; Mon flea market.*

FOOD, WINE & LOCAL CRAFTS

→ **Choptel** This shop should really go under clothing and accessories, but because it's such a Cannes thing, we decided to categorize it as local craft. A Choptel is a little pom-pom that you tie to your cellphone so that you can find it easily in your handbag; draping it over the edge says "Hey, commoners, I've been to Cannes." And it's not just for girls and metrosexuals. If this is your thing, buy one at Jacques Dessange hair salons, or at OngleStar. Did we mention it costs 50€? *4 rue Chabaud.* ☎ *33-6-20-06-61-76. www. choptel.com.*

→ **Les Thés Duval** This place sells 200 kinds of Mariage Frères tea, in tea form, but also in gelée, gingerbread, and gift baskets. The wooden shopfront is remarkable, and the shop is even more so. *16 rue Buttura.* ☎ *04-93-38-54-85. Tues–Sun 9:30am–12:30pm daily 2–6pm*

Side Trips

STE-MARGUERITE

Getting to Ste-Marguerite takes 15 minutes, and boats come and go every hour, from 7:30am to 6:15pm in the summer (until 4:15pm in the winter). The ferry that will take you is the **Trans Côte d'Azur** (☎ **04-92-98-71-30;** www.trans-cote-azur. com; 11€), on the quai Laubeuf.

Already the Romans had discovered the seductive charms of the Ile Ste-Marguerite in the 4th century B.C., having built a fortification there. But after a flood in the first century that covered the island (they think, anyway; it's hard to know these things), the island was left to decrepitude. It remained pretty much empty until Charles de Lorraine built a castle there in 1621, which was used as a prison that housed, notably, the famous *masque de fer,* or Man in the Iron Mask, a prisoner who stayed for 12 years, made famous by novelist Alexandre Dumas. Who was it? No one knows; perhaps it was Louis de Bourbon, or a twin or half-brother of Louis XIV, or Foucquiet the ex-superintendent of finances? Whoever he was, at least he had a view, and it's not like he was missing out on the Croisette scene at that point anyway!

The island also has a little Musée de la Mer, open only for three months in summer, which you can visit for 2€ to 3€. The best part about the iles de Lerins are the acres of forest through which you can amble. You can swim in the mini-inlets, so bring a bathing suit. It's a great day away from the rest of the hubbub.

ST-HONORAT

Getting to St-Honorat takes 25 minutes, and boats come and go every hour, from 7:30am to 6:15pm in the summer (until 4:15pm in the winter). Because it's still a private island, only the **Société Planaria** on the quai Laubeuf will take you there; call them on ☎ **04-92-98-71-38.**

St-Honorat houses one of the oldest abbeys in the entire history of the Christian religion. St-Honorat himself settled there in the year 400 with just a few acolytes. The first tower was built around 1073, and by the seventh century, Lerins was one of Europe's most important monasteries. Even today, monks are still cultivating vines, lavender, rosemary, and other plants, with which they make *lerina,* their liquor, and a wine known as *la vendange des moines.* If you're so moved, you can stay at the monastery, as long as you agree to take a vow of silence.

Nice: La Belle Dame de la Mediterranée

929km (576 miles) directly S of Paris, 32km (20 miles) NE of Cannes

Sure, on first glance, it's easy to dismiss Nice as just another member among the passel of the Côte d'Azur's loud, smarmy resort towns—although it's bigger and filled with more beeping scooters hustling you out of the way. But France's "fifth city" conceals much more than meets the eye, and the benevolent year-round sunshine (2,640 annual hr.) smiling down on "Nissa la belle" makes the crime rate and traffic an afterthought—almost. For years, wealthy retirees populated the bulk of Nice. Today, 50% of the population is under 40. Vibrant and bustling, it's now an art-and-culture town with more museums, hotels, and a busier airport than any other French city after Paris.

Located as it is between the hips of Italy and France, Nice's history necessarily belongs to both, a fact evident in the architecture, accents, and food on display. Phoenician Greeks, Romans, and Saracens left marks on their way through town as well, but after an unfortunate incident involving the Queen of Sicily (death by smothering), the Niçois decided to hand themselves over to the Counts of Savoy. The next couple of centuries saw the Niçois bopping between whomever was experiencing greater prosperity at the time: Louis XIV, the Sicilians, 20 years of the bloody Republic, the Sardinians. Finally, in 1860, after the Treaty of Turin between Napoleon III and the King of Sardinia, Nice became French again. Napoleon made good on his promise to build a town hall, school, roads, dams, and railroads. *Après lui, le déluge:* the touristic development of the Côte d'Azur.

The first of the foreigners who recognized the value of the Côte D'Azur didn't need good roads. Englishmen first trod upon the (then) rocky soil in the mid–18th century, and by 1827, about 500 rich English families were wintering in Nice (too much sun was thought negative, so people came during what today is the off season). The *promenade des Anglais,* which follows the sea from west to east, was in fact built by English subscriptions in 1822. Queen Victoria's 1890 vacation in Nice ensconced it firmly on the map. The Russian aristocracy became enamored of Nice, too, leaving for posterity their spectacular orthodox church and the parc Valrose. Artists such as Matisse in the 1940s; Yves Klein, Christo, and Arman in the 1960s; and the hubbub stirred up around them (the Musée d'Art Moderne et d'Art Contemporain, for instance), added to Nice's appeal as an artistic hub. Although financial controversies and crime have thrust Nice into more headlines than the tourist office would like to admit, *la belle* still welcomes more than four million visitors a year who wouldn't think of allowing eastern European prostitution rings and corruption scandals to affect their even tans.

Getting There

BY AIR

On the west end of the promenade des Anglais, 8km (5 miles) from the town center, is Nice's international airport. **Aéroport Nice-Côte d'Azur** (☎ 08-20-42-22-22; www.nice.aeroport.fr) is the second biggest airport in France, and the views for those flying in are incredible. From there, get to town by bus, which comes every 20 minutes. Taxis cost 25€ to 30€.

BY TRAIN

The train is the best way to get here, considering the traffic around Nice, especially in the summer. The train station (gare SNCF) is in the center of town (av. Thiers), a 15-minute walk from the promenade des Anglais and the beach. The network of Trains Express Regionaux connects Nice to towns all the way west to St-Raphael and east to Vintimille in Italy, following the blue line of the ocean, a beautiful ride. From July to September, you can buy a first-class ticket to any of the trains on this network for 10€, valid all day. Otherwise, the TGV will take you to Paris in 5½ hours, although a reservation is highly recommended, especially during high season. Being the biggest city on the Côte d'Azur, Nice is the one to which most trains coming from other cities in France go; catch one to and from Metz, Dijon, Geneva, Lille, and more (**Gare SNCF Avenue Thiers;** ☎ 08-92-35-25-35). And to think that in 1863, when it was built, the train station was in the middle of the Niçois countryside. Now it's just a 15-minute walk from the sea (it was then, too, but that's just harder to visualize).

BY CAR

The A8 highway and smaller roads—the N7, N98, N202 and the route Napoléon—all lead to Nice. Nice is full of traffic and crazed drivers; this writer had the only car accident of her life in Nice, and the first words from the mouth of the man who hit her were "Oh no, not again!" Even though parking is expensive, the town is walkable, and the

Nice

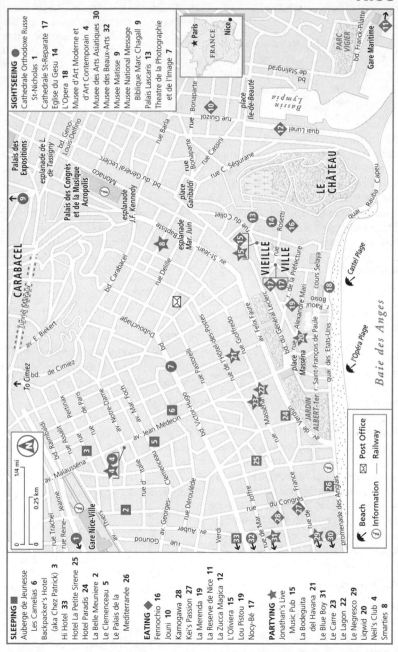

SIGHTSEEING ●

Cathedrale Orthodoxe Russe
St-Nicholas **1**
Cathedrale St-Reparate **17**
Eglise du Gesu **14**
L'Opera **18**
Musee d'Art Moderne et
d'Art Contemporain **4**
Musee des Arts Asiatiques **30**
Musee des Beaux-Arts **32**
Musee Matisse **9**
Musee National Message
Biblique Marc Chagall **9**
Palais Lascaris **13**
Theatre de la Photographie
et de l'Image **7**

SLEEPING ■

Auberge de Jeunesse
Les Camelias **6**
Backpacker's Hotel
(aka Chez Patrick) **3**
Hi Hotel **33**
Hotel La Petite Sirene **25**
Hotel Paradis **24**
La Belle Meuniere **2**
Le Clemenceau **5**
Le Palais de la
Mediterranée **26**

EATING ◆

Fennochio **16**
Jouni **10**
Kamogawa **28**
Kei's Passion **27**
La Merenda **19**
La Reserve de Nice **11**
La Zucca Magica **12**
L'Oliviera **15**
Lou Pistou **19**
Nocy-Bé **17**

PARTYING ★

Jonathan's Live
Music Pub **15**
La Bodeguita
del Havana **21**
Le Blue Boy **31**
Le Carre **23**
Le Lagon **22**
Le Negresco **29**
Liqwid **20**
Neil's Club **4**
Smarties **8**

✖ Post Office
— Railway

🏊 Beach
ⓘ Information

buses easy to navigate. This writer's conclusion: There's no reason to drive.

BY BOAT

Nice is one of the primary ports to and from Corsica, and it's very navigable. In season, several carriers offer up to eight ferries a day. The port is on quai Amiral Infernet (☎ **08-20-42-55-55;** www. riviera-ports.com).

BY BUS

Annoyingly, the bus station, **Gare Routière de Nice** (Promenade du Paillon; ☎ **04-93-80-08-70**), is not that close to the train station. That said, buses are available to take you to pretty much any town on the Côte d'Azur and behind it. Buses are modern, comfortable, and cheap.

Orientation

Anything south of the promenade des Anglais is ocean; anything north, Nice. The center-city starts east of the boulevard Gambetta. It's made up of even blocks until the wide, shop-lined, north-south boulevard Jean-Médecin, through which a tramway is (very slowly) being built. Pedestrian avenues rue Massena and rue de France are busy by day with shoppers and strollers, by night with dolled-up ladies and gents taking in the air before hitting the clubs. Southeast of the boulevard Jean-Jaures is the Vieille Ville, a confusion of charming narrow alleys filled with locals hanging their laundry and selling tourists souvenirs. East of the Vieille Ville is the port, from which the ferries to Corsica push off. Northeast of the train station is Cimiez, a ritzy residential neighborhood that houses most of Nice's museums.

Getting Around

BY PUBLIC TRANSPORTATION

Gas-powered Sunbuses circulate around town, but only until 9pm, when only 4 of the 40 lines keep going. Place Massena is a

good place to catch one. Individual tickets cost 1.30€, or buy a day pass for 4€.

It's not exactly public, but Nice also has one of the little white touristic trains that putt-putts around the city. This one will take you on a circuit—through the flower market, the old city, the view of the port, the castle, belvedere and bay of angels, and the quai des Etats-Unis—before returning you to the starting point opposite the Albert Ier gardens, on the seafront. The trip lasts about 40 minutes and costs 6€. Trains leave every 30 minutes, but don't operate when it's raining. Call ☎ 06-16-39-53-51 for information. Service runs 10am to 6pm April to May, 10am to 7pm June to August, 10am to 6pm September, 10am to 5pm October to March. Closed mid-November to mid-December and for a few weeks in January.

BY BICYCLE

Rent bikes and Scooters at **Energy Scoot** on the promenade des Anglais at the rue St. Philippe. Prices start at 35€ a day (☎ **04-97-07-12-64**). Or try **Nicea Location Rent** on 12 rue de Belgique, near the train station (☎ **04-93-82-42-71**).

BY TAXI

There is a taxi stand on the place Massena and one near the Hôtel Meridien, but these are more operational during the day than they are at night, which is when you want them. But you can always call **Central Taxi Riviera** at ☎ **04-93-13-78-78.**

ON FOOT

Go for a Saturday-morning guided tour of Old Nice. It leaves from the office du tourisme on the promenade des Anglais. Reservation required (12€); call the OT (see phone numbers for tourist offices, below).

Tourist Offices

Nice's tourism office (www.nicetourisme. com) is highly organized, and everyone there speaks English. You can get a museum card for 27€, which will get you into 62 regional museums for a week. Cards are available at the museums as well.

○ **Office de Tourisme:** 5 promenade des Anglais across the boardwalk (☎ **08-92-70-74-07**; Mon—Sat 8am—8pm, Sun 9am—7pm).

○ **Office de Tourisme:** Gare SNCF on the avenue Thiers (☎ **33-08-92-70-74-07**; Mon—Sat 8am—8pm, Sun 9am—7pm).

○ **Office de Tourisme:** Airport, Terminal 1 (☎ **33-08-92-70-74-07**; daily 8am—9pm).

Nice Nuts & Bolts

Car Rental   Rent an old-school Cabriolet from Le Road-Show and tumble around the Côte d'Azur in style. Available: Fiat Spider Europas, Mercedes SLs, Chrisler Le Barons, and so on. For 390€, you get a convertible for two people for a day, a detailed roadbook with a suggested circuit and driving tips to help you through the region, a meal for two including wine and coffee, a snack-stop, gas, insurance, and help on the road (219 bd. du Mont-Boron; ☎ **04-92-04-01-05**; www.azur-roadshow.com). To rent a more ordinary vehicle, you'll find the usual suspects (Ada, Avis, Budget, Europcar, Sixt) at the train station, or near the Hôtel Meridien in the center of town.

Emergencies   If you need help, call ☎ **08-10-85-01-01**.

Exchange Money   Try **Cofima** (SARL) 2 rue de France (☎ **04-93-87-12-31**); **Arin-Sauclieres,** at 9 av. Jean Médecin (☎ **04-93-87-82-62**); or **Change Mediterranée,** at 17 av. Jean Médecin (☎ **04-93-87-99-72**).

Hospitals   Call a doctor at ☎ **08-10-85-01-01** or 08-10-85-05-05. The **Hôpital St-Roche** is on rue Pierre-Devoluy (☎ **04-92-03-33-75**).

Lost Property   Call ☎ **04-93-80-65-50**.

Post Office   The post office is at 23 av. Thiers (☎ **04-93-82-65-00**; Mon—Fri 8am—7pm, Sat 8am—noon).

Pharmacies   There's an all-night pharmacy at 45 av. Jean-Médecin (Mon—Sat 24 hr., Sun 7:30pm—8am). Another on 7 rue Massena is open at the same times.

Sleeping

Rule of thumb: The closer you are to the beach, the more expensive your room will be. Most of the town's affordable sleeping happens around the train station, a neighborhood that lacks charm but does the job. Three words of advice for those coming in high season: reserve, reserve, reserve.

HOSTELS

→ **Auberge de Jeunesse Les Camelias**
The youth hostel is one of the cheapest

places to sleep in Nice, and it ain't bad, either. It's 10 minutes from the station and close to the Old Town, and someone is at the reception desk 24 hours a day. You'll need a FUAJ card, but you can buy one on-site. Rooms have 3, 4, 6, or 8 beds, and bedding is rentable. Reservations are only possible on the Internet (www.fuaj.org) unless you call or come in that day. *3 rue Spitalieri.* ☎ *04-93-80-42-64. 19€ bed. Rate includes breakfast.*

→ **Clair-Vallon** It's like the hostel, only you don't need to be young or have a FUAJ card to stay here. The ambience is more "commune" than "charming" in this hotel near the Cimiez neighborhood, close to many Nice museums and classy shopping. They have a pool, and you can sleep in one of the four-, six-, or eight-person rooms for 15€ including breakfast. Negative reports of the place abound, but did we already mention it costs 15€ per night? *26 av. Scuderi.* ☎ *04-93-81-27-63. 15€ bed. Bus: 15 from the train station. Amenities: Pool.*

CHEAP

→ **Backpacker's Hotel (aka Chez Patrick)** The rooms are the epitome of simplicity, but you didn't come here to stay inside, did you? And they're clean, so no one's complaining. Plus, as befits the name, loads of backpackers congregate here (it seems to have appeared in every guidebook ever published about Nice). *32 rue Pertinax, near the train station. www. chezpatrick.com.* ☎ *04-93-80-30-72. 40€– 45€ double; 18€–21€ per person 3- to 6-person room. Credit cards accepted.*

→ **Hôtel Paradis** One wouldn't expect a hostel that charges 20€ to 40€ per bed to squat between Louis Vuitton and Armani, but there's the Hôtel Paradis. Yes, it may be cheaper to stay uptown, but the location of this place—a 1-minute walk from the beach and a 2-minute walk from the Old Town, plus the fact that you won't have to pay bus or taxi fare to get around—makes the Paradis a winner. You can store luggage for free, use linen and towels for free, rent beach mats for free, and move in and out as you please. *1 rue du Paradis.* ☎ *04-93-87-71-23. www.paradishotel.com. 20€–40€ bed. Credit cards accepted. Amenities: Free Internet. In room: A/C, TV, minibar, safe.*

→ **La Belle Meuniere** Despite being only a hundred steps from the train station, this hotel, in a classy old villa, is elegantly ensconced amid pine and fig trees in a little garden, where the global backpacking

community congregates for picnics. If you're under 26 or a student, you can rent one of the beds in the two communal rooms for 15€ per person. A double with a shower is 50€ (bathroom in the hallway; pay an extra 6€ to have one in your room). *21 av. Durante.* ☎ *04-93-88-66-15. 15€ bed; 50€–56€ double. Closed late Nov to early Feb. Amenities: Laundry, parking, safe.*

DOABLE

→ **Hôtel La Petite Sirene** This quirky little old hotel, named after Hans Christian Andersen's story of the little mermaid, is situated in a quiet backstreet a few minutes off the promenade des Anglais. The 15 rooms are clothed in airy colors and equipped with bathrooms, air-conditioning, television, telephone, and fridge minibar (the penthouse has a kitchen and terrace). The bar specializes in cocktails, and hosts a half-price happy hour from Tuesday through Sunday between 5 and 7pm. *8 rue Maccarani.* ☎ *04-97-03-03-40. www.sirene-fr.com. 76€–152€ single, 112€– 286€ double, 137€–385€ 3- to 4-person penthouse. Credit cards accepted. Amenities: Restaurant/bar; elevator; parking; room service; safe. In room: A/C, satellite TV, hair dryer, Internet, minibar.*

→ **Le Clemenceau** This cutesy little joint is in a great location just north of the place Massena. The rooms look a bit like grandma decorated them, but they're air-conditioned and double-paned, and you can even get a kitchenette if you feel moved to try your own hand at *pan bagnat. 3 av. Clemenceau.* ☎ *04-93-88-61-19. 40€– 60€ double. Credit cards accepted. Amenities: Bar. In room: TV.*

SPLURGE

[MTV] Best ♥ → **Hi Hotel** If the Palais de la Mediterranée takes you back, the Hi Hotel, conceptualized by design wunderkind and Philippe Starck protégé Matali Crasset, takes you forward, into the future. Crasset is interested in "domesticating technology" and puts serious thought into making the beautiful workable, although some of her inventions are clearly prototypes: The shower, for instance, splashes water all over the floor. The panoramic terrace on the roof has a Jacuzzi and water beds, and there is a Turkish bath with massage options. Some rooms are decorated with giant pixels, some have sofas with built-in speakers, some have a wall of bamboo for a shower curtain, some have a gigantic television screen that serves as the door between the bed and the bathroom. Even if you never get to the hotel, I still suggest visiting the website while under the influence. You may never leave. *3 av. des Fleurs.* ☎ *04-97-07-26-26. www.hi-hotel.net. 190€– 680€ double. Amenities: Bar and snack bar; laundry service; limited-mobility room; non-smoking rooms; rooftop pool. In room: A/C, TV, Internet, hair dryer, minibar, safe.*

➼**Le Palais de la Mediterranée** In its glory days, the Palais once catered to Charlie Chaplin, Coco Chanel, Josephine Baker, and even her pig, but it was shut down in 1978 and mostly derelict by 1990. The makers of Taittinger champagne hired the specialists who'd worked on the cathedral in Chartes to renovate it, and boy, what a renaissance. Once you walk past the lofty, buffed lobby, the hotel has 188 Art Deco rooms and suites decorated in blue, ocher, and yellow; sea views; a fancy restaurant; and a glitzy casino. *13–15 promenade des Anglais.* ☎ *04-92-14-77-00. 350€– 470€ double. Credit cards accepted. Amenities: Restaurant; bar; casino; fitness center; limited-mobility rooms; nonsmoking rooms; 2 pools (indoor and outdoor); 24-hr. room service; Turkish bath; solarium; watersports. In room: A/C, TV, dataport, hair dryer, minibar, safe.*

Eating

COFFEE BARS & LIGHT FARE

➼**Fennochio** ICE CREAM Tomato and basil ice cream? Avocado sorbet? Beer, violet, or lavender ice cream? Yes, and yum. The 70-plus flavors on tap are all handmade, from almond to ginger to chewing gum. They're not cheap, but they are dee-licious. Fenoccio is a Nicean institution, so you've got to give it a try. *Place Rossetti.* ☎ *04-93-80-72-52.*

➼**Nocy-Be** TEAHOUSE Buried inside the quiet alleys in old Nice are a handful of oriental-style teahouses that combine an old-school look with a fresh new atmosphere. If you didn't know that tea came in colors, wander down to Nocy-Bye and try red, green, black, and white teas, served in ceramic or silver teapots. You could easily while away an afternoon drinking tea and smoking on the comfy *pouffes. 4–6 rue Jules-Gilly.* ☎ *04-93-85-52-25.*

CHEAP

➼**Kamogawa** JAPANESE Sick of cheese and meat? Cleanse thyself at Kamogawa, where you can get affordable and decent (for France) sushi, sashimi, tempura, chabu bhabu, and sukiyaki. No one's calling it authentic, but when you want that fresh, clean, raw-fish taste, head here. *18 rue de la Buffa.* ☎ *04-93-88-75-88. 15€–30€ per person. Credit cards accepted. Tues–Sun noon– 3pm and 7pm–midnight.*

➼**La Merenda** A stool-and-paper-tablecloth joint, where you should order the stockfish if you want to try something interesting: unsalted cod, dried and prepared with its own swim bladder. The waiters will let you taste it first. *4 rue de la Terrasse. No phone. 30€ per person. No credit cards. Mon–Fri seatings at 7:15 and 9:15pm.*

➼**La Zucca Magica** For a region with such a high quality of fresh vegetables, it's about time a purely vegetarian restaurant

Cuisine Nissarde

Cuisine nissarde has its own wonderful flavor, but it is easily lost among the host of restaurants that cater to tourists satisfied by food that's simply "French," which flattens the sharp regional distinctions that characterize French cuisine from north to south. *Cuisine nissarde* or *niçoise* fits within the broader category of *cuisine provençale,* but has a niche entirely its own. Like the rest of Provence, Nice's climate is warm and dry, with rainfall almost entirely in winter. The cooking has come to reflect that: A common dessert is **tarte aux blettes sucrée,** a sweet pie made with Swiss chard, and the famous **socca** is made with nothing other than chickpea flour, water, olive oil, and the occasional onion. Light, soft *niçois gnocchi* are known as **merde de can** (dog shit), made with Swiss chard and served with a sauce made either with tomato, pistou, or gorgonzola. **Petit farcis** are little stuffed vegetables cooked with a bit of water, oil, sea salt, and herbs such as basil or thyme. Typical local vegetables include zucchini, for which the flower is also utilized (delicious when deep-fried), fennel, artichoke, onion, tomatoes, peppers, eggplant, and other Mediterranean legumes, which are often stewed together into a **ratatouille. Pan bagnat** is like a salade Niçoise stuffed into a bun. **Pissaladiere** is a flat dough covered in cooked onions, topped with garlic, the occasional olive, or anchovy. Some people argue that it's the ancestor of pizza. **Salade niçoise** is a composed salad made with all raw ingredients (except for the hard-boiled egg). There isn't any vinegar involved, and the tomatoes (quartered) must be salted three times and dressed with olive oil. It must also have cucumber, fava bean, green pepper, garlic, onion, olives, anchovies, and basil. If you're interested in learning to cook *niçoise,* think about taking a class with **Rosa Jackson** (**www.rosajackson. com**). She has written a number of articles on *cuisine nissarde,* and she's a wealth of information on the best restaurants, beaches, food shops, and markets of the entire Côte d'Azur. She leads students on market tours, and then takes them back to her apartment in the Old Town to cook a four-course lunch.

did something special to feature them. La Zucca cooks delicious Italian food, subdividing it into five courses: soup, polenta, salad, pasta, and dessert for instance. And you don't pick the menu: The chef prepares five new courses every day. *4 bis quai Papacino (rue de Foresta).* ☎ *04-93-56-25-27. Lunch 17€, dinner 27€. No credit cards. Tues–Sat 12:30–2pm and 7pm–midnight. Bus: 1, 10, or 20.*

➜ **Produce & Flower Market on the Cours Saleya** This is the best place to sample traditional niçoise fare such as *socca* (chickpea pancakes), zucchini-blossom fritters, and *pissaladiere,* an onion tart with olives thought to be the ancestor of pizza. *No credit cards.*

DOABLE

➜ **La Reserve** Everyone's talking about 36-year-old Finnish chef Jouni Tormanen and his revival of the beautiful Belle Epoque Niçoise building, from which he runs La Reserve and its fancier brother **Jouni, atelier du Gout.** Start or end the evening with a drink at the rooftop bar, which has one of the most beautiful panoramic views of the Côte d'Azur. Then move down for one of three meat and fish menus in the splendid dining room, reminiscent of the pre-war glory days of Nice, and enjoy Tormanen's Finnish-influenced French cuisine. *60 bd. Franck Pilatte. ☎ 04-97-08-14-80. Prix-fixe menus average 35€–40€, excluding drinks. Credit cards accepted. Daily lunch and dinner.*

➜**L'Oliviera** Nadim Beyrouti's passion is olive oil, and the simple menu, which changes every night, pairs each dish with a different olive oil. Be your palate rough or refined, you'll be astonunded by the flavors that this simple fruit juice can evoke, from almond to green banana. *8 bis rue du Collet. ☎ 04-93-13-06-45. 25€ with wine.*

➜**Lou Pistou** This place is perfect Provençal in a cute French bistro setting, replete with red-and-white-checked linens. The kitchen hides behind a beaded curtain, and the servers are really nice. Go out on a limb and order the *tripes a la niçoise* in a tomato and white-wine sauce, or the roasted red peppers in garlic and olive oil. Above all, do not—I repeat, do not—leave before trying the lemon tart. *39 rue de la Terrasse. ☎ 04-93-62-21-82. Menus 30€ and 55€. Credit cards accepted. Mon–Fri 7–11:30pm.*

SPLURGE

➜**Jouni** Currently the hottest chef in town, this Finnish chef gets *maître d'hôtel* Giuseppe Serena to buy anything that swims, every morning in San Remo, then grills it *a la plancha*. Jouni seasons everything with olive oil, sea salt, and lemons, and presents it to the 20 diners sitting at *sympathique* wooden tables within terracotta walls. There is a daily risotto, a pasta or two, and a roast, often of pigeon. Reservations are imperative. *10 rue Lascaris. ☎ 04-97-08-14-80. www.jouni.fr. Lunch menu 30€; dinner menus 65€ and 90€. Credit cards accepted. Tues–Sat lunch and dinner.*

Partying

While Nice lacks the club scene of other Riviera towns, it makes up for it in great bars, some of which you can dance in. Nice has loads of students, and you know that means: It's an easy town to party in.

BARS

➜**Jonathan's Live Music Pub** Come sing karaoke here during the Wednesday Night Singing Challenge. On Tuesdays, happy hour lasts all night with a "meter of beer," and live music arrives on weekends. *1 rue de la Loge. ☎ 04-93-80-33-82. No credit cards.*

➜**La Bodeguita del Havana** Cuban-style bar and restaurant in a crazy Latin club situated on two floors. Pros: live music and salsa lessons on Wednesdays and Thursdays from 8:30 to 10:30pm. Cons: mediocre mojitos. *14 rue Chauvain. ☎ 04-93-92-67-24.*

➜**Le Carre** Ah, here's the Riviera you were looking for. Wear your best Eurotrashy sunglasses and smoke your skinny cigarettes while lounging on the zebra-striped couches or dancing to the funk, salsa, or house the DJs throw out. *6 passage Émile Negrin, in the pedestrian zone. ☎ 04-93-88-38-82.*

➜**Le Lagon** If Jonathan ain't your style, try your Idol voice at Le Lagon, where karaoke starts at midnight every night in the purple-and-green disco room. *2 rue Massena. ☎ 04-93-87-76-85.*

➜**Le Negresco** Start the night with a super-classy drink at the Negresco, a temple of polished wood and Belgian tapestry, complete with crystal whisky fountain. It won't be cheap, but it will be unforgettable. *37 promenade des Anglais. ☎ 04-93-16-64-00.*

CLUBS & LIVE MUSIC VENUES

Check out the *Officiel des Loisirs*, sold at newsstands, with details of everything going on around town, or *L'Exces*, which is free and focuses on where to party. For the gay scene, check out the *Lesbian & Gay*

Pride Côte d'Azur publication, free at local newsstands and the tourist office.

➜ **Guest** This spot only gets hot later in the night, but oh, then. The chandeliers and low lighting provide a sexy setting for lots of sinning, Nice-style. *5 quai des Deux Emmanuel.* ☎ *04-93-83-83.*

➜ **Le Blue Boy** At one of the oldest gay clubs on the Riviera, men of every age show up to dance on the blue neon floors. *9 rue Spinetta (near the rue Marechal Joffre). No credit cards.*

➜ **Liqwid** The hottest pre-party spot in the Old Town switches DJs every night. Lounge on the leather and velvet banquettes, and ponder how cool you are. *11 rue Alexandre Mari.* ☎ *04-93-76-14-28.*

➜ **Neil's Club** This is the busiest place in town for live music; check the list next to the door for the schedule of weekly concerts. Cover includes one drink. *10 Cité du Park in the old city. No credit cards.*

➜ **Smarties** This retro-cool lounge plays modern electronic jazz and has DJs on Tuesdays. *10 rue Defly.* ☎ *04-93-62-30-75.*

Sightseeing

Of course you came to Nice for the beaches, the bars, and the food. But Nice has a lot to offer culturally—more than any other towns on the Côte d'Azur.

PUBLIC MONUMENTS

➜ **L'Opéra** A tragic fire in 1881 burned down the old Niçois theater, killing 16 people. Four years later, François Aune (inspired by Charles Garnier) built this rococo masterpiece right behind the promenade des Anglais, curiously facing the cours Saleya area rather than the sea. It makes sense if you remember the fact that back in the day, people didn't give a fig about the sea, figuring both sun and ocean to be bad for the complexion. Anyway, if you get the chance, do go see a concert, opera, or ballet in the Italianate red-velvet interior. If you don't, console yourself by visiting Henri Auer, a few feet away, who continues unbroken the six-generation line of chocolatiers in the Auer family spinning gold for the Niçois. *4 rue St-François-de-Paule. www.opera-nice.org. Shows run Oct–June; admission varies.*

FREE ➜ **Palais Lascaris** In 1648, Jean-Baptiste Lascaris Vintimille bought four houses on the rue Droite and turned them into a palace. During the Revolution, it functioned as barracks. Then it was broken down into apartments, before the municipality purchased it in 1942, in order to restore it to its former glory. The interior is splendidly decorated with the family's coat of arms, an eagle, and a Maltese cross, and you'll get a kick out of the reconstituted 17th-century apothecary, with its collection of flagons and pots. Check out the *trompe l'oeil* frescoes on the ceiling of the top floor. *15 rue Droite.* ☎ *04-93-62-72-40. Free admission. Wed–Mon 10am–6pm. Guided tour at 3pm.*

➜ **Place Rosetti** Fountains and terraces make this the cutest and largest of the plazas in the Old Town, built in 1825 by tearing down old buildings so that people would have a better view of the cathedral. Now, it means you have a better view of both the cathedral and Fenocchio (see "Eating," above).

HISTORIC NEIGHBORHOODS

➜ **La Vieille Ville** It's warm, welcoming, narrow, and adorable, with staircases and ramps in midair connecting random buildings to each other. It's got tiny little plazas, terraced restaurants, and hanging laundry. This part of town was built in the 16th and 17th centuries, but was rehabilitated in the 1950s. Today it remains intelligently and beautifully preserved—and still very much lived in. Start by visiting the cours Saleya, which you can get to from the quai des

Etats-Unis by passing under the arcades des Ponchettes. In the 18th century, the cours Saleya was the town's main artery, and today it houses the town's major market.

→ **Quartier Malonat** Find the chapel of St-Suaire on place Charles-Felix and walk around the neighborhood, checking out the *trompe l'oeil* paintings on houses and the last public laundry in the village. You could actually do your laundry here. *Rue Malonat and rue de l'Ancien Senat.*

MUSEUMS

→ **Musée d'Art Moderne et d'Art Contemporain** The crushed automobile at the entrance just serves as introduction to what you'll find inside: Keith Haring, Robert Indiana, Ellsworth Kelly, and Frank Stella. *Promenade des Arts.* ☎ *04-93-62-61-62. Tickets 4€ adults, 2.50€ students. Tues–Sun 10am–6pm except select holidays. Bus: 3, 5, 6, 16, or 17 to the Promenade des Arts stop; 7, 9, or 10 to the Garibaldi stop; 1 or 2 to Promenade des Arts/Garibaldi stop.*

→ **Musée des Arts Asiatiques** It's a little out of the way but worth the trek, especially since you can hang out in the parc Phoenix. The four cubes of this museum sit on a lake ornamented by swans. Each cube is dedicated to a different Asian civilization: Indian, Southeast Asian, Chinese, and Japanese. You can check out a tea ceremony in the tea pavilion, try your hand at origami, flower arranging, or calligraphy. They also frequently have theater and musical events on. *405 promenade des Anglais.* ☎ *04-92-29-37-00 www.arts-asiatiques.com. Admission 6€. May to mid-Oct Wed–Mon 10am–6pm, late Oct–end Apr Wed–Mon 10am–5pm. Closed Mar. Bus: 9, 10, or 23.*

→ **Musée des Beaux-Arts** Even if you don't think conventional art is your thing, the Degas paintings and Rodin sculptures might convince you otherwise. *33 av. des Baumettes.* ☎ *04-92-15-28-28. 4€ adults,*

2.50€ students. Tues–Sat 10am–noon and 2–6pm.

→ **Musée National Message Biblique Marc Chagall** In brief: You could spend the day ogling the 17 mural-size masterpieces at the Musée Chagall. *16 av. Docteur Menard.* ☎ *04-93-53-87-20. Bus 15 to Cimiez.*

FREE → **Théâtre de la Photographie et de l'Image** In 1910, the *club de l'Artistique*, who had hosted the first Salon de l'Art Photographique in the south of France in 1898, took over this Art Deco village. Over the years, St-Saens, Faure, and others gave concerts there, which the likes of Mata Hari and Puccini came to see. Today, photography hangs in the light, pleasant rooms, and the little theater still occasionally hosts classical concerts. *27 bd. Dubouchage.* ☎ *04-97-13-42- 20. Free admission. Tues–Sun (except certain holidays) 10am–6pm. Bus: 1, 2, 4, 5, 12, 15, 17 or 22, stop at Jean-Médecin.*

CHURCHES

MTV **Best ◉** → **Cathédrale Orthodoxe Russe St-Nicholas** What's an onion-domed orthodox Russian church doing *en plein* Nice? With its bulbous cupolas topped with golden crosses, laid with shiny tile or gold leaf; mosaics; and its Greek-cross silhouette, this may be the most amazing Russian church outside Russia. *Av. Nicolas-II (behind the train station).* ☎ *04-93-96-88-02. 2.50€ to gawk. Summer daily 9am–noon and 2:30–6pm; winter daily 9:30am–noon and 2:30–5pm; spring and autumn 9:15am–noon and 2:30–5:30pm.*

→ **Cathédrale St-Reparate** This cathedral takes its name from a 15-year-old Palestinian martyr whose body, blown to Nice by angels, was apparently found in the year 250. Nissard architect Jean-Andre Guilbert designed the church in the mid–17th century, but couldn't avoid a piece of vaulted stone falling on the head

Matisse & the Colors of the Côte d'Azur

Although he was born up north in the Pas-de-Calais, Matisse spent the latter half of his life in Nice, where he died in 1954. Trips to Corsica and Algeria allegedly turned the artist's thoughts to the use of color, and led him to help birth the fauvist movement—a flattening of forms and accentuation of color (one writer described this as "a kind of contained violence where color seeks to escape a black circle"). Matisse bopped from end to end of the Côte d'Azur, discovering Nice in 1917 but exploring St-Tropez (painting its roof tiles) and Vence (leading to his last masterpiece, the chapelle du Rosaire in Vence). The **Musée Matisse,** housed since 1963 in a 17th-century Genoan house, boasts 187 former belongings of Matisse's, a collection of 95 photographs, and several hundred instances of his work. The ground floor shows little-known examples of Matisse's early years, showing rather banal still lifes, a brief love affair with the Flemish, and how he was informed by Antiquity. Matisse later passes by neo-Impressionist phases with *Les Courges,* pointillism with *La Jeune Fille à l'ombrelle,* and even cubism *(Interieur a l'harmonium).* But it is with the spectacular 1905 portrait of his wife that we get the first stirrings of the personal style that would come to define him. Bright colors emanate in an expression of happiness, *luxe et volupte.* The beginnings of his fauvist tendencies surface in the *Nu au fauteuil.* On the second floor, we see pictures of his Regina workshop and artifacts from it and from his apartment on the cours Saleya. In the next room we'll see where he goes in the 1930s: big paintings like *Polynesie, Nymphe en forêt,* or *Fenetre a Tahiti,* and the cutouts like *Le Nu Bleu.* This was the last phase of Matisse's development, which he believed to be the apotheosis of his career. The third room goes into detail in covering Vence's chapelle du Rosaire, which Matisse so famously immortalized, complete with sketches and models. *164 av. des Arenes.* ☎ *04-93-81-08-08. www.musee-matisse-nice.org. 4€ adults, 2.50€ students. Wed–Mon 10am–6pm. Bus: 15, 17, 20, 22, or 25.*

of the bishop. Witness both an exterior and interior crazily baroque. *Place Rossetti.*

TWO SPECIAL TOURS

Ramparts

Find the rue St-François-de-Paule, the newest street in old Nice, highly patronized by the Russians and English in their heyday. On the west side of this street were the old city ramparts, and right behind it was (believe it), the goose patch, so the birds would raise the alert if anyone attacked. Don't miss the Provençal food shops on rue St-François-de-Paule. **The Moulin a Huile Alziari** stocks beautiful oils, soaps, and fresh olives, as does **Terre des Truffes,** which sells pureed Provençal truffles, black truffles from the Perigord (11

rue St-François-de-Paule; ☎ **04-93-62-07-68**). Matisse and Tchekov used to stay at the Hôtel Beau Rivage at no. 24. Next to the rather ugly church St-François-de-Paule is the chocolate shop **Auer** (no. 7), and behind it the opera (see the opera, above). Robespierre's brother lived at no. 8, and Bonaparte set up quarters at the palais Hongran (no. 2) for 2 weeks in 1796. The pretty Art Nouveau staircase is worth checking out if the doors are open.

The rue Droite—so named not because it was straight (they never are) but because it was the shortest distance between ramparts—bisects the old town from north to south. Start at the Palais Lascaris, then walk down to the Eglise du Gesù, the first big church of the lower town, and stop at Chez Espuno (35 rue Droite) for an old-style *tourte* (if you're lucky, you'll get there just as they've cooked the onions for the *pissaladiere;* the aroma will draw you in for sure). At no. 28, 📺 Best● **Therese** cooks the *socca* in the wood-fired oven here, before she brings it to market on the Cours Saleya. When you get to the rue Benoit-Bunico, you'll see what used to be the Jewish ghetto. A 1430 law ordered that one street in town be reserved for the Jewish citizens. At nightfall, each end of the street would be closed by gates. (Little did police know about the network of underground caves.) The Sardinian king decreed in the 18th century that Jews wear the yellow star, a rule that held until the Revolution. The place Rossetti is adorable, with typical Niçois apartments in varying hues of pleasing colors, and the best ice-cream shop in town, Fenocchio.

Quartier Carabacel

Or instead, stroll the **Quartier Carabacel.** Several calm streets at the bottom of Cimiez have retained their old character. Bourgeois *niçois* lived here first, in the 18th century, but the rich English who settled here took over the beautiful houses when they arrived. Of note is the Imperial Hotel at 8 bd. Carabacel, a beautiful neoclassical house that has become the chamber of commerce at no. 20, and the Langham palace at no. 24. Walk down the avenue Emile-Biekcert, which twists and turns its way down to boulevard Cimiez, and note the friezes and balconies on the Carlton Carabacel (7 montée de l'Hermitage), and the Ermitage, built by Charles Damas, at no. 42.

Another lovely stroll takes place in the gorgeous **Cimiez** neighborhood. Start at 2 bd. Cimiez in front of the Grand Palais, built in 1912 by Charles Dalmas, and admire its neighbor the Majestic (no. 4), built in 1904. Follow the boulevard until the villa

Paradision at no. 24, today Nice's conservatory. You can access the gardens from the avenue Moriez. A polish architect built the villa Surany (no. 35) for a rich Persian, and covered it in multicolored stuccos and friezes. On the other side of the street, the Alhambra (no. 46) has two bulbous minarets and big exotic balconies. The Winter Palace (at no. 84) was built by Dalmas for Polish hoteliers. On boulevard Edouard VII, after a few pretty Italianate villas, you'll suddenly come upon a cute little romantic château known as the manoir Belgrano, whose stained-glass windows and thin, tapering towers are nothing if not medieval. This one was built in 1906 for an Argentinean man, who sold it to an Afghan. Finally, the apotheosis: *l'Excelsior Regina,* 400 rooms built by Biasini, now turned into apartments; fortunately the facade remains unchanged.

Playing Outside

➔ **Beaches** 7km (4½ miles) of beaches, going from the edge of the old port to the international airport. It's gravel, but they're smooth. Seven public beaches are interspersed with sections of private beaches. On the public beaches, you can sit on your own towel for free or rent mattresses, parasols, and chaise longues, use changing rooms, and take freshwater showers. *10€– 12€ half-day; 12€–15€ full day. Bus: 9, 10, 12, or 23 go to the beach.*

➔ **Cimetière Catholique** We're not trying to be morbid by suggesting you stroll through this cemetery, but it really is beautiful. The graven (pardon the pun) sculptures are creative and surprising (check out the hand trying to lift the coffin lid, and the mustachioed men). *Allée François-Arago. Daily 8:30am–5:30pm.*

➔ **Jardin des Arenes** This is where Nice's jazz festival goes down, and why not? We'd listen to anything here. Pines mingle with olive trees, and on sunny days, the *nissards* come down to picnic among the Roman ruins. *78 av. de la Corniche Fleurie. Apr–May 8am–7pm, June–Aug 8am–8pm, Oct–Mar 8am–6pm.*

➜**Parc du Château** Although the army of Louis XIV had laid it to waste at the start of the 18th century, the town of Nice tried to revivify this château in 1821. Think about it: They had all these tourists who didn't want to bathe in the sea or under the sun, so they landscaped to keep themselves busy. Even if today the sun and sea are a greater diversion, this hill still attracts travelers with its green spaces, ideal for picnics or Frisbee.

To get to it, walk up the montée Rondelly (from the place Sainte-Claire, past the chappelle de la Visitation). Alternately, walk up the montée du Château, the rue Segurane, or take the elevator at the end of the quai des Etats-Unis. *The elevator costs .40€. The park is open 9am–8pm in summer, 9am–6pm in spring, 10am–6pm in winter.*

➜**Parc Phoenix** A lovely 6-hectare (15-acre) botanical garden that re-creates various natural settings with surprising ease, from a jungle to the Alps. How do they do it? There's a parrot aviary and a 7-sq.-km (3-sq.-mile) greenhouse that encloses a lush tropical garden filled with orchids, carniforous plants, butterflies, and iguanas. *405 promenade des Anglais. ☎ 04-92-29-77-00. Admission 2€. Mid-Apr to mid-Oct daily 9am–7:30pm; off season daily 9:30–6pm. Bus: 9, 10, or 23.*

➜**Terrasse Frederic-Nietzsche** This is the top of castle hill, where you'll see gorgeous views of the mont Boron, the valley of Peillon, and the sea. If you're there at noon, don't get shocked by the cannon shot, a tradition the Scots Sir Coventry began, so he'd know it was time for lunch. *Colline du château.*

Shopping

CLOTHING & ACCESSORIES

There are two shopping malls in Nice Centre, both on the avenue Jean-Médecin: the Galeries Lafayette and Nice-Etoile, right next to each other on the east side of the street. Can't miss them. Farther on the same avenue are book and record emporium FNAC, and lots of clothing chains.

Luxury shopping is concentrated on the rue Paradis (Sonia Rykiel, Kenzo, Chanel), avenue de Suede (Louis Vuitton, Yves St-Laurent), and the avenue de Verdun (Hermès, Cartier).

➜**La Chapellerie** Hats should really come back in style, and this place has all the classics: Stetsons, berets, the Borsalino. Try one on. *36 cours Saleya. ☎ 04-93-62-52-54.*

MUSIC, BOOKS & MEDIA

➜**L'Atelier de Reliure** For centuries now, the Balloni family has been binding books in the great Italian tradition. In a workshop that smells deliciously of glue and leather, they fix some of the most prestigious books in Europe. If you come at the right time, you might catch a Spanish count looking to repair his rotting family Bible. *20 rue de la Préfecture. ☎ 04-93-62-40-49.*

MARKETS

➜**Marché à la Brocante** This flea market on the Cours Saleya sets up whenever the fruit-and-veg market takes a break. *Mon 8am–5pm.*

➜**Marché de la Liberation** This is the biggest market in Nice, perhaps less picturesque than the one on the cours Saleya, but no less authentic. *Av. Malaussena (farther up the av. Jean-Médecin). Tues–Sun 7am–1pm.*

➜**Marché du Cours Saleya** The first part is a cut-flower market that smells divine; the next bit is a food market that smells even better. *Flowers Sun–Sat 6am–5:30pm*

Moulin a Huile d'Olive Alziari ★★

Olive Oil as Good as 10 Mothers

Like most modern Americans, you probably eat olive oil every day, but do you know anything about it? The region around Nice and especially the river used to be dotted with olive oil mills, but that all changed after the wars and subsequent development of Nice as a big city and tourist destination. Just one of those venerable institutions, however, survived, and until recently **Nicolas Alziari** was still making olive oil, five generations after his great-great-grandfather built the mill. The mill (318 bd. de la Madeleine, 3km (2 miles) north of the intersection of Madeleine and promenade des Anglais; ☎ **04-93-44-45-12;** Mon–Fri 8am–noon and 2–6pm, closed Nov–Mar) was built in 1868 atop the ruins of another mill. Because the river that once powered it is no more than a rivulet today, they use electricity to crush the olives. They still make an effort to continue using traditional methods and craftsmanship, such as the *méthode Génoise,* and to make oil with monovarietal olives.

If you can't make it to the mill, stop by the shop in Old Nice anyway (☎ **04 93 85 76 92;** Tues–Sat 8:30am–12:30pm and 2:15–7pm). Pauline Alziari opened it in 1920 and moved it to its current location at 14 rue St-François de Paule, in front of the town hall, in 1936. Still today, someone comes down from the mill to fill the iron drums with oil every day, and it was sold out of those until 2003, when a rule was made prohibiting the bulk sale of oil.

except Sun afternoon. Produce market Sun–Sat 7am–1pm.

FOOD, WINE & LOCAL CRAFTS

➔ **Le Comptoir des Anges** Boy, it smells good in here: of lavender, jasmine, rose. It's a great place to buy small presents that won't break in transit: soap, lotion, candles, essential oils. 1 rue Dalpozzo. ☎ 04-93-88-09-90. Mon–Sat 10:30am–1pm and 3:30–7pm.

➔ **L'Oliviera** Nadim Beyrouti quit a finance job in London to sell olive oils in Nice, and when you see his tanned skin, relaxed expression, and calm, purposeful manner, you may be tempted to do the same. He's mesmerizing. All the oils he buys come from single producers he values, respects, and supports, and his emphasis is on flavor and quality, not on packaging and the revenues from secondary products such as soap and candles. If you're around at dinnertime, come sample the menu at his restaurant, where each dish is paired with a specific olive oil. 8 bis rue du Collet. ☎ 04-93-13-06-45. www.oliviera. com. Tues–Sat 10am–10pm.

➔ **The Monday Flea Market on the Cours Saleya** The space that houses Nice's gorgeous fruit, vegetable, and flower market from Tuesday to Sunday morphs into a stunning antiques market on Mondays. Wander the aisles of collectible porcelain, vintage jewelry, and Belle Epoque furniture. Arrive early. Cours Saleya. Mon 6am–5:30pm.

➔ **Tout pour la Cave** If you're inspired to start making your own wine, this is the place for supplies. You can also find simpler gear, such as vinegar barrels, gorgeously polished olive-wood rolling pins, *cornichon* tongs, and *confiture* basins. 8–10 rue Catherine-Segurane ☎ 04-93-55-51-19. www.tplc.oxatis.com. Daily 8am–noon and 2–6:30pm.

Grasse: Ain't Just Perfume

906km (562 miles) directly S of Paris, 18km (11 miles) N of Cannes, 23km (14 miles) NW of Antibes

Back in the day, wealthy Grassois used to chuckle richly as they referred to the people of Cannes as "sand eaters." Well, they who laugh last laugh loudest, I guess, as today Grasse is provincial compared to glitzy, glamorous, cosmopolitan Cannes. Happily, it's kept a lot of its old bourgeois charm, while Cannes, on bad days, can feel like an overbrowned tornado of self-involvement.

Grasse first appears in writing during the 11th century, but life appears to have been relatively quiet until the brutal year 1350, when half the population succumbed to the plague. Charles V pillaged the town in 1536, and then there were those pesky Wars of Religion. But gradually things calmed down, and the tanning (leather) trade flourished, then the heyday of perfume, which Grasse spearheaded like nobody's business (more on that below). All that money and excitement made for beautiful *hôtels particuliers,* robust culture, and a vigorous sense of Provençal pride, which attracted the likes of Pauline Bonaparte (Napoleon's sister) and Queen Victoria long before the buses of Germans huffed and puffed their way in.

Before the train was installed last year, to the feverish delight of local residents, travelers largely wrote off Grasse as a day trip for shopping in outlets for discount perfume. But Grasse—the frontier town between the sea and mountains, grittier than Mougins and Valbonne, but with a beautifully preserved medieval center— deserves better. We hope the now-easy access incites people to stay a bit longer.

Getting There

BY AIR

You're a half-hour from the Nice airport. See p. 496.

BY TRAIN

Lucky dogs, you. The **TER Provence-Alpes-Côte d'Azur** train has finally come to Grasse, and you're here to see it. Trains to Mandelieu-La Napoule, Cannes, Nice, and Ventimiglia come and go on any number of journeys every day. The train station is on avenue Pierre Semard; call ☎ **36-35** for details.

BY CAR

You're about 20 minutes north of the Croisette in Cannes, so it's an easy trip up on the RN 85. From Nice, take the D2085. There are parking lots at Vinci Park, Notre-Dame de Fleurs, Martelly, Cours Honoré Cresp, la Foux, and at the Hôtel de Ville-Cathédrale. If you park at Martelly, don't hold a cellphone too close to your ticket, or it will stop working.

BY BUS

The two bus companies that run to Grasse are Sillages **STGA** (☎ **04-93-36-37-37**) and **Rapide Côte d'Azur** (☎ **04-93-36-08-43**). The TAM bus comes to Grasse from Nice approximately every hour, on the ligne 500, passing through St. Laurent, Le Cros, Cagnes, Villeneuve, Roquefort (not *that* Roquefort), Le Rouret, and Châteauneuf on the way. To or from Cannes you want the Ligne 600, which is even more frequent, and the trip shorter.

Orientation

Grasse grows like a mushroom on a rugged boulder; the town is splattered around a series of hills, and the old city is a tight network of steep streets. The Puy, with its imposing cathedral, is the top of town, where the mayor and the bishop once lived. The place aux Aires was the town's urban center, where tanners dipped hides into the canal that once traversed the square, where farmers dried wheat; today, it welcomes a flower and food market.

Getting Around

BY PUBLIC TRANSPORTATION

The new (and free) **La Farandole buses** are as spritzy as a pair of white tennis shoes. They're free, departing every 8 minutes on weekdays, every 15 on weekends, not at all on Sundays. They stop at: the bus station, 11 Novembre, Gambetta, La Roque, Ossola, Bellaud, Carnot, Rastigny, EDF/GDF, Les Caserns, Chasseurs Alpins, Marechal Leclerc, Petit Paris, Molinard, Ste-Lorette, Cours Honoré Cresp, Le Thouron, and then return to the bus station. Call ☎ **04-93-36-37-37** for details.

BY TAXI

There are taxi stands at the place du Cours Honoré Cresp, the Entrée du Nouvel Hôpital (Chemin de Clavary), and the bus station. Call ☎ **08-20-06-60-00.**

Tourist Offices

This may be the most organized, well-documented tourist office in all of France—we love you, Monique! They have outlets at 22 cours Honoré Cresp (Palais des Congrès) (☎ **04-93-36-66-66**) or at 3 place de la Foux (☎ **04-93-36-21-68**).

Grasse **Nuts & Bolts**

Car Rental   Try **Ada,** at 140 av. Sidi Brahim (☎ 04-93-70-31-20); **Budget,** at 2 av. Marechal Leclerc (☎ 04-93-70-80-49); **Europcar,** at 98 av. Georges Pompidou (☎ 04-93-70-89-89); or **Hertz,** on the place Martelly (☎ 04-92-42-34-44).

Crisis Centers   Call the police at ☎ **04-93-40-17-17.**

Emergencies   Dial ☎ **04-93-40-03-00.**

Movie Theater   Catch a flick at **Le Studio** (15 bd. du jeu de Ballon; ☎ **04-93-40-17-10**).

Hospitals   Dial ☎ **04-93-09-55-55.**

Internet   **Webphone,** at 8 place aux Aires (☎ **04-93-40-00-41**), is open daily 10am to 11pm. **Cybercafe "Le Petit Caboulot,"** on the Escalier St-Maxim Isnard (☎ **04-93-40-16-01**), is open Monday through Saturday 8am to noon and 2 to 7:30pm (closed July). **Cyber Moutonne,** in the Quartier des Casernes, at 26–28 av. Mathias Duval (☎ **04-89-64-20-01**), is open Tuesday through Friday 10am to noon and 2 to 7:30pm, Saturday 10am to 4pm and 7 to 10pm. **Web Runner,** at 29 Chemin du Santon, next to the Les Santons shopping center (☎ **04-93-36-78-72**), is open Monday through Friday 9am to noon and 2 to 6pm.

Post Office   There's one at 11 bd. Fragonard (☎ **04-92-42-31-11**).

Sleeping

CHEAP

➜ **Hôtel Panorama** ★ So it won't win any prizes for beauty, but as far as comfort and location, this hotel comes out on top. You can order homemade dinners from room service, and they have comic books you can browse over the wildly decent breakfast. During the Jasminade, or jasmine festival, request a room on the plaza side;

Grasse, Ville du Parfum

How & Why Did It Happen?

Because Grasse's climate is particularly temperate (have you noticed?), the Grassois have been cultivating exotic plants for centuries. The tanning (leather, not skin) tradition in Grasse stretches back to the 12th century, with a large number of families making a prosperous living by tanning, but also growing wheat, pressing olive oil, and cultivating flowers and other tropical products. In the 16th century, scented gloves became highly fashionable in Italy and Spain, and Grasse supplied the demand with perfumed belts, bags, and fans as well. In 1614, by royal decree, the title of "Maître Gantier-Parfumeur," or "Master Glove-Maker-Perfumer, entered the vocabulary. But by 1724, the perfuming industry had detached itself from the tanners and formed its own association. Gardeners grew roses, hyacinths, jasmine, wild oranges, lavender, Moroccan mimosa, and other scented flowers, so that those who bent down to kiss a queenly hand could get an exotic whiff (don't forget, in these days bathing was considered unhealthy—reportedly, Louis XIV allegedly only ever took two real baths in his life, under doctor's orders). In 1759, high taxes effectively ruined the tanning industry, but Grasse's perfume industry had been built up enough in the meantime to support the town.

Perfume is made, in part, from the essential oils contained in plant petals, leaves, stems, roots, grains, fruits, wood, resins, and bark. You know when an orange or a lemon peel spritzes out a wetness and smell? That's the essential oil. The two most important flowers to Grasse's history are jasmine and the Centifolia rose, both of which are celebrated in town festivals that we highly recommend, in August and May, respectively, which correspond to the peak of the harvest periods. Jasmine-cutters work from 5am to 1pm, because as heat diffuses the essence of the flower, it will yield less essence if it gets too hot. One kilo of jasmine essence needs 400 kilos of fresh jasmine; each kilo consists of 8,000 to 10,000 flowers. A very good jasmine-cutter can pick 3 to 5 kilos of jasmine in a morning. The rose Centifolia grows around Grasse because of the gentle microclimate between sea and mountain, the mixture of clay and calcareous soil, and amount of sun.

As the 18th century wore on, instead of declining as a result of the busted-up tanning industry, the Grassois only got richer, as they specialized in perfuming, improving their technology faster than their Parisian competitors could keep up. Well, you know the story: The artisans shut down as the factories opened (giving, however, more people jobs), and industry planted bigger fields of flowers to meet the demand (between 1900 and 1930, jasmine production rose from 600 to 1,400 tons). Today, however, it's a rarity to spot a flower field around Grasse that doesn't serve touristic purposes; cultivation has migrated to less expensive lands. That said, there are still 7 jasmine and 30 to 35 rose Centifolia producers. Furthermore, most of the perfume industry now focuses on producing scents for laundry products and detergents, cleaning products, and insecticides rather than kid gloves. The rest make smells for the dairy, ice cream, cookie, frozen-dinner, soda, and candy industries instead. Sorry to bust the myth, guys, but someone's gotta say it.

you'll be right on top of the parade action without enduring the dousing of eau de cologne. *2 place du cours Honoré Cresp.* ☎ *04-93-36-92-04. 54€–90€ double. Credit cards accepted. Amenities: Elevator. In room: A/C (in some), satellite TV, minibar.*

→**Les Palmiers** ★ A room with a fireplace and garden for 35€ to 50€ a night? Sign us up. This *hôtel particulier* has been turned into a cheap hotel that makes you feel like you're staying at some dear greataunt's house. *17 av. Yves-Baudoin.* ☎ *04-93-36-07-24. 35€–50€ double. Credit cards accepted.*

DOABLE

→**Le Patti-Charm'hôtel** ★★ The outside—a lavender and ocher facade— already looks promising, but the mix of Provençal and other country French decor inside means that the rooms, all different, with especially nice bathrooms, are comfortable, pretty, and entirely modernized. *Place du Patti.* ☎ *04-93-36-01-00. www.hotel patti.com. 70€–100€ double. Credit cards accepted. Amenities: Restaurant/bar. In room: A/C, satellite TV, hair dryer, minibar, safe, stereo, Wi-Fi.*

SPLURGE

→**La Bastide St-Antoine** Okay, it'll have to be a special occasion, and if you sleep here you should really spend almost as much on the awesome dinner at the hotel's restaurant (see "Eating," below). But how many times in your life will you have the chance to sleep in an 18th-century farmhouse surrounded by 400 olive trees and a view of l'Esterel and the baie de Theoule that will leave you clasping your throat? Some of the rooms have a private terrace with Jacuzzi, original 18th-century terra-cotta floors, and fireplaces. *4 av. Henri-Dunant.* ☎ *04-93-70-94-94. 200€–350€ double. Credit cards accepted. Amenities: Bar; boutique; elevator; parking; pool. In room: A/C, plasma TV, Internet, minibar.*

Eating

Grasse specialties show both Provençal and Italian influences and include a zucchini tart (eaten at Christmas), and the delicate MTV Best♬ *fougassette,* a typically Grassoise reinterpretation of Provençal brioche–type olive *fougasse*—only here perfumed with orange blossom instead.

CHEAP

→**Le Café des Musées** A typical Provençal bistro, with a constantly changing menu of homemade specialties, including regional dishes such as quail or *daube,* which you should not leave Provence without trying. Otherwise, try the light salads, the house quiche, and the tasty cakes. *10 place de la Foux.* ☎ *04-93-36-44-88. Main courses 14€–17€. Credit cards accepted. Mon–Tues noon–2pm, Wed–Sat noon–2pm and 7–10pm.*

DOABLE

MTV Best♬ →**Lou Fassum** This is probably the best place in town to discover local fare such as *fassum,* cabbage stuffed with pork and stewed. Also try the mushroom crème, the confited cabbage with dried fruit, or the beautiful cheese plate. *5 rue des Fabreries.* ☎ *04-93-42-99-69. www.lou fassum.com. Menus 19€, 22€, 24€, or 32€. Credit cards accepted. Tues–Sat lunch and dinner.*

SPLURGE

→**La Bastide St-Antoine** Jacques Chibois' 200-year-old Provençal farmhouse serves an array of incredible dishes, including oysters with yucca leaves, fresh crayfish with flap mushrooms, or ice cream made with olives and a hint of olive oil. Reservations are imperative. *48 av. Henri-Dunant.* ☎ *04-93-70-94-94. www.jacques-chibois.com. Prix-fixe lunch 53€–170€; dinner 130€–170€. Credit cards accepted. Daily noon–2pm and 8–9:30pm.*

LA CÔTE D'AZUR (FRENCH RIVIERA)

Tour an Olive Mill

A couple of olive mills near Grasse still operate today. The first two listed are in Grasse, the others in villages nearby.

→ **Moulin a huile de Ste-Anne,** 138 rt. de Draguignan (☎ **04-93-70-21-41**)

→ **Moulin a huile du Rossignol,** 41 chemin des Paroirs (☎ **04-93-70-16-74**)

→ **Moulin a huile de la Brague,** 2 rte. de Châteauneuf (☎ **03-93-77-23-03**)

→ **Moulin a huile Bossi & fils,** Quartier du Bourboutel (☎ **04-93-69-58-59**)

Going Out

Grasse ain't Nice, and it doesn't pretend to be. It does, however, have a number of great cafes (especially on the bd. Jeu de Ballon), a movie theater, a theater, and a big casino.

Sightseeing
PARFUMERIES

In case you haven't noticed, Grasse is a perfume town, and no visit is complete without a tour through at least one of its *parfumeries*. Always competing for attention, the three big players all offer free entry and a guided tour, presenting a relatively equivalent experience. Galimard is the oldest but slightly out of town, Molinard is the next oldest, and Fragonard is the fattest cat in town. Stopping by the tourist office before you go will net you a 10% coupon at any of the distilleries, which is worth doing if you want to bring home gifts.

FREE → **Parfumerie Galimard** Jean de Galimard founded the *maison* in 1747, and the granddaddy of Grasse perfumeries has been kicking ever since. It's slightly out of town. Catch bus no. 600 (Cannes-Grasse line) from the center of Grasse or Cannes. The parfumerie is between the two, 3km from Grasse. *73 rte. de Cannes.* ☎ *04-93-09-20-00. Daily in summer 9am–6:30pm, winter 9am–noon and 2–6pm.*

→ **Studio des Fragrances Galimard** If Galimard impressed you, visit the studio and make your own fragrance. If you run out, they'll keep the formula on file so you can order more. *5 rte. de Pegomas.* ☎ *04-93-09-20-00. 35€ per person to make your own fragrance, plus a 100ml Eau de Parfum. Make an appointment for 10am, 2, or 4pm.*

FREE → **Parfumerie Fragonard** Fragonard has dominated this town since its inception in 1926, set as it is at the center of everything. Its museum has a collection of rare perfume-related objects, and they have a more modern facility on the route de Cannes, surrounded by a suitably fragrant garden. Of course, you can make your own perfume. *L'Usine Historique: 20 bd. Fragonard.* ☎ *04-93-36-44-65. La Fabrique des Fleurs (the newer factory on the outskirts of Grasse): Rte. de Cannes, Les Quatre Chemins.* ☎ *04-93-77-94-30. Both are open in season 9am–6pm, off season 9am–12:30pm and 2–6pm.*

FREE → **Parfumerie Molinard** Open in 1849, this pretty white Spanish tile-roofed abode offers a free guided tour of the factory, scattered with artifacts from Molinard's long and illustrious history. You can make your own fragrance here too, but an added feature at Molinard is that you can also paint your own porcelain plate. We guarantee it'll be ugly. *60 bd. Victor Hugo.* ☎ *04-92-42-33-11. Daily Mar–Sept 9am–6pm; Oct–Feb 9am–12:30pm and 2–6pm; closed Sun.*

→ **Musée International de la Parfumerie** Sadly, this museum is undergoing renovation throughout 2007, but if you're reading this later, come and check out everything about how perfume is made, and how that has changed over history (some of the artifacts in here have been moved over to the Musée d'Art et d'Histoire de Provence for the duration of the renovation). You'll view old Egyptian and Greek perfume flasks, Lalique and Baccarat-stoppered bottles, and Marie Antoinette's travel case. Then go smell the perfumery flowers in the greenhouse. *8 place du cours.* ☎ *04-93-36-80-20. June–Sept 10am–6:30pm, Oct–May 10am–12:30pm and 2–5:30pm; closed Nov.*

➜ **Musée Villa Jean-Honoré Fragonard** This elegant 17th-century country house contains a good deal of paintings by local boy Jean-Honoré Fragonard, and even some *trompe l'oeil* paintings made by his 13-year-old son. *23 bd. Fragonard.* ☎ *04-93-36-52-98. June–Sept 10am–6:30pm, Oct–May 10am–12:30pm and 2–5:30pm; closed Nov.*

OTHER MUSEUMS

➜ **Musée d'Art et d'Histoire de Provence** In the elegant former house of the Marquise de Clapiers-Cabris (what we wouldn't give for a name like that), this museum re-creates daily life in this region from prehistory to the 1950s, through pottery, paintings, clothing, and household objects. Best is the pretty French-style garden and its old rosebushes. Many of the objects from the Musée International de la Parfumerie, closed in 2007 for renovation, are housed here in the meantime, so come take a peep. *2 rue Mirabeau.* ☎ *04-93-36-01-61. June–Sept 10am–6:30pm, Oct–May 10am–12:30pm and 2–5:30pm; closed Nov.*

➜ **Musée Provençal du Costume et du Bijou** This teensy museum down the street from the Fragonard perfumery has an adorable collection of traditional local costumes. *2 rue Jean Ossola.* ☎ *04-93-36-44-65.*

CHURCHES

➜ **Notre-Dame de Puy** Vaulted, imposing, and nice and cool when it's hot out. It's

got Rubens paintings in it and some religious work by Grassois painter Jean-Honoré Fragonard. *Place du Petit Puy. No phone. Daily 9:30–11:30am and 3–6pm.*

TWO SPECIAL TOURS

If you start at the tourist office in the Palais des Congrès, you can walk around the medieval city by following the copper emblems in the street marking the path (you can get a map from the OT). It'll take you about 2½ hours.

For a shorter walk (about 1½ hr.), start at the Cours Honoré Cresp and admire the view. Walk to the rue Jean Ossola and see the 17th-century *hôtel particulier* formerly belonging to the Clapiers-Cabris family. Also on that street are the ancient convent of the Dominicans and their fountain, plus l'Hôtel Luce, where d'Artagnan is said to have stayed. On the rue Gazan, at no. 7, you can admire the Hôtel Gazan de la Peyriere, with the arms of the General Gazan on the walnut-wood door. On the place du petit Puy, the oldest in town, you can admire the cathedral, an example of Roman Provençal architecture. It houses some Rubens paintings (let us know if you figure out how and why they got here; nobody seemed to know) as well as a rare religious theme by local-boy-made-good, Fragonard. Walk through the place Antoine Godeau to the place du 24 août, the site of the first cemetery in town. There's a beautiful view of the Grasse region there. L'Hôtel de Ville, or town hall, now resides in what used to be the old Episcopal palace and its 13th-century tower. Follow the rue de l'Eveche with its 14th-century arcades until the place de l'Eveche, where you'll notice that the arcades of the fountain are ancient vaulted doorways to former caves and storerooms. The place aux Herbes next door is the site of the market; cross it to get to the rue Droite. This was Main Street in medieval

Feeling Fat Yet?

So you've eaten every *chocolate fondant, saucisson sec,* and *tartiflette* from Paris to Nice? Can't blame you; I'm a butter-lover too. Why not take advantage of the athletic opportunities in Grasse (which, after all, means "fatty" in French) to see how the locals burn off all that cream and butter:

→ **Kickboxing & Thai Boxing: Le Tigre Blanc (**Salle Omnisports; ☎ **04-93-36-68-74)**

→ **Kung Fu: Kung Fu Wushu Association ChinaClub** (888 av. de la République, La Roquette su Siagne; ☎ **06-11-39-60-12)**

→ **Running: Grasse Athletic Club** (Stade Perdigon; ☎ **04-93-77-87-38)**

→ **Badminton: Badminton Club de Grasse** (at the Gymnase Canteperdrix, St. Jacques; ☎ **04-93-36-10-46)**

→ **Dance: Centre Artistique de la Danse** (130 av. Pierre Semard; ☎ **04-93-36-97-67)** or **Chorea Danse** (14 bd. Marechal Leclerc; ☎ **04-93-09-02-55)**. Learn Occitan dance at the **Institut d'Occitan** (☎ **04-93-42-79-64)** or at **Lei Baisso Luserno** (☎ **04-93-70-53-18)**.

→ **Horseback riding: Le Club Hippique** (168 rue de Cannes; ☎ **04-93-70-55-41)**

→ **Swimming: Piscine Harjes** (St-Exupery; ☎ **04-93-36-91-61)** or the Olympic-size basin at **Espace Culturelle Altitude** (57 rte. Napoléon; ☎ **04-93-36-35-64;** July–Aug, with spellbinding views of the beaches on the coast)

→ **Tennis: Tennis Club de Grasse** (on the rte. de Cannes—La Paoute; ☎ **04-93-70-02-20)**

→ **Yoga: Yoga de l'energie** (5 rue Jean Ossola; ☎ **04-93-36-83-55)**

times. Like the rue Droite in Nice, it's not straight (despite its name), but rather just the quickest way to cross the town, if you could wade through the donkey carts. The rue de l'Oratoire has the chapelle de l'Oratoire on it, built in 1632; a portal and Gothic window were incorporated in the facade from a now-defunct church that became a perfumery and subsequently a supermarket. Once you arrive at the place aux Aires, look around for no. 27, the Hôtel du Dauphin, which for a long time was the only hotel in town. There is a Provençal market on this square every morning, but initially it was for the tanners to wash leather in, back in the day when a canal passed through the square. The rue Amiral de Grasse will bring you back to the cours Honoré Cresp.

Shopping

CLOTHING & ACCESSORIES

There are two places to go for traditional Provençal embroidery: **Chez Madame Segala** (31 bd. J Crouet; ☎ **06-20-83-87-25)**; and the **Espace Culturel "La Chenaie"** (St-Jacques; ☎ **04-93-09-17-16)**.

MUSIC, BOOKS & MEDIA

→**Tout an'image** Comic books are a French institution. Young and old should check out this shop in the Marronniers shopping mall. Centre Commercial des Marronniers. *6 rue des Grillons.* ☎ *04-93-70-67-40. Tues–Sat 9:30am–12:30pm and 2:30–5:30pm.*

Farther Afield: Gourdon

MTV **Best⧫** **Gourdon** is a charming, if slightly cheesy, medieval citadel-village high above the Gorges du Loup, about 14km (9 miles) from Grasse. It was built to keep an eye out for marauding Saracens. Of note is the 13th-century castle and its beautiful 17th-century gardens, which house an out-of-this-world but ridiculously little-known **MTV** **Best⧫** **Musée des Arts Decoratifs** (Château de Gourdon, Gourdon; ☎ **04-93-09-68-02;** admission 8€; June–Sept daily 11am–1pm and 2–7pm; Oct–May daily 2–6pm), which has some of the coolest furniture ever designed, juxtaposed in the old castle rooms. Majorelle, Mallet-Stevens, and then some—really stunning and worth the detour.

You can hike down to **pont-du-Loup,** via the sentier du Paradis, in 45 minutes, while observing the splendid views of the entire coastline. It's hard going but at least you're not the postman, who used to trek it every day.

FOOD, WINE & LOCAL CRAFTS

Going to Grasse without buying perfume, or at least some kind of fruity-smelling knickknack, is not allowed in France. The immigration officers will ask to see proof of purchase on your way out of the country, and if you can't whip out at least a little bar of soap, they throw you into prison, where you have to eat cheese and *saucisson* until you explode. Seriously.

In addition to the three *parfumeries* listed above, which all have extensive gift shops, check out:

➜ **Espace Terroirs** Olive oil, wines, local aperitifs, raw-milk cheeses, charcuterie, honey, jams, and so on. *45 chemin des Castors.* ☎ *04-93-77-83-23. www.espace terroirs.com. Tues–Sat 9am–6:30pm.*

➜ **Ets. Vallauri** A cute little boutique in the middle of the medieval city with a huge wine cave, where you can taste. *2 rue Dominique Conte.* ☎ *04-93-36-59-25. Tues–Sat 9.30am–7pm.*

MTV **Best⧫** ➜ **Fougassettes Venturini** Come here to try the delicious *fougacettes,* a kind of typical Grassois bread that's delicately flavored with orange blossom. *1 rue Marcel Journet.* ☎ *04-93-36-20-47. Tues–Sat 9am–1pm and 3–6.30pm.*

➜ **Le Palais des Olives** Right at the gates of the medieval city, taste 40 kinds of olive oils, plus tapenades and olives. *Bd. du Jeu de Ballon.* ☎ *04-93-36-57-73. Tues–Sat 10am–1pm and 2:30–6:30pm.*

Monaco & Monte Carlo: Playground of the Rich & Those Who Want to Be Seen Near Them

939km (582 miles) directly S of Paris, 18km (11 miles) E of Nice

Monaco reminds me of a quail egg: tiny, precious, speckled with exquisite color, and pretty much useless if you're looking to eat an omelet. But you're not looking to eat an omelet, are you? In any case, peel this shell with care and don't let the shards cut your fingers.

A little bit Miami and a little bit Milan, Monaco—bigger only than the Vatican—ends up having a style and flavor more cohesive than either. It's the most densely populated country in the world *and* has more millionaires per capita than anywhere else, natch.

After a few days here, that delicate image of a tiny country whose citizens have graduated from the Grace Kelly school of classy glamour cedes somewhat to the more abrupt reality of brats behaving badly and a slew of Midwesterners in slacks who've come to photograph them. But if you've been spending time on the Côte d'Azur, you should be starting to expect that. The beautiful, gentle, and rich: They exist, but the places they frequent are unlikely to end up in a budget-travel guidebook, sorry mate.

No one pays taxes in Monaco, which explains why anyone who has just hit the big time flocks to it: There are now 17 daily flights from London. The revenues from the gambling and hotels pay the city's bills, so if you break it down, you're actually the one footing the bill for Ringo Starr and Shirley Bassey's taxes. What?!

Monaco is one of five European **microstates,** including Liechtenstein, Andorra, San Marino, and the Vatican—remnants of the feudal system that through twists of fate resisted getting swallowed up by the nations that now border them when the maps were being drawn up. Due to the limits on their resources and population obligated by their tiny size, microstates have adopted measures like lowering or eliminating taxes and encouraging investment in order to keep themselves alive. On one hand, this made many of them richer than, well, God (at least the Vatican). On the other hand, it floods their already-tiny space with the most self-centered people alive. Oh, well. Can't say they didn't ask for it.

The first Grimaldi in Monaco was François, who dressed up as a Franciscan monk and seized the fortress on the Rock of Monaco in 1297. Generations later in 1861, after centuries of unrest, the ruling prince, also a Grimaldi, gave up Menton and Roquebrune (95% of the country) to

Telephone Tip

To call Monaco from outside its borders (including other parts of France), dial ☎ **00-377,** followed by the rest of the numbers.

France in exchange for 4 million francs and recognition of Monaco's sovereignty. Several treaties later, it has been agreed that France protects Monaco militarily and economically, and Monaco provides France with tabloid headlines and tax breaks for its rich. This is somewhat of an oversimplification, but you get the point.

All right, we're being a little harsh on this little country. There *are* reasons why its allure has held so many in thrall. Come and discover them—just don't say we didn't warn you.

Last but not least: There is one cop for every 35 Monegasque nationals. Be advised.

Getting There

BY AIR

The coolest way to come into Monaco is by helicopter, and there is a helipad there; in fact helicopters regularly make the trip between Monaco and Nice. Otherwise, the closest airport is Nice, a major French hub 19km (12 miles) away. There's always the option of a private jet, of course. For reservations and quotes, call **Rath Aviation** 24 hours a day at ☎ **33-4-93-90-40-90.**

BY TRAIN

Trains to Monaco come every 30 minutes from Cannes, Nice, Menton, and Antibes, and arrive at the **Gare SNCF** on the avenue Prince Pierre. Call ☎ **08-92-35-35-35** for details. Once you're there, you've still got somewhat of an uphill walk to get to Monte Carlo; take a **taxi,** available from the station or call ☎ **93-15-01-01.**

Monaco

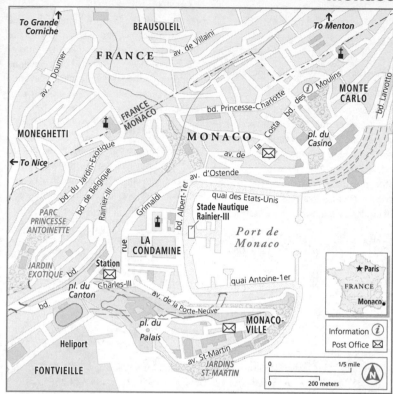

BY CAR

From Paris, take the A6 south to Lyon. At Lyon, connect with the A7 south to Aix-en-Provence and take the A6 south directly to Monaco. From the Riviera, drive from Nice along the N7 northeast.

Orientation

Monaco can generally be divided into six sections, but the whole of it is small enough to walk pretty comfortably, and there are plenty of places to take an easy breather. From west to east: **Fontvieille,** a hip district with a shopping center, beautiful garden, and the famous stadium, Le Sporting; **La Condamine,** just northeast of it, the saddle between the two harbors

of Fontvieille and Hercule; **Moneghetti,** north of that, home to the exotic gardens, hospital, train station, and other useful places; **Monaco-Ville,** all the way to the south, home of the king and his palace; **Monte-Carlo,** where the elegant casino, gardens, and hotels reside; and finally, the **Lavrotto** area, with its long beach. East of that is **Monte Carlo beach,** but it's in France.

Getting Around

BY PUBLIC TRANSPORTATION

Five bus lines wind around Monte Carlo's terraced landscape. You can buy a one-journey ticket for 1.45€, a four-journey pass for 3.50€, an eight-journey pass for

5.60€, or a day card for 3.50€. The buses are reliable and clean, and with luck, you might even see a local on one.

BY BICYCLE

You want a *bike?* In *Monaco?* Poor sod. I'm not deigning to answer that one. Even if you have no pride, the hills are too steep.

BY TAXI

There are taxi ranks at the following locations: at the Casino, avenue de Monte-Carlo; Fontvieille, avenue des Papalins; at the train station on the exit Ste-Devote; at the hospital, avenue Pasteur; at the Larvotto, avenue Princess Grace; at the Métropole, avenue de la Madone; at the Fairmont Monte Carlo, avenue des Spelugues; on the Moulins, place des Moulins; on the Port de Monaco, avenue J. F. Kennedy; at the post office, square Beaumarchais; at the sporting Monte-Carlo on the southeast coast, avenue Princess Grace; at the Terminus, avenue Prince Pierre. Call ☎ **377-93-15-01-01** for 24-hour cab service.

Tourist Offices

Monaco's tourist office, on the boulevard des Moulins, has got its thing *together.* Check it out at ☎ **377-92-16-61-16** or on the Web at www.monaco-tourisme.com

---

Monaco **Nuts & Bolts**

ATMs The country is 2 sq. km (1 sq. mile) and there are 50 banks in it. Plus, everyone takes plastic, *bien sûr.*

Crisis Centers Ambulance ☎ **18**; police ☎ **17.**

Hospitals Go to the **Centre Hospitalier Princess Grace** (av. Pasteur; ☎ **97/ 989-769**).

Internet/Wireless Hot Spots Log on at **Notari Cyberspace** (3 bis rue Basse; Monaco Ville; ☎ **377-92-16-17-62**) or **Achille Informatique** (15 place d'Armes; www.achille.biz; ☎ **37-77-97-70-88-90**).

Laundromats Piece of advice? If you have laundry to do in Monaco, hand-wash it. Or else ask your concierge to.

Pharmacies Get your meds at **Pharmacie Ferry** (1 rue Grimaldi; ☎ **93/392-196**).

Post Office The **Poste Centrale** is located at avenue de l'Hermitage.

Sleeping

Just to warn you, 76% of the rooms in Monaco are rated over three stars, so you'll be hard-pressed to sleep cheaply. But if luxe is what you're looking for, Monaco will do just fine. Our suggestion is to report to the tourist office for a list of every possible place to sleep in the principality. If you tell them what you're looking for, they'll advise you well.

HOSTELS

➔ **Relais International de la Jeunesse de Cap d'Ail** Clearly, everyone here wants to be in Monaco, not Cap d'Ail. That said, the train station is 300m (984 ft.) from the hostel, and Monaco is only 5 minutes away—plus, it's on the water, and you'd be hard-pressed to find real estate as prime and cheap elsewhere. *"Thalassa"* 2. av R. Gramaglia, Cap d'Ail. ☎ 04-93-78-18-58. 15€ bed. Rate includes breakfast and

sheets (in rooms with 4, 6, 8, or 10 beds).
Apr–Oct.

CHEAP

➔**Hôtel de France** Twenty-six perfectly pleasant sun-yellow rooms on a quiet street in La Condamine. What? Are we still in Monaco? Okay, it's basic, but it's *got* the basics: shower, TV, toilet, and a parking lot nearby. *6 rue de la Turbie.* ☎ *377-93-30-24-64. www.monte-carlo.mc/france. 70€ single; 80€–120€ double. Breakfast 9€. Credit cards accepted. Amenities: Bar; limited room service. In room: TV, hair dryer.*

DOABLE

➔**Hôtel Balmoral** This old-school behemoth, over 100 years old, has probably seen a lot go down in its time. It's no longer the glorious homestead it once was, but the rooms have been modernized (although some are much nicer than others, so pick wisely), and the view of the gorgeous Rocher and port d'Hercule hasn't changed. You can take a public elevator down to the port, which will put you in the middle of things very quickly, and if you stay 3 nights or longer, you get free tickets to all the museums in Monaco. *12 av. de la Costa.* ☎ *377-93-50-62-37. www.Hotel-balmoral.mc. 115€–210€ double. Credit cards accepted. Amenities: Restaurant/bar. In room: A/C, TV.*

SPLURGE

MTV ⬤Best⬤ ➔**Fairmont Monte Carlo** This massive elephant of a hotel embodies the Monegasque spirit to the max: The Formula One race passes right under the hotel, for goodness sake. The view of the ocean is unparalleled, and though the hallways are a bit '70s, the rooms are fresh and summery. The concierge, reception, and housekeeping staff are incredible, but the breakfast staff is a band of malcontents. I can't say I blame them, though: No amount of plastic surgery can disguise a hangover, and their customers aren't the type to hold in bad humor (irritated staff notwithstanding, breakfast is still a rip-off). Nevertheless you'll feel like a Grimaldi if you make this your palace. Just leave the keys to the Maserati with the valet staff. *12 av. Des Spélugues.* ☎ *93-50-65-00. www.fairmont.com/Montecarlo. 199€–389€ double. Credit cards accepted. Amenities: 4 restaurants; 2 bars; babysitting; health club; limited-mobility rooms; outdoor pool; sauna; 24-hr. room service. In room: A/C, TV, Internet, hair dryer, minibar, safe.*

Eating

You don't necessarily have to spend money to eat well in Monaco, but it helps. There's a rad little street of restaurants right by the avenue de Citronniers, but you can find good eats all around town.

COFFEE BARS & LIGHT FARE

➔**Marché de la Condamine** Don't waste your time on a stale 13€ croissant at your glitzy hotel breakfast—head straight to the market for rocking local fare and fruit for super cheap. Try the *pan bagnat* at the *bar du marché* or the socca at Chez Roger. Don't bring any kind of pretensions and you'll be just fine. *Place d'Armes. No phone. No credit cards. Daily 7am–1pm.*

CHEAP

➔**Café de Paris** It's cheap enough, but what a rip-off. The *raviolis frais* are about as fresh as Chef Boyardee, and the composed salads taste like they've been sitting in their plates for far too long. That said, this is the best place to watch every tourist in Monte Carlo act really self-conscious. Just try and make eye contact without looking away and blushing yourself. *Place du Casino.* ☎ *377-98-06-76-23. Mains 15€–20€. Credit cards accepted. Daily 7am–1am.*

➔**Sport Aviron Snack Bar** Cheap and worthy. Big pastas for 8€, and stockfish on Fridays. Beautiful views of the port, and a simple clientele blabbing away over their *eaux-de-vies.* Check out the rowing club on the avenue President Kennedy. *3 av. Président J. F. Kennedy.* ☎ *377-93-50-51-30. Main courses 8€. No credit cards. Mon–Sat midnight–3pm.*

DOABLE

➜**Pizzeria Monegasque** Very good pizzas, a roomful of good-looking young Monegasques, and a price tag of about 15€. What could be better? Well, Le Louis XV perhaps, but Pizzeria Monegasque will do. You can also get meat or fish dishes starting at 10€, and on weekends they serve until 11pm—perfect if you're just coming from a show or movie. *4 rue Terrazzani.* ☎ *377-93-30-16-38. Credit cards accepted. Mon–Sat noon–1:45pm and 7:30–11pm (Fri–Sat till midnight).*

SPLURGE

➜**Le Louis XV** At the age of 33, Alain Ducasse became the youngest chef to earn three Michelin stars, which he promised he'd do within 3 years at Le Louis XV. The opulent Versailles-esque dining room is the ultimate in luxury. If spending 192€ on dinner sounds harsh, try the three-course prix-fixe lunch menu for 76€. While dishes such as stuffed sardines or asparagus risotto may sound downright pedestrian for that price, one taste and you'll understand why everyone makes such a commotion. *Hôtel de Paris, place du Casino.* ☎ *92-16-29-76. Main courses 80€–92€; fixed-priced menu 160€–180€. Credit cards accepted. Thurs–Mon 12:15–1:45pm and 8–9:45pm; also June–Sept Wed 12:15–1:45pm.*

Partying

Start the night off with some drinks on the place de Casino; if getting crunk at five ain't your style, there's a Welsh water bar right in front of the Casino with seats that light up.

➜**Bar Americain** If you've been looking for an excuse to wear that tuxedo or that strappy cocktail gown, wait no longer. It's close enough to the Casino to spit on it. You can order your rare armagnac (22€) or 11€ beer while you sneer at the commoners. *Hôtel de Paris, place du Casino.* ☎ *377-92-16-28-64.*

➜**Columbus Bar** If it's four o'clock, you're hot, and you want a fruity cocktail, go to the Columbus, but make sure you look good. In the lobby of the hippest hotel in town, you can rock a fresh fruit martini, spicy mojito, or super-fizzy champagne by the glass (all 15€). Maybe wait until night falls to order one of the many rare whiskies. Oh wait, you're in Monte Carlo. Order now! *23 av. des Papalis.* ☎ *377-92-05-90-00.*

➜**Le Living-Room Club** At the end of the night, head for Le Living-Room, hip for the last 25 years. It opens at 11pm, but Le Living-Room is most bumpin' in the wee hours. Sip your cocktails while you listen to Italian piano music or rock out to French oldies. *7 av. des Spelugues.* ☎ *377-93-50-80-31. Mon–Sat 11pm to early morning.*

CLUBS & LIVE MUSIC VENUES

Okay, I know this is going to be an unexpected recommendation, but don't discount going to see **a philharmonic concert at the Palais Princier.** The orchestra is pretty bad-ass, but most spectacular is the choice of venue. The musicians spill out between twin marble staircases backed by the gorgeous palatial arches. Then, because of course you'll be wearing your tux (jacket and tie are required), you can gamble the night away. Student tickets are only 6€ to 8€, but you must be under 25 with proof (☎ **377-98-06-28-29**). Tickets sold in the atrium of the casino Tuesday through Saturday 10am to 5:30pm, as well as on the eves and days of the concerts. Tickets are also available from the FNAC (see "Music, Books & Media," below) and the Carrefour, which makes it the classiest supermarket I've ever heard of. Finally, check the Internet at www. opmc.mc, www.fnac.fr, and www.monaco-spectacle.com.

Sightseeing

PUBLIC MONUMENTS

➔ **Prince's Palace & State Apartments** The changing of the guard happens daily here at 11:55am sharp. *Place du Palais. June–Sept daily 9.30am–6:30pm; Oct daily 10am–5:30pm.*

MUSEUMS

➔ **Musée National: Automates et Poupées d'Autrefois** In a villa that looks like it could have been designed by Charles Garnier (architect of Paris's Opéra Garnier), this museum houses a magnificent collection of antique mechanical toys and dolls. See the 18th-century Neapolitan crib, which contains some 200 figures. This collection, assembled by Mme de Galea, was presented to the principality in 1972; it originated with the 18th- and 19th-century practice of displaying new fashions on doll models. *17 av. Princess Grace.* ☎ *93-30-91-26. www.monte-carlo.mc/musee-national. Admission 6€. Daily Oct–Easter 10–12:15pm and 2:30–6:30pm; Easter–Sept 10am–6:30pm. Closed Jan 1, May 1, Nov 19, Dec 25, and during the Grand Prix.*

TWO SPECIAL TOURS

Start your walk at Monaco's focal point—the gardens of the grand casino, with impeccably kept flower beds and ornamental lakes adorned with papyrus and waterlilies, which climb gently to the best shopping areas of the city. Walk back down to the port and check out your reflection in the burnished tinted windows of the Maseratis ashore and the gigantic yachts moored in the harbor. It's surely one of the most spectacular ports in the world. Curve around the boulevard Albert Ier and climb up the avenue de la Porte-Neuve until you

Movies in Monaco

It has been said that the best way to learn another language is to watch movies in it. Well, you've been listening to French all day, so maybe the next best thing is watching American movies, subtitled in French. You can do so on the MTV (Best) **biggest open-air cinema screen in Europe,** right by the Musée Oceanographique. Every day in the summer a different film gets projected onto a massive rock face overlooking the sea. Forget about the fact that you're on the roof of a parking lot—there are 450 seats with cushions and a snack bar for your mandatory Magnum munchies. For more infor, call ☎ **377-93-25-86-80** (www.cinemasporting.com).

hit the Prince's palace. If it's nearing nighttime, and there are still seats, you can catch a concert there.

The next walk starts out from the end of the previous one. But doing the whole thing in one go, you might break a sweat, which is unacceptable in Monte Carlo unless you have an entourage around you to fan it away. From the Palais Princier, loop south to see the beautiful building that houses the Oceanographic museum and the adjacent Jardins St. Martin, at the base of which the sea laps gently. Circle back and walk around the Port de Fontvielle, smaller than the Port Hercule but, for all that, no less glam or glitzy. Shoot into the *centre commercial de Fontvieille* and seek out the air-conditioned stores for a short refreshment. Then continue flanking the port to reach the Espace Fontvieille, from which you can sniff the 4,000 roses in the Roseraie Princess Grace. Monaco isn't all that big (that's the point, isn't it?), but if you're tired, catch bus no. 5 or 6 back into town.

Playing Outside

Monaco is rammed with pretty parks so manicured you'll feel like you need one to walk in them. Don't miss the Japanese garden or the Espace Fontvieille and its thousands of roses in the section named after Princess Grace.

Shopping

CLOTHING & ACCESSORIES

Monaco might be the one place on your trip where you'll need to rent a tux, which in French is *"un smoking."*

→**Galleries du Métropole** The smoothies are okay and the bibbed waiters are nice enough, but the real reason to come here is for the rest of the shopping: Christian Lacroix, Kenzo, and the Society Club, an Italianate clothes shop that sports an in-store water bar complemented by huge ashtrays and clerks who don't need to be wearing tuxedos because all you can think about is them not wearing anything. *17 av. Des Spélugues.*

→**Sensi** The people here will tell you how good you look. *10 rue Princesse Caroline.* ☎ 377-97-77-06-80.

→**Stock Griffe** This is where clothes just one season too old come to die, or rather, get adopted. You'll find Prada, Escada, and Pucci at reasonable prices, but you'll have to be a size 0 to fit into them. *5 bis av. St-Michel.* ☎ 377-93-50-86-06.

MUSIC, BOOKS & MEDIA

If you're looking for used bookstores and trendy record shops, Monaco is not the place. That said, essentials can be found at the **FNAC** (Shopping Center Le Métropole; ☎ **377-93-10-81-81;** Mon–Sat 10am–7:30pm).

Okay, I take it back: When I said "used bookstores," I was thinking of the patchouli-exuding, lounge-music-playing trendshops you can stumble upon in Paris.

Markets

If you're lucky, you'll overhear people speaking Monagesque at **La Condamine Market,** on the place d'Armes. It's open daily from 7am to 1pm. The **Monte Carlo Market** is on avenue St. Charles, and is open daily from 7am to 1pm.

But if you want "old" books, check out **Scripta Manent** (Patio Palace, 41 av. Hector Otto; ☎ **377-97-77-51-10;** www. scriptamanent-monaco.com). Bought and sold: ancient books and manuscripts, etchings, lithographies, and old photos. You'll have to make an appointment, though, so come up with a good excuse.

FOOD, WINE & LOCAL CRAFTS

📺 (Best ⬥) →**Comptoir Philatelique de Monaco** Here you can buy rare Monegasque coins, stamps, and old programs and posters from Grand Prix races of long ago. *2 rue Princess Caroline.* ☎ *377-97-70-40-99. www.comptoir-philatelique.com. Mon–Fri 9:30am–noon and 2–6:30pm.*

Festivals & Events

The **Grand Prix de Monaco** in May is an incredible, indelible operation. Car-racing fanatics, celebrities, wannabes, and the mega-rich, frothing at the mouth, all collect to watch the cars race through the streets of the principality. The race itself begins in Condamine, on the boulevard Albert Ier in front of the church, then loops down the avenue d'Ostende and in front of the casino. A series of sharp downhill turns follows, on the avenue des Spelugues, and then the race plunges underground through the bowels of the Fairmont Monte Carlo before thrusting out on the boulevard Louis II along the water. It loops around the Port Hercule, U-turns just west of the quai Antoine, and climbs back onto the boulevard Albert where it started. After completing this hair-raising 3.3km (2-mile) death wish in under 2 minutes, the drivers repeat it a mere 77 more horrifying times.

The race has run every year since 1929—in other words, since before Formula One was Formula One. Although the last person to crash into the harbor was an Austrailian in the '60s, divers known as frogmen stand at attention in case anyone derails.

Every other year, also in May, sees the **Grand Prix Historique,** which for my money out-specials the Grand Prix with its air of old-school gentility and smells of oil-skin and leather. The cars racing it date from 1934 to 1979. Wear a big British hat and shield your eyes from the shining chrome.

A lesser-known but no less exhilarating race hits the streets of Monaco in January: the **Rallye Automobile Monte Carlo,** which outdoes even the Grand Prix in years, starting as it did in 1911, in streets higher up from town, in the Alpine roads surrounding it. Drivers maneuver cars we'd be more likely to find in our driveways than a Ferrari (in recent years, winners have driven a Ford Focus and Subaru Impreza), but we'll let someone else wreck their Corolla, thank you very much. If you're especially lucky, you can catch the bad-ass **Rallye Historique,** where the cars date from between 1955 and 1977.

Even older is the tennis tournament for which enthusiasts flood the city in mid-April: the **Monte Carlo Masters Series,** founded in 1897. **The Jumping International de Monte-Carlo,** in the spring, brings together the best horsemen and horsewomen from around the word to hop over the obstacles on the smallest jumping course in the world. The **Monaco Yacht Show** in September is the only international yacht show devoted to luxury yachting, the biggest European display of so-called "super-" and "mega-yachts." Are you seeing a theme here? You have to be pretty rich to play these sports, and pretty rich to watch them. That said, old boy, they're always a jolly good show. Now just try and get some tickets.

Another notable event: the **International Musical Fireworks Competition** (Concours International de Feux d'Artifice Pyromélodiques) in July.

Corsica

by Nathalie Jordi

A lternately French and Italian in spirit, lush and arid, built-up and run-down, traditional yet buzzing with young travelers, Corsica is a mellow green island with more hidden beauty than you could discover in a decade. Mountainous and rocky, the island exudes a Mediterranean warmth, both in its azure beaches and in the aromatic breeze that blows through its pine trees.

Decent rail and bus systems connect both of Corsica's major towns as well as some more minor destinations, but the best way to explore Corsica is by car. The roads—once you divert from the *nationales* onto the *départementales*—can be hairy, and their hazards are heightened by local driving styles. But if you've been gifted with a calm disposition and steady hand on the wheel, you'll revel in the amazing vistas revealed to you and your travel mates alone. Just prepare to spend your entire trip in second gear.

Local food is terrific, but veer toward home-style places if you want to eat well. As mentioned, the island can't seem to decide whether it's Italian or French (see "Corsica History 101," below), but it retains the loveliest qualities of both cultures: great food and warm people. Wood-fired pizza and local charcuterie are island specialties, but there's a lot of ersatz, industrial stuff around, so use your common sense when you order.

The Best of Corsica

○ **The Best Place to Find Out Where the Party's At (Ajaccio):** Ask one of the waiters at either the **Café Fesch** or **La Part des Anges**—and expect to see them there once their shift ends. See p. 533.

Corsica

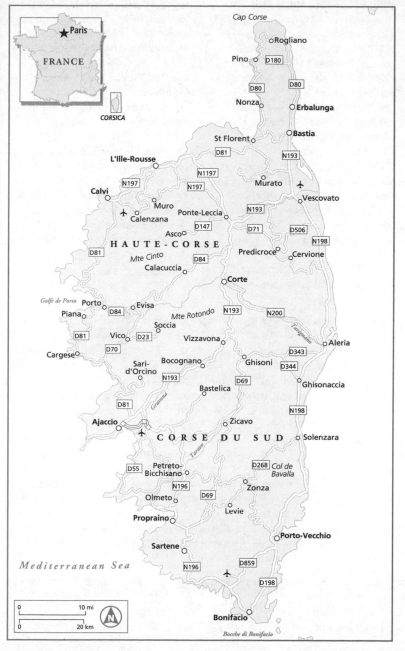

CORSICA

○ **The Best Place to Meet Your Militant Corsican Nationalist One-Night-Stand (Bastia):** You'll need aid deciphering the blackboard menu at **U Tianu,** because it's all written in Corsican, but the Che Guevara look-alike in the corner can help you with that. See p. 539.

○ **The Best Cortesian Circus Tent to Eat Brocciu Under (Corte):** Don't miss **U Museu,** between the citadel and the old city. See p. 548.

○ **The Fort Most Likely to Scare Away Genoans or Anyone Else (Corte): La Citadelle** presides over a rock over-looking the village of Corte. This is not one to mess with. See p. 550.

○ **The Best Place Not to Lose Your Way (Corte):** The **Gorges du Tavignano** may be less famous than the Gorges of Restonica, but they are just as, um, gorgeous. See p. 550.

○ **The Best Staircase Not to Lose Your Footing On (Bonifacio):** The long, long, long flight of steps that leads up to the old town of Bonifacio, perched high on the cliffs overlooking the ocean. See p. 554.

○ **The Best View If You're Dead (Bonifacio):** The white marble **marine cemetery** atop the *bouches de Bonifacio.* Rest in Peace indeed. See p. 554.

○ **The Best Windsurfing Spot (Bonifacio):** The **Bay of Figari,** a few kilometers west of Bonifacio. See p. 554.

○ **The Best Place to Shake What Your Momma Gave You (Bonifacio):** Wear your zebra-print hot pants to **Lollapalooza,** so you match the seat covers in this surprisingly hoppin' joint. See p. 554.

Getting There

You can fly into one of Corsica's four airports: **Ajaccio** (Campo dell'Oro; ☎ 04-95-23-56-56; www.ajaccio.aeroport.fr), **Bastia** (Poretta; ☎ 04-95-54-54-54; www.bastia.aeroport.fr), **Calvi** (St. Catherine; ☎ 04-95-65-88-88; www.calvi.aeroport.fr), or **Figari** (Sud-Corse; ☎ 04-95-71-10-10; www.figari.aeroport.fr).

But the best way to get there is via **Corsica Ferries** (www.corsicaferries.com). It's cheapest to leave from one of the Italian ports, which are closer, but boats depart from France (Nice, Toulon, and Marseille) for Ajaccio, Bastia, Calvi, L'Ile Rousse, Bonifacio, Porto-Vecchio, and Propriano.

The cost of your ferry ticket depends on whether or not you have a car. If you bring a car, make sure to note where you left it; moving ramps change the parking-lot landscape and make it hard to recognize. A cabin (25€, which you can purchase in advance or on board the ship) may be a wise investment if you don't deal kindly with screaming children or dogs running rampant. Show up at least an hour before departure if you have a car; half an hour before if it's just you. Ferries don't wait around, so take these time recommendations seriously. See the website for details.

Corsica History 101

Corsica has only belonged to the French for the past 2 centuries, its previous history involving the English, the Genoans, the Pisans, the Romans, the Phonecians, the

Corsican Tourist Information

Because tourism is such an important part of this island economy, the infrastructure to support it is very well developed. The **Corsican Tourist Information Office** (http://english.visit-corsica.com/corsica_tourism.htm) has outposts throughout the island; agents are very helpful, with plenty of brochures and maps at their disposal, including suggested itineraries maps. Our favorite was the **Route des Sens Authentiques** series: Regional authorities collaborated to show where people can visit artisans making wine, olive oil, cheese, honey, biscuits, jams, jewelry, knives, pottery, chestnut products, charcuterie, and other goods. These maps are awesome but are most applicable to those traveling by car, as most of the craftspeople featured run their businesses from tiny hamlets.

If you're interested in hiking, pick up the very good hiking map available at the tourist office in Corte. You'll find paths, refuges, and leisure options such as paragliding or horseback riding places. The website **www.centru-corsica.com** is terrifically in-depth, with a great deal of additional information (click on the little British flag at the bottom for the English version).

Also, almost every large town in Corsica has a booklet listing all available accommodation options. It's very useful if you're having a hard time finding hotel rooms. One covers all of Corsica, so you can use it the entire time you're there.

Byzantines, and, all the way back, the Romans. In fact, this little green island has lived through only 34 years of independence (1735–69), though it's not for lack of independent spirit. Even today, the Corsican temperament is famously gruff, intemperate, and fiercely devoted to maintaining its individual liberties.

Corsica's infrastructure began developing during the mid–19th century, when many of its roads, bridges, and ports were built. Railroads arrived at the end of that century, but almost all industry ground to a halt during World War I and World War II, when the Corsicans suffered major casualties. Cultivated soil reverted back to brush, and Corsican mines and factories closed one by one as families moved elsewhere in search of a better life. By 1960, the island was in a state of disrepair, with two-thirds the inhabitants it had claimed a hundred years before. Militant separatist parties, such as the Front Regionaliste

Corse and l'Action Regionaliste Corse, rallied to secede from France, which they saw as distant and unresponsive. The 1980s brought about a university in Corte (1981) and universal suffrage (1982), but spats of political violence and separatist discontent still riddled the headlines. Tensions didn't abate until Corsica negotiated with France, between 1999 and 2002, for greater autonomy and 2 billion euros' worth of investment. Today, the island is considered a *collectivite territoriale*, which places it somewhere between France's mainland *départements* and its overseas territories, ensuring it a relatively large degree of autonomy. Tourism's large and meaty hand provides 11% of the nation's income (compared with 6.6% for the rest of France), so Corsica has become very smart about preserving its traditional image and its environment. On the flip side, employment is heavily seasonal and unevenly concentrated.

Ajaccio

151km (94 miles) SW of Bastia, 136km (84 miles) NW of Bonifacio, 82km (51 miles) SW of Corte

Unlike its most famous progeny, Napoleon Bonaparte, Ajaccio has no complex about being petite. It's also more mellow, we'd wager, than any other French provincial capital—with wide, tree-lined avenues, a gorgeous open bay, and perfect year-round temperatures.

Getting There

BY AIR

The **Campo dell'Oro International Airport** is 8km (5 miles) east of Ajaccio's center on the N196 (☎ 04-95-23-56-56; www.ajaccio.aerport.fr). To get into town from there, take a taxi for about 20€ (☎ 06-62-55-71-38) or the number 8 bus, which leaves approximately once an hour from 9am to 11:45pm, takes 20 minutes to get into town, and costs 4.50€. Call ☎ 04-95-23-29-41 for information.

BY TRAIN

Find the **gare SNCF** at ☎ 04-95-23-11-03. Trains leave four times a day for Corte (2 hr., 9.60€) and Bastia (4 hr., 18€); twice a day for L'Ile Rousse (4 hr., 25€) and Calvi (5 hr., 28€).

BY BOAT

The port is on quai l'Herminier (☎ 04-95-51-55-45). You can take a **SNCM** boat from Nice and Marseille, for which you can buy a ticket up to 5 minutes before departure from the port (☎ 04-95-29-66-99; www.sncm.fr) or a **Corsica Ferries** boat from Nice and Toulon (☎ 04-95-50-78-82; www.corsicaferries.com).

BY CAR

Be warned: Parking in town is difficult, especially during the day. You can find parking lots at the place du Diament, quai l'Herminier, and in front of the train station, but they're expensive. There are free spots on the cours Grandval, the cours du Général Leclerc, and in front of the boulevard Lantivy, but you'll have to get there early for them.

BY BUS

The bus station is at quai L'Herminier, near the port. **Eurocorse Voyages** (☎ 04-95-21-06-30) goes to Propriano, Sartene, Porto-Vecchio, Bonifacio, Corte, and Bastia. **Autocars SAIB** (☎ 04-95-22-41-99) leave twice a day for Sagone, Cargese, Piana, Porto, and Ota every day from early July to Sept 15; otherwise, every day except Sundays and holidays. **Ricci buses** (☎ 04-95-51-08-19) go to and from Propriano, Levie, and Zonza every day except Sundays and holidays. In the summer, they go all the way up to the col de Bavella. **Balesi buses** (☎ 04-95-51-25-56) travel to Aullene, Quenza, Zonza, and Porto-Vecchio every day but Sundays and holidays in July and August, and on Mondays and Fridays the rest of the year.

The Best Road out of Ajaccio

You should take the **N81** until you get to the Calanches de Piana, an extraordinary micro-environment that looks like Moab, Utah. It's all jutting red rock and green nubbly brush, and the roads are perilous, but it's a thrilling, gorgeous ride. Go hiking or take a picnic into the Forêt Communale de Piana.

Rental Cars, Motorcycles & Mopeds

You can rent a car from the usual suspects at the airport: **Avis** (☎ 04-95-23-56-90), **Budget** (☎ 04-95-23-57-21), **Hertz** (☎ 04-95-23-57-04). You'll find even more in town: **Avis** is at 1 rue Colonna d'Istria (☎ 04-95-23-92-50), **Budget** is at 1 bd. Lantivy (☎ 04-95-51-21-21), and **Europcar** (☎ 04-95-21-05-49) and **Hertz** (☎ 04-95-21-70-94) are on the cours Grandval, at 8 and 16, respectively.

Rent a scooter or motorcycle from **Corsica Moto Rent**, at 51 cours Napoleon (☎ 04-95-51-34-45); quads or scooters from **General Moto**, rue Colonna d'Istria (☎ 04-95-20-34-21); or mountain bikes, scooters, or motorcycles from **Moto Corse Evasion**, on the montee St. Jean (☎ 04-95-20-52-05).

Orientation

The longest and most important avenue in town is the cours Napoleon, which goes from Charles-Ornano to the north all the way to the place Général de Gaulle. The old city is between the place Général de Gaulle, the place Foch, and the citadel, right above the old fishing port of Tino-Rossi. It encompasses the cathedral, the citadel, and the house Napoleon was born in. Across the place Foch, the rue du Cardinal Fesch is a pedestrian street with a bunch of cute shops, which joins the cours Napoleon right at the train station.

Getting Around
BY PUBLIC TRANSPORTATION

The old city is small enough to walk around, but there are a few buses worth mentioning. The number 8 goes between the bus station and the airport, leaving every hour between 6am and 7:25pm. The number 5 goes along the route des Sanguinaires, stopping at the chapelle des Grecs; beaches of Adriadne, Marinella, and Scudo; and the place Général de Gaulle

every day between 7am and 7pm. Call ☎ 04-95-23-29-41 for more details. Tickets are sold onboard for 1.15€.

BY TAXI

There is a taxi stand on the place Général de Gaulle, on avenue Pascal-Paoli, and on the corner of the cours Napoleon. "Cab companies" on Corsica are car services run by individuals who drive for hire. Relevant numbers: ☎ 04-95-21-00-87; ☎ 04-95-23-25-70; ☎ 06-15-02-60-36.

Tourist Offices

You can find everything you need at this tourist office (3 bd. du Roi-Jerome; ☎ 04-95-51-53-03; www.ajaccio-tourisme. com): maps, hotel guides, and flyers for activities. Open July to August Monday to Saturday 8am to 8:30pm, Sunday 9am to 1pm and 4 to 7pm; September to October and April to June Monday to Saturday 8am to 7pm, Sunday 9am to 1pm; during the rest of the year, it's open Monday to Friday 8am to 12:30pm and 2 to 6pm, Saturday 8am to noon and 2 to 5pm; it's closed Sunday and holidays.

Ajaccio Nuts & Bolts

Crisis Centers **Centre Hospitalier,** 27 av. de l'Imperatrice genie (☎ 04-95-29-90-90). The police station is on rue du Général Fiorella (☎ 04-95-11-17-17).

Internet/Wireless Hot Spots You can check your e-mail for free at the *office de tourisme*. If you're under 25, you can check your e-mail for free at the **Centre U Borgu;** if you're older, it costs 3.80€ per hour (52 rue Fesch; ☎ 04-95-50-13-44; summer Mon–Sat 8am–6pm; rest of the year Mon–Fri 8:30am–9pm, Sat 1:30–7pm).

Laundromats **Quick Wash,** Hôtel Kalliste (51 cours Napoleon; daily 24 hr.). **Lavomatic Diamant** (1 rue du Marechal-Ornano; daily 7am–9pm).

Post Office 13 cours Napoleon (Sun–Fri 8am–6:45pm; Sat 8am–noon).

Sleeping

CHEAP

The cheapest way to sleep in Ajaccio is to camp on the outskirts.

→**Les Mimosas** This camp is only a 15-minute walk from town, totally adequate, and bare-bones cheap. They have hot showers, a snack bar, a laundromat, and a little store. *Rte. d'Alata on the D61.* ☎ *04-95-20-99-85. Apr to mid-Oct 5€ for adults, 2.20€ for a tent, 4.20€ for a caravan, 2.20€ for a car. Even cheaper off season.*

DOABLE

→**Hôtel Le Dauphin** Location-wise, this hotel can't be beat, situated right next to both the train station and the port. There's no elevator, so if you have lots of luggage, ask for a room low to the ground or you might find yourself hauling your bags up five stories. The 39 rooms are practical if not exactly charming, but if you've got an early train or boat, this is the best you'll find for this little money. *11 bd. Sampiero.* ☎ *04-95-21-12-94. www.ledauphinhotel.com. 56€–69€ double. Rates include breakfast. Credit cards accepted. Amenities: Restaurant; parking.*

→**Hôtel Marengo** What the Marengo lacks in accessibility (it's ¾-mile from the town center), it makes up for in charm and hospitality. The 16 rooms are quiet and cool, with sweet balconies. *2 rue Marengo.* ☎ *04-95-21-43-66. www.marengohotel.it. 59€–79€ double. Breakfast 6€. Credit cards accepted. Open Apr–Nov. Amenities:* *Restaurant, elevator, parking. In room: Satellite TV, Wi-Fi.*

SPLURGE

[MTV] Best ● →**Hôtel Demeure Les Mouettes** If you're looking for a splurge in Ajaccio, Les Mouettes is the place to do it. By spring of 2007, the venerable old building will have undergone extensive renovation. All the rooms will be redecorated in 1930s Riviera shades of beige, ecru, and white with bright splashes of color on the walls and carpets, and flatscreens in every room. The hotel has stunning views of the sea, with a pool right on the beach, and offers spa, personal training, boating, and chauffeur services. Enjoy your cocktails and cigarettes on poufy sofas in the shade. *9 cours Lucien Bonaparte.* ☎ *04-95-21-71-80. http://hotellesmouettes.fr. 99€–149€ garden-view rooms; 139€–209€ superior rooms; 149€–259€ privilege suites. Credit cards accepted. Amenities: Restaurant; babysitting; dry cleaning; laundry; parking; pool; private beach. In room: A/C, minifridge, safe, Wi-Fi.*

Eating

COFFEE BARS & LIGHT FARE

→**Boulangerie Galeani** PATISSERIE The best bakery in the city, where Corsican *patisseries* come to life in your mouth. Lemon, raisin, or almond *canistrelli, brocciu beignets, ambrucciata,* and other seasonal fare. We love it. *3 rue du Cardinal Fesch.* ☎ *04-95-21-39-68. Mon–Sat 6am–8pm; Sun 6am–1pm.*

CHEAP

➜ **Chez Gerard** SEAFOOD Walking distance from center city, this *paillotte* (beach hut) serves a very highly recommended, monster portion of *moules marinieres*. Wash it down with some AOC Ajaccio white wine, and you can leave full, drunk, and happy for under 25€. The wind tousles your hair, and the waves beckon you to jump in fully dressed. No one will try to stop you, but at least take your clothes off, or you'll have to walk back to town all sopping wet. *Plage Saint-François. No phone. Main courses 15€. No credit cards. Daily lunch and dinner (no set schedule at this beachside shack).*

➜ **Le Don Quichotte** PIZZERIA Between rue Fesch and the market, this place serves the town's best pizzas, topped with fresh ingredients atop a terrific crust. Eat outside on the terrace and watch the passersby. *Rue des Halles. ☎ 04-95-21-27-30. Menu 12€–20€. Credit cards accepted. Mon–Sat 11am–3pm and 6pm–midnight.*

DOABLE

➜ **U Pampasgiolu** CORSICAN A talented Ajaccian chef serves Corsican cuisine, both old and new, in the old town. Try the *planches,* or wooden boards, heaped with meat or fish. Really fine cooking. *15 rue de la Porta. ☎ 04-95-50-71-52. Main courses 25€–30€. Credit cards accepted. Mon–Sat 7–11pm.*

SPLURGE

📺 Best ⬤ ➜ **Le Bilboq Chez Jean-Jean** SEAFOOD Otherwise known as Chez Jean-Jean, this is the place to go all out, even though there's only one thing on the menu: *spaghettis aux langoustes,* or spiny lobster spaghetti. The langoustines, which literally go from the fishing boat to the cooking pot, come either grilled or cooked with the pasta (insiders say this is the way to get it). While you'll spend 45€ before you even start drinking, the food is exceptional. Owner JeanJean is a former pro boxer, and photos of him in the good old days adorn the walls inside. In the summer, eat outside in the courtyard in the old town. *1 rue des Glacis. ☎ 04-95-51-35-40. 60€, including wine. No credit cards. Mar–May Thurs–Sat 8pm–midnight; June–Oct daily 8pm–midnight.*

Partying

📺 Best ⬤ ➜ **Le Café Fesch** (☎ **04-95-23-22-19**) and **La Part des Anges** (☎ **04-95-21-29-34**) are next-door neighbors on boulevard Lantivy in the old town. They have different owners but switch off nights as the hot spots in town. La Part des Anges has a terrific selection of Corsican wines, which you can sample all night long.

If you go left, you'll get to the casino, inside of which is **l'Entr'acte,** which plays good house music, late. You can dance your cares away after losing all your money.

The best parties happen in *paillotes,* or beach huts, over the summer. The smartest way to find out what's on when is to ask one of the waiters at either the Café Fesch or La Part des Anges, who will probably be in attendance after their shifts end. One particularly good one is at Le Pirate, at Capo di Feno 9km (6 miles) from Ajaccio. They serve grilled seafood and meat, and parties often last until 6am.

Sightseeing

CHURCHES

➜ **La Cathédrale d'Ajaccio** Greek, Roman, and French all at once, the cathedral was built at the end of the 16th century; Napoleon was baptized here in July 1771. If you're lucky to be here in mid-March, don't miss the festivities surrounding the celebration of the Virgin, who allegedly protected the villagers from an outbreak of the plague. *Rue St. Charles. ☎ 04-95-21-05-48.*

Native Son Napoleon

Corsica's most famous native is, no doubt, the redoubtable Napoleon Bonaparte, who is celebrated here in everything from statues to street names to snow globes. The son of petty Corsican aristocrats, Bonaparte was born in Ajaccio in 1769, but he left the island at the age of 9 to attend military school in Brienne. He proved himself a military genius early, rebuffing in 1793 the royalists in Toulon as an artillery chief and defending Corsica from the English in the same year. Following a Parisian coup in 1799, Napoleon declared himself consul, and, several years later, Emperor of the new French republic; he was only 35. Seven years later, he made Corsica the newest French *département,* binding it irretrievably to France. Although Corsicans remain proud of their prodigal son, many wish he'd kept his talents on the island rather than moving to France and swallowing it up.

MUSEUMS

➜**Musée Fesch** Unless you're an art history dork, you might not get how amazing the Fesch's collection of 14th- to 19th-century Italian painting is. It's among the best exhibition of primitive to baroque work in existence, and we have Napoleon's uncle Joseph Fesch to thank for it. While at war with the Italians (with little Napoleon), Fesch accumulated so many Botticellis, Titians, Caravaggios, and Veronesis that he'd amassed 16,000 paintings by the time he died. Okay, if you're still not convinced or just don't like paintings, it's still worth going just to see the 15m (50-ft.) reading room, lined the whole way with more than 40,000 gorgeous old books. *50 rue du Cardinal Fesch. Museum:* ☎ *04-95-21-48-17; www.musee-fesch.com; admission 5.35€; July–Aug Mon 1:30–6pm, Tues–Fri 9am–6:30pm (Fri also 9pm–midnight), Sat–Sun 10:30am–6pm; Oct–Mar Tues–Sat 9:15am–12:15am and 2:15–5:15pm. Library:* ☎ *04-95-51-13-00; free admission; summer Mon–Fri 9am–4:30pm, winter Mon–Fri 10am–6pm.*

➜**Musée d'Histoire de la Corse A Bandera** You probably came to Corsica for its beaches, not its museums, but we couldn't resist slipping this one in, too (it does sometimes rain in Corsica, after all).

This museum tries to cover everything in Corsican history, and it's a veritable bazaar of old costumes, dioramas, guns, and other assorted artifacts. *1 rue du Général-Levie.* ☎ *04-95-51-07-34. Admission 4€ adults, 2.50€ students. May–Oct daily 9am–7pm (Fri until 10pm); Nov–Apr Mon–Sat 9am–noon and 2–6pm.*

➜**Musée National de la Maison Bonaparte** When Napoleon was born here, Ajaccio was actually Genoan. When the island fell to the English in 1793, the Bonapartes fled and the house was pillaged. Four years later, Letizia Bonaparte came home and salvaged it. While no one can really be sure that the house was arranged the same way or even that the furniture is original, the dwelling is adorable and gives an idea of how life was for republic-era petty Ajaccian aristocracy. The coolest thing in the whole building, however, is the family tree made from locks of hair. *Rue Saint-Charles.* ☎ *04-95-21-43-89. Admission 4€ adults, 2.60€ for those 18–25, free for those under 18. Apr–Sept daily (except Mon morning) 9am–noon and 2–6pm; Oct–Mar daily (except Mon morning) 10am–noon and 2–4:45pm. Show up at least a half-hour before close or they won't let you in.*

TWO SPECIAL TOURS

Start out either itinerary with *patisseries,* especially the *pains au chocolat,* from the **Salon de Thé** (☎ 04-95-21-03-70) on the boulevard Roi Jerome. Choose the breakfast menu: tea, coffee, or chocolate, with a croissant or *pain au chocolat,* and juice, for 5.50€. For 2€ more, add a half-baguette with butter and jam.

The Market Tour

Explore the market, which sells attractive-looking fruits and vegetables, Corsican charcuterie and cheeses, and various other food products. Then browse the extraordinary Costa cookshop, established in 1878 and packed with all manner of kitchen equipment. The **Album Librairie** bookshop has stacks upon stacks of local books and maps. It's on the rue Cardinal Fesch and the Piazza di l'Olmes (Mon–Sat 8:30am–12:30pm and 2:30–7:30pm, until midnight on Fri; Sun 8:30am–noon). Walk down past the place Foch, then buckle around the avenue A Serafini until you find the **cours Napoleon** seaside, which buckles around behind the Citadel. Visit the Musée du Capitellu, the Eglise St. Ersame beside it, and then the Cathdrale on the pretty place de Gaulle.

The Imperial City

To tour the imperial city of Ajaccio, start at the **Musée Fesch** on the rue du Cardinal Fesch. Walk down the street a few blocks until you hit the place Foch, where you can pop into the **Salon Napoleonien** at the Hôtel de Ville, or town hall. Check out the Fontaine des 4 lions on the place Foch before continuing on the rue Bonaparte, where you can see the **house Napoleon** was born in. Then follow the rue St. Charles past the rue Roi de Rome until you get to the place de Gaulle. Finish off at the **Grotte Napoleon** on the place d'Austerlitz.

Playing Outside

You'll find two great beaches in town: **Plage de Saint-François** (on the bd. Lantivy and bd. Pascal-Rossini) and the **Plage Trottel** (on the bd. Albert Ier).

Shopping

MUSIC, BOOKS & MEDIA

➜**Au Son Des Guitares** Want to hear Corsicans sing? No, really, some of them are famous for it. Find out why at this old-school bar-cum-concert hall, where you can also buy the music, should you like it. The shows start at 10:30pm, and cover everything from polyphonic chanting to modern Corsican voice. Come in for free, but buy a drink and support the sound. *Rue du Roi de Rome. Call* ☎ *04-95-51-16-47 for reservations. Mon–Fri 7:15pm–2am; Sat–Sun until 3am.*

➜**La Marge** This bookstore bursts at the seams with thousands of books, many of them written on Corsica by Corsicans in Corsican. Awesome. *4 rue Emmanuel Arene.* ☎ *04-95-51-23-67. Mon–Sat 9am–7:30pm.*

FOOD, WINE & LOCAL CRAFTS

➜**U Stazzu** More of the same, but who's complaining? Charcuteries, cheeses, oils, *pâtés,* olives, wines, cheeses. Ask the owner, who is part of a five-generation charcuterie family, about trips to see the production facilities. *1 rue Bonaparte.* ☎ *04-95-51-10-80. Daily 9am–12:30pm and 2:30–7pm; closed Sun in winter.*

➜**Villages Corses** Smack in the center of the capital, this store brings the bounty of the mountains down to the bay. Sample the best charcuteries from Bocognano, canistrelli, olive oils, and honeys. *44 rue Fesch.* ☎ *04-95-51-08-05. Daily 9am–7:30pm.*

Bastia: Fierce Face of the Tyrrhenian

94km (58 miles) E of Calvi, 69km (43 miles) N of Corte, 151km (94 miles) NE of Ajaccio

As Corsica's second-biggest city, Bastia's large commercial port leads many to overlook the beauties of its nooks and crannies. While it would be easy just to stay seaside—which is pleasant enough—you'll get a lot more out of Bastia if you wander up the rocky crags overlooking the city to see the view from above, or wander into the old-school backstreets. This is also probably the best place in Corsica to buy Corsican food products—the best kind of souvenir. You'll find liquor, wine, olive oil, honey, and cheese (but don't even think about transporting the *frommage*).

Getting There

BY AIR

The little **Aéroport Bastia-Poretta** (☎ 04-95-54-54-54) is 20km (12 miles) from the center of town, and you can fly in from most of the big French mainline cities, and also London and Berlin. If you fly in, make sure you get a window seat; the views of the Cap Corse are awesome. From there you can take a 35-minute **bus** (☎ 04-95-31-06-65) into the center of Bastia for 8€ or a **taxi** (☎ 04-95-36-04-05).

BY BOAT

You can buy ferry tickets out of Bastia on the day of travel, or on the Web. **Corsica Ferries** goes to and from Toulon, Nice, Savona, and Livorno. Buy your ticket from the port (5 bis rue du Chanoine-Leschi; ☎ 04-95-32-95-95; Mon–Fri 9am–noon and 2–6pm, Sat 9pm–midnight), or online (www.corsicaferries.com). Alternately, the **SNCM** does the road between Bastia and Marseille (☎ 04-95-54-66-90; Mon–Fri 7:30am–7pm, Sat 8am–noon).

BY TRAIN

Get to Bastia from Ajaccio (trip time: 4 hr., 24€), Corte (2 hr., 11€), or Calvi (3 hr., 18€), up to four times daily. The **train station** is at the top of avenue Marechal-Sebastiani (☎ 04-95-32-80-61).

BY CAR

You can take your car to Corsica on the ferry, which will deposit you in Bastia; take the N193 in and out. If you want to explore Bastia, leave your car at the parking lot in front of the place Saint-Nicolas or the market (11€ per day); driving in town is best left to the insane. You can park for free at the old port or the train station, but they're usually full.

BY BUS

The bus station is at the rue du Nouveau-Port, behind the tourist office. There's no building, only bus stops, but if you have questions, just duck into the tourist office. For Ajaccio, take the **Euro-Corse bus,** which runs every day but Sundays and holidays (☎ 04-95-21-06-30; 19€). Buses to Corte go Monday, Wednesday and Friday from the train station with **Autocars Cortenais** (☎ 04-95-46-02-12; 10€). For Saint-Florent, take the **Autocars Santini** every day other than Sundays and holidays (☎ 04-95-31-03-79; 5€). For Calvi, take the **Beaux Voyages bus** from the train station (☎ 04-95-65-15-02; 15€).

Orientation

You can divide the town into three sea-facing sections. The southern section encompasses the citadel and Terra Nova; the northern part includes Saint-Nicolas and the big square in front of it; and in the middle is the old city, known as Terra Vecchia,

Rental Cars, Motorcycles & Mopeds

You can pick up a rental car either at the airport or in the center of town from **Hertz** (☎ 04-95-30-05-16), **Avis** (☎ 04-95-54-55-46), **Budget** (☎ 04-95-31-77-31), or **Ada** (04-95-54-55-44). Rent a motorbike or scooter from **Corsica Moto Rent** (☎ 04-95-54-55-11). For an all-terrain bike, delivered to wherever you're staying, check out **Objectif Nature,** on 3 rue Notre-Dame-de-Lourdes (☎ 04-95-32-54-34; www.objectif-nature-corse.com; daily 8am–8pm).

and its old port. If you stick around the place Saint-Nicolas, the citadel, and the old port, you'll see what's going on, but it still pays to wander around.

Getting Around

BY PUBLIC TRANSPORTATION

SITB buses will get you anywhere you need to be in Bastia. Lines 1 and 2 traverse the city, line 3 goes to Cardo, line 4 to Miomo and Pietranera, line 5 to Furiani, line 6 to Ville-di-Pietrabugno and San-Martino-di-Lota, line 7 to Figarella, and line 8 to Marana.

BY TAXI

Try either **Taxis Blues** (☎ 04-95-32-70-70) or **Taxis Orange Bastiais** (☎ 04-95-32-

24-24). It costs about 35€ to go to the airport.

ON FOOT

Bastia is small enough to navigate on foot. The main commercial streets are the boulevard Paoli and the rue Cesar-Campinchi. The old port has most of the bars and restaurants in it.

Tourist Offices

The tourist office is at place Saint-Nicolas (☎ 04-95-54-20-40; www.bastia-tourisme.com; Oct–May Mon–Sat 8am–6pm, Sun 8am–noon; June–Sept daily 8am–8pm).

Bastia Nuts & Bolts

Emergencies   Central police station (☎ 04-95-55-22-22). Lifeguards (☎ 04-95-20-13-63).

Hospitals   Route Imperiale, 6km (4 miles) southwest of the city (☎ 04-95-59-11-11).

Internet/Wireless Hot Spots   Your most pleasant bet is **Chez Yves,** where you can munch on a really good sandwich while you check your e-mail anytime from 9am to 10pm for 3€ per hour (4 cours Pierangeli; ☎ 04-95-31-71-69). Or try the **Cyber Café** near the post office (5 av. Mar-Sebastiani; Mon–Fri 9am–7pm, Sat 8am–2pm).

Laundromats   25 rue Luce-di-Casabianca (daily 7am–9pm).

Post Office   Located on avenue Mar-Sebastiani (☎ 04-95-32-80-78; Mon–Fri 8am–7pm, Sat 8am–noon).

Sleeping

CHEAP

Sleeping supercheap in Bastia is not easy, especially during high season. If you're lucky, snag one of the two rooms at **Chez Mme Vignon.** The bathroom is communal, but Mme Vignon is awesome, and the views from her house, overlooking the Cap Corse and the island of Elba, are incredible. The house is 10 minutes from the center of town, and breakfast is included. Because she rocks so hard, Mme Vignon is hard to pin down, so call her for a reservation (20 montee des Philippines; ☎ **04-95-32-23-70;** average double high season 40€; no credit cards).

Or try **M. and Mme Tinti,** who have one double room in an apartment on the boulevard Paoli. Fifty-five euros get you bed and breakfast with your own bathroom (26 bd. Paoli; ☎ **06-29-32-93-66).** Other people offer rooms, but not in the center of Bastia; ask the tourist office for the *Chambres chez l'habitant* handout for more suggestions.

→ **Hôtel Central** If you'd rather be in the center, this is the place to be, in one of these 18 pleasant, clean, warmly decorated wooden rooms, or 6 apartments. The smells from the bakery next door are intoxicating and will lure you out of bed early. If you get a kitchenette room, you can even take the pastries home and toast the bread yourself. *3 rue Miot.* ☎ *04-95-31-71-12. www.centralhotel.fr. Around 55€ double; 80€ room with kitchenette. Breakfast available. Credit cards accepted. Amenities: Bike rental. In room: TV, fans.*

DOABLE

→ **Hôtel Posta Vecchia** Treat yourself to one of the 51 comfortable rooms here for relatively cheap; some have sea views. There is a *pétanque* court right under the windows, so you can watch the games from above. They have parking! *8 rue Posta Vecchia.* ☎ *33-04-95-32-32-38. www. hotel-postavecchia.com. 40€–80€ double, according to the season and quality of the room. Credit cards accepted. Amenities: Parking. In room: A/C, TV.*

SPLURGE

→ **Hôtel Les Voyageurs** This classy three-star hotel is perfectly located between the port and the train station. All the recently renovated rooms are soundproofed and air-conditioned, and boast televisions with more channels (25) than you'll find in most other Corsican hotels. The rooms are peaceful, uncluttered, and simply but artfully decorated. The staff is friendly and professional. *9 av. du Marechal-Sebastiani.* ☎ *04-95-34-90-80. www. hotel-lesvoyageurs.com. 60€–100€ double. Credit cards accepted. Closed mid-Dec to mid-Jan. In room: A/C, TV, Internet.*

Eating

The old port is a popular dining area, and you'll eat decently there, but you'll find better restaurants sprinkled elsewhere. This is one city where you can eat terrifically well without breaking the bank. It has been said that Bastians prefer their meat to fish, but if you're here, indulge in an incredibly fresh Mediterranean *poisson*. Wash it down with the local beer, Pietra, an amber brew made from chestnut flour. These guys also make Corsica Cola, worth a try as well.

COFFEE BARS & LIGHT FARE

→ **Café Au Palais des Glaces** It's hot, you've been walking for hours, and you need a break. Head for the place St. Nicolas—odds are you're there already—and get a homemade ice cream. You can breakfast for 4.50€ and watch young Bastiens and tourists check each other out from the comfort of their wicker chairs. *13 bd. du Général de Gaulle.* ☎ *04-95-31-05-01.*

Daily specials 12€. Credit cards accepted. Mon–Fri 7am–11pm, Sat–Sun 7am–2am.

CHEAP

➜**Chez Carlotti et Fils** PATISSERIE This place is a carb-lovers' dream come true. Enjoy the sublime white-wine or anise-doused *canistrelli*, cheesy *migliacciu*, onion tarts, or big peasant brioches stuffed with *brocciu. 18 bd. Paoli.* ☎ *04-95-31-65-05. Call for hours.*

➜**Claudius** CORSICAN Okay, some of the main dishes here may wander out of the "cheap" category, but because you can get the *plat du jour* for 10€ and this place is so darn rad, I'm listing it so you *go there*. Make sure to eat fish, because it will definitely be good, and sample the delicious 4€ to 5€ desserts. *Port Toga, behind the port.* ☎ *04-95-31-73-54. Plat du jour 10€; a la carte 30€. Call for hours.*

DOABLE

➜**Sol et Mar** SEAFOOD Easy, breezy, beautiful. Choose a fish of the day baked, fried, or poached, for 53€ per kilo (you'll probably only need a quarter of that). Owners Sol(ange) and Mar(io) have created a really adorable eating space; you'll fall in love with it after a couple glasses of Cap Corse. Also highly recommended are the *brocciu* and artichoke ravioli or the crab ravioli. *Quai des Martyrs-de-la-Liberation.* ☎ *04-95-58-14-26. 25€ per person. No credit cards. Mon 7–11pm; Tues–Sun noon–3pm and 7–11pm.*

MTV Best ☻ ➜**U Tianu** CORSICAN We've already mentioned the nationalist thing going on here, but more importantly, you'll eat copiously and well: The menu is 19€ and will stuff you full of charcuteries, meat, cheese, dessert, wine, aperitif, coffee, and liquor. By the time you leave, you'll have drunk enough eau-de-vie to be able to sing along to the Corsican songs playing in the background. *4 rue Monseigneur-Rigo (between the quai des Martyrs and the place du Marché).* ☎ *04-95-31-36-67. Menu 19€. Credit cards accepted. Mon–Sat 7–11pm.*

SPLURGE

➜**Le Caveau du Marin** SEAFOOD For once, even our splurge isn't super expensive. The fish, fresh out of water, will arrive on a platter, and you can pick out your own victims to the tune of 60€ per kilo. Lobster comes with a fatter price tag, but once it's poached or bathed in olive oil and fresh basil, maybe 145€ per kilo won't seem too extreme. Best of all, they have a delicious prix fixe at 20€. *Quai des Martyrs-de-la-Liberation.* ☎ *04-95-31-62-31. Menu 20€. Credit cards accepted. Tues 7–11pm; Wed–Sun noon–2pm and 7–11pm.*

Partying

If by day the best place for a quick nip is on the place Saint-Nicolas, by night you might want to head to **La Marana,** where most of the partying in Bastia goes on. Taking a cab out there is the best place to make sure you come home safely.

➜ **L'Apocalypse** Shake your groove thang to the rolling sounds of the ocean at this local favorite. They host foam parties, lingerie parties, and guest DJs on special nights; at other times, young Bastians rock out to the techno beats on the Apobeach. *Rte. de la Marana-Biguglia.* ☎ *04-95-33-36-83.*

➜ **Le Bouchon** If you're keeping it tame and in town, check out this place. Pick and choose your pleasure off the carefully selected Corsican and international wine list, and talk to the waiters at length about your choice. It's a great place to go for dessert: Try the artisanal gelato made from local flavors such as pine, chestnut, and *brocciu.* The inside is rustic and woodsy, with wobbly tables and lots of schmoozy couples. *4 bis rue Saint-Jean.* ☎ *04-95-58-14-22. No credit cards.*

CORSICA

➔**Le Penalty** Listen to local music as you down a Pietra, the local brew, in this old pub on the corner of place de l'Hôtel de Ville and Stretta Mrg Rigo. *Place de l'Hôtel de Ville.* ☎ *04-95-31-03-47.*

Sightseeing

The **square of Saint-Nicolas** is probably the best place to start your tour of Bastia. An immense rectangle facing the sea, this is one of the biggest piazzas in France, despite the small size of Bastia. Dig the statue of Napoleon as a Roman emperor, gazing toward the Isle of Elba, where Napoleon finished his days, purportedly close enough to smell the maquis of his native land. It's hard to believe the bloody execution of Jean Nicoli happened here in 1943; if you take the cours Pierangeli, you'll see his name on the high school there.

➔**Eglise-Cathédrale de la Canonica** Blink and you'll miss it, randomly placed as it is off the side of the D107 near the Bastia airport. This cathedral, consecrated in 1119, is a gorgeous example of Pisan-Roman architecture. Local stone from the Cap Corse, of different sizes and colors, creates a gorgeous geometric puzzle in yellow, light green, orange, and blue. Check out the Mariana archaeological site nearby as well. Ask about it at the cathedral. *20km (12 miles) north of Bastia, take the N193 toward Borgo, then turn off on the D107 at Crocetta. No phone, no hours (it's a deserted old church).*

➔**Eglise Saint-Jean-Baptiste** This immense neoclassical baroque parish church, financed by the Bastienas, is the biggest church in Corsica. The organs, monumentally placed between beautiful marble and *trompe l'oeil* paintings, are worth a look. *Rue C. Viale-Prela (Terra Vecchia), place de l'Hôtel de Ville.* ☎ *04-95-32-91-66. Sat–Sun 8am–noon and 2–5pm.*

FREE ➔**Oratoire de l'Immaculée-Conception** Resplendent on the place

Saint-Nicolas, next to the Oratoir Saint-Roch, the very appearance of this enormous, solemn baroque church can strike enough fear to make you go confess immediately. When Corsica belonged to England, between 1794 and 1796, the king's throne sat on the oratory. The outside looks austere, but the inside, in shades of scarlet and gold, with frescoed ceilings, is sumptuous. *Rue Napoléon.* ☎ *04-95-32-91-66. Free admission. Sat–Sun 8am–noon and 2–5pm.*

FREE ➔**Village Miniature de René Mattei** Some crazy dude spent 3 years in the 1980s building this mini replica of a Corsican village. It's got chestnut mills, Genoan towers, and old citadel walls. There is an electric train (of course) and the church bells even ring! *Poudriere de la Citadelle.* ☎ *06-10-26-82-08. Free admission. Apr to mid-Oct daily 9am–noon and 2:30–6pm.*

TWO SPECIAL TOURS
Old City

Visit old-school Bastia by getting lost among the narrow alleyways of the old city. Start at the place St-Nicolas, then walk to the **place du Marché,** also known as the place de l'Hôtel de Ville, which is the real entrance to the **Terra-Vecchia** neighborhood. The market is surrounded by high 17th-century buildings, with the old town hall right by it. The east side of the **Eglise St. Jean-Baptiste** is on one side of the market; take a cool break inside. Hit up the **Oratoire de l'Immaculée-Conception** next, on the rue Napoleon, then go around to the old port. It's on the site of the old village of Cardo, made obsolete when steamboats necessitated more room, after 1830. Today, fishing and pleasure boats have taken over, and look best at sunrise. Whether you've gotten up early or are going to bed late, walk to the end of the *jetée du Dragon* to watch the shadows play on the Cap Corse and the Isles of Elba and Montecristo.

The Citadel

The second tour starts at the **Citadel,** to which you come by walking up the boulevard August-Gaudin or by coming down the jardin Romieu. The citadel, built between the 15th and 17th centuries, surveys the town and old port. The Genoans were in charge, and it shows, in the carefully plotted-out blocks that align the military, economic, and administrative centers with the religious quarters. Walk toward the old governor's palace, finished in 1530, which housed the Genoan governors until 1768. At the time of this writing, it was closed to the public, but it's reopening as a **Museum of Baroque Art and Bastian History** in 2007. The rue Notre-Dame will take you to the Eglise Sainte-Marie, where you can see some of cardinal Fesch's amazing art collection, but then take the rue de l'Echeve on the right, which is actually a staircase, toward the oratoire Saint-Croix. Bastia's famous Black Christ, who gets celebrated once a year, lives here. He was allegedly found amid four ethereal lights floating in a fisherman's net. End your tour by relaxing under trees in the jardin Romieu.

Playing Outside

→ **Col de Teghime** You'll need a car to get to the Col de Teghime, 8km (5 miles) southwest of Bastia on the D81. But from this peak at the bottom of the Cap Corse peninsula, smack in between the west and east coasts, you can see the water on both sides and the Agriates desert in the background. It's the best place to watch the sunset and think about how damn lucky you are. Bring a bottle, and don't forget the cork pop.

→ **Jardin Romieu** This is a beautiful spot to take a break when the sun shines too hot. You can sit under the palm, bay, and pine trees and relax for a while. It's near the governor's palace at the old port, to

which it's connected by a giant staircase. *Place du Donjon.*

Shopping

MUSIC, BOOKS & MEDIA

→ **Chorus** This shop stocks both traditional and contemporary Corsican tunes. *11 rue Cesar Campinchi.* ☎ *04-95-32-65-23. Mon–Sat 9:15am–noon and 2:15–7pm; in summer open at 3pm.*

FOOD, WINE & LOCAL CRAFTS

→ **Mattei Cap Corse** Come here for an incredible array of Corsican wine, nut, and cedar liquors, set in splendor. It's the oldest and best boutique in Corsica, with high ceilings and wood floors. Try the house liquor, invented in 1872 by Louis-Napoleon Mattei, who mixed Cap Corse Muscat with macerated orange, quinquina, and who knows what else, to delicious effect. *15 bd. Général-de-Gaulle.* ☎ *04-95-32-44-38. Call for hours.*

→ **U Muntagnolu** This is *the* place for authentic Corsican artisanal food products, as stated by the "no donkey sausage here" sign at the entrance. The usual suspects: raw-milk cheeses, charcuterie from tiny producers, herbs, olive oils, honey, and wine. *15 rue Cesar Campinchi.* ☎ *04-95-32-78-04. Mon–Sat 9am–8pm.*

→ **U Paese** If you've been loving Corsican charcuterie, you'll think you've died and gone to pig heaven at U Paese. Not only that, but you can be sure here that the products are actually artisanal and not ersatz stuff being passed off as such. Try the Alesani hams or the spicy goat's cheeses from Galeria. The divine honeys make great gifts. If you speak a bit of French (or Italian), so much the better, so the staff can enlighten you about the interesting production details. *4 rue Napoléon.* ☎ *04-95-32-33-18. Mon–Sat 9am–noon and 3–7pm.*

CORSICA

Festivals

→ **Fête de la Saint-Joseph** We love food festivals, especially those centered around doughnuts. Why don't we have any of those in the U.S.? Check out the *panzarotti* prepared in honor of Saint-Joseph, the celebree. Then go start up your own doughnut festival back home. *Mar 19.*

→ **Graphic Novel Festival** Check out this popular comic-book festival. (Graphic novels are coming around in the U.S., but the French are generally way more into comic books than we are.) ☎ *04-95-32-12-81. Early Apr.*

→ **Festival of Saint Jean-Baptiste** Bonfires are organized all over town,

especially at the church of Saint Jean-Baptiste, in that saint's honor. *June 23.*

→ **Relief of the Governor Festival** More than 200 people in historical costumes, parading through town? Yes! Be there and watch the re-enactment. Call the folklore preservation society of Bastia (☎ 04-95-32-33-61) for details. *2nd Sat in July.*

→ **The International Chess Competition** This international tournament takes place here in the fall. ☎ *04-95-32-75-91. Oct–Nov.*

→ **Christmas Week** The place Saint-Nicolas gets dressed up in Christmas drag, with a skating rink and artificial village. Buy your Christmas ham here too. *Christmas week.*

Erbalunga

One of the first villages out of Bastia heading north on the D80, Erbalunga serves as a great introduction to the rest of the Cap Corse. Hugging the colorful harbor, this town has become, yes, somewhat gentrified, but it remains precious in ways that Disney could never touch. What today is a sleepy town of local retirees playing *pétanque* under plane trees used to be one of Corsica's busiest ports in the 16th century, meaning that it developed earlier than most of the surrounding villages, which date from the 18th and 19th centuries.

Sleeping & Eating

→ **Chez Antoine** PIZZERIA Simple but tasty pizzas and fresh seafood make this an easy, tasty, and cheap option for those just driving through. You'll have a hard time spending more than 15€. ☎ *04-95-58-29-96. Main courses under 15€. Call for hours.*

→ **Hôtel Castel Brando** Gentility incarnate, this is one of the special châteaux de France. This genteel former *palazzo americano,* then known as Casa Calisti, was originally built by a Corsican who made his

fortune in Santo Domingo. The Pieri family lived there in the late '80s then opened it as a four-star hotel in 1990. They have managed it with panache ever since. You can peep at the sea thorough gorgeous shuttered windows, and the whole town is at your disposal, starting with the kind and friendly concierge downstairs. Rooms, each decorated differently and tastefully, are totally worth the price. There's even a heated pool. *Hôtel Demeure Castel Brando.* ☎ *04-95-30-10-30. www.castelbrando.com. 130€–200€ in season. Credit cards accepted. Open mid-Mar to Oct. Amenities: Wi-Fi in the lobby. In room: A/C, TV, fridge, hair dryer, Internet, safe.*

→ **Le Pirate** SEAFOOD This is Erbalunga's most famous gastronomic destination, and it's beautiful to boot. The fixed-price dinner seems pricey at 55€, but the quality of the food and the impressive wine list parallels what you'd pay twice as much for in Paris or other big French cities: seafood and mountain products that are fresh, simple, and of the highest quality. If it still seems too steep, try the *spuntino* lunch menu for 35€.

Le Cap Corse

If you're flying into Le Cap Corse, you'll see what amounts to Corsica's middle finger, sticking it to France and Italy. Once you land, you won't be surprised to see why this promontory has been so hotly contested by the Genoans, the mainland French, and Corsican natives; from certain peaks inland, you can see the ocean on both sides of this peninsula. What *will* surprise you is how much of this tiny place nevertheless feels unsullied by time, war, and tourism.

In part, this area was populated by adventurers who left to find fortune in the New World or French colonies abroad, occasionally returning to build the statuesque *palazzi americani* that dot the roads. Farmers also lived here, adapting to the rocky, uneven terrain of the peninsula so well that the local economy flourished for 5 centuries based exclusively on olive trees, wine-growing, and a few other crops.

The Cap Corse is divided into 22 *communes* sprinkled with little townships. The peninsula has a tourist office, at the northern exit of Bastia, on the right (☎ **04-95-31-02-32;** www.destination-cap-corse.com; Mon–Fri 9am–noon and 2–5pm). They have information about hiking, beaches, and lodging. Lodging is pricey, but if you're going to treat yourself, this is one good place to do it.

Port de Plaisance. ☎ *04-95-33-24-20. www. restaurantlepirate.com. Lunch menu 29€ and 35€; dinner menu 59€. Credit cards accepted. Mar–Dec Wed–Sun noon–2pm and 7:30–9:30pm.*

📺 Best● →U **Fragnu** SEAFOOD If you have one meal in Erbalunga—or, actually, all of Corsica—let it be here. The 23€ menu gets you a choice of several appetizers. The fish soup, which comes accompanied by garlic, toast, *rouille,* and cheese is a good choice. The *moules marinieres* is a close and excellent second. Third is the fish of the day, caught earlier by Mediterranean fisherman. Finish with beautiful local cheeses or the smooth crème brûlée. The setting is a terrace directly above the crashing waves, and the service is impeccable. Go, go, go. *Erbalunga-Brando 20222.* ☎ *04-95-33-93-23. Menu 23€. No credit cards. Call for hours.*

Playing Outside

Erbalunga's beach is made of smooth flat stones, but if you want sand in your underwear, here are a few options on the Cap Corse.

North of Macinaggio, which is 25km (16 miles) north of Erbalunga, **Cala Francese beach** is a deserted sandy beach with super-smooth water backed by a ruined Genovese tower and Roman vestiges. To get there, park at Tamarone beach in Macinaggio. Walk for 25 minutes, passing the Santa Maria chapel. The beach is a few minutes past that. Otherwise, catch the San Paulu ferry there.

Saleccia beach, east of St. Florent, is reputed to be the most beautiful beach in all of the Mediterranean. Drive to Casta (10km/6 miles), or take the St. Florent shuttle boat (call ☎ **04-95-37-06-04**), which lands in Lotu beach. Then walk northwest on the coast guard path for 20 minutes.

The villages of **Porettu, Castullu,** and **Pozzu** in the hills above Erbalunga are reputed to be of great beauty and worth a drive-by as well.

Corsican Wine

Corsican wine, thought by many as even hairier than its cheeses, has refined itself over the years. Improvements in grape selection, winemaking techniques, and aging have resulted in excellent recent vintages. Best of all, many are really affordable. Native varieties include *niellucciu,* which gives berry and stone fruit notes, or *sciaccarellu,* which is fresh and peppery, or the kicking *vermentinu,* with apple and almond aromas. The Nebbio region is famous for its reds, while the Cap Corse area has simple, pleasant whites and fat muscats. Check out the following wineries, which you can visit if you call ahead.

Route des Vins du Cap (AOC Coteaux et Muscat du Cap Corse)

→ **Domaine de Gioielli** (at Macinaggio) ☎ 04-95-35-42-05

→ **Clos Nicrosi** (Rogliano, near Macinaggio) ☎ 04-95-35-41-17

→ **Domaine de Pietri** (at Morsiglia) ☎ 04-95-35-60-93

Route des Vins de Patrimonio (AOC Patrimonio and Muscat)

→ **Domaine Arena** (at Patrimonio) ☎ 04-95-37-08-27

→ **Domaine de Catarelli** (at Patrimonio) ☎ 04-95-37-02-84

→ **Domaine Orenga de Gaffory** (at Patrimonio) ☎ 04-95-37-45-00

→ **Domaine de Gentlie** (at St. Florent) ☎ 04-95-37-01-54

→ **Domaine de Leccia** (at Poggio d'Oletta) ☎ 04-95-37-11-35

South of Bastia

If you're driving through Corsica, here's a great place to sleep and eat once you've left Bastia, heading south toward Corte or Bonifacio.

→ **Hôtel and Restaurant Accendi Pipa–Campitello** This hotel is in the beautiful middle of nowhere, with a restaurant on-site. Compared to what you'd get for this price in Bastia or Ajaccio, it's a steal. A warren of hallways leads to small but adequate rooms; ask for those flanked by humungous private terraces with views of the pool. Bathrooms are tiny (in one, the "door" to the sink, toilet, and shower doubled as a shower curtain) and not-so-private. If you can't deal with the idea of your travel companions hearing you tinkle, consider staying elsewhere. There is a pool (used for phys ed by the schoolchildren of several local rural communities), and the rooms come with primitive television sets. Although "Campitello" is a part of the hotel name, be warned: It's not in Campitello (a tiny village in the mountains above); rather, it's safely anchored the N193 below. *RN 193.* ☎ *04-95-38-60-31. 122€ double. Credit cards accepted. Amenities: Restaurant, parking. In room: TV.*

Corte: A Stony Face Staring into Space

69km (43 miles) S of Bastia, 83km (51 miles) NE of Ajaccio, 86km (53 miles) SE of Calvi

Corte came as a complete surprise to me. No one told me about it, I just turned a corner and there it was: stony, silent, brilliant in the sun, daring me to penetrate it. Which I did. What did I find? A smattering of adorable restaurants; a quiet, smiling,

Corsica Road Trip

Start on the N193, heading south of Bastia. Detouring onto the D15 toward Campitello will take you onto a tiny, beautiful path that crumbles away to sheer rocky cliffs (hug the mountainside!). Bony cows cross the road deliberately—giving way to cars but in no hurry—to graze on dilapidated soccer fields. This is a good spot to exercise the courtesy of a quick honk as you swing around tight turns; if someone's on the other side, they'll appreciate it (and vice versa; return a honk if you hear one). Don't let the gigantic vultures make you nervous. You can follow the D15 awhile, but eventually you'll want to rejoin the N193.

The mountains flanking the N193 are a spongy green punctuated by boulders. If it's nighttime, stop by the Cesar Palace discothèque, just south of Ponte Vecchia, for a dose of local flavor. You'll see from the bullet-riddled street signs that this area is noted for hunting, especially boar and game birds.

Take the D18 toward Popolasca and drive around the spectacular piney landscape of the Aiguilles de Popolasca. You'll pass little kitchen gardens, aflower with sweet pea and tomato plants, and tiny old villages hanging off cliffs. After the Col de Croce d'Arbitro on the D118, you'll get to Castiglione, which is a dead end. A good amount of hiking trails start from this village of plum and apricot trees, but the pretty stone architecture is worth a detour, even if you won't be getting out of the car. Afterward, take a U-turn to return to the intersection of the D18 and D118.

From that intersection, take the D18 until it intersects the D84. You have the option here, if you take the D84, to go up to the Campu di Neve, a ski station 40km (25 miles) away, or the pretty Col de Vergio. If you continue on the D18, you can stop at **Chez Jacqueline** on the way to Castirla. For 25€, you'll get a plate of terrific Corsican charcuterie (ham, coppa, lonzu, sausage); then *broccio* (goat's cheese) dumplings with anchovies, lasagna, or cannelloni; the meat dish of the day; and then Corsican cheese and dessert. Make sure you request a table under the trees on the patio, although if it's raining the old-school bar will provide consolation (if you're not the one driving, of course).

Continuing along the D18 will take you to the pretty, broken-down chapel of San Michele, pronounced historic by decree in 1958 because of the murals inside. The chapel is temporarily closed, but walking to it will show you a brilliant example of a typical Corsican cemetery, where people are buried in family plots that take the shape of cabinets, with one person per drawer, and adorned with vivid bouquets of fake flowers, portraits, and various religious iconography.

After Castirla, the D18 is much improved, with wider streets and better pavement. The town of Corte, one of Corsica's bigger inland towns, is a great place to while away a couple of hours. Some stunning hiking tours start off here. The tourist office has a helpful orientation bureau with lots of maps. If you go hiking, stay at the **Refuge du Sega,** in the Valley of Tavignano (☎ **06-10-71-77-26;** May 1–Oct 15). You can rent a mattress, shower/toilet, kitchen heater/plates.

hairy community; a bunch of students; a morass of hiking trails. In short, it's a great place to stay a couple of days if you're sick of life in Club Med world.

Corte began in 1419 at the hands of Vincentello d'Istria, Corsican viceroy, who wanted to seize Corsica back from the Genoans. The current citadel, however,

Best Routes In & Out

The *trinichellu,* the little train that has connected the north to the south of the island since 1888, took 40 years to build. Today it's used by everyone from tourists to students coming back to Corte after a summer away. It winds through deserted little stations, woods, and bridges overlooking painful ravines. And it stops, most of the time, for goats that won't budge. To leave, the **N200** toward Aleria takes the prize.

was built by the French in the late 18th century. Corte even served as the capital of the independent Corsican republic founded by Pascal Paoli, which lasted 14 years. The town today serves as the guardian of Corsica's patrimony, both literally and figuratively: It houses the island's only university and its gorgeous anthropology museum.

Getting There

BY TRAIN

Trains run daily to Ajaccio (trip time: 2 hr., 11€) and Bastia (2 hr., 9.70€). By changing at Ponte-Lecchia, you can also get to Calvi and l'Ile Rousse. In July and August, trains go to Vizzavona five times daily for 5.20€. Call the *gare ferroviaire* at ☎ 04-95-46-00-97.

BY CAR

You can only get to Corte on the D18, the D41, the N200, or the N193. This sounds discouraging, but look at a map: Corte is in the middle of the island, and it's pretty easy to reach.

BY BUS

Eurocorse Voyages will take you between Corte and Bastia for 10€ or

Ajaccio (11€). They leave in front of a restaurant called Le Majestic. Call ☎ 04-95-32-01-63. **Autocars Cortenais** go to Bastia Mondays, Wednesdays, and Fridays for 10€ from Le Majestic (☎ 04-95-46-02-12). Get to Porto and Calacuccia by **Autocars Mordiconi** for 19€ from July to mid-September, from Monday to Saturday (☎ 04-95-48-00-04).

Orientation

Corte unfolds from either side of the cours Paoli, which traverses the town. The train station is about a half-mile from the center of town, on the other side of the river. Near the top of the cours Paoli, a few paths lead to the citadel. At the bottom, streets head toward the university and the Tavignano.

Getting Around

BY TAXI OR CAR

You can call **Corsica Taxi** at ☎ 04-95-48-06-29 or **Michel Salviani** at ☎ 06-03-49-15-24. To rent a car, find **Europcar** at the place de la gare, ☎ 04-95-46-06-02.

Tourist Offices

Near the entrance to the citadel (☎ 04-95-46-26-70; www.corte-tourisme.com; off season Mon–Fri 9am–noon and 2–6pm; July–Aug daily 9am–8pm; May–June and Sept Mon–Sat 9am–6pm).

Cash as Cash Can

Because it's a smaller town, places here are less likely to take credit cards, so it's worth mentioning that there are ATMs north of the cours Paoli: Societe Generale, Caisse d'Epargne, Credit Agricole, and Credit Lyonnais. Also, there's one at the post office.

Corte Nuts & Bolts

Emergencies The police station is at the exit of town on the N200 toward Aleria (☎ 04-95-46-04-81).

Hospitals **Hôpital Santos-Manfredi** is on the allée du 9 Septembre (☎ 04-95-45-05-00).

Internet/Wireless Hot Spots **Video Games** (av. du President-Pierucci; ☎ 04-95-47-32-86; daily 7:30am–2am; 4€ per hour). **Le Café du Cours** (22 cours Paoli; ☎ 04-95-46-00-33; www.cafeducours.net; daily 9am–2am; .10€ per minute).

Post Office The post office is on avenue du Baron-Mariani (☎ 04-95-46-81-20; Mon–Fri 8am–12:30pm and 1:30–5pm; Sat 8am–noon).

Sleeping

Finally, some cheap sleeps! As with eating in Corte, sleeping is basic but adequate. Best of all, it won't break the bank.

CHEAP

➜ **Hôtel HR** Okay, this place is ugly, no lie. But you'll pay about 30€ to sleep cleanly, cheaply, and well. The rooms on the side with the garden are much better than the others, and you can get breakfast for 5€. There's a sauna and something resembling a gym room. *6 allée du 9 Septembre. ☎ 04-95-61-02-85. www.hotel-hr.com. 30€ double. Breakfast 5€. No credit cards. Open May–Oct. Amenities: Restaurant, fitness center, laundry, parking, sauna.*

DOABLE

➜ **Hôtel de la Paix** These are some pretty sweet digs, very close to the cours Paoli. Run by the same family since the 1930s, this relatively gigantic hotel divides its rooms into two categories—a "superior with bath'" for 62€, and a "standard with shower" for 53€. The dignified pink facade looks onto the square, and the rooms you see with the blue shutters on that side are the ones to request. *Av. Général-de-Gaulle. ☎ 04-95-46-06-72. 45€–62€ double. No credit cards. Amenities: Restaurant.*

➜ **Hôtel du Nord et de l'Europe** This is the oldest and most charming hotel in Corte. The owners have completely redone the interior without stealing its character. The 16 rooms are huge and comfortable, and the staff is pleasant, helpful, and ready to make local recommendations. The rooms out back have beautiful views of the countryside, but the cours Paoli side rooms aren't bad either. They take credit cards, unlike most other places here. *22 cours Paoli. ☎ 04-95-46-00-68. www.hotel dunord-corte.com. 60€–80€ double. Credit cards accepted. Amenities: Free parking. In room: Satellite TV, hair dryer.*

Eating

Eating in Corte is honest and sensible, with lots of local food in decent portions. Who's complaining?

COFFEE BARS & LIGHT FARE

Right beneath the citadel are a passel of restaurants lining the sides of a cobblestone street called the Rampe St. Croix (intersecting the rue Colonel Ferraci). Particularly cute is **U Passa Tempu,** with Corsican specialties, ice cream, and bar, which faces a fountain. The cours Paoli, Corte's main street, is full of cute cafes and tourist shops, and leads up to the place Paoli, with more of the same.

Corsican Cuisine

For such a small island, the biodiversity of Corsica is seriously amazing; when it comes to food, anyway, the island's intense insularity leads to good effect. And the best thing about it all is that while Corsica's Michelin-starred joints surely hold their own against any on the mainland, you can eat just as beautifully at the most humble roadside restaurants. Make sure you sample the gorgeous *charcuterie* and taste the nutty flavors the island's fat black pigs develop from foraging outside. *Coppa* is a typical Italian sausage made from the cured raw collar or loin of a pig. The meat is marinated in a blend of garlic and red wine, then stuffed inside a large sausage skin. *Lonzu* is like a smoked loin filet, *figatellu* is a dried pork liver sausage, and *prisuttu* is a raw ham.

Try the native boar, *sanglier*, which strolls the maquis eating herbs and roots before ending up in your ragout or roast. Pigeons and partridges *(perdrix)* are prepared in pâtés, and roast goat *(cabri roti)* is a specialty. Seaside, all the fish in the Mediterranean are up for grabs: *rascasse* (scorpion fish), *loup de mer* (sea bream), *rouget* (red mullet), *daurade* (gold bream), *saint-pierre*, *pageot* (Pandora), *grondin* (red gurnard), *langouste* (spiny lobster), *cigale* (sea cricket), *oursin* (sea urchin). Typical dishes include sardines stuffed with *brocciu* (goat's cheese), *pates a la langouste* (spiny lobster pasta), a local variant on bouillabaisse known as *aziminu* (or "Corsican caviar"), or *bottarga* (dried and salted mullet roe).

Corsican olive oil and honey are reputed for their intense aromatics, and indeed each is now blessed with its own AOC certification.

Corsican goat and sheep's cheese can be a little rugged, but try it before you knock it. The island's only AOC cheese, *brocciu,* is made with whey mixed with sheep's milk and salt, then heated and strained. It's eaten between November and June, young and fresh, in every guise. **Remember:** November to June. Out of season, it ain't the real thing.

➔**Chez Marie et Jen-Luc Delair** PATISSERIE Come in season and try Corte's famous *falculelle,* or *brocciu* cakes on a chestnut leaf. The amaretti ain't bad either. If you go outside onto the place Gaffory where the bakery is, you can see the bullet holes from when the Genoans attacked Corte in 1750. *Place Gaffory.* ☎ *04-95-46-03-70.*

CHEAP

➔**Trattoria Casanova** PASTA If you're here in season, you'll be surrounded by Corte's student crowd, shoveling cheap pastas and salads and rocking out to well-selected tunes. Off season, it's a little quieter, but all the better to enjoy the little tables set out on the street, and the daily menus. Very cute waitstaff. *6 cours Paoli.* ☎ *04-95-46-00-79. Menu 12€–15€. Credit cards accepted. Daily 7:30–9:30pm.*

[MTV] (Best ☻) ➔**U Museu** CORSICAN For a real treat of traditional Corsican cooking at very affordable prices, try the restaurant just beneath the Citadel. Sit under a big red circus tent umbrella, and savor the view of the peeling-plaster, blue-shuttered Cortesi buildings and the smells of the blooming flower trees. Sample bizarre-sounding but delicious dishes such as *truite in aiolu* or starling (yes, the little bird) pâté. The menu course includes soup, a main dish, and cheese or dessert. Or you can just go for either an appetizer and a main dish or a main dish and dessert. *Rampe Ribanelle Vieille Ville.* ☎ *04-95-61-08-36. Menu 13€–15€; pizzas 6€–7€. Apr 1–May 31 Mon–Sat 7–10:30pm; June 1–Oct 31 daily 7–10:30pm.*

DOABLE

→**Osteria di l'Orta** CORSICAN Technically, this is on the outskirts of Corte, but because Corte's small enough to walk around (you came here to hike, didn't you?), and the food here is really good, we're including it. You'll have to call ahead, but hotelier/chef Marina will regale you with innovatively reinterpreted Corsican recipes, made with produce from her garden. Don't come finicky, as the menu depends on what she has and feels like making, but if you're open to the experience, you'll be richly rewarded. Get the 35€ menu, which includes 5 dishes and drinks, or a 20€ formula, which is less copious but no less interesting. *Pont de l'Orta, on the northern side of Corte.* ☎ *04-95-61-06-41. www.osteria-di-l-orta.com. Menus 20€–35€. No credit cards. Call for hours.*

Partying

If there are any nightclubs in Corte, you'll have to be hipper than I to find them, because I came across no evidence. That said, one of the great pleasures of being in Corte is escaping the bass beats of the coastal resort towns and chilling with a glass of rose while the sun sets over the mountains. That, you'll have no trouble doing here; try the place Paoli for a start.

You can also go back to the pack of places at the intersection of rue Colonel Ferraci and Rampe St. Croix.

→**Le Grand Café du Cours** *The* cafe in town, where all the young Cortesians come to start their evenings, and hikers come to relax after an arduous day. During the school year, they organize theme parties. *22 cours Paoli.* ☎ *04-95-46-00-33.*

→**Le Rex Lounge** Dominated by students, this bar is a cut above family-style, if you know what I mean. Hip design, hip attitudes, but still pretty low-key; remember where you are. *1 cours Paoli.* ☎ *04-95-46-08-76.*

Menu Translations

If these menu descriptions freak you out, don't worry, Corsica has plenty of recognizable food. But try something every day that you've never heard of, even if it doesn't sound appealing, and you'll be surprised to see . . . how surprised you'll be.

→ *Castagneau avec brocciu et figatellu* chestnut pancake with goat's cheese and dried pork liver sausage.

→ *Migliacci au fromage frais* buckwheat pasta with fresh cheese.

→ *Begnets au broccio et a la farine de chataigne* chestnut dumplings eaten with fresh sheep's cheese, similar to ricotta (if they look like dog turds, don't panic, they're supposed to).

→ *Terrine de sansonnet au myrtes* starling (the little bird) pâté with myrtle berries, a local plant.

→ *Limunata* Corsican lemonade that tastes like San Pellegrino's Limonata and has a label of an earth mother burying her face in Corsica.

Sightseeing

PUBLIC MONUMENTS

➔ **La Citadelle** Although at one point the citadel struck the fear of Corsica into all manner of Genoans, today it houses the university and the tourist office, which makes it slightly less intimidating. No matter, it's still worth visiting. Get to it by walking up one of several ramps off the cours Paoli. The most famous is the rampe Sainte-Croix, from which you'll pass the 17th-century church of Sainte-Croix, with a cool painted ceiling and baroque altar. The other good option is the *rampe du Commandant-Ignace-Montei,* which has an impressive Louis XV-style pyramidal fountain *(la fontaine des Quatres Canons).* Although it looks far older, the citadel was only built in the late 18th century by the French, who provisioned enough rock to build a hospital, political prison, sleeping quarters, and powder magazine. *Off the cours Paoli.*

MUSEUMS

➔ **Museu di A Corsica** Housed in the converted old hospital, the museum was renovated by Italian architect Andrea Bruno with glass and concrete, to superb effect. Start by visiting the galerie Doazan, which displays the artifacts collected by Louis Doazan over 25 years from all over interior Corsica: portraits, taxidermied animals, old Corsican money, and household objects (over 3,000 of them). Then visit the *musée en train de se faire* (museum in progress), which interprets Corsica's living history, past, present, and future. Even those bored by history will be taken aback by the stupendous rocky hillside views through the big windows. Avoid the Jehovah's Witnesses on the way in, unless you want to walk around with a lot of paperwork. *La Citadelle.* ☎ *04-95-45-25-45. Admission 5.30€ adults, 3.80€ students.*

June 20–Sept 19 daily 10am–8pm; Apr–June 19 and Sept 20–Oct 31 Wed–Mon 10am–6pm; Nov–Mar 31 Tues–Sat 10am–6pm.

Playing Outside

➔ **Les Gorges de la Restonica** The hiking trails leading here can get a little busier than those taking you to Tavignano, but there's a reason for that: It's bloody spectacular. The river that runs through it begins at the *lac de Melo* in the *massif du Rotondo* and runs a narrow 15km (9 miles) until it gets to Corte. Bring a picnic and follow it. An excellent choice for bird dorks, it's a habitat for rare raptors and other birds, which you can spot on the trail. The valley has 14 azure lakes that reflect off the stony mountains. If you decide you want to stay forever, visit the information point 2.5km (1½ miles) from Corte on the D263. The Corte tourist office has excellent suggestions for walks and stops along the way. *Information desk 2.5km (1½ miles) from Corte on the D263). No phone. Mid-June to mid-Sept daily 7am–7pm. For more information, call the Corte tourist board (☎ 04-95-46-26-70).*

📺 (Best ✪) ➔ **Les Gorges du Tavignano** You can leave from the citadel and follow the orange-marked path (Mare a Mare Moriani-Cargese) along the river. It's cold but swimmable. Two hours later, you'll get to Rossulinu, where you can either turn around or walk another 3½ hours to the refuge of Sega. *For more information, call the Corte Tourist Board (☎ 04-95-46-26-70).*

Hot Lines for Hikers
....

➔ **Emergencies:** ☎ 04-95-46-04-81

➔ **Weather:** ☎ 08-92-68-02-20

Corsica Road Trip

From Corte, take the N200 toward Aleria, and try not to hit the goats with the chin flaps that look like scrota, lest you become one of the wrecks occasionally visible at the bottom of the valley. There's a really pretty bridge right before Casaperta that overlooks the thick and bubbling Tavignano River flowing through the gorge (you can go kayaking in there). If the sun is shining, the flaky rock reflects the light. Once you get to Aleria, if you want to hit the beach, follow the N200 all the way through. If you want to keep going south, to other beaches, or visit the Fort of Aleria up in the hills, follow the N198. The Etang D'Urbino restaurant on the water serves fresh oysters 10 minutes past Aleria, opposite—get this—the Corsican sheep genetic selection center. The Pasquale Paoli artisan beer brewery is in a stone house with a patriotic mural on the wall just before Mignataja.

Solenzara has lots of restaurants and snack bars with an ocean view, in case you need to recharge your batteries. Here the N198 runs right alongside the coast, opposite soccer fields and cemeteries, and the color of the ocean is dazzling after so much mountainous aridity. Another perfect beach spot is in Tarco, at Chez Jean-Claude, a really cute snack bar with a view.

If you're into self-catering, check out Lecci's terrific fruit and vegetable stand with a good selection of Corsican wines, olive oils, jams, and honeys. Free parking is available by Lecci's beach. For more details, call the **Corsican Tourist Information Office** in Aleria (Casa Luciana; ☎ **04-95-57-01-51**).

Bonifacio: Your Yachting Dream Come True

At the very bottom tip of the island: 28km (17 miles) S of Porto-Vecchio. 54km (33 miles) SE of Sartene

When you're dreaming about your time in Corsica—once you return to your cinderblock dorm or boring cubicle, and you're shaking the snow flurries off the shoulders of your coat—it will likely be images of Bonifacio that float into your brain. This town is so freaking pretty you'll wish you never had to leave, until the waiter comes with your bill, after which you'll immediately reminisce nostalgically about the great taco truck on your corner where fat, tasty burritos only cost 2€. Oh well, balance is everything.

Getting There

BY AIR

Planes leaving the **Aéroport de Figari-Sud Corse** (☎ **04-95-71-10-10**) offer regular service between Paris, Marseille, Nice, and, in season, other big French and European cities. It's 20km (12 miles) from Bonifacio; take the D322, D858, N196, and N198. In July and August, shuttles can take you to Bonifacio from the airport (they cost 8€), but they only go about every 90 minutes, so expect a bit of a wait. Otherwise, you can take a taxi, which is the only off-season option, but that will cost 30€ to 60€, depending on the avarice of your cab driver.

BY CAR

From Ajaccio, take the N192; from Bastia, take the N198. It's super straightforward: Just head south of anywhere you are and you'll get there eventually.

BY BUS

Two to four buses per day run to and from Propriano, Sartene, and Ajacio; and another two to four go to and from Ajaccio, which will pass through Olmeto, Propriano, Sartene, Roccapina, Figari, and Porto-Vecchio. Buses leave from the quai Comparetti; call ☎ 04-95-73-02-15 for details.

Orientation

It's a funny-shaped town, but it's small enough to figure out quickly. If you start out from the bottom, you'll see the marina in front of you, at the end of a long watery inlet. Walk toward the cliffs ahead, and you'll have to climb first the *montée Rastello*, then the *montée St. Roch*, which will take you to the *porte de Genes*. Cars can only go up until the *porte de France*, using the avenue Charles-de-Gaulle.

Getting Around

BY CAR

Don't. Even. Think. About. It. Leave the car at one of the nine parking lots in town, and walk. It costs 1€ to 2€ per hour, but only about 6€ for the whole day.

BY PUBLIC TRANSPORTATION

The only kind available here is the little **tourist train** (☎ 04-95-73-15-07; 5€; runs daily Apr–Oct.), which actually looks sort of fun if you're totally, totally sure you won't run into anyone you know. If you need further justification, just look at how steep the streets are.

Tourist Offices

You'll find two tourist offices here. In the cliffs above, in the **old town,** go to 2 rue Fred-Scamaroni, right after the *porte de France* (☎ 04-95-73-11-88; www. bonifacio.fr). Open July to August daily 9am to 8pm; May to June and September daily 9am to 7pm; October to April 9am to noon and 2 to 6pm.

In the marina below, head to the office located at the end of the marina, near some showers, in a sort of (well-indicated) trailer. The season's calendar of events, posted right outside the old town tourist office is worth a look.

Bonifacio Nuts & Bolts

ATM   It is perhaps worth noting that as there is only one bank in Bonifacio, you might want to make sure you have enough cash before you get there, to last until you leave. Worst-case scenario: In season (when the ATM is most likely to run out), there are a bunch of money-exchange desks around the marina.

Hospitals   Route de Santa-Manza ☎ 04-95-73-95-73.

Police   ☎ 04-95-73-00-17.

Post Office   On place Carrega ☎ 04-95-73-73-73 (Mon–Fri 8am–noon and 2–5:50pm; Sat 8am–noon).

Sleeping

In high season, you'll be lucky to find anywhere at all to stay in Bonifacio, let alone anywhere cheap. If you're going in July or August, make sure you plan ahead and make a reservation. If you get stuck, the tourist office may be able to help you.

CHEAP

→**Hôtel des Etrangers** It has little charm to speak of, but it's perfectly adequate. And don't kid yourself, you won't find anything cheaper in town. At least breakfast is included. *Av. Sylvere-Bohn (at the entrance to town on the N198).* ☎ *04-95-73-01-09. 45€– 75€ double. Credit cards accepted. Open Apr–Oct. Amenities: Parking, safe. In room: A/C, TV.*

DOABLE

→**Hôtel du Roy d'Aragon** The King offers four types of comfort: Comfort, Grand Comfort, Sea Sight, and Suites. All the rooms, simply and pleasantly decorated, have air-conditioning, televisions, and sound-proofing. The ones with a view are worth far more than the ones facing the road, which is not always reflected in the price. *13 Quai Comparetti.* ☎ *04-95-73- 03-99. 50€–90€ double. Credit cards accepted. In room: A/C, cable TV, hair dryer.*

SPLURGE

→**Hôtel La Caravelle** This hotel is perfect for such a topsy-turvy city, with an entrance both at the top and at the bottom of the building. All of the rooms are thematically decorated, with either color-coding or marine or music themes. They have Wi-Fi and parking, air-conditioning, and prices to suit a variety of budgets. *Quai Comparetti.* ☎ *04-95-73-00-03. www.hotel-caravelle-corse.com. 97€–132€ double; 250€– 300€ superior double. Credit cards accepted. Open Apr–Oct. Amenities: Restaurant, elevator, safe. In room: A/C, satellite TV, minibar.*

Eating

It being a tourist town, Bonifacio offers any number of places to eat. Most of them aren't that special for the prices they charge. However, here are a few that rise above.

CHEAP

→**Cantina Doria** BISTRO Big portions of *charcuterie,* lasagnas, or *plats du jour* for under 15€, friendly service, and droves of good-looking young people. Go join them on the wooden banquettes, *bon appétit,* and don't forget dessert. *27 rue Doria.* ☎ *04-95-73-50-49. Main courses 10€– 14€. Credit cards accepted. Mar–Oct daily (call for hours).*

→**Kissing Pigs** BISTRO What used to be a boat shed has been put to much better use as a bistro that serves homemade *charcuterie,* which hangs from the ceiling. It is really hard to believe that in a town this played-out such gems can exist, but believe it, baby, and order a copious plate of *coppa, lonzu,* and *prisuttu,* along with a good Corsican wine from the very serious wine list. *15 quai Banda-del-Ferro.* ☎ *04-95- 73-56-09. Call for prices and hours.*

DOABLE

→**La Main a la Pate** PASTA This is a carb-lover's wet dream, where you can order any shape, any color, and any flavor of pasta, all homemade. Squid-ink fettuccini? Goat's cheese gnocchi? Orange saffron, brown chestnut, and green seaweed spaghetti? Mix and match as you please. *3 montee Rastello.* ☎ *04-95-73-04-50. Main courses 15€–30€; menu 17€. No credit cards. Apr 1 to mid-Nov daily 9am–3pm and 6–10:30pm.*

Partying

Most of the hard-core partying in southern Corsica happens in Porto-Vecchio in the summer, so logically, hard-core partyers

CORSICA

tend to congregate there. You can find a bunch of fun bars on the quai Comparetti.

📺 Best ❷ ➜ **Lollapalooza** It's a far cry from the Lollapalooza we remember from the '90s, but have no shame about ordering the cheesiest cocktail on the menu anyway. If it's too hot to drink outside, set yourself up at the long zinc bar, under the ceiling fans and chandeliers. What? Yeah, you heard right. *25 quai Comparetti.* ☎ *04-95-73-04-54.*

Sightseeing

➜ **Aquarium de Bonifacio** See all the local marine species captured in waters beneath the cave-grotto they're displayed in. Okay, you probably won't want to go out of your way to come here, but it helps that the best bars in Bonifacio are right next door. See the animals; reward yourself. Or better yet, have a few drinks, *then* go see the fishies swim. *71 quai Comparetti.* ☎ *04-95-73-03-69. Apr–Oct 10am–8pm (until midnight in summer).*

➜ **Col Saint-Roch** It'll work out your thighs, but walk up the *montée Rastello,* in front of the Eglise Saint-Erasme, and admire the gorgeous houses hanging onto the cliff face like koala bears. Keep walking along the cliff ledge toward the lighthouse at Pertusato, which will take about 1¹/₂ hours. Notice anything? Yeah! It's absolutely gorgeous here! *Start hike in front of the Eglise St-Erasme.*

PUBLIC MONUMENTS

📺 Best ❷ ➜ **Escalier du Roi d'Aragon** Here's something you *don't* want to experience after a few drinks: the 187 very steep steps that ascend to the upper city. Allegedly the Aragonians carved them by hand to try to seize the city. In fact, locals built them much, much earlier to access the fresh spring at St-Barthelemy, at the top. *Daily 9am–8pm (unless weather is bad). Admission 2€.*

📺 Best ❷ ➜ **Marine Cemetery** On the edges of the cliff atop the swaying aquamarine *bouches* below, Bonifacio's old souls sleep their way to eternity. Eroded marble coffins, adorned by fake flowers, icons, and personal trinkets, combined with the scent of the ocean below, make for a setting that's eerie and comforting at once.

Playing Outside

Bonifacio is an outdoor lover's paradise, with world-class flysurfing, kayaking, and windsurfing (especially good at the 📺 Best ❷ **Bay of Figari,** a few kilometers west of Bonifacio).

Your best bet is to rent kayaking or boarding equipment from **TamTam,** Bonifacio's boating club, on the beach of Santa-Manza (☎ **04-95-73-11-59**). Or, slightly outside of town, try the **Club de Piantarella,** on the plage de Piantarella (☎ **04-95-73-04-89**).

If you want to dive in the gulf of Santa-Manza, try the **Club-Ecole de la Murene** (Immeuble le Magenta; ☎ **04-95-73-54-09**). For diving in the Lavezzi islands, you can check out **Barakouda** on avenue Sylvere-Bohn (☎ **04-95-73-13-02**). The equipment at **Atoll** is fancier, but dives are more expensive (around 40€ before extras like renting equipment). They're on quai Banda del Ferro (☎ **04-95-73-02-83**).

If taking in the view off the port bow is more your style, look into a boat ride with a local operator; options include tours of 1 hour to a day. The view alone is worth it: You can see the **Escalier du Roi d'Aragon** in all its glory, as well as the caves and cliffs of Bonifacio rising up above the blue. An hour costs about 14€, 4 hours are about 25€, but prices are always open to negotiation. Try one of the following operators: **Vedettes Christina** (☎ **04-95-73-13-15**); **Marina Croisieres**

Corsican Market Days

Ajaccio Regional products daily.
Bastia Regional products daily. Textiles Saturday and Sunday.
Bonifacio Regional products Wednesday.
Corte Regional products Friday mornings.
Ile Rousse Regional products daily. Textiles first and third Friday of the month.
Porto-Vecchio Regional products Sunday mornings. Textiles second and fourth Wednesday of the month.
Propriano Regional products first and third Monday of the month. Textiles first and third Monday of the month.
Sartene Regional products Saturday mornings.
St.-Florent Regional products first Wednesday of the month.

(☎ 04-95-73-12-41); or **Vedettes Thalassa** (☎ 04-95-73-01-17; www.vedettesthalassa.com).

Some companies will rent you a boat even without a motorboat license. Try **Piantarella Nautic** on the plage de Piantarella (☎ 04-95-73-51-64) or **Pouss'Vague** on the plage de Santa-Manza (☎ 06-74-41-36-62).

Festivals

→ **Processions de la semaine sainte a Bonifacio** So, this ain't exactly Mardi Gras, but no one can contest that there is something of the carnivalesque about it. Processions wind their way through the city carrying relics and big statues of saints on elaborate baroque supports. *Mar–Apr.*

→ **Fête de Notre-Dame** Go, if only for the free stuffed eggplants, *farcies à la bonifacienne. Sept 8.*

→ **Tour de Corse a la Voile** This 250-mile race follows the Corsican coastline, starting and ending in Bonifacio. ☎ 04-95-73-70-18. Mid-Oct.

Farther Afield of Bonifacio

The area around Bonifacio is absolutely spectacular by car. Whether you're leaving or on your way into Bonifacio, the **Reserve naturelle de la bouche de Bonifacio** is gorgeous, all inlets and sea.

If you're going east on the N198, stop for a picnic at the bay of Rondinara, 7km (12 miles) from Bonifacio. It's surprisingly deserted in the off season; people give way to goats and cows and, best of all, a pristine nature scene with calm and friendly waters. If you turn at the village of Suartone, you can get to the beach.

If you're going west, you'll take perhaps the most scenic road in all of Corsica, the D157 between Bonifacio and Ajaccio. It's twisty and turny but with breathtaking views of the open ocean, jagged coastline, and power lines held off the road by twine. You'll pass Sardene, the self-dubbed "most Corsican of Corsican villages"—where all the shutters facing the sun close once it gets too hot and open again come evening, Propriano and Olmeto are other typically breathtaking Corsican towns. Here are two nearby places to stay, should you be so inclined:

→ **Piaggiola** Warmth, hospitality, and good food from Mr. and Mrs. Paolini will welcome you in this big brick house on a gorgeous piece of property on the D255. Six huge rooms are filled with old furniture;

open the windows for an amazing view of the Gulf of Valinco or the forest. *On the D255. 20166 Porticcio.* ☎ *04-95-24-23-79. 62€ double, including breakfast. Dinner 20€. Credit cards accepted.*

➔**Santa Maria** This old granite house faces the church and the Gulf of Valinco in the middle of Olmeto, which you can reach on the N196. A flight of stairs leads abruptly to rooms that are not particularly charming but functional and clean. The vaulted dining room, an old oil mill, is pleasant enough, but you're missing out if you don't savor your Corsican meals on the lovely blossoming terrace. The 12 rooms are air-conditioned, with bathrooms and televisions. *Place de l'Eglise, Olmeto.* ☎ *04-95-74-65-59. 53€ double in high season; 40€–48€ in low season. Breakfast 6€, dinner 16€–23€. Credit cards accepted.*

The Rhône Valley & French Alps

by *Anna Sussman*

K nown as France's "second city," Lyon is a vibrant, multiethnic gastronomic paradise with a notable historic center. The crown jewel of the Rhône-Alps *département,* it lies at the confluence of the rivers Rhône and the Saone, and it's home to several of France's most beguiling and magnetic natural wonders—some known to all, some to very few. The fertile soil of the Rhône Valley, which produces some of France's top wines; the French Alps, considered the best ski slopes in the country; and the Gorges de l'Ardèche, France's answer to the Grand Canyon, are just a few of the other enchantments you'll find as you make your way around.

The Rhône River is the heartbeat of the region, dancing a sweet little conga line from Lake Geneva (Lac Léman) all the way down to the Mediterranean. Along the way it passes through some spectacular scenery, often overlooked by travelers making their way down to the Côte d'Azur.

The party scene is mellower here than on the Riviera, for the most part, except in world-famous hot spots such as Chamonix-Mont Blanc in the Alps. The culinary scene, however, is raging. Chef/institution Paul Bocuse lives in Lyon; Annecy has a number of experimental, Michelin star–crazed upstarts; and the Savoie and Haute-Savoie boast hearty mountain cuisine that recasts potatoes and cheese in a glamorous new light.

In the Ardèche, families with camper vans and rampaging children make up the bulk of the region's tourists, while the Drome seems to get hardly any tourism at all, especially in relation to Provence, whose lavender fields and medieval towns, are as overrun as a Bombay slum when compared to the Drome—which also has a bunch of lavender fields, medieval towns, and a bewildering array of esoteric little museums. It may be the closest you'll come to the traveler's dream-cliché of an "undiscovered France."

In fact, its Celtic and Roman heritage makes it one of the *first* parts of France to have been "discovered." It became part of the French royal territories in the early Middle Ages, under the Capetians, and has enjoyed a fairly stable and prosperous history since then. Its prosperity was due at first to the rivers, which served as trade routes through the region, but then to the advent of a wine industry, a textiles manufacturing industry, and, more recently, a high-tech and research industry, especially in Lyon and Grenoble.

Whether you hop from city to city taking in the museums and the nightlife, or limit your social interaction to regular visits to local winemakers, this region has much to discover, without the hordes of tourists that descend upon other parts of France.

The Best of the Rhône Valley & French Alps

○ **The Best Place to Fantasize about Becoming a Filipina Dictator and Building a Huge Shoe Collection with Public Funds:** The **Musée International de la Chaussure** in Romans establishes, through its exquisite specimens, why shoes have and always will be shamelessly covetable. See p. 574.

○ **The Best Place to Watch Where You're Going:** The **Gorges de l'Ardèche** are the deepest in France. Easy now. See p. 575.

○ **The Best Place to Rejuvenate, Edith Wharton Heroine–Style:** Upscale **Evian-les-Bains,** with its renowned spas and golf tournament, will put the pep back in your step as it takes the money out of your wallet. See p. 577.

○ **The Best Place to Stay the Night with Someone You Care About (and Wish You Never Had to Leave):** The **Château de Balazuc** in Balazuc, in the Ardèche, is a spectacularly located stone château that's been lovingly (and I don't use the word lightly) restored and decorated by Virginie and Daniel Boulenger. Their sincere hospitality and exquisite taste in furnishings only make a good thing outstanding. See p. 576.

○ **The Best Place to Drink Like a Local:** Le **Sirius**—a bar housed in a boat—has the best music, vibe, and crowd in Lyon. See p. 568.

○ **The Best Place to Sample Real Lyonnais Cuisine: Chez Hugon** is a traditional *bouchon* equally beloved by both guidebooks and locals. See p. 566.

○ **The Best of Antiquity: La Fourvière** hill is the site of Roman ruins, a Museum of Gallo-Roman Civilization, and the ancient amphitheater that plays host to concerts all summer long. See p. 570.

○ **The Best of Highbrow Lyon:** The **National Opéra House** could serve as an emblem of the city, its historic structure crowned by a modern glass cupola designed by starchitect Jean Nouvel. See p. 570.

○ **The Best Way to Burn Off Those** *Tartiflette* **Calories:** An effortless ride on Chambéry's glorious, almost entirely

The Rhône Valley

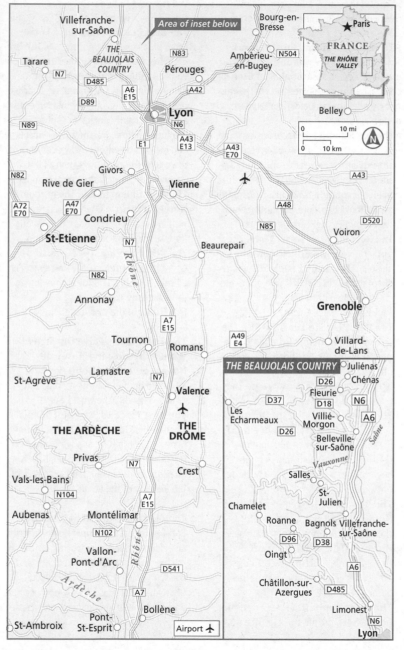

Villefranche-sur-Saône

Area of inset below

Bourg-en-Bresse

Paris

FRANCE
THE RHÔNE VALLEY

Tarare

THE BEAUJOLAIS COUNTRY

N83

Pérouges

Ambérieu-en-Bugey

N504

N7

D485

A6
E15

A42

D89

Lyon

Belley

N6

0   10 mi
0   10 km

N

N89

E1

A43
E13

A43
E70

Givors

Rive de Gier

Vienne

A43

N82

A72
E70

A47
E70

Condrieu

A48

D520

N85

Voiron

St-Etienne

N7

Beaurepair

N82

Rhône

Annonay

A7
E15

Grenoble

Tournon

A49
E4

Romans

Villard-de-Lans

Lamastre

N7

St-Agrève

THE BEAUJOLAIS COUNTRY

Juliénas

Chénas

Valence

D26

Fleurie

N6

THE ARDÈCHE

THE DRÔME

Les Echarmeaux

D37

D18

Villié-Morgon

A6

D26

Belleville-sur-Saône

Privas

N7

Crest

Vauxonne

Salles

Vals-les-Bains

N104

St-Julien

Aubenas

Montélimar

A7
E15

Chamelet

Roanne

Bagnols

Villefranche-sur-Saône

N102

D96

D38

Vallon-Pont-d'Arc

D541

Oingt

A6

Rhône

Ardèche

A7

Châtillon-sur-Azergues

D485

Bollène

Limonest

St-Ambroix

Pont-St-Esprit

Airport ✈

N6

Lyon

flat **bike paths** take you along babbling brooks, to nearby lakes, and always with the Alps keeping an eye over you. See p. 585.

○ **The Best Confusing Cuisine:** Garlic ice cream? Throw your taste buds a surprisingly delicious curveball at **Clos de Sens,** in Annecy, where the chef seems to be smoking something pretty strong. See p. 590.

○ **The Best Cheap Eat: La Montagnette,** in Annecy, has a cozy, wooden chalet atmosphere; inexpensive and filling salads and sandwiches; and a host of Savoyard specialties. Bonus: The friendly owner looks like a more handsome version of Benicio del Toro. See p. 590.

○ **The Best Place to Serve Time:** The former prison in **Annecy,** now a history museum **(Palais de l'Isle),** in the middle of the Thiou canal, is one of the most photographed monuments in France. Say cheese! See p. 591.

○ **The Best Place to Learn to Ski:** The red-suited instructors from the **Ecole de Ski Français,** in Chamonix, are often very handsome, total characters, or have a story to tell. In any case, they'll teach you how to ski. See p. 597.

○ **The Best Place to Forget How to Ski:** The après-ski at **Chambre Neuf,** in Chamonix, and the subsequent two-for-one cocktails happy hour, beginning at 8, will have you walking, not skiing, in zigzags. See p. 597.

○ **The Best Place to Get Something for Nothing:** Refill your plastic water bottle with free unlimited mountain spring H2O from the **municipal fountain** by the Chamonix tourism office. Remember how much you pay for this stuff back home? See p. 594.

○ **The Best Mountain View:** At 3,842m (12,602 ft.) in the air, the **Aiguille du Midi** lookout point in Chamonix may be the highest height you'll ever reach outside of an airplane. See p. 598.

○ **The Best Place to Chat up a Local:** From lunchtime till bedtime, the **Jardin de Ville,** in Grenoble, is buzzing with young people, sitting in groups on benches and carefully manicured strips of grass, smoking, playing instruments, and occasionally juggling. At night in the summertime, free nightly concerts and movie screenings draw everyone in town to see cool movies such as Jim Jarmusch's *Ghost Dog.* See p. 602.

○ **The Best Cheap Sleep:** The 17-room **Hôtel Victoria** in Grenoble is tranquil, well maintained, and has cable TV, all for less than 40€ a night. See p. 600.

○ **The Best Museum:** The **Magasin,** Grenoble's contemporary arts space, is a funky industrial building showing thought-provoking, cutting-edge art from some of the world's leading artists. See p. 603.

○ **The Best Place to Live Out Willy Wonka dreams:** The **Musée de Nougat de Arnaud Soubeyran,** in Montelimar, has the finest nougat in France, possibly the world. See p. 574.

○ **The Best Place to Stop and Snap a Photo:** The **Gorges de l'Ardèche** have been called France's answer to the Grand Canyon. Definitely take a picture, but don't expect your camera to reflect the majesty of the actual place. See p. 575.

○ **The Best Place to Fall in Love:** The **Labeaume en Musique** festival marries an eclectic selection of world music with the breathtaking backdrop of cliffs and trees. If you're staying at the nearby Château de Balazuc, have owner Virginie pack you one of her delicious picnics. See p. 577.

Lyon

431km (268 miles) SE of Paris, 311km (193 miles) N of Marseille

When Munatius Plancus, a lieutenant of Caesar's, colonized what was then called Lugdunum, in 43 B.C., he must have known he was on to something. Marcus Agrippa recognized the city's prime location, at the confluence of the Rhône and Saône rivers, and made it the central hub of the roads that snaked throughout Gaul, and soon thereafter the capital. Today, Lyon is the second largest city in France, and boasts an economic and cultural life second only to Paris. To that, some residents might add that the quality of life even surpasses that of the capital, given Lyon's manageable size and proximity to nature.

In the Middle Ages, Lyon became a banking powerhouse, later a publishing one, and lastly an industrial one, with the emergence of the silk-weaving industry. The Italian merchants who developed the fairs and commercial activity of the city from the late Middle Ages on found a lucrative product in silk, and occupied themselves with forging one of Lyon's most profitable trade ties, with Italy. They settled comfortably in Lyon, leaving a noticeable mark on the city's architecture, their colorful mansions located mostly in Vieux Lyon and reminiscent of Renaissance-era Florentine villas.

As silk production declined, advances made in industry kept pace, and technology and research became the economy's mainstays. André-Marie Ampère, the great physicist after whom the basic unit of electrical current is named, and the Lumière brothers, who are credited with inventing the moving picture, both hailed from here. This prosperous city is keen on finding innovative ways to raise both the quality of life and its international profile, sparing no expense in sponsoring cultural activities, hiring big-name architects, and building elaborate convention centers. Interpol (the police agency, not the band) is headquartered here, and the city boasts a vibrant fashion industry, a thriving cultural life, and, some say, better restaurants than Paris.

Orientation

Lyon is threaded by not one but two rivers, the Rhône and the Saône, which create an island, the Presque'ile, and two banks of remarkably different character. The west bank of the Saône is home to Vieux Lyon, a medieval and Renaissance neighborhood loaded with shops and restaurants, and watched over by the Basilica on La Fourvière hill. It has a small scale and a bustling, crammed feeling. The East bank of the Rhône is home to several administrative buildings, the university quarter, and the city's largest park. Its streets and boulevards are spacious and sprawling, probably because it is not jammed up against a hill. The Presqu'ile, between the two, is easily navigable and eminently walkable. It is mostly flat, except for the Croix Rousse neighborhood, with its steep incline and wonderful views.

Getting Around

Getting from point A to point B in Lyon gives you no fewer than eight options: on foot, or by bike, Cyclopolitain, bus, Métro, funicular, tram, or taxi. The city has an Amsterdam-inspired public bicycle network, Vélo'V, puts over 2,000 sporty red bicycles at your disposal, spread out over stations throughout the city. Buy a short-duration card for 1€ at any of the stations, and pay by credit card, which will then be debited, depending on your usage, at the end of the 7-day validity period. The card costs 1€, but the first 30 minutes on any bike are always free. Then from 30 to 90 minutes, it's 1€; 2€ every hour thereafter. If you're careful to drop your bike off and get a new one before the 30-minute bell goes off, you can cruise the city gratis. The Cyclopolitain is a futuristic rickshaw (an electric tricycle) that costs as little as a bus, 1€ per person per ride. It's a little embarrassing, though, given how slow it goes.

The Métro, bus, and tram services will get you around easily and quickly too. The signs and maps are all clearly marked, and there are stops everywhere you need them to be.

Tourist Office

You can pick up maps and information from the **tourist office** in place Bellecour, in the heart of Presqu'ile (☎ **33-04-72-77-69-69;** www.en.lyon-france.com). The office is open October to June 18 from Monday to Saturday 10am to 5:30pm, closed bank holidays; June 19 to September 30 from Monday to Saturday 9:30am to 6pm, closed bank holidays. **Lyon Citycard** (see "Sightseeing" on p. 568) entitles you to discounts.

Cultural Tips

The Lyonnais have a sort of inferiority complex stemming from their status as a second city, trailing behind Paris in almost every respect. Nothing will warm you faster to the heart of a Lyonnais than a vocal statement of their city's superiority, accompanied by several convincing reasons why. Obvious ones include the cultural life, the restaurants, the slower pace, the ease of movement—but after a day or

two, you will surely have come up with a few reasons of your own.

Sleeping

HOSTELS

Lyon has two hostels, although one is 5km (3 miles) outside of town, also known as a 35-minute bus ride away. The centrally located one (41–45 montée du Chemin Neuf; ☎ **04-78-15-05-50;** fax 04-78-15-05-51; www.lyon@fuaj.org) is halfway up the hill between Vieux Lyon and Fourvière, which blesses it with a panoramic view that can be enjoyed from the common terrace, which is where most of the hostel socializing takes place. This is probably the best thing the hostel has going for it, since the amenities and even basic things like the showers and breakfast are below average. Rooms are 16€ with sheets, and the reception is open daily 7am to 1pm, 2 to 7pm, and 10pm to 1am. Take the funicular up to the top of the hill from the Vieux Lyon Métro station to Les Minimes, or hoof it up the stairs.

CHEAP

➔ **Citotel Dubost** While the rooms are a citotel on the soulless side, this two-star place is about 1 minute from Lyon's Perrache train station. The place is clean, and reception is friendly and English-speaking. It's a great location from which to explore, located near all possible public transport, and 10 minutes' walk from Vieux Lyon and place Bellecour. It's a lovely old building, too; it's a shame they had to redo it with those cottage-cheese-like Styrofoam looking ceilings. *19 place Carnot.* ☎ *04-78-42-00-46.* *55€ single; 60€–65€ double. Amenities: TV; bar; elevator; garage; Internet in most rooms.*

➔ **Hôtel des Savoies** Not far from the Dubost is another two-star doozy, with the same almost-there-but-not-quite decor,

Lyon

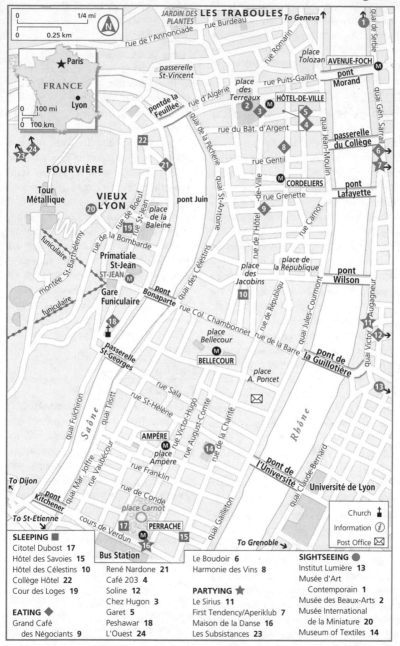

SLEEPING ▪
Citotel Dubost **17**
Hôtel des Savoies **15**
Hôtel des Célestins **10**
Collège Hôtel **22**
Cour des Loges **19**

EATING ◆
Grand Café
des Négociants **9**
René Nardone **21**
Café 203 **4**
Soline **12**
Chez Hugon **3**
Garet **5**
Peshawar **18**
L'Ouest **24**

Le Boudoir **6**
Harmonie des Vins **8**

PARTYING ★
Le Sirius **11**
First Tendency/Aperiklub **7**
Maison de la Danse **16**
Les Subsistances **23**

SIGHTSEEING ●
Institut Lumière **13**
Musée d'Art
Contemporain **1**
Musée des Beaux-Arts **2**
Musée International
de la Miniature **20**
Museum of Textiles **14**

Church ✝
Information ⓘ
Post Office ✉

yet situated in a charming edifice. Like the Dubost, it is unremarkable but for its great location and good value. *80 rue de la Charité.* ☏ *04-78-37-66-94. www.hoteldes savoies.fr. 46€ single; 68€ double. Rates include breakfast. Amenities: TV; phone; private garage.*

DOABLE

→**Collège Hôtel** Even if high school is a period you'd rather not relive, you can't help but be charmed by the genius with which the Collège Hôtel has been appointed. The theme of secondary school runs comprehensively throughout the Hôtel, which is located in the St-Paul section of Vieux Lyon—from the classroom-style desks in the rooms to the antique maps on the walls in the stairwell. Even the elevator's buttons are arranged like a calculator. Small details such as free bottles of water available from a cooler in the hallway, Artemide lamps by the bedside, and a free Internet kiosk downstairs make this place more than just a tastefully done three-star theme hotel. While some rooms are rather small, their spotless modern all-white interiors make them comfortable enough, and the bedding is first-rate. The hotel staff is as friendly and helpful as can be, and the breakfast features some of the tastiest, freshest bread around. *5 place Saint-Paul.* ☏ *04-72-10-05-05. www.college-hotel.com. 105€–140€ double. Breakfast 11€. Amenities: Flatscreen TV; balconies; city views; Internet; parking.*

→**Hôtel des Célestins** Slightly pricier than other two-star hotels, the Célestins boasts a few more amenities than most, and a truly central location, right in front of the spectacular old Italianate theater, Les Célestins. Again, the rooms are nothing to write home about, but the welcome is warm and caring, and their recommendations are well thought out. *4 rue des Archers.* ☏ *04-72-56-08-98. www.hotelcelestins.com/fr/index.*

html. 60€–90€ single; 65€–100€ double, depending on the room and the season. In room: TV, hair dryer, Wi-Fi.

SPLURGE

→**Cour des Loges** This world-class hotel is not just the top address in Lyon, it's the top four addresses in Lyon. Made of an agglomeration of four of Vieux Lyon's most beautiful houses, from the 14th, 16th, and 17th centuries, it is centered around a tranquil and lush garden. Its three floors of Italian-style loggias house a total of 62 rooms, each decorated uniquely and tastefully with the finest antiques. The concierge service and the hotel's restaurant are both top-notch. There's a small indoor pool and a sauna and steam room, so you can stay as beautiful as your surroundings. For American customers, the hotel sometimes offers a 1€ = $1 special, where you will pay the quoted price in dollars, not euros. Check online for availability. *2, 4, 6, 8 rue du Boeuf.* ☏ *33-04-72-77-44-44. From 230€, climbing to a jaw-dropping 590€. Amenities: Cable TV; minibar; Wi-Fi.*

Eating

CAFES & LIGHT FARE

→**Grand Café des Négociants** CAFE Merchants from the nearby livestock fairs used to wrap up their deals here, over 100 years ago, hence the name. Nowadays it's less bargaining than soul-searching, people-watching, and gossiping, as this place fills with lonely poets and their congealing espressos, and chatty young professionals rehashing the events of the previous weekend over salads and dainty appetizers. The outdoor terrace is pleasant but it's the high-ceilinged, luxurious, and gorgeously restored interior that's the draw. *1 place Francisque Régaud.* ☏ *0478425005. www.cafe-des-negociants.com. Main courses 14€–25€. Daily breakfast, lunch, and dinner.*

Lyon Gastronomy

Of Bouchons, Bocuse & Big Mamas

Lyon was always destined to have good food. The surrounding area boasts some of the most fertile, lush land in France, so the produce that comes from the Rhône Valley, and the animals raised on the local farms, are already second to none. The best place to have a sampling of the animals is in a local *bouchon*. These are small restaurants with rustic interiors that serve local specialties, most of them consisting of animal cooked in the fat of more animal, possibly presented with some more animal parts on the side. Fried pork fat, *andouillette* sausage, various kinds of tripe (if you don't know what that is, you probably shouldn't order it), black pudding, and different preparations of ham are all standard on the menu.

For more upscale dining, Michelin man Paul Bocuse maintains a famous and very expensive **L'auberge du pont de Collonges,** 4km (2½ miles) outside of Lyon, on the Saône, in an old family house. Gourmands should make the trek, if there's money and time to be spent. His classic truffle soup, created in 1975, is a whopping 80€ a bowl. No, there's no gold nugget at the bottom. If that's out of your range, try one of his collection of brasseries, one for every direction the compass needle can point, scattered around Lyon proper. These are perfectly delicious and reasonably priced. (See **www.bocuse.fr** for menus, prices, addresses, and reservations.)

Lyon's gastronomic history was formed by a feminist intervention around the first half of the 20th century. At this point, many of the larger upper-middle-class families let go of their personal cooks, and the women of the house stepped in and started up restaurants, serving the dishes the Lyonnais knew and loved, only revved up with a mother's touch. Their restaurants were frequented by everyone, including the most important personages of the time, and they developed recipes that have since become Lyonnais standbys, like hen with black truffle. Mère Guy was the first, succeeded by Mère Filloux and Mère Brazier, Mère Bourgeois and Mère Léa. From their fertile beginnings, Lyon now boasts over a thousand restaurants.

→**René Nardone** ICE CREAM Lyon's best ice cream should be savored in the brilliantly situated outdoor terrace on the bank of the Saône in Vieux Lyon. Alongside the classics are numerous more adventurous flavors like bergamot and blood orange; these change each year, and any and all of them are delicious, as are the prudently composed sundaes. If the prices are killing your appetite, just grab a cone and have a seat on a nearby bench. *3 place Fousseret.* ☎ *04-78-28-29-09. Daily 8:30am–1am.*

CHEAP

→**Café 203** CAFE A weekly rotating art exhibit and 9€ *plats du jour* make this a favorite of locals, particularly students and the culturally inclined, for lunch, coffee, or aperitif. It's named for the Peugeot 203, an old model of which is parked out front. *9 rue du Garet.* ☎ *04-78-42-24-62.*

→**Soline** VEGETARIAN A little New Age haven in the otherwise bleak 3rd *arrondissement,* near the Part Dieu train station, this is one of Lyon's only vegetarian restaurants, serving as something of a counterweight to the numerous pork-heavy *bouchons* all over town. The international cuisine is made with many fairly traded and organic ingredients, and manages to globe-trot with nary a false step. The menu changes each day, offering a handful of delectable choices, such as stir-fried Korean glass noodles or vegetables Provençal, and their culturally appropriate accompaniments. Save room for dessert, especially if the chocolate cake is ruminating on the counter. In the afternoon there is tea service and organic breads. Fifteen minutes from the Institut Lumière, this is a perfect place for lunch or tea before or after a visit or a matinee. *89 rue Paul Bert.* ☎ *0478604043. www.soline.net. Plate with salad 7.50€–8.50€. Mon–Wed and Fri 11:30am–7pm, Thurs evening for dinner.*

DOABLE

[MTV logo] (Best ●) ➜ **Chez Hugon** LYONNAISE The poster child for the Lyonnais *bouchon,* Chez Hugon serves all of the porky, artery-destroying delights that have made Lyonnais cuisine so famous. Owner Arlette Hugon still patrols the premises, making sure everyone's satisfied with their sausages, livers, tongues, and other heartily prepared animal parts. The homemade desserts, *tarte tatin,* flan, and other French classics, are also highly recommended. *12 rue Pizay.* ☎ *04-78-28-10-94. Lunch menu 23€; dinner 23€–33€. Mon–Fri noon–2pm and 7:30–10pm. Closed Aug.*

➜ **Garet** BOUCHON Another highly regarded *bouchon,* this classic restaurant routinely wows patrons with its house specialties, the *andouillettes,* calf's head, and *quenelles.* Friendly and attentive service, traditional *bouchon* decor, and the option of ordering à la carte (a must if you're dining with a vegetarian) make this one a sure shot. *7 rue du Garet.* ☎ *04-78-28-16-94. Mon–Fri noon–2pm and 7:30–10pm.*

➜ **Peshawar** NORTH INDIAN/PAKISTANI One of Lyon's best ethnic restaurants, serving traditional and authentically prepared North Indian and Pakistani cuisine. Try to forget the theme park–like atmosphere evoked by the costumes the waiters are sporting, and focus on the delicious food. *28 rue du Doyenne.* ☎ *04-78-37-06-51. Menus from 13€–27€. Tues–Sat 7:30–10:30pm. Annual holiday late July.*

SPLURGE

➜ **Le Boudoir** FRENCH FUSION At first consideration, the prospect of dinner in a bedroom (the translation of *boudoir*) is less than appealing, especially when the decor really is rather amorous, heavy on the red leather and velvet. But chef Simon Lacassin, who did a stint at the world-famous Taillevent, makes up for the over-the-top theme with his creative and carefully prepared cuisine, with novelties like sesame-crusted tuna steaks, or watercress soup with sautéed escargots. This place is frequented by an upscale crowd in the know, many of them from the surrounding 6th *arrondissement,* one of Lyon's wealthier neighborhoods. During lunchtime, it gets a mix of businesspeople and the leisure class, and after midnight, it turns into a bar and lounge with an in-house DJ playing house and R & B. The converted former train station, Gare des Brotteaux, in which it is located is also home to First Tendency/Aperiklub (see "Partying," below) and one of Bocuse's restaurants, l'Est. *13 place Jules Ferry Gare des Brotteaux.* ☎ *04-72-74-04-41. www.leboudoir.fr. Main courses 15€–26€. Free parking. Mon–Fri noon–2pm; Tues–Wed 8–11pm; Thurs–Sat 8pm–midnight.*

➜ **L'Ouest** BRASSERIE Many of the dishes on Bocuse's brasseries' menus hop from one restaurant to another, but there are enough distinctions between them to merit a visit to more than one. L'Ouest is situated a bit outside of town, on an exceedingly peaceful strip of the Saône in an industrial neighborhood. From the terrace, one looks out onto the river and unspoiled, tree-lined banks on the other side. The interior is slightly more raucous, with large tables usually filled with mirthful groups, the sounds of the open kitchen, and TVs playing music videos. The judiciously prepared salads and creatively sauced and garnished fish dishes are highly recommended, as are the desserts. *1 quai du Commerce.* ☎ *04-37-64-64-64. www. bocuse.fr. Main courses 12€–30€. Métro: Line D to quai de Commerce.*

Partying

BARS & PUBS

Rue Mercière and rue St-Jean are both packed with bars and restaurants and are where most of the city's night owls open up the evening. From there, you can try your hand at getting into some of the exclusive discothèques in boats along the rivers, try some wines at one of the city's many wine bars, or head to Le Sirius or La Fourvière (in summer only) for a concert or live DJ. *Lyon-Poche* is a weekly guide available at newsstands with listings for bars, restaurants and events.

➜ **Harmonie des Vins** Wine, wine, and wine is the specialty here, although there are tapas, charcuterie plates, and *plats du jour* that do harmonize well with the delightful booze. The wine list will have you drunk with excitement over the possibility of more than 300 selections, which the extremely knowledgeable waitstaff is happy to help you navigate. Its cozy wood-walled ambience is very popular in the evenings, so reservations are recommended. *9 rue Neuve.* ☎ *04-72-98-85-59. www. harmoniedesvins.com. Tues–Sat 10am–1am.*

NIGHTCLUBS & LIVE MUSIC VENUES

➜ **First Tendency/Aperiklub** For all intents and purposes, these are the same place, although Aperiklub is a bar and lounge, and First Tendency is a dark sweaty nightclub with a big dance floor surrounded by VIP banquettes. It's the same crowd, the same kind of music, the same prices, and the same sense of self-importance in both places, which are next door to one another in the Gare des Brotteaux. Considered very *branché* by the locals, these places are as Eurotrashy as they come in Lyon. Thursday nights are '80s nights at First, though, and that's fun for everyone. A bottle of champagne starts at 85€, but that's small potatoes for most of the clients here. *13 place Jules Ferry.* ☎ *04-72-69-92-30.*

Best of Fests

Lyon has no shortage of arts festivals. From the excellent **Maison de la Danse** to the rocking **Nuits de Fourvière,** there are world-class artists to be seen here in almost every discipline. Last year's lineup at les Nuits de Fourvière, for example, included Sting, Franz Ferdinand, Cesaria Evora, and The Strokes, all of them performing in the soft light of the illuminated basilica. There are also theater and dance performances, and films (www.nuits-de-fourviere.org). The **Biennale de la Danse** takes place in even-numbered years, and features top performers from around the world (www.biennale-de-lyon.org). Smaller local venues and bars feature mostly French performers and bands, many from around Lyon. Check *Lyon-Poche* for details and listings (www.lyonpoche.com).

📺 (Best ♦) → **Le Sirius** Of the many bar-boats parked on the Rhône, Le Sirius is the best. The DJs here are actually music experts, and technically skilled—not just dudes hired to keep the records (or iPods, as you find these days) spinning. The crowd, a mix of students, 20-somethings, and randoms show their appreciation by turning out in droves, crowding the small dance floor, downstairs bar, and outdoor deck. Depending on the night, you'll find either soul, jazz, funk, hip-hop, salsa, reggae, and something called Funkybeats, but always spun with care and attention. World-class musicians like Gangstarr play here too, so look ahead online to see who's coming up. The small size makes for an intimate atmosphere that's rare for concert-going these days. *Berges du Rhône, in front of 21 quai Augagneur.* ☎ *04-78-71-78-71. www.lesirius.com.*

→ **Maison de la Danse** Lyon's premiere modern and classical dance space hosts world-class companies and esoteric programs from Europe and around the world, including American experimental dance, flamenco, and butoh. To get there take Tram 2 in the direction of Perrache, or buses 23 or 24, to the Bachut-Mairie stop. *8 av. Jean Mermoz.* ☎ *33-04-72-78-18-18. www. maisondeladanse.com.*

Sightseeing

Before you dive headfirst into Lyon's incredibly rich cultural and historical life, consider buying the **Lyon Citycard,** an all-inclusive pass that provides free admission to almost every museum and attraction in the city, as well as free rides on any of the public transport systems (bus, Métro, and funicular); a free cruise down the river; 10% off on the rickshaw (sorry, Cyclopolitain drivers); and 10% discounts at several shops including Richart, the world-famous chocolatier, and Galeries Lafayette. It even carries you into nighttime, with free admission to selected shows at the Lyon National Orchestra and the Guignol Puppet Theater. Whew! The cost is 18€, 28€, or 38€ for 1, 2, or 3 days, respectively.

MUSEUMS

→ **Institut Lumière** What was once the gigantic mansion of Antoine Lumière, father of Auguste and Louis, is now an institute dedicated to the conservation and promotion of film. Auguste and Louis are credited with inventing the cinematic apparatus, and filming the first ever film at the gates of the Lumière factory, on what is now called rue du Premier Film, in homage to this fact. The museum displays many of the apparatuses themselves (yawn), and runs projections of these early films (cool). The ones documenting travels to other countries, especially those that were former French colonies, are particularly fascinating. The Institut also runs a jam-packed schedule of film screenings of movies both great and obscure. *25 rue du Premier-Film.* ☎ *04-78-78-18-95. www.institut-lumiere.org. Admission 6€ adults, 5€ students. Tues–Sun 11am–6:30pm. Take the Métro line D or bus 9, 34, or 65 to Monplaisir-Lumière.*

→ **Musée d'Art Contemporain** Facing the Tete d'Or park in the Cité Internationale, the museum is one of the finest in the region. It mounts many shows in conjunction with Le Magasin (see Grenoble), and they feature top living artists from around the world. The space is large without being overwhelming, and the shows are well curated and well laid out. Next door is a good movie theater. *81 quai Charles de Gaulle.* ☎ *33-4-72-69-17-17 or 33-4-72-69-17-18. www. moca-lyon.org. Admission 5€ adults, 2€ students, free for those under 18. Wed–Sun noon–7pm.*

→ **Musée des Beaux-Arts** One of France's largest collections of art is housed in this 7,000 sq. m (75,347 sq. ft.) museum, formerly the Abbey of our Lady of St-Pierre. From antiquity to the present, its collection is one of the best outside of the Louvre. There's a freely accessible garden in the abbey's cloisters where you can indulge in a picnic. *20 place des Terreaux.* ☎ *04-72-10-17-40. Admission 6€ adults, 4€ students. Tues–Sun 10am–6pm.*

→**Musée International de la Miniature** Their tag line, "Enter into another dimension," is as awful as the museum is wonderful. The building itself, a prestigious and historic landmark, has arcaded open passageways that take you past a sunny courtyard as you go from room to room. The collection is small, like its subject, but takes quite a while to view, since each piece demands that you approach it up close and spend several moments observing the minute details that make this art form so fascinating. The museum has works by miniaturists from all over the world, including China, India, Russia, and the United States. The pride of its collection are the works by founder Dan Ohlmann, which depict famous and not-so-famous places around Lyon. *Maison des Avocats, 60 rue St-Jean.* ☎ *04-72-00-24-77.*

www.mimlyon.com. Admission 7€ adults, 5.50€ students. Daily 10am–7pm; ticket office closes at 6pm.

→**Museum of Textiles (Musée des Tissus)** For a city that built its fortune on silk, it's fitting there should be a museum devoted entirely to textiles. Its creation was modeled after the Victoria and Albert Museum in London, and was one of the first in France to be devoted to "Art and Industry." Its collection has grown to include rare specimens of fashion history, like a pleated tunic from Middle Egypt, and woven portraits of Napoleon the 1st. *34 rue de la Charité.* ☎ *04-78-38-42-00. www. musee-des-tissus.com. Admission 5€ adults, 3.50€ students (includes admission to adjoining Museum of Decorative Arts, which is open 10am–noon and 2–5:30pm). Tues–Sun 10am–5:30pm.*

HISTORIC NEIGHBORHOODS

CROIX ROUSSE For the aerobically inclined, a trek up and around the steep Croix Rousse hill (called "the hill that works," in contrast to La Fourvière) yields a glimpse into Lyon's history as a silk production center, as well as a taste of its future given that this neighborhood is

The Lumière Brothers

It could be said that the Lumière brothers invented the moving picture out of that oldest of motivations: wanting to make Dad proud. It's the same thing that keeps us going on the Little League field, only in this case Antoine Lumière approached his sons, Auguste and Louis, to follow up on Louis's already very profitable invention of the instant dry photographic plate, which had cemented the family fortune. He had noted that some of the brightest minds of the day, Thomas Edison among others, were having trouble getting those darned images up and running. These two brothers were finally able to breathe life into the Golem in the spring of 1895, filming a short movie outside of the gates of their photographic plate factory in Monplaisir. Its title, *Les Sorties des Usines Lumière* (Leaving the Factory), isn't quite as creative as the process that enabled it, but they went on to produce hundreds of others, short and long, that are today viewable in the museum.

being rediscovered by students and others who want to take advantage of the cheap rents. The main road, Montée de la Grand Côte, has residences from the Middle Ages. The high ceilings of the quarter's buildings made it the neighborhood of choice for the city's *canuts,* or silkworkers, who moved in with their towering looms and wove the city into prosperity. The Maison des Canuts, at 10–12 rue d'Ivry, is a small museum devoted to the history of silk production in Lyon, and offers some local textiles for sale. The Gallo-Roman amphitheater, called the Amphitheater of the Three Gauls, is the oldest of its kind, dating from A.D. 19. What is now the Regional Department of Cultural affairs is a former granary, the Grenier d'Abondance, built in 1720 to accommodate enough grain to feed the city's population at that time. In a huge and pastel-colored 17th-century former convent, artists' residence and performance space **Les Subsistances** (8 bis quai St-Vincent; www. les-subs.com) now rocks the neighborhood with a nonstop program of theater, dance, and circus. *Note:* This is perhaps Lyon's least safe neighborhood, so take care when you're walking around at night.

Best LA FOURVIERE HILL The Fourvière Hill is known as "the hill that prays," due to the numerous religious congregations that have flocked to this site since the 6th century. It is mostly a large archaeological park with an outstanding Roman theater and an adjacent Odeon (a theater used specifically for the performance of music) and the Museum of Gallo-Roman Civilization. But it derives its name from the 1896 Fourvière Basilica, dedicated to the Virgin Mary, patron saint of Lyon. As beautiful and holy as it is, it is not immune from ridicule; its imposing silhouette and the four octagonal towers on each corner have given it the nickname "the

upside-down elephant." In the summer, la Fourvière hosts a series of concerts of the Devil's music, rock 'n' roll (and other, perhaps even more sinful strains), called **Les Nuits des Fourvières** (www.nuits-de-fourviere.org).

PRESQU'ILE Inhabited since the Roman times, the Presqu'ile is the narrow body of land cupped by the hands of the Rhône and the Saône on either side. In medieval times, it was the center of economic and printing activity, and it was during this period that the extensive network of *traboules,* or covered passageways, was erected. The small streets and these even smaller *traboules* gave way to the wide avenues and large open spaces dictated by the aesthetics of Napoleon III, who reigned during the mid– to late 19th century. From the 16th century onwards, the neighborhood saw some of its most important buildings spring up or be restructured, namely the Hôtel de Ville; the St-Pierre Abbey, which today houses the Fine Arts museum; the Hôtel-Dieu; the **Best** **National Opéra House;** and Les Célestins, the theater.

The rue de la République, which stretches from place de la République up to the Hôtel de Ville, is one of the longest pedestrian streets in Europe, and one of the busiest, glutted with boutiques, movie theaters, and

Red Cross Art

The **Croix Rousse** neighborhood has a smattering of hipster galleries, some with odd opening hours. The more traditional galleries are gathered around rue Auguste Comte and rue de la Charité in Presqu'Ile. **Galerie El'gah,** 59 Monté de la Grand Côté, is a small white cube space showing work by talented local artists.

department stores. Place Bellecour holds a similar title as one of the largest public squares in Europe, measuring 200 by 310m (656 by 1,017 ft.). The Presqu'ile is still the heart of Lyon's economic and cultural life, although it doesn't have the sweetness of Vieux Lyon.

VIEUX LYON   In 1964, Vieux Lyon was the first historic district in France to become a protected site, a move which was later followed up by UNESCO in 1998, which classified the entire neighborhood as a World Heritage Site. Its mostly Renaissance buildings and mansions, many of them built in the Italian style by wealthy Italian merchants, are punctuated by several medieval churches, namely St-Jean and St-Paul, and medieval homes that were extended and refurbished during the Renaissance. While several of these old mansions have been converted into hotels, the neighborhood is bristling with more restaurants, small shops, and ice cream parlors than you can shake a stick at. In the evening, rue St-Jean over-flows with bar-hoppers bouncing from place to place, and the glow of la Fourvière warms the ambience. It's a wonderful neighborhood to explore day or night. In my opinion, it's the most beautiful in Lyon.

PARKS & GARDENS

➜ **Le Parc de la Tête d'Or** This wonderful landscaped park is 262 acres in size, mak-ing it one of France's largest urban parks. More than 8,800 trees stand guard over a number of treasures, including a rose garden, botanical gardens, exotic plants kept in hothouses, beds of lavender, and a beautiful curvaceous manmade lake. *6th arr.* ☎ *04-72-69-47-60. www.parc-tete-dor. com/leparc.htm. Mid-Oct to mid-Apr daily 6:30am–8:30pm, late Apr–early Oct 6:30am–10:30pm.*

Shopping

Lyon fancies itself a close second to Paris in terms of its fashion savvy. While this is something of a stretch—there are no Colettes to be found in Lyon—there are certainly more than enough places to burn a few (or a few hundred) euros. The neighborhood between place Bellecour and Cordeliers, known as the Carré d'Or district, has over 70 luxury shops, with all the big European names represented. The Part-Dieu shopping mall, across from the train station of the same name, has 260 stores and a huge Galeries Lafayette. But the best and most unique shopping is at the Passage Thiaffait, a little creator's village in the area abandoned by the silk producers, where young up-and-coming local designers, chosen by the municipal-ity, sell their one-of-a-kind pieces.

CLOTHING & ACCESSORIES

➜ **Les Petites** This chic, airy clothing boutique sells cute and very French cloth-ing—flirty, floaty dresses, simple and well-cut cashmere sweaters, silky tops. Nothing revolutionary, but the clothes have just enough details—ruffles, beading, an inter-esting cut—to make them unique. *15 rue Gasparin.* ☎ *04-72-41-76-80. Credit cards accepted. Mon–Wed 10am–1pm and 2–7pm; Thurs–Sat 10am–7pm.*

➜ **Les Petites Années** The French can stand rightfully accused of instilling the fashion bug into their children from their first months; few countries have such a wide and luxurious range of children's clothing brands, some at price points that border on the outrageous. But designer Magali Haond has moved beyond the pre-ciosity of most baby clothes, using an array of African textiles and tropical prints in vivid colors to create baby clothes, pil-lows, and bibs that are unisex by virtue of

Walking Tours

The tourist office has five itineraries, three on foot and two on bike, that take in the following themes: Presqu'ile, a trip back in time; the Heights of Croix Rousse; Secret Streets in Old Lyon; and by bike, Freewheeling by the Rhône; and Adventure biking by the Saône. These pocket-sized sheets are 1.5€ each or 6€ for all five. There's also a free guided tour by bicycle that leaves every weekday at 2pm from place Bellecour in front of the tourist office; book 48 hours in advance by calling ☎ **04-78-83-00-74.**

their originality (nothing pale pink or baby blue in sight) and positively adorable. You'll wish she could make something to fit you or that you could shrink to ¹/₁₀ of your current size. She has a booth at the Sunday market on quai Romain Rolland. *83 rue Duguesclin.* ☎ *04-78-93-25-64. www. lespetitesannees.com. Credit cards accepted. Mon–Wed 10am–1pm and 2–7pm; Thurs–Sat 10am–7pm.*

→ **Maje** A branch of the successful Paris-based line, Maje has the kind of clothes that seem a bit expensive at first, but very soon become wardrobe staples. Soft cotton dresses, delicate underwear, stylish off the shoulder sweaters, and a small collection of accessories. *13 rue Gasparin.* ☎ *04-78-42-92-68.*

→ **Marché de la Création** On Sunday mornings, some of Lyon's most (and, in all honesty, least) talented artisans unfold tables and chairs and peddle their wares alongside the Saône river, on the quai Romain Rolland. You'll find painters, sculptors, fashion designers, jewelers, leather-workers, all ready to answer questions and

enthuse about their products. An exceedingly pleasant shopping experience. *Quai Romain Rolland, 5th arr. No phone. Sun 6am–1:30pm.*

→ **Repetto** Now that ballerina flats, like karate shoes, have been appropriated as streetwear, it's perfectly acceptable for even the most uncoordinated among us to walk into a dance-supply store like Repetto and snap up a pair of ballet-inspired shoes. Besides actual dancewear and shoes, Repetto has a number of styles made for the street—comfortable ballet flats reinterpreted in metallic leathers and soft suedes, with soles that can take on pavement. *36 rue Président Edouard Herriot.* ☎ *04-72-00-28-48. Mon 2–7pm; Tues–Sat 10:30am–7:30pm.*

→ **Shoez Gallery** Not just a shoe store but a hipster hangout and meeting point, this spare, slightly futuristic boutique features the latest and coolest from Nike, Adidas, Converse, New Balance, and brands of the moment like Asics, Tiger, and Birkenstocks in summer. The young people who work and shop here are friendly and not infrequently rather attractive. There's a good T-shirt selection too, so between those and the shoes, there's basically everything a skater, hip-hop head, or indie rocker needs to complement the faded jeans hanging off his or her skinny behind. *15 bis rue d'Algérie.* ☎ *04-78-28-33-78. www.shoez-gallery.com. Tues–Sat 10:30am–1:30pm and 2:30–7:30pm.*

MUSIC, BOOKS & MEDIA

→ **Secondhand Book Market** Every day on the quai de la Pêcherie, a cohort of generally grumpy old men set up their tables and laden them with secondhand books, the nicest of which are extremely expensive. It's fun to browse, but most titles are in French, and rather pricey. *Quai de la Pêcherie, 1st arr. No phone. Daily 9am–9pm.*

Drôme & the Ardèche

The Drôme and the Ardèche lie on either side of the Rhône River—the Drôme to the east, and the Ardèche on its western bank. Both have been members of the French Republic from its earliest days, being among the original 83 *départements* created during the French Revolution on March 4, 1790. Although the regal river ties them together, they in fact have little in common. The Ardèche is one of France's most sparsely populated and economically undeveloped regions, known mostly for its natural sites and agriculture. The Drôme, carved out of the former province of Dauphiné, boasts one of the most rapidly expanding and diverse industrial sectors in France, in addition to its renowned Côtes de Rhône vineyards.

But as a traveler, driving on the meandering roads that run through the two *départements,* taking you from one small village to the next, it's hard to tell the difference. The Ardèche has some stunning geography and some of France's most alluring natural sites. The Drôme has more than its share of vineyards. And both regions boast a number of medieval towns with official classification as "Villages of Character." These small towns, often no more than a dozen streets knotted together by grey stone buildings, are an absolute joy to visit. They often feel, even in the height of summer, like that most elusive of places: undiscovered France.

We recommend that you explore this region, especially the Ardèche, which has very limited infrastructure, by car. This will give you the flexibility to plan your itinerary according to which of the many natural wonders, quirky museums, villages made of 1,000-year-old stones, and wine domains you would like to visit. Or rather, it will give you the flexibility not to plan your itinerary, but rather just to follow your instinct should you see a promising sign on the road. The towns sort of melt into one another, and no museum or winery is very far away, so you'll find tourist offices in one place recommending sights in another. This region has all of the physical beauty and quaint charm of Provence, minus the armies of tourists. Indeed, with its added bonus of some hilariously offbeat museums and unique (and relatively affordable) hotels, some of which are destinations in and of themselves, it's a wonder this area just north of Provence isn't more crowded. Enjoy it while it lasts.

Drôme

This *département* has attractions ranging from the quintessentially French (olive oil, nougat, and Valrhona chocolate) to the absurd (the crocodile farm and the Palais Idéal du Facteur Cheval). Take the A7 motorway if you're in a hurry (all villages and destinations are clearly marked), or the D538, which runs through small villages, off the beaten track.

MIRMANDE

Mirmande is classed as one of the most beautiful villages in France, and you'll find nothing here to argue against that. Fifth-century walls and medieval houses, some later updated with Renaissance windows, are all surrounded by green hills and vineyards in every direction.

➜ **L'Hôtel de Mirmande** This place has nine luxurious and beautifully decorated rooms, their modern simplicity a lovely contrast to the 17th-century building in which they're housed, some with a small terrace looking out over the garden. *No address; just ask for it.* ☎ *04-75-63-13-18. www.hoteldrome.com. 60€–130€ double. Breakfast 10€. Credit cards accepted.*

➔ **Restaurant Margot** FRENCH   A more blissful lunch than one under the vine-covered terrace here would be hard to imagine. It's the kind of small, well-priced restaurant you thought didn't exist any-more, with classic French food and some exotic sensual touches, always prepared with local and seasonal ingredients. The medieval street lined with rose bushes is as delightful a setting as you could possi-bly find. The vaulted interior is also nice, but summer is the best time to hit this place. No address; it's pretty much the only restaurant in town. Just ask for it. ☎ 04-75-63-08-05. *Menus* 19€–24€. *Credit cards accepted. May–Sept daily noon–2:30pm and 7:30–11pm; Mar–Apr and Oct–Dec Wed–Sun noon–2:30pm and 7:30–10pm.*

MONTELIMAR

The town itself is nothing much to speak of, but the fabulous 🎥 Best● **Fabrique et Musée du Nougat d'Arnaud Soubey-ran,** a short drive out of town (Arnaud Soubeyran; ☎**33-04-75-51-01-35;** www.nougatsoubeyran.com; Mon–Sat 8:30am–7pm, Sun 10am–noon and 2:30–6:30pm), is the kind of place you've been fantasizing about since your parents first put Roald Dahl's *Charlie and the Chocolate Factory* into your hands. Instead of Oompa Loompas, the museum and factory employs darling French girls who lead the tour of the premises with enthusiasm and warmth. The boutique is a fantastic place to load up on souvenirs, since this stuff isn't cheap in the rest of France; Arnaud Soubeyran, a master artisanal producer since 1837, is considered the highest quality available. They also have some unique varieties of nougat that are hard to find elsewhere, such as a cinnamon, raison, and a choco-late flavor that is out of this world. Look out for the pretty Loompas walking around with the trays of free samples. Mmm . . . samples.

ROMANS

It's not hard to imagine crooked Filipina ex-dictatress Imelda Marcos dispatching a private plane full of thugs to ransack the treasures at Romans' 🎥 Best● **Musée International de la Chaussure,** where more than 12,000 pairs are stored. Since the 15th century, Romans has been a center of shoemaking and leatherworking, and today it still produces some of France's top luxury brands. Thankfully the museum is often empty, or people would be slipping on the puddles of drool that some of the displays are bound to incite. The historical and ethnographic sections of the museums bring together ancient and dilapidated Egyptian sandals made of papyrus, with minutely embroidered Chinese boots for the golf ball–sized bound feet of 10th-century women. Louis IV's rather tranny-ish boots are also on display.

Before there were shoe brands, and everything got a Made in China stamp, there were ateliers and maisons where women and men could have their foot measured and a custom pair designed to their specifications. The unbelievable detail and creativity illustrated in the sam-ples by such masters as Perugia and Roger Vivier is enough to dampen one's enthusi-asm for the dozens of shoe stores that lined the streets of Romans, offering prod-ucts of our times.

SLEEPING IN THE DROME

➔ **Hôtel Orée du Parc** This three-star hotel has a lovely outdoor swimming pool surrounded by a tranquil garden, in which you can also savor a filling and generous breakfast. The simple, clean rooms are decorated in different color themes, are named after flowers, and come with nice touches such as a plastic beach bag to bring down to the pool. *6 av. Gambetta.* ☎ *33-04-75-70-26-12. www.hotel-oreeparc. com. 77€–108€ single; 80€–111€ double.*

Breakfast 10€. In room: A/C, TV, Internet, minibar, safe, soundproof rooms.

Ardèche

The Ardèche is named after the river that sometimes flows, sometimes trickles, through its narrow (75km/47 miles wide) area. The 📺 Best😊 **Gorges de l'Ardèche,** the area's claim to fame, are punctuated by 25 rapids, which brave canoers and kayakers have flocked to since the 1930s. You can explore the gorges, a series of connected canyons that wind sinuously across the region, on foot, or by road (the D290), with a dozen viewpoints at which to stop and admire the view. The **pont d'Arc** is the most famous, and the **Serre de Tourre** is also one of the most beautiful spots.

The varied and unpopulated terrain lends itself to a number of outdoor activities. Consult with the local tourist board on what is available depending on where you are, and which companies they recommend for a given sport. Canyoning, caving, rock-climbing, canoeing, kayaking, and horseback riding are among the offerings.

Although the Ardèche area has been inhabited by modern humans since the Upper Paleolithic era, as illustrated by the cave paintings at **Chauvet pont d'Arc,** it is currently one of the most sparsely populated areas in France, with an average population density of 50 inhabitants per kilometer (half the national average of 104 per kilometer). This gives it a unique feeling, especially in the summer, when many other parts of the country (including areas very nearby) are overrun with tourists to the point of unpleasantness. Here, avoid the campsites and you'll have the place all to yourself. Two independent guides to the region, in French, include **www.ardeche-evasion.com** and **www. ardeche-online.com.** Because the region is so relatively untouristed, there is little information in English.

Many Romanesque churches were built in the region in the 10th century—at **Ailhon, Mercuer, St-Julien du Serre, Balazuc, Niègles,** and **Rochecolombe.** In the 1500s, the Ardèche became a stronghold of Protestantism, due to the influential missionary Jacques Valery. During the Religious Wars, 50,000 of the region's Protestants left France, many for Switzerland, or suffered forced conversion if they stayed. The French Revolution, and the accompanying Declaration of Human Rights, granted freedom of religion to all its citizens, and the remaining Protestants were finally free to practice their religion in peace. The region is still largely agricultural, with 50% of the population living in a rural environment, as opposed to the national average of 25%. The stone fruits (peaches, apricots, plums, and the like) that grow on the Ardèche's hillsides are legendary.

THE RHÔNE VALLEY & FRENCH ALPS

Chock-Full of Crocs

Unique in Europe, **La Ferme aux Crocodiles** (Les Blachettes; ☎ **04-75-04-33-73;** www.lafermeauxcrocodiles.com) is an 8,000 sq. m (86,111 sq. ft.) farm in Pierrelattes that re-creates a lush tropical setting with more than 400 reptiles. If you're no Indiana Jones, you can visit the gentle, peace-loving giant tortoises, vacationing here from the Seychelles Islands.

Admission is 9.50€, and the farm is open year-round (daily 9:30am–5pm in winter; 9:30am–7pm Mar–Sept).To get there, take exit Montelimar Sud off of A7.

Le Palais Idéal Facteur Cheval

The Drômois are curiously proud of their reputation for being an extremely stubborn lot. The poster child for this stubbornness is local legend Ferdinand Cheval, a postman who toiled night after night for more than 33 years to create, in the end, what is referred to as the world's reference on Art Brut. The **Palais Idéal Facteur Cheval** (at Hauterives; ☎ **33-04-75-68-81-19;** www.facteurcheval. com), is only 26m (85 ft.) long, but consider the fact that it was built with only two hands, belonging to a single man, and that most of the material came from his collection of pebbles that he picked up along his daily mail delivery route (is this bizarre enough for you yet?). Stranger still than the story of its creation is the thing itself; with no architectural or artistic knowledge, Cheval simply built according to a dream that guided him unconsciously in the placement of each stone. The result is Gaudí-esque, but infinitely more concentrated and, without Gaudí's slickness and color, slightly more grotesque.

Open daily 9:30am to 12:30pm; December to January also 1:30 to 4:30pm (Feb–Mar and Oct–Nov until 5:30pm; Apr–June and Sept until 6:30pm; July–Aug until 7pm).

RECOMMENDED WEBSITES

○ **www.chataigne-ardeche.com**: This site has information about the region's prized chestnut.

○ **www.ardeche-wines.com**: This site will help you plan a trip around Ardèche's underexplored vineyards.

○ **www.ardeche-guide.com**: The tourist board's website is one of the few relevant sites in English.

BALAZUC

Also classed among the most beautiful villages in France, medieval Balazuc has been inhabited since the Bronze Ages. Its dramatic location, at the edges of the famous Gorges de l'Ardèche, makes its beauty twice as compelling. Check out the 12th-century Romanesque church, which was built unapologetically on top of the ruins of a former pagan shrine to Belen, the Celtic deity of day and light (and from whom Balazuc derives its name).

MTV **Best ●** → **Château de Balazuc** Poised at the end of a road that drops off into the Gorges, this is quite simply the most exquisite, soulful, and welcoming place in the area—a destination in and of itself. The owners, Virginie and Daniel Boulenger, treat their guests like royalty, or family, or some loving mixture of the two. You could spend hours chatting with them, or simply gazing at the sunset over the ridiculously gorgeous view from the deck, or lingering by the tiny lap pool, or stretched out on the luxurious bed, or immersed in the claw-foot bathtubs in some of the rooms. Each of the four rooms has been decorated with the utmost care— so tastefully it can't be long before the folks at *wallpaper** magazine come a-knockin' (seriously; check out the website photos). The rooms are contemporary and sleek, but personalized with artworks and touches like small glasses of fresh apricots and strawberries, and with all of the original details of the house left intact. If only they offered long-term rates; you'll never want to leave this magical little corner of the world. ☎ 04-75-88-52-67. *www.chateau debalazuc.com.* 95€–105€ *double. Rates include breakfast.*

BOURG ST-ANDEOL

This village has been inhabited for more than 2,000 years, and it's rich with classified historical buildings. One of them, the 18th-century **Hôtel de Digoine** (5 quai Madier de Montjou; ☎ **04-75-54-61-07**; www.digoine.com; 75€–87€ double; breakfast 9€), has been transformed into an outlandish, Patricia Fields-meets-Napoleonic-Orientalist-fantasy bed-and-breakfast. The courtyarded house, with its 5m (15-ft.) ceilings, once belonged to a local silk merchant, and the owners have taken that silk road theme and run far with it, decorating each of the seven rooms as one stop on the way to China, from Venice to Samarkand and beyond. Bolts of fabric and elaborate arrangements of fake flowers in the wildest colors breathe new life into the historic building. The canopied beds and rooms full of antiques are perfect for composing Odalisque portrait sessions. Some look out onto the Rhône river, just across the street, and there's a morning market.

Just outside of town is the **Domaine Coulange** (Quartier St-Ferréol; ☎ **04-75-54-56-26**; http://domain.coulange.free.fr; call for an appointment), a vineyard that has been in the Coulange family since 1723. Currently run by father and daughter Maurice and Christine, it has won many awards in independent wine competitions. Christine will happily give you a tasting and an explanation of the winegrowing process, and you can see the actual pressing take place on-site. An interesting fact, if you've got some spare land on hand: 1 hectare (2½ acres) of vines makes 100 liters of wine per year.

Local olive oil producer **Ingrid Pradal** (Lou Mouli d'Oli, Domaine de la Souteyranne; ☎ **04-75-54-70-54;** www.paroledolive.com; call for an appointment) opens the doors of her little barnhouse and boutique, where she carefully walks guests through the olive oil extraction process.

LABEAUME

📺 Best ⓢ →**Festivale Labeaume en Musiques** This festival could feature an untrained vagrant playing a rusty accordion onstage, and people would still show up, so spectacular is the setting. It takes place in a pebbled concert ground in the open air, with a backdrop of soaring and dramatically floodlit cliffs. Local birds and toads harmonize inadvertently with the performers. A few sausage vendors and other gastronomic producers from nearby farms set up stalls, selling hearty sandwiches on rustic country bread, wine, and cookies. *www.labeaume-festival.org. Tickets 16€–40€, depending on who's playing.*

→**Le Bec Figue** This little bistro, near the church in Labeaume, serves regional charcuterie, tarts, salads, and other country cooking made with the heavenly local produce. *Place de l'Eglise.* ☎ *04-75-35-13-32.*

📺 Best ⓢ Evian-les-Bains

A small town of around 8,000 people built in tiers above Lake Geneva, Evian-les-Bains is best known for its mineral-rich spring water, which reportedly cures arthritis. Imbibed in fine restaurants around the world, Evian water is also the base for healing hydrotherapy treatments and thermal baths that have made this place a popular destination since the Romans set up shop here in 1150, calling it, logically, Aquinanum. It entered its modern incarnation as a wealthy spa resort beginning in the mid-1800s, with the first spa buildings having sprung up in 1839. Since then, the town has developed considerably, while retaining its Belle Epoque architecture and rarified atmosphere.

Now it is best known for its annual golf tournament, the women's Evian Master's, which takes place the last week of July (in 2007 it will run July 25–28). Unless you're rooming with one of the pros, forget trying to find accommodation during this period. It's also a busy convention town, and finding a room during a big convention can be difficult as well. Call ahead to the tourism office when you're planning to visit.

Orientation

Evian is extremely tiny, and has a big lake (the biggest in central Europe) on one side, so it's almost impossible to get lost unless you blindfold yourself. It is built in the shape of an amphitheater, curving to the lake's natural form. Most of the commercial activity of the town takes place around the rue Nationale and the leisure activity alongside the lakefront, where a 3km (2 miles) promenade and Nautical Center rattle with tourists. The **tourist office** is on place d'Allinges (☎ **04-50-75-04-26**; www.eviantourism.com).

Sleeping

HOSTELS & CAMPING

Several campsites are 4km to 9km (2½–6 miles) outside of Evian. Consult the tourist office for details.

SPLURGE

➜ **Evian Royal Palace Resort** A bastion of luxury since 1829, the Evian Royal Palace

Cash Tip

Bring money. This is a town devoted solely to unwinding and leisure, and as we all know, those seemingly effortless activities always seem to have a high price tag. Restaurants, hotels, even grocery stores are all more expensive than usual.

Resort hosts the Master's Tournament each year on its 15-hectare (37 acres) golf course. The spa is considered the best in the city with prices that reflect its reputation. Rooms are well appointed, with large luxurious bathrooms, and the service is outstanding. Besides the spa, there is a gorgeous infinity pool. There are 11—yes, 11—restaurants on the premises, including one for those on a slim-down vacation, which offers "synergistic cuisine" (I think this is code language for "personalized rabbit food"). Les Fresques Royales in the Royal Parc hotel is a gastronomic restaurant that will cost you a pretty penny; try it only if you've been lucky at the casino. *Rive Sud du Lac de Genève.* ☎ *04-50-26-85-00. www.royalparcevian.com. Rooms start at 210€ in low season, and climb steeply from there. Amenities. Hair dryer; Internet; parking; 24-hr. room service. In room: A/C, TV, minibar.*

Eating

➜ **Histoire du Goût** FRENCH Featuring traditional French cuisine with modern, lighter twists, this place tells the "Story of Taste" (as its name translates) best when speaking in the language of wine. Their selection is impeccable, albeit pricey. *1 av. Général Dupas.* ☎ *04-50-70-09-98. http://histoiredegout.ifrance.com/acces.htm. Menus from 18€. Credit cards accepted. Tues–Sun noon–2pm and 7–9pm.*

Partying

➜ **Casino Royal Evian** The casino dates from 1911, when it was built by architect J. A. Hébrard, and was originally called a "gaming club." The Swiss from across the lake come here to cut loose and spend some of that hard-earned banking money on blackjack, baccarat, and roulette, in addition to the usual trashy slot and video poker machines. It's one of the largest in Europe, and has five restaurants. *See Royal Parc hotel review for more info.*

The French Alps

FRANCE
THE FRENCH ALPS
★ Paris

N5

Lausanne

N9

*Lac L éman
(Lake Geneva)* Evian-les-Bains

Thonon-les-Bains

N5

Avoriaz ○

Geneva

Arve ○ Morzine

Annemasse

Rhône

SWITZERLAND

N84

St-Julien

Bonneville ○Flaine

Bellegarde
sur-Valserine

RN201

○ Cluses

N508

A40
E25

Chamonix–Mont Blanc

Annecy

Lac d'Annecy

Seyssel ○

A41

Talloires

N212

Megève

ITALY

*Lac du
Bourget*

RN201

N508

Belley○

N212

Aix-les-Bains

Albertville

A430

Bourg-St-Maurice

Chambéry

N90

Tignes ○

Les Abrets

Moûtiers

Val d'Isère

N75

Voiron

Saint-Pierre-de-
Chartreuse

Isère

Courchevel 1850

Lanslebourg

N532

St-Jean-de-
Maurienne

D902

Grenoble

Airport	✈
Skiing	🎿
Tunnel	) (

0 ___ 25 mi
0 ___ 25 km

Le Bourg-d'Oisans

N91

→ **Le Madison** A small discothèque in the center of town, this is one of your few options for going out, if you're staying away from the den of sin up there in the Royal Parc. No cover, just pay for drinks. *1 rue Clermont.* ☎ *04-50-75-74-68. Fri–Sun 10pm–4am.*

Playing Outside

→ **Steamboat to Lausanne** The Swiss-run Compagnie **Générale de Navigation** runs tours around the lake, by day or by night (night cruise only in summer). They offer a 50% student discount; this might be the only bargain in Evian, so snap it up. *Buy a ticket at the Office du Baigneur, place du Port.* ☎ *04-50-75-27-53. www.cgn.ch/en/home. Around 36€ for the Evian-Lausanne trip.*

NATURAL THERMAL BATHS

The most exquisite spas and baths are in the super fancy hotels; they are open to

Blue Gold

Well before the Royal Casino sprang up, the Count of Laizer hit the jackpot in Evian around 1790. He was strolling on the estate of a man known only as Mr. Cachat, when he stopped at the St-Catherine Fountain to quench his thirst. The water struck him as "light and well-pleasing," and he continued to drink it throughout his stay in the area. As time progressed, he noticed his kidney and liver ailments markedly ameliorated, and he made his health improvements known. Doctors began prescribing the local waters to patients, and Mr. Cachat quickly sprang into action, enclosing his spring and selling the water to ready buyers. Bathing stations sprung up in 1824, and 2 years later the water was being bottled. In 1829, development started in earnest, giving rise to many of the luxury hotels and impressive buildings you can still see today.

guests only. The peons must unwind in the public baths, **Les Thermes d'Evian** (place de la Libération; ☎ 04-50-75-02-30; www. lesthermesevian.com; Jan 3–Dec 23 Mon–Sat), which, at 36€ for a simple day pass, are hardly what I'd call democratic. The day pass includes unlimited time in the fitness center and the thermal Jacuzzi baths. A 63€ pass gets you that plus access to the saunas, steam baths, and two massage sessions. Additional treatments such as facials, special massages such as *reiki,* and nutritional consulting will cost even more. There are weeklong passes that do not include lodging; check the website for more details.

BATHING & SWIMMING

➜ **Centre Nautique Evian-Plage** A large complex with two outdoor heated pools, a reserved lake swimming area, garden, table tennis, 160m (525 ft.) water toboggan area, and water-skiing school. *Av. du Général Dupas* ☎ 04-50-75-02-69. *May–Sept daily 9:30am–8pm.*

Chambéry

If Annecy and Chamonix are the jocks in the class, and Evian the beautiful popular girl, then Chambéry is definitely the nerd. More of a rest station between slopes than a destination in itself, it has a quiet, peaceful way of life, with stunning surroundings and proximity to some of the better ski spots. Furthermore, it has a long history of nerd-dom. Jean-Jacques Rousseau famously made his summer home here, on a green, moist property in the hills called La Charmette, which can today be visited (and envied). Other smarty pants said to have vacationed in Chambéry include Montaigne and Rabelais.

It's easy to see how the laid-back lifestyle, lack of anything pressing to do, and clean Alpine air are conducive to generating ideas that change the course of Western intellectual history. Give anyone long enough to diddle around the cafes and among the natural beauty of the Alps, and she or he is bound to come up with something clever. This thinking is perhaps behind the establishment of numerous scientific research centers and environmental institutions also recently established in Chambéry. Besides its large university, the University of Savoy, it is home to France's National Mountain Institute, a gigantic médiathèque; a scientific, technological, and cultural center called Eurêka; and the largest solar energy production site in

France, whose annual 120,000 KW supply the public electricity network and also power the reservoir system.

Since its heyday as the seat of the House of Savoy, from 1295 to 1563, Chambéry has had a technological edge. The weapons manufactured in Savoy were known as some of the best around, and many of Europe's most fearful armies were fighting with arms bearing a "Made in Savoy" sticker. It was only because the city was *too* open to new ideas that Duke Emmanuel Philbert moved the seat of his duchy to Turin in 1563, afraid that the winds of republicanism would too easily sweep through his capital.

Echoes of Chambéry's intellectual traditions are evident even in the smaller details of everyday life; the quiet streets teem with bookstores, the citizens rally and march when something is bothering them (as was the case during the Israeli invasion of Lebanon this past summer), and it had France's highest rate of public literacy in 2001. Even the walls of the city insist on getting one over on you; notice how many of the architectural details are in fact *trompe l'oeil* paintings.

Getting Around

Chambéry is small and effortlessly walkable, or bikable, as you prefer. In and around the city are over 50km (31 miles) of bike paths, and the bus system, should you need it, runs 24 hours. The many one-way streets make it something of a hassle to drive around; thankfully there is very well-organized and abundant public parking, which should entice you to ditch the car and hit the pavement. The center of the city is anchored by a large arcaded street, the rue de Boigne. It is traversed by several pedestrian shopping streets, the medieval rue Saint Léger, and the rue St-Réal. Notice the labyrinth of small, almost tunnel-like throughways around place Saint Léger linking one street to the next. These passageways and alleys, along with the narrow streets of the old town center, and the feel of nature just next door, are part of what give Chambéry its unique physical atmosphere.

Recommended Websites

- ○ **www.fra.cityvox.fr/bonnes-adresses_chambery/Bonnes Adresses**: User-generated content means authentic reviews from locals, in French.
- ○ **www.chambery-tourisme.com**: The website of the local tourist office is very helpful. From their site you can download a list of the available sports activities.

Cultural Tips

If you read French, pick up a book at one of the city's many bookshops, pull up a chair at a cafe, and start looking smart. If you don't read French, bring your Bridget Jones or Dan Brown and cover it with a tome by local all-star Rousseau. Chambéry is a city of educated, worldly citizens, whose outlooks, knowledge, and opinions reach surprisingly far beyond the mountainous borders of their blissful *département*. Don't think that because it's a small place there's anything provincial about it.

Sleeping
CHEAP

➜ **Art Hôtel** It's not quite clear where the "art" comes in here, since the rooms are as basic and artless as can be. That said, they're clean, simple, and comfortable, and as cheery as a 50€-per-night hotel can be, especially the rooms that look onto the street, which get loads of natural light. All have private baths. The reception staff is friendly, welcoming, and helpful, although sometimes it's just one guy at a time, so be patient. *154 rue Sommeiller.* ☎ *04-79-62-37-26. www.arthotel-chambery.com. 46€–53€*

double; 64€ triple. Breakfast 7€. Amenities: TV; elevator; private parking available; phone.

➜ **Hôtel des Voyageurs** The stairways are dank, the bar downstairs can't decide if "dodgy" or "dingy" should be the operative adjective, and the receptionist couldn't be crabbier (she acts as though you've commanded her to step over hot coals if you ask to see a room). But this is the cheapest lodging in town, and it's in a pretty good location. There are 18 rooms available, including one for four people. It has no real amenities to speak of (unless you count the hostess's good cheer). *3 rue Doppet.* ☎ *04-79-33-57-00. 20€–25€ single; 30€–36€ double. Breakfast 5€.*

➜ **Hôtel-Restaurant Le Lion d'Or** A surprisingly decent hotel directly across the street from the train station, Le Lion d'Or has simple rooms with no bathroom for 29€. The restaurant downstairs, which serves Savoyard specialties and daily specials, isn't half bad, and the prices are very fair. *1 av. de la Boisse.* ☎ *04-79-44-32-75. www.liondor73.com. 29€–39€ single; 49€ double. In room: Some have TV, bathroom, and phone, so specify what you are looking for.*

DOABLE

➜ **Hôtel des Princes** The rooms in the Hôtel des Princes vary in size from large to huge; ask for rooms ending in the number 11, since these are the enormous suites with a loft bed in addition to the double bed downstairs, the large sofa in the living room, and the sitting area. Bathrooms and vestibule are equally spacious, but the old floral curtains and graying bedspreads save it from being too deluxe. Chintzy, not quite regal, antique-looking furniture adds that perfect note of lovable kitsch. It's sort of like a student apartment, decorated on the cheap. If only students' apartments were this large. Skip the very paltry breakfast in favor of a local cafe. For 8.50€ you can get a much better croissant and coffee elsewhere, and even have money left over for an English-language newspaper. *4 rue de Boigne.* ☎ *04-79-33-45-36. www.hoteldes princes.com. 80€–93€ double. Breakfast 8.50€. Amenities: Bar in lobby; elevator; parking available. In room: A/C, TV, free Wi-Fi.*

SPLURGE

➜ **Hôtel-Restaurant Château de Candie** This place was built as a fortress in the 14th century by knights on R and R from the Crusades. The only things it's shielding its residents from now are the minutiae and hassles of daily life. Set in a 6-hectare (15-acre) park a few minutes outside of centre-ville, the lovely grounds are rivaled by the lusciously appointed interiors, which brim with tasteful antiques and indulgent touches such as canopied beds and clawed bathtubs. *Rue du Bois de Candie, Chambéry-Le-Vieux.* ☎ *00-33-04-79-96-63-00. www.chateaudecandie.com. From 110€ double. Breakfast 15€. Duplexes available that sleep 4 or more. Amenities: Restaurant; elevator; parking. In room: TV, Internet.*

Eating

Dining in Chambéry, like most activities here, is a leisurely, pleasurable experience. Chambéry has a few regional specialties to look out for, in particular *Crozets*, small cubes of pasta made from white flour and buckwheat flour. They're a tasty reminder of the era when the House of Savoy encompassed parts of nearby northern Italy as well as France.

CAFES & LIGHT FARE

➜ **Le Réverbère** CREPERIE I've personally never met a crepe I didn't like, but I've never met ones I liked more than those that arrived in front of me piping hot and fragrant with cheese, and later with chestnut puree and whipped cream, at Le Réverbère. It wasn't just the crepes themselves; they were delicious, as could be expected. It was the view I had from my table, of the Château des Ducs artfully illuminated and positively basking in its nighttime beauty, the chapel in front of it rising regally above, and the gentle intrusion of leaves and branches from the large tree shading the dining terrace of this ridiculously well-situated cafe. The pizzas, salads, and crepes are all very tasty, especially the dessert crepes. It's a popular place with the locals for all sorts of obvious reasons, so get here early (around 7pm) for dinner to avoid waiting for a table. *4 place Château.* ☎ *04-79-33-90-68. Daily 11:30am–3pm and 7–10:30pm.*

CHEAP

➔ **L'Atelier** MEDITERRANEAN This place is just outside the main pedestrian area and across from one of the city's nightlife hubs, the Carré Curial. Serving decidedly unrisky Mediterranean cuisine, but at fair prices, l'Atelier is most notable for its relaxed ambience and the attractive, cool, 30-something crowd it draws. During the day, the slightly elevated outdoor terrace is a good place for people-watching, and at night a DJ and a tapas menu enter the picture. The owner often shows the work of local artists in and around the dining rooms. *59 rue de la République.* ☎ *04-79-70-62-39. Menu 14€ lunch, 25€ dinner. Tues–Sat noon–2pm and 7:30–10pm, 6:30pm–1:30am for bar service.*

DOABLE

➔ **Le Sporting** SAVOYARD As the name suggests, there's nothing dainty about the food, the decor, or, come to think of it, the service here at Le Sporting. It's all rib-sticking Alpine cuisine—fondue, *raclette, tartiflette*—of the kind your body craves after a soul-stirring day on the slopes or a bike ride through the woods. Even the salads are enormous and filling. *88 rue Croix d'Or.* ☎ *04-79-33-17-43. www.lesporting-chambery.com. Menus from 13€–27€; main*

courses 14€–22€. Daily noon–2pm and 7–9:30pm.

SPLURGE

➔ **Hôtel-Restaurant Château du Candie** GASTRONOMIC At first glance the prices are rather stupefying. Look a little closer and you'll find several bargains to be had, particularly the weekday lunch menu, which at 28€ is almost a steal, especially if you find yourself relishing it in the terrace overlooking the hotel's garden during the summertime. *Rue du Bois de Candie, chambéry-Le-Vieux.* ☎ *33-04-79-96-63-00. www.chateaudecandie.com. Main courses 34€–43€; menus 28€–69€.*

➔ **Restaurant DZ** GASTRONOMIC Restaurant DZ stands for Dropping Zone. What exactly is cool about this, I have yet to figure out. That aside, this hotel and restaurant is a nice place to stop for lunch if you're on a bicycle excursion to Lake du Bourget, only a few kilometers (a couple of miles) off the path from Chambéry, towards Aix-les-Bains, the famous spa town. The interior is slick and contemporary, with smooth wood tables, bright red chairs, and funky chandeliers that look as though they're dangling flaming rambutans. The summer terrace by the pool is bright and white, the seats barely shaded by white umbrellas, and it's a lovely place to soak up sun as you prepare yourself to get back on the bike trail.

The menu is a bit of a trip, organized as it is into sections called Départ, Suite, and Fin, with a typical départ described as "1st floor, tomato; 2nd floor, eggplant; 3rd floor, mousse of goat cheese." The desserts *(les fins)* are particularly tasty, especially the homemade ice creams and the assortment of crème brûlée. At night, the bar and restaurant turn into a lively disco scene, and the restaurant is often host to the region's glitzier events. The dress code, day or night, is Eurotrash all the way—meaning a lot of open shirt collars, white pants, and sunglasses that enable anyone standing in front of you to adjust their makeup using the lenses. Although most of the clients are businesspeople from nearby companies, no one will look twice at you if you show up dripping sweat with your shorts sticking to the inside of your thighs, so relax and enjoy the food. *Rte. de l'aéroport.* ☎ *04-79-63-80-50-50. www.cervolan.com. Main courses 14€–25€; weekday lunch menu 18€. Mon–Fri noon–2pm; Mon–Sat 7:30–11pm.*

Partying

Chambéry has a lot of bars and several nightclubs, and a lot of students and young people to fill them. The nightclubs are kind of on the scary side, more resembling a bad stereotype of a European discothèque than any place where you would actually want to go hang out. Go only if you are seeking bad music and an air of pretension. The area around rue de la République and the Médiathèque has a lot of small bars, and it's a popular place for weekend bar-hopping. Be sure to try one of the local liqueurs on your evening excursions; *Chambéryzette* and *génépi* are the most famous. The Carré Curial, a complex housing several discothèques in the same neighborhoods as the bars, can be entered at your own risk.

FUNKY BARS

➜ **Le Lounge** Locals congregate at this very chilled out bar for drinks and conversation, since they keep the loungey Hôtel Costes mix-CD kind of music at a civilized volume. The big black leather chairs are quite comfortable. *58 rue St-Réal.* ☎ *04-79-25-88-23. Tues–Sat noon–1:30am.*

➜ **Le O'Cardinal's** One of Chambéry's livelier bars, this place is packed by day with friends chatting in the large outdoor

terrace and solo drinkers engrossed in literature; by night the action moves indoors. The vibe here is really welcoming and casual, the decor a cut above the average pub (cute posters, photographs, and the odd antique), and the music totally tolerable. *5 place Métropole.* ☎ *04-79-85-53-40. Mon 5pm–1:15am; Tues–Sat 8:30am–1:15am.*

Sightseeing

If you do nothing else here, drift around the cobbled streets of the town center, preferably with an ice cream or a piece of cake in hand. The Chambérien, a cake with almonds and coffee-cream, is an appropriate choice. Make sure to hit the alleyways and *traboules* drizzling off of place St-Léger. Take a spin down rue Croix d'Or pausing to see the Charles Dulin theater, modeled after La Scala in Milan, and named after a Chambéry native, a playwright of the early 20th century.

MUSEUMS

If you plan to see more than one of the museums, consider getting a 12€ **Chambéry pass** at the tourist office, which will get you heavy discounts at the Musée de Beaux-Arts, the Musée Savoisien, the Natural History Museum, Les Charmettes (okay, it's free anyway), and Gallery Eureka. In addition, it lowers prices on the little tourist train (which you weren't going to take anyway, right?), on the boats at Lac du Bourget, and on guided tours of the town and the Château des Ducs. Add another 1€ and you can ride the bus 24 hours a day, as many times as you'd like. The pass is valid May 1 to October 31.

➜ **Musée des Beaux-Arts** Many of the big Italian painters are represented here, in particular Uccello, di Fredi, and Luca Giordano (who painted for the Médici family) and others from the 14th to 18th centuries. Their French counterparts, including

Fragonard, strut their stuff as well, as do Northern painters such as Jan van Dornicke. The building, which has housed the museum since 1889, was once a granary. *Place du Palais de Justice.* ☎ *04-79-33-75-03. Free admission 1st Sun of the month. Wed–Mon 10am–noon and 2–6pm.*

FREE ➜**Musée des Charmettes** Reportedly, and understandably, where **Jean-Jacques Rousseau** spent some of the happiest days of his life, Les Charmettes is a 17th-century house, with a beautiful and simple garden, set among fantastically green hills and surrounded by trees. He lived here, surrounded by the nature and botany that he loved so much, from 1736 on, with his companion Madame de Warens, whom he called "Maman." Something kinky going on there? Anyway, the house is now a museum with rotating exhibits, and the bedrooms and original decor have been preserved. On summer evenings in July and August, one can attend a re-enactment of life at Les Charmettes in the 18th century, with out-of-work local actors playing grandly to the roles of the great thinker and his lady friend. Tea and cakes are served afterward. Check with the tourist office for days and times. *890 chemin des Charmettes.* ☎ *04-79-33-39-44. Free admission to the house. Oct 1–Mar 31 10am–noon and 2–4:30pm. Apr 1–Sept 30 10am–noon and 2–6pm.*

MONUMENTS & CHURCHES

FREE ➜**Cathédrale St-François de Sales** A 15th-century Franciscan church that became a cathedral in 1779, with the creation of a bishop's see in Chambéry, the cathedral reportedly holds the **largest ensemble of *trompe l'oeil* paintings** in all of Europe, over 6,000 sq. m (64,583 sq. ft.), to be precise. *Place Métropole.* ☎ *04-79-33-25-00. Free admission. Daily 8am–noon and 2–6:30pm. Treasury mid-May to mid-Sept Sat 5–7pm.*

➜**Château des Ducs** Once the residence of the counts and dukes of Savoy, this complex of medieval buildings is today the home of the town's Préfecture. It can be toured with a guide, who will take you to the treasury tower, the cellar rooms, the semi-circular tower, and the St-Chapelle, with its Gothic arches painted in *trompe l'oeil,* and 15th-century stained-glass windows. This chapel once held the **Holy Shroud,** which moved to Turin in 1578 and has remained there since. *Rue Basse du Château. No phone. Guided tour 4€–5€ with combination guided tour of the old town.*

Playing Outside

Chambéry is conveniently located between three natural parks, Massif des Bauges, Chartreuse, and la Vanoise. Each offers its own dramatic scenery, and a variety of sporting activities, cross-country skiing being one specialty. Chambéry has also invested a great deal in its 📺 Best● **bike paths,** which are flat, smooth, and very well signed. They spread out 50km (31 miles) from the town center, heading towards the surrounding lakes (Lac du Bourget, the largest natural lake in France; Lac d'Aiguebelette; and Le Lac St. André).

CYCLING

➜**Vélostation** This municipally run bike rental at the SNCF train station has a fleet of pretty blue bicycles in great condition. The employees or the tourist office can supply you with a map of bike routes, make recommendations as per your fitness or laziness level, and give you great directions to get onto the paths. *En Gare de Chambéry.* ☎ *04-79-96-34-13. 3€ half-day, 5€ full day, or 3€ full day with Chambéry pass. 300€ deposit. Apr–Oct Mon–Fri 6:30am–7pm, Sat–Sun and holidays 9am–7pm; Nov–Mar Mon–Fri 6:30am–7pm, Sat 9am–7pm; closed holidays.*

Mountain Sports

As the name suggests, **Montania Sport** (6 rue de la Métropole; ☎ 04-79-69-67-82; www.montania-sport.com; Tues–Sat 10am–7pm) has everything you need, for sale or for rent, to explore the mountains in as many modes as there are possible. The experienced staff at the Bureau des Guides will help you plan the adventure of your dreams: Canyoning, hiking, climbing, skiing, and snowshoeing are all available.

HANG GLIDING

The state-certified instructors from the **Aiguebelette Hanggliding School** (Aiguebelette Parapente; ☎ **04-76-37-49-22**; www.aiguebeletteparapente.fr; 3-hr. half-day discovery session 70€) can launch you from a selection of sites around the lake, the third largest such school in France. To get there, take A43 10 min. and get off at exit 12, marked Lac d'Aiguebelette.

Shopping

➜ **La Chant de la Sirène** Entering this rather smelly little record shop is like walking into your friend's garage and finding his cool dad there, poring over his record collection from his teenage years. The records' odor confirms their genuine vintage status, but everything is in great condition. There's reggae, classic French music from the '60s and '70s, rock, soul, '50s American rock, lots of jazz, gospel, and Brazilian music, among other things. The old hippie owner will help you find what you're looking for. *47 place St-Léger.* ☎ *04-79-75-16-55. www.lechantdelasirene.com. Mon 4:30–7pm; Tues–Sat 10am–noon and 3–7pm.*

➜**Laiterie des Halles** Regional cheeses such as Tome des Bauges, Colombier des Aillons, Chevrotin de Vanoise, le Farou, and many others are sitting here under the watchful eye of master *fromager* Denis Provent, who carefully selects the 140 or so cheeses that he displays at any given time. Pick up some edible souvenirs with a bit more shelf life, such as regional pastas with unusual flavors like chestnut and white mushroom. Notice the antique butter churns around the shop. *2 place de Genève.* ☎ *04-79-33-77-17. Tues–Sat 7:30am–12:15pm and 3–7:15pm.*

➜ **La Piste Verte** You can still buy one of Chambéry's most renowned weapons, the Opinel knife, in many a tobacco and gift shop, but this is the original purveyor, with a wide selection. The owner can help you select which model is best for your purposes. We ask that you use it only to attack Savoy's regional cheeses and their ally, the baguette. *172 rue Croix d'Or.* ☎ *04-79-33-57-31. Tues–Sat 9:30am–12:15pm and 2–7:15pm.*

➜ **Le Fidèle Berger** This *salon de thé* dates from 1832, and specializes in chocolate truffles, which were invented in Chambéry in 1828. They run 64€ a kilo, and they're usually not available in the summer, when the heat is too strong for their frail composition of cream and chocolate. Even if you can't locate a truffle, try one of their other chocolaty or buttery treats. *15 rue de Boigne.* ☎ *04-79-33-06-37. Tues–Sat 8am–7:15pm; Sun 8am–12:15pm.*

➜ **Val' Fruits** Every conceivable fruit—both local and in season or exotic and imported, at prices both fair and appalling—is available here. All of the produce is picture perfect, and the staff will help you pick something of just the right ripeness or lay the foundations of a picnic. No ordinary fruit stand; they even have a prize, "Fruitier d'Or 2001," to prove it. *8 rue d'Italie.* ☎ *04-79-85-99-07. Sun 8am–noon; Mon–Sat 7:30am–12:30pm and 2–7:30pm. Sat open continuously through lunch.*

Festivals

In the summer, free concerts, plays, and other performances take place in several venues, most notably at the **Château des** Ducs. They are free, pleasant, and crowded with swaying couples and smiling families. It's usually a mix of French bands and world music, including the ever-popular gospel genre.

Annecy

545km (338 miles) from Paris, 133km (82 miles) from Lyon

Annecy, a city of 130,000, just on the edge of the postcard-perfect Lac d'Annecy, is considered the gateway to the French Alps. Capital of the Haute-Savoie region, it has abundant lodging and dining options, which makes it a logical base for further travel among the spa towns, heading east towards Switzerland or south through the Alps. Like a gateway drug, its laid-back atmosphere and smorgasbord of sporting activities means it can be very addictive and incite you to explore a little deeper.

About midway between Geneva and Chambéry, Annecy was once in fact the capital of the County of Geneva—a status it relinquished when the House of Savoy set up shop here in the 1400s, integrating it into their large territorial holdings, which reached all the way up to what is now northern Italy. As you stare out the window on your train ride through the region, or drive amid the glorious peaks, imagine you're a duke of Savoy and you own all this territory.

There are plenty of options to live it up like royalty here, even if you're not—but be prepared to pay for it. Some of the area's most creative chefs are testing their limits in the kitchen just as strenuously as the bikers huffing and puffing their way uphill on the lake's bike trails, and some accommodations go for a king's ransom. There's a hippie vibe in the air and plenty of young people, bars, and small art galleries, but hotel and restaurant prices are still fairly high. It gets even pricier if you want to indulge in some of the sporting activities—like an exhilarating tandem paraglide over the lake, the price of which (75€ for 20 min.) will leave you feeling crashed and burned like Icarus (with a softer landing, of course).

Long a hub of tourist activity (Henry IV, Louis XII, and Jean-Jacque Rousseau were all fanny-packing around here at one point), Annecy opened its tourist office in 1895—the second official tourist office ever established in France, after Grenoble's. The lake's popularity began to climb in the 1960s, and shows no signs of slowing. Day-tripping kids from Lyon are also a significant portion of the weekend crowd.

The real reason people flock to Annecy is to play outside. There are activities to suit your every whim, although unfortunately not every budget, unless you stick to basics like renting a bike or a kayak. Most of the sporting activities are equipment-heavy and require a trained guide or lessons, which makes them expensive, but the options seem limitless. Water-skiing, paragliding, roller skating (yes, roller skating), sailing, hiking, canyoning, biking, skiing, snowboarding, and more activities are all available depending on the season. The tourism office can help you navigate through the myriad options and choose a nautical or hang-gliding center appropriate for your skill level and budget. See "Playing Outside" (p. 592) for some recommended places.

THE RHÔNE VALLEY & FRENCH ALPS

Orientation & Getting Around

Annecy is small and easy to navigate on foot or with a bike. During the summer the streets are rather flush with tourists, which makes biking a slow and wobbly affair within the town, which is cut through with canals and narrow bridges. However, a bike (or a car) will serve you well for exploring around the lake of Annecy itself. The lake is shaped like a seagull with its wings spread, and its two banks are referred to as the Rive Gauche (Left or West bank) and the Rive Droîte (Right or East bank). Lac d'Annecy is beaded with small towns like Veyrier-du-Lac, Talloires, Sevrier, and Saint-Jorioz. All rather similar in size and feel, each of these towns has its own market day, a few shops, and usually a couple of restaurants right on the lake. Talloires has a reputation as perhaps the most posh of them all, due to its several gastronomic restaurants.

The lake is also ringed with gorgeous mountain ranges. In addition to taking your breath away every time you look at them, they also make excellent places from which to set out on a hike, go skiing, or jump into the air with a pile of fabric on your back (that's paragliding for you). Many of the ski nautique and other sporting centers are located in one of these smaller towns as well, and in between them are little stretches of beach or grass where you can park yourself lakeside and enjoy the water.

If you're driving, beware of traffic, which at times—say, lunchtime in the middle of the summer—gets very bad, since the only way to get around the lake if you don't have your own boat is to take the two-lane road that encircles it, with one lane going each direction. The fact that the road is a closed loop implies that it's impossible to get lost, since you're either going the right way or the wrong way, and

you can always just keep going. However, many of the destinations like restaurants, water-skiing bases, and the like, are off the main road and are poorly marked, so keep an eye out.

Cultural Tips

Annecy is known as a sporty, rich, hippie summer playground. The locals are somewhat protective of their turf, seeing as it's invaded by thousands of tourists, most of them on two wheels, each summer. So don't expect to mingle a lot with the natives, although they are very friendly, if you can find them. It's mostly wealthy Europeans, English, and Americans, doing the usual tourist routines—eating ice cream, sitting in cafes, having lunch at lakeside restaurants, and then, of course, there are the sporting activities.

Sleeping

Spending the night in Annecy ain't cheap. A lot of people are willing to fork out to wake up next to a gorgeous lake with dramatic mountains all around, and not too many hoteliers cut anyone any discounts for this privilege. If you have a car, it might make sense to stay in the less-expensive auberges, not in Annecy proper, but located around the lake. Or, if you have a tent handy, camping is probably the best way to go—the whole point of being here is to be outside anyway, right? Otherwise, you're looking at around 60€ a night per room, to be right smack in the middle of things.

CAMPING

➔ **Europa** This large, 3.2-hectare (8-acre) campsite is only 300m (984 ft.) from Lake Annecy, and has direct access to the cycle path around the lake. It's in Saint Jorioz, between the lake and the mountains, and has its own water park, of sorts, with waterslides, a Jacuzzi, and several heated pools. The site has 210 pitches and several chalets available. *Rte. d'Albertville. 74410 Saint-Jorioz.* ☎ *33-04-50-68-51-01. www.camping-europa.com. Camping 17€–28€ per night per person depending on the season; 5€–6€ supplement per person; 4-person chalet starts at 370€ per week.*

➜ **Le Belvedere** This campsite is a 10-minute walk from Annecy's old town, the beach, and the port of the lake. There are 120 places, of which 80 have electricity available. *Rte. du Semnoz.* ☎ *04-50-45-48-30. 120 places and 2 chalets. Open Apr–Oct.*

➜ **Le Panoramic** This 210-person site has 17 chalets located in a natural park 7km (4 miles) from Annecy and 1.5km (1 mile) from the lake. Le Panoramic even has its own grocery store, in addition to a restaurant and bar, making it almost totally self-contained, like Celebration, Florida—only with the opportunity to play *pétanque. 22 chemin des Bernets.* ☎ *04-50-52-43-09. www. camping-le-panoramic.com. 15€–18€ adults. Open May–Sept.*

HOSTELS

➜ **Auberge de Jeunesse Annecy** Three kilometers (2 miles) from the train station and walking distance from town, this large hostel overlooks the lake, set in front of a coniferous forest. The interior, as usual, is heinous, but in what hostel is that not the case? The setting, on the other hand, is quite spectacular. *4 rte. du Semnoz.* ☎ *04-50-45-33-19. 16€ including sheets and breakfast. Jan 15–Nov 30 reception 8am–midnight and 3–10pm. During winter Sun 8am–midnight. By bus, take Line 6 to "Marquisats," stop "Hôtel de Police" (500m/1,640 ft. from the hostel). By car, exit Annecy Sud, toward the Centre Hospitalier, then follow the signs for the "Auberge de Jeunesse." If you are coming from the lake, take the big avenue close to the Hospital "av. de Tresum," then follow the signs.*

CHEAP

➜ **Roc du Chere** A very cute, very cheap (given the neighborhood!) little hotel in Talloires, run by a couple with excellent knowledge of the area. The rooms are quaintly decorated, though nothing too special, but it's one of the best bargains you'll find in the whole area. The breakfast buffet is generous and includes local cheeses. *Echarvines 74290 Talloires.* ☎ *33-450-60-19-15. www.rocdechere.com. Oct–Apr 30€–39€ double; May 1–Sept 30 36€–46€ double. Rooms for 3, 4, and 7 persons (suite) also available. Breakfast 7€.*

DOABLE

➜ **Hôtel du Palais de L'Isle** This charming three-star hotel in a 17th-century building is outfitted with sleek, modern furniture. For the money, it's one of the best values you'll find in Annecy proper. *13 rue Perrière, Annecy 74000 France.* ☎ *33-04-50-45-86-87. www.hoteldupalaisdelisle.com. 62€–65€ single; 77€–140€ double, depending on the size and view. In room: A/C, cable TV, hair dryer, Internet point, minibar, private bath and WC, soundproof rooms.*

➜ **La Vallombreuse** A six-bedroom guesthouse taking up one wing of a 15th-century manor (the owner and his family live in the other wing) and its adjacent granary, La Vallombreuse is a cozy alternative to a traditional hotel. It has a TV and DVD player in the common living room, in-room phones, a library, a garden, Internet access, and a 16th-century cobblestone courtyard. It is located in Menthon St-Bernard, on the east bank of the lake, about a 10- or 15-minute drive from Annecy. *534 rte. des Moulins, 74290 Menthon-Saint-Bernard Haute-Savoie (Rhône-Alpes).* ☎ *33-04-50-60-16-33. www.la-vallombreuse.com. 73€–98€ a night, depending on the size.*

Eating

The city of Annecy has dozens of restaurants, many of which seem to be serving identical menus of tartiflette, raclette, fondue, pastas, and salads. Assuredly, any place broiling plates of potatoes covered with cheese, onions, and bacon isn't going to do you wrong. Around the lake are many restaurants with terraces on the water. Naturally, they specialize in fish, especially the local fish from the lake, such as fera and *omble chevalier*. Then there are the gastronomic restaurants, which are usually outrageously expensive, and are sometimes, but not every time, worth it.

CHEAP

MTV Best ✪ → **La Montagnette** SAVOYARD With its warm lighting, woody interior, and a hunky friendly owner plus generous salads, inexpensive and creative tartines, and authentic Savoyard cooking, this is one of the most appealing of the many small restaurants on Faubourg Ste-Claire. It has a younger, hipper clientele, and a cute, friendly waitress to boot. If you order the raclette, out comes the whole kitchen: a heavy cauldron of boiled potatoes, a round of cheese as big as a toddler's head, and a brilliant contraption that melts the cheese, bit by bit, as you scrape the gooey parts onto your steaming spuds. The process is every bit as enjoyable as the end result. Or is it the other way around? *22 faubourg Ste-Claire. ☎ 04-50-45-88-78. Mon–Tues and Thurs–Fri noon–2pm and 7–10pm; Sat–Sun 7–11pm.*

→ **Le Rest'O de la Plage** BISTRO On a terrace overlooking a rather dowdy little stretch of sand (it's still on the spectacular lake, with a view of Talloires, but as beaches go, it's quite paltry), Le Rest'O de la Plage serves clean, classic, tasty food in generous portions. The salads are filling, the steaks juicy, and the ingredients—from the fish to the vegetables—very fresh. And you'll eat to the sound of families splashing around in the lake. Try the cold string bean salad with hazelnut oil and sesame seeds. The inside dining room has the same view. Take the coast road, park at the lot for the beach, and follow the signs for the restaurant. *Rte. de la plage, Saint Jorioz. ☎ 04-50-88-24-88. www.lorestaurant.fr. Main courses 11€–16€. May 1–Sept 30 daily noon–2:30pm and 7–10:30pm.*

DOABLE

→ **Auberge du Lac** FISH You have several ways of arriving at Auberge du Lac. By boat, if you roll like that, you can hop right up onto the large dining terrace after docking ostentatiously. On foot, you can enter like everyone else through the main entrance, which is down a small street off the coast road. Once you're safely parked under an awning, dig into big platters of fried fish from the lake, garnished with chubby french fries, and afterwards slip off your summer whites and recline like a toad on the nearby sundeck. The majority of the clients look like big European money (big watches, big hats) who have summer homes here, and there's a fair amount of cigar-smoking and aristocratic chuckling going on. In the winter, there's an indoor restaurant that is part of the adjoining two-star hotel. *Restaurant L'Auberge du Lac, Hôtel La Villa du Port. ☎ 04-50-60-10-15. www.bord-du-lac.com. Main courses 17€–22€; menus from 14€–25€. Closed Nov–Mar.*

SPLURGE

MTV Best ✪ → **Clos des Sens** GASTONOMIC You can almost hear Lou Reed's "Walk on the Wild Side" being piped into chef Laurent Petit's kitchen as he works; there has to be something egging this guy on. Each season, as the menu changes, the offerings get wackier—from conceptual appetizers like a crustless tart (an elaborate mosaic of vegetables) to fig carpaccio accompanied by frozen olive oil. Thanks to his careful ingredient sourcing and impeccable technique, everything still tastes pretty cool. Even a dessert made with vegetables (a mother's dream), a napoleon of eggplant and fennel, has promise in Petit's hands. The interior is elegant, modern, and warmly lit, its sparseness accented by dramatic flowers. The summer terrace is shaded by an unbelievably beautiful tree, pruned to some kind of bonsai-status perfection, and looks out from its hilltop perch onto the city of Annecy below, and the lake beyond. There are also four rooms available in the adjoining guesthouse from 150€–200€. *13 rue Jean Mermoz.* ☎ *33-04-50-23-07-90. www.closdessens.com. Menus from 35€. Tues–Sat noon–2:30pm and 7–10:30pm; Sun noon–2:30pm.*

Partying

BARS

➔**Café Restaurant Bellachia Salah** Known locally as "The Melting Pot," this small bar has good quality music, a rarity in France, and it's full of musicians, artists, and other cool people, some of whom can speak English. It has a neighborhood-y, *Cheers* kind of feel, with its cast of regulars and friendly owner. *4 faubourg Ste-Claire.* ☎ *04-50-51-07-45.*

➔**Finn Kelly's** A typical but popular Irish pub (could you guess from the name?), it has giant screens for watching sports matches, free Wi-Fi, and occasional theme parties. It's near the local French-language school, so there's a constant stream of foreigners passing by for a study break. You can ask for chess or backgammon sets and decks of playing cards; they've got them all on hand. *10 faubourg des Annociades.* ☎ *04-50-51-29-40. www.finnkellys.com.*

NIGHTCLUBS & LIVE MUSIC VENUES

➔**La Macumba** Twelve different "ambiences" spread over seven floors means there's something for everyone here, provided everyone is prepared to lower their standards a bit. Rock, salsa, women-only nights with beauticians, and Chippendale acts are some of the scheduled themed nights. This place will pretty much shatter your cheese-o-meter, but there is potential for a very fun night, especially if you go in a group. Free transport to and from Annecy on weekends on the Macumbabus, an innovative shuttle service to reduce drunk driving in the region. It costs 10€ to get in. ☎ *04-50-49-23-50. www.macumba.net.*

Sightseeing

MUSEUMS & GALLERIES

➔**Musée-Château d'Annecy** This 12th-century stone castle towers above the town of Annecy, reminding the sports enthusiasts that this was once the terrain of noblemen. It has been, throughout the years, residence of Swiss counts and dukes, then a fort, and now a museum—Annecy sure knows how to recycle a building. The museum is kind of a catch-all grab bag of mini-museums, with wings dedicated to religious sculpture, regional crafts, modern art, and temporary exhibits. A highlight is the regional observatory, which has aquariums featuring the different types of fish that bide their time in the lake until the day they land on some tourist's plate. *Place du Château.* ☎ *04-50-33-87-30. Admission 4.70€ adults; .90€ students and guests 12–25; free for children 12 and under. Oct 1–May 31 Wed–Mon 10am–noon and 2–5pm; June 1–Sept 30 Wed–Mon 10:30am–6pm.*

🅼🆅 (Best ◐) ➔**Palais de l'Isle** The Palais de l'Isle has gone through more transformations than Madonna in her heyday, albeit over a matter of centuries, rather than years. It was, since its construction in 1132, the residence of the lord of Annecy, the administrative HQ for the count of Geneva, the town courthouse, the town mint, a jail from the Middle Ages until 1865, and a jail during World War II. Now it is one of Annecy's most popular museums, with rotating exhibits that usually focus on the town's history. *3 passage de l'Ile.* ☎ *04-50-33-87-30. Oct 1–May 31 Wed–Mon 10am–noon and 2–5pm; June 1–Sept 30 daily 10:30am–6pm.*

Playing Outside

RENTING BIKES

→ **Roul' ma Poule** Roul' ma Poule has a ridiculous name, and a huge variety of bikes that range from basic to super sporty, starting at 8€ for a half-day or 12€ for a full day for a 7-speed cruiser, to 24-speed tandem bikes for 28€ a day. Rollerblades are also available. *4 rue des Marquisats.* ☎ *04-50-27-86-83. www.annecy-location-velo.com. Closed Nov–Apr.*

HANG GLIDING

→ **Ecole des Grands Espaces** The guys at Ecole des Grands Espaces are almost worryingly good natured and laid-back—you might want the person between whose legs you will be leaping off of a cliff to have an air of gravity, no? Have no fear; these guys (it's pretty much all guys) definitely know what they're doing up there, and they like to have a good time while they do it. For 20 to 30 minutes of dangling in the air, it costs 75€ to 80€, depending on which ledge you take off from, since they drive you from their base up to one of several Suicide Points. Sorry, Lookout Points. From Annecy, drive towards Talloires, it's in Perroix just after Menthon St-Bernard. *715 rte. de Chaparon.* ☎ *33-4-50-45-95-52. www.parapente-annecy.com.*

→ **Ski Nautique Club Sevrier** This club offers water-skiing and related activities (wakeboarding, wakesurfing, wakeskating, barefoot water-skiing) plus boat rides around the lake. It's pricey but professional. The president of the club, Philippe Girod, is one of the top water-skiers in Europe. Look for signs off the main road; once you approach Sevrier, it's down by the lake (obviously). *Promenade de Borenges.* ☎ *06-84-78-12-89. www.annecyskinautique. com. 23€ for a 10-min. water-skiing lesson plus licensing fee; 145€ for a 1-hr. tour around the lake with a friendly English-speaking guide.*

→ **Takamaka** Sojourners at the youth hostel get a 10% discount at this adventure-tour warehouse. They organize different outdoor sports in the immediate area, as well as the surrounding region, in Lac

Lake Annecy: Deep & Pure

The Lake of Annecy is 18,000 years old, born of melting glaciers. Fourteen kilometers (9 miles) long and up to 3.2km (2 miles) wide at points, it is one of the most attractive lakes in France, providing more than 27 sq. km (11 sq. miles) of water surface, which ranges from clear green to murky dark blue and every shade and opacity in between, depending on the depth (41–80m/134–262 ft.). It has been the beneficiary of a conservation effort that began in the 1950s, when a local doctor noticed the decline in the water's quality and set about reversing the impending contamination. The Lake Association, formed in 1955, created a purifying network of currently several hundred kilometers that treats the water sources as they make their way towards the lake. They have received many prizes for their innovative work.

Leman/Lake Geneva and Evian. According to the website, not only are all of the staff fully accredited, they are also "often very funny." Takamaka also offer adventure

tours to places such as Morocco, but that's another book. *23 faubourg Sainte Claire.* ☎ *33-450-45-60-61. www.takamaka.fr. Mon–Fri 9am–noon and 2–6pm.*

Chamonix

Chamonix these days attracts a lot of British people looking for a good party scene, in addition to the nature lovers it's been drawing since the early 1800s. Winter or summer (but not so much spring or fall), the party is there for the taking, especially in wintertime, when its supremacy as one of France's premiere sporting destinations goes relatively unchallenged. You'll hear as much English (usually with a posh Anglo accent) as you will French, and likewise there is as much beer being swilled as fine wine.

If partying isn't your scene, but skiing is, it is still possible to enjoy a relatively peaceful holiday without encountering all of the debauchery that has become part of Chamonix's reputation. Nearby **Mont Blanc** is the highest peak in western Europe, and dozens of small auberges and B&Bs cater to skiers. Many have their own restaurants. By simply avoiding the bars and louder restaurants and sticking to daytime activities, you can have a perfectly tranquil ski vacation.

Even less taxing than a ski vacation, but still extremely rewarding, is just a simple visit to some of Chamonix's unique natural sites, which are among the most spectacular in Europe, and the third most visited in the world. The 7km-long (4 miles) **Mer de Glace,** and the **Aiguille du Midi,** illustrate the inadequacy of words like "breathtaking." Here, you don't have to do anything more strenuous than looking, appreciating, and inhaling your allotted portion of impossibly fresh Alpine air.

Switzerland and Italy are respectively 16km (10 miles) and 15km (9 miles) away from Chamonix. Both are easily accessible

by road or rail. The Geneva airport is 88km (55 miles) away, making it the closest one.

Orientation

Chamonix, tucked as it is into a valley between **Mont-Blanc** and **Le Brévent,** has remained rather small due to these natural constraints. It is bifurcated by the Arve river, and most of the action is concentrated more or less near the river. The main pedestrian streets are rue du Docteur Paccard, which runs parallel to the Arve, avenue Michel Croz, Allée Recteur Payot, and avenue du Mont Blanc. In and around these streets are the majority of Chamonix's restaurants, bars, shops, and hotels, although some of the more peaceful hotels, both cheap and expensive, are located a bit outside of town. Everything is easily and enjoyably walkable, and you are in fact encouraged to park your car as soon as possible and remain on foot, or use the city's free and environmentally sound public transportation system.

Getting Around

As might be expected of a small community wedged in between overwhelming natural phenomena, Chamonix is acutely aware of its fragile way of life, and has taken great pains to reduce the impact of the ever-increasing waves of tourists who flood its streets, trails, and *pistes* year-round. Part of this effort is a fleet of nonpolluting minibuses called "Mulets" free for all tourists holding a *carte d'hôte,* which is issued to you automatically by your hotel when you arrive. They run every 10 minutes. Transportation on the urban bus system, which makes stops at the ski lift, and on the SNCF rail system between Servoz and Vallorcine, is also free with the guest card.

Tourist Office

The **tourist office** (85 place du triangle de l'Amitié; ☎ **33-450-53-00-24**) of Chamonix is generally swarmed with people, but wait your turn and you'll be rewarded by an exceedingly friendly staff member with a mountain of brochures, maps, and pamphlets to bestow upon you. Here you can also pick up the Multipass Mont-Blanc, which gets you access to all of the sites and excursions of the Compagnie du Mont-Blanc, a locally run tourism cooperative that manages access to the slopes, including the trips up to Aiguille du Midi and Montenvers (also available via www.compagniedumontblanc.fr/index.php). The tourism office is also a reliable place to connect wirelessly to the Internet.

Cultural Tips

There don't seem to be too many locals left in Chamonix, and those that are still here are usually in the hospitality or sporting business. Instead, you'll find that many of the people tending bar or dining at the local restaurants and pubs are British or from elsewhere on the Continent—itinerant folk who came for a holiday, couldn't imagine anywhere more beautiful, and stayed. These friendly souls are usually very generous with their knowledge of the area, and can pour a stiff drink as well.

Recommended Websites

All these websites are thorough and up-to-date guides to Chamonix's activities, accommodations, and restaurants.

- ○ **http://info.chamonix.com**
- ○ **www.compagniedumontblanc. fr/index.php**
- ○ **www.chamonix.net/english/ home.htm**
- ○ **www.chamonix.com**

Drink Up!

Don't forget to fill your water bottle at the fountain near the tourist office with fresh Alpine spring H_2O—the same stuff you'll pay $1.50 for at home.

- ○ **http://skisnowboardeurope. com/chamonix**
- ○ **www.chamonet.com**

Sleeping

HOSTELS

→ **Chamonix Youth Hostel** "Welcome at Chamonix Youth Hostel!!!" screams the website. The enthusiasm level holds in reality; the welcome here is warm, and the solidarity implied by a membership card is taken seriously. Big, tasty dinners are taken together; there's a pub; and a common area is specifically designated for "chilling out." The hostel has its own large collection of ski, snowboard, and snowshoeing equipment, which you can rent for the duration of your stay.

The hostel has views of the Aiguille de Midi and the Glacier des Bossons, Europe's longest ice fall. It is about a 10-minute walk to town or to the Cascade du Dard or the nearby forest. *127 Montée Jacques Balmat, Les Pelerins d'en Haut.* ☎ *04-50-53-14-52. www.fuaj-montagne.org for more hostels in the Alps. 16€ per night. Amenities: Internet; phone; washer/dryer; baggage storage can accommodate bikes/skis overnight. Closed Oct–Nov and 2 weeks in May.*

CHEAP

→ **Hôtel l'Arve** What started as Café de l'Arve four generations ago, at the turn of the century, is now a bustling two-star hotel run by the same family. It's a 10-minute walk from the train station or the tourism office. While the decor could use some help, the amenities are generous for such low prices, and the atmosphere is low-key and welcoming. *60 impasse des Anémones.* ☎ *04-50-53-02-31. www.hotelarve-chamonix.com. 58€–76€ double, depending on size. Credit cards accepted. Amenities: Billiards; elevator; fireplace; parking; sauna and fitness center. In room: Satellite TV.*

DOABLE

→**Hôtel Excelsior** The only two-star hotel in Chamonix with a swimming pool, this place has been run by the Cheilan family for four generations. The rooms are simple, bordering on tasteful, but not quite managing to walk that fine line between modern accoutrements and an old, Alpine building with wooden walls. Still, it's in a lovely location, Les Tines, the last village of the Chamonix valley before the next ski stop, Argentiere. You can arrive by car or bus from Chamonix (4km/2½ miles away), on the road going towards Argentiere. There is an in-house minibus that can be used for a fee, and an on-site restaurant with delicious food. *251 chemin de St-Roch, Les Tines.* ☎ *04-50-53-18-36. www.hotel chamonix.info. 41€–56€/67€–82€ double depending on the season. Breakfast 8€. Credit cards accepted. Amenities: Elevator; parking; pool table. In room: Satellite TV, hair dryer.*

SPLURGE

→**Hôtel Mont-Blanc** There's a very Edith Wharton quality to the pace and style of this grand old four-star hotel that has been sheltering wealthy travelers for over 150 years. One dresses up for dinner; it is customary for guests to pause in the hallway to wish their fellow sojourners a good evening, accompanied by a slight bow; and the place even boasts a piano bar. The location is as convenient as could be, in the middle of Chamonix, and private parking is available. Even with its central location, literally next door to the tourist office, it manages to maintain an air of tranquility. The outdoor pool is heated in winter, although I'd advise forsaking it for the dining room's blazing fireplace and a cup of hot chocolate. Rooms are tastefully done, and from every window the view is stunning. *62 allée du Majestic.* ☎ *04-50-53-05-64. www.bestmontblanc.com. 127€–176€ double. Credit cards accepted. Amenities: Wi-Fi in lobby. In room: Satellite TV, hair dryer, minibar, safe.*

Eating

CAFES & LIGHT FARE

→**Aux Petits Gourmands** PATISSERIE The sights in the window and the smells wafting through the street arrest the unwitting pedestrian and lure her or him inside. This patisserie and *salon de thé* has some of the most comely pastries around, shamelessly on view for the passerby, and at fair prices (1€ for a huge *pain au raisin,* 2.30€ for a slice of quiche). In the summer, an ice-cream cart out front peddles a small selection of delectable homemade flavors; the mint chocolate chip is a standout. *168 rue Paccard.* ☎ *04-50-53-01-59. Daily 7am–7pm.*

CHEAP

→**Le Bivouac** SAVOYARD A local favorite for its consistent Savoyard cooking and fair prices, le Bivouac will stuff you full of cheese, potatoes, cubes of bread speared on long forks, and variations on this theme 7 days a week. *266 rue Paccard.* ☎ *04-50-53-34-08. Main courses 10€–19€. Late Oct to late Nov and mid-May to late June daily noon–3pm and 6–8:30pm.*

DOABLE

→**Elevation 1904** CAFE Although they start serving tasty breakfasts at 7:30am, Elevation 1904 really gets going around 4pm, when it becomes the *après-ski* spot of choice for the young and carefree. Its intimate, low-ceilinged vibe is just sexy enough to warm away any Alpine chills you may have retained. *259 av. Michel Croz.* ☎ *04-50-53-00-52. Burgers and panini under*

10€; beer 2.80€. Credit cards accepted. Daily 7:30am–2am during ski season; daily 7:30am–1am the rest of the year.

➔ **Le Grand Hôtel-Restaurant du Montenvers** SAVOYARD Tartiflette and other Savoyard standbys have never tasted so good as they do here, on an open terrace 1,913m (6,275 ft.) in the air, with the crags and splendor of les Drus and les Grandes Jorasses in full view. Bring a sweater, though, even for a summer lunch. It gets chilly this high up in the air. 35 place de la Mer de Glace. ☎ 04-50-53-87-70.

SPLURGE

➔ **Le Matafan** GASTRONOMIC On the ground floor of the Hôtel Mont-Blanc is a gastronomic restaurant worthy of the appellation. The food here is creative without being showy, or counterintuitive, as haute cuisine sometimes manages to be. The ingredients are superb, the presentation breathtaking, and the combinations always delicious, particularly when it comes to the dessert course. The clientele is mostly wealthy, well-mannered Europeans and Brits who use the seasons as verbs, and have been spending them here for generations. At one table was a little princessy girl no older than 6, yapping on her parents' cellphone (I mean, I'm hoping it's not hers) with the ease and authority of a businesswoman, while her parents worked their way through a roasted rabbit and a plate of foie gras. Best of all, the waiters here may have actually been trained in hospitality, rather than hostility, as their legions of colleagues throughout the rest of France seem to have been. And if you're a wine snob, have a ball with the 20,000 bottle selection they keep on hand. Hôtel Mont-Blanc, 62 allée du Majéstic. ☎ 0-50-53-05-64. Full menu 60€. Credit cards accepted. Daily noon–1:30pm and 7–10pm. Closed May and Oct 15–Dec 15.

Partying

FUNKY BARS

➔ **Le Choucas** This place certainly gets some points for its distinctive decor, which, with its Alpine architecture, cow-hide lined benches, and red lanterns, looks like a cross between a hunting lodge and Carmen Electra's bedroom. They have a well-stocked bar, good selection of beers, and homemade hot wine. There's usually a game or film being shown on the large screen set up inside, and frequent theme parties and live music. 206 rue Paccard. ☎ 04-50-53-03-23. www.lechoucas-chamonix.com.

➔ **The Pub** Maybe you can tell from the name, but there's not a lot of aspiration going on at The Pub. Their attitude is

comiNG in from the cold

Chamonix is almost as famous for its *après-ski* as for its actual skiing; the party scene here is nothing to scoff at. *Après-ski* is the tradition of hitting the bars directly from the slopes, often still dressed in full ski regalia (take the actual skis off, though). Golfers can compare it to the proverbial 19th hole, only it's less about sealing big business deals and reinforcing old-boy networks than it is about warming the @#$%! up after a day spent in the snow. Chamonix has a number of places all offering their own *après-ski* vibe. The chic and trendy ones change with the season—you'll just have to sniff out which one is "in" this year. If you're just looking to warm up as quickly as possible, throw a pot of fondue or an order of raclette into the mix, and you'll be aflush with calories and heat in no time. Repeat process each day until satisfied.

pretty straightforward: We're a pub, we've got booze, want some? *215 rue Paccard.* ☎ *04-50-55-92-88.*

NIGHTCLUBS & LIVE MUSIC VENUES

📺 Best ☝ → **Chambre Neuf** Another breakfast, lunch, and dinner restaurant that warms up into a hot *après-ski* scene and an even hotter night spot, beginning at 8pm when the drinks go two for the price of one until 10. The bar at Chambre Neuf throngs with the town's hipsters floating clouds of Issey Miyake and Giorgio Armani perfumes and colognes so potent it's a wonder Chamonix's environmental experts don't make a fuss about the effect on the ozone layer. They turn out in particular force when there's a DJ or live music going on. *Ground floor of Hôtel Gustavia, 272 av. Michel Croz.* ☎ *33-04-50-53-00-31. www.hotel-gustavia.com.*

→ **La Cantina** The best nightclub for young people, hands down. Good DJs, friendly ambience, cute bartenders, and the people here want to party. *37 impasse des Rhododendrons.* ☎ *33-04-50-53-83-80. www.cantina.fr.*

Playing Outside

Death-defying author Jon Krakauer called Chamonix "the death-sport capital of the world." Indeed, there are certainly a number of risky adventures you can embark on from here, from paragliding to downhill mountain biking to Olympic-level ski trails. The tourism office can help you organize an activity and advise you according to your interests and fitness level.

SUMMER SPORTS

→ **Centre Sportif Richard Bozon** This popular recreation center has a pool, sauna, facilities for tennis and squash, a skating rink, gym facilities, and a climbing hall pack. *214 av. de la Plage.* ☎ *04-50-53-09-07. http:// sports.chamonix.com.*

HIKING

The **tourism office** (Maison de la Montagne, 190 place de l'église; ☎ **33-04-50-53-22-08;** www.ohm-chamonix.com; Mon–Fri 9am–noon and 3–6pm; Sat 9am–noon) has several maps available, some free and some a few euros, that detail the 355km (220 miles) of marked hiking trails running through the mountains. Check at the Office de Moyenne et Haute Montagne, next to the church, for information on weather and safety conditions, if you are concerned.

WINTER SPORTS

The snow here should be referred to as white gold, because it was on this ephemeral stuff that Chamonix's reputation and economy was founded. Ever since the 1820s, travelers have flocked to this unique landscape for some of the best skiing in the world. The 1924 Winter Olympics took place in Chamonix, and brought the town to international prominence. The slopes are just as world-class as they were 90 years ago.

Skiing

All instructors in France must be certified by the 📺 Best ☝ **Ecole de Ski Français,** and you can recognize them by their red snow suits, which dot the white slopes. (The guy with a cigarette hanging out from his 4-day-old beard smelling like stale liquor in a green snowsuit? Probably not certified by them. Stick with the red guys.) They offer lessons at four levels—from "I've never seen a ski before" to "I can do this with my eyes closed backwards but I'd still like some professional instruction." They also have group classes and mini-clinics in snowboarding, and a variety of other ski activities beyond group and private classes (www.esf-chamonix.com).

Sled Dogs

Let these beautiful beasts of burden drag you around on half-day, full-day, and

Organizing a Ski Trip

The easiest and least expensive way to organize a ski trip (besides just showing up at the hostel and plunking down your skis) is through the tourist office (☎ **04-50-53-23-33;** www.chamonix.com). They have a team of people who can guide you through the various options, which range from accommodations in a two-, three-, or four-star hotel, to furnished rentals for stays of a week or more. Depending on how many stars you require, prices can be as low as 156€/person for 3 nights in an all-inclusive hotel accommodation, with breakfast and a 2-day ski pass. An apartment for six people is 215€ per person, per week, with a 6-day ski pass.

night-time excursions. Owners Christophe and Elisabeth will help you determine a route and an itinerary (☎ **04-50-47-77-24;** www.huskydalen.com). A 45-minute ride is 50€ per person; half-day is 100€ per person; full day is 200€ per person with lunch (without extras and drinks).

Snowboarding

Les Grands Montets has a full terrain park, half-pipe, and boardercross just for snowboarders to show off and practice their moves. **La Vormaine** has an area set aside for beginning snowboarders.

Two Ways to See the Slopes

The two most famous observation points in Chamonix are the **Aiguille du Midi** and **Montenvers,** both more than worth a visit. The Aiguille du Midi is accessible by cable car, while the Montenvers site can be reached by a little chugging red train or on foot, if you're an ambitious hiker. The two sites are also connected by a footpath, which takes around 2½ hours to complete. If this isn't vertiginous enough for you, try seeing it all by **helicopter.** Or if you're seeking a more organic experience, try maneuvering around the snow the old-fashioned way, with a few **huskies** pulling your weight. Whatever your vantage point, bring a camera, but don't expect it to capture the grandeur of what you'll see.

MTV **Best** ☉ ➔ **Aiguille du Midi** The cable car that lugs you 3,842m (2,382 ft.) up in the air to the Aiguille du Midi is one of the highest in the world. For 360 degrees around, you'll see the slopes—French, Italian, and Swiss—on which mountaineering history was made. **Restaurant 3842,** claiming to be "the highest Savoyard restaurant of Europe," is at the top, along with a snack bar. *Aiguille du Midi.* ☎ *04-50-53-30-80.*

➔ **Chamonix Mont-Blanc Helicopters** The best vantage of all is the bird's-eye view, from a helicopter. Surprisingly, it's affordable, though brief. ☎ *33-04-50-54-13-82. www.chamonix-helico.fr. Flights 60€ person for 10-min. flight in a 6-person craft; flights of up to 20 min. available.*

➔ **Montenvers** At this panoramic point is a lovely restaurant (see "Eating," above), several smaller snack bars, an ice grotto, and a small museum space displaying crystals and an Alpine fauna exhibition. *Leaves from Gare du Montenvers, place de la Mer de Glace.* ☎ *04-50-53-12-54.*

Shopping

➔ **Boucherie du Mont-Blanc Minié Frères** Stop here for gastronomic souvenirs, particularly local liqueurs, cheeses, and sausages in as many varieties and shapes as you care to imagine, including some twisted into animal shapes, like the balloon figures clowns know how to make.

156 rue de Paccard. ☎ *04-50-53-13-27. www. saveursdesalpes.com. Mon–Sun 8am–12:15pm; Mon–Sat 3:30–7:15pm.*

Grenoble

From the vantage point of the Bastille, a 19th-century fortification high above the city, set into the base of the Chartreuse massif, Grenoble looks as though someone poured it into an empty space between three mountain ranges. It sprawls out across the Isere plain and splashes up the sides of the mountains, not content in its allotted space. This view is deceptive, though. If you've made it this far, you know that the city you traversed to get to the *télépherique* that connects the flat land is not just urban sprawl, but an exciting and quite underestimated city host to a vibrant cultural life and teeming with over 60,000 students (7,000 of them foreign).

The capital of the Isere *département*, Grenoble is a frequent stop on the Tour de France, due to its location at the confluence of three mountain ranges. The Chartreuse to the north, the Vercors to the west, and the Belledonne to the east inspired native son Henri Beyle, better known as Stendhal, to comment that each road ends with a view of a mountain. A funny claim to fame for what is also the flattest city in France.

Grenoble's history dates back to the 3rd century B.C., when the Romans erected a settlement around what was then just a bridge over the Isere River. It changed hands several times until throughout the Middle Ages, coming to rest in the possession of the counts of Vienne, whose title, "Dauphin," came to be associated with the region, known even now as the Dauphiné.

Orientation

While Grenoble suffers from a mild case of urban sprawl, most of the tourist action is concentrated in the old town, which is easily walkable and has an excellent tram system. The tram is how most locals get around.

Recommended Websites

○ **www.38rugissants.com**: Information about the annual experimental world music festival held each November.

○ **www.petit-bulletin.fr**: A comprehensive and up-to-date guide to Grenoble and Lyon.

○ **www.tagattitude.com**: A search engine for events, cultural, sporting, and nocturnal, specifically for 15- to 25-year-olds.

○ **www.eng.cityvox.fr/bonnes-adresses_grenoble/BonnesAdresses**: A regularly updated city guide whose readers post their opinions and ratings.

Cultural Tips

Grenoble is a major scientific research hub, the second largest in France after Paris. Because researchers and students arrive here from all over the world, the city is decidedly cosmopolitan and liberal. One sees people of different ethnic origins mingling together with an ease and comfort that is noticeably different from elsewhere in France.

Sleeping

HOSTELS

➜ **Auberge de Jeunesse** This hostel is 6km (4 miles) outside of town, but if you feel like making the schlep, you'll be rewarded with a refreshingly unique hostel. Located in a 5,000 sq. m (53,820 sq. ft.)

park, it's environmentally sound, has an artists residency program, and a modern design. If you don't feel like taking the bus or tram, or you arrive late at night, the house van can pick you up from the train station for a mere 8€. The staff is very enthusiastic about the programs and qualities of the hostel, and they organize interesting themed parties from time to time (a recent one was "Zen"). *10 av. du Grésivaudan, Échirolles.* ☎ *04-76-09-33-52. www.fuaj.org/aj/grenoble. 17€ with sheets and breakfast. To get there, take bus no. 1 in the direction Claix pont-Rouge to La Quinzaine, or the tram A to la Rampe. From there, it's another 500m (1,640 ft.) away.*

CHEAP

➜ **Hôtel de la Poste** This small, eight-room hotel has a great central location (right near the Victor Hugo tram stop) and very inexpensive rooms. They're as basic as they come, but ideal for the undiscerning traveler on a budget. *25 rue de la Poste.* ☎ *04-76-47-67-25. 27€–32€ double. Credit cards accepted.*

MTV Best ● ➜ **Hôtel Victoria** Super clean, simple, and pleasantly decorated rooms, plus a charming breakfast room with black-and-white checkerboard tiling, make this two-star hotel very good value for the money. Some rooms have private baths. It's conveniently located close to the train station. *17 rue Thiers.* ☎ *04-76-46-06-36. www.hotelvictoriagrenoble.com. 37€–52€ double. Breakfast 7€. Credit cards accepted. Amenities: Parking. In room: TV.*

DOABLE

➜ **Grand Hôtel InterHôtel** This hotel, in a building from the 1800s classified as a historic monument, has 50 decently decorated rooms and a number of nice amenities like 24-hour room service and free e-mail access. The lobby features two grand sweeping staircases that give it a lot of character; unfortunately this character doesn't quite extend all the way into the bedrooms, which are pretty average, if comfortable. It's undergoing renovations and is slated to reopen in May 2007. *5 rue de la République.* ☎ *04-76-44-49-36. www.grand-hotel-grenoble.com. 74€–132€ depending on size. Breakfast 10€. Credit cards accepted. In room: A/C (in some), TV, minibar.*

SPLURGE

➜ **Park Hôtel Grenoble** Grenoble's only four-star hotel is located at the edge of the lovely Parc Paul Mistral, and offers 50 sound-proofed rooms of which 16 are suites replete with Jacuzzi and, often, views onto the park. Somewhat geared towards the business traveler, those lucky schmoes who get put up in places like this on their company's dime, it has an atmospheric bar area with an old-school masculine aura thanks to details like oriental rugs and leather-upholstered chairs, not to mention an emphasis on the wide selection of whiskies. *10 place Paul Mistral.* ☎ *33-476-858-123. www.park-hotel-grenoble.fr/anglais/Hotel-france.htm. 175€–290€ double. Credit cards accepted. In room: A/C, TV, Internet.*

Eating

CAFES & LIGHT FARE

➜ **Adélaïde Cookies** CAFE This tea salon, cafe, and, most importantly, cookie boutique is shamefully near the ice-cream parlor, making consecutive indulgences almost inevitable. Standbys like butter cookies, chocolate chip, and white chocolate are given a run for their money by tempting innovations like chocolate orange, cinnamon, and Nutella. *16 rue des Clercs.* ☎ *04-76-54-87-73.*

➜ **Coup de Pot** ITALIAN/MEDITERRANEAN This tiny little storefront would be called a hole in the wall if it weren't so damn clean and adorable. Serving pasta, soup, and salad, it's one of the cheapest places in town to fill up with something substantial. The gimmick is that the food all comes in pots, but I don't regard that as any detraction from the freshly prepared food, with pasta choices that vary daily depending on what's in season. In summer, the Provençale pasta has eggplant, zucchini, and tomato; in winter you'll see squash and more cheeses. *8 rue Barnave, place Notre-Dame.* ☎ *04-76-41-22-50. Small pot 4€, large pot 5.50€; menus 5€–7€. Credit cards accepted. Tues–Fri 11am–7pm; Mon and Sat 11am–5pm.*

➔ **Maison Gonzalez** ICE CREAM Ice creams flavored with orange flower or red bean; fair enough. But curry or mustard sorbets? I didn't have the courage to try these, or any of the dozen flavors tinged with booze (the Chartreuse variety is an interesting take on the local specialty, and sake is an unusual option), but they must be decent, or this place wouldn't still include them in their repertoire of over 90 flavors. The classic flavors—vanilla, pistachio, and chocolate—are included in that figure. Light snacks, crepes, and tea are also served. *3 rue des Clercs.* ☎ *04-76-03-25-86. Summer Tues–Sat 11:30am–10pm; winter Tues–Sat 11:30am–7pm. Closed Jan.*

➔ **Shaman Café** INTERNATIONAL Locals love the around-the-world-in-12€ lunch buffet at this laid-back cafe that serves dishes from around the world. A typical spread includes Mediterranean-style vegetables, Moroccan couscous, hummus, and an Asian-inspired cucumber salad. The Moroccan mint tea is authentic down to the silver teapot and delicate glass with which it is served, while the sushi is rather . . . less authentic, shall we say? At night, the dark and sexy interior, perhaps inspired by a 19th-century Orientalist painting, warms up the bar scene. *1 place Notre-Dame.* ☎ *04-38-37-23-56. Main courses 12€–16€. Credit cards accepted. Mon–Fri noon–2:30pm and 6pm–midnight; Sat noon–midnight.*

CHEAP

➔ **La Ferme à Dédé** SAVOYARD Slightly over the top in its cutesiness, this extremely popular restaurant is always packed with a hip, young, and smart-looking crowd tucking into hearty mountain cooking. The ravioli with walnut and cream sauce, a regional specialty, is particularly scrumptious here, and the *gratin dauphinois* is bubbling and generously portioned. The red-checked table cloths and original stone walls allude to the "Ferme" in the name, but Dédé is just a fictional character (even though his wrinkly old visage is all over the menu), sorry to disappoint. Get there early (around 7pm) before the waitstaff gets spread thinner than a square of one-ply toilet paper. *1 place aux Herbes.* ☎ *04-76-54-00-33. Menus from 15€–19€; main courses 11€–16€. Credit cards accepted. Daily noon–2:45pm and 7–11:45pm.*

➔ **Le 5** MEDITERRANEAN Art lovers and scenesters dine in the restaurant/cafe on the ground floor of the Musée de Grenoble. The Italian-inspired menu (the owners operate a popular Italian restaurant, Caffe Forte nearby) is enhanced by several inventive salads, such as poppy-seed-crusted tuna atop mesclun and served with pickled ginger and wasabi. *5 place Lavalette.* ☎ *04-76-63-22-12. www.le5.fr. Main courses 11€–16€. Credit cards accepted. Wed–Sun noon–midnight.*

DOABLE

➔ **La Supplice de Tantale** FRENCH/INTERNATIONAL A cozy, 22-seat restaurant serving a seasonally inspired menu complemented by a selection of over 120 wines, this romantic eatery is predictably popular with couples and dates. *13 rue J Jacques Rousseau.* ☎ *04-76-44-28-29. Menus from 25€, 45€ with wine with each course. Tues–Sat noon–1:45pm and 8–10:30pm. Closed 1st 2 weeks in Aug.*

➜**Restaurant du Téléférique** SAVOYARD/ MEDITERRANEAN One of three dining options atop the Bastille, the Restaurant du Téléférique is a summertime standby, with its large terrace overlooking all of Grenoble and as far as Mont-Blanc. The view is enough to make any food taste good, but luckily the chef already knows what he's doing. Savoyard cooking; local specialties such as ravioli with nuts; and pastas, meats, and salads are all on the menu. Don't leave without trying the homemade tarts, especially the lemon meringue, if it's available. *Quai Stéphane Jay.* ☎ *04-76-51-11-11. www. bastille-grenoble.com/fr/contact.htm. Menus 10€–15€ at lunch (the latter includes the round-trip on the telepheric); dinner 30€. Credit cards accepted. Mon–Sat 11am–2:15pm and 7:30–10pm.*

SPLURGE

➜**Chez le Pèr'Gras** FRENCH Tranquil and fine dining under shady trees with a view of three mountain ranges? Where do I sign up? This is the fanciest of the three restaurants at the Bastille, and it serves carefully prepared French food, including a signature all–foie gras menu. Traditionally and simply prepared fresh fish, meats, and—if you order 2 days in advance—frogs' legs, are all available as well, and chef Laurent Gras uses his grandmother's recipe for *gratin dauphinois. Glacis Bastille.* ☎ *04-76-42-09-47. www. restaurant-grenoble-gras.com. Main courses 17€–26€; menus 23€–49€. Credit cards accepted. July–Aug daily noon–1:45pm and 7–10pm; Sept–June daily noon–1:45pm and 7–10pm (closed Sun night); closed Mon Nov and Jan.*

➜**Fantin Latour** GASTRONOMIC A unique gastronomic restaurant with a menu that changes weekly, according to what's at the market and the chef's whims. The setting is one of the finest in Grenoble; in an old *hôtel particulier,* now thoroughly updated with white and grey interiors, punctuated by colorful furniture, and tastefully appointed with luxurious modern fixtures. The landscaped garden is open as soon as the weather permits. *1 rue Générale de Beylié.* ☎ *04-76-01-00-97. www. fantin-latour.net. Lunch menus 30€–40€; dinner menus 70€ for 5 courses; 110€ for 11 courses. Credit cards accepted. Tues–Fri noon–2:30pm and 7–10pm; Sat 7–10pm.*

Partying

The nightlife in Grenoble is pretty decent, given its huge student population. Most of the fun bars are clustered in the area around three almost contiguous squares—place St-André, place Claveyson, and place aux Herbes. In the summer, tables on the outside terraces are cheek to jowl with revelers eyeing their fellow night owls as they make their rounds from bar to bar. During the **Cabaret Frappé Festival** (☎ **04-76-00-76-85;** www.cabaret-frappe.com) in late July, most Grenoblois start the evening at the 📺 Best◉ **Jardin de Ville,** warming up with a free concert or film before tackling the bar scene.

BARS

➜**Café de la Table Ronde** The oldest cafe in Grenoble is just as popular today as it has been for nearly 3 centuries, since its 1739 heyday when it was the center of Grenoble's literary and artistic life. Throughout its history, figures such as Sarah Bernhard, Léon Blum, Gambetta, and Stendhal have all found a place around the table. *7 place St-André.* ☎ *04-76-44-51-41 www.cafetableronde.com.*

➜**Le Basse Terre** Small, narrow, and usually very crowded, this bar specializing in rum and tropical drinks has no problem conjuring up the Caribbean temperatures its decor seeks to evoke. African masks, a ceiling of bamboo reed, and a poster of a smiling, topless, dark-skinned woman with braids and the caption "Black Ladies" get the West Indies vibe about half right. The rum cocktails and beverages macerated with fruit, however, are fully on the mark, as is the music, a nice mix of reggae, hip-hop, and rock. *5 rue Auguste Gaché.* ☎ *04-76-00-02-76.*

➜ **Le 365** This high-ceiling, eclectically decorated bar is nicely crowded on weekdays, and a little too hectic on weekends. The huge baroque candlestick holders, chandeliers, and antique framed paintings make it look like they looted a few churches for their furniture. *3 rue Bayard.* ☎ *04-76-51-73-18.*

NIGHTCLUBS & LIVE MUSIC VENUES

➜ **Le Styx** Le Styx throws its doors open to everyone, especially students and gays, for nightly parties with DJs and occasionally themes. The specialty of the house is vodka, of which there are numerous perfumed varieties (discounted shots during happy hour, 6–9:30pm). The walls are made of stone, and the vaulted ceiling is rather cavelike, but the heavy architecture is lightened by small touches such as candles on every table, and the warm smiles on the waiters' faces. *6 place Claveyson.* ☎ *04-76-44-09-99.*

Sightseeing

MUSEUMS

TV **Best ●** ➜ **Le Magasin** Centre National d'Art Contemporain: This huge, industrial, hangarlike space is a short tram ride away from the town center, in what feels like the Williamsburg of Grenoble, a slightly seedy neighborhood with cheap rents and a lot of students. The building, erected in 1900 by the workshop of Gustave Eiffel to house the Universal Exposition in Paris, was later purchased, packed up, and brought wholesale to Grenoble. The industrialists who bought it used the space to develop hydro-electric power. Later a warehouse, it reached its current incarnation in 1985, and today is one of France's most innovative art centers outside of Paris. The shows often feature original works by prominent artists (Doug Aitken, Kader Attia, Daniel Buren) commissioned exclusively for the Magasin. Shows then travel to major exhibition spaces and museums around the world. The enormous central avenue is called "La Rue," and it is here that most of the site-specific works are installed. Around La Rue are smaller galleries where other temporary exhibits are shown. It's not to be missed, both for its extremely well-curated exhibits and the cool atmosphere of the place itself. *Site Bouchayer-Viallet, 155 cours Berriat.* ☎ *04-76-21-95-84. www.magasin-cnac.org. Admission 3.50€ adults, 2€ students, free for art history students. Tues–Sun 2–7pm. Take tram, line A toward Fontaine-La Poya, to stop Berriat, le Magasin.*

➜ **Musée de Grenoble** Completed in 1994, and designed by talented local architects, the Musée de Grenoble is one of the most enjoyable in France. The layout permits one to walk uninterrupted through gigantic, light-filled rooms that chronologically catalogue the history of Western art through excellent representative works from the 13th through the 19th centuries. A second section of the museum focuses exclusively on art from the 20th century to the present, with an endless number of top-quality pieces from all the big European names like Matisse and Picasso. All of the "isms" are in full effect—Fauvism, surrealism, Impressionism, Abstract Expressionism, New Realism, Minimalism, and Pop Art (ism). *5 place de Lavalette.* ☎ *04-76-63-44-44. www.museedegrenoble.fr. Admission 5€ adults, 2€ students. Wed–Mon 10am–6:30pm.*

FREE ➜ **Musée de l'Ancien Evêché** Housed in a beautiful historic building that was once the seat of the local bishopric, this museum traces the history of the Isere region from pre-historic times to today. The basement retains an original baptistery and crypt from the early days of Christ, when Grenoble was called Cularo. For visits organized by the museum, link to "Museum Publics" on the website. The French or English-language audio guide is free. *2 rue Très-Cloîtres.* ☎ *33-04-76-03-15-25. www.ancien-eveche-isere.fr. Free admission. Mon and Wed–Sat 9am–6pm; Sun 10am–7pm; Tues 1:30–6pm. Closed Jan 1, May 1, and Dec 25. Bus: Route 32, Notre-Dame Musée stop. Tramway: Line B, Notre-Dame Musée stop.*

➜**Musée de la Résistance et de Déportation de Grenoble** This moving museum is dedicated to the French Resistance as it played out in Isere. It includes the Maison des Droits de l'Homme, or House of Human Rights, which hosts exhibitions, discussions, and conferences on human rights issues, sometimes in partnership with NGOs such as Amnesty International. *14 rue Hébert.* ☎ *04-76-42-38-53. www.resistance-en-isere.fr. Mon and Wed–Fri 9am–6pm, Sat–Sun 10am–6pm, Tues 1:30–6pm; July–Aug Wed–Mon 10am–7pm, Tues 1:30–7pm.*

MONUMENTS & CHURCHES

➜**The Bastille** The jewel in Grenoble's crown is the Bastille, a fortress and citadel built between 1823 and 1848. Today it is open to the public and houses a museum, the Musée Dauphinois; an arts space; the soon to arrive Lieu d'Images et d'Arts; and several restaurants. The site itself has been occupied for over 2,000 years, beginning with the Romans in 43 B.C. In the 6th century, the St-Laurent church and the St-Oyand crypt were constructed, and then St. Mary's convent, which is now the museum, in 1622.

Reachable either on foot (around 1 hr. 10 min.) or, more commonly, a 2-minute tram

ride in the famous *boules* (bubbles), it offers spectacular views of the city and its three surrounding mountain ranges from almost any point on the structure. The tram was the first urban one constructed in France, and currently runs on renewable electricity produced by micropower stations in the Alps.

It was constructed by the military leader General Haxo, in order to protect Grenoble from the attacks of the neighboring Savoy duchy. The limestone blocks were shaped on-site, and laid in such a fashion as to provide maximum strength and resistance. The original moat and drawbridge are still there, and around it grows an unusual array of vegetation, with over 200 varieties of trees, Alpine as well as imported Mediterranean, growing on the hill. *Quai Stéphane Jay.* ☎ *04-76-44-33-65. www.bastille-grenoble.com*

➜**Cathédrale de Notre-Dame** The town's largest church has an impressive 15m-high (49 ft.) flamboyant Gothic *ciboria* (covered chalice for the Eucharist wafers) in the choir, which unfortunately suffered some damage during France's period of religious conflict. *Place Notre-Dame.*

Historic Neighborhoods

Downtown Grenoble has a number of beautiful squares and buildings rich with history. A walk devised by the tourist office takes you through the pedestrian area and points out a number of highlights, such as the Roman wall, from the 4th century B.C. On Jean-Jacques Rousseau street, no. 14 marks the house where Stendhal was born. He lived in Grenoble but left for Paris at the age of 17, fed up with his provincial lower-middle-class existence. The place de Grenette, outside of the ancient Roman wall, once hosted fairs and livestock markets, but it was integrated into the city in the 16th century by the duke of Lesdiguières, who commanded the Huguenot armies during the late 1500s. During the Revolution, it played host to the guillotine, which was used relatively minimally (only the heads of two priests rolled). Off of rue Montorge is the lovely Jardin de Ville, where Lesdiguières built the spectacular residence in 1590, which now houses the Stendhal museum in the former drawing rooms. The place St-André is surrounded by impressive buildings, including the church and the old parliamentary building. It was once the seat of political power in Grenoble, when the counts of Albon (the original Dauphins) set up their residence here. Just around the corner is the place aux Herbes, also once used for public executions, a fact that gave it its former nickname, place du Malconseil (Bad Advice Square). Today it hosts a lively fruit and vegetables market from 6am to 1pm Tuesdays through Sundays.

Playing Outside

→ **The Bastille** Several walking trails, hiking routes, and climbs run through and around the Bastille; they take anywhere from 40 minutes on the descent to 4 hours if you plan to walk through the Chartreuse mountains or up to the summit of Mount Jalla. Check with the tourist office (**www. bastille-grenoble.com**) or the gift shop at the Bastille for maps and help in choosing an itinerary. *Quai Stéphane Jay, north bank of the Isere. www.bastille-grenoble.com.*

Shopping

→ **La Noix de Grenoble/Desany** The walnut of Grenoble comes in three varieties—the Franquette, the Mayette, and the Parisienne (sort of like the Nina, the Pinta, and the Santa Maria). It was the first nut to attain the prestigious AOC (Appellation d'Origine Contrôlée; see p. 50) in 1938, an homage to the *terroir* from which it springs. This shop sells everything that humans have managed to derive from the humble walnut—cakes, syrups, oils (great on salads), nougats, and cookies, for starters. There's also an ice-cream stand outside in the summer. *6 bis place Grenette.* ☏ *04-76-03-12-20.*

→ **Marché des Halles Ste-Claire** This covered fruit and vegetables market spills out onto the streets around the building. *Place Ste-Claire. No phone. Tues–Thurs and Sun 6am–1pm; Fri–Sat 6am–7pm.*

Massif Central & Auvergne

by Nathalie Jordi

In the 19th century, novelist George Sand described the Massif Central and Auvergne region as "one of the loveliest spots on earth . . . a country without roads, without guides, without any facilities for locomotion, where every discovery must be conquered at the price of danger or fatigue . . . a soil cut up with deep ravines, crossed in every way by lofty walls of lava, and furrowed by numerous torrents." Of course, it's easier to navigate the terrain today, but you'll still recognize Sand's perspective in the landscape, in many ways unchanged since she limned it.

The Massif Central and Auvergne are resolutely *not* Paris. They are most emphatically *not* the Côte d'Azur. Many compare them to the U.S. Midwest, on the premise that they're some sort of middle ground that connects two coasts of culture, development, and civilization. But reducing them to this level is as dumb as reducing the American Midwest likewise. Sure, economically the Massif Central isn't overly developed. Yes, the cities of the Auvergne are about as exciting as Des Moines. But these characteristics allow for what makes the region special.

The Massif Central is sort of like France's Colorado (if less "granolular"), while the Auvergne, a rural subsection of the Massif, is its Arkansas. If this appeals to you, go—you won't regret a visit here. I found it to be one of the most heartwrenchingly beautiful places I'd seen. If, on the other hand, the thought of French Arkansas makes you shudder, take a deep breath and spread yourself with another layer of suntan lotion—St-Tropez is only a few hours away.

While the Massif Central/Auvergne is enormous, especially in proportion to the rest of France, only a few towns have managed to flourish—if that's what you want to call it—atop its rocky terrain. As the headquarters of Michelin (both the tires and the food guides whose rating system leaves many of the world's best chefs groveling for just one more star), **Clermont-Ferrand** is a bastion of industry yet proud to be parochial in other respects. It flouts its lava-brick cathedral and privileged setting beneath the highest of the volcanoes in the area, the Puy de Dome. **Le Puy,** with its famous lentils and narrow medieval streets, has been charmingly, tastefully restored. But the best places in the Massif Central and Auvergne are yours to discover on your own, preferably by car—mellow **Aurillac,** pretty **Bourges,** the medieval towns of **Besse, Salers,** and **Conques** with its gigantic abbey; the flourishing Saturday morning market in **Brioude;** and the leisurely road to **Chassignolles.**

The Best of Massif Central & Auvergne

○ **The Best Cheese (Clermont-Ferrand):** We can't pick one. Is it rugged, cheddar-like **Salers,** made into 70-pound cloth-bound wheels only in summer from the unpasteurized milk of cows eating mountain herbs on volcanic soil? Is it mellow, resounding, semi-soft **St. Nectaire,** which tastes better in the Auvergne than anywhere else? Is it the famous **bleu d'Auvergne,** creamy and delicate? We'll have them all, please! See p. 613.

○ **The Most Creative Water Taps:** The **fountains of Clermont-Ferrand** provided most of the town's water, given that there are no major, obvious water sources around other than the ones buried underground. See p. 614.

○ **The Most Likely to Terrorize You Into Converting:** The black stone on the imposing **Cathédrale Notre-Dame de l'Assomption,** in Clermont-Ferrand, strikes the fear of God into visitors. See p. 615.

○ **The Most Unlikely Taste Treat:** Try the horsemeat at **Le Cheval'in,** in Clermont-Ferrand. If you're feeling really daring, buy a can of horse fat and cook up a batch of french fries once you get home. No kidding, they will be the most obscenely delicious fries you've ever put in your mouth. See p. 618.

○ **The Best Festival at Which to Stuff Yourself Silly with Sausage:** Experience **La Frairie des Petits Ventres,** in Limoges, on the third Friday in October, when the town's butchers keep up a medieval tradition by cooking a whole lotta meat. Oh, and we love the parade of little children dressed up as turn-of-the-century butchers. See p. 623.

○ **The Best Bar for Miles:** The **Brasserie Bieres Michard** in Limoges makes six different kinds of real beer—unpasteurized, unfiltered, and untouched by CO_2. We'd like one of these in our neighborhood, please. See p. 620.

○ **The Most Random Place to Happen Upon 2,500 Species of Fish:** We're in the *middle* of the country, and the **Aquarium du Limousin** still makes Limoges reek of salty water. Sometimes it's the smallest towns that have the most fun. See p. 621.

○ **The Best Market:** You know you're in Limoges when the market, **Les Halles Centrales,** is covered with 328 panels of porcelain.

○ **The Most Interesting Dynasty in Limoges:** You thought we were going to say porcelain, didn't you? No, the **butchers** in Limoges have a long and interesting history, which you'll notice popping up everywhere as you walk around town. About six powerful families over the generations intermarried in order to keep the money—and the meat—in the same hands.

◦ **The Best Use of 213 Melted Cannons:** The **Rocher Corneille,** upon which you can climb for a lovely view of Le-Puy-En-Velay. Following the siege of Sebastopol during the Crimean War, the cannons used to defend it were melted down to construct a statue of Notre-Dame de France that stands over 15m (50 ft.) atop an eroded volcano. You can climb up to the statue's shoulder. See p. 623.

◦ **The Most Incredible Display of Love for Beans:** The attachment of the *ponotes* (Le-Puy-En-Velay people) to their AOC lentils is amazing. Don't be shy about tasting them, especially since you might otherwise go hungry. See p. 626.

◦ **The Best Epicerie, Surely, in Miles:** We're thrilled to see a high-level food shop like **Le Comptoir Gourmand** in a small town like Le-Puy-En-Velay. Could you visualize one of these in Mystic, Connecticut? See p. 627.

◦ **The Best Party:** Imagine if everyone in your town dressed up in medieval attire and went archery-shooting! That's what you'll find at **La Fête du Roi de L'Oiseau** in Le-Puy-En-Velay. See p. 623.

◦ **The Most Bad-Ass Historical Figure:** **Bishop Gothescalk** pilgrimaged to the western edge of Spain—and was one of the first to make it all the way to Santiago de Compostela and back. Upon his return to Le-Puy-En-Velay, he commissioned construction of the chapelle Saint-Michel, built in 962. See p. 293.

Getting Around the Region

A word of warning: This region is by far easiest to explore in a car (or a bike, if you're really brave and don't mind pedaling uphill). Trains do run here, and getting to Clermont-Ferrand, Limoges, Aurillac, Issoire, Brioude, Vichy, and Le-Puy-en-Velay will be easy enough. Many minor rail routes, however, were replaced by SNCF buses, and many of those were eventually canceled too. Moreover, the most beautiful parts of this region are inaccessible to trains, including massive pine forests, shaven volcano tops, and stone villages whose inhabitants all seem to be over the age of 85.

Clermont-Ferrand: Molten *Je Ne Sais Quoi*

421km (261 miles) directly S of Paris, 323km (200 miles) SW of Dijon, 205km (127 miles) W of Lyon

This black city of industry in a bowl of emerald-green volcanoes is one of the oldest cities in France.

People talk a lot of shit about Clermont-Ferrand. It's dark, dirty, and depressing, they say. True, it's an industrial town proud of its provincial mentality and lifestyle. If you want your France all cobblestoned and pastel, give Clermont-Ferrand a miss. But if contrasts and paradox pique your interest and you don't mind a dash of gritty realism mixed in with your cathedrals, this city has plenty to offer—if you're willing to dirty your nails and scratch its surface. All dressed in black (see "Black Rock," below), it's cool like Johnny Cash.

Massif Central & Auvergne

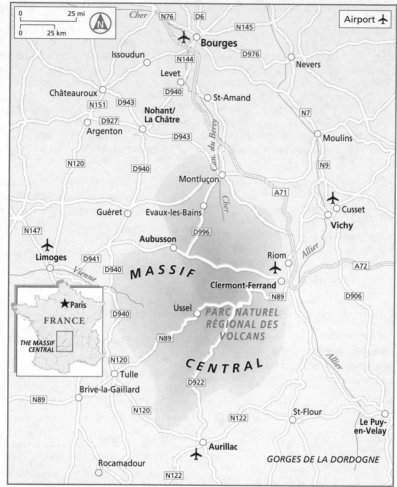

Getting There

BY AIR

The small airport of **Clermont-Aulnat** takes mostly flights from France and surrounding countries. ☎ **04-73-62-71-00.** From the airport you can take a bus to the rail or bus station for 4€.

BY TRAIN

Clermont-Ferrand is a **major train hub** in the region. Since it's smack in the middle of France, you can catch trains from Marseille, Toulouse, Paris, Bordeaux, Grenoble, Dijon, Beziers, and Lyon. One-way from Paris is about a 3¹/₂-hour trip. For schedules, call ☎ **08-92-35-35-35.** The train station is on avenue de l'Union Sovietique.

BY CAR

Paris is 4 hours away; take the A10 south to Orléans, then continue south on the A71. Or if you're coming from Lyon, take the A47

Clermont-Ferrand History 101

Clermont-Ferrand's first claim to fame was as the site of the rabid Battle of Gergovia in 52 B.C., in which the Gauls, led by Vercingetorix (with the help of Asterix and Obelix), temporarily beat the armies of Julius Caesar. Gloating was pointless, however; shortly thereafter, the Romans kicked their butts and renamed the city Augustonemetum. In the 2nd century, A.D., its estimated 15,000 to 30,000 residents made it one of the largest cities of Roman Gaul. Although the Edict of Troyes forcibly joined the two cities of Clermont and Montferrand in 1630, the Montferrandais demanded independence in 1789, 1848, and 1863. It was the construction of the Michelin factories and city gardens in the 20th century that cemented the unification of Clermont and Montferrand.

west to Saint-Etienne, then go northwest on the A89.

BY BUS

Bueses come into the **Gare Routière** on the boulevard François-Mitterrand. For information, call ☎ **04-73-93-13-61.** The station is open Monday to Saturday from 8:30am to 6:30pm

Orientation

The train station is a 5-minute bus ride or 30-minute walk east of the center. It's in a pretty boring neighborhood, but you can escape by taking bus nos. 2, 4, 8, or 14. The

M T V 🖐 Volcanic College Town

While the Auvergne ain't the Côte d'Azur, Clermont-Ferrand is a student town, so a fair amount of partying goes down here. Most of the university students are in the suburb of Les Cezaux south of the center, which you can reach via bus no. 3, 8, or 13 (follow the students). Otherwise, you can find them on the avenue Carnot near rue Paul Collomp, east of the place de Jaude, or on the corner of boulevard François-Mitterand and the boulevard Lafayette.

place de Jaude (where the bus will take you) is the main square in town, with a large shopping center and loads of restaurants and bars. On the side of the square is the mostly pedestrianized center of town, which has the rue Andre Moinier on the north, the avenue des Etats-Unis west, the Cours Sablon east, and the boulevards Leon Malfreyt and Lafayette to the south. The big black cathedral of Notre-Dame overlooks the pedestrianized area, set on the place de la Victoire next to the tourist office.

The best streets to explore are the rue du 11 Novembre, rue de la Boucherie, rue St. Barthelemy, and rue des Gras. It's on the rue St. Barthelemy that you'll find the modern covered market, the Marché St. Pierre.

Getting Around

BY PUBLIC TRANSPORTATION

The new 31-station Clermont-Ferrand tram—which goes by the name of **Translohr** and connects the north and south ends of the cities in 40 minutes—should prove to be the ideal way to get from the 'burbs into town. Town officials call its look *fleur de lave,* a pretty way to say "lava runoff." It runs every 6 minutes; the last train of the day leaves at 1am.

BY TAXI

Call **Taxis-Radio Clermontois** at 26 av. Puy-de-Dome (☎ **04-73-19-53-53**).

Tourist Offices

The Office de Tourisme (☎ **04-73-98-65-00**) is on the place de la Victoire. You can catch a slide-show movie on the history of the Auvergne in their **admission-free museum** in the basement. It's open May to September Monday Friday 9am to 7pm and weekends from 10am to 7pm. From October to April, they're open Monday to Friday from 9am to 6pm, Saturday from 10am to 1pm and 2 to 6pm, and Sundays and holidays from 9:30am to 12:30pm and 2 to 6pm. Another tourist office in the Gare is open weekdays 9:15am to 11:30 am and 12:15pm to 5pm and the same hours on Saturdays from June to September; their number is ☎ **04-73-98-65-00.**

Clermont-Ferrand Nuts & Bolts

Bike Rental   Try **Espace Massif Central** (near the tourist office on the place de la Victoire; ☎ **04-73-42-60-00**; Oct–May Mon–Fri 9am–6pm [Tues open at 10am], Sat 9am–noon and 2–6pm; June–Sept Mon–Fri 9am–6:30pm [Tues open at 10am], Sat 9am–12:30pm and 1:30–6:30pm). Government-organized **Leovélo** is another bike-rental service (37 cours Sablon; ☎ **04-73-90-55-41**).

Crisis Centers   Call ☎ **15** for medical emergencies and ☎ **17** for police.

Hospitals   **Centre Hospitalier Universitaire**, aka CHU (bd. Winston Churchill; ☎ **04/73-75-07-50**).

Internet/Wireless Hot Spots   All of the post offices in Clermont-Ferrand have Internet service. There's also the **Corum Saint-Jean** on 17 rue Gaultier de Biauzat (☎ **04-73-31-57-11**), or the **Mediatheque de Jaude** on 9 place Louis Aragon (☎ **04-73-29-32-52**).

Pharmacies   **Pharmacie Ducher** on 1 place DeLille (☎ **04/73-75-07-50**) is open 24 hours. Otherwise, look for the big neon green cross.

Post Office   **Poste St. Eloy** is on 17 rue Marechal de Lattre-Tassigny (☎ **04-73-30-63-00**; Mon–Fri 8am–7pm, Sat 8am–noon).

Sleeping

CHEAP

➜ **Hôtel Foch** This hotel is in a nice neighborhood near the place Jaude, with a cute little garden. Rooms vary a lot (some with A/C, some without; some butt-ugly, some decent; some loud, some quiet; and so on), so ask to see a few before you commit. They speak English, which is not a given in this part of the world. *22 rue Marechal-Foch.* ☎ *04-73-93-48-40. 37€ single; 42€ double. Credit cards accepted.*

DOABLE

➜ **Hôtel Beaulieu** Comfortable, clean, contemporary, if a bit banal, it's a good choice for those wanting to explore the museums just outside the town center. *13 av. des Paulines.* ☎ *04-73-92-46-99. www. hotel-beaulieu-clermont.com. 53€ double. Credit cards accepted. Amenities: Parking. In room: A/C, satellite TV.*

Eating

Is it because Michelin (and thus, the eponymous red gourmet guides) is based here that this town is so focused on food? Well, this ain't the Mediterranean coast, that's for bloody sure. Cuisine here is cabbage-heavy, cheese-stuffed, with meat at every turn, but *mmm, mmm good!*

CHEAP

➜**Christian Riviere** When people line up for bread, you know you're onto a good thing. Try especially the slowly proofed *tourte de seigle* and the *pain paillasse.* *27 rue du Cheval Blanc. ☎ 04-73-37-38-20. Credit cards accepted. Tues–Sat 6:30am–7pm; Sun 6:30am–noon.*

➜**Fafournoux** It looks like a Greek temple from the outside, but inside it's meat, meat, more meat, and lots of other good stuff. Every day, the butchers go to market early, come back with a load of food, and spend the morning making at least a dozen different preparations. *1 rue St. Pierre. ☎ 04-73-37-16-12. Food is priced by weight, but you can fill up for about 10€. Credit cards accepted. Mon–Thurs 8am–12:30pm and 3–7pm, Fri–Sat 8am–7pm.*

➜**Marché Saint-Pierre** What a pleasure, these French markets. You can stuff yourself silly and walk out only a few euros the poorer. This one, open every day (Sat is the most exciting), has about 40 merchants, including 6 (count 'em!) cheesemakers and two butcher shops, one of which specializes in horsemeat (actually pretty good— give it a chance). Stop by the Trianon chocolate shop for dessert. *Place Saint-Pierre. No phone. Mon–Sat 7am–7:30pm.*

DOABLE

➜**Marché de Nathalie** This cute and funky market-based place is decorated with a surprisingly hip-looking clientele, given that Clermont-Ferrand is a bit parochial. *4 rue des Petits-Gras. ☎ 04-73-19-12-12. Menus from 15€. Credit cards accepted. Thurs–Sat noon–2pm and 7–10pm.*

SPLURGE

➜**Emmanuel Hodencq** Fruits and flowers adorn the beautifully ornate glass-and-wood dining room at Emmaneul Hodenq. You can eat inside or out on the terrace, savoring a *super-terroir* cuisine, rich in flavors and based exclusively on ingredients found at the market. *Place du Marché St-Pierre. ☎ 04-73-31-23-23. www.hodencq.com. Credit cards accepted. Tues–Sat noon–2pm and 7:30–10pm.*

Partying

Most nightclubs are out in the suburbs, and unless you find someone to leave with, you won't have a way home after the buses stop running. But there are some fun cafes and bars in the city center.

➜**Bar d'O** This is the place to get your fill. *Place de la Victoire. ☎ 04-73-91-43-14.*

➜**Le Bam** For a provincial town, Clermont-Ferrand has a surprising number of gay clubs—probably because there aren't many elsewhere in the Auvergne. *2 place Delille. ☎ 04-73-92-57-83.*

➜**Le Distil** A great wine bar (with a decent food menu, too; at least order some charcuterie with your glass) with a relaxed atmosphere. *8 rue de la Préfecture. ☎ 04-73-37-64-15.*

➜**Le Havana Café** Hankering for a mojito or a margarita—and maybe some Latin music at which to shake a tail feather? Look no further than here. *12 rue des Minimes. ☎ 04-73-34-27-51.*

Sightseeing

PUBLIC MONUMENTS

➜**Hôtel de Chazerat** Inspired by antiquity and the fashions of the day, Antoine de Chazerat built this *hôtel particulier* in the 1760s. Constructed from the Volvic stone characteristic of Clermont-Ferrand,

Fromages d'Auvergne & the AOC

We love cheese. We love French cheese. And, specifically, we love ▩ Best◉ **cheeses from the Auvergne.** Having tasted, um, rather extensively, we recommend these few.

→ **Salers:** This is the only French AOC cheese (p. 613) made exclusively on farms, as opposed to in cooperatives, dairies, or factories. Salers can only be made between April 15 and November 15, when the cows are eating grass. Cheese is made twice a day, after each milking (this calls for superhuman cheesemakers; making cheese once a day is hard enough). This always-unpasteurized cheese is gigantic, weighing up to 80 pounds. Some speculate it is an ancestor—or a descendant—of English cloth-bound cheddar. It's best with a handful of cherries, some nuts, and a glass of red Sancerre. Salers is a quintessential example of cheese as an edible expression, or distillation, of the land: grass digested by cows and turned into milk, then turned into cheese and ingested by people.

→ **Cantal:** It's similar in shape, flavor, and make to Salers, but it's made by 30 facilities from the milk of 3,600 producers. You'll see different variations on the theme: Cantal jeune, Cantal entre-deux, and Cantal vieux—these just reference the cheese's age, and thus the intensity of its flavor.

→ **St. Nectaire:** If you frequent fancy cheese shops, maybe you've had this cheese before. If it wasn't anything special, try it again, here. I've tasted St. Nectaire all over Europe and the U.S. and never been that impressed—until I had some in the Auvergne. And then I had some more. Some cheeses just don't travel, so you have to travel to them.

→ **Fourme d'Ambert:** In the tiny village of La Chaulme, there's a 19th-century chapel with a portal upon which seven stones have been carved to represent butter, *saucisson,* ham, eggs, hay, cereals, and the *fourme* that serfs had to provide for their lord every year as tax. Back in the day, all Fourme d'Ambert would've been made in a tiny *jasserie* (at once a stable, cheese-making facility, and house). Separate small cheesemaking facilities for making Fourme came about in the early 1900s, but today most Fourme d'Ambert is made in sizable quantities and pierced with machines rather than knitting needles. Never mind, this creamy blue, with its notes of heather and wild herbs, is still delicious, especially with a Cotes d'Auvergne.

→ **Laguiole:** This is made on the plateau d'Aubrac, at an altitude of between 800m (2,624 ft.) and 1,500m (4,920 ft.). Historically it was made in mountain huts known as *burons,* high above the rest of civilization, where herders-cum-cheesemakers *(buronniers)* made cheese in the summer while the cows were grazing in the *alpages* (mountain pastures). The cows have to be Simmental or Aubrac (local breeds); their milk has to be unpasteurized and collected between May and October from an altitude of higher than 800m. The cheese is enormous (up to 100 lb.), and branded with a bull and its name, as well as an aluminum ID plate. It tastes best between September and March.

→ **Others to look out for:** Perail fermier (soft sheep's milk disc); Pouligny St. Pierre (goat's cheese pyramid matured on straw mats); Valancay (goat's cheese pyramid sprinkled with ash); tome d'Aubrac (used to make aligot); as well as Rocamadour, Bleu des Causses, Fourme de Rochefort, and Pelardon (small soft goat's cheese).

the hotel was first painted white, like many other houses at that time, but it has since reverted to its natural colors. During World War I, it served as a hospital, then later it became a university building, then a tax building, and finally a cultural affairs outpost. *Rue Blaise Pascal.*

➜**Hôtel de Ville** The present incarnation of the Hôtel de Ville was constructed beginning in 1825—or 1826, or 1831, no one can really agree—atop the remains of the Halles Catherine de Médicis had built in the 16th century. Clermont-Ferrand hadn't had much attention paid to it during the Revolution and the Empire period, so this was a way of both beautifying and updating the city. *7 rue Général Pershing.*

MTV Best ● ➜**La Fontaine d'Amboise** This fountain dates back to 1511 and was initially installed in front of the southern portal of the cathedral. The octagonal basin, decorated with beautiful reliefs, shoots water out from eight places, and a Gothic lamp tops the central pillar. A jewel of illustrations—look for the bat, the scenes that depict the evolution of the world, and the kid chasing a lion—the fountain was moved in 1808 to the place Delille, then to the cours Sablon, and then to the rue des Capucins before being placed on the place de la Poterne. *Place de la Poterne.*

MUSEUMS

The **Musée d'Archeologie Bargoin** (45 rue de Ballainvilliers; ☎ 04-73-91-37-31) and the **Musée d'Art Roger Quilliot** (place Louis-Deteix; ☎ 04-73-16-11-30) are good examples of their kind and well worth a visit if you'll be in Clermont-Ferrand for more than a day. We have chosen to focus instead on two more minor but more original museums.

➜**Musée d'Art Roger Quillot** Actually, we take it back, the art museum deserves more of a mention. It ain't the Louvre, but they've made a serious effort to gather all the masterpieces in Auvergnat museums (more than 2,000 works are on display) to present them in this superb building a few kilometers (a couple of miles) northeast of the center. Follow the circle as you follow the development of European art from the 7th to the 20th century. *Place Louis Deteix, Montferrand.* ☎ *04-73-16-11-30. 4.10€ adults, 2.60€ students. Tues–Sun 10am–6pm. Take bus no. 1, 9, or 16 from the place de Jaude or 17 from the train station.*

➜**Musée d'Histoire Naturelle Henri-Lecoq** Gone are the days, we think, when pharmacists roamed their regions collecting the carcasses of animals, digging up minerals, and collecting rocks. Too bad, we think, because the world would be a better place with more of these. Especially the dioramas. *15 rue Bardoux.* ☎ *04-73-91-93-78.*

What's with All the Fountains?

Perhaps you've noticed the lack of a major river in Clermont-Ferrand? For obvious reasons, most French cities revolve around one. Thankfully, the town has no fewer than 22 underground water sources, many of which were medieval subjects of pilgrimage. To coax the water to the surface, engineers of all stripes built MTV Best ● **fountains,** and they have become the city's pride, as well as its water source. Having grown somewhat, Clermont-Ferrand now laments its lack of a river and must divert water toward itself at great cost.

4€ unless you have a student card; free for those under 18. Tues–Sat 10am–noon and 2–6pm (until 5pm Oct–Apr).

➔ **Musée du Tapis et des Arts Textiles** Although carpets are rarely thought of as worthy museum objects, they're prized as art in many parts of the world. On display here are carpets and other textiles from Algeria, Yemen, and other far-flung places. *45 rue Ballainvilliers.* ☎ *04-73-42-69-70. 4.10€ adults, 2.60€ students, free for those under 18. Tues–Sat 10am–noon and 1–5pm; Sun 2–7pm.*

CHURCHES

MTV **Best ☻** **FREE** ➔ **Cathédrale Notre-Dame-de-L'Assomption** This church took 654 years to build. Begun by Jean Deschamps in 1248 atop previous church-like structures built between the 5th and 10th centuries, it was one of the first buildings in town to source black Volvic stone from nearby quarries, which was subsequently used on pretty much every other building in town until the 19th century. The stained-glass windows are remarkable; some were a gift for the marriage of King Philip of Spain and Isabella of Aragon, which happened, somewhat surprisingly, in this church. *Place de la Victoire.* ☎ *04-73-92-46-61. May–Sept Mon–Fri 9am–7pm, Sat–Sun 10am–7pm; Oct–Apr Mon–Fri 9am–6pm, Sat 10am–1pm and 2–6pm, Sun and holidays 9:30am–12:30pm and 2–6pm.*

FREE ➔ **Eglise Notre-Dame du Port** ✶ Begun in the 6th century, this church was destroyed by the Normans in the 9th, and built back up in the Romanesque style in the 12th, from white stone before the quarries at Volvic opened in the 13th. The church's extraordinary proportions relate to the architect's use of the Pythagorean Golden Mean. For a laugh, check out the sanctuary—Adam and Eve's expulsion from the Garden of Eden for eating grapes, as depicted here, rather than an apple. Adam has Eve by the hair, to better kick her in the

BLACK ROCK

The **black volcanic rock** that composes most of Clermont-Ferrand's pre-19th-century buildings came from Volvic, a town more famous today for bottled water than rock. But then again, those two elements go together, don't they? The rock is distinguished by its hardness, somewhere between marble and granite, and the deep pitch it takes on when exposed to the sun.

butt. No kidding. *Rue du Port.* ☎ *04-73-91-32-94. Daily 9am–7pm, until 8pm June to mid-Oct.*

TWO SPECIAL TOURS

Notre-Dame-du-Port

Start at the most logical spot, the **place de Jaude,** then head north on the pedestrianized rue du 11 Novembre, which will take you to the beautiful, **historic rue de Gras;** take a right when you get to it and head east. This will take you to the spectacular **cathedral** on the place de la Victoire. Find the cute **Maison de Savaron,** on 3 rue des Chaussetiers, and have a bite at the creperie downstairs. Keep walking north and you'll reach the **Fontaine d'Amboise,** with the pretty square Pascale nearby. Head east then and you'll get to the other spectacular cathedral in town, the **Eglise Notre-Dame-du-Port.**

Green Clermont-Ferrand

Start at the **place de Jaude,** and walk south, passing the shopping center, until you get to the **rue de Lagarlaye,** where you'll make a left and go straight until you get to the **Jardin Lecoq,** with its **Théâtre de Verdure** and pretty lake (the **Musée Lecoq,** which we like, is on the north side of the park). Head west then, on the **boulevard François-Mitterand,** which will turn into the boulevard Pasteur right around your next stop, the place Gambetta or place de Salins. At the round point of the place Gallieni, take the **rue des Salins,** crossing the boulevard Aristide Briand and following the rue de Bellevue on the other side of it until you get to a little park right between the boulevard Gambetta and the rue des Galoubies. Following the rue des Galoubies will take you to yet another park right in the middle of the Chamalieres district. Cross it, then take the avenue Paul Bert northwest until the best of all, **Parc de Montjoly.** To return to the town center, take the avenue Montjoly until the rue Blatin, and it'll bring you back to the place de Jaude.

Playing Outside

The best thing about Clermont-Ferrand, let's be honest, is its location, cradled in this basin of ancient volcanoes. Make the most of it by visiting the **Park Naturel Regional des Volcans d'Auvergne** (www.parc-volcans-auvergne.com/index.php4) or by spending some time on the extraordinary farms in the area. Visit **www.bienvenue-a-la-ferme.com** and book yourself an appointment for a lesson in cheesemaking or horseback riding.

PARC NATUREL REGIONAL DES VOLCANS D'AUVERGNE

The Auvergne has more than 200 volcanoes. What? You heard right—even the big butte smack in the middle of Clermont-Ferrand is a volcano. Most people imagine ash, lava, and spewing fire when they think of volcanoes. But the most these babies ever do these days is filter water for bottled-water companies, grow grass for moo-cows, and make black bricks for local buildings. In 1977, the French government, recognizing they possessed the most extraordinary collection of volcanoes in Europe (granted, it's not like there's much competition), declared nearly a million

acres of volcanic terrain a national park, encircling within the 186 villages that have made the volcanoes home.

The park includes three volcano ranges: the **Mont Dome** in the north (a minichain of 112 volcanoes), **Mont Dore,** and **Mont du Cantal** in the south. The most notorious and picturesque of the lot is the **Puy de Dome,** just 15km (9 miles) from Clermont-Ferrand. From the top, if you're lucky, you might even see as far east as the Mont Blanc.

Getting Around the Park

Cyclists on the Tour de France compete on the Puy de Dome's 12-degree inclines. And you can experience them on two wheels, too; access to the summit is reserved for cyclists on Sunday and Wednesday mornings from 7am to 8:30am. Of course, you can cycle at other times as well, but every passing car will only make you wish you were in it.

If you're not on a bike, you can ascend the peak via shuttle bus, from the bottom to the top. They run daily in July and August, between 10am to 6pm; and on Saturday and Sunday in May, June, and September from 11am to 6pm. Fares are 3.50€. Even if you've got your own car, you won't be able to drive it during the time the shuttle operates. Besides, the bus is cheaper than the toll to drive up, and the view is obviously better if you don't have to keep your eye on the road. The roads are open only from March to November because of winter snows.

The best way to explore the rest of this region is by car, or, if you're brave enough, by bike. Your chances of busing around are about as good as your chances of hitchhiking—not impossible, but by no means easy or effective. If you have a car, it means you can carry a tent, and camping in the park is a good option—you can do so in the town of Couron, for example, 10km (6 miles) southeast of Clermont-Ferrand on the D21. Otherwise, just drive around the little villages until you find something good, or check a local tourist office for a list of options.

Sleeping in the Park

One very rustic lodging option is to stay in *burons,* or little lodges made of rocks high up in the mountain. At one time, shepherds, goatherds, and cowherds used them in the summer months when the animals were grazing on pasture (some of them are still used for this purpose). To find the park, follow signs from the place de Jaude, or just look up, for goodness sake; the Puy-de-Dome is gigantic and only 15km (9 miles) from Clermont-Ferrand. Call one of the tourist centers below for more information.

Tourist Information

The **main tourist office** (☎ **04-73-65-64-00**) is in Montlosier, Aydat. They have an exhibition on volcanoes and local wildlife, plus guidebooks to local trails. From May to November, they're open daily from 10:30am to 12:30pm and 1:30 to 7pm. July and August hours are extended in the afternoon; open 2:30pm to 7pm. Take the N89 20km (12 miles) southeast to find it.

The **Aurillac Musée des Volcans** (rue Château St-Etienne; ☎ **04-71-48-07-00**) is a museum–cum–tourist information center in the Château St-Etienne, outside Clermont-Ferrand, in the town of Aurillac. From mid-June to mid-September, it's open Monday to Saturday from 10:30am to 6:30pm, and Sunday from 2pm to 6pm. From February to mid-June and from mid-September to October, it's open Monday to Saturday from 10am to noon. To get there, take the N89 to the D922, and go south 90km (56 miles).

Shopping

The only shopping wares we got excited about in Clermont-Ferrand were food-related.

FOOD, WINE & LOCAL CRAFTS

➜ **Couleurs d'Auvergne** ★★ The two sisters who run this shop spent months traveling around the region sourcing the best of it: jams from the Chataigneraie, cheeses, Puy lentils, artisanal beer, and organic honey. Less perishable fare such as Lezoux pottery or Puy lace are also available. *6 rue des Gras.* ☎ *04-73-91-40-39. Mon 2–7pm; Tues–Sat 9:30am–1pm and 2–7pm.*

➜ **Gauthier Frères** This butcher shop will only really appeal to foodies anxious for the next incarnation of the single-estate trend—first coffee, then chocolate, and now meat? Veal from Correze, lamb from Axuria, beef from Chalosse; it doesn't get more fabulously *raffiné* than this! *17 rue de la Boucherie.* ☎ *04-73-37-57-07. Tues–Thurs 6:30am–1pm and 3–7:15pm, Fri–Sat 6:30–7:15pm.*

➜ **La Ruche Trianon** ★ It doesn't look like this place has changed much since the 19th century. And it's très Clermont-Ferrand.

Markets

➜ **Marché Saint-Pierre** (place Saint-Pierre; Mon–Sat 7am–7:30pm) isn't pretty, but the food offerings are extraordinary, with six cheese shops (count them, six!).

➜ **Marché aux Puces** (bd. François-Mitterand and place des Salins; Sun 8am–noon) is a Sunday flea market.

➜ **La Halle St. Joseph** (rue de Courpiere; Fri 7am–1pm and Tues 4–8pm) is a farmer's market in Puy de Dome.

➜ **Place aux Arts** (place des Salins; first Sun of the month, weather permitting) is a monthly contemporary art market.

MASSIF CENTRAL & AUVERGNE

Just try the Volcania—a mix of rum-perfumed ganache and hazelnut paste with raspberries, or the Pascaline, named after Clermontois Blaise Pascale. *26 rue du 11 Novembre.* ☎ *04-73-37-38-26. Tues–Fri 10am–7pm, Sat 9am–5pm.*

📺 Best ♥ →**Le Cheval'in** This is the last butcher shop in town to sell horsemeat. Don't freak out—it's *good*. The shop has been open since 1953 and has worked with the same local farmer for 30 years. The animals are all selected by butchers from the shop. Try the house terrine and various charcuteries. *Marché St-Pierre, place St-Pierre.* ☎ *04-73-37-56-84. Tues–Sat 7am–12:30pm and 2:30–7pm.*

→**Noel Cruzilles** Clermont-Ferrand's Willy Wonka ships his sugared fruits and pavés all over the world—if you've made it all the way here, you might as well check it out and get tempted. It's best if you have a car. *226 av. Jean Mermoz.* ☎ *04-73-91-24-26. Jan–Nov Wed and Fri 8am–noon and 1–3pm; Dec daily 8am–noon and 1–3pm.*

Limoges: It Ain't Just Porcelain

396km (246 miles) S of Paris, 311km (193 miles) N of Toulouse, 93km (58 miles) NE of Perigueux

Limoges is best known for its pottery, but it's endearing for a host of other reasons: its winding streets, its fabulous market, its terrific restaurants (which source their products from the aforementioned fabulous market), its 17 historical monuments, its colorful festivals, its good-looking students, its artists' appeal. We'll stop there and let you see for yourself.

Getting There

BY AIR

Aéroport de Limoges-Bellegarde (☎ 05-55-43-30-30) is about 10km (6 miles) northwest of Limoges towards Saint-Junien on the N141. Only domestic flights land here.

BY TRAIN

The train station, **Gare SNCF des Benedictins** (☎ 08-92-35-35-35), receives direct trains from Toulouse, Bordeaux, Poitiers, Paris, and other closer towns. You're about 3 hours from Paris.

BY CAR

Limoges is 400km (248 miles) from Paris (about halfway between Paris and Toulouse); take the A20. Brive is about 95km (59 miles) away heading south. If you're coming from east or west (Clermont-Ferrand or Bordeaux, for instance), take the N141. From Aubusson, take the D941 west; it's about an hour away.

BY BUS

The **Gare Routière CIEL** (☎ 05-55-45-10-72) is close to the train station.

Orientation & Getting Around

The town, which is situated on the river Vienne's right bank, has historically consisted of two parts: **La Cité** (Vieux Limoges), at the bottom of the hill, and **La Ville Haute** (Le Château) at the top.

BY TAXI

Call **Taxis Verts** (☎ 05-55-37-81-81) or **Limoges Taxis** (☎ 05-55-38-38-38).

Tourist Offices

The tourist office is at 12 bd. de Fleurus (☎ 05-55-34-46-87; www.tourisme limoges.com). From mid-June to mid-September it's open Monday to Saturday from 9am to 7pm, Sunday 10am to 6pm.

Internet Hot Spot

Catch up on news from home at **Point Cyber** (7 av. du Général de Gaulle; ☎ **05-55-79-03-28**), which is open daily.

From mid-September to mid-June it's open Monday to Friday from 9am to noon and from 2pm to 7pm. Ask them about the city tours they organize.

Sleeping

HOSTELS

➜ **FJT Acceuil 2000** It's hardly a welcoming name, and the building's butt-ugly, but at 15€ a night and less than half a mile from center city, who's complaining? *20 rue Encombe-Vineuse.* ☎ *05-55-77-63-97. 15€ bed per night.*

CHEAP

➜ **Hôtel de la Paix** While most people come here for beds, some probably trek all this way to see the phonograph collection. In any case, if you sleep here, make a point of seeing the antiques. Rooms are fresh, simple, and clean. *25 place Jourdan.* ☎ *05-55-34-36-00. 37€–60€ double. Credit cards accepted.*

➜ **Hôtel Familia** Right by the train station, this isn't the prettiest neighborhood in Limoges. But at least it's quiet, and the big rooms make up for the location. *18 rue du Général du Bessol.* ☎ *05-55-77-51-40. 44€ double. Credit cards accepted.*

Eating

You're smack in the middle of France, so eat like it! You won't regret the good Limousin cuisine. Splurge on a good piece of beef.

COFFEE BARS & LIGHT FARE

➜ **Boulangerie des Halles** Damn, it smells good in here. This bakery sells 32 types of bread on weekdays and 42 types on weekends. The most popular are the *tourtiere de Gascogne* and the *pain passion. 13 rue Lanseqt.* ☎ *05-55-34-62-86. Credit cards accepted. Mon–Sat 6am–8pm. Closed Aug.*

➜ **R. Coudert** This is the only place in town for ice cream that didn't come in a plastic wrapper with "Magnum" written on it. They use no colorings or artificial flavorings, so you can really taste the—brace yourself—carrots and tomatoes. It's worth a try. *19 rue Othon-Peconnet.* ☎ *05-55-34-11-89. Credit cards accepted. Tues–Sat 9am–noon and 2–7pm; Sun 9am–noon in season.*

CHEAP

➜ **Les Halles Centrales** This place is yet another example of the fact that the best, cheapest places to eat in town are the markets. And this market is special. Nearly 60 vendors run particularly good-looking stalls, and if you're bored with the French cuisine you've no doubt been eating since day one, check out the Italian and Asian delis in the house. Two bistros in the *halles* allow for a sit-down experience. And don't forget to look up—the decoration here is stunning. *Place de la Motte. Daily 6am–1pm.*

SPLURGE

➜ **Philippe Redon** Right near the market, Philippe Redon, the "finest cook in Limoges," cooks local, seasonal ingredients in a beautiful 19th-century house with an Art Deco interior. *3 rue Aguesseau.* ☎ *05-55-34-66-22. Prix-fixe 42€–63€. Credit cards accepted. Mon–Fri noon–2:30pm; Tues–Sat 7–10pm.*

Partying

Yay! Another **university town,** albeit a small one with a lot of stuffy old china to go around. Ask the tourist office what concerts and events are taking place, or check out *Sortir en Limousin,* on sale at newsstands, which publishes good listings.

BARS, CLUBS & LIVE MUSIC VENUES

➜**Brasserie Bieres Michard** A for-real brewhouse, where you can see the beers fermenting and taste all 6 kinds of artisanal beer, which are way better than beer ought to be. These guys are the last to uphold the tradition of "Limousine" beer, which is not pasteurized, filtered, CO_2ed, or otherwise ruined by "modern," "hygienic" methods. You may never leave. *8 place Denis Dussoubs.* ☏ *05-55-79-37-98.*

➜**Le Recamier** Not only is this club cool and classy, it attracts surprisingly big-name DJs. We like it best when they're just playing jazz, or going all out with funk, house, and disco on weekend nights. *13 rue du Temple.* ☏ *05-55-32-70-32.*

Sightseeing

MUSEUMS

FREE ➜**Musée Municipal de l'Eveche-de-Limoges** This elegant 18th-century structure is filled with Limoges enamels from the 12th century and a few Renoirs (he was a local boy). *Place de la Cathédrale.* ☏ *05-55-45-98-10. June Wed–Mon 10am–11:45am and 2–6pm; July–Sept daily 10am–11:45am and 2–6pm; Oct–May Wed–Mon 10am–11:5am and 2–5pm.*

➜**Musée National de la Porcelaine Adrien Dubouché** This museum holds the largest public collection of Limoges porcelain. Twelve thousand pieces illustrate the changes in ceramics and glass-making over time. *8 bis place Winston Churchill.* ☏ *05-55-33-08-50. http://adrien dubouche.fr. 4€ adults, 2.60€ under 25. July–Aug Wed–Mon 10am–5:45pm; Sept–June Wed–Mon 10am–12:30pm and 2–5:45pm.*

CHURCHES

FREE ➜**Gothic Cathedral of St-Etienne** This is another example of a church that took a dog's age to build; it was begun in the 13th century and finished in the 19th. Personally, we think it's kind of cool that the nave looks so cohesive, given that it took 6 centuries to build. *Place de la Cathédrale* ☏ *05-55-34-53-81. Summer daily 10am–6pm, otherwise 10am–5pm.*

FREE ➜**St-Michel-des-Lions** Built in honor of St. Martial, a local bishop who died in the 3rd century. His skull is supposedly stored in a flamboyant reliquary, and it's removed from storage and exhibited during "Les Ostensions," a religious procession established in 994 that still happens every 7 years. The next one's in 2009. *Place Saint-Michel. No phone. Free admission. Mon–Sat 8am–noon and 2–6pm; Sun 8am–11:45am and 4–6pm.*

ONE SPECIAL TOUR
Quartier du Château

Start at the **place St-Pierre,** and then take the rue St-Martial. This will take you to the **place de la République,** the popular heart of the city, with the ancient **abbey of St-Marital.** Cross the rue Jean-Jaures and take the rue du Clocher, then make a right into the rue Gaignolle. You'll be at the **place du Presidial,** with its pretty *hôtels particuliers* and fountains, most of which used to be wells before more advanced plumbing came into fashion. Continue the rue Ferrerie, then find the rue du Temple and the rue du Consulat, lined with quaint *hôtels particuliers.* The rue du Consulat will lead you to the **Halles,** built in 1869 on the place de la Motte. Right off this is the **rue de la Boucherie,** whose name should make its function obvious—there are still remnants of the now-vestigial medieval butcher shops that lined it. Another medieval remnant is less vestigial—the big party that still takes place in this street every October. The **place de la Barreyrrette** in front of you is the ancient corral where they held the animals before butchering them, until the municipal abattoir was built in 1832. Pass in front of the **Chapelle St-Aurelien,** which the butchers bought at auction in 1795 and still maintain today; cross the place des Bances to get to the rue Haute-Vienne and enjoy a peaceful moment on the **boulevard Louis-Blanc.** A beautiful fountain graces the town hall on the **place Wilson.** Then take a left into the rue du College and a right after the Pavillion du Verdurier, back to where you started.

Playing Outside

📺 Best ◉ → **Aquarium du Limousin**
The Limoges aquarium sits in a cloistered ancient underground water reservoir built under Napoleon III to help the city avoid cholera. On display are 2,500 fish, spread out over a square kilometer. You might find a disproportionate amount of goldfish, but there are also native French species like carp and sturgeon, river fish like piranhas and electric eels, and all manner of ocean fish: sea horses, starfish, sea urchins, and so on. If you put a group together, you can get one of the center's biologists to commentate your visits: Pick a theme such as camouflage and adaptation, pollution and the ecosystem,

or morphology of fish bodies. Sweet. *2 bd. Gambetta (in front of town hall).* ☎ *05-55-33-42-11. www.aquariumdulimousin. com. Admission 6.50€ adults, 4.50€ students. Daily 10:30am–9pm. Bus: 1, 2, 4, or 15 (stop in front of town hall) or 10 (stop at bd. Gambetta).*

→ **Parc des Acrobois Buissiere Galant**
Okay, this adventure park is very clearly aimed at either kids or boys on a bachelor party night, but if you're feeling goofy and want to stretch your legs, check it out. They have rope walks in the trees, little railroads to tool around on in your own railroad car, bow-and-arrow shooting, and pseudo–rock climbing, plus hammocks to take little naps in. *Plan d'eau des Ribieres.* ☎ *05-55-78-86-47. Admission 19€ adults, 17€ students and the officially unemployed. Apr–Sept weekends and holidays 2–6pm; July–Aug 10am–7pm. Reservations encouraged. From Limoges take the N21 towards Perigeux, take a left at Chalus (dir. Buissiere Galant), at Buissiere, take a right following signs for Plan d'eau des Ribieres.*

→ **Parc du Reynou** This habitat is more like a zoo than a park. Choose a nice day to walk around gorgeous century-old flora

Limoges: Okay, It's *Mostly* Porcelain

Limoges is known worldwide for its **medieval enamels on copper** (Limoges enamels), its **19th-century porcelain** (Limoges porcelain), and its Limousain **oak barrels, used for cognac** production. In 1771, kaolinic clay, the fine white clay used for making porcelain, was discovered at nearby Saint-Yrieix-la-Perche. Under the guiding hand of progressive economist Anne Robert Jacques Turgot, Baron de Laune—who had been named the *intendant* of this poor, overtaxed, and isolated area—developed a new ceramics industry, and Limoges porcelain became famous. Most factories producing Limoges porcelain made elaborately molded but all-white wares. These pieces, known as "blanks," often ended up on American soil in the hands of eager china painting students, this being a popular hobby for ladies during the late 1800s. From the mid–19th century to the beginning of the Great Depression, status-conscious American brides extensively used Haviland Limoges dinnerware on well-set tables—explaining the profusion of sets you can spot in antiques malls or your mom's closet.

(cedars, sequoias) and look at the 70 different types of animals chilling in the landscape. You'll need a car: Take the D65 and get off at the Parc du Reynou exit. ☎ 05-55-00-40-00.

Shopping

WHERE TO BUY LIMOGES

The best place to start is the rue Louis-Blanc, otherwise known as *la rue de la porcelaine.*

➔**La Manufacture Bernardaud** There's a good porcelain museum and subsequent showroom where you are free to exercise your credit card. *27 av. Albert-Thomas (take the rue de la Mauvendiere away from the center and walk 15 min.).* ☎ *05-55-10-55-91. Museum admission 4€. Museum hours: June–Sept 9am–11:15am and 1–4:15pm. Store hours: June–Sept daily 9am–7pm; Oct–May Mon–Sat 9:30am–6:30pm.*

➔**La Manufacture Royale Limoges** This is the oldest porcelain house in Limoges (founded in 1797) with, of course, an accompanying shop. It's right across from the port du Naveix. *28 rue Donzelot.* ☎ *05-55-33-27-30 (call for reservations). Oct–June Mon–Sat 10am–7pm; July–Sept daily 10am–7pm.*

MARKETS

➔**Les Halles Centrales** This is one of the more fabulous food markets in France. Don't miss it if you're here. *Place de la Motte. Daily 6am–1pm.*

➔**Marché aux Puces de la Cité** The biggest flea market in the Limousin is open monthly. *Cité neighborhood.* ☎ *05-55-32-46-64. 2nd Sun of the month.*

➔**Marché de la Place** Marceau regional products are sold weekly here. *Place Marceau. Every Sat morning.*

FOOD, WINE & LOCAL CRAFTS

➔**Aux Delices de Mathilde** Before she had the shop, homegirl Mathilde used to sell her products on the local markets. Today, everyone comes here instead. Try the *eaux-de-vie maisons* or any of the other local pates and liqueurs. *8 rue Haute-Vienne.* ☎ *05-55-34-19-32. Tues 2:30–6:30pm; Wed–Sat 9:30am–noon and 2:30–6:30pm.*

➔**Le Pre Gourmand** Oh my God, *rillettes.* Have you tried these yet? Pork + pork fat = one happy guidebook writer. Usually, you have to buy these from a butcher shop, but here they come potted, so you can take them wherever you

---

Assessing Limoges Porcelain 101

So Grandma would be really happy if you brought her back some porcelain. Questions to ask when valuing an item: What is the quality of the decorations? Does it have high-quality hand-painting? Is it signed by the artist? Is it decorated with transfers? Some Limoges pieces were decorated by amateurs, as you saw above. High-quality hand-painting holds more value than unskilled painting, and even some beautifully transferred pieces will be valued more highly than a poorly executed hand-decorated example. Generally, however, collectors prefer hand-decorated items and will pay premium prices for a good one.

Some porcelain collectors focus solely on Haviland products (see above) and ignore other Limoges company names. Others prefer to get a broader range of Limoges items from various other manufacturers. Because there are few fakes on the market, Limoges pieces are a good choice for wannabe collectors who don't want to get ripped off. If you're taking home some Limoges, though, wait until the end of your trip to buy it, so you don't lug home some very expensive shards.

Medieval Meat Fest

MTV Best● La Frairie des Petits Ventres (third Fri in Oct) is a medieval festival that celebrates eating and happens in the rue de la Boucherie (the medieval butcher block)? We are so there. Especially given the thousands of pounds of sausage and ham on offer. Butchers do it *right*.

want. Try also the chestnut beers, and the house specialty—the Saint-Victurniaud, a

chestnut-honey cake. *51 rue Adrien Dubouche.* ☎ *05-55-77-19-73. Tues–Sat 9:30am–12:15pm and 2–7pm.*

➔ **Vinaigreries Delouis** When was the last time you walked into a vinegar shop? Exactly. These guys have been at it since 1885, when they only sold vinegar, but today they also peddle mayonnaises, mustards, and vinegared fruits. The shop mostly sells to restaurants, so you might have to buy in bulk, but wander in anyway. *41 rue de Beaupuy.* ☎ *05-55-77-41-88. Mon–Fri 8:15am–11:45am and 12:45–5pm.*

Le-Puy-en-Velay

541km (335 miles) directly S of Paris, 127km (79 miles) SE of Clermont-Ferrand, 135km (84 miles) SW of Lyon

Although Le Puy counts as part of the Auvergne today, it has a decidedly Occitan flavor—and that's because before the Revolution, it belonged to the Languedocien state. Surrounded by great verdant volcanoes—more peaceful than pugnacious for quite some time—the town has flourished quietly over the years, enriched by the long-standing passage of pilgrims come to visit the three main religious sites in town: the chapelle Saint-Michelle, the Rocher Corneille, and the Cathedral Notre-Dame. You still might even see pilgrims coming through today.

Getting There
BY TRAIN
Most trains to Le Puy come through Saint-Etienne or Saint-Georges d'Aurac, although there are direct ones from Lyon. The train station is on the avenue Charles Dupuy. For information, call ☎ **08-92-35-35-35.**

BY CAR
Get to Le Puy from St-Etienne, southwest on the N88. From Clermont-Ferrand, drive south on the N88 to Lempdes and then southeast on the N102 to Puy.

BY BUS
The **Gare Routière** (☎ **04-71-09-25-60**) is on the place du Marechal Leclerc. Unless you're going to a teensy village outside of Le Puy, though, this won't be very useful information to you. Oh—except if you're coming from a teensy village *into* le Puy.

Orientation
The train station is on the southeast end of town; walk on the avenue Charles Dupuy and turn left on the boulevard Marechal Fayolle to the place du Breuil, the town's center square and location of the tourist office. The park Jardin Henri Vinay and its Musée Crozatier are right around here too, with lots of old men playing petanque. The place aux Laines is a smaller square right behind this; north of the square is the old town. Narrow shopping streets, like the ones around the place du Plot, wind their way uphill to the cathedral. Just north of the cathedral is the rocher Corneille, with its enormous statue of the Virgin Mary with her baby—the emblem of Le Puy, visible from all over town.

Getting Around

Taxis are your best bet here. **Radio-Taxis** (☎ **04-71-05-42-43**) are on place de Breuil. You can even ask them to take you on a tour of the city—45 minutes are 20€. Do you really want to walk all those hills?

Tourist Offices

Le-Puy-en-Velay's **tourist office** (2 place du Clauzel; ☎ **04-71-09-38-41**; www.ot-lepuyenvelay.fr) is incredibly on top of things. From Easter to September 30, it's open every day from 8:30am to noon and from 1:30 to 6:15pm (July–Aug 8:30am–7:30pm). From the 1st of October to Easter it's open Monday to Saturday from 8:30am to noon and from 1:30 to 6:15pm. Sundays and holidays they open from 10am to noon.

They organize tours of the village from July 1 to 31 daily at 3:30pm, from August 1 to 14 daily at 10am and 3:30pm, from August 16 to 31 daily at 3:30pm, and from September 1 to 10 daily at 3pm. Those wanting to partake should meet at the office on the place du Clauzel.

The tours require a minimum of 3 people and cost 5€ per person (free for children under 12). They last about 2 hours. Check out the office's pretty yearly booklet, *Laissez-vous Conter,* which details all the walks: **nature walks** to the nearby ravin de Corbeauf and the Tourbiere du Mont Bar, where well-informed guides describe the region's volcanic activity, geology, flora, and legends; **night tours** that show the village illuminated; special **"wind-mill"** and **"Aeolian" walks** for those the-matically inclined. Some of the tours are even dramatized so that you have the pleasure of watching locals dress up like medievalists and speak in Olde Frenche (we suspect that these are actually quite professional and un-Disney-like).

Sleeping

HOSTELS

➜ **Auberge de Jeunesse** This FUAJ insti-tution is in an ancient convent up in the hills. The rooms aren't much to speak of, but at least they're clean enough, with plenty of beds and a price that can't be beat. *Centre Pierre-Cardinal, 9 rue Jules Valles.* ☎ *04-71-05-52-40. Apr–Sept 7€ per night. Reception Mon–Sat 2–11:30pm, Sun 8–10pm.*

CHEAP

➜ **Dyke Hotel** There are reasons to come here other than just to take a picture of the sign. The rooms are all the same though perfectly adequate. Best of all, they have Wi-Fi. And, for your information, the "dykes" the hotel is named after are local mineral rock formations. For real. *37 bd. du Marechal Fayolle.* ☎ *04-71-09-05-30. 40€ double. Credit cards accepted. Amenities: Wi-Fi. In room: TV.*

DOABLE

➜ **Hôtel Saint-Jacques** Twelve newly renovated rooms have wood floors and fresh coats of paint. Over five stories, the view of the place Cadelade is very pretty, and the staff is helpful and relaxed. *7 place Cadelade.* ☎ *04-71-07-20-40. www.hotel-saint-jacques.com. 43€–65€ double. Credit cards accepted. Amenities: Elevator. In room: TV.*

Eating

You have to like Auvergnat food, if you want to like the food in Le Puy en Velay, but that's not too hard to do. For a town this isolated and open to tourists, the eat-ing is surprisingly good—if you don't get sucked into the tourist traps.

COFFEE BARS & LIGHT FARE

MTV Best ➜ **Yann Sabot** We don't know how this man stands straight, so weighed down with medals is he—from the *patissier* world championships, before he was 25, no less. He can't be much older than that now, so Ponotes (Puy locals) have years to look forward to his macaroons, pineapple mousses, ganaches, and the *Diabolo,* which you'll have to taste to experience. *21 rue St-Gilles.* ☎ *04-71-09-26-41. Tues–Sat 7am–7:30pm; Sun 7am–1:30pm.*

CHEAP

➜ **Le Chamarlenc** We've filed this in the cheap category because the food's of such good value that it belongs here. Carefully selected products, carefully cooked and carefully presented, might be precious if the place wasn't so laid-back and cool. Definitely try the *crème au bleu d'Auvergne* if it's on the menu. *19 rue Raphael.* ☎ *04-71-02-17-72. Menus 13€–19€. Credit cards accepted. Sept–June Tues–Wed 7–10pm, Thurs–Sat noon–2pm and 7–10pm; July–Aug Mon–Sat noon–9pm.*

DOABLE

➜ **Bateau Ivre** Puy lace and Puy lentils: the combo ain't bad. Big oak tables, local food, rustic interior, welcoming service. Try the oxtail terrine and anything with lentils. *5 rue du Portail d'Avignon.* ☎ *04-71-09-67-20. Menus 18€–30€. Credit cards accepted. Call for hours.*

➜ **Comme à la Maison** *My* house isn't like this, but I wish it was. Borrow books to read as you enjoy a drink at the bar, pet the cat, and order a huge portion of really good, home-style food. *7 rue Seguret.* ☎ *04-71-02-94-73. Menus 9€–17€. Credit cards accepted.*

➜ **Lapierre** Right by the Musée Crozatier, along the long sycamore alleys of the Jardin Vinay, organic local food is served without pretension. A bistro interior and friendly service completes the package. *6 rue des Capucins.* ☎ *04-71-09-08-44. Menus 23€–0€. Mon–Fri noon–2pm and 7–10pm.*

Partying

The main place to party in Le Puy is on the place aux Laines or the place du Breuil. "Party," though, is a relative term; it's pretty calm here.

➜ **The King's Head** It's a bit incongruous to see a pub in Le Puy, but the convivial atmosphere and good choice of Belgian, Irish, and English beer will help you get over that real fast. This joint is closed on Sunday. *Place du Marché Couvert.* ☎ *04-71-02-50-35.*

Sightseeing

MUSEUMS

➜ **Musée Crozatier** ★ Contemporary art, stuffed animals, information on volcanoes, and lace, lace, lace—some from the 16th century. *Jardin Henri Vinay.* ☎ *04-71-06-62-40. 3€ adults, 2.25€ students. Mid-June to mid-Sept daily 10am–noon and 2–6pm; Mar to mid-June and mid-Sept to end Sept Wed–Mon 10am–noon and 2–6pm; Feb and Oct–Nov Wed–Mon 10am–noon and 2–4pm.*

CHURCHES

➜ **Cathédrale Notre-Dame** Built first in the 5th century, and then added on through the next, this beautiful half-Christian, half-Arab-looking cathedral on the hillside of Mt. Anis is supported on one side by pillars sunk into the rock. It's at the base of the pinnacle upon which St. Michael's sits, and you can climb up 134 steps for a gorgeous view. *Follow the rue des Tables.* ☎ *04-71-05-98-74.*

➜ **Le Centre d'Enseignement de la Dentelle au Fuseau** This lace collection also runs an instructive tour to show how it's done. *38 rue Raphael.* ☎ *04-71-02-01-68. www.ladentelledupuy.com. 3€. Mon–Fri 9am–11:30am and 1:30–5pm.*

Lace, Lentils & Medicinal Liquor

Le Puy en Velay is known for its lace, lentils, and liquor with a unique flavor and strength that will remind you of the medicine you had to take as a kid. The origins of **lace** in Puy can be traced back to the late 15th century, but it was in the mid-to-late 17th century that the industry had its real heyday. The advent of the industrial age brought—luckily or unluckily, depending on your perspective—special equipment designed to reproduce the delicate lace in mass quantities. Today, the area embraces the new technology but heralds its old-school artisans with pride.

The **green Puy lentil** is another notorious regional export. Grown in the fields around town, its flowers are a pretty white-blue, with curly leaves. The bean takes the color of the soil it's grown in—purplish in volcanic soil, white-ish in calcareous soil. It has its own Appellation Controllée (see the Basics chapter), and the French (or maybe just the people from Puy!) refer to it as *caviar Lyonnais*. The lentils grow best in the microclimate of the upper plateaus of Le Puy, and, so very luckily, suit the two favorite local *plats:* sausages and pork. Many upscale grocery stores in the U.S. now carry Puy lentils.

So you've got your lace napkin on your lap and your plate of sausages and lentils in front of you. What are you going to drink? **Verveine du Velay,** of course! Since 1859, the same "mixologists" have been brewing the same recipe for this green and yellow medicinal-tasting liquor made from 32 different regional plants and herbs.

➔**St. Michel d'Aiguilhe** Built in the 10th century, the chapel also stands on top of a volcanic chimney, like many other buildings around. It spikes up 84m (280 ft.), and you can traipse around what remains of it after centuries of erosion. It's atop the Rocher St. Michel, slightly out of the old part of town. *Atop the Rocher St-Michel.* ☎ *04-71-09-50-03. Admission 2.75€ adults, 2.25€ students. May–Sept daily 9am–6:30pm; Apr and Oct to mid-Nov daily 9:30am–noon and 2–5:30pm; Feb–Mar daily 2–5pm.*

Shopping

MARKETS

I'm a sucker for markets, but the one on Saturday mornings on the **place du Plot** especially rocks.

FOOD, WINE & LOCAL CRAFTS

For Puy lace, try **Lucia Dentelles** (28 place du Plot; ☎ 04-71-09-60-69) or

Specialités du Velay (1 bd. St-Louis; ☎ 04-71-09-09-34).

➔**A la Ville du Puy** Pagès liquors, vervena nougats, lentil beer, local honey, and lentils from three local cooperatives: *décidement,* this shop wants to call itself local! If you speak French, ask Madame Trescarte about what you're buying—she's a veritable font of information on the goods at hand. *12 rue des Tables.* ☎ *04-71-09-50-48. Mar–Oct Mon–Sat 9am–7pm.*

➔**Coulaud** This shop has been run by three generations of bad-ass lady cheesemongers since 1920, and they've been buying at least their Velay from the same cheesemaker ever since. They stock Italian, Spanish, and French cheeses, but specialize in the local sort—cantal, saint-nectaire, *fromage des artisans,* and then some. *24 rue Grenouillit.* ☎ *04-71-09-08-50. Tues–Fri 8am–7:30pm; Sat 7am–7pm.*

Best ❶ → **Le Comptoir Gourmand** French caviar, Thiercellin spices, and even a range of specialty German, Scottish, and Corsican mineral waters set this fancy food shop apart. Of course, they also have the more common Fauchon jams, artisanal beer, and fresh or dried truffles, but that's hardly tragic. *Place du Marché Couvert.* ☎ *04-71-02-69-83. Tues–Sat 9am–12:30pm and 3–7:30pm.*

Elsewhere in the Massif Central & Auvergne

The Massif Central and Auvergne regions compose a large repository of hidden treasures usually too quickly glossed over by those rushing to get from Paris to Nice. It deserves better. Here are a few of our favorites, but keep in mind that while the bigger towns have train stations, this region is much more easily explored in a car, which allows you to stop and start wherever you please. We highly recommend that you check out **www.accueil-paysan.com** to find farmers in the region that you can either stay with and visit, or whose wares you can eat (fruits, meats, or cheeses). Another good website is **www.plusbeauxdetours.com**, which will give you great road-trip ideas.

Aurillac

Aurillac is underrated and worth a visit at any time of the year, despite its reputation as the coldest city in France (Aurillacois argue that the thermometer used by the newscasters is unfairly placed at the top of a mountain). But it would be a capital crime not to go to the **Festival International de Théâtre de Rue,** 4 days in mid-August when the best of the world's street theater comes to Aurillac, along with 100,000 other people. If you're vaguely artistic or have a bit of hippie in you or just like partying in the streets with thousands of other people, come. This festival is one of the best, friendliest, and most fun in France. Obviously, plan ahead, because hotels fill up quickly.

For the other 361 days of the year, Aurillac makes umbrellas, over half of the total produced in France. Today, machines do most of the labor, but in the 1930s the industry employed over 800 people, many of whom just stayed home making umbrellas. This may be another reason people have negative ideas about the weather here.

When you come, walk around the pedestrianized old part of town, just north of the central place du Square (original name!). Take the rue Duclaux to the big place de l'Hôtel de Ville, with its terrific Wednesday and Saturday markets. Follow the rue de Forgerons to the pretty little place St-Geraud, with its 12th-century fountain and church of St. Geraud—check out the ceiling inside with its funky ribs. Once you come out of the church, take the rue de la Fontaine out to the riverbank, and walk along the cours d'Angouleme to the place Gerbert, where you can admire the old *lavoir,* or medieval laundromat.

Brioude

Brioude doesn't show up in many guidebooks, and I stumbled on it kind of randomly, but I loved it. Especially the Saturday-morning market, which I was lucky enough to see on a festival day, with majorettes in lace-up boots and marching bands made up of ancients parading through the windy streets. You can catch a train there from Issoire, but again, you're best off in a car, especially since the roads around here are so really beautiful. If you can, go for lunch or dinner at the **Auberge de Chassignolles** in the cute little village of Chassignolles, 20 minutes east.

Potée Auvergnate & Tango

So, you like road trips? Here's a really great drive. Start in Le Puy en Velay and take the N102 northwest towards Espaly-Saint-Marcel, passing close to Paulhaguet. Right near **Brioude** (see above), take the first exit and continue on the D588. You'll pass lovely alleys of cypress trees, all lined up saluting, and follow the road past Champagnac-le-Vieux, another charming, sleepy little bourg. Make a left and get on the D5, then quickly after, the D56 and the D566 (it sounds confusing, but you'll see it's actually really simple). You'll pass herds of black sheep nuzzling impossibly green grass, assuming you're here in the summer, that is. Five kilometers (3 miles) into the D566, you'll get to **Chassignolles**, where you should stop for the night or at the very least a meal at the brand-new, 10-room **Auberge de Chassignolles** (☎ **04-71-76-33-44; 45€–60€** double). Owner Harry Lester was one of the first chefs at London gastropub institution the Anchor & Hope in Waterloo (this isn't a guidebook to England, but if you're there, *go*). He has now retired to Chassignolles to start his next life as an innkeeper with his lovely partner Ali and their baby son Fred. His cooking is worth flying from London to the Auvergne for, but if you're going down the **A75** between Paris and the South of France, it's only half an hour off the highway—into another world. Next door to the Auberge is—brace yourself—**Pelerin Tango,** a tango school in the Auvergne run by a kind, loopy Dutch couple (www.pelerin.nl). Next door to that is a church, and then a few more houses, and that's all there is to Chassignolles. But then again, that's pretty fabulous. Get back on the D566 and the subsequent D56 and D5 and turn left onto the D588 for 18km (11 miles). Turn right on the D499 and you'll go to La Chaise-Dieu, which means God's Chair. This town is imposing both from far away and up close. Inside the abbey church of Saint-Robert is a fresco of the Danse Macabre, in which Death plucks at the plump bodies of 23 people that supposedly represent the different classes of society. "It is yourself," says the inscription below. The Salle de l'Echo on the place de l'Echo next door is a relic of the days when people afflicted with leprosy or the plague whispered their last confessions to a doctor—standing on the other side of the room (it still works today). Taking the D906 and the N102 will get you back to Le Puy-en-Velay.

Bourges

The "heart of France" moniker gets applied to lots of different places, but in Bourges' case, it holds. The former capital of Aquitaine is today somewhat sleepier than it was in its medieval heyday, but plenty of relics remain, and the town's the better for them. On a wholly different note, Bourges also hosts the excellent Festival Printemps de Bourges music festival for 5 days in April, which really livens up the place. The festival loses money every year, but the town continues to host it anyway. Although only a few well-known artists perform, the draw of the festival is the new talent on show—many famous bands had their first coming-out party here. There are good rail and road connections to Bourges from Tours and Vierzon.

Polignac

Northwest of Le Puy is the charming village of **Polignac,** and 90m (300 ft.) above it the fortress of its former owners, the Polignac family. But before them, this was the location of the temple to the god Apollo in Roman times, where pilgrims made their way to seek advice from the Oracle.

Salers

Sometimes fortune hits a town all of a sudden, and then fortune leaves. And the best part of the fortune is that 400 years later, the story's all still there, written on late-Gothic balconies on charming *hôtels particuliers*. Salers became the administrative center for the highlands of the Auvergne in 1564, housing all of its magistrates before they moved on. This rapid expansion means that the architecture here has remained homogenously pretty, and Salers has a reputation for being *la plus jolie petite ville du Cantal,* or the prettiest little town in the Cantal. Take the cobbled rue du Beffroi uphill into the central place Tyssandier d'Escous, surrounded by the 15th-century mansions of the provincial aristocracy. Note the mullioned windows and carved lintels—how *do* these things last so long, anyway? Things we soldered and superglued in woodshop are already falling apart—and the pretty little turrets of the Maison du Bailliage remain. They make really good cheese here too. See "Fromages d'Auvergne & the AOC," on p. 613. Forget about coming to Salers without a car, unless you like to wait for buses that never come until someone tells you they've canceled the service.

Vichy

The sparkling waters of Vichy are known almost as well as its Nazi occupation, when the town became the site of a de facto French government that was effectively a German puppet state once France surrendered to Germany in 1940. The sparkling water came first. At the end of the 16th century, the baths in Vichy attained renown for their supposed healing powers, further popularized by the Marquise de Sevigne's account of their having cured her hands of paralysis, enabling her to write the letters for which she became famous. After Louis XVI's nieces complained that the waters were muddy and crowded, he built roomier thermal baths in 1787, visited by Napoleon's mom and brother, Princesse Marie-Therese-Charlotte, and all the celebs of the 19th century. The baths were still very popular when, in 1940, having surrendered to Germany, the Etat Français was set up as an alternative government to the one in Paris. It remained the capital of the French State for the 4 years known as the Vichy Regime that most French people would like forgotten. Today, it's the headquarters of l'Oreal. And the town is still famous for healthcare. So if your liver hurts from too much *vin de table* or your stomach's rustling up complaints about the *saucisson,* take any train between Paris and Clermont-Ferrand (Vichy's only 30 min. away from C-F).

Burgundy & the Franche Comté

by Anna Brooke

The atmosphere of Burgundy (Bourgogne) and the Franche Comté is subdued and slow-paced, with sleepy hamlets, castles rising from vineyards, medieval churches, and darling villages remote enough to have remained thoroughly French. Towns such as **Beaune** and **Dijon** (an ideal base for visiting surrounding attractions including the stunning **Abbaye de Fontenay**) are big enough for you to lose yourself in them—yet small enough that you'll never really get lost.

As a dukedom that was separate from the rest of France until after the Revolution, Burgundy was largely unharmed in World War I and World War II; its architecture is remarkably well preserved. The hundreds of old medieval timbered houses with exposed wood beams may remind you of Alsace in northern France.

But it's not the architecture that will leave the biggest impression. Burgundy is reputed for its fine cuisine and wines—easily some of the best in the country. The major growing regions are Chablis, Côte de Nuits, Côte de Beaune, Côte de Chalon,

Mâconnais, and Nivernais. The whites get the most press, but the reds shouldn't be ignored. And don't miss the favorite local aperitif, *kir,* which mixes white wine with liqueur of cassis.

The Franche Comté, where France borders Switzerland, is known as the land of waterways, forests, and mountains. But you could just as well call it the land of cheese and cows. Three of France's most famous *fromages* (Emmental, Mont D'or, and Comté) are made here, from the milk of brown-and-white Montbeliarde cattle, a regional breed you'll spot easily as you pass through this otherwise all-green landscape.

The most happening city here is **Besançon,** where a small student population knocks the average age down by 20 years and keeps the nightlife ticking. And in nearby **Belfort,** the hippest pop-rock festival in France, **Les Eurockéennes,** takes place every summer with an impressive international lineup.

If Burgundy's food, pace, and way of life become too addictive, you could prolong your trip and visit the picturesque, historical settlements of **Auxerre,** with its Flamboyant Gothic cathedral (☎ 03-86-52-06-19); **Vézelay,** a living museum of French antiquity believed to contain the tomb of Mary Magdalene (☎ 03-86-33-23-69); **Avallon,** with its medieval ramparts (☎ 03-86-34-14-19); **Autun,** where Napoleon studied in 1779 (☎ 03-85-86-80-38); **Saulieu,** famous for its food (☎ 03-80-64-00-21); and **Tournus,** a pretty river port (☎ 03-85-27-00-20). These towns aren't covered in this chapter, but the phone numbers refer to the relevant tourist offices, which can supply further information.

The Best of Burgundy & Franche Comté

⟳**The Best Town with Multicolored Rooftops:** From the outside, all looks plain and ordinary in **Beaune,** but on the inside of the Hôtel Dieu, medieval psychedelia has gripped the tiled roof. See p. 647.

⟳**The Best Place to See How Cistercian Monks Lived:** Eight hundred years ago, St. Bernard (a man, not a dog) decided to found an abbey for his monks in a lonely valley. Today, the monks are gone, but **Abbaye de Fontenay** still provides one of the best examples of how the folk lived back then. See p. 651

⟳**The Best Place to Taste Real French Mustard:** Think of **Dijon** and you'll think of mustard. What better place to enjoy this kick-ass condiment than on its home turf. See p. 634.

⟳**The Best Place to Reenact Cyrano de Bergerac (Dijon): La Maison Millière,** one of the oldest mansions in Dijon (now a tearoom), was used in the film version of Edmond Roston's classic, starring everybody's favorite, big-' nosed froggy, Gerard Depardieu. See p. 642

⟳**The Best Photo Op in Dijon:** Hidden behind rows of winding streets are **Les Cours Cachées,** dozens of hidden courtyards that make for some of the prettiest and most unexpected snapshots in town. See p. 646.

⟳**The Best Place to See Roman Besançon:** Old Ceasar's gang just couldn't help building monuments, such as **Porte Noire,** that would withstand the test of time and leave fascinating vestiges of antiquity for us modern folk to gawk at. See p. 658.

○ **The Best Place to Watch Time Go By:** The 12th-century Cathédrale St-Jean has a bell tower, and in the bell tower is the **Horloge Astronomique**—one of the world's most extraordinary clocks, which can tell the time of the tides in eight ports. See p. 658.

○ **The Best Shop for Whiffy but Delectable Local Cheese:** You will find more smelly cheese at **La Cave aux Fromages** than you've seen in your lifetime, along with strings of

wonderful dried sausages, wines, and prepared local specialties. See p. 660.

○ **The Best Place to Get a Diploma in Debauchery: Le Cousty** is a Besançon institution known for its wild parties, cheap drinks, and mad crowds of all ages. See p. 657.

○ **The Best Way to Take in the Town of Besançon:** Yes, **boat trips** are touristy and cheesy, but the boat trips run by Bateaux de Besançon and Vedettes Panoramiques are a fantastic way to see the sights and appreciate Besançon's unusual horse-shoe-shaped topography. See p. 659.

Burgundy's Top 10 Dishes

Throw out your scales! Here's our roster of the best specialties in this region known for its rich, delicious cuisine:

1. Everyone's heard of it; now it's yours for the taking, as authentic as can be—*boeuf bourguignon* (beef stewed in red wine).

2. In second place is *coq au vin*—chicken stewed in (you got it) red wine.

3. Next is *oeufs meurette*—lardoons stewed in (oh, what a surprise) red wine served on a slice of toast, topped with a poached egg.

4. **Dijon mustard** takes fourth place, served with steak and red wine.

5. Next up is *moutarde au lapin*—rabbit in a creamy mustard sauce.

6. Then *clafoutis*—black cherries baked in batter, laced with Kirsch!

7. Potato-lovers will adore the *aligot*—buttery mashed potato with garlic and Cantal cheese.

8. Coming in at number eight are slimy, scrumptious mollusks known here as *escargot* (snails), served in melted garlic butter.

9. Anything made with **Mont d'Or** cheese—a winter treat best eaten scooped out from its wooden box.

10. Last but not least are **black currants**—fresh or in their alcoholic form, *cassis,* served in a *kir.*

Burgundy

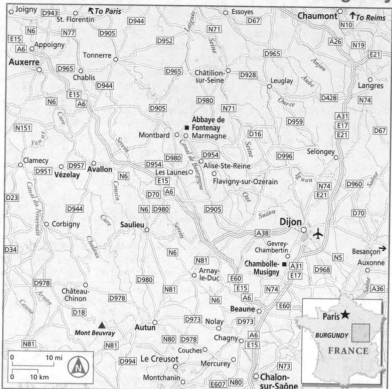

Getting Around the Region

Trains are the best and most efficient way to get around Burgundy, although you may want to rent a **car** or motorcycle for day trips out from Dijon and Besançon. You'll most likely see Burgundy on your way south from Paris. Dijon, just an hour and 40 minutes from Paris's Gare de Lyon, is a great place to get off the train for a day or two and see the countryside and some architecture in this historic part of France. Another good route is via Lyon to Dijon,

with a stopover at Beaune, which lies between the two cities. If you're pressed for time, you can limit your stop in Beaune to only an hour or two. Besançon requires a little more effort to reach from Paris, 2 hours and 40 minutes away, but you can also get there from Lille, in the north, in just over $3^{1}/_{2}$ hours. If you've got a **set of wheels,** take the A6 from Paris to Dijon. From there the A36 and A39 cut through both regions.

Bourgogne Wine-Tasting

Ask the locals about wine, and they will proudly claim that only an authentic Burgundy can satisfy the palate of a connoisseur. It's a bit of an exaggeration in my book, but the wines of Burgundy or Bourgogne are indeed among the world's finest. Being able to taste them in their vineyards is reason enough to visit the region. The reds give you an inner glow from their fruity taste and aromatic bouquet, and, of all the world's whites, a white burgundy is still the one most preferred by gourmands. (And don't worry. Even if your palate is far from seasoned, you'll still have a great time tasting. Maybe you'll even learn what an aromatic bouquet is supposed to smell like.)

After the Roman conquest, it was actually fat, wine-guzzling church bishops who launched the fiefdom's vineyards. They built monuments to the glory of God and to Bacchus—who all but shares the celestial throne in this region. In time, the dukes of Burgundy became known as the "Princes of the best wines of Christianity."

In the years to come, France's most influential citizens sang the praises of Burgundy—Napoleon had a weakness for Chambertin, and Madame de Pompadour claimed she became sex-crazed after drinking Romanée-conti. In 1878, the insect *phylloxera* destroyed the vines, but plants shipped in from the United States were invulnerable to the pest and ended up replacing the Burgundian grapes of yore.

Surprisingly, Burgundy—birthplace of pinot noir and chardonnay—produces only 2% of France's wines. Vineyard acreage is only half of what it was in 1870. Nearly half of the grapes are used to produce red Beaujolais. Burgundies beloved by wine-fanciers the world over include Chablis, Pouilly-Fuisse, Chambertin, Nuits-Saint-Georges, Beaune, Pommard, and others.

As you travel through the region, you'll find that some 150 wine producers or wine traders welcome you to their small cellars to sample their product. These vintners have signed a "Welcome Charter" to guarantee you a friendly reception. Look for this sign on the entrance—BOURGOGNE DECOUVERTE—to know they're opening a bottle for you inside.

📺 Best❷ Dijon: As Mild As Its Mustard

312km (193 miles) SE of Paris. 200km (124 miles) NE of Lyon; pop. 149,867

Yes, this is indeed the birthplace of French mustard, and if you were to describe it in culinary terms, you'd say it was a smooth city, easy on the tongue, with a kick at the end, like its prized product. Dijon is not a feisty place (not in these parts), but being at the core of a communication network linking northern Europe to the Mediterranean, it has an eclectic side that other towns in this region lack.

There is no denying it's an industrial city. Mechanical, automotive, chemical, and food industries fight for space in the outskirts; but it is also historical, with a pretty core littered with medieval and Renaissance buildings (look out for the hidden courtyards), a modern university, and decent nightlife, all within easy reach of Paris.

Dijon

WINE TASTING ●
Le Caveau de la
   Porte Guillaume **28**
Nicot Yves **8**

SIGHTSEEING ●
Auditorium Theatre **4**
Cathédrale St-Benigne **24**
Église Notre Dame **16**
Eglise St-Philibert **23**
Grand Théâtre de Dijon **12**
La Maison Millière **14**
Le Palais des Ducs et des
   Etats de Bourgogne **14**
Musée des Beaux-Arts **13**
St-Michel **10**
Théâtre National
   Dijon-Bourgogne **22**

PARTYING ★
ABC **26**
Atheneum **9**
Foch Strip **29**
L'Atmosphere
   Internationale **31**
L'Avant 2000 Café **32**
Le Carré **2**
Le Caveau
   de l'Univers **20**
Le Chat Noir **5**
Le Zenith de Dijon **3**

EATING ◆
Auger Boutique **25**
Café du Vieux Marché **17**
La Dame d'Aquitaine **19**
Le Germinal **21**
Les Deux Fontaines **7**
Maison Millière **15**
Mulot & Petitjean **18**
Pain Chaud **6**

Church ✝
Information ⓘ

SLEEPING ■
Centre de Rencontres
   Internationals de Dijon **1**
Hotel du Montchapet **30**
Hotel du Nord **27**
Hôtel Wilson **11**

If you're worried about fitting in here, think cool, and think casual. People are more likely to wear old jeans and a scraggy top than feature high-fashion threads worthy of Kate Moss and Co. They're a friendly bunch too. Look lost, and many locals will take their time to help you out.

Dijon isn't a wild party town, but there's plenty to do if you're game to hang out. Several decent bars and brasseries line **avenue Foch** (see "Bars" on p. 641), which

you'll pass on your way from the train station to the Office de Tourisme on place Darcy. For information on local happenings, ask the tourist office for a guide called ***La Chouette.*** It's written by local students from the ESC Dijon business school (www.escdijon.com) and lists their favorite haunts.

While Dijon is worth visiting in its own right, it would be sinful not to use it as a base from which to explore other sites in

Dijon History 101

The great thing about being an invading Roman is that wherever you lay your hat, armor, and toga-clad women, you can call home. So it was that Dijon— built as a fortified stronghold known as Castrum Divionense, along a military road from Lyon to Mainz—soon became home to generations of Romans traveling around the length and breadth of the country. At least when it wasn't being sacked, pillaged, or burned to the ground.

Dijon as we know it today entered the history books in 1015 when the French king Robert the Pious won it over, but a fire in 1137 destroyed practically all evidence of this era. Duke Hugues II rebuilt the city with new fortifications and 11 gates. The last, Porte Guillaume (William gate) was replaced in 1788 with the triumphal arch you can see today on place Darcy.

Next came several centuries as a dukedom. Philip the Bold inherited the duchy of Burgundy from King John the Good and turned the House of Valois into a well-organized, prosperous fiefdom. At this time, Dijon was nothing but a secondary town, bested by Beaune, which was the seat of Burgundy's parliament.

Dijon eventually came into its own under Louis XI who took away much of the dukedom's power but granted some concessions, including the preservation of the parliament, which moved from Beaune to Dijon.

The next major series of urban construction happened in the 17th and 18th centuries, when the architects Jules Hardouin-Mansart (the brainchild of Versailles) and his brother-in-law, Robert de Cotte, rebuilt the ducal palace. Other parliamentarians constructed sumptuous houses and apartments as well, which characterize the city.

The introduction of railways from the 1850s onward linked Dijon to Paris and the Mediterranean, turning it into a desirable, industrializing city. The population then doubled and Dijon became the important regional capital it remains today.

the region. Once you sort out your accommodations, grab a set of wheels or a train timetable and start exploring.

One of the prettiest towns is **Beaune,** the capital of the Burgundy wine country and one of the best-preserved medieval cities in the district, with its girdle of ramparts. If you don't mind forsaking the chance to sunbathe, November is a fine time to visit—though we recommend you invest in an umbrella. On the third weekend of the month, a boozy, 3-day wine festival takes visitors around labyrinths of wine cellars before plying them with the latest vintages. Medieval history junkies will love the picture-perfect **Abbaye de Fontenay,** one of Europe's most unspoiled

12th-century Cistercian abbeys; and then there are the wine tours. Jump on anything with wheels (within reason—shopping trolleys are definitely ruled out), line your stomach, and go on some organized winery visits—that way everyone can have a tipple.

Getting There

BY AIR

Even if your nickname is Icarus, you'll have a hard time getting off the ground in these parts. The nearest passenger airport is Lyon.

BY TRAIN

A total of 25 TGV **trains** arrive from Paris's Gare de Lyon each day. Trains arrive from

Dijon: Five Funky Facts

1. Dijon's national heritage sites encompass 97 hectares (240 acres).
2. An owl *(la chouette)* is Dijon's symbol.
3. Dijon is known as a green city, with 700 hectares (1,729 acres) of parks.
4. Mustard here is called *dijon* because in 1752 a Dijonnais (resident of Dijon), Jean Naigeon, used vinegar to replace *verjuice* (an acid made from unripe grapes that gives mustard its bite), thus creating the form of mustard we know and love today.
5. Dijon is just 200km (124 miles) from Geneva, which makes it an ideal base for visiting Switzerland.

Lyon roughly every hour. For information, check www.sncf.fr or call ☎ 36-35.

BY CAR

The best way to reach Dijon is by **driving**. From Paris, follow A6 southeast to Pouilly-en-Auxois, then go east on A38 to Dijon.

BY BUS

Skip it; catch the train if you aren't able to rent a car.

Orientation

The center of town has many pedestrian-only streets, including the main **rue de la Liberté** (with plenty of shops), which runs on a nearly east-west axis and takes you from the large square by the train station, **place Darcy**, to the **Palais des Ducs** (see "Sightseeing," below) in the center of town. The *centre ville* of Dijon is bordered by wide, tree-lined avenues: **rue du Transvaal** on the south, **boulevard de Brosses** on the north, **boulevard Carnot** and **boulevard Thiers** on the east, and **rue de l'Arquebuse** on the west. The maps of Dijon make it look deceptively easy to navigate; in fact, the streets are so old and curvy that unless you have a homing device to rival Lassie's, you'll probably get lost (and Lassie won't be there to get you out). This does makes the town fun to

cruise around. You constantly feel like you're discovering things, which makes you feel doubly proud when you start to know your way around.

Since Dijon is so small and most of the sights are on or near the pedestrian streets, buses aren't necessary unless you're staying on the outskirts of town.

Getting Around

BY BUS

Dijon has a good bus service (www.divia.fr), but unless you're flagging on your feet or staying out of the city center, you shouldn't have to use it. The main lines across the city center are 3, 4, 5, 6, and 7, which run from approximately 6am to midnight. Lines 1 to 7 also act as night buses. They pass every 20 to 45 minutes. Tickets, which can be bought onboard, cost .95€ and last for 1 hour.

BY BICYCLE

The **Office de Tourisme** rents bikes from their office on rue Darcy (see "Tourist Offices," below) for 12€ (half-day), 17€ (full day), and 50€ (3 days). Dijon is easily navigated by bicycle, but you'll make the most out of your wheels by heading out of town on the wine trail south of the city, or along

Rental Vehicles

To rent a set of wheels, call these guys:

→ **ADA** (109 jean Jaurès; ☎ **03-80-51-90-90;** www.ada.fr; Mon–Fri 8am–noon and 2–6pm, Sat 8pm–noon and 3–6pm)

→ **Allocar** (55 bis av. Jean-Jaurès; ☎ **03-80-41-44-22;** www.allocar.com; call for opening hours)

→ **Avis** (Gare SNCF, 5 av. Mar Foch; ☎ **08-20-61-16-63;** www.avis.fr; Mon–Fri 8am–12:30pm and 2–9pm, Sat 8am–12:30pm and 2–6pm, Sun 5:15–9:15pm)

→ **Europcar** (7 bis cour de la Gare; ☎ **08-21-8058-07;** www.europcar.fr; they also hire scooters)

→ **Hertz** (7 bis cour de la Gare; ☎ **03-80-53-14-00;** www.hertz.fr)

the pretty Canal de Bourgogne, in the west. Call the tourist office for more details.

ON FOOT

Walking is by far the best way to see the city, especially as there are plenty of hidden courtyards for you to discover.

Tourist Offices

You can choose between two **Offices de Tourisme.** The main one is on rue Darcy (☎ 03-80-44-11-44; May–Oct 15 daily 9am–7pm, Oct 16–Apr 30 daily 10am–6pm). The second is at 34 rue des Forges (☎ 08-92-70-05-58; daily 9am–noon and 2–6pm). They sell a series of special passes (the Dijon Pass) for discounts and free entry to some attractions (10€–20€). You can also hire a pocket PC for 3 hours, which will guide you on an hour-long walk around town and spice up your visit with cheesy prerecorded historical re-creations and library footage (ask for details and prices).

Dijon Nuts & Bolts

Emergencies Call ☎ **17** for the police. The firemen answer to ☎ **18.** Ambulances come when you call ☎ **15.**

Hospital We hope you won't need it, but there's an ER at the **Complexe du Bocage Hôpital Général C.H.U.** (1 bd. Jeanne d'Arc; ☎ **03-80-29-30-31**).

Internet/Wireless Hot Spots **Multi Rez** is a great little spot for a surf (21 cours de la Gare Routière; ☎ **03-80-42-13-89;** Mon–Sat 9am–midnight, Sun 2pm–midnight). Access costs 1€ to 4€ an hour.

Laundromats Clean your clothes near the station at **Lavomatiques Dijon** (36 rue Guillaume Tell; no phone; daily 6am–9pm).

Pharmacy **Pharmacie Darcy** is in a handy place near the tourist office (19 place Darcy; ☎ **03-80-43-49-03;** Mon–Fri 8:45am–12:30pm and 1:30–7:15pm; Sat 9am–noon and 2:30–6pm).

Post Office Find it at 15 bd de Brosse (☎ **03-80-50-61-11**).

Supermarkets For a quick food shop, you'll find **Casino** supermarkets at the following addresses: boulevard Clémenceau (north of place de la République), 30 rue d'Auxonne (off place du Président Wilson), and 35 rue Guillaume Tell (near the station).

Taxis Flag a cab in the street or call **Taxi Dijon** (29 bis rue Arquebuse; ☎ **03-80-41-41-12**).

Websites For more information about the region in English, check out **www.burgundy-tourism.com**.

Sleeping

Sleeping in central Dijon won't break the bank, but if money's tight, head out of town.

HOSTELS

→Centre de Rencontres Internationals de Dijon This is one of the cheapest places to stay, a short bus ride away, just north of the center near the university. It was built in the 1970s, consists of two four-story buildings, but makes up for lack of architectural charm with bright, spotless rooms for individual travelers and groups. Some double rooms have showers but not WCs, while some dorm-style rooms, suitable for either four or eight occupants, have neither. There's a patio, a terrace, a community swimming pool literally next door, a self-service restaurant, and a 24-hour reception desk—which means no curfew. *1 bd. Champollion.* ☎ *03-80-72-95-20. www.auberge-cri-dijon.com. 17€ bed; dorm 4–8 people: 21€ twin, 32€ single. Closed Jan. Amenities: Restaurant; Internet; parking; TV. Bus: 4 to Épiray.*

CHEAP

→Hôtel du Montchapet This is a friendly joint right by place Darcy. You can't get closer to the center of town, the tourist office, or the train station. Yes, it looks old-fashioned (the stone wall and furniture will definitely please your grandma), but the welcome is warm, the beds comfortable, and the cost low—which

is what you're looking for, *n'est-ce pas? 26 rue Jacques Cellerier.* ☎ *03-80-53-95-00. www.hotel-montchapet.com. 43€–56€ double. Breakfast 5.40€. Credit cards accepted. Amenities: Bar; free parking. In room: TV.*

DOABLE

→Hôtel du Nord Most lodgings in Burgundy have opted for "traditional charm," and eschewed anything remotely contemporary. This establishment is no exception, although it has made considerable effort to bring the bedrooms into the 21st century, with bright colors, modern furniture, and relatively funky bed covers that match the walls. The restaurant (which serves great traditional grub) and the vaulted wine bar (in the basement; see "Wine-Tasting," below) do fall into the "traditional" category, but knowing that you'll sleep in the 21st century is priceless. *Place Darcy.* ☎ *03-80-50-80-50. www.hotel-nord.fr. 85€–95€ double. Credit cards accepted. Amenities: Bar; restaurant. In room: TV, A/C, clothes press, hair dryer, Internet (Wi-Fi), minibar, safe.*

→Hôtel Wilson If you like staying in places that have soaked up several hundred years' worth of atmosphere, this one's for you. This *ancien relais de poste* (coaching inn) dates from the 17th century. Restored with cute period details, such as old fireplaces and wood ceiling beams, it's not the hippest hotel in town, but it will give you a dose of authenticity you'd be

Gingerbread Straight from the Oven

You knew that Dijon was famous for its mustard, but did you know about its gingerbread? The **Auger boutique** (16 and 61 rue de la Liberté; ☎ **03-80-30-26-28;** Sun–Tues 10am–noon and 2–7pm, Wed–Sat 9am–7pm) has been making the stuff since the 14th century. **Mulot & Petitjean** (13 place Bossuet; ☎ **03-80-30-07-10;** Mon 2–7pm, Tues–Sat 9am–noon and 2–7pm) also makes fantastic gingerbread, including a naughty grownup jam-filled variety, and crunchy *gimblettes* (gingerbread with almonds) for tea.

pressed to find elsewhere. All units have small bathrooms, each with a shower; some have tubs. *Place Wilson.* ☎ *03-80-66-82-50. www.wilson-hotel.com. 70€–91€ double. Credit cards accepted. Parking 9€. Amenities: Bar. In room: TV, Wi-Fi.*

Eating

Burgundy is known as the breadbasket of France. Not because it has bakeries galore, but because it is renowned as having some of the best food in the country. Be prepared to bust your guts in Dijon, and don't forget to sample the mustard.

CAFES & LIGHT FARE

See **Maison Millière** (p. 642) for a tea break. If you're out after hours, stop at **Pain Chaud** (7 av. Garibaldi; ☎ **03-80-73-58-27**), which serves snacks all through the night.

➜ **Havana Café** CUBAN Opposite the covered market, this Cuban-themed cafe is ideal for a quick pit stop, day or night. Wine, beer, and alcoholic and nonalcoholic cocktails (5€) are all on hand, so you can wash down your tapas, salads, or traditional steak frites before sneaking off for a peek around the market. *2 rue Claude-Ramey.* ☎ *03-80-50-05-88. Menus 10€–18€. Credit cards accepted. Mon–Sat noon–2pm; Wed and Sun 7–10:30pm; Thurs–Fri until 11pm; Sat until 11:30pm.*

CHEAP

[MTV] **Best ✿** ➜ **Le Germinal** ★ FROGS' LEGS Frogs' legs are what made French food famous, so when in Dijon, join the throngs and do your best to keep little green amphibians out of the water and on Germinal's plates. They serve them in 11 delicious sauces, but in case you can't stomach the idea, there are other regional specialties to choose from. *44 rue Monge.* ☎ *03-80-44-97-16. Fixed-price menu 11€ lunch, 18€–22€ dinner. Credit cards accepted. Daily noon–1:45pm and 7–10:15pm (until 11pm Fri–Sat). Closed Sun night.*

DOABLE

➜ **Les Deux Fontaines** ★★ TRADITIONAL FRENCH This place hardly needs introduction in Dijon. From the outside, it looks like it's going to be a decent place to dine, but once you're inside, you'll see it's fantastic. Whitewashed walls, old banquettes, and wooden tables smothered in bistro posters create a thoroughly warm and rustic backdrop for some of the best regional dishes in town. If they're on the menu, try the St-Jacques scallops—pure pleasure on a plate. *16 place de la République.* ☎ *03-80-60-86-45. Main courses 25€. Credit cards accepted. Tues–Sat noon–2pm and 7–10pm.*

SPLURGE

➜ **La Dame d'Aquitaine** ★ SOUTHWEST If you fancy some culinary adventure, this is the splurge for you. Step through a porch, and then step back in time as you cross a cobbled courtyard and head down a long, mysterious flight of steps to a groovy 13th-century vaulted dining room.

It's not every day you get to eat in such historic surroundings (check out the stained-glass windows), and it's not every day you get to try southwest cuisine in Burgundy. As the name suggests, recipes here are more at home in Bordeaux (capital of the Aquitaine region) than in Dijon, but when food is this great, who cares where it comes from? Madame *ze* Chef (Monique Salera) rules the roost, and she has a little penchant for duck, so expect a long list of duck dishes such as *magret de canard,* cooked in its skin with capers and foie gras in Armagnac jelly. If you want to spurge on the cheap, come here at lunchtime for the 21€ menu. *23 place Bossuet.* ☎ *03-80-30-45-65. www.bourgogne-restaurants.com/ladamedaquitaine. Fixed-priced lunch 21€, fixed-price evening 29€, 34€, and 42€; a la carte 38€–45€. Mon 7:15–10:30pm, Tues–Sat noon–1:30pm and 7:15–10:30pm.*

Wine-Tasting

See "Wine Tours" in "Playing Outside," below. If you haven't got time to gallivant around vineyards, head to **Le Caveau de la Porte Guillaume** in the Hôtel du Nord (place Darcy; ☎ **03-80-50-80-50;** www.hotel-nord.fr; see above) where you can sample more than 15 sorts of delicious wine from 2€ to 11€ a glass, plus plates of cold meats and cheeses. If you fancy a nightcap, ask for one of their 65 whiskeys.

For a more educational slurp, head to **Nicot Yves** (48 rue Jean-Jacques Rousseau; ☎ **03-80-73-29-88;** Mon–Fri 8am–12:30pm and 3–8pm, Sat 8am–8pm, Sun 8am–12:30pm). The owner is an oenology guru who is particularly attached to his Burgundies, and runs wine-tasting courses in the basement of the shop. He also has a breathtaking collection of whiskeys (that must come with the territory in Dijon), *cassis* liqueur, and some potent but tasty *eaux-de-vie* liquors.

Partying

A few Dijon nightclubs get moving after midnight, but if you want to hang out like a local, go on a bar crawl. It's easy to meet the resident kids—they tend to be students (many international) and seem less involved in their own scenes than the youth in bigger cities. Ask the tourist office for *la Chouette* magazine, which lists the best joints.

BARS

MTV Best ◑ →**L'Atmosphere Internationale** ★ Fancy practicing your Italian, German, or French? Then bring your booty round to this melting pot, where most of Dijon's international students meet for a beer, a boogie, or billiards on one of 12 tables. The mix is such that you could easily end up pocketing a few phone numbers before dancing the night away to lashings of R&B, Latino, techno, and house music. There's an entrance fee for some concerts and discos. *7 rue Audra.* ☎ *03-80-30-52-03. www.atmosphere-internationale.com.*

→**L'Avant 2000 Café** ★★ You can spend hours of fun here just looking at the objects on display. They all date between 1900 and 2000, and you'll be confused as to whether you should be bidding on them or just drinking the beer. It's a good spot for happy hour or some late-night bevies, and it's one of those eccentric gems you'll remember for years. *Rue de Jouvence.* ☎ *03-80-73-45-37.*

→**Le Caveau de l'Univers** Come here with your gay, lesbian, and straight friends for food and frolics in a cool laid-back atmosphere. Your ears are in for a treat too, with tunes from James Brown and other legends, as well as funky, revisited French accordion music. *47 rue Berbisey.* ☎ *03-80-30-98-29.*

M T V 🎵 Fantastic Foch Strip

Despite its nickname, The Foch Strip is not a secret burlesque ceremony performed by plebeian students desperate to get in with Dijon's "it" crowd. Nor does it pertain to the comic strips revered by almost every young person in France. The Foch Strip refers to one very boozy street that stretches from the train station to place Darcy. It's home to some of the best happy hours and beer temples in town. Starting from the Gare SNCF, head toward place Darcy and the first place you'll come across is **Le Paulaner** (no. 1; ☎ 03-80-43-57-60), a busy cafe that buzzes with students and tourists. Next up is karaoke heaven (or hell, depending on your perspective), at **Hunky Dory** (no. 5; ☎ 03-80-53-17-24), where raucous groups of friends battle it out for a slice of stardom and pizza (8€). **Café Leffe** (no. 17; ☎ 03-80-43-51-87) serves dozens of beer types and organizes silly themed parties. And **Au Bureau** (no. 20–22; ☎ 03-80-43-58-33) provides a less wild but still bustling atmosphere and good beer.

CLUBS & LIVE MUSIC VENUES

All-nighters in Dijon revolve more around bars than clubs, but there are a few places for you to shake your booty in. For inspiration, check out this list plus **www.dijon 2night.com**, which lists the latest parties (in French only).

➜ **Le Carré** ★ The only thing square about le Carré (meaning square) is its name. Three huge rooms pump out different sounds. Patrons over 30 crowd one bar, with beats from the '60s through the '90s (drinks 5€–8€). The Paradisio room is big on lighting—eerie greens and mauves—and lashings of house, R&B, and disco for youngsters with attitude (drinks 3€). The Privilège area is a brand-new VIP section where partyers of all ages mix it up (opens in 2007). A free shuttle bus runs from place Darcy and place République on Thursday and Friday nights to and from the nightclub (first bus is at midnight, then every 30 min.; last bus from the club into town is 4:45am). What more can you ask for? *19 rue Marguerite Yourcenar.* ☎ *03-80-74-09-70. www.lecarre.fr.*

➜ **Le Chat Noir** When the black cat *(chat noir)* crosses your path, you'll know you're in for a decent night—if you're under 25

that is. Sprightly young girls whip around the dance floor, shaking their tresses like they've just stepped out of a L'Oreal ad; while young lads, who look like they've only just learned how to shave, watch agog in between dance moves. Resident DJ Pascal spins some house on the first floor, while upstairs in the White Mouse room *(la Souris Blanche)* you can dig DJ Nico's post '70s nostalgia. If you're young and on the make, with eclectic taste in music, this could be your lucky night. Dress smartly, although jeans are allowed. *20 av. Garibaldi.* ☎ *03-80-73-39-57. www.lechatnoir.fr.*

Sightseeing

The best way to take in the sights is on foot: Amble, amble, and amble some more. The tourist sights in Dijon are conveniently concentrated in the old town, so you should be able to squeeze in a good few on the same day.

PUBLIC MONUMENTS

M T V **Best ✿** ➜ **La Maison Millière** Built in 1483 for the tradesman Guillaume Millière, this building has all the giveaway features of late-15th-century architecture: The stone ground floor (today a wonderful tea shop) would have housed a workman's

Soaking Up the Sound

It ain't quite Paris, but Dijon has its fair share of concert venues. Whether you want to experiment with French music, or catch your international favorites on the French leg of their world tour, **le Zenith de Dijon** (Parc de la Toison d'Or, rue de Cochide; ☎ 03-80-72-21-21; www.zenith-dijon.fr; bus: 2 and 7, stop Zenith; www.divia.fr) should be your first port of call. You can check their lineup online or in any FNAC shop (24 rue Bourg; ☎ 03-80-44-80-80). **ABC** (4 Passage Darcy; ☎ 03-80-30-98-99) is a cultural center that organizes regular shows. Whether you make friends with students from the Université de Bourgogne of not, you should go along to the **Atheneum** (esplanade Erasme, part of the uni; ☎ 03-80-39-38-20; www.atheneum.fr; bus: 5, stop Erasme) for its fantastic underground, electronic, and independent music concerts.

atelier. The upstairs overhangs the level below, displaying thick, sculpted wooden beams. Don't forget to look up to the roof, where you can see a bronze statue of Dijon's famous *chouette* (owl), after which the street is named. Once you've drunk a cup of tea here, rent the DVD of *Cyrano de Bergerac,* starring Gerard Depardieu, so you can say you've visited one of the locations in the film. *10 rue de la Chouette.* ☎ *03-80-30-99-99. www.maison-milliere.fr. Tues–Sun 10am–7pm.*

→ **Le Palais des Ducs et des Etats de Bourgogne** ★★ This former Ducal palace is one of the most historic buildings in this ancient province. Capped with an elaborate, multicolored tile roof, the complex is arranged around a trio of courtyards. The oldest section, only part of which you can visit, is the **Ancien Palais des Ducs de Bourgogne,** erected in the 12th century and rebuilt in the 14th. The newer section is the **Palais des Etats de Bourgogne,** constructed in the 17th and 18th centuries for the Burgundian parliament. Today, the palace is La Mairie (town hall); all of its newer sections and much of its older sections are reserved for the municipal government and closed to the public. However, the **Musée des Beaux-Arts** is worth a visit (see below). *Cour de Bar.*

HIGHBROW HAUNTS

Dijon's premier performance venue is the **Grand Théâtre de Dijon** (2 rue Longepierre; ☎ 03-80-60-44-44; www.leduodijon.com), which has just joined forces with the modern **Auditorium Theatre** (11 bd. Verdun; ☎ 03-80-60-44-44; www.leduodijon.com); call ahead for information on operas, operettas, dance recitals, and concerts, or check out their website. The city's second-most visible cultural venue is the **Théâtre National Dijon-Bourgogne** (rue Danton; ☎ 03-80-30-12-12; www.tdb-cdn.com). Tickets for all three theaters cost 6€ to 50€.

CHURCHES

Dijon has an overwhelming number of beautiful churches and cathedrals for such a small town, such as the stunning **Cathédrale St-Benigne** (rue Danton; ☎ 03-80-30-62-44); **Eglise St-Philibert** (closed for restoration but worth looking at from the outside); and **St-Michel** (41 rue Saumaise; ☎ 03-80-63-17-80; www.saint-michel-dijon.com). If you're short on time, head for the **Eglise Notre-Dame** ★★ (place Notre-Dame; ☎ 03-80-28-84-99; www.notre-dame-dijon.net), a block north of the enormous Palais des Ducs. Depending on the direction you're coming from, it

BURGUNDY & THE FRANCHE COMTÉ

DIJON's Hidden Courtyards

Wandering around Dijon is a bit like being on the Starship Enterprise. Like Captain Kirk and Jean-Luc Picard, you'll go where no-one has gone before— or at least feel that way. You have only to peek behind a closed door or venture down a narrow alley to see 📺 Best● **hidden courtyards** that take you by surprise and make you feel like you've happened upon something precious and undiscovered. This is a list of some of the prettiest courtyards in Dijon (some more hidden than others). The trail starts near the Palais des Ducs et des Etats de Bourgogne, so grab a map and keep your camera at the ready.

→ **Rue des Bons Enfants**   No. 4 is the Hôtel Lantin, which houses the Musée Magnin, famous for its 16th- and 17th-century art. Its courtyard will thrill you with its pretty arches.

→ **Rue Amiral Roussin**   No. 23 is the Hôtel Fyot de Mimeure, a private house that opens up its courtyard on weekends (push the porch door to get in). You'll dig the beautiful sculpted Renaissance facade. At no. 29, the privately owned **Hôtel de Bretagne** shows off a cute little courtyard with a novelty balustrade.

→ **Rue Chabot-Charny**   At no. 18, the Hôtel des Lemulier de Bressey (Chambre des Metiers) has two opposing courtyard facades: Renaissance on the rue Chabot Charny side, and Gallo-Roman on the Philippe Pot side. At no. 43–45, the **Hôtel des Barres**'s courtyard and garden (through the archway) are private but generally visible to the public.

→ **Rue Jeannin**   No. 1, **Hôtel Frémyont,** is a private mansion that kindly keeps its gates open most of the time for curious passersby who want to gawk at the arcaded facade, private garden, and well. At no. 8, **Hôtel Rolin** opens up its courtyard midweek. It has a quaint view onto the garden and an ornate entrance. On the same street, look at the courtyards at nos. 13 **(Hôtel de Frasans),** 19 **(Hôtel Pérard de la Vesvre),** and 33 **(Hôtel Arviset puis Jehannin de Chamblanc).**

→ **Rue de la Chouette**   Of all these mansions, the **Hôtel de Vogüe** at no. 8 is the pièce de resistance. Built between 1589 and 1617, it is one of the most decorative and beautiful buildings in Dijon (it inspired the design of many *hôtels particuliers,* private mansions, in the Marais in Paris. Its courtyard will wow you with its intricate stonework.

→ **Rue des Forges**   No. 34 is the **Hôtel Chambellan,** but it is also the tourist office. Once you've gathered info on what to do, admire the flamboyant courtyard (sculpted wood gallery and stunning staircase) by taking a narrow corridor from the street.

looks more like a castle or a Gothic rocket than a church. Inside, the 19th-century stained glass looks to be from the 1200s, and there are plenty of pretty statues of virgins and saints for you to feast your eyes upon. But the real intrigue is on the outside. On one of the central columns, just above eye level, is a softened stone with a little owl carving (see "Stroke of Luck at Notre-Dame," below). Near that spot, a wee salamander carved into the cathedral wall, looks like he might scurry off.

Stroke of Luck at Notre-Dame

According to legend, the architect of Dijon's Eglise Notre-Dame was a young man and a foreigner to Burgundy, and he couldn't come up with the designs necessary to please the locals. Disillusioned, he left town, but found an injured owl at the side of the road and nursed it back to health. To thank the architect, the owl spent each evening circling over typical Bourguignon buildings from which the man could draw inspiration. It worked, and he finally won the deal. Tired, the bird died, but in gratitude for his help, the architect sculpted an owl into the facade of the cathedral. It's a lie, of course; the carving appeared 300 years after the church was built; but it's a nice story, and caressing the owl with your left hand is supposed to make your dreams come true. So get stroking!

MUSEUMS

You've plenty of choices in Dijon: The **Musée Archéologique** (5 rue du Dr-Maret; (☎ **03-80-30-88-54**), has findings unearthed from Dijon's archaeological digs, housed in **L'Ancien Couvent des Bernardines** (a medieval nunnery). The former **Bernadines Monastery** (Monastère des Bernadines; 17 rue Ste-Anne; ☎ **03-80-44-12-69**), is home to two museums. The chapel holds the **Musée d'Arts Sacrés,** devoted to art from regional churches, and the cloister contains the **Musée de la Vie Bourguignonne,** which exhibits folkloric costumes, farm implements, and some 19th- and early-20th-century storefronts from Dijon's center. Admission is free to these museums. All are open Wednesday through Monday 9am to noon and 2pm to 6pm (July–Sept 9am–6pm). The **Musée Magnin** (4 rue des Bons-Enfants; ☎ **03-80-67-11-10;** admission 3€ adults, 2.30€ students; Tues–Sun 10am–noon and 2–6pm) contains an eclectic display of 19th-century antiques, paintings, and art objects that were passed on to the city of Dijon following the death of the owners' last descendant.

FREE → **Musée des Beaux-Arts** ★★
The only part of the old ducal palace that you can visit contains one of France's oldest and richest museums. It boasts exceptional sculpture, ducal kitchens from the mid-1400s (with great chimney pieces), a collection of European paintings from the 14th to the 19th centuries, and modern French paintings and sculptures. The Salle des Gardes, the banquet hall of the old palace built by Philip the Good (Philippe le Hardi), is a sight for sore eyes. The tomb of Philip the Bold, created between 1385 and 1411, is one of the best in France: A reclining figure rests on a slab of black marble, surrounded by 41 mourners. *In the Palais des Ducs et des Etats de Bourgogne, cour de Bar.* ☎ *03-80-74-52-09. Free admission. Temporary expositions cost 3€ each; free admission on Sun. Wed–Mon 10am–6pm.*

Playing Outside

HOT AIR BALLOONING

→ **Survol de Dijon en Montgolfière** ★ If you've money to burn and fancy living the high life (literally), there's no better way to see Dijon and its surroundings than by floating, suspended in the wind, inside a contraption that could deflate and plummet to the ground any second (just kidding). Hot-air ballooning has to be one of the most memorable ways for you see what that owl would have seen when flying over Burgundy; and the advantage of being a human in flight, rather than a bird, is that you can steady your legs with a bottle of local wine and some canapés (pack them yourself before you come). *Information and inscription at the tourist office, place Darcy.* ☎ *08-92-70-05-58. www. dijon-tourism.com. 250€ per person for 1½-hr. flight (up to 8 people).*

WINE TOURS

→ **Wine and Voyages** If you want to get out of town, but don't have your own transport or much time, Wine and Voyages offers two great wine tours that last between 2 and 3 hours. Both leave from in front of the tourist office at place Darcy and take you around some picturesque villages, dotted along the winding vine roads and Route des Grands Crus (vintage wine route), to the wine capital of Nuit Saint Georges. The cheaper tour (50€) provides one cellar visit, and the more expensive one (60€) takes you to two wineries. *Reserve with the tourist office or Wine and Voyages.* ☎ *03-80-61-15-15. http://wineand voyages.com. Tours 50€–60€.*

GARDENS

Every effort has gone into making Dijon as green a city as possible. That's great news if you're looking for a grassy spot upon which to rest your booty after a long day's sightseeing. One of the best parks is **Les Jardins de Ste-Anne** (access rue de Tivoli), which roll out behind the Musée de la Vie Bourguignonne and Musée de l'Art Sacré. There's plenty of grass for kicking a ball around on, and plenty of trees for a read in the shade. The **Cours du Parc** is a mile-long green expanse that leaves place Wilson and follows the Cours du Général de Gaulle to the magnificent **Parc de la Colombière**—a typical French royal park with crisscrossing alleys, smothered in trees (over 6,000). *Daily Oct–Feb 7:30am–5:30pm, Mar until 7pm, Apr–Sept until 8pm.*

Shopping

Now then, what does a cool traveler's shopping list include? Well, when in Dijon, yours may well contain robust regional wines, Dijon mustard, cheese, and the black-currant liqueur *cassis* (try a splash in champagne to make a *kir royale*). For all that, the best shopping streets are rue de la Liberté, rue du Bourg, and rue Bossuet.

FOOD, WINE & LOCAL CRAFTS

The market at **Les Halles Centrales,** rue Odebert, sells fruits, vegetables, and foodstuffs on Tuesday, Thursday, and Friday from 8am to noon, and Saturday from 8am until around 5pm. A separate endeavor that specializes in used clothing, kitchen utensils, housewares, and flea-market castoffs, **Les Marchés autour des Halles** operates along the market's periphery Tuesday and Friday from 8am to noon, and Saturday from 8am to around 5pm.

For a wicked picnic lunch, begin at *the* ultimate mustard shop MTV Best● **La Boutique Maille** ★★ (32 rue de la Liberté; ☎ **03-80-30-41-02**), where you can purchase a lifetime's supply of the many variations on the world-famous condiment. Follow this with a visit to the **Crémerie Porcheret** (18 rue Bannelier; ☎ **03-80-30-21-05**), to pick up several varieties of regional cheese, including *citeaux,* made by the brothers at a nearby monastery. Finish your journey at one of the three locations of **Mulot et Petitjean** (1 place Notre-Dame, 16 rue de la Liberté, or 13 place Bossuet; ☎ **03-80-30-07-10**), where you can pick up a pastry (especially gingerbread) for dessert.

To feed your mind rather than your belly, **Le Consortium** (16 rue Quentin; ☎ **03-80-68-45-55**; www.leconsortium. com) is one of Dijon's most interesting modern-art galleries. If you're feeling rich, you could kit yourself out with a priceless gem (of a contemporary nature, of course).

Festival

→**La Foire Internationale et Gastronomique de Dijon** This is one massive food and wine fest (end of Oct), with over 500 exhibitors all showing off their wares, which include wine, sausages, pâtés, cheeses, regional cakes, breads, mustards, and anything else you can shove down your gullet. Be proud of your gluttony and get your arse down to the Palais des Congrès and Auditorium–Congrexpo. ☎ 03-80-77-39-80. *www.dijon-expocongres. com. Bus: 4 or 7 (from the train station); descend at Palais des Congrès or Congrexpo).*

📺 Best● Beaune: Quaint, Boozy & Multicolored

316km (196 miles) SE of Paris, 39km (24 miles) SW of Dijon; pop. 22,000

The capital of the Burgundy wine country, the charming but very touristy village of Beaune makes a great stop for a few hours, though you likely won't want to spend the night here. It has all the trappings of a small tourist town—steep prices and crowded streets at peak season. But it offers plenty of wine-tasting opportunities (its Burgundy vintages are world famous), and its sites, though few, are worth visiting. Its history goes back over 2,000 years (it was a Gallic sanctuary, then a Roman town and home to the ducs de Bourgogne until the 15th c., when Louis XI annexed it in favor of Dijon), which means that there are plenty of historical buildings (like the **Hospices de Beaune** and adjacent **Hôtel-Dieu,** celebrated for its multicolored roof tiles), cobblestone streets, and a full set of medieval ramparts for you marvel at.

To get into the center from the train station, walk down the main street, avenue du 8 Septembre, which will take you straight into town just past the ramparts. For the very heart of Beaune, follow the signs to the tourist office and the Hôtel-Dieu, which will lead you through the twisty, narrow streets. These two buildings are on **place de la Halle,** the center of Beaune's action. The rest of Beaune consists mainly of small medieval buildings and old wine cellars that look out onto streets so

Beaune History 101

What was first a Gaulish center, and then a Roman station, became the dukes of Burgundy's main residence until the 15th century, when duchy power was transferred to Dijon. When the last duke of Burgundy, Charles the Bold, popped his clogs in 1477, the town refused to let Louis XI annex it and surrendered only after a 5-week siege that cut off all supplies. *Voilà,* the background to centuries of Dijon versus Beaune rivalry, which reached its peak in the 18th century, when the Dijon poet Alexis Piron (1689–1773) wrote some downright rude stuff about the people of Beaune. His works so enraged the locals that he had to be smuggled out of town to avoid being lynched by a ferocious crowd.

It is impossible to separate the history of Beaune from its most celebrated and beautiful building, l'Hôtel Dieu, built in the 15th century to house the sick and needy. Today it is a museum and a wine auction house, which comes to life every year during Les Trois Glorieuses—a 3-day wine festival (see "Three Glorious Days in Winter," below).

Three Glorious Days in Winter

Pull on your winter warmers and visit Baune on the third weekend of November, when the town comes to life for a 3-day festival and wine auction called **Les Trois Glorieuses** (meaning 3 glorious days). Wine buyers and oenophiles from the world over descend to check out the wine stalls offering *dégustations* from 15€ to 30€ for "several" glasses, each of a different wine vintage. There's also access to many spooky labyrinths of caves and wine cellars, which means that with all the free spirits (both kinds), you'll be haunting the streets both above and below ground. The auction is also known as "the greatest charity sale in the world"—an exaggerated title, if you ask me, but all the proceeds go toward modernizing medical facilities and maintaining the Hôtel Dieu.

narrow you'd swear they were pedestrian-only—until a car comes by and rolls over your toes. Look out!

Getting There

If you're **driving,** note that Beaune is a few miles from the junction of four highways—A6, A31, A36, and N6. The narrow streets, however, should make you think twice about coming by car. If Dijon is your base, you'd be better off taking the train, which leaves at least every half-hour and takes just 25 minutes. From Paris's Gare de Lyon, several TGV **trains** run per day (2 hr.). From Lyon, up to seven daily trains per day leave for Beaune (1½ hr.). For info, call ☎ **36-35.**

Tourist Office

The **Office de Tourisme** is at 6 bd. Perpreuil (☎ **03-80-26-21-30;** www.ot-beaune.fr).

Orientation & Sightseeing

Forget Disney: Cobbled, timbered, rampart-surrounded old Beaune is the real deal. It's a bite-size, chocolate-box kinda town that you can explore entirely on foot. The main architectural attraction here is the breathtaking former hospital, **Hôtel-Dieu,** to the north of which lies the **Collégiale Notre-Dame** (place du Général Leclerc; ☎ **03-80-24-53-87;** Easter to mid-Nov), an 1120

Burgundian Romanesque church that contains some remarkable tapestries illustrating scenes from the life of the Virgin Mary. Also by the Hôtel-Dieu is the quaint **place Fleury,** where you should admire the patterns on the roof of the **Hôtel de Saulx** at no. 13. Left off the avenue de la République is rue Friasse, which turns into **rue Maufoux.** Here, you'll find three breathtaking mansions that cry out to be photographed. **No. 16** shows off a stunning Renaissance-style facade with gemel windows; **no. 17,** the Hôtel du Cep, turns on the charm with some magnificent courtyards and 16th-century galleries; and **no. 33,** the Hôtel Thiroux de Saint-Félix, has another funky courtyard (Renaissance), half-timbered galleries, and sculpted stone columns. The Rampart des Dames joins rue Maufoux and should be visited for its **Tour des Dames** (tower), made from bossage-cut stone. It houses a three-story wine cellar within its 7m-thick (23-ft.) walls.

The best shopping streets are rue de Lorraine, rue d'Alsace, rue Mafoux, and place de la Madeleine. For smaller boutiques, stroll down the pedestrian rue Carnot and rue Monge.

MTV **Best ❶** → **Musée de l'Hôtel-Dieu** ★★ What were they on when they built this roof? Piety is the answer. The town's most visible antique building was built by the generous and charitable Nicolas Rolin in 1443 as a hospital for the people of Beaune; and the colorful roof (only visible from the inner courtyard) is historical proof that the 1970s were not the only era to embrace psychedelia. It thrived during the Middle Ages under an order of nuns associated with the famous vineyards of Aloxe-Corton and Meursault and functioned as a hospital until 1971. Today the museum displays Flemish-Burgundian art such as Rogier van der Weyden's amazing 1443 polyptych of *The Last Judgment;* and in the Salle des Pôvres (Room of the Poor), you'll find painted, broken-barrel, timbered vaulting and authentic hospital furnishings. Through donations and legacies over the centuries, the hospital has acquired some 63 hectares (156 acres) of vineyards, and during Les Trois Glorieuses (see "Three Glorious Days in Winter," above) wine festival, it auctions off some of its best vintages here. *Rue de l'Hôtel-Dieu.* ☎ 03-80-24-45-00. *Admission 5.60€. Apr–Nov 19 daily 9am–6:30pm; Nov 20–Mar daily 9–11:30am and 2–5:30pm.*

➜**Musée des Beaux-Arts et Musée Marey** You knew the Frères Lumières invented cinema in 1885 in Paris; well if it hadn't been for Beaune-born physiologist Etienne Jules Marey (honored in the museum), who discovered the principles of moving pictures way before the Lumières brothers, we might not have any movies nowadays at all. The musée's main attractions are rich Gallo-Roman archaeological findings; paintings from the 16th to the 19th centuries, including Flemish primitives; and pieces by Felix Ziem, a precursor of the Impressionists. *6 bd. Perpreuil (Porte Marie de Bourgogne).* ☎ *03-80-24-56-78. Admission (includes Musée du Vin de Bourgogne) 5.40€ adults, 3.50€ students and children, free for children under 12. Apr–Oct daily 9:30am–6pm. Closed Nov–Mar (except 3rd weekend in Nov).*

➜**Musée du Vin de Bourgogne** ★ The entire history of Burgundian winemaking is explained here, in the former mansion of the ducs de Bourgogne. The collection of tools, *objets d'art,* and documents is contained in 15th- and 16th-century rooms. On display in the 14th-century press house is (as you'd expect from the name) a collection of wine presses. While you're there, look out for the 16th-century statue, aptly named *The Virgin Mary with a Bunch of Grapes.* Bet you can't guess what she's holding! *Rue d'Enfer.* ☎ *03-80-24-56-78. Admission (includes Musée des Beaux-Arts et Musée Marey) 5.40€ adults, 3.50€ students. Apr–Nov daily 9:30am–6pm; Dec–Mar Wed–Mon 9:30am–6pm.*

Wine-Tasting

Roll your sleeves up and wiggle your tongue around (it needs to warm up) because Beaune has to be one of the best towns in the region for sampling and buying Burgundy wines. You can tour, taste, and buy at **Marché aux Vins** (rue Nicolas-Rolin; ☎ **03-80-25-08-20;** www.marche auxvins.com), housed in a 14th-century church. Its cellars are in and among the ancient tombs, under the floor of the church. An unusual and well-stocked competitor, selling most of the vintages of Burgundy from a 13th-century convent, is **Cordelier** (6 rue de l'Hôtel-Dieu; ☎ **03-80-25-08-85**). Burgundy's largest cellars (from the 13th, 16th, and 17th c. and over 15,000 sq. m/161,459 sq. ft.) is **Caves Patriarche Père et Fils** (7 rue du Collège; ☎ **03-80-24-53-78;** www.patriarche. com), under the former Convent of the Visitandines. **Sensation Vin** (1 rue d'Enfer; ☎ **03-80-22-17-57;** www.sensation-vin. com) offers hour-long wine-tasting lessons (12€ for 4 wines, 25€ for 8) and weekend courses. The **Vins de Bourgogne Denis-Perret** cellars (40 rue Carnot; ☎ **03-80-22-35-47;** www.denisperret.fr)

group together five major producers, offering some of the most prestigious names around, including the wine that made Madame de Pompadour a sex maniac, Romanée-Conti. And last but not least, if you fancy biking around wine trails, hire a bicycle from **Bourgogne Randonnées** (7 av. du 8 Septembre; ☎ **03-80-22-06-03;** www.bourgogne-randonees.com), from 15€ a day, and follow one of their tours into the wine country.

Sleeping

Sleeping here isn't obligatory (unless you've supped a glass too many), particularly as hotels are expensive in the town center—you have been warned.

➜ **L'Hostellerie de Bretonnière** This is the best bargain in town. It's well run, with quiet rooms, and 5 minutes on foot from the center of town. The inn was built as a postal relay station around 1900 and became a hotel in 1950. In 2004, management enlarged the hotel with the addition of a seven-unit annex in the garden, containing only duplex suites, each rustically outfitted in a style that evokes the traditions of rural Burgundy (ain't that sweet). Rooms are small, but that's fine when you're only staying overnight. *43 rue de Faubourg Bretonnière.* ☎ *03-80-22-15-77. www. hotelbretonniere.com.* 56€–100€ *double. Credit cards accepted. Amenities: Bar; free parking. In room: TV, hair dryer.*

Eating

➜ **La Grilladine** ★ BURGUNDIAN If you want to try pure Bourguignone cuisine, grab a table here. The menu reads like a regional food guide: snails, bouef bourguignon, *coq au vin,* and *oeuf meurette.* And it won't break the bank with fixed-price menus at 14€, 19€, and 27€. Unlike

most other places, smoking and nonsmoking rooms here are very separate—a definite plus. *17 rue Maujoux.* ☎ *03-80-22-22-36. http://lagrilladine.free.fr/Index.htm. Main courses 7€–18€; menus 18€–38€. Credit cards accepted. Tues–Wed 7–10pm; Thurs–Sun noon–2pm and 7–10pm.*

➜ **Le Palais des Gourmets** ★ REGIONAL TEAROOM For a naughty midday bite, you can't beat this sweet little tearoom with regional specialties such as *cassissines* (black currant jelly laced with cassis liqueur), *roulés au cointreau* (cointreau-filled pancakes), and chocolate coins depicting the Hôtel Dieu. *14 place Carnot.* ☎ *03-80-22-13-39. Main courses 4€–7€. Credit cards accepted. May–Sept daily 7am–7:30pm; Oct–Apr Wed–Mon 7am–7pm.*

Partying

To hear solid jazz, flirt with locals, and snag someone older than you, step over to the **Le Raisin de Bourgogne** (164 rte. de Dijon; ☎ 03-80-24-69-48), which fills up early with a 30-something crowd. If you're in the mood for an ale or two, try the English-style **Pickwick's Pub** (2 rue Notre-Dame; ☎ 03-80-22-55-92). For a piano bar and karaoke, why not go to **Why Not** (74 rue de Faubourg-Madeleine; ☎ 03-80-22-64-74). **Opéra-Night** (rue du Beaumarché; ☎ 03-80-24-10-11) plays booming house music and has an immense dance floor, strobe lights, and mirrors revealing every angle imaginable. A competitor is **Disco Jazz Band** (11 rte. de Seurre; ☎ 03-80-24-73-49). Both dance clubs charge a cover of up to 12€. For a funky lounge and wine bar with an ethnic influence and Internet access, pile into **Le Bout du Monde** (7 rue du Faubourg Madeleine; ☎ 03-80-24-04-52).

MTV Best✿ Abbaye de Fontenay ★★: Key to Monastic Past

8okm (50 miles) N of Dijon, 250km (155 miles) S of Paris

The Abbaye de Fontenay is one of Europe's most unspoiled 12th-century Cistercian abbeys—a must for any history-lover visiting Burgundy. You don't have to be contemplating life in the clergy to appreciate the sheer beauty and intrigue of such an edifice either. There is something immediately enchanting and calming about the place, which was declared a UNESCO-protected heritage site in 1981. You can't sleep here, but it's a good idea to take a packed lunch, as the Abbey sometime closes from noon to 2pm in the off-peak season.

Getting There

The least complicated way is by **car.** From Dijon take the A38 and then the D905 to Montbard, from where the Abbey is signposted (6km/4 miles). From Paris take the A6, exit at Bierre-les-Semur, and take the D980 towards Montbard. By **train,** TGVs from Paris to Dijon stop at Montbard (1 hr.;

2 hr. 25 min. if you take a regional train), from where you can get a taxi from place de la Gare (if none are around, call ☎ **03-80-92-31-49**). There are also several trains from Dijon to Montbard (40 min.). Call ☎ **36-35** for more information.

Sightseeing

This beauty is best toured with a guide (Apr to mid-Nov daily 10am–6pm, mid-Nov to Mar daily 10am–noon and 2–6pm; ☎ **03-80-92-15-00**; www.abbayedefontenay. com). Read our text below, though, and you'll be more prepared than a scout on holiday camp, and maybe make the other visitors look like numbskulls!

Your tour starts by the **Porter's Lodge,** the main doorway, surmounted by the abbey coat of arms. Look to the right of the gateway to the first floor, and you'll see a hole that somebody used to call home. Okay, so it was the monk-porter's guard

Abbaye de Fontenay History 101

It all started with St-Bernard, who, after becoming Abbot of Clairvaux, founded three religious communes: Trois-Fontaines in 1115 (near St-Dizier); this one, the Abbaye de Fontenay in 1118; and Foigny in Thiérache in 1121. The reason for his seemingly overzealous building was simple. When Bernard returned to Clairvaux, after having established a hermitage near Châtillon-sur-Seine, he discovered that his successor, Godefroy de la Roche, had done such a good job with recruits that the hermitage could no longer accommodate all the monks. Bernard took the surplus clerics to a secluded valley and set about building Fontenay as we see it today. The abbey became a picture of success, with over 300 monks in residence until the 16th century, when the regime of Commendam (money-grabbing abbots nominated by royal favor) brought about its decline. This, followed by religious wars, gradually led to the abandon of the abbey, until it was sold, after the Revolution, as a paper mill. In 1906 the mill came to new owners who restored it to its former, 12th-century glory. Don't forget to check out the fountains, from which the abbey takes its name; they are very beautiful, in the well-tended gardens.

dog, but even dogs need shelter. He was positioned here to keep watch over the **hostel** (long building on the right), where travelers and pilgrims stayed.

From here, you can walk to the **wayfarers' chapel** (today a library and the lapidary museum) and the **monks' bakery,** which has kept its impressive cylindrical chimney. Head farther right and you'll reach what looks like a mini-château, but is in fact a **dovecote.** The huge tower walls are over a meter (3 ft.) thick and stand as evidence that Fontenay had the right to hunt.

The **Abbey church** is one of the most ancient Cistercian churches preserved in the country. Dedicated by Pope Eugene III in 1147, it was built during the lifetime of St-Bernard (erected 1139–47) with funds from Ebrard, bishop of Norwich in England, who took shelter there. Built like a basilica, in a Latin-cross style with a plain facade, it has a nave with two aisles, a transept, a flat chevet, and seven round-headed windows symbolizing the sacraments of the church. Head to the back of the south transept and you'll find the night staircase that leads to the monks' old **dormitories.**

Comfort was far from the minds of such devout monks: Imagine sleeping on straw mattresses, on the floor, with only a low partition to screen off your snoring neighbor. But the amazing 15th-century ceiling makes up for whatever the dorm lacks in soporific qualities. Thanks to impressive hand-hewn Spanish chestnut beams, it looks more like the inside of a boat than an abbey ceiling.

On the south side of the church, you'll come to the atmospheric, Romanesque **cloisters.** On a sunny day, they provide the ultimate photo opportunity as the alternate pattern of columns and archways casts light and dark shadows on the floor like rail-tracks made of sunlight.

The **chapter-house** has wonderful quadripartite vaulting and waterleaf capitals, and communicates with the eastern cloister. The monks' main scriptorium (workroom) is here, which leads to the warming room—the only heated room in the entire complex (aside from the kitchen, which had fires).

When the monks weren't nursing chilblains or frostbite (only joking, although I wouldn't be surprised), they were out tending to their **medicinal garden,** next to the **infirmary.**

An English gardener was recently brought in to landscape the remaining gardens, and make them easier on the eye for visitors. I'm sure you'll agree the result is charming.

MTV Best ✪ Besançon ★★: Students, Citadels & Cheeses

400km (248 miles) SE of Paris, 241km (149 miles) N of Lyon, 85km (53 miles) Dijon; pop. 118,000

Don't be ashamed, there is nothing wrong with liking bourgeois settlements. For those who get their kicks from harmonious architecture, picturesque river views, fine food, and history, Besançon offers all the chic of yuppiedom without the suffocating snobbism upheld by many other French towns. Yes, the average resident is more likely to have palpitations over Mozart than P. Diddy or the Black Eyed Peas (they've probably never even heard of them), but a handful of students keep popular culture thriving, which means that you can tap into some of the hottest nightlife in the region, and maybe meet a few *kool* kids to exchange cultural notes with. And then there's France's biggest

Besançon History 101

Never talk religion or politics at a dinner party—unless you're recounting Besançon's history (which is inseparable from the Christianization of France) and want to look intelligent in front of your friends and family. Here is the fodder for that conversation: Vesontio, as Besançon was called in Roman days, was converted to Christianity by two Greek missionaries, St-Ferréol and St-Ferjeux, who were decapitated in the amphitheater when they refused to worship pagan gods. Their loss of life didn't prevent Christianity from taking root, however, and when the Emperor Constantine finally converted, Besançon became an important archbishopric. Hugh of Salins was the most significant archbishop here, when in the 11th century he played his political cards right and became second only to the emperor, giving Besançon status as an imperial city with the right to mint money and make its own laws. The St-Etienne church and St-Jean Cathedral both owe their existence to Hugh.

In the 16th century, the Granvelle family made their mark on Besançon in rags-to-riches fairy-tale style. Born as paupers, they managed to save enough money to climb a notch on the social ladder and become artisans. One worked hard enough to become a notary and send his son, Nicolas Perrenot de Granvelle, to university. Nicolas became a man of law, then parliamentary advisor, and finally the chancellor to Charles V. As was customary for such a powerful man, he built a huge house, le Palais Granvelle (contains the Musée du Temps; see p. 659), still visible today.

Strangely, Besançon fell to Spanish rule in 1657, when it was traded (unbeknown to its inhabitants) for Frankenthal in Germany. Louis XIV decided that he wanted it back and led a successful siege with Vauban (brainchild of the Citadelle), and named Besançon capital of the Franche Comté—a title that remains today. God save the Sun King!

rock festival, **Les Eurockéennes,** which takes place an hour away from Besançon, in Belfort. Swarming with international rock stars and French pop bigwigs, it's mandatory for anybody who's ever switched on MTV.

Geographically speaking, Besançon is a gem. Snuggled in the almost perfect ox-bow meander of the River Doubs (pronounced *Doo*), it looks cut off from the rest of the world. It's shadowed by an enormous rocky outcrop, upon which you'll find the town's pride and joy—the citadel, built by the architect Vauban for Louis XIV. Virtually a city in itself, it contains several museums, an aquarium, the largest insectarium in France, a mini-zoo, and a little farm.

The year 2007 is a big one for Besançon. It will be celebrating the tercentenary of Vauban's death by hooking up with 14 other fortified towns built by Vauban, in an attempt to become a UNESCO-protected site. It's great news for you guys, as you might get to take part in the celebrations, including shows and special exhibitions.

Once you've exhausted Besançon's treasures and nightlife, jump in a car and head east to Ronchamp, an old mining town with a must-see church built by Le Corbusier.

Getting There

BY AIR

You could fly to Mulhouse/Bale airport (140km/87 miles away; ☎ 03-89-90-31-11) or even to Geneva in Switzerland (160km/ 99 miles away; ☎ 00-41-22-717-71-11), but you'll still need to hire a car, which will undoubtedly increase cost.

BY TRAIN

The main station is **Gare Viotte,** just beyond the Battant quarter (15-min. walk into the old town). There are frequent TGVs from Paris's Gare de Lyon to Besaçon (2¹/₂–3 hr.) and from Dijon to Besançon (1 hr). Call ☎ **36-35** for more info or consult **www.sncf.com.**

BY CAR

A car is not the most practical thing to be saddled with in the largely pedestrian-only historic center. If you do drive in, take the A39 from Dijon then join the A36 and exit at the 4th junction (Besançon St-Claude). After the roundabout, take the N57 to the town center. From Paris take the A6, then the A31 towards Besançon and Nuits St-Georges, followed by the A36/E60 and, as with Dijon, the N57 into Besançon. Free parking is found at place Battant and place Rivotte; pay parking is near the town hall (Mairie), and at the Parking des Beaux Arts.

BY BUS

Trust me. Take the train.

Orientation

You know me—a sucker for tourist trains. Whether you like them or not, there is no denying that when in Besançon, the brightly colored *train touristique* (leaves from **rue Rivotte** at the foot of the Citadel) is the best way for you to get your bearings, and check out the sights that you'd like to revisit and explore later. Whether you swallow your pride and jump on, or explore the town on foot, the key to staying oriented is to remember that the old town lies inside the ox-bow bend at the foot of the Citadelle. Many streets are restricted to pedestrians (although you should still keep your eyes peeled for stray scooters); and shops and restaurants are mostly found on the **Grande Rue** near the bridges and on the other side of the river in the **Battant** quarter.

Getting Around

BY PUBLIC TRANSPORTATION

Besançon does have a bus service, but you shouldn't have to use it, unless you want to hurry between the train station Viotte and the tourist office, or you've booked a night at the youth hostel (take line 5). Line 10 is a practical central line, which leaves in front of the station and stops right by place de 1ère Armée Française (get off at Délavette). Tickets are sold on board and last for 1 hour (1.10€). For more information, check out **www.ginkobus.com.**

BY BICYCLE

→**Association de la Roue de Sécours** You'd better get here early as there are only 10 bikes available, and this is the only place to rent one in town (apart from the Auberge de Jeunesse, which has three others, whoopee!). You'll be required to leave a 45€ deposit, but then a bike is yours for just 2€ a day. *34 rue Arènes.* ☎ *03-81-83-13-28. Mon–Fri 10am–noon and 2–6pm.*

Tourist Offices

The **Office de Tourisme et des Congrès** is at 2 place de la 1ère Armée Française (☎ **03-81-80-92-55;** www.besancon-tourisme.com). Open November to March Monday to Saturday 9am to noon and 1:30pm to 5:30pm (from 10am Mon); Sunday 10:30am to 12:30pm. In April, May, and October, Monday to Saturday 9:30am to 6pm (from 10am Mon), Sunday 10:30am to 12:30pm; June to September Monday to Saturday 9:30am to 7pm (from 10am Mon), Sunday 10am to 5pm.

Besançon Nuts & Bolts

Emergencies   Ambulance ☎ **15**, police ☎ **17**, fire/paramedic service ☎ **18**. For other emergencies, call **SOS Médecins** (☎ **08-10-41-20-20**).

Internet/Wireless Hot Spots   Besançon is somewhat of a late bloomer when it comes to the Internet. **ID-PC** has at least caught on and offers Internet connections in the town center for 3€ an hour (28 rue République; ☎ **03-81-81-26-25**; Tues–Sat 9:30am–noon and 4–7pm).

Laundromats   The most central place to breath fresh life into your togs is **Salon Lavoir** (54 rue Battant; ☎ **06-71-64-06-15**; Mon–Sat 8am–7pm). Entry is secure, so you'll need to swipe your credit card in order to gain access. From 4€ a wash and 1€ a dry (10 min.).

Pharmacies   A central store for all your drug needs is **Pharmacie de la Poste** (20 rue de la République; ☎ **03-81-81-32-69**; Mon–Fri 9am–12:15pm and 2–7pm, Sat 9am–12:15pm).

Post Office   5 place du 8 Septembre is where you'll find **La Poste.**

Taxis   Give **Radio Telephone** a call on ☎ **03-81-88-80-80.**

Vehicle Rental   **ACB-Location** is a local firm (place Bacchus; ☎ **03-81-81-52-23**; Mon–Fri 8:30am–6:30pm, Sat 9am–6pm). Then there are the usual culprits: **Europcar** (2 av. de la Paix; ☎ **03-81-80-33-39/08-21-80-58-08**; www.europcar.com) and **Hertz** (1 rue Edouard Belin; ☎ **03-81-41-99-29**; www.hertz.fr).

Websites   **www.besac.com** lists all the latest cultural events (in French only).

Sleeping

Imagine waking up in the middle of a historic town surrounded by water, rolling out of bed, and sauntering around picturesque streets. Well that, my dears, is Besançon! If you really want to treat yourself, try to get a room in the center of town. If not, head out for budget options.

HOSTELS

➜**Auberge de Jeunesse les Oiseaux** ★ As with many hostels, staying here necessitates a short bus ride (from the Gare Viotte take line 5, toward Orchamps; get off at Les Oiseaux), but the journey's worth it. Rooms are simple but comfortable: Think whitewashed walls, real duvets on beds, individual WC, and shower. If you're there between October and June, you can take advantage of regular concerts and art

exhibitions—an homage to art appreciated by the many young creative types who stay here. So if you see an artist in your future, don't be shy, and ask a fellow visitor for a game of tennis or a jog around the park. This could be your lucky stay. *48 rue des Cras.* ☎ *03-81-40-32-00. ljt@lesoiseaux àyahoo.fr. 23€ single 1st night, then 18€ consequent nights; 37€ double 1st night, then 31€; 52€ triple 1st night, then 47€. Rates include breakfast. Credit cards accepted. Amenities: 1€ bike hire; canteen; free Internet; free sheets; park; tennis courts.*

CHEAP

➜**Hôtel du Nord** It is hard to believe that the decor in this place was ever in fashion. But in the east of France, sometime during the 1970s, it must have been; it's the only plausible explanation. But let's not linger on shortcomings. Here is a list of reasons to stay at the Hôtel du Nord: price, location, price, location, and did I mention price and location? *8 rue Moncey.* ☎ *03-81-81-34-56. www.hotel-du-nord-besancon.com. 36€–58€ double. Credit cards accepted. Amenities: Bar; parking. In room: TV.*

DOABLE

→ **Charles Quint Hotel** ★★ Goodness gracious me, somebody here has taste. The antique furniture is stylish, yet a light contemporary feel reigns. Rooms are big, with pale walls and views over either the cathedral or the luscious green garden and courtyard out back. Charm leaks from every nook and cranny, and if you can't quite justify a splurge at the Castan (see below), there's no greater place for your money than here. *3 rue du Chapitre.* ☎ *03-81-82-05-49. www.guidesdecharme.com. 82€–125€ double. Credit cards accepted. Breakfast 10€ In room: TV, Internet modem access.*

SPLURGE

→ **Hôtel Castan** ★ If you like play-acting, and want to pretend you're Marie Antoinette, King Louis, or Napoleon, this is the most ostentatious place you could choose in Besançon. It would make the perfect film set for any period movie spanning the Revolution to the 19th century. The Versailles suite is a dream, with duck-egg blue walls, parquet flooring, a floral canapé over the bed, and a marble fountain in the bathroom. Even the standard bedrooms, like the gorgeous Victor Hugo chamber (a 19th-c. room reproduced to perfection), are so lovely you might never want to leave. The hotel looks out onto the gorgeous Square Castan with its Roman columns, breakfast is of the highest order, and staff members are as smiley as they are kind. If you're gonna spend, spend it here. *6 Sq. Castan.* ☎ *03-81-83-01-02. www. hotelcastan.fr. 110€–170€ double. Credit cards accepted. In room: TV.*

Eating

Yum yum, pig's bum, apple pie, and chewing gum! There's food a-plenty here for you epicureans out there.

COFFEE BARS & LIGHT FARE

→ **Baud** PATISSERIE You don't have to be bored to go to Baud (pronounced "bored," ha ha)—you just have to be hungry. This Besançon *patissier* is famous for its sticky delights (cakes, pastries, and ice cream) and takeout dishes. The terrace is a great spot to wind down in—which is unfortunately common knowledge, so be prepared to queue for a table. You won't *regret rien! 4 Grande Rue.* ☎ *03-81-81-20-12. Tues 2–7pm; Wed–Sat 7:30am–noon and 2–6pm.*

CHEAP

→ **La Boîte à Crêpes** ★★ CREPERIE Far from the cries of the Atlantic and Brittany, come here to sample pancakes galore, both sweet and savory, in one of the cheapest eateries in town. Individual crepes (pancakes) go for as little as 2.75€, and the fixed-price menus from 6.10€ to 16€. Needless to say it's popular with students, who keep the atmosphere cheery and sometimes hire out the medieval cellar for parties. *6 rue Ronchaux.* ☎ *03-81-81-38-99. www.laboitea crepes.fr. Menus 6.10€–16€. Credit cards accepted. Mon 6:30pm–midnight; Tues–Sat 11:30am–2pm and 6.30pm–midnight.*

DOABLE

→ **Le Cavalier Rouge** ★ BURGUNDIAN Plain red walls, wooden tables and chairs, and discreet but funky stained-glass windows of horses (made by local artist Amélie Jost), lend a trendy, almost urban edge to this locals' haunt. Food is regional with a twist, depending upon what's in the market that day. There's always a decent glass of wine to make your cheeks shine. *3 rue Mégevand.* ☎ *03-81-83-41-02. Fixed menus 20€, 25€, and 28€. Credit cards accepted. Mon noon–2pm; Tues–Sat noon–2pm and 7–10pm.*

Nightlife at a Glance

The terrace of **Brasserie Rive Gauche** (2 quai Vauban; ☎ 03-81-61-99-57), which overlooks the tranquil waters of the Doubs, is a cool place to start the evening. To drink, eat, and lose track of time, the clock-themed **Le Balancier** (10 min. from the center at 45 av. Clémenceau; ☎ 03-81-53-67) will keep you ticking until 2am. If you like odd-shaped balls, watch rugby matches with fellow fans at the **Kings Park Café** (4 rue des Boucheries; ☎ 03-81-81-29-09). A hip mixed-aged crowd with a penchant for live music, booze, and cow udders (yes, look at the light fittings), pile into the basement of **La Cremerie** (8 rue Claude Pouillet; ☎ 03-81-83-55-00). For untamed karaoke, themed parties, and cheap beer head to **Cactus** (79 rue des Granges; ☎ 03-81-82-01-18). For some serious head-banging, the **Asylum** (18 rue Pasteur; no phone) will thrash your ears with punk-rock, heavy metal, and hard-core.

SPLURGE

➜**Le Chaland** BURGUNDIAN Put on your tailcoat and sea legs, for La Chaland is a classy, pre-war boat, moored on the River Doubs. It affords wonderful riverside views amid irresistibly kitschy yet refined furnishings. Dine here and you'll be joining the likes of Jacques Chirac, Jonny Halladay, and Claude Lelouche, to mention but a few fans. Food is surprisingly contemporary, drawing on traditional dishes and reworking them into modern delicacies. Reservations recommended. *Promenade Micaud near pont Brégille.* ☎ *03-81-80-61-61. www.chaland.com. Fixed-price menus 30€–60€. Credit cards accepted. Daily noon–2pm and 7–10pm (closed Sat lunch).*

Partying

Being a student town, Besançon has plenty of collegiate-type hangouts. But the grownups like to have their share of fun too, so you can party into the wee hours here, whatever your age.

BARS

Most fun happens in bars, many of which hold cheesy themed-nights, which make for a raucous evening. It's best to discover what the theme is before you get there.

📺 Best ✪ ➜**Le Cousty** ★ Who cares if the interior looks like a tatty wood cabin. This place ain't about the decor, it's about having a good time—something you are guaranteed when the locals turn up the heat. Le Cousty has been around forever. The parents of some of the kids here used to come in their heyday, which gives the joint a warm, generational feel that you'll appreciate whether you're homesick or not. When the music and the liquor start flowing, one thing is sure—it's best that mummy and daddy can't see you now. You'll be dancing on the tables like the rest of them, or jumping fully clothed into the inflatable paddling pool they occasionally bring in for really special occasions. *21 rue de Dole.* ☎ *03-81-52-49-94. www.cousty.com.*

➜**Le Pop Hall** ★★ What an atmosphere, what a legend (the decor is made entirely from recycled material), what the hell is that student wearing? Yes, le Pop Hall could go in the Besançon hall of fame for being one of the freakiest bars in town. "Bar" is, of course, the loose term used to describe what is essentially a DIY nightclub, depending on when the punters decide to invade the dance floor. Several themed evenings are organized each month, making this a second home to many an alcoholic university student. *6 rue Proudhon.* ☎ *03-81-83-01-90.*

CLUBS & LIVE MUSIC VENUES

→ **Astoria** You are so fickle! One minute you want house, the next retro pop, and then some '80s rock. Lucky you came to this three-in-one nightclub, where three different dance floors pump out three different sounds. In true sexist style, some evenings are free for the ladies. You, gentlemen, will have to cough up at least 6€, but you do get one free drink for your money. *10 chemin de Mazagran (opposite the tunnel routier de la Citadelle).* ☎ *03-81-51-40-05. www.maribeloisirs.com.*

Sightseeing

If the nightlife hasn't killed your capacity to appreciate non-alcohol-related beauty (nothing's ever as good looking the next day, eh!), you're in for some doozies. Besançon has a fascinating history as a religious hub, a clockmaking center, and a regional capital, which provides numerous sightseeing opportunities.

PUBLIC MONUMENTS

MTV (Best ♥) → **La Porte Noire** Almost all of France was Romanized, but not all that much remains. But Besançon has a surprising number of vestiges, including this one—a Roman triumphal arch, built in the 2nd century, and undoubtedly called the "Black Gate" because of its dark finish. You can still make out some of the sculptures, which were restored in the 19th century, but many have weathered beyond recognition. The nearby place Castan also houses a row of columns that were once part of a nymphaeum, and the remains of the old aqueduct.

→ **Palais Granvelle** ★ Built between 1534 and 1542, this place is pure eye candy. Only one part of the palace, the Musée du Temps (see "Museums," below) can be visited; the rest, including its stately Renaissance facade and grand courtyard, have to be admired from outside. But you can still stroll through the Promenade Granvelle, the palace's shaded gardens, and imagine they are yours.

CHURCHES

→ **Cathédrale St-Jean** ★ The legacy of Archbishop Hugh (mostly built in the 12th c.) is dedicated to St. John the Baptist, and has the distinction of having two apses. The bell tower collapsed in 1729, damaging the Saint-Suaire apse (left of the entrance), so both were rebuilt in the 18th century. If you appreciate religious works, don't miss the Van Loos in the Saint-Suaire area, or Bartolomeo's *Virgin Mary with Saints* in the south aisle. The cathedral is great, but the cherry on the cake has to be the **MTV** Best ♥ **Horloge Astronomique** (astronomical clock) on the bell tower. A work of art, a stroke of genius—call this marvel of mechanics what you will. Built between 1857 and 1860 by A-L Vérité, it comprises 3,000 components, indicates the days and the seasons, the time in 16 places around the world, the tides in eight ports, and the movement of the planets around the sun. Try to get here on the hour to see this awe-inspiring machine chime. *2 rue Chapitre.* ☎ *33-3-81-81-12-76. Guided tours Apr–Sept Wed–Sun 9:50, 10:50, 11:50am, 2:50, 3:50, 4:50, and 5:50pm; Oct–Mar Thurs–Sun at the same times.*

Museums

→ **Musée des Beaux Arts et d'Archéologie** ★ The building—an old grain hall, extended in the 1970s by Louis Miquel (a disciple of Le Corbusier)—is attention-grabbing in itself, but you should still step inside for the collections. Many come from the Granvelle family. There's a fascinating Egyptian section, with a sarcophagus that contains the mummy of Seramon, a display on local finds such as Gallo-Roman mosaics, some

Citadelle & Its Musées

First it was a Roman temple. Then a church dedicated to St-Stephen stood in its place, until the French conquest in 1674, when Vauban tore down everything to built the fortress you see today. The citadel served as army barracks, a military academy, and even a prison, before becoming this cultural metropolis, which attracts thousands of visitors each year.

The **bastions and watch-paths** that run all around the fortress provide the best views—a breathtaking panorama (especially at sunset) over Besançon, the Doubs River, and its surrounding hillsides. At one end lies the **Parc Zoologique**—a vast park containing big cats, monkeys, endangered birds, and a little farm where you can pet goats and sheep. The animals are well cared for, but if you don't like seeing them locked up, you could skip this part of the visit.

The **Musée Comtois** takes up two whole buildings with exhibits on local arts and crafts and Franche Comté folklore; the **Espace Vauban** provides an interesting insight into Vauban's life and Louis XIV's military history. The natural history museum, **le Musée de Besançon,** is great for both little and big kids (that's you), with an **Insectarium** containing spiders, scorpions, and roaches (not for the faint-hearted), and a **Noctarium,** where you can observe nocturnal cuties such as mice and rats. Upstairs there is an **astronomy and meteorology** section and downstairs an **Aquarium,** which imitates the course of the River Doubs and the type of fish found there (trout, perch, carp). A less jovial, but fascinating section is the **Musée de la Résistance et de la Déportation,** which recounts the birth and rise of Nazism, the German occupation of France under the Vichy Régime, and the Liberation. Don't forget to glance at the **Poteaux des Fusillés,** posts that were erected in memory of the French Resistance members killed during the war. ☎ 03-81-87-83-33. www.citadelle.com. Admission 7.80€. Apr–Oct daily; Nov–Mar Wed–Mon. See website for hours.

wonderful art by big-name painters (Bellini, Cranach, and Jacobs), and a relief model of Besançon before the clock tower in the cathedral fell down. 1 place de la Révolution. ☎ 03-81-87.80.49. www.besancon.fr. Wed–Mon 9:30am–noon and 2–6pm. Admission 5€.

➔ **Musée du Temps** Besançon was the mother city of clockmaking from 1793 until the 1920s. This unique museum is a tribute to the craft, with displays on clocks, watches, tools, and techniques used by the industry from the 16th century to today's nano-era. It might not be top of your list, but it's a great way to see the inside of the Palais Granvelle. 96 Grande Rue, Palais Granvelle. ☎ 03-81-87-81-50. www.besancon.fr. May 2–Sept 30 Wed–Sun 1–7pm; Oct 1–late Apr 1–6pm.

A SPECIAL TOUR

There is something magical about the Doubs: the way it meanders around the old town, tickling the quaysides, reflecting the buildings and hillsides in its rippled, silvery stream. You can't help but feel recharged by it all, which makes the 📺 (Best●) boat trips ★ along the river one of the best ways to see the town and relax. Two companies rule the waves: **Bateaux de Besançon** (☎ 03-81-68-13-25; www.sautdudoubs.fr; departure from pont de la République; times vary), which runs all year; and **Vedettes Panoramique** (☎ 03-81-68-05-34; www.vedettes-panoramiques.com; departs from pont de la République; times vary) in July and August.

Playing Outside

In France, the Franche Comté is the region with the most forests. Most of Besançon is surrounded by trees, for a start, so it's no surprise to learn that there's plenty of fun to be had outdoors. Once you've wandered around the **Citadelle's parks,** the **Parc Micaud,** between the pont de la République and pont Bregile, makes for a panoramic stroll along the Doubs. If you feel like reenacting Robin Hood, the dense **Forêt de Chailluz** is a prime spot for robbing the rich, picnicking, or rambling (ask tourist office for details).

Shopping

Wealthy residents mean one thing—shops! Besançon is not a shopaholic's mecca, but it does have ways of making you spend.

CLOTHING & ACCESSORIES

→ **Studio 54** Hipsters of the world, unite! This is where the trendies prowl for urban chic brands such as Homecore, Diesel, and Lady Saoul. Brand rebels will also appreciate the more unknown (for now at least) collections of clothes and shoes. Whether you're a girl or a boy, rich or poor, something in here wants you to buy it. *3 rue Proudhon.* ☎ *03-81-83-04-73.*

MUSIC, BOOKS & MEDIA

→ **L'Occase d'Oncle Tom** When is a nerd not a nerd? When he's at Uncle Tom's, of course. Tom will sell you secondhand CDs, vinyls, and cartoon strips (BDs). Or trade some of your old CDs, vinyls, and cartoon strips against something you really want from his shop. *33 rue Bersot.* ☎ *03-81-61-99-04. Tues–Sat 10am–noon and 1–7pm.*

FOOD, WINE & LOCAL CRAFTS

🅜🅣🅥 (Best♥) →**La Cave aux Fromages** ★ If mice went shopping, they would come here to buy their cheese. If fermented milk gets you salivating, you will be spoiled by the choices at this regional supermarket. For carnivores,

---

ᴍᴛᴠ🅤 Les Eurockéennes

If you're funky and you know it, clap your hands! Then get down to Belfort for the trendiest music festival in France. 🅜🅥 (Best♥) **Les Eurockéennes** (www.eurockeennes.fr) is all about three things: a stage, musical artists from around the world, and thousands and thousands of fans who live like hermits for three days, surfing the crowds and gulping beer to the rhythm of their favorite rock tunes. "But it's in a small French province," you cry. That may well be, but it hasn't stopped the likes of The Strokes, Deftones, Atmosphere, Depeche Mode, and Daft Punk from taking the stage. The setting is dreamlike too. Set right in the middle of a lake, surrounded by fields and forests, it has a sort of New Age hippie appeal about it. The best of nature meets the best of sound, man. Pack a tent and pitch early. Camping is free but there are only 12,000 places. There's a free bus from the campsite to the show ground. The year 2007 promises to be as great as ever, with 3 days of top acts from June 29 to July 1. Advance tickets 36€ to 90€; day of 45€ to 99€ from any FNAC (☎ **08-92-68-36-22;** www.fnac.com), or via www.ticketnet.com.

Getting There: The easiest way is by **train** to Belfort (or Montbeliard). From Paris, trains run direct from Gare de l'Est (4 hr.) and from Gare de Lyon via Besançon (4 hr. 10 min.). From Besançon the journey by TGV takes just an hour. From several major towns in France, **buses** are provided by New East (☎ **08-20-90-06-06;** www.neweastfestival.com).

there are also strings of pink, plump sausages, and sweet lovers can try the various packets of local biscuits. If you can't make it into the shop or want to check out what you can buy before you go in, see their extensive website. *2 rue Gustave Courbet.* ☎ *03-81-81-01-25. www.besac.com/lacaveaux fromages. Mon–Sat 7:45am–12:15pm and 2:30–7:30pm; Sun 10am–12:15pm.*

FESTIVALS

→**Festival International de Musique de Besançon** ★ It has been around forever (well, at least since 1948), celebrating Besançon's favorite highbrow pastime— classical music. Each year in September, orchestras from around the country pluck, blow, and hammer like they've never done before, while young conductors fight for the title of (you got it) Best Young Conductor. On that note, I should mention that 2007 celebrates the 60th anniversary of this festival, so you should expect some extra fun for your money. *Tickets are sold at FNAC (www. fnac.com).* ☎ *08-92-68-36-22 or 03-81-82-08-72. www.festival-besancon.com.*

MTV Best● Ronchamp: Le Corbusier's Masterpiece

Once the pits have closed, former mining towns rarely make the headlines—unless your name is Ronchamp. Three years before the last mine closed in 1958, a Swiss architect let his imagination rip on a hillside overlooking the town. The architect just so happened to be **Le Corbusier** (p. 438), and his imagination created one of the world's most figurative religious edifices in modern history.

→**Notre-Dame du Haut** Le Corbusier's church, made entirely out of concrete, was intended to become a "place of silence, peace, and inner joy." Ronchamp has been on a pilgrimage route since the Middle Ages, so after bombs destroyed its chapel dedicated to the Virgin Mary, in 1944, the locals decided it was time to rebuild it once and for all. From the outside, it looks like some sort of surreal ship—a block that is all angles and curves, in dazzling white and gray. From the inside, the windows become the central focus. Deep set, with colored glass, they cast an eerie haze over the congregational seating area. The altar too is disturbingly *brut*—a square slab, lit up by a funnel of daylight, offset by rough, troglodytic walls. You really should spend an hour here. Compared to the wonderful, yet sometimes repetitive architecture of France's Gothic, medieval, and Renaissance churches, Le Corbusier's chapel will blow your mind. *Association Oeuvre Notre-Dame du Haut, Ronchamp.* ☎ *03-84-20-65-13. www.chapellederonchamp.com. Apr 1– Sept 30 9:30am–6:30pm; Oct 1–Mar 31 10am– 5pm; Nov–Feb 10am–4pm. Admission 2€ adults, 1.50€ students.*

GETTING THERE

By **car** from Paris, take the A4 highway, then the N104 towards Marne la Vallée, followed by the A5 toward Troyes. Toward Troys take the A31 towards Mulhouse, exit at junction 7, and follow the N19 to Ronchamp (4½ hr.). From Besançon take the N57 to the A36 highway and follow signs to Belfort. Take exit 12 and continue along the D47 into Befort, from where you should take the N19 to Ronchamp. **Trains** run from Besançon to Ronchamp via Belfort (2 hr.). Paris's Gare de l'Est trains go via Vesoul and take 4 to 5 hours. Call ☎ **36-35.**

Tourist Office

The **Office de Tourisme** is at 14 place du 14 juillet (☎ **03-84-63-50-82;** www.ron champ.net).

The Champagne Region

by *Anna Brooke*

A fish is to water as a Frenchman is to his bubbly: More than 300 million bottles a year are consumed within France's hexagonal borders alone. And the contents of every batch began life as a grape amid the rolling hills of the Champagne region. (If it ain't from here, it ain't champagne; it's fool's gold, no matter how much it sparkles.) The low-slung, gently trestled vines of pinot noir, pinot meunier, and chardonnay grape plants that hug the chalky soil of Champagne are a testimony to the years of toil and dedication that produce this drink more commonly associated with living for the moment: fruit of a centuries-old love affair between the land, the table, and those who drink at it.

It's hard slog being a winegrower, but it's also highly lucrative; you won't fail to notice that the Champenois folk aren't short of a centime or two. But don't expect to encounter the sort of flashy wealth often associated with bubbly; that image is misleading. Your average wine lord in these parts is far more likely to adorn the gentle knolls of his well-groomed landscape with a modest country home or unassuming

Champagne

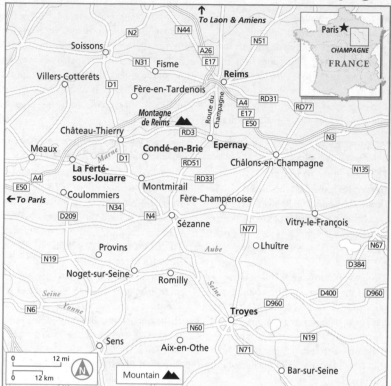

Champagne is a sleepy, deep-green region touching the eastern edge of the Ile-de-France (p. 130).

château than to invite international stars to a diamante palace for an orgy in a champagne-spewing fountain.

Champagne is a sleepy, deep-green region touching the eastern edge of the Ile-de-France (p. 130). It's a prime destination for anyone wishing to swap the hubbub of Paris for some bucolic and (let's face it) boozy sightseeing. The historical towns of **Reims** and **Epernay** are home to the world-renowned champagne houses, great for an informative tipple. A handful of students stoke a flirty nightlife (the liveliest in the region), but don't expect wild hysteria. With a keen

eye and some guidance, you'll find ways to let loose, but something in the air makes partying here tamer than it is farther east, in places like Nancy or Strasbourg.

Reims eats, sleeps, and breathes champagne. Once you've downed enough bubbles to float a submarine, the magnificent Notre-Dame cathedral (a Gothic beauty used for the coronation of every French king since the 9th c.), a handful of museums, and swank restaurants will help you pass the time until the train leaves.

Epernay is best discovered as a day trip from Reims or Paris. Its main street, avenue de Champagne, is a veritable Sunset Boulevard of champagne production. From the outside, big, 19th-century châteaux line the road. On the inside, steps lead deep underground to champagne cellars that twist and turn their chalky expanses into endless tunnels (p. 677).

If nature calls after so many hours in champagne cellars (I mean the outdoors, not your bladder), rent a car and head for the **Forêt d'Orient** (p. 689), with its lakes and nature trails near Troyes. Or follow the champagne trail (see "Reims" on p. 665 or "What's All the Fizz About?" on p. 675) across meadows and over streams into the heart of the vineyard country. It's beautiful and peaceful—and the ultimate way for you to get a flavor of life as it's lived in Champagne.

The Best of the Champagne Region

○ **The Best Place to Imitate a Gothic Gargoyle:** Look up at the **Notre-Dame Cathedral,** in Reims, and decide which stone monster looks most like you. No, not the smiling angel—the one with the devil's eyes, ha ha ha! See p. 673.

○ **The Best Champagne House History:** One of the world's very first filmed publicity stunts, for **Mercier** (now in Epernay), involved a champagne barrel so big that houses had to be knocked down for it to pass through the street. And that's not the half of it. See p. 678.

○ **The Best Place for Stained Glass and Sausages (Troyes):** You're right—they really don't go together: One cuts your gums to pieces and the other won't keep the rain out. But you'll find them both in abundance in **Troyes.** See p. 681.

○ **The Best Boogie Parlor (Reims):** Mirror, mirror, on the wall, which club is the best of all? **Le Soa,** of course—a cool basement venue with lashings of house, R&B, and disco. See p. 672.

○ **The Best Religious Edifice that Isn't the Cathedral (Reims):** It's not every day you can see the tomb of a real saint. In the **Basilique St-Rémi** lies—you guessed it—Saint Rémi, who baptized Clovis and started a fetish for coronations in the cathedral. See p. 673.

○ **The Best Place to Get High on Bubbles (Reims):** In the capital of French champagne, you can't get more anachronistic than **Maison de Pommery,** an Elizabethan English–style champagne house. But the buildings are impressive, and the champagne's not half bad. See p. 675.

○ **The Best Place to Eat Your Last (Reims):** To guarantee your place in chocolate heaven, you have to suffer death by chocolate. If Reims is to be your last stop on earth, hurry to **La Petite Friande** and *RIP* open the wrappers. See p. 676.

○ **The Best Place to Admire Fauvist Paintings (Troyes):** For art lovers, the **Musée d'Art Moderne** is a reason in itself to visit Troyes: an Episcopal palace with hundreds of paintings by big names such as Matisse, Roussel, and Modigliani. See p. 688.

○ **The Best *Andouillette* (Troyes):** Follow your nose and you're bound to end up at **Au Jardin Gourmand,** where the most unromantic of sausages is served in the most romantic of courtyards. See p. 685.

○ **The Best** *Pause-Café* **by the Cathedral (Troyes):** Di Marco is easily the greatest newspaper illustrator France has ever known. The **Petit Café du Musée Di Marco,** attached to a tiny museum on his work, serves great coffee and sells funky black-and-white postcards of his drawings. The view of the cathedral is pretty cool from here, too. See p. 685.

○ **The Best Wow-Factor from Stained Glass (Troyes):** I know the **Cathédrale St-Pierre-et-St-Paul** is yet another cathedral, but you must come to admire the 16th-century windows. Bold and colorful, they look brand new, even abstract, and way ahead of their time. Look out for the "Mystical Wine Press," which gruesomely depicts Jesus's blood being squeezed out by a press and turned into wine. See p. 688.

○ **The Best Nerd Haunt for a Quirky Present (Troyes):** For a pittance, take home the car of your dreams—in your pocket, at **Auto-Stradale,** a vintage toy-car shop. See p. 689.

Getting Around the Region

Is it a bird? Is it a plane? No, it's definitely a bird. Getting to Champagne by air is impossible. (Paris has the closest airport.) That leaves you with two choices: rail or road. If you opt for the high-speed TGVs, trains leave from Paris all day and take just 1½ hours to both Reims and Troyes—although thanks to a new high-speed line around the east of France, Reims to Paris will take just 45 minutes from June 2007 (www.tgvesteuropeen.com). Epernay is just a 40-minute train ride away from Reims. Note that you can't actually get from Reims to Troyes by rail without passing via Paris. The region's main *autoroute* is the A26 from Calais (then the A5 for Troyes) and the A4 from Paris, which cuts through Champagne towards Alsace.

Reims: Bursting the Bubble

140 NE of Paris, 30km (19 miles) N of Epernay, 130km (81 miles) N of Troyes; pop. 191,000

The city of Reims (pronounced *rahns*) isn't quite as effervescent as the stuff it's famous for. The graying buildings in the city center, many from the 1950s (Reims was heavily bombed in World War I and World War II), lend a stern edge to an otherwise stately array of architecture. Once you've toured the champagne cellars (**Mumm, Tattinger, Pommery, Piper-Heidsieck,** and **Veuve Clicquot** are all here; see p. 674), you probably won't want to spend more than a day sightseeing. But if you've got the budget, this is a fine place in which to free your inner epicurean. A handful of posh restaurants and ritzy bars make ideal distractions for anyone wishing to fly the highlife. And if your finances are more grounded, you can join the swarms of students who keep the local beer industry alive and kicking in cheaper pubs. For all-nighters, Reims has the reputation of having the best clubs in

Reims History 101

Reims has changed hands more times than it has had hot dinners. First up were the Romans, who stole it from the Rème tribe when Julius Caesar decided to conquer the whole of Gaul. The only remnants of this era are the ruined arches of the **Porte Mars** (roman gate; see p. 672), north of the center.

The city was Christianized in the 3rd century, before Attila the Hun burned it to the ground in the mid–5th century. It was rebuilt just in time for Clovis (founder of the French nation; see p. 750) to be baptized in the cathedral by St-Rémi, the Bishop of Reims, in A.D. 498. According to legend, Clovis was anointed with oil sent from heaven (the holy ampula) by a white dove. For centuries, this episode became the symbol French monarchs used to claim the divine right to rule.

After a futile invasion in the late 14th century, the English finally got their sticky mitts on the city when Isabeau de Bavière's polemical **Treaty of Troyes** (p. 681) handed it to them on a silver platter in 1420. But the occupation was to be short-lived as Joan of Arc escorted Charles VII to the cathedral for coronation in 1429, kissing the silly man's feet and reinstating Reims to the French.

During the Prussian invasions of the 1870s, Reims became the HQ of the German Governor General. It was then heavily bombed during World War I and World War II, but it was here on August 7, 1945, that General Eisenhower and the Allies received the unconditional surrender of the Wehrmacht, putting and end to World War II and Nazi domination.

Champagne (though between you and me, they couldn't blow the top off the partyometer). If you're dead set on getting jiggy here, tell yourself there's nothing in life that champagne can't fix, and drink some. It'll see you through at least until morning.

Once you've explored the cellars, tasted the wines, and had several bottles giftwrapped, you may wonder where to head next. If you're short on time, the absolute must-see is the magnificent **Cathédrale de Notre-Dame,** adorned with its famous smiling angels. The culture-thirsty will also dig the **Basilique St-Rémi, Musée de Beaux Arts, Palais du Tau, Ancien Collège des Jésuites,** and the **Salle de Reddition.** And you can't pass by without sampling one of Reims's famous desserts— a pink, finger-shaped cookie called a *biscuit de Reims* (best enjoyed dunked in champagne) or a champagne-filled, corkshaped chocolate. Did I say "or"? To hell with that—scoff both.

Talk of the Town

Five Words of Champenois

So your French is a little rusty, but you don't want to blow your cover? Here are five words so specific to the Champagne region that most other French people won't even know what you're talking about.

1. *Arganer* (pronounced Arganneh): to work

2. *Argoter* (pronounced Argotteh): to work badly

3. *Banette* (pronounced Banet): a free-hanging woman's apron

4. *Bibi* (pronounced Bibi, as it reads): a piece of cork that supports the bottles

5. *Cossier* (pronounced Coziaye): a wine producer (a person)

Reims

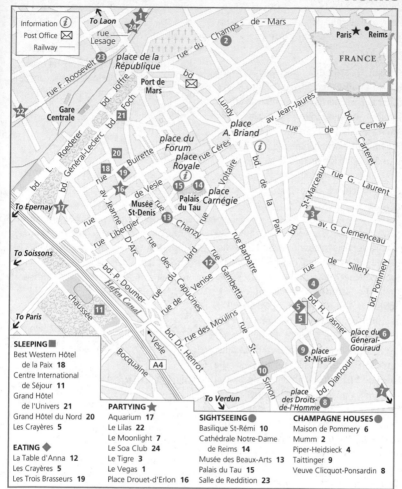

SLEEPING ■
Best Western Hôtel
  de la Paix **18**
Centre International
  de Séjour **11**
Grand Hôtel
  de l'Univers **21**
Grand Hôtel du Nord **20**
Les Crayères **5**

EATING ◆
La Table d'Anna **12**
Les Crayères **5**
Les Trois Brasseurs **19**

PARTYING ★
Aquarium **17**
Le Lilas **22**
Le Moonlight **7**
Le Soa Club **24**
Le Tigre **3**
Le Vegas **1**
Place Drouet-d'Erlon **16**

SIGHTSEEING ●
Basilique St-Rémi **10**
Cathédrale Notre-Dame
  de Reims **14**
Musée des Beaux-Arts **13**
Palais du Tau **15**
Salle de Reddition **23**

CHAMPAGNE HOUSES ●
Maison de Pommery **6**
Mumm **2**
Piper-Heidsieck **4**
Taittinger **9**
Veuve Clicquot-Ponsardin **8**

One great day trip from Reims is Epernay. There you'll find **Moët & Chandon** and **Mercier** champagne houses, which easily offer the best tours in France—and yet more opportunities for going underground.

If you're traveling by car, or if you fancy cycling or hiking, don't miss the **Montagne de Reims champagne trail** (p. 680). This forested plateau around Epernay and Reims affords the best way to take in the beauty of the vine-studded region around the main towns.

Getting There

BY TRAIN

Train is by far the best way to get to Reims. This will be especially true in June 2007 when the new high-speed line opens, dramatically reducing travel time in the east of France. From Paris, trains depart from

Gare de l'Est roughly every 1'/₂ hours, and about five arrive from Strasbourg daily. There are regular departures from Reims to Epernay. For info, call ☎ 36-35.

BY CAR

By road, take the A4 highway (toward Marne La Vallée/Metz) from Paris to Reims (1'/₂ hr.). For Epernay, turn off the A4 at junction 21 and follow the signposts. Finding a parking lot in the center can be difficult, but most champagne houses have limited parking for visitors. Once the tour is over, look out for the blue-and-white P signs, which indicate public parking lots.

Orientation

As far as cities go, Reims isn't huge, so walking between attractions isn't a hassle. Most of the champagne houses (Pommery, Piper-Heidsieck, Taittinger, and Veuve Cliquot-Ponsardin) sit near **place St-Niçaise** and **place Général Gouraud** in the south, which means you won't have far to stagger between visits. Mumm champagne, with its must-see Foujita Chapel, sets itself apart in the north near the **Hôtel de Ville.** The main shopping district is around the Notre-Dame Cathedral, so you can spend and repent to your heart's desire. Nearby streets to sin in are the long **rue Vesle,** the **cours Langlet,** and **place Druot d'Erlon,** with the largest concentration of bars and restaurants in the city. The fine arts museum (Musée des Beaux-Arts), Palais du Tau, and several other attractions also lie around the cathedral.

Getting Around

BY BUS

Unless you stay in the youth hostel, you shouldn't have to hop on a bus. But then again, this is Champagne, and your arms are probably numb from slogging around bottles. If so, it's good to know that two useful lines slice through the city center to the station: Line A and Line F (get off at Gare SNCF). Line K gets you to the hostel from the Gare (see "Hostels," below). Tickets are sold onboard for .90€ one-way. Their offices are at 6 rue Chanzy (☎ 03-26-88-25-38; www.tur.fr; stop: Théâtre). Print a map from the website or ask the tourist office.

BY BICYCLE

Reims is not a haven for cyclists, given that roads can get jam-packed with car traffic. But if you're short on time or have a death wish, **Centre International de Séjour** (p. 669) can rent you a bike. **Chausée Bocquaine** (☎ 03-26-40-52-60) charges 10€ for a half-day, 15€ a day, 20€ a weekend, plus a 76€ deposit or your passport. Open daily 8am to 11pm.

ON FOOT

One of the best ways to see the town is to follow the tourist office's audio-guided tours (see below).

Tourist Offices

No one here knows you, so who cares if you've got a giant audio guide stuck to your face? You'll learn all about the cathedral and the Palais de Tau, plus you'll burn a few calories on the 6km (4-mile) "discover Reims" street tour. Prices range from 5€ to 19€. Stop by the **Office de Tourisme** at 2 rue Guillaume-de-Machault (☎ 03-26-77-45-25; www.reims-tourisme.fr).

Reims Nuts & Bolts

Emergencies Dial ☎ **17** for the police, ☎ **18** for the fire service, and ☎ **15** for the SAMU (ambulance service).

Internet/Wireless Hot Spots Reims's only cybercafe is **Clique et Croque,** 27 rue de Vesle, passage du Commerce; ☎ 03-26-86-93-92; www.cliqueetcroque.com; Mon–Sat 10am–midnight, Sun 2–8pm; 4€ per hour or .07€ per min.).

Post Office Lick a few stamps at **La Poste,** 8 place Drouet d'Erlon; Mon noon–7pm, Tues–Fri 10am–7pm, Sat 10am–5pm).

Taxis If you sip one glass too many call **Les Taxis de Reims** (Cours de la Gare, bd. Joffre; ☎ 03-26-47-05-05; open 24/7) or **Les Nouveaux Taxis de la Marne** (20 rue Jacquart; ☎ 03-26-02-15-02; open 24/7).

Useful Websites A handy supplement to the tourist office is **www.reims.fr**. For more information on champagne trails, consult **www.tourisme-en-champagne. com**, and **www.lemonocle.com** is a mini-guide to the trendiest bars and clubs in Reims.

Vehicle Rental Give **Europcar** a buzz on (☎ 08-25-35-83-58; www.europcar. com). They're at 76 bd. Lundy. The pickup point is a 10-minute walk from the Gare SNCF.

Sleeping

In case all that champagne starts making you sleepy, you'll find plenty of hotels in Reims.

HOSTELS

➜ **Centre International de Séjour** The cheapest joint in Reims—surprise, surprise—is out of the city center. But it compensates for its remote location by being in a park and by not imposing curfews. The hostel is quite bland but offers some single rooms (some with individual bathrooms), and all prices include breakfast and sheets. This is also the only place in Reims where you can rent bikes (see "By Bicycle," above). From the Gare SNCF, catch bus line K toward Croix Rouge and get off at Comédie. *Chaussée Bocquaine, Parc Léo Lagrange.* ☎ *03-26-40-52-60. www.cis-reims.com. 15€– 18€ dormitory; 23€–31€ individual room. Credit cards accepted.*

CHEAP

➜ **Grand Hôtel du Nord** Once a 19th-century relay station for the postal service, this hotel has newly renovated guest rooms with high ceilings and contemporary decor. The hotel lies in a great spot in a pedestrian-only zone in Reims's historic core, a 10-minute walk from the cathedral and steps from the rail station. In true archaic French fashion, all but five rooms have showers; the rest have tub/shower combos. Two steps from the entrance, place Drouet-d'Erlon has plenty of boutiques, cafes, and bars. The hotel is also near the Basilica and other museums. *75 place Drouet-d'Erlon.* ☎ *03-26-47-39-03. www.hotelreims.com. 55€–59€ double. Credit cards accepted. Parking 5€. Amenities: Some nonsmoking rooms. In room: TV, dataport, hair dryer.*

DOABLE

➜ **Best Western Hôtel de la Paix** It might be part of a chain, between the train station and the cathedral, but it's the only modern hotel in France with its own medieval chapel (built for Benedictine nuns in the 1200s) overlooking its garden and pool. Rooms are unremarkable, in simple contemporary style with sterile furnishings, but they are clean, tidy, and air-conditioned. The hotel's Taverne de Maître Kanter (☎ **03-26-47-00-45**) serves top tucker daily at lunch and dinner. Expect regional delights such as sauerkrauts, fish, grills, oysters, and casseroles. *9 rue Buirette.* ☎ *800/528-1234 in the U.S. and Canada, or 03-26-40-04-08. www.best western-lapaix-reims.com. 95€–120€ double. Credit cards accepted. Amenities: Restaurant; bar; outdoor pool; parking 10€; some nonsmoking rooms. In room: A/C, TV, beverage maker, dataport, hair dryer, minibar.*

➜**Grand Hôtel de l'Univers** The decor here is rather plain, rooms are small, and some rooms don't have showers. However, it is in the heart of town, across from the train station, and you can start your day with breakfast in the American-style piano bar, where an automated piano plays melodies whenever you press a button (reason alone to stay here for a certain sort of traveler). *41 bd. Foch.* ☎ *03-26-88-68-08. www.hotel-univers-reims.com. 68€–72€ double. Credit cards accepted. Amenities: Restaurant; bar; laundry service; limited-mobility rooms. In room: TV, dataport, hair dryer, minibar, safe.*

SPLURGE

➜**Les Crayères** ★ There is no better place to stay or dine than here—one of the finest châteaux in eastern France. This is your chance to grab your Guccis or Pradas (even the fakes—if you sleep here no one will guess they're not real) and dress up like there's no tomorrow. Imagine that you are lord of the 5.6-hectare (14-acre) park, before commenting on the merits of staying in a château of this caliber, with its 5.5m (18-ft.) ceilings, paneling, and luxurious furnishings. The guest rooms, with terraces and all the trimmings, are the stuff of country-manor magazines, and they're usually available when a champagne mogul isn't in residence. Leave space in your bag for the deluxe toiletries in the bathrooms, and fill up on gourmet grub in Reims's best restaurant (see "Eating," below). *64 bd. Henri-Vasnier.* ☎ *03-26-82-80-80. www.lescrayeres.com. 275€–475€ double; 390€–475€ suite. Credit cards accepted. Closed Dec 20–Jan 11. Amenities: 4 restaurants; bar; babysitting; dry cleaning; laundry service; limited-mobility rooms; limited room service; nonsmoking rooms; tennis court. In room: A/C, dataport, hair dryer, minibar, safe.*

Eating

Whether or not champagne's involved, eating in Reims can be an expensive affair. But it's also an affair to remember. *Bon appétit!*

CAFES & LIGHT FARE

Whether you want to pop your pants or grab a light bite, **place Drouet-d'Erlon** offers everything a starving tourist could desire. Just steer clear of menus labeled *menu touristique* unless you want to join coachloads of fellow tourists and get ripped off.

CHEAP

➜**Les 3 Brasseurs** ★★ REGIONAL CUISINE When you've gotten sick of champagne and canapés, beeline to this beer temple, and beef out on heavy, soul-satisfying staples of *Flammekueches* (a pizza-like specialty from Alsace), sauerkraut, and *steak frites*. There's something distinctly Germanic about the whole experience, from the decor down to the six beers home-brewed in the restaurant. The cheap prices and great atmosphere have made it a favorite hangout for students. They sell their own beers, glasses, and T-shirts from

Dʀɪɴᴋ Pɪɴᴋ!

When you order champagne in Reims, you might be handed a pink, finger-shaped naughty known as a *biscuit rose de Reims*. These cookies date from medieval times (Joan of Arc reportedly offered a few to Charles VII), when bakers, not wishing to waste the heat in their ovens, invented a cake that would cook slowly, at a low temperature. The word *biscuit* comes from this period, as the cookies had to be twice *(bis)* baked *(cuit)*, to ensure that they were hard on the outside and fluffy in the middle. They're made from eggs, sugar, flour, and vanilla, plus natural red food colorant called *carmin* (or cochineal), which was added to disguise the black speckles left behind by the vanilla, giving them their rosy hue. It is French custom to dip them in champagne, so get dunkin'! To buy some, go to **La Maison Fossier** (see "Shopping," below).

an on-site boutique (if you can call a cubbyhole in the wall a boutique). *73 place Drouet d'Erlon.* ☎ *03-26-47-86-28. www.les3 brasseurs-reims.com. Fixed menus 12€ lunch, 15–17€ all day. Credit cards accepted. Daily 11:45am–midnight.*

DOABLE

→**La Table d'Anna** FRENCH If you're looking for something a little fancy that won't break the bank, try this cutesy resto overlooking Reims's music school. The menu depends on what's in the local market, but you should expect artistically presented dishes like calf's liver pan-fried with apples, or Reims's ham in a mustard and grape sauce. Puddings are typically French (think apple pie and crème brûlée) and delicious, and the wine list looks out beyond the horizons of Champagne with some excellent Bordeaux and Bourgogne (Burgundy) bottles. *6 rue Gambetta.* ☎ *03-26-89-12-12. www.latableanna.com. Fixed menus 13€ lunch, and 19€, 28€, and 37€ evening. Credit cards accepted. Tues–Sat noon–2:30pm and 7–10pm; Sun lunch.*

SPLURGE

Ⓜ️ Best ☻ →**Les Crayères** ★ MODERN FRENCH No restaurant in the champagne country equals this one. And as if that weren't recommendation enough, the

hyper-upscale *maison bourgeoise* (aka mini-château) is to die for too (see "Sleeping," above). The cuisine here has always been a magnet for champagne barons in the area, so put on your glad rags if you want to fit in. Chef and culinary artist Thierry Voisin's cuisine is sublime. What's more, he's part of a new cooking movement among young French chefs that is trying to renew France's reputation on the world food scene (p. 99). If it's on the menu, begin your repast with a ravioli stuffed with escargots or the celestial *trilogie*—that is, three different preparations of foie gras, including one presented *au naturel*. Follow up with wild turbot and grilled lobster or the earthy roast duck with honey vinegar sauce. Are you salivating yet? You should be! *64 bd. Henri-Vasnier.* ☎ *03-26-82-80-80. Reservations required a few days in advance for weekday dinners, at least a month in advance for weekend dinners. Fixed-price menu (including red bordeaux and champagne) 210€. Credit cards accepted. Daily 12:15–2pm and 7:15–10pm.*

Partying

Reims has the most vibrant nightlife in the region, and the best place to start is **place Drouet-d'Erlon,** where you'll find a string of clubs and **bars.** This is a university town after all, so when the champagne tycoons aren't looking, chase the students to the best venues or follow our lowdown.

For a beer and a heavy dose of noise and rowdy students, head to the **Glue Pot** (no. 49; ☎ **03-26-47-36-46**). At **Au Bureau** (no. 80; ☎ **03-26-40-33-06**), a mixed-age crowd congregates in an Irish-style pub that has more than 120 types of beer. In the exotic **Au Lion de Belfort** (no. 37; ☎ **03-26-47-48-17**), stuffed heads of hippos, elephants, and the like keep watch. On a warm evening, head to the biggest terrace in Reims at **Le Gaulois** (no. 2; ☎ **03-26-47-35-76**). For some funky sound, choose **Le Royalty**'s DJ nights or themed parties (no. 67; ☎ **03-26-88-52-88**) and for somewhere swish, grab a cocktail at **L'Apostrophe** (no. 59; ☎ **03-26-79-19-89**); I highly recommend the strawberry daiquiri and *coco shake vanille*.

Other places to try include the **Aquarium** (93 bd. Général-Leclerc; ☎ **03-26-47-34-29**), which attracts a mixed-age crowd of students and 25- to 40-year-olds. **Le Tigre** (2 bis av. Georges-Clemenceau; ☎ **03-26-82-64-00**) is a fun venue decorated with old French cars placed like artwork against the brick walls and mirrors. **Le Moonlight** (4 rue Cerisaie; ☎ **03-26-85-32-11**), a 1,200-sq.-m (12,917-sq.-ft.) mega-discothèque near the canal, churns out techno, house music, and French golden oldies. And if you have a mocking eye and want a serious laugh, **Le Vegas** (19 rue Lesage; ☎ **03-26-84-93-13**; www.levegas.fr; tickets 39€–44€) is Reims's poor take on a Paris cabaret, complete with ventriloquists, magicians, and 50-year-old voyeurs with their wives. Everybody wears jeans in these clubs and, unless otherwise mentioned, the cover is usually 9€ to 12€.

➔ **Le Lilas** ★ Hey, everybody, *lesbifriends!* Here in this heteroclite bar for homosexuals, the crowd tends to be young, hip, and boozy; the music varied and loud (there's a bar and a dance floor); the decor kitschy (think naked statues, flowery banquettes, and glittery tables); and the overall experience oodles of fun. Don't forget to try the house cocktail, **le Lilas**; it's made with vodka and tastes like jelly beans. Drinks cost 8€. *75 rue des Courcelles.* ☎ *03-26-47-02-81.*

🅜 ⓑ Best ❤ ⒻⓇⒺⒺ ➔ **Le Soa Club** ★ This is a pretty hip place as far as Reims goes. In fact it has almost enough glitter to convince you you're not in the provinces. Deep in the basement, resident DJ Tom Rich gets the walls vibrating to a palatable mix of house and R&B, while pretty young Champenois folk wiggle away on the dance floor or flirt like crazy in smooth, concave, '70s-style chairs. On Thursday nights, it's free entry and happy hour until closing. The rest of the time, you get in free before 1am. After 1am 12€, including 1 drink. *15 rue Lesage.* ☎ *03-26-40-34-35. www.soaclub.com.*

Sightseeing

As you've probably realized by now, Reims's main attractions are the gorgeous Gothic spires of the Cathédrale Nôtre-Dame and the mossy cellars of the many champagne houses. After an awe-inspiring, if not spiritual, spin around the cathedral, a visit to one of Reims's champagne houses should bring you back to more worldly pleasures (or perhaps you should drink and then get spiritual). Just about all the houses have English-language tours of their cellars, but only some feature a complimentary tasting at the end of the tour.

MONUMENTS

➔ **Porte Mars** If it wasn't for these vestiges in the north of town, built to honor the emperor Augustus, you could easily forget that Reims was once an important Roman city. The arches date from before the 3rd century A.D. but were incorporated into the city's medieval defenses before they disappeared in the 18th century. If you've 20/20 vision, see if you can make out the sculptures under each arch. They are supposed to represent Jupiter, Leda, and Romulus and Remus (the founders of Rome), but they may as well be your uncle Jack with no clothes on, for all you can see of them. From here, take nearby **rue de Mars** and gaze at the fantastic champagne-themed mosaic at no. 6.

CHURCHES

MTV **Best ◕** **FREE** → **Basilique St-Rémi** ★★ You'd do best to visit this church (Reims's oldest, dating from 1007) before the cathedral, so this one doesn't disappoint by comparison. Less dramatic than the cathedral, it is no less lovely; it just doesn't have the same wow-factor. It is an example of classic medieval French masonry, and the complex houses the former royal abbey of St-Rémi, who was the guardian of the holy ampula used to anoint the kings of France (p. 666). The abbey now functions as a museum, with an extensive collection covering the history of Reims, regional archaeology, and military history. Architect Louis Duroché designed the majestic ornamental front of the main quadrangle and the Grand Staircase (1778), where you can see a portrait of the young Louis XV looking debonair in his coronation robes. The church also contains a Romanesque nave leading to a magnificent choir crowned with pointed arches. The nave, the transepts, one of the towers, and the aisles date from the 11th century. The portal of the south transept is in early-16th-century Flamboyant Gothic style, and some of the stained glass in the apse is from the 13th century. Don't miss the tomb of St. Rémi. It looks stunning dolled up in elaborately carved Renaissance figures and columns. *53 rue St-Simon. Basilique* ☏ *03-26-85-31-20. Free admission. Daily 8am–7pm. Musée* ☏ *03-26-85-23-36. Admission 3€ adults. Mon–Fri 2–6:30pm; Sat–Sun 2–7pm.*

MTV **Best ◕** **FREE** → **Cathédrale Notre-Dame de Reims** ★ Following Clovis's baptism here by St-Rémi in A.D. 498, all the kings of France—from Louis the Pious in 815 to Charles X in 1825—were crowned in this beautiful cathedral. It was painstakingly restored by contributions from John D. Rockefeller after World War I bombs almost wiped it off the face of the earth (it escaped World War II relatively unharmed). It is laden with amazing statuettes of smiling angels. If you like stained glass, you'll also love its three western facade portals. A rose window above the central portal is dedicated to the Virgin. The right portal portrays the Apocalypse and the Last Judgment, and the left, martyrs and saints. *Place du Cardinal-Luçon.* ☏ *03-26-47-81-79. Free admission. Daily 7:30am–7:30pm.*

MUSEUMS

FREE → **Ancien Collège des Jésuites** ★ This is a great place to visit if you can fit it in. Founded in 1606 when Henry IV granted the Jesuits authorization to build a chapel, it was used as a hospital in the 18th century. A 300-year-old vine (brought from Palestine by one of the Jesuit fathers) still bears fruit. The grand *refectoire* (refectory) is full of wonderful 17th-century wooden carvings, there is a pretty Renaissance-style staircase that leads to an old library containing over 18,000 books that were evacuated to Paris during World War I, and the underground cellar and Gallo-Roman gallery (12th c.) is a feast for the eyes. One of the wings houses the town's planetarium. *1 place Museux.* ☏ *03-26-35-34-70. Mon–Fri 2–6pm. The planetarium follows the same opening times but has a charge (call for details).*

→ **Musée des Beaux-Arts** You may not have come to Reims to look at German princes, but this fine provincial gallery contains more than a dozen portraits of them by both "the Elder" and "the Younger" Cranach. Housed in the 18th-century buildings belonging to the old Abbaye St-Denis, they're not the only highlights either. You can see the *toiles peintes* (light painting on rough linen) that date from the 15th and 16th centuries and depict the *Passion du Christ* and *Vengeance du Christ*. Paintings and furniture from the 17th and 18th centuries are in the salles Diancourt and Jamot-Neveux, and there's an excellent series of 27 tree-shaded walks by Corot. *8 rue Chanzy. ☎ 03-26-47-28-44. Admission 3€ adults, free for students; free to all 1st Sun of the month. Wed–Mon 10am–noon and 2–6pm. Closed Jan 1, May 1, July 14, Nov 1 and 11, and Dec 25.*

→**Palais du Tau** Built in 1690 as the residence of the bishops of Reims, this stone mansion beside the cathedral contains many statues that, until recently, decorated the cathedral facade. (The ones there now are mostly copies.) Also on display are holy relics associated with Reims, including a 12th-century chalice for the communion of French monarchs and a talisman supposedly containing a relic of the True Cross that Charlemagne is said to have worn. *Place du Cardinal-Luçon. ☎ 03-26-47-81-79. Admission 6.10€ adults, 4.10€ students and ages 18–25. May–Sept Tues–Sun 9:30am–6pm;*

Oct–Apr Tues–Sun 9:30am–12:30pm and 2–5:30pm.

📺 Best ☻ →**Salle de Reddition** There's not that much to see, but everyone should pass by such a historical spot at least once in their lifetime. On May 7, 1945, the Germans surrendered to General Eisenhower in this structure, which was once a schoolhouse near the railroad tracks. Maps of the rail routes line the walls of the rooms, exactly as they did on the day of surrender. *12 rue Franklin-D-Roosevelt. ☎ 03-26-47-84-19. Admission 3€. Wed–Mon 10am–noon and 2–6pm. Closed May 1 and July 14.*

CHAMPAGNE CELLARS

Champagne cellars can be dangerous places in Reims. Just because there aren't any monsters or ghosts doesn't mean that you shouldn't watch your step. *Some* cellars are so huge (up to 28km/17 miles long) that you could easily go down and never resurface. During the German siege of 1914 and throughout the war, people lived and even published a daily paper in them, so who knows what still lies down there. The cellars are open year-round, but are most interesting during the fall grape harvest. After that, the wine is fermented in vats in the caves, then bottled with a small

The chapel that champers Built

Choose friends wisely: You need a doctor for when you're ill, a lawyer for when they sue you, and an artist for when you need to design a champagne label and build a chapel. In 1964, the president of Mumm champagnes, Réné Lalou, invited his friend, Japanese painter Leonard Foujita, to create the famous Rose de Champagne, which adorns Mumm's champagne bottles today. Then he commissioned him to build and design the walls of the **Chapel of Notre-Dame de la Paix** (33 rue du Champ de Mars; ☎ **03-26-40-06-96**; admission 3€; May–Oct Thurs–Tues 2–6pm; closed bank holidays) in the Mumm gardens. The result—a tiny, Roman-style church with intricate frescoes of blue, gold, green, and yellow—is a credit to Foujita's name, and all the more impressive when you think that he was 80 when he painted them. In 1966, Lalou gave the chapel to the city of Reims, and it's now one of the most visited sights in town.

What's All the Fizz About?

The love of that effervescent mystery called champagne is nothing new. During the Renaissance, the only thing François I of France and Henry VIII of England could agree on was a preference for bubbly. Napoleon carted cases of the stuff to his battlefronts. Casanova used it to liven up his seductions, Mme de Pompadour employed it to tempt the Sun King, and Talleyrand imported cases of it to the Congress of Vienna for a different sort of seduction—procuring more favorable peace terms.

But without a complicated series of additives, double fermentations, cooling at precise temperatures, and turnings and twistings, champagne would be plain old table wine. We should all raise our glasses to Dom Pérignon (1638–1715), the Benedictine monk who initiated the technique of adding sugar and yeast to the still wine, causing it, after years of fermentation, to foam.

The best champagne grapes grow in vineyards that meander like narrow ribbons along the bottomlands south of Reims. French vintners consider the best regions the Côte des Blancs, Montagne de Reims, and Vallée de la Marne; these are also the names of the three *Routes du Champagne*—signposted wine roads extending through the area.

By law, only sparkling wine made in France's Champagne region deserves the term champagne. Bubbly made elsewhere is technically sparkling wine produced by the *méthode champenoise*. In the U.S., each state has its own laws about this—in one state you can call your bubbly champagne, while in another you cannot. But don't try that in France—you'll face lengthy litigation. Just ask Yves St-Laurent, who once had the effrontery to name a perfume *Champagne*.

---

amount of sugar and natural yeast. The yeast feeds on the sugar and causes a second fermentation, which produces those fabulous bubbles. The winegrowers wait until the sparkle has "taken" before they remove the bottles to racks or pulpits. For about 3 months, *remueurs* (migrant workers) turn them every day on "riddling desks," which brings the impurities (dead yeast cells and other matter) toward the cork. Eventually the sediments are removed, and the wine receives its proper dosage of sugar, depending on the desired sweetness. The process takes 4 or 5 years and takes place in caves that are 30m (98 ft.) deep, where the temperature is a constant 50°F (10°C).

MTV **Best** ❧ → **Maison de Pommery**
Madame Pommery was one of those rare French people to love the English—well, at least their architecture. To make sure that her cellars stood out from the crowd, she built them in an Elizabethan-English style, complete with gardens. An eerie 116-step stairway leads to a maze of galleries dug into the chalk (linking 120 chalk mines used in the Gallo Roman period); the complex is more than 18km (11 miles) long and 30m (98 ft.) below ground. Various stages of champagne-making are demonstrated—fermentation and riddling desks—and the end product is for sale in the gift shop. *Place du Général-Gouraud.* ☎ *03-26-61-62-55. www.pommery.com. Admission 7.50€. Reservations required. Daily 9:30am–7pm.*

→ **Mumm** Mumm's tour doesn't bubble with energy, but you do get to try a few glasses at the end (that's the reason you came here, *n'est-ce pas?*). The gardens contain the wonderful Foujita Chapel (see

"The Chapel that Champers Built," above). It all starts with an educational but yawn-inducing video on champagne production. They further dull your senses with an in-house museum exhibiting casks and illustrating the ancient role of the vintner, before they revive you with a guided tour in a labyrinth of tunnels and storage cellars in the chalky bedrock. If you had a euro for every bottle down there, you'd be set for a couple lifetimes—there are 25 million of them. *34 rue du Champ-de-Mars.* ☎ *03-26-49-59-70. www.mumm.com. Tours (in English) 7.50€; with wine-tasting 13€–18€. Reservations required. Mar–Oct daily 9:30–10:50am and 2–4:40pm. The rest of the year by appointment only.*

➔**Piper-Heidsieck** This might be one of the oldest champagne houses in the world (established in 1785), producing a vast number of vintages. There is also something markedly vintage about its 1940s-style blue-and-white main building. Once underground, you get to whiz around the cellars in a cool electric-powered car known as *une nacelle* (it holds five passengers). Then you'll have plenty of champers to knock back before you buy a bottle or two in the gift shop. They dug the cellars directly into the chalky substrata through the 19th century, and they hold more than 13 million bottles. *51 bd. Henri-Vasnier.* ☎ *03-26-84-43-44. www.piper-heidsieck.com. Admission 7.50€*

adults. Mar–Dec 1 daily 9:30–11:45am and 2–5pm.

➔**Taittinger** A sad year for Taittinger was 2005, when the American company Starwood Capital Group took over the family-run business (the Taittinger's since 1930). Lucky for you, the visit is as good as ever. You'll explore Romanesque cellars, dug from the site of Gallo-Roman chalk mines in use from the 4th to the 13th century, watch a short film, and learn anecdotes about Reims, the champagne-making process, and Taittinger family lore. *9 place St-Nicaise.* ☎ *03-26-85-84-33. www.taittinger. com. Admission 7€. Mar to mid–Nov Mon–Fri 9:30am–noon and 2–4:30pm, Sat–Sun 9–11am and 2–5pm; Mid-Nov to Mar Mon–Fri 9:30am–noon and 2–4:30pm.*

➔**Veuve Clicquot–Ponsardin** Feminists of the world, unite to toast this bubbly! In 1866, matriarch Nicole Ponsardin, at the age of 27, inherited the Clicquot champagne company from her husband. After adding her name to the brand (*veuve* means widow), she remained firmly in control of business. She even invented "riddling"—turning champagne bottles to remove sediment—a method still used in champagne production everywhere. Come here and you'll visit some of the 26km (16 miles) of underground galleries as part of guided tours that last 75 to 90 minutes. *1 place des Droits-de-l'Homme.* ☎ *03-26-89-53-90. www.*

The Sweetest of Them All

This is where you'll find the region's best sweets. The best *biscuits rose de Reims* are made at **La Maison Fossier/Biscuits Fossier** ★★, which has just celebrated its 250th birthday. It is like walking into Barbie-land, where all the cakes are pastel pink. If you are a pistachio fan, you must try the pistachio biscuit—creamy pistachio ice cream, encircled by pink Reims biscuits topped with whipped cream (25 cours Langlet; ☎ **03-26-40-67-67**; www.biscuits-fossier.com). For chocolate and candied specialties, there is nowhere better than 🎵 Best 🌟 **La Petite Friande** ★★, which will take you one step closer to heaven with liqueur-filled chocolate champagne bubbles and corks (15 cours Langlet; ☎ **03-26-47-50-44**).

veuve-clicquot.com. Admission 7.50€. Reservations required. Apr–Oct Mon–Sat; Nov–Mar Mon–Fri (check hours when you call for reservations or book online).

Shopping

To part with some dosh, head to the cathedral area and nearby **rue de Vesle, cours Langlet,** and **place Drouet d'Erlon.** You'll find a mishmash of boutiques, high-street stores, and champagne shops.

FOOD, WINE & LOCAL CRAFTS

➔ **Le Marché aux Vins, Pérardel** This place stocks one of the most comprehensive inventories of champagne in Reims, with 150 types of bubbly from more than 100 companies. They include many superb brands for 12€ to 27€ per bottle that are virtually inaccessible outside France. If your palate is feeling experimental, buy some lesser-known brands such as Deutz, Billecart Salmon, Henriot, Guy Charlemagne, and Erick de Sousa. *3 place Léon-Bourgeois* ☎ *03-26-40-12-12. www. perardel.com. Mon–Fri 9am–12:30pm and 2pm–7:30pm; Sat 9am–7:30pm.*

Epernay: It's Gotta Lotta Bottle

113km (70 miles) E of Paris, 70km (43 miles) N of Troyes; pop. 46,000

When the world gets you down, think of Epernay: On the Left Bank of the River Marne, it has stood in the path of every French war since the 6th century. It has been destroyed dozens of times, yet it has risen like a Phoenix from the ashes to stand proud as the epicenter (along with Reims) of France's champagne production. It is an inspiration to us all—one that should be toasted, tear on cheek, with some bubbly from the cellars.

The town is a fascinating world of upstairs–downstairs. Upstairs (street level), the main avenues display stately neo-Renaissance mansions. But downstairs, deep in the belly of the earth, lie more than 322km (200 miles) of chalk tunnels filled with the liquid cash that paid for the luxurious architecture overhead. Epernay might have only one-sixth of Reims's population, but it produces almost as much champagne, which means there are some seriously wealthy dudes out there. Keep your eyes peeled if you're single, and you just might meet a champagne heir or heiress (presuming they're not living it up in Paris). You're in the wrong place, however, if you're looking for a youth subculture. The only thing to do here is visit champagne cellars and stock up for your next picnic.

Getting There

Epernay's rail station is right by the main avenue de Champagne on **place Mendés France** (east). More than 10 **trains** arrive each day from both Reims and Paris ☎ **36-35. Bus** travel is highly impractical, so you should think about **driving.** From Reims take the E51 and from Paris take the A4 toward Reims and turn off at Junction 21.

Tourist Office

The **Office de Tourisme,** at 7 av. de Champagne (☎ **03-26-53-33-00;** www.ot-epernay.fr) can advise on all the champagne houses and give information and maps on the Routes de Champagne.

Orientation & Sightseeing

As soon as you arrive, head straight to avenue de Champagne, where you'll find

Epernay History 101

Many centuries ago, long before grapes were grown here, a small settlement called Sparnacum (meaning "thorny collectivity" in Latin) emerged from the bogs and the brambles. By the 5th century, the town had become Epernay (from the French word *épine,* or thorn), although most of the brambles had been cleared away, and tanners had taken root alongside the river. In 1024, the town became the property of the Counts of Champagne. From then on, it was demolished, pillaged, or razed more than 25 times. Epernay was hit seriously during World War I, which wiped out more than two thirds of the population. After heavy bombing in World War II, the Germans settled in until General Patton liberated the town on August 28, 1944. With such a violent past, it's a wonder that the 19th-century champagne houses are still standing. But they are, and if they could smile they'd probably be smirking.

the tourist office (no. 7) and all the cellar visits. Just below the train station is the **place de la République,** the town's central square. The pedestrian zone around **place des Arcades** and **place Hughes-Plomb** houses the town's best bakeries and delis, where you can buy picnic staples. To reach these squares, walk west from place de la République along **rue Général-Leclerc** and turn south along **rue Saint-Thibault.** You certainly won't need any public transportation here, and you'll find plenty of other stores selling gifts, clothes, antiques, and books along the way.

CHAMPAGNE CELLAR TOURS

MTV Best ♥ →**Mercier** ★★ This place offers an insightful journey into bubbly lore in Epernay (see "Mercier through the Grapevine," below). You'll see the world's largest champagne barrel, descend 30m (98 ft.) inside a panoramic lift that displays champagne-making techniques along the way, and then enter a vast network of tunnels on a laser-guided train that will take you right back to childhood. More than 15 million bottles lie fermenting here. A highly protected *glacière* (cave) contains Mercier's best vintages from 1923 onward. You won't be able to taste anything in

there, but you will be rewarded with a glass of champagne at the end of the tour. *70 av. de Champagne.* ☎ *03-26-51-22-22. www. champagne-mercier.fr. Admission 6.50€. Mid-Mar to mid-Nov daily 9:30–11:30am and 2–4:30pm. Closed Feb 16, Mar 15, Nov 14, and Dec 11.*

MTV Best ♥ →**Moët et Chandon Champagne Cellars** This tour tops Mercier's as the best tour in Epernay. You can practically smell the wealth of the place, founded by Jean Remy Moët in 1743. It was a favorite of Napoleon, who, legend has it, used to lug cases around for consumption before battle—except of course at Waterloo, and look what happened there. The video presentation is so cheesy it could give you mental indigestion, but English-speaking staff members lead the tours, spinning wonderful anecdotes and making sure you don't get lost in the 28km (17 miles) of spooky tunnels. At the end of the tour, you receive a glass of bubbly—a fine reward for a fine tour. *20 av. de Champagne.* ☎ *03-26-51-20-20. www.moet. com. Admission 8€ (1 glass), 17€ (2 glasses), and 21€ (3 glasses). Daily Apr to mid-Nov 9:30–11:30am and 2–4:30pm. Mid-Nov to late-Dec Mon–Fri 9:30–11:30am and 2–4:30pm.*

Mercier through the Grapevine

One of the world's first filmed publicity stunts advertised **MTV** **Best❂** **Mercier champagne.** Involving a giant barrel, a hot-air balloon, and the Eiffel tower, it caused a stir in the 19th century.

It all started in 1858 with Eugène Mercier, a 20-year-old with no money and grand ideas. Champagne houses were multiplying at a speed rivalled only by the rate at which the upper classes were drinking bubbly. Eugène decided that his fortune lay in the local vintage, and after 17 years of hard slog, he'd acquired a property on avenue de Champagne, built an 18km (11-mile) wine cellar beneath the house, thrown bucket loads of parties, and confirmed his name as a serious businessman.

When the 1889 World Exhibition came to Paris, he wanted fairgoers to taste his wine. But how was he to get it there? The answer lay in a 20-ton champagne barrel, so big it took 24 bulls and 18 horses to pull it all the way from Epernay. Containing the equivalent of 200,000 bottles, it was so wide Mercier had to buy 5 Parisian buildings in order to demolish them, to allow the barrel to pass freely down the street. He also felled trees along the quai d'Orsay, and some poor Hungarian restaurateur had to take the roof off his restaurant. But by Bacchus, the work paid off. Mercier won second prize for his effort—second only to Gustave Eiffel's tower.

Eleven years later, the Mercier bubble hadn't burst; it had gotten bigger. For the 1900 Paris Exposition, he provided precisely 3,723,821 onlookers with the first ever filmed publicity. Crafted by the pioneering Lumières brothers, it took 2 years to make. For want of *lumière* in the cellars, they had to shoot it outside.

The real pièce de résistance, however, was a gigantic hot-air balloon. Mercier asked his aviation friend Louis Vernanchet to whip up a 2,500m (8,200-ft.) cube balloon, so that he could float his public high above the Château de Vincennes in Paris for a panoramic slurp. Needless to say, the concept, well, took off. More than 10,000 Parisians took the joy ride for 5 francs a head.

Eugène Mercier sipped his last four years later in 1904, and control passed on down the family vine. Mercier Champagne is now owned by conglomerate L.V.M.H., which has put a stopper in the notion of wild extravagance.

Sleeping

DOABLE

➜**Les Berceaux** ★ This place is aptly named (*berceaux* means cradles): After such a busy day in champagne cellars, you'll need a cozy place to cradle your head. Besides the 29 comfy rooms upstairs (TV, tub/shower combo in bathroom), the fantastic restaurant here serves up vast quantities of Champenois cuisine (think suckling lamb roasted on a spit and snails

More Bubbly

A number of stores represent a variety of champagne houses. Two of the best are **La Cave Salvatori,** 11 rue Flodoard (☎ **03-26-55-32-32**), and **Le Domaine des Crus,** 2 rue Henri Dunant (☎ **03-26-54-18-60**), known for a staggering array of bubbly.

in champagne sauce). The food is delightful, but be warned it's 46€ to 61€ for the
fixed-price menu. *13 rue des Berceaux.*
☎ *03-26-55-28-84. www.lesberceaux.com.
77€–86€ double. Credit cards accepted.*

Eating

There's Les Berceaux if you can splurge
(see "Sleeping," above). Otherwise, consider these.

DOABLE

➔ **Le Théâtre** ★ This chic-looking joint
next door to the theater offers some
decently priced food. Eat at one of their
well-dressed tables and rub shoulders
with Epernay's artsy crowd, discussing the
highs and lows of the play they've just
seen, while tucking into mouthwatering
dishes such as hare terrine, or lobster with
leek compote. Decor is a funky mix of gray
walls and orange lampshades, which make
you feel like you've stepped into a 1970s
Bond movie. *8 place Mendés France.* ☎ *03-
26-58-88-19. www.epernay-rest-letheatre.com.
Fixed-price menu 15€ lunch, 22€, 28€, and
44€. Mon and Thurs–Sat noon–2pm and
7–10pm; Tues–Wed and Sun noon–2pm.*

Partying

After so much champagne, why stop when
the sun sets? Start out at the chic cafe and
bar **Le Progrès** (5 place de la République;
☎ **03-26-55-22-72**). For a glass of wine or
even Scotch (a novelty in this wine-crazed
region), **Le Chriss Bar** will do you proud
(38 rue de Sézanne; ☎ **03-26-54-38-47**). A
place that rocks later into the night, sometimes with live music, is **Le Garden Club**
(5 av. Foch; ☎ **03-26-54-20-30**), which
has a Parisian atmosphere.

Playing Outside

What better way to see the Champagne
region than with the wind rushing past your
car windows (that's right, turn the A/C off
and pretend you're in a convertible). You'll

whiz around like there's no tomorrow,
through green pastures into luscious vineyards selling some of the world's finest
champagnes. Take the RN51 out of Epernay
toward Reims and follow the **Montagne de
Reims** circuit (follow signs for ROUTE DE
CHAMPAGNE)—a forested plateau between
Epernay and Reims and the best place to
experience the beauty of this undervalued
region. This is where you'll find the smaller
producers who often give tours or let you
taste a few glasses in the shop. Don't miss
this list of places to see in between stops:

First up is **Dizy Champillon,** which has
a fantastic view over the vines of the
Marne Valley; **St-Imoges** has a 16th-cen-
tury church and a Franco-British cemetery
from World War I; in the forest at
Germaine, a backwoodsman's house features a mini exhibition on forestry in the
area; **Ludes** contains the vestiges of a castle and has a pretty medieval and
Renaissance church; you can visit the subterranean galleries of an old feudal castle
at **Mailly-Champagne; Verzenay** has a
windmill and a 19th-century lighthouse;
Verzy is famous for its eerie forest with
trees that have been growing in an
umbrella shape, towards the ground, since
the 6th century; **Villers-Marmery** has
another windmill and a Merovingian
cemetery; **Trépail** also has a windmill and
an old wash house; the church towers at
Ambonnay date from the 11th and 12th
centuries; boozy old **Bouzy** is famous for
its red wines, which Tallyrand called
"wines of the civilized world" (see "French
History 101" in the Nerd's Guide to French
Wine & Culture); **Tauxières-Mutry** has a
Roman church; and **Ay** is a historical village with half-timbered houses where
Henry IV had his own wine press.

It is also possible to attack the Route de
Champagne by bike or on foot. You should
follow the sentiers de Grandes Randonnées
(or GRs), running along the top of the

northern plateau of Montagne de Reims. Prepare yourself for a winding, hilly affair. Ask Epernay's **Office de Tourisme** for more info (☎ **03-26-53-33-00**).

Troyes ★★: Shaped Like a Champagne Cork

150km (93 miles) SE of Paris; pop. 61,000

On your way into Troyes, don't be put off by the unattractive buildings and utilitarian atmosphere. So what if the outskirts are about as appealing as the ring of scum around a footballer's bath? It's what's in the middle that counts. And it's a fine middle, especially if you like history.

Troyes is a cultural wallflower. Shy and overshadowed by Reims, it let itself go for a while. Even now, despite a hefty urban-renewal program, it doesn't reveal its qualities willingly. You have to want to find them, to make an effort to see things by sauntering in and out of its medieval alleys, side streets, and courtyards. The beauty of Troyes is in its authenticity. It charms you unhurriedly with dinky museums, gorgeous churches (with dramatic stained glass), traditional half-timbered Champenois architecture, and friendly locals.

Troyes is the least champagne-orientated of the region's cities, but for the fact that it's shaped like a champagne cork. It's a freak of medieval urban planning, but a

Troyes History 101

Troyes got a map reference in 22 to 21 B.C., following the construction of la Voie d'Agrippa, a huge Roman road linking Milan to Boulogne-sur-Mer. Built on the site of an old Gaul fortress, Tricasses (as it was known then) was evangelized in the 3rd century then thrust into the spotlight around 450 when Attila the Hun invaded France. Pillaging everything he found in his path, he burned Reims to the ground. But when he got to Troyes, the priest St-Loup offered himself as a hostage in exchange for the town. Attila was so impressed with Loup's selflessness he spared the city.

In the 900s, after centuries of religious control, Troyes passed to the counts of Champagne, who gave the capital a necessary spring cleaning: Henry I ordered the construction of 13 churches and 13 hospitals (the Hôtel-de-Dieu still stands). His poetry-spurting grandson, Thibaut II, created les Foires de Troyes, a huge trade fair that contributed to the city's renown and prosperity.

On May 21, 1420, the city fell to the archenemy (the English), following Isabeau de Bavière's (Charles VI's wife) royal blooper. She signed a treaty with Henry V of England so that his marriage with Catherine de France would make him rightful heir to the French throne after Charlie's death. Thank heavens for feisty Joan of Arc, who delivered the city back to the French in 1429.

By the 16th century, the creative juices were really flowing. While the rest of France was under the influence of the Italian art schools, Troyes was pigheadedly sticking to its own methods. The result is a school of Troyen sculpture, painting, and glass-making—still the pride of residents today.

By the 18th century, productivity went undercover, where it stayed: The country's first stocking factory came to be in 1745, and undies remain a prime source of revenue round here to this day.

Five Quirky Facts about Troyes

1. Medieval Troyes was the prosperous city to which we owe the troy weight, used to weigh precious stones and gems.

2. It was the birthplace of the Knight's Templar. The founder of the order, Hugues de Payns, was born here around 1070.

3. If a medieval resident were to come back to life, he'd be able to find his way around the historical center. Most streets retained their medieval names and look the same.

4. Troyes is home to Europe's first "Craft University," where youngsters are trained in the skills of restoration.

5. The city contains 10,000 sq. m (107,639 sq. ft.) of original stained glass from the 12th through to the 17th centuries.

fun touch that reminds you where you are every time you look at the street map.

It's also the birthplace of the bonnet and has been the capital of the French textile and hosiery industry since the Middle Ages. Nowadays, the tradition continues (excellent news if extortionate Paris prices have rendered your wallet inactive) in a mini metropolis of designer and high street factory stores located a short bus ride away in the suburbs (p. 689).

I've already mentioned the smelly *andouillette* tripe sausage, and I'll keep mentioning it so you summon up the guts to try one. Practically every restaurant in Troyes serves them, so you have no excuses. And hey, it's no more gross than eating frogs' legs or snails right?

Getting There

BY AIR

Unless you own a pair of wings, leave air travel here to the birds.

BY TRAIN

Troyes is 1½ hours from Paris. The last train back to the capital is at around 10pm, but confirm at **www.sncf.com** or ☎ 36-35, unless you want to fork out for a hotel.

BY CAR

From Paris to Troyes, take the A4 then the N104 (follow Marne La Vallée), followed by the A105/A5b, and follow the signs to Troyes (1 hr. 55 min.). From Reims to Troyes, get on the A4 toward Epernay, and you will see signs for Troyes (1 hr. 20 min.).

BY BUS

As in much of France, where the trains are so fast and frequent, skip the bus.

Orientation

Capped by the Seine and sliced in half by the man-made Bassin de la Préfecture (a standing canal), Troyes' champagne-cork *centre ville* is separated into two segments. From the station, the **body** of the cork is the first part you'll come across. This contains most of the pedestrianized, medieval streets and shops. The **head** of the cork, across the canal, is dominated by the cathedral, modern art museum, and student quarters around rue **de la Cité.** You'd have to be as bird-brained as a blind, deaf, dumb carrier pigeon to get lost in the center. All the attractions are marked on brown-and-white panels, and the tourist office map is seriously accurate.

Getting Around

ON FOOT

By far it's best to see the city on foot, with all its narrow alleys. You can cover the whole cork (from head to body) in 20 minutes, but you should build in time for obligatory pit stops on cafe terraces.

BY BICYCLE

Foil the crowds with a bike from the **Hôtel des Comptes de Champagne** (56 rue de la Monnaie; ☎ **03-25-73-11-70;** www. comtesdechampagne.com), which offers the only bike rentals in town. Prices range from 8€ half-day to 12€ day (2€ reduction if you sleep at the hotel; see p. 684) plus a 250€ deposit that you recoup at the end.

BY BUS

You won't have to brave public transport in Troyes unless you're shopping in factory outlet stores in the suburbs. Buses (TCAT; ☎ **03-25-78-30-30**) leave from place de la Halle in the body of the cork. Line 1 (toward pont Ste-Marie, get off at Magasins) takes you to the McArthur Glen mall (www. mcarthurglen.fr), and line 2 (toward Bréviandes, get off at Magasins de l'Avenue) goes to Marques Avenue mall. Tickets are sold onboard for 1.20€ each way. See "Shopping" on p. 689.

BY TAXI

Taxi Troyens (☎ **03-25-78-30-30**) cabs line up in front of the station, but unless it's raining hard, you shouldn't need one.

Tourist Offices

Troyes has two offices. From the station, the nearest is 50m (164 ft.) away, at 16 bd. Carnot (☎ **03-25-82-62-70;** Mon–Sat 9am–12:30pm and 2–6:30pm, Nov 1–Mar 31 Sun 10am–1pm). The second is in the pedestrian-only sector, at rue Mignard (☎ **03-25-73-36-88;** Sept 16–June 30 Mon–Sat 9am–12:30pm and 2–6:30pm, Sun 10am–noon and 2–5pm; July 1–Sept 15 daily 10am–7pm). They organize guided tours in French (except on Fri evenings at 6pm from the office on rue Mignard). If your language skills aren't up to scratch, opt for an audio tour, which will help you understand what you're looking at. For more information, check out **www. tourisme-troyes.com**.

Troyes Nuts & Bolts

Emergencies Ambulance ☎ **15**, police ☎ **17**, fire/paramedic service ☎ **18**. The main police station is **Commissariat de police nationale de Troyes,** 4 bd. 1er R. A. M. (☎ **03-25-43-51-00**).

Hospitals If you forget you're not a snake and swallow your *andouillette* whole, the **Centre Hospitalier** may well save your life (101 av. Anatole France; ☎ **03-25-49-49-49;** www.ch-troyes.fr).

Internet/Wireless Hot Spots The only Internet cafe in town is funky **Cyber-café le Poincarré,** with state-of-the-art laptops. The decor is publike, with dark colors and wooden beams. Goldfish swim in an old pump, they host regular jazz concerts, and Anas the Rottweiler wanders from table to table in search of affection (27 av. Raymond Poincarré; ☎ **03-25-81-63-44**). Open daily 10am to 1:30am. Cost is 2€ an hour.

Pharmacies   Pharmacie de la Gare tends to stay open the longest (2 bd. Carnot; ☎ **03-25-73-03-57;** Mon–Sat 9am–7:30pm).

Vehicle Rental   Ada (25 rue des Noës; ☎ **03-25-73-41-68;** www.ada.fr) is recommended by the tourist office for car hire in and around Troyes.

Sleeping

Troyes is tiny and so close to Paris that many visitors opt not to stay here. But you could do a lot worse than the champagne cork with hotels in 16th-century buildings as a less expensive base from which to explore the surrounding Champagne countryside. In summer, it's smart to book in advance.

HOSTELS

→**Auberge de Jeunesse de Troyes-Rosières** It's common to bunk with strangers in youth hostels, and this place is no exception, with rooms for three to eight people. But an everlasting friendship might be lurking on the bed below yours, and then you could go out together and spend all the money you're saving here on museums, out-of-town shopping sprees, or bang-up meals. The auberge is clean and tidy, a short bus ride away from the center. To get there, take Line 8 from place de la Halle (toward Château de Rosières) and get off at Liberté. Who knows, by the end of the night, you and your newfound buddy might be whispering sweet nothings into each other's ears. (For maximum impact, avoid "I wish I hadn't eaten that second *andouillette*" and opt for "We'll always have Troyes.") *Chemin Ste-Scholastique, Rosières.* ☎ *03-25-82-00-65. www.fuaj.org. Troyes-rosieres@fuaj.org. 12€ bed (sheets included). Breakfast 3.40€. Amenities: Breakfast; meals available; kitchen; parking; tents available.*

CHEAP

→**Hôtel des Comptes de Champagne** ★★ Four traditional Champenois houses were cobbled together to make this hotel. The result is utterly charming, and you won't find a cuter bed for your money anywhere else. From the blue and pink half-timbered lobby, to the 29 individually decorated rooms, this place oozes the 16th-century charm Troyes is famous for. Breakfast is yummy, the staff is smiley and helpful, and this is the only place where you can rent a bike. *56 rue de la Monnaie.* ☎ *03-25-73-11-70. www.comtesdechampagne. com. 35€–57€ double; 63€–81€ triple. Breakfast 6€. Credit cards accepted. Amenities: Bike-hire; champagne at wholesale prices (box of 6); parking 6€. In room: TV.*

DOABLE

→**Le Royal** Next to the train station, Le Royal lacks the character of the historical quarter (think unimaginative, hotel-chain-like furniture), but it's just a 5-minute stroll from lots of action. Rooms are clean, modern, reasonably priced, and there's a bar with cheesy PVC armchairs for a sneaky tipple after hours. *22 bd. Carnot.* ☎ *03-25-73-19-99. www.royal-hotel-troyes.com. 80€–100€ double. Breakfast 10€. Credit cards accepted. Amenities: Restaurant; bar. In room: A/C, TV, Internet.*

SPLURGE

→**La Maison de Rhodes** ★★ You're an avid historian? An Indiana Jones fan? A Dan Brown convert? If you've answered "yes" to any of these questions, the Knights Templar has captured your imagination at least once in your lifetime, and that means that you must stay here. This half-timbered dwelling (next to the cathedral) has foundations dating back to the 12th century and once belonged to the Knights Templar of the order of Malta. I'm not promising that you'll find the elixir of life or the Holy Grail in your room, but you'll certainly be enchanted by all you see: exposed stone walls, ocher fabrics, spotless bathrooms, restored fireplaces, a medieval garden, a cobbled courtyard—all with quirky medieval touches. If you're looking for intrigue, luxury, and romance, you can't beat this glorious, family-run *lieu de charme*. *18 rue Linard Gonthier.* ☎ *03-25-43-11-11. www.maisonderhodes.com. 135€– 192€ double, 215€–225€ suite. Breakfast 17€. Credit cards accepted. Amenities: Restaurant; parking 12€.*

Eating

Besides the *andouillette*, Troyes is also a wonderful place in which to try Champagne's other regional *plats*. Being near to Alsace, it bears a distinct German influence, and it is not unusual to see sauerkraut on menus. Many dishes include sauces made from champagne, which is an open invitation for you to order a glass of bubbly on the side.

CAFES & LIGHT FARE

➔ **Le Victoria** TEA HOUSE   Your arms are aching from all those shopping bags, your throat is dry, and you're longing for a decent cup of tea. Look no farther than Le Victoria. In the shopping area, in the body of the cork, this funky tea boudoir smells like grandma's homemade cakes. In fact, you can watch the cakes being made behind the bar at the back. The front area sells tea and tea-related trinkets; the back lounge cuts you off from the rest of the world; and the basement, with 16th-century brick arches, makes for some atmospheric slurping. If you're there in summer, ask for a tea cocktail or an ice cream. *34 rue du Général Saussier.* ☎ *03-25-73-37-95. Cakes 3.50€; salads 9€. Credit cards accepted. Mon–Thurs 9am–7pm; Fri–Sat 9am–11pm.*

[MTV] [Best ♦] ➔ **Petit Café du Musée Di Marco** ★ CAFE   Before you saunter

around the cathedral, stop off at Troyes' most eccentric cafe for a snack or a hot drink (salads and sticky buns 10€–15€). Attached to the upstairs museum, it pays homage to Angelo di Marco, France's great newspaper illustrator. You can't really call it underground, but there's definitely an artsy feel to its slick gray walls and posters of Di Marco's drawings. The museum (5€) is eerie and portrays the dark universe of French crimes and disasters. If you're fed up with pretty landscape postcards, grab a few black-and-white ones here; they won't show where you've been, but they depict a less-known (if not morbid) side of French culture. *61 rue de la Cité.* ☎ *03-25-40-18-27. Daily 10am–6:30pm. Credit cards accepted.*

CHEAP

[MTV] [Best ♦] ➔**Au Jardin Gourmand** CHARCUTERIE   If it's warm outside, request a table in one of Troyes' most romantic courtyards. If there's no room there or it's raining, a seat inside will do. The most important thing is for you to be comfortable, because it's here you'll be sampling the momma of all sausages; the stinky, pinky queen of tripe; the fat rascal of offal; the pride of every Troyen butcher—the *andouillette*. There are over 11 different sauces with which you can disguise the taste, from simple mustard to elaborate champagne and foie gras. In case you can't stand the thought, the menu offers excellent meat and fish options as well. *31 rue Paillot de Montabert.* ☎ *03-25-73-36-13. Menus from 17€–25€. Andouillettes from 12€–20€. Credit cards accepted. Mon– Sat noon–2pm and 7:30–11pm.*

DOABLE

➔ **Estelle & Olivier** ★ TAPAS   The last thing you'd expect to find in a town far from the cries of the sea and the sun is a Basque tapas bar. But that is what has

All for Offal & Offal for All

If I were to tell you that *andouillettes* were the food of kings and that the destiny of an entire city was once irrevocably altered by their treacherously smelly entrails, you'd be forgiven for thinking I was two pigs short of a sausage. Yet in Troyes, this is exactly the sort of historical tripe the locals love to boast about. What's more, it's all true. In 828, Louis II was crowned king in Troyes and celebrated his new title with a banquet of *andouillettes*. Then in 1560, the French Royal army breached the city walls to take Troyes from the governor of Champagne, the Duke de Guise. All was going well until the soldiers caught wind of a smell wafting from behind the cathedral. Rushing to its source, they discovered *andouillette* sellers and threw themselves onto the food. Caught red-handed by de Guise's army, the greedy men were driven out of town. Nowadays, the only people to relish such sizzling tales are members of the AAAAA (the Association Amicale des Amateurs d'Andouillettes Authentiques or Friends of the Authentic Andouillette Association). They are the musketeers of sausage, defending the quality of every single one of the 20 million *andouillettes* served each year.

made Estelle & Olivier a household name in Troyes. There are dozens of different *tapas* (15€ each) including vegetarian options, delicious bruchettas, and wild main courses such as antelope or coconut scallops 23€); surprising wine (Olivier trained in oenology and serves 35 wines and 30 champagnes); and surprising vibes (salsa, flamenco, mojitos, and Cuban cigar nights). On student nights, tapas and wine are just 12€. Otherwise expect to pay around 30€. *32 rue de Turenne.* ☎ *03-25-76-68-30. Credit cards accepted. Tues–Sat 10am–3pm and 5–9pm (until midnight Fri–Sat and when the clients don't want to leave).*

SPLURGE

Save the big bucks for your next stop. Food in Troyes is great without your having to spend a fortune.

Partying

Troyes isn't great for all-nighters. But if you decide to linger, head for the main student quarter along rue de la Cité and the medieval lanes around place Alexandre Israël.

The late-night venue for students and other locals is **Le Bar Tabac** (24 rue de la

Cité; ☎ **03-25-80-59-15;** daily 7:30am–3am; beer 1.50€) near the cathedral. From the outside, it looks like nothing at all, but on the inside it sells the cheapest beer in Troyes. Another student institution is the **Gainz'Bar** (39 rue de la Cité; ☎ **03-25-80-60-76;** daily 1am–3am; beer 1.60€). Just like the Gitane smoking music icon it's named after (Gainz'Bar refers to Serge Gainsborough), the bibulous locals sit around looking cool on nicotine and alcohol. Back down in the body of the cork **Le Bougnat des Pouilles** (29 rue Paillot-de-Montabert; ☎ **03-25-73-59-85;** daily 6pm–3am) attracts a more grownup crowd with its reputable wines, jazz, and world music concerts. **Le Squat VIP** (38 rue Voltaire; ☎ **03-25-74-28-85;** Tues–Sat nights) is a small nightclub that resonates to the sound of house and pop. For a great gay bar, head to **Le Furious** (80 rue Général de Gaulle; ☎ **03-25-73-58-96;** Mon–Sat 1pm–3am). If you're looking for a concert, check out **La Maison du Boulanger** (42 rue Paillot-de-Montabert; ☎ **03-25-43-55-00;** Mon–Fri 9am–noon and 2–6pm, Sat 10am–noon and 2–5pm; www.maisonduboulanger.com), which maintains Troyes' cultural agenda in all the arts. If you're in town around the end of August, don't miss the **Kills Party Festival** (www.kills party.com), which hosts live music, DJs, and art expos in a few bars around the center. Sponsored by Troyes' student radio, it's the most upbeat thing you'll find in these parts.

Sightseeing

You don't have to be majoring in history to appreciate Troyes, but a keen interest in it certainly helps. Once you've done the modern art museum, moseyed around a few churches, checked out the stained glass, and eaten an *andouillette*, the only thing left to do is admire the 16th-century, half-timbered houses.

MONUMENTS: A GUIDED TOUR

Start at **place Alexandre Israël,** near the **Hôtel de Ville** with its Louis XIII facade, and head for rue Champeaux. Medieval folk liked narrow streets, and rue Champeaux is extraordinarily wide for the era. That's good news if you like cafe terraces, but given that you just started your walking tour, you should crack on towards the **La Maison du Boulanger** cultural center, on the corner of rue Paillot-de-Montabert (see "Partying" on p. 686). Once you've checked out what's on, admire the astonishing half-slated tower on the corner. **La Tourelle de l'Orfève** owes its name to the profession of its first medieval owner, who was a goldsmith (or *orfève*).

Now head toward the St-Jean church and take **rue Mignard** back towards rue Champeaux. The building in front of you is **l'hôtel Juvénal-des-Ursins,** built in 1526. It bears the family name of Jean I, King Charles VII's magistrate, who was born in Troyes. Next up is the most narrow street in town, la **Ruelle des Chats (Cat Alley).** On the left is the **cour du Mortier d'Or,** which was painstakingly renovated using

original materials and techniques. Go to the end of the Ruelle des Chats to **rue Charbonnet,** where you'll find the **Hôtel de Marisy.** Built in 1531, this stone building has a cute little Renaissance-style tower, decorated with figurines and coats of arms.

Turn left down **rue des Quinze Vingts** and right down **rue de la Monnaie.** At no. 32–36 you'll come across **l'hôtel de la Croix d'Or.** Built in the typical *Damier* style (brick-and-chalk checkerboard-pattern masonry) in the early 16th century, it was home to Nicolas Riglet, mayor of Troyes. From here, go back and turn right down **rue J. Ursins,** which leads to **rue Turenne,** where you should have a gander at the pretty Renaissance facade of no. 55, **l'Hôtel de Chapelaines.** Constructed between 1524 and 1536, it was home to a wealthy dyer whose descendants became the noble barons de Chapelaines (amazing what money can buy).

Now take rue Général-Saussier and turn left down rue de la Trinté. No. 7, the **Hôtel de Mauroy,** is a banquet for the eyes. It houses the Musée de l'Outil, but you should have a peek at the courtyard even if you don't visit the museum. It's got wooden tiles, Damier brickwork, a five-sided tower, and Corinthian-style columns supporting the wooden gallery. This was the city's first bonnet factory in 1745, where orphans were trained in the textile trade. Next door is the 16th-century **Maison des Allemands,** which sheltered German traders when they came to the Foire de Troyes.

Back on rue Général-Saussier there's more intrigue than first meets the eye: The Knights Templar command posts were at nos. 1 and 3, and Napoleon Bonaparte stayed in the house at no. 11. Go back and turn right down **rue Montée des Changes,** cross **rue Emile Zola,** and down the little alley straight ahead. This leads to the end of your historical voyage in **place du Marché-au-Pain,** the old merchants' quarters. You'll find plenty of drinking holes around here for a glass of bubbly or an ice cream.

CHURCHES

With eight churches to visit, you could easily go into ecclesiastical overload. Stick to the cathedral, and then decide whether you have time or energy for some of these other highlights: The **Basilique St-Urbain** (place Vernier; ☎ 03-25-73-37-13) has more wonderful stained glass. The **Eglise Ste-Madeleine** (rue de la Madeleine; ☎ 03-25-73-82-90) is famous for its flamboyant *jubé* (1508–17), carved by Jean Gailde using Troyen techniques. **L'Eglise St-Pantaléon** (rue Turenne; ☎ 03-25-82-62-70) has a wooden vaulted ceiling and a collection of statues from convents destroyed during the Revolution. **L'Eglise St-Jean** (rue Urban IV; ☎ 03-25-82-62-70) is closed to the public but can be admired from the outside. The **St-Nicolas church** (rue Jeanne D'Arc; ☎ 03-25-71-75-41) was rebuilt after a fire in 1524. The **Eglise St-Rémy** (place St-Rémy; no phone) has a wonderful lead bell, and the most colorful tiled roof in Troyes belongs to the **Eglise St-Nizier** (rue Simart; ☎ 03-25-82-62-70).

📺 **Best ❷** ➔ **Cathédrale St-Pierre-et-St-Paul** You know how it is with medieval builders: One minute they're following the architect's plans, the next they've forgotten to build an entire tower. At least that's what it looks like from the outside of the cathedral, with its solitary 66m-high (216-ft.) tower to the left of a gap that looks decisively like it needs filling. The cathedral was built between the 13th and 17th centuries, and the second tower was indeed never finished. But none of that matters once you get inside and start looking at the stained glass. Each section dates from a different period: The Choir part is from the 13th century and depicts popes, emperors, and virgins with intense, warm colors. The nave's windows date from the 16th century and look more like paintings than pieces of glass. A talented bloke called Martin Chambiges made the mighty Rose window on the facade in 1546 (he also did Beauvais and Sens cathedrals). It shows the patriarchs with God the Father, but most of it is hidden by the whopping 18th-century organ. In the fourth chapel on the left, take a look at the gory *Mythical Press.* Finished in 1625, it shows Christ being crushed by a wine press. His blood runs down into a golden cup while a huge vine tree erupts from his chest to support his 12 apostles. *Rue de la Cité.*

MUSEUMS

Like any small town in France, Troyes has its fair share of museums. **La Maison de l'Outil** (read: the tool museum) in l'Hôtel de Mauroy is particularly interesting, so ask the tourist office for more information. The jewel in the crown has to be **Le Musée d'Art Moderne,** next door to the cathedral.

📺 **Best ❷** ➔ **Le Musée d'Art Moderne** ★★ In 1976, a couple called Pierre and Denise Lévy did a generous thing. They gave their personal art collection to the town of Troyes. With more than 2,000 pieces, the collection contains works by some of the world's greatest 19th- and 20th-century artists. Needless to say, many items are by fauvist painters (the term *fauve* was adopted in 1905 to describe a style that frequently used bright colors and strange forms and lacked perspective), but there's also a pre-fauvist section and a fascinating tribal arts room. Whether or not you know your Picassos from your Lacroixs, there's no denying that so many big names in one building outside of Paris is damned impressive. Check out eye candy by Matisse, Roussel, Modigliani, Courbet, Degas, Derain, Soutine, Seurat, and the list goes on.

Playing Outdoors

The handy thing about Troyes is that it is right next door to the **Parc de la Forêt d'Orient**, a natural park containing a trio of artificial lakes created in the 1960s to regulate the flow of the Seine: Lac de la Forêt d'Orient, with its large beach and sailboat rentals; Lac Temple-Auzon, which lures fishermen; and the most fun-filled lake of all, Lac Amance, where in the summer you can rent boats or take water-skiing lessons. The park sprawls across 68,000 hectares (170,000 acres) of low rolling hills and lush meadows, encompassing nearly 50 small towns dotted with traditional Champenois buildings. In the northeast is a 480-hectare (1,200-acre) bird sanctuary, plus a 32-hectare (80-acre) animal reserve stocked with stag, wild boar, and deer. Literally hundreds of miles of hiking trails cut through this forest, going past the lakes and heading south to the Valley of the Seine. Along these trails, you'll pass dozens of champagne vineyards as well as cider houses (did I forget to mention that this is an apple-growing region as well?). Hunting season lasts from October to February, so if you go at this time, be sure to wear bright colors like chartreuse or sunflower yellow, and definitely don't show up if you look like a bull moose.

For more information you should contact the **l'Office de Tourisme Intercommunal des Grands Lacs et de la Forêt d'Orient** (Maison du Parc; ☎ 03-25-43-38-88; daily July–Aug 10am–6pm; Apr–Oct 10am–noon and 2–6pm; Nov–Mar 1–5pm). They will advise you on sites of interest, provide maps (including some on bird-watching, botany, and geology), and give you a list of companies that run activities (cycling and hiking associations, sailing, and so on). You could also consult **www.pnr-foret-orient.fr**, but it is in French only.

Shopping

CLOTHING & ACCESSORIES

Troyes has been the center of the textile industry for centuries, so you can expect to find a clothes shop or two in the town center. For designer bargains, jump on the bus (see "Getting Around: By Bus " on p. 683) and head to Troyes' famous factory outlet stores in the suburbs.

➜ **Marques Avenue** South of the city, this shop stocks a mainly French range of wares: La City, Promod, Caroll (for women), Cardin, Café Coton, and Chevignon (for men). *114 bd de Dijon* ☎ *03-25-82-80-80. Mon–Sat 10am–7pm (from 2pm on Mon).*

➜ **McArthur Glen** The newest kid on the shopping block stocks everything from well-known designer wear like Versace, Ralph Lauren, Nike, and Burberry, to lesser known brands such as Mexx, Morgan, and Naf Naf. *10150 pont Ste-Marie.* ☎ *33-03-25-70-47-10. www.mcarthurglen.fr/destockage-en/troyes/index.php. Mon–Sat 10am–7pm.*

MUSIC, BOOKS & MEDIA

📺 Best ✪ ➜ **Auto-Stradale** ★ It doesn't sell books, music, or media-related stuff, but I had to find somewhere to list this Aladdin's cavern for geeks. Stepping into this shop is like entering a mystical car graveyard, where every vehicle belonged to a Lilliputian. Gulliver around here is Laurent, a mad eccentric who likes to eye up pretty girls over his thick-rimmed glasses. He knows everything there is to know about every car that rolls through his door, and he'll sell you anything you see as long as it doesn't come from his private collection behind the counter. *7 rue de la Cité.* ☎ *03-25-81-12-18. Official hours: Fri–Wed 10am–12:30pm and 2:30–7pm. Real hours: "I'll come in when I feel like it."*

→ **Tempo Vinyls** So you're looking for a 1986 vinyl of the Beastie Boys? You might just track it down here, along with a pile of others. From inside its graffiti-clad walls, Tempo boasts records on techno, house, house-tek, hard core, tribe, jungle, drum & bass, R&B, groove, rap, break beat, party beat, and anything else that has a pulse. You can even find a cassette or two. *28 rue*

Clémenceau. ☎ *03-25-40-06-13. Tues–Sat 2–4pm.*

FOOD, WINE & LOCAL CRAFTS

I couldn't end the chapter without slipping in one more *andouillette* reference. If you want to cook your own, head to **La Boucherie Moderne** (Halles de l'Hôtel de Ville; ☎ **03-25-73-32-64**), where you'll find some of the best in the country, made by Gilbert Lemelle, a certified sausage friend and member of the AAAAA (see "All for Offal & Offal for All" on p. 686).

Alsace-Lorraine

by Anna Sussman

Some of the towns and cities in Alsace-Lorraine are so charming it's understandable why the Germans and French feuded for so long in the hope of capturing a few of them. The regions' common history as disputed territories, however, does not translate to any strong sense of solidarity between them. Joined at the hip by the Vosges Mountains and a hyphen, the contiguous regions of Alsace and Lorraine are in fact two distinct entities, and locals today don't appreciate outsiders' inability to distinguish between them.

In 1918, as the German empire crumbled, the population got fed up and declared its independence. Unfortunately, freedom required having more weapons than the fledgling republic had. After barely more than a week, France snatched it up again, invading and occupying Mulhouse, Colmar, Metz, and Strasbourg, and solidifying French control over the region until World War II.

Under the Nazis, Germany took control of the region and forced local young men to serve in the German Waffen-SS, or else. When the French regained hold of Alsace-Lorraine in 1945, its reintegration into France was problematic, as many of the region's residents had engaged in repression towards their fellow French citizens. Naturally, the French government wanted to wipe out all traces of what had just taken place and banned the German language from all parts of society, from street names to the educational system. As one sees from wandering the streets and exploring the restaurants, however, German influence still dominates. Streets are lined with narrow, several-story houses criss-crossed with wooden beams, and the restaurants propose sauerkraut, *flammekuechen,* and a selection of very sturdy German sausages.

Despite French suppression, Alsatians often speak the German dialect in addition to French, which is not the case in Lorraine. When Louis XIV annexed the region in 1648, he began a process of Frenchification that stuck, and the cities in Lorraine consequently feel distinctly more French than their counterparts across the Vosges. Nancy and Metz, the two capitals of the region, are both sophisticated cities endowed with the straight avenues and large parks that one associates with French urban planning.

Both regions offer the chance for exquisite and/or hearty dining—especially Alsace, where the delicacy *pâté de foie*

gras, or fattened goose liver, was invented. In fact, the term *à l'alsacienne* usually means that foie gras is somewhere on the plate (failing that, a pile of sauerkraut). Quiche Lorraine—a round pastry shell filled with eggs and cream and studded with bacon (and sometimes cheese and onion)—is Lorraine's regional contribution to the fine annals of rib-sticking cuisine. Alsace-Lorraine is one of the few regions in France where you can unabashedly order an excellent local beer with your meal, although it is famous for its fresh fruity white wines, such as Gewürztraminer and Riesling, as well. After the meal, savor one of the fine *eaux-de-vie* made from regional fruits, particularly the mirabelle plum, the cherries of the Ajol valley, and the raspberries of Alsace, used to make *framboise,* a costly and refined after-coffee drink. Lorraine is also the source for Vittel water, one of France's most popular bottled mineral waters.

The Best of Alsace-Lorraine

○**The Best Change of Pace from Sauerkraut: Les Temps des Délices,** a romantic restaurant in Colmar with a lovely open-air deck, boasts an Italian chef in the kitchen with an obvious passion for preparation, presentation, and fresh, seasonal ingredients—outdone only by his passion for his Alsatian wife, with whom he owns the restaurant. Feel the love. See p. 711.

○**The Best Romantic Canalside Dining:** Nestled right up against one of Petite Venise's tiny canals, **Caveau St. Pierre Restaurant** is Colmar's most intimate, romantic restaurant. The water floats past; the bridge, bedecked with planters bursting with flowers, hovers in the background; and there's

nothing between you and your loved one except a big plate of sausage. See p. 710.

○**The Best Reminder to Be Grateful for Modern Medicine:** The order of St. Anthony—which commissioned the **Isenheim Altarpiece,** at the Musée d'Unterlinden in Colmar—was famed for its ability to treat *ergotism,* or rye-fungus. Thankfully that's not much of a problem these days, and pilgrims can just admire the Antonites' taste in art, namely Matthias Grünewald's masterpiece, completed in 1516. See p. 712.

○**The Best Achingly Cute Tradition:** Each holiday season, from the end of November until the very end of December, Colmar gets even more twee with its atmospheric **Christmas markets** (www.noel-colmar.com), featuring local crafts, arts and antiques, children's toys, and food products. See p. 714.

○ **The Best Place to Waste a Few Hours in Pursuit of Leisure:** The **Parc Pépinière** in Nancy is a sort of Platonic ideal of a park with mini-golf, bike lanes, wandering peacocks, and a snack stand selling artisanal ice cream. See p. 722.

○ **The Best Method of Learning Bible Stories Like an Illiterate 13th-Century Peasant:** Study the facade carvings on Strasbourg's magnificent **cathedral.** See p. 704.

○ **The Best Place to Strike an Iconic Pose:** Next to Auguste Rodin's *The Thinker* at Strasbourg's **Musée d'Art Moderne et Contemporain.** See p. 703.

○ **The Best Reminder of the Human Capacity for Senseless Death and Destruction:** The **Ossuaire** near Verdun, a World War II memorial under which are buried the bones of 130,000 unknown soldiers. The bottom of the building is glass, which allows a glimpse of piles and piles of skeletal remains. Never again? See p. 724.

○ **The Best Attempt at Time Travel:** The good folks at **A la Table du Bon Roi Stanislas** do their damnedest to transport diners back in time by serving recipes straight from the cookbook of Stan's personal chef, which they

found in the municipal library. I say "attempt" because you should do all you can to keep yourself in the present—this delicious cooking merits your full attention. See p. 720.

○ **The Best Time to See Another Dimension of Mulhouse:** In mid-July, local music venue La Noumatrouff hosts the **Festival Bêtes de Scène** (☎ 03-89-32-94-10)—probably just as much to prove that Mulhouse knows how to party as to give everyone something fun to do. Esoteric genres like *gnawa* music from North Africa and instrumental trance means there's something for everyone.

○ **The Best Proof That the Show Must Go On:** The **Opéra-Théâtre** (☎ 03-87-75-40-50; http://opera.ca2m.com). in Metz has been entertaining folk with ballets, operas, and operettas since 1752.

○ **The Best French Seinfeld Character:** The Soup Nazi's Continental counterpart in Metz, **Patrick Grumberg** (☎ 06-08-31-11-04) is anything but a Nazi. He's Jewish, to start, and exceptionally friendly, serving more than a dozen delicious soups at his stand under the covered market.

○ **The Best Beer Bar:** It's a chain, but **Les Frères Berthom** (24 rue du Palais; ☎ 03-87-75-25-52) in Metz still offers the best selection of artisanal beers and a lively, atmosphere with warm lighting and friendly waiters.

ALSACE-LORRAINE

Getting There & Getting Around

Getting around Alsace and Lorraine is fairly easy. Tourist offices in most Alsatian towns and cities can provide you with itineraries for visiting the region's wineries by car or by bike, and the train runs frequently between all the major towns and cities, although less frequently to some of

the smaller destinations such as Verdun, the site of several World War II memorials. See each city, below, for details.

The **Strasbourg-Entzheim Airport** (Aéroport International Strasbourg; ☎ 03-88-64-67-67; www.strasbourg.aeroport. fr), 15km (9¹⁄₃ miles) southwest of the city center, receives daily flights from many European cities, including Paris, London, Rome, Vienna, Moscow, and some destinations in North Africa and Turkey.

Strasbourg

It's difficult to come up with a negative statement about Strasbourg. The city has so many things going for it: magnificent and varied architecture, kick-ass museums, sophisticated shopping, major student life, and a big old river flowing through it. People tend to think of Strasbourg as a place where important European stuff goes down, and the assumption is understandable: The European Parliament meets there once a month for 4 days at a time. The rest of the time it meets in Brussels, with some remaining business conducted in Luxembourg.

If this unusual setup is reminiscent of a custody ruling in an ugly divorce case, it's because that's rather how it came about. The French and Germans fought over the region of Alsace for hundreds of years, most recently and violently in World War II, when it was effectively part of Germany. After the war ended and the Council of Europe formed in 1949, Strasbourg, by then handed back to the French, was chosen as its seat, to symbolize a future of European cooperation rather than strife.

The name of the city more or less means "town where lots of roads meet." Rail lines and rivers converge here, too. Thus, it has always been a prosperous mercantile center, and this prosperity is no less evident now than it was in the past. Strasbourg is still an important manufacturing and engineering hub, with 50,000 students and a growing number of tourists, as the word spreads about the city's many attractions. The shopping here is abundant and top of the line, as are the restaurants.

And did we mention the cathedral? It's Strasbourg's other claim to fame—a Gothic masterpiece in pink sandstone that took nearly 300 years to build. This was the city's crown jewel, erected during its golden era, when it was an independent republic, self-governing and self-important. A center for humanist scholarship, it was also a hub of Lutheran activity and book publishing, like nearby Basel. If they had been making college yearbooks back then, you would be able to look up Goethe sporting an embarrassing haircut, since he attended the German Lutheran university here.

Even throughout the tug of war between France and Germany that began in 1681, when King Louis XIV annexed the city, and didn't end until 1944, Strasbourg has maintained its own culture and spirit. The pace here is brisk but easy, it's small in size but very cosmopolitan, and the people are sophisticated without being snobby. Again, it's hard to find anything bad to say about Strasbourg.

Getting There

The **Strasbourg-Entzheim Airport** (Aéroport International Strasbourg; ☎ **03-88-64-67-67**; www.strasbourg.aeroport. fr), 15km (9¹/₃ miles) southwest of the city center, receives daily flights from many European cities, including Paris, London, Rome, Vienna, Moscow, and some destinations in North Africa and Turkey.

At least nine **trains** a day arrive from Paris's Gare de l'Est (trip time: 4¹/₂ hr.); the one-way fare is 40€. From Nancy, there are 13 trains a day (trip time: 90 min.); the fare is 19€ one-way. For information and schedules, call ☎ **08-92-35-35-35.**

A high-speed TVG train to Paris is in the works. In summer 2007, it will whisk you from the capital to Strasbourg and back in 2 hours.

Alsace-Lorraine

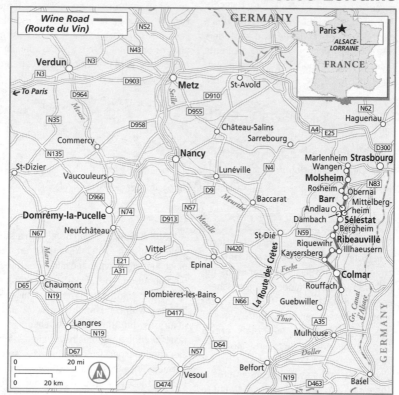

Orientation

Although it is the biggest city in the region, Strasbourg is easy to get around both on foot and with public transport—in particular their smooth-running, prompt, clean, and spacious tram system. Because it's flat, it's also easy to bike, although some of the more crowded neighborhoods, such as the area around the cathedral, are a hassle to get around. For the most part, though, wide pedestrian lanes and bike lanes make it a safe and enjoyable place to ride.

Most of the tourist activity is concentrated in the historic area around the cathedral and the several squares nearby, on what is called the Grande Ile. It was one

By **car,** the giant A35 crosses the plain of Alsace, with occasional references to its original name, the N83. It links Strasbourg with Colmar and Mulhouse.

You can get from the airport to the town center by using **shuttle buses** and **city trams.** They run at 30-minute intervals in the morning and every 15 minutes in the afternoon. The one-way cost is 4.90€. Take a shuttle bus to the south side of Strasbourg, to a junction point known as Baggersee. From there, you'll continue to the town center on tram line A. Combined travel time is between 35 and 40 minutes each way. For information, call ☎ 03-88-77-70-70.

of the first city centers to be classified in its entirety as a heritage site by UNESCO. The city is cleaved by the River Ill, which encircles the Grande Ile and meanders into canals throughout the romantic Petite France neighborhood. The university campus (and, therefore, some of the student life) is a bit southeast of the center. The European institutions are near the large Parc de l'Orangerie, northeast of the old center. It's all easy to reach by bus, tram, bike, or on foot. There is also an adequate number of public parking lots scattered throughout the city.

Strasbourg Nuts & Bolts

Emergencies Fire ☎ 18; police ☎ 17.

Hospital **Civil Hospital,** place de l'Hôpital (☎ 03-88-11-67-68).

Post Office **La Poste,** 4 av. de la Liberté (☎ 03-88-52-31-00).

Sleeping

Strasbourg has some surprisingly affordable hotels, although you won't run into any visiting European dignitaries in the hallways. Even the moderate hotels here are often a good value for the money, with a lot of romance and atmosphere. Some of the bigger international hotels are a bit outside the center, and although Strasbourg has a good tram system, it's always better to stay in the center of town. There's a lot to see, and you won't want to waste time getting to and from the hotel.

HOSTELS

➔ **Ciarus** Ciarus is a rare find—a hostel that doesn't require four municipal bus transfers in order to reach it. As hostels go, it's pretty expensive; you'd almost do as well to find a cheap hotel. But if you like the hostel atmosphere, this place has plenty of it and plenty of room—it sleeps 285 guests, over four floors. Management throws a crepe party several times a week, and there's an in-house discothèque. Reception is open from 6:30 to 10pm, and the building is fully accessible for travelers with special needs. *7 rue Finkmatt.* ☎ *33-03-88-15-27-90. www.ciarus.com. From 17€ bunk bed in 6- to 8-person room; 40€ private room.*

CHEAP

➔ **Hôtel Kléber** A cheap hotel with a tangible aesthetic bent? Yes, right on the place Kléber, smack in the middle of things (and about 9m/30 ft. from a tram stop), is this darling, intimate hotel in a historic building with renovated interiors. It isn't luxurious, but the decor is cheery and tasteful enough. Rooms have themes: You can choose from "fruity ambience," "spicy harmony," or "sweet atmosphere." To be honest, these ridiculous names sound a lot nicer in French, as do the names of the rooms themselves: Mirabelle, Noisette, Meringue. All of this gimmicky nomenclature basically refers to the color scheme of the rooms, which are compact, clean, and lovely. They could have stepped it up a little on the breakfast. Save your 7€ for a few *viennoiserie* and a cup of coffee from a cafe or *boulangerie. 29 place Kléber.* ☎ *33-03-88-32-09-53. www.hotel-Kléber.com. 50€–82€ double. Credit cards accepted. In room: Flatscreen TV, Internet.*

➔ **Hôtel Michelet** With only 17 rooms, low prices, and an unbeatable location, this little nugget fills up fast, so book as far ahead as possible. The rooms are nothing extraordinary, but it's right on one of

Strasbourg's busiest commercial streets, a few minutes from the cathedral and many of the museums. If you book online, you'll also get free breakfast. *48 rue du Vieux Marché aux Poissons.* ☎ *03-88-32-47-38. www.hotel-michelet.com. 28€–32€ single with sink, 41€ with shower, 42€ with shower and toilet; 38€–49€ double. Breakfast 5€. Pets accepted.*

DOABLE

→**Beaucour Romantik Hôtel** Even if they spell romantic with a k, the folks over here at the Hôtel Beaucour do seem to know a thing or two about romance. The three-star hotel is hidden away, down a little side street, just across the river from the major action. There are four single rooms, each with a shower cabin, but most of the rooms are for two, with canopied beds, frescoed walls, wood beams, and warm lighting. All the rooms except the singles have a Jacuzzi bathtub. *5 rue des Bouchers/5 rue des Boeufs.* ☎ *33-03-88-76-72-00. www.hotel-beaucour.fr. 65€–181€ double. Breakfast 12€. Credit cards accepted. Pets welcome. Amenities: Dry cleaning/laundry; paying parking across the street; room service. In room: A/C, TV, hair dryer, minibar, Wi-Fi.*

→**Hôtel Cathédrale** This hotel is working the classy angle (check out the classical music and opera that kick in when you access the website). Indeed, it's in a gorgeous three-star hotel in a Renaissance building, in Strasbourg's most desirable location, facing the cathedral. Cathedral-side rooms are most expensive, but all are nicely done with top-quality linens, and some have original architectural details, such as half-timbered walls (those wooden beams that form triangle patterns) and French windows.

You couldn't be any closer to all of Strasbourg's sites, and complimentary bicycles here will help you cover even more ground faster. *12–13 place de la Cathédrale.* ☎ *03-88-22-12-12. www.hotel-cathedrale.fr. 75€–150€ double. Credit cards accepted. In room: AC, cable TV, minibar, safe, Wi-Fi.*

SPLURGE

→**Régent Petite France** The building dates from the 1700s, but the Régent Petite France features slick, contemporary rooms and a zen, modern reception area jazzed up with snazzy, self-conscious lighting. It would be right at home in New York or Los Angeles, but the actual location, directly on the River Ill, means you'll be lulled to sleep by the sound of rushing water. It has four stars, prices to reflect that, and clients whose every round of hotel bar cocktails speaks to the fact that their company (or government) is picking up the tab. *5 rue des Moulins.* ☎ *33-03-88-76-43-43. www.regent-hotels.com. 169€–255€ double; 249€–370€ suite. Rates include breakfast. Credit cards accepted. Pets 20€; parking 20€. In room: AC, cable TV, minibar, Wi-Fi.*

Eating

CAFES & LIGHT FARE

→**Christian** ICE CREAM Centrally located on the main tourist drag in front of the cathedral, this place is thronged in summer with tourists and locals clamoring for homemade ice cream. Flavors are daredevil, such as vanilla with tapenade, which is strangely not gross at all, and raspberry-basil sorbet. In winter, go for a savory onion tart or a rich cup of hot chocolate. Year-round, treat yourself to the buttery and very French pastries, or the fanciful chocolates and truffles (ginger, cardamom, and coriander with Madagascar chocolate is one of their latest creations), which ornament the windows as beautifully and self-consciously as mannequins in an

ALSACE-LORRAINE

Alsatian Menu Reader

Confused by the sudden appearance of German on the menu? It's not a bad thing, either linguistically or gastronomically. For starters, you can finally get yourself a decent beer here in Alsace, which pairs perfectly with the umpteen renditions of sausage you're going to see on the menus around town.

Actually, the Germanic menu terms are often Alsatian, which is its own official language. To the perturbation of French and German officials who have each tried in their turn to eliminate the language from the public sphere, locals persist in speaking it (often in addition to the other two languages).

Other Alsatian specialties—*flammekueche,* or *tarte flambée,* sauerkraut, and *baeckeoffe*—are equally abundant. Once you familiarize yourself with the lingo, the only problem you'll have is deciding which Alsatian mouthful to order.

Baeckoffe   Boiled meat and potatoes marinated in white wine
Bibeleskäs   Soft white cheese with shallots and fried potatoes
Choucroute   Refers to both the dish and the vegetable, which can be garnished with grilled saveloy or fish
Fleischkiechle   Spicy meatballs
Fleischnecke   ("meat snails") Boiled beef rolled in lasagna-type pasta
Grumbeerekiechle   Potato flat cakes
Kassler   Smoked pork filets
Knepfle   Dumplings made of mashed potatoes, egg yolks, and flour
Kougelhopf   Tall, sweet pastry for breakfast or afternoon tea
Lewerknepfle   Pig's liver dumplings
Presskopf   Parsleyed pork headcheese
Rustcherla (or Rustchala)   Traditional little flat-bottomed glass
Saumagen (or Saumawe)   Stuffed pork stomach
Schiffala   Shoulder of pork marinated in white wine
Spätzle   Alsatian noodles
Stammtisch (or table d'hôte)   The regulars' table in a wine cellar
Sueri Nierli   Veal or pork kidneys cooked in vinegar
Wädele   Small pork knuckle
Winstub   Wine cellar (*wistub* in the "High Rhine" region)

upscale department store. Spices are all stone-ground on a regular basis to preserve their freshness, and many of the fruits are grown on the Christian family's property in the Vosges mountains. Don't expect warm and benevolent service—this place is top of the line, they know it, and they've got little to prove to anyone. The second location, on rue de l'Outre (☎ 03-88-32-04-41), is a little more laid-back. *10 rue Mercière.* ☎ *03-88-22-12-70.*

www.christian.fr. Ice cream 1.50€ per scoop. Credit cards accepted. Mon–Sat 7:30am–6:30pm.

CHEAP

→**Flam's** FLAMMEKUECHE   It's a chain, yes, but it's also a great way to get cozy with the Alsatian pizza known as *flammekueche*. In its most basic incarnation, it's a thin, square-shaped, pizza-like dough topped with cream, cheese, onions, and smoked bacon, baked until it's bubbly and golden. You should eat it immediately—read: You can't eat it cold the next morning like Neopolitan pizza—because that tasty gooey cream congeals into disgusting curds once it cools. But chances are the *flammekueche* won't last long enough to lose its steam anyway; these things are pretty addictive. Can you find anything wrong with the dough + cream + cheese + onions + bacon formula? Neither can I. They've put a creative spin on the basic *flammekueche*—such as the Indian spiced chicken version, that may or may not have taken its cues from Domino's or Pizza Hut. They also serve vegetarian *flammies* and dessert flamsters, such as apple and cinnamon, plus a monthly novelty flam that's always in rotation.

The flammeroonies (it's hard to stop riffing on a prefix like flam) are available a la carte or as part of a fixed-price menu with all-you-can-eat flammin'. It's a bargain if you haven't eaten all week. The decor is a little cheesy—with red and yellow walls and a kind of trying-to-be-hip-doctor's-office feel to it—but it's easy to overlook once you start eating. *29 rue des Frères.* ☎ *03-88-36-36-90. www.flams.fr. Flammekuech 5.50€–8€ a la carte; all-you-can-eat 12€–18€. Credit cards accepted. Daily 11am–midnight.*

➜ **L'Epicerie** TARTINES This place is almost too cute for its own good. It's one of those ludicrously charmingly decorated cafe-restaurants with a ludicrously good-looking, young, and carefree clientele that serves tasty food for not too much money. The specialty of the house is the *tartine*—a slice of bread that in the right chef's hands is a blank canvas for an extensive oeuvre of one masterpiece after another. This chef dresses it up with creative combinations

like brie, honey, and nuts, and other sweet and salty combinations, in addition to classic meat and cheese and veggie mixes.

The shabby chic decoration includes a smattering of antique boxes and other retro '60s gear dotted around the restaurant. The centerpiece is a large communal table where you should plop yourself down and make a friend or two, if you can stand the smoke. The lighting is warm and flattering, which ups your chances of achieving the aforementioned. The desserts have a bad rep, but the sweet *tartines* are a sure shot. *6 rue du Vieux Seigle.* ☎ *03-88-32-52-41. Tartines 3.50€–5.20€; salads and soups 2€–3€. Credit cards accepted. Daily 8am–1pm.*

➜ **Poêles de Carottes** VEGETARIAN Are you tired of seeing big wieners everywhere? There's hope for you yet, at this popular vegetarian restaurant on a quiet but animated side street in Petite France, facing a square where semi-talented but endearing musicians and street performers set up shop on summer evenings. Since it attracts tree-hugging, everyone-loving, scruffy-bearded types in sensible shoes (and the chic French version of these types), the patrons are very friendly. This trait hasn't trickled up to the waiters yet, but it may just happen soon.

So the atmosphere is lovely, and the food is pretty decent as well. The menu—full of pizzas, stir-fries, Asian-ish noodle dishes, pastas, salads, and loose interpretations on the burrito—leaves a lot of room for customer creativity. You can add different vegetables or other ingredients for small extra fees. To some, this may signal a careless chef who hasn't taken the time to compose a menu. To others, tired of fascist French waiters who consistently veto requests for substitutions, this may seem a blessing.

ALSACE-LORRAINE

You'll see on almost every table a plate of something oozing goopy cheese. That's the stuffed bread—a big slice of chewy *ciabatta* filled with mozzarella and pesto (or, again, a loose interpretation of pesto) and another ingredient of your choice. I had the cumin seeds, and against all odds it tasted good (albeit like something I might have put together at 3am studying for finals that doesn't really fit into any cuisine but hits the spot anyway).

In the summer, get there early, because the terrace fills up by around 7:30pm, and sitting inside isn't half as nice as sitting on the square and watching a guy swallow fire or belt out charmingly mediocre tunes. *2 place des Meuniers.* ☎ *03-88-32-33-23. www. poelesdecarottes.com. Main courses 8€–13€. Credit cards accepted. Mon–Sat noon–2:30pm and 7–10:30pm.*

DOABLE

→**Chez Yvonne** ALSATIAN Another must-see on the Strasbourg *winstub* circuit, Chez Yvonne keeps a running list of the heavy-hitters who have feasted at her red-and-white-checked tablecloths. French actors, comedians, journalists, and big name intellectuals (and pinups) such as Bernard Henri Lévy, plus the many diplomats and *chefs d'état* who are passing through on European Union business, make up the pantheon of stars into which you can gently insert yourself.

The food is *winstub* fare done especially well; the *coq au Riesling* comes with plenty of creamy boozy sauce for sopping up with bread after the tender chicken has disappeared, and the region's star cheese nestles nicely into a bed of puff pastry in a very well-done *feuilleté of munster*. The decor looks like it has held steady since the place opened—in 1873. *10 rue du Sanglier.* ☎ *03-88-32-84-15. www.chez-yvonne.net. Main courses 12€–25€. Credit cards accepted. Daily 6pm–midnight.*

→**La Place** BRASSERIE This combination bar, restaurant, brasserie, and cafe is most of all a pleasant place to sit on a sunny afternoon and fill your stomach or quench your thirst at moderate prices. The small menu features fairly creative French cooking with hints of Italian influence. There's a good selection of carpaccios and tartares, as well as salads, local dishes, and vegetarian options. The starter dishes come in two sizes and prices. It's a bit of a place to see and be seen—as the French call it, the *tu m'as vu* (have you seen me?) crowd. The magazine pickings on the wall rack inside reflect that—you'll find hipster magazines devoted entirely to sneakers, and music and culture rags too. *3–5 place des Tripiers.* ☎ *03-88-22-22-20. Small starters 4€–8€; starters 8€–13€; main courses 12€–20€. Credit cards accepted. Mon–Sat lunch noon–4pm, cocktails 4–7pm, dinner 5–11pm.*

→**Restaurant Maison Kammerzell** ALSATIAN/FRENCH For convenience's sake, it's hard to beat Restaurant Maison Kammerzell, located right on the place de la Cathédrale. Unlike many of the other tourist traps hovering around the magnificent Gothic cathedral, this restaurant is actually renowned for the food, which is traditional Alsatian and French. The three-fish *choucroute* (a novelty in this town, where sauerkraut is usually served with animals that walked rather than swam) and the homemade foie gras come highly recommended.

The 15th-century quarters are very cool looking. The stone arcades were once a market, where the succession of rich merchants who owned the building also plied their wares with great success. The rest of the house, a gingerbread fantasy, was built in 1589 by a cheese merchant, Martin Braun. A grocer, Phillippe Kammerzell, later purchased the place, which still bears his name. *16 place de la Cathédrale.* ☎ *03-88-32-42-14. www.maison-kammerzell.com. Main courses from 14€; menus 29€–45€. Credit cards accepted. Daily 7am–11pm.*

➔**Winstub Le Clou** ALSATIAN This *winstub* around the corner from the cathedral is a Strasbourg classic—everyone from the grocer to the hotel clerk to the tourist office personnel will recommend this place for a solid meal of Alsatian specialties, particularly the meats, sausages, and *choucroute,* or sauerkraut, dishes. The interior is decorated in classical winstub fashion, meaning a lot of wood and not too much natural light. But it's a pleasant atmosphere, with lots of Strasbourgeois regulars, satisfied-looking tourists, and lone businessmen gorging themselves on the hearty food and fine wines.

The menu ranges from French classics such as steak with green pepper sauce and different preparations of foie gras, to Alsatian specialties such as veal head with vinaigrette (which I wish I could report to be delicious, if I'd had the *cojones* to sample it). *3 rue du Chaudron.* ☎ *03-88-32-11-67. Fax 03-88-21-06-43. Main courses 12€–23€. Credit cards accepted. Mon–Tues noon–2pm; Mon–Sat 7:30–10pm; Thurs–Sat noon–2pm.*

SPLURGE

🅜 ⬤Best◗ ➔**Au Crocodile** FRENCH If you've got it—"it" meaning "big wads of cash"—here's where to flaunt it. Au Crocodile is sporting two Michelin stars, and it's definitely in the mood to keep them—having lost one several years ago in a very public episode that thankfully didn't drive the chef to suicide, as Michelin star-deprivation in France has been known to do. (Chef and owner Emile Jung has posted a heartbreaking letter on the restaurant's website, in which he laments that "words cannot describe our pain" upon hearing of the loss of the Michelin star.) The fixed-price

menus are a relative bargain, and you'll eat well, even if the options are fairly limited. This food deserves a blinged-out bottle of wine, and the menu has plenty. It's proper gastronomy—meaning delicate subtle flavors and textures (lemon foam, chestnut flan), innovative combinations (pineapple risotto and masala curry), and very French and time-consuming preparation (duck liver cooked in a salt crust—a Crocodile classic). Just be sure to savor everything slowly, especially as this will delay the arrival of the gigantic bill. *10 rue de l'Outre.* ☎ *33-03-88-32-13-02. www.au-crocodile.com. Appetizers 16€–75€; main courses 39€–75€. Prix-fixe lunch 57€–112€; prix-fixe dinner 86€–127€. Credit cards accepted. Tues–Sat noon–1:30pm and 7:30–9:30pm; closed July and Dec 24–early Jan.*

Partying
FUNKY BARS

➔**Académie de la Bière** Have you ever wished your high school had been a beer academy instead of a regular educational institution? It may be too late for that fantasy to come true, but there is always this lovely bar. Within its warm, all-wooden interior, servers will be happy to provide you with a few lessons in tasty beer and tutoring in *flammekueche* as well, should you require it. With its broad selection of beers on tap and music at a reasonable volume, it's a great place to start the evening—especially because prices are a bit lower before 9pm. *17 rue Adolphe-Seyboth.* ☎ *03-88-22-38-88.*

➔**Au Brasseur** Mmmm . . . microbrews and *flammekueches.* Au Brasseur makes four beer varieties on tap, with flammos to match, served at all hours of the day. The quality of the beer exceeds that of the food, but no one ever said pub grub needs to shine. *22 rue des Veaux.* ☎ *03-88-36-12-13.*

➜ **Brasserie de la Lanterne** *Conviviale* is how the patrons of this small, lively bar describe it, without fail. It's one of the last few microbreweries in downtown Strasbourg (also see Au Brasseur, above). Huge copper brewing vats line the wall to the right. They serve four varieties of beer at a time, made in house, to a crowd of mostly students, both nerdy and chic, and every gradation in between. Cute, friendly bartenders will explain to you the beer-making process, should you desire to know the method behind the madness. *3 rue de la Lanterne.* ☎ *03-88-32-10-10.*

➜ **La Perestroïka** Yes, it's beer country, but there's room for a vodka bar nonetheless. For a different kind of hangover than the one you've been getting thus far in Alsace, hit La Perestroïka for a wide selection of vodkas, and the exclusive artisanal beer made with mountain spring water. It's a few minutes outside of the town center on foot, on the ground floor of the Hôtel Le Grillon. *2 rue Thiergarten.* ☎ *03-88-75-05-45.*

CLUBS & LIVE MUSIC VENUES

➜ **La Laiterie** This is the top spot for live music, from U.S. acts like Yo La Tengo to offbeat music acts and soirees that feature everything from French pop, to dub, to "reggae conscious," to "grind core brutal death metal," (whatever those are). The crowd is as varied as the music, and there is definitely something for everyone here, depending on the night. Check the website or the free monthly *Spectacles* for concert listings, and book your ticket online or pick one up at Virgin.

It's a 15-minute walk from the train station. Take a right out of the station, and it's down the fifth street on your right. Or take the tram lines B or C; the place has its own stop. Get off at La Laiterie and take a right at the light, then your first right. *13 rue du Hohwald.* ☎ *03-88-23-72-37. www.artefact.org.*

➜ **La Salamandre** There's nothing snobby or upscale about La Salamandre, it's just a place to get drunk, listen to some rockin' cheesy music and make your best attempt to burn off some calories from all the *flammekueche* and beers that have made their way to your gut. Themed evenings like salsa or all-white clothing night, and student nights (Thurs, usually) make it a popular place for people just looking to have an earnest, unpretentious good time. *03 rue Paul Janet.* ☎ *03-88-25-79-42. www.lasalamandre-strasbourg.fr.*

Sightseeing

Church and state sit comfortably side by side in Strasbourg. Home to one of Europe's most famous cathedrals, and also to the institutions of the European Union (part-time, at least), Strasbourg has attractions for the layman and the pious alike. If politics and churches aren't your thing, you'll also find several historical museums and a seriously great modern art museum, on the square named after native son Hans Jean Arp, overlooking the foamy magnificence of the rushing Ill River.

If you need help organizing your cultural agenda or want an in on the art gallery scene, stop by the **Boutique Culture** (10 place de la Cathédrale; ☎ **03-88-23-84-65**), which is sort of a municipally run tourist office promoting local cultural life, including concerts and theater events. You can buy tickets there.

MUSEUMS

➜ **Musée Alsacien (Alsatian Museum)** A sweet little ethnographic museum dedicated to the crafts and daily objects of Alsatian life from the 13th to 19th centuries. You'll find the typical local costumes, pottery, and other bits and pieces of not terribly interesting handiwork, interspersed with really original pieces such as the beautiful old tiled ovens that middle-class and wealthier families had in their homes. There are tableau scenes too, showing the objects not just in isolation but as they might have been used once upon a time. The re-created pharmacy looks like just the kind of place that would have been pushing snake oil and eye of newt back in the day. This year marks its 100th anniversary. It's partially wheelchair accessible. *23–25 quai Saint-Nicolas.* ☎ *03-88-52-50-01. Admission 4€. Wed–Mon 10am–6pm.*

⚫ Best ◑ →**Musée d'Art Moderne et Contemporain (Museum of Modern & Contemporary Art)** Strasbourg's modern and contemporary art museum has a worthwhile collection of art dating from the 1890s to the present. The family of Strasbourg native Hans Jean Arp started the city's collection with a gift of around thirty pieces from Arp and his wife, Sophie Taeuber-Arp, over the years from 1920 to 1973, after which the museum began actively collecting. In addition to temporary exhibits by both famous artists and young, up-and-coming rebels from Europe and elsewhere, there are some classics like Rodin's *The Thinker,* 1 of over 20 copies known to have been made from the original mold.

The lively and only mildly snooty scene at the Art Café on the first floor is a fun place for a break between exhibits or for a post-museum pick-me-up. To show they've spared no expense, down to the last detail, they hired the architect who did the Café Marly at the Louvre to design this sleek space with its huge floor-to-ceiling glass wall that looks onto the river Ill. Wheelchair accessible. *1 place Hans Jean Arp.* ☎ *03-88-23-31-31. www.musees-strasbourg.org/F/musees/mamcs/mamcs.html. Admission 5€ adults, 2.50€ students. May 1–Sept 30 Tues–Sat*

11am–11pm; Oct 1–Apr 30 11am–7pm (Thurs until 10pm).

→**Musée de l'Oeuvre Notre-Dame** The quiet soothing interior garden of this 14th century building is reason enough to visit this museum, dedicated to the art of the Middle Ages and Renaissance in the Lower Rhine region. It was for many years the administrative site in charge of maintaining funds and directing the construction of that big old cathedral across the way (you know the one I'm talking about?), and its rooms were at one point lodging for the cathedral's architects, masons, and stone cutters.

The museum has a small but high-quality selection of religious art, ironwork, wood sculpture, and a room of wonderful stained-glass windows. The German artists of the region for the most part worked in a haunting, stylized manner, and the sculptures especially have a tortured and refreshingly creepy manner about them. Be warned: Close proximity to a stained-glass window engenders a new level of appreciation for all the ones you've been kinda glancing at in French churches so far. It's a privilege to see these delicately worked masterpieces up close, without craning your neck. *Note:* It's not wheelchair accessible. *3 place du Château.* ☎ *03-88-52-50-00. Admission 4.50€. Tues–Sun 10am–6pm.*

→**Palais Rohan** One of Strasbourg's finest edifices, this building was constructed beginning in 1732 by Robert de Cotte, then the king's architect, for the then-Cardinal of Strasbourg. Now it houses three museums on three floors: In the basement is the **Musée Archéologique (Archaeology Museum),** with artifacts dating from 600,000 B.C.; on the ground floor is the **Musée des Arts Décoratifs,** with tapestries, home furnishings, and timepieces way too sumptuous for a man of

God; and on the second floor (they call it a first floor) is the **Musée des Beaux-Arts (Fine Arts Museum)**. If you love big, over-done French houses, you'll enjoy strolling through the triumvirate of museums in this very spectacular building. *2 place du Château* ☎ *03-88-52-50-00. Admission 4€ adults, 2.50€ students. Wed–Mon 10am–6pm.*

GALLERIES

There is a lively gallery scene in Strasbourg, although few of the galleries have ground-floor space.

FREE → **Gallery Zoo** This gallery dedicated to young talent frequently hosts mini-events (and a large portion of Strasbourg's hipsters) at its openings. Check website for schedule. *19 rue Thiergarten.* ☎ *06-83-75-00-10. http://galeriezoo.free.fr. Free admission. Wed–Sat 3–7pm.*

MONUMENTS & CHURCHES

FREE → **The Cathedral** Whole books have been written about this cathedral, with good reason. The pink sandstone confection is gasp-inducing and doesn't have a bad angle. Begun in 1176, its 142m (466 ft.) spire was completed in 1439. The 250 years in between gave the many craftsmen who toiled at it ample time to weave the figures and ornamental decorations that give the facade its impressive beauty and complexity. It features figures representing Virtue kicking the keisters of those representing Vice, and scenes and personages from the life of Christ, all in such great profusion it's difficult to appreciate unless you travel very slowly with your eyes (or seek out a tour guide).

Inside are a number of free things to gawk at (lavishly decorated chapels, baptismal fonts, an organ from the Middle Ages) and two you'll have to cough up for. It costs 4.40€ (2.20€ for students) for the privilege of scaling 332 steps to the top of the spire. And why would you do such a

thing? Because on a clear day you can see as far as the Black Forest in Germany, and to the Vosges mountains. *Pas mal.* It's 1€ to get a close look at the Astronomical Clock, completed in 1547, with its little spectacle of automatons that represent the different stages of life. Called a masterpiece of the Renaissance, it takes lightbulb jokes to a whole new level: How many mathematicians, artists, Swiss watchmakers, technicians, craftsmen, sculptors, painters, and automaton-makers did it take to make the Astronomical Clock? *Place de la Cathédrale.* ☎ *03-88-24-43-34. Apr–Sept daily 9am–7:30pm (until 10pm June–Aug); Oct–Mar daily 10am–5:30pm; closed Jan 1, Jan 5, and Dec 25. Tickets sold at postcard stand 9am–11:30am, then at the desk of the south porch 11:50am–12:20pm. Admission 3€. Free admission to tower 1st Sun of the month.*

FREE → **The European Institutions** For 4 days each month, European parliamentarians pack their bags and head to Strasbourg for a week of vigorous debate, lawmaking, and expensive hotel rooms courtesy of the European taxpayer. Visits are possible when the parliament is in session for up to 1 hour on a first-come, first-served basis (call ☎ **03-88-17-20-07** for the schedule). The **Palais de l'Europe** is used by the Council of Europe. You can visit on free 1-hour weekday tours, which you may reserve a day ahead (☎ **03-88-41-20-29;** www.coe.int). During one of the four yearly Parliamentary Assembly sessions, you can sit in as three dozen countries squabble about agricultural subsidies and the other scandalous issues tearing modern Europe apart. Then there's the (hear, hear!) **European Court of Human Rights** (☎ 03-88-41-24-32; www.europarl.eu.int/abc/visit/visit_en.htm), in a futurist building by architect Richard Rogers. Two to five morning court sessions take place each month. Space permitting, visits are allowed. Check "pending cases" on the website to see if you stand a chance of coming face to face with the war criminal of the moment.

HISTORIC NEIGHBORHOODS

Strasbourg's entire **Grand Ile** was classified as a UNESCO World Heritage site in 1988, one of the first times a whole neighborhood has taken that honor. Besides the monumental cathedral, you can visit a number of smaller medieval churches such as St-Thomas, St-Pierre le Vieux, and St-Pierre le Jeune, and wander among the half-timbered houses, most notably the Maison Kammerzell just across from the cathedral. The pedestrian walkways are broken up by large squares, notably the places Gutenberg, Kléber, and Broglie. The Petite France neighborhood is another treasure, with its narrow streets overlapped by canals. All around, of course, are plenty of stores and cafes. The tourist office has a Walkman tour that's 6€ or 3€ for students, which lasts 1½ hours. Or you can arrange a tour with an accredited guide.

THE GERMAN NEIGHBORHOODS

To the north and east of Strasbourg are neighborhoods built from the 1870s to 1906 by Otto Back, the German mayor of the city at that time, whose ambition was to make Strasbourg a "window onto the new German empire." The buildings blend Florentine Renaissance principles with Berlin baroque elements, but the overall effect is one of strength and monumentality.

BREWERIES

The Kronenbourg and Heineken breweries both open their doors and taps to tourists. `FREE` → **Heineken Brewery** Free 2-hour tours available. Call for times and reservations. *4 rue Saint Charles, Schiltigheim.* ☎ *03-88-19-57-55. Take bus no. 4 northbound to Schiltigheim Mairie stop.*

→ **Kronenbourg Brewery** By reservation only Monday through Saturday. *68 rte. d'Oberhausbergen.* ☎ *03-88-27-41-59-68. Tour 5€. Tram stop Ducs d'Alsace.*

Playing Outside

CYCLING

You can rent bikes from **Vélocation** for 5€ per half-day or 8€ per full day, from two locations: **10 rue des Bouchers** (☎ 00-33-3-88-24-05-61; www.velocation. net; open summer: Mon–Fri 9:30am–12:30am and 1:30–7pm, weekends and holidays 9:30am–midnight and 2–7pm; open winter Mon–Fri 10am–5pm and closed weekends and holidays). Or **4 rue du Maire** (☎ 00-33-3-88-23-56-75; www. velocation.net; summer Mon–Fri 9:30am–7pm and weekends and holidays 9:30am–midnight and 2–7pm; winter Mon–Fri 9:30am–7pm and Sat 9:30am–midnight and 2–6pm).

BOATING

Strasbourg Fluvial/Batorama (☎ 33-03-88-32-75-25; tickets 7€ adults, students 3.50€; Mar 31–Oct 29 8am–10pm; Oct 30–Mar 30 9am–5pm) runs boat tours which leave from behind the Palais des Rohan.

MUNICIPAL BATHS

Strasbourg has a rather funky (strictly in the aesthetic sense) **municipal bathhouse** (10 bd. de la Victoire; ☎ 03-88-25-17-58; www.strasbourg.fr; admission 3€ adults, 1.55€ students). With its original Art Nouveau fixtures, it has two good-size swimming pools and Roman baths (all of which are open at odd hours, so check with the tourist office or call before arriving). While the lighting is fluorescent—as is usually the case in "municipal" structures, the building itself is rather marvelous. It's a treat to bathe in an original 1908 Art Nouveau bathhouse when many of these

The Route de Vin

Alsace-Lorraine's wine route, which you can reach by train, bus, car, or bicycle from any of the major cities and towns, takes you through picturesque hamlets such as Kayserberg, Obernai, Molsheim, Turckheim, and many others. Once you're on it, you can even walk from one town to another, on marked paths that run through the vineyards in the Vosges mountains. The tourist office in any of the larger towns can help you plan your trip. Ask for brochures or check **www. alsace-route-des-vins.com**.

For full-on indulgence (beyond multiple daily wine-tasting), consider spending a night or two in a restored château. Many of the ruined castles that dot these hills are now luxurious hotels, where you can live like royalty for less than princely sums. The **Château d'Isenbourg** (Rouffach, Alsace; ☎ 33-03-89-78-58-50; www.isenbourg.com; from 115€ double), 10 minutes outside of Colmar, for example, was once one of the royal residences of the Austrasian ruling family. Its vaulted cellar floor dates from the 1300s. It also has its own winery, and breakfast is served on a terrace overlooking the vineyards. Like its former residents, it rules. The glorious **Château de l'Ile** (4 quai Heydt, Strasbourg; ☎ 33-03-88-66-85-00; www.chateau-ile.com; from 180€ double), has a renowned spa, and an in-house sommelier who will guide you towards some of the region's finest pickings.

For a healthier adventure (less wine-tasting, more hiking), you'll find guesthouses in the mountains from which you can launch a nature escapade or two into the surrounding pine forests. These places are a more laid-back affair—meaning no coiffed women with small dogs sitting poolside. They are usually built with local materials, and are cozy and family run. **Le Refuge du Grand Tetras** (www.les-sapins-bleus.com; 10€–11€ per person in shared 15-bed room; rates do not include breakfast) and **Le Chant des Sources** (www.les-sapins-bleus.com; 46€ double, 21€ single bed in shared room without sheets; rates include breakfast) are both run by the same owner, Marc Dumoulin, who can help you plan your hikes or bike trips into the wild.

buildings in France and around Europe are now being used for other purposes, such as museums and cultural centers.

GARDENS

FREE → **Botanical Garden** A fairly self-explanatory attraction, Strasbourg's botanical gardens are a nice place to picnic and see students from the nearby university frolicking and courting one another in between classes. The most interesting thing about the garden is a secret buried in the soil: Germans used the site as a cemetery in the 1870s, meaning that rotting corpses are nourishing the growth of the 6,000 species of plants and flowers flourishing there today, some of which are experimental varieties grown for research purposes in conjunction with university students. *28 rue Goethe.* ☎ *03-90-24-18-65. Free admission. Summer Mon–Fri 8am–7:30pm, Sat–Sun 10am–7:30pm; spring and autumn Mon–Fri 8am–6pm, Sat–Sun 10am–6pm; winter Mon–Sat 8am–noon and 2–4pm, Sun 2–4pm.*

Shopping

Most of the fancy European brands have their flagships around rue des Hallebards and rue de la Haute Montée, but small boutiques that specialize in everything from cheese to candles to soaps are everywhere; it's just a matter of sniffing them out. Fresh fruit and vegetables are sold at the market in place Broglie on Wednesdays and Fridays, and during the winter the Christmas markets, an Alsatian tradition, take over the city. All over the Grand Ile, in many of the squares, markets specialize in one or more products, such as the one in the place du Gare that is colonized entirely by bakers and confectioners. What a first impression, huh? Others include the wine market in the Couronne d'Or area, or the book fair near place Gutenberg.

→ **Edouard Artzner** If all the hype about globalization and mass consumption has you worried that one day everything will be made in Chinese sweatshops, fear not. Here is a little place where tradition rules. The Edouard Artzner foie gras has been made the same way for over 2 centuries (allowing for some technological innovation), according to a recipe passed down from generation to generation. Their promotional literature reassuringly boasts that "all the livers are sorted one by one, by hand, before being selected by the chef to be included in one of our foie gras." (Who has that enviable job of sorting livers by hand, I wonder?)

Upstairs from the boutique, which also sells a variety of prepared foods, perfect for picnicking, is a casual restaurant where you can try the foie gras in different preparations, or grab a reasonably priced breakfast. *7 rue de la Mésange.* ☎ *03-88-32-05-00. www.edouardartzner.com. Mon 3–7pm; Tues–Fri 9am–7pm; Sat 8:30am–6:30pm.*

→ **La Sphère** An elegant, bright boutique selling several long racks of trendy, cute basics for women, from labels such as Antik Batik, Blue Cult, DKNY, Le Coq Sportif, and the like. The style is very French—not too daring but chic nonetheless. *1 rue des Orfèvres.* ☎ *03-88-75-50-35.*

→ **Mulhaupt** France abounds with bakeries all serving what seem like the ultimate in tarts, éclairs, and the like, but Mulhaupt is a cut above the rest. With two locations in Strasbourg, it has won numerous pastry contests and awards for its spectacular sweets. The pastry is over on rue de Vieux Marché aux Poissons. Chocolate, spice bread, coffee, tea, and other prepared goods are for sale at the boutique on rue Temple Neuf. Certain products (jams, *pain d'épices*, liqueurs) are available online, should you develop an addiction. *18 rue du Vieux Marché aux Poissons.* ☎ *03-88-23-15-02. www.mulhaupt. fr. Tues–Thurs 8:45am–12:15pm and 1:30–6:30pm; Fri 8:30am–12:15pm and 1:30–6:30pm; Sat 8:30am–12:30pm and 1:30–6:30pm; Sun 8:30am–noon. Closed holidays and Aug 1–15. Second location: 5 rue du Temple Neuf.* ☎ *33-03-88-23-15-02. www.mulhaupt.fr. Tues–Fri 10am–12:30pm and 1:30–6:30pm; Sat 9:30am–12:30pm and 1:30–6pm; closed July 18–Aug 21.*

→ **Pain d'Epices** A sort of museum of spice breads, Pain d'Epices sells over a dozen varieties of the region's hallmark dessert. Owner Mireille Oster has found room in her shop and her kitchen to perfect tradition, as in the traditional seven-spice variety, and blow the roof off with radical experimental flavors such as spelt and banana. The bread is available as cookies, in heart shapes, or in the classic loaf shape, for slicing and serving with foie gras. *14 rue des Dentelles.* ☎ *03-88-32-33-34. www.paindesoleil.com.*

→ **Wanamana Shoes** If the phrase "cult sneakers" makes any sense to you, then you won't be confused by this bubble of a shop, where hard-to-find Nikes, Chuck Taylors, Asics, Birkenstocks, and other footgear lie in wait for the too-cool-for-school collectors who crave them. *13 rue du Dôme.* ☎ *03-88-75-00-36.*

ALSACE-LORRAINE

ALSACE-LORRAINE

MTV Best● Colmar

This wonderfully intact medieval and Renaissance town is among France's most romantic. In fact, even the legend of its preservation—it was one of the few towns in Alsace that didn't get bombed to smithereens during World War II—is rooted in romance. The wife of the French General de Lattre de Tassigny was particularly fond of Colmar, and begged her husband to protect it. He asked the Allies to lay off a little with the heavy machinery and take their business elsewhere. So it was that a horrible battle was fought just 10km (6 miles) outside of Colmar, in which more than a thousand U.S. soldiers died, but the city was left intact.

Their deaths were not in vain. In February of 1945, Colmar was at last liberated, one of the last important towns in the region to be so. It's understandable why the Germans wanted desperately to keep their grubby hands on it. The medieval and Renaissance town center is bursting at the seams with architectural gems and rich ornamental details, making it one of the most visually unique pedestrian areas in France.

It's also one of the largest pedestrian areas in Europe, which means that you can wander around with your head in the clouds, taking in charming details such as the painted and wrought-iron signposts, with little fear of oncoming traffic. Do keep a watch out for the train ride that shuttles among the sights at an embarrassingly slow speed. You could probably outpace it walking backward on your hands, but it's still a slight hazard.

Besides that, the main hazards in Colmar are the dangerous abundance of good food, romantic streets, and high-quality pastries.

Colmar is not exactly a throbbing center of frenzied youth culture. Most of the visitors here, with the glaring exception of cyclists in neon spandex passing through, appear to have sired at least two generations. The younger locals, few and far between, are mostly teenagers who look just about ready to get the hell out of their postcard-perfect town and move to a bigger city. So don't come looking for wild nights and high-decibel revelry. Colmar is about history, picturesque streets, and quiet dinners.

The **tourist office** is at 4 rue des Unterlinden (☎ **03-89-20-68-92;** www.ot-colmar.fr; Mon–Sat 9am–noon and 2–6pm, Sun and holidays 10am–1pm, closed Dec 25–Jan 1).

Getting There & Getting Around

If you're **driving,** take N83 from Strasbourg; trip time is 1 hour. Because of the narrow streets, we suggest that you park and walk. Leave the car in the Champ-de-Mars, or in the underground place Rapp for a fee of around 12€ per hour, northeast of the railway station, then walk a few blocks east to the old city; or park in the lot designated PARKING VIEILLE VILLE, accessible from rue de l'Est at the edge of the Petite Venise neighborhood, and walk a few blocks southeast to reach the old city. **Trains** link Colmar to Nancy, Strasbourg, and Mulhouse, as well as to Germany via Strasbourg, across the Rhine. Nine trains per day arrive from Paris's Gare de l'Est (trip time: 4–6 hr.); the one-way fare is 50€. For information, call ☎ **08-92-35-35-35.**

Sleeping

CHEAP

→**Maison Martin Jund** This centrally located family-run guesthouse offers fine organic wine-tastings from the family's vineyards, in addition to the six double rooms, two of which are available year-round. All have shower and sink, and many have a toilet, kitchen, and TV as well. The best part? Their low, low rates. *12 rue de l'Ange.* ☎ *03-89-41-58-72. www.martinjund. com. 30€–45€ double. Credit cards accepted. Parking available.*

DOABLE

→ **Hostellerie Le Maréchal** Four stars for under 100€? That's less than 25€ a star. Snatch up this (relative) bargain fast—the huge and lovingly decorated rooms in this family-run hotel are often booked far in advance. Choose from 30 rooms, each named after a different classical composer, and outfitted with Louis XV, Louis XVI, or Louis-Philippe decors. All have air-conditioning, and many have canopied beds. If you pay a little extra, you can even get yourself a Jacuzzi. The location could not be more romantic, smack in the middle of the Petite Venise area, in a house from 1565. *4–6 place de Six Montagnes Noires.* ☎ *03-89-41-60-32. www.le-marechal.com. 80€–90€ single; 95€–135€ double. Credit cards accepted. In room: TV, hair dryer, minibar, safe, Wi-Fi.*

→ **Hôtel Amiral** A fairly priced hotel also located in the charming Petite Venise area, with clean, modern-ish rooms. Some of them have retained architectural details—such as exposed brick walls, wooden floors, and old wooden ceiling beams—from the past, when the building was a malt house. *11a bd. du Champ de Mars.* ☎ *03-89-23-26-25. www.hotel-amiral-colmar.com. 55€ double. Credit cards accepted.*

Eating

CAFES & LIGHT FARE

→ **Jadis et Gourmande** TEA HOUSE The desserts are the real draw at Jadis et Gourmande, a self-described *salon de thé* that serves a small menu of salads,

tartines, and savoury tarts as preludes to a dessert repetoire that's second to none, especially given the price. The homemade tarts, made with seasonal ingredients, are always a brilliant choice, especially the rhubarb meringue one, if it's available. A tiny bit of pastry cream mixed with the rhubarb filling slightly offsets the sourness and blends wonderfully with the sweet, airy meringue topping. Taste the chocolate *liegois*—vanilla and chocolate ice creams with tepid chocolate poured over top, and you'll be singing *ooh la la.* Ask to sign the guestbook that owner Sophie keeps, and join the big cuddly international family of Jadis fans. *8 place du Marché aux Fruits.* ☎ *03-89-41-73-76. Tarts and desserts 3.50€– 7€; hot dishes and salads 8€–13€. Mon 11am–6pm; Tues–Sat 8:30am–6pm.*

→ **Le Croissant Doré** CAFE The slightly senile old women running the show here just add to the place's character, which is so quaint it's almost cloying. A jumble of antique teapots and old samovars decorate the place, which offers a wide assortment of herbal infusions and classic black teas to go along with the *viennoiserie* and savory tarts. It doesn't get much more idyllic than the few tables outside, where you can relax in front of the cheery pink storefront and watch the tourists and locals trundle by. *28 rue des Marchands.* ☎ *03-89-23-70-81. Tea 2.50€; tarts 6.50–7€. Tues–Sun 8am–7:30pm.*

CHEAP

→ **Restaurant-Winstub Pfeffel** ALSATIAN Okay, okay. It's right next door to the tourist office, in front of the Unterlinden Museum, and looks right onto the starting point of the tourist train rides. Is it touristy? Well, yes. Does this mean they serve all day, with no irritating break from 3 to 7 in the afternoon? Thank goodness, yes. And, most importantly, is it good? Absolutely. The Alsatian fare is solid—consistent though

Pity the Goose in France

Foie gras, or fatty liver, is one of those delicacies that only the French could have thought up, in their constant prowl for new ways to ingest lipids. But they didn't exactly invent overweight poultry. The French had always fed their geese what was on hand, but when Germans came to the more fertile regions of eastern France, they spoiled the species with a far richer diet than was possible in Germany, where the soil is poorer. Thankfully, the French had a modest proposal for these chubby little birds. In the late 1700s, Jean Joseph Close, the Norman chef of the Marchal de Contades and governor of Alsace, cooked the first antecedent of what is today called *pâté de foie gras*. He took the goose liver, mixed it with chopped veal and lard, stuck a truffle in the center, and surrounded the whole thing with crust. Knowing a moneymaker when he saw it, he retired in Alsace, where the fat livers were abundant, and marketed his product.

Unfortunately, these Alsatian geese had it coming. Larger and built lower to the ground than the common French goose, the ash or farm goose, the Strasbourg goose is practically born destined for a small sealed jar. It has a loose fold of skin on its belly, providing a pouch just waiting to be filled up with extra pounds, and due to its anti-athletic build, has a hard time working off the weight. Put one of these bad boys on an all-carb, force-fed diet (they are customarily fed on noodles) and watch him balloon! At the time of its death, a goose's liver can weigh up to 2¼ pounds and make up ¹⁄₁₀ of its body weight. Pity the French goose, that gets none of the milk and massages of the spoiled Kobe cow, Japan's signature fatty delight. Just cold noodles and a glorious afterlife. If you've wondered why Chicago banned the delicacy, now you know.

with nothing ethereal about it. Muenster cheese and sausages are in frequent rotation on the menu, and believe it or not, this is cause for celebration. The former makes a star appearance on the *feuilleté de Munster,* an oval of rich puff pastry filled with the locally made cheese and baked to oozy, salty decadence. The generous salads on the menu are rather beside the point, but make fine options for those whose last visit to the cardiologist did not bring such good tidings. *1 rue Rampart.* ☎ *33-03-89-41-45-71. www.restaurant-pfeffel.fr. Menus 10€–36€. Daily 11am–until closing (at owner's discretion). Closed in winter; reopens in early Mar (exact dates and times vary; call for details).*

➜ **Winstub La Petite Venise** ALSATIAN Impress your friends at home by telling them you ate *roïgabreldi.* What? It's just a fancy, Alsatian name for potatoes cooked with onions and white wine, but it sounds adventurous. Winstub La Petite Venise specializes in tasty, rib-sticking Alsatian fare, such as the aforementioned *roïgabreldi* and *fleischkierler* (slowly cooked medallions of meat), and other dishes involving booze, meat, and potatoes, with the occasional appearance of cheese and puff pastry. The interior is homey and cozy, and it's run by a local couple, Christelle and Arnaud. *4 rue de la Poissonerie.* ☎ *03-89-41-72-59. Main courses 5€–12€. Credit cards accepted. Mon–Tues and Thurs–Sat noon–2pm and 7–10pm.*

DOABLE

🎵 Best ● ➜ **Caveau St. Pierre** ALSATIAN If this were any other town, Caveau

St-Pierre would have had the market cornered on romantic. This being Colmar, however, there's still plenty to go around, although this restaurant does have way more than its fair share. First of all, you have to stroll through the charming Petite Venise area to get there, and make your way down a little side street until you've turned the corner and—there it is. Perched right on the bank of a small canal, as intimate as can be, this place is made for couples, although that doesn't stop families from coming. The food is standard Alsatian—heavy on the meat and sauerkraut—and the desserts are very good. *24 rue de la Herse.* ☎ *03-89-41-99-33. Menus 13€–22€; a la carte 20€. Credit cards accepted. Tues–Sun noon–2pm and 7–10pm. Closed in winter until mid-Feb (dates vary; call for details).*

SPLURGE

➡ **JY's** FRENCH FUSION Another strong contender for best canalside view, JY's is one of Colmar's only dining establishments that even hints at being aware of the 21st century. Chef and owner Jean-Yves Schillinger has resisted the temptation to outfit his restaurant like a human-scale gingerbread house, and instead summoned a high-end Parisian interior decorator, Olivier Gagnaire (ever heard of Hôtel Costes? there you go), to bring the place fully into the present tense. The cuisine is contemporary, as is the minimalist gray, white, and orange decor, but it's far more colorful. And the clientele is a lot like the decor—tasteful and understated, across a range of middle-aged Eurotrash, elegant couples, or well-behaved families.

Schillinger has earned himself a bright shiny Michelin star with his thoughtfully composed dishes such as fried soft shell crabs with a citrus emulsion and tomato and satay sauce. If this sounds like too much action for a few crispy little crabs, it's surprisingly not. The citrus emulsion, which looks and sounds as though it is in danger of tasting like lemony-fresh dishwashing foam, is actually an unobtrusive bubble bath of delicate and refreshing citrus that just enhances the richness of the perfectly seasoned crabs, each no bigger than a credit card. Skip the appetizer medley, which travels a bit too randomly across the globe, and concentrate on the more intelligently done main courses. Desserts are even better. You'll drive yourself crazy attempting to discern how the puff pastry for the apple tart manages to be so thin yet have so many crisp buttery layers. Or, more likely, you'll have finished it before you even notice the enigma. Dress nicely and book ahead. *17 rue de la Poissonnerie.* ☎ *03-89-21-53-60. www.jean-yves-schillinger.com. Main courses 28€; 4 plates 47€; 6 plates 63€. Credit cards accepted. Mon 7–10:30pm; Tues–Sat noon–2:30pm and 7–10:30pm.*

📺 Best ● ➡ **Les Temps des Délices** ITALIAN In the mood for a proper bowl of pasta—not another side order of spaetzle? Les Temps des Délices is a cure-all for all cravings Italian. The menu runs the gamut from southern to northern Italian cooking, but the focus on fresh ingredients is constant; the menu changes every 2 months to reflect the season's offerings. The pastas are all homemade and authentic, like the classic Sicilian combination of eggplant, basil, and tomato with shavings of ricotta salata. The ingredients are of a dazzlingly high quality, like the *mozzarella di bufala* that melts in your mouth, and they are cooked and presented with care and attention. This is no "choose your pasta, then your sauce" kind of joint; it's authentic Italian cooking. The setting is as classy as the food—a romantic terrace set above street level and surrounded by trees. Let Angélique, the gentle hostess and co-proprietor, guide you through the menu or order the *menu scoperta,* her husband the chef's choice. The desserts are equally delightful. *23 rue d'Alspach.* ☎ *03-89-23-45-57. Main courses 6€–23€; menus 35€. Credit cards accepted. Tues–Sat noon–3:30pm and 7–9pm.*

Partying

Aside from a few pubs and bars on the Grand Rue, the scene is pretty bleak. It's not a big university town, or really a big town full stop. Most of the evening action revolves around strolling the gorgeously illuminated streets, licking an ice cream, and pausing for occasional deep meaningful gazes into your significant other's eyes.

➔ **Le Pelican Fou** This lively two-level bar had just opened at the time of writing, but it already seemed to have gotten it right. It's one of the few places in Colmar with people under 30, and the upstairs lounge area has a great graffiti painting of—you guessed it—a crazy pelican on the wall. *33 Grand Rue.* ☎ *03-89-24-25-60. www. jet8.org and www.pelican-fou.com.*

➔ **Les Arcades** A lively but basic bar, with nothing much to recommend it save for that it's one of the few venues with decent music—a DJ plays soul, blues, and rock on the weekends—and it hosts live bands once a month. *88600 Bruyeres.* ☎ *03-89-41-00-00.*

Sightseeing

MUSEUMS

➔ **Musée Bartholdi** Statue of Liberty sculptor Frédéric-Auguste Bartholdi was born in Colmar in 1834. This small, memento-filled museum is in the house where he was born. It has Statue of Liberty rooms containing plans and scale models,

and documents related to its construction and other works regarding U.S. history. Bartholdi's Paris apartment, with furniture and memorabilia, has been reconstructed here. The museum supplements its exhibits with paintings of Egyptian scenes that Bartholdi collected during his travels in 1856. *30 rue des Marchands.* ☎ *03-89-41-90-60. Admission 4.10€ adults, 2.50€ students and children 12–18. Wed–Mon 10am–noon and 2–6pm. Closed Jan–Feb, May 1, Nov 1, and Dec 25.*

[MTV] (Best ❂) ➔ **Musée d'Unterlinden (Under the Linden Trees)** This former Dominican convent (1232), the chief seat of Rhenish mysticism in the 14th and 15th centuries, became a museum around 1850, and it has been a treasure house of the art and history of Alsace ever since.

The jewel of its collection is the **Issenheim Altarpiece (Le Retable d'Issenheim),** created by Würzburg-born Matthias Grünewald, "the most furious of realists," around 1515. His colors glow, and his fantasy will overwhelm you. One of the most exciting works in German art, it's an immense altar screen with two-sided folding wing pieces—designed to show the Crucifixion, then the Incarnation, framed by the Annunciation and the Resurrection. The carved altar screen depicts St. Anthony visiting the hermit St. Paul; it also shows the Temptation of St. Anthony, the most beguiling part of a work that contains some ghastly birds, weird monsters, and loathsome animals. The demon of the plague is depicted with a swollen belly and purple skin, his body blotched with boils; a diabolical grin appears on his horrible face.

Other attractions include the magnificent altarpiece (dating back to 1470) of Jean d'Orlier by Martin Schongauer, a large collection of religious woodcarvings and stained glass from the 14th to the 18th centuries, and Gallo-Roman lapidary collections, including funeral slabs. The armory collection contains ancient arms from the Romanesque to the Renaissance, featuring halberds and crossbows. *1 rue d'Unterlinden.* ☎ *03-89-20-15-50. www.musee-unterlinden. com. Admission 7€ adults, 5€ students and children 12–17. Apr–Oct daily 9am–6pm; Nov–Mar Wed–Mon 9am–noon and 2–5pm. Closed national holidays.*

MONUMENTS & CHURCHES

➔**Eglise des Dominicains** Since this Gothic church has been desanctified, the management has been running a brisk business off the renowned triptych inside, The *Virgin in the Rosebush* by Martin Schongauer, painted in 1473. *Place des Dominicains.* ☎ *03-89-24-46-57. Admission 1.30€ adults, 1€ students. Apr–Dec daily 10am–1pm and 3–6pm.*

FREE ➔**Eglise St-Martin** ★ In the heart of Old Colmar is a collegiate church begun in 1230 on the site of a Romanesque church. It has a choir erected by William of Marburg in 1350 and a steeple that rises to 70m (230 ft.). *Place de la Cathédrale.* ☎ *03-89-41-27-20. Free admission. Daily 8am–6pm. Closed to casual visitors during Mass.*

➔**Temple St-Mathieu** This Protestant church has a dirty little secret—its 14th-century Gothic choir area once served as a Catholic hospital chapel, from 1715 to 1937. Just beyond the rood screen is the Protestant nave. The wall paintings date back to the 13th century, and the stained-glass windows from the century following.

HISTORIC NEIGHBORHOODS

More than 45 buildings in Colmar are classified as historical monuments, so you'll find impressive architecture almost everywhere you look. The tourist office has maps and proposed itineraries that will cover just about all the buildings of interest, but a few neighborhoods are impossible to miss. In general, the region's houses are built to maximize living space on lots as small as possible, since in the olden days, people paid taxes on the area of their ground floor. This led to a lot of vertical construction, or at least what was possible given the engineering and construction capacities of the day. But this queer policy explains the somewhat haphazard and irregular quality of some of the houses.

If you start at the tourist office, in the **place d'Unterlinden,** take a right onto the rue des Tetes, and marvel at the many-headed beast that is the **Maison des Têtes (House of Heads).** It was built in 1609 in the Rhenish Renaissance style, and features 105 heads on its facade. The building, now a fancy hotel and swank restaurant, once served as a wine exchange, so one can only imagine what kind of stories those heads could tell if they weren't made of stone. Then turn left onto rue des Boulangers, which, although it was probably named centuries ago, still features a number of bakers plying their wares. Despite the delicious smells, save your money and your appetite for **Patisserie Jean,** at the end of the street on 6 place de l'Ecole (☎ **03-89-41-24-63**). Grab a home-made ice cream (in a home-baked cone) or one of the tarts of the day and keep walking, veering right onto rue des Marchands.

Here you'll see the famous **Maison Pfister,** built in 1537 by a hatmaker, Louis Scherer, who also luckily happened to have a hand in some silver mines in Val de Liepvre. Although the ornamentation—which features allegories from the Old and New Testaments and the seals of Germanic

ALSACE-LORRAINE

emperors—takes its cue from Renaissance humanist culture, the architecture is medieval, particularly the staircase turret, irregularly set windows, and wooden gallery. The mixture isn't exactly harmonious, but it's definitely interesting and very well preserved.

Continuing on this street, you'll pass the **Ancienne Douane,** or Koïfhus, which was once the political and economic nerve center of the city, because all who passed through Colmar were required to stop there and pay their taxes. At the time of its construction, in 1480, Colmar lay on two main commercial arteries—a road leading from Italy to Flanders, and one from the Champagne to the Danube regions. This Gothic and Renaissance building saw visitors from all sides, and served as a warehouse, market, and customhouse. Note the huge doors—merchants astride their horses trotted right inside without bothering to dismount. Now it is often the site of intimate concerts during the festivals. Past the Ancienne Douane is the **Quartier des Tanneurs,** which consists mainly of the rue des Tanneurs, and which leads you to Petite Venise.

The canals of **Petite Venise** were once used by farmers who grew their goods just outside Colmar and rowed them into town to sell, along with fisherman who merely sunk their netted hoops into the water and waited for the aquatic merchandise to roll in. Now they're a tourist's playground, both as scenic background for some of Colmar's most romantic restaurants, and as the byways for relaxing boat rides (see "Playing Outside," below).

Playing Outside

CYCLING

→ **Colmarvélo** Run by the city, this bike shop offers very fair prices on rentals.

Place Rapp. ☎ *03-89-41-37-90. 3€ nonresidents. Apr–May and Oct daily 9am–noon and 2–7pm. June–Sept 30 Mon–Tues and Thurs–Fri 8:30am–noon and 2–8pm. Wed and Sat–Sun 8:30am–8pm.*

BOAT RIDES

Seeing Colmar by boat is actually quite pleasant, however touristy. The 30-minute commentated rides are operated by two different companies that follow similar routes along the canals. You'll be in groups of five to eight people, depending on what kind of crowds turn up, but it's still romantic. Both leave from the Petite Venise area: **Association des Bateliers de la Lauch** (embark at the corner of rue de la Poissonerie and rue de Turenne; ☎ **03-89-23-59-31**), or **Sweet Narcisse** (embark at the foot of pont St-Pierre; office 12a rue de la Herse; ☎ **03-89-41-01-94;** www.sweetnarcisse.com). They're open from April to September.

Shopping

→ **Arts et Collections d'Alsace** If you want a casserole dish to make some authentic Alsatian stew, this is the place to get it. Some of the motifs are actually rather cute, like the navy and yellow polka-dot ceramics, but most of the merchandise veers toward the grandma birthday gift aesthetic (for Grandma, not even from Grandma). For the stew, you'll need three kinds of meat—pork, mutton, and beef—and it needs to slow-cook overnight. *1 rue des Tanneurs.* ☎ *03-89-24-09-76.*

📺 Best ● → **Christmas Markets** From November 25th to December 31st, Colmar bedecks itself heavily with lights, holiday decorations, and even an ice-skating rink for the little ones. But the real draw is the shopping—five different picturesque locations scattered through old town, with hundreds of vendors displaying local gastronomic delicacies, handmade crafts, imported goods, arts and antiques, and a market dedicated to children's toys and goodies. *www.noel-colmar.com.*

SOUVENIRS

The best souvenirs from Alsace are edible. Unless you fell in love with the local stew, and want to lug around an authentic earthenware crockpot, stick with the more portable local specialties—*pain d'épices* and foie gras—and you'll have wonderful gifts for your friends and family. Assuming, that is, that they make it all the way home, and don't mysteriously disappear en route (burp).

➡ **Fortwenger** If you hadn't heard of *pain d'épices* before you arrived in Colmar, Fortwenger will do its best to ensure that you've become acquainted before you leave; their delightful products appear in almost every souvenir shop. Literally "spice bread," *pain d'épices* can manifest itself in many forms. Always made with honey and a mélange of yuletide spices—mainly cinnamon, ginger, anise, cardamom, cloves, and black pepper—it can take the shape of a mildly sweet loaf, to be served in slices as an accompaniment to foie gras. Or it can take the form of sweet cookies, frosted with thin icing, or dipped in chocolate, or shaped like Santa or a star—you get it. Head straight to the original outpost, on rue des Marchands, where the selection is the greatest: more than 50 variations on *pain d'épices* alone, and more than 400 types of food products for sale at any given moment. If you fall hard for these cookies, arrange for a factory tour (for groups of 20 or more); reserve by calling ☎ **03-88-08-96-06.** *Store: 32 rue des Marchands.* ☎ *03-89-41-06-93. www. fortwenger.fr. Mon–Fri 9:30am–12:30pm and*

1:30–7pm (6:30pm after July 14); Sat–Sun and holidays 10am–6pm.

➡ **La Fromagerie St-Nicolas** You're hard-pressed to pick a clunker here, but the specialties of the house are Munster, from the nearby and eponymous town, and raw milk cheeses. A nice selection of cheeses is a good alternative for making a picnic if foie gras is out of your league. *18 rue St-Nicolas.* ☎ *03-89-24-90-45. www. fromagerie-st-nicolas.com. Mon 2–7pm; Tues–Fri 9am–12:30pm and 2–7pm; Sat 9am–7pm.*

➡ **Les Foies Gras de Liesel** Their recipe for foie gras calls for "a pinch of talent and plenty of love." If only it were that simple. Making foie gras is a lot more complicated and heinous than you would think (see "Pity the Goose in France," above). Eating it, on the other hand, requires little more than some elbow grease to twist open the jar, and a loaf of crusty bread on which to smear the creamy stuff. Savoring it, well, that takes slightly more effort—maybe some chutneys or jams to bring out the sweetness, and a good bottle of wine to wash it down never hurt. All of these things, except the bread and the elbow grease, are for sale at Les Foies Gras de Liesel, which has been engaged in the white-market duck and goose organ trade for 20 years. *3 rue Turenne.* ☎ *03-89-23-88-29. www.alsacefoiegras.com. Main courses 30€–70€. Credit cards accepted. Tues–Sat 9:30am–12:30pm and 3–7pm.*

MARKETS

➡ **Covered Market** This market erupts on Thursdays in this beautiful old sandstone building from 1865, which is used as a parking lot the rest of the week (lucky cars). Rumor has it that it will be held several times per week beginning in 2007. *Place de l'Ancienne Douane and rue des Tanneurs. Thurs 7am–1pm.*

Nancy

Of all of the schlocky tourist slogans I've come across, Nancy's actually made sense: "Delightful Nancy," the city's chosen appellation, rings true, loud and clear. A few days here are enough time to take in all the sights, but take them in at a snail's pace. Leave plenty of time for Nancy's many parks, gardens, and cafes lining the people-watching paradise that is place Stanislas.

The visual landscape of Nancy is elegant and upscale, rather like a whole town designed like a fancy department store. Because it was once the country's second-most prominent Art Nouveau production center, the city is dotted with houses sporting original Art Nouveau architecture, stained-glass windows, and other details. The main square, place Stanislas, was recently renovated to bring it back to its 18th-century glory, and its gilded railings and light stone pavement are every bit as majestic as the Polish king who built it. The historic town center is unnervingly picture-perfect; the apparent absence of poverty or even an eyesore or two makes it seem a bit out of touch with reality. You may find yourself wondering: Why do the shops only sell designer clothes? Where are all the supermarkets to get a cheap bottle of water? How come everyone has such nicely ironed clothes? The short answer is that Nancy does brisk business in the services sector—IT, finance, logistics, and health. There's also a bustling, 48,000 student-strong university life, making it a research hub, and more women in the workforce than on average in France. The shorter answer is: Don't worry about it. Just enjoy the passing of life as it traipses across place Stanislas.

It was through the efforts of Good King Stanislas (as he's known locally) that the city, to some degree, is the beautiful bubble it appears to be. But first off—what in the !$ä# was a Polish king doing ruling the then-Duchy of Lorraine? Around the middle of the 18th century, King Stanislas found himself pretty hard up. Deposed, broke, and none-too-powerful, he readily accepted an offer from his son-in-law, Louis XV, to become the Duke of Lorraine. Louis XV, who was married to Stan's daughter Maria, had no interest in having a loser for a father-in-law, casting about Europe in exile. So, coasting on the appointment (and, one can assume, the funds) from his son-in-law, Stanislas enthusiastically took up his new post, setting in motion a number of charitable institutions, such as a public hospital, a public school, and a communal granary. His most enduring contributions, however, are the architectural ones: the place and several parks and gardens, which, along with its rich Art Nouveau history, allow the city to claim its rightful title of "Delightful Nancy."

Nancy is home to 45,000 students, so you'll find a mixed bag of people here. Most of the local population seems to fancy themselves *bcbg (bon chic, bon genre),* however, and shamelessly so. A dab of hair gel and a collared shirt go a long way in this town, especially in the nicer cafes, clubs, and restaurants around the square, where the noses hover in the air at a slightly higher altitude than in the rest of the city.

Getting There

Trains from Strasbourg arrive every hour (trip time: 1 hr.); the one-way fare is 20€. Trains from Paris's Gare de l'Est pull in about every 2 hours (trip time: 3 hr.); the one-way fare is 40€. For information and schedules, call ☏ **08-92-35-35-35.** If you're **driving** to Nancy from Paris, follow N4 east (trip time: 4 hr.).

Tourist Office

Nancy's **tourist office** (place Stanislas; ☎ 03-83-35-22-41) is at the corner of rue Stanislas and rue des Dominicains, right on the place Stanislas. It boasts a five-star rating from the French government, for whatever that's worth. I think it means that they're particularly helpful, and this may be true. The staff is friendly, knowledgeable, and totally at your service.

Sleeping

HOSTELS

→**Château de Rémicourt** Head for the hills, literally, if you're going to be hostelling it in Nancy—the youth hostel is located in a 9-hectare (22-acre) park, a 10-minute drive outside of town, atop a lush green hill. While the rooms are typical of any other hostel in France—clean, bright, *sans caractère*—they do come wrapped in a 16th-century exterior, on grounds so lovely that many people hold their weddings here. So check ahead to make sure there are no festivities when you plan on coming. The château also has a sunlit little courtyard, where the usual hostel activities go down—late night bottles of wine, the inevitable guitar, and the billionth iteration of the "So where are you from?" conversation. Two buses run here, but rather infrequently, so you may be stuck cabbing it back and forth to town. Still, you're hard-pressed to find another château in France to accommodate you for this price. *149 rue de Vandoeuvre. ☎ 03-83-27-73-67. 16€ per person double; 14€ per person triple. Family rooms available.*

CHEAP

→**Hôtel de Guise** The wrought-iron staircase and cheerfully black-and-white-tiled floor of the lobby echo, albeit less grandly, the aesthetic of nearby place Stanislas. This hotel, charming and intimate, is in the 17th-century home of a former nobleman. The spacious rooms are each decorated uniquely, and the breakfast room, which was formerly part of an abbey, illustrates many examples of original Louis XIII interior design. While maintaining the delightful historicity of the building, the foundations of which were laid in the 1600s, the owners have made sure to bring the plumbing into this century. The wisteria in the garden also has miraculously made it into this century; it has been blooming each spring for more than 130 years. *8 rue de Guise. ☎ 33-03-83-32-24-68. www.hoteldeguise.com. 48€–59€ standard room single or double; from 105€ larger and 3-person rooms; prices rise by 2€–3€ in May and June. Amenities: Internet; meeting room; parking. In room: TV.*

DOABLE

→**Hôtel des Prélats** The three-star Hôtel des Prélats is the ideal place to live out Grimm Brothers' fantasies of living like royalty, at relatively fair prices. The lush decor—stained-glass windows in each room and luxurious canopied beds—will go a long way towards making you feel like the princess or prince that you always knew you were. Wiggle around and see if you can feel the pea underneath the mattress. Then head down the sweeping spiral staircase for breakfast in a glass-ceilinged room looking onto the garden. The hotel shares a wall with the cathedral next door and dates from the 17th century. *56 place Mgr Ruch. ☎ 54-58-84-92. www.hoteldesprelats.com. 84€–179€ double. Credit cards accepted.*

SPLURGE

→**Grand Hôtel de la Reine** If it's good enough for Marie Antoinette and Czar Alexander, is it good enough for you? She stayed here en route to meet her future husband, Louis XVI, and who's to say your future mate isn't sitting out there on the square? Designed and built in the 1750s by Emmanuel Héré, the architect to King

Stanislas, this hotel was home to a number of successive local big cheeses before it was transformed into a hotel at the turn of the 19th century. Now, the website claims, it is proud to welcome a thoroughly modern host of "famous artists, statesmen, and athletes." The location is unsurpassed—it's right on the place Stanislas. In fact, its facade is an integral part of the harmonious square. The breakfast room looks onto the square, as do several salons, where people once gathered for Belle Epoque evenings of lightweight debauchery and stimulating conversation. Less of that is going on these days than daytime drinking by businessmen on expense accounts, but it's still the nicest place in town to shack up, if this is how you roll. *2 place Stanislas.* ☎ *33-03-83-35-03-01. www.hoteldelareine.com. 145€–360€ double. Amenities: Dry cleaning; 24-hr. reception; valet parking. In room: A/C, TV.*

Eating

Nancy left its mark on the cookbook pages of history with the *baba au rhum,* a soft spongy brioche-like cake, studded with dried fruits, baked in a round mold, and then showered with rum and sometimes sugar syrup. Oozing booze as it does, it's often served with a shot of extra rum on the side and, ideally, a poof of chantilly or scoop of vanilla ice cream. The name comes from the Polish *babka,* a similar dessert that got a lot better when King Stan's chef gave it the French treatment and doused it in alcohol.

Restaurants like **A la Table du Bon Roi Stanislas** and **Brasserie Excelsior** serve *baba,* as well as fine and very French cooking. Several trendy restaurants around place Vaudémont, just off of place Stanislas, offer more contemporary menus that run the usual gamut of big tasty salads, pizzas, pastas, and some French main courses. These restaurants make for great people-watching as well as eating, especially in the summer at lunchtime, when the youngish and stylish turn out in droves to eat, meet, and greet.

If the three restaurants huddled in place Vaudémont were siblings, **Le Régent** would be the middle child, the one who got a cool job in graphic design or at a hipster magazine, and became kind of a yuppie. Across the square is the youngest, going through a Radiohead and vintage clothes phase. **Le Vaudémont** is the eldest, with very little to prove, having grown up with all the attention. Having all sprung from the same parents, however, their cooking differs very little.

LIGHT FARE & SNACKS

→ **Hôtel California** If you're looking to grub for less than 5€, look no further than this divey snack bar and cafe, which owner Rachid has also optimistically categorized as a *brasserie.* The "specialties"—as he insists on calling them—are cheeseburgers and shish kabob. Haute cuisine it may not be, but it's definitely cheap, and Rachid is definitely a hoot. Algerian by birth, he speaks English and Spanish in addition to Arabic and French, so his wisecracking will come at you from four angles. Hôtel California is just outside the city center, about a 10-minute walk away from place Stan, in what may one day be the Williamsburg of Nancy. At the moment, this street boasts two of these slightly grubby cafes, and attracts a lovely medley of cute boys who may or may not engage in the sport of skateboarding, and old men who may or may not engage in the activity of bathing, such is the reek of stale smoke they emit. At night it morphs into a bar, with blues and country music providing an aural complement to the cacti painted on the sign outside. The place oozes character and authenticity day or night, so be sure to stop by. *22 av. du XXeme Corps.* ☎ *03-83-32-20-44. Main courses 5€–10€. Mon–Sat 7am–10pm.*

CHEAP

➜**Aux Delices du Palais** SALADS This place could have been airlifted out of New York City's East Village, Wizard of Oz–style, and dropped down in Nancy like a sack of United Nations–donated rice. The eclectic mishmash of chairs, cheap plastic patterned tablecloths, and low, starving artist-style prices are a refreshing change from the slightly Eurotrashy joints on the place Vaudémont. The menu is extensive but rotates mainly around a truckload of classic salads such as beet and goat cheese, Greek salad, and smoked salmon and capers salad. A dozen-plus *plats du jour* span the globe from Mexican beef fajitas (I can't vouch for a Frenchman making a fajita) to Moroccan *tajine* with honey and dried fruits (this sounds preferable). It only seats 32 people, with a few extra tables outside in the warm months, so it can get crowded. Aperitifs and a range of French desserts—the usual suspects, such as *tarte tatin, île flottante, chocolate mousse*—are also available. *69 Grand Rue.* ☎ *03-83-30-44-19. Salads 6€; sandwiches 4.50€. Credit cards accepted. Mon–Fri noon–1:30 and 6–9:30pm; Sat 6–9:30pm.*

➜**L'Artichaut** CAFE Ah, don't you love these little cafe-restaurant-art-gallery medleys? Here's another one, serving up tasty sandwiches and inexpensive menus to Nancy's artsy crowd. The restaurant occasionally hosts a live band or two, so check with a waiter to see if there are any upcoming gigs. *3 rue St-Nicolas.* ☎ *03-83-31-22-17. Lunch menus 12€–15€; sandwiches and starters 6€–7€; main courses 10€–13€. Credit cards accepted. Tues–Thurs noon–2:30pm; Fri–Sat noon–2:30pm and 7:30–10pm.*

DOABLE

➜**Le Régent Restaurant** FRENCH/MEDITERRANEAN Bar Le Régent seems to attract a more local crowd, especially young urban professionals—oops, that spells "yuppie"—on their 2¹/₂-hour lunch breaks. (And the French wonder why their economy is going down the crapper?) Notice how the heavy cigarette smoke provides more cover from the midday than do the sun umbrellas, every table is dotted with one pair of designer sunglasses per capita, and even the men order Diet Coke. I sat next to two greasy-haired teenagers in Energie and Diesel T-shirts who sat down, lit up, and immediately commenced ogling and commenting on the female clientele, which made for an entertaining soundtrack to my meal. The objects of their narrative were, for the most part, dressed to kill in tight dresses and high heels, but also accompanied by dates—leaving me to wonder if the boys' sexual prowess was thus far strictly verbal.

Try not to let the amusing mating rituals unfolding in front of you distract from the food, as I nearly did. The ingredients are top-notch—the fruity olive oil on the salads, for example, was so green and flavorful it breathed new life into a plate of crudités, shining especially brightly on the thinly sliced mushroom and parsley salad. The other items on the menu—risottos, French dishes, and other generically Mediterranean options—are equally solid. The service situation is similar to that at Le Vaudémont—either there was a general strike that day, and the two guys I saw were the scabs who crossed the line, or the management won't spring for that mythical "third waiter" who would go so far as to lighten the load on the other two existing servers. That said, the waiters were as graceful as could be given the pressure they were under. Successful men wearing designer sunglasses on hot dates aren't always the most patient of customers. *1 place Vaudémont.* ☎ *03-83-32-96-79. Lunch menu 15€; dinner menu 20€–38€; main courses 12€–21€. Credit cards accepted. Mon–Sun 10am–2am, closed Sun night.*

ALSACE-LORRAINE

MTV (Best**❷**) → **Restaurant a la Table du Bon Roi Stanislas** POLISH/FRENCH Treat the budding gastronome in you to an evening at the "table of the good King Stanislas." This romantic little restaurant's entire menu comes from the private recipe book of the former king's chef. This translates into regional Polish and French dishes. It's extremely difficult to picture the fat old king turning down one of their finely selected cheese plates, or delicately composed salads with dressings light as air. And it's easy to picture the King demanding second and third helpings of their desserts, especially the beautifully presented *blanc-manger,* an almond milk mousse served with cassis fruit jellies and a compote of dried peach. Whew! *7 rue Gustave Simon.* ☎ *03-83-35-36-52. www.tablestan.free.fr. Main courses 8€–38€. Credit cards accepted. Lunch Tues and Thurs–Sun; dinner Mon–Sat.*

SPLURGE

→ **Brasserie L'Excelsior** BRASSERIE Go-Go-Gadget Time Warp-Machine! What do you know? It worked. Rewind to 1911, when the Brasserie l'Excelsior opened its large wooden doors to an excited public, eager to see the Art Nouveau masterpieces rumored to be inside. They weren't disappointed by the 10 stained-glass dividers by local master Jacques Gruber, the 300 Daum lamps, and the sweeping staircase by Jean Prouvé, and nor should you be. While a few renovations in 1928 gave the place a more Art Deco feel, the food has more or less remained the same for the past century. French classics such as salad of mâche with truffle oil and local goat cheese, steak tartare with fries, and crème brûlée are the mainstays. It's good stuff— all of it—but don't let it keep you from appreciating the historic decor. Feel free, silly as it may seem, to wander around the restaurant just to have a look at some of

the details, but keep an eye out for the people carrying plates of hot food. *50 rue Henri Poincaré.* ☎ *03-83-35-24-57. www.brasserie-excelsior.com. Main courses 20€–30€. Credit cards accepted. Daily 8am–11:30am; 3–6:30pm for tea; late evening meals begin at 10pm.*

Partying

Like everything else about Nancy, nightlife is a pretty upscale affair, with the exception of a few more chilled-out wine bars, one student-oriented bar, and the two cafe/bars outside of the *vielle ville.* The nightclubs around place Stan are considered the most *branché* by the local populace, but they may strike you as generic, loud, throbbing-techno meet markets. The Grand Rué, which begins at place Vaudémont and carries on for several blocks, is the place to barhop, since it's home to a number of small bars with different decors, themes, and alcoholic offerings, and you're bound to find one that's up your alley—or at least get drunk trying.

If you're going to hit one of the bigger clubs, you'll probably have to kill some time at the smaller bars anyway, since the nightclubs don't get going until around midnight. Or park yourself at one of the cafes around place Stan and while away a few hours people-watching.

FUNKY BARS

→ **Le Cyrano** This casual cozy wine bar on the Grand Rue offers two dozen wines to try by the glass, or a far greater selection if you go for a bottle. The bottles are served in little yellow buckets, one more charming touch in this rustically decorated, warmly lit bar. If you tipped back a glass (or bottle) too many, settle your stomach with hearty *tartines* or *gratins,* bread or potatoes over which owner Frances Roosselet melts a variety of cheeses and other tasty ingredients. *7 Grande Rue.* ☎ *03-83-36-65-69.*

➜Varadero In case you were wondering where the students without the no-limit credit cards were hiding, this is it. Varadero is small, crowded, smokier than smoky, but it has a great, relaxed, and unpretentious vibe. Even the Latin-house medley music doesn't seem to bother the patrons, who are too busy asking each other for lights and making other awkward forays into lighthearted flirtation to notice, anyway. Take a break from all the grape juice with one of their creative drinks, such as Gloss, a shot of cherry and ginger liqueurs, or choose from a catch-all range of pan—South American cocktails. *27 Grande Rue. ☎ 03-83-36-61-98. http:// levaradero.com. Mon—Sat 8pm—2am.*

NIGHTCLUBS

➜Bar la Place Do you want to hear, over and over, from a robotic voice at way too many decibels that "You're a sexy f**k"? Then by all means make your way to Bar la Place, Nancy's premiere gay-friendly nightspot, where techno and explicitly sexual lyrics are the order of the night. The bass is so strong you'll think your cell-phone is vibrating the entire time you're in there, and the red leather stools are populated by patrons who know the lyrics to these techno songs by heart. Maybe that's a lot to give them credit for, since each song only has one, or at most two lines. The wall-to-wall window, with its view

over a gently lit place Stan, could almost trick you into thinking you're not being suffocated by smoke and the smell of sweaty flailing bodies. Almost. *7 place Stanislas. ☎ 03-83-35-62-63.*

➜Les Caves du Roi It is highly, *highly* doubtful that any Roi ever kept caves like this—unbearably loud, creepy techno music, dark vampirish decor, and darkness so deep that were it not for the bleached whiskers and knee patches of the clientele's jeans, one might have trouble discerning where the other patrons are standing. Still, this is considered the cool dude place to be, among the students dressed in all their tight black clubbin' getup, huddled outside, waiting for some unknown summons from below. *9 place Stanislaus. ☎ 03-83-35-24-14. www.lescaves nancy.com.*

Sightseeing

Nancy is *way* into its Art Nouveau heritage, as well it should be. Besides a gorgeous Musée des Beaux-Arts, most of Nancy's best sight-seeing relates back to the Art Nouveau scene, be it a visit to the breath-taking Ecole de Nancy museum, or a taxi ride with a recorded commentary that zings you around town to see some of the outstanding buildings and architectural details and to stop and take pictures (arrange through the tourist office). And

Jazzpulsations

Worst Name for the Best Festival

The name that manages to simultaneously conjure up Kenny G, repulsion, and a heartbeat in the wrist is a terrible and misleading label for what is actually a pretty cool festival. While jazz plays a part, it's more eclectic than anything else. The 2006 lineup featured a range of acts from the enchanting Brazilian munchkin Cesaria Evora, to indie favorites Gotan Project, to hip-hop legends Gangstarr. It's conveniently held over 2 weeks in October, so you don't have to miss all the summer festivals to catch this one (**www.nancyjazzpulsations. com**).

be sure to take a good hard look at the elaborate 18th-century gold-and-black wrought-iron gates around place Stan. These are some impressive gates.

FREE → **Ecole de Nancy** If you're a fan of Art Nouveau—think of the sultry Métro signs in Paris—then this museum (free Wed for students) will rub you the right way. The theory behind the practice of Art Nouveau was that everyday objects, from desks to bathtubs to lamps, should reek of beauty and art. This guiding philosophy of aesthetic excess, of which Nancy native Emile Gallé was a proud spokesman and practitioner, inspired masterpieces such as the piano on the first floor, with its gracefully dying swans carved in wood. Most of the works take inspiration from nature, in subject matter (flowers, trees, seasons, animals); as source material (over 600 kinds of wood, mostly imported from South America, were being used at the height of production, and glass—originally sand—was another important material); and in the way their curves and sinuous shapes echo the flowing lines of the natural world.

The museum is in the 19th-century villa of local big shot Eugène Corbin, who donated his impressive collection of Nancy School works to the city in 1935. The house itself is an Art Nouveau masterpiece, and if the stunning bathtub on the second floor doesn't provoke embarrassing levels of covetousness, the interior courtyard gardens surely will. *36–38 rue du Sergent Blandan.* ☎ *03-83-40-14-86. 6€ adults, 4€ students; free Wed for students. Wed–Sun 10:30am–6pm (1st Sun of the month 10:30am–1:30pm), tours Fri–Sun at 3pm.*

FREE → **Musée des Beaux-Arts** Free for students on Wednesdays, Nancy's fine arts museum is in an 18th-century building right on place Stanislas, housing a worthwhile selection of European paintings and sculpture from the 14th to 21st centuries. Of

particular interest is the Daum crystal collection, an ode to Nancy's local pride and joy. *3 place Stanislas.* ☎ *03-83-85-30-72. Admission 6€ (free Wed for students). Wed–Mon 10am–6pm.*

Playing Outside

HIRING BIKES

Cyclotop (www.cyclotop.net) rents bikes by the hour (3€), half-day (6€), or full day (8€), with a small discount for students. There are four locations around Nancy, so choose the one that is most convenient. An 80€ deposit is required.

PARKS

Nancy is renowned for its parks and gardens, which date from medieval times, as in the case of the **Citadelle Gardens,** to the contemporary water garden. According to the tourist office, the municipal gardens produce 330,000 flowering plants every summer, with 185,000 joining the party in spring and fall. Flower children should head for the **Dominique Alexandre Godron Gardens,** where thousands of plant varieties are labeled on view. For a good all-around park, hit the **Parc Pépinière,** which is tricked out with just about every park amenity you can imagine. There's a merry-go-round, a rose garden, small friendly animals (like goats, sheep, a ram, and a pony), popcorn and waffle stands, a snack bar/brasserie with serious ice cream in flavors such as lavender and vanilla pecan fudge, peacocks strolling around like they own the place, and miniature golf.

PICNICS

If you haven't ventured too far outside the city center, then the covered market, and the clothing market behind it, may be the only place in Nancy where you'll see any multicultural action. This place gets a stream of immigrants who come for the decent prices on produce and meats. If you make it past the initial butcher's displays of dead skinned rabbits stretched out on their backs like a scene out of Indiana Jones, you'll find several cheesemongers and pâté hawkers selling their goods at affordable rates. So grab what looks good to you, fill it out with some fresh bread from a boulangerie and a few tomatoes or cucumbers, and head to your park of choice.

Shopping

Rue Gambetta and **rue des Dominicains** are lined with one small boutique after another, each carrying more or less the same selection of high-end European brands such as Sonia Rykiel, Diesel, Chloe, and so on. There's also a flagship Daum store, selling the world-famous crystal products at factory-direct prices, around 30% less than elsewhere in France. The actual factory outlet has slightly damaged items at almost half off, and it's 5 minutes away from the flagship on place Stan. One problem though: While they're not made-in-China knockoffs, they don't have the "Daum" signature. Cheaper, more portable, and more delicious souvenirs are available at Maison des Soeurs Macarons, where local specialties such as *macarons* and *bergamot* candies have been made and hawked for over a century.

➡ **Hall du Livre** The Hall du Livre carries mostly French books, but a vast selection of them. The English offerings are fairly limited, although the store is still fun to browse, and the music and magazine sections are decent. *38 rue St-Dizier.* ☎ *03-83-35-53-01. www.halldulivre.fr. Mon–Sat 9am–8pm; Sun 11am–7pm.*

➡ **Maison des Soeurs Macarons** Here you can taste the sweets that were once reserved exclusively for royalty—the famous *bergamot* candies of Nancy. In 1750 King Stanislas, for all his benevolence,

selfishly proclaimed that these sweets, his favorites, could be consumed only by the bluest of bloods. In 1857, they came back into public circulation, and now they make an appearance with almost every cup of coffee served or restaurant bill presented in town. The *macarons,* which are a tad drier and less almond-y than most, are based on a recipe developed in 1793 by a pair of Benedictine nuns who were hard up for cash and got into the baking business. This sidewalk bake sale turned into the plush little business you see today. *21 rue Gambetta.* ☎ *03- 83-32-24-45. www.macaron-de-nancy.com. Mon 2–7pm; Tues–Sat 9:30am–12:30pm and 2–7pm.*

➡ **Pierre Koenig** Mmmm, chocolate! This place will bring out your inner Homer Simpson, such is its tempting selection of pralines and handmade chocolates. The specialty of the house is the Baton Gourmande, a stick of praline made with hazelnuts, almonds, and pistachios, covered with a layer of dark chocolate and then dusted with powdered sugar. You can serve it in slices like a piece of sausage, although it begs to be picked up and gnawed at until you feel it melting in your hand. *42 rue des Dominicains.* ☎ *03-83-35-18-36. mag.na@chocolats-koenig.com. Mon–Sat 10am–noon and 2–7pm.*

HOOK a BOOKWORM

If you love to speak and read French, make Nancy a top priority on weekends in September, when it hosts one of France's biggest book fairs, **La Livre sur Place.** More than 400 authors and 120,000 visitors—there have to be some cute ones in there somewhere—come to stock up on books, trade highbrow criticism, and chase some tail.

→**Punk Records** The name might refer more to the owner, a crusty but kindly old relic from the 1970s, than to the musical selection. The merchandise encompasses a number of genres but generally includes recent titles from all kinds of nifty indie bands, as well as classics you've been looking for from bands such as Duran Duran and the Stones. It's worth a browse. *27 rue des Maréchaux.* ☎ *03-83-36-79-56. Mon 2–6:30pm; Tues–Sat 10am–noon and 2–6:30pm.*

Verdun

Verdun is one of the nine towns referred to as *Le Zone Rouge,* or "The Red Zone," which was among the hardest-hit areas of France during World War I. In the last 2 years of the war, an astonishing 800,000 soldiers were killed here, most of them French, but also a number of Germans and Americans. And all that went down way before smart bombs and collateral damage were part of the military picture. Its own special tragedy, *l'enfer de Verdun,* or the hell of Verdun, took place from February 1916 to August 1917, during which time the town was attacked with artillery, flame-throwers, and poison gas.

Around the town, which is also renowned, although far less so, for its production of the sugar-covered almonds called *dragées,* are sites and memorials commemorating the lost soldiers and the tragedy and horror of warfare in general. Among the most moving and gruesome is L'Ossuaire de Douaumont (Douaumont Ossuary), which houses the bones of 130,000 unknown soldiers, French and German.

Getting There

Two **trains** arrive daily from Paris's Gare de l'Est; you'll have to change at Châlons-en-Champagne. Several daily trains also arrive from Metz, after a change at Conflans. The one-way fare from Paris is 35€; from Metz it's 12€. For train information and schedules, call ☎ 08-92-35-35-35. Driving is easy; Verdun is several miles north of the Paris-Strasbourg autoroute (A4).

Tourist Office

The **Office de Tourisme** is on place de la Nation (☎ **03-29-86-14-18;** fax 03-29-84-22-42; www.verdun-tourisme.com). It's closed on bank holidays.

Sightseeing

→**Mémorial de Verdun** This memorial museum is in the now nonexistent town of Fleury, one of the nine towns in the area destroyed during the war. It stands on the site of its long-gone train station. It features a number of relics from the war, such as military costumes, photographs, and weapons, all of which, in combination with a film screened in English, give something of a feel of what the war was like. The most resonant objects on display are in the section on the trench art—soldiers on the front engraved things like their cutlery and even leaves—which has a deeply personal element. The shards of stained glass from destroyed churches are also pretty brutal. *Musée Mémorial de Verdun.* ☎ *03-29-84-35-34. www.memorial-14-18.com. Admission 7€ adults; 3.50€ students. Opening hours vary; see website.*

📺 **Best ☻** →**Ossuaire de Douaumont (Douaumont Ossuary)** This long, dark hall built of somber grey stone is one of the most moving of the many memorials erected around France's many battlefields. On the walls and ceiling are the names of some of the soldiers whose bodies were never found; families of these soldiers each contributed a small amount of money to commemorate their sons' sacrifices to the war.

Beneath the edifice is the ossuary. Its glass walls allow the visitor a face-to-face confrontation with what mass death actually looks like. Pile upon pile upon pile of still-white bones fill up the windows, the sheer volume of them almost numbing the viewer to their actual meaning and the history behind their presence. Stop to think about how many of those bones make one person, and then envision how many are lying buried there, names and provenances unknown. ☎ 03-29-84-54-81. www.verdun-douaumont.com. Daily Dec and mid-Feb 2–5pm; Nov and Mar 9am–noon and 2–5pm; Apr 9am–6pm; May–Aug 9am–6:30pm; Sept 9am–noon and 2–6pm; Oct 9am–noon and 2–5:30pm. Closed Jan to mid-Feb (school holidays).

Mulhouse

This industrial city, whose name sort of rhymes with "more booze," would have long ago been wiped off the tourist map if it weren't for a quartet of ass-kicking museums that pay homage to, rather than apologize for, its industrial past. For much of its history, from 1515 on, Mulhouse was allied with the cantons of Switzerland, before it voted to join France in 1798. At this point, it had already become a prosperous and important center of trade and manufacturing, due to its ideal location on two of the Rhine's tributaries, the Doller and the Ill; the development of a local textile and textile-printing industry; and, many say, the strong work ethic of its Calvinist and Protestant community.

In joining France at this time, Mulhouse suavely and strategically benefited from Napoleon's blockade on English goods, which left the Continental market wide open and desperate for Mulhouse's textiles and other industrial goods. As the city's walls were demolished in order to accommodate the growth of its industries and its population, premonitions of France's socialist future blossomed in Mulhouse. To counter the possibility of Dickensian misery, worker's unions and social services charities formed to make sure the laborers retained their health and humanity and didn't degenerate into grubby exploited "hands" like their British counterparts. This, despite the fact that many of the city's sons were sent to Manchester to study their industries, and the construction of the worker's quarter took its inspiration from Manchester's urban planning.

Unlike Colmar, which was almost entirely preserved throughout World War II, Mulhouse lost a good deal of its historic buildings to heavy bombardment during the Liberation. Utilitarian '60s architecture dominates the landscape today. This has led to the well-intentioned, but rather forlorn practice of painting trompe l'oeil exteriors on the walls of buildings around town, in particular the tourist office, that re-create the original architecture like a set design for a 5th-grade school play. The tourist office, housed in a 16th-century building that was once the hôtel de ville, is at the heart of the small remaining old city, in place de la Réunion. It's the best place to start exploring the town. Besides this place, and several pedestrian walkways lined with branches of the usual French chains—Pinkie, Monoprix, and the like—there's not a whole lot of street life. You're better off spending your time (2 days and 1 night should be enough) at the very worthwhile museums, and then blowing this taco stand and moving on to

ALSACE-LORRAINE

somewhere more scenic—or using it as a less-expensive base from which to visit Colmar, 43km (27 miles) north.

Orientation

Mulhouse, at least the part of it that's not post–World War II urban sprawl, is small and easy to navigate on foot. It's divided into two parts: the Old Town, around place de la Réunion, and the New Town, around place de la République, where the city's rich industrialist families once lived. All of the museums are either within walking distance from your hotel, or an easy bus or tram ride away. The swank new tram system is in fact the current pride of the city (www.tram-train.net), and even has its own mascot, Max. It will take you almost everywhere you need to go, specifically between the train station, the town centers, and the Automobile Museum. Bicycles are fairly superfluous due to Mulhouse's puny size, and the rides out of town aren't particularly scenic. However, in case you must rent one, they are available from **Locacycles** (10 av. du Général Leclerc; ☎ **33-03-89-89-45-25-98**).

How to Fit in with the Locals

I suggest you pretend to have studied engineering or chemistry or one of the other hard sciences, and have a riveting conversation about the direction of research in the field of something you just made up. If lying's not your thing (fair enough), sing the well-deserved praises of the town's museums.

Tourist Offices

There are two tourism offices in Mulhouse—one at 9 av. Foch (☎ **33-03-89-35-48-48**) and the other at place de la Réunion (☎ **33-03-89-66-93-13**)—a sign of their egotism, optimism, or ambition; it's hard to tell which. Whichever it is, they're a good place to grab some information on the museums and a few extra pointers on getting around by public transport. They often offer packages in conjunction with hotels.

Mulhouse Nuts & Bolts

Emergencies Call SAMU at ☎ 15.

Hospital **Moenchsberg Hospital** (av. du Dr. Laennec; ☎ **33-03-89-64-64-64**).

Laundromats Try **Laverie GTI** (1 bis rue des Halles; ☎ 33-06-62-86-55-43), **Lavomatique** (25 rue Thénard; ☎ **33-06-62-86-55-43**), or **Laverie GTI** (65 av. de Colmar; ☎ **33-06-62-86-55-43**).

Police Call ☎ 17.

Post Office Located at 3 place du Général De Gaulle (☎ **33-03-89-56-94-11**).

Sleeping

There are a number of cheap hotels near the town center, all of which are perfectly serviceable and probably your best bet, as this is not a romantic destination for lovers or a city in which solitary travelers will want to linger. Save your money for the charming nearby town of Colmar, with its dearth of inexpensive accommodations.

HOSTELS

The Mulhouse youth hostel (37 rue de L'Ilberg; ☎ 03-89-42-63-28; bus no. 1 or 2 to the youth hostel stop) is standard-issue fare: it's a short bus ride out of town, features sterile rooms, and boasts some sporting grounds. While it has a capacity for 100 people, it's hard to imagine this place full. Maybe that's because the reception is closed every day from noon until five. The whole place takes a long winter break each year too, from the end of December until mid-January. You'll pay 12€ for a bed and sheets, 15€ with breakfast. Lunch or dinner is available for 9€.

CHEAP

→**Hôtel de Bâle** Run of the mill but less tackily decorated than its nearby counterparts, the Hôtel de Bâle has some of the cheaper rooms in town, probably due to its almost total lack of amenities (there *is* a place to plug in a razor, fear not), charm, or distinction. Still, given the utilitarian nature of a visit to Mulhouse, this place fits the bill just fine. Its location, like the others on this street, is ideal—right between two tram stations, a hop away from the town square, and next to a market and patisserie. *19–21 passage Central.* ☎ *03-89-46-19-87. www.hoteldebale.com. 50€ double. Credit cards accepted.*

→**Inter Hôtel Salvator** Another hotel as dreary as the city it serves, the Salvator has the all the same things going for it (and against it) as its neighbor the Bâle, with the slight variation that it offers the possibility to communicate with the outside world, in the form of Internet and telephone access. This (and the bar downstairs) might come in handy, especially for the single traveler, as this town can get pretty lonely. *29 passage Central.* ☎ *03-89-45-28-32. www.hotel salvator.fr. 60€–80€ double. Credit cards*

accepted. *Closed Dec 24–Jan 2. Amenities: Bar. In room: A/C, TV, Internet.*

DOABLE

→**Hôtel du Parc** Where was this place when Mulhouse's other hotels were being built? The city's most inviting and top-rated hotel, this Art Deco–themed four-star is a standout amid a sea of drab and depressing cheapies. Although the rooms don't exactly scream taste, they're light years classier (Greek marble bathrooms, ahem) than the ones going for half the price at the Salvator, and the lobby actually maintains some of its former glory from the days when it was the property of the illustrious, subsequently disgraced Schlumpf family. If for some inexplicable reason Mulhouse inspires you to splurge (and at 91€ for a basic room, it's something of a doable-splurge hybrid), this is the only place worth splurging on. *26 rue de la Seine.* ☎ *03-89-66-12-22. www.hoteldu parc-mulhouse.com. 91€ single; 450€ suite. In room: TV, minibar, Wi-Fi.*

Eating

→**Maurer Frères** CHARCUTERIE Follow the scent of grilling meat down the rue de Sauvage to this little *traiteur* who benevolently erects an outdoors stand selling big, juicy, tasty sausages for less than 10€. *12 rue de l'Industrie. No phone. www.maurerfreres.fr. 7.85€–9.85€.*

→**Pâtisserie Helfter** BAKERY Right between the two cheapo hotels on passage Central, this lovely bakery and *boulangerie* carries the usual assortment of those things for which we love French people: croissants, baguettes, tarts laden with this and that. There are also homemade chocolates and ice cream. If you're staying in one of the cheapies, this place could go a long way toward making your sojourn more enjoyable. *27 passage Central.* ☎ *03-89-56-00-88. www.helfter.fr. Daily 7:30am–5pm.*

Revenge of the Nerds

The Rise of Mulhouse's Industrial Giants

Samuel Kœchlin, Jean-Jacques Schmalzer, Jean-Henri Dollfus, and Jean-Jacques Feer were the dot.com geeks of their time. In 1746, these four men built the city's first workshop for fabric printing, which, within 40 years, would become the city's economic lifeblood. As a small city with no chance of expansion—neither east, where it would bump into Switzerland, nor west, where it would collide with France—Mulhouse was an ideal location for this kind of industry, which required very little land to make a buck. Toward the close of the 18th century, the city had more than 25 textile manufactures, and it was literally bursting at the seams. In 1798, the old ramparts came tumbling down, and the captains of industry began constructing a new neighborhood to house themselves and their workers. They modeled their residences after Louisiana plantation houses, with colonnades but hopefully no slaves, since this American port city launched the boats carrying the cotton on which Mulhouse's fortunes were founded.

In 1826, the leading industrialists of the time started the Société Industrielle de Mulhouse (SIM), with the aim of documenting existing technology, promoting further scientific innovation, and, in what today might seem like an error of inclusion, protecting their workers' health and rights. It was, in effect, a sort of small-scale and genuine version of today's World Trade Organization, guided by a Protestant and liberal sense of ethics, rather than cutthroat neoliberalism.

Through their endowments, Mulhouse became a center of scientific learning as well as manufacture: Libraries, university faculties, and, later, museums were created and maintained by the generosity of the Society, in their efforts to archive and promote industrial research. We have them to thank for the

→ **Pum Thaï Restaurant and Cooking School** THAI Two words: Who knew? If you've been waiting for Mulhouse to throw you a curveball, this is it. Fresh, authentic, sparkling clean Thai food served from an open kitchen. The modern, hip, but not overdone interior, white and black with touches of orange, is a refreshing change from the usual overly enthusiastic ethnic restaurant decor. No elephant tchotchkes and hand-me-down posters from the Thailand tourism board distract from the food at this place. The owners—a wife-and-husband team from Phuket, Thailand, and Alsace, respectively—have created an inexpensive restaurant that's always packed with well-to-do-looking families, groups of friends, business lunchers, and couples on dates. In fact, this restaurant is one of four—there are two other branches in Thailand, and one more in France. The noodle and rice dishes are excellent, and the green, yellow, red mini-rainbow of curries more than satisfactory. In fact, you'd be hard-pressed to find a more subtly spiced green curry outside of Paris. Don't skip dessert—the sticky coconut rice with mango slices almost outdoes the main courses, and wash it all down with a glass of creamy Thai iced tea or iced chrysanthemum tea. *7 rue du Mittelbach.* ☎ *33-389-46-05-56. www.pumthaifoodchain.com. Main courses 6.50€–9.50€. Credit cards accepted. Mon–Sat noon–1:30pm and 7–9:30pm (until 10pm Fri–Sat).*

delicious **Museum of Textile Printing** (14 rue Jean-Jacques Henner; ☎ 03-89-46-83-00), which began in 1857 as the Museum of Industrial Design.

No one-trick pony, Mulhouse soon added chemistry and engineering, and later auto manufacture, to its list of "Things we do really well and make people pay for." Today, the Mulhouse factory of automaker Peugeot is among the largest employers in the region of Alsace. It's not Peugeot, however, that we have to thank for the National Automobile Museum. While they did manufacture some of the cars within, the museum itself is the unlikely outcome of the conflict between a greedy textile magnate and his outraged workers (come to think of it, maybe it is likely, given the involvement of outraged French workers).

The scrooge of the story, Fritz Schlumpf, was a self-made wool tycoon whose success allowed him to indulge his lifelong passion for fancypants cars. When his empire dwindled in the 1970s, and his company faced bankruptcy, his workers stormed what was then the recently defunct woolen mill, now the museum. Instead of finding old weaving machines collecting dust, however, they were staring at 400-some of the fanciest and rarest cars on the planet. A bigger smack in the face they likely could not have imagined.

Luckily, their looting instincts were inexplicably restrained, and they decided to expose the collection to public view. For the first 2 years of its operation, during which more than 800,000 people stampeded the premises, the union of workers oversaw its operations, while earning over 3 million francs in the process. In 1979, the museum's management was turned over to a consortium of public and private entities, and the Société of industrialists could once again reclaim its good name.

Partying

📺 **Best ●** → **Le Noumatrouff** Even industrialists and chemistry majors need to kick back sometime. Here's where they go to catch a beer and listen to a very, very wide-ranging selection of live acts, most of whom hail from France, but represent most of the musical genres in the spectrum. Weepy singer-songwriters, sweaty punk bands, metal, hip-hop, electro, and a United Nations of performers have all graced the stage here, and continue to do so, in their turns. In mid-July, La Noumatrouff hosts the La Bêtes de Scène festival, which is equal parts eclectic and international. Check the website for their monthly program. *57 rue de la Mertzau.* ☎ *33-03-89-32-94-10. www.noumatrouff.com.*

Sightseeing

Mulhouse's only draw for the tourist is its fabulous museums. The theme of the pie, of which they all take a slice, is Industry with a capital I. The best of the best are the automobile, wallpaper, textile printing, and train museums, each of which do a wonderful job of presenting not only the topic at hand but the personages involved, making the giant clankings of trains and the polished bodies of 1940s cars seem a lot more human. All these museums, and a truckload more, are part of **www.museumspass.com**, where you can buy a short pass for 28€ that's valid for 1 month and gets you 4 days of unlimited visiting.

→ **Le Musée de l'Impression sur Etoffes** This museum, which narrates the process and history of fabric printing, is a must for fashion buffs. The tour starts with a room filled with exquisite textiles from India, illustrating the patterns that later became all the rage in Europe, and led to the lucrative industry on which Mulhouse's prosperity is based. Drizzled among the fabric samples are curiosities such as old cans and bottles of chemicals, machinery, and documents, all relics donated by the SIM, whose first brainchild, the Industrial Design Museum, grew to become this place. Be sure to take a glance at the six-page royal edict dating from 1726, which politely offered the death penalty to anyone caught importing Asian products, a measure that gives protectionism a whole new name. Seems that Western leaders feared cheap Asian imports long before Wal-Mart stepped on the scene with its sweatshop goodies. *14, rue Jean-Jacques Henner. ☎ 03-89-46-83-00. Fax 03-89-46-83-10. accueil@musee-impression.com; www.musee-impression.com. Admission 6€ adults, 3€ students, and special-needs travelers; 2€ kids 12–18; free for kids under 12. Tues–Sun 10am–noon, 2–6pm. Closed Jan 1, May 1, and Dec 25.*

➔ **Cité de l'Automobile Musée Nationale (National Automobile Museum)** You usually think of collections and museums as things that you view or visit. This is not one of those kinds of collections. The exterior, with its tinsel-like hangings of car bodies, is the first indication that this is no ordinary museum. Even those with an aversion to cars, and the macho truck-show persona that car-loving connotes, can't help but fall for the row

upon row of shiny, colorful but, above all, *sexy* vehicles in front of them, from mini-models made for spoiled royalty (the current king of Morocco, Mohammed VI, for example, used to cruise around in a half-scale Bugatti 1928 Type 52) to some Rolls-Royces that will make your bosoms heave. In addition to the 400 cars on display, there are also a number of informational movies, some extremely likable talking robots who work in a Peugeot factory, and a rotating exhibition space with car-related contemporary art on display (generally skippable). The museum is also a good place for intergenerational mullet sightings, as it's full of the kind of families who in America might be at the Monster truck rally with cans of Bud in hand. *192 av. De Colmar. ☎ 33-3-89-33-23-21. www.collection-schlumpf.com. Admission 11€ adults, students 8€. Hours vary widely by season; see website for details.*

➔ **Cité du Train** What could have been merely Disneyland-style fun for the whole family is actually a responsible and thoughtful look at the history of the French railway system, SNCF, in all of its roles: as the first enabler of mass tourism (who predicted Eurailing way back when?); as the symbol of modernity; and, very soberingly, as the major non-human factor in France's deportation of Jews in World War II. All this, plus sound-and-light shows, too. *2 rue Alfred de Glehn. ☎ 33-3-89-42-83-33. www.citedutrain.com. Admission 10€ adults, 7.5€ students; with entry to National Automobile Museum: 16€ adults, 12€ students. Hours vary; see website.*

The Nerd's Guide to French Wine & Culture

French Wine 101

Wine tasting should be part of any trip to France, one of the world's greatest wine-producing nations. And we're going to bet that you're all fairly expert wine *drinkers, n'est-ce pas?* But when you're not used to *tasting* the stuff, it can be intimidating to stand face-to-face with someone who has devoted a lifetime to the fermentation of grape juice. Well, fear not—this guide aims to give you a foundation in wine-tasting, highlighting the main wine-growing regions, common tasting etiquette, and the grape varieties used to make the most delicious nectar in the world.

Wine Basics

Despite popular belief, in France, the culture of the vine goes back to a time way before the Romans—even if they are responsible for spreading the lore and practice of winemaking throughout the country. Every single grape can be traced back to a variety called **Vitis vinifera,** cultivated in Asia centuries before Europe cottoned on to the benefits of making and drinking wine. But over time, the French did learn to "domesticate" the vine, selecting the best varieties and crossing them with others to create new ones. Today there are thousands of different grape varieties *(cépages),* yet only a few dozen (like Cabernet Sauvignon and chardonnay, which are world famous) have the qualities required for fine wine-making. In some regions, just one grape variety is used to produce all wine. In Burgundy, for instance, the pinot noir grape is behind every single bottle of red. In other areas, such as Bordeaux, the best wines are made using a clever combination of grapes, chosen and dosed very carefully, to ensure that the right "personality" is given to the wine. Although other countries such as the U.S., Australia, Germany, Italy, Mexico, Argentina, Australia, New Zealand, Spain, and South Africa produce great bottles, French wine still has the edge of being on every wine list in the world's greatest restaurants. Well, lucky you. When you're in France you won't have to scale the world's expensive restaurants to see what all the fuss is about: Just choose your region, book a tour, and open yourself up to the new world that awaits your taste buds.

The Wine Regions

France has 10 principal winegrowing regions. The most famous are Bordeaux, Burgundy, Champagne, Alsace, and the Loire, but you'll also find great *vin* in Provence and Corsica, the Jura and Savoie, the Southwest, Languedoc-Roussillon, and the Rhône.

ALSACE The vineyards of Alsace lie across an almost uninterrupted 100km (62-mile) stretch between Strasbourg and Mulhouse in the east of France, along the German border. The area is wooded and hilly, often affording breathtaking views over the Rhine and Germany's Black Forest. It would be too cold for wine-growing here were it not for the Vosges hills that protect it from the cold and rain. In fact, thanks to its geography, Alsace has some of the best weather in the country, typically benefiting from warm springs, dry and sunny summers, long and mild autumns, and cold winters. Alsace's proximity to Germany explains why some of the grape varieties (Riesling and Gewürztraminer) are also used by German wine-growers. Alsace is famous for its white wine, although it does use pinot noir grapes for its small red wine production.

BORDEAUX Bordeaux is practically a synonym for wine châteaux. Head out of town in any direction and you'll find yourself in the middle of endless vineyards, dotted with the vintner's stone houses and farms (often modest—wine château does not mean turrets and drawbridges). This is where the road signs read like a wine list: Graves, Sauternes, Saint-Julien, Pauillac, and St-Emilion; and where four out of five bottles are red wine. Bordeaux is known not only for the quality of its full-bodied wine but also for the number of bottles it produces. With 115,000 hectares (284,171 acres) of vineyards, its wine-growing surface is four times larger than the Napa Valley in California, and it produces around 660 million bottles every year.

BURGUNDY Burgundy is a vast region, yet only a relatively small area is cultivated for wine. That doesn't stop the liquor from being famous—no mean feat when you consider that Burgundy's climate is particularly unpredictable. If the summer is too wet, pinot noir grapes won't mature correctly, or if September is too cold and wet (which happens frequently), a whole crop can be annihilated. For a good crop, Burgundy's vines need a temperate spring (no frost), a warm month of June (for blossoming), a warm summer with an occasional shower, and a hot and dry September. The main producing areas are the Côte d'Or (that contains famous wine villages like Nuit-Saint-Georges), the Côte Chalonnaise farther south, the Mâconnais region around the town of Mâcon, and Beaujolais (the only region not to use pinot noir grapes). Other grape varieties used in Burgundy include Gamay for reds and chardonnay for whites.

CHAMPAGNE Who hasn't heard of this? The austere, windy plains of Champagne (which has given its name to the drink) have been creating great wines ever since medieval times, and way before Dom Pérignon accidentally created the bubbles. The bubbles, in fact, occur during the wine's second fermentation, when a mixture of sugars, yeasts, and wines are added, thus creating carbonic gas that gets trapped inside the bottle. The region, which expands some 145km (90 miles) northeast from Paris, is rich in chalky soil and covers around 35,000 hectares (86,487 acres) of land. The Montagne de Reims, a wooded plateau south of Reims, is a main grape-growing area, as are the vineyards in the Vallée de la Marne and la Côte des Blancs.

JURA The **Jura** produce wines from grape varieties that are little-used elsewhere in the east of France—a phenomenon due to the surrounding mountains, which have insulated the region from external influences. You'll be hardpressed to find a more continental climate than in the Jura, where winters are freezing (well below zero), summers hot and sunny (with just the right amount of rainfall), and autumns long and mild. Soils tend to be chalky and clayey. All this combines to create wines with some of the "strongest" personalities in France. As for the **Savoie,** the endless cereal fields and rolling pastures lend yet another facet to wines from this region. Vineyards radiate out from towns such as Chambéry up to the Lake Léman, producing mainly white wine and sparkling wine called Mousseaux (made primarily from Molette and Roussette grape varieties). The climate is often hard in the mountains, with frequent snow, but the microclimates around the lakes, combined with rich mineral deposits in the clayey limestone soils, tend to counterbalance any unfavorable conditions.

LANGUEDOC-ROUSSILLON The vineyards of the **Languedoc-Roussillon** cover a massive stretch along the Mediterranean coast from the Pyrenees to the Rhône Delta. Not only does this part of France create a bumpin' 40% of all French wine, it also makes some of the best. Practically every bottle receives an AOC seal of approval (see "Wine Basics," above)—not bad when you consider that only 20 years ago wine from this region was heavily criticized by experts. The Mediterranean climate is ideal for grapes: Winters are mild, summers warm and dry, and the rain that does fall in winter and spring tends to bring enough moisture for the whole year. The cépages that best respond to this region are Carignan, Cinsaut, and Grenache grapes.

LOIRE VALLEY The **Loire Valley's** vineyards follow the lengthy course of the River Loire and its confluents the Cher, the Indre, the Allier, and the Vienne. The principal biggies (or the ones you've probably heard of) are the white wines Pouilly and Sancerre, known for their crisp, fruity flavor (the soil in this region contains a lot of limestone and clay, which provides ideal conditions for white grapes), but the Loire also produces plenty of highly drinkable reds (such as Saumur), rosés (from Anjou), and sparkling wines. The Basse Loire is also famous for a light, sweet wine called Muscadet (also nicknamed the melon of Burgundy), served as an aperitif.

PROVENCE Provence is land of the rosé *par excellence;* however, since 1975, some delicious red wines have come out of this region. It is one of the largest wine-growing parts of the country (covering the area from the Var to the Bouches-du-Rhône, the Alps, and the Mediterranean). Thanks to gravelly, well-drained soils, generous sunshine, and refreshing winter showers, it has all the right conditions for making wine. Its geography also protects it from the gusts of the Mistral, Provence's (in)famous wind. Over 60% of all wine produced here is rosé (against 35% red), something that other regions criticize, saying that rosé is a fine drink, but only in the summer.

CORSICA The wines from the island of **Corsica** owe their characteristics to the sea and the mountains. Indeed the rocky ridges that cover this "island of beauty" have divided the country into little valleys, within which each winegrower has developed his own techniques and grape varieties. Corsica has its own microclimate: It can be Mediterranean, subtropical, or temperate according to the seasons—yet combined with the sea air, mountains, and complexity of the landscape, conditions are particularly adapted to viticulture.

FRENCH WINE & CULTURE

RHONE VALLEY The north of the **Rhône Valley** receives a continental climate (mild springs and warm summers), and the south gets more Mediterranean weather (plus the cold Mistral wind from the north). As a result the wines produced here (both red and white) vary tremendously according to where the grapes are grown. Red wines grown in the north tend to be either simple and light, or full-bodied and meaty, compared to reds in the south that are fruitier and have spicy undertones. Much of the Rhône Valley is sloped, so although the soil (which contains silex, limestone, sand, and chalk) is often eroded away, the plants receive plenty of sunshine and are less affected by seasonal mist and frost.

SOUTHWEST The **Southwest** refers to the area around Bergerac, Cahors, the Pyrenees, and Quercy—a vast expanse that churns out a wide variety of wine (mainly reds), and roughly corresponds to the ancient province of Gascony. The vines follow the course of the rivers: Bergerac—the Dordogne; Cahors—the Lot; Gaillac—the Tarn; and Fronton, Buzet, and Marmandais—the Garonne. Inevitably, Bordeaux's wines have influenced wines from the Southwest, but the local *vignerons* (winegrowers) have recently spent a lot of time cultivating new *cépages,* creating a palette of grape varieties exclusive to the area. Once again soils tend to be chalky, gravelly, and clayey, and the region's main climatic advantage is the mild winters.

Grape Varieties *(Cepages)*

Don't get your knickers in a twist, but understanding grape varieties is not easy. In fact, it is so complex that a whole science, *L'Ampélographie* (Ampelography), has been given over to it—and even then, things aren't as straightforward as you'd think. Beaujolais wine, for example, is primarily made from a grape variety called Gamay. However, after centuries of mixing and cloning, hundreds of Gamay varieties exist. They are all "translated" as Gamay, even if the original Gamay is the only one true Gamay. Got it? This makes knowing exactly which variety has gone into making each wine very difficult indeed. This task is further complicated by the fact that experts count over 5,000 official grape varieties in the world, which actually equates to more than 40,000 different varieties.

Don't worry, we're not going to bore you with all 40,000, but we will give you the lowdown on the main varieties used in French red and white wines.

REDS

Red wines are made from red grapes whose juice is without color. The color appears when the grapes are crushed, thus transferring the pigment from the flesh, skin, and pips to the liquid.

CABERNET FRANC This *cépage* is similar to Cabernet Sauvignon (no surprise there), and it has grown on land around Bordeaux since the 15th century. It also likes the soils along the Loire Valley, producing some excellent fruity wines that can be enjoyed young, although the best vintages should be kept for a long time.

CABERNET SAUVIGNON The most famous grape in the world is actually a cross between Sauvignon Blanc and Cabernet Franc grapes. It is mainly used in wines from Bordeaux and the Médoc, and they tend to create excellent, full-bodied, spicy wines that should be stocked for a good few years in a cellar to bring out the celebrated flavors.

GAMAY Well, you already know that it is the principal grape for Beaujolais wines. It is also known for its acidity and low tannin content, often producing fruity, floral reds. Gamay grapes are mostly cultivated along the Loire.

GRENACHE This *cépage* originated in Spain and came to France in the 14th century. Grenache make wines that are high on alcohol and low on acidity, and it's more often than not mixed with other grape varieties such as Syrah.

MERLOT These famous Bordelais grapes like the chalky-clayey soils of the right Bank of the Garonne River, St-Emilion, and Pomerol. They produce subtle, fruity wines with undertones of black currant and plum.

PINOT This is a very old variety rumored to come from Burgundy. You could say it is genetically unstable, as it has fathered many different *cépages* (pinot noir, Meunier, Gris, Blanc, to name but a few). It is also highly affected by growing conditions. In Burgundy, for instance, it can produce a totally different wine every 500m (1,640 ft.). Pinot grapes are also used in Champagne and Alsace.

SYRAH How does the song go? "Que syrah syrah. Whatever will be, will be"? Well, you can bet your bottom dollar that whatever will be, will be delicious, dark in color, with decent legs, and peppery with violet undertones. Many wines on the Mediterranean use Syrah grapes.

WHITES

Most white wines are produced from the juice of white grapes; however, some red grapes can produce white wine when pressurized under the right conditions. Champagne, for instance, is often made from red pinot noir and Pinot Meunier grape varieties.

CHARDONNAY Everybody raise a glass to chardonnay, another world-famous *cépage*. It came to be thanks to some bright spark in Burgundy who decided to cross the mediocre, medieval Gouais Blanc variety (from the Jura and Franche Comté) with the pinot noir. What a fusion! Chardonnay is known for its aromas such as brioche, fresh butter, nuts, grilled bread, pineapple, and exotic fruits, and it's hardy enough to adapt to climatic and soil changes.

CHENIN This *cépage* is best at home in the Loire, but it has exported well to South Africa, where it is called Steen. It is a versatile grape that produces standard table wines as well as fizzy Crémant and the occasional vintage.

GEWÜRZTRAMINER This is the ultimate aromatic grape (*gewür* means spices in German) used in Alsace since 1870. It is a branch of the Sauvignon Blanc family, whose grapes are pink in color. Wines are sweet, exotic, spicy in flavor, and velvety in texture. Some of the most expensive Gewürztraminer wines come from "late" harvests called *vendanges tardives,* where the grape is picked just before it rots, giving extra body and sweetness to the final liquor.

MUSCAT These grapes form a huge family that probably originated in Asia. Many wines in Alsace are made from a variety of this *cépage,* the most common being le Muscat d'Alexandrie. Its wines tend to be very dry and aromatic.

RIELSING This variety began life in Germany, but some experts argue that the Romans brought it to France. Nevertheless, you'll only find it in vineyards in Alsace nowadays, where it produces excellent wines (dry, elegant, lemony whites) that rival chardonnay.

SAUVIGNON This limestone-loving *cépage* has been around the Loire and Bordeaux regions for centuries. It makes crisp, dry wines, best enjoyed young. Sauvignon grapes are used exclusively to make Sancerre and Pouilly wines in the

Loire, as well as the occasional white from Bordeaux, but otherwise it is mixed with Sémillon varieties.

SEMILLON This southwestern grape is rarely used alone, but it adds body and texture when mixed with other grape types. Sauterne wines in particular use sémillon grapes.

Environmental Influences

Grapes need plenty of care and attention if they're going to make it off the branch and into the bottle. Four factors play a crucial role in wine-making, and all have to be just right if unappetizing grape-mush is to become one of the most sought-after gastronomic delights.

TERROIR

In French, the notion of *terroir* means much more than just its literal translation, the "land." The term *terroir* incorporates all the geological factors that influence vine-growing: the geology of the soil and earth (even bedrock) and the geographical configuration of the area around the vines. The quality of a *terroir* is judged by its capacity to support vines. They grow best in poor soil (gravel, limestone) with good drainage, plenty of sunshine, and little wind.

CLIMATE

Grapes are plants (obviously) and like all green stuff need a balance of water and sunlight and heat. All over the globe, vines grow best when they are situated between 35° and 50° latitude, which is why Europe is particularly well situated for viticulture. Grapes generally like mixed weather in spring and autumn; long, dry summers (so the grapes can mature); and long, cold winters during which they can rest. In terms of rainfall, they like 500 to 700 ml of water per year, and anything over that can jeopardize their growth.

CEPAGE

Each grape variety gives a different savor and aroma to the wine. Some tastes (like Gewürztraminer and pinot noir) are instantly recognizable, even to the most amateur tester; others can be identified by their tannin, like Cabernet Sauvignon and Syrah. However, a grape only comes into its own when it is grown in the right geographical area with an appropriate climate. For example, the pinot noir in Burgundy yields some of the most prestigious wines *(Grands Crus)* in the world, but if it were cultivated in Bordeaux, you'd be lucky to get any wine at all.

HUMAN INTERVENTION

You got it. Without the men and women of the winegrowing world, we would not have any wine to drink: Grapes would remain grapes, and parties would be much less fun. It is humans who look after the vine from the moment it is planted, to the moment the grapes are picked, fermented, bottled, and sold. And not just anyone could do the job either. A good wine producer knows vines better than he knows himself. He watches their every move for months, intervening when necessary to ensure that the bunches mature as they should. In fact, you could say that a winegrower needs to be a farmer, a gardener, and a chef, all at the same time, as it is ultimately the grower's personality that will give the finishing touches to the wine.

Tasting Etiquette

So you've got the basics; now you're ready to sample the stuff. But how do you go about it without looking like a dork or getting blind drunk? Well, unlike in other areas of life, whether you spit or swallow is not a matter of choice: When tasting wines "seriously," you spit. Traditionally you taste wine on an empty stomach, so if you were to swallow every mouthful, you'd be

Mythical Wines

Every century produces wines so exceptional that they become priceless. Since 1975, five annual harvests have produced these "legendary" wines. Impress your mates by rolling out this quick list. And if you happen to come across any, snap it up quickly—providing you have a few thousand to spare.

→ 1975 Clos de Goisses
→ 1978 Rayas
→ 1982 Pétrus
→ 1982 Château le Pin
→ 1982 Château Léoville-Las-Cases
→ 1985 Dom Pérignon
→ 1989 Château Haut Brion

on the floor before you had time to say *"Un autre, s'il vous plaît"* (another one, please). Now that that little conundrum is clear, here are a few tidbits.

THE "EYE" OF THE WINE

First things first—how does it look in the glass? By observing its color, shine, and legs (the liquid residue left on the side of the glass when you swirl the wine), you can already tell a lot about its age, personality, even how good it will taste. It is best to look at the wine by holding the glass against a white background or a light. The wine is then described in terms of its color (usually associated with precious stones: ruby, metals; copper, flowers; rose, poppy; fruits, lemon and cherry) and intensity (dark, light, pale, and so on). Once you get really good, it is possible to tell which *cépages* have been used to make the wines.

Observing the "legs" is the last step of the "visual" examination. Turn your glass slowly and see how the residue sticks to the sides. The residue (legs) determines the texture and strength of the wine. The longer the legs stay on the side, the richer the alcohol or sugar content. A wine that is lower in alcohol or sugar appears more fluid and runny.

THE "NOSE" OF THE WINE

Hold your horses—you're not quite ready to taste it yet. First you have to identify the wine's "bouquet" or "nose" (aromas). By smelling it you can also tell a lot about what it's going to taste like, its age, and quality. Wine-tasting is all about playing on the senses, and this step is designed to activate your "olfactive" memory.

The term "nose" describes all of the odors that characterize the wine. To get a good whiff, choose a tulip-shaped glass, fill it a third of the way up, and make sure the wine is served between 46° and 64°F (8°–18°C) depending on the type. Too cold and you won't make out the odors—too warm and you'll only breathe the alcohol vapors (a pleasant experience, but one that defeats the purpose).

You'll need to smell the wine three times to get the best impression. With the first sniff, you'll smell the wine's initial bouquet—a volatile aroma that disappears almost as soon as the wine is poured. Then swirl the wine around in the glass to oxygenate it. The aim of the second "nose" is to identify the wine's aromatic personality (the force and intensity of the smell). Swirl again and then sniff the wine a third time. Notice how the odors change as the various elements come into contact with the air. This third "nose" is designed to help you note the aromatic evolution of the wine—its strength and persistence.

LA DEGUSTATION: SWILL & THEN SPIT!

Right then, now you're ready to taste the stuff *(la dégustation)*. But beware: Tasting is a lot more complicated than a simple sip,

FRENCH WINE & CULTURE

How to Open a Bottle

You mightn't know it, but how you open the bottle in France is as important as how you drink the wine. If you don't want to make a faux-pas at the dinner table, follow this quick list of instructions:

1. Using a knife, cut around the foil covering the cork, just below the ring of the bottle.
2. Remove the upper part of the foil you have just cut to prevent the wine from coming into contact with the metal.
3. Rub the neck of the bottle with a cloth: Don't be put off if there's mould on the bottle; it simply proves that it was stocked in a cellar.
4. Push the corkscrew right into the middle of the cork, taking care not to pierce the cork at the bottom end.
5. Take out the cork and listen to the pop.
6. Once removed, squeeze the cork to check its elasticity—the older the cork, the harder it is to press. Then smell the cork, which should have absorbed some of the odor from the wine. This is the best way to tell whether the wine is drinkable or has been "corked" (gone off). A wine that has gone off will leave a vinegar-like smell on the cork.

swill, and spit-out. You've probably seen people tasting wine on TV and wondered why they pull such ridiculous faces and make such impolite slurping noises. The answer is that you have to. The idea is to get the wine to cover every millimeter of your mouth to awaken all of your gustative potential and release the wine's aromatic molecules. The only way of doing this is unfortunately (and I apologize for the vulgarity) to make your mouth look like an asshole, as you suck in air through the tiny opening, before blowing your cheeks in and out to swill it around.

Although you'll taste the wine in one fell swoop, there are three different stages you should note while the wine is in your mouth. They will help you determine the overall personality of the wine. First, there's the **attack:** Take a sip as you would normally and then ask yourself, what is your first impression? Does it hit hard in the mouth (a strong attack) or have a mild taste (a weak attack)? A good attack is one that is precise and pleasant. Next up is the **middle of the mouth** step. This is when the asshole look comes into play as you swirl the wine around your mouth for a few seconds, before sucking in a bit of air in order to activate the aromatic molecules that will allow you to taste the spectrum of flavors in the wine. Finally **spit** the wine out into the spittoon, and count how many seconds the taste (or memory) of the wine stays in your mouth. This length of time is known as a *caudalie* (from the Latin "cauda" which means "tail"). One *caudalie* equals 1 second of taste in the mouth. The longer the *caudalie,* the better the quality of the wine. The trick here is not to confuse the aromatic elements with the sensations left behind by the tannin or alcohol. Now and only now are you ready to give your opinion and describe what you tasted and the sensations the wine gave you.

French Art 101

Prehistoric, Celtic & Classical Art (25,000 B.C.–A.D. 500)

After Stonehenge in England, Europe's most famous prehistoric remains are France's **Paleolithic cave paintings.** Created 15,000 to 20,000 years ago, they show off mind-blowing hunting scenes and abstract shapes. Whether the paintings served in religious rites or were simply decorative is anybody's guess.

WHERE TO SEE IT

Cave Art

The **caves at Lascaux,** known as the Sistine Chapel of prehistoric art, have been closed since 1963, but experts have created a replica, Lascaux II (p. ###). For the real deal, visit **Les Eyzies** (p. ###), nearby, with several interesting caves.

Celtic & Classical Art

You'll be hard-pressed to find much art from **Celtic** (ca. 1,000 B.C.–A.D. 125) and **Roman** (A.D. 125–500) Gaul. Most items in France's **archaeology museums** include small votive bronzes, statues, jewelry, and engraved weapons and tools. Burgundy, however, preserves the most of Celtic Gaul, including sites at **Dijon.** For Roman Gaul, whip your booty down south to **Nîmes** (p. 358) and **Arles** (p. 461). You'll also find some sculptures in Paris's **Musée de Cluny** (p. 117).

Romanesque Art (900–1100)

The art of early medieval France was largely church-related, and because Mass was in Latin, images were used to communicate the Bible's lessons to the mostly illiterate people. For those who couldn't read, **bas-reliefs** (sculptures that project slightly from a flat surface) were used to illustrate key tales that inspired faith in God and fear of sin (the Last Judgment was a particular favorite). Chapels were built to house silver and gold **reliquaries** displaying bits of saints to which worshipers could pray. Saintly **statues** also began appearing on facades, though this became more of a Gothic convention.

WHERE TO SEE IT

Sculptures & Statues

For reliefs of *Christ and the Evangelists,* by Bernard Guildin, go to the crypt of **St-Semin** in Toulouse (p. ###); and don't miss the wonderfully detailed facade frieze and statues of **St-Pierre** in Angoulême.

Bayeux Tapestry (1066–1077)

The most notable example of Romanesque artistry is the Bayeux Tapestry, 70m (230 ft.) of embroidered linen telling the story of William the Conqueror's defeat of the English (p. 214).

Gothic Art (1100–1400)

France is literally dripping in Gothic art, although most is (as you'll probably notice) ecclesiastical. Church facades and choir screens were festooned with **statues and carvings,** and the French became masters of **stained glass.** Many painterly conventions began on windowpanes or as elaborate designs in **illuminated manuscript** margins, which developed into altarpieces of the colorful, expressive **International Gothic** style of posed scenes and stylized figures. With a keen eye and a bit of practice, you can tell Gothic painting and sculpture from the figures that tend to be more natural than in the Romanesque styles. One could also say that they are also highly stylized, flowing, and rhythmic, as the features and gestures were usually exaggerated for symbolic or emotional emphasis.

WHERE TO SEE IT
Sculpture & Statues

The best-preserved examples are at the cathedrals of **Chartres** (p. 140) and **Reims** (p. 673). **Strasbourg** also boasts one of the most elaborate Gothic portals and rose windows in France.

Stained Glass

All of the above churches (especially **Chartres**) contain some of the most stunning stained glass in Europe—though first prize goes to Paris's **Ste-Chapelle**. See p. 112.

Painting

Burgundy was the first French area to embrace the High Gothic painting style of its Flemish neighbors. The great **van der Weyden** left works in **Dijon** and **Beaune** as well as at the **Louvre**. **Enguerrand Quarton** was the most important French painter of the period. One of his only documented paintings is at the **Musée de l'Hospice** in Villeneuve-lez-Avignon, although most scholars also attribute to him the **Louvre's** *Villeneuve Pietà* (1460).

Unicorn Tapestries (1499–1514)

Now in Paris's **Musée de Cluny** (p. 117), these gorgeous tapestries shine brightly as a statement of medieval sensibilities and sensualism.

Renaissance & Baroque Art (1450–1800)

Renaissance means "rebirth"—in this case, that of classical ideals. Humanist thinkers rediscovered the wisdom of ancient Greece and Rome, while artists strove for naturalism, using newly developed techniques like linear perspective. The French had little to do with this movement, which started in Italy and was picked up only in Germany and the Low Countries. However, many Renaissance treasures are in French museums, thanks to collectors such as **François I**.

In fact you'll have to wait until the 17th-century **baroque** for a few French masters to emerge. This period is hard to pin down. In some ways it was influenced by a religious version of Renaissance ideals, but in others it looked back to the classics for inspiration and concentrated on contrasts of light and dark. **Rococo**, for instance, is later baroque art gone all frothy and chaotic.

WHERE TO SEE IT

Paris's **Louvre** abounds with Renaissance works by Italian, Flemish, and German masters, including **Michelangelo** (1475–1564) and **Leonardo da Vinci** (1452–1519). Leonardo's *Mona Lisa* (1503–05), perhaps the world's most famous painting, hangs there. See p. 73.

WHO'S WHO OF BAROQUE & ROCOCO ART

○ **Nicolas Poussin (1594–1665):** He painted many mythological scenes that foreshadowed the Romantic movement. It has also been said that his love of painting nature influenced Impressionists such as Cézanne.

○ **Antoine Watteau (1684–1721):** A rococo painter of colorful, theatrical works, Watteau began the short-lived *fête galante* style of china-doll figures against stylized landscapes of woodlands or ballrooms.

○ **François Boucher (1703–70):** Louis XV's rococo court painter, Boucher studied Watteau and produced decorative landscapes and genre works.

○ **Jean-Honoré Fragonard (1732–1806):** Boucher's student became a master of rococo pastel scenes and painted pink-cheeked, wispy, genteel lovers frolicking among billowing trees. His famous *The Bathers* hangs in the Louvre.

FRENCH WINE & CULTURE

Neoclassical & Romantic Art (1770–1890)

As the baroque got excessive and the rococo got cute, and as the somber Counter-Reformation got serious about imposing limits on religious art, several artists, such as Jacques-Louis David, looked to the ancients. Viewing new excavations of Greek and Roman sites such as Pompeii and Paestum and growing (revolutionary) interest in Greek democracy led the artists of this enlightened era to create a **neoclassical** style that emphasized symmetry, austerity, clean lines, and classical themes, such as depictions of historical or mythological scenes.

The **Romantics,** on the other hand, felt that both the ancients and the Renaissance had gotten it wrong and that the Middle Ages were the place to be. They idealized tales of chivalry and held a deep respect for nature, human rights, and the nobility of the peasantry, as well as a suspicion of progress. Their paintings were heroic, historic, and (melo)dramatic.

WHO'S WHO OF ROMANTIC & NEOCLASSICAL ART

○ **Jacques-Louis David (1744–1825):** David dropped the baroque after study in Rome exposed him to neoclassicism, which he brought back to Paris and displayed in such paintings as *The Oath of the Horatii* (1784) and *Coronation of Napoléon and Joséphine* (1805–08), both in the **Louvre.**

○ **Jean-Auguste-Dominique Ingres (1780–1867):** Ingres trained with David, from whom he broke to adapt a more Greek style. He became a defender of the neoclassicists and the Royal French Academy and opposed the Romantics. His *Grand Odalisque* (1814) hangs in the Louvre.

○ **Théodore Géricault (1791–1824):** One of the early Romantics, Géricault

painted *The Raft of the Medusa* (1819), which served as a model for the movement. This large, dramatic history painting also hangs in the **Louvre.**

○ **Eugène Delacroix (1798–1863):** Painted in the Romantic style, his *Liberty Leading the People* (1830), in the Louvre, reveals experimentation in color and brush stroke.

○ The **Barbizon School:** This group of landscape painters, founded in the 1830s by **Théodore Rousseau** (1812–67), painted from nature at Barbizon, where the **Musée Ganne** is devoted to Rousseau's works. The paintings of **Jean-François Millet** (1814–75), who depicted classical scenes and peasants, hang in his studio nearby and in Paris's Musée d'Orsay. You'll find works by **Jean-Baptiste-Camille Corot** (1796–1875), a sort of idealistic proto-Impressionist, in the Louvre.

Impressionist Art (1870–1920)

A favorite for many folk, Impressionism was an alternative to the formal, rigid neoclassicism and idealized Romanticism that rankled some late-19th-century artists interested in painting directly from nature. Seeking to capture the fleeting *impression* of light reflecting off objects, they adopted a free, open style characterized by deceptively loose compositions; swift, visible brushwork; and often, light colors. For subjects, they turned away from the historical depictions of previous styles to landscapes and scenes of daily life. Unless specified below, you'll find some of their best works in Paris's **Musée d'Orsay.**

WHO'S WHO OF IMPRESSIONIST ART

○ **Edouard Manet (1832–83):** His groundbreaking *Picnic on the Grass* (1863) and *Olympia* (1863) weren't Impressionism proper, but they helped inspire the movement with their realism, visible brush strokes, and thick outlines.

○ **Claude Monet (1840–1926):** The Impressionist movement began with an 1874 exhibition in which Monet showed his loose, Turner-inspired *Impression, Sunrise* (1874), now in the **Musée Marmottan.** One critic focused on it to lambaste the whole exhibition, deriding it all as "Impressionist." Far from being insulted, the show's artists adopted the word for their movement. Monet's *Water Lilies* hangs in Paris's **Musée de l'Orangerie.** You can visit his studio and gardens at **Giverny,** north of Paris.

○ **Pierre-Auguste Renoir (1841–1919):** Originally Renoir was a porcelain painter, which helps explain his figures' ivory skin and chubby pink cheeks.

○ **Edgar Degas (1834–1917):** Degas was an accomplished painter, sculptor, and draftsman—his pastels of dancers and bathers are memorable.

○ **Auguste Rodin (1840–1917):** The greatest sculptor of the Impressionist era, Rodin crafted remarkably expressive bronzes, refusing to idealize the human figure as had his neoclassical predecessors. The **Musée Rodin,** his former Paris studio, contains, among other works, his *Burghers of Calais* (1886), *The Kiss* (1886–98), and *The Thinker* (1880).

Post-Impressionist Art (1880–1930)

Few experimental French artists of the late 19th century were considered Impressionists, though many were friends with those in the movement. The smaller movements or styles are usually lumped together as post-Impressionist.

Again, you'll find the best examples of their works at Paris's **Musée d'Orsay,** although the pieces mentioned below by Matisse, Chagall, and the Cubists are in the **Centre Pompidou.**

WHO'S WHO OF POST-IMPRESSIONIST ART

○ **Paul Cézanne (1839–1906):** Cézanne adopted the short brush strokes, landscapes, and light color palette of his Impressionist friends, but his style was more formal and deliberate. He sought to give his art monumentality and permanence, even if the subjects were still lifes (*Nature Morte: Pommes et Oranges*, 1895–1900), portraits (*La Femme a la Cafetière*, 1890–95), and landscapes (*La Maison du Pendu Auvers-sur-Oise*, 1873).

○ **Paul Gauguin (1848–1903):** Gauguin could never settle himself or his work, trying Brittany, where he developed **synthetism** (black outlines around solid colors), and hopping around the South Pacific, where he was inspired by local styles and colors, as in *Femmes de Tahiti sur la Plage* (1891).

○ **Georges Seurat (1859–91), Paul Signac (1863–1935),** and **Camille Pissarro (1830–1903):** These artists developed **divisionism** and its more formal cousin, **pointillism.** Rather than mixing yellow and blue together to make green, they applied tiny dots of yellow and blue right next to one another so that the viewer's *eye* mixed them together to make green. Seurat's best work in the Orsay is *Le Cirque* (1891), though the lines are softer and subjects more compelling in the nude studies called *Les Poseuses* (1886–87).

○ **Henri de Toulouse-Lautrec (1864–1901):** He's most famous for his work with thinned-down oils, which he used to create paintings and posters of wispy, fluid lines, anticipating Art Nouveau. He often depicted the bohemian life of Paris (dance halls, cafes, and top-hatted patrons at fancy parties), as in the barely sketched *La Danse Mauresque* (1895); the pastel *Le Lit* (1892) shows his quieter, more intimate side.

○ **Vincent van Gogh (1853–1890):** A Dutchman, van Gogh spent most of his career in France. He combined divisionism, synthetism, and a touch of Japanese influence and painted with thick, short strokes. Never particularly accepted by any artistic circle, he is the most popular painter in the world today, even though he sold only one painting in his life. The Orsay contains such works as *Le Chambre de Van Gogh à Arles* (1889), a self-portrait (1887), a portrait of his psychiatrist *Docteur Paul Gachet* (1890), and *La Méridienne* (1889–90).

○ **Henri Matisse (1869–1954):** Matisse took a hint from synthetism and added wild colors and strong patterns to create **Fauvism** (a critic described those who used the style as *fauves,* meaning "wild beasts"), such as *Interior, Goldfish Bowl* (1914). He continued exploring these themes even when most artists were turning to cubism. When his health failed, he assembled brightly colored collages of paper cutouts (such as the Pompidou's *Sorrow of the King,* 1952). You'll find several of his works in the **Musée Matisse** in Nice. His masterpiece, the **Chapelle du Rosaire** (1949–51), a chapel he designed and decorated, is near Vence.

○ **Georges Braque (1882–1963)** and **Pablo Picasso (1881–1973):** French-born Braque and Spanish-born Picasso painted objects from all points of view at once, rather than using tricks like perspective to fool viewers into seeing three dimensions (in the Pompidou, Braque's *Man with Guitar,* 1914, and Picasso's 1907 study for *Les Demoiselles d'Avignon*). The result was called **cubism** and was expanded upon by the likes of **Fernand Léger** (1881–1955; *Wedding,* 1911) and the Spaniard **Juan Gris** (1887–1927; *Le Petit Déjeuner,* 1915). Braque developed the style using collage (he added bits of paper and cardboard to his images), while Picasso moved on to other styles. You can see work from all of Picasso's periods at museums dedicated to him in **Paris, Antibes,** and **Vallauris,** where Picasso revived the ceramics industry.

○ **Marc Chagall (1889–1985).** This Hasidic Jewish artist is hard to pin down. He traveled widely in Europe, the United States, Mexico, and Israel; his painting started from cubism and picked up inspiration everywhere to fuel a brightly colored, allegorical, often whimsical style. You'll find a museum devoted to him in **Nice,** several of his stained-glass windows in the **Cathédrale Notre-Dame d'Amiens,** his painted ceiling in Paris's **Opéra Garnier,** and *To Russia, the Asses and the Others* (1911) in the Pompidou.

French Architecture 101

While each architectural era has its distinctive features, some elements, floor plans, and terms are common to many of the eras.

From the Romanesque period on, most **churches** consist of either a single wide **aisle** or a central **nave** flanked by two narrow aisles. The aisles are separated from the nave by a row of **columns,** or more accurately by square stacks of masonry called **piers,** connected by **arches.** Sometimes in structures from the

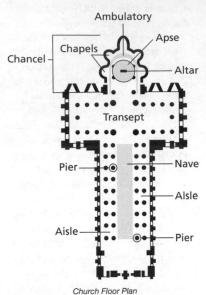

Church Floor Plan

Some churches, especially those built after the Renaissance, when mathematical proportion became important, have a **Greek Cross** plan, with each axis the same length—like a giant plus sign (+). Very few buildings (especially churches) were built in one particular style. Massive, expensive structures often took centuries to complete, during which time tastes would change and plans would be altered.

Ancient Roman Architecture (125 B.C.–A.D. 450)

Provence was Rome's first transalpine conquest, and the legions of Julius Caesar quickly subdued the Celtic tribes across France, converting it into Roman Gaul. Roman architectural innovations include the load-bearing arch and the use of concrete, brick, and stone.

Nîmes preserves from the 1st century B.C. a 20,000-seat **amphitheater,** a **Corinthian temple** called the "Square House," a fine **archaeology museum,** and the astounding **pont du Gard,** a 47m-long (158-ft.), three-story aqueduct made of cut stones fitted together without mortar.

From the Augustan era of the 1st century A.D., **Arles** preserves a 25,000-seat **amphitheater,** a rebuilt **theater,** and a decent **museum.** The nearby **Glanum** excavations outside St-Rémy-de-Provence (which houses its **archaeology museum**) offer a complete, albeit highly ruined, glimpse of an entire Roman provincial town, from a few pre-Roman Gallic remnants and a 20 B.C. arch to the last structures sacked by invading Goths in A.D. 480.

Romanesque and Gothic eras, you'll see a second level, the **clerestory,** above these arches (and hence above the low roof over the aisles) punctuated by windows.

This main nave and aisle assemblage is usually crossed by a perpendicular corridor called a **transept,** placed near the far, east end of the church so that the floor plan looks like a **Latin Cross** (shaped like a crucifix). The shorter, east arm of the nave is called the **chancel;** it often houses the stalls of the **choir** and the **altar.** If the far end of the chancel is rounded off, it is termed an **apse.** An **ambulatory** is a curving corridor outside the altar and the choir area, separating them from the ring of smaller chapels radiating off the chancel and apse.

Pont du Gard, Nîmes

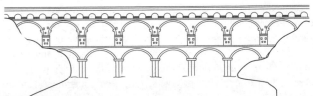

Romanesque Architecture (800–1100)

Romanesque churches were large, with a wide nave and aisles to accommodate the faithful who came to hear Mass and worship at the altars of various saints. To support the weight of all that masonry, the walls had to be thick and solid (meaning they could be pierced by only a few small windows) and had to rest on huge piers, giving Norman churches a dark, somber feeling.

Some of the features of this style include **thick walls, infrequent and small windows, huge piers,** and **rounded arches.** These load-bearing architectural devices allowed architects to open up wide naves and spaces, channeling the weight of the stone walls and ceiling across the curve of the arch and into the ground through the columns or pilasters.

The **Cathédrale St-Bénigne** in Dijon was the first French Romanesque church, but of that era only the crypt remains. The **Cathédrale St-Pierre** in Angoulême has a single large nave, a rounded apse with small radiating chapels, and a pair of transept mini-apses.

Gothic Architecture (1100–1500)

By the 12th century, engineering developments freed architecture from the heavy, thick walls of the Romanesque and allowed ceilings to soar, walls to thin, and windows to proliferate. The Gothic was France's greatest homegrown architectural style, copied throughout Europe.

Instead of dark, relatively unadorned Romanesque interiors that forced the eyes of the faithful toward the altar, the Gothic interior enticed the churchgoers' gaze upward to high ceilings filled with light. The priests still conducted Mass in Latin, but now peasants could "read" the stories told in stained-glass windows.

The squat, brooding exteriors of the Romanesque fortresses of God were replaced by graceful buttresses and soaring spires, which rose from town centers like beacons of religion.

Some identifiable Gothic features include:

○ **Pointed arches:** The most significant development of the Gothic era was the discovery that pointed arches could carry far more weight than rounded ones.

○ **Cross vaults:** Instead of being flat, the square patch of ceiling between four columns arches up to a point in the center, creating four sail shapes, sort of like the underside of a pyramid. The X separating these four sails is often reinforced with ridges called **ribbing.**

Cross Vault

○ **Flying buttresses:** These free-standing exterior pillars connected by graceful, thin arms of stone help channel the weight of the building and its roof out and down into the ground. Not every Gothic church has evident buttresses.

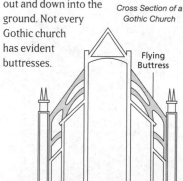

Cross Section of a Gothic Church

Flying Buttress

FRENCH WINE & CULTURE

○ **Stained glass:** The multitude and size of Gothic windows allowed them to be filled with Bible stories and symbolism portrayed in colorful patterns of stained glass. The use of stained glass was more common in the later Gothic periods.

○ **Rose windows:** These huge circular windows, often the centerpieces of facades, are filled with elegant tracery and "petals" of stained glass.

○ **Tracery:** Lacy spider webs of carved stone curlicues grace the pointed ends of windows and sometimes the spans of ceiling vaults.

○ **Spires:** These pinnacles of masonry seem to defy gravity and reach toward heaven.

○ **Gargoyles:** These are drain spouts disguised as wide-mouthed creatures or human heads.

○ **Choir screen:** Serving as the inner wall of the ambulatory and the outer wall of the choir section, the choir screen is often decorated with carvings.

Cathédral Notre-Dame de Chartres

The statuary, spire, and some 150 glorious stained-glass windows of the **Cathédrale Notre-Dame de Chartres** (1194–1220) make it a must-see, while the **Cathédrale Notre-Dame de Reims** (1225–90) sports more than 2,300 exterior statues and stained glass from 13th-century rose window originals to 20th-century windows by Marc Chagall. **Paris's Notre-Dame** cathedral (1163–1250) has good buttresses, along with a trio of France's best rose windows, portal carvings, a choir screen of carved reliefs, and spiffy gargoyles (many of which are actually 19th-century neo-Gothic). The *sine qua non* of stained glass is Paris's **Ste-Chapelle** (1240–50).

Renaissance Architecture (1500–1630)

In architecture as in painting, the Renaissance came from Italy and was only slowly Frenchified. And as in painting, its rules stressed proportion, order, classical inspiration, and precision to create unified, balanced structures.

Some identifiable Renaissance features include **a sense of proportion, a reliance on symmetry, the use of classical orders** (this specifies three types of column capitals: Doric, Ionic, and Corinthian), and **steeply pitched roofs.** They often feature **dormer windows** (upright windows projecting from a sloping roof).

The Loire Valley is home to many Renaissance **châteaux.** Foremost is the Loire's **Château de Chambord,** started in 1519, probably according to plans by Leonardo da Vinci (who may have designed its double-helix staircase). In contrast, the **Château de Chenonceau,** home to many a French king's wife or mistress, is a fanciful fairy tale built in the middle of a river.

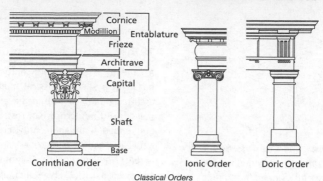

Corinthian Order · Ionic Order · Doric Order

Classical Orders

Classicist & Rococo Architecture (1630–1800)

While Italy and Germany embraced the opulent baroque, France took the fundamentals of Renaissance **classicism** even further, becoming more imitative of ancient models. This represents a change from the Renaissance preference of finding inspiration in the classic era.

During the reign of Louis XIV, art and architecture were subservient to political ends. Buildings were grandiose and severely ordered on the Versailles model. Opulence was saved for interior decoration, which increasingly (especially from 1715–50, after the death of Louis XIV) became a detailed and self-indulgent **rococo** (*rocaille* in French). Externally,

rococo is noticeable only in a greater elegance and delicacy.

Rococo tastes didn't last long, and soon a **neoclassical** movement was raising structures, such as Paris's **Pantheon** (1758), that were even more strictly based on ancient models than the earlier classicist designs had been.

Some identifiable features of classicism include **highly symmetrical, rectangular structures** based on the classical orders; **projecting central sections** topped by triangular pediments; **mansard roofs,** with a double slope, the lower longer and steeper than the upper, which became a defining feature and French trademark developed by **François Mansart** (1598–1666) in the early 17th century; **dormer**

Château de Chambord

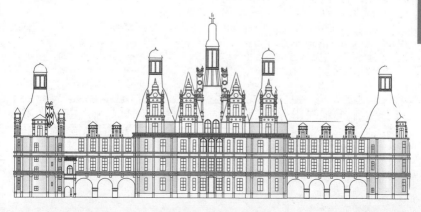

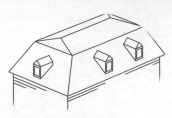

Mansard Roof

windows; and *oeil-de-bouef* ("ox-eyes"). These small, round windows poke out of the roof's slope.

Mansart built town houses, châteaux, and churches (**Val-de-Grâce** in Paris; the **Palais du Tau** in Reims) and laid out Dijon's **place de la Libération**. But the Parisian architect is chiefly remembered for his steeply sloping namesake, "**mansard**" roofs.

Louis Le Vau (1612–70) was the chief architect of the Louvre from 1650 to 1670 and of the **Château de Vaux-le-Vicomte** (1656–61) outside Paris, a gig that put him and his collaborators—including Mansart, interior decorator **Charles Le Brun** (1619–90), and the unparalleled landscape gardener **André Le Nôtre** (1613–1700)— on Louis XIV's radar and landed them the commission to rebuild **Versailles** (1669–85). Versailles is France's—indeed, Europe's—grandest palace.

Rococo architecture is tough to find. In Paris, seek out Delamair's Marais town house, the **Hôtel de Soubise** (1706–12), and the prime minister's residence, the **Hôtel Matignon** (1721), by Courtonne. For rococo decor, check out the **Clock Room** in Versailles.

19th-Century Architecture

Architectural styles in 19th-century France began in a severe classical mode. Then architects dabbled with medieval revival, delved into modern urban restructuring, and ended with an identity crisis torn between Industrial-age advancements and Art Nouveau organic. The 19th century saw several distinct styles, including:

○ **First Empire:** Elegant neoclassical furnishings—distinguished by strong lines often accented with a simple curve— during Napoleon's reign.

○ **Second Empire:** Napoleon III's reign saw the eclectic Second Empire reinterpret classicism in a dramatic mode. **Baron Haussmann** (1809–91), who cut broad boulevards through the city's medieval neighborhoods, restructured Paris.

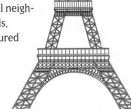

Tour Eiffel, Paris

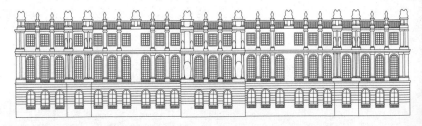

Château de Versailles

○ **Third Republic/early industrial:**
Expositions in Paris in 1878, 1889, and
1900 were the catalysts for constructing
huge glass-and-steel structures that
showed off modern techniques and the
engineering prowess of the Industrial
Revolution. This produced such Parisian
monuments as the **Eiffel Tower (Tour
Eiffel)** and **Basilique du Sacré-Coeur.**

○ **Art Nouveau:** Architects and decorators rebelled against the Third Republic
era of mass production by stressing the
uniqueness of craft. They created asym-
metrical, curvaceous designs based on
organic inspiration (plants and flowers)
in such mediums as wrought iron,
stained glass, tile, and wallpaper.

Napoleon spent his imperial decade
(1804–14) refurbishing the **Palais de
Fontainebleau** in First Empire style. The
ultimate paean to the classical was the **Arc
de Triomphe** (1836), Napoleon's imitation
of a Roman triumphal arch.

In the Second Empire, Napoleon III commissioned **Baron Haussmann** in 1852 to
remap Paris according to modern urban-
planning theories—clearing out the tan-
gles of medieval streets to lay out **wide
boulevards** radiating off **grand squares**
(the **Etoile** anchored by the Arc de
Triomphe is his classic).

In 1889, the French wanted to show how
far they had come since the Revolution.
They hired **Gustave Eiffel** (1832–1923)
to build the world's tallest structure, a
temporary 315m-high (1,051-ft.) tower
made of riveted steel girders. Everyone
agreed it was tall; most thought it was ugly.
Its usefulness as a radio transmitter saved
Eiffel's tower from being torn down.

Art Nouveau was less an architectural
mode than a decorative movement, though
you can still find some of the original Art
Nouveau Métro entrances designed by
Hector Guimard (1867–1942) in Paris. (A
recently renovated entrance is at the Porte
Dauphine station on the no. 2 line.)

20th-Century Architecture

France commissioned some ambitious
architectural projects in the last century,
most of them the ***grands projets*** of the
late François Mitterrand. Most were considered controversial, outrageous, or even
offensive. Other than a concerted effort to
break convention and look stunningly
modern, nothing unifies the look of this
architecture—except that foreigners
designed much of it.

Britain's **Richard Rogers** (b. 1933) and
Italy's **Renzo Piano** (b. 1937) turned architecture inside out—literally—to craft the
eye-popping **Centre Pompidou** (1977),
Paris's modern-art museum. Exposed
pipes, steel supports, and plastic-tube
escalators wrap around the exterior.

Chinese-American maestro **I. M. Pei**
(b. 1917) was called in to cap the Louvre's
new underground Métro entrance with
glass pyramids (1989), placed smack in

FRENCH WINE & CULTURE

Centre Pompidou, Paris

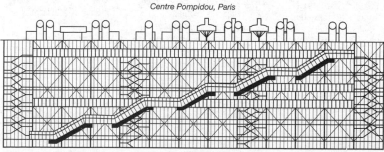

the center of the Palais du Louvre's 17th-century courtyard.

In 1989, Paris's opera company moved into the curvaceous, dark-glass mound of space of the **Opéra Bastille** (1989), designed by Canadian **Carlos Ott**. (Unfortunately, the acoustics have been lambasted.)

French History 101

The Way We Were— Early Gaul

By the time those Gaul-bashing Romans finally got their sticky mitts on France, their empire's boundaries extended deep into the forests of the Paris basin and up to the edges of the Rhine. In 52 B.C ol' Julius Caesar colonized an island in the middle of the Seine (today's Ile de la Cité, founded by Celtic settlers, the Parissi) and called it Lutetia (Paris to you and me).

Back down south, as the Roman Empire declined, Roman armies retreated to colonies that had been established along a strip of the Mediterranean coast. These included Montpellier, Arles, and Nîmes, which retain some of the best Roman monuments in Europe today.

But, history is full of irony. After years of ruthless Christian killing, the Romans finally converted and left the legacy of Christianity behind for Europe to embrace. The Roman Church, for all its abuses, was a guardian of civilization during the anarchy following the Roman decline, even if Rome viewed the Christianity adopted by many chieftains as heretical.

When Clovis (king of Gaul's Franks and founder of the Merovingian dynasty) converted to Catholicism, he cleverly swung the approval of the pope, the support of the archbishop of Reims, and the loyalty of many Gallic tribes who'd grown disenchanted with anarchy (what a winner!). In fact, you could say that Clovis's baptism is the beginning of a collusion between the Catholic Church and the French monarchy that would flourish until the French Revolution in 1789.

Clovis popped his clogs in 511, and his kingdom was split among his heirs (the Merovingian dynasty), an act that would bring about over 250 years of feudalism. Compared, however, to the enlightened colonization of the Romans, this quasi anarchic reign is known as the Dark Ages.

The Cool Carolingians

From the wreckage of the intrigue-ridden Merovingian court emerged the Carolingians. After halting several Muslim

FRENCH WINE & CULTURE

Dateline

- **121 B.C.** Them rascally Romans establish the province of Gallia Narbonensis to guard overland routes between Spain and Italy; its borders correspond roughly to today's sunny Provence.
- **58–51 B.C.** Old Jules (Julius Caesar) conquers Gaul (roughly today's north-central France).

- **52 B.C.** The Romans build Lutetia, later Paris, on an island in the Seine.
- **2nd century A.D.** Christianity arrives in Gaul.
- **485–511** Under Clovis I, the ferocious Franks defeat the Roman armies and establish the Merovingian dynasty.
- **768** Charlemagne (768–814) becomes the Frankish king and establishes the Carolingian

dynasty, ruling all the land between northern Italy, Bavaria, and Paris.

- **800** Charlemagne is crowned Holy Roman Emperor in Rome (no more arguing with him, mate!).
- **814** Charlemagne dies; his empire breaks up.
- **1066** Dastardly William the Conqueror (of Normandy) invades England and conquers King Harold's army at the Battle of Hastings,

invasions, their empire stretched from the Pyrenees to deep in the German forests, encompassing much of modern France, Germany, and northern Italy. Heir to all this was France's pride and joy, Charlemagne. Crowned in Rome on Christmas Day 800, he created the Holy Roman Empire. But despite ol' Charlie's magnetism, cultural rifts formed in his sprawling empire, most of which was divided at his death between two of his three squabbling heirs. Charles of Aquitaine annexed the western region; Louis of Bavaria took the east. Historians credit this division with the development of modern France and Germany as separate nations, even if these "new" countries were invaded by Vikings from the north, Muslim Saracens from the south, and Hungarians from the east.

Piggy in the Middle Ages

As if things weren't juicy enough already, when the Carolingian dynasty died out in 987, Hugh Capet, comte de Paris and duc de France, began the Middle Ages with the establishment of the Capetian dynasty. In 1154, the annulment of Eleanor of Aquitaine's marriage to Louis VII of France and her subsequent marriage to Henry II of England placed the western half of France under English control—an act that would bring about centuries of Anglo-French rivalry. This too was a period of growth, both architecturally (vast forests and swamps were cleared, often by Cistercian monks, and Gothic cathedrals were begun) and socially (the population grew, social order settled, and marriages created alliances among the ruling families, doubling the size of the territory controlled from Paris, a city increasingly recognized as the country's capital). Wily Philippe II (reigned 1179–1223) infiltrated more prominent families with his genes than anyone else in France, successfully marrying members of his family into the Valois, Artois, and Vermandois. He also craftily won Normandy and Anjou back from the English.

Louis IX (St. Louis) emerged as the 13th century's most memorable king. Admittedly he ceded most of the military conquests of his predecessors to the English, was a religious fanatic, and died of illness in 1270 in a boat off Tunis, but it was under his rule that the world received the architectural wonders of Notre-Dame and the Sainte-Chapelle in Paris.

During the 1300s, the struggle of French sovereignty against the claims of a rapacious Roman pope tempted Philip the Fair to support a pope based in Avignon. During one of medieval history's most

depicted in the Bayeux tapestry, see p. 214.

- ■ **1140** The first example of Gothic architecture is completed in the form of St-Denis Cathedral.
- ■ **1270** Don't cry now, but Louis IX (St. Louis) dies, along with most of his army, in Tunis on the 8th Crusade.
- ■ **1309** Philip the Fair establishes the Avignon papacy, which lasts nearly 70 years

and almost abolishes Rome's papal domination.
- ■ **1347–51** The bubonic plague (Black Death) kills a whopping 33% of the population.
- ■ **1431** There's no such thing as smoke without fire! The English burn feisty Joan of Arc at the stake in Rouen for resisting their occupation of France.

- ■ **1453** The French drive the English out of all of France except Calais; the Hundred Years' War ends.
- ■ **1515–47** France captures Calais after centuries of English rule.
- ■ **1562–98** Religion—the eternal source of war: Catholics fight Protestants; Henri IV converts to Catholicism and issues the

FRENCH WINE & CULTURE

continues

bizarre episodes, two popes ruled simulta-neously, from Rome and from Avignon. They competed for control of Christendom until political intrigue turned the tables in favor of Rome, and Avignon relinquished its claim in 1378.

The 14th century saw an increase in the wealth and power of the French kings and overall prosperity, but the Black Death took hold in 1348, killing an estimated 33% of Europe's population, decimating the population of Paris, and setting the stage for the exodus of the French monarchs to safer climes in such places as the Loire Valley.

Next up came the Hundred Years' War, during which the power-craving English crossed the Channel in an attempt to grab the throne. They managed to control almost all of the north (Picardy and Normandy), Champagne, parts of the Loire Valley, and the huge region called Guyenne, until the feisty (and very young) Joan of Arc (aged 19) stepped in and rallied the French troops, settling Charles VII on the throne in Reims's cathedral. But the English soon put a stop to her shenanigans by declaring her a heretic and burning her at the stake in 1431. Her death was not entirely in vain, as the French did manage to drive the discontented English out, leaving them only the Norman port of Calais.

In the late 1400s, Charles VIII married Brittany's last duchess, Anne, unifying France with its Celtic-speaking western outpost (everyone say "aahh"!). But the greatest credit goes to François I. In the early 1500s, he strengthened the monar-chy (financially and politically) and hus-banded the arts into a form of patronage that French monarchs would approve for centuries.

Meanwhile, the rivalry between Protestantism and the Catholic Church escalated into widespread civil strife. In 1572, Catherine de Médicis ordered the St. Bartholomew's Day Massacre of hundreds of Protestants. Henri IV, tired of the blood-shed and fearful that a Catholic Spain would meddle in the conflicts, converted to Catholicism in 1593. Just before being stabbed by a half-crazed monk, he issued the Edict of Nantes in 1598, granting free-dom of religion to Protestants in France.

Bye, Bye, Feudalism

By now all but a few vestiges of feudalism were gone from France. In 1624, Louis XIII appointed a Catholic cardinal, the duc de Richelieu, as his chief minister. You could easily argue that Richelieu wanted to be king himself. He amassed enormous power, practically running the country until his death in 1642. His sole objective

Edict of Nantes, granting limited rights to Protestants.

- **1643–1715** France's most famously extravagant ruler, Louis XIV, the Sun King, develops a powerful army, but wars in Flanders and court extravagance sow the seeds of decline.
- **1763** The Treaty of Paris effectively ends French power in North America.

- **1789–94** The most famous event in French history: The French Revolution. Peasants storm the Bastille on July 14, 1789, followed by the terri-ble Reign of Terror.
- **1793** Don't lose your head, but poor Louis XVI and Marie Antoinette are guillotined.
- **1794** Robespierre and the leaders of the Reign of

Terror also have their heads chopped off by Mr. Guillotine's famous contraption.

- **1799** The toughest short man in French history, Napoleon, enters Paris and unites opposing factions. He sets out to conquer neigh-boring countries, and his victories in Italy solidify his power in Paris.

was investing the monarchy with total power—he committed a series of truly horrible and gory acts trying to attain this goal and paved the way for the eventual absolutism of Louis XIV.

Louis XIV was a mere whippersnapper of 9 when he ascended to the throne, but thanks to his Sicilian-born chief minister, Cardinal Mazarin, the Sun King (called such after his emblem—the sun) was the most powerful monarch Europe had seen since the Roman emperors. The estimated population of France at this time was 20 million, as opposed to 8 million in England and 6 million in Spain (zoze French loveurs!). French colonies in Canada, the West Indies, and America (Louisiana) were stronger than ever. The economy and the arts flourished, as did a sense of aristocratic style that's remembered with bittersweet nostalgia today. Louis's palace of Versailles is one of the most flamboyant monuments in French history.

Under the orders of the ambitious Sun King, France conducted a series of expensive wars that, coupled with high taxes and bad harvests, stirred up much discontent, although the Atlantic ports, especially Bordeaux, grew and prospered with France's success in the West Indian slave and sugar trades.

Revolution & the Rise of a Short Guy Named Napoleon

In the 18th century, the Enlightenment (an intellectual movement headed by great thinkers such as Rousseau and Voltaire) was instructing the world on the struggle against absolutism, religious fanaticism, and superstition. When the "people" overthrew authority in 1789 by storming the Bastille Prison in Paris, Europe would never be the same again. On August 10, 1792, troops from Marseille, aided by a Parisian mob, threw the dim-witted Louis XVI and his Austrian-born queen, Marie Antoinette, into prison. After months of bloodshed and bickering among competing factions, the two monarchs were executed by the infamous guillotine, named after its inventor, Monsieur Guillotin.

France's problems got worse before they got better. In the ensuing bloodbaths and reigning terror (La Terreur), thousands of heads rolled off the guillotines, providing the most heroic and horrible anecdotes in French history. From this era emerged the Declaration of the Rights of Man, an enlightened document published in 1789; its influence has since been cited as a model of democratic ideals.

When the country's in ruin and the streets run with blood, who you gonna

FRENCH WINE & CULTURE

- **1804** Megalomaniac Napoleon crowns himself emperor in Notre-Dame de Paris.
- **1805–11** Napoleon and his armies successfully invade most of Europe.
- **1814–15** All good things come to an end: Napoleon fails to take Russia and abdicates. But old habits die hard, especially at Waterloo,

in 1815, when he is defeated by the archenemy, the English. He's exiled to Ste-Helena and dies in 1821.

- **1830–48** Eighteen years of monarchial reign, this time with Louis-Philippe.
- **1848** Another revolution topples Louis-Philippe's crown, and Napoleon III (nephew of Napoleon I) is elected president.

- **1851–71** President Napoleon (modestly) names himself Emperor Napoleon III.
- **1863** An exhibition of paintings marks the birth of Impressionism.
- **1870–71** The streets of Paris run with blood as the city falls to Franco-Prussian invaders. France gives up

continues

call? The very short and very brilliant Napoleon Bonaparte, of course. Only his militaristic fervor could reunite France and bring an end to the chaos. A political and military genius who appeared on the landscape when the French were sickened by the anarchy following their Revolution, he restored their tarnished national pride. In 1799, at the age of 30, he entered Paris and was crowned First Consul and Master of France.

Napoleon was a great fighter, and his victories made him the envy of Europe. In fact he almost managed to conquer the whole of Europe. Had it not been for an infamous retreat from Moscow during the winter of 1812 that reduced his army to tatters, as 400,000 Frenchmen died in the Russian snows, he might have made it. The combined armies of the English, Dutch, and Prussians finally defeated the man at Waterloo. Exiled to the British-held island of Ste-Helena in the South Atlantic, he died in 1821, probably the victim of an unknown poisoner.

The Bourbons & the Second Empire

Question: When your emperor lets you down, what do you do? Answer: Reinstate the monarchy—but with reduced powers of course. In 1814, following the destruction of

Napoleon and his dream, the Bourbon monarchy was reestablished with Louis XVIII, an archconservative, and a changing array of leaders who included the prince de Polignac and, later, Charles X. A renewal of the ancient regime's oppressions, however, didn't sit well in a France that had already spilled so much blood in favor of egalitarian causes (there's a surprise).

In 1830, after censoring the press and dissolving Parliament, Louis XVIII was removed from power after more uprisings. Louis-Philippe, duc d'Orléans, was elected king under a liberalized constitution. His reign lasted for 18 years of prosperity, during which England and France more or less collaborated on matters of foreign policy (unbelievable!). The establishment of an independent Belgium and the French conquest of Algeria (1840–47) were to have resounding effects on French politics a century later. It was a time of wealth, grace, and expansion of the arts for most French people, though the industrialization of the north and east produced some of the 19th century's most horrific poverty.

Yet another revolution in 1848, fueled by a financial crash and disgruntled workers in Paris, forced Louis-Philippe out of office, and yet another Napoleon (Napoleon I's nephew, Napoleon III) saved

Alsace-Lorraine but manages to colonize North Africa and Southeast Asia, if not a little aggressively.

■ **1873** Who said the Hundred Years' War was over? France loses the Suez Canal to the British, and a financial scandal wrecks an attempt to dredge it.

■ **1889** The most phallic and controversial of all edifices,

the Eiffel Tower, is built for Paris's Universal Exhibition and the centennial of the Revolution.

■ **1914–18** World War I. French casualties exceed 5 million.

■ **1934** After years of massive economic growth, the Great Depression arrives, and clashes of left and right spur a political crisis.

■ **1936** Germans march into the demilitarized Rhineland, and France decides to do nothing.

■ **1939** France and Britain guarantee Poland, Romania, and Greece protection from Nazi aggressors. Germany invades Poland, and France declares war.

■ **1940** Marshal Pétain's Vichy government collaborates

the day by becoming president. Appealing to the property-protecting instinct of a nation that still wore the scars of upheavals less than a century before, he initiated a repressive government in which he was awarded the status of emperor in 1851. This was an era of rebirth: The clergy gained in status, steel production began, a railway system and Indochinese colonies were established, new technologies fostered new kinds of industry, the bourgeoisie flourished, and Baron Georges-Eugène Haussmann radically altered Paris by demolishing medieval slums (and the occasional palace) in favor of the grand, uniform boulevards the world knows today.

But by 1866, an industrialized France began to see the Second Empire as more of a hindrance than an encouragement to expansion. The dismal failure of colonizing Mexico and the increasing power of Austria and Prussia were setbacks to the empire's prestige. In fact, in 1870, the Prussians defeated Napoleon III at Sedan and held him prisoner with 100,000 of his soldiers. Paris was besieged by a new enemy that once again brought bloodshed and tears to the capital.

When the Prussians finally withdrew, peace and prosperity slowly returned.

France refound its mojo, a mania of building occurred, the Impressionists revolutionized the art world, and writers such as Flaubert redefined the French novel into what today is still regarded as the most evocative in the world. The world's most famous edifice, the Eiffel Tower, was also built as part of the 1889 Universal Exposition.

By 1890, a new corps of satirists (including Emile Zola) had exposed the country's wretched living conditions and the underlying hypocrisy of late-19th-century French society. The 1894 Dreyfus Affair exposed the corruption of French army officers who had destroyed the career and reputation of a Jewish colleague (Albert Dreyfus), falsely and deliberately punished for treason. These ethnic tensions would lead to further divisiveness into the 20th century.

The Wicked World Wars

You've all studied it, now here they are: World War I and World War II. International rivalries, thwarted colonial ambitions, and conflicting alliances led to World War I (1914–18), which, after decisive German victories for 2 years, degenerated into the mud-slogged horror of trench warfare. Mourning between 4 and 5 million casualties, Europe was afflicted

with the Nazis, and Paris falls to Germany on June 14. General de Gaulle forms a government in exile in London to direct French resistance fighters.

- **1944** On June 6, the Allies invade the Normandy beaches. Some of the war's bloodiest battles are fought, and other Allied troops invade from the south. Paris is liberated in August.

- **1946–54** Yet more war—but this time in Indochina. The French withdraw from Southeast Asia, and North and South Vietnam are created.

- **1954–58** Algeria revolts and wins subsequent independence from France, but the bloodshed is fierce, and refugees flood into France. The Fourth Republic instated

since the Revolution collapses.

- **1958** De Gaulle comes out of retirement and initiates the Fifth Republic, calling for a France independent from the United States and Europe.

- **1968** Students riot in Paris, and de Gaulle resigns.

- **1981** François Mitterrand becomes the first Socialist

continues

with psychological scars that have never healed. But after the Allied victory, economic problems, plus demoralization stemming from years of fighting, encouraged the growth of socialism and communism. The French government, led by a vindictive Georges Clemenceau, demanded every centime of reparations it could from a crushed Germany. The humiliation associated with this has been cited as the origin of the German nation's almost obsessive determination to rise from the ashes of 1918.

The worldwide depression had devastating repercussions in France. Poverty weakened the Third Republic to the point where coalition governments rose and fell more regularly than waves in a storm. The crises reached a crescendo on June 14, 1940, when Hitler's armies marched down the Champs-Elysées, and newsreel cameras recorded French people openly weeping. The Nazis occupied the north of France, and a puppet French government was established at Vichy under the authority of Marshal Pétain. The immediate collapse of the French army is still viewed as one of the most significant humiliations in modern French history, and it is still difficult to broach the subject of occupation and collaboration today, even with the young kids.

Pétain and his regime cooperated with the Nazis in shameful ways. Not the least of their crimes included the deportation of more than 75,000 French Jews to German work camps. Pockets of resistance fighters (le maquis) waged small-scale guerrilla attacks against the Nazis throughout the war, and free-French forces continued to fight along with the Allies on battlegrounds such as North Africa. Charles de Gaulle, the irascible giant whose personality is forever associated with the politics of his era, established himself as the head of the French government in exile, operating first from London and then from Algiers.

One of the most documented and inspirational battles of World War II took place on June 6, 1944, in France. The largest armada in history (mainly British and American soldiers) landed on the beaches of Normandy. Paris rose in rebellion before the Allied armies arrived, and on August 26, 1944, Charles de Gaulle entered the capital as head of the government. The Fourth Republic was declared even as Nazi snipers shot their evil last from scattered rooftops through the city.

The Postwar Years

Talk about being fickle: Plagued by the bitter residue of colonial policies that France had established during the 18th and 19th

president since World War II.

- **1989** Bicentennial of the French Revolution; centennial of the Eiffel Tower.
- **1993** Conservatives topple the Socialists, as Edouard Balladur becomes premier.
- **1994** Old wounds are healed as France becomes linked to England via the

Channel Tunnel (aka the Chunnel).

- **1995** Jacques Chirac wins the French presidency and declares a war on unemployment; his popularity wanes and much unrest follows; terrorists bomb Paris several times, but Chirac remains.
- **1997** Strict immigration laws are enforced, causing

strife for many African and Arab immigrants and dividing the country. French voters elect Socialist Lionel Jospin prime minister.

- **1998** "They are the champions my friends": France hosts and wins the Socca World Cup.
- **2000** The euro (Europe's single currency) is officially introduced. France gives

centuries, the Fourth Republic witnessed the rise and fall of 22 governments and 17 premiers. Thousands of French soldiers died on foreign soil as colonies in North Africa and Indochina rebelled. Quelling just one revolt in Madagascar cost 80,000 French lives. After a bitter defeat in 1954, France ended the war in Indochina and freed its former colony. It also granted internal self-rule to Tunisia and (under slightly different circumstances) Morocco.

With Algeria, however, the story was different. The country rebelled against French rule in 1958, an event that signaled the end of the Fourth Republic. De Gaulle had to be called back from retirement to initiate a new constitution, the Fifth Republic, with stronger executive controls, but to almost everyone's dissatisfaction, de Gaulle ended the Algerian war in 1962 by granting independence. Streams of *pieds-noirs* (French-born residents of Algeria recently stripped of their land) flooded back into metropolitan France, often having to settle in makeshift refugee camps in Provence and the Languedoc.

As you've probably guessed by now, France is a country that thrives on crisis, and in 1968, yet more social unrest came about when a violent coalition hastily formed between the nation's students and blue-collar workers. Their fierce demonstrating led to the collapse of the government, and de Gaulle resigned. Power passed to his second-in-command, Georges Pompidou, and his successor, Valérie Giscard d'Estaing, both of whom continued de Gaulle's policies.

What Remains: France Today

Emperors, kings, fascists, heroic right-wingers—France had seen 'em all. But since World War II it hadn't seen a socialist leader until François Mitterrand took center stage in 1981 with a majority of 51%. In response (or retaliation?), many wealthy French transferred their assets out of the country, much to the delight of banks in Geneva, Monaco, the Cayman Islands, and Vienna. Though reviled by the rich and ridiculed for personal mannerisms that often seemed inspired by Louis XIV, Mitterrand was re-elected in 1988. During his two terms, he spent billions of francs on his *grands projets,* all controversial architectural additions (such as the Louvre's pyramid, Opéra Bastille, Cité de la Musique, and the Grande Arche de la Défense) that have nudged their way into Paris's permanent and well-loved skyline.

FRENCH WINE & CULTURE

legal status to unmarried couples (both gay and hetero).

■ **2002** France renounces its beloved Franc and switches to the Euro.

■ **2004** New 782 million euro (over $1 billion) terminal collapses at Charles de Gaulle Airport outside Paris, killing four.

■ **2005** Social unrest in the poor suburbs of almost all major towns ignites mass debates on how to fight social inequalities and immigration problems.

■ **2006** Students demonstrate against the CPE (first job contract), which they deem too restrictive. Unemployment hovers at around 9%, and the country prepares itself for the presidential elections in 2007.

In April 1993, voters dumped the Socialists and installed a conservative government. Polls cited corruption, unemployment, and urban insecurity as reasons for this, but either way, the Conservative premier Edouard Balladur had to "cohabit" the government with Mitterrand, whom he blamed for the country's economic problems. Diagnosed with terminal cancer near the end of his second term, Mitterrand continued to represent France with dignity, despite his illness. The battle over who would succeed him was waged against Balladur with epic rancor by Jacques Chirac, survivor of many terms as mayor of Paris. The papers had a field day over their mutual dislike for one another, and on his third try, on May 7, 1995, Chirac finally won the presidency with 52% of the vote. But Chirac's popularity faded in the wake of unrest caused by an 11.5% unemployment rate, a barrage of terrorist attacks by Algerian Muslims, and an economy struggling to meet European Union entry requirements.

A wave of terrorist attacks in 1995 brought an unfamiliar wariness to Paris. Six bombs killed 7 people and injured 115. Algerian Islamic militants, the suspected culprits, may have brought military guards to the Eiffel Tower, but they failed to throw France into panic.

Next up, it was France's turn to infuriate the world. Throughout 1995 and early 1996, they enraged everyone from the members of Greenpeace to the governments of Australia and New Zealand by resuming the policy of exploding nuclear bombs on isolated Pacific atolls. It continued until public outcry, both in France and outside its borders, exerted massive pressure to end the tests. This is another touchy subject amongst the French youth of today.

In 1999, yet more changes were in store as France joined other European countries in adopting the euro as its standard of currency. The new currency accelerated the creation of a single economy comprising nearly 300 million Europeans, with a combined gross national product approaching $9 trillion, larger than that of the United States. France kissed *au-revoir* to its French franc forevermore in 2002 and watched as the introduction of the euro caused prices to rise.

Just before the new millennium, on October 13, 1999, the French Parliament passed a new law giving legal status to unmarried (heterosexual and homosexual) couples. The law allows couples to enter into a union and be entitled to the same rights as married couples in such areas as housing, inheritance, income tax, and social welfare.

In the winter of 2003, Mother Nature delivered devastating floods to southwest France, killing residents and inundating much of the region in rising waters and "acres of mud." Roads and railways were submerged, and thousands of people were forced to flee their homes. Marseille, for example, was declared a disaster area.

On a more ominous note, attacks against Jews in France reached their highest level since World War II. An increase in anti-Semitic acts coincided with heightened tensions in the Middle East. Jewish schools, temples, and cemeteries were attacked. Slogans denouncing Jews were regularly spray-painted on school walls and over Jewish cemeteries. The year of 2003 witnessed the stabbing of a rabbi in Paris and the beating of Jewish youths with metal bars at an antiwar protest in Paris.

Washington's decision to invade Iraq in 2003 drove a wedge between the United States and its ally, and George W. Bush became one of the most unpopular American presidents ever in the eyes of the French. When he arrived in Paris in June 2004, thousands of antiwar and

FRENCH WINE & CULTURE

anti-Bush protesters marched through the streets of Paris. Bush declared, "We have great relations with France," but an opinion poll released the same week showed that an astonishing 78% of the French people no longer trusted the policies of the United States.

In 2005 the E.U. held a referendum on the introduction of a European constitution. France, founder of the E.U., shocked the polls by voting *Non*. Yet the negative vote was interpreted by many not as a refusal of Europe but as a display of general discontent over Chirac's policies. This disgruntlement would also come to a head in suburbs all around the country with riots and demonstrations.

The first half of 2006 saw yet more unrest—this time from students demonstrating against employment laws. And the latter half was overrun with speculation on the presidential election campaigns for 2007's general elections. Bye-bye, Chirac!

Recommended Books, Films & Music

Books

Books on all aspects of French history and society range from the very general—such as the section on France in the *Encyclopedia Americana,* International Edition (Grolier), which presents an illustrated overview of the French people and their way of life—to the specific, such as Judi Culbertson and Tom Randall's *Permanent Parisians: An Illustrated Guide to the Cemeteries of Paris* (Chelsea Green), which recounts the lives of many famous people who are buried in Paris.

HISTORY

If you want to astound your mates with your in-depth knowledge of French history, brush up by reading *History of France,* by Guillaume de Bertier de Savigny and David H. Pinkney (Forum Press), which offers a comprehensive history with illustrations and plenty of obscure but interesting facts.

Paris: The Biography of a City (Viking) was written by Colin Jones, a historian at Britain's University of Warwick, and moves from prehistoric tribal habitation to modern times, recounting a lusty saga of one of the world's greatest cities and how rulers, economic factors, religion, and even violence shaped what Paris is today.

Two books about French life and society in the 17th century are Warren Lewis's *The Splendid Century* (William Morrow) and Madame de Sévigne's *Selected Letters,* edited by Leonard W. Tancock (Penguin), which contains witty letters to her daughter during the reign of Louis XIV.

For something more modern, move into the 20th century with *Pleasure of the Belle Epoque: Entertainment and Festivity in Turn-of-the-Century France,* by Charles Rearick (Yale University Press), which depicts public diversions in the changing and troubled times of the Third Republic.

One unusual approach to French history is Rudolph Chleminski's *The French at Table* (William Morrow), a funny, honest history of why the French know how to eat better than anyone else.

TRAVEL

In *The Flâneur: A Stroll Through the Paradoxes of Paris* (Bloomsbury), Edmund White wants the reader to experience Paris as Parisians do. Although hard to translate, a *flâneur* is someone who strolls, loafs, or idles.

BIOGRAPHY

Hugh Ross Williamson brings Catherine de Médicis to life in his *Catherine de Médici*

FRENCH WINE & CULTURE

(Viking Press), combining text with illustrations from the 16th century. This queen of France was the dominant personality during her nation's religious wars and the mother of three kings of France, a queen of Spain, and a queen of Navarre.

Representing a different era are *A Moveable Feast* (Collier Books), Ernest Hemingway's recollections of Paris in the 1920s, and Morley Callaghan's *That Summer in Paris: Memories of Tangled Friendships with Hemingway, Fitzgerald and Some Others* (Toronto Macmillan), an account of the same period. Another interesting read is *The Autobiography of Alice B. Toklas*, by Gertrude Stein (Vintage Books). It's an account of 30 years in Paris.

One critic called *Simone de Beauvoir*, by Deirdre Bair (Summit Books), a biography "*à l'Americaine*—that is to say, long, with all the warts of its subject unsparingly described." The story of the great feminist intellectual was based in part on tape-recorded conversations and unpublished letters. *Colette: A Life*, by Herbert R. Lottman (Little, Brown), is a painstakingly researched biography of the French writer and her fascinating life—which included not only writing novels and appearing in cabarets but dabbling in lesbianism and perhaps even collaborating with the enemy during the Nazi occupation.

THE ARTS

Much of France's beauty can be found in its art. Three books that approach France from this perspective are *The History of Impressionism*, by John Rewald (Museum of Modern Art), a collection of documents—both writing and quotations by the artists—illuminating this period in the history of art; *The French Through Their Films*, by Robin Buss (Ungar), an exploration of the history and themes of over 100 films; and *The Studios of Paris: The Capital of Art in the Late Nineteenth Century*, by John Milner (Yale University Press). Milner describes the forces that made Paris one of the most complex centers of the art world in the early modern era.

Nightlife of Paris: The Art of Toulouse-Lautrec, by Patrick O'Connor (Universe), is an enchanting 80-page book with lively anecdotes about the hedonistic luminaries of Belle Epoque Paris, with paintings, sketches, and lithographs by the artist.

Olympia: Paris in the Age of Manet, by Otto Friedrich (Harper-Collins), draws its inspiration from the artwork in the Musée d'Orsay. From there the book takes off on an anecdote-rich chain of historical associations, tracing the rise of the Impressionist school of modern painting but also incorporating social commentary on such issues as the pattern of prostitution and venereal disease in 19th-century France—nice!

FICTION

The *Chanson de Roland*, written between the 11th and 14th centuries, is the earliest and most celebrated of the "songs of heroic exploits." *The Misanthrope* and *Tartuffe* are two masterful satires on the frivolity of the 17th century by the great comic dramatist Molière. François-Marie Arouet Voltaire's *Candide* is a classic satire attacking both the philosophy of optimism and the abuses of the *ancien régime*.

A few of the masterpieces of the 19th century are *Madame Bovary*, by Gustave Flaubert (Random House), in which the carefully wrought characters, setting, and plot attest to the author's genius in presenting the tragedy of Emma Bovary; Victor Hugo's *Les Misérables* (Modern Library), a classic tale of social oppression and human courage set in the era of Napoleon I; and *Selected Stories*, by the master of short stories, Guy de Maupassant (New American Library).

Honoré de Balzac's *La comédie humaine* depicts life in France from the fall of Napoleon to 1848. *The Vagabond,* by Colette, evokes the life of a French music-hall performer.

For an American's take on the City of Light, try Henry James's *The Ambassadors* and *The American.* From a different era is *Tropic of Cancer,* the semi-autobiographical story of Henry Miller's years in Paris. One of France's leading thinkers, Jean-Paul Sartre shows individuals struggling against their freedom in *No Exit and Three Other Plays* (Random House).

For a more contemporary (and lighter) read, try *Me Talk Pretty One Day* by David Sedaris. He sums up French culture, as told from the viewpoint of an American tourist, in a remarkably hilarious way. Or check out *Paris to the Moon* by Adam Gopnik, an engaging tale about an American living in Paris.

Of course, you'll run into mentions of *The Da Vinci Code* during your travels. Both the movie and the book were panned by most reviewers. Still, it's fun to read about or see the places you'll be visiting, and the Louvre is featured predominantly in both.

Films

Definitely check out some movies by New Wave directors like François Truffaut and Jean-Luc Godard before coming to Paris. Don't expect action-packed adventures, but you will glimpse wonderful, atmospheric scenes that will give you an idea of how the city looked in the '50s and '60s.

More recent must-sees include the French flick *Amelie* (by Jean-Pierre Jeunet), which was mostly shot in the picturesque Montmartre district, and American films like *French Kiss* (by Lawrence Kasdan) or *Before Sunrise* (by Richard Linklater)—all of these will surely put you in a romantic mood. If suspense is more your genre, *Ronin* (by John Frankenheimer) is an action movie with thrilling car-chase scenes throughout the streets of Paris, and *Cache* (by Michael Haneke) is a psychological thriller set in Paris.

For biting social commentary, rent *Le Placard* (by Francis Veber) with Gérard Depardieu, Daniel Auteuil, and Thierry Lhermitte, a funny movie that deals with the issue of homosexuality in French society. Hard-hitting *La Haine* (by Mathieu Kassovitch) was made in 1995 (starring the then relatively unknown Vincent Cassel, before he got in with Monica Belluci, that is) but foreshadows the 2005 riots in the Parisian ghettos.

Music

Listen to some classic Edith Piaf—a French torch singer and icon of the people's Paris in the 1940s—and you'll be instantly transported to the streets of Paname (Paris's nickname). It'll be hard to avoid hearing her most famous song, "La Vie en Rose," while you're in the City of Light.

For something truly authentic, give any song by Hungarian-born Joseph Komas a whirl. Together with his French poet friend Jacques Prévert, they wrote some of the most influential popular *chansons* of the 20th century. Mention "Les Feuilles Mortes" and you're bound to get an "ahh" from any French person (check out www.zigzag-territoires.com to download a recent classical version of the songs).

Often thought of as the French Elvis Presley, Johnny Halladay has remained one of the country's top performers since the 1960s. He's probably best known outside of France for his film roles, though, such as in 2003's *The Man on the Train*.

Serge Gainsbourg, a French poet, singer/songwriter, actor, and director, achieved similar success across the arts. He started out singing *ye-ye pop* (light French pop music) but branched out to produce some of the most influential concept albums to have come out of France. The French have always put an accent on "good text" in their songs, and Gitane-smoking Serge knew how to manipulate the language of lurve in ways rarely experienced since. Current Parisian artists bent on resuscitating "la Chanson Française" (French Chanson) à la Gainsbourg are Bénabar (www.benabar.com), Albin de la Simone (www.albindelasimone.com), Charlotte Gainsbourg (yep—Serge's actor-daughter with British actress Jane Birkin; www.charlottegainsbourg.net), Vincent Delerm (www.vincentdelerm.com), and Mickey 3-D (www.mickey3d.com), to name but a few.

Today, France's biggest exports are electro-pop bands like Daft Punk (www.daftpunk.com), Air, and French rap, which has come a long way since the '80s when MC Solar ruled the charts—current bands like NTM boast uncompromisingly sharp rhymes and tight beats.

The French have also had their fair share of Classical composers. For some 19th-century operetta, pop into any music shop and seek out Offenbach's *Vie Parisienne,* or *Orphée aux Enfers,* known for their satirical and highly poignant social commentary.

Survival French

English	French	Pronunciation
Yes/No	Oui/Non	wee/nohn
Okay	D'accord	*dah*-core
Please	S'il vous plaît	seel voo play
Thank you	Merci	*mair*-see
You're welcome	De rien	duh ree-*ehn*
Hello (during daylight)	Bonjour	bohn-*jhoor*
Good evening	Bonsoir	bohn-*swahr*
Goodbye	Au revoir	o ruh-*vwahr*
What's your name?	Comment vous appellez-vous?	ko-*mahn*-voo-za-pell-ay-*voo?*
My name is	Je m'appelle	*jhuh* ma-pell
How are you?	Comment allez-vous?	kuh-mahn-tahl-ay-*voo?*
So-so	Comme ci, comme ça	kum-*see,* kum-*sah*
I'm sorry/excuse me	Pardon	pahr-*dohn*

GETTING AROUND/STREET SMARTS

English	French	Pronunciation
Do you speak English?	Parlez-vous anglais?	par-lay-voo-zahn-*glay?*
I don't speak French	Je ne parle pas français	jhuh ne parl pah frahn-*say*
I don't understand	Je ne comprends pas	jhuh ne kohm-*prahn* pas
Could you speak more loudly/more slowly?	Pouvez-vous parler plus fort/plus lentement?	Poo-*vay* voo par-lay ploo for/ploo lan-te-*mahn?*
What is it?	Qu'est-ce que c'est?	kess-kuh-*say?*
What time is it?	Qu'elle heure est-il?	kel uhr eh-*teel?*
What?	Quoi?	kwah?
How? or What did you say?	Comment?	ko-*mahn?*
When?	Quand?	kahn?
Where is?	Où est?	oo *eh?*
Who?	Qui?	kee?
Why?	Pourquoi?	poor-*kwah?*

English	French	Pronunciation
here/there	ici/là	ee-*see*/lah
left/right	à gauche/à droite	a goash/a drwaht
straight ahead	tout droit	too-*drwah*
Fill the tank (of a car), please	Le plein, s'il vous plaît	luh plan, seel-voo-*play*
I want to get off at	Je voudrais descendre à	jhe voo-*dray* day-son-drah ah
airport	l'aéroport	lair-o-*por*
bank	la banque	lah bahnk
bridge	le pont	luh pohn
bus station	la gare routière	lah *gar* roo-tee-*air*
bus stop	l'arrêt de bus	lah-*ray* duh boohss
by means of a car	en voiture	ahn vwa-*toor*
cashier	la caisse	lah kess
cathedral	le cathedral	luh ka-tay-*dral*
church	l'église	lay-*gleez*
driver's license	le permis de conduire	luh per-*mee* duh con-*dweer*
elevator	l'ascenseur	lah-sahn-*seuhr*
entrance (to a building or a city)	une porte	ewn port
exit (from a building or a freeway)	une sortie	ewn sor-*tee*
gasoline	du pétrol/de l'essence	doo pay-*trol*/de lay-*sahns*
hospital	l'hôpital	low-pee-*tahl*
luggage storage	la consigne	lah kohn-*seen*-yuh
museum	le musée	luh mew-*zay*
no smoking	défense de fumer	day-*fahns* duh fu-may
one-day pass	le ticket journalier	luh tee-*kay* jhoor-nall-ee-*ay*
one-way ticket	l'aller simple	lah-*lay* sam-pluh
police	la police	lah po-*lees*
round-trip ticket	l'aller-retour	lah-*lay* re-*toor*
second floor	le premier étage	luh prem-ee-*ehr* ay-*taj*
slow down	ralentir	rah-lahn-*teer*
store	le magasin	luh ma-ga-*zehn*
street	la rue	lah roo
subway/ underground/Tube	le Métro	luh *may*-tro
telephone	le téléphone	luh tay-lay-*phone*
ticket	un billet	uh *bee*-yay
toilets	les toilettes/les WC	lay twa-*lets*/les vay-*say*

SHOPPING TERMS

English	French	Pronunciation
How much does it cost?	C'est combien?/Ça coûte combien?	say comb-bee-*ehn?*/sah coot comb-bee-*ehn?*
That's expensive	C'est cher/chère	say share
Do you take credit cards?	Est-ce que vous acceptez les cartes de credit?	es-kuh voo zaksep-*tay* lay kart duh creh-*dee?*
I'd like to buy	Je voudrais acheter	jhe voo-*dray* ahsh-*tay*
aspirin	des aspirines/des aspros	deyz ahs-peer-*een*/deyz ahs-*proh*
gift	un cadeau	uh kah-*doe*
map of the city	un plan de ville	uh plahn de *veel*
newspaper	un journal	uh zhoor-*nahl*
phone card	une carte téléphonique	uh cart tay-lay-fone-*eek*
postcard	une carte postale	ewn cart pos-*tahl*
road map	une carte routière	ewn cart roo-tee-*air*
stamp	un timbre	uh *tam*-bruh

HOTEL TERMS

English	French	Pronunciation
I'd like	Je voudrais	jhe voo-*dray*
a room	une chambre	ewn *shahm*-bruh
the key	la clé (la clef)	la clay
Are taxes included?	Est-ce que les taxes sont comprises?	ess-keh lay taks son com-*preez?*
balcony	un balcon	uh bahl-*cohn*
bathtub	une baignoire	ewn bayn-*nwar*
hot and cold water	l'eau chaude et froide	low showed ay fwad
Is breakfast included?	Petit déjeuner inclus?	peh-*tee* day-jheun-*ay* ehn-*klu?*
room	une chambre	ewn *shawm*-bruh
shower	une douche	ewn dooch
sink	un lavabo	uh la-va-*bow*
suite	une suite	ewn sweet
We're staying for . . . days	On reste pour . . . jours	ohn rest poor . . . jhoor

NUMBERS & ORDINALS

English	French	Pronunciation
zero	zéro	*zare*-oh
one	un	uh
two	deux	duh
three	trois	twah
four	quatre	*kaht*-ruh
five	cinq	sank

English	French	Pronunciation
six	**six**	seess
seven	**sept**	set
eight	**huit**	wheat
nine	**neuf**	noof
ten	**dix**	deess
twenty	**vingt**	vehn
forty	**quarante**	ka-*rahnt*
fifty	**cinquante**	sang-*kahnt*
a hundred	**cent**	sahn
a thousand	**mille**	meel

THE CALENDAR

English	French	Pronunciation
Sunday	**dimanche**	dee-*mahnsh*
Monday	**lundi**	luhn-*dee*
Tuesday	**mardi**	mahr-*dee*
Wednesday	**mercredi**	mair-kruh-*dee*
Thursday	**jeudi**	jheu-*dee*
Friday	**vendredi**	vawn-druh-*dee*
Saturday	**samedi**	sahm-*dee*

FOOD & MENU READER

English	French	Pronunciation
I would like	**Je voudrais**	jhe voo-*dray*
to eat	**manger**	mahn-*jhay*
Please give me	**Donnez-moi, s'il vous plaît**	doe-nay-*mwah*, seel-voo-*play*
a bottle of	**une bouteille de**	ewn boo-*tay* duh
a cup of	**une tasse de**	ewn tass duh
a glass of	**un verre de**	uh vair duh
a cocktail	**un apéritif**	uh ah-pay-ree-*teef*
the check/bill	**l'addition/la note**	la-dee-see-*ohn*/la noat
dinner	**le dîner**	luh dee-*nay*
a knife	**un couteau**	uh koo-*toe*
a napkin	**une serviette**	ewn sair-vee-*et*
a spoon	**une cuillère**	ewn kwee-*air*
a fork	**une fourchette**	ewn four-shet
Cheers!	**A votre santé!**	ah vo-truh sahn-*tay!*
fixed-price menu	**un menu**	uh may-*new*
Is the tip/service included?	**Est-ce que le service est compris?**	ess-ke luh ser-*vees* eh com-*pree?*
Waiter!/Waitress!	**Monsieur!/ Mademoiselle!**	muh-*syuh*/mad-mwa-*zel*
wine list	**une carte des vins**	ewn cart day *van*
appetizer	**une entrée**	ewn en-*tray*

English	French	Pronunciation
main course	**un plat principal**	uh plah pran-see-*pahl*
tip included	**service compris**	sehr-*vees* cohm-*pree*
wide-ranging sampling of the chef's best efforts	**menu dégustation**	may-*new* day-gus-ta-see-*on*

MEATS

English	French	Pronunciation
beef stew	**du pot au feu**	dew poht o *fhe*
marinated beef braised with red wine and served with vegetables	**du boeuf à la mode**	dew bewf ah lah *mhowd*
chicken	**du poulet**	*dew poo*-lay
rolls of pounded and baked chicken, veal, or fish, often pike, usually served warm	**des quenelles**	day ke-*nelle*
chicken, stewed with mushrooms and wine	**du coq au vin**	dew cock o *vhin*
frogs' legs	**des cuisses de grenouilles**	day cweess duh gre-*noo*-yuh
ham	**du jambon**	dew jham-*bon*
lamb	**de l'agneau**	duh lahn-*nyo*
rabbit	**du lapin**	dew lah-*pan*
sirloin	**de l'aloyau**	duh lahl-why-*yo*
steak	**du bifteck**	dew beef-*tek*
filet steak, embedded with fresh green or black peppercorns, flambéed, and served with a cognac sauce	**un steak au poivre**	uh stake o *pwah*-vruh
double tenderloin, a long muscle from which filet steaks are cut	**du châteaubriand**	dew sha-tow-bree-*ahn*
stewed meat with white sauce, enriched with cream and eggs	**de la blanquette**	duh lah blon-*kette*
veal	**du veau**	dew voh

FISH

English	French	Pronunciation
fish (freshwater)	du poisson de rivière, or du poisson d'eau douce	dew pwah-*sson* duh ree-vee-*aire*, dew pwah-*sson* d'o *dooss*
fish (saltwater)	du poisson de mer	dew pwah-*sson* duh *mehr*
Mediterranean fish soup or stew made with tomatoes, garlic, saffron, and olive oil	de la bouillabaisse	duh lah booh-ya-*besse*
herring	du hareng	dew ahr-*rahn*
lobster	du homard	dew oh-*mahr*
mussels	des moules	day moohl
mussels in herb-flavored white wine with shallots	des moules marinières	day moohl mar-ee-nee-*air*
oysters	des huîtres	dayz *hwee*-truh
shrimp	des crevettes	day kreh-*vet*
smoked salmon	du saumon fumé	dew sow-*mohn* fu-*may*
tuna	du thon	dew tohn
trout	de la truite	duh lah tru-*eet*

SIDES/APPETIZERS

English	French	Pronunciation
butter	du beurre	dew bhuhr
bread	du pain	dew pan
goose liver	du foie gras	dew fwah *grah*
potted and minced pork products, prepared as a roughly chopped pâté	des rillettes	day ree-*yett*
snails	des escargots	dayz ess-car-*goh*

FRUITS & VEGETABLES

English	French	Pronunciation
cabbage	du choux	dew *shoe*
eggplant	de l'aubergine	duh loh-ber-*jheen*
grapes	du raisins	dew ray-*zhan*
green beans	des haricots verts	day ahr-ee-coh vaire
lemon/lime	du citron/du citron vert	dew cee-*tron*/dew cee-tron vaire
potatoes	des pommes de terre	day puhm duh *tehr*
potatoes au gratin	des pommes de terre dauphinois	day puhm duh *tehr* doh-feen-*wah*

Language of Lurve

The Seducer's Guide to French

English	French	Pronunciation
Your eyes are like stars	Vos yeux brillent comme des étoiles	vose yeuh bree comm dez ay-*twaalles*
Will you sleep with me tonight?	Voulez-vous coucher avec moi ce soir?	voo-*lay* voo coo-*shay* avek mwa suh *swaar*
I think I love you	Je pense que je t'aime	jhu pahnse kuh jhu *taim*
Kiss me darling	Embrasse moi mon amour	om-*brass* mwa mon ah-*moor*
You are so beautiful (handsome)	Que tu es belle (beau)	kuh two *eh* bell (bow)
A condom	un préservatif	unn pray-ser-vah-*tiff*
A rubber	une capote	oune kaa-*potte*
I won't have sex unless you wear a condom	Je ne te ferai pas l'amour si tu ne mets pas un préservatif	jhu nuh tuh fair-*ray* pah lah-*moor* sea two nuh meh pahs unn pray-ser-vah-*tiff*
You make me horny	Tu m'excites	two mex-*seet*
That feels good	C'est bon!	seh *bohn*

English	French	Pronunciation
french fries	des pommes frites	day puhm *freet*
spinach	des épinards	dayz ay-pin-*ar*
strawberries	des fraises	day *frez*

BEVERAGES

English	French	Pronunciation
beer	de la bière	duh lah bee-*aire*
milk	du lait	dew *lay*
orange juice	du jus d'orange	dew joo d'or-*ahn*-jhe
water	de l'eau	duh *lo*
red wine	du vin rouge	dew vhin *rooj*
white wine	du vin blanc	dew vhin *blahn*
coffee (black)	un café noir	uh ka-fay *nwahr*
coffee (with cream)	un café crème	uh ka-fay *krem*
coffee (with milk)	un café au lait	uh ka-fay o *lay*
coffee (decaf)	un café décaféiné (slang: un déca)	un ka-fay day-kah-fay-*nay* (uh *day*-kah)
coffee (espresso)	un café espresso (un express)	uh ka-fay e-*sprehss-o* (un ek-*sprehss*)

SURVIVAL FRENCH

English	French	Pronunciation
tea	**du thé**	dew *tay*
herbal tea	**une tisane**	ewn tee-*zahn*

DESSERTS

English	French	Pronunciation
cake	**du gâteau**	dew gha-*tow*
cheese	**du fromage**	dew fro-*mahj*
thick custard dessert with a caramelized topping	**de la crème brûlée**	duh lah *krem* bruh-*lay*
caramelized upside-down apple pie	**une tarte Tatin**	ewn tart tah-*tihn*
tart	**une tarte**	ewn tart
vanilla ice cream	**de la glace à la vanille**	duh lah *glass* a lah vah-*nee*-yuh
fruit, especially cherries, cooked in batter	**du clafoutis**	dew kla-foo-*tee*

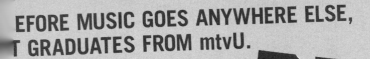

EFORE MUSIC GOES ANYWHERE ELSE,
T GRADUATES FROM mtvU.

EW ARTISTS, VIDEOS AND CONCERT
OURS - IF IT'S MUSIC, WE'VE GOT IT.
UT THAT'S NOT ALL: STUDENT FILMS,
ILLER INTERNSHIPS, JOB
PPORTUNITIES, CONTESTS THAT
UMPSTART CAREERS, CAMPUS
VENTS AND MUCH MORE!
mtvU ENHANCES YOUR ENTIRE
COLLEGE EXPERIENCE.

TUNE IN ALL SEMESTER LONG.

M T V U

NOW YOU CAN WATCH mtvU 24/7 AT mtvU.COM

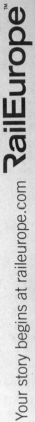

RailEurope™

Your story begins at raileurope.com